P9-BYD-885

THE GREEN GUIDE

R. Mattès/MICHELIN

Germany

Director	David Brabis
Chief Editor	Mike Brammer
English Edition	Alison Hughes
Practical Points	Alison Hughes, Philippa Smith, Natacha Brumard, Michael Hertlein, Blandine Lecomte, Annika Melcher
Mapping	Alain Baldet, Michèle Cana, Christelle Coué, Jean-Pierre Michel
Picture Editors	Catherine Guégan, Geneviève Corbic
Editorial Assistance	Philippa Smith
Lay-out	Rudolf Diratzouyan, Frederic Sardin
Graphics	Christiane Beylier
Cover	Agence Carré Noir
Production	Pierre Ballochard, Renaud Leblanc
Marketing	Ellie Danby
Sales	John Lewis (UK), Robin Bird (USA)
Public Relations	Gonzague de Jarnac, Paul Cordle
Contact	The Green Guide Michelin Travel Publications Hannay House 39 Clarendon Road Watford Herts WD17 1JA United Kingdom ☎ (01923) 205 240 Fax (01923) 205 241 www.ViaMichelin.com TheGreenGuide-uk@uk.michelin.com
Advertising	Manchette Publicité 4, rue Rouget de Lisle 92 793 Issy les Moulineaux Cédex France ☎ +44 1 40 93 23 93

NB

While every effort is made to ensure that all information printed in this guide is correct and up-to-date, Michelin Travel Publications (a trading division of Michelin Tyre PLC) accepts no liability for any direct, indirect or consequential losses howsoever caused so far as such can be excluded by law.

The Green Guide: Spirit of Discovery

Leisure time spent with The Green Guide is also a time for refreshing your spirit, enjoying yourself, and taking advantage of our selection of fine restaurants, hotels and other places for relaxing: immerse yourself in the local culture, discover new horizons, experience the local lifestyle. The Green Guide opens the door for you.

Each year our writers go touring: visiting the sights, devising the driving tours, identifying the highlights, selecting the most attractive hotels and restaurants, checking the routes for the maps and plans.

Each title is compiled with great care, giving you the benefit of regular revisions and Michelin's first-hand knowledge. The Green Guide responds to changing circumstances and takes account of its readers' suggestions; all comments are welcome.

Share with us our enthusiasm for travel, which has led us to discover over 60 destinations in France and other countries. Like us, let yourself be guided by the desire to explore, which is the best motive for travel: the spirit of discovery.

Contents

R. Mattes/MICHELIN

May tree.

/Munich Tourist Office

Fairground in Munich.

/Lindau Tourismus

Lindau.

R. Mattes/MICHELIN

Germany produces some delicious white wines.

Maps and Plans

Companion publications

Michelin map 718 Germany
– a practical map on a scale of 1:750 000 which shows the German road network and indicates isolated sites and monuments described in this guide;
– with index of place names.

Michelin Tourist and Motoring Atlas Germany/Austria/Benelux/Switzerland/Czech Republic
– spiral-bound atlas on a scale of 1:300 000 for Germany;
– with index of place names and town maps.

Michelin regional maps (541-546)
– maps on a scale of 1:350 000 with detailed road mapping and maps of the main towns.

City plans:
Berlin in map format (33)
Berlin in spiral atlas format (2033)

Travelling to Germany
Michelin Tourist and Motoring Atlas Europe – A4 spiral (1136), A3 spiral (1129), A3 paperback (1135)
– the whole of Europe on a scale of 1:1 000 000 in one volume;
– major roads and 73 town plans and area maps;
– highway code of every country.

www.ViaMichelin.com
Internet users can access personalised route plans, Michelin maps and town plans, and addresses of hotels and restaurants featured in The Michelin Guide Deutschland.

Thematic maps

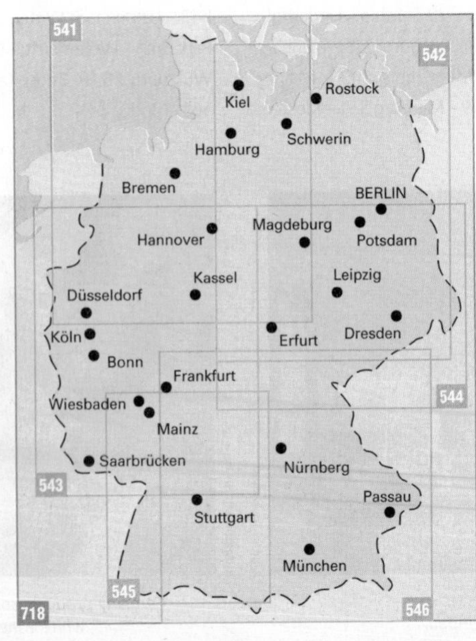

Town plans

Regional maps and tours

Museums, monuments and sites

Key

Selected monuments and sights

 Tour - Departure point

Catholic church

Protestant church, other temple

Synagogue - Mosque

Building

Statue, small building

Calvary, wayside cross

Fountain

Rampart - Tower - Gate

Château, castle, historic house

Ruins

Dam

Factory, power plant

Fort

Cave

Troglodyte dwelling

Prehistoric site

Viewing table

Viewpoint

Other place of interest

Special symbols

Park and Ride

Covered parking

19 Federal road (Bundesstraße).

Sports and recreation

Racecourse

Skating rink

Outdoor, indoor swimming pool

Multiplex Cinema

Marina, sailing centre

Trail refuge hut

Cable cars, gondolas

Funicular, rack railway

Tourist train

Recreation area, park

Theme, amusement park

Wildlife park, zoo

Gardens, park, arboretum

Bird sanctuary, aviary

Walking tour, footpath

Of special interest to children

Abbreviations

J	Law courts (Justizgebäude)
L	Provincial government (Landesregierung)
M	Museum (Museum)
POL.	Police (Polizei)
R	Town hall (Rathaus)
T	Theatre (Theater)
U	University (Universität)

The German letter ß (eszett) has been used throughout this guide.

Highly recommended ★★★
Recommended ★★
Interesting ★

Additional symbols

Symbol	Meaning
	Tourist information
	Motorway or other primary route
	Junction: complete, limited
	Pedestrian street
	Unsuitable for traffic, street subject to restrictions
	Steps – Footpath
	Train station – Auto-train station
S.N.C.F.	Coach (bus) station
	Tram
	Metro, underground
	Park-and-Ride
	Access for the disabled
	Post office
	Telephone
	Covered market
	Barracks
	Drawbridge
	Quarry
	Mine
B F	Car ferry (river or lake)
	Ferry service: cars and passengers
	Foot passengers only
③	Access route number common to Michelin maps and town plans
Bert (R.)...	Main shopping street
AZ B	Map co-ordinates
►►	Visit if time permits
	Admission times and charges listed at the end of the guide

Hotels and restaurants

Symbol	Meaning
	Price categories:
	Budget
	Moderate
	Expensive
20 rm	Number of rooms
€120/185	Price of single/double room including breakfast.
€5.50	Price of breakfast when not included in the room price.
half-board or full-board €79	Price per person, based on double occupancy (half or full board obligatory)
€15/30	Restaurant: minimum/maximum price for a full meal (not including drinks)
	Major credit cards not accepted.
P	Car park for customers.
	Swimming-Pool
	No-smoking rooms available. Restaurant partly or wholly reserved for non-smokers.
	Rooms with wheelchair access.

The prices correspond to the higher rates of the tourist season

Principal sights

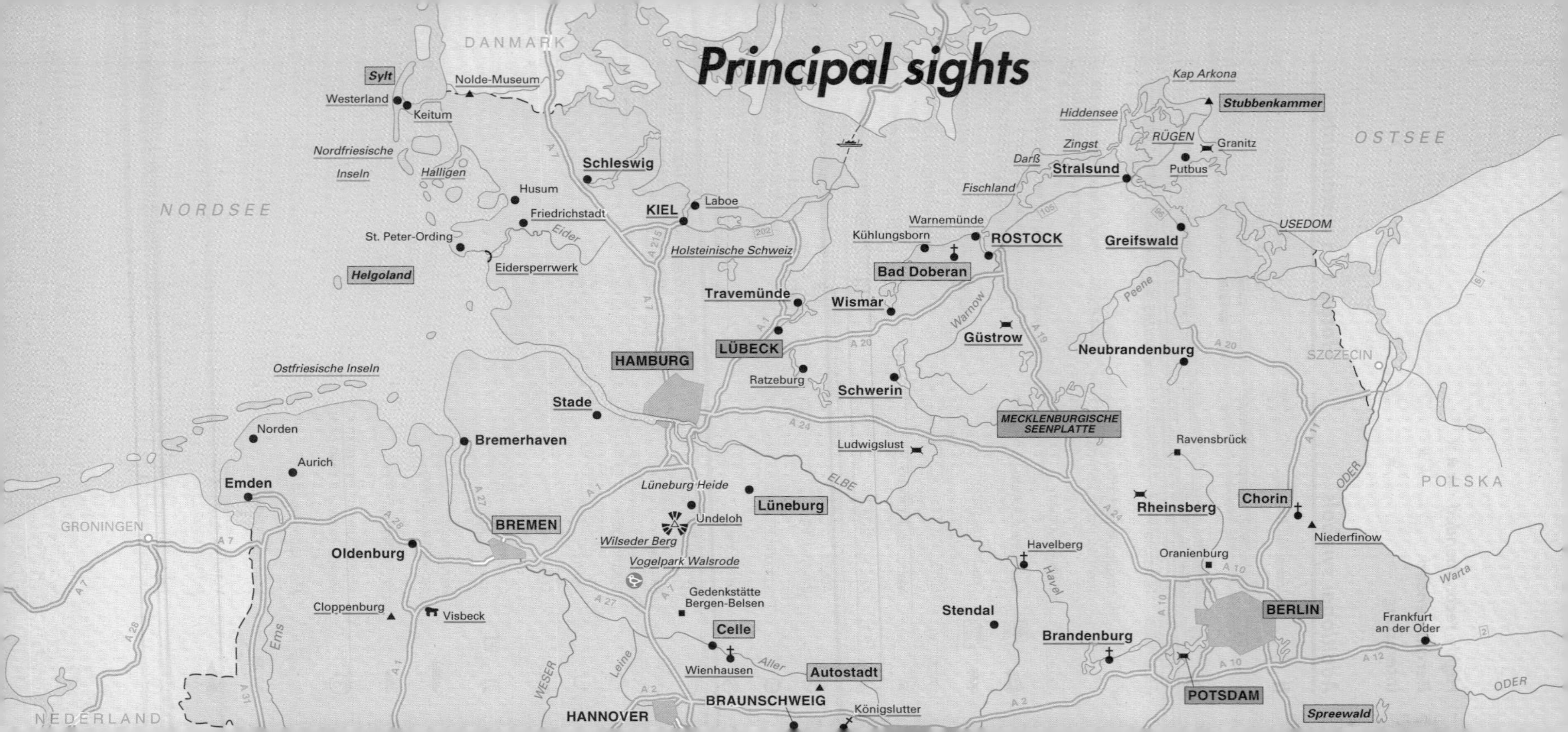

Tecklenburg
Hameln
Hildesheim
Wolfenbüttel
Lübbenau
Branitz
Goslar
Halberstadt
Wittenberg
Hülshoff
Münster
Lemgo
Hämelschenburg
Bielefeld
ARNHEM
Wernigerode
Quedlinburg
Dessau
Wörlitz
Einbeck
Anholt
Vischering
Vornholz
Corvey
Höxter
Harz
Landsberg
Lembeck
RHEIN
Lippe
Weser Valley
ELBE
Saale
HALLE
Bautzen
Göttingen
Soest
Moritzburg
Görlitz
LEIPZIG
Meissen
ESSEN
DORTMUND
Wilhelmsthal
DRESDEN
St. Marienthal
Neuenburg
Pillnitz
Zittauer Gebirge
DUISBURG
KASSEL
Hann. Münden
Naumburg
Bad Kösen
Oybin
Rührgebiet
Sauerland
Unstrut
Freiberg
SÄCHSISCHE SCHWEIZ
Königstein
Buchenwald
Weimar
DÜSSELDORF
Attahöhle
ERFURT
Jena
CHEMNITZ
Fulda
Gotha
Eisenach
Augustusburg
Zons
Bad Berleburg
Altenberg
Eder
KÖLN
Weiße Elster
Werra
Oberhof
Ilmenau
Rudolstadt
Annaberg-Buchholz
Marburg
MEUSE
Augustusburg
AACHEN
Kornelimünster
Oberes Saaletal
Thüringer Wald
Saalburg
Erzgebirge
Ohře
BONN
Rur-Dam
Lahn
Fulda
Wasserkuppe
Klingenthal
PRAHA
Lahntal
Arnsburg
Bad Münstereifel
Wetzlar
LIÈGE
Limburg
Rhön
Coburg
Maria Laach
Münzenberg
ČESKÁ REPUBLIKA
Monschau
Koblenz
Taunus
Friedberg-Bad Nauheim
Frankenwald
Nürburgring
Bad Ems
BELGIQUE
Großer Feldberg
Wallfahrtskirche Vierzehnheiligen
Fichtelgebirge
Eltz
LORELEY
FRANKFURT am Main
Eifel
Main
Eberbach
Sanspareil
Luisenburg
Maare
Moselle
Bayreuth
RHEINTAL
WIESBADEN
Bamberg
Manderscheid
Fränkische Schweiz
PLZEŇ
MAINZ
Volkach
Kirchberg
Rüdesheim
Ebrach
MOSELTAL
Bingen
WÜRZBURG
Regnitz
Vitava
Darmstadt
Gößweinstein
Bernkastel-Kues
RHEIN
Neuhaus
Main
Weißenstein
GRD DUCHÉ
Hunsrück
Bad Kreuznach
Trier
Otava
Pegnitz
Worms
Idar-Oberstein
NÜRNBERG

NEDERLAND
BELGIQUE
ČESKÁ REPUBLIKA
HANNOVER
BRAUNSCHWEIG
Autostadt ★★
Wolfenbüttel ★★
★ Hildesheim
MAGDEBURG ★★
POTSDAM ★★★
Wittenberg
Dessau
Wörlitz ★★
Halberstadt
★ Wernigerode
Quedlinburg ★
Harz ★★
★★ Goslar
★ HALLE
LEIPZIG ★
Branitz ★★
Bautzen
★ Görlitz
Zittau
★ Moritzburg
★ Meissen
DRESDEN ★★★
Bad Schandau ★
SÄCHSISCHE SCHWEIZ ★★★
Freiberg ★
CHEMNITZ
Annaberg-Buchholz ★
★ Neuenburg
★ Bad Kösen
Naumburg ★★
★★ Weimar
★ ERFURT
Jena
★ Eisenach
★★ Thüringer Wald
★ Coburg
Kulmbach
Fichtelgebirge ★
Luisenburg ★★
Bayreuth ★
★★ Wallfahrtskirche Vierzehnheiligen
★★ Bamberg
Osnabrück
Enschede
Bielefeld
Münster
ARNHEM
ESSEN
DORTMUND
DUISBURG
DÜSSELDORF
KASSEL
★★★ KÖLN
★ AACHEN
Augustusburg ★★
BONN ★
LIÈGE
★★ Monschau
★ Bad Münstereifel
★ Maria Laach
★★ Eltz
Koblenz ★
RHEINTAL ★★★
★ MAINZ
WIESBADEN
FRANKFURT am Main
PRAHA
PLZEŇ
Aller
Ems
WESER
Leine
Weser
Lippe
RHEIN
MEUSE
Rur
Eder
Fulda
Werra
Lahn
Moselle
Main
Unstrut
Saale
ELBE
Weiße Elster
Neisse
Oder
Ohře
5
6
7

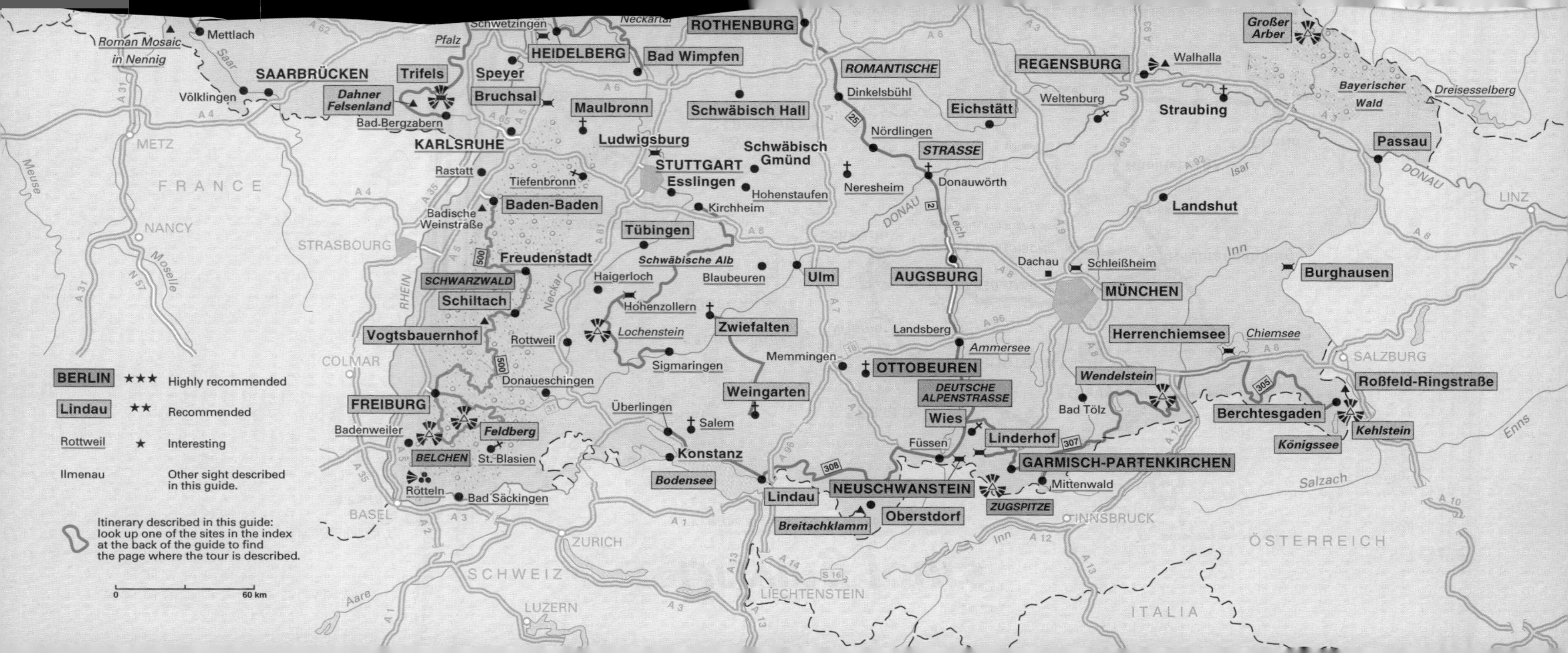
BERLIN ★★★ Highly recommended
Lindau ★★ Recommended
Rottweil ★ Interesting
Ilmenau Other sight described in this guide.
Itinerary described in this guide: look up one of the sites in the index at the back of the guide to find the page where the tour is described.
0
60 km
ROTHENBURG
HEIDELBERG
Bad Wimpfen
SAARBRÜCKEN
Trifels
Speyer
Bruchsal
Dahner Felsenland
Maulbronn
Schwäbisch Hall
ROMANTISCHE
STRASSE
REGENSBURG
Eichstätt
Straubing
Großer Arber
Bayerischer Wald
Dreisesselberg
Walhalla
Weltenburg
Passau
KARLSRUHE
Ludwigsburg
STUTTGART
Schwäbisch Gmünd
Esslingen
Hohenstaufen
Kirchheim
Neresheim
Donauwörth
Nördlingen
Dinkelsbühl
Landshut
Baden-Baden
Tübingen
Schwäbische Alb
Haigerloch
Hohenzollern
Lochenstein
Blaubeuren
Ulm
AUGSBURG
MÜNCHEN
Dachau
Schleißheim
Burghausen
Freudenstadt
SCHWARZWALD
Schiltach
Vogtsbauernhof
Rottweil
Zwiefalten
Sigmaringen
Landsberg
Ammersee
Herrenchiemsee
Chiemsee
Memmingen
OTTOBEUREN
DEUTSCHE ALPENSTRASSE
Wendelstein
Weingarten
Donaueschingen
Überlingen
Salem
FREIBURG
Feldberg
Badenweiler
BELCHEN
St. Blasien
Rötteln
Bad Säckingen
Konstanz
Bodensee
Lindau
NEUSCHWANSTEIN
Breitachklamm
Oberstdorf
Wies
Füssen
Linderhof
GARMISCH-PARTENKIRCHEN
ZUGSPITZE
Mittenwald
Bad Tölz
Berchtesgaden
Königssee
Kehlstein
Roßfeld-Ringstraße
Roman Mosaic in Nennig
Mettlach
Völklingen
Bad-Bergzabern
Rastatt
Tiefenbronn
Badische Weinstraße
Schwetzingen
Neckartal
Pfalz
METZ
NANCY
STRASBOURG
COLMAR
BASEL
ZURICH
LUZERN
INNSBRUCK
SALZBURG
LINZ
FRANCE
SCHWEIZ
LIECHTENSTEIN
ÖSTERREICH
ITALIA
Meuse
Moselle
Saar
RHEIN
Neckar
DONAU
Lech
Isar
Inn
Salzach
Enns
Aare

Driving tours

For descriptions of these tours, turn to the Practical Points section following.

1 Hamburg and Schleswig-Holstein: 550 km / 342 mi (6 days)
2 Baltic Sea, Mecklenburg-Vorpommern: 650 km / 380 mi (7 days)
3 Bremen, Hamburg and Lower Saxony: 550 km / 342 mi (5 days)
4 Berlin and Brandenburg: 600 km / 373 mi (6 days)
5 Harz, Thuringia, Saxony-Anhalt and Leipzig: 750km / 466 mi (7 days)
6 Saxony (Dresden), Zittau and Erzgebirge: 650 km / 380 mi (7 days)
7 Palatinate, Rhineland and Moselle: 950 km / 570 mi (9 days)
8 Nuremberg and Franconia: 650km / 380 mi (7 days)
9 Baden-Württemberg and Lake Constance: 850 km / 510 mi (8 days)
10 Munich and the Bavarian Alps: 650 km / 380 mi (7 days)
0 60 km
GRD DUCHÉ
LUXEMBOURG
Trier ★★
Bernkastel-Kues ★
Idar-Oberstein
Darmstadt
★★ WÜRZBURG
Weißenstein ★
★ Worms
Bergstraße
Main
★ Bad Mergentheim
MANNHEIM
HEIDELBERG ★★
ROTHENBURG ★★★
NÜRNBERG ★★
Pegnitz
★ Speyer
SAARBRÜCKEN
Saar
★★ Trifels
Bruchsal ★★
★★ Schwäbisch Hall
Dinkelsbühl ★
Weißenburg
REGENSBURG
Maulbronn ★★
ROMANTISCHE STRASSE ★★
Eichstätt ★★
Otava
Vitava
METZ
★ KARLSRUHE
Ludwigsburg ★
★ Nördlingen
DONAU
Isar
Passau
FRANCE
★ Rastatt
Baden-Baden ★★
STUTTGART ★
LINZ
STRASBOURG
SCHWARZWALD ★★★
Neckar
Bad Urach
AUGSBURG ★★
Inn
★★ Tübingen
Ulm ★★
MÜNCHEN ★★★
Burghausen ★★
★ Freudenstadt
Zwiefalten ★★
Lech
RHIN
Schiltach ★★
★ Chiemsee
Vogtsbauernhof ★★
Bad Schussenried
★★ Herrenchiemsee
Ruhpolding ★
SALZBURG
★★ FREIBURG
Landsberg ★
Donau
Donaueschingen ★
★ Schliersee
Titisee ★★
ROMANTISCHE STRASSE ★★
Weingarten ★★
Berchtesgaden ★★
Feldberg ★★
Ravensburg
★ Bad Wiessee
Wendelstein ★★
Enns
Meersburg ★
BELCHEN ★★★
★ Füssen
DEUTSCHE ALPENSTRASSE ★★★
★ Konstanz
★★★ NEUSCHWANSTEIN
★★ Bodensee
GARMISCH-PARTENKIRCHEN ★★★
Salzach
BASEL
Lindau ★★
★★★ ZUGSPITZE
ZURICH
INNSBRUCK
ÖSTERREICH
LIECHTENSTEIN
Aare
LUZERN
SCHWEIZ
ITALIA

Beach at Fischland peninsula.

T. Krieger/MICHELIN

Practical Points

Planning your Trip

Useful Addresses

Tourist Organisations

Information on travel arrangements and accommodation and a variety of brochures are available from the **German National Tourist Office**. For on-line information refer to www.germany-tourism.de, the German National Tourist Office website.
Most German cities have websites, the addresses of which are generally composed of the city name, eg www.karlsruhe.de is the website for Karlsruhe.

Chicago: German National Tourist Office Chicago, PO Box 59594, Chicago, IL 60659-9594, ☎ (773) 539-6303, fax (773) 539-6378, gntoch@aol.com, www.cometogermany.com

Johannesburg: German National Tourist Office, c/o Lufthansa German Airlines, PO Box 412246, Craighall, 2024 Johannesburg, ☎ (011) 325 1927, fax (011) 325 0867.

London: German National Tourist Office, PO Box 2695, London W1A 3TN, ☎ (020) 7317 0908, ☎ 09001 600 100 (24hr brochure line, calls cost 60p/min), fax (020) 7317 0917, gntolon@d-z-t.com, www.germany-tourism.co.uk

New York: German National Tourist Office, 122 East 42nd Street, New York, NY 10168-0072, ☎ (212) 661-7200, toll-free (800) 651-7010, fax (212) 661-7174, www.cometogermany.com

Sydney: German National Tourist Office, GPO Box 1461, Sydney NSW 2001, ☎ (02) 8296 0488, fax (02) 8296 0487, gnto@germany.org.au

Toronto: German National Tourist Office, 480 University Avenue, Suite 1410, Toronto, ON, M5G 1V2, ☎ (416) 968-1685, fax (416) 968-0562, info@gnto.ca, www.cometogermany.com

Cultural Organisations

The Goethe-Institut websites for each of the cities below can be accessed via www.goethe.de

Goethe-Institut Johannesburg, 119 Jan Smuts Ave, Parkwood 2193, Johannesburg, ☎ (011) 442 3232, fax (011) 442 3738.

Goethe-Institut London, 50 Princes Gate, Exhibition Road, London SW7 2PH, ☎ (020) 7596 4000, fax (020) 7594 0240.

Goethe-Institut New York, 1014 Fifth Avenue, New York, NY 10028, ☎ (212) 439-8700, fax (212) 439-8705.

Goethe-Institut Ottawa, 47 Clarence Street, Suite 480, Ottawa, ON, K1N 9K1, ☎ (613) 241-0273, fax (613) 241-9790

Goethe-Institut Sydney, 90 Ocean Street, Woollahra, NSW 2025, ☎ (02) 8356 8333, fax (02) 8356 8314.

Embassies and Consulatess

In Australia

Embassy of the Federal Republic of Germany, 119 Empire Circuit, Yarralumla ACT 2600, ☎ (02) 6270 1911, fax (02) 6270 1951, info1@germanembassy.org.au, www.germanembassy.org.au

Consulate General of the Republic of Germany, Sydney, 13 Trelawney Street, Woollahra NSW 2025, ☎ (02) 9328 7733, fax (02) 9327 9649, info@sydney.diplo.de

In Canada

Embassy of the Federal Republic of Germany, 1 Waverley Street, Ottawa, ON, K2P 0T8, ☎ (613) 232-1101, fax (613) 594-9330, germanembassyottawa@on.aibn.com, www.ottawa.diplo.de
Postal address: PO Box 379, Postal Station "A", Ottawa, ON, K1N 8V4

Consulate General of the Federal Republic of Germany, 77 Bloor Street West, Suite 1703, Toronto, ON, M5S 1M2, ☎ (416) 925 28 13, fax (416) 925 28 18, www.germanconsulatetoronto.ca
Postal address: Consulate General of the Federal Republic of Germany Postal Station "P" Box 523 Toronto, ON, M5S 2T1

In South Africa

Embassy of the Federal Republic of Germany, 180 Blackwood Street, Arcadia, Pretoria 0083, ☎ (012) 427 89 00, fax (012) 343 94 01, germanembassypretoria@gonet.co.za
Postal address: PO Box 2023, Pretoria 0001

Consulate-General of the Federal Republic of Germany, 19th Floor, Safmarine House, 22 Riebeek Street, Cape Town 8001, ☎ (021) 405 30 00, fax (021) 424 94 03, info@germanconsulatecapetown.co.za
Postal address: PO Box 4273, Cape Town 8000

In the United Kingdom

Embassy of the Federal Republic of Germany, 23 Belgrave Square, London SW1X 8PZ, ☎ (020) 7824 1300, fax (020) 7824 1449, www.german-embassy.org.uk

Consulate General of the Federal Republic of Germany, 16 Eglinton Crescent, Edinburgh EH 12 5DG, Scotland, ☎ (0131) 337 2323, fax (0131) 346 1578

IN THE UNITED STATES

Embassy of the Federal Republic of Germany, 4645 Reservoir Road NW, Washington, DC 20007-1998, ☎ (202) 298-4000, www.germany-info.org

Consulate General of the Federal Republic of Germany, 871, United Nations Plaza (1st Avenue @ 49th Street), New York, NY 10017, ☎ (212) 610-9700, fax (212) 610-9702, www.germanconsulate.org/newyork

IN GERMANY

American Embassy, Neustädtische Kirchstraße 4-5, 10117 Berlin, ☎ 030-8 30 50, fax 030-2 38 62 90, www.usembassy.de

American Consulate-General, Willi-Becker-Allee 10, 40227 Düsseldorf, ☎ 0211-7 88 89 27, fax 0211-7 88 89 38

Australian Embassy, Wallstraße 76–79, 10179 Berlin, ☎ 030-88 00 88-0, fax 030-8 80 08 82 10, www.australian-embassy.de

Australian Consulate-General, Grüneburgweg 58–62, 60322 Frankfurt am Main, ☎ 069-90 55 80, fax 069-90 55 81 09

British Embassy Berlin, Wilhelmstraße 70-71, 10117 Berlin, ☎ 030-20 45 7-0, www.britischebotschaft.de

British Consulate-General, Yorckstraße 19, Düsseldorf 40476, ☎ 0211-94 48-0, fax 0211-48 81 90

Canadian Embassy, Friedrichstraße 95, 10117 Berlin, ☎ 030-20 31 20, fax 030-20 31 25 90, www.kanada-info.de

Consular Services Section, Canadian Embassy, Friedrichstrasse 95, 10117 Berlin, ☎ 030-2031-2470, fax 030-2031-2457

South African Embassy, Tiergartenstraße 18, 10785 Berlin, ☎ 030-22 07 30, fax 030-22 07 31 90, www.suedafrika.org

Wannsee.

J. Gläser/Presse- und Informationsamt des Landes Berlin

South African Consulate-General, Sendlinger-Tor-Platz 5, 80336 München, ☎ 089-2 31 16 30, fax 089-23 11 63 63

TOURIST INFORMATION ON SITE

Tourist offices – Tourist offices are marked on the town plans in this guide by the ℹ symbol. The address and telephone number of the tourist office is found under 'Location' in the descriptive part of the guide.

Formalities

DOCUMENTS

Passport – Visitors entering Germany must be in possession of a valid national passport. Citizens of European Union countries need only a national identity card. In case of loss or theft, report to the embassy or consulate and the local police.

Driving licence – A valid national or international driving licence is required to drive in Germany and third-party insurance cover is compulsory; it is advisable to obtain an International Insurance Certificate (Green Card) from your insurer. If you are bringing your own car into the country, you will need the vehicle registration papers.

HEALTH

British citizens should apply to their local post office for an E111 Form (application form available from the post office), which entitles the holder to emergency treatment for accidents or unexpected illness in EU countries. Non-EU residents should check that their private health insurance policy covers them for travel abroad, and if necessary take out supplementary medical insurance with specific overseas coverage. All prescription drugs should be clearly labelled, and we recommend that you carry a copy of the prescription with you.

Seasons

THE BEST TIME

Whatever the season, the weather in Germany is subject to enormous variation. The period when you are most likely to find good weather extends from May to October (and it may even be too hot during high summer in Baden-Württemberg and Bavaria). Autumn and spring, when tourist sights are less crowded, can be the perfect time to discover the country. In any case, it is sensible to pack some waterproof clothing whenever you plan to go. Before you leave, don't forget to find out about any festivals, fairs or other events which may considerably increase the number of visitors in certain towns and make finding a room difficult (see 'Events and Festivals' at the end of this chapter). Skiers will find snow-covered slopes from the end of November until the end of February.

Public holidays

1 Jan, **6 Jan** (in Baden-Württemberg, Bayern and Sachsen-Anhalt only), **Good Fri**, **Easter Day**, **Easter Mon**, **1 May**, **Ascension**, **Whit Sun** and **Mon**, **Corpus Christi** (in Baden-Württemberg, Bayern, Hessen, Nordrhein-Westfalen, Rheinland-Pfalz, Saarland, Sachsen, Thüringen and those communities with a predominantly Roman Catholic population only), **15 Aug** (in Roman Catholic communities in Saarland and Bayern only), **3 Oct** (Day of German Unity), **31 Oct** (Reformation Day, celebrated in the new Federal States, ie Brandenburg, Mecklenburg-Vorpommern, Sachsen, Sachsen-Anhalt and Thüringen only), **1 Nov** (in Baden-Württemberg, Bayern, Nordrhein-Westfalen, Rheinland-Pflaz and Saarland only), **Buß- und Bettag** (Day of Repentance and Prayer, usually third Wed in Nov, observed in Sachsen only), **25**, **26** and **31 Dec**.

Time Differences

In winter, standard time is Greenwich Mean Time + 1 hour. In summer the clocks go forward an hour to give Summer Time (GMT + 2 hours) from the last weekend in March to the last weekend in October.

Special Needs

A book entitled *Handicapped-Reisen Deutschland* (€14.80, plus postage) is published by FMG-Verlag GmbH, Postfach 2154, 40644 Meerbusch, ☎ 02159-815622, fax 02159-815624, www.fmg-verlag.de. It lists 890 wheelchair-friendly hotels, apartments and youth hostels with wheelchair facilities, giving detailed information for wheelchair users. A similarly helpful publication is Reise-ABC (€5, plus postage) published by Bundesverband Selbsthilfe Körperbehinderter e.V., Postfach 20, 74236 Krautheim, ☎ 06294-4281-0, fax 06294-4281-79, www.bsk-ev.de. Disabled motorists should take note that a disabled car badge/sticker does not entitle them to unrestricted parking, as it does in the UK (local disabled residents are granted special parking permits only in exceptional circumstances). Apart from this, Germany is on the whole a well-equipped country for disabled visitors.

Transport

Getting there

By air

Various international airline companies operate regular services to one or all of Germany's international airports (Berlin, Bremen, Dresden, Düsseldorf, Frankfurt/Main, Hamburg, Hannover, Köln/Bonn, Leipzig, München, Münster/Osnabrück, Nürnberg, Saarbrücken, Stuttgart). The international German airline **Lufthansa** can be contacted on the following numbers:

Australia, ☎ 1300 655 727
Canada, ☎ 1-800 563 5954
South Africa, ☎ 0861 842538
UK, ☎ 0870 8377 747
USA, ☎ 800 399-5838, 800 645-3880

Information about flights to and in Germany can also be obtained, and reservations made, on their website at www.lufthansa.com.

Budget airlines **Ryanair** and easyJet also fly to several destinations in Germany from various cities in Europe. They are both ticketless airlines. Ryanair serves Berlin, Hamburg, Düsseldorf, Leipzig, Erfurt, Friedrichshafen and Karlsruhe/Baden from London Stansted airport. For information and reservations, visit www.ryanair.com or contact one of their European call centres. They can be contacted on ☎ 0871 246 0000 (£0.10/min) from within the UK, on ☎ 01 90 170 100 in Germany (€0.62/min), and on ☎ +353 1 249 7700 from the rest of the world. Web-based airline **easyJet** flies to Berlin, Cologne/Bonn, Dortmund and Munich from various airports in the UK. Fares are quoted one way and discounts granted for online booking. For information and reservations, visit www.easyjet.com, or call ☎ 0871 7500 100 in the UK for departures within two weeks.

By car

When driving to the Continent the ideal ports of entry for Germany are Cuxhaven (from Harwich, 19hr sailing), Rotterdam (from Hull, 11hr sailing), the Hook of Holland (from Harwich, 3hr 40min by fast ferry), Zeebrugge (from Hull, 11hr sailing) and Calais (from Dover, 1hr 15min sailing; or Folkestone via the Channel Tunnel, 35min crossing). From these ports there is a wide choice of routes using motorway or national roads into Germany.

Michelin offers motorists and motorcyclists a free route planning service on the Internet, at www.ViaMichelin.co.uk For a proposed journey, you can determine possible stopovers between departure point and destination, and define your required route using various criteria (such as time, distance, use of motorways, road tolls etc). You are given information on mileage, journey time, hotels and restaurants along the way (selected from the Michelin Red Guide), and map extracts that can be printed out.

Cuxhaven to Berlin 404km/251mi.

Rotterdam to Berlin via Hannover 698km/434mi.

Hook of Holland to Munich via Bonn, Mainz, Stuttgart and Augsburg 845km/525mi.

Zeebrugge to Munich via Karlsruhe, Stuttgart and Augsburg 853km/530mi.

Calais to Cologne via Aachen 417km/259mi.

By coach

Eurolines serves many cities in Germany from the UK. The coaches are all well-equipped for maximum comfort, with air conditioning, WC, TV/video, reclining seats etc. Journey times can be quite long (from London Victoria it takes around 18hr to Berlin, 19hr to Munich and 13hr to Cologne), but tickets are inexpensive, especially when booked in advance (a 30-day advance return to Berlin costs around €76).

The **Eurolines Pass**, valid for 15, 30 or 60 days allows you to travel for a set price between a choice of 35 cities across Europe, with internal connections in Germany available between Frankfurt and Munich (low/high season prices for adults from €219/€287 for a 15-day pass to €390/€490 for a 60-day pass). A **Mini Pass** is also available for travel between London, Cologne and Paris (cost from €107).

There are discounts for children, youths (under 26) and senior citizens. Children under 4 travel free.

For information and reservations, call ☎ 08705 143219 in the UK, or visit the Eurolines website at www.eurolines.co.uk.

G. Schneider/Press- und Informationsamt des Landes Berlin

By train and by sea

The principal travel routes by rail and sea are from:

London Victoria or Charing Cross Station, via Dover and Calais (sailing: 1hr 15min);

London Liverpool Street Station, via Harwich and the Hook of Holland (sailing: 7-9hr) or Cuxhaven (on the mouth of the River Elbe, sailing: 19hr);

London to Brussels via Folkestone and Calais (the Channel Tunnel), travel time to Brussels 2hr 20min;

Hull to Rotterdam (sailing: 11hr).

For details of rail tickets, see Getting around – By train below.

Getting Around

By car

Driving Regulations – Traffic in Germany drives on the right. Drivers in cities in which trams operate should be extra careful when looking to check that the road is clear before crossing tramlines. The maximum speed permitted in built-up areas is 50kph/31mph. On the open road the maximum increases to 100kph/62mph. There is no official limit on motorways *(Autobahnen)*, but drivers are recommended not to exceed 130kph/81mph. There is a compulsory speed limit of 80kph/50mph on roads and motorways for vehicles with trailers. In Germany careless or reckless driving is considered a serious offence and fines can be stiff. The maximum limit for level of alcohol in the blood is 0.5ml/g.

German motorways (signposted 'A' for *Autobahn*) are toll-free and are well equipped with service areas. These are usually open round the clock and provide the following facilities: petrol, spare parts and accessories, washrooms, toilets, public telephones, refreshments, accommodation and first-aid equipment.

Important Warning Signs:

Anfang	beginning	*Rechts einbiegen*	turn right
Ausfahrt	exit	*Links einbiegen*	turn left
Baustelle	roadworks, building site	*Rollsplitt*	gravel chippings
Einbahnstraße	one-way street	*Stau*	hold-up, traffic jam
Ende	end	*Unfall*	accident
Einfahrt	entrance	*Umleitung*	diversion
Gefahr	danger	*Verengte Fahrbahn*	road narrows
LKW	HGV; truck	*Vorfahrt*	priority
PKW	private car	*Vorsicht*	Look out!

City centres are very often reserved for pedestrians. It is possible to park in one of the many covered car parks *(Parkhaus)*.

It is compulsory to wear a seatbelt in the back as well as in the front of the car. Children under the age of 12, or less than 1.5m/4ft 11in tall, are required by law to be seated and fastened in a suitable child car seat; there are fines for non-compliance. It is a legal requirement to carry the regulation red emergency triangle, for warning other motorists of a breakdown or enforced roadside halt, and a first-aid box (including disposable gloves and rescue blanket).

In Germany emergency services are always given priority and drivers should pull over to the side of the road.

Emergency telephone numbers:
Police: 110
Fire brigade: 112

Breakdown Service – For 24-hour breakdown service on motorways and main roads, call ☎ 01 80/2 22 22 22 (or ☎ 22 22 22 from mobile phones). This is taken care of on main roads and motorways throughout Germany by the ADAC (www.adac.de), and also by the Auto Club Europa in the eastern part of the country (☎ 01 802/34 35 36). Roadside breakdown services can be called from one of the emergency phones – small arrows on the posts along the road indicate the direction of the nearest emergency phone.

On-the-spot repairs are free, as only the cost of replacement parts or towing is charged. Motorists ringing this service should ask specifically for the "Straßenwachthilfe" (road patrol assistance).

The Michelin Guide Deutschland lists the numbers to use to contact the ADAC service in all big towns.

Petrol – The following grades of petrol (gas) are available in Germany:
Super Plus Bleifrei: Super unleaded (98 octane)
Normal Bleifrei: Standard unleaded (95 octane)
Diesel

Leaded petrol is no longer available in Germany. A lead substitute additive can be purchased at petrol stations for vehicles requiring leaded petrol and added to the fuel tank.

Car Hire – Cars may be hired only if the driver is over 23 and has held a driving licence for more than one year.

The major car hire firms have offices at airports and main stations and in large towns. Also remember that it is generally cheaper to arrange car hire before travelling to Germany. Some useful numbers include:
Avis: ☎ 0 18 05/55 77 55, fax 0 18 05/21 77 11, www.avis.com
Europcar: ☎ 0 18 05/80 00, fax 0 40 52/01 82 610, www.europcar.com
Hertz: ☎ 0 18 05/33 35 35, fax 0 61 96/93 71 16, www.hertz.com
Sixt: ☎ 0 18 05/25 25 25, www.e-sixt.com

By train

Tickets and Fares – Germany's leading transport organisation, **Deutsche Bahn (DB)** provides a quick and reliable means of transport. Most cities are served by DB's high-speed train, the InterCityExpress, or InterCity/EuroCity (IC/EC) services; regional centres are connected by a modern fleet of Regional Express trains.

Special offer tickets: **Euro Domino** – for 3-8 days' unlimited travel all over Germany (available for adults, youths and senior citizens); **Bahncards** – 25% or 50% discount for frequent travellers to Germany; **InterRail** – the classic European rail pass for unlimited rail travel for 16 days (1 zone), 22 days (2 zones) or 1 month (global pass).

Savertickets and discounted fares for groups and mini groups are also available.

Children under fourteen may travel for free, if accompanied by their parents or grandparents.

NightTrain services and Motorail bookings are also available.

For further information and reservations, apply to:
Deutsche Bahn UK Booking Centre, ☎ 0870 243 5363 (Mon-Fri 9am-5pm), sales@bahn.co.uk, www.bahn.co.uk.

Information can also be obtained from Deutsche Bahn's website, www.bahn.de (for English text, select the "Int. Guests" option).

Rail Europe, 178 Piccadilly, London W1, ☎ 08705 848 848 (brochure hotline: ☎ 08708 30 60 30), www.raileurope.co.uk
DER Travel Service, 18 Conduit Street, London W1S 2XN, ☎ 020-7290-1111, fax 020-7629-7442, sales@dertravel.co.uk, www.dertravel.co.uk

By bus

The bus can be a handy way of travelling round certain regions of Germany (like the Harz) or in areas where there is no train service. Bus stations are generally found near to railway stations. For information on prices and timetables, contact **Deutsche Touring Gmbh**, Am Römerhof 17, 60486 Frankfurt am Main, ☎ (069) 79 03 50, www.deutsche-touring.com

By air

There are numerous internal flights in Germany, most of them operated by Lufthansa (☎ 0180-5 83 84 26, www.lufthansa.com). Local airports, such as Augsburg or Kiel are served by smaller airlines. **Deutsche BA** (☎ 01805/35 93 22, www.flydba.com) is Lufthansa's main competitor and the German wing of British Airways and often has more competitive rates than the national carrier.
It's worthwhile noting that it normally costs at least €130 for a return flight between 2 German towns in economy class with Lufthansa (not including special offers). Children up to the age of 11 can take advantage of savings of between 33% and 50% of the price of the ticket.

Where to Stay

Addresses in the guide

The **Directory** sections in the main text of the guide list a selection of hotels chosen for their value for money, location or character. We have tried to cater for all budgets. However, please note that certain regions (like the Bavarian Alps or the Black Forest) are more expensive than others and that there is sometimes a huge gap between accommodation prices in a large city like Munich or Berlin and those of smaller towns. Wherever you plan to stay, it is a good idea to reserve your accommodation in advance. Be aware that during festivals, fairs and other cultural events it is almost impossible to find last-minute accommodation: finding a room in Bayreuth during the festival, for example, is impossible without a reservation. If you wish to stay in Munich during *Oktoberfest* you will need to reserve at least 6 months in advance.
Our selection of hotels, guesthouses and hostels is divided into three price brackets and does not include breakfast; any variation on this (VAT or breakfast included in the price) is pointed out. Please note that in regions and cities popular with tourists, there is often a significant difference in price between high and low season, so please check rates before you go ahead with a reservation. For each hotel, the first figure refers to the price of a single room, the second figure to the price of a double room.

Our selection is divided into three price brackets:
- **Budget**, represented by a ⊖ symbol (€60 or under for a room): modest but generally comfortable hotels
- **Moderate**, represented by a ⊖⊖ symbol (rooms from €60 to €90): pleasant establishments
- **Expensive**, represented by a ⊖⊖⊖ symbol (rooms for over €90): hotels which, although pricey, are particularly charming, guaranteeing a memorable stay

The importance of reserving your room in advance cannot be emphasised enough, particularly in regions which are especially popular with tourists (Berlin, Southern Germany), during the period between May and October. Tourist information offices offer lists of local accommodation, including self-catering accommodation, rural guesthouses and castle hotels and are able to reserve rooms on your behalf. Breakfast in hotels normally consists of a large buffet.
The **ADZ (Allgemeine Deutsche Zimmerreservierung)**, Corneliusstraße 34, D-60325 Frankfurt am Main. ☎ (069) 74 07 67, fax (069) 75 10 56, is a German room reservation service, able to reserve rooms in hotels, guesthouses and hostels throughout Germany. Reservations can be made up to 5 weeks in advance. A deposit may be required. English spoken.

Bed and Breakfast-"Garni"

The sign *Zimmer frei* outside private houses indicates that guestrooms are available. Final prices quoted usually include tax, service charges, breakfast etc.

Camping

With around 2 200 campsites, Germany is has plenty of scope for camping. Most are closed between November and April, but 400 remain open all year. Allow around €2.50 to €5 to pitch a tent. More information is available from **Deutscher Camping-Club**, Mandlstraße 28, 80802 München, ☎ (089) 380 14 20, www.camping-club.de, or from **ADAC**, Am Westpark 8, D-81373 München, ☎ (089) 767 60, www.adac.de

Youth hostels-Jugendherbergen (JH)

Germany has more than 600 youth hostels. To obtain the list of establishments and an international hostelling card, contact **Deutsches Jugendherbergswerk**, Hauptverband, Bismarckstraße 8, D-32756 Detmold, ☎ (052 31) 740 10. It is possible to book accommodation online at www.djh.de. A bed in a dormitory costs around €15 to €25.

Self-catering

Renting a flat for a short period of time is common practice in Germany. Local tourist information offices normally have information on availability.

Farms

This type of accommodation is particularly well developed in Bavaria and in the wine-growing regions. A guide to farms with accommodation, *Urlaub auf dem Bauernhof* (price €9.90), is edited by DLG-Verlag, Eschborner Landstrasse 122, 60489 Frankfurt, ☎ 069/24 788-451, www.dlg-verlag.de

Castle hotels

A list of hotels and restaurants to be found in castles and other historic buildings is available from **European Castle Holidays GmbH**, Erika Köther Str. 56, D-67435 Königsbach, ☎ (06321) 96 84 87, www.european-castle.com or from **Gast Im Schloss**, Postfach 1428, 65527 Niedenhausen, ☎ (6127) 99 90 98, www.gast-im-schloss.de

The Michelin Guide Deutschland

For a more exhaustive list of hotels consult *The Michelin Guide Deutschland* which provides a whole host of details on Germany's hotels and restaurants.

Where to Eat

We offer a selection **restaurants** chosen for their location, atmosphere or originality. They are also divided into three categories: **Budget**, represented by a ⊖ symbol (meals for under €20), **Moderate**, represented by a ⊖⊖ symbol (meals between €20 et €40) and **Expensive**, represented by a ⊖⊖⊖ symbol (meals for over €40).

Bremer Touristik-Zentrale

The Michelin Guide Deutschland

The Michelin Guide Deutschland has a selection of 1 700 restaurants. Minimum and maximum prices are given for each establishment, along with practical information.

German cuisine

German food is more varied and better balanced than is generally supposed, and the composition and presentation of meals are in themselves original. Breakfast **(Frühstück)** – and there is plenty of it – includes cold meats and cheese. Lunch **(Mittagessen)** usually begins with soup, followed by a fish or meat main course always accompanied by a salad (lettuce, cucumber, shredded cabbage). **Imbisse**, small fast-food concerns, are to be found everywhere, in town or at the roadside. These offer the traditional **Bratwurst** (grilled sausage), sometimes accompanied by a potato salad, and usually washed down with beer (often on draught, **Bier vom Faß**). In the afternoon, you can stop for a break in one of the many coffee-houses, which offer a large selection of cakes, such as **Schwarzwälder Kirschtorte** (Black Forest cherry cake) or **Käsekuchen** (cheesecake). They also serve the somewhat lighter fruit tarts and the famous **strudel**, a mixture of fruit wrapped in crisp pastry. The coffee served with these pastries is always accompanied by cream **(Kaffeesahne)**. For the evening meal **(Abendessen)**, which the Germans take early, there will be a choice of cold meats **(Aufschnitt)** and cheeses served with a tremendous variety of breads.

Although each region has its own specialities, certain dishes are served all over the country: **Wiener Schnitzel** (veal cutlet fried in breadcrumbs), **Eisbein** (salted knuckle or shin of pork), **Sauerbraten** (beef in a brown sauce) and **Gulasch** (either in the form of soup or as a stew).

Beer and Wine – Germans are justifiably proud of their national beverage, produced by nearly 1 200 breweries throughout the country. Brewing techniques respect a purity law *(Reinheitsgebot)* decreed in 1516, whereby nothing but barley, hops and plain water may be used in the fabrication of beer (with the addition, today, of yeast).

German vineyards cover 69 000ha/170 500 acres, extending from Lake Constance to the Siebengebirge, and from Trier to Würzburg. The growers produce a great variety of wines from a wide range of grapes – as the visitor may discover in most bars and restaurants, sampling them by the glass *(offene Weine)*. Notable among the **white wines** – 80% of production – are the vigorous Rieslings of the Middle Rhine and those of the Moselle, Saar and Ruwer rivers, aromatic and refreshing; the high quality, delicate wines of the Rheingau; full-bodied and elegant Nahe wines; the potent wines of Franconia, verging sometimes on the bitter; and the many and varied wines of Baden and Württemberg. Among the **red wines**, particularly choice examples come from Rheinhessen and Württemberg, not forgetting the vigorous, well-balanced reds of the Palatinate and, above all, the wines of the Ahr, paradise of the Spätburgunder. Be sure to make the most of the inviting **Weinstuben** (wine cellars or wine bars) during your stay, where the best wines can be tasted by the glass.

Ph. Gajic/MICHELIN

Regional specialities

BAVARIA AND FRANCONIA

Leberknödel: Large dumplings of liver, bread and chopped onion, served in a clear soup.

Leberkäs: Minced beef, pork and liver, cooked in the form of a loaf.

Knödel: Dumplings of potato or soaked bread.

Haxen: Veal or pork trotters.

Schlachtschüssel: Breast of pork, liver sausage and black pudding, served with pickled cabbage and dumplings.

Rostbratwürste: Small sausages grilled over beechwood charcoal.

BADEN-WÜRTTEMBERG

Schneckensuppe: Soup with snails.

Spätzle: Egg-based pasta in long strips.

Maultaschen: Pasta stuffed with a mixture of meat, calves' brains and spinach.

Geschnetzeltes: Slices of veal in a cream sauce.

RHINELAND-PALATINATE

Sauerbraten: Beef marinated in wine vinegar, served with potato dumplings.

Reibekuchen: Small potato pancakes with apple or blueberry sauce.

Hämchen: Pork trotters with pickled cabbage and mashed potato.

Saumagen: Stuffed pork belly with pickled cabbage.

Schweinepfeffer: Highly seasoned, spicy pork in the form of a ragout, thickened with blood.

Federweißer: Partially fermented new wine, customarily accompanied by an onion tart.

HESSEN AND WESTPHALIA

Sulperknochen: Ears, trotters and tail of pork, served with pickled cabbage and pease pudding.

Töttchen: Ragout of brains and calf's head, cooked with herbs.

Pickert: Sweet potato cakes with raisins.

THURINGIA

Linsensuppe mit Thüringer Rotwurst: Lentil soup with Thuringian sausages.

SAXONY

Rinderzunge in Rosinen-Sauce: Calf's tongue in a grape sauce.

Dresdener Stollen: Raisin cake.

LOWER SAXONY AND SCHLESWIG-HOLSTEIN

Aalsuppe: Sweet-and-sour soup, made of eels, prunes, pears, vegetables, bacon and seasoning.

Labskaus: Favourite sailor's dish, basically beef, pork and salted herrings with potatoes and beetroot, served with gherkins and fried egg.

Buntes Huhn: Salt beef on a bed of diced vegetables.

Services

Concessions

For budget accommodation, refer directly to the Directory for each town; these list addresses divided into three price categories, including a budget category (⊖, rooms for less than €60).

Discounts

BY TRAIN

See above *(Transport – Getting around)* for information on reductions offered by Deutsche Bahn.

BY AIR

Often purchasing a ticket in advance will give you a cheaper fare. Several airlines, including Lufthansa, operate Frequent Flyer programmes that entitle passengers to free tickets once they have accumulated a certain number of air miles. Lufthansa's website lists special offers and discounts are given for online bookings. For flying between European cities, easyJet and Ryanair offer very low fares.

Discounts for young people under the age of 26

BY AIR

Many airlines give discounts for children and adults under 26. Children under the age of 2 usually travel free.

The KaDeWe in Berlin.

Ph. Gajic/MICHELIN

BY TRAIN

See the "Getting around – By train" section above.

Practical Information

Emergencies

Medical emergencies/First aid ☎ 112

Traffic accidents ☎ 110

Emergency telephones are available along the hard shoulder on motorways. There are also alarm buttons on S-Bahn and U-Bahn platforms.

Health

Make sure before you leave that you have adequate health insurance cover. The cost of medical treatment given in Germany is reimbursed for all European Union citizens (pick up an **E111** from any main post office or travel agent).

Medication for minor problems can be obtained from a **pharmacy** (signs with a red A for *Apotheke*). When they are closed, the pharmacies display the names of doctors on duty and emergency pharmacies.

It is also advisable to check whether you have **repatriation** insurance cover (check whether this is included in your car insurance or with your bank card).

Money

The euro has been the unit of currency in Germany since the beginning of 2002. Citizens of countries that are not part of the euro zone can change currency at airports and banks, as well as in some stations and hotels.

BANKS

Banks are closed on Saturdays and Sundays. They are open during the week from 9am to 12pm and from 1pm to 3.30pm (sometimes to 6pm). Bureaux de change *(Wechselstuben)* are usually open longer.

a. D17
b. N202
c. D30

Which road will get you there?
To find out, simply open a Michelin map!

The Michelin Atlases and new NATIONAL, REGIONAL, LOCAL and ZOOM map series offer clear, accurate mapping to help you plan your route and find your way.

CREDIT CARDS

Traveller's cheques and the main international credit cards (including Visa and Eurocard-Mastercard) are accepted in almost all shops, hotels and restaurants. You can also use these cards to withdraw money at cash dispensers.

In the event of loss or theft of your card, call the following numbers immediately: **Visa** ☎ (0800) 81 49 100, **Eurocard-Mastercard** ☎ (069) 79 33 19 10, **American Express** ☎ (069) 97 97 10 00

POST

Yellow is the trademark colour of the post office in Germany. Most post offices are open Mondays to Fridays from 8am to 6pm and on Saturdays from 8am to 12pm. Some of them, particularly at stations and airports in the big cities, are open longer. They are generally indicated in the Directory sections in this guide. Domestic postal rates apply to all of the countries in the European Union as well as to Turkey and Switzerland.

TELEPHONE

The international dialling code for Germany is **49**, so from the UK, for example, you would dial 00 49 + local dialling code **omitting** the initial 0 + subscriber's number

International dialling codes from Germany: 00 44 for the UK; 00 353 for Ireland; 00 1 for the USA and Canada; 00 61 for Australia; 00 27 for South Africa.

National directory enquiries ☎ 11 833

International directory enquiries ☎ 11 834

Public telephones: phonecards *(Telefonkarten)* for the increasingly card-operated public telephones can be bought at post offices and newspaper kiosks. Some phones also take bank cards.

Note that phone calls from hotel rooms are generally expensive.

Mobile phones with a Europe or World package are very handy for making calls within the country (the GSM 900 and GSM 1800 networks ensure global roaming). Please note that it is illegal to use your phone while driving.

ELECTRICITY

Voltage is 220 V and appliances use two-pin plugs.

NEWSPAPERS

Regional daily newspapers are widely read in Germany. The conservative *Frankfurter Allgemeine* and Munich's *Süddeutsche Zeitung* have a broad readership throughout Germany. Berlin's most popular daily paper is the *Tagesspiegel*, but the *Berliner Zeitung* and the *Tageszeitung* are also popular with readers in the capital. Among the national newspapers, the sensation-seeking daily *Bild* has a print run of over 5 million copies. *Die Welt* offers better quality news, *Focus* and *Der Spiegel* are excellent weeklies, and *Stern* and *Bunte* belong more to the tabloid category.

The main foreign newspapers are, of course, available at airports, stations and the larger newspaper kiosks.

TELEVISION

Germany has two national state television channels, **ARD** and **ZDF**. There are also regional channels such as Cologne's Westdeutscher Rundfunk (WDR) and Munich's Bayrischer Rundfunk (BR), and the Franco-German cultural television channel **Arte**. Numerous private channels have schedules that include soap operas, sitcoms and game shows. Although most of them target the general public (RTL 2, PRO 7, SAT 1 etc), there are some theme channels, such as the music channel VIVA – the German equivalent of MTV – and the sports channel DSF.

SHOPPING

On the whole, shops open between 9am and 10am, and close between 6.30pm 8pm. On Saturdays they close at 4pm (except for grocer's, butcher's and baker's shops, which close between 1pm and 2pm). Some bakeries open on Sunday mornings.

Sightseeing

The "Selected Sights" section gives the opening times and admission charges for monuments, museums, churches etc. On account of the ever-increasing cost of living and frequent variations in the opening times of these monuments, this information should only be used as a rough guide. It is intended for tourists who are travelling on their own and are not entitled to any reduction. With prior agreement, groups can obtain special conditions as regards both times and charges. Enquire at the ticket office before purchasing your tickets; age-related reductions, in particular, are available.

It is always a good idea to make enquiries by phone before setting off since certain monuments may be temporarily closed for restoration. Visiting conditions for churches are only specified if the interior is of particular interest, if there are set opening times or if there is an admission charge. Churches can generally not be visited during services. If a church is open only during services, visitors should behave with all due respect.

Museums

Museums are usually closed on Mondays. Art museums often have a late-night opening one evening per week. But remember, ticket offices close between 30min to 1hr before closing time.

Ideas for your Visit

Touring by car

For those who would like to do a tour by car over several days, we suggest ten itineraries which are shown on the map of touring programmes **at the front of this guide.**
You can also refer to the map of principal sights and read the in-depth descriptions in the "Selected Sights" section.

Hamburg and Schleswig-Holstein 1

550km/342mi-tour leaving from Hamburg – This tour through the Länder of Hamburg and Schleswig-Holstein provides an opportunity to explore the far north of Germany, a region with a glorious Hanseatic past. The country's second largest city, **Hamburg is a bustling port** set on the banks of the Elbe estuary; its central districts are ideal for a stroll, and the particularly well-stocked museums will be much appreciated by art lovers. A mere 70km/43mi from Hamburg is **Lübeck**. This delightful town in northern Germany has been on UNESCO's World Heritage list since 1987. Remarkably preserved, it boasts an exceptional collection of houses and monuments from many different periods. Not far from Lübeck, **Travemünde,** on the shores of the Baltic Sea, is renowned for its sandy beach, its very long seafront promenade and its casino. The tour continues northwards with the next port of call **Kiel, the gateway to Scandinavia.** Capital of Schleswig-Holstein, Kiel is an old maritime town steeped in a cheerful yet stylish atmosphere. The route then takes a northwesterly direction along the Baltic coast to **Schleswig**, an ideal place to relax and explore. Heading westwards, from one sea to the other, you will soon reach the island of **Sylt** and the North Frisian islands. The fragile sandy shores of these wild islands are pitted against the North Sea in a constant battle against marine erosion. Lastly, the peaceful seaside town of **Husum**, birthplace of the writer Theodor Storm, offers all the attractions of a modern tourist resort.

Salzspeicher in Lübeck.

J. Bouraly/MICHELIN

Baltic Sea, Mecklenburg-Vorpommern 2

650km/380mi-tour leaving from Neubrandenburg – This itinerary will give you a glimpse of a little-known Germany that is both wild and captivating. The town of **Neubrandenburg has a surprise in store with its** imposing medieval ramparts, miraculously spared by the Second World War. The journey continues westwards through the **Mecklenburg lake district, a well-preserved region and** one of the least populated in Germany. With countless lakes and a wide range of activities on offer, it will certainly appeal to nature lovers. **Schwerin** is without a doubt one of the most pleasant towns in northern Germany. Its refined architecture and the majestic charm of its castle set atop an island facing the old town add to the appeal of this city full of character. Our itinerary takes us north out of Schwerin and up to the coast. **Wismar**, with its red-brick buildings, provides an excellent introduction to the Baltic coast. The town's historic centre was classed a UNESCO World Heritage site in 2002. Dotted along the coast, the towns of **Bad Doberan**, **Rostock** and **Stralsund** are all worth a visit on your way to the island of **Rügen** with its surprising variety of landscapes; bands of dunes, land reclaimed from the sea, salt meadows, cultivated fields, endless mudflats (Watt, or Wadden) and prehistoric tumuli. It is, like the neighbouring island of **Usedom**, a very popular holiday destination, with pleasant seaside, health and spa resorts. Last stop on the itinerary is **Greifswald**, whose very old architecture reveals a Scandinavian influence.

Bremen, Hamburg and Lower Saxony 3

550km/342mi-tour leaving from Bremen – The bustling town of **Bremen is a true delight.** A large port and city of artistic interest where the Weser Renaissance style flourished, it has a number of parks and a charming riverside promenade. After a stop in **Hamburg**, 125km/78mi to the northeast *(see description in itinerary* 1 *)*, we invite you to explore **Lüneburg**, which owes its longstanding prosperity to salt. The town constitutes the gateway to the vast expanse of the **Lüneburg Heath**. In the face of the increasing advances of agriculture, attempts are being made to preserve this wild environment with its picturesque copses of birch, pine and juniper; from mid-August to mid-September, the carpet of heather in bloom is a magnificent sight. To the south of the Lüneburg Heath stands the aristocratic city of **Celle**. There are many reasons to stop here; treasures from the old city, a magnificently restored ducal palace, and a folklore and history museum to name but a few. For car fanatics, a trip to **Autostadt** – a vast automobile complex set up by Volkswagen about 60km/37mi from Celle – is a must. Here you will find generously landscaped areas of park and water, dotted with architecturally striking buildings. A stop in **Braunschweig** is followed by a leisurely look around the beautiful city of **Wölfenbuttel** with its exceptional collection of Renaissance houses. Further west, after **Hildesheim**, **Hannover** awaits with **its waterways** *(Maschsee)*, city forest and famous Herrenhausen gardens.

Berlin and Brandenburg 4

600km/373mi-tour leaving from Neubrandenburg – After a look around **Neubrandenburg** *(see description in itinerary* 2 *)*, head south to explore Schloß **Rheinsberg** where Frederick the Great, by his own admission, spent the best years of his life. Germany's vibrant capital is located 90km/56mi further south. The buzzing city of **Berlin** offers a wealth of culture and a very lively night-life. This amazing metropolis – one of the most extensive and among those with the largest number of parks and

© Partner für Berlin/FTB-Werbefotografie

Schloß Sanssouci, Potsdam.

gardens on the Old Continent – seems to be experiencing a new golden age. Another town marked by the personality of Frederick the Great, who held a brilliant and cosmopolitan court here, **Potsdam** is a genuine "Rococo treasure" of universal appeal. Carry on westwards and, after the small town of **Brandenburg** set in the heart of the Havelland (an area of scattered lakes), stop off at **Tangermünde** enclosed within its late 14C ramparts. **Stendal**, just a few kilometres away, was until the mid-16C the most important town in the Brandenburg March, before the ravages of the Thirty Years' War dealt it a fatal blow. Several monuments typical of Gothic brick architecture from this period of prosperity can still be seen. Further north you can admire the beautiful cathedral of **Havelberg**, a pretty town set on the banks of the River Havel. The itinerary ends with a foray into the picturesque **Mecklenburg lake district.**

Harz, Thuringia, Saxony-Anhalt and Leipzig 5

750km/466mi-tour leaving from Leipzig – This route will take you back into Germany's past, where – particularly in the 18C – literature and music flourished. **Leipzig** is a city of artistic interest that can be proud of its exceptional musical heritage; Bach, Wagner and Mendelssohn all lived here at one time and it remains very much in the foreground of the German music scene. Around 60km/37mi south, **Naumburg** stands among hills cloaked in vineyards and forests. The town is renowned in particular for its exceptional Romanesque-cum-Gothic cathedral. **Weimar**, **Jena**, **Erfurt** and **Eisenach** are all names with strong connotations in German culture, through their association with figures such as Luther, Goethe and Schiller. Offering a pleasant distraction from the "cultural pilgrimage", the

Thuringia Forest and, further north, the Harz mountains take you right to the very heart of nature. The countless activities on offer here include hiking, mountain biking, canoeing, skiing and rock climbing.

Saxony (Dresden), Zittau and Erzgebirge 6

650km/380mi-tour leaving from Dresden – Saxony is one of the regions which have played a key role in Germany's history. A city of art and culture, **Dresden** attracts an ever increasing number of visitors. A long and ongoing reconstruction effort has restored its Baroque treasures, making it once again "the Florence of the Elbe". **Swiss Saxony** stretches out to the south of Dresden; with its impressive sandstone cliffs and long gorges gouged from the rock, this region is one of Germany's most spectacular natural wonders. The towns of **Görlitz** and **Bautzen** provide an opportunity to stop off in Sorbian country. An ethnic minority in Germany, occupying the region of Lusace which straddles the Länder of Saxony and Brandenburg, the Sorbians have long belonged to the kingdom of Bohemia. Not only do they still speak their language, but they have also kept alive many traditions, such as the decoration of eggs at Easter and the wearing of the Sorbian national costume and tall embroidered headdresses. Heading northwards, you will come to **Branitz**, a stone's throw from Cottbus where Prince Hermann von Pückler-Muskau built a palace and – indulging his passion for garden design – a fabulous park. Covering an area of 90ha/222 acres, the park alternates open spaces, groups of trees, individual specimens, ditches and pools. Heading back down to Dresden, you will stop at **Schloß Moritzburg** and **Meissen**, renowned for its porcelain. Further south, near the Czech border, **Annaberg-Buchholz** boasts one of the most impressive examples of Flamboyant Gothic style in Saxony: St Annen-Kirche.

Palatinate, Rhineland and Moselle 7

950km/570mi-tour leaving from Cologne – Not far from the borders with Belgium, Luxembourg and France, this very long route from Cologne to Heidelberg encompasses some of the major sights of western Germany. The Rhine valley is full of surprises; alternating vineyards and rocky outcrops dominated by lofty castles, the route from **Koblenz** to **Rüdesheim** or **Bingen** affords some magnificent views. Take a stroll around the historic centre of **Mainz** with its maze of little alleyways and old houses, some of them inhabited by craftsmen. After **Darmstadt**, take the **Bergstrasse** southwards to the fascinating town of **Heidelberg**, a symbol of German Romanticism, whose hillside castle leaves a lasting impression. One of Germany's great forest regions, the Palatinate mountains are also a remarkable zoological and botanical reserve. The eastern part is blessed with an incredibly mild microclimate enabling the cultivation of exotic fruits. Some of the region's towns, such as **Speyer**, **Worms** and **Trier** are former Roman colonies and the oldest towns in Germany. From Trier to Koblenz, the winding course of the **Moselle** takes you on a journey dotted with picturesque villages, castles and vineyards. Cruises, hiking and cycling are among the activities on offer during this part of the tour. **Monschau**, on the road to **Aachen** in the northwest, is next on the agenda. This charming village, which went by the name of Montjoie until 1919, nestles at the end of a winding gorge of the River Rur. As for **Cologne**, with its two black spires reaching skywards, its multitude of churches, colourful little houses, numerous museums, trade fair and exhibition venues etc, it has a great deal to offer.

Nuremberg and Franconia 8

650km/380mi-tour leaving from Nuremberg – This itinerary provides a chance to explore the age-old sights of northern Bavaria. It begins with **Nuremberg**, an old bronze casters' and gold-beaters' town and one of the most beautiful medieval cities in Germany. Further south, **Eichstätt** is now a "Mecca" of uncompromising contemporary architecture, exemplified by the new *Pädagogische Hochschule* and the university's summer residence. Passing through river valleys and fertile hills, the Romantic Road recalls at every stage some aspect of the past that could only belong to the history of Germany. As the route unfolds, it evokes life in the great medieval cities **(Nördlingen**, **Dinkelsbühl**, **Rothenburg)**. In Würzburg, what remains of the grandeur acquired in the mid 17C under three prince-bishops of the Schönborn family can be seen in the town's Baroque churches and the splendid Residenz Palace. After **Bamberg**, the town with which, according to the results of a survey, the Germans feel the strongest connection, our Bavarian route touches the region of Thuringia and passes through **Coburg**, where a stop at the **Vierzehnheiligen Church** is recommended. This pilgrimage church is a Baroque masterpiece which may surprise even those who are least enamoured of this style. The interior layout reflects the boldness of the architect Balthasar Neumann, and the wealth of decoration is truly captivating. **Bayreuth**, last stop on the tour, will be a high point for fans of Wagner's music and admirers of the Rococo style.

Baden-Württemberg and Lake Constance 9

850km/510mi-tour leaving from Freiburg – Southeast Germany has an astonishing number of remarkable tourist attractions. It is hard to remain untouched by the relaxed atmosphere of **Freiburg**, an old university town whose paved alleyways beg to be explored. The **Black Forest** is steeped in legend and offers a surprising variety of scenery for such a small region. Add to that its picturesque villages, a passion for cuckoo clocks and the possibilities of hiking in summer and skiing in winter, and it is easy to see why this mountainous region has become one of Germany's most popular tourist destinations. Passing through towns such as the elegant spa resort of **Baden-Baden**, which attracts a wealthy clientele all year round, and **Karlsruhe**, the route takes you up to **Bruchsal**. This town has inherited a sumptuous 18C palace which houses an original museum entirely devoted to mechanical musical instruments. A few kilometres southeast of Bruchsal stands **Maulbronn Abbey**; built in 1147, it was one of the earliest Cistercian foundations in Germany. The school established here since the Reformation (1557) has seen the flowering of such diverse scientific, literary and philosophical talents as those of Kepler, Hölderlin and Hermann Hesse. The road south leads to **Tübingen** and **Ulm**. Tübingen's labyrinth of narrow sloping streets lined with old half-timbered houses combined with its animated student life create a relaxed and happy atmosphere away from the throng of tourists. In Ulm, you can take a stroll between the canals and the Danube and admire the town's extraordinary cathedral. The Upper Swabian Plateau is dotted with Baroque churches whose dazzling decoration and architecture combining light effects and symmetry are in perfect harmony with the

R. Chéret/MICHELIN

Kloster Bebenhausen, Tübingen.

landscape. **Zwiefalten** and **Weingarten** are two superb illustrations of the Baroque style that flourished so extensively in southern Germany. The tour ends with the magnificent **Lake Constance**, regarded by the Germans as their very own "Riviera".

Munich and the Bavarian Alps 10

650km/380mi-tour leaving from Munich – A tour through this region, with its magnificent alpine scenery and wealth of culture, will undoubtedly be a high point in your exploration of Germany. The country's second most popular tourist destination after Berlin, **Munich** – Bavaria's vibrant capital – is a prosperous and lively city. Art lovers will delight in its fabulous museums and Baroque churches. A little over 100km/62mi to the east, on the Austrian border, **Burghausen** was the biggest fortress in Germany in the Middle Ages. Its defence system, reinforced at the beginning of the 16C in the face of a threatened invasion by the Turks, stretches for around 1km/0.6mi. The much-travelled **German Alpine Road** starts at **Berchtesgaden**, whose basin forms a salient on the German border that penetrates deeply into Austria. This route allows travellers not only to enjoy the superb Bavarian mountain scenery but also to visit such famous monuments as the castles of Ludwig II – including **Neuschwanstein** – and the Wieskirche. At **Füssen**, the Alpine Road joins up with the Romantic Road, plunging the traveller into the Baroque splendour of the episcopal courts and imperial towns such as **Augsburg**.

P. Gajic / Michelin

- a. ✗✗ *A comfortable restaurant*
- b. ✿ *A very good restaurant in its category*
- c. ☺ *Good foot at moderate prices*

Can't decide?

Find out more with the Michelin Guide Collection!

- A collection of 12 titles
- 20 000 restaurants around Europe
- 1 600 town plans
- The best addresses in every price category

Discover the pleasure of travel with the Michelin Guides.

Historic Routes

Very clearly signposted, these "thematic" itineraries provide an original means of crisscrossing the country and getting to know it better. They include:

Baden Wine Route (Badische Weinstraße), from Baden-Baden to Lörrach.

Castle Road (Burgenstraße), from Mannheim to Bayreuth and then on to Prague (975km/605mi in total).

Franconian Wine Route (Bocksbeutelstraße): five different routes leaving from Würzburg.

German Avenues (Deutsche Alleenstraße), from Sellin on Rügen Island to Goslar.

German Holiday Route (Deutsche Ferienstraße Ostsee-Alpen), which links the Baltic Sea (Puttgarden) with the Alps (Berchtesgaden).

German Wine Road (Deutsche Weinstraße), from Bockenheim/Palatinate to Wissembourg/Alsace.

Half-timbered Buildings (Deutsche Fachwerkstraße), six routes through Lower Saxony and Hessen.

Old Salt Road (Alte Salzstraße), from Lüneburg to Lübeck.

Romanesque Road (Straße der Romanik), circuit leaving from Magdeburg.

Romantic Road (Romantische Straße), from Würzburg to Füssen.

Silver Route (Ferienstraße Silberstraße), from Zwickau to Dresden.

Thuringian Classical Route (Klassikerstraße Thüringen), circuit from Meiningen.

Upper Swabian Baroque Route (Oberschwäbische Barockstraße), from Ulm to Lake Constance.

Weser Renaissance Route (Straße der Weser-Renaissance), from Hann. Münden to Bremen.

Sport and Leisure

Parks

National Parks

Germany's 13 national parks will certainly appeal to travellers who prefer nature to culture. Further information is available from **Europarc Deutschland**, Marienstraße 31, D-10117 Berlin, ☎ (030) 28 87 88 20, fax (030) 288 78 82 16, www.europarc-deutschland.de

Bavaria: Bavarian Forest (Bayerischer Wald), Berchtesgaden.

Schleswig-Holstein: Schleswig-Holstein mudflats (Wattenmeer).

Lower Saxony: Lower Saxon mudflats (Niedersächsisches Wattenmeer), Harz.

Hamburg: Hamburg mudflats (Wattenmeer).

Saxony-Anhalt: Hochharz.

Mecklenburg-West Pomerania: Jasmund, Müritz, Vorpommersche Boddenlandschaft.

Saxony: Swiss Saxony (Sächsische Schweiz).

Brandenburg: Lower Oder valley (Unteres Odertal).

Thuringia: Hainich.

Theme Parks

The following list includes some of the best known and most popular of Germany's amusement parks.

Sports

For nature lovers and outdoor sports fans alike, Germany's varied landscapes provide an ideal setting for all sorts of activities. Some very useful information in this respect can be found at www.germany-tourism.de (under Travel Tips, Outdoor Vacation).

Hunting

For information on hunting in Germany, contact **Jagdschutz-Verbandes**, Johannes-Henry-Straße 26, 53113 Bonn, ☎ (02 28) 94 90 620, www.jagd-online.de

Cycling

Cycling can be a very practical, economic and pleasant way to explore some of the regions of Germany. Information is available from the Bund **Deutscher Radfahrer e.V.**, Otto-Fleck-Schneise 4, 60582 Frankfurt Am Main,

Park/Place	☎ website	Nearest motorway exit (number)
Bavaria-Filmstadt/ Geiselgasteig (Bayern)	(089) 64 99 20 00 www.bavaria-filmtour.de	A 99: Oberhaching (4)
Churpfalzpark Loifling/Cham (Bayern)	(099 71) 303 40 www.churpfalzpark.de	A 3: Straubing (106)
Erlebnispark Schloß Thurn/ Heroldsbach (Bayern)	(091 90) 92 98 98 www.schloss-thurn.de	A 73: Baiersdorf Nord (10)
Erlebnispark Tripsdrill/Cleebronn-Tripsdrill (Baden-Württemberg)	(071 35) 99 99 www.tripsdrill.de	A 81: Mundesheim (13)
Erlebnispark Ziegenhagen/ Witzenhausen (Hessen)	(055 45) 246 www.ziegenhagen-hessen.de/ Erlebnispark/ erlebnispark.html	A 75: Hann.-Münden (75)
Europa-Park/Rust (Baden-Württemberg)	(0180) 577 66 88 www.europapark.de	A 5: Ettenheim (57)
Fränkisches Wunderland/Plech (Bayern)	(092 44) 98 90 www.wunderland.de	A 9: Plech (46)
Freizeit-Land/Geiselwind (Bayern)	(095 56) 92 11 92 www.freizeit-land.de	A 3: Geiselwind (76)
Filmpark Babelsberg/Potsdam (Brandenburg)	(0331) 721 27 55 www.filmpark.de	A 115: Potsdam-Babelsberg (5)
Fort Fun Abenteuerland/ Bestwig-Wasserfall (Nordrhein-Westfalen)	(029 05) 811 23 www.fortfun.de	A 46: Bestwig (71)
Hansa-Park/ Sierksdorf (Schleswig-Holstein)	(045 63) 47 40 www.hansapark.de	A 1: Eutin (15)
Heide-Park/Soltau (Niedersachsen)	(051 91) 91 91 www.heidepark.de	A 7: Soltau-Ost (44)
Holiday Park/ Haßloch (Rheinland-Pfalz)	(018 05) 00 32 46 www.holidaypark.de	A 65: Neustadt-Süd (13)
Phantasialand/Brühl (Nordrhein-Westfalen)	(022 32) 362 05 www.phantasialand.de	A 553: Brühl-Süd (2)
Potts Park/ Minden-Dützen (Nordrhein-Westfalen)	(0571) 510 88 www.pottspark-minden.de	A 2: Porta Westfalica (33)
Ravensburger Spieleland/Weitnau (Bayern)	(075 42) 40 00 www.spieleland.com	A 96: Wangen-West (5)
Safari- und Hollywood-Park/Schloß Holte-Stukenbrock (Nordrhein- Westfalen)	(052 07) 95 24 25 www.safaripark.de	A 2, then A 33: Stukenbrock-Senne (23)
Sea Life Constance (Baden-Württemberg)	(075 31) 12 82 70 www.sealife.de	A 81 or A 98, then B 33
Serengeti-Safaripark/ Hodenhagen (Niedersachsen)	(051 64) 979 90 www.serengeti-park.com	A 7: Westenholz (7)
Taunus-Wunderland/ Schlangenbad (Hessen)	(061 24) 40 81 www.taunuswunderland.de	A 66: Wiesbaden-Frauenstein (2)
Vogelpark Walsrode/Walsrode (Niedersachsen)	(051 61) 60 440 www.vogelpark-walsrode.de	A 27: Walsrode-Süd (28)
Warner Bros. Movie World/Bottrop-Kirchhellen (Nordrhein-Westfalen)	(020 45) 89 98 99 www.movieworld.de	A 31: Kirchhellen-Feldhausen (40)

☎ (069) 967 80 00, www.bdr-online.org. The German National Tourist Office also publishes a brochure containing 30 tourist routes for cyclists.

Horseriding

Lists of equestrian centres can be obtained from regional tourist offices. You can also contact the **Deutsche Reiterliche Vereinigung**, Freiherr-von-Langenstrasse 13, 48231 Warendorf, ☎ (02581) 636 20, www.pferd-aktuell.de

Golf

There is no shortage of golf courses in Germany. For information, contact the **Deutscher Golf Verband e.V.**, Viktoriastraße 16, 65189, ☎ (0611) 99 02 00, Wiesbaden, www.golf.de. Prices are from €25 to €50 for a one-day pass during the week, and from €30 to €70 on Saturdays and Sundays.

Fishing

Information from the **Verband Deutscher Sportfischer e.V.**, Siemensstrasse 11-13, 63071 Offenbach, ☎ (069) 87 37 70, www.vdsf.de

Walking

The Federation of German Mountain and Walking Clubs can provide details on hikes organised by regional associations and also publishes guides and maps. Contact details: **Verband Deutscher Gebirgs- und Wandervereine e.V.**, Wilhelmshöher Allee 157-159, D-34121 Kassel, ☎ (0561) 93 87 30, www.wanderverband.de. The German Alpine club (Deutsche Alpenverein, DAV), Von-Kahr-Straße 2-4, 80997 München, ☎ 0 89/14 00 30, fax 0 89/1 40 03 11, www.alpenverein.de, gives useful information on routes and accommodation in the mountains. Their Alpine information centre (Alpine Auskunft) at the same address, can be contacted on ☎ 0 89/29 49 40, Mon-Fri 8am to noon, Mon-Wed 1pm to 4pm and Thurs 1pm to 6pm for details on mountain refuge opening times, weather reports, guides and maps. For the Alpine weather forecast, call ☎ 0 9001 29 50 70.

Canoeing and Kayaking

Those interested in canoeing and kayaking or rafting can contact the **Deutscher Kanu-Verband e.V.**, Bertaallee 8, 47055 Duisburg, ☎ (0203) 99 75 90, www.kanu.de

Winter Sports

Although the Alps and the Black Forest remain the most popular skiing areas in Germany, there are a large number of upland sites where, depending on the snow cover, skiing is possible. These include the Harz mountains, the Thuringian Forest, and the Eifel, Sauerland and Swabian Alp (Schwäbische Alb) ranges.

Hamburg Tourismus GmbH

Sailing on the Aussenalster, Hamburg.

Sailing

Sailing is a widely practised sport in Germany; over 180 sailing schools are scattered along the shores of the North Sea, Baltic Sea and many inland lakes. Information can be obtained from the **Verband Deutscher Sportbootschulen**, Varlar 86, 48720 Rosendahl, ☎ (2541) 98 03 03, www.sportbootschulen.de or from the German Sailing Federation, the **Deutscher Seglerverband**, Gründgenstrasse 18, 22309 Hamburg, ☎ (40) 632 00 90, www.dsv.org

- a. *Charming guesthouse*
- b. *Room for 45€ or less per night*
- c. *That little extra, not to be missed*

Can't decide ?

Then simply open a copy of Michelin Guide Charming Places to Stay in France !

- Hotels and guesthouses offering value for money
- Regionally based selection
- Establishments offering wining and dining breaks
- Establishments offering activity breaks
- Regional maps with establishments pinpointed for easy reference

The pleasure of travel with Michelin Maps and Guides.

Health and Wellbeing

The frantic pace of modern life is driving an increasing number of people to seek a few days' peace at one of Germany's spa resorts. Not only are **spas** used for the treatment or prevention of certain illnesses, but they are also an ideal place to recharge your batteries.

Spas have access to mineral water with medicinal properties – a declared public utility – and they also have health services and proper facilities for applying the necessary treatments. They are usually to be found in beautiful natural settings and are an interesting alternative for those wishing to have a quiet holiday, enjoy nature and get back into shape.

The numerous spas scattered throughout Germany uphold a tradition which dates back to Roman times.

Information on all of the country's spa resorts can be found on www.baederkalender.de.

Books

History and Biography

A Concise History of Germany – Mary Fulbrook (Cambridge University Press)
A History of Germany 1815-1985 – W Carr (Edward Arnold)
Hitler, A Study in Tyranny – A Bullock (Perennial)
The Last Days of Hitler – HR Trevor-Roper (Macmillan)

The Arts

Outline of European Architecture – N Pevsner (Penguin)
Bauhaus – F Whitford (Thames & Hudson)
Early Medieval Art: Carolingian, Ottonian, Romanesque – J Beckwith (Thames & Hudson)
The Expressionists – WD Dube (Thames & Hudson)
The Weimar Years: A Culture Cut Short – J Willett (Abbeville Press)

Literature

The Lost Honour of Katharina Blum – Heinrich Böll
The Caucasian Chalk Circle; Threepenny Novel; Mother Courage – Bertolt Brecht
Auto da Fé – Elias Canetti
The Riddle of the Sands – Erskine Childers
The Tin Drum; The Flounder; From the Diary of a Snail; Mein Jahrhundert – Günter Grass
The Glass Bead Game; Narcissus and Goldmund; Steppenwolf – Hermann Hesse
Die Architekten – Stefan Heym
Tales of Hoffmann – Ernst Theodor Amadeus Hoffmann
Buddenbrooks; The Magic Mountain – Thomas Mann
The Adventures of Baron Münchhausen – Rudolph Erich Raspe
All Quiet on the Western Front – Erich Maria Remarque
Kindheitsmuster – Christa Wolf
Goethe the Poet and the Age: Revolution and Renunciation (1790-1803) – Nicholas Boyle

Travel and Modern German Society

A Time of Gifts – P Leigh Fermor (Penguin)
A Traveller's Wine Guide to Germany – K Brady Stewart et al (Interlink Publishing Group)
A Tramp Abroad – M Twain
Deutschland: A Winter's Tale – H Heine
Germany and the Germans – J Ardagh (Penguin)
Goodbye to Berlin – C Isherwood (Hunter Publishing)
The Simon & Schuster Guide to the Wines of Germany – I Jamieson (Simon & Schuster)
The Germans – GA Craig (Plume Books)
The Origins of Modern Germany – G Barraclough (WW Norton & Company)
Three Men on the Bummel – JK Jerome
Vanishing Borders – M Farr (Penguin)
Winter – L Deighton

- a. ***Muséum National d'Histoire Naturelle (Paris)***
- b. ***Natural History Museum (London)***
- c. ***Museum für Naturkunde (Berlin)***

Can't decide ?
Then immerse yourself in the Michelin Green Guide !

- Everything to do and see
- The best driving tours
- Practical information
- Where to stay and eat

The Michelin Green Guide: the spirit of discovery.

Events and Festivals

Listed below are the main events and festivals which take place in Germany. More details can be obtained from tourist information centres.
See also under 'Festivals' in certain blocks in the Directory section.

1 January

New Year's Day International Ski Jump, part of the Four Jump Tournament	**Garmisch-Partenkirchen**

Sunday before Shrove Tuesday

"München narrisch" Carnival	**Munich**

Shrove Monday

Rosenmontagszug: procession and street carnival	**Cologne, Düsseldorf, Mainz**

Shrove Monday and Tuesday

Narrensprung Carnival: elaborate traditional costumes and expressive wooden masks; Dance of the Fools	**Rottweil**

Maundy Thursday to Easter Monday

Traditional Sorbian Easter Egg Market	**Bautzen**

Easter

Sorbian Easter Egg market	**Oberlausitz**

30 April/1 May

Walpurgisnacht: Witches' Sabbath Festival	**Various towns in the Harz region**
Marburg townspeople and students sing in the month of May	**Marbourg**

End of April to end of May

International May Festival: theatre, music	**Wiesbaden**

Mid-May to mid-September every Sunday at noon

Rattenfängerspiel: pageant retracing the legend of the Pied Piper	**Hamelin**

Friday after Ascension

Blutritt: mounted cavalcade in honour of the Holy Blood	**Weingarten**

Early May to early June

Classical Music Festival	**Schwetzingen**

Second half of May

International horse racing at Iffezheim	**Baden-Baden**

Whitsun

Kuchen und Brunnenfest: dance of the salt-workers in traditional 16C costume	**Schwäbisch Hall**
Meistertrunk: performance of the legend of the "Long Drink" and re-enactment of the Thirty Years War by locals in period costume	**Rothenburg ob der Tauber**

Tourist-Information Rottweil

The Dance of the Fools, Rottweil.

Whit Monday

Pingstritt: mounted cavalcade — **Kötzting**

Whit Tuesday

Historische Geißbockversteigerung: auctioning of a goat (period costumes; folk dancing; local fair) — **Deidesheim**

Corpus Christi

Solemn procession through the decorated town — **Munich**

Mühlheimer Gottestracht: procession of boats along the Rhine — **Cologne**

Procession through flower-decked street — **Hüfingen**

Last Saturday of May

Wildpferdefang: capture and auction of young stallions — **Merfelder Bruch**

14 days after Whitsun, from Friday to Monday

Salatkirmes: Salad Fair commemorating the introduction of the potato to the Hessen region; traditional local costumes — **Schwalmstadt**

1st weekend in June and September, 2nd weekend in July

Castle illuminations (firework displays) — **Heidelberg**

June-August

Summer Music Festival: concerts of classical music in the Cistercian abbey — **Chorin**

Festival of Drama and Opera in the abbey ruins; theatre, opera — **Bad Hersfeld**

June to September (every 5 years, next: 2007)

Documenta: world's largest international exhibition of contemporary art — **Kassel**

Last week of June

Kiel Week: international sailing regatta; local festival — **Kiel**

Last weekend of June

Bergparade in historical costumes — **Freiberg**

Four Sundays from end of June to mid-July (every 4 years, next: 2005)

Fürstenhochzeit (Landshut Royal Marriage): historical pageant in period costume — **Landshut**

During summer months

Mecklenburg-Vorpommern Summer Music Festival, held in historic houses, castles and churches — **Various places in Mecklenburg-Vorpommern**

July to August

Schleswig-Holstein Music Festival — **Various places in Schleswig-Holstein**

1st weekend in July

Spreewald Festival: Sorbian folklore and traditions — **Lübbenau**

Early July

Archers' Festival: procession of archers — **Hannover**

Mid-July (every 4 years, next: 2008)

Fischerstechen (Fishermen's Festival) — **Ulm**

3rd weekend in July (Saturday, Sunday, Monday)

Kinderzeche: commemorating the saving of the town by a deputation of children (historical costumes) — **Dinkelsbühl**

Penultimate Monday in July

Schwörmontag: river procession on the Danube — **Ulm**

3rd Sunday and Monday in July

Tänzelfest: historical procession by schoolchildren — **Kaufbeuren**

Last Saturday in July and 1st Sunday in August

Summer music festival — **Hitzacker**

End of July to end of August

Bayreuther Festspiele: Wagner Opera Festival — **Bayreuth**

July-August

Festival on the cathedral steps — **Erfurt**

Der Rhein in Flammen (The Rhine Ablaze): illumination of the river valley from Braubach to Koblenz — **Koblenz-Oberwesel, St Goar**

2nd Saturday in August

Seenachtsfest: evening lakeside festival — **Constance**

2nd week in August

Der Drachenstich (Death of the Dragon): pageant of the legend of St George, in period costumes — **Furth im Wald**

Saturday after 24 August

Schäferlauf: shepherds' race (barefoot over a field of stubble) — **Markgröningen**

Last week in August

International horse racing at Iffezheim — **Baden-Baden**

September

Festival with firework display — **Rothenburg ob der Tauber**

End of September to beginning of October

Cannstatter Volksfest: popular local fair — **Bad Cannstatt**

The two weeks leading up to the first Sunday in October

Oktoberfest: Beer Festival. The largest popular festival in the world attracts nearly 6 million people to the Bavarian capital every year. — **Munich**

1st and 2nd weekend in October

Weinlesefest: Wine Fair and election of the Queen of Wine — **Neustadt an der Weinstraße**

Last 10 days in October

Bremer Freimarkt: largest popular fair in northern Germany — **Bremen**

Sunday before 6 November

Leonhardifahrt: similar celebration to that at Bad Tölz (below) — **Benediktbeuern**

Munich Tourist Office

Oktoberfest.

6 November (St Leonard)

Leonhardifahrt: prior to a Mass in honour of St Leonard, gaily decorated horse-drawn carts process through town to the church — **Bad Tölz**

Advent

Christkindlesmarkt: Christmas market (Christmas tree decorations and gifts); seasonal performances by children — **Nuremberg**

24 December and New Year's Eve

Weihnachtsschießen und Neujahrsschießen: Christmas and New Year shooting matches — **Berchtesgaden**

The Chiemsee.

Insights and Images

Germany Today

Germany is a highly decentralised federal state whose human, political and administrative facets reflect very individual traits that are rooted in its history. This brief, factual portrait highlights some of the aspects peculiar to the German nation and to life in Germany today.

Population

With over 82 million inhabitants, Germanyis the most highly populated country in the European Union. It has been in demographic decline for about 25 years and is experiencing an accelerated ageing of the population (the average age – over 39 – is the highest in Europe). Nearly 90% of Germans live in towns with more than 2 000 inhabitants, and the western part of the country has by far the highest population densities. Although immigration has, since the 1970s, provided a significant additional source of labour, the tightening of legislation has considerably reduced the influx of people from abroad. Over 7 million foreigners have now settled in Germany, including at least 2 million Turks and 1 million people from the former Yugoslavia.

The Reichstag in Berlin.

A Federal State

Subdivided throughout history into different regions that were largely autonomous, owing allegiance to no single capital (prior to 1945 Berlin was only capital of the Reich for just over 70 years), Germany has naturally gravitated towards a governmental structure that is federal in origin. Today it is a highly decentralised state whose Länder or regions have been granted considerable powers.

The **Basic Law** established in 1949 guarantees the liberty of the individual and defines the institutions of the Republic, a state of law founded on democratic principles. The Federal Parliament is composed of two chambers: the **Bundestag**, a national assembly of 656 members elected by universal suffrage, is invested with legislative power, chooses the Chancellor, and controls the government; the **Bundesrat**, a federal council comprising members drawn from the local governments administering the Länder, is concerned with certain aspects of legislative power, particularly when they affect the Länder. The Bundesrat also exercises a certain degree of control over the government, with the government being required to submit all bills to it.

© Partner für Berlin/FTB-Werbefotografie

The **Chancellor** holds executive power and is elected by the members of the Bundestag, to whom he is accountable. He is invested with wide-ranging powers and defines the broad lines of government policy. The government introduces laws (adopted by the Bundestag) and is also responsible for their implementation. The role of the Federal President **(Bundespräsident)** is essentially representative. It is he who concludes treaties with foreign states, decides upon or revokes the appointment of judges and federal functionaries as well as federal ministers suggested by the Chancellor. Lastly, the supreme judicial authority of the Federal Republic is the **Constitutional Court**, which sits in Karlsruhe. It ensures compliance with the Basic Law and is the guardian of constitutional principles. It also acts as arbitrator in disputes between the Federal Government and the Länder.

The Länder: regions with extensive powers

The Federal Republic comprises 16 Länder, 11 of which formed the old West Germany plus the five added in 1990 which were re-constituted from the 15 districts of the former East German Democratic Republic (the East German Länder had been abolished in 1952). Each Land organises its constitution within the terms of the Basic Law. The Länder also have a legislative assembly **(Landtag)** elected by universal suffrage and an executive body consisting of a council of ministers with a President **(Ministerpräsident)**. Although areas involving the sovereignty of the state, such as foreign affairs, defence or monetary policy, fall under the responsibility of the Federal Government alone, the Länder still possess very broad powers; they have exclusive jurisdiction over education and culture, and they are actively involved in the areas of justice and the economy.

The Länder.

An economic giant

After the Second World War, the economy of West Germany made a spectacular recovery, generally referred to as an **"economic miracle"** *(Wirtschaftswunder)*. Indeed, the considerable reconstruction effort, backed by American aid under the Marshall Plan, together with a judicious fiscal and monetary policy, propelled the West German economy to third place worldwide, behind the United States and Japan. Good relations between employers and trade unions and a powerful banking system also helped to maintain this exceptional growth. The **"social market economy"** (liberalism allowing state intervention to correct the perverse effects of the market) long provided the context of this development, which was also stimulated by a favourable economic climate.

Despite the strong development of service-sector activities, industry remains the cornerstone of Germany's economic strength. The industrial sector, which represents around one third of Gross Domestic Product, consists of large international groups with varied activities (Thyssen-Krupp, Bayer, Hoechst, Siemens, Bosch, BMW, Volkswagen etc) and countless small but dynamic companies.

The **reunification** of the two Germanies in 1990 was an enormous challenge; the very high cost of the economic integration of the former German Democratic Republic had an immense impact on the competitiveness of the Federal Republic. The "upgrading" of the new Länder (in particular the modernisation of the infrastructures and industrial plants) together with social support for employees in the East put a great strain on the federal budget. However, the massive investments made by the Federal Government – which, in 1995, had to resort to increasing taxation in the West – and the structural aid from Europe finally allowed the East to make the transition from a planned economy to a market economy. The cost of the reunification partly explains why, in spite of an effective policy of restraint, **budget deficits** remain high in Germany and are still a bone of contention with Brussels. Today, with a **high rate of unemployment** (9.8% in 2002) and a **very slow rate of growth** (+0.6% in 2001 and +0.2% in 2002), the German economy appears to be running out of steam.

Politics dominated by the bipartite system

Since 1949, two parties – the CDU and the SPD – have dominated political life in the Federal Republic. A rare alliance between these two groups came about in 1966 with the formation of the "great coalition" *(Große Koalition)*. One of the most significant recent developments in German politics is, without a doubt, the rise of the ecology party, Die Grünen.

The Christian Democratic Union **(CDU)** has a slightly more right-wing Bavarian offshoot, the CSU. The conservative CDU-CSU and their liberal allies from the FDP won the majority of votes in the 1949 elections, and **Adenauer** became Chancellor. The party returned to power in 1982 under the aegis of **Helmut Kohl**, who was reelected Chancellor four times (1983, 1987, 1991 and 1994).

The Social Democrat Party **(SPD)** rallied to the market economy and the Atlantic Alliance in 1959, leaving Marxist theory behind. They came to power for the first time in 1969 led by **Willy Brandt** in an alliance with the liberals, then again in 1974 under **Helmut Schmidt**. More recently, they claimed victory in the 1998 elections under the leadership of **Gerhard Schröder**. Chancellor Schröder owed his 2002 reelection to the SPD's alliance with the Greens.

The liberal **FDP** party, capable of making alliances with either of the two main parties, has for a long time acted as referee on the political chessboard. Chairman of the party, **Guido Westerwelle**, is the archetypal dynamic young politician.

Successor of the SED, East Germany's former communist party, the Party of Democratic Socialism **(PDS)** has a considerable following in the new Länder. It did, however, suffer a considerable setback after the 2002 elections, when it dropped below the 5% mark.

In 1983, **Die Grünen** entered the Bundestag. Their 1998 alliance with the SPD enabled their leader, **Joschka Fischer**, to take up office as Foreign Secretary in Schröder's government.

M. Hertlein/MICHELIN

The Holstentor at Lübeck.

Regions and Landscapes

At the heart of Europe, bordered by the Alps to the south and by the Baltic Sea to the north, Germany is virtually without natural frontiers to the east and the west. Such a lack of barriers, and the subsequent accessibility to outside influences has had a profound effect on the country's history and civilisation.

The red-sandstone cliffs of the island of Helgoland.

Three large natural regions

In the **north**, the immense **Germano-Polish Plain**, formed by the glaciation of the Quaternary Era, owes the fact that it was scarcely touched by the Hercynian and Alpine mountain-building movements to the resistance of its crystalline bedrock. In the **centre**, during the Primary Era, the formidable Hercynian folding created a complex of minor massifs – now smoothed by erosion and for the most part wooded – separated by geographic depressions. The most important of these Hercynian massifs are the Black Forest, the Rhenish schist massif, and – encircling Bohemia – the Böhmerwald, the Bavarian Forest, the Erzgebirge (Ore Mountains) and the Sudeten Mountains. On the edges of this Hercynian zone accumulated the coal-bearing deposits of the Ruhr and Silesia which led to the industrial expansion of the 19C.
The sedimentary basin of Swabia-Franconia, its vast area drained by the Main and the Neckar, offers a less dramatic landscape; abutting the Black Forest to the west and the Swabian Jura to the south, the limestone plateau is patterned with lines of hills sculpted according to the resistance of the varied strata.
In the **south**, the Alpine portion of Germany is delimited by the **Pre-Alps**, where the debris torn up and crushed during the final exertions of Quaternary glaciation formed the Bavarian plateau – a huge area stretching in a gentle slope as far as the Danube.

Northern Germany

Lower Rhine Valley and Westphalia – Lush, green and flat, protected from flooding, the plain of the Lower Rhine, with its cosy houses, brings to mind the landscape of the neighbouring Netherlands. There is similar scenery around Münster, on the Westphalian plain, where the farmlands patterned by hedges and trees offer the additional attraction of many moated castles (Wasserburgen).
Great Northern Plain – Despite its apparent monotony, this enormous area (which extends eastwards into Poland but is confined, so far as Germany is concerned, between the Ems and the Oder) does offer a certain variety of landscapes.
In the south, below the Weser and Harz foothills, the Börde country lies between the Weser and the Elbe – a region covered by an alluvial topsoil whose fertility is

Bremer Touristik-Zentrale

legendary. Farms and market gardens flourish in this densely populated zone, which is favoured also with mineral deposits rich in iron and potassium. Further north, on either side of the Elbe, is the Geest – a region of glacial deposits (sand, gravel, clay) with little to recommend it geographically, since it was covered by the Scandinavian glaciers right up to Paleolithic times. This has resulted in poor drainage and soils that are too sandy; between Berlin and the Baltic, the Mecklenburg plateau is scattered with shallow lakes interspersed with morainic deposits that bear witness to the prolonged glacial presence. The Spree and the Havel, meandering through the flatlands, supply the lakeland regions of the Spreewald and Potsdam.West of the Lower Weser, and in the Worpswede neighbourhood north of Bremen, peat bogs (Moore) alternate with very wet pastureland. Most of the peat moors are now under cultivation, after drainage using Dutch methods. The nature reserve south of Lüneburg, however, has preserved for all time a typical stretch of the original moorland.

The Baltic Coast – The German section of the Baltic Coast, which stretches from Flensburg all the way to the Stettin Haff, is a murrain landscape, which, in addition to very flat parts also has a few elevations that rise above the 100m/320ft mark. Because of the relatively limited tidal differences of the on average 55m/180ft deep Baltic Sea, the coastline has only been subject to little change. That's why numerous cities with long traditions have evolved here. Between the bays of Lübeck and Kiel lies the Holsteinische Schweiz (Holstein Switzerland), the hilly and lake-dotted remainders of a ground and end moraine from the Ice Age. The arms of the sea, which are the fjords and bays left over from the glaciers of the last Ice Age, cut deep into the land and form excellent natural harbours. Their banks are lined with beaches, forests and little fishing villages. Further to the east, the Baltic Coast is marked by shallow, water-filled inlets from the post-Ice Age period. Four islands lie offshore, the largest is the water-washed Rügen.

North Sea Coast – Because of the winds and waves, the North Sea Coast between the Netherlands and Denmark is constantly undergoing change. The tides (every 12hr 25min 53s) raise and lower the water level by 2m/6.4ft to 3m/9.6ft. Several island groups lie out off shore in the „Watt„, a 5x30km/3x18mi strip of land that is washed by the sea when the tide is in, but is above sea level at ebb times. The Watt ecosystem is home to nearly 2 000 species, from sea lions to almost invisible creatures 1/10 of a millimetre in size. A strip of marshland created over centuries lies along the coast. Once upon a time, the tides used to bring in animal and plant particles together with find sand, which formed a fertile base for agriculture in the

Lindau in Bavaria.

marshlands. Behind this is the less fertile, hilly "Geest". Broad moors have formed in the depressions, some of which have been turned over to farming. Germany's two largest seaports, Hamburg and Bremen, lie at the inner ends of the funnel-shaped Elbe and Weser estuaries.

Central Germany

The Rhenish Schist Massif – This ancient geological mass, cut through by the Rhine – the only real channel of communication between the north and south of the country – the Lahn and the Moselle, comprises among others the highlands known as the Eifel, the Westerwald, the Taunus and the Hunsrück. They share the same inhospitable climate and the same evidence of volcanic activity as the crater lakes, known as the Maare, of the Eifel plateau.The Eifel will be familiar to motoring enthusiasts as the home of the Nürburgring Grand Prix race circuit. The Upper Sauerland, a thickly wooded, mountainous region (alt 841m/2 760ft), with its many dams, acts as a water reserve for the Ruhr industrial area.

Mountains of Upper Hessen and the Weser – Between the Rhenish schist massif and the forest of Thuringia (Thüringer Wald) lies a confused amalgam of heights, some of them volcanic (Vogelsberg, Rhön), and depressions which have been used as a highway, linking north and south, by German invaders throughout the ages.

Between Westphalia and the north, the Weser Mountains – extended westwards by the Teutoburger Wald – form a barrier that is breached at the Porta Westfalica, near Minden. Further to the east, the Erzgebirge (Ore Mountains) form a natural frontier with the Czech Republic.

Harz Mountains – This relatively high range (alt 1 142m/3 747ft at the Brocken) has a typical mountain climate, characterised by heavy snowfalls in winter.

Southern Germany

Plain of the Upper Rhine – Between Basle and the Bingen Gap, a soil of exceptionally fertile loess, accompanied by a climate which combines light rainfall, an early spring and a very hot summer, has produced a rich agricultural yield (hops, corn and tobacco) and a terrain highly suitable for the cultivation of vines. The whole of this low-lying, productive tract has become a crossroads for the rest of Europe, which is why certain towns – Frankfurt, for instance – have profited internationally from their development.

Black Forest – This crystalline massif (alt 1 493m/4 899ft at the Feldberg), which overlooks the Rhine Gap, is relatively well populated. The region's healthy climate

H. Spiering/MICHELIN

and many thermal springs, with their attendant, highly reputed spa resorts, draw large numbers of tourists here every year.

Swabian-Franconian Basin – Franconia, formed by vast, gently undulating plateaux, is bordered to the south-east by the small limestone massif of the Franconian Jura which produces Germany's finest building stone, and to the north and north-east by the heavily wooded crystalline ranges flanking Bohemia and Thuringia.Swabia, once ruled by the kings of Württemberg, offers a great variety of landscapes – barred to the south by the blue line of the Swabian Jura, which rises to 874m/2 867ft. Small valleys, enlivened by orchards and vineyards, alternate here with the gentle slopes of wooded hillsides.

The Alps and the Bavarian Plateau – The Bavarian Alps and the Alps of Allgäu offer impressive contrasts between the sombre green of their forests and the shades of grey colouring their rocks and escarpments, which make an impressive sight when seen against the backdrop of a brilliant blue sky. The Zugspitze, the highest point in Germany, reaches an altitude of 2 962m/9 720ft.Torrents such as the Isar, the Lech, the Iller and the Inn, gushing down from the mountains throughout the ages, have carved out wide corridors with broad, flat floors suitable for the cultivation of the land and the development of towns (Ulm, Augsburg and Munich).

Thuringian windmills.

J. Bouraly/MICHELIN

From Germanic tribes to the Federal Republic

Long divided into a number of autonomous states, Germany was slow to achieve unity. This nation of great diversity, which was for a long time marked by feudalism and whose regions still hold considerable powers, is today one of the main spearheads of European unity.

Willy Brandt in 1966.

The Origins

The earliest evidence of human life on German territory today is the lower jaw bone dating back over 500 000 years of the so-called Homo heidelbergensis, which was discovered near Heidelbergin 1907. The Middle Palaeolithic Age (200 000-40 000 BC) is considered the age of the Neanderthal Man *(see DÜSSELDORF: Excursions)*. The first „modern people„, the Homo sapiens, who lived from fishing, hunting and gathering, lived during the Late Palaeolithic, an epoch of the Stone Age within the last Ice Age. During the Neolithic Era, people began to settle in village-like communities, where they lived for a while, grew plants and began raising animals.

The last prehistoric period, the Iron Age, began around 1000 BC, following the Bronze Age, thus named because that material was widely used to make implements, weapons and jewellery. The Iron Age is divided up into the La Tène Culture and the Hallstatt Culture. Economic and political power started becoming more concentrated, evidence from graves suggests a stratified social system.

La Tène Culture

The name for this cultural epoch supported by Celtic tribes (5C-1C BC) originated at an excavation site on Neuenburg Lake in Switzerland. Over 2 500 objects were found there including grave furnishings and treasures. The focal area of the La Tène Culture is in southwestern Germany, along the northern edge of the Alps and in the Main-Moselle area. Protective forts for the people grew into city like settlements, the first north of the Alps. The advance of Germanic tribes and the expansion of the Roman Empire brought the La Tène Culture to an end.

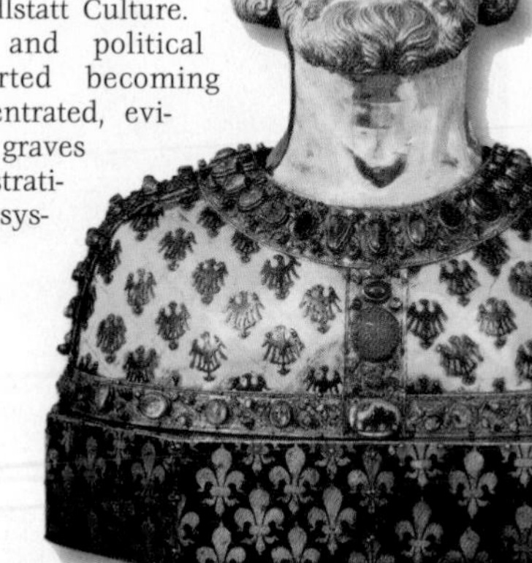

Charlemagne

Bildarchiv Preussischer Kulturbesitz

Germans and Romans

In the first millennium before Christ, Germanic tribes began resettling towards Central Europe. The occurrence and extent of this movement was under the auspices of numerous population groups of various origins and cultural levels living in the area between the northern German flatlands and the central mountain ranges. The first written reference to „Germania„ is in the works of the Roman author Poseidonius (1C BC). Julius Caesar, too, used this term in his *De Bello Gallico* to describe the non-Gallic regions north of the Alps.
The wars conducted by the Kimbers and the Teutons against the Romans around 100 BC were the first military conflicts between German tribes and the Roman civilisation.
The expansion of the western German tribes was stopped by Caesar's conquest of Gaul (58-55 BC). The aims of foreign policy until Emperor Augustus also covered the inclusion of Germania into the Roman Empire all the way to the Elbe, an objective that was never met.
During the 1C AD, the **Limes** was built, a 550km/330mi fortified line that sealed the Roman sphere of influence from the Rhine to the Danube. Skirmishes did break out every now and then, but there were also alliances, trade and cultural exchanges. New towns arose where the Roman camps stood and at river crossings (eg Cologne, Koblenz, Regensburg).
Late Antiquity, Germanicism and Christianity merged to become the Western European Middle Ages. In the 2C-3C AD, the large tribes like the Franks, the Saxons and the Allemanni joined forces. The military kingdoms of the age of mass migration gave way to early medieval states formed by units of individuals.

- **AD 9** – Three Roman legions under General Varus are annihilated by Germanic troops under the command of the Cheruscan prince **Arminius**, which results in the Romans relinquishing their bastions on the right bank of the Rhine.
- **314** – One year after announcing the Edict of Tolerance, Emperor Constantine establishes the first bishopric on German territory in Trier.
- **375** – Beginning of the *Völkerwanderung*, the "movement of the peoples": The Huns drive the Goths (East Germans) to the west. The former „Imperium Romanum„ falls apart to form partial empires.
- **800** – End of the West Roman Empire brought about by Odoaker, the East German general. He is in turn murdered by the Ostrogoth Theodorich.

The Frankish Empire

The tribal union of the Franks – a West German tribe in the estuary of the Rhine – expanded slowly towards the south. These erstwhile confederates of Rome (settled allies), developed into the most important factor at the beginning of the Middle Ages thanks to the creation of large powers introduced by the Merovingians around 500. Their king, Clovis I, mopped up the final remains of the West Roman Empire and converted to Christianity. In the 7C, the Merovingians lost their hegemony to the dynasty later referred to as the Carolingians, who had been the highest officials (major-domos) of the royal household under the Merovingians.

Emperor Charles IV and seven prince electors (armorial, c 1370)

Since the 8C, the general term *thiutisk* had developed from a linguistic derivation of the word for tribe to describe the peoples speaking Germanic languages – as opposed to Latin or later French. There was still no supra-regional language spoken to the east of the Rhine, the area that considered itself the Frankish Empire until the 11C. In the 10C, the term „Regnum Teutonicorum„ appeared for the first time as the name for the ruling association of a number of tribes in the Eastern Frankish Empire. During the 11Cand 12C it slowly established itself as a term.

• **751** – Pope Zacharias agrees to the deposition of the last of the Merovingian kings, Childeric III, in favour of the palatine Pippin. Three years later the Pope places Rome under the protection of the Frankish kings.

• **768** – Charlemagne becomes the ruler. He conquers, amongst others, the Lombards, divides up Bavaria and defeats the Saxons after a long war.

• **800** – Coronation of Charlemagne in Rome. The emperor thus legally assumes sovereignty over the former empire.

• **843** – The Treaty of Verdun divides the Carolingian Empire amongst Charlemagne's grandchildren. The East Frankish Kingdom is given to Ludwig the German. The final division of the Carolingian Empire, that paved the way to Germany and France, is determined by the treaties of Mersen (870) and Verdun/Ribemont (879-80).

• **911** – The East Franks elect the Frankish duke Konrad to become their king, thereby separating themselves from the West Franks.

Charlemagne's Empire

After being crowned Emperor in St Peter's Cathedral in Rome in 800, Charlemagne stepped in the shoes of the Roman emperors. His empire stretched from the Spanish border to the Elbe, from Rome all the way to the English Channel. Besides the „Carolingian Renaissance„, as this Golden Age was called, the most important aspect of his reign was the setting up of a working administrative structure. In disposing of the independent duchies and the tribal states, Charlemagne introduced a county constitution. At the top of each administrative district stood an officer of the king chosen from the Frankish Imperial aristocracy, which ensured the coherence of the empire. The vulnerable borders were secured against attack by setting up border marches under margraves invested with special powers. Emissaries with royal powers watched over the Imperial administration. The king constantly travelled through the empire and visited the „Pfalzen„, which grew into major economic and cultural centres, or used the „guesting„ option in the Imperial monasteries.

Bildarchiv Preussischer Kulturbesitz

The Holy Roman Empire

The Roman-German Empire consisted of an elective monarchy. The elected king – who also had to have hereditary rights – became emperor only after being crowned by the Pope. From the 11Conwards, the emperor could rely on being king of not only Germany and Italy, but also of Burgundy. An especially "German" Imperial concept gave way to a Roman-universal idea of an emperor, a fact underscored as of 1157 by the additional title *sacrum Imperium*. During the time of the Staufer dynasty, in the mid 13C, the claim to rule in Italy came to an end. In the 15C, the term "Holy Roman Empire of the German Nation" was finally established, implying the politically active community of the German Imperial estates, who acted as a counterweight to the emperor.

Ruling this huge empire, which during the High Middle Ages stretched from Sicily all the way to the Baltic, was extremely difficult without the benefit of central administrational organs and the technical, financial and military wherewithal. By granting land and various privileges (e.g. customs rights), responsibility for the administration, security and expansion of the empire was placed in the hands of the Imperial aristocracy.

Beginning in the second half of the 11C, the **Investiture Controversy** pitted the Pope against the Emperor on the issue of the right to invest the bishops. This weakened the empire and shook up the Christian world. The dispute was ended by the Concordat of Worms (1122), which proclaimed that ecclesiastical dignities had to be separated from bestowed worldly goods. The position of the bishops became similar to that of the princes, since they became vassals of the empire.

Over time, these vassals of the Emperor gradually accumulated more and more power owing to the establishment of heredity of the fiefs and regalia, which in the long term weakened the empire; this paved the way to the rise of numerous small and some larger territorial states, such as Bavaria and Saxony. The regional ruling of the princely territorial states replaced the personal union state resulting in the federal structure that remains typical of Germany to this day.

- **962** – In Rome, Otto the Great revives the Imperial title and the Pope crowns him emperor. The Saxon duke had already been crowned king in 936. The Otto dynasty rules until the death of Henry II in 1024, and is followed by that of the Salians (Franks).
- **1073** – Pope Gregory VII elected. This church reformer disputes the legitimacy of secular power of decision in affairs of the church. The dramatic crux of the conflict was the penitent journey to Canossa (1077) by King Heinrich IV to receive absolution from the Pope, who had excommunicated him.

The Golden Bull

Beginning in the 10C, the number of electors for the king began to decline, while at the same time the election itself became more regulated legally and formalised. Finally, in 1356, the Golden Bull promulgated an Imperial law to regulate the election of the king, defining an institutional framework and limiting the power of the empire. Thenceforth, the king would be elected by a college of three religious electors (the Archbishops of Mainz, Cologne and Trier) and four secular ones (the Kings of Bohemia, the Margrave of Brandenburg, the Duke of Saxony and the Palatine of the Rhine), and then later crowned emperor. The election was to take place in Frankfurt/Main, and the coronation in Aachen, confirmation by the Pope was no longer necessary. This law, announced by the Luxembourg emperor **Charles IV** is considered the empire's first constitution and a basis for a federal system of state. The power of the electors grew, because they were granted even more extensive privileges, such as the indivisibility of the electoral territories, sole jurisdiction and sovereignty over the land and the securing of dynastic heredity.

Der Pſalter.

CI.

Wol dem der nicht wandelt im rat der Gottloſen/noch trit auff den weg der ſünder/Noch ſitzt da die Spötter ſitzen.
Sondern hat luſt zum Geſetz des HERRN/Vnd redet von ſeinem Geſetze tag vnd nacht.
Der iſt wie ein bawm gepflantzet an den waſſerbechen/der ſeine frucht bringet zu ſeiner zeit/Vnd ſeine bletter verwelcken nicht/vnd was er machet/das gerett wol.
Aber ſo ſind die Gottloſen nicht/Sondern wie ſprew/die der wind verſtrewet.
Darumb bleiben die Gottloſen nicht im b gerichte/noch die ſunder jnn der Gemeine der gerechten.
Denn der HERR kennet den weg der gerechten/Aber der gotloſen weg vergehet.

(Spötter) Die es fur eitel narheit halten/was Gott redet vnd thut.

b (Gerichte) Das iſt/ſie werden weder ampt haben/noch ſonſt jnn der Chriſten gemeine bleiben/ja ſie verweben ſich ſelb/wie die ſprew vom korn

CII.

Warumb toben die Heiden/Vnd die leute reden ſo vergeblich?
Die Könige im lande lehnen ſich auff/vnd die Herrn ratſchlahen miteinander/Wider den HERRN vnd ſeinen geſalbeten.
Laſſet vns zureiſſen jre bande/vnd von vns werffen jre ſeile.
Aber der im Himel wonet/lachet jr/Vnd der HERR ſpottet jr.
Er wird eineſt mit jnen reden jnn ſeinem zorn/Vnd mit ſeinem grim wird er ſie ſchrecken.
Aber ich

Bildarchiv Preussischer Kulturbesitz

Luther's Bible, 1534.

• **1152-90** – Rule of the Staufer emperor Frederick I Barbarossa, who once again strengthened Imperial power *(Restauratio Imperii)* – and who captured the duchies of Bavaria and Saxony from the Guelph duke Henry the Lion *(see BRAUNSCHWEIG)* after a long dispute – and did what he could to limit papal power to the religious sector.

• **1212-50** – Frederick II stays in southern Italy and Sicily for much of his reign, the area north of the Alps held little interest for him. Two Imperial edicts (1220-31) confirm the power over the territories of the secular and religious princes.

• **1254-73** – The years extending between the death of Konrad IV and the election of Rudolf of Habsburg are known as the Interregnum. It was a time of lawlessness and rule by force under „foreign„ kings and anti-kings, which once and for all took away the typically high Middle Ages power and universal meaning of the empire.

The Late Middle Ages

After the Interregnum, the power of the Habsburgs grew. The dynasty succeeded in building up tremendous family power, and by the 15C they had consolidated that power – though now and then the powerful Luxembourgs, Nassaus and Wittelsbach families also succeeded in slipping a king onto the throne. The emperors got

The Hanseatic League

The Hanseatic League existed between the mid 12C and the mid 17C. Its basic structure had already been outlined by around 1300, an alliance of 30 larger and numerous smaller cities to safeguard their joint interests in shipping and trade. This union of cities went through its Golden Age in the 14C under the leadership of Lübeck. At that point it included over 100 cities and was the most significant economic force in northern Germany. After the Thirty Years War, the Hanseatic tradition only continued in Hamburg, Lübeck and Bremen.

into the habit of trying to have a son elected king during their lifetime in order to keep the highest ranking in their own dynasties. But during the Renaissance, the Imperial crown surrendered its holiness.
During the Late Middle Ages, the "Hoftage", the Imperial meetings, became the **Reichstag** – a meeting of the good 350 secular and religious Imperial estates – signalling the beginning of the sharp dualism between the emperor and his estates that followed. At the Reichstag in Worms (1495), fundamental reform decisions were passed that created the preconditions for transforming the Reich into a unified legal and pacified territory. The proclamation of the „Ewiger Landfrieden„ (Eternal Peace in the land) prohibited all feuds and personal justice, creating a new legal basis. A Permanent Imperial Chamber Court was there to implement it and ensure compliance. After a long debate between Emperor Maximilian I and the Imperial Estates, a reform of the Imperial finances was pushed through raising the „Common Penny„, a combination of wealth tax, income tax and poll tax. Later Reichtags divided up the empire into supra-regional administrative units – the Reichskreise, or Imperial districts. In 1663, the Permanent Reichstag was set up in Regensburg.
Inspired by the ideas of the Humanists, the concept and consciousness of a „German nation„ began to arise on a political as well as a cultural level, which was legitimised thanks to the rediscovery and collection of literary monuments, such as „Germania„ by Tacitus. Until around 1500, it was the *"deutsche Lande"* (German lands) that were always mentioned, but around that time, the term "Deutschland" in the singular cropped up for the first time.

- **1273** – After a warning from the Pope, the electors chose Count Rudolf of Habsburg (dynastic power in the Breisgau, Alsace and Aargau, amongst others) to be king.
- **1346-78** – Charles IV of Luxembourg in power as the most important ruler of the Late Middle Ages.
- **1386** – Founding of the University of Heidelberg, the oldest in Germany.
- **1414-18** – Council of Constance; the largest church meeting of the Middle Ages until then.
- **1438** – After the death of the last of the Luxembourg emperors, the electors chose the Habsburg duke Albrecht V to become King Albrecht II.
- **c 1450** – Invention of book printing with movable type by Johann Gutenberg from Mainz; flourishing and spread of Humanism.
- **1452** – During a military campaign by Frederick III, the last coronation of an emperor in Rome takes place.
- **1493** – Maximilian I becomes king. As of 1508 he is the „elected Roman Emperor„. His successors adopt the Imperial title immediately after the royal coronation in Aachen, thereby avoiding the difficult and dangerous journey to Rome along with their courts.
- **1519-56** – Emperor Charles V, Maximilian's grandchild, gathers the greatest amount of power during his term (in terms of size, population and wealth) since the Carolingians.

The Reformation and the Thirty Years War

In 1503, **Martin Luther** (1483-1546) entered the Augustinian monastery of Erfurt. A dedicated cleric, he was tormented by the problem of salvation. Appointed Professor of Theology, he found in the Holy Scriptures (c 1512-13) his answer: "We cannot earn forgiveness for our sins through our deeds, only God's mercy justifies us in our faith in it." Man's salvation, therefore – Luther argued – lies entirely within the gift, or Grace, of God. This concept led him to attack the Church's dealing in indulgences and, on 31 October 1517, he nailed 95 "theses" condemning such practices and reminding the Faithful of the primordial importance of the sacrifice on the Cross and the Grace of God on the doors of Wittenberg Church.
Luther was denounced in the court of Rome, refused to recant, and in 1520 burned the Papal Bull threatening him with excommunication. Subsequently he attacked the institutions and hierarchy of the Church and objected to the primacy of the clergy in spiritual matters, arguing the universal priesthood of Christians conferred by baptism.

Regensburg Tourismus

Napoleon at Regensburg, 23 April 1809.

Refusing to recant once more before the Diet of Worms (1521), where he had been summoned by Charles V, he was then placed under a ban of the Empire. His works were also condemned.

The patronage of Frederick the Wise, Duke of Saxony, enabled him to continue work on a translation of the Bible considered to be the first literary work in modern German. The Edict of Worms was confirmed in 1529 – and even hardened by an additional ruling forbidding any religious reform.

The Council of Trent (1545-63) resulted in the renewal of Catholicism and the Counter Reformation, which was resolutely supported by the Emperor. The internal struggles of the Protestants and the feud between Rudolf II and his brother Matthias put an end to the Peace of Augsburg. The Protestant Union led by the Electorate of the Palatinate now faced the Catholic League with the Duchy of Bavaria at its head. The Bohemian Rebellion of 1618 led to the outbreak of the Thirty Years War, which began as a religious conflict among the estates and soon engulfed all of Europe.

The war, which was almost exclusively fought on German territory, devastated huge tracts of land, caused general havoc, left the cities in piles of rubble and ash and finally ruined all economic life in the countryside. By the end of the war, only the individual territorial states showed some form of gain in authority at the cost of the empire, whose significance dwindled.

- **1530** – Invited by Charles V to meet in Augsburg; theologians of the opposing faiths fail to agree, and Melanchthon draws up in the name of the Lutherans the "Confession of Augsburg" which becomes the charter of the new Protestantism.
- **1555** – The Peace of Augsburg established a compromise, and Lutheran Protestantism was officially recognised as an equal to Catholicism. The empire thereby lost its sovereignty over religious matters to the territories. The basic pronouncement, *Cujus regio ejus religio* – to each state the religious faith of its people – is one of the legal principles of the religious peace.
- **1618** – The Bohemian estates refuse to recognise the Archduke Ferdinand, the successor of Emperor Matthias, as the Bohemian king. Instead, they elect the Protestant Elector Frederick V from the Palatinate to be their ruler. After the Defenestration of Prague in May (when the King of Bohemia's representatives were thrown out of a window by Bohemian nobles protesting about reduction of their privileges), the situation became more tense and ultimately led to the outbreak of the Thirty Years War.
- **1618-23** – The first phase of the war (Bohemian-Palatinate War) is decided by the defeat of Frederick V at the battle of Weifler Berg in 1620 against an army commanded by Tilly.
- **1625-29** – Phase two (the Danish-Dutch War) ends with Denmark's Protestant soldiers being defeated by Imperial troops under Wallenstein.
- **1630-35** – Sweden enters the war on the Protestant side (Swedish War). King Gustav Adolph II dies in the battle near Lützen.

• **1635-48** – France, under the leadership of Richelieu, now begins to participate actively in the alliance with Bernhard von Weimar (French-Swedish War). Previously France had avoided open war against the Habsburg countries – whom she felt encircled by – and had simply paid subsidies.
• **1648** – Peace of Westphalia: peace treaty in Münster and Osnabrück after five years of negotiations *(see MÜNSTER)*. An eighth elector is created for the Rhineland Palatinate after it becomes known that Bavaria will be allowed to keep the electoral position it took from the Palatinate during the war.
• **1688-97** – Palatinate War of Succession. Louis XIV lays claim to the left bank of the Rhine; French troops under Louvois devastate the Palatinate.

The Rise of Prussia

In 1415, Burgrave Frederick of Hohenzollern was granted the Electorate of Brandenburg. The Duchy of Prussia, 203 years later also came under the authority of his dynasty. Frederick William (1640-88), the Great Elector, turned the small country into the strongest, best governed northern German state thanks to successful power policies, deprivation of the estates' power, a centralised administration and the creation of a standing army. He also extended the country by adding eastern Pomerania, which he received in the Peace of Westphalia. After the revocation of the Edict of Nantes in France, thousands of Huguenots fled to Brandenburg and built up the economic basis for the rise of Berlin.
His grandson, King Frederick William I continued the good works by laying the foundations to the Prussian military and official

PRUSSIAN REFORMS: THE REVOLUTION FROM ABOVE

The reforms already prepared by the General Land Law of 1794, were initially set in motion by Baron von Stein, and, after his dismissal, by Baron von Hardenberg. The two men went about installing new structures for government and society virtually by decree and with almost revolutionary energy. Abolition of serfdom by the Edict of 1807 was of particular importance, as was the lifting of guild compulsion and the introduction of a free crafts market. Educational reforms followed, resulting in the founding of the University in Berlin by Wilhelm von Humboldt (1810) and a military reform. Other reforms included the emancipation of the Jews and the modernisation of the administration.

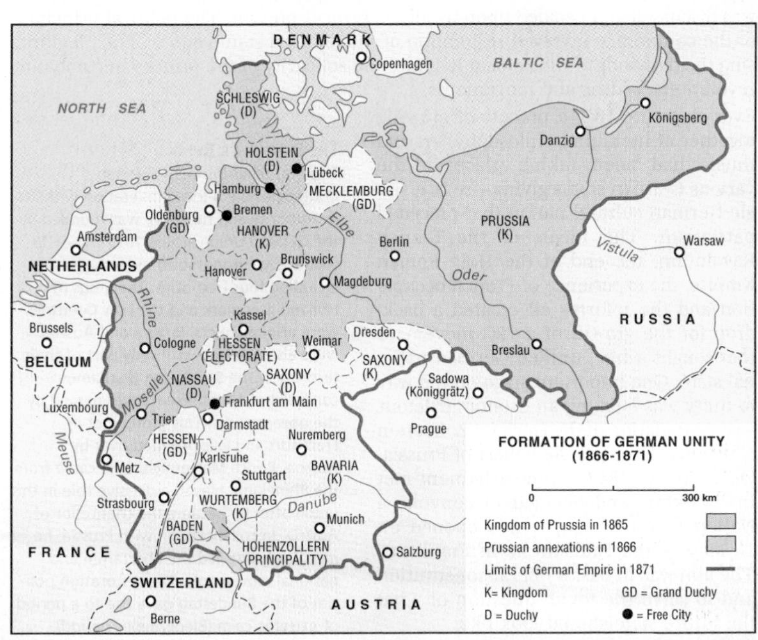

state. Fulfilment of one's duty, industriousness, economy and strict discipline on the part of the soldiers were some of the aspects of this state inspired by the "Soldier King".

His son, **Frederick the Great** (1740-86), took the throne in a country with an exemplary administration, and within a few years, he turned it into the second power of the empire. The Silesian War and the Seven Years War won him Silesia, and the division of Poland extended his power eastwards. This connoisseur and lover of music and literature, the friend and correspondent of Voltaire, was considered an „enlightened ruler„ and had a high reputation among European scholars especially at the beginning of his incumbency. The rule of "Old Fritz" left Prussia with a well organised administration and a close relationship between the king and the nobles, which all formed the cornerstone of Prussian power.

- **1701** – Elector Frederick III is crowned Frederick I King of Prussia in Königsberg.
- **1740-48** – War of Austrian Succession/Silesian Wars: The legality of the Pragmatic Sanction (1713) pronounced by Charles VI is disputed. The war is triggered by Frederick II's troops marching into Silesia.
- **1756-63** – The Seven Years War, during which Prussia joins forces with England against the Emperor, France and Russia. By the end of the war, Prussia was the fifth European power; the system of power will guide Europe's fate until the outbreak of the First World War.

The Way to a German National State

Since 1792, war had raged between France and the other powers of Europe. The Peace of Lunéville, signed in 1801, resulted in the loss of the territories of the left bank of the Rhine. The Decision of the Deputation of German Estates (1803) destroyed the political and legal foundations of the old Empire: Dissolution, secularisation and harmonisation of almost all religious and smaller states and of most of the Imperial towns. The beneficiaries were Bavaria, Prussia, Baden and Württemberg. They gained territory, and the latter two were even given Elector ranking. Sixteen of the south and western German states left the Imperial Union and founded the Confederation of the Rhine in 1806 in Paris under the protection of France.

At the **Congress of Vienna** (1814-15), the geographical reorganisation of Europe was discussed and decided upon by all the princes present. The political principles of the conference involved restoration of the political status quo of 1792, legitimising the demands of the Ancien Régime, and solidarity of the princes in combating revolutionary ideas and movements.

Ever since the 18C, a process of growing together of literature, philosophy, art and music had been taking place in the various German states giving rise to a single German cultural nation that preceded patriotism. The ideals of the French Revolution, the end of the Holy Roman Empire, the experience of French occupation and the reforms all created a backdrop for the growth of a 19C movement that sought a free, unified German national state. One important stage on the way to unity was – taking an economic detour – the foundation of the German Zollverein (Customs Union) at the behest of Prussia. On 31 March 1848, a pre-Parliament met in Frankfurt and decided to convoke a National Convention, which opened on 18 May in the Paulskirche in Frankfurt. The aim was to pass a liberal constitution and to solve the tough question of what the future state should look like.

The Deutscher Bund

The Deutscher Bund, or German Confederation, a loose federation with little authority and function, was founded by the German Union Act of 1815 out of 39 (politically autonomous) individual states – including four free cities. The kings of Holland, Denmark and the Low Countries were also members. Prussia and Austria were also involved with only part of their territories. The Bundestag (Parliament) consisted of 11 representatives named by the governments. This group met in Frankfurt and was presided over by Austria. Prince Metternich, who came from the Rhineland, played a decisive role in this union after he became the chancellor of Austria. In collaboration with Prussia, he mercilessly crushed the libertarian and national movements. The restoration policies of the Bundestag gave rise to a period of extreme calm (Biedermeier period).

On the table were the greater German solution, with the Habsburg empire under Austrian leadership, and the smaller German solution, ie without Austria, but with a Hohenzollern emperor at the top.
The latter was finally voted in. However, the Prussian king Frederick William IV refused the Imperial crown brought to him by a delegate from the Paulskirche Parliament.
Otto von Bismarck, appointed Minister-President of Prussia in 1862, needed no more than eight years to bring about unification under Prussian rule. With the loyalty of an elite bourgeoisie born through the advances of industrialisation and science at his back – and also with the neutrality of Napoleon III – he aggressively pursued a policy of war. After joining Austria in defeating Denmark in 1864, Prussia then declared war on her German ally and defeated the Imperial troops at the battle of Sadowa. This ended Austrian-Prussian dualism for good. A year later, Bismarck created the North German Alliance, consisting of all German states north of the River Main: Hannover, Hessen and Schleswig-Holstein already belonged to Prussia. The Franco-Prussian War of 1870-71 completed the task of unification.
- **1806** – Napoleon marches into Berlin. Emperor Francis II of Austria surrenders the Roman-German Imperial Crown ending the Holy Roman Empire of the German nation going back to Charlemagne.
- **1813** – Prussia commands the Coalition in the Wars of Liberation against Napoleon, who is defeated in the Battle of Nations at Leipzig.
- **1814-15** – Congress of Vienna: foundation of the German Confederation; Holy Alliance between Russia, Prussia and Austria.
- **1819** – The Decisions of Karlsbad include press censorship, prohibitions of the fraternities, monitoring of the universities.
- **1833-34** – Founding of the German Customs Union (Zollverein), an economic unification of most German states – except Austria – under Prussian leadership.
- **1835** – First German railway line is opened between Nuremberg and Fürth.
- **1848** – Unrest in France in February spreads to Mannheim first and then, in March, to all German states. But the "March Revolution" quickly turns into a bourgeois reform movement.

The German Empire (1871-1918)

The immediate cause of the Franco-Prussian War of 1870 was the claim by the House of Hohenzollern (Leopold von Hohenzollern-Sigmaringen) to the Spanish throne. Bismarck succeeded in kindling national pride on both sides of the border. France then declared war on Prussia. The southern states united with the states of the North German Union led by Prussia. The German princes all stood against France as they had signed secret alliances with Prussia. After the victory of Sedan (2 September), the southern states opened negotiations with Prussia on the issue of German unification.
The first years following the founding of the German Reich in 1871 were marked by an exceptional economic boom, also known as the **Gründerzeit**. One reason for this was the 5 billion francs in reparations that the French had been forced to pay. Combined with the advantages of the larger boundary free economic area and measures to standardise coins, measures and weights, this gave rise to rapid growth in the financial, industrial, construction and traffic sectors.
- **1871** – On 18 January, William I is crowned German Emperor in the Mirror Room of Versailles. Imperial Germany, enlarged by the acquisition of Alsace-Lorraine, remains in theory a federation – but it is in fact under Prussian domination. Germany is transformed from an agricultural to an industrial economy.
- **1888** – William II succeeds after his father Frederick III's brief reign.
- **1890** – After numerous altercations, the Emperor forces Bismarck's resignation. The demographic explosion, added to overheated industrial development leads the Emperor to play dangerous power politics. The Emperor's unabashed expansionary policies and dangerous foreign policy decisions provoke the enmity of England, Russia and France.

The First World War and the Weimar Republic

Erupting into an international atmosphere crackling with tension, the assassination of the Austrian Archduke Ferdinand and his wife at Sarajevo on 28 June 1914 unleashed a chain reaction. Austria-Hungary's declaration of war against Serbia mobilised the great powers of Europe. Germany's plans for a war on two fronts originated with a former chief of the General Staff named Von Schlieffen. Ignoring Belgium's neutrality, German troops moved into France. The advance was halted at the River Marne, and the war of attrition began in the trenches. On the eastern front German troops under General Hindenburg occupied large sections of Ruscian territory.

- **1914** – Germany declares war on France and Russia on 3 August.
- **1917** – An armistice is agreed with Russia, shattered by Revolution. The USA enters the war, after Germany had declared indiscriminate submarine warfare.
- **1918** – On 28-29 October, the sailors of the German naval fleet at Wilhelmshaven began a mutiny, and the revolution that had been brewing in Germany finally erupted, with workers' and soldiers' councils springing up throughout the land. However, the revolution was suppressed by the provisional government under Friedrich Ebert with the support of military supreme command. On 9 November, William II abdicated and Philipp Scheidemann proclaimed the republic. Two days later, Matthias Erzberger signed the armistice at Compiègne.

After the November revolution, which dwindled in early 1919 due to the unrest caused by the Spartacists, the model of a liberal democratic state with a strong president was able to get established. On 11 August 1919, Germany adopted a Republican Constitution in Weimar, where the National Convention was meeting. This „republic without republicans„ had to shoulder the heavy burden of assuming the obligations of the Treaty of Versailles, which took effect in 1920: this meant accepting responsibility for the war, the diminution of national territory (losing important agricultural and industrial areas), loss of colonies, demilitarisation and a very high level of reparations.

The only truly republican parties accepting the constitution, the SPD (Social Democrats), the Centre Party and the DDP (German Democratic Party) had a parliamentary majority after 1920. All in all, the Weimar Republic had 16 governments; every eight and a half months on average, the government changed. Galloping inflation broke out fairly soon, brought about by an economic crisis, by difficulties in getting the industrial sector working again and by high government debt: the bourgeoisie was ruined, all financial assets that had not been invested in land or real estate were worth nothing.

Germany experienced fairly tranquil years from 1924 to 1929, even though the republic did have to deal with major internal and external burdens. In spite of continuously high unemployment figures, an economic upswing did take place, thanks to the Dawes Plan agreeing more manageable yearly reparation payments, the end of the occupation of the Ruhr area and high influx of capital – thanks to the commitment of American investors. Germany was even accepted into the League of Nations (1926) during the incumbency of Chancellor and Foreign minister Gustav Stresemann. A year earlier in Locarno, Germany and France signed a pact pledging not to use violent means to revise borders – a corresponding agreement could not be signed for the eastern borders.

However, the Weimar Republic was then swept into the world economic crisis of 1929. High foreign debt, sharp decline in exports, inflation and dramatic unemployment figures all led to the rise of radical political parties, especially the German National Socialist Worker's Party, after 1930. They presented a concept that states that to solve the social problems, a „Volksgemeinschaft„, ie a people's community, based on race was needed. The Nazi storm-troops and Communist groups increasingly fought it out in the street. The social elite and the business community saw in Adolf Hitler a bulwark against Communism: on 30 January 1933, almost 10 years after his first attempt to seize power, Hitler was named Chancellor of the Reich by President Von Hindenburg; it was the end of the Weimar Republic.

- **1919** – The National Convention meets in Weimar, Friedrich Ebert (SPD) is named its first President (11 February); Versailles Peace Treaty is signed (28 June).

• **1923** – Occupation of the Ruhr region on 11 January by France, because Germany has fallen behind on reparation payments, followed by passive resistance in the Ruhr. The NSDAP (the National Socialist German Workers' Party) attempts a coup in Munich on 8-9 November led by Adolf Hitler, who had joined the party in 1919. The coup is foiled, Hitler is sentenced to jail, but released in 1924.
• **1925** – After the death of Friedrich Ebert, the former Field Marshall General Paul von Hindenburg is elected President of the Republic.
• **1930** – After an electoral defeat in the Reichstag (Parliament) come a number of presidial cabinets (Brüning, Von Papen, Von Schleicher), ie governments without parliamentary majorities.
• **1932** – At the Reichstag elections in July, the NSDAP becomes the strongest party with almost 38% of the votes. Together with the Communists, the Nazis have an absolute majority, which lets the radical parties block any parliamentary majorities they please.

The Nazi dictatorship and the Second World War

No sooner had the NSDAP taken power under the leadership of Hitler than it began to organise a totalitarian dictatorship and eliminate all democratic rules. In a climate of propaganda, intimidation and terror on the part of the SA, SS and Gestapo, all parties, associations and social organisations were liquidated or dissolved, with the exception of the churches. The NSDAP was declared the sole legal party. Opponents were thrown into concentration camps and murdered. Via the process of taking power and standardising society, the party penetrated every single level of state government, from local to national. A kind of coexistence did remain which was marked by competing authorities and rivalries that remained one of the main characteristics of the Nazi state. Art and literature were subjected to censorship: "Degenerate art" was banned, forcing numerous artists into exile.
The Nuremberg Laws promulgated at the Reich party rally (September 1935) endowed the persecution of the Jews with final, systematic, racist characteristics: prohibitions, loss of civil rights and mass arrests were the instruments of the anti-Semitic ideology. As early as 1 April 1933, the NSDAP had ordered a "boycott of the Jews" and thus initiated the gradual exclusion of Germany's 500 000 Jews from public life. In the night of 9-10 November 1938, the Nazis organised a pogrom ("Reichskristallnacht"): synagogues, Jewish apartments and shops were damaged or destroyed.
The improved worldwide economic situation helped reduce the number of unemployed as did a programme of public works (motorways, drainage schemes) that had already been planned earlier, a policy of rearmament, and the recruitment of young people into para-governmental organisations. In 1942, the National Socialist Reich stood at the zenith of its power: materially speaking and otherwise, many Germans had profited up until that point.

Landesarchiv Berlin/Presse- und informationsamt des landes Berlin

Airlift during the blockade of Berlin in 1948.

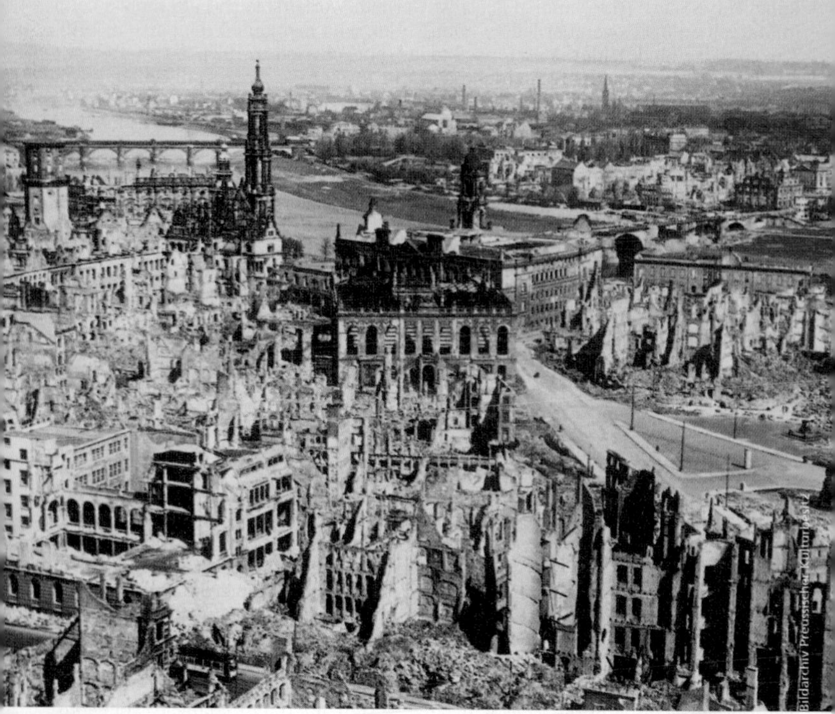
Bildarchiv Preussischer Kulturbesitz

Dresden in ruins, 1949.

The assault on Poland on 1 September 1939 launched the **Second World War**. Preparations for an annihilation war had already been going full steam since 1936. The aim was to do away with other peoples and build up a greater European area dominated by „Aryan„ Eurasians. But the war reached German civilians as soon as the British and the Americans began dropping explosive and incendiary bombs on war-related and residential targets. By the end of the war, Germany lay in ruins, the bulk of the inhabitants were suffering from under-nourishment and millions had been driven out of the eastern regions. With the liberation of the concentration camps, the world at large discovered to its horror with what cruelty and meticulousness the Nazis had actually carried out their policy of genocide against the Jews.

Germany from post-war 1945 to the present

• **1945** – Germany and Berlin are divided into four zones of occupation. According to the agreement, American and British forces pull out of Saxony, Thuringia and Mecklenburg and redeploy in the western sector of Berlin. At the Potsdam Conference *(see POTSDAM)* the victorious powers decide to demilitarise and denazify Germany, make it into a democracy and administer it jointly.
• **1946** – Amalgamation of the British and American zones (bi-zone).
• **1948** – End of the Four-Power administration of Germany after the Soviet delegate leaves the Allied Control Council (20 March). Soviet blockade of the western sectors of Berlin, the city is supplied by the airlift.
• **1949** – Creation (23 May) of the Federal Republic in the three western zones. The Soviet zone becomes (7 October) the German Democratic Republic. Under the leadership of Konrad Adenauer, Chancellor until 1963, and Ludwig Erhard, Minister of Economic Affairs, the Federal Republic enjoys a spectacular economic rebirth and re-establishes normal international relations.
• **1952** – Soviet leadership offers to create a single, neutral, democratic Germany, a reunification initiative which fails.
• **1961** – Construction of the "Berlin Wall" (12-13 August).
• **1972** – Signature of a treaty between the two Germanies, a milestone in Chancellor Willy Brandt's (chancellor from 1969-74) policy of openness towards the East (*Ostpolitik*).

• **1989** – Citizens of East Germany occupy West German embassies in Prague, Budapest and Warsaw with the aim of travelling to West Germany. Ever since the opening of the border between Austria and Hungary, a veritable mass migration begins. On 4 November, the largest demonstration ever takes place in East Berlin, involving over one million people. On the night of 9-10 November, the internal German border is opened, the Wall is broken through. On 7 December, the Round Table meets for the first time as an institution of public control, with representatives from the political parties and the citizens' movements.

• **1990** – Treaty of reunification drawn up; on 3 October the German Democratic Republic joins the Federal Republic of Germany according to Article 23 of the Basic law. On 2 December, the first joint German parliamentary elections take place.

Keen to achieve rapid reunification, on 28 November 1989 West German Chancellor **Helmut Kohl** put forward a ten-point plan providing for the initial constitution of a confederation. On 3 October 1990 (now a public holiday) the Parliament sitting in the Reichstag in Berlin ratified the treaty of reunification. Helmut Kohl won the elections in December 1990, and, in 1991, the Bundestag chose Berlin as capital of the reunified country. With the withdrawal of the last occupying troops in 1994, Germany became a totally sovereign state. It set its sights on the construction of Europe of which – to Helmut Kohl's mind – France and Germany together must form the cornerstone. After the Federal President's move to Berlin, the Parliament followed suit in 1999. On 19 April the new Plenary Room of the Reichstag building, crowned by a dome designed by British architect Sir Norman Foster, was inaugurated.

The reunification, which had been carried out at great speed on the political level, was to cause considerable problems in the economic and social domains; a drop in competitiveness, high rates of unemployment in the new Länder, and increased taxation in the West to finance the "upgrading" of the East fuelled growing discontent. These problems arising from the refound unity of the two Germanies partly explain the poor performance of Helmut Kohl's CDU-CSU party in the 1998 legislative elections; it was Social Democrat **Gerhard Schröder** who claimed victory and went on to form a coalition government with the Greens. Taking control of a sector of Kosovo as part of the KFOR in 1999, Germany began to take a greater role on the international scene. In a difficult socio-economic climate and with the crucial aid of the Greens, Gerhard Schröder was re-elected in 2002.

© Landesarchiv Berlin

The fall of the Berlin Wall, 1989.

Elements of Architecture

Religious architecture

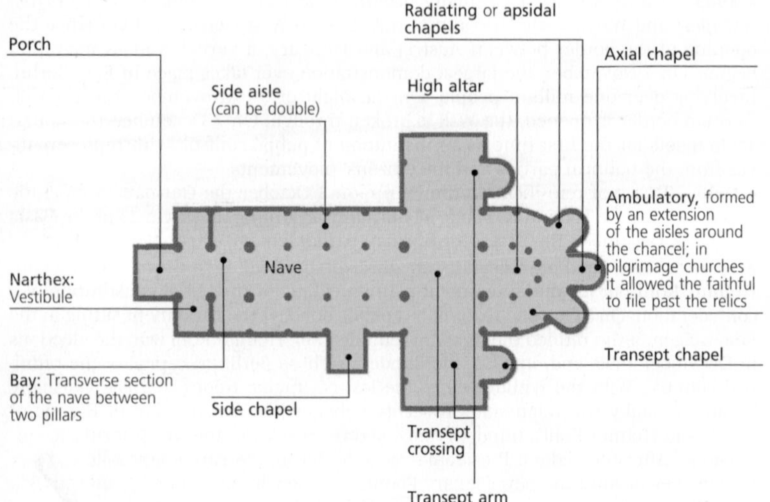

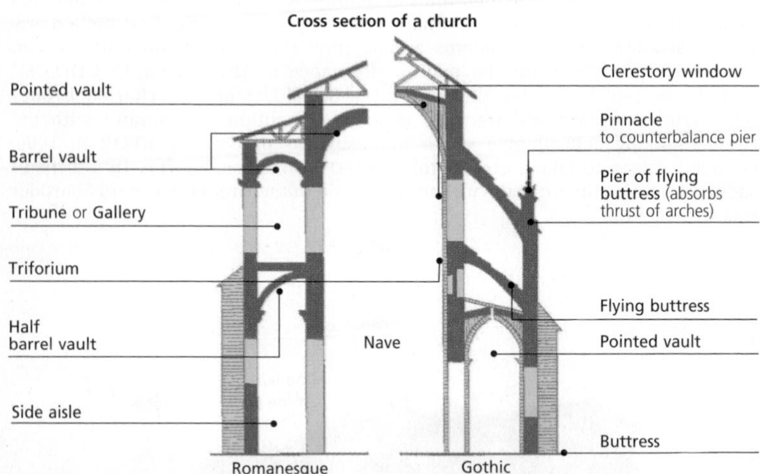

Hall Church

Unlike a basilica, a hall church has aisles the same height as the central nave and covered with one roof their windows let light inside the edifice.

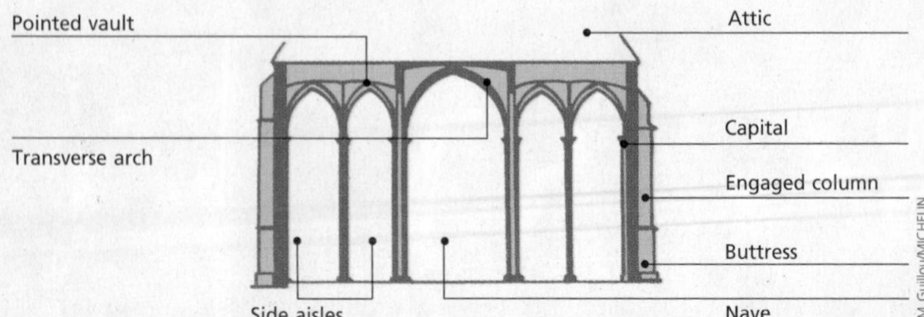

SPEYER – East End of the Cathedral (11C)

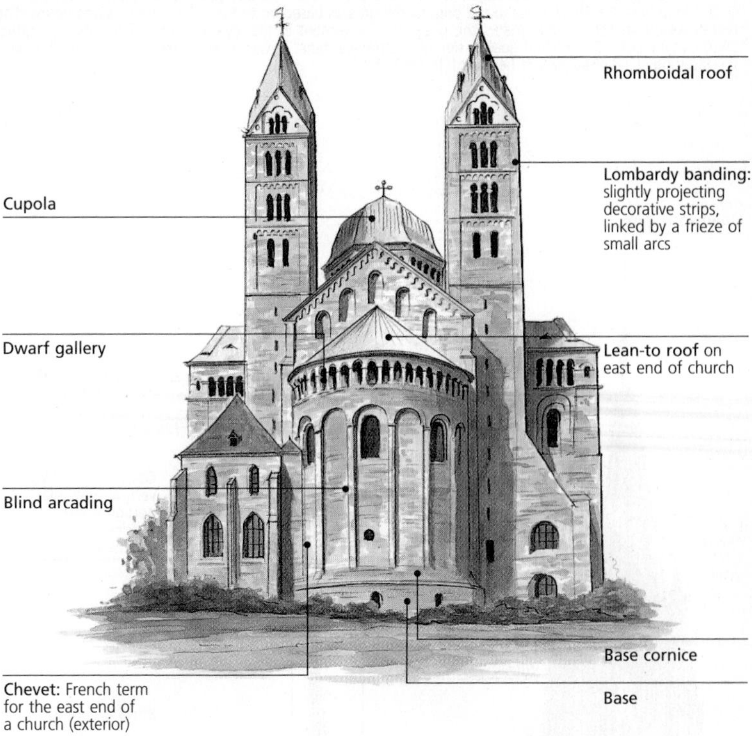

Rhomboidal roof

Lombardy banding: slightly projecting decorative strips, linked by a frieze of small arcs

Cupola

Dwarf gallery

Lean-to roof on east end of church

Blind arcading

Base cornice

Base

Chevet: French term for the east end of a church (exterior)

FREIBURG – Cathedral Altar (14C-16C)

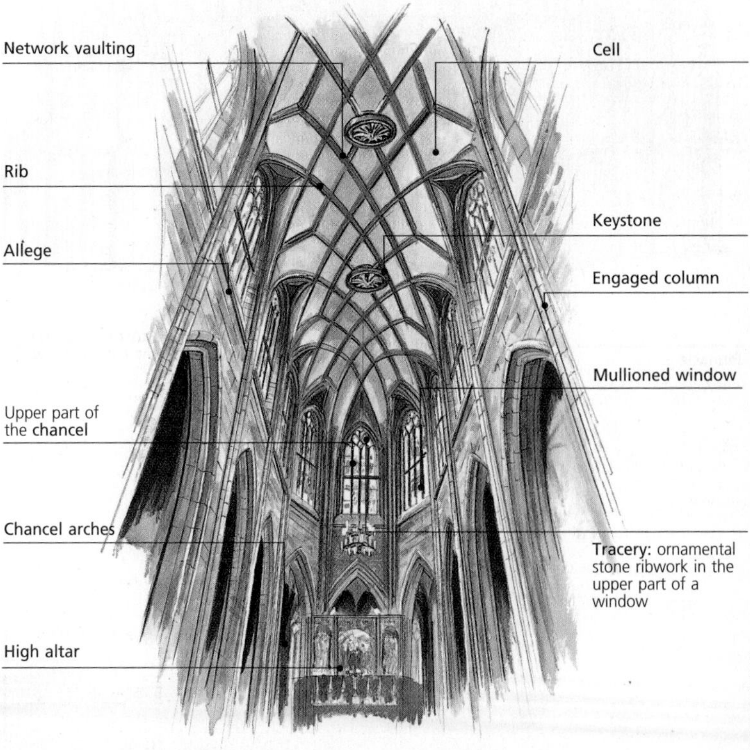

Network vaulting

Cell

Rib

Keystone

Allège

Engaged column

Mullioned window

Upper part of the **chancel**

Chancel arches

Tracery: ornamental stone ribwork in the upper part of a window

High altar

R. Corbel/MICHELIN

COLOGNE CATHEDRAL (1248 to 1880), South façade

The construction of the cathedral began in 1248 and took more than 600 years to complete. It was the first Gothic church in the Rhineland and the original design was based on those in Paris, Amiens and Reims. The twin-towered western façade marks the peak of achievement in the style known as Flamboyant Gothic. Stepped windows, embellished gables, slender buttresses, burst upwards, ever upwards, slimly in line with the tapering spires that reach a height of 157m/515ft.

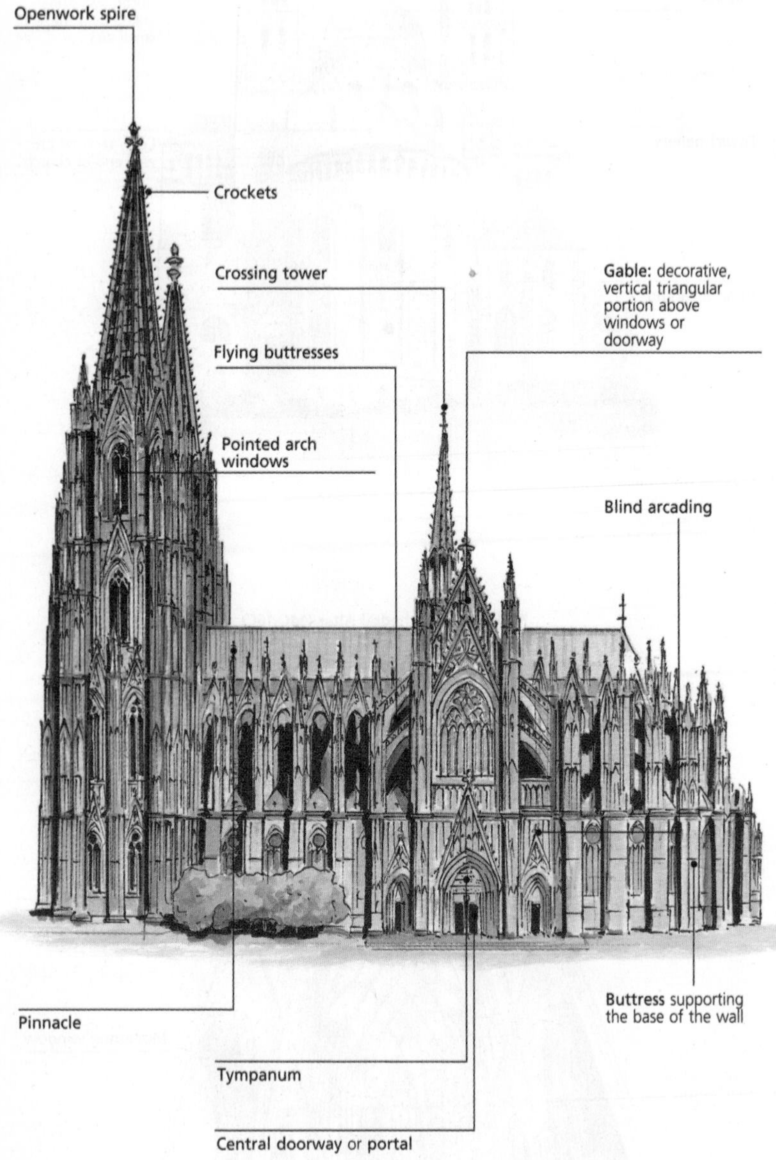

R. Corbel/MICHELIN

Schloß BRUCHSAL – Garden façade (18C)

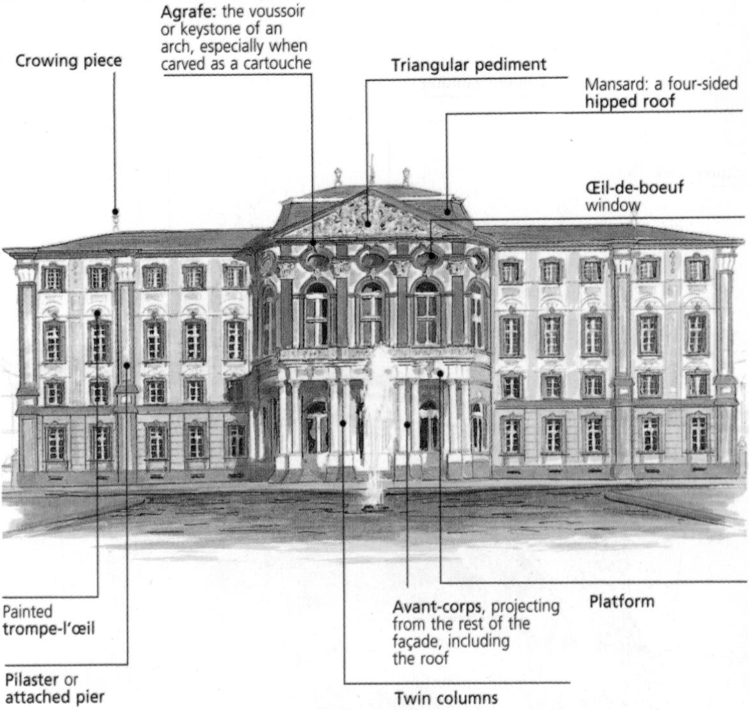

Crowing piece

Agrafe: the voussoir or keystone of an arch, especially when carved as a cartouche

Triangular pediment

Mansard: a four-sided **hipped roof**

Œil-de-boeuf window

R. Corbel/MICHELIN

Painted **trompe-l'œil**

Pilaster or **attached pier**

Avant-corps, projecting from the rest of the façade, including the roof

Platform

Twin columns

POTSDAM – Sanssouci Palace and Park (Georg Wenzelaus von Knobelsdorff and Friedrich II, 1745-47)

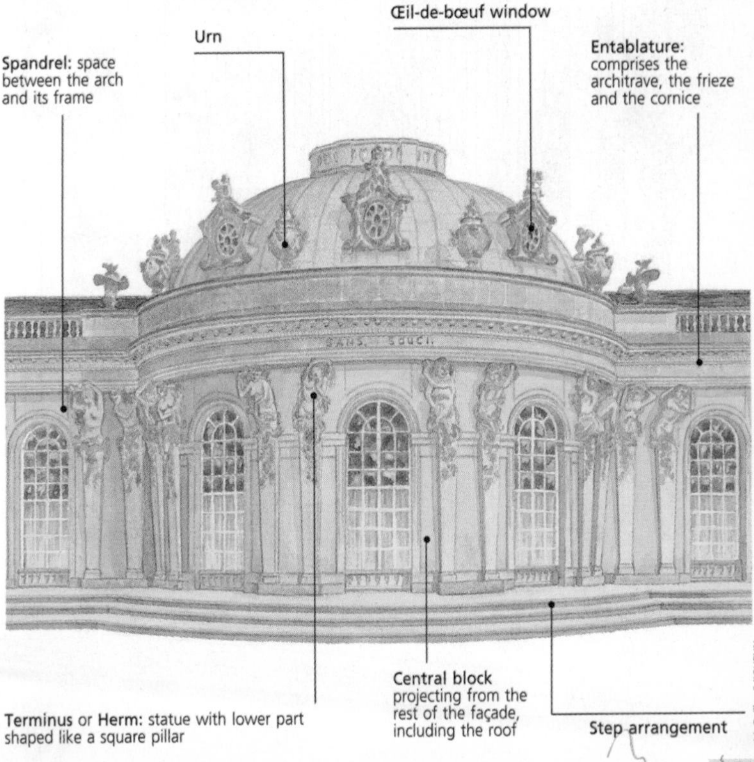

Œil-de-bœuf window

Urn

Spandrel: space between the arch and its frame

Entablature: comprises the architrave, the frieze and the cornice

SANS SOUCI

M. Guillou/MICHELIN

Terminus or **Herm:** statue with lower part shaped like a square pillar

Central block projecting from the rest of the façade, including the roof

Step arrangement

OTTOBEUREN Abbey Church (18C)

Ottobeuren is characteristic of other Bavarian churches with its dazzling ornamentation and plays of light and symmetry.

"Uncle Tom's Cabin" estate (Bruno Taut, Hugo Häring, Otto Rudolf Salvisberg, 1926-32)

Designed to house 15 000 people, this estate built under the supervision of Martin Wagner, does not convey an impression of monotony. There is a U-Bahn Station in its centre as well as a shopping centre and a cinema.

Philharmonie (Hans Scharoun, 1960-63) and Chamber Music Hall (Edgar Wisniewski, from a drawing by Scharoun, 1984-88)

In 1957, during a congress, H Scharoun expressed his wish to build "an adequately shaped hall for music making, where listening to music would be a common experience". The audience sits round the orchestra, which occupies the very heart of the arena.

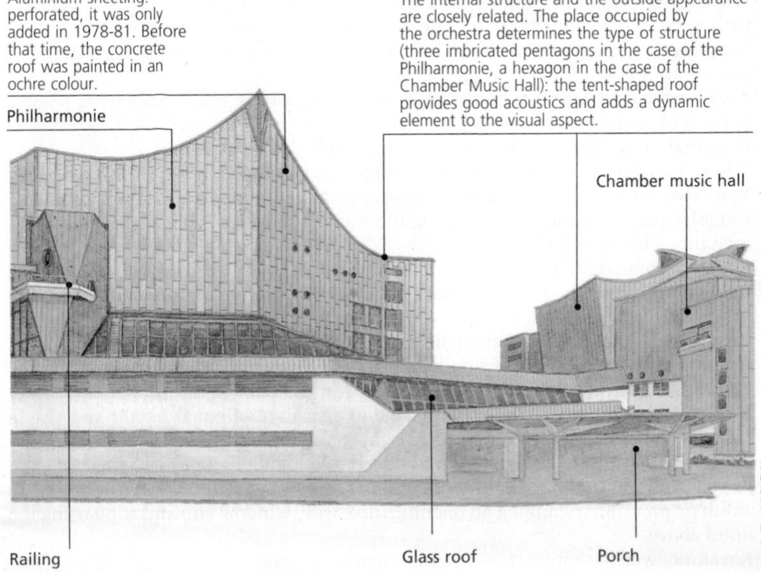

M. Guillou/MICHELIN

Glossary of Architecture

Absidiole or **apsidiole chapel**: small apsidal chapel opening on the ambulatory of a Romanesque or Gothic church.
Aisles: lateral divisions running parallel with the nave.
Ambulatory: formed by an extension of the aisles around the chancel; in pilgrimage churches it allowed the faithful to file past the relics.
Apse: rounded or polygonal end of a church; the outer section is known as the chevet.
Archivolt: ornamental moulding around the outside of an arch.
Atlantes (or **Telamones**): male figures used as supporting columns.
Atrium (or **four-sided portico**): court enclosed by colonnades in front of the entrance to a early Christian or Romanesque church.
Basilica: rectangular religious building, built on the Roman basilica plan with three or five aisles.
Bossage: architectural motif or facing made of bosses, uniformly projecting blocks on the outer wall. They are surrounded by deep carving or separating lines. Bossage was in vogue during the Renaissance.
Buttress: external mass of masonry projecting from a wall to counterbalance the thrust of the vaults and arches.
Capital: crowning feature of a column, consisting of a smooth part, connecting it to the shaft, and a decorated part. There are three orders in classical architecture: Doric, Ionic (with double volute), and Corinthian (decorated with acanthus leaves). The latter is often found in 16C-17C buildings.
Chancel: part of the church behind the altar set aside for the choir, furnished with variously decorated wooden stalls.
Chevet: French term for the east end of a church (exterior).
Choir screen or **rood screen**: partition separating the chancel from the nave.
Ciborium: canopy over an altar.
Console (or **corbel** or **bracket**): element of stone or wood projecting from a wall to support beams or cornices.
Corbelling: projecting course of masonry.
Corbie gable: triangular section crowning a wall, with steps on the coping.
Cornice: in classical architecture, projecting ornamental moulding along the top of a building. Also designates any projecting decoration around a ceiling.
Cross (church plan): churches are usually built either in the plan of a Greek cross, with arms of equal length, or a Latin cross, with shorter transept arms.
Crossing: central area of a cruciform church, where the transept crosses the nave and choir. A tower is often set above this space.
Crypt: underground chamber beneath a church, where holy relics were placed. Often a chapel or church in its own right.
Diagonal arch: diagonal arch supporting a vault.
Drum: circular or polygonal structure supporting a dome.
Embrasure: recess for a window or door, splayed on the inside.
Entablature: in classical architecture, the section above the columns consisting of architrave, frieze and cornice.
Gable: decorative, triangular section above a portal.
Gallery: in early Christian churches, an upper story opening on the nave. Later used in exterior decoration.
Grotesque: fanciful ornamental decoration inspired by decorative motifs from Antiquity. The term comes from the old Italian word *grotte*, the name given to the Roman ruins of the *Domus Aurea*, uncovered in the Renaissance period.
Hall-church: church in which the nave and aisles are of equal height and practically the same width, communicating right to the top.
High relief: sculpture with very pronounced relief, although not standing out from the background (half-way between low relief and in-the-round figures).
Jamb or **pier**: pillar flanking an opening (doorway, window etc) and supporting the lintel above.
Keystone: wedge-shaped stone at the crown of an arch.

D. Scherf/MICHELIN

Gothic architecture

The gradual emergence of the Gothic style (13C) – The French style of Gothic architecture struggled to free itself of the austere Romanesque forms and did not begin to flourish in Germany until the mid 13C. Architecture then reached new heights of refinement, producing such masterpieces as the cathedral in Cologne with its vast interior, two tall slender towers framing the façade in the French style and its soaring pointed vaulting. Also inspired by the French Gothic style are the cathedrals of Regensburg, Freiburg im Breisgau, Magdeburg and Halberstadt. A further manifestation of the predominance of French architecture can be seen in the establishment of Cistercian monasteries between 1150 and 1250. Their churches, usually without towers or belfries and often later modified inside in the Baroque manner, were habitually designed with squared-off chancels flanked by rectangular chapels. The abbey of Maulbronn is one of very few Cistercian complexes preserved in almost its entirety still extant in Europe.

The originality of German architecture – This first emerged in the use of brick. Indeed, in the north of the country the most imposing edifices were brick built, complete with buttresses and flying buttresses. Typical of this brick Gothic style (known in German as Backsteingotik) are the Nikolaikirche at Stralsund, the Marienkirche in Lübeck, the town halls of those two cities, Schwerin Cathedral and the abbey church at Bad Doberan.

The other German specificity throughout the Gothic period is the adoption of a new layout inspired by Cistercian architecture and manifested in the **hall-churches** *(Hallenkirche)*. In these buildings, the aisles are now the same height as the nave – which therefore has no clerestory windows – and separated from it only by tall columns. In the Elisabethkirche in Marburg, the three aisles are separated by thin supports, giving an impression of space and homogeneity.

Late Gothic Architecture *(Spätgotik)* – This very long period (14C, 15C and 16C) witnessed the widespread construction of hall-churches, including Freiburg cathedral, the Frauenkirche in Munich and the Georgskirche, Dinkelsbühl. The vaulting features purely decorative ribs forming networks in the shape of stars or flowers in stark contrast to the austerity of the walls. St Annenkirche at Annaberg-Buchholz epitomises this artistic virtuosity, free of all constraints.

Secular Architecture in the Late Middle Ages – Commercial prosperity among merchants and skilled craftsmen in the 14C and 15C led to the construction in town centres of impressive town halls and beautiful gabled and half-timbered private houses, frequently adorned with painting and sculpture. Examples of such architecture are still to be seen in the old town centres of Regensburg, Rothenburg ob der Tauber, Goslar and Tübingen.

The Renaissance

The Renaissance (1520-1620) is no more than a minor episode in the history of German architecture. Long held at bay by the persistence of the Gothic style, it was finally eclipsed by the troubles of the Reformation. Renaissance-style buildings are therefore very rare in German towns, except in Augsburg with its beautiful mansions lining Maximilianstaße and its town hall designed by **Elias Holl** (1573-1646), who was responsible for the most important buildings of the Renaissance in Germany.

Southern Germany shows a marked Italian influence: elegant Florentine arcading, for instance, was used by Jakob Fugger the Rich as decoration for his funerary chapel at Augsburg (1518); the Jesuits, building the Michaelskirche in Munich (1589), were clearly inspired by their own Sanctuary of Jesus (Gesù) in Rome; and in Cologne, the town hall with its two-tier portico reflects Venetian influence.

Northern Germany, on the other hand, was influenced by Flemish and Dutch design. In the rich merchants' quarters, many-storeyed gables, such as those of the Gewandhaus in Brunswick, boast rich ornamentation in the form of obelisks, scrollwork, statues, pilasters etc. The castles at Güstrow and Heidelberg and the old town of Görlitz are important examples of Renaissance architecture, while the buildings of Wolfenbüttel, Celle, Bückeburg and Hameln are steeped in the particular charm of the so-called "Weser Renaissance" *(see HAMELN)*.

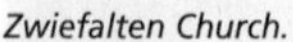

Zwiefalten Church.

M. Hertlein/MICHELIN

The splendours of Baroque architecture

After the disruption of the Thirty Years' War (1618-48), the ensuing revival of artistic activity provided an opportunity for the principalities to introduce Baroque architecture by welcoming French and Italian architects. Characterised by an irregularity of contour and a multiplicity of form, the Baroque style seeks, above all, the effect of movement and contrast. Taken to its extreme, it was soon saturated by Rococo decoration, which originated in the French *Rocaille* style; this style was originally secular and courtly but subsequently used in religious buildings.

From the mid 17C, Baroque influence was felt in southern Germany, encouraged by the Counter-Reformation's exaltation of dogmatic belief in Transubstantiation, the cult of the Virgin Mary and the saints, and in general all manifestations of popular piety. The aim was to achieve an emotional response from the spectator. This exuberance did not spread to Protestant Northern Germany.

The Masters of German and Danubian Baroque – There were exceptionally talented individuals in Bavaria who displayed equal skill across a variety of techniques, and who tended to prefer subtle ground plans, such as a round or elliptical focal shape. **Johann Michael Fischer** (Dieflen, Zwiefalten and Ottobeuren), the **Asam brothers** (Weltenburg and the Asamkirche in Munich) and **Dominikus Zimmermann** (1685-1766, Steinhausen and Wies) were the virtuosi of this Bavarian School; their vibrant creations are covered by a profusion of Rococo decoration.
The Baroque movement in Franconia, patronised by the prince-bishops of the Schönborn family, who owned residences in Mainz, Würzburg, Speyer and Bamberg, was closely linked with the spread of similar ideas in Bohemia. The Dientzenhofer brothers decorated the palaces in Prague as well as the one in Bamberg. Perhaps the greatest of all Baroque architects was **Balthasar Neumann** (1687-1753), who worked for the same prelates, and whose breadth of cultural knowledge and creativity, enriched by his contact with French, Viennese and Italian masters, far surpassed that of his contemporaries. One of his finest creations was the Vierzehnheiligen Church near Bamberg, where he managed to combine the basilical plan with the ideal of the central plan. In Saxony, the Zwinger Palace in Dresden – joint masterpiece of the architect **Matthäus Daniel Pöppelmann** (1662-1736) and the sculptor Permoser – is a consummate example of German Baroque with Italian roots. The refinement of the Rococo decor in Schlofl Sanssouci at Potsdam is even more astonishing given the reputed Prussian tendency towards austerity, but is explained by the periods of study undertaken in France and Italy by **Georg Wenzeslaus von Knobelsdorff** (1699-1753), official architect and friend of Frederick the Great.

Churches – A sinuous movement, generally convex in line, animates the façades, while the superposition of two pediments, different in design, adds vitality to the whole. They are additionally adorned with twin domed towers. Inside, huge galleries stand above the lateral chapels, at the height of pilaster capitals with jutting abaci. Chapels and galleries stop at the level of the transept, giving it a much greater depth. Clerestory windows, opening at the level of the gallery, allow plenty of light to enter.
Bohemian and Franconian Baroque is typified by **complex vaulting**, round or oval bays being covered by complicated structures in which the transverse arches bow out in horse-shoe shape, only to meet in their keystones.
Illusion is the keyword as regards the often **Rococo** decoration, using the effects of the white stucco, coloured marble and gilding. The numerous paintings and sculptures enhance this celebration of the sacred.

The monumental altarpiece or reredos – This becomes the focal point of the church. Reminiscent of a triumphal arch, in carved wood or stucco, it frames a large painting and/or a group of statuary (Ottobeuren Abbey Church). Columns twisted into spiral form accentuate the sense of movement which characterises Baroque art, and back lighting from a hidden source, with its striking contrasts of brightness and shadow, is equally typical of the style.

Palaces – The one-storey construction of these country residences was often lent additional importance by being built on a raised foundation. The focal point was a half-circular central bloc with the curved façade facing the garden.
Monumental stairways with several flights and considerable theatrical effect are often the centrepieces of the larger German castles and palaces built in the 18C. The staircase, embellished with arcaded galleries and a painted ceiling, leads to the first floor state room which rises majestically to a height of two storeys. Such elaborate arrangements characterise many of the great abbeys of this period, often complemented by that other ceremonial room, the library.

From neo-Classicism to neo-Gothic

The ideal of an original austerity – From 1750 on, Winckelmann's work on the art of Antiquity, and the excavations taking place at Pompeii, threw a new light on Greco-Roman architecture. At the same time, the example of Versailles inspired in Germany a new style of court life, particularly in the Rhineland and the Berlin of Frederick II. Many French architects were employed by the Electors of the Palatinate, of Mainz, of Trier and of Cologne; mainly, they produced plans for country mansions with names such as Monrepos ("my rest") or Solitude. Other German

architects, such as **Carl Gotthard Langhans** (1732-1808), were instrumental in the transition from the Baroque to the neo-Classical style (Brandenburg Gate and the Charlottenburg theatre in Berlin).
Features such as unadorned pediments, balustrades at the base of the roofs, columned porticoes at the main entrance, all indicate a desire for unobtrusive elegance. A new fashion arose, in which architects favoured the Doric style coupled with a preference for the colossal – pilasters and columns of a single "order" no longer stood one storey high but always two.
The interior decoration, carried out with a lighter touch, confined itself to cornucopias of flowers mingled with Rococo motifs that were now a little more discreet (garlands, urns, vases and friezes of pearls).
Architecture was now responding to a demand for rationality that had emerged in reaction to the Late Baroque and Rococo styles.
Karl-Friedrich Schinkel (1781-1841) – Appointed state architect by Frederick William III in 1815, he designed many buildings, including the Neue Wache, Altes Museum and Schauspielhaus in Berlin. In a refined approach using elements inspired by Antiquity, this great exponent of Romantic Classicism constantly sought to blend his constructions in with their surroundings. The grandiose style of his buildings with their long neo-Classical colonnades, the dramatic contrasts of light and the use of Gothic elements are typical of the Romantic trend.
The 19C and the neo-Gothic – By 1830, the neo-Classical movement had become sterile; it was superseded, except in Munich, by a renewed interest in the Gothic which became, for the Romantics, emblematic of "the old Germany".
At the same time, the **Biedermeier** style – lightweight, cushioned furniture with flowing lines, glass-fronted cabinets for the display of knick-knacks – corresponding perhaps with the later Edwardian style in England, was popular in middle-class homes between 1815 and 1848.
The year 1850 marks the beginning of the **Founders' Period** *(Gründerzeitstil)* with E. Ludwig and A. Koch in pursuit of a more up-to-date style. But the wealthy industrialists fell for pretentious medieval or Renaissance reproductions, also to be found in public buildings such as the Reichstag in Berlin.
19C architecture was thus characterised by a great diversity of styles.

20C movements

In the late 19C, artists began exploring new avenues in a desire to move away from past styles and into the modern age. **Art nouveau** or **Jugendstil**, a European movement, became the vogue in Germany. The architects' idea was to create a complete work of art that would be accessible to all, combining structure, decoration and furniture. This ideal, based on cooperation with industry, its methods of production and the use of the new materials (glass, iron, cement) that it was promoting, resulted in the fundamental concept of an industrial aesthetic, brought to the fore by such pioneers as Peter Behrens, **Mies van der Rohe** and **Walter Gropius**.
This style flourished mainly in Munich, Berlin and Darmstadt (with the Mathildenhöhe artists' colony). The artists' commitment, expressed within the Secessions (Munich 1892, Berlin 1899), was coupled with a political demand for independence.

The Jewish Museum, Berlin.

H. Champollion/MICHELIN

© Wallraf-Richartz-Museum, Cologne

"Virgin and Rose Bush" by Lochner

The Bauhaus – In 1919, Walter Gropius founded the **Bauhaus** Weimar: 1919-25, Dessau: 1926-32), a school of architecture and applied arts which radicalised the movement for modernisation, displaying an even greater interest in industrial production. The quest for unity between art and technique was a fundamental element. Architecture remained, in principle at least, the preferred form of expression since it combined structure and decoration and enabled application of the principles of functionality and rationality *(see DESSAU and WEIMAR)*. The movement instigated modern reflections on architecture and habitat and lent its vocabulary to modern design.
The school, which was critical of society, was closed in 1933 by the Nazis, who adopted a pompous and monumental style of architecture that was intended to reflect the strength of their power. It was, in most cases, to be destroyed.
At the end of the war, the reconstruction effort inspired a wide variety of architectural creations. Architects such as Dominikus Böhm and Rudolf Schwartz were among the craftsmen who were brought to light by this renewal of interest in sacred work, many of their designs being markedly austere.
New concepts, too, characterised the construction of municipal and cultural enterprises such as Hans Scharoun's Philharmonia in Berlin and the Staatsgalerie in Stuttgart by British architect James Stirling – buildings of an architectural audacity only made possible by the development of entirely new materials and construction techniques. Architectural creation is still very much alive in Germany today, particularly in Berlin with centres such as Friedrichstrasse or Potsdamer Platz – showcases of the avant-garde – and creations such as the Jüdisches Museum, completed by Daniel Liebeskind in 1998.

Germany's great painters and sculptors

15C

In the fields of painting and architecture, Germany remained for a long time attached to the Late Gothic tradition, which denied the realism so sought after in Italy. The country was divided into a large number of local schools under Dutch influence. Now came the time to seek an outlet for emotional expression and give vent to the religious concerns that marked the end of the Middle Ages.

Stefan Lochner (c 1410-51) – This leading master of the Cologne School perpetuated the tradition of international Gothic, giving it a lyrical and refined touch with his sweet expressions and an exquisitely delicate palette. The use of gold backgrounds afforded him a certain amount of leeway as regards the requirements of perspective. (*Adoration of the Magi*, Cologne cathedral; *Virgin and Rose Bush*, Wallraf-Richartz-Museum, Cologne).

Veit Stoß (c 1445-1533) – Sculptor, painter and engraver with a distinctive, powerful style; one of the greatest woodcarvers of his age. His figures were generally of a pathetic nature (*Annunciation*, Lorenzkirche, Nuremberg; *Reredos of the Nativity*, Bamberg Cathedral).

Tilman Riemenschneider (c 1460-1531) – Sculptor of alabaster and wood, he was master of an important studio where he created many altarpieces. His intricate works are executed with great finesse and richness of expression (*Tomb of Henry II* *the Saint*, Bamberg Cathedral; *Adam and Eve*, Mainfränkisches Museum, Würzburg; *Altarpiece to the Virgin*, Herrgottskirche, Creglingen).

The Master of St Severinus (late 15C) – The intimacy and iridescent colours of his works reflect Netherlandish influence (*Christ before Pilate*, Wallraf-Richartz-Museum, Cologne).

The Master of the Life of the Virgin (late 15C) – Painter of original works, influenced by the Flemish artist Van der Weyden (*Scenes from the Life of the Virgin*, Alte Pinakothek, Munich; *Vision of St Bernard*, Wallraf-Richartz-Museum, Cologne).

Engraving – First emerging in Germany around 1400, this art form was espoused by the greatest German masters. One of the pioneers was the unidentified engraver **Master E.S.**, known by the monogram with which he signed his engravings, whose work dates from between 1450 and 1467. Copperplate engraving techniques were later perfected and were best demonstrated by virtuosi such as **Martin Schongauer** (c 1450-91), whose designs were later followed by Albrecht Dürer.

© Wallraf-Richartz-Museum, Cologne

"Mary Magdalene" by Cranach

16C

The German Renaissance did not emerge until the 16C, with Dürer. The observation and idealising of nature resulted in works of increasing precision and refinement. The Danube School showed a new interest in landscape, encouraging its development as a genre, while Holbein breathed new life into the art of portrait painting with his striking realism.

Matthias Grünewald (c 1480-1528) – An inspired painter of the Late Gothic period, producing works of great emotional intensity capable of expressing the pain of humanity (***Crucifixion***, Staatliche Kunsthalle, Karlsruhe; *Virgin and Child*, Stuppach parish church).

Albrecht Dürer (1471-1528) – The greatest artist of the German Renaissance, he was fascinated by the art of Antiquity and the Italian Renaissance, with which he was able to combine a Nordic gravity. Based in Nuremberg, Dürer produced woodcuts achieving some magnificent light effects and a very broad range of greys (*The Apocalypse*). The religious scenes and portraits he painted are of an extraordinary intensity (*The Four Apostles*, *Self-Portrait with Cloak*, Alte Pinakothek, Munich; *Charlemagne*, Germanisches Nationalmuseum, Nuremberg).

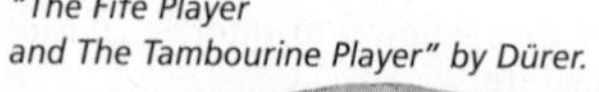

"The Fife Player and The Tambourine Player" by Dürer.

© Wallraf-Richartz-Museum, Cologne

R. Mattes/MICHELIN

Atlantes in the Zwinger Palace, Dresden.

Lucas Cranach the Elder (1472-1553) – Official painter to the prince-electors of Saxony and master of an important studio, he was the portraitist of the most eminent men of the Reformation, most notably of his friend Luther. His works reflect a strong sense of the wonders of nature, allying him with the painters of the Danube School. As court painter in Wittenberg, he produced religious paintings inspired by Lutheran ideas. The more Expressionist works of his youth gave way to paintings full of grace and nobility, typical of the refinement towards which 16C German art was heading. (*The Electors of Saxony*, Kunsthalle, Hamburg, *The Holy Family*, Städel museum, Frankfurt; *Portrait of Martin Luther*, Germanisches Nationalmuseum, Nuremberg).

Albrecht Altdorfer (c 1480-1538) – Leading member of the Danube School and one of the founders of landscape painting. His use of chiaroscuro creates dramatic and moving works, with the focus on landscapes shrouded in mystery (*Battle of Alexander*, Alte Pinakothek, Munich).

Hans Baldung Grien (c 1485-1545) – His complex compositions feature dramatic lighting effects, unusual colours and tortured movement (Altarpiece: *The Coronation of the Virgin*, Freiburg Cathedral).

Hans Holbein the Younger (1497-1543) – Painter of German merchants and subjects from court circles and the high aristocracy, he breathed new life into the art of portrait painting. His subjects are depicted with incredible precision in skilfully composed settings that illustrate their office. His compositions, both solemn and realistic, mark a definitive departure from the Gothic tradition (*Portrait of the Merchant Georg Gisze*, Gemäldegalerie, Berlin).

17C and 18C

Italian influence remained very much in evidence during these two centuries. Court circles played host to many French and Italian artists who introduced an increasingly exuberant Baroque style.

Adam Elsheimer (1578-1610) – Elsheimer's often small scale mythological and biblical paintings reflect a combination of Italian influence and a concept of landscapes peculiar to Flemish and German painting. At the same time as Caravaggio, he experimented with the power of light in the evocation of nature, notably in his dramatic nocturnal landscapes (*The Flight into Egypt*, 1609, Alte Pinakothek, Munich).

Andreas Schlüter (c 1660-1714) – This master of Baroque sculpture in northern Germany and talented architect produced some very powerful works (*Statue of the Great Élector*, Schloß Charlottenburg, Berlin; *Masks of Dying Warriors*, Zeughaus, Berlin).

The Merians (17C) – A family of engravers specialising in plates illustrating German towns.

Balthasar Permoser (1651-1732) – Sculptor to the Court of Dresden, Permoser studied in Rome, Vienna and Venice. His masterful works reflect the exuberant style of the Italian Baroque, particularly at the Zwinger (*Wallpavillon* and *Nymphenbad*, Zwinger, Dresden).

Antoine Pesne (1683-1757) – This French-born painter in the service of the Prussian court became the portraitist of Frederick II, who admired his colouristic talent. He produced a great number of portraits and some mythological ceiling paintings and murals (*Portrait of Frederick II and his sister Wilhelmina,* apartments of Schloß Charlottenburg, Berlin).

Joseph Anton Feuchtmayer (1696-1770) and Johann Michael II Feichtmayr (1709-72) – These members of a family of German painters and sculptors helped to perpe-

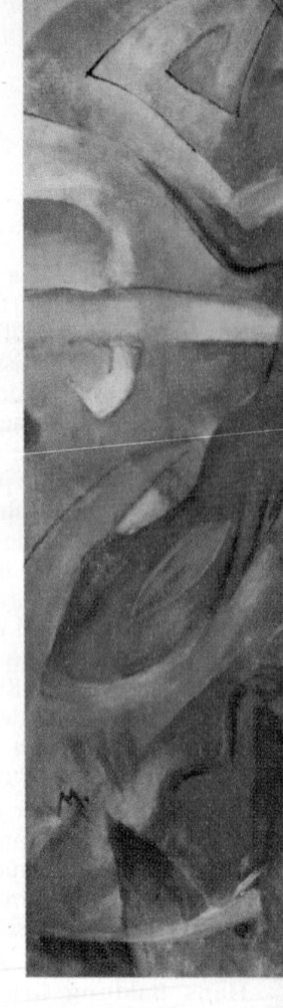

tuate the Rococo style with their fanciful compositions (decoration of the abbey churches of Ottobeuren and St Gallen).

Matthäus Günther (1705-88) – A pupil of CD Asam, master of Rococo painting in southern Germany, Günther is famous for his decoration of many churches in Swabia and Bavaria (Amorbach, Rott am Inn).

19C

The 19C was first of all dominated by the **Biedermeier style** (1815-48) which glorified middle-class values and a certain way of life, as perfectly illustrated by the genre painting of GF Kersting. Then came the time for rebellion. Romanticism called the classical values into question, launching a dialogue between reason and feeling. Realism and Impressionism, which both originated in France, allowed German artists to express certain budding socialist ideas. All of these various forms of artistic expression came in response to the moral crisis of modern Europe.

Caspar David Friedrich (1774-1840) – German Romantic painter whose landscapes were represented as manifestations of the divine and places of wonderment ideal for meditation (*The Monk by the Sea*, *The Cross on the Mountain*, Alte Nationalgalerie, Berlin; *Rambler Above a Sea of Clouds*, Kunsthalle, Hamburg).

Friedrich Overbeck (1789-1869) – Member of the Lucas Brotherhood, he was the most important member of the group of **Nazarenes** who occupied the abandoned monastery of San Isidoro in Rome in 1810. Advocating a form of painting that glorified moral values in a reaction against neo-Classicism, they revived medieval art and sought the purity of the early Italian and Flemish masters of the 15C. (*Italia and Germania*, Neue Pinakothek, Munich).

Adolf von Menzel (1815-1905) – Representative of German Realism, initially illustrating anecdotal themes and later producing powerful portrayals of the industrial world, tempered by the influence of Impressionism (*Rolling Mill*, Nationalgalerie in Berlin).

Wilhelm Leibl (1844-1900) – Master of German Realism, he was influenced by Courbet and mostly painted scenes of village life (*Three Women in Church*, Kunsthalle, Hamburg; portrait of *Mina Gedon*, Neue Pinakothek, Munich).

Adolf von Hildebrand (1847-1921) – German sculptor based in Munich, whose measured taste in monumental sculpture, inspired by the most austere Greek style, was in contrast to the excesses of most 19C artists. (*Wittelsbach Fountain*, Munich).

Max Liebermann (1847-1935) – Greatly influenced by French Realism and Naturalism, he painted the universe of peasants and workers in all its harsh reality. Later, under the influence of Impressionism, he allowed light to suffuse his already rich palette. He led the Berlin "Sezession" movement in 1899, advocating freedom and realism as opposed to the patriotic insipidness of the court painters (*Jewish Street in Amsterdam*, Wallraf-Richartz-Museum, Cologne).

20C

The Expressionism which marked the beginning of the century gave way to a new form of revolt and glorification of subjective feeling. The shock of the First World War and the ensuing social crisis plunged art into a period of darkness and disillusionment. Political and social dissent were embodied in a succession of new avant-garde movements. More than ever before, art was driven by a desire to change society and expose its failings.

EXPRESSIONISM – German Expressionism introduced an emotionally charged, often violent or tragic vision of the world to modern painting. The movement owed much to Van Gogh and the Norwegian painter Edvard Munch (1863-1944), whose work had a marked influence in Germany. In Dresden and then in Berlin, the **Brücke (Bridge) Group** united from 1905 to 1913 such painters as Erich Heckel, Ernst Ludwig Kirchner and Karl Schmidt-Rottluff, whose work, with its use of pure colour, recalls that of the Fauves in France. See the works of **Emil Nolde** (1867-1956) at Seebüll, and of Expressionism in general at the Brücke-Museum, Berlin.

DER BLAUE REITER (The Blue Rider Movement) – Association of artists founded in Munich in 1911 by **Wassily Kandinsky and Franz Marc**, later to be joined by **August Macke** and **Paul Klee**. Although the work of the artists involved differed

Kämpfende Formen by Franz Marc.

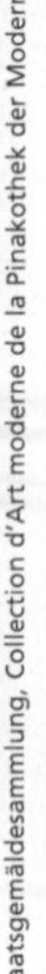

widely, they were united by a general aim to free art from the constraints of reality, using bold colours and untraditional forms, thus opening the way to abstraction (*Deer in the Forest* by **Franz Marc**, Orangerie Staatliche Kunsthalle, Karlsruhe; *The Dress Shop* by **August Macke**, Folkwang-Museum, Essen). The movement broke up during the war.

The BAUHAUS – This movement, which united all art forms, attracted a host of avant-garde painters and sculptors including Klee and Kandinsky, Oskar Schlemmer, Laszlo Moholy-Nagy, **Lyonel Feininger** and **Joseph Albers**.

NEUE SACHLICHKEIT (New Objectivity) – An artistic movement affecting all the arts which grew up in the early 1920s, aiming to produce a realistic illustration of social facts and phenomena. It corresponds to the awareness of the harsh and distressing post-war situation. The pioneers of this movement were **Otto Dix** and **George Grosz** (*War* by **Otto Dix**, 1932, Albertinum in Dresden). The Dada movement, present in Cologne and Berlin, and in Hannover with **Kurt Schwitters**, used art for political ends. On the sidelines of these movements, **Max Beckmann** (1884-1950), who was also deeply affected by the war and its consequences, shared his very bleak view of humanity.

Second half of the 20C – The Nazi regime brought an abrupt end to these artistic experiments labelled as "degenerate art", replacing them with a neo-Classical style glorifying race, war and family. This "Nazi art" died out at the end of the Reich in 1945.

Social Realism, an official art form which served the regime's ideology, was predominant in East German painting until the 1960s-70s. The painters of Leipzig in particular won international acclaim, among them Bernhard Heisig, Wolfgang Mattheuer, Willi Sitte and Werner Tübke. In East Germany in the years leading up to reunification, non-conformist artists were also given the opportunity to express themselves.

The 1960s saw a turning point in German artistic creativity. **Gruppe Zebra** took up the credo of New Objectivity against German Abstract art, while the members of **Gruppe Zero** (Heinz Mack, Otto Piene, Güntheb Uecker concentrated on using kinetic art to transform thoughts into material objects. In the 1970s, **Joseph Beuys**, together with the artists of the school of **Constructivist Sculpture** in Düsseldorf, strove to create a direct relationship between the artist and the viewing public in his Happenings and Performances, and to redefine the role of art and the artist in contemporary society (**Neue Nationalgalerie** in Berlin; **Hessisches Landesmuseum** in Darmstadt; **Staatsgalerie** in Stuttgart).

From the 1980s, a new generation of German artists managed to break through onto the international scene with "new Fauves" *(Neue Wilde)* **Georg Baselitz** and **Markus Lüpertz** developing a new form of Expressionism, **Sigmar Polke**, closer to pop art, and **Anselm Kiefer**, with his focus firmly on German history.

Literature and Philosophy

German literature, from the reign of Charlemagne up to the present day, has demonstrated an enduring vitality, constantly breaking with tradition and inventing new forms of expression. In the wake of Goethe's monumental influence in the 18C, the best authors have been guaranteed international renown.

From the Middle Ages to the 17C

German literature in the Middle Ages was written in a great variety of dialects. Largely drawing on the oral tradition, it was characterised by lyrical poetry and genres that can be described – not in any pejorative way – as popular: plays, ballads, songs and epics. One of the earliest works, dating back to Charlemagne's reign, is the **Lay of Hildebrand** (820), of which only a 68-line fragment has survived. The national folk saga of the **Nibelungen**, an anonymous work from the late 12C, draws on the sources of Germanic mythology and celebrates the heroic spirit that faces up to trials and tribulations without ever giving up. One of the big names in courtly epics was **Wolfram von Eschenbach;** his poem *Parzifal* (c 1200), which recounts the quest for the Holy Grail, revolves around themes of religious and chivalrous life. The 14C was an age of mystic literature, with writers such as **Meister Eckhart**. In a departure from the dryness of scholastic teaching, he sometimes forsakes Latin to discuss religious topics in powerful and eloquent German.

Satire took centre stage in the 16C (*The Ship of Fools* by **Sebastian Brant** appeared in 1494) along with folk songs and the poetry of the Meistersingers. **Hans Sachs** (1494-1576), a poet-cum-cobbler from Nuremberg, was a prominent figure in the latter genre, which provides the theme of Wagner's opera *Tannhäuser*. **Luther**'s contribution during this period also marked a turning point; his hymns and translation of the Bible (1534) paved the way for the writing of literary works in modern German. The late 16C witnessed the publication of the *Faust Book* (1587) by **Johann Spies**, a work of remarkable depth which draws the captivating portrait of a man driven by an unquenchable thirst for knowledge which distances him from God.

The ravages of the Thirty Years' War (1618-48) profoundly marked the collective psyche; 17C literature bears echoes of this traumatic time. Among the recurrent themes of these often edifying works is the vanity of human things and man's need to find God in order to ensure his salvation. *Adventurous Simplicissimus* (1669) by **Grimmelshausen** (1622-76) is a picaresque novel whose hero, having experienced the suffering of war, finally chooses a life of retreat and meditation.

"Aufklärung" (Age of Enlightenment)

The 18C marked the beginning of the golden age of German literature, as its influence began to extend well beyond the German-speaking countries. The spotlight was now on philosophical and moral themes, the flourishes of language belying a pursuit of the natural. The influence of **Leibniz** (1646-1716), whose Theodicy in French and Latin uses rational arguments to justify evil and show that we live in "the best of all possible worlds", still remains very strong. The rationalist

Jakob and Wilhelm Grimm.
J. P. Anders/Bildarchiv Preussischer Kulturbesiitz

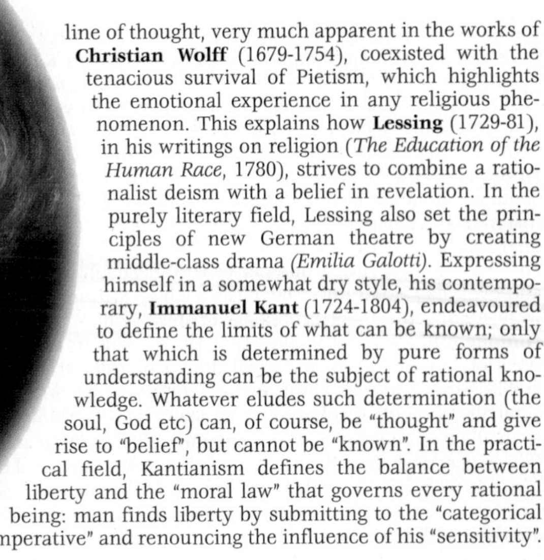

line of thought, very much apparent in the works of **Christian Wolff** (1679-1754), coexisted with the tenacious survival of Pietism, which highlights the emotional experience in any religious phenomenon. This explains how **Lessing** (1729-81), in his writings on religion (*The Education of the Human Race*, 1780), strives to combine a rationalist deism with a belief in revelation. In the purely literary field, Lessing also set the principles of new German theatre by creating middle-class drama *(Emilia Galotti)*. Expressing himself in a somewhat dry style, his contemporary, **Immanuel Kant** (1724-1804), endeavoured to define the limits of what can be known; only that which is determined by pure forms of understanding can be the subject of rational knowledge. Whatever eludes such determination (the soul, God etc) can, of course, be "thought" and give rise to "belief", but cannot be "known". In the practical field, Kantianism defines the balance between liberty and the "moral law" that governs every rational being: man finds liberty by submitting to the "categorical imperative" and renouncing the influence of his "sensitivity".

"Sturm und Drang" and Classicism

In reaction to the strict rationalism of the Aufklärung, the **Sturm und Drang** (Storm and Stress) movement, encompassing authors such as **Herder** (1744-1803) and **Hamann** (1730-88), exalts freedom, emotion and nature. Poetry, "the mother tongue of the human race", takes pride of place and the past is revisited, with particular emphasis placed on folk songs. The works of the young **Goethe** (1749-1832), such as *The Sorrows of Young Werther*, bear witness to the influence of Sturm und Drang. However, Goethe – poet and universal genius – soon tempered this fashionable enthusiasm with a move towards the **classical humanist** tradition. As the leading light of German literature prior to the emergence of the Romantic trend, in which he never became involved, he penned a great number of works. These notably include classical dramas (*Iphigenie auf Tauris*, *Egmont*, and *Torquato Tasso*), novels (*Elective Affinities*, *Wilhelm Meister's Apprenticeship*), and *Faust (Parts I and II* – 1808 and 1832), which contain the quintessence of Goethe's philosophy. After settling in Weimar in 1775, Goethe was joined by Herder, **Wieland** and **Schiller** (1759-1805). The historical dramas of the latter, a poet and dramatist of genius, are undisguised hymns to liberty (*Don Carlos*, *Wallenstein*, *Wilhelm Tell*).
Two major literary figures emerged during the transitional period between Weimarian Classicism and actual Romanticism: **Hölderlin** (1770-1843), a tragic, lyric author (*Hyperion*, *The Death of Empedocles*) with a passion for Ancient Greek civilisation, produced some powerful odes before sinking into madness at the age of 36. The novelist Johann Paul Friedrich Richter (1763-1825), better known as **Jean Paul**, had a creative imagination although a somewhat laboured style.

19C: between Romanticism and Realism

The **Romantic movement**, which reflects certain deep-rooted aspects of the German character, charts the individual soul's quest for the infinite in all its forms. Besides literature, it incorporates the fine arts, philosophy, politics and religion. First Jena, then Heidelberg and Berlin were centres from which the movement blossomed. After initially being theorised by the **Schlegel brothers**, the Romantic doctrine was put into powerful poetic form by **Novalis** (1772-1801); a poet and mystic, Novalis exalts the art and religion of the Middle Ages and his "Blue Flower" symbol comes to represent the Absolute, or object of Romantic longing (*Heinrich von Ofterdingen*). While in the process of theoretical elaboration, budding Romanticism was exposed to the influence of post-Kantian idealist philosophers, in particular **Fichte** (1762-1814), **Schelling** (1775-1854) and **Hegel** (1770-1831). It also reflects a heightened interest in popular literature, often seeking inspiration in the sources of myths and legends, as can be seen in the tales of the **Brothers Grimm** (1812) or

the more disturbing tales of **Hoffmann** (1776-1822). On the sidelines of the Romantic movement, the playwright **Heinrich von Kleist**, who tragically committed suicide in 1811, wrote some remarkable plays, notably *The Prince of Homburg* (1810), a play about a man of action led away by his dreams.
The exuberant idealism of Romanticism was succeeded by a search for greater realism. An outstanding figure and "defrocked Romantic" poet of the *Loreley*, **Heinrich Heine** (1797-1856), treats the naivety of his age with bitter irony and enthuses about St Simonian ideals. **Hebbel** (1813-63), a fine psychologist, wrote plays often inspired by biblical or mythical subjects, focusing on conflict between the individual and the existing moral order (*Judith, Herodes und Mariamne, Agnes Bernauer*). Towards the mid 19C, a number of writers sought to bring literature closer to life and everyday experience; novelists such as **Stifter** (1805-68) and **Keller** (1819-90) were among the main exponents of this "Realist" trend. Some of them, such as **Fontane** (1819-98) and **Raabe** (1831-1910), focus on the social and political conditions of human existence. Social drama is brilliantly illustrated by **Hauptmann** (1862-1946), a prolific author whose Naturalist writing is at times allegorical and symbolic, drawing inspiration from legend and mythology (*The Atrides Cycle*).
In the field of philosophy, **Schopenhauer** (1788-1860), pessimistic theorist of the will to live, describes the will as reality's true inner nature, and this will as suffering (*The World as Will and Idea,* 1819); he had a crucial influence on the thinking of authors such as Nietzsche, Freud and Wittgenstein. Political thought, moreover, took a new direction with **Karl Marx** (*The Communist Manifesto* was published in 1848); rejecting Hegelian idealism, Marx, who was both a philosopher and an economist, developed the theory of "historical materialism", a powerful conceptual tool enabling the analysis of human societies according to their historical development. Together with **Engels**, Marx cofounded "scientific socialism", in opposition to so-called "utopian" socialism, and launched the modern international workers' movement.

The modern period

Friedrich Nietzsche, who died in 1900, belongs as much to the history of philosophy as to the history of literature. His tremendous influence over the history of literature and western thought is still in evidence today. His fundamentally life-affirming philosophy called, with great lyricism, for mankind to surpass itself (*Thus Spoke Zarathustra*, 1886).
Focusing on the often irreconcilable duality of the mind and the senses, the irrational and the rational, the works of **Thomas Mann** (*Buddenbrooks, The Magic Mountain*) and **Hermann Hesse** (*Der Steppenwolf*) bear the stamp of Nietzscheism; the sanatorium in Davos in *The Magic Mountain* symbolises the "disease" that runs rife in decadent European societies. In this struggle between life force and morbid instincts, the shadow of Thanatos hangs over our western civilisations. The Czech-born German language writer **Franz Kafka** (1883-1924) differs from these authors in both style and thought; his nightmarish novels (*The Trial, The Castle, America*) contain a vision of a dehumanised world dominated by anxiety and the absurd. The works of Vienna-born **Stefan Zweig**, one of Kafka's contemporaries, were of a much less tortured nature. This highly cultivated man, citizen of the world, traveller and translator proved in his best short stories (*Amok, Conflicts, The Royal Game*) to be a remarkable story teller with humanist sympathies.
The early 20C also witnessed a revival in the field of poetry. **Stefan George** (1868-1933) published poems which, in their formal perfection, ally him with the French Symbolists, while the Austrians **Rainer Maria Rilke** (1875-1926) and **Hugo von Hoffmannsthal** (1874-1929) reach the peak of lyrical impressionism.
The 1930s and 40s were marked by an intensified search for the meaning of life; spurred on by Husserlian phenomenology, **Heidegger** and, to a lesser degree, **Jaspers**, put the question of being back at the heart of philosophy. Based on our essential finiteness, Heideggerian existentialism distinguishes between an existence marked by a sense of being and an "inauthentic" existence that has been led astray into the impersonal self.
The world of theatre was dominated by **Bertolt Brecht** (*The Threepenny Opera, Mother Courage, Galileo*). A committed socialist, he rejected the "theatre of illusion", advocating the alienation effect: the spectator must observe the action on stage with a critical eye and be able to decipher the methods by which the strong exploit the weak.

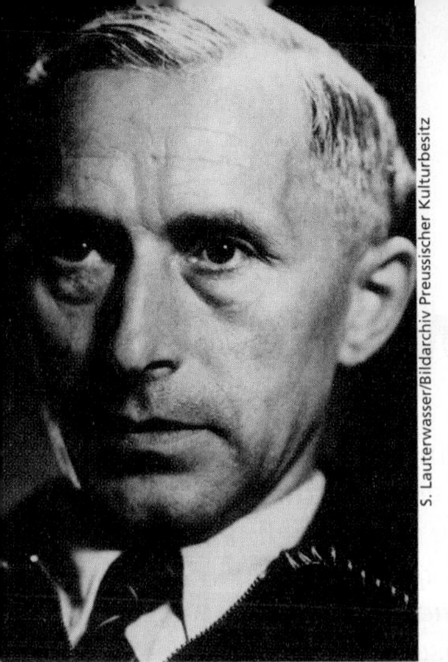
S. Lauterwasser/Bildarchiv Preussischer Kulturbesitz

Ernst Jünger in 1949.

National Socialism forced numerous poets and writers into exile (Walter Benjamin, Alfred Döblin, Lion Feuchtwanger, Else Lasker-Schüler, Thomas and Heinrich Mann, Carl Zuckmayer, Stefan Zweig). **Gottfried Benn** (1886-1956) withdrew into silence, while **Ernst Jünger** (1895-1998) courageously published his novel *On the Marble Cliffs* in 1939: "...Such are the dungeons above which rise the proud castles of the tyrants... They are terrible noisome pits in which a God-forsaken crew revels to all eternity in the degradation of human dignity and human freedom."

Post-1945 literature

Twelve years under National Socialist rule had broken the flow of literary creation in Germany, necessitating repair work in this domain too. The association of authors known as **Gruppe 47** (after the year of its founding), which centred around **Hans Werner Richter** and **Alfred Andersch**, was instrumental in putting Germany back onto the map as far as world literature was concerned. This loosely associated group of writers served as a forum for reading, discussion and criticism, until its last conference in 1967, exerting a lasting and formative influence on the contemporary German literary scene. Authors associated with Gruppe 47 included **Paul Celan**, **Heinrich Böll** (Nobel Prize winner in 1972), **Günter Grass** (Nobel Prize winner in 1999), **Siegfried Lenz**, **Peter Weiss** and **Hans Magnus Enzensberger**. By the end of the 1950s, works of international standing were being published: Günter Grass' masterpiece *The Tin Drum* is an extraordinary novel in the tradition of Celine; **Uwe Johnson**'s *Speculations about Jacob*, **Heinrich Böll**'s *Billiards at Half Past Nine* and **Martin Walser**'s novel *Marriages in Philippsburg*. Increasing politicisation was what finally put an end to Gruppe 47's activities. Authors not associated with Gruppe 47 were hard at work also; **Arno Schmidt** developed a very original and high-quality body of work, while **Wolfgang Koeppen** produced some wickedly satirical novels on contemporary society.

In the world of theatre, dominated initially by the dramatic theory of Bertolt Brecht, a new band of writers began to make their presence felt, with works by **Tankred Dorst** (*Toller*, 1968), **Peter Weiss** (*Hölderlin*, 1971) and **Heinar Kipphardt**. **Rolf Hochhuth** was particularly successful with his "documentary dramas" in which he examines contemporary moral issues (*The Representative*, 1963), and **Botho Strauß**, the most widely performed modern German dramatist, has won international acclaim with plays such as *The Hypochondriac* (1972), *The Park* (1983) and *Final Chorus* (1991).

The political division of Germany was also reflected in German literature. In the old East German Republic, the leadership viewed literature's *raison d'être* as the contribution it might make to the socialist programme for educating the masses. The Bitterfelder Weg, a combined propaganda exercise and literary experiment launched at the Bitterfeld chemical factory in 1959 as part of the East German Republic's cultural programme under Walter Ulbricht, was intended to unite art and everyday life and break down class barriers. Poetry was the literary form least easily subject to the censorship of the Communist Party and the state, and poets such as **Peter Huchel**, **Johannes Bobrowski** and **Erich Arendt** produced some remarkable work. From the early 1960s the prose work of **Günter de Bruyn**, **Stefan Heym** (d 2001) and **Erwin Strittmatter** was widely appreciated. **Anna Seghers**, who returned from exile in America after the war, was considered to be the greatest East German writer of the older generation, while rising star **Christa Wolf** began to win acclaim in both Germanies. Important contributions to the theatre were made by playwrights **Ulrich Plenzdorf**, **Peter Hacks** and above all **Heiner Müller** (*The Hamlet Machine,* 1978).

Any overview of German-language literature since the Second World War must, of course, acknowledge the enormous contribution made by **Max Frisch** and **Friedrich Dürrenmatt**, of Switzerland, and **Ilse Aichinger**, **Ingeborg Bachmann** and **Thomas Bernhard** of Austria.

J. Quast/© Bayreuther Festspiele GmbH

Music

Germany and the German-speaking world in general have made a considerable contribution to western music. After reaching an initial high point in the 18C with the Baroque period, German music was propelled back into the limelight by the genius of composers such as Beethoven and Wagner. Modern experimentation since the emergence of the twelve-tone system testifies to the continuing vitality of German music.

From Minnesingers to Meistersingers

In the 12C and 13C, feudal courts constituted the main forum for musical expression. The **Minnesänger**, who were often noble knights, such as **Wolfram von Eschenbach** and **Walther von der Vogelweide**, drew inspiration for their songs from French lyric poetry. They would perform their love songs before the nobility, accompanying themselves on the lute.

The Meistersingers or Mastersingers of the 14C-16C preferred a more sedentary lifestyle and organised themselves into guilds. They introduced polyphony to German music and clearly set the musical forms of their art. Anyone wanting to become a Meistersinger had to prove himself in a public contest. Among the prominent figures of the time was **Heinrich von Meißen** (1250-1318) who marked the transition from Minnesang to the poetry of the Meistersingers. **Hans Sachs** (1494-1576), a cobbler by trade and an ardent supporter of Luther, was also a very prolific poet; many of his compositions were turned into protestant chorales. Sachs later became the subject of Wagner's opera *The Mastersingers of Nuremberg*.

From the Renaissance to the 17C

In the wake of the Reformation, German music began to develop an individual identity with the emergence of the chorale, the fruit of the collaboration between **Luther** and **Johann Walther** (1496-1570). *"Ein' feste Burg ist unser Gott"* (*A Mighty Fortress is Our God*) composed by the two men in 1529 was reworked by Bach. Originally a hymn with a simple melody, the chorale – sung in the vernacular – soon opened up to the secular repertoire, embracing popular genres of music. It subsequently gave rise to the German cantata and oratorio.

Religious music maestro, **Heinrich Schütz** (1585-1672) managed to produce a skilful combination of German and Italian elements. He composed the first German opera, *Dafne*, a work which was sadly lost. *The Seven Words of Christ* (1645) shows the influence of Monteverdi who, along with Gabrieli, was one of Schütz's masters.

The second half of the 17C witnessed a proliferation of organ schools, one of the most famous of which was based in Nuremberg. An inspiration for Bach who is said to have walked hundreds of kilometres to hear him play in Lübeck, **Dietrich Buxtehude** (1637-1707) organised the first concerts of sacred music. **Johann Pachelbel** (1653-1706) was the great master of the organ school in southern Germany; the only surviving piece of his work is the *Canon*.

Tannhäuser at the Bayreuth Festival.

Bach and Baroque music

His consummate skill as a composer, his genius for invention and his mastery of counterpoint enabled **Bach** (1685-1750) to excel in every kind of music he wrote. Based in Weimar until 1717, he then spent several years at the court of Köthen, during which he composed *The Brandenburg Concertos*. In 1723, he was appointed "Cantor" at St Thomas' School, Leipzig. Bach's duties included the composition of a cantata for every Sunday service, as well as the supervision of services at four other churches. He also taught Latin and voice and still found time left over to write his own instrumental and vocal works. His masterpieces include *The Well-Tempered Clavier* (1722 and 1744) and the *St Matthew Passion* (1727).

A brilliant court composer, influenced by his travels in Italy, **Georg Friedrich Händel** (1665-1759) excelled in both opera and oratorio (*The Messiah*, 1742). Born in Halle, he was organist at the town's cathedral for a while, before pursuing his career at the Hamburg opera. Based in England from 1714, he spent most of the last forty years of his life in London, and even obtained British nationality.

Händel's friend, **Georg Philipp Telemann**, (1681-1767) was influenced by French and Italian composers, and was himself a particularly prolific composer. He turned from counterpoint to harmony and composed chamber music and church music as well as operas. Telemann was godfather to Bach's second son, **Carl Philipp Emmanuel** (1714-88), who popularised the sonata in its classic form.

From the Mannheim School to Beethoven

In the mid 18C, the musicians of the **Mannheim School**, under the patronage of Elector Palatine Karl Theodor, helped establish the modern symphonic form, giving a more prominent role to wind instruments. Influenced by the innovations from Mannheim, **Christoph Willibald Gluck** (1714-87) undertook a "reformation of opera", producing refined works where the lyrics took pride of place; he provoked the enthusiasm of the innovators – and the horror of fans of traditional, Italian-inspired opera – by staging, in Paris, his *Iphigenia in Aulis* and *Orpheus*. This period was also marked by the appearance in Germany of the **Singspiel**, a type of popular opera in which dialogue is interspersed with songs in the form of Lieder. Mozart's *Magic Flute* (1791) and Beethoven's *Fidelio* (1814) are excellent examples of this genre later identified with operetta.

The contribution of Viennese Classicism during the second half of the 18C proved to be crucial. **Joseph Haydn** (1732-1809) laid down the classical form of the symphony, the string quartet and the piano sonata. **Wolfgang Amadeus Mozart** (1756-91) perfected these forms and created some truly immortal operas (*The Marriage of Figaro*, *Don Juan*).

Born in Bonn, **Ludwig van Beethoven** (1770-1827) went to Vienna to study under Haydn and Antonio Salieri. With his innovative harmonisations, he developed a highly individual style and transformed existing forms of music, heralding the Romantic movement. The depth of his inspiration, ranging from pure introspection to a wider belief in the force and universality of his art, emanates from his work with extraordinary power, perhaps most particularly in his symphonies, moving and majestic works. It was in 1824, when he had already been suffering from total and incurable deafness for five years, that Beethoven's magnificent *Ninth Symphony* – inspired by one of Schiller's odes – was performed for the first time.

Romantic music and Wagner

Franz Schubert (1797-1826) brought Romantic music to its first high point. He focused much creative energy on the Lied (song), blending folk and classical music in a unique style.

Carl Maria von Weber (1786-1826), created Germany's first Romantic opera, *Freischütz* (1821), paving the way for the characters of Wagnerian drama. It was a resounding success when first performed in Berlin, certainly due in part to the use of folk songs. As for the lofty world of **Felix Mendelssohn-Bartholdy** (1809-79), it was far removed from the forces of evil that inhabit the *Freischütz*. Although espousing classical music forms, Mendelssohn, who was a conductor, pianist and founder of the Leipzig Conservatory, also reveals a Romantic influence.

Robert Schumann (1810-56), passionate and lyrical in turn, but brought up in the Germanic tradition, strives to reconcile a classical heritage with personal expression. A talented music critic (he founded the *Neue Zeitscrhift für Musik* newspaper in 1834), he initially wrote for piano alone (*Carnival, Scenes from Childhood*). Then, spurred on by his admiration for Schubert and the advice of his friend Mendelssohn, he began to compose Lieder *(Dichterliebe)*, subsequently turning his attention to symphonies and chamber music. A close friend of Schumann whose wife Clara he loved with a passion, **Johannes Brahms** (1833-97) exemplified a more introverted style of German Romanticism. After long being accused of formalism, he was rediscovered in the 20C, notably thanks to the influence of Schönberg (*Brahms the Progressive*).

Crowning glory of the German Romantic movement, the work of **Wagner** (1813-83) revolutionised the opera genre. Wagner claimed that music should be subservient to the dramatic action, being there to create "atmosphere" and a "backdrop of sound" without which the opera's message could not be fully conveyed. Orchestration thus becomes of paramount importance. Libretto and plot unfold continuously, to preserve dramatic reality. Wagner introduces the use of "leitmotifs" – musical phrases used recurrently to denote specific characters, moods or situations – making them essential to the continuity of the action. *Lohengrin* was first performed in 1850 in Weimar, under the supervision of **Franz Liszt**.

Designed by Wagner himself as a stage for the performance of the entire work (Gesamtkunstwerk), the Bayreuth Theatre was inaugurated in 1876 with *The Ring of the Nibelung* (*Rheingold, Walküre, Siegfried* and *Götterdämmerung*). The fruit of 22 years' work, the magnificent first public performance of *The Ring* lasted 18 hours. Although its artistic success was undeniable, the Bayreuth episode ended in financial ruin for the composer. *Parsifal*, Wagner's last opera, revolves around the theme of redemption through sacrifice, and was first performed in Bayreuth in 1882.

At the end of the 19C, **Gustav Mahler** (1860-1911), Czech-Austrian composer and creator of the symphonic Lied, and **Hugo Wolf** (1850-1903) developed a new musical language which forms a bridge between Romanticism and dodecaphony.

Richard Strauss (1864-1949) excelled in orchestra music (*Thus Spoke Zarathustra*), uniting a certain harmonic audacity with a dazzling and multifaceted style.

Contemporary music

Contemporary musical experimentation is derived principally from the Austrian school of atonal, or serial (especially 12-note systems) music, represented by **Arnold Schönberg** and his two main disciples **Alban Berg** and **Anton von Webern**. Introducing a new method of composing music, the twelve-tone system was first revealed to the public by Schönberg in 1928 in the *Variations for Orchestra.* Berg applied his master's innovation to lyrical drama *(Lulu)*, while Webern, turning his back on Romanticism, focused on the concision of form. The brilliant **Paul Hindemith** (1893-1963), initially influenced by Romanticism, remained untouched by Schönberg's innovations; in a break with German tradition, he forged a path of his own between atonality and dodecaphony.

Carl Orff (1895-1982), creator of the Orff Schulwerk, propounded innovative ideas about music education. His highly original theatrical compositions combine drama, speech and song in a fascinating rhythmic framework: his powerful collection of secular songs with infectious rhythms, *Carmina Burana* (1937), soon gained international renown. The compositions – mainly opera and ballet music – of **Werner Egk** (1901-83), a student of Carl Orff, reveal the influence of Igor Stravinski and Richard Strauss. As for **Kurt Weill** (1900-50), influenced at the beginning of his career by the atonal composers, he returned under the impact of jazz to tonal music, and composed *The Threepenny Opera* (1928) in collaboration with Brecht.

Although **Wolfgang Fortner** (1907-87) was influenced initially by Hindemith, he nonetheless later turned to modal 12-tone serial music. His mature works introduce electronic elements into his musical compositions.

Bernd Alois Zimmermann (1918-70) perceived past, present and future as one, and the multiple layers of reality are reflected in his composition technique. Quotations and collage were particularly important to him. His major work is the opera *The Soldiers*.

From 1950, a younger generation of musicians developed the potential of electronic music under the aegis of **Karlheinz Stockhausen** (b 1928). **Hans Werner Henze** (b 1926) created expressive operas, in which modernity and tradition, and atonality and tonality are combined. **Wolfgang Rihm** (b 1952), a student of Fortner, like Henze, also mixes traditional stylistic elements with new techniques in his extremely complex musical language.

Münich Tourism Office

Munich Philharmonic Orchestra in concert.

Cinema

After producing a number of masterpieces during the Expressionist period of the 1920s, German cinema fell into a decline from which it did not emerge until the 1960s. Although now struggling to make its mark in the face of American productions, it has managed to produce some remarkable international award-winning works.

Fritz Lang's Metropolis.

The golden age of Expressionism

The creation in 1917 of UFA (Universum Film Aktiengesellschaft), a production company of considerable means which, from 1921, was directed by producer **Erich Pommer**, led to some lavish productions. The Expressionism that was apparent in literature, theatre and painting also seeped into film production in the troubled post-war political and social scene. Deliberately turning its back on Realism, it often revelled in angst-ridden atmospheres, cultivating an exaggeration of forms and contrasts; it was typified by the use of chiaroscuro lighting effects and the geometric stylisation of the decor. Very few works could actually be classed as purely Expressionist, but among them is **Robert Wiene**'s masterpiece *The Cabinet of Dr Caligari* (1919), which was well-received in the United States and France. Nevertheless, Expressionism was a great source of inspiration for German cinema in the 1920s; this period was dominated by the films of **FW Murnau** (*Nosferatu the Vampire*, 1922; *The Last Laugh*, 1924; *Faust*, 1926) and **Fritz Lang** (*Dr Mabuse*, 1922; *Metropolis*, 1925). Lang's German work reached its high point in 1931 with *M*, the director's first talking picture. Initially entitled *Murderers Among Us* (the title was changed under pressure from the Nazis), *M* paints the picture, in all its harsh reality, of a diseased society which, unable to cure its own ills, seeks scapegoat sinners on whom to place the blame. *The Last Will of Dr Mabuse* in 1932 attracted Nazi censure. Soon after being invited by Goebbels to supervise the Reich's film production, Lang went into exile, first moving to Paris and then to California, where he pursued his film-directing career.

The 1920s in Germanyalso witnessed a shift towards Realism and away from the dominant Expressionist trend. Examples of this new trend include the films of **GW Pabst** (*The Joyless Street*, 1925; *Diary of a Lost Girl*, 1926; *Lulu*, 1929) and **Josef von Sternberg**'s *The Blue Angel* (1930) starring **Marlene Dietrich** and **Emil Jannings**.

An abrupt halt

The promising surge of German cinema after the First World War was sadly stopped in its tracks with the arrival of the Third Reich. Many actors and directors went into exile. The Nazis turned cinema into a tool to serve the regime's ideology; filmmaker

Leni Riefenstahl (1902-2003) stands out in the generally disappointing and inartistic genre of propaganda films, with her productions of amazing cinematic beauty, such as *The Gods of the Stadium*, a glorification of the 1936 Berlin Olympics.
The period immediately after the Second World War was a cultural desert. While "Socialist Realism" prevailed in East Germany, film production in the Federal Republic of the 1950s was of poor quality. Only a few films, such as *The Last Bridge* (1954) and *The Devil's General* (1955) by **Helmut Kaütner**, managed to escape the pervasive mediocrity. The 1962 **Oberhausen Manifesto**, signed by 26 young filmmakers, signalled the birth of a new cinematographic language; the long-awaited revival was here at last.

The revival of the 1960s and beyond

In the 1960s and 1970s makers of "New German cinema" rose up in the wake of the French *nouvelle vague*, seeking to distance themselves from old-style cinema with its run-of-the-mill commercial superficiality. Films made by **Werner Herzog**, **Volker Schlöndorff** (*Young Törless*, 1966) and **Alexander Kluge** (*Artists at the Top of the Big Top: Disorientated*, 1968) quickly met with success. It was not long – the mid 1970s – before this younger generation had reestablished German cinema on an international scale. **Volker Schlöndorff** made *The Lost Honour of Katharina Blum* (in collaboration with **Margarethe von Trotta**, 1975), and *The Tin Drum* (1979). **Werner Herzog** went on to explore a fantastic, often quite exotic world in *Aguirre, Wrath of God* (1972), *Nosferatu the Vampyre* (1979), and *Fitzcarraldo* (1982). Among the prominent figures in the **Munich School** of filmmaking were **Rainer Werner Fassbinder** (1945-82), who also worked in television, and who was responsible for a considerable number of excellent films (*Fear Eats the Soul (Angst essen Seele auf)*, 1973; *The Marriage of Maria Braun*, 1978; *Berlin Alexanderplatz*, a 14-part television series, 1980), and **Wim Wenders** (*The American Friend*, 1977; *Paris, Texas*, 1984; *Wings of Desire*, 1987; *Buena Vista Social Club*, 1999). Important and innovative women film directors include **Margarethe von Trotta** (*Rosa Luxemburg*, 1986; *Das Versprechen*, 1995). Wolfgang Peterson's fantasy world in *The Neverending Story* (1984) was a resounding commercial success. **Edgar Reitz** won international acclaim with his film epic *Heimat* (1984) and its sequel *Heimat 2* (1993). However, West German cinema was, and still is, characterised by a strongly individual narrative feel which perhaps makes it less approachable to outsiders. One refreshing filmmaker worthy of note is **Doris Dörrie** who, with *Men... (Männer)* (1985) and *Bin ich schön?* (1998), reduced the Zeitgeist to a humorous point. Other successful films include **Caroline Link**'s 1996 *Jenseits der Stille* and **Tom Tykwer**'s 1999 *Lola rennt* (*Run Lola Run*). However, German film today rarely crosses the borders of the German-speaking world, and hits such as **Wolfgang Becker**'s *Goodbye Lenin*, which won the Best European Film award at the 2003 Berlin Film Festival, remain few and far between.

Cinema in the former East German Republic

It is difficult to summarise East German cinema, since like all other art forms it was compelled by the state to fulfil a didactic function. Thus a number of films were made taking literary classics as their theme, since directors felt unable to confront issues relevant to contemporary East Germany. **Konrad Wolf** made his mark on three decades of East German filmmaking, with films such as *Sterne* (1958), which won him recognition worldwide. In *Solo Sunny* (1979), he put the case for individualism, thus paving the way for a breakthrough in the East German film industry. **Egon Güntheb** made the highly successful *Der Dritte* (1971), while the greatest hit of the East German Film Industry Cooperative (DEFA) was **Heiner Carow** with *Die Legende von Paul und Paula* (1973). 1984 was a particularly fruitful year, with **Hermann Zschoche**'s *Hälfte des Lebens*, **Iris Gusner**'s *Kaskade Rückwärts*, and **Helmut Dzuiba**'s *Erscheinen Pflicht*. One of the leading East German filmmakers of the 1970s and 1980s was **Rainer Simon** (*Das Luftschiff*, 1982; *Die Frau und der Fremde*, 1985). Finally, **Lothar Warneke** studied the problems of everyday life faced by his fellow citizens, and endeavoured to dismantle rigid ideological points of view (*Bear Ye One Another's Burdens (Einer trage des anderen Last)*, 1988).

Schloß Moritzburg to the north of Dresden.

Selected Sights

Aachen★

Aix-la-Chapelle

The hot springs of Aachen, already famous in the time of the Celts, were transformed into thermal baths by the Romans ("Aquae Grani"). Under Charlemagne, Aachen became the capital of the Frankish Empire and thirty princes were crowned King of Germania in the cathedral.
Today, the city is an important industrial centre with a renowned college of technology. Aachen is located close to Belgium and The Netherlands and has a charming cosmopolitan atmosphere.

Location

Population 245 000. Michelin map n° 543 N 2 – Nordrhein-Westfalen. Situated among the northern foothills of the Ardennes (Hohes Venn), close to the Belgian border, Aix-la-Chapelle is the most westerly town in Germany. It is easily accessible by road from Cologne, Düsseldorf or Liège in Belgium.

Elisenbrunnen, Friedrich-Wilhelm-Platz, D, 52062 Aachen, ☎ 0049-241/1802960 and 1802961; www.aachen.de

Surrounding area: see MONSCHAU (38 km to the south), KÖLN (70 km to the east by A4), EIFEL (Bad Münstereifel is located 74 km to the southeast).

Background

Charlemagne (747-814) – King of the Franks from the year 768, Charlemagne (known as Karl der Große to the Germans) chose Aachen as a permanent site for the Frankish Court – which until then had had no fixed abode. In AD 800, Charlemagne was crowned Holy Roman Emperor. He then conquered the Saxons and the Bavarians, consolidating his frontiers north of the Pyrenees to resist invasions by Moors, Slavs and Danes. Charlemagne's court became a fountainhead of wisdom, culture and Christianity, which spread throughout his realm. The emperor brought to the West the treasures of Latin civilisation and culture as well as the advantages of a centralised government with statute laws and a uniform administration. Charlemagne was buried at Aachen, in the Octagon of the Palatine chapel (Pfalzkapelle).

The Imperial City – Between 936 and 1531, thirty princes were crowned King of Germania in the cathedral at Aachen. In 1562 the town lost the status of Coronation City to Frankfurt am Main *(see FRANKFURT AM MAIN)*.

Special Features

CATHEDRAL DISTRICT

Cathedral ★★ (Dom)

♿ *Supervised opening times: every day 11am-7pm, Sun, from 12.45pm. No charge. Treasury (Domschatzkammer) (access via Klostergasse): Open Mon 10am-1pm, Tue-Sat 10am-6pm, Sun 10am-9pm. Closed 1 Jan, Monday before Shrove Tuesday, Good Friday, 25 Dec. €2.50. ☎ (0241) 47 70 91 27; www.aachendom.de*

The 74m/242ft high tower of the cathedral is at the heart of the town. Charlemagne's Palatine chapel (Pfalzkapelle), built around 800, consists of an octagonal domed central section surrounded by a 16-sided gallery modelled on the Byzantine palace churches. It was the first construction of this type seen north of the Alps. The Gothic chancel, started in 1355, was consecrated in 1414, on the 600th anniversary of the Emperor's death. The Aachen cathedral was the first German construction to be placed on the list of UNESCO's World Heritage Sites.

Exterior – *Starting at the Katschhof (north side), walk around the cathedral.* One after another the chapel of St Nicholas (pre-1487), the chapel of Charles-Hubert (1455-74), with its Flamboyant portal, and finally the chancel (standing at a height of 51m/167ft to the tip of the cross) bearing 19C statues between the clerestory windows, come into view.

From the Münsterplatz *(south side)*, there is a good view of the largest remnant of the Carolingian church, crowned now with a 16-sided cupola dating from the 17C. Also on this side are three chapels: dedicated to St Matthew (1414) and St Anne (pre-1449), both Gothic, and the Hungarian chapel (1756-1767). The Carolingian entrance hall (west building) on the cathedral courtyard is closed by bronze doors embellished with lions' heads (c 800).

Directory

Where to Eat

Ratskeller – *Markt 40 – ☎ (0241) 350 01 – www.ratskelleraachen.de – ♿ – €13/50.* This smart restaurant is located in an old groined vault in the historic town hall, which gives onto the marketplace. The welcoming hosts and the pleasant atmosphere add up to a pleasant environment for trying out some traditional food.

Zum Schiffgen – *Hühnermarkt 21-23 – ☎ (0241) 335 29 – www.zum-schiffgen.de – Booking advised – €13/35.* A clean, well-run establishment which welcomes locals and newcomers alike. Traditional regional specialities are on the menu. Charming view of the nearby town hall from the terrace on the edge of the pedestrianised zone.

Where to Stay

Haus Press – *Trierer Straße 842-844 – ☎ (0241) 92 80 20 – fax (0241) 9280211 – www.haus-press.de – P – 15 rm: €26/79 – Restaurant: €12/18.* Small unpretentious family-run hotel. Functionally-equipped rooms with interesting furniture; some furnished with up to 3 beds. Regional cuisine on offer in the restaurant.

Forsthaus Schöntal – *Kornelimünsterweg 1 – BUS €16/33 – Southeast of the town centre, towards the Kornelimünster Abbey Church – ☎ (0241) 60 14 59 – fax (0241) 607365 – www.forsthaus-schoental.de – Closed Wed. – P – Booking advised – 10 rm: €40/60 – restaurant €20.40/35.30.* Clean and well-maintained establishment located in a brick house. The functionally-designed rooms are furnished in light-coloured pine. The Biergarten situated behind the restaurant is a pleasant place to sit in summer.

Going out

Café Molkerei – *Pontstr. 141 (to the northeast of Markt) – ☎ (0241) 489 82 – Open every day, 10am-2am, Fri-Sat until 3am.* This studenty café is situated in a former dairy in the heart of a working-class district of Aachen. Breakfast is served every morning and in the evening the delicious cocktails attract aficionados.

Magellan – *Pontstr. 78 (to the northeast of Markt) – ☎ (0241) 4 01 64 40 – Sun-Thu, 10am-1am, Fri-Sat, 10am-2am.* This café-bar/restaurant is particularly pleasant in the summer months due to its shady terrace. From Monday to Friday, between 11am and 3pm, Turkish cuisine in the form of dishes of the day and set menus is served at a very reasonable price. At the bar, choose from around 40 different cocktails.

Van den Daele Alt Aachener Kaffee- und Weinstuben – *Büchel 18/Körbergasse (near the Couven-museum) – ☎ (0241) 3 57 24 – www.van-den-daele.de – Mon-Sat, 9am-6.30pm, Sun 10am-6.30pm – Closed 25 Dec and 1 Jan.* This unusual café-cum-restaurant has been built at the point where four old buildings meet. The establishment's various rooms are worth having a look round. While here try the town's speciality, Printen (a type of gingerbread), or rice biscuits *(Milchreisfladen)*.

Interior – The octagon is surrounded by a two-storey ambulatory with bronze grilles dating from the Carolingian period masking the spaces between the columns on the upper level. The dome is richly decorated with 19C mosaics. From the centre hangs a magnificent **chandelier★★** in copper, donated by Emperor Frederick I Barbarossa (1165). To the right of the two piers in front of the chancel is a 14C statue of the Virgin of Aachen. Modern stained-glass windows illuminate the Late Gothic chancel aisle. On the right, above the door leading to the sacristy, is the **Ambo of Henry II★★★** – a small pulpit in gilded copper, decorated with precious stones (early 11C). The Carolingian high altar is adorned with a **Pala d'Oro★★★** – a sumptuous, gold altar front decorated with scenes from the Passion and Christ in Majesty (c 1020). Behind the altar is the **Shrine of Charlemagne★★★** (Karlsschrein: 1200-15), a reliquary containing the bones of the Emperor which is masterfully hand-worked in gilded and embossed silver. In the entrance bay of the chancel aisle is the precious **Shrine of Mary** dating from 1238.

On the upper floor of the west yoke is the **Throne of Charlemagne★** *(only visible during the guided tour; gathering point in the cathedral's treasury)*. This perfectly intact throne is made of plain, assembled marble slabs. After being elected and consecrated, 30 Roman-German kings climbed upon this throne and were officially enthroned. Over time, thousands of pilgrims have squeezed through the narrow aperture underneath the throne to take part in the Aachen Shrine Pilgrimage (Aachener Heiligtumfahrt), which has been held every seven years since 1349 (next pilgrimage is 2007).

Domschatzkammer★★★

Access via Klostergasse. The Treasury is one of the most important north of the Alps and is also a unique collection of precious items culled from the history of the cathedral. It consists of more than 100 outstanding artworks displayed in five thematic sections. Highlights include: the silver and gold Bust Reliquary of Charlemagne (post-1349) donated by Karl IV; the Cross of Lothair (c 1100), encrusted

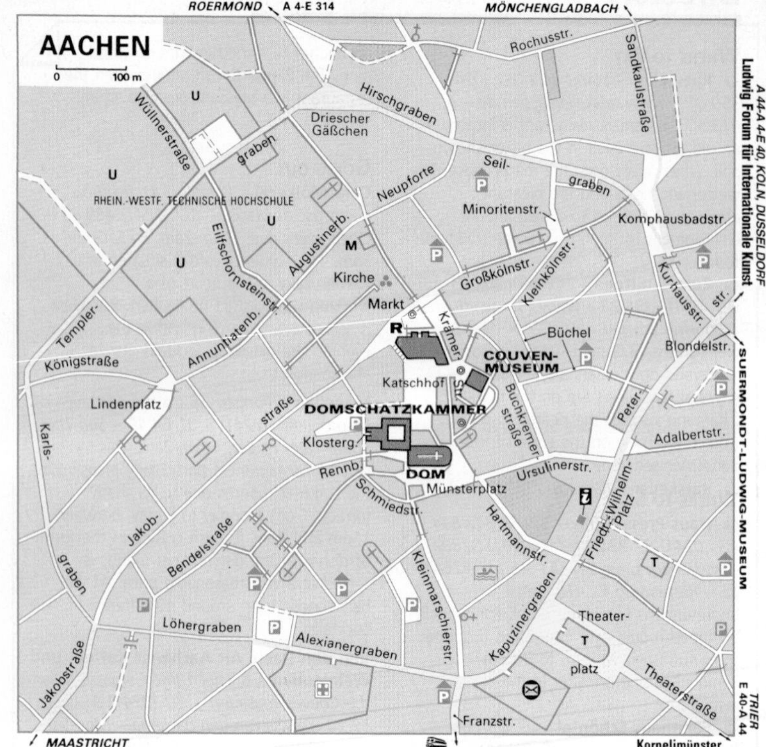

with precious stones; the Aachen Altarpiece (c 1520); and a unique ivory situla (c 1000), a ritual vessel for holy water. The rich collection of textiles has as its centrepiece the Cappa Leonis (14C), used as a coronation mantle.

Rathaus

♿ *10am-1pm, 2-5pm. Closed 1 Jan, Carnival, Good Friday, 1 May, Ascension, 1 Nov, 24-26 and 31 Dec, and during special events. €1.50.* ☎ *(0241) 180 29 60; www.aachen-tourist.de*
The town hall was built in the 14C, on the site of Charlemagne's palace, of which the squat Granus tower remains on the corner of Krämerstraße. The façade of the tower, decorated with statues of the kings and emperors crowned at Aachen, overlooks the market place, with its **fountain** and **statue of Charlemagne**.
The Peace Treaty of 1748, which ended the War of Austrian Succession, was signed in the Baroque **White Room** *(Weißer Saal)*, inside the town hall. The **Council Chamber** *(Ratssaal)* is clad with panelling executed in 1730 by a master woodworker of Liège.
The **Coronation Chamber** (Krönungssaal), with its ogive vaulting, is the venue for the annual awarding of the Aachen Charlemagne Prize for best efforts towards the unification of Europe.
▶▶ Couven-museum★ (domestic life in Aachen), Suermondt-Ludwig-Museum★ (art from the present to Antiquity) – Ludwig-Forum für Internationale Kunst (international art).

Excursions

Kornelimünster

10km/6mi SE. This suburb of Aachen, with its slate-roofed, blue and grey stone houses, in the valley of the Inde is typical of small towns in the Eifel region. The old abbey church of **Kornelimünster★** is an unusual construction with five naves (14C-16C), dating back to a Benedictine church of the Carolingian period. The galleries above the chancel *(east side)* were added in the 17C, the octagonal Kornelius chapel in the early 18C. The furnishings in the Gothic interior (ogive vaulting, painted ceilings) are essentially Baroque; note particularly the Baroque **high altar**, subsequently modified (c 1750) by JJ Couven in the Rococo style. On the left there is a stone statue of St Kornelius (c 1460). The church also contains a rich collection of **relics★**.
There is a fine **view** of the church, the abbey and the town from the Romanesque-Gothic **church of St Stephanus** (in the graveyard above to the north).

Deutsche Alpenstrasse★★★

German Alpine Road

One of the attractions of this splendid scenic route is the fact that it allows the traveller both to enjoy the splendours of mountain scenery and to visit such renowned monuments as the Wieskirche and the castles of Ludwig II of Bavaria. When passing through the pretty villages of the region, where villagers continue to live the simple alpine life of their ancestors, stop to sample some local culinary or cultural traditions, or head off for a walk among the alpine flowers.

Location

Michelin Map n°s 545 X 13 to 18, n°s 546 X 14 to 22 – Bayern. From Lake Constance (Bodensee) to the edge of Salzburg, this scenic route runs through ever-changing high mountain country of alpine lakes and steep, treeless mountainsides. The route

Directory

Where to Eat

⊖ **Ratskeller** – *Rathausstraße 2 – 83727 Schliersee – ☎ (08026) 47 86 – Closed Mon – ⊭ ♿ – €11.50/13.50.* This restaurant has three rooms, all furnished and decorated in a rustic style. If traditional food is up your street, you'll love this pleasingly simple and good-value establishment.

⊖⊖ **Obere Mühle** – *Ostrachstraße 40 – 87541 Hindelang – ☎ (08324) 28 57 – Closed Tue – ⊭ – €23/39.* This pleasant country-style restaurant dates from 1433 and is set in a former windmill. Regional cuisine and wood-fired dishes are served in a spick-and-span setting. Look out for the demonstration cheese dairy adjoining the restaurant.

⊖⊖ **Freihaus Brenner** – *Freihaus 4 – 83707 Bad Wiessee – ☎ (08022) 820 04 – info@freihaus-brenner.de – €26.50/48.* A mountain restaurant with an attractive view over Lake Tegernsee. The comfortable dining rooms, with wooden ceilings, exposed beams and prettily-curtained windows make this make this a most pleasant setting for a meal.

Where to Stay

⊖ **Gästehaus Weißes Rössl** – *Dorfstraße 19, 83242 Reit im Winkel – ☎ (08640) 982 30 – fax (08640) 5297 – www.weissesroessl-riw.de – Closed 3 weeks after Easter and from mid Oct to 20 Dec – ⊭ P ⊁ – 20rm: €25/68 – ☕ €8.* This well-kept and centrally-located hotel offers holidaymakers clean and comfortable rooms. The dining room where breakfast is also served has a country feel to it. The establishment also offers a sauna and gym.

⊖ **Gasthaus Zum Stern** – *Dorfstraße 33, 82487 Oberammergau – ☎ (08822) 867 – fax (08822) 7027 – Closed Wed – P – Booking advised – 13rm: €26/52 ☕ – Restaurant €11/35.* This typical Bavarian hotel dates from the start of the 17C and has simple, well-cared for rooms. In the plain, country-style dining room light meals and well-seasoned three course dinners are served with equal charm. Pleasant *Biergarten* in summer months.

⊖ **Alpengasthof Winkelmoosalm** – *Dürrnbachhornweg 6, 83242 Reit im Winkel – ☎ (08640) 974 40 – fax (08640) 974444 – www.winkelmoosalm.com – Closed Nov-Dec – P ♿ – 18rm: €33/118 – Restaurant €12.40/22.* A good place to know about for tourists and skiers alike. On offer are well-maintained rustic guestrooms and a bright restaurant with panoramic views serving organic dishes.

⊖ **Alpengasthof Hirsch** – *Kurze Gasse 18, 87541 Hindelang-Bad Oberdorf – ☎ (08324) 308 – fax (08324) 8193 – www.alpengasthof-hirsch.de – Closed 3 weeks in Nov – P ⊁ ♿ – 25rm: €35/120 – ☕ €7.50 – Restaurant €9.50/14.80.* Centrally-located, family-run hotel. Comfortable, modern guestrooms, some with kitchenette, others with lounge area, are on offer. Exuberant, country-style restaurant.

⊖ **Gasthof Fischerwirt** – *Linderhofer Straße 15, 82488 Ettal – ☎ (08822) 63 52 – fax (08822) 3568 – www.zum-fischerwirt.de – Closed from Nov to mid-Dec and for 2 weeks at Easter – P – 10rm: €40/58 ☕ – Restaurant €12.80/24.50.* If you're looking for a traditional, pleasant hotel, look no further. The simply-decorated guestrooms are particularly charming and the restaurant serves uncomplicated and reasonably-priced regional specialities.

⊖ **Terrassen Hotel Isnyland** – *Dengeltshofen 290, 88316 Isny-Neutrauchburg – ☎ (07562) 971 00 – fax (07562) 971040 – www.terrassenhotel.de – P ⊁ – Booking advised – 28rm: €48/112 ☕ – Restaurant €19/37.* A peaceful establishment set on a hill with themed, light-coloured guestrooms. All rooms have a balcony and the dining areas all look out towards the valley.

⊖⊖ **Hotel Lederer am See** – *Bodenschneidstraße 9, 83707 Bad Wiessee – ☎ (08022) 82 90 – fax (08022) 829200 – hotel@lederer.com – Closed from Nov to mid-Dec – P ⛱ – 104rm: €68/192 ☕ – Restaurant €20/36.* Four houses, built in the local style make up this pleasant hotel sitated in the heart of a fantastic park with a unique view of the lake. Bright, convivial, country-style restaurant, also with views over the lake.

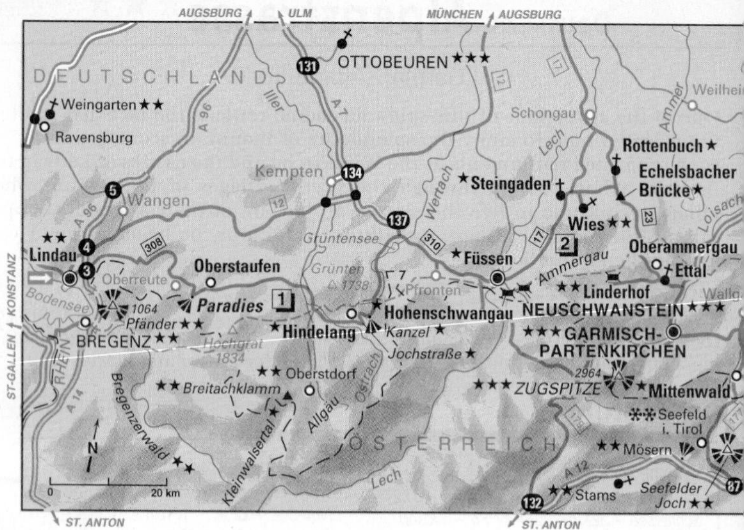

crosses the foothills of the Allgäu and the Bavarian Alps, passing on the way such heights as the Zugspitze (2 964m/9 724ft) and the Watzmann (2 712m/8 898ft). The trip follows the southern border of the country in an area dominated by ski resorts, traditional little villages with flower-filled balconies and churches and castles perched high on the mountainside. To cover the whole itinerary of 310mi/500km, allow three days.

Surrounding area: see ROMANTISCHE STRASSE (meets the German Alpine Road at Füssen), KONSTANZ, CHIEMSEE (to the north of the final part of tour 4 below).

Tours

THE ALLGÄU★ 1

From Lindau to Füssen 112km/70mi – half a day

This part of the tour features not Bavarian but Alemannic civilisation. The farmers of this region have made their mountain countryside into the great cheese manufacturing area of Germany.

Lindau★★ *see LINDAU*

Paradies

Engineers have given this name to a viewpoint between Oberreute and Oberstaufen, built halfway around a sweeping curve from which, far off to the southwest, the distant Appenzell Alps in Switzerland (Säntis and Altmann) can be seen.

Oberstaufen

This charming resort, at the foot of the Hochgrat massif (1 834 m/6 017ft), has some interesting ski slopes.

The road now climbs the alpine valley of the Iller, which runs to the foot of Grünten, the 'guardian' of the Allgäu.

Hindelang★

Together with its neighbour, Bad Oberdorf, this flower-decked village is a holiday centre and spa (sulphurous waters) from which mountain walks can be enjoyed in summer, and skiing on the slopes of the Oberjoch in winter.

Above Hindelang, the climb of the **Jochstraße★** affords a variety of views over the jagged limestone summits of the Allgäu Alps. From the **Kanzel★** viewpoint, almost at the summit, admire the panorama embracing the Ostrach Valley and the surrounding mountains.

Descending on the far side, the road crosses the valley of the Wertach, skirts the Grüntensee and passes near the large Pfronten ski resort before it arrives at Füssen.

Füssen★ *(voir FÜSSEN)*

THE AMMERGAU★ 2

From Füssen to Garmisch-Partenkirchen. 95 km/59mi – a day.

The road bypasses the outcrop of the Ammergau Alps to the north and then crosses a stretch of country that is seamed and broken up by the moraines deposited when the ancient Lech glacier withdrew. This rolling countryside is punctuated by the "onion" domes crowning the belfries of village churches.

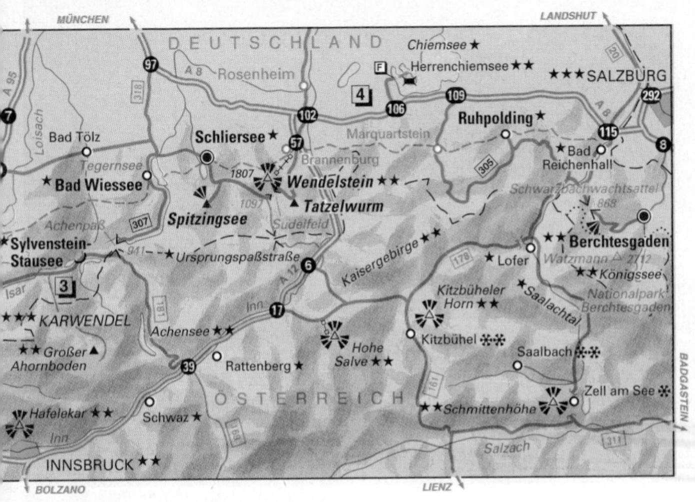

Hohenschwangau and Neuschwanstein★★★ – *See NEUSCHWANSTEIN*

Steingaden

The former abbey of the Steingaden Premonstratensians, founded in the 12C, still boasts its remarkable minster, though the **abbey church★** was modified in the 18C in the Baroque style. Only the outside, with its massive towers and Lombardy arcading, still has its original, thick-set Romanesque appearance.

The Gothic entrance is enriched with a painted genealogy of the House of Welf, the original founders of the abbey. The sobriety of the stuccowork embellishing the whole of the chancel contrasts sharply with the brightness of that in the wide nave, which is enhanced by finely painted motifs. Furnishings in both the Baroque and Rococo styles – pulpit, organ loft, altarpieces, statues – lend the interior a certain theatrical quality, as if symbolising the triumph of decoration over architecture.

Wieskirche★★ *See WIESKIRCHE*

Rottenbuch

First built as an Augustinian monastery, the **Mariä-Geburts-Kirche★** (Church of the Nativity of the Virgin) was entirely remodelled in the Baroque and Rococo styles in the 18C.

The stucco here embodies the virtuosity of the School of Wessobrunn, of which Joseph and Franz Schmuzer were among the masters. Frescoes by Matthäus Günther harmonise perfectly with the extravagantly sculpted decor. The pulpit, organ loft and altars by Franz Xaver Schmädl are heavily adorned with statues and giltwork in pure Rococo tradition.

Echelsbacher Brücke★ (Echelsbacher Bridge)

Since 1929, this audacious reinforced concrete structure has spanned the Ammer gorge, which at this point is 76m/250ft deep. Walk to the middle of the bridge to get the most impressive view of the gorge.

Oberammergau★

This small town of peasants and craftsmen, encircled by the wooded foothills of the Ammergau, owes its fame to the internationally-renowned Passion Play, which is performed only once every 10 years (next performance: 2010). The play, involving 1 100 amateur actors drawn from the local population, lasts an entire summer's day. The tradition derives from a vow made by the inhabitants in 1633, after a plague epidemic had miraculously been cut short.

Linderhof★★ *See Schloß LINDERHOF*

Ettal

A blossoming of the Benedictine tradition, added to local veneration of a statue of the Virgin attributed to Giovanni Pisano, explain the vast dimensions of Ettal Abbey, founded by the Emperor Ludwig IV "the Bavarian" in 1330.

The sole example of its kind in Germany, the original **abbey church** was a Gothic building with a polygonal floor plan. The present construction is due to the Baroque architect Enrico Zucalli, who built the façade and the chancel (1710-26). Joseph Schmuzer of the School of Wessobrunn *(see above)* added the dome after the church was gutted by a fire in 1774. The **frescoes** on the inside of this dome, a masterpiece of Rococo, are the work of Johann Jakob Zeiller.

T. Krieger/MICHELIN

Hindelang seen from the Jochstrasse.

The road now rejoins the Loisach Valley. To the south, the Wetterstein range appears, with the summits of the Zugspitze, the Alpspitze and the pyramid peak of the Dreitorspitze. Carry on to Garmisch-Partenkirchen.

THE UPPER ISAR VALLEY AND THE LAKE DISTRICT★ 3

From Garmisch-Partenkirchen to Schliersee. 105 km/65mi – 1 day.

Mittenwald★ *See GARMISCH-PARTENKIRCHEN excursions*

At Wallgau, the route joins the upper valley of the Isar *(toll road as far as Vorderriß)*, a wild, bleak stretch of open country.

Sylvenstein-Staudamm (Sylvenstein Dam)

Built to regulate the excessive flooding of the Isar, this earthwork dam with its waterproof core has created a huge reservoir, from which water is drawn off to supply an underground power station.

The road crosses the wooded Achenpaß (going 2km/1.2mi into Austria) and then plunges down towards the Tegernsee.

Bad Wiessee★

An elegant resort, both a fashionable holiday centre and a major spa (iodine, sulphur, fluorine springs), Bad Wiessee is pleasantly situated on the shores of Lake Tegernsee in cultivated, green, semi-Alpine surroundings.

Schliersee

Beside the lake of the same name, this small community – together with the town districts of Fischhausen, Neuhaus and Spitzingsee *(see itinerary below)* – offers holidaymakers interesting possibilities for a short stay. The **St Sixtus Parish Church★** (Pfarrkirche) is a former Collegiate of the Chapter of Our Lady in Munich, rebuilt in the Baroque style between 1712 and 1714. Both the frescoes on the vaulting and the delicate stucco were executed by Johann Baptist Zimmermann (1680-1758), brother of the architect of the Wieskirche *(see WIESKIRCHE)*.

THE SUDELFELD AND THE CHIEMGAU MOUNTAINS★ 4

From Schliersee to Berchtesgaden. 172km/107mi – one day

Spitzingsee

A little less than 1mi from the summit, the steep access road offers a fine overall view of the Fischhausen-Neuhaus plain and Lake Schliersee. Soon afterwards, the road comes to a stop by the Spitzingsee.

Shortly (3km/2mi) before Bayrischzell, the road passes the lower terminal of a cableway leading to the summit of the Wendelstein.

Tatzelwurm-Wasserfall

– *15min there and back on foot.* From the "Naturdenkmal Tatzelwurm" car park, a footpath leads to this impressive cascade.

Wendelstein★★

There are two ways of getting to the summit of the Wendelstein. Either take the cableway from Bayrischzell-Osterhofen terminal *(journey time about 7min)*, or take the **rack-railway**, Wendelstein-Zahnradbahn, leaving from the lower station at Brannenburg-Inntal *(journey time about 25min)*.

Ruggedly grinding its way up increasingly steep slopes, the little train finally reaches an altitude of 1 738m/5 702ft. The rest of the climb is on foot up a path carved out of the bedrock. The summit (1 838m/6 030ft) is crowned by a solar observatory and a chapel built in 1718. *From the valley station at Brannenburg. Summer: 9am–5pm; Winter: 9am-4pm. Departures every hour. Journey time: 30min. Enquire about closure periods. Return fare (round trip) €22.50. ☎ 080 34/30 80; www.wendelsteinbahn.de*
Going back 230 million years, the Wendelstein was a coral reef lying many hundreds of miles south of its present location. It has been declared a "Geo-Park" because of its quite singular geological makeup, and there are four geological trails (Geo-Wanderwege) that have been indicated with explanatory panels for visitors to follow. We particularly recommend the Gipfelweg, a circuit of the summit which takes about 2hr 30min.
The **panorama★★** visible from the top encompasses, from east to west, the mountains of the Chiemgau, the Loferer and the Leoberger Steinberge, the Kaisergebirge range with its jagged peaks, and the glacial crests of the Hohe Tauern.
From the Wendelstein terminal, our route winds down the valley of the Inn and then follows the Munich-Salzburg motorway, which skirts the southern shore of the ***Chiemsee★****. After Marquartstein, the road passes through a succession of tortuous, steep-sided valleys, running out finally above the Reit Basin, at the foot of the Zahmer Kaiser.*
Turning back towards the east, the Alpenstraße cuts through a long corridor past a series of dark-watered lakes.

Ruhpolding★

This resort, very popular with holiday-makers, is well known for upholding local traditions, crafts and folklore. The most precious artwork in the parish church of **St George** is a Romanesque statue of the Virgin Mary dating from the 12C housed in a golden casing on the right-hand side altar.
The drive across the Schwarzbachwacht pass gives ample opportunity to appreciate the striking contrast between the rather austere wooded valley of the River Schwarzbach and the open Alpine pastures on the Ramsau slopes. The drive down into the valley towards Ramsau gives several fine ***panoramas★★****, revealing the "teeth" of the Hochkalter biting into the white surface of the Blaueis (the only glacier in Germany, along with the Höllentalferner, in the Zugspitze massif) and the Watzmann. The German Alpine Road ends at Berchtesgaden.*

Berchtesgaden★★ *See BERCHTESGADEN*

Annaberg-Buchholz★

After the discovery of significant lodes of silver and tin ore on the Schreckenberg (Fear Mountain) in 1491 and 1496, Annaberg and Buchholz – which were governed by different families and were only united in 1945 – experienced an economic boom; at the peak period, 600 mines were pumping wealth into the capital of the Erzgebirge (Ore Mountains). In the 16C, as the silver yield diminished, lace production replaced mining as Annaberg's most important industry. Today the town's principal tourist attraction is its magnificent and flamboyantly Gothic cathedral.

Location

Population 24 000. Michelin map nos 544/546 O 22, local map see ERZGEBIRGE – Sachsen. Annaberg-Bucholz is located in the Erzgebirge region of Saxony, about 60 mi/100km to the southwest of Dresden and near the border with the Czech Republic.
ℹ *Markt 1, 09456 Annaberg-Buchholz, ☎ (037 33) 42 51 39.*
Surrounding area: see Chemnitz (20mi/32km to the north; see DRESDEN excursions), Freiberg (32mi/51km to the northeast; see DRESDEN excursions), DRESDEN (106 km to the northeast), SÄCHSISCHE SCHWEIZ (tour departing from DRESDEN), ERZGEBIRGE.

Worth a Visit

St-Annen-Kirche★★

Built between 1499 and 1525, this church with three naves is one of the most successful and impressive examples of Saxony's Flamboyant Gothic style. Twelve tall, thin pillars soar into the ribs of the vaulting, which consists of seven looping stars in a row and each yoke is covered by a "blossom baldaquin". This superb vault composition was the work of Jakob Heilmann from Schweinfurt. The parapets of the galleries on the side walls are embellished with scenes from the Old and New Testaments.

At the far end of the church, in the left-hand wall, is the **Schöne Tür★★** ("beautiful door"), a brilliantly multicoloured portal originally designed for another church. It was made by Hans Witten in 1512. The **pulpit★★** (1516) is the work of the sculptor F Maidburg. Note the relief figure representing a miner. A similar reference to Annaberg's old activity lies in the painted panels to be found behind the **Miners' Reredos★** (Bergmannsaltar, c 1520). Placed in the left-hand chapel of the chancel, these depict the various stages of work in a mine of that period.

Erzgebirgsmuseum mit Besucherbergwerk

Museum: open Jan to Nov Tue–Sun 10am–5pm; in Dec open also on Mon. Mine: opening times as for museum; guided tours only (1hr; last tour of mine at 3.30pm). Closed 24 Dec. €5.50 (museum and mine). ☎ (037 33) 234 97.

This museum retraces local history, in particular that of the mining industry, and contains varied collections of local crafts and folklore.

Annexed to the museum is the **Im Gößner** mine, which went into production at the height of Annaberg's economic prosperity c 1498 and from which silver was extracted for a quarter of a century. *The entrance shaft is in the courtyard of the museum. The section open to the public is 260m/285yd long and is reached via metal steps.*

Technisches Museum Frohnauer Hammer

Guided tours (50min) daily 9am–12pm and 1–4pm. Closed 1 Jan, 24, 25 and 31 Dec. €3. ☎ (037 33) 220 00; www.annaberg-buchholz.de

Once a flourmill, this old building was turned into a workshop for the minting of coins when silver was discovered in the region; it was subsequently transformed into a blacksmith's **forge**. Hydraulically-operated bellows and power-hammers (100, 200 and 300kg/220, 440, 660lb) can be seen there today.

Excursions

Erzgebirge★ *see ERZGEBIRGE*

Augsburg★★

Tacitus described Augsburg as "the most splendid colony in the province of Rhaetia". Not for nothing do the arms of this city on the German Romantic Road feature a pine cone, ancient symbol of fertility. In the 17C and 18C, local crafts and in particular outstanding silversmith work reached an all-time peak, with its excellent reputation spreading throughout Europe.

The city has been home to numerous famous artists: Hans Holbein the Elder (d 1525), Hans Burgkmair (1473-1531), and Martin Schongauer, the son of Augsburg-born goldsmith Konrad Peutinger. The city can also lay claim to Mozartian fame, as the composer's father was born here. The twentieth century is also represented on the city's roll-call by the famous dramatist Bertolt Brecht.

Modern Augsburg is an important industrial centre and intersection for communications. However the city of the German Renaissance which bears the hallmark of architect Elias Holl (1573-1646) continues to enchant visitors with its beauty.

Location

Population 265 000. Michelin map nos 545, 546 U 16 – Bayern. Augsburg is one hour from Munich by the A 8 and 30 minutes by train. The river Lech, a tributary of the Danube, crosses the town, and is canalised in the lower town. Augsburg is the third largest town in Bavaria and an important industrial centre and intersection for communications.

ℹ *Bahnhofstraße 7, 86150 Augsburg, ☎ (0821) 50 20 70*

Surrounding area: see ROMANTISCHE STRASSE, MÜNCHEN (41mi/66km to the east), ULM (46mi/74km to the west), OTTOBEUREN (56mi/89km to the southwest).

Background

Roman origins – Founded in 15 BC by Drusus and Tiberius, the stepsons of Emperor Augustus, Augsburg is, along with Trier and Cologne, one of the oldest cities in Germany. It became a trading centre on the road to Italy and, at the fall of the Roman Empire, an Episcopal See. By the end of the 13C it was a Free Imperial City and the seat of the Diet.

Directory

Where to Eat

⊜ **Zur alten Feuerwache** – *Zeugplatz 4 – ☏ (0821) 51 16 85 – zuraltenfeuerwache@t-online.de* – ♿ – *€15/25.* This pleasant restaurant is situated opposite the 16C arsenal of Augsburg. There is a large Biergarten to the front of the establishment suitable for a relaxing bite.

⊜⊜ **Die Ecke** – *Elias-Holl-Platz 2 – ☏ (0821) 51 06 00 – restaurant.dieecke@t-online.de – €27.50/46.* Located in a one of the town's historic buildings, this restaurant brings together rustic and modern styles. The dramatist Bertolt Brecht was a regular in days gone by.

Where to Stay

⊜ **Unterbaarer Hof** – *Ulmer Straße 218 – Tram 2 – ☏ (0821) 43 13 00 – fax (0821) 4866540 – www.unterbaarer-hof.de* – P – *6rm: €30/55* ☕ – *Restaurant €7.90/16.40.* A good hotel with modern guestrooms and a huge self-catering apartment. The wooden furnishings and pleasant décor give the dining room a country feel and traditional cooking is served here for a very reasonable price.

⊜ **Hotel garni Georgenrast** – *Georgenstraße 31 – Tram 2, Fischertor – ☏ (0821) 50 26 10 – fax (0821) 5026127 – Closed from Christmas to Twelfth Night – 24 rm: €35/60* ☕. Clean and simple guesthouse situated in a relatively quiet side street about 1km from the town-centre. The smallish guestrooms are well maintained with plain, light-coloured furnishings.

Taking a Break

Caféhaus Eber – *Philippine-Welser-Str. 6 (opposite the town hall) – ☏ (0821) 3 68 47 – www.cafe-eber.de – Open Mon-Sat, 8am-6pm.* You are guaranteed to be spoilt for choice at this confectionery shop: delicious tarts vie with chocolates for space in the shop window. Try some of these goodies in the tea-room on the first floor or, in good weather, on the terrace on the Rathausplatz. Lunch is available between 11am and 2pm.

Stadtmarkt – *Annastr. 16 (accessible also from Fuggerstr. 12) – ☏ (0821) 3 24 39 22 – Mon-Fri 7am-6pm, Sat 7am-2pm.* Everything is available from the market stalls here. Stave off hunger with a snack from a cold meat stall *(Fleischhalle)* or grocery stall *(Viktualienhalle)*. Cafés, restaurants and a crêperie are also to be found here. A farmers' market is held here in the morning.

Going Out

Der Weinbäck (Laxgangs Weinstuben) – *Spitalgasse 8 – ☏ (0821) 3 79 11 (Reservations: ☏ 50 26 80) – www.weinbaeck.de – Mon-Sat 5pm-1am – Closed Sun and bank holidays and 25 Dec to 1 Jan.* Choose wine by the glass from a large selection of mostly German *crus* to enjoy with a seasonal set menu, all served in historic 16C cellars (or in the charming courtyard in summer months). The home-made bread comes free of charge.

The Fuggers – At the end of the 15C, Augsburg – which already had a population of 50 000 – became a centre of high finance and banking. This was due to the Fuggers and the Welsers, two local dynastic families who – so it was said – shared the known world between them so far as money and trade were concerned. History has preserved the name of Jakob Fugger the Rich (1459-1529), renowned as the Empire's banker and even better known as the financier of the Habsburgs. He was powerful enough to deliver a haughty rebuke to Charles V himself, reminding him that: "It is well known that, without my help, Your Majesty would no longer wear the crown of the Holy Roman Empire." The debt of the Habsburgs to their Augsburg bankers, never settled, has been estimated at four million ducats.

The Augsburg Confession – In 1530 Charles V, disturbed by the growing strength of the Reformation in many states of the Empire, called an Imperial Diet at Augsburg with the hope of dissipating the religious troubles. The Protestants, inspired by Luther, thereupon proclaimed in a celebrated "Confession" the basic tenets of their belief. The statement was rejected, and it was not until the **Peace of Augsburg** in 1555 that Protestants in Germany won the freedom of worship.

The name of the town was once more inscribed in the history books in 1686 with the creation of the Augsburg League – an alliance between the Habsburgs and Prussia aimed against Louis XIV, who had revoked the Edict of Nantes.

Worth a Visit

Rathausplatz

The **town hall** is a vast Renaissance building built by Elias Holl between 1615 and 1620, and rebuilt from the original plans after extensive damage received in 1944. Two onion-domed towers frame a pediment adorned with the traditional pine cone. Inside, the town hall's Golden Room *(Goldener Saal)*, with its restored coffered ceiling, can be visited *(visits take place, 10am-6pm, €2)*.

AUGSBURG

Street	Grid
Annastraße	Y
Bahnhofstraße	YZ
Bürgermeister-Fischer-Straße	Y 5
Dominikanergasse	Z 8
Frauentorstraße	Y 12
Fuggerstraße	Y 13
Grottenau	Y 16
Haunstetter Str.	Z 18
Hoher Weg	Y
Karlstraße	Y
Karolinenstraße	Y 22
Lechhauser Str.	Y 23
Leonhardsberg	Y 24
Margaretenstraße	Z 25
Maximilianstraße	Z
Mittlerer Graben	Y 27
Perlachberg	Y 32
Predigerberg	Z 33
Rathausplatz	Y 34
Unterer Graben	Y 39
Vorderer Lech	Z 43
Wintergasse	Y 44

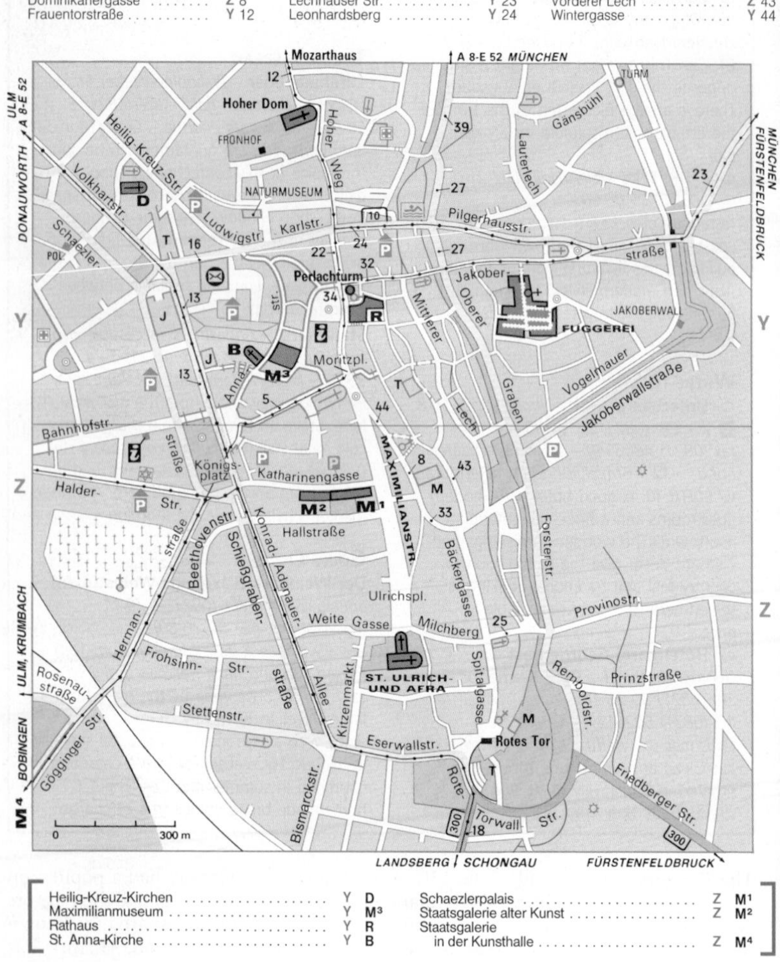

The **Perlachturm**, on the left, was originally a Romanesque watchtower. It was expanded three times over the course of the centuries. When the Alps can be seen from the top of it, a yellow flag is flown *(tower visits in high season)*.

St Anna-Kirche

Luther came to Augsburg in 1518 to defend his reformist thesis and stayed in this 14C Carmelite monastery. The church became Protestant in 1525 and the rooms where Luther stayed have been turned into a museum *(Lutherstiege)*. The **Fugger Funeral Chapel★** *(Fuggerkapelle)* at the heart of the church is exceptional: a Catholic enclave in an otherwise Protestant church, it is the first example of Renaissance architecture in Germany. Note the three works by Lucas Cranach the Elder in the east chancel.

Fuggerei★

This name was bestowed in 1519 on the quarter founded by Jakob Fugger the Rich to house the town's poor. The eight streets in the Fuggerei are lined by 53 gabled houses. The district has its own church and its own administration. Each evening the four gateways to the quarter are closed, as they always have been. This housing settlement, the first of its kind in the world, still welcomes citizens in need as it did in the 16C, charging them only a token rent but placing on them the moral obligation of praying for the souls of the founders.

Dom

The cathedral was rebuilt in Gothic style in the 14C. Outside, note the Gothic south door to the chancel or **Virgin's Door★★** *(Jungfrauen-Portal)*, and also the Romanesque bronze **panels★** *(Türflügel)* dating from the first half of the 11C. They are embellished with 32 bas-relief sculptures illustrating scenes and characters from the Old Testament and mythology (provisionally displayed within the cathedral at

T. Krieger/MICHELIN

The town hall and the Perlachturm

the present time). Inside the church, the tall nave is flanked by double side aisles. The chancel, at its eastern extremity, has a double ambulatory with Gothic chapels added. Four of the altars in the nave are adorned with panel **paintings★** *(Tafelgemälden)* by Holbein the Elder (on the left: *Birth of the Virgin Mary* and *Entry Into the Temple*; on the right, *The Offering Refused* and *The Presentation*). The clerestory windows on the south side of the nave contain stained-glass **Windows of the Prophets★** (*Prophetenfenster* – 12C) which are very rigid in style. The alabaster panes surrounding them are modern.
In front of the cathedral can be seen remains of the Roman city.

Maximilianstraße★

Lined by mansions and private houses built by the wealthier burghers of Augsburg during the Renaissance, this street offers one of the most majestic vistas of Old Germany. Many façades have been extensively restored. Three bronze Renaissance fountains adorn the street.

Städtische Kunstsammlungen★ (Municipal Art Gallery)

Entrance: Maximilianstraße 46. ♿ Open every day except Mon, 10am-5pm. Art collections: Wed, 2pm-4pm. Closed 24, 25 and 31 Dec. €3, no charge on the first Sun of the month. ☎ (0821) 324 41 02.
The Schaezler-Palais galleries (1767) are the first to be passed through. Paintings by masters of German Baroque are on display here. The enormous **banqueting hall★★** *(Festsaal)* is noteworthy for a ceiling lavishly decorated with Rococo frescoes and stuccowork, and wall panelling adorned in the same style.
Beyond this, a second **gallery**, the *Staatsgalerie Alter Kunst* exhibits paintings by 15C and 16C Augsburgan (especially) and Swabian masters, including a votive portrait of *The Schwarz Family* by Hans Holbein the Elder and the famous *Portrait of Jakob Fugger the Rich* by Albrecht Dürer.
Works by Van Dyck, Tiepolo and Veronese can be seen on the second floor.

Münster St Ulrich und Afra ★

This former Benedictine abbey lies adjacent to a Protestant church of the same name. The juxtaposition of the two churches, one Catholic, one Protestant, each with the same name, is characteristic of Augsburg. The two **Heilig-Kreuz-Kirchen** are another example.
The large basilica was founded in 1474 and is of late-Gothic style with Renaissance and Baroque additions. The core of the building, high and impressive, is separated from the three aisles by a fine Baroque screen. The ribbed vaulting is well lit by the clerestory windows and at the far end are three Baroque altars. At the transept crossing note the bronze group of the *Crucifixion* dating from 1607.
Among the chapels on the north side, St Simpert's is furnished with a Gothic baldaquin and a balcony surmounted by terracotta **Statues of the Saints★**.

▶▶ *Maximilianmuseum* (Augsburg art and craftwork) – *Mozarthaus* (Mozart's father's house) – Walk along the ramparts and *Rotes Tor* – *Staatsgalerie in der Kunsthalle★* (19C and 20C German art) – *Augsburger Puppenkiste* (Puppet Theatre, *reservation required*).

Baden-Baden★★

From Brahms to Queen Victoria, some of the richest and most famous people of the 19C have enjoyed the baths and casinos of Baden-Baden. A spa resort since Antiquity and a gambling centre for the last 150 years, the town attracts well-heeled visitors to this day. However, you don't have to be a member of high-society to appreciate its luxury, history and atmosphere.

Location

Population: 53 000. Michelin map nº 545 T 8 – Baden-Württemberg. Situated between the Black Forest and the Baden vineyards, in a sheltered position in the Oos Valley, Baden-Baden is 60km/37mi from Strasbourg on the A 5-E 52.

ℹ *Kaiserallee 3, 76530 Baden-Baden,* ☎ *(072 21) 27 52 00.*

Surrounding area: see RASTATT (8km/5mi to the north), KARLSRUHE (40km/25mi to the north), or one of the tours in the SCHWARZWALD.

Directory

Getting About

Baden-Baden is linked to the Karlsruhe public transport network by city line S 4 or regional line R 3. Information on the network and on ticket prices from **Baden-Baden-Linie** (Beuernerstraße 25, ☎ *(072 21) 27 76 38)* or from the town hall office (Jesuitenplatz, ☎ *(072 21) 27 73 52)*.

Airport – Baden-Baden Airport (10 km to the southeast of the town, by the A 5, Baden-Baden exit, towards Iffezheim, follow the "Baden-Airpark" signs) has several flights a day to and from Berlin. *Information* ☎ *(072 29) 66 20 00 or www.baden-airport.de*

Sightseeing

A guided tour of the main sites is available in English, ☎ *(072 21)27 52 41* for information.

Tourist bus – The City-Bahn Baden-Baden tours the town all year round (45min round trip, €4.50).

Where to Eat

⊖ **Yburg** – *Burgruine 1 –* ☎ *(07223) 95 75 43 – www.burggaststaette-yburg.de – Closed Jan-Feb, except weekends – – €6.50/14.50.* This establishment has pleasant views over the Rhine river plain and is popular with tourists. Good choice of traditional dishes in the restaurant.

⊖ **Hildegard's** – *Am Verfassungsplatz –* ☎ *(07221) 337 55 – www.hildegards.de – €17/28.50.* Richly-coloured paintings adorn the walls of this agreeable restaurant-bistro. There are plenty of dishes to choose from and afterwards, round off the evening by propping up the longest bar in town!

Where to Stay

⊖ **Haus Rebland** – *Umwegerstraße 133, 76534 Baden-Baden – Varnhalt –* ☎ *(07223) 520 47 – fax (07223) 60496 – www.hausrebland.de – Closed from mid-Nov to mid-Dec – P – 24rm: €50/90 – Restaurant €13/18.* Located among the vineyards of Varnhaltet, this family-run establishment's guestrooms all have balconies and are functionally furnished in light wood. Rustic restaurant with country feel and pretty views over the Rhine valley.

⊖⊖ **Hotel Bayrischer Hof** – *Lange Straße 92 – BUS 201 –* ☎ *(07221) 935 50 – fax (07221) 935555 – www.hotel-bayrischerhof.de – P – 38rm: €70/130.* This hotel is located opposite the Festival Theatre *(Festspielhaus)*, and it would be difficult to find a more conveniently situated establishment – the town's sights are all virtually on the doorstep. Functionally-furnished guestrooms.

Petite Pause

Café König – *Lichtentaler Straße 12 –* ☎ *(07221) 2 35 73 – info@chocolatier.de – café: 9.30am-6.30pm, confectionery and pastry shop: 10.30am-6pm.* Try cakes and sweets from the neighbouring confectionery and pastry shop within the gilded walls of this café. Also available are savoury snacks or even a full-scale lunch. In summer months, enjoy all these delicacies on the terrace under the shade of the giant lime tree.

Eiscafé Capri – *Sophienstr. 1b –* ☎ *(07221) 2 37 51 – Mon-Sat, 8am-midnight (winter: 8pm), Sun, from 9am – Closed Jan.* It's impossible to resist choosing from the impressive list of home-made ice-creams and cakes. In the summer the terrace is at the heart of the action in Baden-Baden.

Going Out

In der Trinkhalle – *Kaiserallee 3 (in the west aisle of the Trinkhalle, entrance at the back of the building) –* ☎ *(07221) 30 29 05 – www.in-der-trinkhalle.de – 10am-2am.* Very chic café-bar with leather armchairs offering a large selection of drinks and light snacks. After a busy day exploring the town, the tranquil terrace with views of the spa park is all the more welcome.

T. Krieger/MICHELIN

Baden-Baden.

Background

Spa – The restorative powers of the waters at Baden-Baden were already known in Roman times. In the 12C, the town became the seat of the Zähringer branch of the Margraves of Baden. In the 16C, the great Paracelsus, one of the founders of modern pharmacy, came here to take care of the Margrave. Today, two spa complexes offer treatments and relaxation with cold and hot baths, whirlpools, steamrooms, etc *(open every day, price depends on the length of stay and choice of treatments).* The **Friedrichsbad** is a neo-Renaissance style palace built in 1877 with a Belle Époque ambience. The **Caracalla-Therme** (named after the Roman Emperor who came frequently to Baden-Baden to cure his rheumatism) is a more modern complex, geared to relaxation and leisure.

Casino – By the 19C, a casino launched by the Frenchman Jacques Bénazet, a theatre and opera house (opened in 1862), and a racecourse organised by the Paris Jockey Club had transformed the town into the summer capital of Europe.

Worth a Visit

Lichtentaler Allee★★

This, the most beautiful promenade in Baden-Baden, runs beside the River Oos, flowing here over an artificial bed. The shade of the esplanade has seen many a historical figure: Napoleon III, his wife the Empress Eugénie, Queen Victoria, Bismarck and Dostoevsky, to name a few, strolled along here. In 1861, an unsuccessful attempt was made here on the life of the then King of Prussia, later Kaiser Wilhelm I.

Originally the shade was provided uniquely by oaks, planted more than 300 years ago, but other species of tree and numerous ornamental shrubs have since been added. On the left, beyond the swimming pool, is the **Gönneranlage★**, a pretty little park

Kurhaus

Guided visits of the casino take place every 30min until 11.45am. €4. To use the Casino, you need to show your passport, pay an entrance fee and be suitably dressed.

Despite its name, bathing no longer goes on behind the white Corinthian columns of the Kurhaus built by Friedrich Weinbrenner (1821-24). Instead, glittering balls and concerts are held here and the casino takes up one wing of the building. Notable are the four **gaming rooms★** designed in 1855 by Bénazet in the style of the French royal chateaux. Nearby in the same park is the Drinking Hall *(Trinkhalle)*, embellished with murals illustrating the legends of the Baden countryside.

Stadtmuseum im Baldreit★ (Town Museum)

Lichtentaler Allee 10. Open Tue to Sun, 10am-6pm (-8pm, Wed). Closed 1 Jan, Easter Mon, Whit Mon, 24, 25 and 31 Dec. €1. ☎ (072 21) 93 22 72, stadtmuseum@.baden-baden.de. Two thousand years of the history of the town are presented using archaeological documents and historical artefacts. Note especially the locally-produced porcelain (in production between 1771 and 1778), reconstructions of the town as it was in the 19C and pieces of religious art.

BADEN-BADEN

Street	Grid
Burgstraße	BY 3
Eichstraße	CZ 6
Gernsbacher Straße	BCY 8
Goetheplatz	BZ 10
Hirschstraße	BY 18
Kaiser-Wilhelm-Straße	BZ 19
Konrad-Adenauer-Platz	BZ 23
Kreuzstraße	BZ 24
Lange Straße	BY 25
Lichtentaler Straße	CZ 28
Ludwig-Wilhelm-Platz	CZ 30
Luisenstraße	BY
Markgrafenstraße	CZ 32
Marktplatz	CY 33
Merkurstraße	CZ 35
Prinz-Weimar-Straße	CY 38
Sonnenplatz	CY 42
Sophienstraße	CY
Steinstraße	CY 43
Willy-Brandt-Platz	CY 47

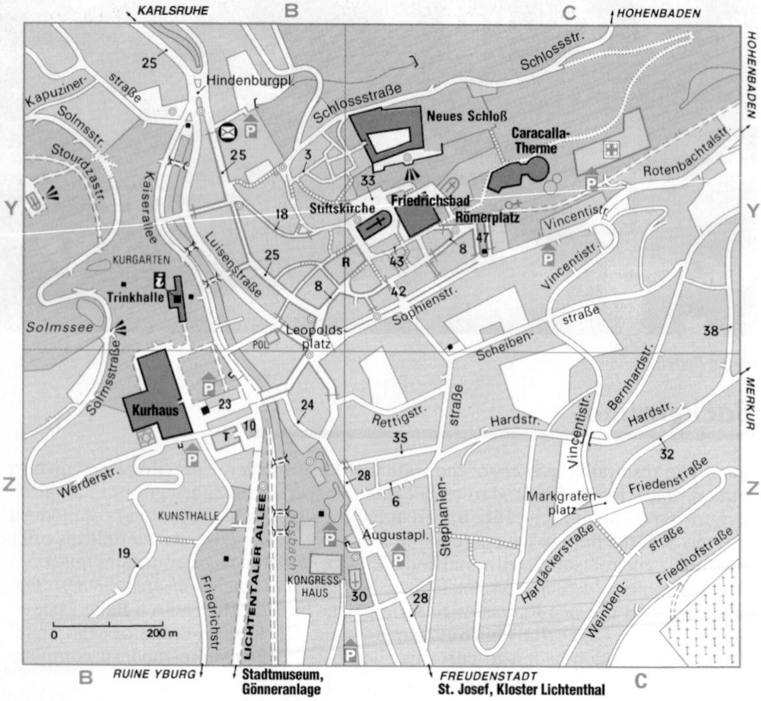

Neues Schloß (New Castle)

The castle was built in the 16C by the Margraves of Baden, incorporating parts of an earlier building. In the mid 19C it was modified again, with the result that the present building reflects several different architectural styles. Until 1918, it was the summer residence of the Margraves of Baden. The castle is private property but the gateway building houses an annexe of the town museum. From the terrace there is a pleasant view over the town and towards the Stiftskirche.

Stiftskirche (Collegiate Church)

The Margraves of Baden were all buried in this church from the 14C to the 18C. The chancel contains a wealth of artfully decorated tombs ranging from the Late Gothic to the Rococo period, including that of Margrave Leopold Wilhelm (left, late 17C), and of **Ludwig the Turk** (right, 1753). On the end wall of the chancel is the eye-catching sandstone **Crucifix★**, a 1467 masterpiece by Nicolaus Gerhaert von Leyden and an outstanding example of late medieval sculpture. Another must is the filigreed Late Gothic tabernacle (late 15C) at the entrance to the chancel.

Römische Badruinen (Roman Baths)

Beneath the Römerplatz, excavations have unearthed the ruins of a Roman bathhouse (note particularly the hypocaust underfloor heating system). *Closed until further notice due to renovation (details not available at time of going to press). ☎ (072 21) 27 52 06; www.baden-baden.de*

Excursions

Yburg Ruins★

6km/3.5mi SW. Leave by Friedrichstraße.

From the tower *(110 steps)* there is a vast **panorama★★** over the Rhine plain, with the Baden vineyards in the foreground.

Merkur

2km/1.2mi E. Leave by Markgrafenstraße or take bus 204 or 205 from Leopoldsplatz. A funicular railway runs from 10am to 10pm. Round trip: €4.

The **broad view★** takes in Baden-Baden, the Rhine Valley to the west, the Murg Valley to the east and (on a clear day) the Vosges.

▶▶ Altes Schloß Hohenbaden (4 km/2.5mi to the northeast, at Ebersteinburg)

Tours

Baden Vineyards★

34km/21mi, 2hr. Leave the town on Kaiser-Wilhelm-Straße then Fremersbergstraße. Follow the signposts marked "Badische Weinstraße".

The **Badische Weinstraße★★★** winds sinuously from village to village through the vineyards on the lower slopes of the Black Forest.

At Altschweir, leave the Wine Road to get to Altwindeck.

Burg Altwindeck★

This ancient fort, built on a circular plan, has been transformed into a restaurant with panoramic views. From its precincts there is a wide **view★** of the plain.

Rejoin the Wine Road and head towards Kappelrodeck.

Sasbach

15min on foot there and back. Leave the car opposite the Hotel Linde and walk into the park.

An obelisk and plinth with inscriptions in German, French and Latin mark the spot where, in 1675, a fatal cannon-ball ended the glorious career of **Marshall Turenne** – the French hero charged by Louis XIV with the defence of Alsace against the Imperial forces, during the conquest of Franche-Comté.

Oberkirch★

This beautiful town is surrounded by orchards, vineyards and forests and retains charming half-timbered houses dating from the 17C.

If you wish, carry on for 150km/94mi until Basel (Switzerland).

SCHWARZWALD-HOCHSTRAßE (BLACK FOREST CREST ROAD)

See SCHWARZWALD.

Badenweiler★

A peaceful and pleasant village of orchards and vineyards, Badenweiler has been known for its thermal waters and gentle climate since time immemorial. This spa and holiday town attracts people seeking rest and recuperation, or relief of rheumatic and articulatory complaints or cardiovascular problems.

Location

Population: 3 400. Michelin map nº 545 W 7 – Baden-Württemberg. Badenweiler lies on a slope at the mouth of a valley in the southern foothills of the Black Forest with a view both of the Rhine Valley and the Vosges.

Ernst-Eisenlohr-Straße 4, 79410 Badenweiler, ☎ (076 32) 79 93 00.

Surrounding area: see FREIBURG IM BREISGAU (36 km/22mi to the north), Bad SÄCKINGEN (46 km/29mi to the southeast), SCHWARZWALD.

Worth a Visit

Kurpark★★ (Spa Park)

The rolling parkland abounds in sub-tropical plants and splendid trees: cedars and cypresses mingle with enormous sequoias. The park also contains the impressive ruins of some **Roman baths**, the largest and best-preserved north of the Alps. A climb up to the ruins of the old fort brings with it a fine **view★** of the resort, the Rhine Valley and the Vosges.

Excursions

Blauen★

8km/5mi SE; 2hr 30min on foot or 15min drive. From the viewing tower, rising above the woods at the top of a hill, there is a remarkable **panorama★★** over the plain – the parallel ribbons of the Rhine and the Grand Canal of Alsace can be seen clearly – and the tree-covered humps of the Vosges. The bare summit to the northeast is the Belchen. On a clear day the Swiss Alps appear in the south.

Schloß Bürgeln★
10km/6mi south. This gentleman's residence, set in beautifully kept, terraced gardens, was built in 1762 for the abbots of St Blasien. The property overlooks the last undulations of the Black Forest, several reaches of the Rhine, and part of the city of Basle. Inside, there are beautiful examples of stuccowork in the Rococo style. *Guided tour (40min), Mar-Nov: Wed-Mon, 10.30am-6pm. €3. ☎ (076 26) 237.*

Burg Rötteln★★
The ruins of this fortress extend over 300m/1000ft and are all that remains of a complex constructed in the 14C and destroyed during the Palatinate War of Succession at the end of the 17C. The Oberburg, the defensive nucleus of this fortress, is reached by a series of ramps and a drawbridge. The Green Tower (Grüner Turm), which overlooks the whole complex, has been restored and modified into a look-out tower. From the tower, the view includes the Wiese Valley (which eventually fades into the outskirts of Basle), the wooded massif of the Blauen *(see above)* in the Basle Jura, the gentler slopes of the Black Forest and, far off on the horizon, the Swiss Alps.

Bamberg★★

Beyond any other town, the German people feel themselves most closely attached to the town of Bamberg, according to a recent survey, and it's not difficult to see why. Established in the Middle Ages, transformed in the 17C and 18C in the new Baroque style under the Schönborn bishops and spared wartime bomb-raids, it today counts 2 300 listed buildings that span the Romanesque to the Baroque periods. The UNESCO paid its respects by putting Bamberg on the World Heritage List in 1993.
The sculptor Tilman Riemenschneider (1460-1531) and the Dientzenhofer family, draughtsmen of distinction, were the most famous products of the city. Among Bamberg's many gastronomic specialities visitors should sample carp (Karpfen) prepared to a traditional local recipe, and "smoked beer" (Rauchbier).

Location
Population: 70 000. Michelin maps n°s 545, 546 Q 16 – Bayern. Bamberg is surrounded by seven hills and lost in the Franconian countryside. The River Regnitz and the Main-Danube Canal both bisect the town: the historic centre is in the upper part of the town.
🅸 *Geyerswörthstraße 3, 96047 Bamberg, ☎ (0951) 87 11 61.*
Surrounding area: see Wallfahrtskirche VIERZEHNHEILIGEN (32 km/20mi to the north), BAYREUTH (65 km/40mi to the east), NUREMBERG (63 km/39mi to the south), or take the ROMANTISCHE STRASSE to Volkach (66 km/41mi to the west).

Little Venice.

M. Hertlein/MICHELIN

BAMBERG

Äußere Löwenstraße	CY 2
Am Kranen	BZ 3
Bischofsmühlbrücke	BCZ 5
Dominikanerstraße	BZ 8
Domstraße	BZ 9
Geyerswörthstraße	CZ 12
Grüner Markt	CZ 13
Hauptwachstraße	CZ 15
Herrenstraße	BZ 18
Judenstraße	BZ 20
Karolinenstraße	BZ 23
Lange Str.	CZ
Luitpoldbrücke	CY 26
Luitpoldstraße	CY
Maximiliansplatz	CY
Mittlerer Kaulberg	BZ 30
Nonnenbrücke	CZ 32
Obere Karolinenstraße	BZ 33
Obere Königstraße	CY 34
Obere Sandstraße	BZ 36
Residenzstraße	BZ 40
Richard-Wagner-Str.	CZ 44
St-Getreu-Str.	BZ 45
Schillerplatz	CZ 47
Schönleinsplatz	CZ 48
Untere Brücke	BZ 52
Untere Königstraße	CY 54
Unterer Kaulberg	BZ 55

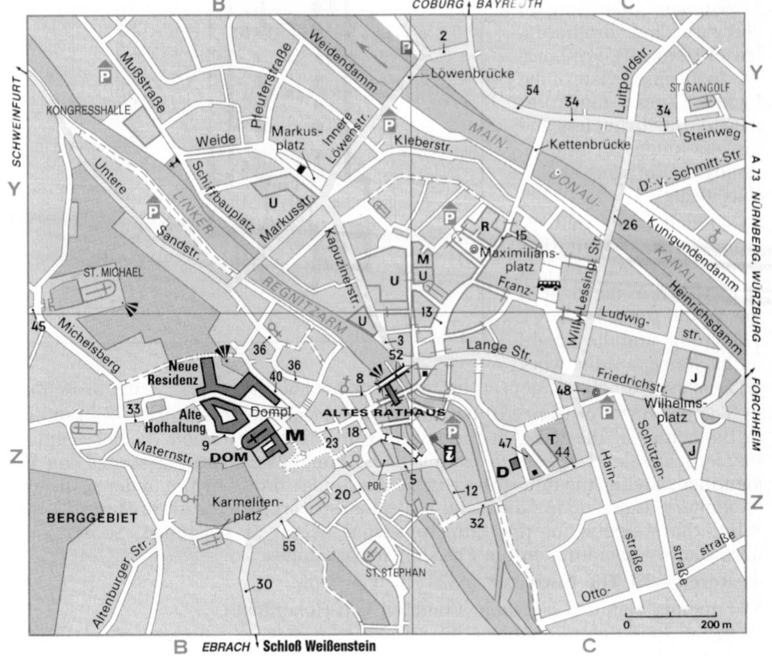

[Diözesanmuseum .... BZ **M**   E.T.A. Hoffmann-Haus .... CZ **D**]

Special Features

THE OLD TOWN *2hr.*

Kaiserdom★★

The Cathedral of St Peter and St George, completed in 1237, is transitional Gothic in style and characterised by its two apses. The older of the two, the Georgenchor *(ahead)*, stands raised upon a terrace with a fine balustrade, its cornices worked in a chequered pattern; the Peterschor *(hidden to the back)*, is entirely Gothic. Four towers quarter the two choirs. The design, inherited from the original Ottonian edifice *(see Art and Architecture)*, exemplifies the reticence of the Empire's powerful ecclesiastical institutions when faced with the innovations of French Gothic.

The finest of the cathedral entrances is the *Fürstenportal* **(Princes' Doorway)**, on the Domplatz. It comprises 10 recessed arches supported on fluted, ribbed or chevroned columns which alternate with statue-columns representing prophets with apostles on their shoulders.

Enter the church through the Adamspforte. This doorway is decorated with diamond and dogtooth carving (the statues which used to adorn it are in the Diocesan Museum). The progression from Romanesque to Gothic is at once apparent: two choirs, noticeably raised because of the crypts built beneath them, enclose a single nave whose walls – with no galleries – attest to the conservatism of the prevailing style. Underneath the first choir *(near the entrance)*, the crypt is huge: three Romanesque naves with impressive ribbed vaulting supported on powerful columns. Beneath the second choir *(at the back of the church)* is the tomb of the Bamberg archbishops, whose basic features are those of the re-excavated western crypt of the original cathedral of Heinrich.

Among the masterpieces of German Gothic sculpture on view are:

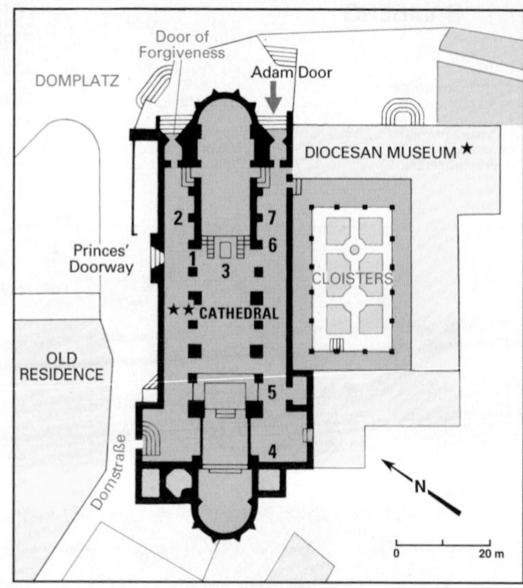

1) Equestrian statue of **The Knight of Bamberg★★★** *(Bamberger Reiter)*, a 13C representation of an unidentified king (possibly St Stephen, first King of Hungary and brother-in-law of Henry II), symbolising an idealised view of the Middle Ages, much as Bayard, the "blameless and fearless knight" of France, stands for the same chivalrous ideals.

2) Celebrated statuary group, **The Visitation** (note the features of St Elizabeth to the right of the central statue of Mary). The group, and the Knight on his horse, are the work of an artist strongly influenced by the French School, particularly that of Reims.

3) The **tomb★★★** of Henry II the Saint and Cunegunda *(St Heinrichs Grab)* stands in the centre of the nave, at the entrance to the eastern choir. It took Tilman Riemenschneider 14 years to complete the tomb. The following scenes can be identified, circling the tomb *(clockwise)*: Cunegunda's ordeal by fire under suspicion of adultery; Cunegunda's dismissal of dishonest workmen; death of Henry II the Saint; the weighing of the Emperor's soul before St Lawrence; St Benedict miraculously operating on the Emperor for gallstones.

4) **Reredos of The Nativity★** (1523) by Veit Stoß.

5) Funerary statue of a bishop (Friedrich von Hohenlohe).

6) Statue representing the Church.

7) Remarkable statue symbolising the Synagogue, in the form of a blindfolded woman.

Alte Hofhaltung (Old Residence)

The courtyard is open until dusk. This was formerly the episcopal and Imperial palace (10C-11C). Its façade, with carved gables, oriel window and corner turret date, along with the doorway, from the Renaissance. The delightful inner **courtyard★★** *(Innenhof)* is bordered by half-timbered Gothic buildings with steeply sloping roofs and picturesque, flower-decked wooden galleries. It houses the Historical Museum (art and culture in the town's history).

Neue Residenz (New Residence)

♿ Guided tour (45min). Apr-Sep: 9am-6pm; Oct-Mar: 10am-4pm. €3. ☎ (0951) 51 93 90; www.schloesser.bayern.de.

This palace, the largest building in Bamberg, comprises four main blocks: two, bordering the Obere Karolinenstraße, were constructed in the early 17C and are Renaissance in style; the two wings on the Domplatz are Baroque. They were started in 1695 by the architect Leonard Dientzenhofer, on the orders of Lothar Franz von Schönborn, Prince-Elector of Mainz and Bishop of Bamberg.

On the first floor, works of the German masters are on view (Master of the Life of the Virgin, Hans Baldung Grien etc). On the second floor, the Imperial apartments are among the finest in the palace, with beautiful parquet floors, Baroque furniture and authentic Gobelins tapestries. The **Emperors' Hall** *(Kaisersaal)* is outstanding for its portraits and its allegorical frescoes. From the palace rose garden, there is a fine **view★** of the town and the former Benedictine abbey of St Michael.

Follow the Karolinenstraße to the lay quarter of the old town, built on the banks of the River Regnitz. Take time to explore some of the adjoining streets, particularly around Jugenstraße (note the statues of the Virgin Mary on the house corners).

Altes Rathaus★ (Old Town Hall)

Standing alone on an islet in the river, this unusual building was remodelled in the 18C. In addition to the town hall proper, with its façades decorated with a perspective fresco, there is a bridge tower and a small half-timbered house, known as the Rottmeisterhaus, balanced on one of the bridge's pontoons leading to the islet. From the Untere Brücke – the bridge at the lower end of the islet – there is a good **view** of half-timbered cottages in the fishermen's district or "Little Venice" *(Klein Venedig)* along the riverbank.

The Bamberg Christmas Crib Circuit

Many people choose to visit the town in winter, during the Advent period (and up to 6 January) to take advantage of a particularly seasonal attraction on offer here – the Bamberg Christmas Crib Circuit (Bamberger Krippenweg), which takes in 30 or so churches, museums and squares featuring highly original, decorative crib scenes.

The circuit begins in the cathedral with the altar to the Virgin Mary by Nürnberg master Veit Stoß, and continues to the *Maternkapelle* and the *Obere Pfarre*, in which the scenes portrayed include events from the Annunciation to the Wedding at Cana. There is an astonishing variety of cribs on display – the enormous crib in Schönleinsplatz with life-size figures in traditional local costume and the lovingly arranged figures (over 200 of them) in the crib scene at St Martin's – each with its own unique charm to commend it. The tiny crib in the church of St Gandolf can be examined through a viewer.

Leaflets on the Bamberg Christmas Crib Circuit are available from the Bamberg Tourismus und Kongreß Service, Geyerswörthstraße 3, 96047 Bamberg.

►► Diözesanmuseum★ *(religious art and pieces relating to the cathedral)* – E.T.A.-Hoffmann-Haus, *(home of the author of The Tales)*.

Directory

Where to Eat

Historischer Brauereiausschank Schlenkerla – *Dominikanerstraße 6 – BUS 26 – ☎ (0951) 560 60 – www.schlenkerla.de – Closed Sun – €11/16.* This beautiful half-timbered building is a little piece of Bamberg's history: Franconian specialities are served here and smoked beer *(Rauchbier)* is brewed on the premises and drawn directly from the barrel, in the traditional manner.

Würzburger Weinstuben – *Zinkenwörth 6 (west of Schönleinsplatz) – ☎ (0951) 2 26 67 – Closed Tue evening and Wed – €20.50/35.* This *weinstube* is located in a half-timbered building in the heart of the town centre. Wines from Franconia and traditional dishes are served here: in the summer months, enjoy the refreshments on the terrace in the shade of hundred-year-old chestnut and lime trees.

Where to Stay

Romantik Hotel Weinhaus Messerschmitt – *Lange Straße 41 – ☎ (0951) 278 66 – fax (0951) 26141 – hotel-messerschmitt@t-online.de – Closed 17-23 Feb – 19 rm: €52/140 – Restaurant €26/39.* This yellow and white-fronted hotel is located at the start of the main shopping street. The guestrooms are well equipped with rustic or modern furniture. There is also a restaurant with charming terrace which gives onto a courtyard with fountain.

Barock-Hotel am Dom – *Vorderer Bach 4 – ☎ (0951) 540 31 – fax (0951) 54021 – Closed Feb and 24-27 Dec – ♿ – 19 rm: €62/87.* This hotel has been in operation since 1520 and was given an elegant Baroque façade in 1740. Located right next to the cathedral with a welcoming ambience. Breakfast is served under a Gothic vault.

Taking a Break

Café im Rosengarten – *Domplatz (in the Neue Residenz) – ☎ (0951) 98 04 00 – Open from Easter to mid-Oct, 10am-6pm.* Delicacies from the Graupner pastry shop at Lange Str. 9 are served in the rather formal pavilion or on the pleasant rose garden terrace. Those with a sweet tooth will feel at home here...

Going Out

Plenty of bars are to be found in Austr. (west of Grüner Markt) and Obere Sandstr.

Klosterbräu – *Obere Mühlbrücke 1-3 (to the southeast of Judenstr.) – ☎ (0951) 5 22 65 – www.klosterbraeu.de – Mon-Fri, 10.30am-11pm, weekend, 10am-11pm.* Choose from a large selection of speciality beers in this the oldest brewery in the town, with beautiful country-style rooms imbued with nostalgia for old times. Local cuisine is also available. Terrace available in summer.

Palais Schrottenberg – *Kasernstr. 1 (between Dominikanerstr. and the Regnitz) – ☎ (0951) 95 58 80 – www.palais-schrottenberg.de – Sun-Fri, 9am-1am, Sat, 9am-3am.* Built in the 18C by Johann Dientzenhofer, the café-bar offers a choice of style and ambience: Baroque-style lounge, modern winter garden, sushi bar (Fri-Sat from 6pm) or an internal courtyard.

Excursions

Schloß Pommersfelden★

21km/12mi south. Open every day except Mon, 10am-5pm. Closed Good Fri, 24, 25 and 31 Dec. €2. ☎ (0951) 50 23 16. Also known as **Weißenstein**, this building was designed by Dientzenhofer and Hildebrandt and built for Bishop Lothar Franz von Schönborn between 1711 and 1718; it quickly became one of the most outstanding examples of a Baroque palace in Germany.

A rapid tour permits the visitor to admire the **galleried state staircase★**. The paintings on the ceiling represent the Olympian gods and the four quarters of the globe. On the ground floor, an artificial grotto opening onto the garden perpetuates a Renaissance tradition. The marble hall on the first floor, lined with stucco pilasters, is decorated with frescoes by Rottmayr.

A longer visit would include the Elector's apartments with their small painting gallery and a hall of mirrors.

Ebrach★

35 km/22mi west. The **Old Abbey** (currently used as a prison), founded in 1127 as the first Cistercian monastery to the right of the Rhine, was extensively remodelled in the Baroque fashion, first by JL Dientzenhofer and then by Balthasar Neumann. The ground plan of the abbey **church★** – which was built between 1200 and 1285 in Early Gothic style with a right-angled ambulatory – with its flat-ended chancel was directly inspired by that of Cîteaux (the first abbot of Ebrach was closely tied to St Bernard, who was active in that Burgundian monastery). A rose window 7.6m/25ft in diameter illuminates the façade. Inside, there are fine Rococo railings, two Baroque organs in the choir, and a Renaissance altarpiece *(north transept)* to St Bernard.

Coburg★

46 km/29mi north. The brilliant beginnings of the dukes of Saxe-Coburg have meant that the Renaissance has left an indelible mark on the town. Coburg's townscape, surmounted by a mighty fortress, dates to this period. The town does not fail to surprise with beautiful façades encircling the market place *(Marktplatz)* and the **Gymnasium Casimirianum★** *(opposite the Moritzkirche)* which dates from 1605.

Veste Coburg (Fortress) – *Open Tue-Sun, 10am-5pm (Apr-Oct) and 1-4pm (Nov-Mar). Closed Shrove Tue, 24, 25 and 31 Dec. €3. ☎ (095 61) 879 79; www.kunstsammlungen-coburg.de.* This complex, which can be seen from afar, is one of the largest fortresses in Germany with a triple ring of fortified walls. The original castle dated from the 11C, but the present structure is 16C, the epoch of Johann Casimir, first duke of Coburg. In the museum are **art collections★** *(Kunstsammlungen)* consisting mainly of the possessions of the dukes of Coburg and fine examples of their kind in Europe, including paintings by Albrecht Dürer and Lucas Cranach. In the central wing *(Carl-Eduard-Bau)*, there is a display of decorative arts, with notably the largest collection of Venetian glassware in Europe and an exhibition of engravings.

The Noble Dynasty of Saxe-Coburg

In a history of intrigue and diplomacy spanning many centuries, the noble dynasty of Saxe-Coburg was either directly related to or married into nearly all the royal families of Europe: the Belgian, Portuguese, Russian, Swiss and Bulgarian royal families. The marriage between Edward, the Duke of Kent, and the Coburg Princess Victoire produced Queen Victoria; she, in turn, married a cousin: Prince Albert of Saxe-Coburg.

Schloß Ehrenburg – *Guided tour (50min – hourly), Tue-Sun, 9am-5pm (Apr-Sep) and 10am-3pm (Oct-Mar). Closed 1 Jan, Shrove Tue, 1 Nov, 24, 25 and 31 Dec. €3. ☎ (095 61) 80 88 32; www.sgvcoburg.de.* This castle was the official residence of the dukes of Coburg from 1547 to 1918. Only the south block facing the Steinstraße remains from the original Renaissance palace built in 1547. After a fire in 1690 the castle was rebuilt and tts interior features elements of the Baroque, although the façade facing the Schloßplatz was remodelled in the early 19C in the English neo-Gothic manner. The castle rooms are adorned with sumptuous furniture in the Empire and Biedermeier styles and stuccowork by Italian masters is on view in several rooms and in the chapel. There is also an art gallery containing works by German and Dutch masters.

Bautzen★

Bautzen owes much to its site – it is built on a rocky outcrop skirted by the winding course of the Spree. The town has managed to retain its old-fashioned charm, despite wars and other vagaries of history. There is an especially picturesque view of the town from the bridge (Friedensbrücke), combining the cathedral (Dom St Peter), the castle (Ortenburg), a network of narrow streets and an ancient fountain which serves as an emblem for the municipality.

Location

Population: 44 000. Michelin map nº 544 M 27 – Sachsen. The Spree surrounds the old town and Bautzen has developed along this bend in the river. The town is reached by the A4 motorway which links Dresden and Görlitz.

ℹ Hauptmarkt 1, 02625 Bautzen, ☎ (035 91) 420 16.

Surrounding area: see GORLITZ (40 km/25mi to the east), DRESDEN (64 km/40mi to the west), SÄCHSISCHE SCHWEIZ.

Background

Sorbian Town – There are many **Sorbian** families in Bautzen – descendants of a western Slav people settling between the Elbe and the Neisse (mainly in south Brandenburg and east Saxony) after the migrations of the 6C. The Sorbian language (a Slavic language related to Czech and Polish) is still taught in local schools and numerous folk traditions – the decoration of eggs at Easter, the wearing of tall embroidered headdresses, the use of Sorbian national costume for festivals and holidays – promote the identity of this ethnic minority.

Worth a Visit

Hauptmarkt

The old market square is surrounded by fine burghers' houses and a three-storey town hall – built around 1730 by Johann Christoph Naumann. Its asymmetrically positioned tower is crowned by a wonderful helm roof. Reichenstraße leads from the market square to the **Reichenturm** (Tower of the Rich), a 56m/179ft leaning tower that offers an excellent view of the city. *Open from Apr-Oct, 10am-5pm. €1.20. ☎ (035 91) 46 04 31; www.bautzen.de*

Tourist information available at the Fleischmarkt, behind the Town Hall.

Dom St-Peter★

This hall-church with three naves (1213-1497) is the sole place of worship in the region to be used both by Roman Catholics and by Protestants (Catholic Masses in the chancel; Protestant services in the main nave). Construction began at the beginning of the 13C. In the middle of the 15C the southern part of the structure was enlarged, and the Late Gothic windows date from this period – construction of the hall choir gave rise to the elbow in the axis, which is clearly visible from within and without. In 1664, the 85m/279ft tower was crowned with a Baroque cupola. Inside the cathedral, note the large wood **Crucifix** (1714) by **Balthazar Permoser**, the **Baroque high altar** (1722-24) by G Fossati in the chancel, with figures of the saints by JB Thomae and an **altar painting** by GA Pellegrini *(St Peter Receiving the Keys)*, and the Princes' Loggia (1674) in the Protestant section.

Follow the road that runs past the cathedral as far as the monastery.

Those parts of the **monastery** that remain standing date from 1683. The southern façade with its imposing portal (1753-55) is particularly fine. The armorial bearings of the monastery are displayed in the rounded pediment indicated.

Now follow the Schloßstrasse.

This charming street with restored, mainly Baroque houses leads straight to Ortenburg Castle.

Schloß Ortenburg

Where Ortenburg stands today, there once stood a fortified complex that was completed around AD 600 and was expanded as a frontier fort in 958 by Heinrich I. Two devastating fires in the early 15C destroyed the construction. The Hungarian king Matthias Corvinus had the fortress rebuilt from scratch in Late Gothic style between 1483 and 1486 (the Lausitz region was a Hungarian province from 1469 to 1490). A portrait in relief of the Hungarian king can still be distinguished on the tower of the north wing. The Thirty Years War also left profound scars, which were removed by renovations that were performed after 1648. In the midst of the Baroque Age, in the year 1698, three Renaissance gables were added to the castle, a veritable anachronism.

Sorbisches Museum / Serbski Muzej

♿ *Open Apr-Oct, Mon-Fri, 10am-5pm, Sat-Sun, 10am-6pm; Nov-Mar: 10am-4pm, Sat-Sun, 10am-5pm. Closed 24 and 31 Dec. €2.50. ☎ (035 91) 424 03.*

Situated in the former Salt House, an annex of Ortenburg castle added in 1782, the **Sorbian Museum** illustrates the history, culture and way of life of the Sorbians from the 6C to the current day.

Town ramparts★

The medieval ramparts are very well maintained and shape the silhouette of the town. A walk along the town walls provides visitors with an idea of what it must have been like in the Middle Ages. The ruins of the **Nikolaikirche** and the cemetery of the same name are especially worth a visit.

Alte Wasserkunst★

Apr-Oct: 10am-5pm; Feb-Dec: 10am-4pm; Jan: Sat-Sun, 10am-4pm. €1.50. ☎ (035 91) 415 88; www.bautzen.de. This formidable defensive and water tower has been standing since 1558. Although it is difficult to believe, it actually supplied the town with water up to 1965. The workings of this technical monument, with its seven storeys and an impressive pumping system, are extremely interesting.

Excursions

FROM BAUTZEN TO HERRNUT

31 km/19mi (along the B 178)

König-Friedrich-August-Turm★ in Löbau

Southwest of Bautzen on the Herwigsdorfer Straße. Open May-Sep, 9am-8pm (-10pm, Sat and Sun); Oct-Apr, 10am-6pm (-8pm, Sat and Sun). May be closed during bad weather. Use the car park outside the nature reserve or obtain a special permit for the trip from Löbau-Information, Altmarkt 1. €1. ☎ (035 85) 45 01 40; www.loebau.de

The 28m/92ft high **cast-iron viewing tower** is the only one of its kind in Europe. Some 6 000 individual grey cast-iron parts and a total weight of 70t combine to produce a filigree masterpiece. Three platforms, heights 12, 18 and 24m/39, 59 and 78ft, afford the visitor a wonderful view.

Obercunnersdorf ★

Turn right 3km/1.8mi south of Löbau. The entire village is a protected monument, as it is a self-contained development of post-and-beam frame houses. Some of the 250 or so houses are open to visitors.

Herrnhut

The town has acquired world renown through the Evangelical brotherhood of the same name. The members of this community, which was founded in Mähren in 1457, were persecuted for their beliefs, took refuge here in 1772 and founded the town. This resulted in the self-contained method of building described as "Herrnhuter Baroque". A folklore museum documents the educational work of the brethren, which is still continued in 22 countries on five continents.

Bayreuth★

Bayreuth is the Holy Grail to Wagner fans and the Wagner opera festival attracts many visitors to Bayreuth every year in August. The composer was not the only one to leave his mark on the town: the Margravine Wilhelmina, one of the most cultivated women of the 18C, transformed Bayreuth into a cultural centre and showcase for an original style of Rococo. Situated close to the unusual landscape of Swiss Franconia, Bayreuth is ideally placed for an exploration of the surrounding area on foot or by car.

Location

Population: 73 000. Michelin map nº 546 Q 18 – Bayern. Built between the wooded heights of the Fichtelgebirge and the curious, desolate landscape of Swiss Franconia, Bayreuth is located in the north of Bavaria. The big A 9 motorway which links Munich to Berlin runs near the town.

🅱 *Luitpoldplatz 9, 95444 Bayreuth, ☎ (0921) 885 88.*

Surrounding area: see Oberes SAALETAL (80 km/50mi to the north along the A 9), Wallfahrtskirche VIERZAHNHEILIGEN (56 km/35mi to the west), NUREMBERG (80 km/50mi to the south along the A 9).

Background

Princess Wilhelmina – The Margravine Wilhelmina, daughter of the King of Prussia, sister of Frederick the Great and lifelong friend of Voltaire, was one of the most cultivated women of the 18C. She could have married royalty, but it was decided instead that she should marry Margrave Friedrich of Brandenburg-Bayreuth. Finding him rather a dull man, she gathered cultivated figures around her, creating a more stimulating environment in which her talents might flower.

Her life (1709-58) marked the most brilliant period in Bayreuth's history. A gifted artist, writer, composer, and patroness of the fine arts, the Princess was responsible for the blossoming of "Bayreuth Rococo" – a highly personal style whose garlands and flowers differed markedly from what was then in vogue.

er**Wagner and the festival** – Wagner moved to Bayreuth in 1872, attracted to the town by the famous opera house which had been built by Princess Wilhelmina. He brought his wife Cosima, daughter of the Hungarian composer **Franz Liszt**. Wagner's music was stimulated by admiration for his father-in-law and it is often said that many of Wagner's masterworks would never have seen the light of day

Directory

Where to Eat

⊜ **Oskar – Das Wirtshaus am Markt** – *Maximilianstr. 33 – ☎ (0921) 5 16 05 53 – www.oskar-bayreuth.de – 8-1am – €15/19.* Situated in the former town hall, this restaurant is furnished in both modern and traditional styles. Different rooms with varying degrees of intimacy, a pretty winter garden and a terrace are at your disposal. On the menu are typically Bavarian specialities.

⊜⊜ **Zur Sudpfanne** – *Oberkonnersreuther Straße 6 – 95448 Bayreuth-Oberkonnersreuth – 3km/2mi to the southeast along Nürnberger Straße – ☎ (0921) 528 83 – sudpfanne@sudpfanne.com – €32/44.* The façade of this establishment mixes old brick with modern glass. Inside, the restaurant has rustic-style décor.

Where to Stay

⊜ **Grunau Hotel** – *Kemnather Str. 27 (continuation to the east of Wieland-Wagner-Str and Königsallee) – ☎ (0921) 7 98 00 – fax (0921) 7 98 01 00 – www.grunau-hotel.de –* P ♿ *€50/120* ☕. Located on the upper floor of a commercial complex to the east of the town-centre. Guestrooms are modern, spacious, quiet and comfortable and guests can use the fitness centre at a discounted rate.

⊜⊜ **Goldener Anker** – *Opernstraße 6 – ☎ (0921) 650 51 – fax (0921) 655 00 – info@anker-bayreuth.de – Closed from Nov-mid-Jan – 35rm: €65/180* ☕ *– Restaurant €30/60.* Each guestroom in this traditional hotel has its own style of décor, but they are all large rooms. Traditional cuisine is served in the establishment's restaurant.

Taking a Break

Café Funsch – *Sophienstr. 9 – ☎ (0921) 6 46 87 – www.funsch.de – 8.30am-6.30pm – Closed for 2 weeks after Whitsun and at Christmas.* This tearoom has a terrace on to the pedestrianised part of town and a menu offering delicacies to everyone's taste. The shop sells little marzipan figures that make good souvenirs.

Café Orangerie – *Eremitage 6 (4 km/2.5mi to the east of the town along Wieland-Wagner-Str.) – ☎ (0921) 79 99 70 – Apr/May-Oct (depending on the weather): 11am-6pm.* The magnificent terrace of this tea room is the ideal place for refreshment after a wander around the park of the castle. As the name suggests, this establishment is situated in the orangery and is only 5 minutes' walk from the castle. There is also a restaurant with a *Biergarten* should you feel the need for something a little more substantial.

Going Out

Sinnopoli – *Badstr. 13 – ☎ (0921) 6 20 17 – www.sinnopoli.de – Mon-Sat, 8-1am, Sun and bank holidays, 9-1am.* Tastfully decorated bar. On the menu: a large choice of tasty home-made pasta. There is a "happy hour" between 5 and 7pm. More than 40 cocktails, both alcoholic and non-alcoholic, are available at the bar. A beautiful garden is open during the summer.

if it had not been for the influence of Liszt. The writer and composer of *Parsifal* and *Song of the Nibelung*, Richard Wagner searched on his many wanderings for the ideal place to present his works. With the support of Ludwig II of Bavaria, he had the Festival Theatre *(Festsplielhaus)* built to his own design; at the time the building was revolutionary, as much for the space given to spectators as for its outstanding acoustics.

Wagner held the first festival of his lyrical pieces here in 1876. After his death in 1883, the tradition continued under the stewardship of Cosima and, subsequently, his son Siegfried, his grandson Wieland (d 1966) and Wolfgang Wagner, who is the current director.

Worth a Visit

Markgräfliches Opernhaus★

♿ *Apr-Sep: 9am-6pm; Oct-Mar: 10am-4pm. Closed 1 Jan. Shrove Tue, 24, 25 and 31 Dec. €3.50. ☎ (0921) 759 69 22.*

The Margravine Wilhelmina built this theatre in 1748 as a venue for the opera and ballet performances of the troupe under her patronage. The austere façade, hemmed in between 18C townhouses, gives no clue to the richness of the interior decoration. This was the largest opera house in Germany until 1871. The interior, constructed entirely of wood, attains with the stage and apron an astonishing depth of 72m/236ft. There used to be no seats in the stalls, as that part of the auditorium was reserved for dancing.

The **decoration**, by Giuseppe Galli Bibiena, a brilliant artist from Bologna, is of an exuberant richness. The reds, greens and browns harmonise perfectly with the abundance of gilded stuccowork which winds around the columns, frames medallions and festoons the candelabra hanging over each box.

BAYREUTH

Am Mühltürlein	Y 3
Bahnhofstraße	Y 4
Balthasar-Neumann-Str.	Z 5
Bürgerreuter Str.	Y 7
Erlanger Str.	Y 8
Friedrich-von-Schiller-Str.	Y 10
Josephsplatz	Y 14
Kanalstraße	Y 15
Kanzleistraße	YZ 17
Karl-Marx-Str.	Y 18
Ludwigstraße	Z 20
Luitpoldplatz	Y 22
Markgrafenallee	Y 24
Maximilianstraße	Y
Muncker Str.	Y 26
Nürnberger Str.	Z 28
Opernstraße	Y 30
Richard-Wagner-Str.	YZ 32
Schulstraße	Y 33
Sophienstraße	Y 35
Wieland-Wagner-Str.	Z 36
Wilhelminenstraße	Z 38
Wittelsbacherring	Z 39
Wölfelstraße	Y 40

Richard-Wagner-Museum	Z M1
Schloßkirche	Y A

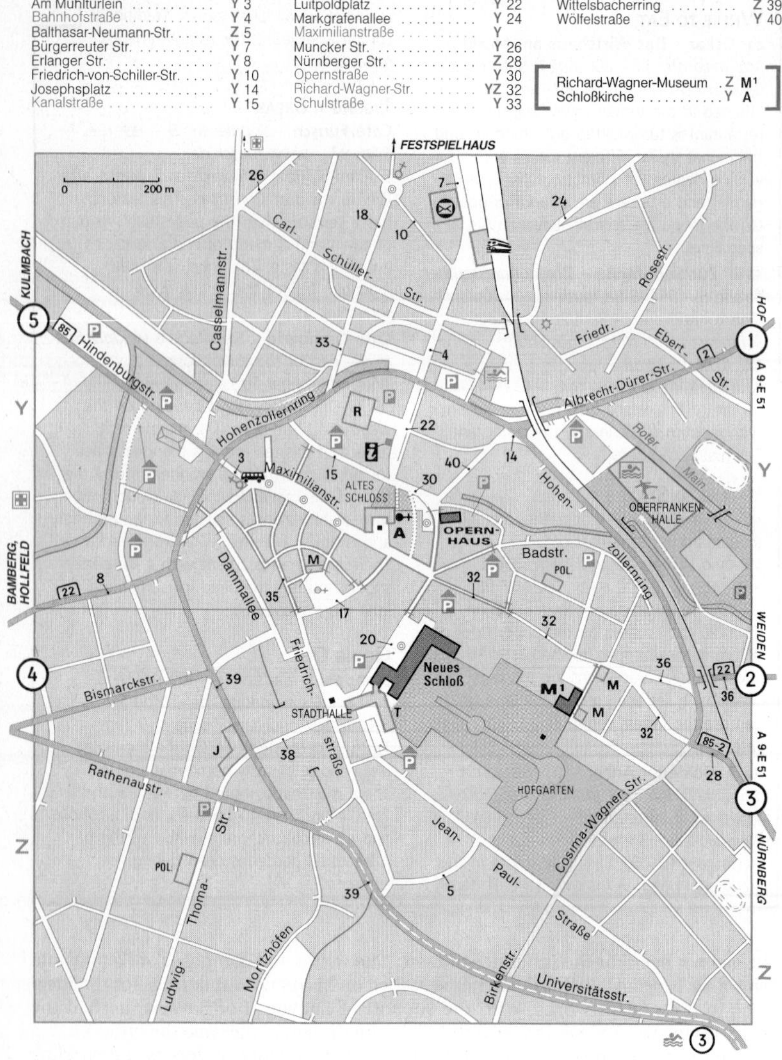

Neues Schloß (New Palace)

♿ *Open Apr-Sep: 9am-6pm; Oct-Mar: 10am-4pm. Closed 1 Jan, Shrove Tue, 24, 25 and 1 Dec. €2.50. ☎ (0921) 75 96 90.*

Wishing to make Bayreuth into a second Potsdam, Wilhelmina created this palace between 1753 and 1754, unifying and remodelling a number of existing buildings. The fascinating elegance of the **interior decoration★** owes much to the stucco-master Pedrozzi, greatly influenced by the Princess, whose delight in the airy, flowery Rococo style is everywhere in evidence. Wilhelmina, whose private apartments were on the first floor of the north wing, concerned herself particularly with the decor of the Mirror Room, the Japanese Room and the old Music Room.

Attending the Bayreuth Festival

From 25 July until 28 August, Bayruth reverberates to the sound of Wagner. Hotels within ten kilometres of the town tend to be fully booked throughout this period and many of the 60 000 hotel rooms are often reserved up to seven years in advance. Bookings can only be made by post and the lucky few who do get a room (often after several attempts) have to endure poor seating and stifling heat while listening to the master's marathon operas. But each year spellbound enthusiasts are overwhelmed by the exceptional programme.

Write to Bayreuther Festspiele, Kartenbüro, Postfach 100262, D-95402 Bayreuth. Information and programme (in German) on www.festspiele.de. Prices change from one year to the next but are comparable to the usual cost of tickets to the opera. During the festival some unused tickets are available for purchase on the day of the performance. But note that queuing for these tickets normally starts at 6 in the morning...

On the ground floor of the north wing is a **museum of Bayreuth porcelain** *(Museum Bayreuther Fayencen).*

Richard-Wagner-Museum ★

Open every day, Apr-Oct: 9am-5pm, (-8pm, Tue and Thu); Nov-Mar: 10am-5pm. Closed 1 Jan, Easter Sunday, Whitsun, 24 and 25 Dec. €4. ☎ (0921) 757 28 16; www.wagnermuseum.de

Haus Wahnfried (House of Supreme Peace), in which the composer lived from 1874 onwards, and which was owned by his family until 1966 is still one of the main centres of Wagnerian pilgrimage. The only remaining original feature of the house is the façade. Collections on display in the museum evoke the maestro's life and work (furniture, manuscripts, pianos and death mask) as well as the history of the Bayreuth Festival (construction of the Festival Theatre, costumes and scenery). Richard Wagner and his wife Cosima lie buried in the garden. The tomb of Liszt, Wagner's great friend and father-in-law, who died during one of the first festivals in 1886, is in the Bayreuth cemetery (Stadtfriedhof – *entrance on Erlanger Straße*)

Bayer Verwaltung der Staatl, Schlösser, Gärten und Seen

The sumptuous Markgräfliches Opernhaus in Bayreuth

Schloß Eremitage (Hermitage Palace)★

4km/2.5mi east by ② on the town plan.

♿ Guided tour (25min) from Apr to mid-Oct: 9am-6pm. €2.50. ☎ (0921) 759 69 37.

The Hermitage was the pleasure palace of the Margraves of Brandenburg-Bayreuth and was a gift from her husband to The Margravine Wilhelmina, who proceeded to transform it. The **old castle** *(Altes Schloß)*, surrounded by geometric flowerbeds, was built in 1715 and remodelled by the Margravine, in 1736. There is a particularly interesting, if only for its somewhat original decoration, **Chinese Mirror Cabinet** *(chinesisches Spiegelkabinett)* in which Wilhelmina wrote her memoirs. The **Schloßpark★**, is laid out in the manner of an English garden. Note the curious lower grotto opening onto the inner courtyard, and the hermitage of the Margrave Friedrich. Nearby is the artificial ruin of a theatre constructed in 1743.

The new palace *(Neues Schloß)*, designed on a semicircular plan, was rebuilt after 1945. In the centre, the Temple of the Sun contains an image of Apollo in his golden chariot.

▶▶ Schloßkirche – Festspielhaus *(access via Karl-Marx-Straße)*

Excursions

SWISS FRANCONIA★★ (Fränkische Schweiz) AND SANSPAREIL 1

Round tour of 105km/65mi – allow one day

Southwest of Bayreuth, far from the main road and rail routes, an undulating plateau gashed by deep valleys forms the northern extremity of the Franconian Jura. Heavy erosion of this porous limestone shelf has resulted in a landscape of dolomitic relief, pitted with many caves.

Tüchersfeld

The houses of this village are dispersed among an astonishing series of rocky pinnacles.

Pottenstein

The castle, a former residence of the elector-bishops of Bamberg, overlooks the town. There are many natural curiosities (gorges, caves etc) in the neighbourhood.

Teufelshöhle

Guided tour (45min). Mar-Oct: every day, 9am-5pm; Nov-Feb: Tue and Sat-Sun, 10am-3pm (26 Dec-6 Jan: every day). Closed 24 and 25 Dec. €3.50. ☎ (092 43) 708 41; www.teufelshoehle.de

Some parts of the Devil's Caves are large enough to hold a church. The stalactites and stalagmites of the caves are impressive, particularly in the *Barbarossadom* (Cathedral of Barbarossa) and the exit through a maze of towering Jura cliffs is most picturesque.

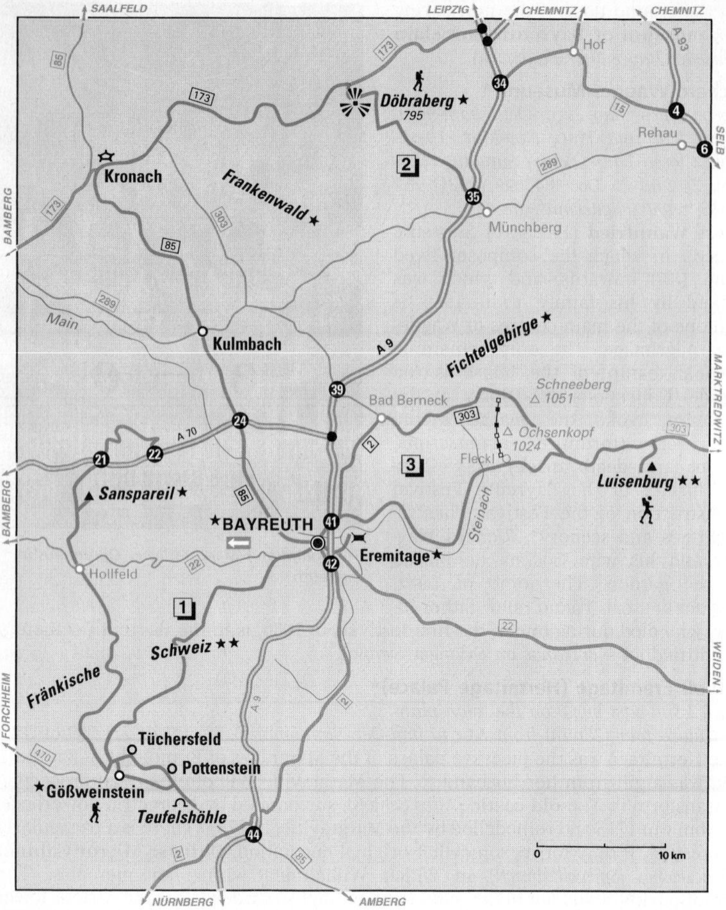

Gößweinstein★

The Circuit of **Marienfelsen** *(about 45min there and back on foot, leaving the castle to follow the signposts: Marienfels-Schmitt-Anlagen)* leads, through undergrowth strewn with picturesque rocks, to several fine **viewpoints★★** over the deep valley of the Wiesent.

In the village, the Pilgrimage Church (Wallfahrtskirche), built between 1730 and 1739 by Balthasar Neumann, contains on the upper part of the high altar an early 16C Gothic group of the Trinity.

Sanspareil ★

After the completion of the hermitage in Bayreuth, Margravine Wihelmina and Margrave Friedrich turned their attention to an old hunting estate, converting it into an impressive **rock garden★** which they named Sanspareil ('without equal'). At the edge of the grove stands an Oriental building, fitted out in the Bayreuth Rococo style making it an example of Frankish court art. Further architectonic features of this 17ha/42 acre park include caves, grottoes and ruined theatres.

Burg Zwernitz – *north of Sanspareil.* The earliest documentary evidence of the castle dates from 1156. From 1338, the fortress was the property of the Hohenzollern, then in 1810 it fell to Bavaria. It contains furnishings, and a selection of cutting and stabbing weapons from the 16C-18C. There is a good **view** from the keep. ♿ *Open Apr-end Sep, every day except Mon, 9am-6pm. €2.50. ☎ (0921) 759 69 75.*

THE FRANCONIAN MOUNTAINS★ 2 (Frankenwald)

Round tour of 125km/78mi – allow 5hr

Döbraberg★

45min there and back on foot. Climb to the look-out tower (795m/2 608ft).

The majestic **panorama★** extends as far as the mysterious depths of the Thuringian Mountains in the north, and the Fichtelgebirge in the south, which enclose the Hof Basin.

Kronach

Festung Rosenberg (16C-18C), one of the largest medieval fortresses in Germany, towers over the small town of Kronach and the wooded heights of the Frankenwald. The fortress houses the Franconian Gallery, a daughter museum to the Bavarian National Museum. It exhibits medieval and Renaissance Franconian art, including works by **Lucas Cranach the Elder** who was born in Kronach (?1472).

Kulmbach

Town plan in the Michelin Guide Deutschland.

This industrial town, once the seat of the Hohenzollern Margraves of Franconia, is famous today for its strong beers *(Echt Kulmbacher, Bayrisch Gfrorns).*

The Plassenburg★, an impressive medieval fortress in an excellent state of preservation, surprises the visitor with the contrast between the defensive look of its exterior buildings and the delightful elegance of its **Renaissance courtyard★★** surrounded on three sides by tiered galleries. Various collections are on display in the refurnished apartments, the most interesting being that of **tin soldiers★** from the Deutsches Zinnfigurenmuseum, the largest collection of its kind in the world with more than 300 000 pieces grouped in 150 dioramas. ♿ *Apr-Oct: 9am-6pm; Nov-Mar: 10am-4pm. Closed 1 Jan, 24, 25 and 31 Dec. €3. ☎ (092 21) 958 80; www.kulmbach.de*

THE FICHTELGEBIRGE★ 3

Round tour of 92km/57mi – allow about 5hr

The **panoramic route★** follows the Steinach Valley, penetrating deeply into the pine-covered granite massif of the Fichtelgebirge. Above Fleckl, a cable-car climbs the **Ochsenkopf** (1 024m/3 360ft), one of the highest peaks in the massif, which is crowned by a television tower.

Luisenburg★★

This labyrinth of enormous granite boulders, in situ or fallen, eroded into round shapes or piled on top of each other, can be walked through along a pine-shaded, hilly path *(blue arrows indicate the way up, red the way down)*. Several look-out points along the way afford varying views of the Fichtelgebirge. Goethe, then minister to the court of Weimar and a geology enthusiast, was the first to explore the cave scientifically in 1785.

Return to Bayreuth on road n° 303, which passes through the small spa of Bad Berneck.

Berchtesgaden★★

Journey's end on the German Alpine Road (Deutsche Alpenstraße) and departure point for many other tourist excursions, Berchtesgaden is intensely busy throughout the summer. The development of the area is linked with the importance of an Augustinian priory, which became a pivot of the Bavarian political machine at a time when the grasping archbishops of Salzburg were becoming too demanding. Berchtesgaden was chosen as a holiday retreat by Adolf Hitler, who built his notorious "Eagle's Nest" sanctuary on the Kehlstein.

Location

Population: 8 200. Michelin map n° 546 X 22 – Local map see Deutsche ALPENSTRASSE – Bayern. The basin of Berchtesgaden is enclosed on three sides by the mountain chains of the Watzmann, the Steinernes Meer and the Hagengebirge, the whole complex forming a salient that penetrates deeply into Austria. The town is dominated by the bulk of the Watzmann (2 712m/8 900ft).

🅱 *Königsseer Straße 2, 83471 Berchtesgaden, ☎ (086 52) 96 70.*

Surrounding area: see Deutsche ALPENSTRASSE (Berchtesgaden is the last stop on this tour), CHIEMSEE (67 km/41mi northwest), BURGHAUSEN (76 km/48mi north).

Worth a Visit

Schloßplatz★

This triangular-shaped square is the heart of Berchtesgaden. On the western side are the so-called Getreidekasten, the former granary, remodelled and furnished with an arcaded gallery in the 16C. The Lombard influence manifests itself in the façade of the **Church of St Peter and St John** *(Stiftskirche St Peter and Johannes)*, where an alternation of stone in different colours makes a decorative pattern. The towers

Directory

Where to Stay

Neuhäusl – *Wildmoos 45, 83471 Berchtesgaden – 7 km east – ☎ (08652) 94 00 – fax (08652) 64637 – neuhaeusl@berchtesgaden.com – Closed 20 Apr-1 May, 15 Nov-15 Dec – P – 26rm: €46 – Restaurant €15/23.50.* A well-cared-for, rustic hotel: make the most of the magnificent alpine countryside by day, and at night, enjoy the comfort of the well-furnished guestrooms and apartments.

Hotel Fischer – *Königsseer Straße 51, 83471 Berchtesgaden – ☎ (08652) 95 50 – fax (08652) 64873 – www.hotel-fischer.de – Closed in Mar and from end Oct to mid-Dec – P – 54rm: €48.50/138 – Restaurant €13/16.50.* A few minutes on foot from the town centre, this hotel is a practical option for those interested in leisure activities. Guestrooms are simple and well presented, and most of them have a balcony or terrace. Ski instruction is available by reservation.

Alpenhotel Denninglehen – *Am Priesterstein 7, 83471 Berchtesgaden – 7 km east – ☎ (08652) 978 90 – fax (08652) 64710 – info@denninglehen.de – Closed 1-18 Dec, 15-30 Jan – P – 24rm: €68/126 – Restaurant €18/32.* Remotely situated and surrounded by mountains, guests are welcomed into a country-style hotel with rustic painted furniture. Winter sports are available locally.

were rebuilt in the last century after a fire. The interior of the building is distinguished by early-16C network vaulting in the nave, and by a chancel some 200 years older, much higher and of a purer Gothic style.

Schloß (Palace)

Guided tour (50min). From Whitsun to mid-Oct: every day except Sat, 10am-1pm, 2pm-5pm; from mid-Oct until Whitsun: Mon-Fri at 11am and 2pm. €7. ☎ (086 52) 94 79 80; www.haus-bayern.com

At the time of the commendatory prelates, the monks' priory did indeed become a sumptuous palace. From 1923 onwards, it was the home of the Crown Prince Rupert, former Commander-in-Chief of the Bavarian forces during the First World War and head of the House of Wittelsbach until his death in 1955. The Prince embellished the palace with furniture and art treasures. The palace museum exhibits interesting collections of weapons, French Gobelins tapestries and Nymphenburg porcelain. German wood sculptures of the 15C and 16C, including two altar images by Tilman Riemenschneider, are also on view.

Guided visit – Conserving its Romanesque galleries on three sides, the 13C cloister has a variety of columns – circular, polygonal or twisted, garnished with latticework, plant designs and capitals with foliated scrolls. The dormitory *(Dormitorium)* is a fine early Gothic hall with two aisles contains examples of religious art, including 12 magnificent busts from the choir stalls of Weingarten Basilica (1487). Worth special attention are the two Renaissance rooms on the first floor (Italian furniture of the 15C and 16C), and the row of eight interconnected Seigneurs' rooms (Herrenzimmer) which offer an attractive glimpse into the 19C and its Biedermeier style. The highest terrace, reached along a beautiful rose garden, offers an open view of the Watzmann.

Salzbergwerk★

Guided visit (1hr). From May to mid-Oct: every day, 9am-5pm; from mid-Oct to Apr: Mon-Sat, 12.30-15.30pm. Closed 1 Jan, Shrove Tue, Good Fri, 24-26 and 31 Dec. €12.50. ☎ (086 52) 600 20; www.salzbergwerk-berchtesgaden.de

The working of the Berchtesgaden salt mines, begun in 1517, brought prosperity to a region which was once very poor. The salt rock is washed by fresh water and the resulting brine (*Sole*), containing 27% salt, is piped to Bad Reichenhall to be refined.

The tour, in miner's overalls, includes a trip through the galleries in a small train, and the crossing by raft of an illuminated underground lake.

A room arranged as a salt museum exhibits the machinery, based on the hydraulic pump, invented by the engineer Georg von Reichenbach in 1817 for raising the brine to the pipeline.

Berchtesgaden Tourismus

Winter in Berchtesgaden.

Excursions

Obersalzberg★★ and the Kehlstein

4km/2.5mi, there is a shuttle service by bus between Obersalzberg and the Kehlstein from mid-May to mid-Oct. €13.50 there and back. For details of timetables ☎ (086 52) 96 70

After the abortive putsch of 1923 and the end of his prison sentence, **Adolf Hitler**, linked by friendships and family ties to the region, settled in Obersalzberg. When the Nazis seized power in 1934, the new Chancellor started an increasingly ambitious plan to enlarge and enhance the chalet (Berghof) which he had acquired. Subsequently, the sanctuary of "the lonely man of Berchtesgaden" became the stage for a number of expertly manipulated diplomatic receptions.

The greater part of the Berghof buildings were destroyed in an American air raid on 25 April, 1945, prior to their capture on 4 May by a detachment of the French 2nd Armoured Division operating with the 101st US Airborne Division.

Obersalzberg – With the exception of the Platterhof – a "People's Hotel" where the faithful could be lodged, at Hitler's behest, for the nominal sum of a single mark – the ruins of all the other buildings comprising the Nazi sanctuary have been razed. A **documentation centre on the history of National Socialism** was opened here in 1999. *(Dokumentationszentrum zur Geschichte des Nationalsozialismus).*

Kehlstein★★ – The bus climbs an impressively narrow **road★★★** blasted from the bedrock on the craggy spur of the Kehlstein. At the end of the road *(reserve seats for the return journey)*, a lift ascends the final 100m/328ft. On the summit there is now a tearoom *(Teehaus)* on the premises of the old Eagle's Nest *(Adlerhorst)* – which Hitler was given by the Nazi party as a 50th birthday present, but where he went to stay only rarely.

The **panorama★★** *(climb a little higher up the crest)* extends over the neighbouring peaks and, on the far side of Salzburg, the rolling, rounded Pre-Alps of the Salzkammergut, can be seen hard against the massif of the Dachstein, glittering with small glaciers.

Königssee★★

5 km/3mi south. Boat trips all year round, leaving approx every 30min. Allow 1hr45, plus at least 1hr for possible short trips ashore. Cruises stop at St Bartholomä in low season. €12; www.bayerische-seenschifffahrt.de This long, narrow lake, with its dark waters and steep banks, is one of the most romantic sites in Bavaria. Dominated on the west by the giant escarpments of the Watzmann, and the rocky base of the Steinernes Meer to the south, the lake narrows at St Bartholomä, making a picturesque **scene★**, where visitors can go ashore to admire the pretty **chapel of**

St Bartholomä with its triple apse and explore the interesting old houses. From the landing-stage at Salet, a 15min walk brings the visitor to the **Obersee**, below the Teufelshörner at the circular end of the valley. From here the Röthbach falls, hurtling down from a height of 400m/1 312ft, can be seen.

The cable car from Jenner to Königssee *(30min climb, €13.50)* offers unrestricted **views** over the lake and surrounding peaks.

Numerous walks and hikes can be undertaken locally. The Königssee natural park tourist centre, situated in the former station next to the car park, has information on hiking in the area.

Roßfeld-Höhenringstraße★★

Round tour of 29km/18mi E of Berchtesgaden (anti-clockwise) – about 1hr 30min. Toll: €1.50 per person. (086 52) 96 70; www.berchtesgadener-land.com The **Roßfeld road**, which is open all year round, reaches the lip of the crest and runs above the Austrian valley of the Salzach. It overlooks the Tennengebirge. The Dachstein, still recognisable by its glaciers, fills in the background. On the other side of the ridge there is a wonderful view of the countryside around Berchtesgaden and Salzburg and of the great massive of the Hoher Göll, the Kehlstein and the Untersberg.

From the Hennenkopf car park, it is only a few minutes' climb to the beacon and the Hennenkopf Cross at 1 551m/5 089ft. The road plunges down from the crest after the Roßfeldhütte (Inn) and winds through the charming, wooded valleys of the Oberau region.

Hintersee★

12km/8mi west. The road climbs the narrow Ramsau Valley to reach this lake framed by the steep-sided domes of the Reiteralpe and the Teeth of Hochkalter. The eastern shore, and the "enchanted forest" *(Zauberwald)* bordering it, together with the shady banks of the rapids feeding the lake, are a popular destination for ramblers.

Bergstrasse

This road running at the foot of the low, scrub-covered hills of the Odenwald has given its name to a strip of sunny escarpments sloping towards the Rhine Valley. Orchards flourish on this fertile tract, and its ideal position assures the marketing of fruit earlier than anywhere else in the region. The old villages and small towns of the Bergstraße are surrounded by typical Rhineland scenery.

Location

Michelin map n° 543 R 10 – Baden-Württemberg and Hessen. Spanning Hessen and Baden-Württemberg, the Bergstrasse runs north from Heidelberg to Darmstadt following a course parallel to the A 67 motorway, which it meets at Frankfurt.

Surrounding area: see HEIDELBERG, DARMSTADT, WORMS (50km/31mi to the northwest of Heidelberg), FRANKFURT AM MAIN (32km/20mi to the north of Darmstadt), MAINZ (34km/21mi to the northwest of Darmstadt).

Tour

FROM HEIDELBERG TO DARMSTADT

58km/36mi – about 3hr.

Heidelberg★★ – *see HEIDELBERG*

Weinheim

Hemmed in to the north and the east by ridges up to 400m/1 300ft, Weinheim is the first town on the Bergstraße to feel the coming of spring. The town was given civic rights in 1264 and developed from an agricultural community to the large seat of local government it is today. The old town has a remarkable number of old houses, including the attractive Altes Rathaus (old town hall) on Marktplatz (about 1577) and the Büdinger Hof *(Judengasse 15-17)*. The former Schloß (castle), which serves as the town hall today, abuts the castle park, which is in English style and boasts Germany's largest cedar tree. Adjacent to the park is the 50ha/124 acres **Exotenwald★** (Exotic Forest), which was laid out between 1872 and 1884 and boasts a wonderful variety of species. The ruins of Burg **Windeck** and the **Wachenburg** (castle completely restored at the beginning of the 20C) are enthroned above the town.

Heppenheim an der Bergstraße

The **Marktplatz★**, or *Großer Markt*, owes its charm to two wooden buildings with corner oriel windows: the Liebig pharmacy and the 16C town hall. The square is dominated by a vast neo-Gothic church, nicknamed "the Bergstraße Cathedral".

Lorsch

Of the great abbey founded in 774, there now exist at the east end of the town only the church narthex and the **Torhalle★**, a triumphal arch in Carolingian style, which has now been added to the list of Unesco World Heritage sites. Above the columns with their composite capitals is an impressive wall adorned with blind, cowled bays and sandstone marquetry in red and white. The old abbey buildings house a **museum complex** *(Museumszentrum Lorsch)* with sections on the history of the abbey and on local folklore, as well as a tobacco museum. Behind the church, there is a wide view of the Rhine plain in the direction of the Odenwald. ♿ *Guided tour (1hr). Open Tue-Sun, 10am-5pm. Closed 1 Jan, Shrove Tue, 24 Dec. €3. ☎ (062 51) 10 38 20; www.kloster-lorsch.de*

Behind the church, the view extends over the Rhine plain towards the Odenwald.

Bensheim

This "town of flowers and wine" is justly proud of its pretty **old town** *(Altstadt)*. Beautiful half-timbered houses are to be found principally in the Marktplatz, and along the Haupstraße and the Wambolterhofstraße. In a sheltered valley is the **Fürstenlager★★**, once the summer residence of the Landgraves of Hessen. The park surrounding the building (Herrenhaus) is planted with tropical trees and studded with pavilions and symbolical monuments in the late 18C style. A little further north, **Auerbacher Schloß** commands a view over the whole region. *10am-5pm. No charge. ☎ (062 51) 729 23; www.schloss-auerbach.de*

Darmstadt – *see DARMSTADT*

Berlin★★★

The vibrant, forward-looking and ever-changing city of Berlin never ceases to amaze with its enduring capacity for innovation and reinvention. Its dynamism is immediately apparent in the urban landscape, where the countless avant-garde structures that have been built – and there are more in the pipeline – are creating a brand new city made of stone, glass and concrete. This amazing metropolis, one of the most extensive and among those with the largest number of parks and gardens on the Old Continent, seems to be experiencing a new golden age. Its location at the heart of Europe and the restoration of its status as German capital since 1991 are at the root of its growing international influence. A city of artistic interest with prestigious museums, Berlin offers a wealth of culture and an exciting night-life that are second to none.

Location

Population: 3 500 000. Michelin maps 542, 544 I 23/24 – Michelin city plan 33 – Berlin.
Berlin developed on the banks of the River Spree in the heart of the great Brandenburg plain, on land covered in forest, with areas of sand and marsh. With a total surface area of 889km^2/556sq mi (eight times the size of Paris), the city stretches out over 45km/28mi from east to west and 38km/24mi from north to south. Greater Berlin has spread, incorporating villages, and now has a multipolar structure. The outer districts are residential areas (Dahlem, Grunewald, Pankow) or industrial zones (Charlottenburg/Spandau, Köpenick, Tempelhof). The integration of the districts of Marzahn (1979), Hohenschönhausen (1985) and Hellersdorf (1986), where new towns were built during the era of the former German Democratic Republic, marked the last extension of the city, which has been unable to expand to the west.

Europa-Center, Budapester Straße, 10787 Berlin, ☎ (030) 25 00 25.
Surrounding area: see POTSDAM (30km/19mi southwest), the SPREEWALD (Lübbenau is 93km/58mi southeast via the A 13), Lutherstadt WITTENBERG (107km/67mi southwest via the A 9), WÖRLITZER PARK (114km/71mi southwest, also via the A 9), the MECKLENBURGISCHE SEENPLATTE (Röbel is 141km/88mi northwest), MAGDEBURG (152km/95mi west).

Background

Historical notes – The German capital originated from two villages which can be traced back to the 13C: Cölln and Berlin were small towns built respectively on a sandy island and on the east bank of the River Spree, both inhabited by fishermen and travelling merchants. It was the Hohenzollern Electors of Brandenburg who were politically responsible for the evolution of Berlin as a capital city. The first castle to be constructed on Cölln was completed in 1451. Nineteen years later it became the permanent residence of the Hohenzollern family.

The Great Elector (1640-88) – **Frederick-William of Brandenburg** found Berlin largely deserted at the end of the Thirty Years' War. The great commander, who had in 1675 succeeded in beating the Swedish army at Fehrbellin, was also a very capable administrator. He had spent his youth in Holland and, emulating the Dutch, he constructed quays along the banks of the Spree and established many laws which made Berlin a healthy and well-governed town. The construction of a canal between the Spree and the Oder further encouraged trade, but Frederick-William's most important contribution was to open Berlin to the French Huguenots after the Revocation of the Edict of Nantes in 1685. The arrival of a massive contingent of new townspeople – approximately one Huguenot for every five Berliners – transformed the city, and the influx of craftsmen, theologians, doctors, scholars, among others, strengthened Berlin's influence on its neighbours.

Berlin in the Age of Enlightenment (18C) – The first King of Prussia, Frederick I, built the palace of Charlottenburg for his wife, Sophie-Charlotte. He entrusted the work to Andreas Schlüter, an architect and sculptor of genius (c 1660-1714) who had worked mainly at the Royal Palace and the Arsenal. Frederick was succeeded by **Frederick-William I** (1713-40), known to history as the **Soldier-King** because of his punctilious administration and a policy of systematic recruitment which laid the foundations of Prussian military power. He was less interested in the embellishment of Berlin than in making it more powerful. He ordered a new town, Friedrichstadt, to be laid out beyond the old city bastions. Draconian measures accelerated the development and peopling of the district, which is cut by such wide arteries as Leipziger Straße, Friedrichstraße and Wilhelmstraße (now Toleranzstraße), the Whitehall of the Reich.

Frederick II the Great (1740-86) continued this civic effort, adding monuments along the famous Unter den Linden and the Forum Fridericianum (Bebelplatz). To fulfil his ambitions, he enlisted the aid of Knobelsdorff (1699-1753), an architect who drew inspiration as much from the Rococo tradition (Sanssouci) as from the Antique (Opera). The evolution towards neo-Classicism continued until 1835. The monuments of Berlin were finally completed by the Brandenburg Gate (1789) and the *Neue Wache* (1818), among others.

19C Berlin – Berlin found its soul for the first time when the high patriotism inaugurated by the professors of the university, founded in 1810 by Wilhelm von Humboldt, was allied to the King of Prussia's call to arms in 1813 when he joined the Allies against Napoleon. The city benefited from the growing prestige of the Prussia and, as a favoured subject, was at the forefront of its Industrial Revolution, under the forceful direction of such great advisers as August Borsig, "the locomotive king", Werner von Siemens (1816-92), the pioneer electrical engineer and Emil Rathenau, the founder of the giant AEG. Although official architectural projects produced prestigious, not to say triumphalist, buildings such as the Reichstag, the number of green spaces also increased as the residential suburbs moved westwards towards Grunewald forest. By 1871, Berlin had become the capital of the Empire and numbered almost one million inhabitants.

Greater Berlin – In 1920 the city united, under a single administration, six urban suburbs, seven towns, fifty-nine villages and twenty-seven demesnes to form a unit of four million inhabitants.

Despite the upheavals from which Germany was still suffering, the 1920s was an exciting period in Berlin, intellectually and artistically in particular. Berlin newspapers set the tone for newspapers all over Germany. Films made in Berlin won international acclaim thanks to such great directors as Ernst Lubitsch, Fritz Lang *(Metropolis,* and later *M)*, Carl Mayer, Georg Wilhelm Pabst and the actors Emil Jannings and Marlene Dietrich (*The Blue Angel, Nosferatu* etc). The theatre, rejuvenated by Max Reinhardt (1873-1943), also flourished. In 1928 Bertolt Brecht and Kurt Weill's *The Threepenny Opera* was premiered in what was called the Theater am Schiffbauerdamm. Their collaboration brought together much of the best of the artistic and cultural spirit of 1920s Berlin: subversive, innovative, confident and cosmopolitan in its outlook. The blossoming of this talent was violently interrupted by the advent of the Hitler regime, when, along with the persecution of the Jews, a wealth of the country's artistic and literary heritage was banned or destroyed in the name of the campaign against "degenerate art" – that is to say all schools of writing, painting and sculpture judged by the Nazis as "decadent" and "un-German".

The Taking of Berlin – The final communiqué of the Yalta Conference in February 1945 announced that Berlin would be occupied after the war by the major powers. From 21 April to 3 May, the German capital was a battlefield: the Red Army commanded by Generals Zhukov and Koniev against the remnants of the German army. The Soviet troops advanced through the defence lines, destroying everything above ground, including 120 of Berlin's 248 bridges.

At last, able to crawl out of their hiding places, the inhabitants learned of the final capture of the Reichstag and Hitler's suicide (30 April 1945).

Berlin Divided – After the German surrender had been signed in Berlin on 8 May, the four victorious allies – Great Britain, the United States, France and the Soviet Union – took over the administration of Greater Berlin. Political developments in the (eastern) Soviet Sector, which the Soviets saw as the potential kernel of a future People's Democratic Republic, nevertheless very rapidly began to hinder the municipal administration as a whole. Political pressures, vetoes, and various incidents built up an increasing tension. Municipal councillors unaligned with the concept of State Socialism walked out of the City Hall and formed a rival council at Schöneberg. The Soviet representatives gave up their seats in the allied organisations. From 1948 onwards, the eastern sector found itself administratively isolated. The Berlin Blockade, provoked by Russian opposition to a currency reform introduced in the western sectors, was beaten by an airlift of supplies from the West (26 June 1948 to 12 May 1949). The split was aggravated by the proclamation in the east of the German Democratic Republic on 7 October 1949. Strike-breaking and the suppression of an anti-Soviet uprising on 17 June 1953 confirmed the rulers' determination to impose Communist order on the eastern

H. Champollion/MICHELIN

Großer Müggelsee.

zone, and the influx of refugees into West Berlin increased still further. On 13 August 1961 the eastern authorities ruled out all communication between the two parts of Berlin and, in spite of East German leader Walter Ulbricht's famous denial, the construction of the Wall began a few days later, following the exact theoretical borderline of the Soviet zone. From then on, on either side of a concrete barrier 160km/100mi long and 4m/13ft high, bristling with barbed wire, watchtowers and sentry posts, the two parts of the city evolved separately, cut off from their ideological opposite. Attempts to pass from East to West through this hermetically sealed cordon ended more often than not in tragedy.

The "Fall" of the Wall – A night of wild celebration, especially around the Brandenburg Gate, followed the official "opening" of the Berlin Wall during the evening of 9 November 1989: the eastern authorities, bowing to increased pressure from public protest movements, had finally agreed to re-establish the right of free passage between the two Germanies. In June 1991, the Bundestag voted that Berlin should become capital of the united Germany. For all the rapid reshaping in the capital, the two halves of the once-divided city still have their differences. For some, "socialist" town-planning is an ugly reminder of the political system which produced it, but others, for whom it represents forty years of their identity and experience, have more ambivalent feelings: what to change, and how much to change it, remain controversial questions. The traces of the Wall, in the mind as much as on the ground, will only fade slowly.

An Outdoor City – Berlin, the biggest city in Germany, covers a huge area. Devastated in the last months of the war, the capital lost much of its historical heritage, but thanks to the famous architects (Le Corbusier, Scharoun, Jean Nouvel, Liebeskind and others) involved in its reconstruction, a modernistic city, served by broad arteries linking different quarters separated by vast green belts, has emerged from the ruins of 1945. The River Havel has been widened in its course through the woods to form lakes (Tegeler See, Stößensee, Großer Wannsee). More than one third of the city's surface is covered by forests, parks and waterways.

A Lively Cultural Scene – The city deservedly enjoys a worldwide reputation for the quality and diversity of its cultural scene, and particularly for its music, theatre and film festivals. Before the Second World War, the city's life was concentrated around the Potsdamer Platz and the Friedrichstraße. Today the liveliest part of Berlin is around the Kurfürstendamm ("Ku'Damm"), the Gedächtniskirche (memorial church) and the Alexanderplatz complex. Night-life on the **Kreuzberg** hill has something of a cosmopolitan, anti-establishment flavour, while the rapidly reviving Prenzlauer Berg district, alive with bars, shops and cultural events, also has a cool, subtly alternative atmosphere. During the past 300 years, Berlin has welcomed a large number of immigrants (French Huguenots after the Revocation of the Edict of Nantes, refugees from Poland, and Bohemia). All have contributed a little to the character of a "typical" Berliner: lively and tolerant, approaching the world with a sardonic sense of humour. After Theodore Hosemann in the Biedermeier period, Heinrich Zille (1858-1929) caught this character exactly in a series of spicy sketches satirising the everyday life of Berlin's "little people". Because of this intermixture of populations, Berlin restaurants offer – along with such Brandenburger specialities as pig's knuckles (*Eisbein*) with sauerkraut and pease-pudding – a great variety of dishes from international cuisine. Berliners term a tankard of lager beer a "Berliner Molle", and a light beer with a dash of raspberry syrup or woodruff a "Berliner Weiße mit Schuß".

The Green Guide Berlin, with plenty of accommodation, eating out, entertainment and shopping suggestions, is recommended for a more in-depth tour of the city.

Walking About

HISTORIC CENTRE★★

The itinerary starts from the Reichstag and then follows the celebrated Unter den Linden ("under the lime trees"), which runs from Schlossplatz to Pariser Platz. Most of the great monuments of the former Prussian capital are set around this avenue, which was once a path taken by the Prince-Electors to the Tiergarten hunting reserve.

Reichstag★★

This massive neo-Renaissance style palace by Paul Wallot was inaugurated in 1894 and has housed the sessions of the new Diet of the Empire (an assembly elected through universal suffrage) ever since.

At Goering's instigation, it was gutted by a fire in 1933 and heavily damaged in 1945 during the Battle of Berlin. In 1954 the famous cupola was dynamited. The building was restored during the 1970s, albeit without the cupola. On 4 October 1990, it housed the inaugural session of the Parliament of reunified Germany. In 1995 the artists **Christo** and **Jeanne-Claude** wrapped the Reichstag in silver plastic sheeting which was left in place for a fortnight. Finally, building work began again, this time based on the design of British architect **Sir Norman Foster**. He came up with a glass cupola whose complete lightness stands in sharp contrast to the massive building beneath it. Supported by twelve columns, it draws light into the Plenary Hall by way of a mirrored spindle. An exciting thing is being able to access the cupola via a ramp that leads to a **Panorama Platform★★**, which has proved extraordinarily popular with visitors.

On 19 April 1999, the Members of Parliament were able to convene in plenary session in the new Reichstag for the first time.

From the Reichstag go along Eberstraße towards the Brandenburg Gate.

THE FUTURE HOLOCAUST MEMORIALS

The memorial planned to honour the memory of the six million Jews exterminated by the Nazis was the subject of great debate in Germany. In the end, the plans of Jewish American architect (of German extraction) **Peter Eisenman** were chosen. The memorial will stretch over two hectares (five acres) near the Brandenburg Gate and the Reichstag, and consist of 2 700 concrete pillars of differing heights. There will also be an information centre. The inauguration is due to take place on 8 May 2005, marking the sixtieth anniversary of the German capitulation.

Sir Norman Foster's lofty Reichstag dome.

M. Hertlein/MICHELIN

Directory

Telephone prefix – 030.

Tourist information – *Berlin Tourismus Marketing GmbH*, Am Karlsbad 11, ☏ 25 00 25 (room reservations) or 0190 01 63 16 (Info Hotline), Mon-Fri 8am-7pm, Sat-Sun 9am-6.30pm. Information office: Europa-Center, Budapester Straße 45, Mon-Sat 10am-7pm, Sun 10am-6pm; Brandenburg Gate, south wing, Mon-Sun 10am-6pm; Tegel airport, opposite gate 0, Mon-Sun 5am-10.30pm; KaDeWe, Reisecenter (travel centre) ground floor, Mon-Fri 8.30am-8pm, Sat 9am-4pm.

The fortnightly city magazines *Zitty* and *Tip* and the monthly *Berlin-Programm* provide information on events of all kinds. Berlin's major dailies have a weekly insert featuring a calendar of events. Tickets are available up to three weeks before the performance at *Berlin Tourismus Marketing*. The numerous theatre box offices are the best place to buy tickets when in town.

Post offices with special opening times – Post office 120 at Joachimstaler Straße 8 is open Mon-Sat 8am-midnight and Sun 10am-midnight, post office 519 at Tegel airport, main hall, is open Mon-Fri 8am-6pm, Sat-Sun 8am-1pm. (Deutsche Post AG, ☏ 62 78 10.)

Daily papers – *Berliner Morgenpost, Tagesspiegel, Berliner Zeitung (or bz), Die Tageszeitung (taz).*

Internet – www.berlin.de; www.berlinonline.de; www.berlin-info.de; www.d-berlin.de; www.berlinculture.de; www.gotoberlin.de; www.city-berlin.com

Transport

Airport – Berlin has 3 airports. For general flight information ☏ 0180 500 01 86.

Tegel (TXL), northwest of Berlin, handles much of the international traffic. Bus nos. 109 and X9 (going to *Zoologischer Garten*) will take you to the city centre from the airport. The Jet Express Bus TXL runs between Tegel and the Mitte district (notably Potsdamer Platz, Friedrichstraße and Unter den Linden).

Public Transport

The BVG (Berliner Verkehrs-Betrieb) is the umbrella organisation for trams, buses and underground trains in Berlin, ☏ 1 94 49 or 24hr hotline ☏ 0180 599 66 33 (offices open Mon-Fri, 5.30am-8.30pm and Sat, 8.45am-4.15pm).

Transportation for the region around Berlin and the S-Bahn are operated by the VBB (Verkehrsverbund Berlin-Brandenburg) in conjunction with the BVG, ☏ 25 41 41 41 Mon-Fri 8am-8pm, Sat-Sun 9am-6pm. Information is available at the BVG-Pavillon on Hardenbergplatz (Bahnhof Zoo) 6.30am-8.30pm and at many U-Bahn and S-Bahn stations. Berlin and its environs (eg Potsdam) are divided into three fare zones (A, B and C). For rides within the city, you need a ticket for Zone AB. Tickets are available in all U-Bahn and S-Bahn stations, in trams, at ticket vending machines and from bus drivers. Tickets must be stamped in order to be valid.

Normal fare (valid 2hr) €2.10 (€2.35 for the 3 zones ABC); day ticket (valid from the time of punching until 3am next morning) €6 (€6.20 for the 3 zones) and the 7-day ticket (7 Tage Karte) €22 for 2 zones, €23 for 3 zones.

The **Welcome Card** (valid 72hr) costs €21 and lets an adult with up to three children under the age of 14 use the entire VBB network; it also gives discounts for selected theatres, museums, attractions and city tours. The card is available at BVG outlets and at the information offices of the *Berlin Tourismus Marketing*.

The heavy construction activity in Berlin can lead to delays and to some detours in local transport.

Useful Tip: Bus number 100 that shuttles between Bahnhof Zoo and Alexanderplatz passes by many of Berlin's sights.

Internet – www.bvg.de; www.vbbonline.de; www.berliner-verkehr.de

Sightseeing

City tours – *Severin & Kühn* (☏ 880 41 90), *Bus-Verkehr-Berlin* (☏ 885 98 80), *Berliner-Bären-Service* (☏ 35 19 52 70; www.sightseeing.de) and *Berolina* (☏ 88 56 80 03; www.berolina-berlin.com) all drive the City-Circle: 2hr tours with explanations via headphones leave every 30min beginning at 10am. You can join or leave the tour at various places. Departure from Kurfürstendamm (between Joachimsthaler Straße and Fasanenstraße) and Alexanderplatz in front of the Forum-Hotel. Severin & Kühn run the Große Berlin-Tour: 3-4hr tours at 10am and 2pm.

City walking tours with various historical, topical and contemporary themes are offered by: *Kulturbüro* (☏ 444 09 36; www.stadt-fuehrung.de), *art:Berlin* (☏ 28 09 63 90) and *Stattreisen* (☏ 455 30 28; www.stattreisen.berlin.de).

Boat tours – *Stern- und Kreisschiffahrt* (☏ 536 36 00) offers rides through the historic centre of the city beginning in the Nikolaiviertel (1hr); tours through the inner city by way of the Spree and Landwehr canals (3hr 30min) beginning at the Jannowitzbrücke and Schloßbrücke; and rides on the Havel from Wannsee to Potsdam/Lange Brücke (1hr 15min).

Eating Out

Diekmann – *Meinekestraße 7 – 10719 Berlin-Charlottenburg – ☏ (030) 883 33 21 – www.j-diekmann.de – Closed Sun lunchtime – Reservation necessary – €10/41.* With its wooden flooring, simple chairs and old-style décor this restaurant somewhat resembles a boutique of colonial products and has an air of nostalgia. Quick lunch menus available.

Nußbaum – *Bundesplatz 6 – Bundesplatz – (030) 854 50 20 – Closed Christmas Eve – Reservation recommended – €12.50/24.50.* For robust traditional cuisine "just like home", head to the Wilmersdorf district. Nußbaum is located on the very lively Bundesplatz.

Mutter Hoppe – *Rathausstraße 21 – Alexanderplatz – (030) 24 72 06 03 – www.prostmahlzeit.de/mutterhoppe – €16/30.50.* This typical old-style restaurant is very near the Nikolaiviertel, rebuilt in historic style. The rustic layout, with old bars and photographs, is somewhat nostalgic. Traditional live music on Fridays and Saturdays from 8pm.

Marjellchen – *Mommsenstraße 9 – (030) 883 26 76 – Closed Sun – €19.50/39.* Pleasant, typical Berlin restaurant serving substantial dishes from eastern Prussia and Silesia. The Marjellchen has inherited its grandmother's recipes. A real rustic, homely setting.

Zander – *Kollwitzstraße 50 – 10405 Berlin-Prenzlauer Berg – Senefelderplatz – (030) 44 05 76 79 – www.gourmetguide.com/zander – Closed Sun – Reservation recommended – €27/46.* This restaurant with its simple décor spreads over two storeys. Its charm lies in its wooden flooring and dark wooden chairs. Modern cuisine with different dishes served every week.

Bamberger Reiter – *Regensburger Straße 7 – (030) 218 42 82 – Closed Sun and Mon – €28/48.* Delicious dishes to delight fans of Austrian food. The elegant rustic décor tastefully combines beautiful wood, sparkling mirrors and various accessories.

Lutter und Wegner – *Charlottenstraße 56 – (030) 202 95 40 – €29/44.50.* This sandstone-fronted corner house is near the Gendarmenmarkt. Inside, dark wood panelling gives the establishment a tavern-style character. Three big columns painted by modern artists illustrate this restaurant's motto: "wine, women and song".

Borchardt – *Französische Straße 47 – (030) 20 38 71 10 – veranstaltung@gastart.de – Closed Sun – €30.50/52.* With its impressive columns and their gilded capitals, stuccoed ceilings and refined furniture, it is hardly surprising that this is one of the most chic restaurants in town. People come here to see and be seen. Seasonal, French-style cuisine.

The Turkish market in Kreuzberg.

H. Champollion/MICHELIN

Harlekin – *Lützowufer 15 – (030) 254 78 86 30 – info@esplanade.de – Closed from 1st-6 Jan, Aug, Sun and Mon – €45/65.* Markus Lüpertz's Harlekin dominates the dining area in this restaurant. The glass-fronted kitchen enables diners to watch the team of chefs and the pots. Creative dishes to admire and sample.

Kaiserstuben – *Am Festungsgraben 1 – (030) 20 61 05 48 – info@kaiserstuben.de – Closed 3 weeks in Jul/Aug, Sun and Mon – €46/57.* This little restaurant with its simple elegance, high white-stucco ceilings and classic menu, is on the first floor of a magnificent palace.

Where to stay

Hotel Am Anhalter Bahnhof – *Stresemannstraße 36, 10963 Berlin-Kreuzberg – (030) 251 03 42 – Fax (030) 2514897 – www.hotel-anhalter-bahmhof.de – 33rm: €35/100.* A no-frills establishment in a very central location near Potsdamer Platz, with a bus stop on its doorstep. Basic rooms, some with showers, but very clean and cheap.

Hotel Künstlerheim Luise – *Luisenstraße 19 – (030) 28 44 80 – Fax (030) 28448448 – www.kuenstlerheim-luise.de – Reservation necessary – 47rm: €48/149 – €7 – Restaurant €18.* This very classical municipal palace built in 1825 – now a listed building – today houses a unique hotel where a number of artists have had a hand in the decoration of the rooms. More basic, cheaper rooms with showers are also available. The Wein Guy restaurant is adjacent to the hotel.

Transit-Loft Hotel – *Greifswalder Straße 219, 10405 Berlin-Prenzlauer Berg – 2, 3, 4 – access via Immanuel kirchstraße – (030) 48493773 – Fax (030) 44051074 – www.transit-loft.de – 47rm: €59/69.* Since August 2001, this converted factory building right in the heart of Berlin's Szenebezirk (theatre district) has housed a two-storey "hotel for young people". The rooms are basic but very well-kept and equipped with modern furniture.

Am Wilden Eber – *Warnemünder Straße 19, 14199 Berlin-Zehlendorf – Podbielskiallee – (030) 89 77 79 90 – Fax (030) 897779999 – www.hotel-am-wilden-eber.de – 15rm: €60/85.* A simple hotel with well-kept, identical and fairly quiet rooms, and a small swimming pool and sauna in the basement.

Hotel Econtel – *Sömmeringstraße 24 – Mierendorffplatz – (030) 34 68 10 – Fax (030) 34681163 – www.econtel.de – 205rm: €80/98 – €3 – Restaurant €17.80/34.* This establishment near the city centre is particularly suitable for groups and offers a choice between three categories of room: Economy, Business or Comfort. Mickey Mouse face painting available for children. Schloß Charlottenburg is a stone's throw away.

Hotel Berlin-Plaza – *Knesebeckstraße 63 – (030) 88 41 30 – Fax (030) 88413754 – www.blueband.de – Reservation recommended – 131rm: €81/180 – Restaurant €13/16.50.* This hotel stands in a very desirable central location in a street near the Ku'damm. The rooms are modern and functional.

Hotel Hackescher Markt – *Große Präsidentenstraße 8 – (030) 28 00 30 – Fax (030) 28003111 – info@hackescher-markt.com – 31rm: from €120 – €15.* A recent building with an old-style façade in Berlin's new Szeneviertel (theatre district). Spacious rooms with pale wooden furniture. Despite the hotel's central location, the rooms with terrace are very quiet since they face the small inner courtyard.

Grand Hotel Esplanade – *Lützowufer 15, 10785 Berlin-Tiergarten – (030) 25 47 80 – Fax (030) 254788222 – info@esplanade.de – 386rm: from €225 – €20.* This big hotel has been engulfed by the cultural life of this district and resembles an exhibition of modern interior decoration. Collection of paintings by the "Berliner Wilden". Very modern luxury rooms.

Hotel Adlon – *Unter den Linden 77 – (030) 226 10 – Fax (030) 22612222 – adlon@kempinski.com – 336rm: from €300 – €29.* A living legend! In 1997, it once again became possible to stay in this magnificent restored building near the Brandenburg Gate and the Unter den Linden avenue. The rooms, the suites and the three restaurants – all pure luxury.

Cafés

Café am Schiffbauerdamm – *Albrechtstraße 13 (Mitte) – Friedrichstraße – (030) 28 38 40 49 – from 10am.* A very pleasant atmosphere suffuses the bright rooms and terrace of the Café am Schiffbauerdamm, set in a quiet street in Friedrich-Wilhelm-Stadt. Cakes and tarts, sandwiches and light or copious meals are served.

Café Ephraim's – *Spreeufer 1 (Mitte, near Mühlendamm) – Klosterstraße – (030) 24 72 59 47 – from 12pm.* A real gem of a café in the Nikolaiviertel, with "Gründerzeit"-style furniture (late 19C) and a warm atmosphere. Customers can also sit outside on the banks of the Spree. Berlin specialities, home-made cakes and tarts served here.

Telecafé – *Panoramastraße 1a (Mitte, near Alexanderplatz) – Alexanderplatz – (030) 2 42 33 33 – www.berlinerfernsehturm.de – Panorama: Mar-Oct: 9am-1am; Nov-Feb: 10am-midnight – Telecafé: Mar-Oct: 9am-1am; Nov-Feb: 10am-midnight.* This café in the television tower (208m/682ft off the ground) rotates full-circle in 30min, allowing customers to admire the view over the whole of Berlin.

H. Champollion/MICHELIN

Café terrace on the banks of the Spree.

Going out

Useful Tips – The "scene" in Berlin is very decentralised; there are numerous areas and streets where there is plenty going on *(further details in The Green Guide Berlin – Potsdam)*: in Charlottenburg around Savignyplatz and on the Ku'Damm; in Schöneberg around Winterfeldplatz; in Kreuzberg around Chamissoplatz, on Oranienstraße and Wiener Straße and along the Landwehrkanal; in Berlin-Mitte at Friedrichstraße, in the Nikolaiviertel and around the Hackescher Markt, and in Prenzlauer Berg around Kollwitzplatz and along Kastanienallee.

Clärchen's Ballhaus – *Auguststraße 24-25 (Mitte) – Weinmeisterstraße – (030) 2 82 92 95 – www.claerchens-ballhaus.de.* This traditional dance hall in the Spandauer Vorstadt district has belonged to the same family since 1913. The atmosphere is good and the music ranges from old classics to the latest hits. On Wednesdays there is a beginner's tango class. The dance hall is also open on Fridays and Saturdays.

Oxymoron – *Hackesche Höfe/Rosenthaler Straße 40-41 (Mitte) – Weinmeisterstraße – (030) 28 39 18 86 – www.oxymoron-berlin.de – 10am-1am. Club: Wed-Sat from 9pm.* Located in the first of the Hackesche Höfe's courtyards, in the daytime the Oxymoron is a restaurant and tea room (from 11am) with a bar, and at night an upmarket disco (on Wednesdays from 8pm and Fridays and Saturdays from 11pm). Fashion shows and concerts are also sometimes held here.

925 Loungebar – *Taubenstraße 19 (Mitte) – Tram Hausvogteiplatz, Stadtmitte – ☎ (030) 20 18 71 77 – Open from 5pm.* A cocktail bar at the Gendarmenmarkt: the rooms, furniture and lighting are all red. This place is named after its bar made of 925 sterling silver.

Die Tagung – *Wühlischstraße 29 (east of Warschauer Straße) – 10245 Berlin-Friedrichshain – Tram Frankfurter Tor – ☎ (030) 29 77 37 88 – www.die-tagung.de – Open from 7pm.* The appeal of this dark and slightly dilapidated bar lies in its décor consisting of various odds and ends from the former East Germany: busts, signs and posters of all kinds are to be found in every nook and cranny.

Müller-Lüdenscheid – *Szredskistraße 45 (between Schönhauser and Prenzlauer Allee; south of Danziger Straße) – 10435 Berlin-Prenzlauer Berg – Tram Eberswalder Straße – ☎ (030) 44 04 92 24 – Open every day except Mon, from 6pm.* This pleasant, well-lit wine bar offers over 150 different wines, many of them sold by the glass and most of them German.

Universum Lounge – *Kurfürstendamm 153 – 10709 Berlin-Charlottenburg – Tram Adenauerplatz – ☎ (030) 89 06 49 94 – from 3pm.* A new bar in Kurfürstendamm, in the same building as the Schaubühne. Coloured leather seats, teak panelling and, everywhere you look, pictures of the universe and man's first steps on the moon. The copper bar and slightly rounded room hug the curves of Erich Mendelssohn's building.

Zillemarkt – *BleibBerustraße 48a (running parallel between Leibniz- and Uhlandstraße) – 10623 Berlin-Charlottenburg – S Savignyplatz – ☎ (030) 8 81 70 40 – www.zillemarkt.de – 10am-1am.* Traditional décor (William II watches over the customers) with small tables of undressed wood, a bar lit by old lamps and a charming little beer garden at the back.

Culture

Useful Tips – Every other month Berlin Tourismus Marketing publishes the *Berlin Kalender*, which can be bought for €1.20 at the BTM information offices at the Brandenburg Gate, KaDeWe and the Europa-Center (both in Tauentzienstraße). The magazines *Tip*, *Zitty* and *Prinz* also provide information on events of all kinds and are available at the city's bookshops and kiosks.

Shopping

Useful Tips – The city's main shopping streets are Kurfürstendamm, Tauentzienstraße (with department stores Europa-Center and KaDeWe), Friedrichstraße, and Fasanenstraße in the city centre. The most prestigious shopping arcades are Leibnizkolonnaden (between Leibniz- and Wielandstraße), Potsdamer Platz Arkaden, Friedrichstadtpassagen (with Galeries Lafayette) and the Hackesche Höfe.

Department stores – Kurfürstendamm, Tauentzienstraße and the Potsdamer Platz arcades are where the most famous department stores are to be found: *KaDeWe*, Tauentzienstraße 221, a gigantic selection in a luxurious setting; *Galeries Lafayette*, Friedrichstraße 207, good variety in amazing architectural surroundings. Exclusive shops are located on Fasanenstraße and Friedrichstraße.
A special shopping address is the **Hackeschen Höfe** (Rosenthalerstraße/Sophienstraße, www.hackesche-hoefe.com), with eight courtyards containing art galleries, fashion boutiques, antiques shops, restaurants and bars, a cinema and even a cabaret.

Art galleries – In the west half of the city these have collected around Savignyplatz (Charlottenburg), on Fasanenstraße (Charlottenburg), and on Pariser Straße (Wilmersdorf); in the east part of the city between Oranienburger Straße and Rosa-Luxemburg-Platz.

Antiques – The antique dealers are mainly on Eisenacher Straße, Kalckeruthstraße and Fasanenstraße, around Bleibtreustraße, Pestalozzistraße, and Knesebeckstraße, as well as around the Friedrichstraße station.

Flea markets – Großer Berliner Trödel- und Kunstmarkt (flea and art market), Straße des 17. Juni (Charlottenburg), Sat-Sun 11am to 5pm; flea market in Wilmersdorf, Fehrbelliner Platz, Sat-Sun 7am to 4pm; art and antiques market on Museumsinsel, Sat-Sun, 11am to 5pm.

Markets – Market on Winterfeldplatz, Wed and Sat 8am to 1pm; weekly Turkish market, Maybachufer (Neukölln), Tue and Fri noon to 6.30pm.

Brandenburg Gate★★ (Brandenburger Tor)

This triumphal arch, the very emblem of Berlin, was for almost three decades the symbol of the city's division: the structure was integrated into the Wall, which followed a north-south axis here towards the Potsdamer Platz.
There is a vast perspective westward towards Straße des 17 Juni and the Victory Monument *(Siegessäule)*, and eastward towards the Unter den Linden.
Six Doric columns support an antique-style entablature. Inspired by the Propylaea of the Parthenon, the gate was built by Carl Gotthard Langhans in 1788-91 and surmounted by the famous Victory Quadriga of Gottfried Schadow (1793). The original group, a post-war reconstruction, was removed to Paris after one of Napoleon's campaigns and returned to Berlin in 1814. After much debate, the Quadriga was re-endowed with its iron cross and eagle, warlike attributes designed by Schinkel at the behest of King Frederick William III.

134) 134)

Brandenburg Gate, symbol of Berlin.

Unter den Linden★★

The famous avenue "under the lime trees", conceived by the Great Elector Frederick William in 1647, is bordered from the Friedrichstraße intersection onwards by monuments of the 17C and 19C. The original lime trees that shaded Unter den Linden were cut down in 1658. Four rows were replanted in 1820.

Take the Charlottenstraße southwards to the Gendarmenmarkt.

Gendarmenmarkt★★

This is undoubtedly the most beautiful square in Berlin, named after the Soldier-King Frederick William I's "Gens d'Armes" regiment, which had stables here.

In this square, the Schauspielhaus, an elegant theatre built by Schinkel in 1821, is bounded on the south side by the German cathedral, **Deutscher Dom★**, and on the north by the French cathedral, **Französischer Dom★**. Both early-18C churches had domes added by Karl Gontard during the reign of Frederick the Great. The German cathedral houses the exhibition "Fragen an die deutsche Geschichte" (Questions for German History), and the French cathedral the Hugenottenmuseum (Huguenot Museum).

Schauspielhaus★★ (Theatre) – This is the work of Karl Friedrich Schinkel, whose principal inspiration was Greek Antiquity; evidence of this is the portico supported by six pillars. After being destroyed during the Second World War, the theatre was rebuilt between 1980 and 1984 in compliance with the rules of classicist architecture. Although the interior is not an exact reproduction, the concert halls are truly magnificent.

The monument of Schiller standing in front of the main staircase is an 1871 work by the Berlin sculptor Reinhold Begas.

Take Französischestraße up to St Hedwigs-Kathedrale, set back from Bebelplatz.

Forum Fridericianum★★ (Bebelplatz)

This large complex was part of Frederick II's plans for the development of the city. The Forum Fridericianum (also known as Friedrichsforum or Lindenforum) was intended to give the Prussian monarchy unprecedented artistic and scientific influence in Europe. *Designed by* Knobelsdorff, who planned to level the fortifications, the site was to hold an opera house, an academy dedicated to the sciences and a castle with a ceremonial courtyard. The opera house was the only building to be completed according to the original plans, since the king was increasingly drawn to the residential town of Potsdam. A library was built instead of the science academy, on a smaller site than originally planned. The castle was

The Huguenots, France's Contribution to Berlin

In 1685, in response to Louis XIV's Revocation of the Edict of Nantes, the Great Elector Frederick William of Brandenburg issued the Edict of **Potsdam** granting asylum to French Calvinists. A huge propaganda campaign was held in France itself and in Frankfurt-am-Main, where 100 000 Huguenots passed through in the space of 20 years. There were 15 000 in Brandenburg, including 6 000 in Berlin (one quarter of the population), who were responsible for the development of the **Friedrichstadt area**. Until the 19C, the French community had its own ecclesiastical and legal organisation.

The incentive was not purely demographic. This community was to have a long-lasting influence in various areas, with the emergence of about fifty trades, the creation of factories and the rapid growth of the textile industry, the acclimatisation of fruit and vegetables and the introduction of new dances such as the cotillon, gavotte and minuet.

replaced by a palace for the king's brother, Prince Heinrich of Prussia, and **St Hedwigs's cathedral** was built in the southwest corner. According to Friedrich Nicolai's description of Berlin in 1786, the Forum – formerly known as *Opernplatz* – was one of the most beautiful squares in the world. The changes made since then have shattered the harmony of space and volumes. In the 19C an imperial palace and a Dresdner Bank building were added to the complex. In the 20C, the opera house was extended both upwards and sideways and several storeys were added to the bank. It was St Hedwigs-Kathedrale that suffered the most from these transformations, which deprived it of its vital space, and the works caused a general outcry, some people describing them as an insult to "the architectural dignity of Berlin's greatest square". In 1994, Micha Ullman created the **Versunkene Bibliothek** (the sunken library) on the underground route of the tramway which used to pass beneath the square. This glass-fronted room with its empty shelves commemorates the book-burning on Bebelplatz which took place on 10 May 1933.

St Hedwigs-Kathedrale – According to recent research, Georg Wenzeslaus von Knobelsdorff drafted the plans for this Catholic church, which was built between 1743 and 1773. It was closely modelled on the Pantheon in Rome. Since Frederick II had been victorious in capturing Silesia, the church was dedicated to St Hedwig, the patron saint of Silesia. It was badly damaged during the Second World War and largely rebuilt between 1952 and 1963.

Staatsoper Unter den Linden★ – *Opposite St Hedwig's cathedral on Bebelplatz.* Built by Knobelsdorff between 1740 and 1743 on the site of the "Forum Fridericianum", the Opera House was the only one of three originally planned buildings to be completed. It burned down in 1843; Langhans' reconstruction follows the original plans. Destroyed again during the Second World War, the State Opera House was rebuilt by Richard Paulick in historicist style between 1951 and 1955.

Humboldt-Universität – *On Unter den Linden, opposite the Opera House.* The palace of Frederick II's brother, Prince Heinrich, built by Johann Boumann the Elder in 1753, was transformed into a university in 1810. On the left side of the entrance, a statue of one of its founders, Wilhelm von Humboldt, faces that of his brother, the geographer Alexander von Humboldt, on the other. Some prestigious figures have passed through the doors of this university, which now takes 20 000 students: Fichte was the first rector; Hegel, Einstein and Planck taught here; and Heine and Marx studied here at one time. A famous equestrian statue of Frederick the Great made by Christian Daniel Rauch between 1840-51 stands in the centre of the avenue.

Alte Bibliothek★ (Old Library) – *Opposite Humboldt-Universität.* Designed by Georg Friedrich Boumann in the Viennese Baroque style for the royal book collection, this library was inaugurated in 1780.

Take Charlottenstraße southwards to the Gendarmenmarkt.

Neue Wache (New Guardhouse)

This small, exquisitely proportioned memorial, designed by Schinkel in 1818, is in the form of a temple with Doric columns, wedged between two massive pillars.

It was consecrated in 1966 as a Monument to the Victims of Fascism and Militarism. Since 1993, it has been designated the leading memorial for Germany, a "place of remembrance for the victims of war and violence". In the middle of a striking open space, the interior houses an enlarged reproduction of the sculpture by Käthe Kollwitz: *Mother with Dead Son.*

Zeughaus★★ (Arsenal)

♿ *Open Wed-Mon, 10am-6pm. Closed 24-26 and 31 Dec €5.* ☎ *(030) 20 30 40; www.dhm.de*

Berlin's most important Baroque edifice, erected between 1695 and 1706. It houses the **Deutsches Historisches Museum★★** *(German Historical Museum)*, which will probably remain closed until 2006; the collections have been transferred to the Kronprinzenpalais *(Unter den Linden 3)*. During this period, the museum will be subjected to a comprehensive technical renovation programme and will be extended with a light-filled exhibition hall designed by the American architect and Gropius student Ieoh Ming Pei.

Friedrichswerdersche Kirche★ (Friedrichswerdersche church)

♿ *Open Tue-Sun, 10am-6pm. €3, free admission 1st Sun of each month.* ☎ *(030) 20 90 55 66; www.smb.spk-berlin.de.* This impressive brick church was built from 1824 to 1830 following the designs of Karl Friedrich Schinkel. It houses the **Schinkelmuseum★**, with sculptures by this multi-talented artist, who left his mark on the cityscape in a way that none other has. There is also various literature on Schinkel's work as well as works from Berlin's classicist period.

Cross the Spree and carry on to the Museumsinsel (described below in "Special Features"). On the left stands Berlin Cathedral.

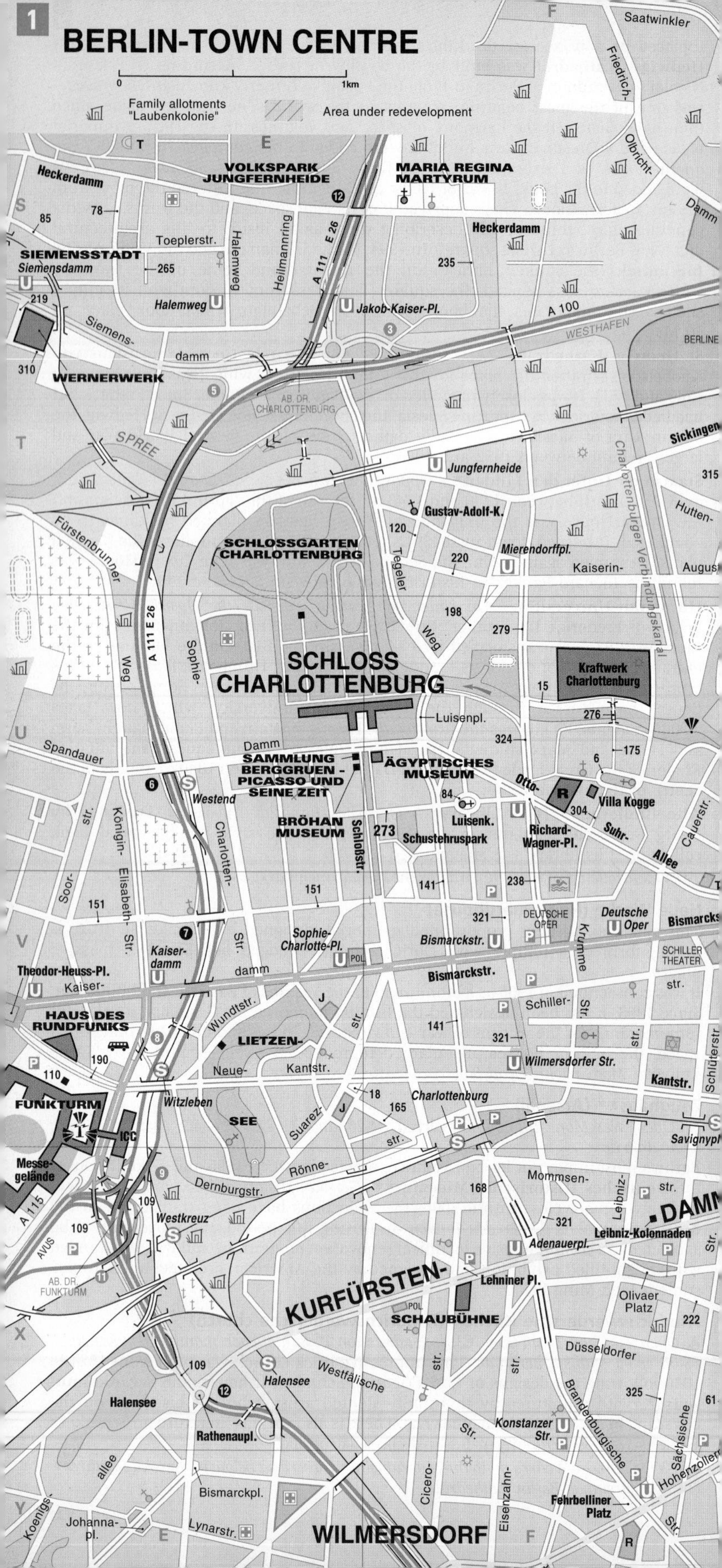

1
BERLIN-TOWN CENTRE
0
1km
Family allotments "Laubenkolonie"
Area under redevelopment
VOLKSPARK JUNGFERNHEIDE
MARIA REGINA MARTYRUM
Heckerdamm
SIEMENSSTADT
Siemensdamm
Halemweg
Jakob-Kaiser-Pl.
WERNERWERK
Jungfernheide
Gustav-Adolf-K.
SCHLOSSGARTEN CHARLOTTENBURG
Mierendorffpl.
SCHLOSS CHARLOTTENBURG
Kraftwerk Charlottenburg
Luisenpl.
SAMMLUNG BERGGRUEN - PICASSO UND SEINE ZEIT
ÄGYPTISCHES MUSEUM
Westend
BRÖHAN MUSEUM
Schlosstr.
Luisenk.
Villa Kogge
Richard-Wagner-Pl.
Schustehruspark
Sophie-Charlotte-Pl.
Bismarckstr.
Deutsche Oper
DEUTSCHE OPER
SCHILLER THEATER
Theodor-Heuss-Pl.
Kaiserdamm
HAUS DES RUNDFUNKS
LIETZEN-SEE
Wilmersdorfer Str.
Kantstr.
FUNKTURM
ICC
Messe-gelände
Witzleben
Charlottenburg
Savignypl.
Westkreuz
Adenauerpl.
Leibniz-Kolonnaden
KURFÜRSTENDAMM
Lehniner Pl.
SCHAUBÜHNE
Olivaer Platz
Halensee
Rathenaupl.
Konstanzer Str.
Fehrbelliner Platz
Bismarckpl.
Johanna-pl.
WILMERSDORF

2
WEDDING
MOABIT
TIERGARTEN
KULTURFORUM
SCHÖNEBERG
Plötzensee
Gedenkstätte Plötzensee
GOETHE-PARK
Universitätsklinikum Rudolf Virchow
Leopoldpl.
Alte Nazareth-kirche
M 14
16
Luxemburger Str.
Amrumer Str.
Trift-str.
Müller-str.
Nordufer
Föhrer Str.
BERLIN-SPANDAUER-SCHIFFAHRTSKANAL
WESTHAFEN
Westhafen
KANAL
GROSSMARKT
Beusselstr.
Quitzow-str.
Siemens-straße
Birkenstr.
Perleberger Str.
Heide-str.
Lehrter Str.
Kruppstr.
FRITZ-SCHLOSS-PARK
POSTSTADION
Rathenower Str.
REFORMATIONSKIRCHE
AEG TURBINEN FABRIK
Wiclefstr.
Bremer Str.
Stromstr.
HEILANDSKIRCHE
Turmstr.
Ottopl.
J1
Seydlitzstr.
Invaliden-str.
St. Johannis
Alt-Moabit
Haus am Wasser
HANSA-VIERTEL
Moabiter Brücke
Gotzkowskybrücke
Levetzowstr.
LANDES-BILDSTELLE
Helmholtzstr.
Bellevue
Hansapl.
Q1
Schloß und Park Bellevue
Moabiter Werder
BUNDESKANZLERAMT
ENGLISCHER GARTEN
Bundespräsidialamt
Lutherbrücke
Franklinstr.
Salzufer
Bachstr.
Ernst-Reuter-Platz
KPM
Technische Universität
Tiergarten
Straße des 17. Juni
SIEGESSÄULE
Großer Stern
Rousseauinsel
Schleuseninsel
Neuer See
A2
HOCHSCHULE DER KÜNSTE
ZOOLOGISCHER GARTEN
NORDISCHE BOTSCHAFTEN
MEXIKANISCHE BOTSCHAFT
A3
M6
M9
M7
LANDWEHR-KANAL
Rauchstr.
Reichpietsch-ufer
KAISER-WILHELM-GEDÄCHTNISKIRCHE
BAUHAUS-ARCHIV
Steinpl.
C4
IHK
SAVIGNYPL.
T8
STILWERK
Kant-Dreieck
Synagoge Fasanenstraße
Europa-Center
Lützow-pl.
Kurfürsten-damm
Tauentzien-str.
Wittenbergpl.
22
URANIA
Magdeburger Pl.
Kurfürsten-str.
Potsdamer Str.
M10
The Story of Berlin
Uhlandstr.
Augsburger Str.
KADEWE
Kleiststr.
Nollendorfpl.
Kurfürstenstr.
FASANENSTR.
Universität der Künste
BUNDESHAUS
Motzstr.
Bülowstr.
LUDWIGKIRCHPL.
Spichernstr.
Nachodstr.
Ansbacher Str.
Viktoria-Luise-Pl.
Winterfeldtpl.
Pallas-str.
KIRCHE AM HOHENZOLLERNPL.
Hohenzollernpl.
Hohenstaufen-str.
Kleistpark
Güntzelstr.
Bundesallee
Goltzstr.
Luther-str.
Eisenacher Str.
Grunewaldstr.
Bayerischer Pl.
Pfalzburger Str.
Uhland
St. Matthäus-Kirchhof I

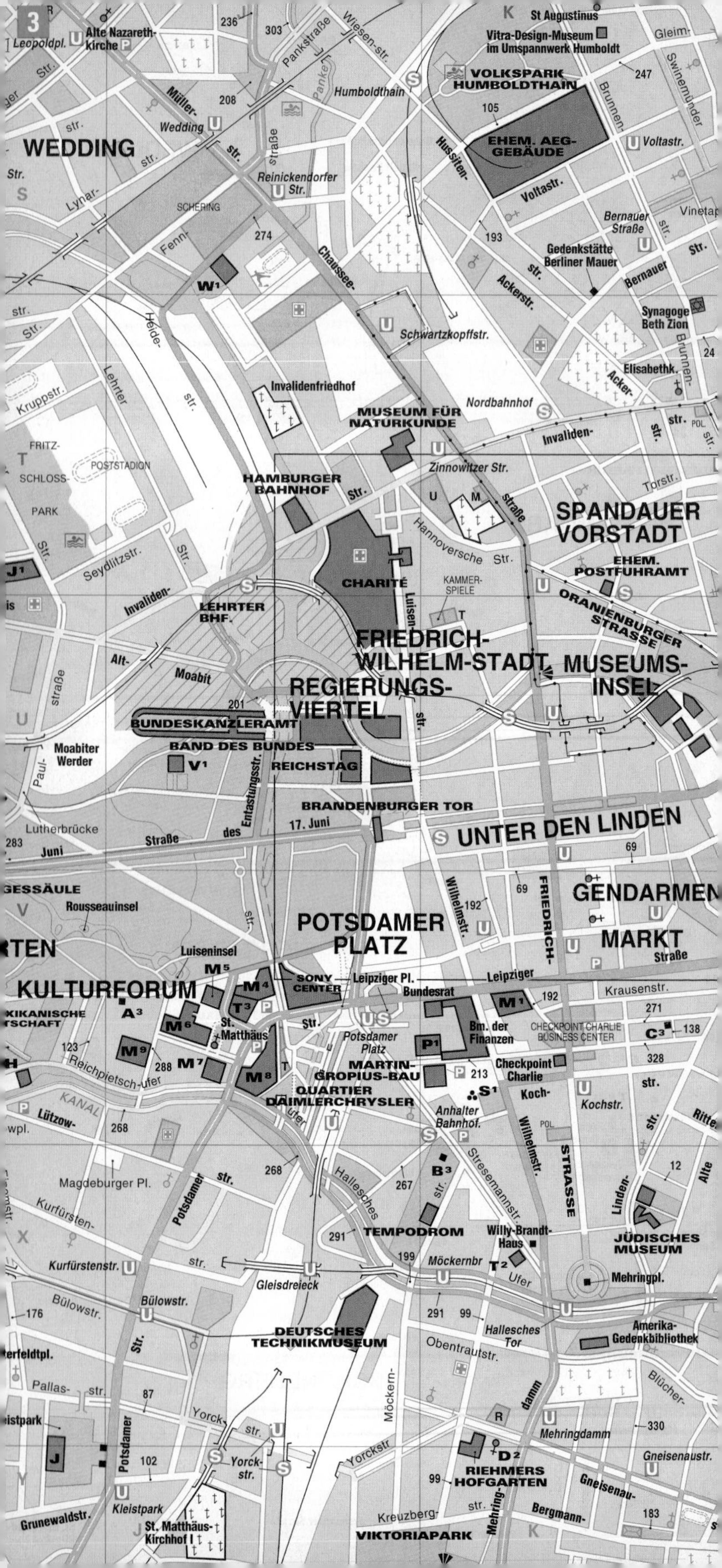
3
WEDDING
VOLKSPARK HUMBOLDTHAIN
EHEM. AEG-GEBÄUDE
Gedenkstätte Berliner Mauer
Synagoge Beth Zion
Invalidenfriedhof
MUSEUM FÜR NATURKUNDE
HAMBURGER BAHNHOF
SPANDAUER VORSTADT
EHEM. POSTFUHRAMT
ORANIENBURGER STRASSE
CHARITÉ
KAMMER-SPIELE
LEHRTER BHF.
FRIEDRICH-WILHELM-STADT
MUSEUMSINSEL
REGIERUNGSVIERTEL
BUNDESKANZLERAMT
BAND DES BUNDES
REICHSTAG
BRANDENBURGER TOR
UNTER DEN LINDEN
GENDARMENMARKT
POTSDAMER PLATZ
SONY CENTER
KULTURFORUM
St. Matthäus
Bundesrat
Bm. der Finanzen
CHECKPOINT CHARLIE BUSINESS CENTER
Checkpoint Charlie
MARTIN-GROPIUS-BAU
QUARTIER DAIMLERCHRYSLER
Anhalter Bahnhof
TEMPODROM
Willy-Brandt-Haus
JÜDISCHES MUSEUM
Mehringpl.
DEUTSCHES TECHNIKMUSEUM
Amerika-Gedenkbibliothek
Hallesches Tor
Gleisdreieck
RIEHMERS HOFGARTEN
VIKTORIAPARK
St. Matthäus-Kirchhof I
Kleistpark
Rousseauinsel
Luiseninsel
Moabiter Werder
Lutherbrücke
Straße des 17. Juni
Magdeburger Pl.
Leopoldpl.
Alte Nazareth-kirche
St Augustinus
Vitra-Design-Museum im Umspannwerk Humboldt
Elisabethk.
Nordbahnhof
Zinnowitzer Str.
Schwartzkopffstr.
Humboldthain
Reinickendorfer Str.
Voltastr.
Bernauer Straße
Kochstr.
Kurfürstenstr.
Bülowstr.
Möckernbr.
Mehringdamm
Gneisenaustr.
Yorckstr.
POSTSTADION
FRITZ-SCHLOSS-PARK
SCHERING

4
PRENZLAUER BERG
Gethsemanek.
Stargarder
42
GROTERJAHN-BRAUREI
MAX-SCHMELING-HALLE
F.-L.-JAHN-SPORTPARK
STADION
Schönhauser
Pappelallee
Eberswalder Str.
58
Prenzlauer Allee
Erich-Weinert-Str.
126
Ostseepl.
Grell-Str.
ZEISS-GROSSPLANETARIUM
Greifswalder Str.
Storkower Str.
Greifswalder Str.
Anton-Saefkow-Str.
Ernst-Thälmann-Park
Danziger Str.
Prenzlauer
KULTUR-BRAUEREI
217
Schwedter Str.
Arkonapl.
144
285
130
KOLLWITZ-PL.
Kollwitz-
250
Prenzlauer Berg Museum
184
JÜDISCHER FRIEDHOF
Schönhauser Allee
Greifswalder str.
Hufelandstr.
Kniprode-Straße
Danziger str.
POL.
Senefelderpl.
64
Volkspark am Weinberg
HERZ-JESU-KIRCHE
Torstr.
Am Friedrichshain
297
FREIZEIT-PARK
VOLKSBÜHNE
Volkspark Friedrichshain
Frieden-
Braun-Str.
Mollstr.
Liebknecht-Str.
Otto-
Pl. der Vereinten Nationen
Landsberger Allee
ALEXANDERPLATZ
FERNSEHTURM
Karl-
Mollstr.
Landsberger straße
ERLINER OM
Gruner str.
Alexander-str.
Schillingstr.
KARL-MARX-ALLEE
Straße
STRAUSBERGER PL.
Strausberger Pl.
Schillingstr.
SCHLOSS-PLATZ
ROTES RATHAUS
NIKOLAI VIERTEL
Stralauer Str.
Singer-str.
Lichtenberger
Weberwiese
FRANKFURTER TOR
FRIEDRICHSHAIN
Holzmarkt-
Andreas-str.
82
FISCHER-INSEL
MÄRKISCHES MUSEUM
Inselstr.
196
Ostbahnhof
str.
Seydelstr.
Heinrich-Heine-Str.
Annenstr.
Sebastian-
Jakobstr.
Köpenicker
Mühlenstraße
SPREE
St. Michael
118
Engel-damm
Straße
St. Thomas
EAST SIDE GALLERY
ORANIEN-STR.
Moritzpl.
E¹
Mariannen-platz
229
60
327
OBERBAUM-BRÜCKE
300
207
300
Oranienpl.
F²
KREUZBERG
Adalbert-
Heinrichpl.
Lausitzer Pl.
Schlesisches Tor
Wrangelstr.
Ritterstr.
Wassertorpl.
277
Görlitzer Bahnhof
277
Prinzen-Str.
Prinzenstr.
Kottbusser Tor
159
157
Fraenkelufer
LANDWEHRKANAL
Wiener Str.
Görlitzer Park
Reichenberger Str.
Plan-ufer
Paul-Lincke-Ufer
Maybach-ufer
94
Schönleinstr.
Kottbusser Damm
Urban-
156
Pflüger str.
Graefe-str.
Südstern
LANDWEHR-KANAL
115

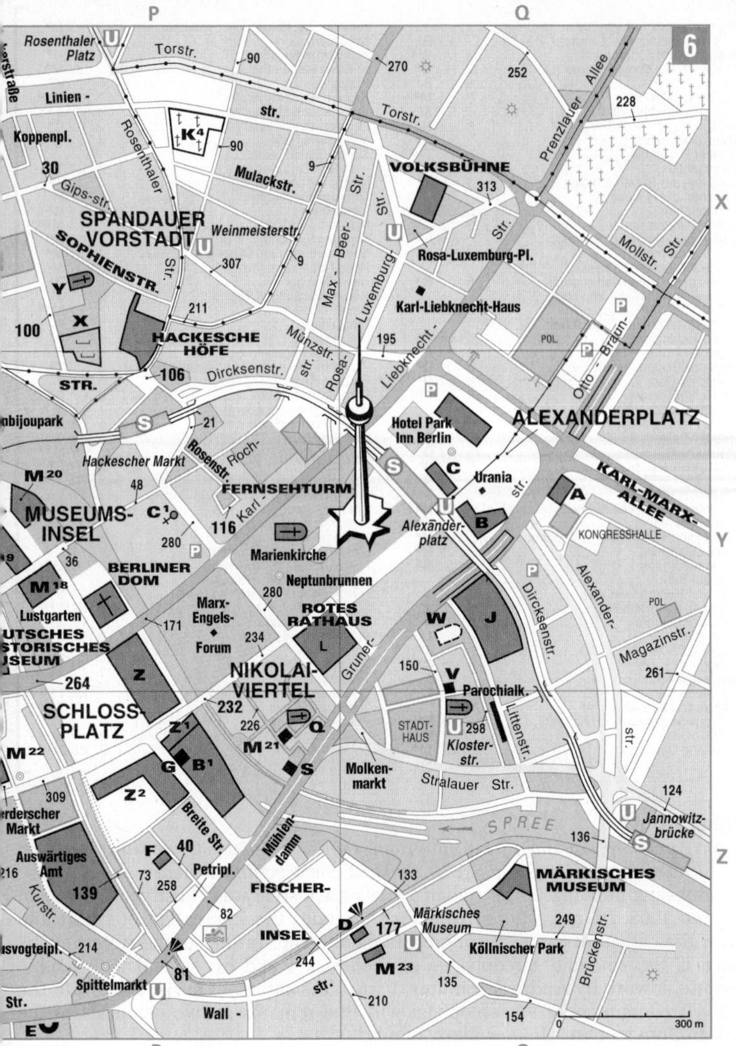
P
Q
6
Rosenthaler Platz
Torstr.
Linien - str.
Koppenpl.
Gips-str.
Rosenthaler Str.
Mulackstr.
Weinmeisterstr.
SPANDAUER VORSTADT
SOPHIENSTR.
HACKESCHE HÖFE
Dircksenstr.
Münzstr.
Max - Beer - Str.
Rosa - Luxemburg - Str.
VOLKSBÜHNE
Rosa-Luxemburg-Pl.
Karl-Liebknecht-Haus
Liebknecht - Str.
Prenzlauer Allee
Mollstr.
Otto - Braun - Str.
ALEXANDERPLATZ
Hotel Park Inn Berlin
Urania
KARL-MARX-ALLEE
KONGRESSHALLE
Alexanderplatz
Monbijoupark
Hackescher Markt
Rosenstr.
Roch-
FERNSEHTURM
Karl-
MUSEUMSINSEL
BERLINER DOM
Marienkirche
Neptunbrunnen
Marx-Engels-Forum
ROTES RATHAUS
Lustgarten
Gruner-
Dircksenstr.
Alexander-str.
Magazinstr.
NIKOLAIVIERTEL
SCHLOSSPLATZ
Parochialk.
STADTHAUS
Klosterstr.
Littenstr.
Molkenmarkt
Stralauer Str.
SPREE
Jannowitzbrücke
Breite Str.
Mühlendamm
Petripl.
FISCHERINSEL
MÄRKISCHES MUSEUM
Märkisches Museum
Köllnischer Park
Brückenstr.
Auswärtiges Amt
Kurstr.
Spittelmarkt
Wall - str.
0
300 m
X
Y
Z

Name	Map	Grid	Key
Abgeordnetenhaus von Berlin (ehem. Preußischer Landtag)	3	KV	P^1
Abspannwerk Scharnhorst.	3	JS	W^1
Akademie der Künste (Tiergarten)	2	HU	Q^1
Alexanderhaus	6	QY	B
Alte Nationalgalerie	6	PY	M^{20}
Alter Jüdischer Friedhof	6	PX	X
Altes Museum	6	PY	M^{18}
Abhalter Bahnhof	3	KX	B^3
Berliner Ensemble	5	OY	T^{10}
Berolinahaus	6	QY	C
Botschaft der Republik Indien	3	JV	A^3
Botschaft der Russischen Föderation	5	OZ	A^1
Bundesministerium des Justiz	5	OZ	G^6
Bundesministerium für Bildung und Forschung	5	OX	G^7
Bundesminiterium für familie, Senioren, Frauen und Jugend	5	OZ	G^5
Bundesminsterium für Verkehr, Bau- und Wohnungswesen	5	NX	G^3
Bundesminsterium für Wirtschaft und Technologie	5	NX	G^4
Charlottenburger Tor	2	GV	A^2
Deutsche Guggenheim	5	OZ	Q^2
Deutscher Dom	5	OZ	N^1
Deutsches Theater	5	NX	T^{13}
Dorotheenstädtischer und Französischer Friedhof	5	OX	K^3
Ephraim-Palis	6	PZ	S
Ermelerhaus	6	QZ	D
Franziskaner-Klosterkirche	6	QY	W
Französischer Dom	5	OZ	N
Friedrichstadtpalast	5	OY	T^{11}
Friedrichswerdersche Kirche	6	PZ	M^{22}
Garnisonsfriedhof	6	PX	K^4
Gedenkstätte Deutscher Widerstand	3	JV	M^9
Gemäldegalerie	3	JV	M^6
Gouverneurhaus	5	OZ	G^2
Görlitzer Park	4	MX	
Haus der Kulturen der Welt (ehem, Kongreßhalle)	3	JU	V^1
Haus des Lehrers	6	QY	A
Hebbel Theater	3	KX	T^2
Heckmannhöfe	5	OX	K^2
Heiliggeistkapelle	6	PY	C^1
Kammergericht	2	HY	J
Kammerspiele	5	NX	T^{14}
Katholische Akademie und Kirche St. Thomas von Aquin	5	NX	K^1
Knoblauchlaus	6	PZ	M^{21}
Komische Oper	5	OZ	T^{16}
Kreditanstalt für den Wiederaufbau	5	OZ	Q^3
Kreuzberg	4	LX	
Kronprinzenpalais	6	PZ	H^1
Kunstgewerbemuseum	3	JV	M^5
Kunsthof	5	OX	K^5
Käthe-Kollwitz-Museum	2	GX	M^{10}
Künstlerhaus Bethanien	4	MV	E^1
Ludwig-Erhard-Haus	2	GV	C^4
Marheinike-Halle	4	MX	F^2
Maxim-Gorki-Theater (ehem. Singakademie)	5	OY	T^{18}
Metropol-Theater	5	OY	T^9
Mohrenkolonnaden	5	OZ	P
Mossehaus	3	KV	C^3
Museum für Kindheit und Jugend	6	QZ	M^{23}
Museum für Kommunikation Berlin	5	KV	M^1
Musikinstrumenten-Museum	3	JV	M^4
Neue Nationalgalerie	3	JV	M^7
Neuer Marstall	6	PZ	Z^1
Neues Kriminalgericht	2	HT	J^1
Neues Museum	6	PY	M^{19}
Nicolaihaus	6	PZ	F
Nicolaikirche	6	PZ	Q
Palast der Republik	6	PY	Z
Philharmonie, Kammermusiksall	3	JV	T^3
Podewil-Palais	6	QY	V
Prinzessinnenpalais	5	OZ	G^1
Rathaus (Chalottenburg)	1	FU	R
Reiterdenkmal Friedrichs II	5	OZ	D^1
Ribbeck-Haus	6	PZ	G
Robert-Koch-Museum	5	NY	M^{17}
Schadowhaus	5	NY	C^2
Schauspielhaus	5	OZ	T^{15}
Sophienkirche	5	PX	Y
Spittelkolonnade	6	PZ	E
St. Bonifatius	3	KY	D^2
St. Hedwigs-Kathedrale	5	OZ	F1
Staatsbibliothek-Preußischer Kulturbesitz (Kulturforum)	3	JV	M^8
Staatsbibliothek-Preußischer Kulturbesitz (Unter den Linden)	5	OY	B^2
Staatsoper Unter den Linden	5	QZ	T^{17}
Staatsratsgebäude	6	PZ	Z^2
Stadtbibliothek	6	PZ	B^1
Stadtgericht	6	QY	J
Theater des Westerns	2	GV	T^8
Tierarzneischule (Altes Anatomiegebäude)	5	NX	T^{12}
Topographie des Terrors	3	KV	S^1
Villa Von-der-Heydt «Stiftung Preußischer Kulturbesitz»	2	HV	H
Zuckermuseum	2	HS	M^{14}

Berliner Dom★

♿ *Open Apr to Sep, 9am-8pm, Thu, 9am-10pm, Sun 12 noon-8pm; Oct to Mar, 9am-7pm, Sun, 12 noon-7pm. €5.10. ☎ (030) 20 26 91 52; www.berliner-dom.de*

This imposing building in the Italian Renaissance style was constructed between 1894 and 1905. Its magnificent **interior★★** exudes the impression of might and power; the cathedral can seat congregations of 1 500. In the southern part of the church is the splendid sarcophagus of Frederick I and his second wife Sophie Charlotte, a work by Andreas Schlüter. Part of the cathedral **crypt** is open to the public. It contains over 90 sarcophagi with the remains of five centuries of the Prussian-Brandenburg Hohenzollern family.

At this point it is possible to prolong your walk to take a look at the modern districts via Karl Liebknechstraße.

Alexanderplatz★

The name of this square derives from Tsar Alexander's visit to Berlin in 1805. An important public transport junction and immense commercial centre, the square – known as "Alex" by locals – acts as a focus of city life in the eastern sector of Berlin. It was completely destroyed during the Second World War and mostly rebuilt in the austere style of socialist architecture. The **Marienkirche** (late 14C: 15C Danse Macabre fresco in the tower; Baroque pulpit by Schlüter) looks flimsy indeed at the foot of the 365m/1 198ft **Fernsehturm★** (Television Tower). The revolving sphere at the top of the tower houses a restaurant and a panoramic viewing platform.

South of the square stands the **Rotes Rathaus★** (Red Town Hall), built from 1861 to 1869 entirely of bricks and sporting a 97m/318ft tower.

Nikolaiviertel★ (St Nicholas Quarter)

With its narrow cobbled streets and its old taverns, this quarter of restored period houses – including the **Knoblauch house★** (Knoblauchhaus – *Poststraße 23; open Tue-Sun, 10am-6pm. Closed 24 and 31 Dec. €1, free admission on Wed. ☎ (030) 27 57 67 33; www.stadtmuseum.de*) and the **Ephraim palace★** (Ephraim-Palais – *between Poststraße and Mühlendamm; ♿ Open Tue-Sun, 10am-6pm. Closed 24 and 31 Dec. €3, free admission on Wed. ☎ (030) 24 00 21 21; www.stadtmuseum.de*) – between the Rathaus and the Spree, and between the Rathausstraße and Mühlendamm, seems like a country town transported to the heart of the city.

The quarter is dominated by the neo-Gothic bell-towers of the **Nikolaikirche★**, the oldest church in Berlin. The old Romanesque basilica, with its Gothic chancel (1379), was transformed into a brick-built Gothic hall-church after the great fire which ravaged the city in 1380. Inside, **museum** exhibits explain the construction of the church and its significance as a creative hub and burial place of major Berlin personalities. Its interior decoration includes remarkable tombs and sacred paintings and sculptures ranging from the Gothic period to the 18C.

TIERGARTEN DISTRICT★

The oldest park in the city stretches almost 3km/2mi from Ernst-Reuter-Platz to the Brandenburg Gate. Originally a royal hunting reserve, then a military exercise area, it was transformed – thanks to the celebrated landscape architect Peter Joseph Lenné (1789-1866) – into a delightful English-style park. The Hanse residential quarter, a model of town planning which lies to the north, was reconstructed in 1957 by 14 world-famous architects. The **Kulturforum** complex stretches out to the southeast.

Siegessäule (Victory Column)

Open Apr to Oct, 9.30am-6.30pm, Sat-Sun, 9.30am-7pm; Nov to Mar, 9.30am-5.30pm. Closed 23 and 24 Dec. €2.20. All of 67m/220ft high, this landmark monument, surmounted by a Victory, commemorates the Prussian campaigns of 1864, 1866 and 1870 against Denmark, Austria and France. From the top (285 steps), there is an aerial **view★** of the Spree, the Hanse complex, the Tiergarten, the Brandenburg Gate, Unter den Linden, the Berlin Rathaus and the 12km/8mi perspective that extends to the shores of the Havel.

Schloß Bellevue

Built in the neo-Classical style by Boumann in 1785, this was the summer palace of Frederick the Great's younger brother, Prince Augustus-Ferdinand. Today it is the official residence of the President of the Republic.

Behind the castle there is a 20ha/50-acre park, the western sector being laid out in the English fashion.

Zoologischer Garten★★★ (Zoological Gardens)

Main entrance: Hardenbergplatz. ♿ Summer: 9am-6.30pm; rest of the year: from 9am to nightfall. €9. ☎ (030) 25 40 10; www.zoo-berlin.de. Situated in the heart of Berlin, this zoo, with 14 000 creatures from more than 1 400 species, is one of the largest in the world.

The Aquarium *(entry via the zoo or directly from Budapester Straße)* displays an important collection of approximately 650 species. On the first floor are the widely renowned crocodile hall and the terrarium. *♿ Open 9am-6pm. €9. ☎ (030) 25 40 10; www.aquarium-berlin.de*

KNAUTSCHKE THE SURVIVOR

The end of the war was a difficult time for the animals at the zoo; the locals were using them for food, just as they were using trees from the Tiergarten for heat. One writer, Stefan Reisner (*Stadtfront, Berlin West Berlin*, 1982), recalls his father returning home with a camel's hump which he melted in a frying pan. However, the hippopotamus Knautschke was more fortunate. He stayed underwater during the final days of the conflict, re-emerging a true hero once the bombardments were over.

KURFÜRSTENDAMM DISTRICT★

Kurfürstendamm★★

In the 16C, the Kurfürstendamm was no more than a simple path allowing the Prince Electors to reach the Grunewald hunting lodge. It was Bismarck who transformed it, between 1882 and 1886, into the prestigious thoroughfare known to Berliners today as the "Ku'Damm". Along its 3.5km/2mi length, the boulevard unites the cafés, restaurants, theatres, cinemas, galleries and fashion boutiques that make this area the centre of cosmopolitan high life in the capital.

Kaiser-Wilhelm-Gedächtniskirche★ (Kaiser Wilhelm Memorial Church)

♿ Open 9am-7pm. Free admission. ☎ (030) 218 50 23; www.gedaechtniskirche.com

This neo-Romanesque church was built between 1891 and 1895 as a memorial to the Emperor Wilhelm I. It was badly damaged during the Second World War, but the ruins were preserved as a reminder of the horrors of conflict and have become a symbol of Berlin. The shattered tower has been incorporated in a modernistic complex (1959-61) of pierced concrete modules in polygonal form, lit by 20 000 blue glass windows designed by Gabriel Loire and made in Chartres.

The former entrance beneath the tower has been arranged as a **Memorial Hall**. An exhibition traces the history of the church, recalls the victims of the war, and pleads for reconciliation. On the ceiling and walls, **mosaics★** (1906) to the glory of the Hohenzollerns and the Empire are in a good state of preservation.

Tauentzienstraße

This is the fashionable shopping street where the **"KaDeWe"**, said to be the largest department store in Europe, is situated. The abbreviation stands for Kaufhaus des Westens: Big Store of the West. Behind the Gedächtniskirche is the **Europa-Center**, a shopping and business complex which also offers restaurants, cinemas and the

famous cabaret "Die Stachelschweine" (The Porcupines). The water-clock on the Blumenhof is by the Frenchman Bernard Gitton. From the roof of this building, 100m/328ft above the street *(lift to the 20th floor then staircase for the last two storeys)* there is a fine **view★** over the centre of the city.
The fountain in the square between the Gedächtniskirche and the Europa-Center, with its bronze scelptures and exotic figures, symbolises the terrestrial globe. Berliners call it simply "**Wasserklops**" (the "water meatball").

Special Features

MUSEUMSINSEL★★★ (MUSEUM ISLAND)

Created at the instigation of Frederick William III at the beginning of the 19C, this museum complex between the Spree and the canal stands on the site of Berlin's former sister town, Cölln, which was first mentioned in 1237. A competition was launched for the redesign of the Museumsinsel. The winning project will involve reconstruction of the Neues Museum – destroyed during the Second World War – by English architect David Chipperfield. It will take over the Egyptian Museum collections. Famous German architect Oswald Mathias Ungers won a further competition to extend the Pergamonmuseum. The plan is ultimately to connect all the museums on the island (with the exception of the Alte Nationalgalerie) in an Archaeological Promenade by 2010.

Pergamonmuseum★★★ (Pergamon Museum)

Entrance Kupfergraben. ♿ Open every day except Mon, 10am-6pm, Thurs 10am-10pm. €6, free admission 1st Sun of each month. ☎ (030) 20 90 55 66; www.smb.spk-berlin.de. Built between 1909 and 1930, according to the plans of Alfred Messel who died before the works began, and under the supervision of Ludwig Hoffmann, this is the island's most recent museum. Particularly renowned for its monumental reconstructions, it is divided into three sections (we indicate, for each one, the main centres of interest).

Collection of Antiquities★★★ *(Antikensammlung)* – **Altar of Pergamon★★★**, a masterpiece of Hellenistic art, dedicated to Zeus (2C BC); richly ornate gateway to the Milet market★★ (2C AD); Greek and Roman sculptures; objets d'art and mosaics.

Middle East Museum★ *(Vorderasiatisches Museum)* – **Processional Way and Ishtar Gate★★** from ancient Babylon, 580 BC (rooms 8 and 9); Plinth of Asachadon, 7C BC (room 3); brick façade of the Temple of the Goddess Irmin at Uruk (Sumerian period); bas-relief sculptures of the Temple of Assurnasirpal II at Kalchu, 9C BC (rooms 10 and 11).

Museum of Islamic Art★★ *(Museum für Islamische Kunst)* – Façade of Omayyade Castle, Mchatta (8C), east Jordan; painted and lacquered panelling from a house in Aleppo (early 17C); miniatures (15C-17C).

Alte Nationalgalerie★★ (Old National Gallery)

Entrance Bodestraße. ♿ Open every day except Mon, 10am-6pm, Thurs 10am-10pm. €6, free admission 1st Sun of each month. ☎ (030) 20 90 55 66; www.smb.spk-berlin.de. This building, designed by Friedrich August Stüler, (1864-74), exhibits paintings and sculptures from the 19C. After being closed for renovation for four years, it reopened to the public in December 2001.

In the upper exhibition gallery, where the visit begins, the display includes works from the time of Goethe until Late Romanticism (among others: **Caspar David Friedrich**, Waldmüller, Blechen, Schinkel). The middle floor displays the works of Feuerbach, Böcklin, Marées, Leibl, Liebermann, the French Impressionists, and German and Flemish historical scenes. On the lower floor exhibits include Realism with the focus on Berlin painters and sculptors (**Adolph Menzel**, Krüger, Schadow) and Realist landscapes (Constable, Courbet).

Bode-Museum★★

Entrance Monbijoubrücke. Closed for restoration until 2005. This splendid neo-Baroque edifice completed in 1904 at the tip of Museumsinsel has been closed since mid-1999 for a thorough renovation and restructuring of the interiors. The idea is now to make the best of the outstanding potential of the building, with its three exhibition floors and four interior courtyards. When it is reopened in 2005, the Bode-Museum will house the entire reunited **Sculpture Collection** including the **Museum of Late Antique and Byzantine Art** (Museum für Spätantike und Byzantinische Kunst), as well as the **Numismatic Collection**, which portrays the history of coins and money.

Altes Museum★★ (Old Museum)

♿ Open Tue-Sun, 10am-6pm. Closed Easter and Pentecost, 24, 25 and 31 Dec. €6, free admission 1st Sun of each month. ☎ (030) 20 90 55 66; www.smb.spk-berlin.de
Berlin's first public museum, built by Schinkel between 1824 and 1830. The main entrance, which is 87m/285ft high and boasts 18 Ionic columns, is a masterpiece of neo-Classical art. Inside, note particularly the frescoes decorating the cupola

The Altes Museum on Museumsinsel, Berlin's first public museum.

(rotunda). The building, severely damaged during the war, was reconstructed between 1951 and 1966; the granite basin (7m/23ft diameter) in front of the museum was originally intended for the inside of the rotunda.

Nowadays, the ground floor houses the **Antikensammlung** (Collection of Antiquities), specifically the smaller items (the monumental works are located in the Pergamonmuseum). The tour of Ancient Greek art and cultural history begins with the marble idols from the Cyclades (3rd millennium BC). It then covers the Archaic Period (7C-5C BC), Hellenism and finally the Roman Empire.

The **Antique jewellery** (Antiker Schmuck, located in two treasure chambers) is fascinating as well. It includes the gold discoveries from Vettersfelde (c 500 BC), from Tarent (3C BC) and the **Hildesheimer Silberfund★★★** (Hildesheim Silver Hoard) from the Roman era.

The upper storey is used for temporary exhibitions.

The Museums of Berlin

The Altes Museum, the first museum to grace Berlin, was built in 1830 by Karl Friedrich Schinkel. It was followed during the rule of Frederick William IV by the Neues Museum and Nationalgalerie on the Museumsinsel. Wilhelm von Bode, director of the Berlin museums from 1906 onward, made a major contribution to the further organisation of the city's collections, using his energy and far-sightedness to bring them to the attention of connoisseurs worldwide.

Reconstruction of the destroyed museums began after the Second World War. The collections had either been protected from destruction or confiscated by the victorious powers. Some had been pillaged. The post-war situation, with Germany divided and the city under Allied control also resulted in the dividing of the museum collections. When the German Reich vanished so did Prussia, and it was then formally dissolved by Law no 46 of the Allied Control Council passed in 1947. Prussia's heritage was kept in both halves of Germany. The Stiftung Preußischer Kulturbesitz (Foundation for Prussian Cultural Property) was founded in the west in 1957, while the heritage in the east gathered at the traditional spot: the "Museumsinsel".

After the unification of Germany in 1990, the administration of Berlin museums was also unified in 1992 under the umbrella of the Stiftung Preußischer Kulturbesitz – Staatliche Museen zu Berlin.

KULTURFORUM IM TIERGARTEN AND SURROUNDING AREA

The Kulturforum was designed, in the late 1950s, to become the cultural centre of West Berlin, thus constituting a counterpart to the Museumsinsel in the eastern part of the city. Not far from the vast Potsdamer Platz, it now stands in the heart of the reunified capital.

Gemäldegalerie★★★ (Picture Gallery)

♿ *Open every day except Mon, 10am-6pm, Thurs 10am-10pm. Closed Easter and Pentecost, 24, 25 and 31 Dec. €6, free admission 1st Sun of each month.* ☎ *(030) 20 90 55 66; www.smp.spk-berlin.de*

The collection was born from the collecting passion of the Great Elector (1620-88) and Frederick the Great (1712-86). However, it was **Wilhelm von Bode**, director of the Gemäldegalerie beginning in 1890, who so indefatigably pushed for new acquisitions, so that by the outbreak of the First World War, a comprehensive collection of European painting from the 13C to the 18C had been brought together. The transfer of the picture gallery to the Kulturforum and, in the summer of 1998, the converging of the collections from the Bode-Museum and the Dahlem-Museum, put an end to 50 years of division and provisional states. In spite of losses to the war (400 paintings were destroyed), the collection today is still considered one of the finest in the world.

The modest building was conceived by the architects Heinz Hilmer and Christoph Sattler in such a way that all the rooms receive light from above. The 53 rooms are arranged in a horseshoe around a central foyer and provide space for over 1 100 paintings. The Study Gallery *(Studiengalerie)* on the ground floor displays other valuable works.

The works are presented in chronological order and arranged by school. The schools are listed below along with some of the artists and paintings on display:

Rooms I-III, Galleries 1-4: German School, 13C-16C (Late Gothic/Renaissance), notably illustrated by Martin Schongauer *(The Birth of Christ)*, Lucas Cranach the Elder (*Venus und Amor, Adam and Eve*), Hans Holbein the Younger *(The Merchant Georg Gisze)*, Albrecht Dürer (*Portrait of Hieronymus Holzschuher*).

Rooms IV-VI, Galleries 5-7: Dutch School, 15C-16C (Late Gothic/Renaissance: Gérard David, Hans Memling, Hugo Van der Goes, Jan Gossaert, Jan Van Eyck, Quentin Metsys and Pieter Bruegel the Elder, including his famous painting *The Netherlandish Proverbs*).

Rooms VII-XI, Galleries 8-19: Flemish and Dutch Schools, 17C (Baroque). This is an extremely impressive section; among the artists represented here are Peter Paul Rubens *(Child with a Bird, Virgin and Child)*, his pupil Anthony van Dyck (*Portrait of a Wealthy Genoan Couple*), Matthias Stomer *(Esau Sells his Birth Right)*, Rembrandt *(Self-portrait, Moses Shatters the Decalogue, Susanna and the Two Old Men, The Man with the Golden Helmet)*, Jacob van Ruisdael *(Oaks by the Lake with Water Lilies)*, Jan Bruegel the Elder *(Flower Bouquet)*, Frans Hals *(Singing Child with Flute)*, Jan Vermeer van Delft *(The Glass of Wine)*.

Galleries 20-22: English, French and German Schools, 18C (Rococo/Neo-Classicism), with works by Thomas Gainsborough *(The Marsham Children)*, Antoine Watteau *(The Dance)*, Jean-Baptiste-Siméon Chardin *(The Painter)*, Antoine Pesne *(Frederick the Great as Crown Prince)*.

Rooms XII-XIV, Galleries 23-26, 28: Italian School, 17C-18C (Baroque/Mannerism); French School, **17C; Spanish School, 16C-17C** (Mannerism/Baroque). Exhibits here include Francesco Guardi *(Canal Grande in Venice)*, Canaletto *(Canal Grande with View of the Rialto Bridge)*, Velázquez *(Portrait of a Lady)*, Caravaggio *(Amor as Victor)*, Claude Lorrain *(Ideal Roman Landscape)*, Nicolas Poussin *(Self-portrait)*, Georges de La Tour *(Peasant Couple Eating Peas)*.

Rooms XV-XVII, Galleries 29-32: Italian School, late 15C-16C (Late Renaissance/Mannerism). This part of the museum contains works by Correggio *(Leda with the Swan)*, Parmigianino *(Christ's Baptism)*, Titian *(Venus with the Organist, Portrait of a Bearded Young Man)*, Tintoretto *(Virgin and Child*), and several paintings by Raphael (including the *Madonna Terranuova*).

Gallery 34: miniatures, 16C-18C, including *Katharine of Bora* (Martin Luther's wife) by Lucas Cranach the Elder.

Room XVIII, Galleries 35-41: Italian School, 13C-late 15C (Gothic/Early Renaissance), including Botticelli *(Saint Sebastian, Virgin Enthroned)*, Giovanni Bellini, Andrea Mantegna *(Representation of Christ in the Temple)*, Fra Angelico *(The Day of Judgement)*, Lorenzo Monaco *(The Last Supper)*.

Study Gallery. Top-quality paintings from all schools are also exhibited here, including some very beautiful still-life paintings: Jan Fyt: *Still-life with Fish and Fruit*; Jan Davidsz de Heem: *Still-life with Fruit and Lobster*; Pieter Claesz: *Still-life with a Drinking Vessel and Fruit.*

5-7-9

The three-naved foyer of the Gemäldegalerie, a wonderfully designed space, boasts a single work of art: a sculpture by the American conceptual sculptor Walter De Maria entitled *The 5-7-9 Series*. It consists of 27 polygonal, highly polished steel staffs ordered in three rows in a granite water basin. The pentagonal, heptagonal and nonagonal staffs have been put together according to all kinds of mathematical combinations. This work of art is a good conclusion to a visit to the Gemäldegalerie, as it makes the viewer come down to earth, test his or her imagination or merely pause and rest.

Kunstgewerbemuseum★★ (Museum of Decorative Arts)

Matthäikirchplatz. ♿ Open every day except Mon 10am-6pm, Sat-Sun 11am-6pm. Closed Easter and Pentecost, 24, 25 and 31 Dec. €3, free admission 1st Sun of each month. ☎ (030) 266 29 02; www.smb.spk-berlin.de

This is the Kulturforum's oldest museum. The spacious interior layout and the clear presentation make for a very pleasant visit. The museum houses a magnificent collection of works in silver and gold and has an annex in Schloß Köpenick. It gives a very good insight into decorative art from the Middle Ages to contemporary industrial design.

Gallery I *(ground floor)* is devoted to the Middle Ages. Just inside the entrance, the Enger-Herford (Westphalia) **Treasure of Dionysius★** is displayed. This includes a remarkable reliquary purse encrusted with precious stones (second half of the 8C). In the centre of the gallery, the **Guelph Treasure★★★** is displayed, including a reliquary in the form of a Byzantine church with a dome (Cologne c 1175).

Gallery II *(ground floor)*: Italian furniture and majolica from the 14C to the 16C, Venetian glassware from the 16C to the 17C; **Gallery III** *(ground floor)*: **Lüneburg's municipal silver★★★** (Late Gothic and Renaissance) and jewellery from Nuremburg; **Gallery IV** *(first floor)*: the splendid **Pommern Cabinet★** and its contents; Gallery V *(first floor)*: 17C-18C porcelain from China and Germany, Gallery VI *(first floor)*: Biedermeier and Jugendstil objets d'art, panelled glass cabinet from Schloß Wiesentheid in Franconia (1724); Gallery VII *(first floor)*: porcelain, earthenware (glazed) and glass from the Jugendstil (Art Nouveau) and Art Deco periods. Galleries IX and X *(basement)* exhibit the largest existing permanent collection of international design in Germany, including furniture.

Kupferstichkabinett und Sammlung der Zeichnungen und Druckgraphik★ (Prints and Drawings Collection)

Matthäikirchplatz. ♿ Exhibition: open every day except Mon, 10am-6pm, Sat-Sun 11am-6pm. Studiensaal: open every day except Mon, 9am-4pm. Closed 24, 25 and 31 Dec. Prices vary depending on the exhibition, free admission 1st Sun of each month; Studiensaal: free admission. ☎ (030) 266 20 02; www.smb.spk-berlin.de

The collection dates back to 1652, when the Great Elector purchased 2 500 drawings and watercolours. This subsequently led to the creation of an **internationally renowned Museum of Prints and Drawings** which now boasts around 1 100 000 drawings, watercolours, gouaches and pastels from the 14C to the 20C, along with 540 000 prints from the late Middle Ages to the present day. The collection of drawings by old German and Dutch masters – including 80 by Rembrandt – is truly unique. In the consultation room, visitors can ask to see works from the collection without having to wait too long. Several temporary exhibitions are organised every year.

The Matthäikirchplatz has been home to the Kunstbibliothek, a particularly richly stocked art library. Part of its function as a public reference library includes hosting special exhibitions.

Neue Nationalgalerie★★ (New National Gallery)

Potsdamer Straße 50. ♿ Open every day except Mon, 10am-6pm, Thurs 10am-10pm, Sat-Sun 11am-6pm. €6, free admission 1st Sun of each month. ☎ (030) 20 90 55 66; www.smb.spk-berlin.de. This steel and glass structure, designed in 1968 by Mies van der Rohe, houses paintings and sculptures from the 20C.

The collections include important work from the European Classical Modern art movements and the American art of the 1960s and 1970s. The exhibition begins with the forerunners of **Expressionism** and the impressive gallery of work by artists of the **Brücke** provides the first of many highlights. There follow numerous works by Lovis Corinth, Oskar Kokoschka, Wilhelm Lehmbruck and Ernst Barlach. French Cubism is represented by Picasso and Juan Gris. Other Classical Modern artists with work on display include members of the **Bauhaus** (Schlemmer, Kandinsky), George Grosz, **Paul Klee** and the Surrealist **Max Ernst**. Group Zero, the New Realists, and American painters provide the high points of contemporary art. Among the sculptures gracing the interior of the gallery and the terrace, note *The Washerwoman* by Renoir, Calder's *Heads and Tails*, and the elegant statue of *Maja* by Gerhard Marcks.

Works from the second half of the 20C are displayed in the **Hamburger-Bahnhof: Museum für Gegenwart** (Hamburg Train Station: Contemporary Art Museum).

Philharmonie★★★

Herbert-von-Karajanstraße 1. ♿ Guided tour (1hr) for individuals at 1pm. Meeting point: stage door. Closed 24-26 and 31 Dec. Free for individuals, admission charge for groups. ☎ (030) 25 48 81 56; www.berliner-philharmoniker.de

The roof of this boldly asymmetrical building by **Hans Scharoun** (1963) is in the form of a giant wave. The Berlin Philharmonic Orchestra, directed from 1954 to 1989 by **Herbert von Karajan**, plays here – the musicians sit in the middle of the auditorium, surrounded by tiered rows of seats that can accommodate up to 2 200 people. Von Karajan's successor, **Claudio Abbado**, passed the baton to Sir Simon Rattle in September 2002. The **Chamber Music Hall** (1988), built beside the Philharmonia by Scharoun and his pupil Edgar Wisniewski, can seat an audience of 1 150. Here, the roof is shaped like a tent. The **Musical Instruments Museum★** *(Musikinstrumenten-Museum)* is housed in an annexe *(Tiergartenstraße 1)*, also designed by Scharoun and Wisniewski. Keyboard instruments, strings and percussion dating back to the 16C can be seen in this museum. *♿ Open every day except Mon, 9am-5pm, Sat-Sun 10am-5pm. Closed 1st Jan, 1st May, 24, 25 and 31 Dec. €3, free admission 1st Sun of each month. ☎ (030) 25 48 11 78; www.sim.spk-berlin.de*

The massive **National Library★** *(Staatsbibliothek Preußischer Kulturbesitz)*, which faces the Neue Nationalgalerie and houses some 3.7 million volumes, is also the work of Scharoun. It is worth a visit if only to admire the interior. The reading room provided the setting for a beautiful scene in Wim Wenders' *Wings of Desire*.

Gedenkstätte Deutscher Widerstand (Monument to German Resistance)

Stauffenbergstraße 13-14. Open every day except Mon, 9am-6pm (Thurs 8pm), Sat-Sun 10am-6pm. Closed 1st Jan, 23-26 and 31 Dec. Free admission, free guided tour Sun at 3pm. ☎ (030) 26 99 50 00; www.gdw-berlin.de. The monument stands on the site of the former army headquarters. This is where Claus Schenk, Count of Stauffenberg, had his office, which served as the planning centre for the attempted overthrow of Hitler on 20 July 1944.

An exhibition describes German resistance to the Nazis.

Potsdamer Platz★★

A legendary place in the Berlin of the inter-war years, this square was, for a long time, the busiest crossroads in Europe. Split in two by the Wall when the city was divided, it was left as waste ground until some private investors restored it to its former glory after the reunification. In 1990, Sony became the second largest investor in Potsdamer Platz after Daimler-Chrysler.

H. Champollion/MICHELIN

A showcase of Berlin's avant-garde architecture: the Sony Center on Potsdamer Platz.

DAHLEM MUSEUMS – INTERNATIONAL ART AND CULTURE★★★

The former seigneurial domain of Dahlem, strewn with villas in the style of English cottages, adapted to their Brandenburg setting by **Hermann Muthesius** (1861-1927), remains a leafy residential suburb. Endowed with a vast university, whose buildings – though low-rise – are not a natural match for the villas, this district is of particular interest on account of its remarkable set of museums. The great amount of space left after the Gemäldegalerie moved to the Kulturforum and the collections of the Museum of Islamic Art were brought together in the Pergamonmuseum, was ideal for the collections of the Ethnographic Museum, the Museum of Far Eastern Art and the Museum of Indian Art. These three museums, together with the Museum of European Cultures, are now officially known as **Museen Dahlem – Kunst und Kulturen der Welt** (Dahlem Museums – International Art and Culture).

Ethnologisches Museum★★★ (Museum of Ethnography)

Lansstraße entrance. ♿ Open every day except Mon, 10am-6pm, Sat-Sun 11am-6pm. €3, free admission 1st Sun of each month. ☎ (030) 20 90 55 66; www.smb.spk-berlin.de. The collections in this museum, comprising some 400 000 objects, are among the most impressive of their kind in the world.

Ancient American Cultures Section★★★ – **Religious and secular Aztec statuary** (human sacrifice cup); pre-Inca cloths in multicoloured designs and anthropomorphic ceramics from Peru. **The Gold Room★★★** displays magnificent jewels and exquisitely engraved cult objects dating from the 7C BC to the 11C AD.

Oceania Section★★ – Among the exhibits gathered during sea voyages in the Pacific since the end of the 18C, some by Captain James Cook's expeditions, note the painted **masks** and **wooden sculptures** from New Guinea, the spectacular **Oceanian boats**, and the magnificent ochre and red feathered cloak of the king of Hawaii.

Southern Asia★ – Exhibits from south-east Asia, India and Sri Lanka, including masks, puppets and Chinese shadow theatre figures evoke the culture of this region. Indonesia is represented by a sizeable collection of carved and painted figures used in religious ceremonies and textiles.

North and West Africa Section★★ – The most interesting objects in this collection include **terracotta heads from Ife** (Nigeria), **bronzes** from the ancient kingdom of Benin, and Berber jewellery. There are also some interesting wooden sculptures from Cameroon.

Museum für Indische Kunst★★ (Museum of Indian Art)

Lansstraße entrance. This museum's permanent exhibition is divided into three sections: the Indian subcontinent, south-east Asia and the Silk Road – covering India, of course, but also Pakistan, Afghanistan, Sri Lanka, Nepal, Tibet, Myanmar and Vietnam. The highlight of this museum is the **Turfan collection★★** (named after an oasis in Chinese Turkestan) with its wall paintings, statues, fabrics and manuscripts, together with the reconstruction of the cave temple known as the "Cave with the Ringbearing Doves".

Museum für Ostasiatische Kunst★ (Museum of Far-Eastern Art)

Lansstraße entrance. This museum reopened in 2000 with twice as much exhibition space. It is devoted to China, Japan and Korea and displays include items made of bronze, wood, ivory, lacquer and ceramic dating from the third millennium BC to the present.

Museum Europäischer Kulturen★ (Museum of European Cultures)

Im Winkel 6/8. ♿ Open every day except Mon, 10am-6pm, Sat-Sun 11am-6pm. €3, free admission 1st Sun of each month. ☎ (030) 20 90 55 55; www.smb.spk-berlin.de

The Museum of Folklore was founded by Virchow in 1889. After the Second World War, a second museum of folklore and ethnology was created in the western part of the city. In 1992, the two were merged together in the Dahlem museum buildings. The museum collects items from folk culture from the 16C to the present. Following refurbishment, it reopened to the public in the summer of 1999, and offers a wide-ranging programme of exhibitions (special exhibitions, cultural family days, Easter and Christmas market). *The tour starts on the upper floor.*

1st floor – Under the heading "Cultural Contacts in Europe", the theme of the permanent exhibition is the evolution of the images in European culture, beginning with the wonderful artistry of individually created religious artworks, printed images as the basis for paintings on the walls of living rooms, furniture and other household items, all the way to the mass commodities of our times.

Ground floor – Images are first of all presented in the light of three monotheist religions: Judaism, Christianity and Islam. The focus then moves to religion's role in society in the 19C and 20C.

SCHLOß CHARLOTTENBURG★★★

Allow one day for the tour.

♿ Silverware room (Silberkammer), crown gallery (Kronkabinett) and apartments of Frederick William IV: open every day except Mon, 9am-5pm, Sat-Sun 10am-5pm. €2. ☎ (0331) 969 42 02; www.spsg.de

Charlottenburg was originally the favourite retreat of Queen Sophie-Charlotte, wife of Frederick I, who set up the first literary court in Brandenburg and Prussia here in 1695. With the philosopher-mathematician Leibniz she founded a scientific society in 1700. After her untimely death in 1705, the palace at Liezenburg was renamed Charlottenburg in her honour. What had been a small summer residence in 1695 was soon enlarged, and a dome was added in 1710. The modern, gilded figure of Fortune on top of this cupola serves as a weather vane. Charlottenburg was abandoned by the Soldier-King, but Frederick II had a new east wing added by Knobelsdorff, whose columned portico was the sole decorative motif. Later, Queen Louise, the wife of Frederick William III, lived in the palace. Since the serious damage it sustained during the Second World War, Schloß Charlottenburg has been rebuilt as new and most of the interior restored.

In the **Cour d'honneur★** stands an equestrian statue of the Great Elector, the masterpiece of Andreas Schlüter (1703).

Historic Apartments★★

Ground floor of central block (Altes Schloß). Guided tours: 1hr. ♿ Guided tour: every day except Mon, 9am-5pm, Sat-Sun 10am-5pm. Closed 24, 25 and 31 Dec. €8. ☎ (0331) 969 42 02; www.spsg.de. The tour begins in a room containing two models showing the palace and gardens in the 18C (Baroque gardens) and early 19C (after conversion to an English style landscape garden by Lenné).

The three small rooms in the **Mecklenburg Apartment** feature superbly carved overdoors. Do not miss the chimneypiece in the bedchamber.

The official function rooms stretch along a length of 140m/460ft overlooking the gardens. They are adorned with family portraits of the Houses of Hohenzollern and Hanover, and contain finely lacquered furniture and Sophie Charlotte's harpsichord. Note also the bathroom near the king's bedchamber. The famous **Porcelain Room★★** (1706) houses a magnificent collection of Oriental porcelain, reconstituted after the Second World War and housed in wall niches and on ledges and display tables. The **Palace Chapel★** (*Schloßkapelle* – 1706) is occasionally also used as a concert venue. Above the royal pew is an enormous crown carried by two allegorical figures, with the Prussian eagle above it.

The fine free-standing **staircase** by Eosander, architect of the palace extension after 1702, was the first of its kind in Germany.

The Crown Prince's Silverware

This masterpiece of 20C German craftsmanship was a gift from 414 Prussian cities on the occasion of the marriage of Crown Prince William, son of William II, to Duchess Cecilia of Mecklenburg-Schwerin in 1904. Completed in 1914, the dinner service never belonged to the couple. Following the Hohenzollerns' abdication, it became the property of the Berlin Senate and is now on long-standing loan to Schloß Charlottenburg. It was taken to the USA for a short while at the end of the Second World War, when it was known as the "Hohenzollern silver". The dinner service originally contained 2 600 pieces for fifty place settings on a 16m/53ft-long table. Most of the napkins and glasses (there were five different kinds) have disappeared. Terrines, plates and salad bowls are on display on a magnificent sideboard behind the table. A working group of six people, including architects, sculptors and the director of the Museum of Decorative Arts, supervised the creation of the dinner service, which is in classical and *Jugendstil* style. The statuettes are charming and the figures monumental: elephants surmounted by an obelisk, equestrian statues and candelabra, all part of a long tradition of royal dinner services.

Climb the staircase to view the first floor of the central block.

The upper round room overlooking the main courtyard is adorned with elegant chandeliers; the upper oval room, decorated with mirrors, offers a fine view of the gardens.

The **former apartments of Frederick William IV**, the last king to be a regular visitor here, and his wife Elisabeth contain hardly any furniture. The painting entitled *Parade along Unter den Linden in 1837* by Franz Krüger recognisably features some of this famous avenue's most important buildings. The adjoining rooms exhibit part of the Schlobitten Collection (a seat of nobility in East Prussia that no longer exists) including paintings, tapestries, porcelain, goldsmiths' work and medallions. The **Crown Prince's silverware★★** is particularly interesting; this was given by the Prussian cities to Crown Prince William, son of William II, on the occasion of his betrothal to Cecilie of Mecklenburg-Schwerin in 1904. The Prussian crown jewels are on display in the **crown gallery** *(Kronkabinett)*.

New Wing★★ (Knobelsdorff Wing)

East of the central block. ♿ Open every day except Mon, 10am-6pm, Sat-Sun 11am-6pm. €5. ☎ (0331) 969 42 02; www.spsg.de. The staircase leads to the **White Room** *(Weißer Saal)* on the left, used by Frederick II as a dining room and throne room. The ceiling painting is a modern work by Hann Trier which replaced a work by Antoine Pesne destroyed in 1943.

The 42m/138ft long **Golden Gallery★★** is a large music room and dance hall in the style of "Frederician Rococo": it has been restored to its original glowing pale green, pink and gold colours.

The following rooms, Frederick II's apartments, with white and gold Rococo decor, contain important works of art from French painting of the 18C, a particular favourite of the king. These include ***Gersaint's Signboard★★★*** (1720) in the concert hall and ***Embarkation for Cythera★★★***, both by Watteau. Note also the fine Frederician furniture.

Winter apartments★ – This is where Frederick II's successors (Frederick William II and his daughter-in-law Louise, wife of Frederick William III) had their winter quarters in the late 18C and early 19C. These south-facing rooms are good examples of the rigidly disciplined elegance of early Prussian neo-Classicism. The charming **Queen Louise's Bedchamber★** is decorated in harmonious mauve tones and draped in white net. This was executed for the royal family by Schinkel (1810). The last room in this series of rooms contains a fine collection of **portraits★** of women by court painter Antoine Pesne. The three rooms on the garden side are decorated in magnificent Rococo style. A glass case in the library contains a selection from Frederick II's priceless collection of snuffboxes.

On the ground floor a model shows **Berlin Palace**, blown up in 1950 on the orders of the East German authorities. In the adjoining room are Baroque tapestries with Chinese scenes and parts of Frederick the Great's collection of **antiques**.

The **Chinese Gallery and Chinese Room**, which were part of Frederick William II's summer apartments, overlook the gardens. Frederick William III's rooms contain paintings with scenes from the Napoleonic Wars, including Jacques-Louis David's famous portrait of Napoleon on horseback.

West Wing (Great Orangery) – This Orangery wing was built by Eosander between 1701 and 1707. The architect of the old theatre (built 1788-91) at the west end of the orangery was Langhans. Directly opposite stands the Small Orangery, now a café and restaurant.

Museum für Vor- und Frühgeschichte★ (Museum of Prehistory and Early History) – *♿ Open every day except Mon, 9am-5pm, Sat-Sun 10am-5pm. Closed Easter and Pentecost, 24, 25 and 31 Dec. €3, free admission 1st Sun of each month. ☎ (030) 20 90 55 66; www.smb.spk-berlin.de.* Excellent dioramas and exhibits from archaeological digs give an overview of the history of Europe. An entire floor has been devoted to exhibitions about the Iron Age, the Hallstatt Culture,

Lausitz Culture, La Tène Culture and to the Ibero-Celts. The Roman Empire, Late Antiquity, the Middle Ages and Eurasia's Ages of Bronze and Iron are also well represented.

Schloßgarten★★

Landscaped in English style under Frederick William II, this green space is an oasis of tranquillity amid the bustle of the city. To the west, at the end of a yew and cypress walk, is a small **mausoleum★** in the form of a temple, built in 1810 by Heinrich Gentz. It contains the tombs of Frederick William III, Queen Louise, the Emperor Wilhelm I and Queen Augusta.

The New Pavilion★ (Schinkel Pavilion) *(between the east end of the Knobelsdorff Wing and the castle bridge)* was built by Schinkel in 1824 as a summer residence for Frederick William III. It was designed following Italian models. Almost all the interior decoration was also designed by Schinkel, but this was destroyed in the Second World War. The outstanding works of art, including paintings by Caspar David Friedrich, K Blechen and E Gaertner, now testify to the importance of the age of Schinkel and his contemporaries in Berlin.

North of the lake, in the direction of the Spree, is a **Belvedere★** designed by Langhans. It houses a **historic exhibition★** of the Royal Berlin Porcelain Manufactory founded by a citizens' initiative and then taken over by the king in 1763. It gives an outline of the development of Berlin porcelain from Rococo to Biedermeier.

AROUND SCHLOß CHARLOTTENBURG

Stüler Buildings

Schloßstraße 1, opposite the palace. The two domed buildings on either side of Schloßstraße were erected by Friedrich August Stüler between 1851 and 1859 as guard barracks for the royal bodyguards. The Berggruen Collection is housed in the western building, the Egyptian Museum is still located in the eastern one.

Sammlung Berggruen★★ – Picasso und seine Zeit (Berggruen Collection – Picasso and his Times)

In the western Stüler Building. ♿ Open every day except Mon, 10am-6pm. €6, free admission 1st Sun of each month. ☎ (030) 20 90 55 66; www.smb.spk-berlin.de. The collection belonging to the former Parisian art dealer Heinz Berggruen comprises mostly works by Picasso. All aspects of his œuvre are displayed: tableaux (*The Yellow Pullover*, 1929); sculptures (*Head of Fernande*, 1909), drawings and gouaches. There are also works by Cézanne, Van Gogh, Matisse, Braque, Laurens, Giacometti and African tribal art. Virtually the whole of the second floor is devoted to **Paul Klee** who was greatly admired by Heinz Berggruen; over fifty of the artist's works are on display here, including *Stadtartiger Aufbau (Urban Structure)*, a 1917 watercolour, *Betrachtung beim Frühstück* (1925, watercolour), and the painting *Klassicche Küste* (1931).

Ägyptisches Museum und Papyrussammlung★★★ (Egyptian Museum and Papyrus Collection)

In the eastern Stüler Building. Open Tue-Sun 10am-6pm, closed Easter and Pentecost, 24, 25 and 31 Dec. Ticket valid in all Preußischer Kulturbesitz museums €6, free admission 1st Sun of each month. ☎ (030) 34 35 73 11; www.smb.spk-berlin.de. Berlin's ancient Egypt collection is one of the best and most comprehensive in the world. It was founded in 1828 during the reign of King Frederick William III, on Alexander von Humboldt's recommendation. The division of Berlin resulted in the collections being shared between the Stüler Building in the western sector and the Bode-Museum on Museumsinsel (currently closed) in the eastern sector. The two collections will finally be reunited in 2009, when the Neues-Museum reopens.

The exhibits from the time of Pharaoh Akhenaton, king of Egypt between 1353 and 1336 BC, are among the highlights of the museum. The collection focuses on treasures found at **Tell-el-Amarna**, **Amenhotep IV-Akhenaton's** capital. The Deutsche-Orient-Gesellschaft, which excavated the site between 1911 and 1914, concentrated on the southern part and uncovered many private houses. All of the objects that were unearthed and which are now on display give a remarkable insight into the life of the people of Amarna. A particularly large number of finds were made at the **workshop of Thutmose**, one of the king's temple and palace sculptors. The exhibits reveal the working methods of an Egyptian artist and emphasise the uniqueness of this period in the history of ancient Egypt.

Amenhotep IV-Akhenaton's Revolutions

Upon his accession to the throne, **Amenhotep IV** – son of Tiy and Amenhotep III – imposed the idea of a single god. All other gods were set aside in favour of the representation of **Aton**, the disk of the sun whose rays terminate in human hands holding the hieroglyph that signifies life *(Ankh)*. **Amenhotep** changed his name to **Akhenaton, "One Useful to Aton"**, set up court in Tell el-Amarna and banned all worship, priests and temples related to other gods, thereby offending a rich and powerful clergy.

The reign of his son-in-law **Tutankhamen**, who abandoned Tell el-Amarna after two or three years, marked the end of this revolution.

The highlights of the museum are the impressive ebony **head of Queen Teje★★** (1355 BC), the unusually expressive **Green Head of a Priest★** (c 300 BC) and the world-famous **Bust of Queen Nefertiti★★★** (painted plaster over limestone – 1350 BC). This miraculously preserved bust was uncovered in Thutmose's workshop and served as a model for future effigies of the queen (which explains why only one eye was inlaid). The colours of this near-perfect piece accentuate the sovereign's enigmatic and sacred presence.

Bröhan Museum★ (Bröhan-Museum)

Schloßstraße 1a. ♿ Open every day except Mon, 10am-6pm. Closed 24 and 31 Dec. €4. ☎ (030) 32 69 06 00; www.broehan-museum.de. This exhibition, based on a private collection, presents arts, crafts and industrial design, including Jugendstil and Art Deco. Note, in particular, furniture from the French cabinet-makers in the 1920s (JE Ruhlmann), the art of French glassmakers (Marinot and Gallé), and the porcelain. Do not miss, either, the paintings of the Berlin Secession.

Gipsformerei der Staatlichen Museen – *Sophie-Charlotten-Straße 17-18.* The national museums' replica workshop, which contains some 6 500 figures, is located near Schloß Charlottenburg. It is one of the largest in the world, alongside those of the British Museum and of the Louvre, France. *♿ Exhibition-salesroom: open every day except Sat-Sun, 9am-4pm, Wed 9am-6pm. Closed on all public holidays. Free admission. ☎ (030) 326 76 90.*

Worth a Visit

Museum für Kommunikation Berlin★ (Museum of Berlin Telecommunications)

An der Urania 15, Leipziger Straße 16. ♿ Open every day except Mon, 9am-5pm, Sat-Sun 11am-7pm. Free admission. ☎ (030) 20 29 40; www.museumsstiftung.de. The museum has a wonderful setting in the historic building of the former Reichspost Museum. This magnificent edifice from the Wilhelminian days, which was the world's first postal museum when it was built, presents the past, present and future of communications.

Berlin German Transport and Technical Museum★★ (Deutsches Technikmuseum Berlin)

Trebbiner Straße 9. ♿ Open every day except Mon, 9am-5.30pm, Sat-Sun 10am-6pm; Mon, Easter and Pentecost 10am-6pm. Closed 1st May, 24, 25 and 31 Dec. €3. ☎ (030) 90 25 40; www.dtmb.de. Technical progress is presented as part of the cultural evolution of mankind in a series of vivid displays, housed in what was formerly the main Anhalt goods depot. Air and space travel, road traffic and maritime transport are all represented, along with the application of technology to the media, photography and energy production. A particularly impressive **Railway Section★★** includes a selection of locomotives, some of them dating back to the very earliest rail transport. In the **Spectrum**, 250 experiments demonstrate scientific phenomena to visitors.

Hamburger Bahnhof (Hamburg Station) – Museum of Contemporary Art★★ (Museum für Gegenwart Berlin)

Invalidenstraße 50-51. ♿ Open every day except Mon, 10am-6pm, Sat-Sun 11am-6pm. €6, free admission 1st Sun of each month. ☎ (030) 20 90 55 66; www.smb.spk-berlin.de. Hamburg Station, the oldest of Berlin's first generation of railway stations to have survived, was built in 1845-47. It was closed in 1884 and later became the home of the Transport and Construction Museum, for which it had a striking purpose-built metal hall added to it. This is now the focal point of the new museum designed by architect Paul Kleihues, which houses works of art from 1960 onwards. The core of it is made up of the private collection of Dr Erich Marx.

The great hall contains works by Anselm Kiefer (*Census*, 1991), Richard Long (*Berlin Circle*), Mario Merz and Günther Uecker. The long gallery houses superb works by Cy Twombly, Robert Rauschenberg and Andy Warhol. A whole room is devoted to Joseph Beuys and his installations (*Biennale-Installation Tramstop*, 1976).

Käthe-Kollwitz-Museum★ (Käthe Kollowitz Museum)

Fasanenstraße 24. Open every day except Tue, 11am-6pm. Closed 24 and 31 Dec. €5. ☎ (030) 882 52 10; www.kaethe-kollwitz.de. A broad survey of the works of the talented, Berlin-born graphic artist and sculptress Käthe Kollwitz (1867-1945). Her series of engravings *The Weavers' Revolt* (1893-98) and *The Peasants' War* (1903-08), the woodcuts titled *War* (1920-1924) and *The Proletariat* (1925), as well as the self-portraits and the late series of lithographs labelled *Death*, all mark milestones in the Kollwitz career. Well-known posters from the 1920s such as *Nie wieder Krieg (No More War)* underline the artist's political and humanistic commitment. The sculptures are exhibited on the upper floor, among them the *Muttergruppe (Mother Group)* in bronze (1924-37).

Martin-Gropius-Bau★★ (Martin Gropius Building)

Stresemannstraße 110. ♿ *Open every day except Tue, 10am-8pm. €5-7 depending on the exhibition.* ☎ *(030) 25 48 60; www.gropiusbau.de.* This neo-Renaissance building in the form of a cube (1881), inspired by Schinkel's Academy of Architecture, was originally conceived by Martin Gropius (great uncle of Walter Gropius) and Heino Schmieden as a home for the Royal Museum of Decorative Arts. Its reconstruction, after heavy war damage, was begun in 1978. Its highly refined decoration of ceramics, mosaics and stone friezes is reminiscent of an Italian palace.

The interior, with its majestic columned hall, is a living proof of the expertise of Prussian designers during the Founders' Period or Gründerzeit.

Topographie des Terrors (Topography of Terror)

♿ *May-Sep: 10am-8pm; Oct-Apr: 10am-6pm. Closed 1st Jan, 24 and 31 Dec. Free admission.* ☎ *(030) 25 48 67 03; www.topographie.de*

Adjacent to the Gropius building lies an area known as the Prinz-Albrecht-Gelände. From 1939 on, this was the Reich security and secret police centre, grouping the headquarters of the SS, the Gestapo and the SD (*Sicherheitsdienst*: Security Service). In the 1980s, on what had been considered just a stretch of wasteland, the foundations of the centre's prison building were unearthed.

In 1992 a competition was called for a new building for the planned international documentation centre and meeting place of the "Topographie des Terrors" Foundation. The winner was the Swiss architect Peter Zumthor. Until completion of the new building, an open-air exhibition can be visited on the site of the Niederkirchnerstraße excavations.

Viktoria-Park★

In the middle of this district is the highest "natural" piece of ground (66m/216ft) in the city. The hillock is surmounted by Karl Friedrich Schinkel's monument to the "Wars of Liberation". There is a panoramic view of Berlin from the terrace.

Luftbrückendenkmal (Airlift Memorial)

In the Tempelhof district, Platz der Luftbrücke. The three west-facing arcs of this structure symbolise the three air corridors still open to the Allies during the Berlin Blockade to supply the city with its necessities.

Jüdisches Museum Berlin★★ (Jewish Museum)

Lindenstraße 9-14. ♿ *10am-8pm, Mon 10am-10pm. Closed on Jewish festivals of Rosh Hashanah (Jewish New Year) and Yom Kippur (Day of Atonement), 24 Dec. €5.* ☎ *(030) 308 78 56 81; www.jmberlin.de*

The American architect Daniel Libeskind designed this spectacular lightning-shaped museum, which opened at the beginning of September 2001. This veritable labyrinth, with empty rooms that lead nowhere, is in itself a symbol for the annihilation of the Jewish-German culture. A brilliant use of architectural space adds immediacy and poignancy to the exhibits themselves.

The Jewish Museum designed by Daniel Liebeskind.

H. Champollion/MICHELIN

The permanent exhibition traces the history of the Jews in Germany from the earliest documents to the present. The significance of the Jews for the development of Berlin from the 18C to the 20C is given a special accent in the presentation, with emphasis on the Shoa, the Holocaust during the Nazi era. A special section is also devoted to the present day, showing the growth of Berlin's Jewish community following an influx of people from Russia in particular.

The Jewish Museum also owns the neighbouring building, the old Supreme Court *(Altes Kammergericht, Lindenstraße 14)*, where ETA Hoffmann was once employed.

The Wall

The border complex known simply as the "Berlin Wall" divided the city's western districts from the eastern half and from the surrounding area. Watchtowers, barbed wire and self-shooting gadgets have all long gone; on the erstwhile deathstrip, construction sites, parks or wild growth have appeared. Only few traces remain of the once divided city, such as the watchtower at the *Schlesisches Tor*, used as a museum for "Forbidden Art", or walled-in house entrances at Heidelberger Straße in the Treptow district. Remains of the actual wall can only be seen in a few places.

The longest stretch of the wall is the "East Side Gallery" in Friedrichshain. The graffiti art completed by various artists in the 1990s is in poor shape these days. More central is the bit of wall in the shadow of the former Prussian House of Parliament between the Detlev-Rohwedder-Haus (built as Göring's Reichs Air Ministry) and the grounds of the "Topography of Terror". As in no other place, the various eras of the last century of Berlin history converge here.

Bernauerstraße remains a symbol of the inhumanity of the wall. In 1998, the **Berlin Wall Memorial** (Gedenkstätte Berliner Mauer) was opened on land from the cemetery of the Sophie Community (corner of Bernauerstraße/Ackerstraße).

Museum Haus am Checkpoint Charlie (Berlin Wall Museum)

Kochstraße 6, on the corner of Friedrichstraße. 9am-10pm. €7. ☎ (030) 253 72 50; www.mauermuseum.de. Documentation on the building of the Berlin Wall and attempts to cross it, as well as on the movements for human and civil rights are on display. All kinds of extraordinary means were used to reach the west: on board a tractor, hidden in the boot of a car, in the battery and heating compartment or in a suitcase, using ladders, even via a chairlift suspended from a cable; many attempts came to a tragic end. The official figures state that 80 were killed, but the real total may have been as many as several hundred.

Märkisches Museum (March Museum)/Stiftung Stadtmuseum Berlin★ (Foundation City Museum of Berlin)

Open every day except Mon, 10am-6pm. Closed 24 and 31 Dec. €4, free admission on Wed. ☎ (030) 30 86 62 15; www.stadtmuseum.de

This picturesque complex of buildings gathered around two interior courtyards was built between 1899 and 1908 borrowing from the typical Gothic and Renaissance architecture of the March of Brandenburg. The museum displays the historical and cultural development of Berlin from the first traces of a prehistoric settlement to the immediate present. Three floors of special exhibitions on various aspects of Berlin history will be shown until completion of extensive renovation activities. A copy of the larger-than-life 1474 figure of Brandenburger Roland, symbol of civic liberties and privileges, stands in front of the entrance to the museum.

Kunstgewerbemuseum★★ (Museum of Decorative Arts)

In Schloß Köpenick (Schloßinsel); www.smb.spk-berlin.de/e. A visit to this museum takes the visitor into the old-world provincial charm of the "green" Köpenick suburb, southeast of the city centre and far from the hectic bustle of international tourism. The museum is situated in a Baroque mansion built between 1677 and 1689 by the Dutch architect Rutger von Langerfeld. The 16C-19C furniture is especially interesting. Note also the **panelled room★** from Haldenstein castle (Switzerland, 16C) and the writing **pulpit★** by David Roentgen (Neuwied, 1779), on which the marquetry represents the Seven Liberal Arts of Frederick II.

The **Treasury★** contains jewellery and 16C gold plate and Baroque silverware. Also of interest is the great silver **sideboard★★** from the Knights' Room in the old Castle of Berlin (made by J Ludwig and A Biller, the famous silversmiths of Augsburg, between 1695 and 1698).

Großer Müggelsee★★

Leave by Lindenstraße. The largest of the Berlin lakes. From the terrace at the top of the tower: broad view of the surrounding lakes and woods.

Botanischer Garten★★ (Botanical Gardens)

Königin-Luise-Straße 6/8. ♿ Nov-Jan: 9am-4pm; Feb: 9am-5pm; Mar and Oct: 9am-6pm; Sep: 9am-7pm; Apr and Aug: 9am-8pm; May-Jul: 9am-9pm. Closed 24 and 31 Dec. €4. ☎ (030) 83 85 01 00; www.bgbm.org/bgbm. Its 43ha/106 acres make it one of the world's largest botanical gardens – vegetation from the temperate zone of the northern hemisphere, planted out geographically from mountains to plains. There are rare species (trees and shrubs) in the Arboretum, while 16 greenhouses display a wealth of tropical and subtropical plants on a total of 6 000m²/64 000sq ft.

The **Botanical Museum★** *(Botanisches Museum)* shows the evolution of flora in all its diversity. Numerous utility plants are shown, as are funeral offerings discovered in Ancient Egyptian tombs. *♿ 10am-6pm. Closed 24 and 31 Dec. €1. ☎ (030) 83 85 01 00.*

Brücke-Museum★

Bussardsteig 9. ♿ Open every day except Tue, 11am-5pm. Closed 24 and 31 Dec. €4. ☎ (030) 831 20 29; www.bruecke-museum.de. This museum contains works by members of the **Brücke**, the most important school of German Expressionists.

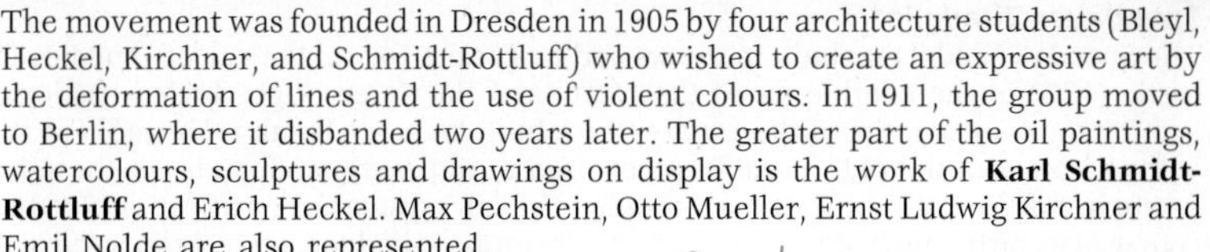
The movement was founded in Dresden in 1905 by four architecture students (Bleyl, Heckel, Kirchner, and Schmidt-Rottluff) who wished to create an expressive art by the deformation of lines and the use of violent colours. In 1911, the group moved to Berlin, where it disbanded two years later. The greater part of the oil paintings, watercolours, sculptures and drawings on display is the work of **Karl Schmidt-Rottluff** and Erich Heckel. Max Pechstein, Otto Mueller, Ernst Ludwig Kirchner and Emil Nolde are also represented.

Grunewald★★

A hunting reserve of the prince-electors in the 16C, this mixed forest covers an area of 3 100ha/745 acres. The Grunewald is bounded on the east by a chain of small lakes, interspersed with residential areas. Beside one of these lakes, the Lake of Grunewald, is the elegant **Jagdschloß Grunewald★**, a hunting pavilion built in 1542 by Caspar Theyss for the Prince Elector Joachim II. The original small Renaissance pavilion was converted some 160 years after its construction into the Baroque style for King Frederick I of Prussia. The building overlooks a courtyard surrounded on three sides by outbuildings *(Jagdzeugmagazin)* and bordered by ancient beech trees. *From mid May to mid Oct: open every day except Mon, 10am-5pm; guided tours only from mid Oct to mid May: Sun at 11am, 1pm and 3pm. €2. ☎ (0331) 969 42 02.*
Inside the pavilion are interesting pieces of furniture and an art gallery with German and Dutch works from the 15C to 19C.
The western boundary of the Grunewald is formed by **Lake Havel★★**. Beside this runs the picturesque Havelchaussee road, which leads, a little further south, to the beaches of the **Wannsee★★**, a favourite place for Berlin bathers in warm weather.

Pfaueninsel★★ (Peacock Island)

Access by boat, leaving from the landing-stage at the end of Nikolskoer Weg (service on demand).
Landscaped gardens studded with small, picturesque buildings offer a perfect example of late-18C taste on this isle on the Havel. The shaded park is an ideal place for a quiet stroll.
The **castle★** (1794-97), left incomplete in accordance with the taste for "ruined" follies at the beginning of the Romantic period, displays souvenirs of Queen Louise in a number of salons panelled and floored with exotic woods. *Apr-end Oct: guided tour (30min) every day except Mon, 10am-5pm. €3. ☎ (0331) 969 42 02.*

Funkturm★ (Radio Tower)

♿ Open every day except Mon, 10am-11pm. Closed 1st Jan and 24 Dec. €3.60. ☎ (030) 30 38 29 96. This 150m/492ft structure, known to Berliners as the "Beanpole", is indissolubly linked to the city and has become its mascot. At a height of 126m/413ft there is a viewing platform, reached by a lift, which offers a **panorama★★★** of Berlin.

Olympia-Stadion★ (Olympic Stadium)

☎ (030) 30 06 33. Open daily; summer, 10am-7pm, winter 10am-4pm; restricted opening before and after match days and other events. Closed 23 Dec-1 Jan. €2. Guided tours available
The top of the campanile affords the best view of this stadium made of reinforced concrete, which seated 120 000 spectators. "Too small", according to the Führer, who would have preferred this harmoniously designed structure to be made of stone, a more noble material.
The stadium is accessed via a vast avenue leading up to two towers. Monumental statues represent Nazi ideals. The architect **Werner March** made skilful use of the lie of the land and sunk the stadium, which appears to be quite low from the outside (17m/56ft); add to that a further 12m/39ft below ground level. Behind the building stood the May field *(Maifeld)* where 500 000 people could gather to listen to Hitler's speeches.

Bauhaus-Archiv★ (Bauhaus Archives)

Klingelhöferstraße. ♿ Open every day except Tue, 10am-5pm. Closed 24 and 31 Dec. €5. ☎ (030) 254 00 20; www.bauhaus.de. The building housing this museum was constructed in 1979 after the original designs of **Walter Gropius**, the founder of the Bauhaus *(see the "Art and Architecture" chapter and DESSAU)*. The Bauhaus School is known predominantly for its work in the field of architecture, but it exerted a strong influence too on the plastic arts; through the everyday objects it designed, it was the precursor of contemporary design.
In this museum, apart from industrial products and craftwork, one can see sculptures and paintings (including montages) by Schlemmer, Moholy-Nagy, Feininger, Kandinsky and Klee, as well as models, experimental typography for posters and adverts, and drawings from the Bauhaus School.

Gedenkstätte Plötzensee (Plötzensee Memorial)

♿ Mar-Oct: 9am-5pm; Nov-Feb: 9am-4pm. Closed 1st Jan, 23-26 and 31 Dec. Free admission. ☎ (030) 26 99 50 00. The memorial to victims of the Nazi regime occupies the former execution chamber in Plötzensee prison. Between 1933 and 1945 over 3 000 prisoners were killed here, dying under the guillotine or by hanging.

Spandauer Zitadelle★

The Spandau citadel was built in the second half of the 16C on the site of a medieval castle (12C) at the confluence of the Havel and the Spree. Right-angled bastions occupy the four corners of the square, brick-built keep – a break with tradition in comparison with the old, round bastions used until that time. Spandau is the sole example north of the Alps of this so-called "Italian" system of fortification. In the course of its turbulent history, the citadel has been assaulted successively by Swedish, Austrian, French, Russian and Prussian troops, but it is best-known as a state prison. A drawbridge leads to the gateway. Armorial bearings painted on the pediment represent the different provinces of Prussia.

Juliusturm (Julius Tower) – *Skirt the right-hand side of the building. Open every day except Mon, 9am-5pm, Sat-Sun 10am-5pm. Closed 1st Jan, 1st May, 3 Oct, 24, 25 and 31 Dec. €2.50. ☎ (030) 354 94 42 00.* Sole remnant of the original castle, this 32m/105ft keep has become the emblem of Spandau. It was here, in 1874, that the authorities stored the 120 million DM in gold demanded from France as war reparations after the defeat of 1870. The entrance is guarded by an impressive system of bolts. Inside the tower, 145 steps lead to a lookout point with a panoramic view. A **Museum of Local History** *(Stadtgeschichtliches Museum Spandau)* has been installed inside the citadel *(entrance via the footbridge)*. On the northern side of the citadel are 13C and 14C Jewish gravestones, which were salvaged from the Spandau Jewish cemetery sacked in 1510.

St-Nikolai-Kirche★

In Spandau. ♿ From beginning of Jan to end Nov: open every day except Fri, noon-4pm, Sat 11am-3pm, Sun 2-4pm. Free admission. ☎ (030) 333 56 39. This hall-church is one of the last brick-built Gothic buildings still standing in Berlin. The entrance to the north chapel in the polygonal choir is surmounted by a handsome Crucifixion Group (1540) in polychrome carved wood. The magnificent Renaissance **altar★** (painted limestone and stucco) was a gift from the military architect, Count Rochus de Lynar. Note the gilded Baroque pulpit, which is finely carved, and the baptismal fonts cast in bronze (1398).

►► Volkspark Friedrichshain – Kirche Maria Regina Martyrum – Schloß Tegel★ (Humboldt-Schloß) (*Adelheidallee 19-20*).

Excursions

Potsdam★★★

19km/12mi W. See POTSDAM.

Oranienburg

31km/19mi N. The Concentration Camp of **Sachsenhausen**, now a memorial – *Gedenkstätte und Museum Sachsenhausen* – dates from 1936. More than half of the 200 000 people imprisoned there perished. The various aspects of the history of the concentration camp are shown in changing and permanent exhibitions at the original sites. The **Museum Baracke 28**, which opened in 1997, is a special exhibition on the fate of the Jewish prisoners.

A tour of the camp *(follow the plan distributed at the entrance)* gives some idea of the implacable organisation of the Nazi concentration system, whose cynical approach is exemplified by the slogan still above the entrance gates: *"Arbeit macht frei"* (Work brings Freedom). Film screening for visitors. *♿ From mid Mar to mid Oct: open Tue-Sun, 8.30am-6pm; from mid Oct to mid Mar: open Tue-Sun, 8.30am-4.30pm. Closed 1st Jan, 24, 25 and 31 Dec. Free admission. ☎ (033 01) 20 02 00.*

Frankfurt an der Oder

90km/56mi E via ① on plan.

This former Hanseatic city founded in the 13C has been the seat of the **European University of Viadrina** since 1991. A third of all student places are awarded to students from neighbouring Poland, which can even be reached on foot from here over the town's bridge. Since nearly 70% of Frankfurt an der Oder was destroyed in the Second World War, many monuments have been rebuilt, including important examples of the brick Gothic style, namely the Rathaus (town hall), St Marienkirche and the Carl Philipp Emanuel Bach concert hall (a former Franciscan abbey). In April 2001 the Kleist-Forum, designed as a cultural and conference centre by Klaus Springer, was opened to the public. It is named after the town's most famous son, **Heinrich von Kleist** (1777-1811), most famous for his plays and novellas. There is also a museum *(at Faberstraße 7)*, dedicated to him, documenting his life and work.

Kloster Chorin★★ (Chorin Abbey)

71km/44mi north of Berlin. ♿ Apr-Oct: 9am-6pm; Nov-Mar: 9am-4pm. €3. ☎ (03 33 66) 703 77.

The majestic ruins of Chorin Abbey stand framed against a backdrop of trees on the banks of the Amtssee. The original abbey, financed by the Margraves of Brandenburg, was built from 1273 by Cistercian monks from the abbey at Lehnin (*see POTSDAM "Excursions"*). The abbey was dissolved in 1542, and over the next few centuries parts of it fell into disrepair or were converted for another purpose. In 1825, the architect Karl Friedrich Schinkel drew the attention of the King of Prussia to the historical interest of the ruins and persuaded him to start a project to save the site. Now partially restored, Chorin Abbey is one of the finest examples of a brick building in northern Germany. This peaceful site hosts a festival of classical music during the summer.

Church – The monks from Lehnin adopted the same basilical ground plan with three naves at Chorin, but with one or two modifications on their home church. The sanctuary was extended by the addition of a heptagonal apse, the nave no longer featured twin bays, the transverse and cross ribs were supported on clustered columns rather than piers, and the rectangular pillars are softened by slender engaged colonettes. As it now stands, the building is missing its south wall. The west front, with a very strong vertical articulation, combines severity and elegance: flanked by two staircase turrets are three windows, separated by buttresses and surmounted by a rose window, while the upper section of the façade features an attractive array of gables and blind arcading.

Conventual buildings – *Currently under restoration.* The west wing, reserved for the lay-brothers (brothers devoted to manual work), and the east wing, reserved for the clerics (as was the south wing, which is no longer extant), are original.

The abbot's residence, brewery and the remains of a mill are also open to visitors.

Schloß Rheinsberg★

87km/54mi northwest of Berlin. Apr-Oct: open every day except Mon, 9.30am-5pm; Nov-Mar: open Tue-Sun, 10am-12.30pm, 1pm-4pm. €5. Guided tour (50min), Nov-Mar:Tue-Sun, 10am-12.30pm, 1pm-4pm. Closed 24, 25 and 31 Dec. Guided tour of palace and grounds €7.50. ☎ (0339 31) 72 60.

Just as the town of Rheinsberg is associated with German writer **Kurt Tucholsky** (1890-1935), the beautiful palace on the banks of Lake Grienerick is inseparably linked with Frederick II, or **Frederick the Great**, although he only lived here for four years. These were, in his own words, the best four years of his life. He had serious differences of opinion with his authoritarian father, which led to an attempted flight to England (1730) and the execution of his friend Katte who had helped him in this attempt. Frederick's imprisonment, at his father's orders, ended when the prince agreed to become engaged to Elisabeth-Christine of Brunswick. As a result, Frederick William I purchased the estate of Rheinsberg for his son in 1734 and furnished him with sufficient funds for converting the old 16C castle.

The Brandenburg architect Johann Gottfried Kemmeter designed the Baroque structure with three wings. The Crown Prince and Georg Wenzeslaus von Knobelsdorff, who took over direction of the site in 1737, were also involved in the planning.

It was here that the young Frederick, in the company of his friends and in line with the growing philosophical idea of benign, enlightened rule, came to the conclusion that the Prince should be the "chief servant of his country". Thereafter began his correspondence with Voltaire, which lasted, on and off, until the latter's death in 1778. In Rheinsberg, the architect Knobelsdorff, the painter Antoine Pesne and the sculptor Friedrich Christian Glume created a style which was subsequently to reach its zenith in the Rococo of Charlottenburg and Sanssouci.

From 1752 to 1802, the palace was used as a residence by Prince Heinrich, Frederick II's brother.

During Prince Heinrich's time, under the management of Georg Friedrich Boumann the Younger, the corner buildings were built. An obelisk was erected opposite the palace in honour of the Prussian Generals who fell during the Seven Years' War. Up until the German reunification, the palace was used as a sanatorium. Its complete restoration is currently in progress, but some thirty rooms can be visited. The central building was the work of Knobelsdorff. The roof parapet bears four statues, allegories of Rhetoric, Music, Painting and Sculpture.

Facing the garden, the side wings, which are linked by a colonnade, end in round towers.

Interior – The hall of mirrors, the Bacchus Room and the anteroom, with magnificent ceiling paintings by Antoine Pesne, are remarkable. There is a large number of paintings in the red room and bed chamber in Princess Amalie's quarters. The Ferdinand apartment was designed in 1767 based on plans by Carl Gotthard Langhans.

The palace also houses the **Kurt Tucholsky Memorial**.

Grounds – The garden dates back essentially to plans by Knobelsdorff and Johann Samuel Sello, and took account of Frederick II's particular interest in garden culture. The aim was to combine kitchen and pleasure gardens. Prince Heinrich had the park extended on the other side of Lake Grienerick (this side affords a lovely view of the palace).

Bernkastel-Kues★

Bernkastel-Kues is formed of two towns straddling the Moselle and is in the largest single wine-growing region of Germany, which spreads over the slopes flanking a wide bend in the Moselle (Moselschleife) and continues as far as Graach and Zeltingen. The grapes are 95% of the Riesling variety. Many visitors come during the first week in September to celebrate the grape harvest.

Location

Population: 7 200. Michelin map n° 543 Q 5 – Rheinland-Pfalz. Bernkastel-Kues is in the heart of the Middle Moselle *(Mittelmosel)* around 50km/30mi northeast of Trier. There is a magnificent view of the half-timbered houses of the little town from the ruins of Landshut fortress.

Gestade 66, 54470 Bernkastel-Kues, ☎ (065 31) 40 23.

Surrounding area: see IDAR OBERSTEIN (37km/23mi south), MOSELTAL (tour includes Bernkastel-Kues), TRIER (49km/31mi southwest), EIFEL (Manderscheid is 73km/46mi north).

Worth a Visit

Markt★

Old houses, most of them half-timbered, surround this small, sloping square in the middle of which is the 17C **St Michael fountain** *(Michaelsbrunnen).*

Cusanusstift (St Nikolaus-Hospital)

On the Kues side of the river. Chapel and cloisters: Open Sun–Fri, 9am-6pm, Sat, 9am-3pm. No charge. Guided tours of library on Fri at 3pm and additionally Apr to Oct on Tue at 10.30am. €4. ☎ (065 31) 22 60.

Founded in 1447 by **Cardinal Nicholas of Kues** (or Nikolaus Cusanus) (1401-64), a humanist and theologian, the hospice was built to house people in need. The number of lodgers was restricted to a symbolic 33 – the age of Christ at his death – a tradition still respected today.

Admire the Late Gothic cloister, the chapel with its fine 15C reredos, and the copy in bronze of the cardinal's tombstone (the original is in Rome, at San Pietro in Vincoli). Note the fresco depicting The Last Judgement *(to the left of the entrance)* and the **tombstone of Clara Cryftz**, the prelate's sister.

The **library** houses almost 400 manuscripts and early printed works, in addition to astronomical instruments used by the founder.

Excursion

Burg Landshut

3km/2mi southeast towards Longkamp and uphill to the right. The **castle**, built on a rocky promontory, was the property of the archbishops of Trier from the 11C. It has been in ruins ever since the War of the Orléans Succession.

From the ruin there is a fine panoramic **view**★★ over the bend in the Moselle, above which even the steepest slopes are planted with vines.

Bodensee★★

Lake Constance

With the immensity of its horizons, sometimes lost in the summer haze, and a climate mild enough for tropical vegetation in the more favoured sites, Lake Constance, or the Bodensee as it is known to German speakers, attracts a multitude of German holidaymakers, who regard it as their local "Riviera". Attracted by the clear waters, medieval towns and numerous cruises, tourists flock here in good weather. The lakeside roads offer numerous vistas of the lake with the Alps, in clear weather, as an impressive background.

Location

Michelin map n°s 216 folds 9 to 11 and 545 W 10/X 13 – Baden-Württemberg. The Bodensee is filled by the Rhine as it finishes its tiring crossing of the Alps. The lake is on the border with Switzerland and Austria. With a maximum depth of 252m/827ft, it has its own microclimate which is particularly conducive to the cultivation of fruit. With an area of 53 000ha/210sq mi, the lake is only marginally smaller than Lake Geneva, the biggest of the Alpine waterways.

Directory

Where to Eat

Winzerstube zum Becher – *Höllgasse 4 – 88709 Meersburg – (07532) 90 09 – Closed for 3 weeks in Jan and Mon – €22/40.50.* This place has been welcoming thirsty visitors since 1610! Pleasantly rustic establishment with its own history: it has belonged to the same family for over 120 years.

Where to Stay

Gasthof Auer – *Stockacher Straße 62, 78359 Orsingen-Nenzingen – (07771) 24 97 – fax (07771) 2497 – Closed for 1 week at the end of July – P – 5rm: €28/64.* A hotel typical of the village with painted façade and decorated shutters. The interior has been kitted out with sober good taste. A large choice of traditional dishes is on offer and a few simple, well-presented guestrooms are available.

Landgasthof und Hotel Zum Sternen – *Schienerbergstraße 23, 78345 Radolfzell – Moos-Bankholzen – (07732) 24 22 – fax (07732) 58910 – www.zum-sternen.de – P – Reservation – 18rm: €36/75 – Restaurant €12/25.* The guestrooms of this renovated half-timbered hotel with modern extension contain light-coloured wooden furniture, some of them with kitchenette. In the restaurant, country cooking and regional specialities are on the menu.

Hotel Kreuz – *Grasbeurer Straße 2, 88690 Uhldingen Mühlhofen – (07556) 933 60 – fax (07556) 933670 – www.hotel-kreuz-bodensee.de – P – Reservation – 45rm: €37/72 – Restaurant €14/21.* This family-run hotel is located in a side street. Warm, rustic interior with well maintained guestrooms furnished with light wood.

Gästehaus Schmäh – *Kapellenstraße 7, 88709 Hagnau – (07532) 62 10 – fax (07532) 1403 – www.gaestehaus-schmaeh.de – P – 17rm: €42/80.* This well cared for guesthouse is situated in a quiet residential area, between the main street and the lake. Very clean guestrooms, all furnished in simple and rustic oak. Sun-worshippers will adore the lawn.

Seehof – *Unterstadtstraße 36, 88709 Meersburg – (07532) 433 50 – fax (07532) 2406 – www.hotel.seehof.mdo.de – Closed from mid-Nov to mid-Mar – P – 24rm: €49/100.* This hotel is located in the lower town, next to the lake. Modern, functional guestrooms are available. The perfect base for interesting excursions in the surrounding area.

Taking a Break

Strandcafé – *Strandbadstraße 102 – 78315 Radolfzell – (07732) 16 50 – Open every day 11am-midnight.* This modern, glass-fronted building is made attractive by its position on the lakeside. Both from inside and from the terrace, there are superb views over the lake.

A wide choice of boat services provides many possibilities for cruises and excursions; the most frequent of these services run from the ports of Constance, Überlingen, Meersburg, Friedrichshafen, Lindau and Bregenz *(see The Green Guide Austria)*. The islands of **Reichenau★**, on the Untersee, and **Mainau★★**, on the Überlingersee, are described under *KONSTANZ:* Excursions.

Surrounding area: see KONSTANZ, SALEM (8km/4mi north of Birnau), SIGMARINGEN (72km/45mi north of Konstanz), SCHWÄBISCHE ALB (tour includes Sigmaringen).

Boats on the lake with Uberlingen in the background.

T. Krieger/MICHELIN

FROM ÜBERLINGEN TO LINDAU

56 km/35mi – allow 4hr

Überlingen★ *(see ÜBERLINGEN)*

Birnau

The present church was built between 1746 and 1750 on a terrace overlooking the lake, the Cistercians of **Salem** *(see entry)* having entrusted the work to Peter Thumb, Master of the Vorarlberg School, with the help of Joseph Anton Feuchtmayer for the stuccowork and Gottfried Bernhard Göz for the frescoes. The building's Rococo charm is most evident in the architectural design, the painted decoration of the interpenetrating oval spaces and curved surfaces over the single aisle, the flattened dome above the chancel, and the cupola surmounting the apse. Halfway up the walls, an elegant gallery is supported on corbels, the bosses of which are embellished with Rococo cartouches. Pilgrims venerate the early-15C Virgin above the tabernacle on the high altar.

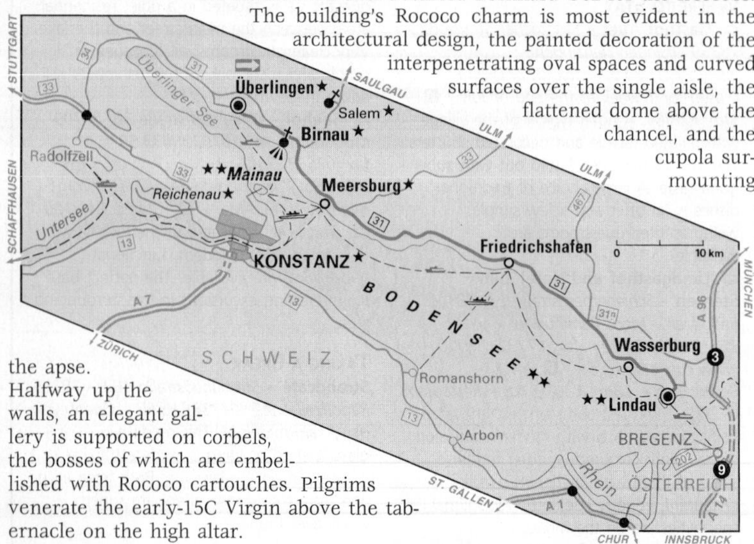

Meersburg★

This former residence of prince-archbishops Meersburg is now a picturesque village, set in a privileged position among the vineyards and orchards and perched on a plateau with views over the lake. The stylish upper town (Oberstadt) is centred on the **Marktplatz★**, from which the **Steigstraße★**, bordered by half-timbered old houses, offers delightful views of the lake.

Annette von Droste-Hülshoff, a poet born in Westphalia in 1797, died in 1848 in her apartments in the Meersburg, the so-called Altes Schloß, where she had lived for 7 years. This massive medieval construction with circular rooms, dungeons and walls up to 3m/10ft thick dominates the little town. It was purchased in 1838 – and saved from total ruin – by Josef von Laßberg, an Antiquity specialist and the brother-in-law of Annette von Droste-Hülshoff, who came to live here in 1846. The two small tower rooms where she wrote some of her finest poetry can be visited. The memory of the author of the *Judenbuche (The Jew's Beech)* is honoured both here and in the Droste-Museum *(Fürstenhäusle, Stettener Straße)*. From the terrace of the **New Castle** *(Neues Schloß)*, a Baroque castle with pink façade, there is a **panorama★** of Lake Constance and the Säntis massif.

The itinerary continues along the "Grüne Straße" (the Green Route), between orchards of apple trees, whose fruit (in particular the Jonagold variety) is exported throughout Europe.

Friedrichshafen

Friedrichshafen, the second largest town on Lake Constance after Constance itself, is an important and lively port. Friedrichshafen also likes to be called the "Fair and Zeppelin town", in praise of its importance as an industrial centre and the birthplace of the dirigible. The lakeside offers one of the longest and prettiest promenade-quays. The Baroque **church** *(Schloßkirche)*, situated to the extreme west of the promenade, near the castle (still occu-

THE BODENSEE SEEN FROM A ZEPPELIN: EXCLUSIVE ENJOYMENT

Dirigibles are once again being built in Friedrichshafen. In September 1997, the Zeppelin Neuer Technologie (NT) undertook its maiden journey. The airship sails at speeds of up to 130kmh/78mph, 97 years after the very first Zeppelin journey. It is small in comparison to its predecessors: 75m/240ft long with a volume of about 8 200m³/268 000cu ft. The LZ 129 Hindenburg was 245m/784ft long and had a volume of 200 000 m³, which is over 6.5 million cu ft. This 12-seater is available to well-heeled tourists for a sightseeing trip over the Bodensee. Flights take place from March to September and last 1 hour. The price is around €335, increased by 10% at weekends; it's a good idea to book ahead.

pied by the ducal Wurtemberg family), is worth a detour. Friedrichshafen is the point of departure for boat excursions to the Rhine falls in Schaffhausen or to the "flower island" of Mainau and the stilt houses in Unteruhldingen *(see Überlingen)*.

Zeppelin-Museum – ♿ *Open May to Oct, Tue-Sun, 10am-6pm; Nov to Apr, Tue-Sun 10am–5pm. Closed 24 and 25 Dec. €6.50. ☎ (075 41) 380 10; www.zeppelin-museum.de.* This museum located at the eastern end of the promenade in the former harbour train station is devoted to Count Ferdinand Zeppelin (1838-1917) who developed the dirigibles named after him in Friedrichshafen. Part of the legendary "Hindenburg", which exploded in Lakehurst in 1937, has been reconstructed, allowing visitors to grasp to some extent the dream of technology and luxury which it represented.

An art department housing works from the Middle Ages to contemporary times is attached to the museum. It portrays the interaction between art and technology.

Wasserburg am Bodensee

This much-visited village is squeezed onto a narrow peninsula jutting out into the lake. Appreciate it on foot, walking to the tip of the promontory, from where there are views of both sides of the bank, and in the distance, the peaks of the Alps.

Lindau★★ *(see LINDAU IM BODENSEE)*

Bonn★

In 1949, Bonn was chosen as the capital of the new West German Federal Republic, to the surprise of many Germans. Its modest size and supposed provincial character even lent it the nickname of "the federal village". No longer a major European capital, Bonn has a calm and welcoming atmosphere and is rich in museums. Bonn's most famous son, Beethoven, is celebrated in many ways and in particular during the town's annual international Beethoven Festival.

Location

Population: 308 000 – Michelin map n° 543 N 5 – Nordrhein-Westfalen. Bonn is placed at the gateway to the romantic Middle Rhine region, at the foot of the Seven Mountains range *(Siebengebirge)*. The town is accessible from Cologne by the A 555 or A 59 motorways. The whole town, including the Rhine and the surrounding countryside, can be seen from the **Alter Zoll**. The **view★** of the river and the Siebengebirge range *(see below)* is particularly attractive in late afternoon and early evening. From the foot of the bastion, riverside promenades beckon those with time for a leisurely stroll *(this is the departure point also for boat trips)*.

🅱 *Windeskstraße. 1 (Münsterplatz), 53103 Bonn, ☎ (0228) 77 50 00.*

Surrounding area: see BRÜHL (22km/14mi north), KÖLN (29km/18mi northwest), EIFEL (Bad Münstereifel is 39km/24mi south).

Background

Origins – The site has been inhabited since it was a camp for Roman legionaries, but it was not until the 16C that the town became important as the residence of the electors and archbishops of Cologne. In the 18C, the fortifications were transformed into a Baroque residence.

Capital of the Federal Republic of Germany – After **Konrad Adenauer** was nominated the first federal Chancellor on 23 May 1949, he pressed for the "sleepy little town" of Bonn to become the provisional capital of the new Republic. The town fulfilled that role for 50 years and became in the process a true seat of government. The parliamentary buildings were located in a well-off residential area on the banks of the Rhine, to the southeast of town. Embassies flourished and numerous museums were inaugurated. Since the reunification of Germany and the transfer of the Federal Government to Berlin in the autumn of 1999, huge sums of money have been spent redefining the nature of the city. As well as playing host to several international bodies, including 12 UN organisations, Bonn is now a peaceful university town with a lively cultural life.

Beethoven's formative years – Precursor of the great stream of Romantic music, **Ludwig van Beethoven** (1770-1827) was born and grew up in the neighbourhood around the church of St Remigius *(St. Remigius-Kirche)*. At 13, Beethoven was already an accomplished musician, playing violin, viola and harpsichord in the orchestra attached to the brilliant Court of the Elector. At the

Directory

Where to Eat

⊖⊖ **Bistro Kaiser Karl** – *Vorgebirgsstraße 50 – ☎ (0228) 69 69 67 – Closed for 1 week during Carnival and for 2 weeks in August, Sat lunchtime and Sun – €27.50/43.* The attraction of this *Jugendstil* bistro lies mostly in its décor: decorated ceilings and magnificent chandeliers, mirrored walls and beautiful brasserie-style windows giving on to a terrace.

Where to Stay

⊖⊖⊖ **Sternhotel** – *Markt 8 – ☎ (0228) 726 70 – fax (0228) 7267125 – info@sternhotel-bonn.de – Closed from 24 Dec until beginning of Jan – – 80rm: €100/165* . Located close to the former town hall, this hotel with its beautiful façade is part of the history of the town. Conformable guestrooms with every convenience in a quiet but central location.

age of 22 the fervent admirer of Mozart and Haydn left Bonn for good to follow in their footsteps, arriving in Vienna with only his virtuosity at the piano as an asset.

The **Beethovenhalle**, a bold example of modern architecture, is the impressive setting for Bonn's annual international Beethoven Festival. The architect was Siegfried Wolske.

Walking About

Beethovenhaus (Beethoven's Birthplace)

Bonngasse 20. Open Apr-Oct: Mon-Sat, 10am-6pm, Sun, 11am-4pm; Nov-Mar: Mon-Sat, 10am-5pm, Sun, 11am-4pm. Closed 1 Jan, Mon before Shrove Tue, Good Fri, Easter Mon, 24-26 Dec. €4. ☎ (0228) 981 75 25; www.beethoven-haus-bonn.de

Beethoven was born in this house in the old town of Bonn in 1770. It has been a museum since 1890, showing authentic documents relating to the life and opus of the great composer. These include portraits of Beethoven and his friends, original hand-written documents, his instruments (grand piano, string instruments), his listening horns and life and death masks.

Go down Bonngasse towards the Markt.

Altes Rathaus (Town Hall)

Markt. A charming Rococo building (1738) with a pink and grey façade and a fine outside staircase with two flights.

Leave the Rathaus and head south.

Kurfürstliche Residenz (Electors' Residence)

A few feet from the cathedral. The lawns of the Hofgarten park make a fine setting for this long Baroque building (1697-1702). Since 1818 the palace has housed the university.

Münster★ (Cathedral)

Münsterplatz. The former Stiftskirche St Cassius und Florentius grew out of a place of worship dating from the second half of the 3C. The 11C-13C is what marks the architecture of the church today; stylistic elements from the Romanesque and Gothic eras are harmoniously interwoven.

The Romanesque baptismal font and the Romanesque stone carvings at the stairway to the choir are worthy of especial note, as is the graffito (c 1200) drawing depicting the Madonna standing between St Cassius and Florentius. A fresco painted about 100 years later shows the Virgin Mary's welcome in heaven. The sacristy was built in 1619, whilst the rest of the furnishings are mostly from the Baroque period or the end of the 19C.

Under the high chancel is a three-naved crypt (1040) with a shrine to the martyrs. The atmospheric Romanesque **cloister★** (c 1150) is considered one of the best-preserved examples from the period in Germany.

From the Kurfürstliche Residenz, take the Poppelsdorfer Allee, a large chestnut-lined avenue.

Poppelsdorfer Schloß

Meckenheimer Allee 171. The design of this castle was entrusted to the French architect **Robert de Cotte**. It was built between 1715 and 1753. The outer façade, with its three wings, reflects a classical French influence, while the inner courtyard, bordered by a semicircular colonnade, is more Italian in style. At the back, on level ground where a moat once flowed, are the university's **Botanical Gardens**.

From the castle, explore the surrounding streets and university district where different faculty buildings alternate with beautiful houses on tree-lined avenues *(in particular Mozartstrasse).*

BONN

Am Alten Friedhof .... BZ 2
Am Hof .... CZ
Am Neutor .... CZ 3
Belderberg .... CY 7
Bertha- von-Suttner-Platz .... CY 9
Bottlerplatz .... BZ 10
Brüdergasse .... CY 12
Budapesterstr. ....BYZ 14
Fritz-Schroeder-Ufer .... CY 15
Gerhard-von-Are-Straße .... BZ 16
Kasernenstraße .... BY 20
Markt .... CZ 23
Martinsplatz .... CZ 24
Mülheimer Platz .... BZ 27
Münsterplatz .... BZ 28
Münsterstraße .... BZ 29
Oxfordstraße .... BY 31
Poppelsdorfer Allee .... BZ 32
Poststraße .... BZ 34
Rathausgasse .... CZ 36
Remigiusplatz .... CZ 38
Remigiusstraße .... CZ 40
Sternstraße .... BCZ 43
Sterntorbrücke .... BY 45
Thomas-Mann-Str. .... BZ 46
Welschnonnenstraße .... CY 48
Wenzelgasse .... CY 49
Wilhelmstraße .... BY 50

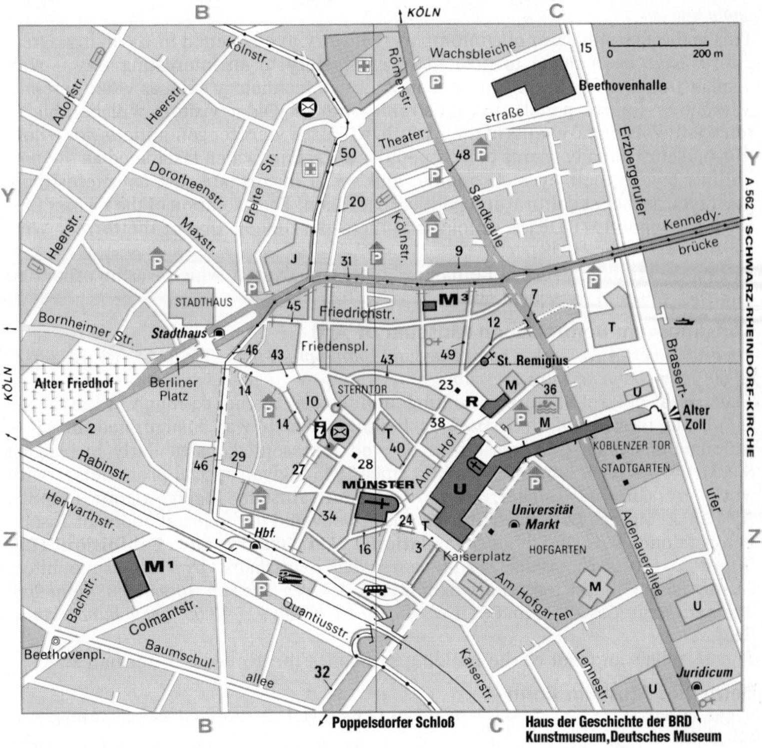

Beethovenhaus .... CY M³
Kurfürstliche Residenz .... CZ U
Rathaus .... CZ R
Rheinisches Landesmuseum .... BZ M¹

Alter Friedhof

Bornheimer Strasse. Artists, scholars and celebrities are buried here in the **old cemetery**. One can visit the graves of Robert and Clara Schumann, Beethoven's mother, Ernst Moritz Arndt, August Wilhelm von Schlegel, and others.

August Macke Haus

Bornheimer Strasse 96. Auguste Macke (1887-1914) lived in Bonn from 1910 until 1914 and over the course of these five years produced impressive pictorial works with Impressionist and Fauvist influences. Inside the neo-classical residence (1878) are some examples of Macke's work, as well as a history of Rhenish Expressionism.

Worth a Visit

Rheinisches Landesmuseum★

This museum offers an overview of the history, culture and art of the Middle and Lower Rhine region, from prehistory to the present.

The **Prehistoric Section** *(Urgeschichtliche Abteilung, 1st floor)* shows the skull of the celebrated Neanderthal Man, interesting artefacts from the Stone and Bronze Ages and La Tène culture (weapons, metalwork, jewellery found in tumuli etc).

The department of **Roman Antiquities★** *(Römische Abteilung)* is particularly well endowed. Note the Altars to the Matrons, a cult popular with Roman soldiers stationed in the Rhinelands.

A masterpiece of Roman craft is the **Sun God Mosaic** (c 250 AD), which shows the Sun God in his chariot, surrounded by the signs of the Zodiac. Large memorial stones, such as that for Marcus Caelius found at Xanten (early 1C AD) illustrate funerary cults.

Pride of place in the **Frankish Section** is reserved for a reconstruction of a chieftain's tomb (c 600 AD).

The section from the **Middle Ages to the Present** displays arts and crafts from the Romanesque era to the 19C. Well represented are Romanesque sculpture and above all the **Gothic panel paintings** and **Dutch painting** of the 16C and 17C.

Haus der Geschichte der Bundesrepublik Deutschland★ (Museum of the Federal Republic of Germany)

Adenauerallee 250. ♿ Open Tue-Sun, 9am-7pm. No charge. ☎ (0228) 916 50; www.hdg.de

This is the first museum of contemporary history to be opened in Germany. Great efforts have been made to present recent history in an interesting way – with displays making full use of modern audio-visual technology such as video screens, interactive control panels and electronic buttons. Older visitors will be able to retrace the historical events of their youth, while the younger generations, for whom this museum already seems to be a popular attraction, watch fascinated as the past unfolds before their eyes. Economic and social history are just as interestingly portrayed as recent cultural and political evolution. The evolution of the former East German Republic (DDR) is unfolded at the same time as that of the former West German Republic (BDR).

During construction work, a Roman cellar was uncovered, which was incorporated into the museum *(basement level)*.

Kunstmuseum Bonn★ (Bonn Museum of Art)

Friedrich-Ebert-Allee 2. ♿ Open Tue-Sun, 10am-6pm, (-9pm, Wed). €5. ☎ (0228) 77 62 60; www.bonn.de/kunstmuseum

The appeal of Axel Schulter's exciting architecture lies not so much in the façade as in the interior of this spacious building, which was inaugurated in 1996. Among the exhibits, Expressionism is well represented, particularly by August Macke who lived in Bonn. German art since 1945 is given special prominence, with works by Günther Uecker, Gerhard Richter, Anselm Kiefer, Georg Baselitz, AR Penck, Marcus Lüpertz. Three rooms are devoted to the installations of Joseph Beuys alone. The neighbouring **National Art Gallery and Exhibition Hall** *(Kunst- und Ausstellungshalle der Bundesrepublik Deutschland)* by Viennese architect Gustav Peichl houses temporary exhibitions. *♿ Open Tue-Sun, 10am-7pm, (until 9pm Tue and Wed). Closed 24 and 31 Dec. €6.50. ☎ (0228) 917 12 00; www.bundeskunsthalle.de*

The 16 pillars in front of the building symbolise the 16 Federal German states.

Deutsches Museum Bonn

Ahrstraße 45. ♿ Open Tue-Sun, 10am-6pm. Closed during Carnival period, Shrove Tue, Good Fri, 1 May, 24, 25 and 31 Dec. €4. ☎ (0228) 30 22 55; www.deutsches-museum-bonn.de

This museum, which is an offshoot of the famous museum of this name in Munich, has as its theme "Research and Technology in Germany since 1945", a particularly exciting period in the history of technology. Technological advances in both the former West and East Germanies are covered here. Modern media presentations, video and videophones present a comprehensive picture of German technology and its combination of tradition and innovation.

►► Zoologisches Forschungsingsinstitut und Museum Alexander Koenig (Museum of Natural History and Alexander Koenig Museum), Frauenmuseum (Museum of Women), Arithmeum, Ägyptisches Museum (Egyptian Museum), Freizeitpark Rheinaue (Rhine Leisure Park).

Rocket-carrier by Daimler-Benz, Deutsches Museum Bonn

Deutsches Museum, Bonn

Excursions

Bonn is a sprawling town with ill-defined limits. Beyond the central districts, the town developed southwards (Popepelsdorf, Kessenich, Dottendorf, Gronau, Hochkreuz) and engulfed areas like Beuel on the other side of the Rhine or Bad Godesberg to the south.

Schwarz-Rheindorf★

Leave by the Kennedy bridge. This two-storey **chapel★** in Romanesque style was consecrated in 1151. The lower chapel contains expressive murals with scenes from the Book of Ezekiel. The upper chapel has a throne for the emperor like its model, the Pfalzkapelle in Aachen.

Bad Godesberg

Town plan in the Michelin Guide Deutschland.

This residential suburb south of the city was the seat of foreign embassies until the government moved to Berlin. It is home to some enchanting villas and parks (Redoute-Park, Draischbrunnen).

The **riverside walk** between the Rhine ferry landing-stages is very popular. The Petersberg Hotel and the Drachenfels ruins overlook the heavy flow of traffic on the river. The ruins of Godesburg Castle, built in the 13C by the prince-electors of Cologne, stand on a basalt outcrop in the town centre. From the keep, there is a fine panoramic **view★** of the city, the Bonn depression northwards as far as Cologne, and the Siebengebirge massif.

Telephone for information on opening times, ☎ (0228) 31 60 71.

Siebengebirge★

The Seven Mountains massif, which reaches an altitude of 460m/1 472ft and is the Rhine's northernmost wine-growing region, rises opposite Bad Godesberg on the eastern bank of the Rhine. Its name comes from the seven prominent summits that were once almost all crowned by castles. These hills and volcanic cones, surrounded by Germany's oldest nature reserve, are favourites with local day-trippers and holidaymakers in search of that old romantic Rhine feeling. There's plenty of that atmosphere in the towns and culturally significant buildings such as the chancel ruin of Heisterbach Monastery and in the picturesque inns and wine establishments.

At the foot of the range, bordering the Rhine, are the localities of **Bad Honnef-Rhöndorf** (house of Konrad Adenauer) and **Königswinter**, from where a funicular rises to the jagged **Drachenfels★** ruins. It was here, so the legend has it, that Siegfried, the hero of the *Nibelungenlied (see Rheintal)*, slew the dragon and then bathed in its blood to render himself invulnerable.

From the terrace, near the ruins of the castle tower, the visitor can admire a vast **panorama★★** comprising (from left to right) the Weserwald and Eifel plateaux, Bad Godesberg, Bonn, and finally Cologne.

Funicular: Operates May to Sep 9am–7pm every 30min; Jan, Feb and Nov (up to and including Buß- und Bettag, or the third Wed in Nov) departures depending on demand Mon–Fri noon–5pm, Sat–Sun 11am–6pm (hourly); Mar and Oct 10am–6pm (every 30min); Apr 10am–7pm (every 30min). Return (US: round trip): €8. ☎ (022 23) 920 90; www.drachenfelsbahn-koenigswinter.de

Remagen

23km/14mi south. Leave by the Adenauerallee. Passing Mehlem, one sees on the right the ivy covered ruins of Rolandsbogen, and, on the left, the island of **Nonnenwerth**, linked to it by legend.

The origin of the small town of Remagen goes back to a Roman fortified camp. Finds from that period are exhibited in the **Roman Museum** (Römisches Museum) at *Kirchstraße 9*, the former 16C Knechtstedener Chapel. Remagen became famous when its **bridge** across the Rhine fell into American hands almost intact on 7 March 1945 – the first time the Americans had been able to establish a bridgehead east of the river. Then days later, the bridge collapsed under the weight of armoured vehicles. The remaining towers are today the site of a **Peace Museum**, Friedensmuseum, tracing the history of the bridge and the battles of March 1945. In the town itself, see the **parish church**: its outer wall is furnished with **double Romanesque doors** – a carriage entrance and one for pedestrians. The reliefs which decorate the arches represent sirens and fantastic beasts. *Open May to mid-Nov: daily, 10am–5pm; May-Oct: daily, 10am–6pm. €3.50. ☎ (026 42) 201 59; www.bruecke-remagen.de*

Schloss Branitz

The former Branitz estate had belonged to the family since 1696 when Hermann von Pückler-Muskau took up permanent residence here. He had just had to sell Muskau, but was unable to abandon the great passion of his life, garden design. Future generations reaped the benefits, since in Branitz Park he created a jewel in garden design.

Location

Michelin maps n° 544 K 27 – Brandenburg. Branitz is less than 5km/3mi east of Cottbus, a merchant settlement which grew up at the point where the Salzstraße from Halle to Silesia crosses the Spree.

Surrounding area: see SPREEWALD (Lübbenau is 37km/23mi to the west), BAUTZEN (77km/48mi south).

Worth a visit

SCHLOSS AND PÜCKLER-PARK BRANITZ★★ *Tour: 3hr*

Schloß Branitz

Open Apr to Oct daily 10am–6pm; Nov to Mar Tue-Sun 11am–5pm. Closed 24 and 31 Dec; stables (Marstall) Nov to Mar. €3.50. ☎ (0355) 751 52 25; www.pueckler-museum.de

The proceeds from the sale of Muskau enabled Prince Pückler to have the **palace**, built in 1772 by Gottfried Semper, converted and sumptuously fitted out. Large parts of the structure and fittings remain, such as the dining room furniture and the library. Pückler's love of Oriental and exotic styles is evident on the first floor. Some rooms house an art gallery featuring paintings by **Karl Blechen**, the Romantic painter born in Cottbus.

In front of the palace are the former Tudor-style royal **stables**, in which temporary exhibitions are housed, and the Cavalier's House, which is used today as a café. An attractive bower courtyard, with terracotta reliefs based on designs by Bertel Thorvaldsen and cast zinc figures, extends between these two buildings. On the side facing the garden it opens out into a terrace featuring two bronze griffins.

Park

The park covers an area of 90ha/222 acres, into which the elevations, watercourses and lakes had to be incorporated, since the river landscape as a framework did not already exist here as it did in Muskau. The soil from the excavation of the lakes was piled up to form hills and pyramids. Pückler placed particular emphasis on the alternation between open spaces, groups of trees and individual specimens, ditches and pools.

The terrace and park of the luxurious Branitz estate, laid out by the extravagant Hermann, Prince of Pückler-Muskau.

R. Chéret/MICHELIN

Impoverished prince seeks financial backing

"A garden in the grand style is simply a picture gallery, and pictures need frames".

Hermann, Prince of Pückler-Muskau was born in Muskau in 1785. He was a spendthrift throughout his life, and even while young he accumulated such debts that the family estate came under threat. His father's desperation was such that he even attempted to have his son legally declared incapable of managing his own affairs.

Hermann first discovered his true calling during some lengthy trips, in particular when he came upon the magnificent parklands of England. As a result he started designing the Muskau estate park in 1815. He worked on this project for 30 years.

His marriage for money (in 1817) to Lucie von Hardenberg, who was nine years his senior, was harmonious, although the Prince divorced her a few years later, in order to marry for money once again (this time the marriage did not actually take place), since he had of course used up all his first wife's money for Muskau Park. Despite all their troubles, the pair remained inseparable until Lucie's death in 1858.

When he had to part from Muskau in 1845, at the age of 60, following the threat of its seizure, he took up a new project, Branitz Park, on which he worked for the remaining 25 years of his life.

Tumulus

Prince Pückler had quite individual views on living and dying. He wanted his corpse to be decomposed using caustic soda, potash and lime. In accordance with his wishes, his remains were interred in the 11m/36ft high tumulus in the pyramid lake, which was covered in wild vines.

Braunschweig

Brunswick

The second city of Lower Saxony in population terms, Brunswick was already considered a thriving industrial region at the beginning of the Industrial Revolution, and it remains so to this day. After its destruction in October 1944, the inner city was rebuilt according to modern urban concepts, but some noteworthy sights can still be seen today.

Location

Population: 250 000. Michelin map nos 542, 544 J 15 – Niedersachsen. Located to the south of the Lüneburger Heath, the town of Brunswick is reached from the A 2 motorway which links Hannover and Berlin.

ℹ *Vor der Burg 1, 38100 Braunschweig,* ☎ *(0531) 27 35 50.*

Surrounding area: see WOLFENBÜTTEL (11km/7mi southeast), CELLE (52km/32mi northeast), HANNOVER (63km/40mi west).

Background

The Lion of Brunswick – In 1166, having boosted the House of Guelph to the summit of political power in Germany, Henry the Lion, Duke of Bavaria and Saxony, settled permanently in Brunswick. Frederick I Barbarossa, offended at Henry's meteoric rise, summoned him before the Diet. When "the Lion" refused to appear, he stripped him of everything except his personal properties between the Upper Weser and the Lower Elbe. Henry the Lion died in 1195. The lion sculpture on Burgplatz, the first large free-standing sculpture to be installed north of the Alps, dates from that period.

Till Eulenspiegel Country – Memories of the famous jester and buffoon, **Till Eulenspiegel**, spread far and wide from the beginning of the 16C by storytellers and minstrels, are especially cherished in his native Brunswick. He was born c 1300 in Schöppenstedt, 23km/14mi southeast of the city, where there is a small museum in his honour.

A Cultured Court – Brunswick ceased being a princely residence after the death of Henry the Lion, but the Court was reinstated in 1753 by a younger branch of the House of Brunswick. In 1807, after its conquest by Napoleon, the region was added to the short-lived kingdom of Westphalia.

Patrons of the arts were numbered among the later Brunswick princes: it was Karl II who invited Goethe to stage the first performance of *Faust* in the city in 1828.

Walking About

TOWN CENTRE

Brunswick grew up around 5 distinct districts **(Altstadt, Hagen, Altewiek, Neustadt and Sack)**, each one with its own constitution, town hall and market; the modern-day town retains some traces of its old structure.

The majority of the sights are found in the fully reconstructed town centre, which is best explored on foot.

Altstadtmarkt

One steps back in time when visiting this district, where the old municipal institutions of Brunswick's merchant quarter can be seen. The **old town hall** *(Altstadtrathaus)* is built with stepped gables, the two wings set at right angles to one another (13C-15C). The buttresses of buildings facing the square support statues of the princes of Saxony and the House of Guelph. In the middle of the Poststraße is the **Drapers' Hall** *(Gewandhaus)*, the building with the town's most decorated gable (Late Renaissance). Four principal floors rise above the street, and these are surmounted by four further pediment levels.

Martinikirche

St Martin's, the Hanseatic church at Altstadtmarkt, is the burghers' counterpart to Brunswick cathedral. For centuries it was the city's richest church and now offers us a kind of mini-history of German religious art, both inside and out. It begins in the Romanesque period with 12C towers, continues with the Gothic period (transept façade from 1320, St Anne altar of 1434). The wealthy furnishings begin in the Renaissance and end in the Baroque age with the high altar (1722-25). The group of epitaphs from the 16C and 17C suggests the connection to the powers that be, with monuments to mayors, jurists and officers. Indeed, St Martin's represents the power and pride of the Hanseatic League and its merchants as no other church in northern Germany.

Dom★ (Cathedral)

The Westwerk supports two octagonal towers, linked the whole way up by a Gothic bell gable dating from 1275. This general design was later copied by other churches in the city. The original Romanesque church built at the time of Henry the Lion has groined vaulting. The aisles on the north side create a Late Gothic hall with spiral columns turned in alternate directions. The choir and transept are decorated with 13C painted murals. Note especially: the seven-branched c 1180 **candelabrum★** *(Bronzeleuchter)* in the choir, a donation by Henry the Lion; and the impressive cross (c 1150) by Master Imervard in the northern side nave whose **Christ★** is clothed in a rigidly pleated robe with sleeves. Another Romanesque work of art is the **Marian Altar**, which was consecrated in 1188. An outstanding example of Saxon sculpting is the **tomb** of Henry the Lion and his second wife, Matilda of England, located in the central nave. In the main crypt beneath the chancel, an independent three-naved church, are the tombs of the Guelph princes.

Herzog-Anton-Ulrich-Museum★

♿ *Open Tue-Sat, 10am-5pm (1pm-8pm, Wed). Closed 1 May, 24, 25 and 31 Dec. €2.50.* ☎ *(0531) 122 50; www.museum-braunschweig.de*

Established in 1754, the museum of art and decorative arts possesses a collection of remarkable paintings *(1st floor)* with German, Flemish and Dutch masters represented, including Rembrandt, Rubens, Van Dyck, Vermeer, Cranach the Elder and Holbein. Biblical subjects, popular at the time of the Reformation, are to the fore. The 2nd floor is given over to an exhibition of sculpture and various works of decorative art.

▶▶ Medieval Art Collection in the Burg Dankwarderode.

Excursions

Königslutter am Elm

20km/12.5mi east. On the fringe of the lovely beech forests of the Elm, Königslutter is renowned for its former abbey *(Abteikirche)* better known as the **Imperial Cathedral★** *(Kaiserdom)*. This is a Romanesque basilica with three naves and five apses. The principal nave is embellished with a fine, Lombard-inspired, **carved decoration★★** (the hunting frieze). The north doorway is original: it comprises three lobes upheld by twisted columns, each supported by a lion. Kaiser Lothar, the patron and founder of the Kaiserdom, who laid the cornerstone together with his wife Rihenza, is buried in the church.

The north gallery of the **cloister★** consists of two Romanesque naves with groined vaulting resting on elaborate fluted, trellised and chevroned columns.

Autostadt★★

32km/20mi northeast in Wolfsburg, north of town centre. ♿ Open Apr to Oct, 9am-8pm; Nov to Mar: 9am-6pm. Closed 24 and 31 Dec. €14. ☎ (08 00) 288 67 82 38; www.autostadt.de

This 25ha/62 acre theme park built by the Volkswagen company right by its headquarters boasts generously landscaped areas of park and water dotted with architecturally striking buildings. Everything here revolves around the motor car – its history, the values associated with it, and visions for its future.

Entering the Autostadt via the **KonzernForum** plunges the visitor into an interactive world of state-of-the-art technology, with films, simulators and virtual installations.

In the **KonzernWelt**, four special screens present the company's philosophy. The interactive **AutoLab** demonstrates the manufacture and technology of motor vehicles by means of live experiments. The **ZeitHaus** is a museum of the history of the automobile with numerous models polished to perfection, including John Lennon's Beetle. Naturally, pride of place is given to the success story of Volkswagen as a marque. The **MarkenPavillions** show the individual marques under the Volkswagen company umbrella. The image of the marque is translated into sounds and images to appeal to senses and emotions. For example the speed and performance of the Lamborghini Diablo is communicated in a gripping show with powerful light and sound effects (110 decibels). Skoda and Seat, on the other hand are presented with the emphasis more on poetry and folklore. The 360° spherical screen in the Volkswagen pavilion is particularly impressive. The **KundenCenter,** with towers **(AutoTürmen)** illuminated by night, contains cars fresh from the production line and ready for collection.

There are special facilities for children of all ages, and supervision is provided. This town with a difference also offers a number of restaurants, cafés and shops, along with a five-star hotel. It is also possible to take a guided tour around the VW factory from Monday to Friday *(1hr, included in admission fee, request tour when buying entry ticket).*

Helmstedt

41km/25mi east

This small town with its numerous picturesque half-timbered houses was the seat of a university until 1810. A memento of this is the richly ornamented **Juleum★**, built in the Renaissance style at the end of the 16C and once the university's main building *(access from the pedestrian zone via Neumärker Straße and Collegienstraße).*

Helmstedt-Marienborn was once the most important border crossing point inside Germany, and three monuments here illustrate the bizarre conditions that once prevailed along the Iron Curtain: the **Zonengrenz-Museum** in Helmstedt itself *(Südertor 6; ♿ Open Mar: Wed, 10am-noon, 3-5pm, Thu, 3-6.30pm, Fri, 3-5pm, Sat-Sun, 10am-5pm. No charge. ☎ (053 51) 121 11 33; www.helmstedt.de)*, the **Grenzdenkmal Hötensleben** *(16km/10mi S of Helmstedt via Schöningen)*, where the original border installations have been preserved over a distance of 350m/390yd, and the actual border crossing point, which has been transformed into the **Gedenkstätte Deutsche Teilung Marienborn★** *(access via A 2, towards Berlin)*, an impressive archive and documentation centre. *♿ Open Tue-Sat, 10am-5pm. Donation. ☎ (0394 06) 920 90; www.grenzdenkmaeler.de*

Bremen★★

Bremen is a pleasantly bustling town famous for its Beck's beer and popularised by the Brothers Grimm. Bremen itself is Germany's oldest maritime city. It had market rights from 965; in 1358 it joined the Hanseatic League; in 1646 it was declared a Free Imperial City; and direct trading with America began as early as 1783. By tradition it is a cotton and coffee town, its Cotton Exchange ranks with Liverpool's as a world authority. Bremen is also a town of culture, where the Weser Renaissance architectural style blossomed; there are numerous parks as well as a charming promenade along the river.

Location

Population: 550 000. Michelin map n° 541 G 10 – Bremen. Bremen, at the inner end of the Weser estuary, and Bremerhaven, its outer harbour 59km/37mi downstream, together form a remarkable port system.

ℹ *Am Bahnhofsplatz, 28195 Bremen, ☎ (0421) 30 80 00.*

Surrounding area: see OLDENBURG (48km/30mi west on the A 28), LÜNEBURGER HEIDE (Undeloh is 62km/39mi east), HAMBURG (126km/79mi northeast on the A 1).

Background

Die Bremischen Häfen (The Harbours) – The Bremen harbour group (including Bremen City and Bremerhaven) provides employment directly or indirectly for about a third of the city's population. With a turnover of over 304 million tonnes, these harbours are the largest in Germany after Hamburg.

Bremen specialises in the importation of raw materials. By far the most important of its activities is however the handling of container transport and cars. Each year more than a million containers pass through the Wilhelm-Kaisen-Terminal, Europe's largest container transhipment terminal, and over one million motor vehicles go through the docks. The harbour group of Bremerhaven is Europe's leading port for the turnaround of vehicles.

♿ *Tours leave from the quay by the St Martinikirche. Duration of trip: 1hr 15min. Departures Apr to Oct daily at 11.45am, 1.30pm, 3.15pm and 4.45pm; Nov-Mar, Sat-Sun at 1.30pm and 3.15pm. €8. ☎ (018 05) 10 10 30; www.bremen-tourism.de*

Coffee bean city

Bremen's close links with coffee date back over three centuries. The first ever coffee house in German-speaking countries was built here in 1673, before those in Vienna and Hamburg. Half of all the cups of coffee drunk in Germany are brewed from beans imported via the port at Bremen.

Walking About

OLD BREMEN *Allow 2hr*

Marktplatz★★

The market square, its wide expanse surrounded by the finest buildings in the city, lies in the heart of the old town. The centre is marked by a giant 10m/33ft statue of **Roland** beneath a Gothic canopy (1404). The knight bears the sword of justice and a shield adorned with the Imperial eagle.

The **Schütting**, an elegant 16C building, used to house Bremen's Guild of Merchants. The decoration of its façade shows a Flemish influence.

Rathaus★

Guided tour (45min) Mon-Sat, 11am, noon, 3pm and 4pm, Sun 11am and noon. €4. ☎ (018 05) 10 10 30; www.bremen-tourism.de

The main building is Gothic, its upper floors crowned by decorative gables – part of a 17C transformation in the Weser Renaissance style.

The three-storey principal façade rises from an arcaded gallery emphasised by a richly carved balustrade. Above this, tall windows alternate with statues of Charlemagne and the Seven Electors (copies: the Gothic originals are in the Focke-Museum). Three Renaissance gables embellish the top floor.

At the corner of the west wing is a bronze group by the modern sculptor Gerhard Marcks representing the *Animal Musicians of Bremen* (a pyramid formed by an ass, a dog, a cat, and a cockerel) – characters from a popular fairy tale by the Brothers Grimm.

Interior – A splendid spiral **staircase★★** *(Wendeltreppe)* in carved wood (1620) adorns the first-floor Council Chamber. The room's Renaissance decoration recalls connections with the law courts *(The Judgement of Solomon)* and with the sea (models of boats). The **Guildhall** *(Güldenkammer)* – a small council chamber renovated between 1903 and 1905 by Heinrich Vogeler – is noteworthy for its sumptuous leather wall hangings enriched with gold.

The Bremer Rathauskeller *(entrance on the west side)* serves exclusively German wines from 600 different vineyards.

St Petri-Dom★

In general, the cathedral presents much the same massive appearance as it did in the 11C, but traces of the 16C and 19C rebuilding are clearly evident in the exterior detail.

Pannekoekschip Admiral Nelson.

M. Hertlein/MICHELIN

Where to Eat

Paulaner's – *Schlachte 30 – ☎ (0421) 169 06 91 – www.paulaners.de – Booking advised – €8/14.* A pleasant, country-style establishment with efficient but friendly service. Riverside establishment with beautiful Biergarten. Bavarian dishes feature on the menu.

John Benton Restaurant – *Am Markt 1 – ☎ (0421) 32 30 33 – Closed 24 Dec – ♿ – €14.70/24.* This popular address is spread over two floors in the heart of the old town. Beautiful views of the cathedral from the terrace. Various meat dishes.

Cargo – *Schlachte 18 – ☎ (0421) 165 55 99 – www.cargo-bremen.de – Reservation required – €21.70/27.90.* A trendy establishment situated on the promenade along the Weser. The restaurant covers two floors with modern, understated décor. Extensive choice of dishes on the menu and cocktails at the bar.

Where to Stay

Bölts am Park – *Slevogtstraße 23 – ☎ (0421) 34 61 10 – fax (0421) 341227 – 16rm: €35/83 – Restaurant €15.70/21.70.* As its name indicates, this quiet little guesthouse is in the park. Well-looked after guestrooms and a lovely breakfast room with views of the small back garden.

Hotel Buthmann – *Löningstraße 29 – ☎ (0421) 32 63 97 – fax (0421) 3398816 – www.hotel-buthmann.de – 10rm: €45/75.* This little guesthouse is situated close to the station. Its guestrooms are clean, well-cared for and furnished in wood, with plain décor. The reasonable rates are another advantage.

Park Hotel – *Im Bürgerpark – ☎ (0421) 340 80 – fax (0421) 3408602 – relax@park-hotel-bremen.de – 150rm: from €155.* The luxury and exclusive nature of this place are obvious as soon as you enter the sumptuous domed lounge of this former country house. The individually-decorated suites are particularly splendid and the fitness centre has a Turkish bath and heated outdoor pool.

The richly-decorated Town Hall

Bremer Touristik-Zentrale

Taking a Break

F. L. Bodes – *Bischofsnadel 1-2 (alleyway which leads from Wallanlagen to Domshof) – ☎ (0421) 32 41 44 – www.bodes.de – Tue-Thu, 8am-6pm, Fri, 8am-6.30pm, Sat, 8am-3pm – Closed Sun, Mon, and bank holidays.* Fish shop and snack bar a stone's throw from the town centre. Try seafood and fish à la carte, choose from the blackboard menus or make your selection directly from the stalls. It's best to avoid lunchtimes *(between 11.30am and 2pm)* when it can get extremely busy.

Konditorei Knigge – *Sögestr. 42-44 – ☎ (0421) 1 30 60 – www.knigge-shop.de – Mon-Sat 9am-6.30pm, Sun 12-6pm.* Bremen's classic tearoom, decorated in various styles. House specialities include the "Bremer Klaben", a type of fruitcake.

Going Out

Useful tip – In Bremen, most of the cafés, bars, restaurants and little bric-a-brac shops are located in the historic Schnoor district, to the south of the cathedral. The Schlachte, on the right bank of the Weser, is a Mecca for gastronomes. There are also plenty of bars here, many of which have a terrace looking on to the river.

Café Frei'tag – *Böttcherstr. 3-5 – ☎ (0421) 32 09 95 – open every day from 10am (food served: 11.30am-8.30pm).* This elegant café-bar is modern in design is situated in the Robinson-Crusoe House on the famous Böttcherstraße. In summer the terrace is the perfect place to sit back and people-watch.

Pannekoekschip Admiral Nelson – *Schlachte Anleger 1 – ☎ (0421) 3 64 99 84 – www.admiral-nelson.de – Food served: Fri-Sat, 12-10pm, Sun-Thu, 12-9.30pm; Nov-May: every day except Mon.* Ahoy there! Friendly 'pirates' serve sweet or savoury thick pancakes on this three-masted ship.

Salomon's – *Ostertorstr. 11-13 – ☎ (0421) 2 44 17 71 – www.salomons-bremen.de – 9-2am.* The bar-restaurant is situated in a wing of the 19C Law Courts. Reasonably-priced dishes are served here Monday to Saturday from 11.30am-3pm. In summer months there is a beautiful terrace in the interior courtyard of this historic building.

Culture

Useful tip – The monthly magazines *Mix* (free, available from restaurants and bookshops), *Bremer* and *Prinz* (available to buy from bookshops or from newspaper stands in the town) are helpful when planning an evening in Bremen.

Shopping

Useful tip – The elegant shopping thoroughfares of Lloydpassage, Domshof Passage and Katharinen-Viertel in the heart of the town are great for a stroll. Independent little boutiques are located in the historic Schnoor district *(see Going Out)*.

BREMEN

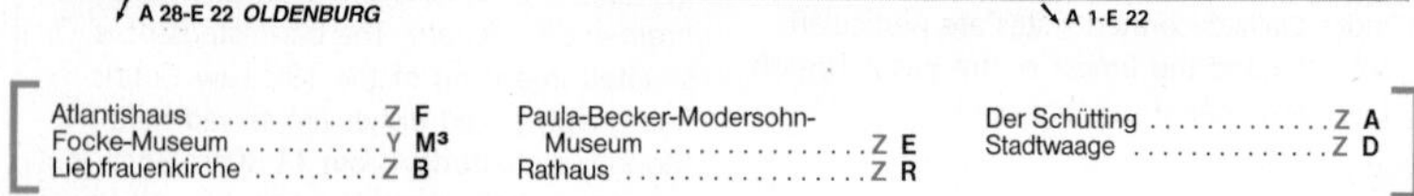
Atlantishaus . . . . Z F
Focke-Museum . . . . Y M³
Liebfrauenkirche . . . . Z B
Paula-Becker-Modersohn-Museum . . . . Z E
Rathaus . . . . Z R
Der Schütting . . . . Z A
Stadtwaage . . . . Z D

Inside, against the first left-hand pillar of the raised chancel, stands a fine 16C **Virgin and Child★**. Among the 16C carvings on the organ balustrade can be seen, in the middle, the figures of Charlemagne and Willehad, the first Bishop of Bremen. Beneath the organ loft, the 11C western crypt houses Romanesque capitals and a magnificent bronze **baptismal font★★** (*Taufbecken*, c 1220). A small organ by Gottfried Silbermann also stands here, the only one outside Saxony. The eastern crypt, which dates from the age of the early Salian Franks boasts important capitals adorned with chessboard ornamentation and mythological animals.

The **cathedral museum** *(Dom-Museum)* displays items recovered from tombs beneath the nave.

The inner courtyard leads to the **Lead Cellar** *(Bleikeller)*, which displays eight mummified bodies in glass coffins. The mummification is a result of the extremely dry air in the cellar.

Pfarrkirche Unserer Lieben Frauen (Church of Our Lady)

The plain interior of this hall church (construction began in 1229), bare of decoration except for the 1709 chancel, is relieved by rounded ogive vaulting dating to the construction period. The four main stained-glass windows, on biblical themes, were executed between 1966 and 1979 by Alfred Manessier.

The market place in the heart of the old town, dominated by an immense statue of Roland.

The church has a simple **crypt** with a groined vault and a single central pillar dating from the preceding church (St Veit), which has been traced to 1020 and therefore represents the oldest built-up space in Bremen.

Stadtwaage (Weigh-House)

A lovely 16C building constructed with alternating layers of brick and embossed stone.

Böttcherstraße★

This narrow street, running from the Marktplatz to the River Weser, was built between 1923 and 1933 by the industrialist Ludwig Roselius, who had made his fortune in the coffee trade. While architects Runge and Scotland took the local building style as their inspiration, Bernhard Hoetger gave free rein to his imagination, drawing on the Expressionist style with Jugendstil (Art Nouveau) and Art Deco overtones. The tall, gabled buildings of this highly original street house art galleries, shops and museums. Between two of the gables, a porcelain carillon chimes at noon, 3pm and 6pm *(in summer, on the hour between noon and 6pm).*

Paula-Modersohn-Becker-Museum★ – *Böttcherstraße 6-10. Tue-Sun, 11am-6pm. €5. ☎ (0421) 336 50 66; www.pmbm.de.* The Paula Modersohn-Becker house was built by Bernhard Hoetger and provides the ideal setting for the display of paintings, drawings and graphic work by Modersohn-Becker (1876-1907), one of the pioneers of modern art.

The **Museum in the Roselius-Haus** *(Museum im Roseliushaus)*, a merchant's mansion dating from 1588, contains luxurious furnishings, paintings and craftwork from the 12C to 19C. Works from Lucas Cranach the Elder's studio and a Lamentation group by Tilman Riemenschneider are the high points of this collection built up by Roselius.

Atlantishaus – This 1931 block, decorated with the signs of the zodiac, has an unusual spiral staircase made of concrete and glass.

Not far away, beyond the Martinistraße, on the banks of the Weser, is the 13C-14C **hall-church of St Martin** *(St-Martinikirche).*

Worth a Visit

Schnoorviertel★

The cottages in this quarter, once the homes of fishermen and their families, are all that remains of Old Bremen. In styles ranging from the 15C to the 19C, they have all been restored and are now used as art galleries, antique shops, restaurants and craft boutiques. The narrow streets of the quarter, popular with tourists, are very busy after dark.

Kunsthalle★ (Art Gallery)

♿ *Open Tue-Sun, 10am-5pm (Tue until 9pm). Closed 24 and 31 Dec. €5. ☎ (0421) 32 90 80; www.kunsthalle-bremen.de*

An outstanding collection of 19C and 20C French and German art is the main attraction here. On display are works by: Courbet, Delacroix and the Barbizon School; Menzel, Leibl, Beckmann; the French Impressionists and their German counterparts; artists of the Worpswede School *(see below)*. Earlier periods of European art are illustrated by 15C Old Masters, and by Rubens, Rembrandt, Tiepolo, up to Picasso. In the print room (Kupferstichkabinett) are over 230 000 prints and drawings of exceptional quality from Dürer's day to the present.

Focke-Museum★★

Leave via the Rembertiring. ♿ *Open Tue-Sun, 10am-5pm (-9pm, Tue). Closed 1 Jan, Easter Sun, Whitsun, 1 May, Ascension, 3 Oct, 24, 25 and 31 Dec. €3.50. ☎ (0421) 361 35 75; www.bremen.de/info/focke*

This regional museum nestled amid parkland covers the artistic and cultural evolution of Bremen and its surroundings. It houses all these treasures from 1 000 years of Bremen history in four historic buildings and one modern main house.

The newly opened Main House (Haupthaus) holds some particularly noteworthy objects in the entrance hall underlining some topics that have remained important to Bremen to this day: the Bremen house, the Weser, Bremen silverware, car and shipbuilding. This is followed by a chronological tour up to and including the present. Shipping and trade are just one aspect of the maritime history of this ancient Hanseatic town.

The prehistoric collections from the region can be seen in a thatched annex. A farmhouse – a Lower German hall house from Mittelsbüren built around 1586 – on the museum grounds is devoted to the inland areas of Bremen. The Tarnstedter Scheune (Tarnstedt Barn) shows the products of rural work.

Haus Riensberg also belongs to the museum *(right from the lane leading to the Focke-Museum)*. This house built in the second half of the 18C was once an estate and summer residence for upper class Bremen families. It displays the collections covering bourgeois lifestyle and collections extending beyond the local region to cover Fürstenberg porcelain and European glass art.

►► Wallanlagen★ *(rampart promenade)* – Übersee-Museum *(ethnographic collections)* – Neues Museum Weserburg *(collectors' museum with contemporary art)* – Universum Science Center *(Wiener Straße 2)*.

Excursions

Worpswede

24km/15mi north – about 1hr 30min. Leave Bremen by the Rembertiring. Isolated at one time in a desolate landscape of peat moors, the village of Worpswede attracted at the end of the 19C a colony of artists, notable among whom were Paula Modersohn-Becker, her husband Otto Modersohn and the poet Rainer Maria Rilke. Since then, galleries, studios and craft workshops have multiplied. Odd, asymmetrical buildings such as the Worpswede Café and the Niedersachsenstein First World War Memorial illustrate the avant-garde ideas and innovations of the architects allied to the group.

Bremerhaven

58km/36mi north. Bremen's deep-sea port was founded at the mouth of the Weser estuary in 1827. Half of the German national fishing fleet is based here, but Bremerhaven is first and foremost an important container port *(see "The Harbours" above)*.

►► Deutsches Schiffahrtsmuseum★★ *(national maritime museum)* – Technikmuseum U-Boot Wilhelm Bauer *(submarine museum)* – Zoo am Meer *(aquarium)*.

Schloß Bruchsal★★

Bruchsal, residence of the last four prince-bishops of Speyer, is blessed with a pretentious Baroque palace reconstructed after its destruction in March 1945. Maximilian von Welsch was the architect of this vast complex, built in 1722 on the orders of the Prince-Bishop Damian Hugo von Schönborn. As well as the palace, there is an unusual and entertaining museum devoted to mechanical musical instruments.

Location

Michelin map n° 545 S 9 – Baden-Württemberg. Twenty kilometres/12.5mi north of Karlsruhe, on the edge of the rolling hills of the Kraichgau, the castle complex comprises around 50 dwellings or annexes; the main road from Karlsruhe to Heidelberg runs through the extensive grounds.

Surrounding area: see KARLSRUHE (20km/12.5mi south), Kloster MAULBRONN (24km/15mi east), SCHWARZWALD (the forest begins 30km/19mi south of Bruchsal), SPEYER (35km/22mi north), HEIDELBERG (38km/24mi north).

Worth a Visit

Central Block

♿ *Open every day except Mon. 9.30am-5pm. €3.50. ☎ (072 51) 74 26 61; www.schloesser-und-gaerten.de*

Pride of place here is held by a magnificent **staircase**★★ with an oval well designed by Balthasar Neumann in 1731. Rococo stucco decorates the dome above it. The **state apartments** have items from the original furnishings on display, such as silver and porcelain tableware and portraits of the prelates.

The Gartensaal – a vaulted room with a marble floor – opens onto the park *(Hofgarten)*. When they were at their best, blazing with formal flowerbeds in the French manner, the **gardens** boasted a broadwalk that extended as far as the river, 16km/10mi away.

Museum mechanischer Musikinstrumente★★

In the main building. Guided tour of about 1hr, with demonstration of instruments. ♿ Open every day except Mon. 9.30am-5pm. €4, including castle visit. ☎ (072 51) 74 26 61; www.schloesser-und-gaerten.de

This department of the Regional Museum derives from a private collection and includes about 200 instruments ranging from the 18C to the 20C, most of them worked by cylinders, pricked-out metal or cardboard, or rolls of paper. The guided tour is enchanting: a recital is performed on each instrument after an explanation of how it functions. Cinema organs, "Barbary organs", and pianolas (mechanical pianos operated by perforated "piano-rolls") are also represented. Note particularly the "household" organs and orchestrions (in 19C England Aeolian Orchestrelles – machines resembling an oversize upright piano, complete with manual keyboard and stops for different "voices" – wind-operated by means of pedals). Examples from Leipzig and the Black Forest are well represented here.

Städtisches Museum

Southern part of the main block, on the attic floor. ☎ (07251) 74 26 61.

The museum is divided up into five areas: the palaeontological collection, which also contains minerals from Bruchsal and its surrounding area; the prehistoric department with regional finds from the Late Stone Age to the end of the Middle Ages; the Bruchsal penal system; the numismatic and medal collections of the former state of Baden, the Palatinate and the prince-episcopate of Speyer.

Brühl

Brühl developed around a fortress which acquired municipal status in 1285. After the destruction of the fortress by foreign troops, its foundations were used for the construction in the 18C of the Augustusburg Palace. Brühl is widely known for this masterpiece of Rococo, which has been placed on UNESCO's World Heritage List.

Location

Population: 41 500. Michelin map n° 543 N 4 – Nordrhein-Westfalen. Brühl is situated on route 265 a few miles to the south of Cologne (directly linked to Cologne by the B51)

🅱 *Uhlstraße 1, 50321 Brühl, ☎ (022 32) 793 45.*

Surrounding area: see KÖLN (13km/8mi north), BONN (22km/14mi south), KOBLENZ (90km/56mi south).

Background

SCHLOSS AUGUSTUSBURG★★

Allow at least 1 hr.

♿ *Feb-Nov: Guided tour (1hr) every day except Mon. 9am-noon, 1.30-4pm, Sat-Sun, 10am-5pm. €4. ☎ (022 32) 440 00; www.schlossbruehl.de*

The Rococo palace was built for Clemens August, illustrious member of the House of Wittelsbach. August became a bishop at the age of 19, but showed more interest in the material than the spiritual world. Hawking was his passion and he decided to build a hunting lodge. When he became the Archbishop and Elector of Cologne four years later, this project evolved into a palace, where he could hold court in magnificent style. From 1725 to 1768, Westphalian master-builder Johann Conrad Schlaun and Bavarian court architect François de Cuvilliés contructed a sumptuous Rococo castle. A splendid staircase was built to fill visitors with wonder, with a superb ceiling trompe l'œil, giving the impression of a cupola. The gardens were designed by a pupil of Lenôtre.

Staircase★★

The Würzburg court architect **Balthasar Neumann** produced one of his most beautiful compositions in this splendid staircase. The marble stuccowork, used in abundance, is in shades of greyish-green and yellowish-orange. Four powerful, vivacious supporting figures are grouped around each pillar and hold up the vault. The **ceiling fresco★** by Carlo Carlone is in celebration of the prince and of the House of Wittelsbach.

Interior★★

A good two dozen rooms can be visited.

Large new suite: This suite comprises a garden room with ceiling fresco by Carlo Carlone, a dining room with gallery and elaborate ceiling and wall paintings, a magnificent **audience chamber★**.

Summer suite: The rooms in this suite are all on the ground floor and were intended for use on hot summer days. In order to reinforce the airy impression, the floors are covered in blue and white tiles from Rotterdam, which are laid in attractive patterns.

Yellow suite: The yellow suite was principally used by Clemens August as his private residence. Cuvilliés designed the rooms in the Régence style.

Garden★

The French style garden designed by Lenôtre student Dominique Girardet, with reflective lakes and elaborately decorative beds gradually gives way to a country park that was designed around 1840 by Peter Joseph Lenné.

SCHLOSS FALKENLUST★

Some 2.5km/1.5mi from Schloß Augustusburg. Go past the lake and along Falkenluster Allee. A 20min slide show with synchronised sound provides an insight into the history of the building and the appointments of this castle.

Feb-Nov: Open Tue-Sun, 9am-noon, 1.30-4pm, Sat-Sun, 10am-5pm. €3. ☎ (022 32) 121 11; www.schlossbruehl.de

This captivating little two-storey Rococo palace with its belvedere and lantern roof is designed in an absolutely symmetrical shape.

Inside, the small **japanned room★** with its lacquered paintings is most impressive. The staircase is covered with blue and white tiles right up to ceiling height. Particularly remarkable is the small **mirrored room★**, a miniature masterpiece with its blue-edged panels and gilded carved frames.

Excursion

Phantasialand★

On the southern edge of the town. ♿ *Open Apr to mid-Oct: 9am-6pm; mid-Oct to early Nov: 9am-9pm. €24.50. ☎ (022 32) 362 00; www.phantasialand.de*

The 28ha/69 acre leisure park, which is famous for its rides, offers many attractions within four themed areas: log flumes with drops of up to 16m/52ft, one of the world's largest indoor roller-coasters, a monorail jet, a **Wild West stunt show**, and an exciting simulated space flight. The **Wintergarten-Show★** (book places at the Wintergarten ticket office) is magic in motion: one of the best attractions features great illusions with white tigers.

►► Schloßkirche.

Burghausen★★

The dukes of Bavaria, who became lords of Burghausen in the 12C, made it into the biggest fortress in Germany: the defence system, reinforced at the beginning of the 16C in the face of a threatened invasion by the Turks, stretches for more than 0.8km/0.5mi. Above the old town is the castle, built on a quite exceptional site★★ – a long, narrow, rocky spur separating the Salzach from the Wöhrsee.

Location

Population: 19 000. Michelin map n° 546 V 22 – Bayern. Burghausen lies within a curve of the River Salzach, where it forms the frontier between Bavaria and Austria.
Rathaus, Stadtplatz 112, 84489 Burghausen, ☎ (086 77) 24 35.
Surrounding area: see PASSAU (83km/52mi northeast), LANDSHUT (75km/47mi northwest), CHIEMSEE (61km/38mi southwest), the eastern section of the Deutsche ALPENSTRASSE (Berchtesgaden is 76km/48mi south).

Directory

Where to Eat

Fuchsstuben – *Mauthnerstraße 271 – ☎ (08677) 627 24 – Closed end of Aug to mid-Sep, Sun evenings and Mon – €19/36.* A handy establishment, located in the heart of the old town. The tastefully-decorated dining room has a terracotta floor and is filled with German antique-style furniture.

Where to Stay

Bayerische Alm – *Robert-Koch-Straße 211 – ☎ (08677) 98 20 – fax (08677) 982200 – info@bayerischealm.de – P – 23rm: €60/98 – Restaurant €22.50/36.* For a holiday among the pastures with views of the Salzach, don't hesitate to try this intimate, country-style establishment, with Alpine-style balconies. Charming rustic restaurant covering two floors and with pleasant terrace on to the garden.

Worth a Visit

Burg★★ (Castle)

Allow about 2hr 30min walking and sightseeing. Leaving the car in the Stadtplatz, follow the road which circles the cliff at the southern extremity of the spur and pass beneath the Wöhrenseeturm. Beyond the lake, a steep path leads to the outer line of fortifications. From here, the ramparts stepped up the Eggenberg hill, on the far side, are visible. The *Georgstor*, or **St George's Gate**, is set in the innermost ring of battlements, which protect the last small medieval courtyard at the castle's centre. There are two museums in the main block.

Staatliche Sammlungen (Municipal collections) – The former ducal apartments house original 15C-17C furniture and an interesting collection of late Gothic panel paintings by the Bavarian School. From the observation **platform** *(62 steps, access from the second floor)*, there is a splendid panoramic **view★** of Burghausen, the Salzach and the surrounding hills.
The Gothic **chapel** *(in the same wing)* has elegant star vaulting. *Open Apr to Sep, 9am-6pm, Oct to Mar, 10am-4pm. €2.50. ☎ (0871) 924 11 44.*

Stadtmuseum (Municipal Museum) – This is installed in the apartments once reserved for the duchess *(west side of the main block)*. The main exhibit traces the history of Burghausen. It includes collections of local folk art, craftwork and country furniture. *Open from mid-Mar to end Apr and Oct, 10am-4.30pm; May to Sep, 9am-6.30pm. €1.30. ☎ (086 77) 651 98.*

Returning directly to the Stadtplatz via the **Burgsteig** *(a ramp between the castle entrance and the Georgstor)*, there is a particularly fine **view** of the old town.

Excursions

Marienberg

4km/2.5mi south. Here there is a Rococo pilgrims' church (1764) which is almost square in plan. Inside, the dome over the central part of the building is adorned with a fresco painted by Martin Heigel: a boat (symbol of the Church) lies beneath the Holy Trinity, surrounded by celebrated members of the Founding Fathers. Note the ornate high altar.

Städt, Verkehrs- u. Kulturamt, Burghausen

Burghausen, dominated by its castle, for many years the largest fortress in Germany.

Raitenhaslach

6km/4mi south. Red-marble tombstones enshrining the memory of abbots from the 15C to the 18C can be seen in this 12C Cistercian church, which was modified in the Baroque style in the late 17C. The life of St Bernard of Clairvaux is illustrated in the fine **ceiling paintings★★** (1739) by Johannes Zick of Lachen, near Ottobeuren (1702-62).

Numerous interesting tombstones (15-18C) of former abbots.

Tittmoning

16km/10mi south. On the west bank of the Salzach, across the water from Austria, Tittmoning preserves the remains of its medieval fortifications and a castle which was once the residence of the prince-bishops of Salzburg. Two old fortified gateways give access to the wide **Stadtplatz**, which is bordered by houses with ridge roofs masked by perpendicular copings. Brightly painted façades, some decorated with gilded figures, wrought iron signs, oriel windows and emblazoned fountains add considerable style to the ensemble.

Altötting

21km/13mi northwest. This pilgrimage centre consecrated to the Virgin is one of the oldest in Bavaria and draws more than 700 000 people to the town each year. The Miraculous Virgin, a black Madonna, is housed in the octagonal **Holy Chapel** *(Heilige Kapelle)*.

In the late Gothic **Parish Church** *(Stiftskirche)*, there are two fine pieces in the Treasury *(Schatzkammer)*: a splendid Flemish ivory crucifix dating from 1580, and a masterpiece of goldsmith's work (c 1404) – a small gold horse, originally given to Charles VI of France by his wife, Isabella of Bavaria. Johann Tzerklaes, Count of Tilly (1559-1632), a famous general on the side of the Catholic League in the Thirty Years War, is buried in the crypt *(entrance through the cloister)*.

Celle★★

Formerly the official residence of the Dukes of Brunswick-Lüneburg, Celle retains the air of an aristocratic retreat. Its carefully preserved centre of half-timbered houses has miraculously escaped war damage over the centuries. There are many reasons to stop off here: the treasures of the old town, the magnificent restored ducal castle or the Folklore museum – elegant Celle has much to offer.

Location

Population: 74 000. Michelin maps n°s 541, 542, 544 I 14 – Niedersachsen. Celle is located in the Lüneburg Heath, a region filled with charming little villages and with plenty of opportunities to explore the countryside.

Markt 14-16, 29221 Celle, ☎ (051 41) 12 12.

Surrounding area: see HANNOVER (41km/26mi southwest), BRAUNSCHWEIG (52km/32.5mi southeast), LÜNEBURGER HEIDE (89km/56mi north).

Walking About

OLD TOWN★★

Allow 1hr to explore the historic centre of Celle.

The largely pedestrianised old town of Celle has many half-timbered houses particularly in the Neue Straße, the Zöllnerstraße, the Poststraße (note the richly carved Hoppenerhaus, which dates from 1532) and the narrow Kalandgasse, near to the church (**Alte Lateinschule**, 1602).

Rathaus

The pale roughcast town hall is in different Renaissance styles. The north gable, built in 1579 by craftsmen who came from the banks of the Weser, is heavily scrolled and bristles with fantastic pinnacles *(the Weser Renaissance style, see HAMELN).*

Directory

WHERE TO EAT

⊖⊖ Weinkeller Postmeister von Hinüber – *Zöllnerstraße 25 – ☎ (05141) 284 44 – info@weinkeller-celle.de – Closed for 3 weeks in Jul and Aug, Sun and Mon – €25/33.* This historic half-timbered house surprises with its stylish interior. The Weinkeller is a beautifully rustic taverna in the brick cellar with huge wooden tables.

WHERE TO STAY

⊖ Hotel Am Hehlentor – *Nordwall 62 – ☎ (05141) 885 69 00 – fax (05141) 885 69013 – info@hotel-am-hehlentor.de – P – 16rm: €53.* This wonderful half-timbered house is typical of the old-fashioned charm of the old town. The well-kept interior is rather modern and in summer months, breakfast can be enjoyed in the interior courtyard, among the plants.

Where to Visit

Schloß★

Guided tour (50min). Open Apr to Oct: Tue-Sun, 11am-3pm; Nov to Mar: Tue-Sun, 11am and 3pm. Closed 24 and 25 Dec. €3. ☎ (051 41) 123 73.

Construction of the castle began in 1292 and it initially served as fortification for the town. Modified in the Renaissance style in 1530, it was given a Baroque look at the end of the 18C. The unfortunate Queen Caroline Mathilde of Denmark was exiled, and died, here in 1775 at the age of 24.

This rectangular fortress is flanked by massive corner towers. The eastern façade, overlooking the town, features dormer windows topped by rounded pediments – a characteristic of the Weser Renaissance style.

The castle **chapel★** *(Hofkapelle)* is Renaissance in origin; its galleries are partly open and partly glazed in. The chapel was modified in the late 16C by the Flemish painter Martin de Vos (1532-1603), whose *Crucifixion* adorns the altar. Nearby is the **Schloßtheater**; built in 1674 to an Italian design and said to be the oldest court theatre in Germany, it is still in action today with its own theatre company.

A permanent exhibition from the Bomann Museum in the eastern wing documents the history of the kingdom of Hanover.

Bomann-Museum★

Schloßplatz. ♿ Open Tue-Sun, 10am-5pm. €2.50. Closed 24, 25 and 31 Dec. ☎ (051 41) 123 72. The rich collections in this interesting museum cover the folklore of Lower Saxony and the history of the town of Celle. In the centre of the local history section is also a display on the history of the former kingdom of Hanover.

Stadtkirche★ (Church)

This dark and originally Gothic church was considerably renovated in rich Baroque style by Italian stuccoworkers between 1676 and 1698. Especially noteworthy are the 1613 **altar**, which combines Renaissance features with Baroque elements, the 1565-66 Fürstenstuhl (Prince's Seat) beneath the organ and the 1610 baptismal font. The remains of dukes from the Celle branch of the House of Guelph lie in the **princes' vault** beneath the chancel. The commemorative stones are above in the chancel itself.

►► Synagogue (*Im Kreise 24*).

Excursions

Kloster Wienhausen★

10km/6mi south. ♿ Guided tour (75min; leaves hourly). Apr to Sep: Tue-Sun at 10am, 11am, 2pm, 3pm, 4pm and 5pm, Sun 12noon-5pm; beginning of Oct to mid-Oct: last tour, 4pm. Closed Good Fri. €3.50. ☎ (051 49) 357.

This Cistercian abbey, founded in 1233 by Henry the Lion's daughter-in-law Agnes of Meissen, has been occupied since the Reformation by a small community of Protestant canonesses. Among the piously preserved relics are a stone statue (1280) of the founder, and 13C wooden figures of the Virgin of Wienhausen and Christ Resurrected. The **Nuns' Choir** is embellished with fine early-14C **mural paintings★**.

Once a year, for 11 days only, starting on the Friday after Whitsun, the convent holds an exhibition of its famous tapestries (1300-1500), woven by the nuns in medieval times.

Chiemsee★

Known as the "Bavarian Sea", the Chiemsee (pronounced Keem-zay) is the largest of the province's lakes, with a surface area of 82km/32sq mi. Its calm waters lie between gently sloping, rush-covered banks. Two islands, not far from the west bank, are worth a visit. They are named the Herreninsel (gentlemen's isle) and Fraueninsel (ladies' isle). On the former is an extraordinary palace, which took Versailles for inspiration; on the latter, an abbey.

Location

Michelin map nº 546 W 21 – Bayern. The foothills of the Bavarian Alps are clearly visible to the south, with their peaks in the background. Summer resorts popular with water sports enthusiasts line the banks of the lake, in particular **Prien**, the busiest, and **Seebruck**.

The Salzburg-Munich motorway runs close to the Chiemsee's flat, marshy southern extremity, but it is from the northern bank, between Rimsting and Seebruck, that the most interesting vistas – with the Alpine peaks as a dramatic backdrop – can be seen.

Surrounding area: see Deutsche ALPENSTRASSE (itinerary along the south bank of the Chiemsee), WASSERBURG (27km/17mi northwest), BURGHAUSEN (61km/38mi northeast), and Ludwig II's other castles: LINDERHOF and NEUSCHWANSTEIN (134km/84mi and 154km/96mi southwest).

Worth a Visit

THE ISLANDS

From the motorway (Bernau exit), approach the lake from the west, and make for the **Prien-Stock landing-stage.** *Allow 15min for the trip to the Herreninsel, €5.70 return trip; for a combined ticket for Herreninsel and Fraueninsel, allow 75min, €6.80. Boats leave every half hour.*

Boat trips around the lake: all year leaving from the Prien-Stock landing-stage: €6.80, return trip. ☎ (080 51) 60 90; www.chiemsee-schifffahrt.de

T. Krieger/MICHELIN

Boats with the village of Seebruck in the background.

Herreninsel

The parks, woods and forests and as well as the numerous paths of the "Gentlemen's Isle", make this island an excellent place to explore on foot. Excavations have revealed traces of an 8C monastery. The young **King Ludwig II of Bavaria** bought the whole of this island in 1873 to save it from a systematic deforestation, but also because he wanted to build a sumptuous palace there.

Schloß Herrenchiemsee★★ – *20min on foot from the landing-stage. ♿ Guided tours (30min, available in English). Visitors to Schloß Herrenchiemsee should be prepared to queue for at least an hour in high season. From Apr to beginning Oct daily 9am-5.15pm; beginning Oct to end Oct daily 9.40am-4.40pm; Nov to Mar 9.40am-3.40pm. Closed 1 Jan, Shrove Tue, 24, 25 and 31 Dec. €6.50. ☎ (080 51) 688 70.* Construction on the **Neues Schloß** (New Palace) in the paradisiacal solitude of this generally forest-covered island started in 1878 and continued until 1885. Ludwig II's visit to Versailles in 1867 had greatly strengthened his admiration for Louis XIV, "the Sun King", and his Court; the palace on his island would be a replica of Versailles. The death of the King on June 12, 1886, who had spent only one week in the palace, put an end to the dream – by which time 20 million DM had already been spent and the royal coffers were empty.

Directory

Where to Eat

⊖⊖ **Kloster-Wirt** – *Frauenchiemsee 50 – Access by boat from Gstadt – ☎ (08054) 77 65 – www.klosterwirt-chiemsee.de – ⊭ – €22/45.* This fairly touristy establishment is situated immediately next to a landing-stage, and is thus ideally placed for a pleasant break. The neat restaurant offers traditional dishes as well as cakes and tarts.

Where to Stay

⊖ **Gruber-Alm** – *Almweg 18, 83370 Seeon-Seebruck – ☎ (08667) 696 – fax (08667) 1445 – www.gruber-alm.de – P – Booking advised – 19rm: €30/71 ☕ – Restaurant €17/40.* This simple hotel is situated on a little hill with views to Chiemgau and the Alps. Some of its guestrooms have beautifully decorated ceilings. The rustically-furnished dining room of this hotel-restaurant has traditional dishes on the menu.

⊖ **Hotel Alter Wirt – Bonnschlößl** – *Kirchplatz 9, 83233 Bernau am Chiemsee – ☎ (08051) 890 11 – fax (08051) 89103 – info@alter-wirt-bernau.de – P ⊭ – 41rm: €40/97 ☕ – Restaurant €12/27.50.* This renovated country house hotel is situated in the middle of a beautiful park. Its guestrooms are furnished with rustic-style and varnished, Baroque style furniture.

⊖ **Hotel Zur Linde** – *83256 Chiemsee – On the Fraueninsel – ☎ (08054) 903 66 – fax (08054) 7299 – hotel.linde.fraueninsel@t-online.de – Closed 8 Jan-15 Mar – 14rm: €55/110 ☕ – Restaurant €14/35.* If you fancy visiting an island, this could be just the hotel to stay in. Dating from 1396 and in olden times the haunt of artists, this hotel is located in the heart of a pedestrianised area. The historic dining room, still with its original layout, adds yet more character to the place.

The resemblance between the original and the copy is striking: the Latona fountain stands in the middle of formal French-style gardens; the huge façade is adorned with columns and crowned by a flat roof with balustrade in the Italian style; the apartments include a **State Bedroom★** and a **Hall of Mirrors★**, both of which are magnificent.

The southern wing of the building houses the **König Ludwig II Museum** *(entrance charge included in Schloß Herrenchiemsee ticket)*, which documents the fairytale king's life. The museum is an interesting place to spend some time before the start of the guided tour.

Museum Augustiner Chorherrenstift – A chapter of Augustinian canons was installed on the island around 1130; this fell into decline during the Reformation, then enjoyed a revival in the 17C, when intensive building work took place (notably the construction of the Collegiate Church). Some of the old monastery buildings now house a **museum** tracing the history of the island.

Fraueninsel

Although it is small, this islet boasts a charming fishing village and an ancient **Benedictine monastery** whose 13C church was rebuilt in the Gothic style in the 15C. The interior is decorated in Baroque style with a high altar dating from 1694. A particularly striking feature of the church is its free-standing octagonal bell-tower, whose foundations date from the 11C and were once used as a refuge. The onion-dome was added in 1626.

Darmstadt

Darmstadt has long been renowned also as an intellectual and cultural centre, thanks to the endeavours of a succession of enlightened princes who were lovers of art, particularly Jugendstil, at the beginning of the last century. Numerous institutions continue the tradition today, in particular the German Academy of Language and Poetry (Deutsche Akademie für Sprache und Dichtung), and the Institute of Industrial Design (Rat für Formgebung). The town is a pleasant place to take a break while exploring the region.

Location

Population: 138 000. Michelin maps n°s 543, 545 Q 9 – Hessen. The former capital of the Grand Duchy of Hesse-Darmstadt, lies close to the Odenwald massif, around 30km/19mi south of Frankfurt on the A5 motorway.

Luisen-Center, Luisenplatz 5, 64283 Darmstadt, ☎ (061 51) 13 27 81 and opposite the central station, Hauptbahnhof ☎ (061 51) 13 27 82.

Surrounding area: see FRANKFURT (32km/20mi north), MAINZ (34km/21mi north-west), WIESBADEN (40km/25mi northwest), HEIDELBERG (64km/40mi south).

Worth a Visit

Hessisches Landesmuseum★

♿ Open Tue-Sun, 10am-5pm, (-8pm, Wed); Sun, 11am-5pm. Closed 1 Jan, Good Fri, 1 May, Ascension, Corpus Christi, 24, 25 and 31 Dec. €2.50, no charge after 4pm. ☎ (061 51) 16 57 03; www.hlmd.de

The main block houses an outstanding selection of **medieval altar paintings** (Ortenberg and Reidberg), along with works by Stefan Lochner, Lucas Cranach the Elder and Dutch painters. Other exhibits include craftwork **(carved ivory)**, 19C German painting, a Jugendstil collection, a natural history collection and the famous **Werkkomplex of Beuys** (1949-69). The annexe is devoted to German Impressionism and Expressionism, and also contemporary art.

Mathildenhöhe

This is one of the most unusual places in the town, with its terraces, pergolas and Russian chapel. The ensemble is typical of the architecture of Art Nouveau seeking new forms of expression. This is the site on which the Grand Duke Ernst Ludwig founded, in 1899, a colony of artists known as the Künstlerkolonie. It united painters, sculptors and architects who sought to work together in search of a "total art". Outstanding representatives included Joseph Maria Olbrich, Peter Behrens and the sculptor Bernhard Hoetger.

In 1901 the dwellings and workshops grouped near the Russian chapel were the centre of an exhibition titled "A Document on German Art". The **Wedding Tower** *(Hochzeitsturm)*, built in 1908 to celebrate the marriage of the Grand Duke, overlooks the whole site. Inside are two beautiful mosaics celebrating Love.

Verkehrsamt Darmstadt

Mathildenhöhe: A temple to Art Nouveau centred on a Russian chapel.

Schloß

Guided tours (1hr) Mon-Thu, 10am-1pm and 2-5pm, Sat-Sun 10am–1pm. Closed 1 Jan, Easter Sun, Pentecost, 24, 25 and 31 Dec. €2.50. ☎ (061 51) 240 35. The former residence of the Landgraves, in the town centre, comprises two separate buildings: the New Castle (*Neuschloß*, 1716-26), a Rémy Delafosse design with its symmetrical façade fronting the market place; and the Old Castle (*Altschloß*, 16C and 17C), an edifice with voluted gables and the family coat of arms on the gateway which leads to an inner courtyard.

In the *Schloßmuseum*, family collections on view include splendid carriages, furniture, silver and, in the picture gallery, Holbein the Younger's *Darmstadt Madonna*.

Prinz-Georg-Palais

Open Mon-Thu, 10am-1pm and 2-5pm, Sat-Sun 10am-1pm. Closed 1 Jan, Shrove Tue, Easter, 1 May, Pentecost, 24, 25 and 31 Dec. €2.50. ☎ 0 61 51/71 32 33; ☎ (061 51) 71 32 33. This onetime summer residence of the Landgraves (built in 1710) houses the priceless grand-ducal porcelain **collection★**; almost all the pieces were gifts from the royal and imperial families of Europe. The table services and ornaments belong to the ducal family and constitute one of the largest collections of porcelain from the ducal factory at Kelsterbach, as well as from other German and Russian factories.

The **Prinz-Georg-Garten** has been preserved as a work of art of landscape gardening. It is a unique example in Hessen of a historical garden laid out in formal geometric patterns following late-18C principles of landscape gardening. The garden is roughly 2ha/5 acres in area and contains both useful and decorative plants arranged in formal flowerbeds divided by clipped yew borders. It features a number of charming ornamental elements (summer house, tea pavilion, ponds etc) and an orangery.

Jagdschloß Kranichstein

5km/3mi northeast. Open Apr to Oct Wed-Sat 1-6pm, Sun 10am–6pm; Nov to Mar Wed–Sat 2–5pm, Sun 10am–5pm. Closed 24 Dec-6 Jan. €2.70. ☎ (061 51) 71 86 13. The **hunting museum★** in this small hunting lodge has assembled an interesting collection of weapons, trophies and pictures.

Dessau

As well as being famous as the centre of Bauhaus architecture, in the 18C, Dessau was also the birthplace of neo-Classical architecture, a style copied throughout Europe. Dessau was heavily bombed during the Second World War and was largely rebuilt in the socialist architectural style, with rather austere results. The town is not, however, without charm and visitors will particularly enjoy the landscaped gardens created by Prince Leopold III.

Location

Population: 81 000. Michelin map n° 544 K 20 – Sachsen-Anhalt. Situated between the Elbe and the Mulde, Dessau developed along major trading routes. The town is accessed by the A9 motorway which links Berlin and Munich.

Zerbster Straße 2c, 06844 Dessau, ☎ (0340) 204 14 42.

Surrounding area: see WÖRLITZER PARK (Wörlitz is 17km/11mi east), WITTENBERG (32km/20mi northeast), MAGDEBURG (63km/39mi northwest), HALLE (53km/33mi south).

DESSAU

Akazienwäldchen	BY 2
Bertolt-Brecht-Straße	CX 3
Carl-Maria-von-Weber-Straße	CX 5
Eisenbahnstraße	BY 8
Erdmannsdorffstraße	BY 10
Ferdinand-von-Schill-Straße	BCX 12
Flössergasse	CX 14
Friedrich-Naumann-Straße	CY 15
Friedrich-Schneider-Straße	CX 16
Hausmannstraße	BX 18
Humboldstraße	CX 20
Johannisstraße	CX
Kleiststraße	BX 21
Kornhausstraße	AX 23
Liebknechtstraße	ABX 25
Marktstraße	CY 26
Mendelssohnstraße	CX 28
Mozartstraße	CX 29
Richard-Wagner-Straße	CX 30
Schwaberstraße	BX 32
Steinstraße	CX 33
Wallstraße	CY 34
Wörlitzer Straße	CX 37
Zerbster Straße	CXY

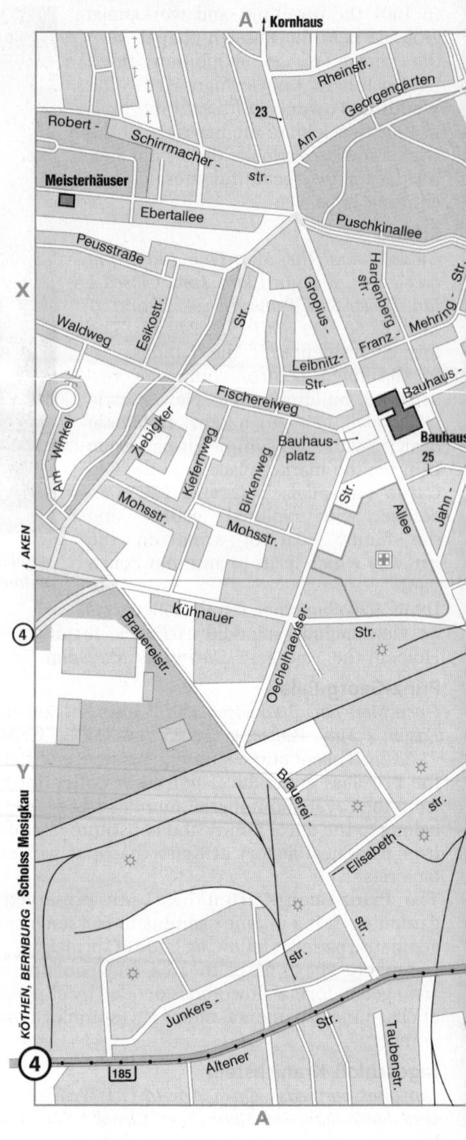

Background

A Colourful Local Figure – Founded in the 12C, Dessau developed rapidly and in 1474 the town became the seat of a collateral line of the princes of Anhalt. Prince Leopold I von Anhalt-Dessau (1676-1747) was an independent-minded character who married the daughter of an apothecary in the face of considerable opposition. His 50 year rule was characterised by a lively building and colonisation policy.

Directory

Where to Eat

Das Pächterhaus – *Kirchstraße 1 – 06846 Dessau-Ziebigk – ☎ (0340) 650 14 47 – maedel@paechterhaus-dessau.de – Closed Mon – €20/27.* This partially ruined, half-timbered house was built in 1743 and has been restored with enthusiasm. Pleasant reasonable cooking served in an unusual, but elegant setting.

Where to Stay

City-Pension – *Ackerstraße 3a – ☎ (0340) 882 30 76 – fax (0340) 8825017 – city-pension-dessau@t-online.de – 24rm: €41/64* . This hotel is located close to the town centre and has light and airy guestrooms, functionally equipped. Watch the hustle and bustle of the town while enjoying breakfast.

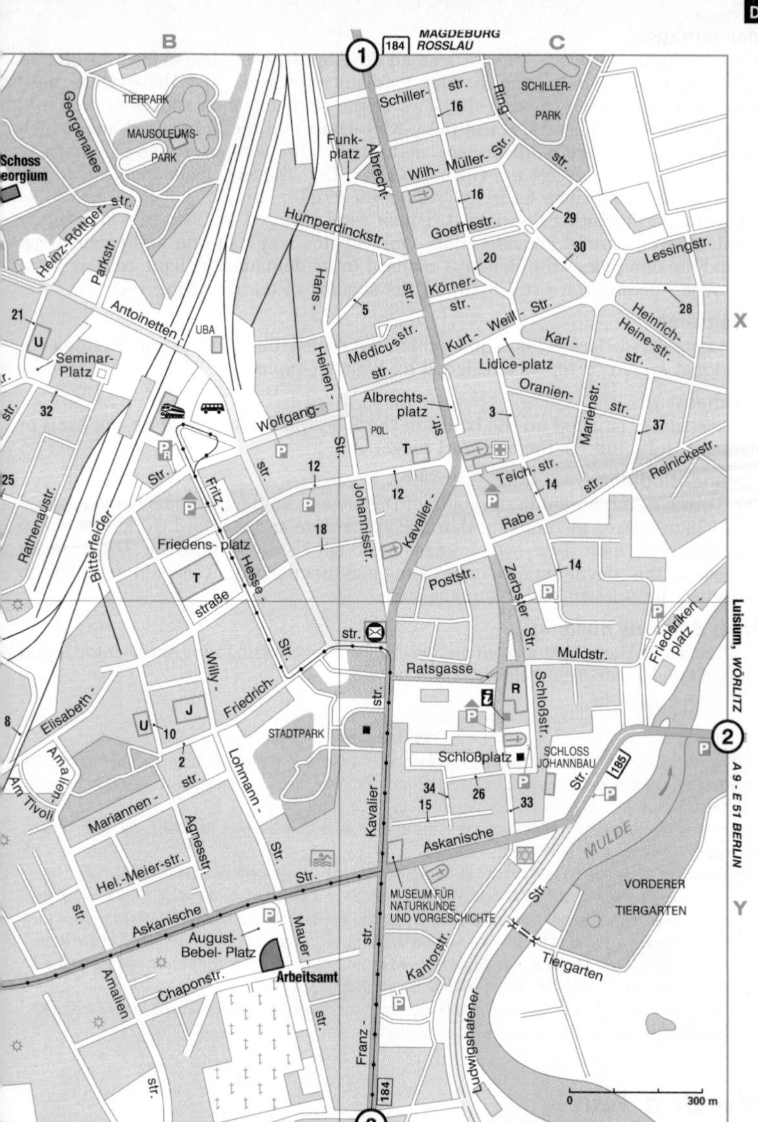

The "Gartenreich" – His grandson, Leopold III Friedrich Franz (1740-1817), made the Elbe meadows into a garden landscape which was quite unique within Europe, extending it as far as **Wörlitz★★** *(see WÖRLITZER PARK)*. The enlightened Prince pursued his reforms, to the benefit of the 36 000 inhabitants of the area, with considerable zeal. He had taken progressive England as his model, and made every effort to renew and modernise agriculture, dike-building and manufacturing: so it was that a forward-looking state, albeit one of little political influence, arose in the shadow of powerful Prussia.

Special Features

THE BAUHAUS LEGACY

Since a great number of Bauhaus buildings have survived in Dessau, UNESCO made the town a World Cultural Heritage Site in 1996.

Bauhausgebäude

Open daily, 10am-6pm. Closed 24 and 31 Dec. €4. ☎ (0340) 650 82 51. The "Design Academy" built on the basis of plans by Walter Gropius was opened in 1926 and displays all the features of the so-called Bauhaus style: cubic blocks, an absence of visible supports at the corners of the building and glazed façades.

Meisterhäuser

Walter Gropius drew up plans for a small development of a house for himself and three semi-detached houses for the Bauhaus professors and these were built between 1925-26 on a wooded site. Two of the semi-detached houses remain and are open to the public: the **Kandinsky-Klee-Haus** and the **Feiningerhaus**, which now houses the **Kurt Weill Centre**, dedicated to the composer who was born in Dessau in 1900. *Feiningerhaus: Open mid Feb to Oct, Tue-Sun, 10am-6pm; Nov to mid Feb, Tue-Sun, 10am-5pm. €4.10. ☎ (0340) 661 09 34.*

It is well worth visiting the houses, which were restored in 1994, in which every detail is given careful consideration. Only in this way can one appreciate what ground-breaking ideas the Bauhaus realised in its demand for "light and air", at a time when people were still living in the shadow of the departing 19C.

Arbeitsamt

On August-Bebel-Platz. This semicircular flat-roofed building, a fine example of functional architecture, was designed by Walter Gropius in 1928.

Kornhaus

The restaurant situated on the banks of the Elbe was built in 1929 on the basis of plans by Hermann Baethe and Carl Fieger.

Törtenensiedlung

The Törten development to the south of Dessay was built by Gropius between 1926 and 1928 to relieve the housing shortage at the time and to afford workers a cheap opportunity to own their own homes. Although hardly any of the 314 terraced houses in this development have remained unchanged, it is still possible to recognise the unmistakable Bauhaus style.

Other Bauhaus buildings

Stahlhaus and Haus Fieger *(both on Südstraße)*, Konsumgebäude *(Am Dreieck 1)* and Laubenganghäuser *(Peterholzstraße)*.

Das Bauhaus

The most important art school of the 20C was founded in Weimar in 1919 as a "State Bauhaus", in which architecture, painting and sculpture, including all ancillary trades, were to be taught. Its first Director was **Walter Gropius**.

As soon as the elections in 1924 brought extreme right-wing Conservatives to power, the days of the Bauhaus in Weimar were numbered.

Dessau was finally selected as a new base by the Bauhaus Masters. They were able to realise their plans here in a whole range of buildings and objects. This was the start of a period of fruitful work, during which the ideas associated with the new style of living took shape in the Bauhaus workshops. In 1932 however the Bauhaus in Dessau was closed following a decision by the municipal council, at the instigation of the Nazis. The director at the time, **Mies van der Rohe**, resolved to move to Berlin and to continue to run the Bauhaus as a private school, but this too was closed by the Nazis on 12 April 1933.

This act sealed the fate of the institution, although its revolutionary ideas were internationally accepted. It is impossible to imagine 20C international architecture without the Bauhaus.

Worth a Visit

Georgium

Open Tue-Sun, 10am-5pm. Closed 24 and 31 Dec. €2.60. ☎ (0340) 61 38 74. The palace built by Friedrich Wilhelm von Erdmannsdorff for Prince Johann Georg lies in the broad George gardens. The Georgium houses a picture gallery, the Anhaltische Gemäldegalerie, an excellent collection of German paintings from the 15C to the 19C, with works by Lucas Cranach the Elder (princes' altar) and Hans Baldung Grien, Frankfurt painting from the 18C and Dutch artists from the 15C to the 17C.

Excursions

Luisium

In Waldersee, via ②, 4km/2.5mi east of Dessau. Guided tours (1hr) May to Sep, Tue-Sun 10am-6pm; Apr and Oct, Tue-Sun 10am-5pm. €4.50. ☎ (0340) 64 61 50; www.gartenreich.com

The attractive little neo-Classical palace designed by Friedrich Wilhelm von Erdmannsdorff was built for Princess Luise von Anhalt-Dessau between 1774 and 1778. The rooms are decorated with ceiling paintings and murals in gentle colours and enchanting compositions. This little architectural gem nestles in a generously proportioned, atmospheric country park, with views of most of the park buildings which are modelled on Greco-Roman times. The great house stands in the centre of the "garden kingdom", the crowning glory of which is **Wörlitz Park★★** *(see WÖRLITZER PARK)*.

Schloß Mosigkau★

On ④, B 185, around 5km/3mi southwest of Dessau. Guided tours (1hr) May to Sep, Tue-Sun 10am–6pm; Apr and Oct, Tue-Sun, 10am-6pm. €4.50. ☎ (0340) 64 61 50; www.gartenreich.com

The summer residence, built between 1752 and 1757, was used as a home by Princess Anna Wilhelmine, the unmarried daughter of Leopold I. The two-storey three-winged building is a successful example of the Rococo style, and forms a particularly attractive ensemble with its garden. The rooms in the castle are richly furnished with silk and damask hangings, panelling, white inlaying and stucco ceilings, affording a bright picture of the 18C. The **Gartensaal★** is particularly interesting with its remarkable collection of paintings by Flemish and Dutch masters.

Wörlitz Park★★ *see WÖRLITZER PARK*

Bad Doberan

This small spa town developed between 1800 and 1825 for the visitors of the neighbouring Baltic spa town of Heiligendamm. At the time, Bad Doberan was the summer residence of the Mecklenburg court. The oldest hippodrome in Germany is here and the town is famous for its horse races which take place in July and August. The principal sight is the superb Gothic brick cathedral (Münster).

Location

Population: 12 400. Michelin map nº 542 D 19 – Mecklemburg-Vorpommern. Bad Doberan developed around a Cistercian monastery, a few kilometres from the Baltic. To get to the town from Rostock, follow the 105 road. From the A 20 motorway, take exit 13.

Alexandrinenplatz 2, 18209 Bad Doberan, ☎ (0382 03) 621 54.

Surrounding area: see ROSTOCK (16km/10mi east), WISMAR (75km/47mi west), MECKLENBURGISCHE SEENPLATTE (accessible by the A 19)

Special Features

MÜNSTER★★

♿ Open May to Sep, Mon-Sat 9am-6pm, Sun 11.30am-6pm; Oct, Mar and Apr, Mon-Sat 10am-5pm, Sun 11.30-5pm; Nov to Feb, Tue-Sat 10am-4pm, Sun 11.30am-4pm. Closed 1 Jan, Good Fri and 25 Dec. €1.50. ☎ 03 82 03/6 27 16.

The former Cistercian monastery church, which was built between 1294 and 1368 and is one of the most beautiful examples of the north German brick Gothic style. In accordance with the architecture of the Order, a mighty window decorates the towerless western façade. Flemish style chapels radiate out from the chancel with its ambulatory. The only decoration in this building, whose clear lines are so characteristic of the Cistercian order, is the clover-leaf arched friezes made of black glazed stone under the roof.

Interior

Brick also dominates here, toned down by the colourful painted triforium between the archway and the clerestory. Ogive vaulting covers the three naves of the basilica, which radiates harmonic slenderness. The sumptuous decor reflects the church's significance as the place of burial of the Mecklenburg dukes. The **high altar★**, a filigree Lübeck wood carving dating from the year 1310, shows Old and New Testament scenes. The rood altar dating from 1370 and the mighty **triumphal cross★** which is part of it (depicted as the Tree of Life) have Christ on one side (for the lay-brothers) and Mary on the other (for the monks). The Late Gothic needle-shaped oak **tabernacle★**, which must be the oldest in Germany, originates from the same period. The candelabra of Our Lady features a charming Madonna with a crescent moon (symbolising chastity) in a glory; this outstanding work dates from the year 1290. Two side-aisle **windows** with 14C Gothic stained glass are also worth a closer look.

Tombs of the Mecklenburg ducal house stand in the chapels around the chancel.

Excursions

It is possible to get to the Baltic spa resorts of Heiligendamm and Kühlungsborn by means of the **"Molli Schmalspurbahn"**. This narrow gauge railway, affectionately referred to as the "Molli", has been in operation since 1886. *Allow around 10min for the journey to Heiligendamm from Bad Doberan station, and 40min for Kühlungsborn.*

Heiligendamm

6.5km/4mi northwest. Heiligendamm was founded by the Duke of Mecklenburg in 1793. The architecture is typical of spa resorts of the period; the main building was built in 1814-16, and the many elegant houses along Prof-Vogel-Straße bear witness to the luxurious past of this town where the wealthy came to "take the waters".

Kühlungsborn★

14 km northwest. A beach resort and spa, Kühlungsborn has become one of the most popular holiday destinations on the Baltic coast, thanks to the miles of beaches and the vast pine forest.

Donaueschingen★

The Danube starts in Donaueschingen where two streams are united, giving rise to the German proverb "Brigach und Breg bringen die Donau zuweg", which roughly translates as, "from small streams great rivers flow". Donaueschingen owes its fame to the annual Festival of Contemporary Music, founded as the Donaueschingen Music Festival in 1921, which draws musicians and music-lovers worldwide.

Location

Population: 20 800. Michelin map nº 545 W 9 – Baden-Württemberg. In the middle of the Baar, a fertile basin between the Black Forest and the Swabian Jura, Donaueschingen stands at the confluence of two rivers which form the Danube, the Breg and the Brigach.

ℹ Karlstraße 58, 78166 Donaueschingen, ☎ (0771) 85 72 21.

Surrounding area: see ROTTWEIL (31km/19mi north), FREIBURG IM BREISGAU (54km/34mi west), SCHWARZWALD.

Worth a Visit

Source of the Danube

The monumental fountain *(Donauquelle)* was built in the castle park in the 19C. It is considered the official source of the Danube, which has another 2 840km/1 775mi to flow until its estuary, after having flowed through or along the border of 13 different countries: Germany, Austria, Slovakia, Slovenia, Hungary, Croatia, Bosnia, Serbia and Montenegro, Bulgaria, Romania, Moldova and the Ukraine.

Fürstenberg-Sammlungen (Princely Collections)

Open Mar-Nov, 10am-1pm, 2pm-5pm, Sun, 10am-5pm. Closed 1 Nov. €5. ☎ (0771) 865 63. Am Karlsplatz. The exhibitions on geology, mineralogy, paleontology and zoology have a special place among collections of natural history in Germany, as the presentation and the furnishings date to the founding days of the museum (1868).

Gemäldegalerie★ (picture gallery) – *Second floor.* Works by 15C and 16C Swabian masters and, above all, the very fine **Altarpiece of The Passion★★** *(Passionsaltar)* by Hans Holbein the Elder. Pictures by Cranach the Elder. Contemporary art is represented by some outstanding items such as works by Anselm Kiefer.

Schloß

Guided tour (40min). May to Aug: 11am and 2.30pm. €10. ☎ (0771) 8 65 63. The home of the Fürstenbergs, a well-proportioned building of 1723 remodelled in the 19C, retains the luxurious amenities of the period, enriched now with gold and silver plate, porcelain and fine Beauvais and Brussels Gobelins tapestries.

▶▶ Pfarrkirche *(parish church, Grüningen).*

R. Chéret/MICHELIN

The source of the Danube.

Dresden★★★

The cultural and artistic city of Dresden attracts an ever increasing number of visitors. It was not so long ago, however, that the magnificent "Florence of the Elbe" was a scene of total devastation; on the night of 13-14 February 1945, just a few weeks before the armistice, the Allies carried out an air raid which killed at least 35 000 and almost completely destroyed the old Baroque town. The arduous reconstruction effort, still ongoing today, has allowed Dresden to rise from its ashes and once again show its true face to the world – that of an outstanding capital of culture. The celebrations to mark Dresden's 800th anniversary in 2006 will provide an opportunity to spotlight the splendour of this beautiful city, undoubtedly one of Europe's finest.

Location

Population: 490 000. Michelin map 544 M 25 – Sachsen. Dresden enjoys an exceptional location in the heart of Saxony, on the banks of the Elbe and at the gates of "Swiss Saxony" *(Sächsische Schweiz).* The Czech border is less than 50km/31mi away to the south. The A 4, A 13 and A 14 motorways converge near the town, which also boasts an international airport.

Prager Straße, 01069 Dresden, ☎ (0351) 49 19 20.

Surrounding area: see SÄCHSISCHE SCHWEIZ (our suggested touring programme begins in Dresden), MEISSEN (23km/14mi northwest), BAUTZEN (64km/40mi north-east), GORLITZ (107km/67mi northeast), LEIPZIG (113km/70mi west).

M. Hertlein/MICHELIN

The Elbe and the brilliantly reconstructed Baroque town

Background

"The Florence of the Elbe" – Originally a Slav town, germanised in the 12C by the Margraves of Meißen, Dresden remained a possession of the Albertine succession from the partition of Saxony in 1485 until 1918.

The major development of the city took place during the first half of the 18C, in the reigns of the Electors **Augustus II the Strong** and his son Augustus III. Drawn by these powerful patrons of the arts, many artists from Italy, and particularly from Venice, were regular visitors at the court of Dresden. The magnificent Baroque ensemble of the Zwinger, the Japanese Palace and the Hofkirche (the Court church), as well as outstanding collections of paintings and objets d'art date back to this period. In addition to these treasures, Dresden – also the cradle of German Expressionism – boasts works by many 19C and 20C German painters. The 19C was a time of great economic development; numerous industries and factories were set up on the outskirts of the city, encouraged by the railway (the Dresden-Leipzig line was inaugurated in 1839) and steam navigation on the Elbe.

The Night of the Apocalypse – A few months before the end of the Second World War, on the night of 13-14 February 1945, Dresden was the target of one of the Allies' most destructive air raids, designed to break the morale of the population. Three successive waves of Lancaster bombers left the blackened skeletons of the city's principal monuments emerging from a waste of smoking ruins, and a death toll of between 35 000 and 135 000. Seventy five per cent of the city was destroyed. The strategic stakes of this large-scale military operation were low, and the extent of the

DRESDEN

Albertbrücke	X 2	Josephinenstr	Z 23	Reichpietschufer	X 40
Augustusbrücke	Y 4	Königstr.	X	Rothenburger Straße	X 42
Brühlsche Terrasse	Y 6	Königsbrücker Str.	X 24	Schlesischer Pl.	X 44
Carolabrücke	Y 8	Kreuzstr	XY 25	Schloßstr.	Y 45
Dr.-Külz-Ring	YZ	Leipziger Str.	X 28	Schweriner Straße	Y 46
Hansastr	X 15	Marienbrücke	X 29	Sophienstr	Y 47
Hauptstr	X 19	Neumarkt	Y 33	Theaterplatz	Y 52
Holländische Str.	Y 20	Neustädter Markt	X 34	Waisenhausstr	Z 53
		Ostra-Ufer	X 36	Wilsdruffer Str.	Y
		Postplatz	Y 39		

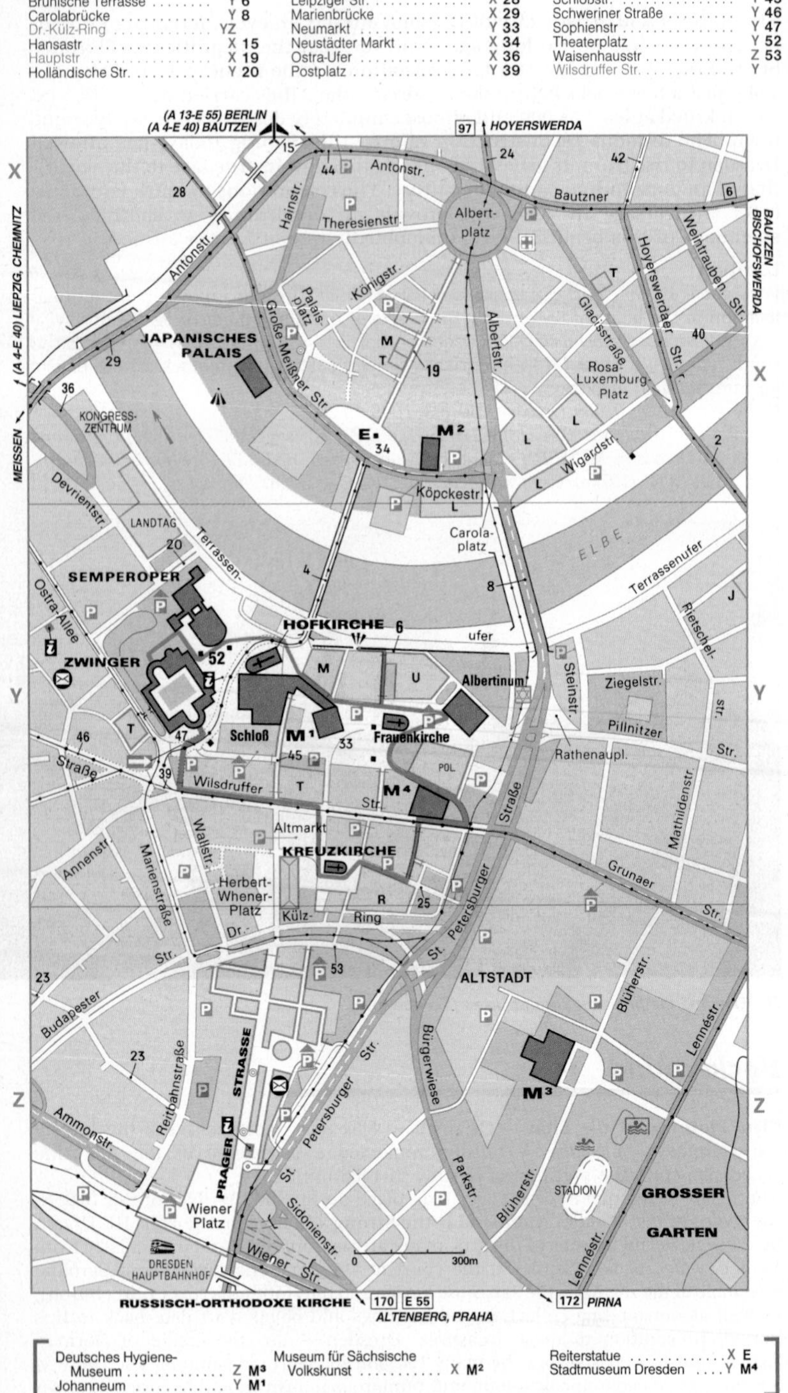

Deutsches Hygiene-Museum	Z M³	Museum für Sächsische Volkskunst	X M²	Reiterstatue	X E
Johanneum	Y M¹			Stadtmuseum Dresden	Y M⁴

allied deployment to strike a city which was at that time full of refugees has since been the source of much debate. Restoration of Dresden's historic patrimony – in particular the miraculous reconstruction of the Zwinger – and the rebuilding of residential quarters traversed by wide new thoroughfares have given the town a special quality marrying modern urbanism with this ancient heritage. The **Prager Straße★**, linking the old town with the quarter around the railway station, is the most typical example of this contemporary town planning, with imposing modern blocks on each side of a broad pedestrian mall.

Directory

Telephone prefix – 0351

Tourist information – *Dresden Werbung & Tourismus GmbH*, ☎ 49 19 20, *Fax 49 19 21 16*, Mon-Fri 8am-7pm, Sat-Sun 9am-4pm. Information offices: Schinkelwache am Theaterplatz, Mon-Fri 10am-6pm, Sat 10am-4pm and Sun 10am-2pm; Prager Straße 2a, Mon-Fri 9am-7pm, Sat 9am-2pm. The city magazines *SAX-Das Dresdner* (monthly) and *BLITZ! Dresden* (free of charge) provide information on all events taking place in Dresden. The *Kulturkalender*, which appears monthly and is available in hotels, at tourist information offices and cultural venues, is also a good source of information. Tickets and maps available from *Dresden Werbung und Tourismus*, ☎ *49 19 22 33*.

Post offices with special opening hours – *Postamt 1, Königsbrücker Straße 21-29 – Mon-Fri 6.30am-7pm, Sat 6.30am-1pm.* Another, more central post office can be found near the tourist information office at Prager Straße 72.

Daily papers – *Sächsische Zeitung, Dresdner Neueste Nachrichten*.

Internet – www.dresden-tourist.de; www.cityguide-dresden.de; www.dresden-online.de; www.dresden.de

Getting About

Dresden's historic centre is essentially a pedestrian and bicycle zone. Most of the sights and museums are concentrated within a limited area and are easily accessible on foot. The city is efficiently served by a network of 18 tram lines as well as by buses and regional express trains *(S-Bahn DB)*.

Dresden has two railway stations: the *Hauptbahnhof* (Am Hauptbahnhof 4) south of the old town and the *Bahnohf Neustadt* (Schlesischer Platz 1). Most trains stop at both stations.

Airport – ☎ *+881-33-60*. Dresden's international airport is less than 10km/6mi north of the Elbe. An Airport City Liner runs to the city centre and central station every 30min (€4). It is also possible to travel to the city centre by S-Bahn (S2); direct line to the central station.

Public Transport The network of the *Dresdner Verkehrsbetriebe* (DVB) is clear and well-structured, ☎ 857 10 11, Fax 857 10 10, round the clock. Information is available at the service centres at the main railway station *(Hauptbahnhof)*, Mon-Fri 7am-7pm, Sat 8am-6pm, Sun 9am-6pm; Postplatz, Mon-Fri 7am-8pm, Sat 8am-6pm, Sun 9am-6pm; Pirnaischer Platz and Albertplatz, Mon-Fri 7am-6pm, Sat 9am-4pm. The DVB is integrated into the *Verkehrsverbund Oberelbe* (VVO), which also covers the region known as "Swiss Saxony" *(Sächsiche Schweiz)*, the eastern Erzgebirge mountains and parts of the Oberlausitz area, Info-Hotline ☎ *01 80/24 519 98*, Mon-Fri 7am-8pm, Sat-Sun 8am-7pm. Tickets at the service centres, vending machines at the stations and in the tram stations and buses; normal fare is €1.50 (1hr). There are 4 geographical price zones. One-day passes *(Tageskarte)* can be purchased, worthwhile if you plan to make several trips. Family/group tickets *(Familientageskarte)* are also available.

Internet – **VVO**: www.nahverkehr.sachsen.de, **DVB**: www.dvbag.de

The **Dresden-City-Card** for €18 (valid 48hr) lets an adult (plus any children under 6) use all buses and trams and Elbe ferries in Dresden, plus free entry to 12 museums of the State Art Collections (Old Masters Gallery, Gallery of 19C and 20C Painters, Porcelain Collection, Green Vault Collections etc) and discounts for other museums; also includes discounts for certain tours of the city by coach and boat.

The **Dresden-Regio-Card** for €29 (valid 72hr) includes free rides on the S-Bahn trains along the Elbe to eg Meißen, Pirna and Königstein, discounts for rides on various narrow-gauge trains, and discounts at the region's main museums. The two cards are available at tourist offices, in numerous hotels and in the service centres of the DVB.

Sightseeing

City tours by coach – *Dresden Tour*, ☎ *899 56 50*: 1hr 30min tours, every 30min. First departure 9.30am, last one at 5pm. Tickets cost €18 and are valid all day long. Departure Augustusbrücke/Schloßplatz and 11 other stops such as Königstraße, Frauenkirche and Dr.-Külz-Ring. The *Dresden Tour* ticket includes the following benefits at no extra cost: guided tours of the Zwinger and Grauenkirche, evening city tour and night watchmen's beat. The *Super Dresden Tour* includes, besides the bus tour, a walk through the city's historic centre (departure from Augustusbrücke daily 10.30am, 12pm, 1.30pm, Nov-Apr Sat only). Theme tours on foot are organised by *igeltours – Dresdens andere Stadtführung*, ☎ *804 45 57, Fax 804 45 48*, www.igeltour-dresden.de.

Boat trips – The *Sächsische Dampfschiffahrts GmbH und Co. Conti, Elbschiffahrts*, ☎ 86 60 90, Fax 866 09 88, offers rides on the Elbe in authentic old paddle-wheel steamers and in modern ships between Meißen and "Swiss Saxony". Tickets cost €9, half price for children. Trips last around 1hr 30min. Departures every day at 11am, 1pm and 3pm. Pick-up and drop-off point: Terrassenufer under the Brülsche Terrasse.

Where to eat

Le Maréchal de Saxe – *Königstraße 15 – ☎ (0351) 810 58 80 – ♿ – €8.50/30.* This café-bar-restaurant occupies part of the Arts Centre *(Kulturrathaus)*, in the heart of a shopping street lined with cafés in the new town. Dark wood, gleaming tables, a pleasant setting and friendly service. Fish and seafood specialities.

Historisches Fischhaus – *Fischerhausstraße 14 (5km/3mi northeast of the city centre; follow Bautzner Straße) – (0351) 89 91 00 – www.fischhaus-dresden.de – Mon-Fri midday-midnight, Sat 11am-midnight, Sun 11am-11pm – – Reservation recommended – €15/25 – 8rm: €69/86.* In a leafy setting on the outskirts of town, this traditional establishment serves dishes depending on the catch of the day. Specialities include fish, naturally, but also game. Idyllic garden to enjoy in summer.

Luisenhof – *Bergbahnstraße 8 – 01324 Dresden-Weißer Hirsch – (0351) 214 99 60 – gastronomie@luisenhof.org – €16/33.* Set in a historical building from 1895, this panoramic restaurant is known as "Dresden's balcony" on account of its unique view. Distinctive modern decoration and large glass façade. Very pleasant terrace shaded by trees.

Kurhaus Kleinzschachwitz – *Berthold-Haupt-Straße 128 – 01259 Dresden-Kleinzschachwitz – Tram 1 – (0351) 200 19 96 – www.kurhaus.net – Closed from 2nd week in Jan to end of Jan – – Reservation recommended – €17.50/30.40.* This renovated restaurant, true to the original, is located in the residential district and is noted for its beautiful architecture. Inside is a cosy dining room. A few attractive, comfortable rooms also available. A pleasant place to stop on the banks of the Elbe, opposite Schloß Pillnitz.

Opernrestaurant – *Theaterplatz 2 (1st floor) – (0351) 491 15 21 – gastro.theaterplatz@t-online.de – Closed 16 Jul-24 Aug – €21/29.50.* Set in an annex to the Semperoper (Dresden opera house), this restaurant serves a variety of dishes. Before or after an evening at the opera, you can choose between the ground-floor café and the classic dining-rooms upstairs. Pleasant view.

Alte Meister – *Theaterplatz 1a – (0351) 481 04 26 – info@altemeister.net – €23/29.50.* This restaurant has bright, high-ceilinged rooms, one with a white vaulted ceiling supported by columns decorated with frescoes; the atmosphere is laid back and the terrace affords a view of the opera house and square.

Gourmet-Restaurant – *Merbitzer Straße 53 – (0351) 425 50 – info@pattis.net – Closed 2 weeks in Jan, 2 weeks in Aug, Sun and Mon – €49/62.* Set behind the Jugendstil-style reconstructed façade of the romantic Hotel Pattis, this restaurant features a magnificent interior: an intricately-worked ceiling, paintings and tastefully laid tables give this former ballroom an air of luxury.

Caroussel – *Rähnitzgasse 19 – (0351) 800 30 – info@buelow-residenz.de – €57/70.* Patrons can enjoy the tasteful decor – porcelain, an earthenware stove and paintings – and Stefan Hermann's excellent cuisine. You can also have a drink on the pleasant glass-roofed terrace with its pale wicker chairs and pastel tones.

Where to stay

Gästehaus Mezcalero – *Königsbrücker Straße 64 – (0351) 810770 – Fax (0351) 8107711 – www.mezcalero.de – P – 23rm: €15/60.* Beautifully decorated Mexican-Aztec-style establishment. The rooms are all personalised and some have mezzanine beds. Dormitories for small groups.

Hotel Zum Nußbaum – *Wirtschaftsweg 13 – (0351) 4273690 – Fax (0351) 4210354 – www.hotel-nussbaum-dresden.de – P – 15rm: €47/76 – Restaurant €15/25.* A pleasant hotel in an intimate setting. Functional, well-kept rooms with modern furniture, and a restaurant with terrace. Bus and rail links to the town centre very close by.

Hotel Goldener Apfel – *Schulweg 3, 01326 Dresden-Pillnitz – BUS 83 – (0351) 26 16 60 – Fax (0351) 2616613 – www.goldener-apfel.de – P – 12rm: €48/90.* Since 1999, this former village school dating back to 1840 has housed a hotel with fitness centre (sauna, massages, hydrotherapy and oxygenotherapy). The accommodation here is practical, polished and reasonably priced. Breakfast is served in the historic tea tavern.

Landhaus Lockwitzgrund – *Lockwitzgrund 100, 01257 Dresden-Lockwitz – (0351) 271 00 10 – Fax (0351) 27100130 – tkaiser@landhaus-lockwitzgrund.de – P – 12rm: €50/80 – Restaurant €16.50/30.* The romantic Lockwitzgrund welcomes you in a pleasant, restful setting: comfortable rooms in country-house style with many of the original farmhouse features. Attractively decorated rustic-style restaurant with a friendly atmosphere.

Gasthof Coschütz – *Kleinnaundorfer Straße 1 – BUS 72 – (0351) 401 03 58 – Fax (0351) 401384 – gasthof-coschuetz@t-online.de – P – booking necessary – 11rm: €55/90 – €7.50 – Restaurant €15/45.* This hotel has been run by the same family for four generations. The few rooms are well-equipped and comfortable. Authentic-style restaurant decorated with paintings and wooden furniture. Two terraces to enjoy in summer.

Martha Hospiz – *Nierizstraße 11 – (0351) 817 60 – Fax (0351) 8176222 – marthahospiz.dresden@t-online.de – Closed 22-27 Dec. – – 50rm: €76/118.* Traditional evangelical church establishment, the Martha Hospiz offers elegant rooms with classic honey-coloured furniture, some in Biedermeier style. Some rooms are reserved for disabled guests. Pleasant restaurant, once a coal cellar and potato store.

Hotel Schloß Eckberg – *Bautzner Straße 134 – ☎ (0351) 809 90 – Fax (0351) 8099199 – email@hotel-schloss-eckberg.de* – P – *84rm: €85/210* – *Restaurant €27/46.* A grand park and comfortable rooms – some containing precious antiques, others more modern – make this hotel, comprising a neo-Gothic castle and *Kavaliershaus*, an interesting place to stay. The classic, tasteful restaurant fits in perfectly with the historic rooms.

Hotel Bayerischer Hof – *Antonstraße 33 – ☎ (0351) 82 93 70 – Fax (0351) 8014860 – info@bayerischer-hof-dresden.de – Closed 23-27 Dec.* – P – *50rm: €95* – *Restaurant €14/31.* This former library, now a chic, tasteful hotel, offers spacious, elegant rooms equipped with beautiful cherrywood furniture and decorated with old paintings. The restaurant is also in the classic style.

Taking a Break

Café Schinkelwache – *Theaterplatz 2 – ☎ (0351) 4 90 39 09 – www.restaurant-dresden.de – 10am-midnight.* This old watchtower built by the famous German neo-Classical architect Friedrich Schinkel stands between the Zwinger, the castle and the opera house.

Café Toscana – *Schillerplatz 7 (5km/3mi east of the old town on the banks of the Elbe) – ☎ (0351) 310 07 44 – Mon-Sat 9am-7pm, Sun 11am-7pm.* This classic tea room with winter garden and terrace boasts a lovely view of the *Blaues Wunder* bridge and a 12m/39ft-long cake buffet. Savoury specials also available.

Dresdner Molkerei Gebrüder Pfund – *Bautzner Straße 79 – ☎ (0351) 8 10 59 48 – Mon-Sat 10am-6pm, Sun and public holidays 10am-3pm, café-restaurant: 10am-8pm.* The dairy shop is entirely covered in hand-painted tiles (1892). Customers can sample dairy and cheese products. Café-restaurant on the 1st floor.

Going Out

Useful Tips – Cafés, bistros and restaurants abound in the old town and inner Neustadt, at the junction of Alaunstraße and Luisenstraße. The "alternative"/youth scene is mainly in the Neustadt area (east bank of the Elbe north of Albertplatz), domain of the punks who certainly don't go unnoticed.

Ballhaus Watzke – *Kötzschenbroder Straße 1 (prolongs Leipziger Straße to the west) – ☎ (0351) 85 29 20 – www.watzke.de – 11am-midnight.* Restaurant on the banks of the Elbe, set in a historical building where grand balls used to be held on the 1st floor. The superb view of the old town from the beer garden is known as "Canaletto's View" since it was immortalised in a painting by the master.

Brauhaus am Waldschlösschen – *Am Brauhaus 8b (2km/1.2mi east of Albertplatz; follow Bautzner Straße) – ☎ (0351) 81 19 90 – www.waldschloesschen.de – 11am-1am.* Probably the most attractive brasserie in town. Along with the three types of beer brewed here, cocktails and traditional dishes are served in a tasteful, rustic decor. Piano music Monday to Saturday from 8pm. Splendid views of the Elbe from the beer garden.

Frank's Bar – *Alaunstraße 80 (north of Albertplatz between Rothenburger Straße and Königsbrücker Straße) – ☎ (0351) 8 02 67 27 – 8pm-3am.* A pleasant little bar with a quiet atmosphere and, on the menu, over 200 cocktails, with or without alcohol, sweet or dry, strong or weak... You may need some advice.

Italienisches Dörfchen – *Theaterplatz 3 (on the corner of Augustusbrücke and Terrassenufer) – ☎ (0351) 4 98 16 60 – www.italienisches-doerfchen.de – 10am-midnight (food served until 11pm).* Tea room with a terrace overlooking the Elbe, café on the ground floor and restaurant upstairs. Customers can sample the delights of the establishment in magnificent rooms decorated with beams, stuccowork and frescos on the ceiling.

Winzerstube Zum Rebstock – *Hauptstraße 17 – ☎ (0351) 5 63 35 44 – www.winzerstube-zum-rebstock.de – Mon-Sat 12pm-10pm, Sun 2-10pm.* Both a Weinstube and a wine shop, serving wines from the Bad Kreuznach region and Meißen as well as dishes to accompany them. Quiet, restful terrace with a view of a magnificent Baroque pavilion.

Culture

Useful Tips – The *Theater.Konzert.Kunst – Kulturkalender für Dresden* and *Dresdner – Kulturmagazin* provide information on cultural events. These magazines are published once a month and are distributed free of charge by Dresden Werbung und Tourismus GmbH. Other monthlies such as *SAX – Das Dresdner Stadtmagazin* and *Prinz* are available from bookshops and newspaper kiosks. Interesting information can also be obtained from www.dresden.de (follow the links Tourismus then Veranstaltungen).

Shopping

Eseful Tips – Dresden's main shopping streets are Prager Straße (with department stores), Wilsdruffer Straße and Altmarkt in the old town, Königstraße (exclusive boutiques) and Hauptstraße.

Kunsthofpassage Dresden-Neustadt – *Alaunstraße 70 (north of Albertplatz between Rothenburger Straße and Königsbrücker Straße; access also via Görlitzer Straße 21-25) – ☎ (0351) 8 02 67 04 – www.kunsthof.com.* Between Alaunstraße and Görlitzer Straße are a series of rear courtyards, many with unusual façades decorated according to different themes. Here you can browse around the craft shops or stop for a drink at one of the bars.

Neustädter Markthalle – *Metzer Straße 1 (level with Hauptstraße 36; access via Ritter- and Metzer Straße) – ☎ (0351) 8 11 38 60 (museum) – www. automobilmuseum-dresden.de (museum) – Mon-Fri 8am-8pm, Sat 8am-6pm; museum: 10am-7pm, entry €3.80.* Traditional fare alongside international specialities at the stalls in this historic covered market. An entertaining exhibition on the 1st floor presents the history of automobile manufacture in the German Democratic Republic between 1945 and 1990. Many original vehicles on display.

Art galleries and antique dealers – These are to be found mostly in the Neustadt, on Königstraße and Hauptstraße, and in the quarter between Bautzener Straße, Königsbrücker Straße and Alaunplatz.

Flea markets – *Elbemarkt, Käthe-Kollwitz-Ufer/Albert-Brücke*, May-Oct 9am-2pm; World Trade Center, Ammon-/Freiberger Straße, second Sunday of every month, 8am-4pm.

Markets – Altmarkt, mornings from 8am, daily except for Sun. The Spring Market *(Frühlingsmarkt)* is held here in May, the Autumn Market *(Herbstmarkt)* in Sep and the famous *Striezelmarkt* in Dec.

Walking About

HISTORIC CENTRE★★★ (ALTSTADT)

The Elbe runs through Dresden, dividing it into two very distinct parts. The old town *(Altstadt)* south of the river is dominated notably by the outlines of the Zwinger, Semperoper and Hofkirche. In the north, the new town stretches out around Albertplatz.

Semperoper★★ (Semper Opera House)

Built between 1871 and 1878 by **Manfred Semper**, a personal friend of Richard Wagner, based on plans designed by his father Gottfried – Professor of Architecture at Dresden, responsible for the previous edifice, destroyed by fire in 1869 – the present opera house owes its form to the Italian Renaissance. The tiered façade comprises two storeys of arcades, surmounted by a third in recess. Each side wall is furnished with twin niches, occupied on the left by statues of Shakespeare and Sophocles, on the right, Molière and Euripides. Famous conductors such as Karl Böhm appeared at the Semperoper, where nine operas by Richard Strauss, including *Der Rosenkavalier*, were performed for the first time.

Cross Theaterplatz eastwards towards the Hofkirche.

Ehemalige Katholische Hofkirche★★ (Cathedral)

This enormous basilican edifice, the largest church in Saxony, was built between 1738 and 1755 by the Italian architect Chiaveri on the orders of Augustus III. This followed the conversion of the Albertines to Roman Catholicism, the condition of their accession to the Polish throne. The building, strongly influenced by Italian Baroque, is dominated by an 86m/282ft bell-tower and decorated with statues of the saints and apostles, mainly on the attics. The nave is separated from the side aisles by a circular ambulatory which opens on to four oval chapels. Above the high altar, a fine painting (1765) by Anton Raphael Mengs depicts the Ascension. The pulpit was executed by Permoser in 1722, while the organ was the last work (1750-55) of the master craftsman **Gottfried Silbermann**. The crypt contains the tombs of several kings and princes of Saxony, as well as the heart of Augustus the Strong, whose body lies in Cracow cathedral.

A Line of Organ Builders

Gottfried Silbermann (1683-1753) served his apprenticeship in Strasbourg in the workshops of his brother Andreas, who created the famous organs of Ebersmunster in Alsace. In 1710, Gottfried settled in Freiberg, where he designed instruments with remarkable tone. Of the 51 organs attributed to him, the ones in Freiberg are the most noteworthy.

His nephew Johann Andreas also went into the trade and designed 54 organs in the Upper Rhine region.

Schloß

The Renaissance palace, once the official residence of the Court, is in the process of being restored. That part of the exterior façade linking the west wing to the Johanneum is covered by a colossal mosaic, The **Procession of Dukes**★ (*Fürstenzug*, 102m/335ft). Originally created by the painter Wilhelm Walter using the sgraffito technique, this monumental painting representing the dukes of the house of Saxe-Wettin was transferred in 1906 on to 25 000 squares of porcelain from Saxony. The work, which miraculously survived the 1945 bombardments unscathed depicts 35 margraves, prince electors and kings over a period of around one thousand years.

J. Bouraly/MICHELIN

The Procession of Dukes of Saxe-Wettin, an immense mosaic covering one of the palace façades

The **Langer Gang★** which connects the Johanneum to the George building is a long gallery formed by a series of Tuscan arcades enclosing the stable courtyard.
The **Johanneum** (left of the *Schöne Pforte* entrance, a gateway in the Renaissance style) was itself once used as the stables. It now houses a Transport Museum *(Verkehrsmuseum)*, where collections of vintage cars and motorcycles join a display outlining the evolution of public transport.

Leaving the Johanneum, cross the Neumarkt towards the Frauenkirche.

Frauenkirche

This mighty building now covered in scaffolding, was built from 1726 and was the principal work of the architect George Bähr. The famous 95m/312ft high 23.5m/77ft diameter dome, which so characterises the silhouette of the town, was completed in 1738. The place of worship was the most important testimony to Protestant church building, right up until it fell victim to the air attacks of 13 and 14 February 1945. The sea of flames heated up the sandstone to such an extent that it burst and the eight pillars were no longer able to bear the weight of the 5 800t stone dome. On the morning of 15 February it collapsed with such force that the floor of the church was broken open. The ruin of the Frauenkirche symbolised the destruction of the town and stood as a witness and memorial until after the reunification of Germany.
The restoration work should be completed on time for the celebrations marking the 800 year anniversary of the founding of Dresden in 2006. The **crypt**, with its stone altar by the English artist Anish Kapoor and the tomb of the master builder George Bähr, was completed in August 1996.
So-called restoration concerts are held on Saturdays. The church will seat 2 200 and is set to become an "international meeting place".

Go onto the Brühlsche Terrasse laid out on the site of ancient fortifications: this pleasant promenade, very popular in summer, offers an interesting **view★** *of the Elbe and the Neustadt quarter, on the river's east bank. Then turn back and cross the Neumarkt heading towards the Stadtmuseum (currently closed) and cross Wilsdrufferstraße to reach the new Town Hall.*

Neues Rathaus (New Town Hall)

This early 20C neo-Renaissance building surmounted by a golden statue of Hercules stands behind the Kreuzkirche. No organised tours.

The Restoration of the Frauenkirche

Throughout the communist period, the ruins of the Frauenkirche constituted a war memorial. The restoration work finally began in 1993, after a good deal of procrastination, not least due to the immense costs involved.
A few figures serve to indicate the scale of this project: 8 390 façade, wall and ceiling blocks, one quarter of its total surface, were found in the rubble of the Frauenkirche, but only 10% of them were undamaged. In addition there are 90 000 back-up blocks available, which will of course also be used in the construction together with damaged but still usable blocks. It has been possible to locate, survey and photograph the blocks, with the aid of 10 000 old photographs of the original building plans, before they are assigned to their final location. They are recorded in a database which includes 90 000 electronically stored pictures.

Kreuzkirche★

The original church, the city's oldest (early 13C), was remodelled in the Baroque style after its destruction during the Seven Years' War.

The damage inflicted during the Second World War has been repaired on the outside of the church, but the inside strikes visitors with quite a shock since it has so far only been roughly plastered over. The Kreuzkirche is home to the Kreuzchor, a famous 400-voice male choir.

►► Yenidze: west of the old town. This former tobacco factory now resembles a mosque and houses a number of restaurants – **Stadtmuseum Dresden★**: this museum (currently closed, probably reopening in 2005), retraces the stages of Dresden's development and the principal facts of its history, through original objects and documents.

NEUSTADT★ (NEW TOWN)

This part of Dresden, largely spared by the air raids in 1945, stands on the site once occupied by *Altendresden* (Old Dresden) which was destroyed by fire in 1685. When the district was rebuilt – in stone – it was renamed New Town *(Neustadt)*.

The **Hauptstraße,** which links the Albertplatz and the Neustädter Markt – dominated by the gilded **equestrian statue★** of Augustus the Strong – was the object of a tasteful restoration scheme which managed to preserve several 18C dwellings. With its rows of plane trees and numerous shops, it is one of the best places in town for a stroll.

The Neustadt quarter, where the styles of the residences range from Baroque via neo-Classicism to buildings from the Gründerzeit period of rapid industrial expansion, is becoming increasingly popular among both residents and tourists.

If you are coming from the historic centre of Dresden, you can reach the old town by the Augustusbrücke. Turn right into Köpckerstrasse to reach the Museum of Saxon Arts and Crafts.

Museum für Sächsische Volkskunst★ (Museum of Saxon Arts and Crafts)

Open every day except Mon, 10am-6pm. €3. ☎ (0351) 491 46 19. This collection is located in the oldest Renaissance building in the city, the 1568 Jägerhof (Hunters Court). It displays works mainly of Saxon folk art, painted furniture, works of pottery and basketry, blue prints and tableware, as well as Saxon and Swabian folkloric costumes and lacework, toys and carvings from the Erzgebirge and Christmas decorations.

Turn back along Köpckerstrasse and cross the Neüstadtermarkt towards the Japanese Palace.

Japanisches Palais★ (Japanese Palace)

Built between 1715 and 1737 under the direction of Pöppelmann, this huge quadrilateral was designed to display Augustus the Strong's collection of Meißen tableware. It now houses the Museum of Ethnology and the Museum of Prehistory. Note the oriental-style roofs of the corner pavilions. On the side nearest the Elbe, there is a pleasant garden with a **view★** of the river's west bank.

Pfunds Molkerei

Bautzner Straße 79. This dairy, founded by the Pfund brothers in 1880, is an attraction in itself. Wine, milk and numerous varieties of cheese of various origin are sold here. But the shop is decorated with an amazing array of multicoloured ceramic tiles – a truly magnificent sight.

►► Großer Garten★ – Russisch-Orthodoxe Kirche★ – Deutsches Hygiene-Museum.

Worth a Visit

ZWINGER★★★

A tour of this 18C Baroque palace, built by Augustus the Strong, will be among the highlights of any trip to Dresden. After suffering severe damage in the 1945 bombardments, the building was painstakingly reconstructed and now houses five museums, including the Old Masters Gallery.

The best view of the whole complex is gained if you go in via the Glockenspielpavillon on Sophienstraße.

Augustus the Strong's original idea was to build, on the site of a former fortress, a simple orangery. But his architect, **Matthäus Daniel Pöppelmann** (1662-1736), brought such breadth of vision to the project that it ended up as an enormous esplanade surrounded by galleries and pavilions. The main appeal of this jewel of German Baroque lies in the harmonisation of architectural work with sculptures from the studio of **Balthasar Permoser** (1651-1732), a Bavarian artist strongly influenced by his visits to Italy.

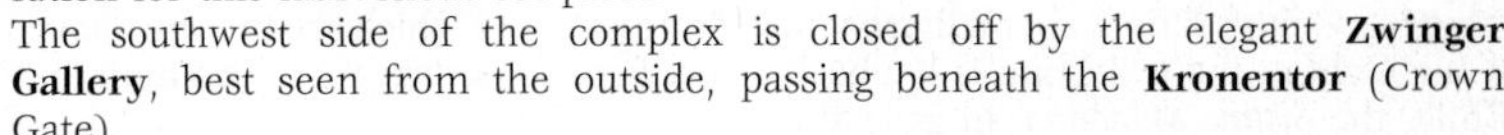

The huge rectangular courtyard has two semi-elliptical extensions which include the **Wallpavillon★★** (Rampart Pavilion) and the Glockenspielpavillon (Carillon Pavilion). It is in the former that the intimate relationship between sculpture and architecture most admirably expresses itself. Not a single transverse wall breaks up the soaring lines of these verticals animated by the exuberance and vigour of atlantes with the face of Hermes, drowned in a sea of vegetation. Crowning the pavilion, **Hercules Carrying the World –** with which Augustus the Strong identified – is the only work personally signed by Permoser.
Steps from the Wallpavillon lead to the terrace on which Pöppelmann's **Nymphenbad★★** (Bath of the Nymphs) can be seen. It was undoubtedly in Italy that the artist found inspiration for this marvellous set piece.
The southwest side of the complex is closed off by the elegant **Zwinger Gallery**, best seen from the outside, passing beneath the **Kronentor** (Crown Gate).
This latter, embellished with statues representing the four seasons, is crowned by an onion-shaped dome, which terminates in four eagles supporting the Polish crown. The Semper Gallery, built in 1847 by **Gottfried Semper** (1803-79), occupies the northeast side of the Zwinger reserved since 1728 for the exhibition of the royal collections.
Of the Baroque ensemble as a whole – two-storey pavilions linked by one-storey galleries – the Anglo-German critic Sir Nikolaus Pevsner wrote: "What exultation in these rocking curves, and yet what grace! It is joyful but never vulgar; vigorous, boisterous perhaps, but never crude... of an inexhaustible creative power, with ever new combinations and variations of Italian Baroque forms placed against each other and piled above one another."

Gemäldegalerie Alte Meister★★★ (Old Masters Gallery)

Semper Gallery, west wing. Open every day except Mon, 10am-6pm. Closed 25 Dec. €6. ☎ *(0351) 491 46 19.* This collection of paintings built up by Augustus II the Strong and his successor Augustus III is one of the best of its kind in the world. The most important masters from the Italian Renaissance and the Baroque period as well as Dutch and Flemish painters from the 17C are represented.

Ground floor:

Galleries 1-4 contain tapestries after sketches by Raphael and numerous *vedute* (townscapes which are detailed and realistic enough for the town in question to be identified) by Bernardo Bellotto, otherwise known as Canaletto, who painted Dresden and Pirna with extraordinary precision of detail in the mid-18C, to the extent that many of his paintings were used as a guideline during the reconstruction of Dresden after the Second World War.
Galleries 5-6 house paintings by Dresden masters.

1st floor:

Galleries 101-102: Works by Silvestre and Canaletto.
Galleries 104-106 and 108-111: Flemish and Dutch painting from the 16C-17C. Rembrandt's *Self-portrait with Saskia* (Gallery 106), Rubens' *Bathsheba*, and Vermeer's *Girl Reading a Letter by the Window* (Gallery 108).
Gallery 107: Paintings by the Early Netherlandish (Jan van Eyck is represented by a marvellous triptych) and Early German (masterpieces by Holbein, Cranach the Elder and Dürer) schools.
Gallery 112: 17C French painting (Claude Lorrain, Nicolas Poussin).

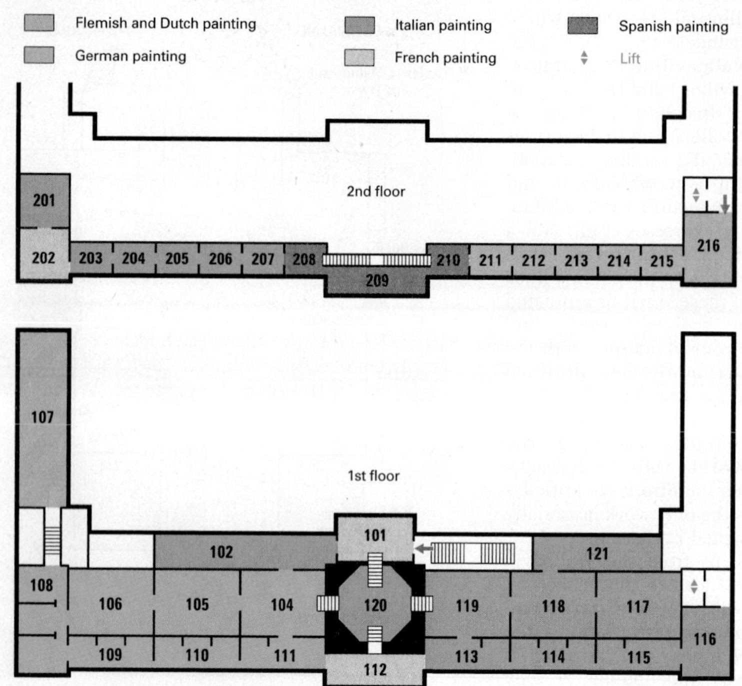

Galleries 113-121: 16C Italian painting. Works by Veronese, Tintoretto, Giorgione *(Sleeping Venus)*, Titian, are on display in galleries 117-119 which are lit from above. A highlight of the collection is Raphael's most famous portrayal of the Virgin and Child, the *Sistine Madonna,* in gallery 117.
Gallery 116: Paintings by Botticelli, Mantegna and Pintoricchio *(Portrait of a Boy)*.

2nd floor:

Gallery 201: pastel painting. Jean-Étienne Liotard's *Chocolate Girl* is particularly captivating. World's largest collection of works by Rosalba Carriera (75 pastels).
Gallery 202: 18C French painting.
Galleries 203-207: 18C Italian painting with works by Tiepolo and Crespi.
Galleries 208-210: Spanish painting (El Greco, Murillo, Zurbarán, Velázquez).
Galleries 211-216: 17C and 18C German painting. The exhibition reaches the threshold of the 19C in gallery 216.

Porzellansammlung★★ (Porcelain Collection)

Entrance on Sophienstraße. ♿ Open every day except Mon, 10am-6pm. Closed 25 Dec. €5. ☎ (0351) 491 46 19. This gallery displays not only unique products of the famous factory at **Meißen**, but also porcelain acquired by Augustus the Strong from Japan and China. Do not miss the "dragoon vases", for which the prince paid with 600 dragoon soldiers in 1717, or the life-size porcelain figures from Meißen on the upper floor (first half of the 18C). There is also space devoted to **Johann Friedrich Böttger**, a potter who profited from the discovery of kaolin deposits nearby to create (1708) in Europe a porcelain modelled on that of the Far East.

Rüstkammer★★ (Armoury)

Semper Gallery, east wing. Open every day except Mon, 10am-6pm. Closed 25 Dec. €3. ☎ (0351) 491 46 19. Even those not particularly interested in armour will appreciate this fascinating exhibition of what must be among the finest handcrafted armour, which was collected by the princely dynasty of the Wettiner. This abundant inventory includes 1 300 objects from the 15C to the 19C. The **suits of armour** are most impressive, and include the work of one of the most famous Augsburg armourers, Anton Peffenhauser. There is also a unique display of children's armour, worn by the little princes during children's jousting tournaments at the Saxon court.

Mathematisch-Physikalischer Salon★★ (Salon of Mathematics and Physic)

Northwest corner pavilion. Open every day except Mon, 10am-6pm. Closed 25 Dec. €3. ☎ (0351) 491 46 19. The inventive genius of scientists is documented in the clocks and instruments of the 16C to 19C. The display includes sun, sand, oil, artistic and automatic clocks, standing clocks, wall clocks, table clocks and pocket watches as well as marine chronometers.

There are also some remarkable measuring, optical, astronomic and meteorological instruments.

On the way to the **Theaterplatz** – note the equestrian statue of King John (1854-73) in the centre of the square – the road passes the **old town watchtower** *(Altstädter Wache)*, which was designed by Karl Friedrich Schinkel.

ALBERTINUM★★★

This neo-Renaissance style building was built at the behest of King Albert in 1884, on the foundations of the former arsenal. It now houses three interesting museums: the Gallery of 19C and 20C Painters, the Green Vault Collections, and a sculpture and coin collection.

Gemäldegalerie Neue Meister★★★ (Gallery of 19C and 20C Painters)

Open every day except Thur, 10am-6pm. Closed 25 Dec. €6. ☎ (0351) 491 46 19; www.skd-dresden.de

A visit to these rooms permits the visitor to gauge the richness and diversity of German art from the Romantics (Casper David Friedrich, *Two Men Contemplate the Moon*) to the Biedermeier (Carl Spitzweg, *The Hook and Line Fisherman*); from the Bourgeois Realists (Adolf von Menzel) to the so-called "Deutsch-Römer" (Arnold Böcklin, Wilhelm Leibl) and the painters of Jugendstil. The German Impressionists are represented by their leading lights: Max Liebermann, Max Slevogt and Lovis Corinth.

The **Brücke** movement, spearhead of German Expressionism, was born in Dresden at the beginning of the 20C. The group, a spin-off from Fauvism, is notably represented by Karl Schmidt Rottluff and Max Pechstein.

Two triptychs illustrate in a gripping way the "revolutionary" German school operating between the wars: *War* (1929-32) by **Otto Dix**, a denunciation without concession of the cruelty and folly of the warlike mentality; and *The Thousand-Year Reich* (1935-38) by **Hans Grundig**. The remaining rooms are devoted to painters from the former German Democratic Republic.

Grünes Gewölbe★★★ (Green Vault Collections)

Open every day except Thur, 10am-6pm. Closed 25 Dec. €6. ☎ (0351) 491 46 19.

This treasury is unequalled on a global scale and is a must-see in the programme of any visitor to Dresden. The masterpieces of goldsmiths' work and jewellery collected by Augustus the Strong were originally kept in a room in the palace at Dresden that earned the nickname "Grünes Gewölbe" (Green Vault) because of its colour. The name stuck, although the collection has been housed in the Albertinum since the Second World War.

Among the many outstanding exhibits, be sure to see the works by the court jeweller **Johann Melchior Dinglinger**: including the *Court State of the Grand Mogul*, *Diana's Bath* and the famous *Moor with the Emerald Step*.

Due to lack of space, only half of the treasures of Augustus II are on display. When restoration work is finished on Dresden palace, the treasures of the Green Vault will be returned to their original place.

Staatl. Kunstsammlungen Dresden

Green Vault Collections – Diana's Bath (1704)

Excursions

Schloß Moritzburg★

14km/9mi northwest, via Hansastraße. Open Apr-Oct: 10am-5.30pm; Nov-Mar: guided tours only (1hr) every day except Mon, 10am-4pm. Closed 24 and 31 Dec. €4.10. ☎ (0352 07) 87 30; www.schloss-moritzburg.de

Built by the Duke Moritz on one of the Royal Saxon Hunting Reserves in 1542-46, this was originally designed to be no more than a simple hunting lodge in the Renaissance style. However, it was considerably refashioned between 1723 and 1736 by Matthäus Daniel Pöppelmann, at the request of Frederick Augustus I (1670-1733), who had wanted to transform it into a Baroque château. Adjoining the present striking edifice, with four wings and imposing ochre and white corner towers (the colours of the Baroque in Saxony), are an artificial lake and a large park.

Schloß Pillnitz★

15km/9.5mi east, via Bautznerstraße. Bergpalais (Kunstgewerbemuseum), May-end Oct: open every day except Mon, 10am-6pm; Wasserpalais, from May to end Oct: open every day except Tue, 10am-6pm. €4. ☎ (0351) 491 46 19; www.skd-dresden.de

Pöppelmann, favourite architect of the electors, was responsible for this pleasure palace too. Designed between 1720 and 1724, the Riverside Palace *(Wasserpalais)* was originally built on the east bank of the Elbe. The Late Baroque predilection for Chinese motifs is apparent in the roof treatment. The park was transformed into an English-style garden in 1778. The banks of the Elbe offer attractive riverside walks; the islet opposite the gardens is a bird reserve, inhabited by grey herons.

Freiberg★

37km/23mi south. Set at the foot of the Erzgebirge mountain range, Freiberg was the largest town in Saxony during the Middle Ages. For a long time its underground mineral resources were the source of its wealth (silver, copper, lead, zinc, fluorspar, heavy spar and agate). Although today all the mines are disused, the town is nevertheless proud of its mining past and cultivates its traditions, such as the annual mining parades.

Cathedral★★ – This Late Gothic hall-church was built between 1490 and 1501 and replaced an earlier Romanesque building. ♿ *Guided tour (45min). May-Oct: at 10am, 11am, 2pm, 3pm and 4pm, Sun at 11.30am, 2pm, 3pm and 4pm; Nov-Apr: at 11am, 2pm and 3pm, Sun at 11.30am, 2pm and 3pm. €2. ☎ (037 31) 225 98; www.freiberger-dom.de.*

The **tulip pulpit★★** is a masterpiece of religious art. It was produced by master sculptor Hans Witten c 1505 and in fact represents a tree of life, the steps climbing up its trunk.

The harmonious shape and the delicate angel figures of the **organ★★** are beautiful indeed, but the actual sound of the instrument, which is considered to be **Gottfried Silbermann**'s masterpiece, with its three keyboards, 45 stops (sets of pipes) and 2 674 pipes, is quite breathtaking. He combined Saxon and French musical traditions to create this organ, producing as a result a tone of exceptional quality.

The magnificent eight-stepped **golden entrance portal★★** was erected in around 1230 for the church's Romanesque predecessor. The tympanum depicts the enthroned Madonna and the adoration of Christ by the Magi *(explanatory leaflet available)*. Although it was originally edged in colour, in particular in gold, only the name still bears witness to its early colour.

The **mortuary chapel★** is also worth a visit. The chancel was converted in the 16C into the burial place of the Albertine line of the house of Wettin, and was reworked in the Mannerist style. The tomb of Elector Moritz of Saxony (1563) is the first Renaissance tomb in Saxony and is the work of the sculptor Antonius Van Zerroen from Antwerp.

Schloß Augustusburg★

75km/46.5mi southwest. The Elector of Saxony, Augustus I, built this hunting lodge (c 1570) on top of Schellenberg hill (515m/1 690ft). In the chapel, the high altar is adorned with a painting by Lucas Cranach the Younger (1571) showing the Elector surrounded by his 14 children. The castle houses a Museum of Game and Ornithology and a Motorcycle Museum.

Chemnitz

80km/50mi southwest. Known as "Saxony's Manchester", Chemnitz became home to the first cotton mills from 1800 and also boasts some Gothic and Renaissance treasures. Between 1953 and 1990, the town was known as Karl-Marx-Stadt.

Brückenstraße – The impressive apartment blocks and office buildings of the modern town are centred around this street and the Straße der Nationen (Avenue of Nations), which it crosses. The imposing **Karl-Marx monument** (12m/40ft high), of Ukrainian granite, designed by Lew Kerbel in 1971, stands in front of a huge plaque bearing in several languages the last words of the Communist Manifesto: *"Workers of the world, unite!"*.

Altes Rathaus (Old town hall) – Painstakingly rebuilt after 1945, this building has a fine Gothic façade, remodelled at the beginning of the 17C. There is a Renaissance doorway at the foot of the tower. To the east stands the Neues Rathaus (new town hall) built at the beginning of the 20C.

Fine Arts Collection – German painting and sculpture of the 19C and 20C (Dresden Romantic School, German Impressionism and Expressionism). *Open every day except Mon, 12pm-7pm. Closed 24 and 31 Dec. €4. ☎ (0371) 488 44 24.*

Schloßkirche (Castle Church) – Once part of a Benedictine abbey founded in 1136, this building was transformed into a hall-church at the beginning of the 16C.

Swiss Saxony★★★ *(see SÄCHSISCHE SCHWEIZ)*

Meißen★ *(see MEISSEN)*

Düsseldorf★

This onetime fishing village is today one of the country's most important economic centres. Capital of the Rhineland-Westphalia Land and fashion capital of Germany, Düsseldorf is a place where people like to be seen, particularly on Königsallee with its succession of prestigious boutiques. Although the city shines essentially in its financial and industrial activities, it also affords many opportunities for a pleasant stroll along the banks of the Rhine.

Location

Population: 570 000. Michelin map 543 M 4 – Nordrhein-Westfalen. Düsseldorf stands on the east bank of the Rhine, at its confluence with the Düssel. The city is at the heart of a major motorway junction, linking it notably to Cologne, Duisburg, Essen and Dortmund. Düsseldorf is only one hour away from Paris by Thalys (1 service per day). The city also has an international airport.

Immermannstraße 65b, 40210 Düsseldorf, ☎ (0211) 17 20 20.

Surrounding area: see ESSEN (37km/23mi north), KÖLN (39km/24mi south), AACHEN (81km/50mi southwest).

Background

City of the arts – Düsseldorf first acquired city status in 1288 from the Count of Berg after the Battle of Worringen. In 1380 it was chosen as the official residence of the dukes of Berg. Four centuries later, the family of the prince-electors of the Neuburg-Palatinate settled there and the fame of the city spread. This was largely due to the energy and intelligence of the family's most famous member, Johann Wilhelm (1679-1716). Patron and apostle of the Baroque, Jan Wellem, as he was known, surrounded himself with a brilliant court of musicians, painters and architects who transformed Düsseldorf into a true city of the arts. A large part of his collection is now the pride of the Alte Pinakothek in Munich.

In 1806 Düsseldorf came under Napoleonic rule and in 1815 it seceded to Prussia.

The Head Office of the Ruhr – Seat of one of Germany's most important stock exchanges, Düsseldorf is not only one of the country's principal banking and financial centres but also administrative capital for most of the Rhineland industries. All these functions are exemplified in the Dreischeibenhaus (Thyssen Building).

The World of Fashion – Exhibitions, fairs and collections of haute couture several times a year maintain Düsseldorf's reputation as a "minor Paris" and fashion capital of Germany. Dhe CPD (Collections Premiere Düsseldorf) is the largest fashion trade show in the world, with over 2 000 exhibitors from over 40 countries. Everything that is elegant in the town centres on the graceful **Königsallee★** (popularly known as "the Kö"), with its boutiques and arcades built on either side of the old moat.

Düsseldorf and the Rhine

Düsseldorf Marketing & Tourismus GmbH

Directory

Where to Eat

⊖⊖ **Rheinturm Top 180** – *Stromstraße 20 – 40221 Düsseldorf-Unterbilk – ☎ (0211) 848 58 – rheinturm@guennewig.de – €33/49.* The lift takes less than a minute to reach this unusual restaurant 172m/564ft up in the air. It rotates slowly, allowing diners to enjoy a superb view of the city.

⊖⊖⊖ **Berens am Kai** – *Kaistraße 16 – 40221 Düsseldorf-Unterbilk – ☎ (0211) 300 67 50 – info@berensamkai.de – Closed 1-7 Jan, Sat lunchtime, Sun and public holidays – €50/74.* A modern restaurant set in an office building next to the landing stage at the harbour. Concrete walls and columns and chrome chairs with black cushions highlight the refined decoration. Splendid view of the Rhine through the impressive glass façade.

Where to Stay

⊖⊖ **Hotel Merkur** – *Mörsenbroicher Weg 49, 40470 Düsseldorf-Mörsenbroich – ☎ (0211) 159 24 60 – Fax (0211) 15914625 – hotel-merkur-garni@t-online.de – Closed from Christmas to the beginning of Jan. – P – 30 rm: €69/129.* A pleasant hotel with functional, well-kept rooms, almost all of them equipped with cherrywood furniture. The Hotel Merkur stands in a quiet location in a side street near the city centre, and has its own parking spaces.

⊖⊖ **Fashion Hotel** – *Am Hain 44, 40468 Düsseldorf-Stockum – ☎ (0211) 439 50 – Fax (0211) 4395200 – hotel@fashion-duesseldorf.de – Closed 24-31 Dec – P – 38 rm: €75.* A haven of peace and quiet despite being right next to the centres of business and industry. Comfortable rooms with rustic furniture plus some brand new rooms in a private house.

Taking a Break

Eis-Café Pia – *Kasernenstr. 1 – ☎ (0211) 326 233 – 10am-11pm – closed from mid Oct to mid Feb.* Probably the best Italian ice cream in town. You may have to queue, but it's certainly worth the wait. Hot and cold drinks also served in the café.

Going Out

Useful Tips – The old town is known as the longest bar in the world on account of the succession of countless bars, pubs and restaurants between Ratinger Straße and Karlsplatz. But don't make the mistake of ordering a Kölsch in Düsseldorf – here the beer that reigns supreme is the brown ale known as "Altbier".

Op de Eck – *Grabbeplatz 5 (in the Kunstsammlung Nordrhein-Westfalen building) – ☎ (0211) 32 88 38 – www.op-de-eck.de – Fri-Sat 11am-2am, Tue-Thur and Sun 11am-1am, Mon 5pm-1am.* This café-restaurant has a concave glass façade and modern design interior. On the menu: international specialities, home-made cakes and sorbets, and a good selection of wines and cocktails. A good place for a snack at any hour of the day.

Uerige – *Bergerstr. 1 (between Karlsplatz and Marktplatz) – ☎ (0211) 86 69 90 – www.uerige.de – 10am-midnight – closed Carnival Monday and 25 Dec.* The place to come if you want to try Altbier – the atmosphere is unique. Casks serve as tables, and in summer the patrons of all ages spill out into the street.

The Far East – Düsseldorf plays an increasingly important role in economic relations linking Germany with the Far East. Japanese firms alone have 300 branches in the city. This strong Oriental presence is reinforced by the existence of the Japanese Cultural Center in the Immermannstraße, the Taiwan Trade Center, near the central station, and a Japanese cultural centre in the Niederkassel district.

Walking About

Old Town (Altstadt)

This riverside quarter, with its taverns and bars jam-packed from the earliest hours of the evening, is known as "the biggest boozer in Europe". It is here that the "Radschläger" – local street urchins and buskers who perform outdoor acrobatics for a few pennies – can be found.

The **Bolkerstraße**, birthplace of Heinrich Heine (no 53), is the busiest and liveliest of the city's pedestrian precincts. The neighbourhood is equally linked with the story of the tailor Wibbel, who attended his own funeral after switching identities to escape a prison sentence. This folklore legend is recalled by the figures of the Schneider-Wibbel-Gasse carillon clock, which operates at 11am, 1pm, 3pm, 6pm and 9pm.

Marktplatz

Separated from the Rhine only by the Altes Rathaus (late-16C town hall), this square is embellished with the bronze equestrian statue (early 18C) of the famous Jan Wellem. There is a good view of the river from the Burgplatz adjoining this square to the north, in the shadow of the Schloßturm, a free-standing tower.

DÜSSELDORF

Street	Ref.	No.
Am Wehrhahn	EY	3
Berliner Allee	EZ	
Blumenstraße	EZ	7
Bolkerstraße	DY	8
Citadellstraße	DZ	13
Corneliusstraße	EZ	15
Elberfelder Str.	EY	21
Ernst-Reuter-Platz	EZ	23
Fischerstraße	EY	27
Flinger Str.	DY	28
Friedrich-Ebert-Str.	EZ	29
Grabbeplatz	DY	32
Graf-Adolf-Str.	EZ	
Heinrich-Heine-Allee	EY	42
Hofgartenrampe	DY	45
Jan-Wellem-Platz	EY	51
Königsallee	EZ	
Marktplatz	DY	68
Martin-Luther-Platz	EZ	69
Maximilian-Weyhe-Allee	EY	70
Mühlenstraße	DY	73
Ratinger Str.	DY	88
Schadowplatz	EY	90
Schadowstraße	EY	91
Schneider-Wibbel-Gasse	DY	95
Schulstraße	DZ	96
Schwanenmarkt	DZ	97
Tonhallenstraße	EY	101
Vagedesstraße	EY	104
Venloer Str.	EY	105

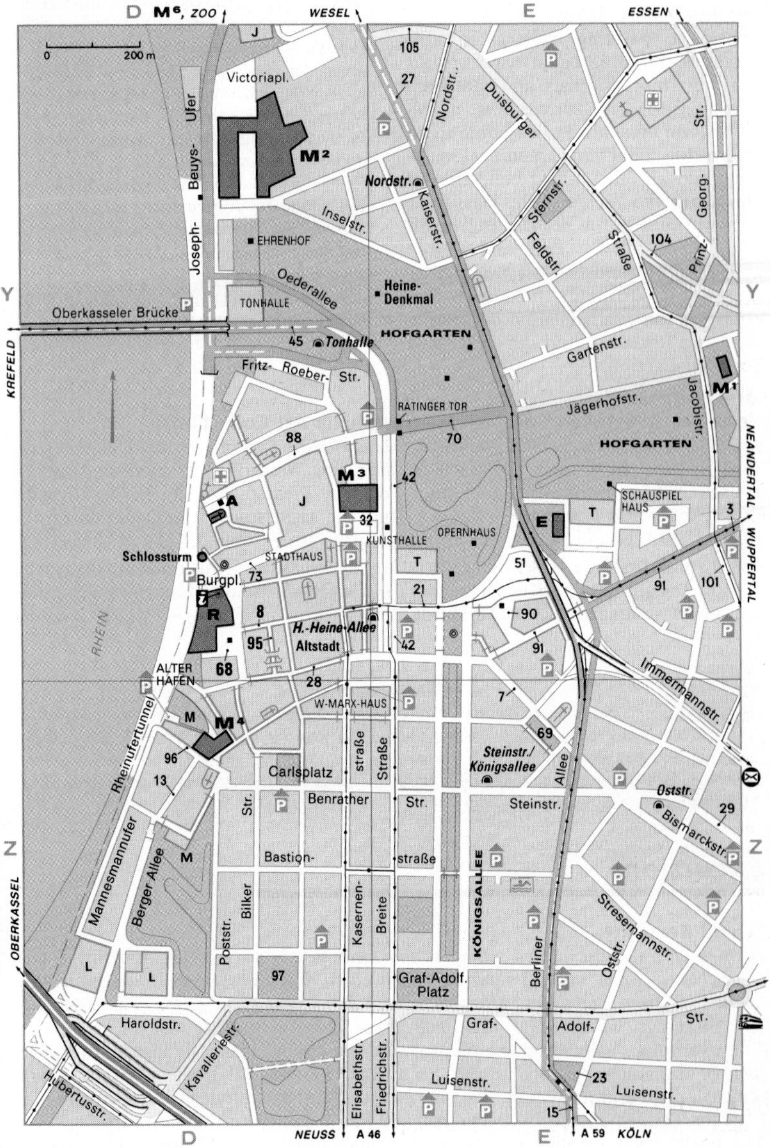

Sight	Ref.	Key
Altes Rathaus	DY	R
Dreischeibenhaus	EY	E
Goethe-Museum	EY	M1
Hetjens-Museum	DZ	M4
Kunstsammlung Nordrhein-Westfalen	DY	M3
Lambertuskirche	DY	A
Löbbecke-Museum und Aquazoo	DY	M6
Museum kunst palast	DY	M2

Hofgarten and Schloß Jägerhof★

The Hofgarten park forms a shady continuation of the Königsallee, northwest towards the riverside museum quarter and east as far as Schloß Jägerhof. This delightful building, onetime home of the Electors' Master of the Hunt, dates from the 18C. The French architect Nicolas de Pigage contributed to the plans. Today the mansion houses the **Goethe-Museum★**, which displays the author's manuscripts, autographs, drawings and engravings. Napoleon Hill, in the park, is crowned with a small Maillol bronze entitled *Harmony* – in fact a modest monument to Heine.

Worth a Visit

Museum Kunst Palast★ (Fine Arts Museum)

♿ *Open every day except Mon, 11am-6pm. From €2.50, depending on the exhibition.* ☎ *(0211) 899 62 50.* Romantics of the Düsseldorf School dominate the important painting gallery in this museum. There is equal exposure for German Impressionists and members of the German Expressionist movement. The museum is also home to an interesting collection of medieval sculpture, and an outstanding collection of **glassware**★★ which includes glass from Roman times to the present from both Europe and the Far East, and a large amount of Jugendstil glassware. Other museum departments include an Oriental section (with Islamic decorative arts and textiles) and an extensive design collection.

POETRY AND MUSIC IN THE 19C

Heinrich Heine (1797-1856), son of a Bolkerstraße merchant, lived in Düsseldorf throughout his youth, deeply impressed by the presence of the French and the personality of Napoleon. A poet who was also a willing pamphleteer, eternal traveller, defender of liberalism, a Francophile and a genuine European, Heine once described himself as "a German nightingale which would have liked to make its nest in Voltaire's wig".

Among the musicians who have given Düsseldorf its enviable reputation as an artistic centre are Robert Schumann and Felix Mendelssohn-Bartholdy. **Schumann** (1810-56) was appointed conductor of the municipal orchestra in 1850. Living for four years in a house in the Bilker Straße, he was already seriously in prey of a nervous illness, attempting to drown himself in the Rhine in 1854. His friend **Mendelssohn** (1809-47) brilliantly directed the city's Rhine Festival. He made his first journey to England in 1829, conducting his own *Symphony in C Minor* at the London Philharmonic Society.

Kunstsammlung Nordrhein-Westfalen★ (Rhineland-Westphalia Art Collection)

♿ *Open every day except Mon, 10am-6pm, Sat-Sun 11am-6pm. €6.50.* ☎ *(0211) 83 81 10.* Designed by the Danish architects Dissing and Weitling, this modern building houses a 20C art collection including works by Picasso, Braque, Léger, Chagall, Ernst, Beuys and **Paul Klee** – who was the Fine Arts Professor in Düsseldorf from 1930 to 1933. Ninety-two of the artist's pictures are exhibited.

▶▶ Lambertuskirche – Schiffahrt-Museum im Sclossturm (this museum also gives a good insight into the city's history) – Hetjens-Museum/Deutsches Keramik-Museum★ – Aquazoo-Löbbecke-Museum★.

GASTRONOMY

It is in the taverns typical of the old town that regional specialities can best be appreciated: *Blutwurst mit Zwiebeln* (black pudding with onions); *Halve Hahn* (caraway cheese eaten with strong local mustard); and *Röggelchen* (small rye bread rolls). On Friday evenings, there is a tradition of eating *Reibekuchen*, a kind of savoury potato cake. *Altbier*, the still, dark brown ale of the region, is brewed in Düsseldorf.

Excursions

Schloß Benrath★

10km/6mi southeast. Town plan in the current edition of The Michelin Guide Deutschland. From mid Mar-end Oct: open every day except Mon, 10am-6pm, Wed 10am-8pm; from Nov to mid Mar: open every day except Mon, 11am-5pm. Closed 24, 25 and 31 Dec. €4. ☎ *(0211) 892 10 03; www.schloss-benrath.de*

This exemplary Late Baroque building was designed by Nicolas de Pigage from 1755 to 1770 as a country palace for the Prince Elector of the Palatinate. Two subsidiary wings flank a central pavilion. The interior is decorated in a style which is transitional between Rococo and Early Classicism, and has elegant late-18C furniture.

The **park**★, planted with many trees, was also designed by Pigage and laid out in the formal French style. It extends west as far as the Rhine.

Neandertal

14km/9mi east, via Am Wehrhahn. The deep and steep-sided valley of the Düssel owes its name to the Calvinist poet Joachim Neander (1650-80), who liked to use it as a retreat. It was here, in a grotto since destroyed, that the famous skeleton of Neanderthal Man, 60 000 years old, was discovered in 1856. A plaque on a triangular rock *(on the right-hand side of the road, 3km/2mi beyond the motorway underpass)* marks the site of the cave.

Neanderthal Museum – *Talstraße 300.* ♿ *Open every day except Mon, 10am-6pm. Closed 24, 25 and 31 Dec. €6.50.* ☎ *(021 04) 97 97 97.* This museum, not far from the Neandertal excavation site, gives an overview of the history of human evolution. There is a striking reconstruction of our ancestor: from a skull, a computer was able to calculate how the features would have looked. Silicon and modern technological skill were then combined to create a life-size model of prehistoric man.

Kloster **Eberbach**★★

The former Cistercian abbey is the only sister foundation of Clairvaux in Germany apart from Himmerod in the Eifel. The abbey still emanates the peace and isolation sought proper to a Cistercian community. With its white walls, sloping roofs and neatly laid-out gardens, this is another world where wine is produced according to secular techniques.

Location

Michelin map nº 543 P 8 – Hessen. The abbey grew up at the bottom of a small valley, on the northern side of the Rheingau, on the edge of the vineyards.
Surrounding area: see WIESBADEN, MAINZ, RHEINTAL.

Worth a Visit

Abbey Church

♿ *Apr-Oct, 10am-6pm; Nov-Mar, 10am-4pm, Sat-Sun, 11am-4pm. Closed 24 Dec-1 Jan. €3. ☎ (067 23) 91 78 10; www.klostereberbach.net*
Built in two stages, in 1145-60 and then 1170-86, it is a Roman cross vaulted basilica with three naves; its austere appearance is characteristic of Cistercian architecture. Gothic chapels with beautiful tracery windows were built on the south side between 1310 and 1340. Remarkable **tombs**★ dating from the 14C to the 18C.

Abbey Buildings

These are grouped around the **cloister**★, which was built in the mid-13C and 14C. Only the portal remains of the monks' refectory which was built before 1186. Rebuilt in 1720, the room is impressive, with a magnificent stucco ceiling by Daniel Schenk from Mainz (1738).
The lay brothers' refectory contains a collection of mighty **winepresses**★★, documenting the wine-producing tradition of the abbey which has endured for over 800 years. The oldest press dates from the year 1668.
The **monks' dormitory**★, which is around 85m/279ft long and which dates back mainly to the period around 1250-70, is remarkable. The double-naved, ribbed vaulted room was built with a slightly rising floor, and the columns were shortened accordingly, so that it appears longer than it is. The **chapter-house**, with beautiful star-ribbed vaulting from 1345 and stylised plant decoration dating back to 1500, was built prior to 1186.
The dormitory leads to the **abbey museum** *(Abteimuseum)* on the upper floor, which contains a display on the history of the abbey and of the Cistercian Order.

The Name of the Rose

After three months' preparation, the cameras began to roll at Eberbach in November 1986, for the one-month filming of the monastic whodunnit *The Name of the Rose* set in the year 1327. Word has it that director Jean-Jacques Annaud chose the Cistercian abbey from a list of 300 abbeys. Alongside Cinecittà near Rome, Eberbach was the main setting for the film shoot of the Benedictine abbey that features in Umberto Eco's novel. The dispute between the papal envoy and the Franciscan monk William of Baskerville, played by Sean Connery, was filmed in the chapter-house, where monastic law was once laid down. The scriptorium was reconstructed in the monks' dormitory. In the film, sentences were passed by the Holy Inquisition where now people gather to taste wine, in the monastery cellar. The abbey church and hospice (which appeared as the refectory) also feature in the film.

Eichstätt★★

Eichstätt, a small episcopal city and seat of a Catholic university, owes its Baroque character to its reconstruction after the Thirty Years War: only the cathedral survived the burning of the town by the Swedish army. But Eichstätt is also a centre of uncompromising, contemporary architecture, such as the new Pedagogical University and the refurbishing of the Summer Residence as a university building.

Location

Population: 13 000. Michelin map nos 545, 546 T 17 – Bayern. Eichstätt lies on a meander in the midst of the Altmühl Valley natural park. Many of the roofs are covered with limestone slabs (from Solnhofen) peculiar to the region.
ℹ *Kardinal-Preysing-Platz 14, 85072 Eichstätt, ☎ (084 21) 988 00.*
Surrounding area: see ROMANTISCHE STRASSE, NÖRDLINGEN (65km/41mi west), NUREMBERG (79km/49mi north), REGENSBURG (99km/62mi east).

Directory

Where to Eat

Schmankerlwirtshaus Gasthof Krone – *Domplatz 3 – ☎ (08421) 44 06 – www.krone-eichstaett.de – €15/30.* Located in the heart of the old town near the cathedral, this corner house has dark wooden furnishings and plain, country-style décor. Regional specialities are on the menu.

Where to Stay

Hotel Zum Hirschen – *Brückenstraße 9, 85072 Eichstätt-Wasserzell – ☎ (08421) 96 80 – fax (08421) 968888 – info@hirschenwirt.de – Closed in Jan – P – 40rm: €38/60 – Restaurant €13/24.* This well-kept hotel is an ideal departure point for excursions into the Altmühltal natural park. Comfortable guestrooms, lawn and games area and restaurant with winter garden, serving Franconian specialities.

Worth a Visit

Dom★

The nave and the eastern chancel date from the 14C, though large parts of them are Romanesque, Early Gothic or Baroque. The main entrance is via a Gothic door in the north side decorated with polychromatically set statues. The west face is Baroque. Inside, the most fascinating feature is the late-15C **Pappenheim Reredos★★**, almost 9m/30ft high and of Jura limestone, in the north aisle. The representation of the *Crucifixion* with its attendant figures is a masterpiece of religious sculpture. In the west chancel is a seated statue of **St Willibald** (Bishop of Eichstätt in the 8C) as an old man, an early 16C work.

Mortuarium★ – *Access through the south transept.* This funerary chapel, forming the west wing of the cloister, is a late-15C Gothic hall with two naves. Handsome **tombstones** pave the floor. A twisted column ends each line of pillars supporting the groined vaulting. The so-called "Beautiful Column" is very finely worked. Four stained-glass **windows** in the east wall are by Hans Holbein the Elder (c 1500). There is a 16C *Crucifixion* on the south wall by Loy Hering.

Diözesanmuseum – *Upper floor, above the chancel. Apr-Oct, Wed-Fri 10.30am-5pm, Sat-Sun, 10am-5pm. Closed Good Fri. €2, no charge Sun and bank holidays. ☎ (084 21) 502 66.* The long history of the diocese is illustrated by means of pictures, maps, vestments, liturgical accessories and statues in stone and wood. In the Bishop's Room, note St Willibald's Chasuble, the oldest liturgical vestment in the see – thought to be a Byzantine work dating from the 12C.

Reliquaries, chalices, monstrances and other examples of religious art are on view in the treasury.

Cloister★ – This element was a 15C addition to the cathedral (1420-30). The stone tracery of the windows is richly decorated.

EICHSTÄTT

Domplatz
Freiwasserstraße 3
Gabrielstraße 4
Herzoggasse 5
Kapuzinergasse 8
Loy-Hering-Gasse 10
Luitpoldstraße
Marktgasse 12
Marktplatz
Ostenstraße
Pater-Philipp-Jeningen-Platz 13
Spitalbrücke 17
Walburgiberg 20
Weißenburgerstraße 23
Westenstraße
Widmanngasse 25

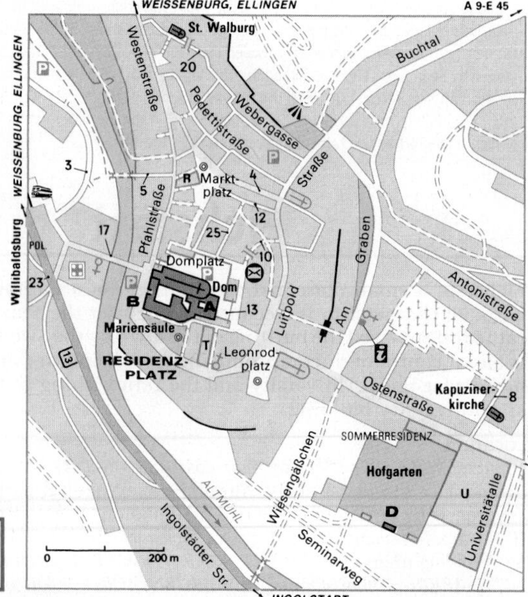

Fürstbischöfliche Residenz B
Kreuzgang A
Muschelpavillon D

Residenzplatz★

Despite its irregularly shape, the square nevertheless displays a striking unity *(the southeast corner is the best place from which to obtain a general view)*. Lawns carpet the centre; Rococo palaces surround it. The south side is bordered by four imposing houses with decorated gables and entrances guarded by atlantes. Facing them is the southern wing of the Residence and, on the west side, the former Vicar-General's mansion. The **Virgin's Column** in the immediate foreground *(Mariensäule)* rises from a fountain surrounded by cherubs.

The main entrance to the **Former Episcopal Residence** opens on to a magnificent staircase with a Baroque banister and painted ceiling.

Willibaldsburg

Access via route B 13 and the Burgstraße. This 14C castle, unfinished until the beginning of the 17C, occupies a dominant position on a height overlooking the river in the western part of the town. Inside the castle, note the **well** *(Tiefer Brunnen)*, 75m/246ft deep *(access through the courtyard)*.

From the top of the crenellated tower *(98 steps)* there is a view of the fortifications, the town and the river.

Jura-Museum★ – ♿ *Open Apr-Sep, Tue-Sun, 9am-6pm; Oct-Mar, Tue-Sun, 10am-4pm. Closed 1 Jan, Shrove Tue, 24, 25 and 31 Dec. €3. ☎ (084 21) 29 56.* The geological history of the Franconian Jura is traced in this museum. Most of the fossils on display (ammonites, crustaceans, fish, reptiles and dragonflies) were discovered in the limestone beds of neighbouring Solnhofen. The museum's prize exhibit is the complete fossilised skeleton of an Archaeopteryx (prehistoric ancestor of birds). A link between the reptile and the bird in the evolution of species, this extremely rare example was found in 1951 near Workerzell, northwest of Eichstätt.

Museum für Ur- und Frühgeschichte (Museum of Early History) – *Apr to Sep, Tue-Sun, 9am-6pm; Oct to Mar, Tue-Sun, 10am-4pm. Closed 1 Jan, Shrove Tue, 1 Nov, 24, 25 and 31 Dec. €3. ☎ (084 21) 894 50.* The exhibits here chart the history of settlers and settlements in the valley of the Altmühl from the epoch of hunters and crop-gatherers to the Middle Ages. Note especially the objects found in archeological digs which relate to iron-working during the Hallstatt civilisation, the collection of Ancient Roman artefacts and a double grave from the Merovingian period.

►► Summer Residence Garden *(Hofgarten,* Rococo shell pavilion★) – *Kapuzinerkirche* – St Walburg Church.

Excursions

Weißenburg

24km/15mi northwest. At the limit of the Ancient Roman province of Rhaetia, Weißenburg was an important garrison town. The **Roman Baths★** *(Römische Thermen)*, discovered in 1977 and a **Roman Museum** *(Römermuseum)* – note particularly the fine collection of **bronze★**, and the *Porta decumana*, a perfectly reconstructed fortified gateway, in the Kastell Biriciana – testify to its significant past. Weißenburg's historical **old town** centre is worth a visit for the 15C Gothic town hall and the market square *(Marktplatz)*, Luitpoldstraße (the Holzmarkt or Wood Market) with its elegant merchants' houses.

The **Ellinger Tor**, to the north of the town, is an interesting gateway once part of the surrounding 14C ramparts. The **Andreaskirche** has an elegant Late Gothic chancel built at the beginning of the 15C. Near the church, on Martin-Luther-Platz, is the **Imperial City Museum** of Weißenburg museum *(Reichsstadtmuseum Weißenburg)* located in historic walls. It documents the history of the city with special emphasis on the Imperial period – a title that Weißenburg held until 1802.

Ellingen

3 km/2mi north of Weißenburg. This locality owes its fame to the Teutonic Knights, whose Commander for Franconia was based in this small town from the 13C until Napoleon's dissolution of the Order in 1809.

The **castle** *(Schloß)* (1718-25) comprises an inner courtyard framed by four imposing wings, one of which is entirely occupied by the church. The huge twin-flight **main staircase★** is worth seeing. There is a small museum covering the history of the rise of the Teutonic Order. ♿ *(see the ticket office) Guided tours hourly. Apr to Sep, Tue-Sun 9am-5pm; Oct to Mar, Tue-Sun 10am-3pm. €3. ☎ (0981) 953 83 90.*

Neues Fränkisches Seenland

North of Weißenburg. The building of the Rhine-Main-Danube Canal and the channel linking the waters of the Danube and Altmühl has created an area with three lakes (Altmühl-, Brombach- and Rothsee), north and west of Weißenburg, which is ideal for relaxation and recreation.

Eifel★

The Eifel massif runs alongside the border with Belgium and Luxembourg, between Aachen and Trier and offers the visitor picturesque wooded valleys. There are no motorways or big urban areas; instead, the small roads snake their way through the forests passing small villages among the trees.

Location

Michelin map nº 543 O P 4 – Nordrhein-Westfalen and Rheinland Pfalz. Straddling the Länder of Rheinland-Pfalz and Rheinland-Westfalen, the Eifel massif is flanked by a great plain to the north, the Rhine to the East, the Moselle to the south and the Belgian border to the West.

Surrounding area (distances from Bad Münstereifel): BONN (39km/24mi northeast), KÖLN (49km/31mi northeast), AACHEN (74km/46mi northwest), RHEINTAL, MOSELTAL.

Directory

Where to Eat

⊖⊖ Weinhaus an der Rauschen – *Heisterbacher Straße 1 – 53902 Bad Münstereifel – ☎ (02253) 84 25 – Closed 2 weeks in Jul and Mon – ⊭ – €24.50/38.* This half-timbered house was built in 1553 and is in the historic town centre, next to the Erft waterfall *(Erftwasserfall)*. Furnished in light wood and rattan, with pretty décor, a fireplace and exposed beams, this establishment has a decidedly rustic air.

Where to Stay

⊖ Pension Oos – *Lieserstraße 16, 54550 Daun-Gemünden – ☎ (06592) 29 09 – fax (06592) 7890 – www.pension-oos.de – Closed Nov to mid-Mar – ⊭ P – 6rm: €26/42 ☕.* As well as its simple, well-kept guestrooms, this pension has a living room and small kitchen with fridge available for use by guests. Leisure pursuits available locally include swimming, sailing and visiting the volcanic craters nearby.

⊖ Hotel Seemöwe – *Am Obersee 10, 52152 Simmerath-Einruhr – ☎ (02485) 271 – fax (02485) 1356 – www.hotel-seemoewe.de – Closed Jan and Feb – P ⊭ ♿ – 50rm: €41/74 ☕ – Restaurant €12/15.* Good hotel on the edge of the lake (Obersee), with functional, but clean and well-cared for guestrooms. Country-style restaurant offering cuisine with a traditional flavour. Terrace.

⊖⊖ Burg Adenbach – *Adenbachhutstraße 1, 53474 Bad Neuenahr-Ahrweiler – ☎ (02641) 389 20 – fax (02641) 31714 – www.burghotel-adenbach.com – Closed Mon (Restaurant) – P ⊭ – Booking advised – 7m: €70/110 ☕ – Restaurant €15.50/32.* This hotel is set in a romantic medieval castle and has beautiful, comfortable guestrooms with large bathrooms. The restaurant has its own attractions: the stone walls give it historic appeal. Feasts worthy of a medieval gathering are served in the cellars.

Background

Natural environment – The Eifel, geographically an eastward extension of the Ardennes, is the largest and most complex of the Rhineland schist massifs. An undulating plateau at an average altitude of 600m/1 970ft, the region is deeply gashed by the Ahr, the Rur and the Kyll rivers, which meander through picturesque wooded valleys.

The **Upper Eifel** *(Hocheifel)*, in the centre, shows traces of ancient volcanic activity, with basalt crests (Hohe Acht: 747m/2 450ft), tufa deposits, hot springs and lakes *(Maare)*.

The **Schnee-Eifel**, the most rugged and isolated of the four parts, forms a sombre barrier along the Belgian frontier, northwest of Prum. Much of it rises to 700m/2 300ft.

The **North Eifel**, a landscape of moors and forests cut by deep valleys, is romantic and attractive. The touristic Seven Lakes sector extends in the northwest to the Upper Fagnes *(Hohes Venn)*, a marshy tableland belonging more to the Ardennes than the Eifel.

The **South Eifel**, bordering Luxembourg's "Little Switzerland", is a region of picturesque valleys with small villages among the trees.

Ahr Wines – The vineyards bordering this river, planted with Burgundian stock on schist slopes, produce dark-red wines late in the season, which are at their best when drunk almost warm. This is Germany's northernmost wine-producing region.

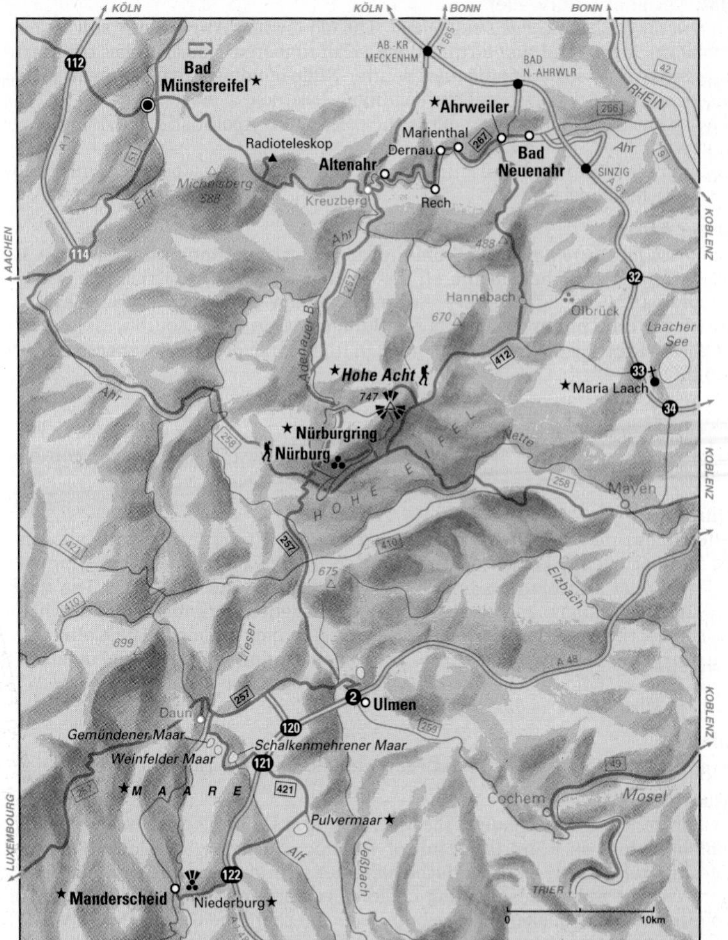

Tour

FROM BAD MÜNSTEREIFEL TO MANDERSCHEID

145 km/90mi – one day.

This excursion follows the valley of the Ahr with its popular resorts, climbs to the rolling, forested immensity of the Upper Eifel, and then snakes between the volcanic lakes of the Maare.

Bad Münstereifel

Surrounded by massive **ramparts★** *(Stadtbefestigung)*, the town still boasts a quantity of old houses and monuments. The **Stiftskirche St Chrysanthus und Daria** is an outstanding abbey church recalling St Pantaleon in Cologne because of the two towers flanking its 11C Romanesque west front.

A few miles east of Münstereifel, the road passes, on the left, a giant **radio-telescope**, rejoins the Ahr at Kreuzberg and continues along the winding valley. The telescope is 100m/328ft in diameter and its parabolic depth is 21m/69ft.

Altenahr

On a site between two bends in the river, Altenahr is an excursion centre dominated by the scattered ruins of the 12C **Burg Are**. There is an attractive view from the upper terminal of the chair-lift.

The valley, in which vineyards now alternate with rock outcrops, plays host to a number of wine producing villages: Rech, on either side of its Roman bridge; Dernau with its "wine fountain"; Marienthal and its ruined convent.

Bad Neuenahr-Ahrweiler

Plan in the Michelin Guide Deutschland. The old town of **Ahrweiler★** still retains its medieval gates and its fortifications. Half-timbered houses line the narrow, pedestrian-only streets of the town centre. While building a road a Roman villa was discovered that was in excellent condition. It is now a museum.
The spa at Bad Neuenahr produces the celebrated "Apollinaris" sparkling mineral water.
Leaving Ahrweiler, the road climbs swiftly towards the forest before it runs out over a rolling highland area.

Hohe Acht★

30min on foot there and back. From the viewpoint at the top of the tower *(75 steps)* erected at the highest point of the Eifel (747m/2 451ft), there is a superb panorama★★ to delight the eye – a vast landscape slashed by deep valleys above which the only prominent points are Nürburg Castle to the south-west and, in the opposite direction, the ruins of Olbrück in front of the distant Siebengebirge (Seven Mountains).

Nürburg

30min on foot there and back. A much-restored ruin in the middle of a rugged **landscape★** which can be admired to the best advantage from the top of the keep.

Nürburgring★

The famous motor racing track is named after the Nürburg ruin, which lies inside its northern loop. Famous events such as Formula 1, motorcycle Grand Prix, International Touring Cars and Super Touring races are held here. The track is 4.542m/2.82mi long, and has 14 bends and a height differential of 56m/184ft. The Erlebnispark Nürburgring is entirely devoted to motor racing. The **Collection of Nürburgring Legends★**, numerous veteran and racing cars, is housed in one of the halls. ♿ *Open daily, 10am-6pm. Closed Mondays from Nov to mid-Apr, 24 and 25 Dec. €10. ☎ (026 91) 30 26 02.*

Ulmen

A pretty volcanic crater lake between the village and a ruined castle.

Maare★

The ancient volcanic region of the Maare starts at Daun. The relatively small lakes which distinguish it are the result of volcanic activity in the Upper Eifel in the Tertiary era. Gas pressure produced explosions, forming craters with neither cone nor lava but only a surrounding circle of cinders. Water collected within these craters and created lakes that are both deep and calm: the **Gemündener Maar**, the **Weinfelder Maar** (also known as the **Totenmaar**, or 'lake of the dead'), the **Schalkenmehrener Maar** and the almost perfectly circular **Pulver Maar★**. *Follow the brown signposts with the word "Maare".*

Manderscheid★

In Manderscheid go to the **Niederburg★** ruins. From the top of the castle keep, there is a fine **view★** over the village to the Oberburg ruins and the Lieser Valley. Drive to the Pension Burgenblick car park and from here take the footpath which leads to the **viewpoint★★**, the so-called Kaisertempelchen (little Imperial temple) overlooking the Oberburg and Niederburg ruins.

Einbeck★

In the Middle Ages, no less than 700 small breweries in this former Hanseatic town supplied the whole of Germany with "Einpöckisches Bier" (from which the modern name Bockbier is derived). Situated between the Harz mountains and the Weser, Einbeck still retains part of its medieval fortifications, but a more attractive heritage is a collection of almost 400 half-timbered 16C houses, richly decorated with multicoloured carvings.

Location

Population: 29 400. Michelin map n°s 543, 544 K 13 – Niedersachsen. Einbeck is between the Harz massif and the Weser valley. The town is easily reached along the A 7 motorway which links Hannover to the north and Hann. Münden to the south.
🅱 *Rathaus, Marktplatz 6, 37574 Einbeck, ☎ (055 61) 161 21.*
Surrounding area: see HILDESHEIM (54km/34mi north), THÜRINGER WALD.

Walking About

OLD TOWN★

Allow one hour.

There is a remarkable collection of half-timbered houses in the town centre of Einbeck. Most of these dwellings are near the old market place.

Marktplatz★★

Note first of all the two houses on the corner of the Münsterstraße: the Brodhaus (1552), and especially the *Ratsapotheke* (1590), an impressive building which, like most of the old houses, has ventilated attics which served as lofts for hops and barley. Opposite is the town hall *(Rathaus)*, its three projecting fronts crowned with unusual pointed roofs. The well-preserved façade of the ancient **Ratswaage** (Weigh-House) exhibits an embellishment typical of the burghers' houses in Einbeck: fan-shaped, palm-leaf motifs, beaded and twisted mouldings to frame doors and traverses, friezes festooned with garlands.

Tiedexerstraße★★

Start behind the church tower (Marktkirche). The gables and façades on either side of this street offer an especially pleasing perspective.

Marktstraße

Note particularly the **Eickesches Haus★★** *(no 13 in the street, on the corner of the Knochenhauerstraße).* Erected between 1612 and 1614, this wooden construction ignores the traditional local style and imitates the stone mansions of the Renaissance. Carved panels represent the virtues and the artistic muses in an allegorical cycle; statues and expressive masks adorn the uprights and the beam-ends.

Excursions

Bad Gandersheim

22km//14mi northeast. The birthplace of Roswitha von Gandersheim, Germany's first (10C) poetess, is better known today as a hot spring and salt-water spa. The twin octagonal towers of the cathedral★, buttressing the 11C central façade, overlook the historic town centre. Inside are two very fine altars, one 15C and the other 16C. Around the market place are many well-preserved half-timbered houses (especially those dating from the 16C) and the Renaissance town hall, which adjoins the Moritzkirche.

Alfeld

24km/15mi north.

It is above all the Alte Lateinschule which makes a detour to this town on the banks of the Leine worthwhile.

Today this half-timbered old school building, which dates from 1610 and is adorned with carved figures, is the site of a local museum (Stadtmuseum) with an annexe featuring a collection of exotic stuffed animals. The dioramas display animals that are either extinct or in danger of extinction. *Open Tue-Fri, 10am-noon, 3pm-5pm, Sat-Sun, 10am-noon; May to Sep, also open Sun, 3-5pm. Closed bank holidays. No charge. ☎ (051 81) 70 31 81.*

Eisenach★★

Martin Luther called Eisenach "my dear town" and the Wartburg fortress is a place dear to many Germans, symbolising the very spirit of German civilisation and history. The town plays host to Lutherans and Bach lovers from around the world. The town is also famous for producing Wartburg cars, which were very popular in the former East German republic.

Location

Population: 44 500. Michelin map nº 544 N 14 – Baden-Württemberg. A former East German town near the border which divided the two Germanies, Eisenach is on the northwestern edge of the Forest of Thuringia.

ℹ Markt 2, 99817 Eisenach, ☎ (036 91) 792 30.

Surrounding area: see ERFURT (61km/38mi east), WEIMAR (77km/48mi east).

EISENACH

Street	Grid	No.
Alexanderstraße	BY	
Altstadtstraße	CY	4
Am Hainstein	BZ	5
Am Klosterholz	AY	7
Am Roten Bach	AY	9
August-Bebel-Straße	ABY	12
Barfüßerstraße	BZ	13
Burgstraße	BZ	14
Christianstraße	AY	15
Clemdastraße	BY	18
Ernst-Böckel-Straße	BCZ	19
Frauenberg	BZ	21
Gabelsbergerstraße	CY	22
Georgenstraße	BY	25
Goldschmiedenstraße	BY	26
Grimmelgasse	BZ	28
Hainweg	BYZ	27
Heinrich-Ehrardt-Pl	BY	29
Hinter der Mauer	BY	30
Johannisstraße	BY	31
Johann-Sebastian-Bach-Straße	CZ	33
Karlstraße	BY	
Klostenweg	BZ	35
Kupferhammer	BY	34
Langensalzaer Straße	CY	37
Luisenstraße	CZ	36
Markt	BY	38
Naumannstr.	BY	39
Nicolaistraße	BY	41
Querstraße	BY	40
Reuterweg	BZ	42
Schmelzerstraße	BY	43
Sommerstr.	BY	44
Stedtfelder Straße	AY	45
Theaterpl.	BY	46
Waisenstraße	BCZ	47
Werneburstraße	BY	48
Werrastraße	AY	50
Wilhem-Rinkens-Straße	BY	51

Rathaus	BY	R

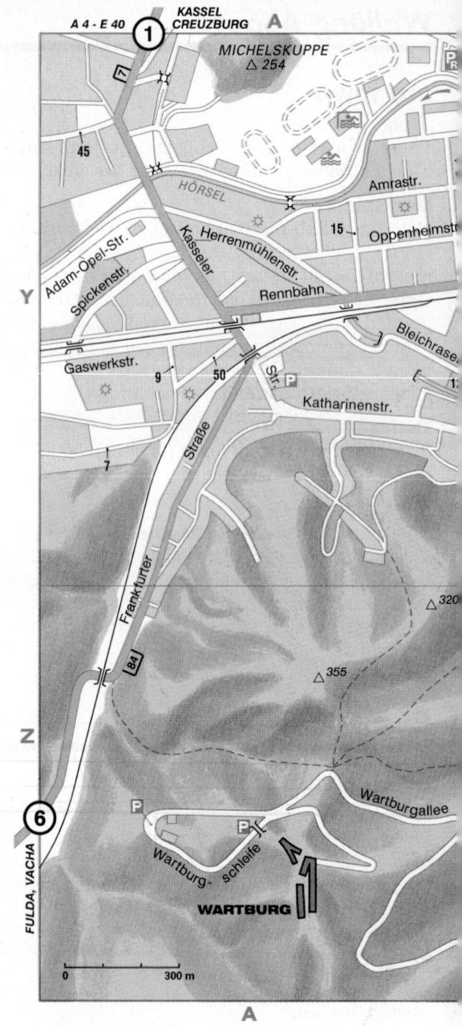

Background

At the Heart of Germany – At the beginning of the 13C, the Minnesänger (troubadours) took part in the legendary contests in the Wartburg – a custom which inspired Wagner's opera *Tannhäuser*. It was at Eisenach that **Martin Luther** studied and in the Wartburg that he later translated the New Testament under the patronage of the Duke of Saxony. **Johann Sebastian Bach** was born here in 1685, when the town was the seat of the dukes of Saxe-Eisenach, who were obliged to relinquish it in 1741 to the house of Saxe-Weimar.

In 1817, the Wartburg fortress was the site of a manifestation by student corporations designed to stimulate patriotism and progressive ideas. Fifty years later (1869) the "Eisenach Declaration" marked the creation by August Bebel and Wilhelm Liebknecht of the German Social Democrat Party.

Directory

Where to Stay

Hotel St. Peter – *Am Petersberg 7 – ☎ (03691) 87 28 30 – fax (03691) 872831 – www.stpeter-eisenach.de – P – 13rm: €36/50 – Restaurant € 11.25/17.50.* This little hotel has well-kept guestrooms and modern furnishings and is on the edge of the town. Dark wood and neat décor give the restaurant a rustic feel. There is also a Biergarten.

Auf der Wartburg – *at the Wartburg (shuttle to the hotel) – ☎ (03691) 79 70 – fax (03691) 797100 – info@wartburghotel.de – Closed 6 Jan to 6 Feb. – P – 35rm from €110.* Above and beyond its location, one night in this tastefully restored hotel is a never-to-be-forgotten experience. The Landgrafenstube restaurant has a rustic atmosphere.

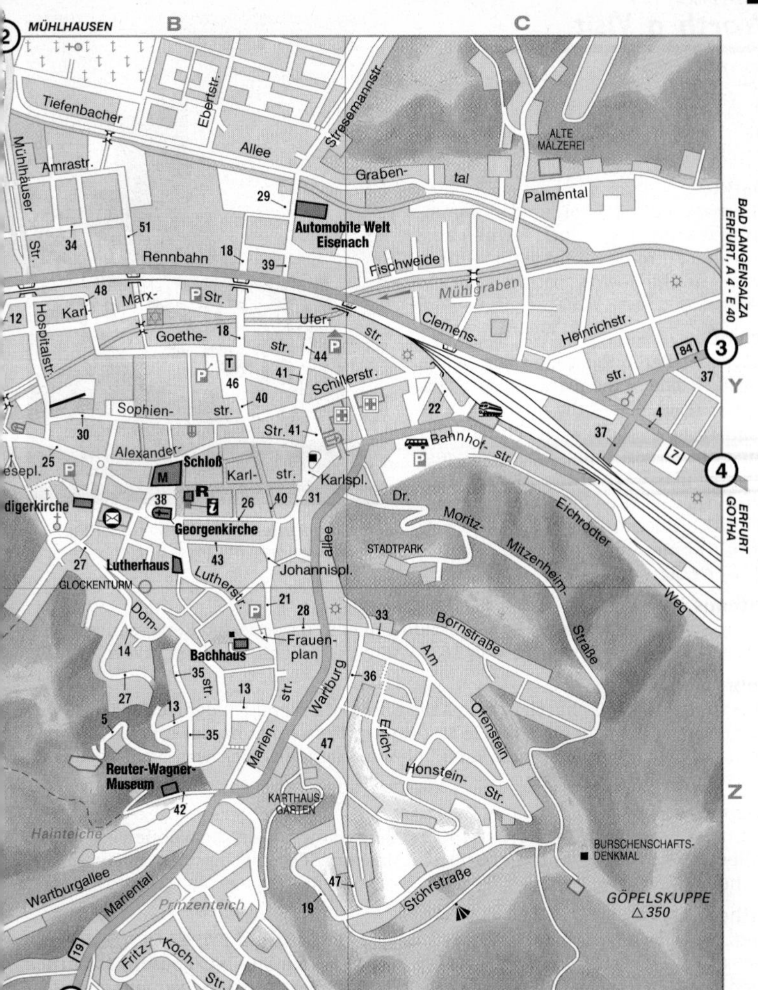

Special Features

THE WARTBURG★★ *Allow 2hr*

Leave the car in one of the car parks (fee payable) half way up the hill, from where it is a 15min walk up to the fortress. Alternatively, take the bus from the market place. Guided tour (1hr). Mar-Oct, 8.30am-5pm; Nov-Feb, 9am-3.30pm. €6. ☎ (036 91) 25 00; www.wartburg-eisenach.de

The Wartburg was formerly the seat of the Landgraves of Thuringia. Since 2000, the site has appeared on the UNESCO World Heritage list. It is more than worthy of the distinction: an exceptional historical site, well worth a visit for any visitor spending time in Eisenach.

Perched on a rocky spur, the fortress combines elements from several different periods. The visitor passes first beneath the porch of an entrance lodge, the oldest parts of which date from the 12C. Beyond this, the **outer courtyard** *(Erster Burghof)* is framed by half-timbered buildings erected in the 15C and 16C. A second, inner courtyard leads to the most interesting parts of the fortified complex. On the left, the **Palais★**, where the Landgraves lived, piles three storeys one upon the other, the whole garnished with early-13C arcading.

The fortified wall and south tower give a panoramic **view★** of Eisenach, the Forest of Thuringia and the Rhön foothills.

The one-hour guided tour *(available in English)* of the apartments is well worth while. It includes a visit to the **Hall of the Troubadours**, with Von Schwind's huge fresco illustrating episodes from the epic jousts of the Minnesänger in the Wartburg.

The tour ends in the **Wartburg Museum**, which displays selected works from the Wartburg foundation's collections. There are several paintings by Lucas Cranach the Elder.

Following the watch-path, the last thing to see is **Luther's Room** *(Lutherstube)*.

Worth a Visit

Ask for the free leaflet on Eisenach in English, which is available from the Tourist Office (on the market place).

Markt

The market place is bordered by administrative buildings and townhouses. In the centre is a fountain with a statue of the town's patron saint, St George.

Schloß

The sober Baroque façade seals off the northern side of the market place. This former residence of the dukes of Saxe-Weimar now houses the **Thuringian Museum** (porcelain, faience and regional glassware of the 18C and 19C; paintings and drawings from the 19C and 20C; Rococo banqueting hall). ♿ *Open Tue-Sun, 10am-5pm. €2. ☎ (036 91) 67 04 50.*

J. Bouraly/MICHELIN

Wartburg Fortress where memories of the Troubadours mix with those of Luther.

Rathaus

The town hall is a three-storey 16C building in both Baroque and Renaissance styles, restored after a disastrous fire in 1636. Note the (slightly) leaning tower.

Georgenkirche

This triple-aisle 16C church contains the tombs of several Landgraves of Thuringia. Luther preached here on 2 May 1521, despite the fact that he was officially banned from the Holy Roman Empire, and Johann Sebastian Bach was baptised in this church on 26 March 1685.

Predigerkirche

The church, an Early Gothic (late-13C building), now houses the **wooden sculpture collection★** formerly in the Thuringian Museum. The carvings date from the 12C to the 16C.

Lutherhaus

Open Apr-Oct, 9am-5pm; Nov-Mar: 10am-5pm. Closed Good Fri. €2.50. ☎ (036 91) 298 30; www.lutherhaus-eisenach.de. It was in this fine late-14C house that **Luther** lived between 1498 and 1501, while he was a student at the School of Latin. The display includes historical rooms, paintings and literature retracing the history of the Reformation.

Bachhaus

From the Lutherhaus, return along the Lutherstraße as far as the Frauenplan. ♿ *10am-6pm. €4. ☎ (036 91) 793 40; www.bachhaus.de.* The house at no 21 Frauenplan is believed to have been the **birthplace** of the great composer. The interior of the house provides fascinating insights into the lifestyle of a late-17C burgher. Manuscripts, scores and portraits recall not only Johann Sebastian Bach but also several other members of the family, all of them composers.

Automobile Welt

♿ *Open Tue-Sun, 10am-5pm. €2.10. ☎ (036 91) 772 12.*

The premises of a savings bank *(Rennbahn 6)* next to the former automobile factory are home to a small exhibition documenting the history of the Wartburg car; first manufactured here in 1955, the last one rolled off the production line in 1991. On the factory premises themselves *(Friedrich-Naumann-Str 10)* a new exhibition was opened at the end of 2001, entitled **Automobile Welt Eisenach**. This presents the history of car manufacture at the Eisenach works (1896-1991), inextricably linked with the names Wartburg, Dixi, and BMW (which manufactured its cars here between 1928 and 1940), and also with the social and cultural history of the age.

►► Fritz-Reuter- und Richard-Wagner-Museum.

Excursion

The Forest of Thuringia★★ *(see THÜRINGER WALD)*

Emden

Emden is a pleasant town which has been tastefully reconstructed following the Second World War. Many of the inhabitants are employed at the town's huge Volkwagen factory. Art lovers will definitely want to stop here: Emden has some remarkable museums, including the Kunsthalle, a gallery of contemporary art. The town is also a good departure point for tours of the East Frisian islands.

Location

Population: 51 000. Michelin maps nº 541 F 5 – Niedersachsen. Emden is located at the mouth of the Ems and faces the Netherlands. The Ems river has been dyked and the Dortmund-Ems and Ems-Jade canals have enabled the town to regain its position as the chief maritime port of Lower Saxony.

🅱 *Alter Markt 2a, 26721 Emden, ☎ (049 21) 974 00.*

Surrounding area: see OLDENBOURG (84km/52mi southeast), BREMEN (131km/82mi east), OSTFRIESISCHE INSELN.

Worth a Visit

Ostfriesisches Landesmuseum★ (Museum of the East Frisian Islands)

In the former town hall. Open Tue-Sat, 10am-5pm. Closed until late 2005 for renovation. Re-opening date undecided at time of writing. €3.50. ☎ (049 21) 87 20 58.

Items excavated in peat bog digs, models of the port and fishing boats and paintings by the Dutch School evoke the colourful history of the town.

Pride of place is given to the collection of the former **Rüstkammer★★**: weapons and armour of the burgher militia from 1500 to the 18C. From the bell-tower, there is a view of the harbour and surrounding countryside.

Port

Ratsdelf. The oldest section is the **harbour gateway** *(Hafentor)* built in 1635 and bearing the Latin inscription *"God is Emden's bridge, harbour and sailing wind"*. In the historical harbour basin you can see several **museum ships** *(Museumsschiffe)*.

Pelzerhaus

Pelzerstrasse. This building dating from c 1585 with the Renaissance façade is one of the few houses in the town centre that survived the bombs of the Second World War.

Kunsthalle in Emden – Stiftung Henri und Eske Nannen

Hinter dem Rahmen 13; northwest of town. ♿ Open Tue-Sun, 10am-5pm, Tue, 10am-8pm, Sat and Sun, 11am-5pm. Closed 24 and 25 Dec. €5, no charge on 3 Oct. ☎ (049 21) 97 50 50. The post-modern red-brick building houses the sizeable collection of works of art by the German Expressionists and Neue Sachlichkeit, gathered together during his lifetime by founder of *Stern* magazine Henri Nannen, who was born in Emden. The exhibition includes contemporary painting and sculpture.

Tour

ALONG THE STÖRTEBEKERSTRASSE

156km/97mi. Allow one day.

The **Störtebeker route** takes its name from Klaus Störtebeker, a legendary pirate infamous throughout the Baltic Sea *(see Insel RÜGEN)*.

Leave Emden along the Abdenstraße to the west.

Krummhörn

This area of bogs that has been inhabited for millennia is marked by *Warfendörfer*, or "Warf" villages. A "Warf" is a hill or mound artificially put up to protect people from floods. The churches built of volcanic tufa and brick were erected at the highest point of the **Warf** from which the network of streets gathered, connected by radial avenues (the "Lohnen").

Rysum

This particularly noteworthy Warf-village has a church containing a Late Gothic organ from the 15C which is considered the world's oldest playable organ.

Pewsum

The sight to see in Pewsum is the romantically located Manningaburg (late 15(surrounded by a moat and boasting a collection on East Friesian fortresses an chiefs. In the Middle Ages, the heads of powerful family dynasties – who, thank to land ownership and success in trade, had achieved positions of power in the Eas Friesian villages – were called chiefs.

Pilsum

The cruciform church in Pilsum, with its mighty crossing tower, is one of the best-kept and most beautiful Late Romanesque religious buildings (c 1200) in the region.

Greetsiel

This charming and picturesque fishing and artist village has a typical East Friesian look, with a fleet of crab catchers, carefully restored gable houses, lighthouse and its two 'twin' windmills.

Norden

On the *Marktplatz* stands the imposing **Ludgerkirche**, built in fits and starts between the 13C and 15C. It has a Romanesque nave and a free-standing bell-tower. Inside is the Late Gothic sacristy and the heavily decorated Baroque organ by Arp Schnitger (1868-92) with a wonderful sound. On the other side of the plaza is the palace-like Mennonite church. Beyond the B 72 is the old town hall *(Altes Rathaus)* from the 16C with the **museum of local culture** *(Heimatmuseum)* and the **East Friesian Tea Museum** (*Ostfriesisches Teemuseum* – with a comprehensive documentation on the history of tea). Haus Schöningh on Osterstraße, a richly decorated patrician house from the Renaissance, which was built in 1576, deserves special attention.

Dornum

Of the three chief's fortresses of Dornum built before 1400, only two were rebuilt after the town's destruction in 1514, one of which is the Beningsburg. The castle, a four-winged Baroque construction, stands in the midst of an extensive park.

Esens

The Late Classicist **Magnuskirche** (built 1848-54) in the charming little rural town of Esens, is Ostfriesland's largest church. The attentively worked, grandiose sandstone sarcophagus inside belonging to the knight of Sibet-Attena, who died in 1473, is particularly impressive. The **Holarium** on *Kirchplatz* teaches its visitors something about holography, and lets them delve into the magic of three-dimensional images and sculptures.

Neuharlingersiel

This fishing village is not only the oldest (first mentioned in documents in 1693) but also one of the most beautiful ports of the North Sea coastline. The **Buddelschiffmuseum** (a bottled-ship museum) is worth visiting.
Drive back to Emden via Esens and Aurich.

Erfurt★

Erfurt is a peaceful, captivating town dominated by numerous steeples and bell-towers. Its historic centre is one of the best preserved in Germany. Half-timbered houses and Renaissance-style buildings have been carefully restored. This university town has attracted many important people; Luther, Goethe, Schiller, Herder and Bach, among others, are closely associated with the town's history.

Location

Population: 197 300. Michelin map n°° 544 N 17 – Thüringen. Erfurt is sitated in the heart of the state of Thuringia, between Gotha and Weimar, and has been its capital since 1990.
🅱 *Benediktsplatz 1, 99084 Erfurt, ☎ (0361) 664 00.*
Surrounding area: see WEIMAR (21km/13mi east), EISENACH (61km/38mi west), THÜRINGER WALD (itinerary leaves from Eisenach).

Background

A trading town for East and West – In the year 742, St Boniface from England founded a bishopric at Erfurt, which was soon joined to that of Mainz.

From the Middle Ages onward, the town's position on the important trade route linking the Rhine with Russia lent it such commercial consequence that it was incorporated into the Hanseatic League in the 15C: Erfurt thus became an essential part of the connection uniting Central Europe with the powerful ports of the north. The trade of woad, the only plant at the time capable of producing the colour blue, secured the town's prosperity in the 15C and 16C.

Spirituality and Humanism – The numerous steeples and bell-towers rising above the roofs of the town bear witness to the religious activity in Erfurt under the influence of the archbishop-electors of Mainz.

The influential Christian mystic **Master Eckhart** was born near the town and was established in Erfurt as Provincial of Saxony. Two centuries later came another young man who was to present an even more radical challenge to religious thinking. **Martin Luther** studied philosophy at the university – considered to be the cradle of German Humanism – entered the Augustine monastery in 1505 and left six years later to establish himself in Wittenberg.

Directory

Where to Eat

⊖ Köstritzer "Zum güldenen Rade" – *Marktstraße 50 – ☎ (0361) 561 35 06 – www.gourmetguide.com/koestritzer zum gueldenen rade* – ♿ – *€16/45.* This restaurant is situated in the old town, not far from the town hall. Stone walls, plenty of wood and paintings form a pleasant ambience. In pleasant weather, there is a summer garden and interior courtyard. A separate building houses an old mill.

⊖⊖ Alboth's Restaurant – *Futterstraße 15 – ☎ (0361) 568 82 07 – Closed Sun and Mon and for 3 weeks in Jul and Aug – €26/45.* This chic, well-presented restaurant is set in one of the town's historic houses: dark wood ceilings and smart décor in the dining room. Varied menu with good wine list.

Where to Stay

⊖ Hotel Erfurtblick – *Nibelungenweg 20 – ☎ (0361) 22 06 60 – fax (0361) 2206622 – hotel-erfurtblick @gmx.de* – P ⅹ – *11rm: €50/75* ☕. Well-kept hotel-guesthouse with light and airy guestrooms and a pleasant atmosphere. Pleasant garden with water feature. Pleasant view of the town from the breakfast room and terrace.

⊖ Der kleine Nachbar – *Weimarer Straße 16, 99867 Gotha – ☎ (03621) 40 07 95 – fax (03621) 28841 – www.derkleinenachbar.de* – P ⅹ – *9rm: €32/50* ☕ *– Restaurant €8/12.* This small guesthouse has plain and simple rooms which are immaculately kept. Well served by public transport with quick and easy access to the historic centre of Gotha.

Walking About

AROUND THE DOMPLATZ

The Domplatz is dominated by the two imposing edifices of the Mariendom (Cathedral) and the Severikirche. In the centre, an obelisk commemorates a visit in 1777 by the Archbishop of Mainz.

Dom St-Marien★★

The original Romanesque basilica, built in 1154 on a hill occupied by the citadel, was added to in the mid 14C – a portal at the entrance to the north transept, the so-called Triangle Portal; a soaring Gothic chancel at the east end. A century later, the Romanesque nave was replaced by a nave in the Flamboyant Gothic style, with broad side aisles.

Triangle portals★★ – The north entrance consists of two doors set obliquely and supporting elegant statuary groups – on the northeast the Apostles at Work, a group recalling the French master-masons; on the northwest side, the Wise and Foolish Virgins showing Magdeburg influence.

Interior – There are several works of art worthy of attention: the Romanesque Altar of the Virgin (1160); the **statue candelabra★** known as "the Wolfram" (1160); the tombstone of the Count of Gleichen and his two wives; the intricately worked choir stalls (14C). The stained-glass **windows★** above the choir (c 1370-1420) shed light on everyday medieval life through their depiction of episodes from Old and New Testament and the lives of various saints.

Severi-Kirche★

Formerly the Benedictine monks' abbey church of St Paul and of the Augustines, this Early Gothic building is of the hall type, with five naves. The **sarcophagus★** of the saint (c 1365) is in the southernmost aisle.

Cross the Domplatz and take the Marktstraße.

AROUND THE FISCHMARKT

Fischmarkt (Fish Market)

Inside the imposing neo-Gothic *Rathaus* are **frescoes★** which illustrate the lives of Luther, Faust and Tannhäuser. On the north side of the square there is a fine three-storey Renaissance building, *"Zum Breiten Herd"*.

ERFURT

Anger .... B
Bahnhofstraße .... B
Dalbergsweg .... A 13
Domstraße .... A 15
Fischmarkt .... A
Löberstraße .... B 22
Mainzerhofstraße .... A 24
Marktstraße .... A
Meienbergstraße .... B 27
Moritzwallstraße .... A 28
Regierungsstraße .... A 34
Schlösserstraße .... AB 36
Schlüterstraße .... A 37
Walkmühlstraße .... A 40
Wenigemarkt .... B 42
Willy-Brandt-Platz .... B 43

Angermuseum ...... B M¹
Rathaus .... A R

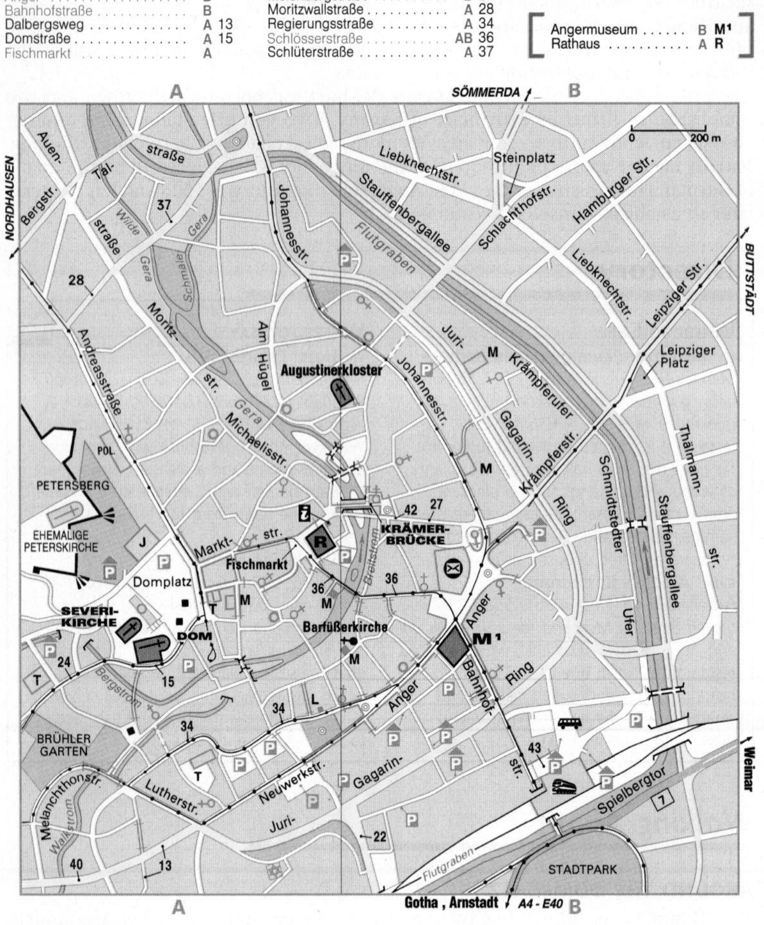

Krämerbrücke★

This bridge, built in 1325, similar to the Ponte-Vecchio of Florence, is the only bridged street north of the Alps on which the houses are inhabited. The narrow, half-timbered houses with their steeply pitched roofs date from the 16C to the 19C, but give the bridge something of a medieval air.

Angermuseum★

Anger 18. Closed for restoration work, but a few rooms open for temporary exhibitions. ☎ (0361) 55 45 60.

This museum in the middle of the city is located in a Baroque building dating from 1706 (the erstwhile weighing and packing house). The focal point of the museum is the exhibition of medieval art from Thuringia: among its highlights are 14C and 15C **altarpieces★★**, including the Augustineraltar, a **Pietà★★** by the Master of St Severinus' sarcophagus and paintings by Hans Baldung Grien depicting the Creation. In the gallery is a collection of 18C-19C German landscape painting. Porcelain and faïence produced in the workshops of Thuringia are a prominent feature of the craftwork on display. Note the gem of the museum – a mural by Erich Heckel, entitled *Life of Man* (1923-24).

►► Augustinerkloster – Barfüßerkirche.

Excursions

Arnstadt

16km/10mi south. A small Thuringian town dating from the 8C, but known above all for the fact that **Johann Sebastian Bach** stayed there from 1703 to 1707, when he was organist at the parish church, which today bears his name. There is a **Local History Museum** *(Museum für Stadtgeschichte: Open Mon-Fri, 8.30am-4.30pm,*

Sat-Sun, 9.30am-4.30pm. €3. ☎ (036 28) 60 29 78) outlining the history of the town and displaying mementoes of the composer and literary exhibits in the house named "Zum Palmbaum" on one side of the market place *(Am Markt)*.
In the old cemetery (*Alter Friedhof*, Bahnhofstraße) are the graves of more than 20 members of the Bach family.
In the **New Palace** (*Neues Palais*, August-Bebel-Straße), see the collection of marionettes and **dolls★** *(Mon plaisir Puppensammlung)*, the Brussels tapestries of the Renaissance period, and the **porcelain★** from Meissen and the Far East. *Open Apr to Oct, Tue-Sun, 8.30am-5pm, Nov to Mar, Tue-Sun, 9.30am-4.30pm. Closed Good Fri. €3. ☎ (036 28) 60 29 33)*

Gotha

The town won worldwide renown through the publication of the Gotha Almanac on the genealogy of the aristocracy. The market square, surrounded by beautiful town houses dating from a variety of periods, stretches as far as the ducal palace. In the lower part of the town, on the Hauptmarkt, stands the *Rathaus*, an elegant Renaissance building (1567-74), with an eye-catching, richly ornate north façade and beautiful doorway. The massive bulk of the Friedenstein palace, set back slightly from the main line of sight, dominates the town.

Schloß Friedenstein

Open May to Oct, Tue-Sat, 10am-5pm; Nov to Apr, Tue-Sat, 10am-4pm. €4. ☎ (036 21) 22 21 32.
This austere Early Baroque palace, which has three wings, was begun in 1643 under Ernst I the Pious, and finished in 1655. An arcaded gallery around the inner courtyard is the only decorative feature. However, the visitor is amply compensated for this by the palace interior, which consists of more than 30 rooms decorated in the Baroque, Rococo and Classical styles, with fittings that verge in parts on the absolutely sumptuous. Note in particular the original stucco ceilings (late 17C), the beautiful marquetry flooring, and the fine quality furniture (from the workshop of Abraham Roentgen among others).
The palace houses numerous collections built up over the centuries by the Gotha dynasty with some later additions.
The art collection includes 17C Dutch and Flemish painting, while specialising in 15C and 16C German works. Note the paintings by **Lucas Cranach the Elder** and the charming ***Gotha Lovers*★**, painted by the Master of the Housebook in 1484, the first ever separate double portrait in German painting. The Gotha altarpiece is also a magnificent work, comprising 157 panels depicting the life of Christ, making it one of the most heavily illustrated of its kind in German art.
The palace also houses a collection of works by French sculptor **Jean-Antoine Houdon** (1741-1828), the richest after that in the Louvre. The **collection of Egyptian and Antique art** testifies to the enthusiasm of its collector. Finally, the visitor to the palace should not miss the **Ekhof-Theater** (1774).

Schloßpark

The extensive palace gardens, landscaped in the English style, with a number of beautiful old trees and an orangery built from 1747 to 1767, make a pleasant place for a stroll.

Erzgebirge★

Known as the Ore Mountains, this medium-height massif owes its name to the many veins and deposits of silver, tin, cobalt, nickel and iron – a natural wealth which brought prosperity to a number of small towns such as Zwickau, Annaberg and Schneeberg.
The stretch of the mountain range which lies in Germany features the impressive summit of the Fichtelberg, at 1 214m/3 950ft. Landscapes that are both open and wooded, reservoir lakes, forests criss-crossed by footpaths and picturesque holiday villages combine to make the region particularly attractive to visitors.
The itinerary described below, which explores the western part of the range, follows the Czech frontier to start with.

Location

Michelin maps n°s 544, 546 O 21, 22 – Sachsen. The ridge of peaks marking the frontier with the Czech Republic reaches a modest maximum height above sea level of 750m/2 461ft, and the relatively high altitude of the valley floors frequently makes it feel more like an upland plateau than a mountain range.
Surrounding area: see Oberes SAALETAL (Saalburg is 65km/41mi west of Klingenthal), DRESDEN (106km/66mi northeast of Annaberg-Bucholz), BAYREUTH (106km/66mi southwest of Klingenthal).

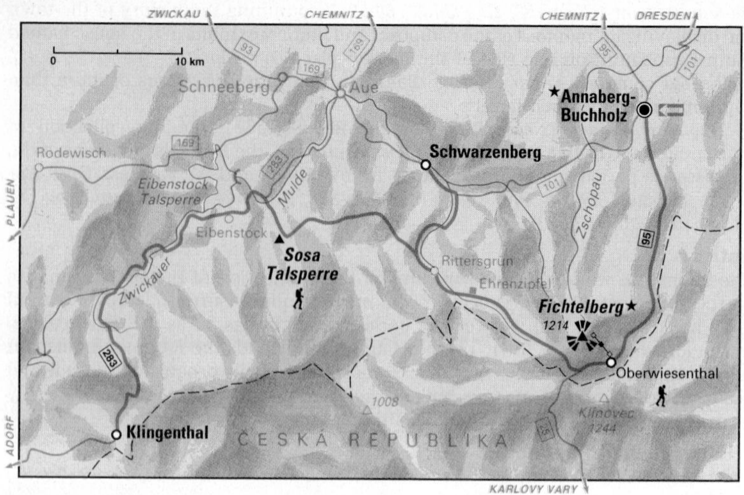

Tour

FROM ANNABERG-BUCHHOLZ TO KLINGENTHAL

81km/50mi (93km/58mi via Schwarzenberg) – 3hr
Leave Annaberg-Buchholz (see entry) on road no 95 in the direction of Oberwiesenthal.

Fichtelberg★

Towering above the health and winter sports resort of **Oberwiesenthal**, this peak is identifiable from far off by the meteorological equipment adorning its summit. The top is reached by ski lift or on foot *(30min there and back. Leave the car in the car park 455m/500yd after the lower ski-lift terminal)*. A vast **panorama★** opens out when the top is reached, showing all of the surrounding country and, away in the south, the silhouette of Mount Klinovec in the Czech Republic. At 1 214m/3 950ft, this is the highest peak of the Erzgebirge.

From Oberwiesenthal to Ehrenzipfel there is a pretty forest road which follows the course of a river. At Rittersgrün, one can either take the detour via Schwarzenberg or continue along the direct route.

Schwarzenberg

Resting on a crag, this officially protected old town is nestled around its castle and church. The fortress, which was founded in 1150, was turned into the elector's hunting lodge in 1555-58. Nowadays it harbours the "Schloß Schwarzenberg" museum. Next to it stands the Baroque **St Georgenkirche★** (1690-99), a single-naved church with an impressive wooden ceiling and a richly carved trinity pulpit. A beautiful wrought-iron grille separates the nave from the altar space.

Sosa-Talsperre

From the car park, walk to the kiosk and then the promontory. This small lake and its dam are in an idyllic forest setting.

The road follows the northern bank of the reservoir formed by the Eibenstock barrage and then (Road 283) climbs the winding valley of the Zwickauer Mulde before it runs into Klingenthal.

Klingenthal

Built at the end of the 16C as a mining community, this town is better known for the musical instruments made here since the mid-17C. The Baroque church "Zum Friedenfürsten" is worth visiting.

Frankfurt am Main★★

Financial and commercial capital of Germany, Frankfurt has more skyscrapers than any other city in Europe; many big international companies, government organisations and financial institutions are based here. Nowadays it is largely renowned for its trade fairs and shows of all kinds, and one sometimes forgets that this is also Goethe country and that, for over two centuries, the coronation of the kings and emperors of the Holy Roman Empire in Germany took place here. Its research institutes, university, opera, theatres and an ever increasing number of museums have turned Frankfurt into the modern scientific and cultural metropolis of the HessenLand.

Location

Population: 650 000. Michelin map 543 P 9, 10 – Hessen. Frankfurt stands at the crossroads of the country's north-south and east-west communications. It is at the heart of a major motorway junction, notably at the intersection between the A 3 (Cologne-Nuremberg), and the A 5 from Karlsruhe. It takes around 2hr to reach the city from Cologne, 2hr 30min from Nuremberg.

Hauptbahnhof, 60329 Frankfurt am Main, ☏ (069) 21 23 88 49.

Surrounding area: see DARMSTADT (32km/20mi south), WIESBADEN (41km/26mi west), MAINZ (42km/26mi west), RHEINTAL (Rüdesheim is 66km/41mi west).

G. Marth/Tourism + Congress GmbH Frankfurt a. M.

A German Manhattan.

Background

The second coronation city – Built in the 8C on the site of an old Roman camp, Frankfurt became the emperor's place of residence and capital of Franconiaone century later. In 1152, Frederick I Barbarossa engineered his election as Emperor of Germania at Frankfurt, thus inaugurating a tradition which was to be ratified by the Golden Bull of the Emperor Charles IV in 1356. Two centuries later, in 1562, the town replaced Aachenas the **coronation place** of the rulers of the **Holy Roman Empire** – a privilege it retained until the dissolution of the Reich in 1806.

The Young Goethe – Johann Wolfgang von Goethe was born in Frankfurtin 1749. The great writer preserved the memories of the city of his birth throughout his life and described them in his memoirs *(Aus meinem Leben)*. It was here that he enjoyed his most prolific period as a writer, between 1772 and 1775, producing among other great works *Die Leidendes jungen Werthers* in only four weeks.

Capital of Finance and Economy – In the 16C Frankfurtwas granted the right to mint money. The money market rapidly flourished and the **stock exchange** was founded. German banks dominated the economy in the 18C; in the 19C they acquired a worldwide reputation thanks to financiers such as **Bethmann** and above all **Rothschild** (1744-1812) whose sons, "the Five Frankfurters", established branches in Paris, London, Viennaand Naples. Profiting from such an economic climate, industries were not long in establishing themselves in the city. Chemicals and pharmaceuticals remain the most active today. The first Autumn Fair was held in 1240. The Spring Fair was added in 1330. Since the war the Fur Fair *(Pelzmesse)*, the Motor Show *(Automobilausstellung)* and the famous Book Fair *(Buchmesse)* have confirmed Frankfurtas the country's commercial capital.

Election of the Emperors

In the Holy Roman Empire in Germany, the title of emperor did not pass from father to son. In order to be elected, the candidate had to belong to one of the sovereign families. And so it was that the crown passed between Franconians (Salian dynasty), Saxons (Ottonians), Bavarians and Swabians (the Hohenstaufens). However, the emperors would make gifts and grant privileges to the dukes, counts and high prelates who belonged to the Diet in order to keep the title in their family. In 1356, the Golden Bull limited the number of Electors to seven, three of whom from the clergy (the Archbishops of Mainz, Cologneand Trier) and four laymen (Duke of Saxony, Margrave of Brandenburg, Count Palatine, King of Bohemia).

Directory

Telephone prefix – 069.

Tourist information – For room reservations: *Tourismus + Congress GmbH, ☎ 21 23 88 00, Fax 21 23 78 80*, Mon-Fri 8.30am-5pm. Information offices: Tourist Information Hauptbahnhof, central station entrance hall, Mon-Fri 8am-9pm, Sat-Sun 9am-6pm, *☎ 21 23 88 49*; Tourist Information Römer, Römerberg 27, Mon-Fri 9.30am-5.30pm, Sat-Sun 10am-4pm; City Info Zeil, Mon-Fri 10am-6pm, Sat 10am-4pm. The city magazines *Journal Frankfurt* (in newsagents), *Fritz* (free of charge) and *Welcome to Frankfurt* (in German) provide information on all events. Ticket sales (only on location) at the *Tourismus + Congress GmbH*.

Post offices with special opening times – The post office on the Zeil is open Mon-Fri 9.30am-8pm, Sat 9am-4pm; the branch office at the train station (Hauptbahnhof, 1st floor) is open Mon-Fri 7am-7.30pm, Sat 8am-4pm, and at the airport daily 7am-9pm.

Newspapers – *Frankfurter Allgemeine Zeitung, Frankfurter Rundschau, Frankfurter Neue Presse*.

Internet – www.frankfurt.de; www.rhein-main.net; www.frankfurt-am-main.de; www.frankfurt-online.net; www.frankfurt-tourismus.de

Getting About

It is quite easy to get around Frankfurt, especially since much of the city centre is a pedestrian zone. The best way to get around is therefore on foot.

Public Transport

The **RMV** (Rhein-Main-Verkehrsbund) is responsible for all public transport services, trams, buses, U-Bahns and S-Bahns, and regional trains in the greater Frankfurtregion: *☎ 2 73 07 62*, Mon-Fri 8am-6pm, Sat 9am-4pm. The **VGF** (Verkehrsgesellschaft Frankfurt am Main) manages the local public transportation of the city of Frankfurt: *☎ 1 94 49* Mon-Thu 8am-5pm, Fri 8am-1pm. Information: on the traffic island of the Hauptwache, Mon-Fri 9am-8pm, Sat 9am-4pm, also at Konstablerwache, Passage B level and other underground (U-Bahn) and S-Bahn stations. The tariff rate 3 is for all rides inside Frankfurt. Normal fare is €1.90, between 9am-4pm €1.53, day ticket €4.35 (valid until the last ride of the day, and can be used to travel to the airport). Tickets are available at vending machines or from the bus drivers. Tickets are not available in the U-Bahn, S-Bahn or tramcars.

Ebbelwei-Express.

Lechthaler/Tourism + Congress GmbH Frankfurt a. M.

Internet – www.rmv.de; www.vgf-ffm.de

The **Frankfurt Card** costs €7.50 (valid for one day) and €11 (valid for two days) and can be used for the RMV network within city limits including the airport. It also gives a 50% discount to 15 museums and other attractions, such as the zoo and the airport terraces, also 25-30% for selected boat and coach rides. The Frankfurt Card is available in many travel agencies, at tourist information offices and in both terminals at the airport.

Tip: For S-Bahn rides to the airport you need a ticket at tariff rate 4.

Where to Eat

Steinernes Haus – *Braubachstraße 35 – Tram 4+5 – ☎ (069) 28 34 91 – www.steinernes-haus.de – Open 11am-11pm – Reservation necessary – €15/40.* This pleasant, rustic-style establishment is around 500 years old and one of the oldest in Frankfurt. It is surrounded by art galleries. Typical Frankfurtcuisine and specialities grilled on lava stone can be sampled here.

Lorsbacher Thal – *Große Rittergasse 49-51 (street heading southeast from Deutschherrnufer near the Alte Brücke) – ☎ (069) 61 64 59 – www.lorsbacher-thal.de – Tue-Sat 4pm-midnight, Sun noon-11pm – 🚭 ♿ – €15.50/21.*
A particularly friendly establishment serving *Äppelwoi* (dry cider). The restaurant and its lovely garden are slightly hidden from view in a rear courtyard. Copious traditional fare in a pleasant and original setting.

Toan – *Friedberger Anlage 14 – ☎ (069) 44 98 44 – €19/33.50.* Excellent Vietnamese restaurant in the Nordend district (next to the zoo), with pleasant garden terrace.

Bauer – *Sandweg 113 – ☎ (069) 40 59 27 44 – info@gebrueder-bauer.de – Closed Sat and Sun lunchtime – 🚭 – €25/29.* This fashionable establishment, set in a residential quarter near the city centre, attracts people of all ages. The Bauer brothers concoct varied dishes in a plain, bistro-style setting.

Meyer's Restaurant – *Große Bockenheimer Straße 54 – ☎ (069) 91 39 70 70 – info@meyer-frankfurt.de – Closed 1st-5 Jan and Sun – €30/43.* A little bistro-restaurant on the edge of the pedestrian zone, on the corner of the old opera house. You can cast an eye over the kitchen at the back of the restaurant; the dishes served here have a maritime flavour.

Restaurant-Café "Zum Schwarzen Stern" – *Römerberg 6 – (069) 29 19 79 – www.schwarzerstern.de – – Reservation recommended – €30/50.* Goethe once wrote that one could study the most varied styles of building in Frankfurtjust by looking at this beautiful half-timbered house. This remains true today, since the *Schwarzer Stern* was rebuilt after the war to resemble the original establishment as closely as possible. Pleasant, rustic decor.

Ernos Bistro – *Liebigstraße 15 – (069) 72 19 97 – Closed 20 Dec-4 Jan, 26 Jul-17 Aug, Sat-Sun (except fair days) – €51/74.* A friendly, bistro-style rustic establishment set in a villa in the bank district. High-quality French cuisine.

Tiger-Restaurant – *Heiligkreuzgasse 20 – (069) 92 00 22 25 – info@tigerpalast.com – Closed 14 Jul-26 Aug, Sun and Mon – €57.50/87.* This restaurant, with walls covered in photographs of performers, offers creative cuisine which appeals to more than just the theatre crowd who gather here after the show (the variety theatre is in the same building). The beautiful brick vaulting contributes to the special atmosphere.

Where to Stay

Hotel-Pension Gölz – *Beethovenstraße 44 (south of Palmengarten and northwest of the central station) – (069) 74 67 35 – Fax (069) 746142 – www.hotel-goelz.de – Closed Dec – €36/99.* A stone's throw from the city centre and exhibition centre, this family-run hotel set in a 19C villa has spacious double rooms and some more basic single rooms (including two with bathroom on the landing).

Kolping Hotel Frankfurt – *Lange Straße 26 – Ostendstraße – (069) 29 90 60 – Fax (069) 29906100 – www.kolpinghotel-frankfurt.de – – 41rm: €45/135 – restaurant €15.* This simple, functional hotel is in the heart of the city centre, very near the Allerheiligentor and under the same roof as the Kolping training institute and youth hostel. The exhibition centre, airport and central station are within easy reach by S-Bahn.

Hotel Wiesbaden – *Baseler Straße 52 – (069) 23 23 47 – Fax (069) 252845 – 39rm €45/150.* A small, simple, clean and comfortable hotel next to the station. Rooms are well-kept and inexpensive.

A Casa Bed&Breakfast – *Varrentrappstraße 49 – Messe – (069) 97 98 88 21 – Fax (069) 97988822 – www.hotel-acasa.de – Closed from end of Dec to beginning of Jan – – 6rm: €59/155.* A small English-style Bed & Breakfast set in an old villa. The charming rooms, each one personalised and tastefully decorated, have each been given a name, adding to the family atmosphere of the establishment.

Hotel Hamburger Hof – *Poststraße 10 – (069) 27 13 96 90 – Fax (069) 235802 – www.hamburgerhof.com – – 66rm: €65/225.* An inexpensive, comfortable hotel near the station.

Liebig-Hotel – *Liebigstraße 45 – (069) 72 75 51 – Fax (069) 727555 – hotelliebig@t-online.de – Closed 22 Dec-2 Jan – – 20rm: €98/175 – €12.* Small hotel in a villa in the bank district with particularly charming and luxurious rooms; Italian- and English-style furniture, beautiful fabrics, and old-fashioned bath taps. A smart, very well-run establishment.

Steigenberger Frankfurter Hof – *Bethmannstraße 33 – (069) 215 02 – Fax (069) 215900 – frankfurter-hof@steigenberger.de – – 332rm from €355 – €23.* This grand hotel from 1876, traditional residence of the Steigenbergs is truly magnificent. The Weißfrauenflügel wing in particular has been superbly renovated. Luxury reigns throughout, from the elegant lobby to the modern, tasteful rooms.

Hilton – *Hochstraße 4 – (069) 133 80 00 – Fax (069) 13381338 – sales frankfurt@hilton.com – – 342rm: from €429 – €24 – restaurant €25.* Access to this modern hotel is via a spartan, atrium-style lobby. Transparent lifts lead to the rooms, which have all mod cons. The city's old swimming pool – a listed building – has been tastefully incorporated into the establishment.

Taking a Break

Useful Tips – Große Bockenheimer Straße (known as the *Fressgass* or "eatery alley") is a good place to go for a quick bite to eat. It offers a wide selection of restaurants.

Café im Liebighaus – *Schaumainkai 71 – (069) 63 58 14 – 11am-8pm, Sat 11am-6.30pm, Sun 10am-8pm.* This little self-service (except Sun) café set in the Museumof Sculptureis an ideal place for a break, with its very peaceful, idyllic terrace. Buffet of home-made salads and cakes.

IMA-Multibar – *Kleine Bockenheimer Straße 14 – (069) 90 02 56 65 – www.ima-multibar.com – Mon-Wed 11am-8.30pm, Thu-Sat 11am-1.30am.* Creative and interactive little fast-food restaurant with a family welcome. Traditional recipes from various countries, fresh produce guaranteed.

Kleinmarkthalle – *Hasengasse 5-7 – www.kleinmarkthalle.de – Mon-Fri 7.30am-6pm, Sat 7.30am-4pm.* It's hard to resist all the regional and international specialities that are on offer on the 80 stalls of this covered market. Make up your own picnic or sample snacks on the spot.

Sandwicher Fastgoodfood – *Katharinenpforte 6 (street heading north from the crossroads between Kleiner Hirschgraben and Bleidenstraße) – (069) 13 37 92 26 – info@sandwicher.de – Mon-Fri 10am-11pm, Sat 10am-8pm.* Here you can choose your own bread and sandwich filling. Ready-made sandwiches also available, to eat in or take away. This fast-food chain also has outlets at Reuterweg 63 and Westendstraße 27.

Wacker's Kaffee – *Kornmarkt 9 (street heading south from the crossroads between Kleiner Hirschgraben and Bleidenstraße) – ☎ (069) 28 78 10 – www.wackers-kaffee.de – Mon-Fri 8am-7pm, Sat 8am-6pm.* Over 30 varieties of roasted coffee and around 60 varieties of tea are available at this little establishment. Small snacks also served. From October, "Frankfurter Bethmännchen" – an almond-paste based speciality – are available.

Zarges – *Kalbächer Gasse 10 – ☎ (069) 29 90 30 – 8.30am-11pm (until 8pm in winter).* Delicatessen where you can choose your own sandwich filling. The upstairs restaurant has a reasonably-priced "Fast Lunch" menu (11am-6pm) with a choice of 4 or 5 different dishes every day.

Going Out

Useful Tips – One of the most lively quarters is the Alt-Sachsenhausen area on the south bank of the Main. Around the "Große Rittergasse" (south of Deutschherrnufer), are a large number of traditional restaurants which serve the famous *Äppelwoi* (dry cider), and a great variety of bars.

Café Hauptwache – *An der Hauptwache 15 – ☎ (069) 21 99 86 27 – Mon-Sat 10am-1am (food served until 11pm).* Built in 1729-30, Frankfurt's main guardhouse was entirely renovated after being destroyed during the Second World War. Since 1905 it has housed a café which now has a modern look; it also has a lovely terrace.

Euro Deli – *Neue Mainzer Straße 60-66 – ☎ (069) 29 80 19 50 – www.euro-deli.de – Mon-Fri 4pm-1am (Tue until 2am).* This red and black yuppie bar is in the economic heart of the city. Patrons are mainly businessmen, but the theme evenings (after 6pm) attract a young crowd: After-Work-Party on Tuesdays and Gastro-Trade-Market on Thursdays.

Harry's New-York Bar – *Walther-von-Cronberg-Platz 1 (take Deutschherrnufer towards Offenbach; in the Main Plaza hotel) – ☎ (069) 66 40 10 – www.main-plaza.com – 5pm-3am.* This classic bar with its quiet atmosphere follows the tradition of Harry MacElhone, who, in 1911, inaugurated Europe's first cocktail bar in Paris. Piano music, and terrace in front of the hotel in summer.

Jazzkeller – *Kleine Bockenheimer Straße 18a – ☎ (069) 28 85 37 – www.jazzkeller.com – Wed and Thu from 9pm, Fri and Sat from 10pm, Sun from 8pm – concerts from €8; discotheque €5.* A German institution. Since 1952, the greatest jazz legends, such as Louis Armstrong and Frank Sinatra, have appeared here. Newcomers also perform. "Cool Music Mix" discotheque on Fridays.

Krüger/Tourism + Congress GmbH Frankfurt a. M.

Culture

Useful Tips – The tourist information office distributes a free programme of events, the *Veranstaltungshinweise...* (followed by the month), in its offices, the central station and the Römer. The magazines *Prinz* (monthly) and *Journal Frankfurt* (fortnightly) are available from bookshops and newspaper kiosks, and information can also be found at www.frankfurt-tourismus.de or www.frankfurt-rhein-main.de

Shopping

Useful Tips – Frankfurt's main shopping street (with department stores) is the Zeil – including, among others, the passage called Les Facettes. This is just a short way away from the exclusive shops in the streets around the Große Bockenheimer Straße ("Fressgass") and Goethestraße. In Sachsenhausen interesting shopping opportunities are found at Schweizer Straße, in Bockenheim at Leipziger Straße. The antique dealers have settled in the Pfarrgasse in the vicinity of the cathedral.

The fact that the EU decided in favour of Frankfurt as the headquarters for the European Central Bank is enhancing its undisputed reputation as Germany's financial metropolis.

City Life – Despite its cosmopolitan character (one inhabitant in four is foreign), this "metropolis on the Main" has managed to preserve a typical Hessian atmosphere. It is around the **Hauptwache**, a square dating from 1729 at the junction of the Roßmarkt and the Zeil, that the life of Frankfurtis at its busiest. The Zeil is said to be the most shopped-in street in Germany. To the north, the quarter known as the Westend, a tranquil, shady residential area from the Bismarckera, fights to stave off the encroaching office blocks of the commercial centre. Cafés, cabarets, bars, and restaurants, often exotic, are grouped around the central station, while the taverns of the Alt Sachsenhausen quarter, on the south bank of the Main, specialise in the celebrated **Äppelwoi** or **Ebbelwei** (slightly bitter cider), and *Handkäse mit Musik* (a small yellow cheese with onions and vinegar sauce).

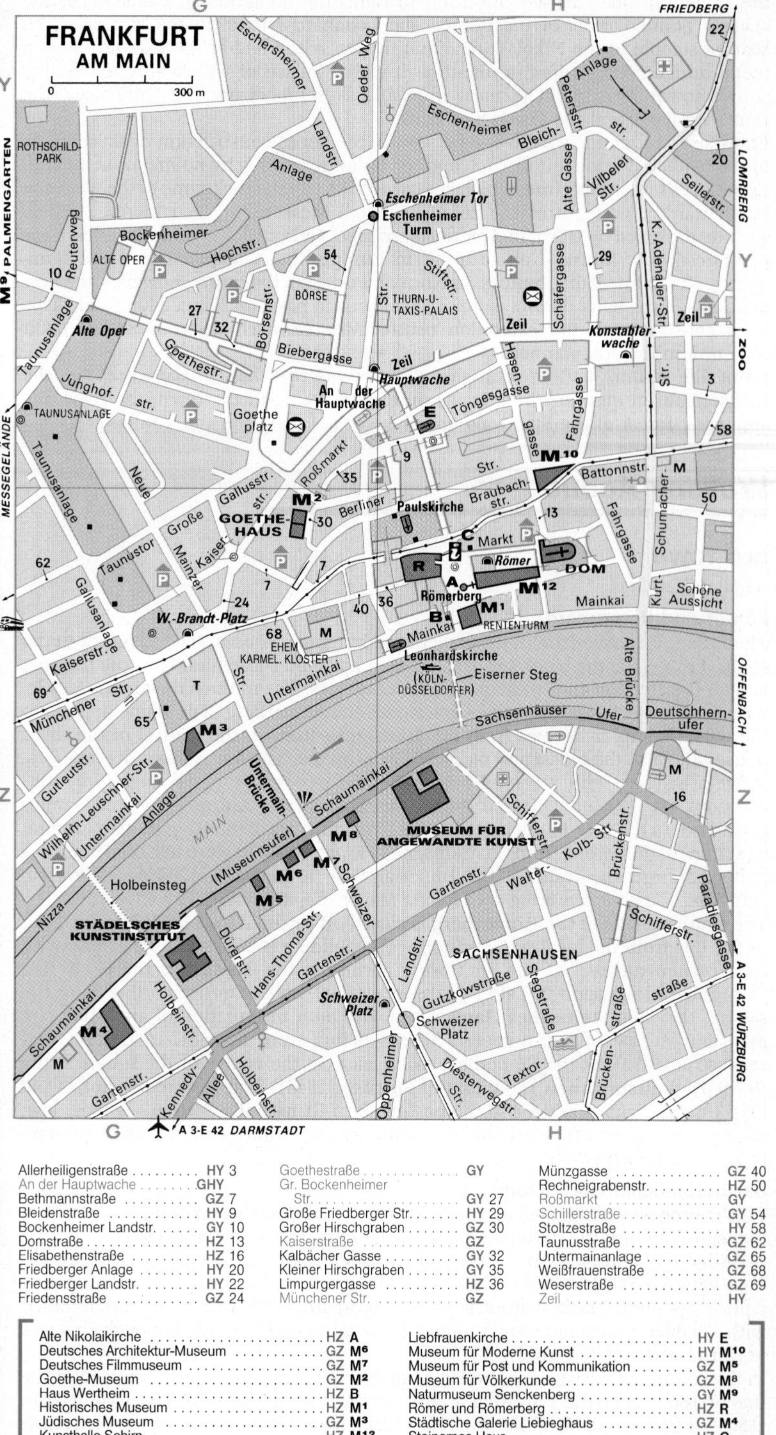

Allerheiligenstraße . . . . HY 3
An der Hauptwache . . . . GHY
Bethmannstraße . . . . GZ 7
Bleidenstraße . . . . HY 9
Bockenheimer Landstr. . . . . . GY 10
Domstraße . . . . HZ 13
Elisabethenstraße . . . . HZ 16
Friedberger Anlage . . . . HY 20
Friedberger Landstr. . . . . HY 22
Friedensstraße . . . . GZ 24
Goethestraße . . . . GY
Gr. Bockenheimer Str. . . . . GY 27
Große Friedberger Str. . . . . . HY 29
Großer Hirschgraben . . . . GZ 30
Kaiserstraße . . . . GZ
Kalbächer Gasse . . . . GY 32
Kleiner Hirschgraben . . . . GY 35
Limpurgergasse . . . . HZ 36
Münchener Str. . . . . GZ
Münzgasse . . . . GZ 40
Rechneigrabenstr. . . . . HZ 50
Roßmarkt . . . . GY
Schillerstraße . . . . GY 54
Stoltzestraße . . . . HY 58
Taunusstraße . . . . GZ 62
Untermainanlage . . . . GZ 65
Weißfrauenstraße . . . . GZ 68
Weserstraße . . . . GZ 69
Zeil . . . . HY

Alte Nikolaikirche . . . . HZ **A**
Deutsches Architektur-Museum . . . . GZ **M6**
Deutsches Filmmuseum . . . . GZ **M7**
Goethe-Museum . . . . GZ **M2**
Haus Wertheim . . . . HZ **B**
Historisches Museum . . . . HZ **M1**
Jüdisches Museum . . . . GZ **M3**
Kunsthalle Schirn . . . . HZ **M12**
Liebfrauenkirche . . . . HY **E**
Museum für Moderne Kunst . . . . HY **M10**
Museum für Post und Kommunikation . . . . GZ **M5**
Museum für Völkerkunde . . . . GZ **M8**
Naturmuseum Senckenberg . . . . GY **M9**
Römer und Römerberg . . . . HZ **R**
Städtische Galerie Liebieghaus . . . . GZ **M4**
Steinernes Haus . . . . HZ **C**

A General View – The old town, almost entirely destroyed in 1943-44, lay within a green belt on the site of former fortifications razed in 1805. The Eschenheimer Turm still stands however as a well-preserved example of the medieval defence system. The tower dates from 1428. After 1945, a small kernel of the old town was reconstructed around the Römerberg.

The contrast between its modest silhouettes and those of the business quarter skyscrapers is at its most striking when seen from the southern end of the **Untermainbrücke** river bridge. Between the apse of the old Carmelite church and the cathedral, one can see (from left to right) the dome of the Paulskirche, the sharply pointed roofs of the Römer, the Leonhardskirche on the riverside, the soaring steeple of the Nikolaikirche and finally, at the end of the Eiserner Steg (a metal bridge), the Saalhof, a one-time Imperial Palace of which only the Gothic corner tower remains. The most imposing skyscrapers are the FairTower, the Deutsche Bank and the Dresdener Bank.

Frankfurt's economic wealth can be seen in the dense construction of skyscrapers in the bank and trade fair district, and the building craze is by no means at an end. Frankfurt's famous **skyline**, which has earned the city the nickname of the "German Manhattan", now features the 265m/870ft tall **Messeturm**, clad in red Swedish granite, designed by German-American architect Helmut Jahn, and the tallest – for the foreseeable future – office block in Europe, the headquarters of the Commerzbank (259m/850ft), built by Sir Norman Foster. In the future, however, the new buildings in the bank district will not be allowed to pass the 200m/640ft mark. This is in contrast with the exhibition centre *(Messegelände)*, where a 340m/1088ft MillenniumToweris planned.

From the 120m/394ft **Henninger Turm** *(leave by the Paradiesgasse)*, in the Sachsenhausen quarter, there is a **panorama★** taking in the town, the river, the sprawling forest of the Stadtwald and the wooded massif of the Taunus.

Walking About

OLD TOWN

Allow half a day.

Römer and Römerberg

The Römer is a collection of three medieval burghers' houses, reconstructed in the 1980s. From 1405 the block served as a town hall, and subsequently as the banquet hall for the election and coronation of the emperors. The most characteristic façade, with three stepped Gothic gables, overlooks the Römerberg. The name applied to the whole complex derives from the **Haus zum Römer**, the central of the three houses and also the oldest and most richly decorated. The four statues of emperors, above a balcony with a carved balustrade and beneath Imperial eagles, are 19C additions. A graceful pierced Renaissance stairway adorns the small inner courtyard. In the 19C, to celebrate the 1 000-year history of the Holy Roman Empire, 52 statues of emperors, from Charlemagne to Franz II (1806) were installed in niches hollowed from the walls of the Imperial Hall *(Kaisersaal)*. ♿ *Open 10am-1pm, 2pm-5pm. Closed when being used by the Mayor. €2.* ☎ *(069) 21 23 49 19.*

The southern side of the **Römerberg** is closed off by the **Alte Nikolaikirche**, built in the 13C from the local red sandstone. The building is crowned by a gallery with four corner turrets. In the southwest corner is the **Haus Wertheim**, a fine half-timbered mansion in Late Renaissance (1600) style. On the north side of the square, the 1464 **Steinernes Haus** was clearly built in imitation of an Italian city mansion. A row of half-timbered houses dating from the 15C to the 18C (all reconstructed) flank the Römerberg to the east. In the centre of the square is the **Gerechtigkeitsbrunnen** (Fountain of Justice) (1543). The restored sector of old Frankfurt is right next door to the post-modern **Kunsthalle Schirn** – a long, low, domed cultural centre, stark and uncompromising, where exhibitions of contemporary art are organised.

Bartholomäuskirche★ (Dom)

This church was designated a cathedral after it had been chosen first as the election and subsequently the coronation site of the emperors (1356 and 1562).

A Gothic hall-church with a nave and two side aisles and a wide transept, it was built between the 13C and the 15C on a hill previously occupied by a Carolingian edifice. Its outstanding feature is the tall **west tower★★** *(Westturm)*, ornamented with a gabled polygonal crown topped by a dome and lantern, although this was not in fact completed until 1877.

In the columned peristyle erected in front of the tower in neo-Gothic style after the fire of 1867, note the outstanding grey-sandstone sculpture of **The Crucifixion** (1509) – the work of the Mainz artist Hans Backoffen. Inside, the finely worked **choir stalls★** are due to a master craftsman from the Upper Rhine (c 135). The **mural paintings**, which date from 1427, are the work of a Master of the Cologne School. They illustrate the legend of St Bartholomew. In a niche on the south side of the chancel is the tombstone (1352) of Count Günther von Schwarzburg, unsuccessful rival to the Emperor Charles IV for the title of King of Germania. A door alongside leads to the chapel (*Wahlkapelle*: early 15C) where the seven Electors of the Holy Roman Empire in Germany made their final choice.

In the opposing chapel (north chancel) is the **Altar of Mary Sleeping** *(Maria-Schlaf)*, which dates from 1434. Sole remaining altar from the church's original interior furnishings, this too is the work of the Cologne School. It represents the twelve

Apostles grouped around the bed of the dying Mary. The large **Descent from the Cross** hanging on the west wall of the north chancel was painted by Anthony van Dyck in 1627.

Dommuseum★ (Cathedral Museum)

♿ *Open every day except Mon, 10am-5pm, Sat-Sun 11am-5pm. Closed 1st Jan, 24, 25 and 31 Dec. €2. ☎ (069) 13 37 61 86.* This very small museum has been installed in what remains of the Gothic cloister. Besides the cathedral treasure *(Domschatz)* that is presented there, consisting of precious goldsmith works and splendid vestments from the high Middle Ages to the historicist period, the Late Merovingian tomb of a young girl merits special attention. West of the cathedral is an **Archaeological Garden** *(Historischer Garten)*, where the remains of Roman and Carolingian and Baroque fortifications can be seen.

Museum für Moderne Kunst★ (Modern Art Museum)

♿ *Open every day except Mon, 10am-5pm, Wed 10am-8pm. €5, free admission on Wed. ☎ (069) 21 23 04 47.* The Viennese architect, Hans Hollein, has achieved a spacious custom-built gallery in spite of the rather cramped and awkwardly shaped site. The imaginatively designed interior is surprisingly large and makes an ideal setting for the mainly contemporary art collection, the basis of which is formed by Darmstadt collector Karl Ströher's collection, acquired by the city of Frankfurt in 1980 and constantly augmented since. Artists of the New York School (Claes Oldenburg, Andy Warhol) are represented, as are German contemporary artists (Joseph Beuys, Mario Merz, Katharina Fritsch, and Gerhard Richter with his oppressive *Stammheim Cycle*). There is also a collection of photography. Every six months, six to eight of the museum's galleries are rehung, giving the museum collection the impression of being in perpetual motion.

Leonhardskirche

The outer aspect of this 15C Gothic church denies its Romanesque basilican origins. Two octagonal towers remain at the east end, along with the fine carvings of **Master Engelbert's Doorway** – although these can only be seen from inside (north aisle) now, as aisles were subsequently added on either side.

The central nave, almost square, is surrounded on three sides by a gallery. Fine stained-glass windows illuminate the chancel. Left of the chancel are a superbly carved reredos representing scenes from the life of the Virgin, and a painting by Holbein the Elder depicting the Last Supper. The baptismal chapel is in the north aisle.

Paulskirche

It was in this circular building dating from the beginning of the Classic era (again, reconstructed) that the German National Assembly, elected after the revolution of March, sat from 1848 to 1849. The church houses an exhibition devoted to the history of the German democratic movement.

Goethe-Haus★ and Goethe-Museum

Open Apr-Sep: 9am-6pm, Sat-Sun 10am-4pm; Oct-Mar: open every day except Sat-Sun, 9am-4pm. Closed 1st Jan, 24, 25 and 31 Dec. €5. ☎ (069) 13 88 00; www.goethehaus-frankfurt.de

"The house is spacious, light and tranquil, with free-standing staircases, large vestibules and several windows with pleasant views of the garden" – it was thus that Goethe described the paternal home.

The room in which the poet wrote – reconstructed like the rest of the house after 1945 – is as it was in his lifetime; even a silhouette of Charlotte Buff, the object of his youthful passion, hangs there. A separate exhibition shows the lifestyle of the Goethe family in 18C Frankfurt and has documents pertaining to Goethe's early work.

The **Museum** adjoining Goethe's birthplace has been arranged as a painting gallery of his era (Late Baroque to Romantic), and is otherwise devoted to his life-long close relationship with the visual arts. The works include paintings by, among others, Tischbein, Graff, Hackert, Fuseli and Friedrich.

Worth a Visit

Museumsufer

An impressive series of museums stretches the length of the Schaumainkai, the south bank of the Main, between the Eiserner Steg and the Friedensbrücke. The creation and development of projects such as the Museum of Applied Arts and the Museum of Architecture, started in the 1980s and now enjoying worldwide renown, has been skilfully integrated within this residential area attractively interspersed with green spaces.

Städelsches Kunstinstitut and Städtische Galerie★★ – ♿ *Open every day except Mon, 10am-5pm, Wed and Thu 10am-8pm. Closed 24 and 31 Dec. €6, free admission on Tue. ☎ (069) 605 09 80.* This stronghold of art houses an important collection of outstanding works by **old Masters**: Holbein the Elder *(Christ's Family Tree)*, Grünewald, Altdorfer, Dürer, van Eyck (*Lucca Madonna*), Fra Angelico, Mantegna, and Botticelli. Subsequent centuries are represented by works by Vermeer *(The Geographer)*, Rembrandt, Frans Hals, Rubens *(Betrothal of St Catherine)*, Tiepolo, Elsheimer, Poussin and Watteau. German works from the age of Goethe include the memorable meditation of *Goethe in the Roman Countryside*, painted by Johann Heinrich Wilhelm Tischbein in 1787. French Impressionism is represented by Renoir and Monet *(The Breakfast Party)*. Max Liebermann stands for German Impressionists. German Expressionists exhibited include Beckmann, Kirchner and Marc. Matisse and Picasso represent that part of the modern movement influenced by Fauvism and the Cubists. There are also works reflecting Surrealism, the Bauhaus and contemporary art (Dubuffet, Bacon, Tapiès).

Museum für Angewandte Kunst★ (Museum of Applied Arts) – ♿ *Open every day except Mon, 10am-5pm, Wed 10am-8pm. €5, free admission on Wed. ☎ (069) 21 23 40 37.* The museum building (1985) was designed by the New York architect Richard Meier and integrated within the design is a classically styled villa dating from 1803. In the well-lit building, the shape and material of the exhibits is shown to good advantage. This is particularly true of the furniture collection: pieces from the Middle Ages, carved Renaissance and Baroque cupboards and chests, jewel-encrusted commodes and cabinets as well as Jugendstil items. The glassware collection (15C and 16C Venetian work) is particularly interesting. The Islamic department contains mainly porcelain and carpets. The Far East department displays glossy porcelain and lacquerwork. Crafts from the Rococo and Classical periods include a remarkable porcelain collection (Meissen, Berlin, Nymphenburg, Vienna and Sèvres). There is also a book and calligraphy section.

Städtische Galerie Liebieghaus/Museum alter Plastik (Liebig Museum of Sculpture) – Here there are fine examples of sculpture from different civilisations, spanning Ancient Egypt (head of a dignitary from the Middle Kingdom), the Middle Ages (Virgin and Child, Trier, 11C) and works by Tilman Riemenschneider to the Classical era. *Open every day except Mon, 10am-5pm, Wed 10am-8pm. €4, free admission on Wed. ☎ (069) 21 23 86 15.*

Deutsches Filmmuseum★ (German Cinema Museum) – This museum displays various inventions from the early days of photography and the history of the cinema (Edison's Kineto-scope, 1899). In the section on film production, the history of the cinema and genres visitors get a glimpse behind the scenes of both silent movies and those with soundtracks. A small working cinema shows newsreels, publicity shots and shorts several times a day. ♿ *Open every day except Mon, 10am-5pm, Wed 10am-8pm, Sat 2-8pm. €2.50, free admission on Wed. ☎ (069) 21 23 88 30.*

Zoo★★

♿ *Open summer: 9am-7pm; winter: 9am-5pm. Closed 25 Dec. €7. ☎ (069) 21 23 37 35.* The Frankfurt zoo is famous for its rare species (over 5 000 examples of 600 species), which are encouraged, successfully, to reproduce. The bird section, with its huge free-flight aviary, is particularly colourful. Penguins, reptiles, fish and insects inhabit the Exotarium. In the **Grzimek-Haus**, darkened by day, nocturnal animals such as the desert fox can be observed.

Naturmuseum Senckenberg★ (Senckenberg Natural History Museum)

Leave by the Bockenheimer Landstraße. Open 9am-5pm, Wed 9am-8pm, Sat-Sun 9am-6pm. €5. ☎ (069) 754 20.

Opened in 1821, this museum is distinguished by its remarkable **Department of Palaeontology★★** *(ground floor)*. Fossils from the Lower Jurassic (Lias) are on display in the entrance hall, most discovered near Holzmaden, in Württemberg. They include ichthyosaurus, sea crocodiles and crinoids.

In the **Hall of Dinosaurs**, the skeletons of huge beasts from the Secondary Era are on view: diplodocus, iguanodon.

There is a display of objects found in **Jurassic digs** – most of them near Solnhofen, on the banks of the Altmühl (archeopteryx, pterodactyl). The evolution of man is traced with the aid of numerous artefacts. A window into the geological past is provided by the perfectly preserved fossils from the archaeological dig at Messel near Darmstadt.

An interesting collection of stuffed animals and slide shows complete this visit of Germany's largest natural history museum.

Palmengarten★ (Tropical Gardens)

Leave by the Bockenheimer Landstraße. ♿ *Open Feb-Oct: 9am-6pm; Nov-Jan: 9am-4pm. €3.50. ☎ (069) 21 23 66 89.* These botanical gardens include a large area given over to various greenhouses, containing tropical plants, palms, Alpine plants etc and also exotic plants such as orchids, cacti and bromeliaceae (pineapples). The Palm House ating from 1869 is the oldest botanical building in Europe. These tropical gardens re home to a great variety of ornamental plants and flowers (roses), Alpine plants, nd species of tree. The greenhouses contain precious tropical and subtropical lants.

▶▶ Historisches Museum – Liebfrauenkirche – Jüdisches Museum – Museum für Kommunikation Frankfurt am Main – Deutsches Architektur-Museum – Museum der Weltkulturen.

Excursions

Offenbach

Town plan in the current edition of The Michelin Guide Deutschland. 7km/5mi east. Leave on the Deutschherrn-Ufer. This town on the south bank of the Main is the centre of the German leather industry (International Leather Fair twice a year).

Deutsches Ledermuseum/Deutsches Schuhmuseum★★ (Leather and Shoe Museum) – *Frankfurter Straße 86. ♿ 10am-5pm. Closed 1st Jan, 24, 25 and 31 Dec. €3. ☎ (069) 829 79 80.* The Leather Museum contains some interesting collections of articles made from leather, especially vellum and hides, and the display covers the use of leather in various domains such as sport, travel and leisure.

The **Shoe Museum** in the same building presents a history of foot fashion in all its variety, from Ancient Egyptian and Roman sandals to modern footwear. The section on shoes as works of art is particularly interesting.

Friedberg★

28km/17mi north on the Friedberger Landstraße. This is an attractive example of a medieval community with two distinct centres: the town enclosed within the Imperial castle and the bourgeois town grouped at the foot of the church, at either end of the main street *(Kaiserstraße)*.

The castle *(Stauferburg)* erected by Frederick Barbarossa in 1180 together with its outbuildings still has the air of a small, self-sufficient town. The ramparts, now a promenade, have been made even more attractive with bays of greenery and look-out points. **Adolf's Tower★** *(Adolphsturm, 1347)* overlooks the assembled buildings.

The **Jewish Baths★** *(Judenbad, 13C)* – at Judengasse 20, in the bourgeois sector – consist of a deep, square well with a dome, which served originally for ritual ablutions required by Jewish law. The **church** *(Stadtkirche)* is a 13C-14C building with a typically Hessian exterior – transverse attics with separate gables jutting from the roof above the aisles. Inside, an unusually tall **ciborium★** (1482) stands in the chancel. On the left of the rood screen is the **Friedberg Madonna** (c 1280).

Tour

The Taunus★

Round tour of 62km/39mi – 4hr. The Taunus is limited in extent, but reaches at the Großer Feldberg a greater height (880m/2 997ft) than any of the other Rhineland schist massifs. The area is covered by magnificent forests, and there are many mineral springs.

Königstein im Taunus★ – *Open Apr-Sep: 9am-7pm; Mar and Oct: 9.30am-4.30pm; Nov-Feb: 9.30am-3pm, Sat-Sun: 9.30am-4pm. €1.50. ☎ (061 74) 20 22 51.* Here, on a height isolated from the main Taunus slopes, is a ruined **castle** *(Burgruine)* with impressive foundations: round 16C bastions and 17C projecting defences. Climb the keep *(166 steps)* for a bird's-eye view of the small town and the surrounding woods. This spa town boasts a certain number of old buildings, such as the 13C town hall, which give it character. There is also a series of buildings dating from the late 19C and early 20C.

Großer Feldberg★ – *163 steps. From 9am, Sun from 8am. Closes at nightfall. Closed 31/2 weeks in Nov. €1.60. ☎ (061 74) 222 19.* The tower and antennae of an important telecommunications centre top this height. From the tower's observation platform *(Aussichtsturm)* visitors can enjoy an immense **panorama★★** including the Westerwald tableland to the northwest, the Wetterau depression to the northeast and in the southeast, the plain of the Lower Main invaded by the outskirts of Frankfurt. In good weather, it is possible to make out the spires of the cathedrals of Cologne and Strasbourg.

Saalburg – This is a complete Roman fortress camp in the middle of the forest, reconstructed on the orders of Kaiser Wilhelm II on the Limes (fortified lines marking the northern limit of Roman occupation). Note the external trenches and in the inner courtyard, buildings which now house a Roman museum.

Bad Homburg vor der Höhe★ – *Town plan in the current edition of The Michelin Guide Deutschland.* In 1840, the opening of a casino by the Blanc Brothers transformed this little spa into one of Europe's gaming capitals. But the establishment was obliged to close its doors in 1872.

Today the life of most visitors centres on the **Spa Park★** *(Kurpark)*, where pavilions containing the health-giving springs are dispersed over shady lawns.

The **castle**, dominated by the tall White Tower – a remnant of the original fortress – was successively the residence of the Landgraves of Hesse-Homburg, then the summer palace of the Prussian kings (who became, after Wilhelm I in 1871, the emperors of Germany).

A well-known exhibit in the castle is the artificial limb of Friedrich II (1633-1708) known locally as "the silver leg" because the joints of the wooden limb are fashioned from the precious metal. Friedrich II was immortalised in Kleist's play, *The Prince of Hombourg.*

Freiburg im Breisgau★★

Set among the hills of the Black Forest. Freiburg is one of the most attractive cities in southern Germany, with its five-hundred year-old university and the little streets of its old town. The successive wars have left intact the beautiful cathedral and the many historic sites, make the "free" town an important tourist site.

Location

Population: 230 000. Michelin map nº 545 V 7 – Baden-Württemberg. Mid-way between Basel and Strasbourg, on the Rhine plain, Freiburg is on the A 5 which leads to Karlsruhe *(130km/81mi north).*

Rotteckring 14, 79098 Freiburg, ☎ (0761) 388 18 81.

Surrounding area: see BADENWEILER (36km/22mi southwest), Bad SÄCKINGEN (71km/44mi southeast), SCHWARZWALD (tour leaves from Freiburg).

Background

Freiburg was founded in the 12C by the dukes of Zähringen who conferred upon it a number of special privileges; this is the origin of its name, literally "free town". From 1368 to 1798 the city was under Habsburg rule. After secularisation and the French revolution it was handed over to Baden in 1805. In the second half of the 19C, Freiburg won renewed importance as a place of research and learning thanks to its university.

Residents and visitors alike enjoy its mild, sunny climate. There are little streams ("Bächle") running in open gullies beside the streets of the old town, fed by fresh water from the nearby Black Forest; they give the town centre a relaxed and cheerful atmosphere, only enhanced by the restrictions on cars which leave the centre free for pedestrians, cyclists and trams.

Special Features

Münster★★

Brochure in English available at the entrance.

All that remains of the original Romanesque building, on which work began in c 1200, is the transept crossing and the two "Cockerel Towers" flanking it. The octagonal towers are surmounted by Gothic superstructures. The technical progress characterising the Gothic period was reflected as building continued westwards culminating in the erection of the splendid tower which crowns the west façade. This feature, with its multiplicity of planes intersecting at sharp angles, is one of the few church towers in Germany to be wholly completed in the Middle Ages. In 1354, work started on the construction of a new chancel, but the grandeur of the design and the severity of the times were such that this huge addition was not finished and consecrated until 1513. The ambulatory, typically German in concept, has fan vaulting in keeping with its Late Gothic style.

North side – Above the door which leads to the chancel, the tympanum, carved c 1350, illustrates the theme of Original Sin, while the archivolt depicts the Creation of the World according to Genesis. On the right of this, note the rare representation of the Creator resting on the seventh day.

West Tower★★★ – On the plain, square base of this stands a pierced octagonal belfry surmounted by a delicate open-work spire of stone. Four sharply jutting projections form a star at the foot of the tower house, the Sterngalerie. The gargoyles here are worth a closer look.

South side – Statues of the Apostles and the Old Testament kings stand on the buttresses of this richly ornate façade. A Renaissance porch shelters the south door.

Enter the church by this door and head towards the west porch and doorway.

West porch and doorway – Late-13C figures crowd this main entrance. On the left wall, facing the door, Satan, beguilingly disguised as "the Prince of this world", leads a procession. He is followed by his victim, sparsely clothed in a goat skin, the Wise Virgins, and a number of biblical characters. The Foolish Virgins decorate the right wall. Behind them are figures representing the arts of painting and sculpture, and statues of St Margaret and St Catherine.

S. Ollivier/MICHELIN

The cathedral tower and the finely worked masonry of its spire.

The doorway itself, flanked by statues representing the Church (left) and the Synagogue (with eyes covered; right) is entirely occupied by the mystery of the Redemption. The tympanum is unusual in that it portrays scenes from Christ's earthly life and an interesting Last Judgement.

Nave – Moderately tall, the nave is embellished with graceful galleries, their blind, trefoil arcades decorating the aisle walls from end to end. Furnishings and statuary include:

1) the Virgin at the pillar (1270-80), worshipped by two angels;

2) a Late Gothic pulpit with rustic themes (1560); the sculptor himself is represented in a window beneath the stairway;

3) a statue (originally recumbent, remodelled in the 17C) of Berthold V, last of the dukes of Zähringen who founded the town;

4) the Holy Sepulchre, dating from c 1330, behind a delicate Gothic grille;

5) in the three windows of the south transept, 13C stained-glass medallions, the oldest in the cathedral;

6) a 1505 group sculpture, the Adoration of the Magi.

Chancel – ♿ *Open Apr to Oct, Tue-Sun, 10am-noon, 2.30-5pm; Sat 10am-noon only. €1. ☎ (0761) 20 27 90.* Very well lit, the chancel invites appreciation of the skilful design of the ambulatory vaulting combined with that of the widely spaced side chapels. Among the many works of art note:

a) a Rococo baptismal font by JC Wenzinger in the Stürzel Chapel;

b) the Oberried altarpiece (1521) in the Universität Chapel. The two side panels, the Nativity and the Adoration of the Magi, are by Hans Holbein the Younger;

c) in the Second Kaiser Chapel: an altarpiece from Schnewlin depicting on the central panel the *Rest during the Flight to Egypt* by Hans Wydyz. The side panels are from the Baldung Grien studio;

d) reverse of the large Baldung Grien altarpiece: a painting of the Crucifixion;

e) the Böcklin Chapel: the Romanesque Locherer Crucifix in beaten silver by Böcklin;

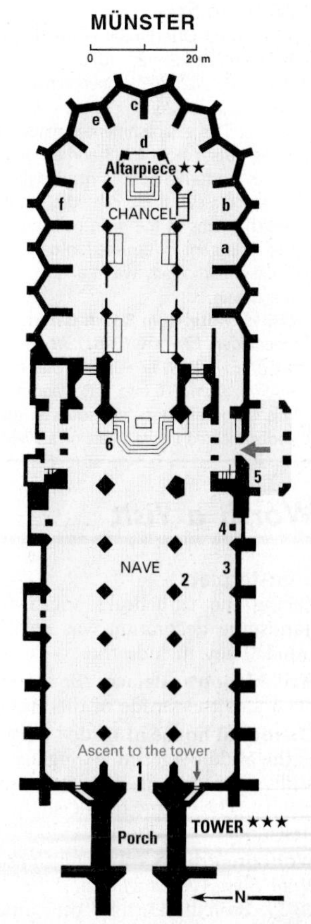

f) an altarpiece in the Locherer Chapel by Sixt von Staufen (1521-24). The carved part depicts the Virgin with her sheltering cloak.
The **altarpiece★★** *(Hochaltar)* by **Hans Baldung Grien** (1512-16), which portrays the Coronation of the Virgin on the central panel;
Ascent of the West Tower *(Turmbesteigung) – Outside wall, southern side. Open Apr to Oct, 9.30am-5pm, Sun, 1-5pm; Nov-Mar, Tue-Sun, 9.30am-5pm, Sun, 1-5pm.* The first section of stairway leads to the tower room, and then, after a further climb, visitors reach the upper platform beneath the beautiful perforated spire. From here there are **views★** over the city, with the Kaiserstuhl and the Vosges just visible in the distance.

Directory

Where to Eat

⊖ Hausbrauerei Feierling – *Gerberau 46 – ☎ (0761) 24 34 80 – www.feierling.de – 11am-midnight (-1am, Sat); Biergarten open 11am-11pm – ⌿ – €13/18.* Since 1989, this micro-brewery has produced its own beers from organic ingredients. Have a look at the copper stills from the gallery. Regional cuisine is served here and in the biergarten, on the other side of the road.

⊖⊖ Schlossbergrestaurant Dattler – *Am Schlossberg 1 (follow Wintererstraße or take the Schlossberg cable-car) – 79104 Freiburg-Herdern – ☎ (0761) 317 29 – info@dattler.de – Closed Tue – €24/44.* This popular eating place is worth a visit for the altitude of its location. The view over the roofs of Freiburg and the Kaiserstuhl is magnificent!

Where to Stay

⊖⊖ Hotel Oberkirchs Weinstuben – *Münsterplatz 22 – ☎ (0761) 202 68 68 – fax (0761) 2026869 – oberkirch@t-online.de – Closed Jan – 26rm: €86 ☕ – Restaurant €29/44.* This establishment is made up of a house dating from 1738 and a hotel – the rooms are furnished in a rustic-style. There is a good view of the cathedral from certain rooms of the main building. The restaurant is furnished in dark wood is particularly warm and welcoming.

⊖⊖⊖ Hotel Zum Roten Bären – *Oberlinden 12 – ☎ (0761) 38 78 70 – fax (0761) 3878717 – info@roter-baeren.de – 25rm: from €103 ☕ – Restaurant €24/36.* This is one of the oldest hotels in the town and is located in the heart of a lively district. Since it has been modernised and extended, it is well equipped to meet the needs of modern-day travellers. For centuries, guests have enjoyed Swiss-influenced cusine in the restaurant.

Taking a Break

Markthalle – *Kaiser-Joseph-Str. 233 (via Grünwälderstr. and Fressgässle) – ☎ (0761) 38 70 00 – www.freiburger-markthalle.de – Mon-Fri 7am-7pm, Sat 7am-4pm.* Here you will find a multitude of stalls offering a range of international flavours – Afghan, Chinese or Portuguese, among others – to take away or to eat in. Fresh fruit, vegetables and even fish are also available.

Going Out

Kagan – *Bismarckallee 9 (in the building next to the central station; take the lift) – ☎ (0761) 7 67 27 66 – www.kagan-lounge.de – café: 10-1am; club: Fri-Sat, 10-5am, Wed-Sun, 10-3am.* From the café-bar situated on the 17th floor, there is an exceptional panoramic view of the town. The club was designed by the German-American designer Valdimir Kagan. Large choice of drinks and snacks available (Friday is sushi day). The club on the 18th floor has salsa evenings on Sundays from 9pm.

UC-Café – *Niemensstr. 7 (between Bertoldstr. and Kaiser-Joseph-Str.) – ☎ (0761) 38 33 55 – uc-cafe@t-online.de – 8-1am, Sun from 10am – closed 1 Jan.* A maple shades the terrace of this popular café in Freiburg's pedestrian zone. A mix of clientele stops here for coffee and snacks.

Worth a Visit

Münsterplatz

Facing the cathedral's south front across this square stand buildings whose handsome decoration was designed with municipal or ecclesiastical prestige in mind. They include the:

Archbishop's Palace *(Erzbischöfliches Palais)* – A fine wrought-iron balcony decorates the façade of the archiepiscopal palace (1756).

Historical house of trade★ *(Historisches Kaufhaus)* – The centre of commercial life in the Middle Ages, this roughcast red structure features watchtowers on either side with pointed roofs. It is covered with glazed tiles and supported by an arcaded gallery. The Gothic façade shelters statues of the Habsburg emperors (1530) on the first floor.

Wentzingerhaus – *Ticket includes entrance to the Augustinermuseum. Open Tue-Sun, 10am-5pm. Closed 24 and 31 Dec. €2, no charge first Sun of the month. ☎ (0761) 201 25 15.* Built in 1761 by the famous local painter and sculptor Johann Christian

FREIBURG IM BREISGAU

Auf der Zinnen . . . . Y 2
Augustinerplatz . . . . Z 3
Bertholdstraße . . . . Y
Eisenbahnstraße . . . . Y 7
Eisenstraße . . . . Y 9
Europaplatz . . . . Z 12
Fahnenbergplatz . . . . Y 13
Franziskanerstraße . . . . Y 14
Friedrichring . . . . Y 16
Gerberau . . . . Z
Greiffeneggring . . . . Z 19
Habsburgerstraße . . . . Y 20
Herrenstraße . . . . YZ 24
Holzmarkt . . . . Z 26
Kaiser-Joseph-Straße . . . . YZ
Münsterstraße . . . . Y 30
Oberlinden . . . . Z 31
Platz der Alten Synagoge . . . Y 32
Rathausgasse . . . . Y 33
Salzstraße . . . . YZ 38
Schiffstraße . . . . Y 40
Schusterstraße . . . . Z 43
Schwabentorplatz . . . . Z 45
Schwabentorring . . . . Z 47
Schwarzwaldstraße . . . . Z 49
Turmstraße . . . . Y 54
Universitätsstraße . . . . Y 55
Unterlinden . . . . Y 57
Werthmannplatz . . . . Z 59

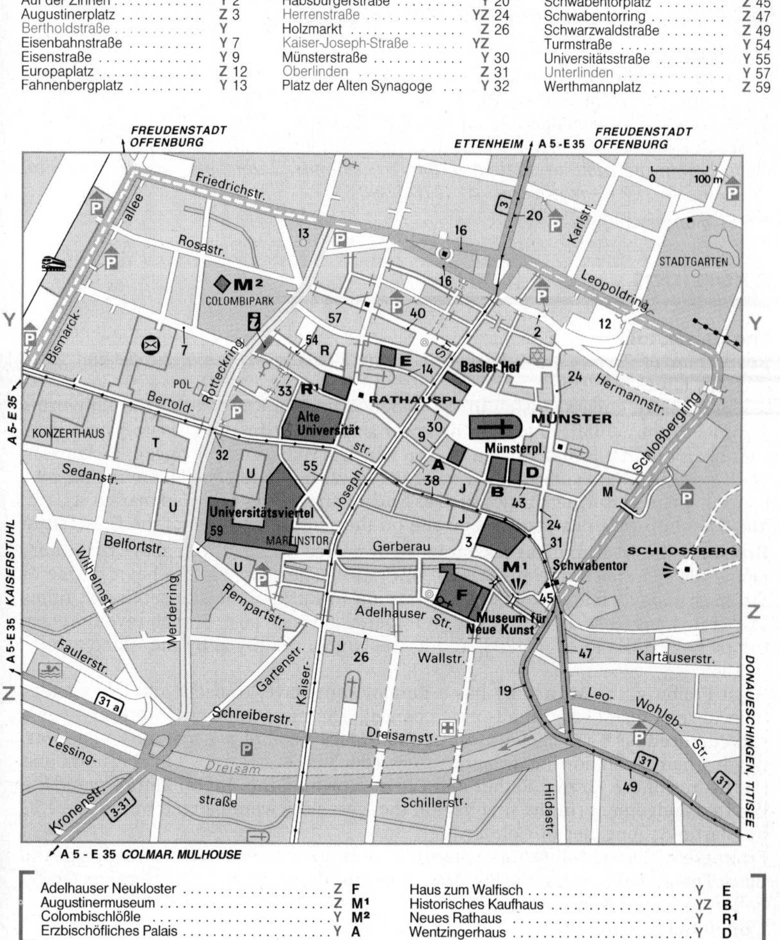

Adelhauser Neukloster . . . . Z F
Augustinermuseum . . . . Z M¹
Colombischlößle . . . . Y M²
Erzbischöfliches Palais . . . . Y A
Haus zum Walfisch . . . . Y E
Historisches Kaufhaus . . . . YZ B
Neues Rathaus . . . . Y R¹
Wentzingerhaus . . . . Y D

Wentzinger as his own residence, this mansion completes the layout of the square. A magnificent Baroque staircase adorns the interior which now houses the museum of local history *(Museum für Stadtgeschichte)*.

Rathausplatz★

The town hall square is a pleasant sight, with its flowered balconies and fountain with the statue of Berthold Schwarz, a Franciscan said to have invented gunpowder in Freiburg in 1350.

Neues Rathaus★

Two 16C burghers' houses, once the heart of the old university, were linked in 1901 by a central arcaded portion.
The oriel window at the corner of Rathausgasse is decorated with carvings illustrating the *Lady and the Unicorn*.

Haus zum Walfisch

Of the original 1516 construction, there remains today an oriel which forms a canopy above a richly ornamented Late Gothic doorway.

Augustinermuseum★★

Open Tue-Sun, 10am-5pm. Closed 24 and 31 Dec. No charge. ☎ *(0761) 201 25 31.* The most interesting part of this museum is the **Medieval Religious Art Section★★** *(Mittelalterliche Sakralkunst)*, housed in the church of an old Augustinian monastery and adjacent ground-floor galleries. Among the special treasures are the altarpiece panel (once at Aschaffenburg) depicting the miracle of the Virgin Mary and the Snow, painted in 1519 by Matthias Grünewald and works by Lucas Cranach the Elder and Hans Baldung Grien, as well as an impressive 14C crucifix. The statuary, in particular, includes admirable 14C and 15C pieces.

Schwabentor *(Swabian Gate)*

From this remnant of the town's medieval fortifications, sightseers can walk down through the picturesque but poor Insel quarter to the quays bordering the Gewerbekanal, once the preserve of Freiburg's fishermen and tanners.

Schloßberg★

On this last foothill of the Black Forest, woods now replace Zähringen Castle which was destroyed in the 18C by the French. The climb, either in the cable-car *(from Stadtgarten cable-car station)* or on foot *(pathway starts from the Schwabentor)*, also offers fine views of the cathedral and has panoramic views from the summit *(20min on foot from the cablecar station). Cable-car: summer, 11am-7pm; winter: Wed-Sun, 11.30am-5pm. €3.60 return trip. ☎ (0761) 398 55.*

▶▶ Colombischlößle.

Exursions

The Kaiserstuhl★

Round tour of 73km/45mi – allow 3hr. Leave Freiburg on Lessingstraße and go to Breisach via Gottenheim.

A small volcanic massif rising in the Baden plain, the Kaiserstuhl (the Emperor's Throne: 538m/1 765ft) enjoys on its lower slopes a warm, dry climate particularly suitable for orchards and vineyards. The wines of Achkarren, Ihringen, Bickensohl and Oberrotweil are considered among the finest in the region. The tour goes past charming wine-growing villages such as **Endingen★**, with its fine old market square, and **Burkheim★**, in its picturesque site on the south-west slope of the Kaiserstuhl

Breisach – Breisach and its rock, crowned by a large church, tower above the Rhine, facing the twin town of Neuf-Brisach in France. The rock was the heart of one of the most redoubtable systems of fortification in Europe, the site serving at times as a French bridgehead, at times as an Imperial advance post. French revolutionary troops sacked the town in 1793, and it was largely destroyed by the Allied armies in 1945.

As at Freiburg, the **Münster★** has a Romanesque nave, transept and two smaller twin towers, together with a Gothic chancel. The most important work of art is a carved **reredos★★** (1526) with an extraordinarily complex decoration of leaves, flowing hair and billowing draperies from which emerge a crowd of cherubim and the figures of the Eternal Father and Christ crowning the Virgin. Murals depicting the Last Judgement (in the first bay on the west side) were painted in the late 15C by Martin Schongauer of Colmar.

From the cathedral hill (Münsterberg) there is a good view★ of the heights of the Black Forest to the south, the Sundgau peak (in Alsace), the Vosges from the Grand Ballon to Upper Königsburg Castle and, quite close, the Kaiserstuhl.

Upper Black Forest★★★ *(See SCHWARZWALD)*

Füssen★

The old town of Füssen, dominated by its castles, is surrounded by the remains of its fortified wall and watchtowers. The town attracts a lively number of tourists – it is on the Romantische Strasse and the castles of Neuschwanstein and Hohenschwangau are close at hand. The town's pedestrianised centre is particularly pleasant in the evening.

Location

Population: 16 500. Michelin map nos 545, 546 X 16 – Bayern. Located in the Königswinkel ("royal corner"), near to the Austrian border, Füssen is surrounded by lakes (Forggensee, Hopfensee, Weißensee) and has beautiful views over the Tyrol peaks.

Kaiser-Maximilian-Platz 1, 87629 Füssen, ☎ (083 62) 938 50.

Surrounding area: see Schloß NEUSCHWANSTEIN (4km/1mi east), Deutsche ALPEN-STRASSE, ROMANTISCHE STRASSE, WIESKIRCHE (25km/16mi north).

Worth a Visit

Ehemaliges Kloster St Mang

Open all year, Tue-Sun, 11am-4pm (2-4pm, Nov to Mar). €3. Ticket valid for the chapel, the abbey buildings and the museum collecctions (free entry to the parish church).

A Benedictine foundation, St Mang harks all the way back to the work of St Magnus (who died in 750) in Füssen. It was rebuilt in the Baroque style during the 18C and secularised in 1802.

Directory

Where to Eat

⊖ **Zum Schwanen** – *Brotmarkt 4 – Closed Mondays from Nov to mid-Dec, Sundays and Mondays from Jan to Apr. – ☎ (08362) 61 74 –* ⊭ *– €15/29.* This well-run hotel is in the old part of town. The welcoming hosts serve specialities from the Allgäu in a simple environment with a slighty rustic feel.

Where to Stay

⊖ **Hotel Eiskristall** – *Birkstraße 3 – ☎ (08362) 50 78 12 – fax (08362) 507810 – www.hotel-eiskristall.de –* **P** *– Booking advised – 32rm: €44/72* ☕ *– Restaurant €14/35.* Travellers will find this plain and well cared for establishment on the outskirts of Füssen, immediately next to the skating rink. Functional guestrooms furnished in light-coloured wood. The town centre is easily accessible on foot.

⊖ **Hotel Geiger** – *Uferstraße 18, 87629 Füssen-Hopfen am See – ☎ (08362) 70 74 – fax (08362) 38838 – info@hotel-geiger.de – Closed Nov to mid-Dec –* **P** *– 24rm: €48/120* ☕ *– Restaurant €17.50/34.50.* This hotel has been in the hands of the same family for many years. It is on the lakeside promenade and makes the ideal place for exploring the idyllic Hopfensee. The country style restaurant with its winter garden has beautiful views over the lake.

⊖⊖ **Hotel Sonne** – *Prinzregentenplatz 1 – ☎ (08362) 90 80 – fax (08362) 908100 – www.hotel-sonne.de –* **P** ⊭ *– 32rm: €75/105* ☕. This family hotel with pretty façade is situated in the heart of the old town. Comfortable, modern rooms. Wonderful views of the Kaiser-Maximilian-Platz from the café-restaurant on the 1st floor.

Parish Church (Stadtpfarrkirche)

Rebuilt between 1701 and 1717, this church displays a remarkable unity, for Johann-Jacob Herkomer, born in the parish, was not only the architect but also the painter and stuccoworker. The Romanesque crypt in front of the high altar has frescoes from around AD 1000 that portray the two holy men Magnus and Gallus.

St Anne's Chapel (St Anna Kapelle)

Access via the Museum der Stadt Füssen. The oldest part of the abbey (830); within the chapel, there is a striking **Dance of Death★** (*Totentanz*, c 1602) by a local painter. There is also a group in the Gothic style portraying the Holy Family.

Abbey Buildings

Open all year, Tue-Sun, 11am-5pm (1-5pm, Nov to Mar). €2.50. ☎ (083 62) 90 31 46. The abbey buildings were also planned by Herkomer as a grandiose symmetrical Baroque complex in Venetian Baroque style. The Museum der Stadt Füssen, reached across the main quadrangle, is housed in the former state apartments of the abbey (banqueting hall, refectory, library etc) and contains displays on the history of the abbey itself including an excavated medieval cloister. There is also an interesting exhibition of string instruments, illustrating the evolution of the manufacture of violins and lutes locally.

Hohes Schloß

The ramp leading up to the castle entrance starts behind the parish church. In the late 15C, the castle was the summer residence of the prince-bishops of Augsburg. The apartments housing the local museum, in particular the Knight's Hall (Rittersaal) with its sumptuous octagonally coffered ceiling, display a collection of Swabian painting from the 15C to the 18C. The surrounding property has been transformed into a public park (Baumgarten), picturesque and peaceful, affording unexpected views of the Säuling escarpment (alt 2 047m/6 716ft).

Lechfall

0.5km/550yd south. The river Lech leaves the Alps in Füssen and hurls itself tumultuously over a ledge in a small, rocky gorge. The falls are spanned by a footbridge.

Forggensee

This reservoir lake, as well as the many other little lakes to be found on the outskirts of Füssen, is a pleasant place to walk and swim.

Fulda

The town's name is closely connected to the history of Christianity in Germany. But Fulda is not so much dominated by its medieval buildings, as by its Baroque core, with the cathedral, the palace and the mansions of the nobility harking back to the town's religious past when the prince-bishops were the guardians of the tomb of St Boniface. Fulda is a pleasant town with plenty of green spaces.

Location

Population: 63 200. Michelin map nos 543, 544 O 13 – Hessen. Fulda is the economic and cultural centre of the region of eastern Hessen, a few kilometres from the borders with Thuringen and Bavaria.

ℹ *Schloßstraße 1, 36037 Fulda, ☎ (0661) 10 23 46.*

Surrounding area: see EISENACH (100km/62mi northeast), FRANKFURT AM MAIN (102km/64mi southwest), WURZBURG (108km/66mi south), THÜRINGER WALD (tour starts in Eisenach).

Background

St Boniface, the Apostle of Germany – Wynfrith, an English missionary from a monastery in Exeter, was sent by Pope Gregory II in the 8C to preach the gospel to the heathen Germans. The Pope gave him the Latin name "Bonifatius" or Boniface, meaning "he who does good deeds". Boniface charged Sturmius with building a monastery in Fulda. Work began on 12 March 744 and it became Boniface's favourite monastery. In 754, Boniface was proselytising in Friesland when he was murdered at Dokkum. His corpse was brought back to Fulda and buried in the monastery.

The Benedictine abbey, especially under the rule of Abbot Raban Maur (822-42), became a centre of religious devotion, art and scholarship and was responsible for the production of Germany's earliest literary works. *The Lay of Hildebrand,* a heroic epic of which only a fragment survives, was copied by two Benedictine monks in c 820.

An economic and religious centre – At the end of the Middle Ages, after a long period of prosperity, Fulda Abbey entered a period of decline. The town experienced a new period of growth at the end of the 17C thanks to the prince-bishops who decided to build the cathedral, a new castle, a university, a hospital and a palace for the aristocracy. The town's particularly coherent Baroque architectural style is a result of this time.

Worth a Visit

Dom (Cathedral)

From the beginning of 1704, this church was rebuilt in a style inspired by Italian Baroque by the architect Johann Dientzenhofer. Pilgrims still worship the tomb of St Boniface, which lies in a crypt (Bonifatiusgruft) beneath the high altar. At the base of the **funerary monument★**, an 18C alabaster bas-relief represents St Boniface.

The reliquaries of the saint, the head reliquary and his sword, are conserved in the museum (**Dommuseum** – *access to the left of the cathedral, ♿ Open Apr to Oct, Tue-Sun, 10am-5.30pm, Sun 12.30-5.30pm; Nov-Mar, Tue-Sun, 10am-12.30pm, 1.30-4pm, Sun, 12.30pm-4pm. Closed mid-Jan to mid-Feb, from Good Fri to Easter Sun and Pentecost, 24 and 25 Dec. €2.10. ☎ (0661) 872 07*), which also displays an important collection of liturgical vestments from the Baroque period. Baroque art is also represented by a splendid silver altar. There is a good collection of medieval artefacts.

Michaelskirche★

This church, built around an early-9C rotunda, with a stout, square tower, overlooks the cathedral forecourt. The crypt, in which the vaulting rests on a single pillar, is Carolingian. The rotunda itself is supported on eight columns marking the outline of an impressive well-head.

Schloß

This formerly Renaissance construction was extended and rebuilt in 1706-21 to serve as a **residence** for the prince-bishops of Fulda according to blueprints by Johann Dientzenhofer. Their apartments and the Imperial and Princes' Halls – both heavily decorated with stucco and paintings – are part of the Historical Rooms.

A collection of Fulda porcelain is also on display. The mirror room with its splendid Rococo furnishings is considered one of the high points. A stroll though the palace garden leads to the **Orangery** (1724), accessed by way of an oval free-standing stairway. Half way up there is a monumental **"Floravase"**, a superb Baroque ornate masterpiece by Humbach dating from 1728.

Excursions

Probsteikirche St Peter

4km/2.5mi, plus 30min walking and sightseeing. Leave Fulda by the Petersberger Straße and road no 458. Follow the Petersberg signposts to the foot of the rock on which the church is built, and leave the car there. A vast **panorama★** is commanded from the summit: to the east is the Rhön massif *(see below)*, the Milseburg spur and the rounded dome of the Wasserkuppe; south-west, behind Fulda, lies the Vogelsberg.

The Romanesque sanctuary built on this impressive **site★** was largely remodelled in the 15C. It contains five 12C **low-relief sculptures★★** – Christ in Glory and the Virgin on either side of a triumphal arch; St Boniface, Carloman and Pepin the Short (Charlemagne's brother and father). Mural paintings from the 9C decorate the Carolingian crypt.

Schloß Fasanerie or Adolphseck

6km/4mi south. Open Apr to Oct, guided tour (45min) Tue-Sun, 10am-5pm. €5. ☎ (0661) 948 60. Constructed between 1739 and 1754 by Prince-Bishop Amand von Buseck, this Baroque mansion with an expansive park owes to the Landgraves and Electoral Princes of Hesse its interior style, decoration and furnishing. The museum offers visitors an impressive overview of 18C and 19C decorative arts and the evolution of noble lifestyles from the Baroque age. It also houses a fine collection of porcelain.

Tour

The Rhön

Round tour of 104km/65mi southeast of Fulda – allow 4hr.

The remnants of an enormous extinct volcano, the Rhön massif's craggy summits tower above its bleak moorlands, up to a height of 1 000m/3 280ft. These heights, swept by strong winds, have made the area a favourite among the organisers of gliding clubs.

Gersfeld – The most central resort in the Rhön district, Gersfeld has a Protestant **church** (1785) with interestingly placed furnishings: the grouping of organ, altar and pulpit in a single compact ensemble symbolises liturgically the Lutheran reform.

Kreuzberg★ – From the Calvary – at 928m/3 044ft after a steep uphill climb – there is a splendid **view★** of the massif. The Wasserkuppe can be seen to the north.

Wasserkuppe★★ – From the gliding centre, climb to the summit (950m/3 116ft), following the fencing on the left. The **panorama★★** extends as far as Fulda and the Vogelsberg.

Garmisch-Partenkirchen★★★

This is Germany's great winter sports resort, famed as the site of the fourth Winter Olympics in 1936 and the World Alpine Ski Championships in 1978. Worthy of its international reputation, the resort lies in an open mountain basin at the foot of the Wetterstein range, from which the massive silhouettes of the Alpspitze, the axe-shaped Waxenstein, and of course the Zugspitze, Germany's highest peak, stand out.

Despite its modest altitude (720m/2 362ft), favourable meteorological conditions assure the resort a regular winter snowfall. This, coupled with an excellent infrastructure, makes it a first class winter sports resort.

Location

Population: 26 500. Michelin maps n°s 545, 546 X 17 – Bayern. The many surrounding peaks measuring more than 2 000 m make an impressive setting for the two adjacent towns of Garmisch and Partenkirchen. They are also on the Deutsche Alpenstrasse, less than 15km/9mi from Austria.

🅸 *Dr.-Richard-Strauß-Platz, 82467 Garmisch-Partenkirchen, ☎ (088 21) 18 06.*

Surrounding area: see Deutsche ALPENSTRASSE, Schloß LINDERHOF (26km/16mi west), WIESKIRCHE (45km/28mi west).

Worth a Visit

St-Martin Alte Kirche

Garmisch. The parish church stands on the west bank of the River Loisach, in a picturesque neighbourhood where the old chalets have been carefully preserved. The interior embraces two equal naves, where a single central column supports Late Gothic vaulting. A large number of 15C and 16C murals have been uncovered and restored (note especially a huge representation of St Christopher and scenes from the Passion).

Wallfahrtskirche St Anton

Partenkirchen. To the octagonal nave of this 1708 pilgrim's sanctuary, a second nave, oval in shape, was added in 1734-36 by Joseph Schmuzer. The dome above this is decorated with frescoes by JE Holzer.

Philosophenweg (Philosophers' Way)

Partenkirchen. The park of St Anton-Anlagen is the departure point for this panoramic walk which offers fine, clear **views**★ of the surrounding massifs – including the Zugspitze visible behind the Waxenstein.

Excursions

Zugspitze★★★ *(for access and description, see ZUGSPITZE)*

Wank★★

20min cable-car ride. May to Sep, 8.45am-5pm; Oct and Nov, 8.45am-4.30pm. Leaves every hour. €16.50 round trip. ☎ (088 21) 79 70; www.zugspitze.de. Leaves from the Schützenhaus guesthouse, north of Partenkirchen.

From the summit (1 780m/5 840ft) there is a comprehensive view of the Wetterstein chain and Zugspitze peak – and a vertiginous appreciation of the Garmisch-Partenkirchen basin far below and the pre-Alps. At the summit, there is a 3km/2mi panoramic footpath *(gentle gradients, parts cleared in winter)* with free terraces.

Partnachklamm★★

About 1hr30min there and back, of which 5min are in a cable-car. Remember to take rainwear.

From the Partenkirchen ski stadium, go to the lower terminus of the Graseck cable-car. The upper station is at the Forsthaus Graseck

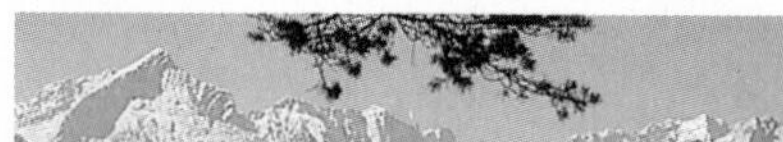

Garmisch-Partenkirchen and the Zugspitze massif.

Kurverwaltung, Garmisch-Partenkirchen

Directory

Where to Eat

⊜ **Postkeller und Alte Braustub'n** – *Innsbrucker Straße 13 – 82481 Mittenwald – ☎ (08823) 17 29 – www.postkeller-mittenwald.de – Closed Mon – ♿ – €10.50/14.* The brewery next door ensures that the taps never run dry in the large dining room on the first floor. On the menu is regional cuisine washed down with local beers.

⊜ **Zur Schranne** – *Griesstraße 4 – ☎ (08821) 16 99 – Closed Tue – ♿ – €13.80/19.* An establishment very typical of the region: sample Bavarian cuisine, served in particularly hearty portions. A covered terrace is also available.

Where to Stay

⊜ **Gästehaus Brigitte** – *St.-Martin-Straße 40 – ☎ (08821) 739 38 – fax (08821) 79125 – bzaja@web.de – P ♿ – 11rm: €26/66 ☕.* This spotlessly clean guesthouse is near the lower cable-car station. Tennis courts, footpaths, and the Olympic skating rink are just around the corner.

⊜ **Gästehaus und Hotel garni Edlhuber** – *Innsbrucker Straße 33, 82481 Mittenwald – ☎ (08823) 13 89 – fax (08823) 94138 – www.mittenwald.de/edlhuber.html – ⊭ P – 16rm: €40/63 ☕.* This friendly, family-run hotel is located at the foot of the Karwendel massif, in the middle of the countryside, is the ideal place to get away from it all. Comfortable guestrooms and professional reception.

Taking a Break

Konditorei-Café Thron – *Marienplatz 13 – ☎ (08821) 522 60 – www.konditorei-thron.de – 8.30am-7pm.* Just the presentation of the huge choice of pastries, tarts and chocolates will get your mouth watering. Prince Regent's cake (Prinzregententorte), wine-cream roulades (Weincremerouladen) and flaked cream (Flockensahne) are just a few of the specialities of this pastry shop cum tea room.

hotel, and from here a footpath leads up to the gorges. The route, carved from the solid rock, passes two spectacular bottlenecks amid the thunder of falling water and clouds of spray. At the Partnachklamm inn, the path rejoins the upward route. It is possible to make the same trip in wintertime, when the route will be decorated with a huge frieze of icicles.

Eibsee★

8km/5mi west. The calm waters of this lake occupy a superb forest site. It lies at the foot of the Zugspitze, at an altitude of 1 000m/3 280ft. A footpath *(2hr walk)* circles the lake.

GARMISCH-PARTENKIRCHEN

Street	Grid
Am Kurpark	X 7
Bahnhofstraße	X 10
Ferdinand-Bath-Straße	X 15
Hauptstraße	X
Hindenburgstraße	X 18
Mittenwalder Str.	X 27
Münchner Str.	X 30
Parkstraße	X 32
Promenadestraße	X 35
Rießerseestraße	X 37
Von-Brug-Str.	X 46
Wildenauer Str.	X 48
Zugspitzstraße	X

Mittenwald★

20km/12mi east. Mittenwald, a community of violin makers on the old Augsburg-Verona trade route, still suffers from heavy traffic today. This is due to the large number of excursions possible in the nearby Kranzberg and Karwendel massifs, and to the beauty of the town itself. The **painted houses★★** lining the pavements of the main street are especially noteworthy.

If Mittenwald, as Goethe said, is "a living picture-book", a monument outside the church recalls that the town also has a place in the world of music. The memorial honours Matthias Klotz (1653-1743), who returned from Cremona in 1684 with a lute and, as an ex-pupil of Stradivarius, introduced the manufacture of stringed instruments to Bavaria despite the fact that it was then in the midst of an economic depression. A dozen artisans, a technical school, and a museum, the Geigenbau- und- Heimatmuseum, carry on that tradition today. *Open from end Dec to end Oct, Tue-Fri, 10am-1pm, 3pm-6pm, Sat and Sun, 10am-1pm. €2.50. ☎ (088 23) 339 81.*

Görlitz★

Görlitz became extremely prosperous during the 15C and 16C, in particular through textile manufacture and trade in woad, and the town was largely spared during the Second World War, so that its huge legacy of 3 500 listed houses represents a major commitment and a challenge. Visitors will be pleased to see that the pearl of Lower Silesia is regaining its old shape, colour and splendour.

Location

Population: 65 000. Michelin map nº 544 M 28 – Sachsen. Görlitz has spread out along the west bank of the Neiße, which has formed the frontier with Poland since 1945.

Obermarkt 29, 02826 Görlitz, ☎ (035 81) 475 70.

Surrounding area: see BAUTZEN (45km/28mi west), DRESDEN (107km/67mi west), SÄCHSISCHE SCHWEIZ.

Walking About

OLD TOWN★

Most of the town's sights are concentrated around two interesting squares, the Obermarkt and the Untermarkt, which dominate the historic centre of Görlitz.

Obermarkt

On the north side of this square, fine Baroque houses have been preserved between the Reichenbacher Turm, a fortified gateway to the west, and the Dreifaltigkeitskirche to the east. Flamboyant **Gothic stalls★** are worth looking at inside the church. At no 29 *(the Tourist Information Centre)*, the façade, including an entrance framed by sculpted columns, is adorned with impressive stuccowork.

Dreifaltigkeitskirche

♿ *May-Sep: 10am-6pm, Sun 12pm-6pm; Oct: 10am-5pm. ☎ (035 81) 40 21 73.*

A high, slim tower with a Baroque cupola is a major feature of the Holy Trinity church in the Obermarkt. The interior with its two naves (15C) is extremely narrow and extends into the long chancel which dates from 1371 to 1381. Visitors will be impressed by the choir **stalls★** (1484), with the chronicle of the Franciscans above them. The Baroque high altar, which dates from 1713, was created by Caspar Gottlob von Rodewitz, a student of Permoser. The pulpit with the twelve Apostles is a work from the Late Renaissance era.

The **Barbarakapelle** houses some valuable works of art, for example the **Maria altarpiece★** (c 1510), a Late Gothic masterpiece. It depicts the Virgin Mary encircled by a glowing halo and also relates the Christmas story. When closed, the hinged panels of the altarpiece represent Christ's Passion. The burial group was created by Hans Olmützer in 1492, whilst the poignant Christ at peace (late 15C) is ascribed to a south German master.

Untermarkt★

Formerly the town's chief trading centre, the market place is overlooked by the tower (1378) of the **Rathaus** (town hall) (BX R). Note, on the corner of the Brüderstraße, the outside staircase (1537-38) encircling an elegant statue (a copy) representing Justice. To the right of the building's Renaissance doorway, a Late Gothic (1488) sculptured plaque displays the armc of Matthias Corvinus, King of Hungary. The central part of the town hall dates from Renaissance times, while the neo-Gothic additions are less than a century old.

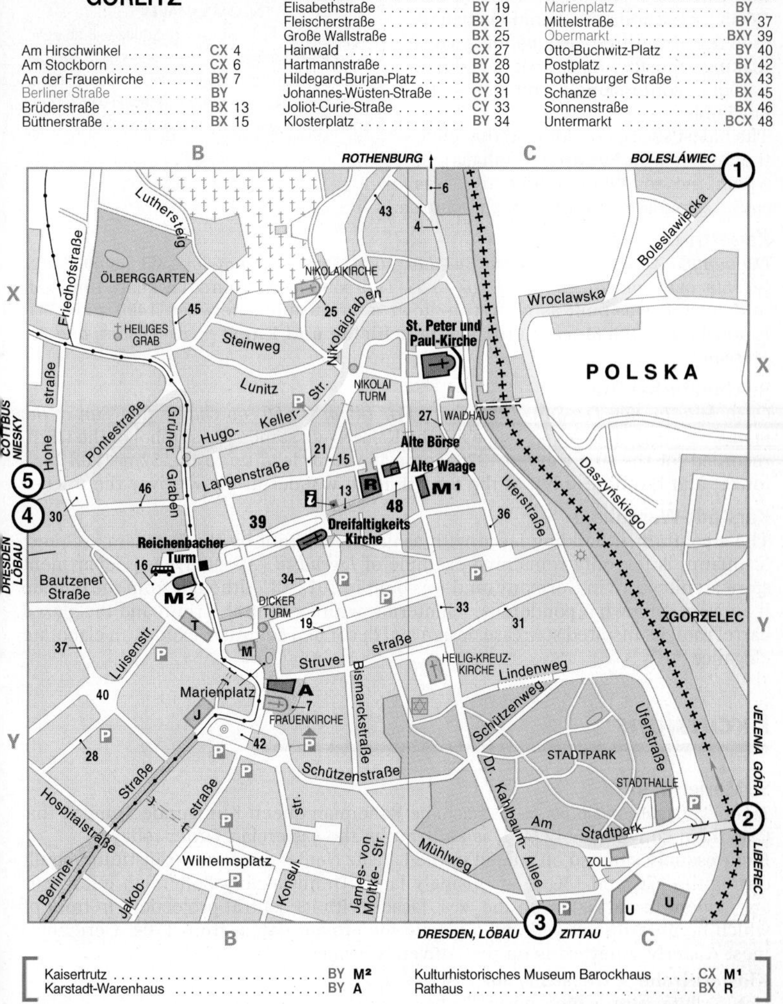

In the middle of the market, the **Alte Börse** (old exchange) (BX), with its entrance surrounded by allegorical figures, is the oldest Baroque monument in the town. Dating from 1706, the exchange is adjacent to the **Alte Waage** (Weigh-house) (BX), which combines three Renaissance upper storeys with a Baroque base at street level.

Kulturhistorisches Museum (Museum of Cultural History)

At Neißstraße 30. This imposing Baroque mansion (1727-29) at the south-east corner of the square houses an interesting collection of art, 16C to 19C decorative arts and beautiful Renaissance and Baroque furniture. There is a particularly fine collection of glassware on display. A collection of 18C rustic **cupboards and cabinets★** on the second floor is distinguished by the interesting painted decoration of the exhibits. The print room contains prints and graphic work from the 16C to the 20C.

St-Peterskirche★

♿ *Open May to Sep, 10.30am-5pm, Sun, 12.30pm-5pm; Oct, 10.30-4pm, Sun, 12.30-4pm; Nov to Apr, 10am-4pm, Sun, 12.30pm-4pm. No charge. ☎ (035 81) 40 21 73.*

The mighty five-naved sandstone building of this place of worship, with its steep copper roof, towers high above the Neiße. It was built over a period of 75 years, being completed by the end of the 15C. Some Late Gothic additions were made to the Late Romanesque west portal (1235) of its predecessor.

Interior – The three central naves form a high, airy open space with a beautiful star vault. The windows are decorated with ornate tracery. The **pulpit**, which dates from 1693, with its gilded acanthus leaves, supported by a charming statue of an angel, is quite magnificent. The Baroque high altar (1695) was completed by Georg Heermann in sandstone and marble stuccowork. The altarpiece depicts the Ascension. The **great organ** was built by Eugenio Casparini, Andreas Silbermann's tutor, in 1703. The organ front, by the Görlitz artist Johann Conrad Buchau, is crowned by three groups of angels making music. A set of elaborate Baroque confessionals completes the ensemble.

The oldest secular building in the town, the former **woad house** (Waidhaus), in which the sought-after blue dye was stored, stands to the right of the church.

"SILESIAN HEAVEN"

With a bit of luck, visitors to Görlitz will be able to sample *Schlesisches Himmelreich*, a typical Silesian sweet and sour dish, prepared from pickled pork and dried fruit and served with a light lemon sauce and white bread dumplings.

Kaisertrutz

Demianiplatz. Open May to Nov, Tue-Sun, 10am-5pm, Fri, 1pm-8pm. €3.50; no charge first Sun of the month. ☎ (035 81) 67 13 55. This solid-looking circular keep, 19m/62ft in diameter, was built as part of the town's fortifications between 1490 and 1541. It now houses the **Museum für Stadtgeschichte und Kunst** *(Local History and Art Museum).*

Reichenbacher Turm

Open May to Nov, Tue-Sun. 10am-5pm, Fri, 1-8pm. €1.50, no charge first Sun of the month. ☎ (035 81) 67 13 55. Opposite the Kaisertrutz stands the symbol of the town, recorded for the first time in 1376. Some 165 steps lead up to the 52m/170ft high tower, and the little room at the top affords a wonderful **view★** over the town.

Karstadt-Warenhaus

The steel-framed building faced with ashlar stone, built by the Potsdam architect Schmann, is the only remaining example of *Jugendstil* (Art Nouveau) department store architecture in Germany, and was built in 1912-13. Although from the outside it appears somewhat ponderous, its interior, with its central atrium and the glazed barrel roof, its inspired staircase design and decorated columns, exudes an elaborate elegance.

Excursions

St-Marienthal★

15km/9mi south via B 66, in Ostritz. The Bohemian queen Kunigunde founded this Cistercian convent in 1234. It is still run by the Cistercian Order today.

Picturesquely situated on a bend in the Lausitz Neiße, the convent institution built during the 17C and 18C is surprisingly large. Unmistakably Bohemian influences are evident in particular on the west façade with its central projection, in front of which lie an artesian well and a plague monument dating from 1704. Germany's most easterly vineyard is on the convent's estate.

Klosterkirche – Unusually for Cistercian architecture, which normally has only a roof turret, this church has a tower. The interior with its groined vaulting was painted in the narrative Romanesque style in 1850 by Nazarenes.

Zittauer Gebirge★

35km/22mi south via the B 66. This mountain range extends for 20km/12mi in a southeast-northwest direction, forming an abrupt barrier towering over the Zittau Basin. A favourite region for rock climbers, mountaineers and winter sports enthusiasts, it is also noted for such spas as Lückendorf, Oybin and Jonsdorf, and the trips that can be made from them. The highest peaks in the range – Lausche (793m/2 602ft), Hochwald (749m/2 457ft) and Jonsberg (681m/2 234ft) – are steep phonolithic (clinkstone) cones protruding from sandstone bedrock. This juxtaposition of sandstone and limestone heights with the remains of volcanic and igneous eruptions is characteristic of the Zittau mountains.

R. Chéret/MICHELIN

Karstadt-Warenhaus, Görlitz

Goslar★★

A popular weekend destination among Germans, Goslar is a former Free Imperial City which was once part of the Hanseatic League. The town exhibits its long and rich history in a large grouping of half-timbered houses and important monuments around its medieval centre. The old town and the Rammelsberg ore mines were designated a World Heritage Site by UNESCO in 1992.

Location

Population: 46 000. Michelin map n°°544 K 15 – Niedersachsen. Goslar lies on the northwestern rim of the Harz National Park and makes an ideal starting point for exploring the massif.

Markt 7, 38640 Goslar, ☎ (053 21) 780 60.

Surrounding area: see HARZ, WOLFENBÜTTEL (36km/22mi north), BRANSCHWEIG (46km/29mi north), HILDESHEIM (51km/32mi west).

Background

The mines – A former Free Imperial City, Goslar owed its prosperity to the mineral wealth of the Harz, and particularly to the **Rammelsberg** mines, worked during the Middle Ages for lead and silver. The city's commercial importance reached its height in the 15C and 16C, when profit accrued also from the vast surrounding forests which provided timber for the metal smelters. It was during this period that the fine houses of the city centre were built.

Religious controversy between the Free City and the dukes of Brunswick, who owned the mines, brought an economic decline in the mid 16C. Today tourism is Goslar's principal industry; the **Hahnenklee-Bockswiese district** is a very popular winter sports destination.

Directory

Where to Eat

Les petites maisonnettes – *Am Siechenhof 12 – Closed 1-7 Jan, Tue and Sat noon – ☎ (05321) 188 88 – info@les-petites-maisonettes.de – €36.* This restaurant has a country feel and is set in a half-timbered house. The cosy décor gives this place a warm ambience and the terraced garden makes the restaurant particularly pleasant in the summer months.

Where to Stay

Hotel Die Tanne – *Bäringer Straße 10 – ☎ (05321) 343 90 – fax (05321) 343934 – www.die-tanne.de – 25rm: €43/89 .* The shale frontage of this establishment which is classed as a historic monument conceals comfortable rooms. Explore the little backstreets nearby.

Walking About

THE OLD TOWN★★★ (ALTSTADT) *allow 3hr*

The old town of Goslar is largely pedestrianised, making it a pleasant place to wander round.

Beginning on Marktplatz (see town plan).

Marktplatz★

The market square, dignified and austere in appearance, is surrounded by houses protected by slate cladding. Its architectural prestige derives from two Gothic buildings: the Kaiserworth and the Rathaus, behind which soar the spires of the 12C **Marktkirche**. In the centre of the square there is a **fountain** *(Marktbrunnen)* with two bronze basins (1230) surmounted by the crowned Imperial eagle with outstretched wings. On the gable of a house opposite the Rathaus there is a chiming **clock** which animates four different scenes *(at 9am, noon, 3pm and 6pm)* representing the history of mining in the Harz mountains from the Middle Ages to the present day.

Rathaus★ (Town Hall)

Following the medieval custom, this 15C building was designed with an open hall at street level, an arcaded gallery opening onto the Marktplatz.

On the south side, an exterior staircase leads to the first floor **State Room** (*Diele*). The lower part of the roof is masked by an ornate balustrade alternating with decorative gabling.

Huldigungssaal★★ (Chamber of Allegiance)

11am-4pm. Closed 24 and 31 Dec. €2. ☎ *(053 21) 757 80.*

This room, transformed into the **Municipal Council Chamber** in 1490, was magnificently decorated c 1520. Along the walls, beneath delicately carved upper panelling, Roman emperors alternate with sibyls in Renaissance costume; on the ceiling, scenes from the childhood of Christ are surrounded by figures of the Prophets and Evangelists. Concealed behind a door is a tiny chapel containing paintings of the Passion and an arm-reliquary (c 1300) of St Margaret.

Hotel Kaiserworth

Built in 1494, this Gothic edifice, now a hotel, is embellished with a turreted oriel and Baroque statues of emperors beneath baldaquins. On a gable ridge, at the foot of an allegorical statue of Abundance, a grotesque figurine of **The Ducat Man** *(Dukatenmännchen)* vividly illustrates Goslar's ancient right to mint coins.

J. Bouraly/MICHELIN

Restaurant opposite the Marktkirche.

Carved Half-timbered Houses★★ (Fachwerkhäuser)

The Schuhhof, a small square to the northwest of the Rathaus, is entirely surrounded by half-timbered buildings, those on the right resting on arcades.
Further on, a passageway on the left leads to the narrow Münzstraße, which in turn passes an old staging inn, **Am Weißen Schwan** and then the **Alte Münze** (Old Mint). Transformed today into a restaurant, this timbered building dates from 1500. The fine house on the corner of the Münzstraße and the Marktstraße, with its splendid two-storey oriel, was constructed in 1526.
Facing the Marktkirche is the huge pointed roof of the **Brusttuch**, also dating from 1526, which was built for a rich mine owner and decorated, according to Renaissance taste, with a host of biblical, mythological and legendary characters and motifs. Not far away, the tall gable of the **Bäckergildehaus** (Bakers' Guild Hall), built between 1501 and 1557, rises into view.
The **Renaissance houses** at the Marktstraße-Bäckerstraße crossroads are adorned with friezes of the fan motif, so often found in Lower Saxony *(no 2 Bäckerstraße)*, or a row of blind arcades *(no 3 Bäckerstraße)*.
Turn into Bergstraße which leads to the Marktkirche.

Siemenshaus

♿ *Open Thu and Fri, 9am-12noon. Closed bank holidays. No charge.* ☎ *(053 21) 238 37.* An impressive half-timbered house built in 1693 by Hans Siemens, ancestor of the founder of the celebrated industrial firm of the same name. There is a particularly fine tiled entrance hall (Däle), and a picturesque interior courtyard.

Worth a Visit

Stiftskirche Neuwerk★

This former collegiate church was built in 12C-13C. The tall polygonal towers are among the most elegant ever built for a Romanesque church. The exterior decoration of the apse is exceptionally elaborate.
Heavily ribbed, pointed vaulting characterises the interior. The former rood screen decorated with six low-relief sculptures dating to 1230-40, with figures (Christ, the Virgin, the four Apostles) whose clothing and artistic design appear manifestly Gothic, is used as an organ loft in the west. The Late Romanesque painting in the choir is particularly noteworthy.

Pfarrkirche Peter und Paul★

Entrance on the Frankenberger Plan.
Later modifications had minimal impact on the Romanesque character of this three-nave cruciform basilica built in the 12C.
The pillars and vaults of the interior are richly decorated with stone carvings. The work on the columns of the western choir, borrowed from those at Königslutter *(see BRAUNSCHWEIG: Excursions)* is particularly fine. Over the choir and upper loft are

GOSLAR

Astfelder Straße	Y 2
Breite Straße	Y
Brüggemannstraße	Y 8
Fischermäkerstraße	Y 19
Fleischscharren	Y 23
Hoher Weg	Z 37
Hokenstraße	Y
Kaiserbleek	Z 42
Königstraße	Z 45
Marktstraße	Z
Münzstraße	Y 52
Obere Kirchstraße	Y 58
Petersilienstraße	Y 61
Rammelsberger Straße	Z 63
Rosentorstraße	Y 66
St-Annenhöhe	Z 69
Schielenstraße	Y 71
Schreiberstraße	Z 74
Schuhhof	Y 76
Worthstraße	Z 82

Alte Münze	Y Z
Alter Gasthof Am Weißen Schwan	Y A
Bäckergildehaus	Z Y
Brusttuch	Z B
Eckhaus-Münz- Marktstraße	Z V
Goslarer Museum	Z M²
Kaiserworth	Z S
Mönchehaus	Y M¹
Pfarrkirche Peter und Paul	Z F
Rathaus	YZ R
Renaissancehäuser	YZ W
Siemenshaus	Z C
Stift zum Großen Heiligen Kreuz	Z K

murals painted in the early 13C. The 12C altar bears a splendid Baroque retable dating to 1675, which, like the 1698 chancel, originated in the Goslar woodcarving workshop of Heinrich and Jobst Heinrich Lessen.

Kaiserpfalz (Imperial Palace)

♿ *Open Apr to Oct: 10am-5pm; Nov to Mar: 10am-4pm. Closed 24 and 31 Dec. €4.50.* ☎ *(053 21) 757 80.* The palace, originally built for Kaiser Heinrich III in the 11C and reduced to ruins with the passage of years, was rebuilt and restored between 1868 and 1879. Ambitious historical paintings in the gigantic **Reichssaal** *(on the first floor)* chart the significant events affecting Saxony when Goslar was still an Imperial residence.

Beyond the Reichssaal is the early-12C **Palatine Chapel of St Ulrich**, where the plan passes, in elevation, from that of a Greek cross to that of an octagon. Inside the chapel is the tomb of Heinrich III, whose heart is preserved in the plinth. The recumbent effigy of the ruler dates from the 13C.

Mönchenhaus★ (Monks' House)

A **museum** of modern art, housed in an ancient half-timbered house (1528), displays works by Beuys, Hundertwasser, Serra and de Kooning. In the garden are sculptures, with an interesting Calder mobile.

Rammelsberg

Southwest of town, via Clausthaler Straße and Rammelsberger Straße. Guided tour (1hr to 4hr depending on the tour) 9am-6pm. Closed 24 and 31 Dec. From €5.50. ☎ *(053 21) 75 01 22; www.rammelsberg.de*

Over the centuries the Rammelsberg mines with their rich deposits of non-ferrous metals have been largely responsible for Goslar's prosperity. The mines were worked continuously for at least 1 000 years, if not longer, giving up almost 30 million tons of ore during this period. During the museum visit, the Roeder gallery and other parts of the mine can be explored on foot or in a mining train. The mining museum and the public mine of Rammelsberg are connected, ie the mine can be visited above and below ground.

►► Stift zum Heiligen Kreuz – Breites Tor★ – Goslarer Museum – Zwinger.

Excursions

Grauhofer Kirche★

3km/2mi. Leave Goslar by the Okerstraße.

Augustinian friars from Grauhof monastery (founded in 1527) employed an Italian architect to build this church in 1701. It was completed in 1717. Of particular interest are a pulpit in the form of a boat (1721), the splendid organ case, which dates from 1737, and the choir stalls in exotic woods, where 56 separate scenes represent the life and philosophy of St Augustine.

Harz Mountains★★ – *See HARZ.*

Greifswald★

Greifswald dates from the foundation of Eldena Abbey. There is documentary evidence that the town had already been granted rights as early as 1250. Once it joined the Hanseatic League in 1281, Greifswald appears to have flourished. The construction at this time of three large parish churches, whose silhouettes still grace the town's skyline, provides evidence of its prosperity. In fact, Greifswald was to continue to expand and prosper for the next four centuries. The city boasts a considerable number of historic buildings, having been largely spared from destruction during the Second World War. Its charming appearance, with a distinctly Scandinavian flavour, will no doubt stand it in good stead for its future development.

Location

Population: 54 000. Michelin map n°°542 D 23 – Mecklenburg-Vorpommern. Built on the banks of the river Ryck, Greifswald is on the Baltic coast, with Stralsund to the northwest. The town is about halfway between the islands of Rügen and Usedom.

Rathaus am Markt, 17489 Greifswald, ☎ (038 34) 52 13 80.

Surrounding area: see STRALSUND (33km/20mi northwest), ROSTOCK (91km/57mi west), MECKLENBURGISCHE SEENPLATTE, Insel RÜGEN, Insel USEDOM.

Background

Swedish Rule – Following the peace treaty of Osnabrück, West Pomerania, and with it Greifswald, passed into Swedish hands. The Swedes proved not to be oppressive rulers, exercising leniency for nigh on 200 years and granting the town an unusual degree of autonomy for the age. From 1815, when West Pomerania became part of Prussia, a busy period of construction began, to which the numerous well-preserved burghers' houses still testify.

The Greatest German Romantic Painter – Caspar David Friedrich, the epitome of the German Romantic artist and a revolutionary landscape painter, was born in Greifswald in 1774 (his birthplace at no 57 Lange Straße was destroyed by fire in 1901). Although he left Greifswald at the age of 20 (to settle in Dresden), he remained deeply attached to the town of his birth; Greifswald, and especially the ruins of Eldena Abbey, feature in many of his works. Friedrich's most famous land- and seascapes, at dusk or daybreak, show his mastery of light to great effect and are suffused with symbolism of the transitory nature of human existence; rarely, if ever, had intense and subjective emotions been committed to canvas in this way before. As evocations of mankind's place in the greater spiritual and natural world, between isolation and a sense of history or destiny, his works still bring to life much of the spirit and aesthetic of German Romanticism.

Worth a Visit

THE OLD TOWN★

Marktplatz★

To the west of this square stands the **Rathaus** (1738) with its distinctive curved, Renaissance style gables; the roof turret is nonetheless in the Baroque style. The arcades along the east gable, which were built according to medieval model, were uncovered in 1936. Around the square stand a number of architecturally interesting houses, the most noticeable of which is **no 11★**: this early 15C building with its ornately decorated crow-stepped gable is one of the most beautiful examples of north German Gothic architecture in brick.

Marienkirche★

♿ *Open May to Oct, daily, 10am-5pm, Sat 10am-12 noon, Sun, 11am-12 noon; Nov to Apr: 12 noon-1pm, Sun, 11am-12 noon. Closed Easter Mon and Pentecost, 1 May, 3 and 31 Oct.* ☎ *(038 34) 22 63.* This hall-church with three naves has no chancel. The elegantly structured east gable with its ornate tracery alleviates the somewhat heavy, stocky appearance of the rest of the brick church, which is known affectionately as "podgy Mary" by locals. Construction of the church was begun in 1280 and lasted into the 14C. Inside there is a beautiful carved **pulpit★** dating from 1587, the work of Joachim Mekelenborg from Rostock. There are Late Gothic frescoes from the 15C, including one which depicts a whale caught in the fishing village of Wieck in 1545.

Dom St-Nikolai★

♿ *Open Apr-Sep, 10am-6pm, Sun, 11am-1pm; Oct, 10am-4.30pm, Sun, 11am-1pm; Nov to Mar, 10am-3pm, Sun 11am-1pm. €1.50.* ☎ *(038 34) 26 27.* The cathedral is dwarfed by its tower, which is almost 100m/328ft in height and takes the form of a square base flanked by four small round towers, supporting a two-storey octagonal tower with blind double windows decorated with tracery. The crowning glory is a Dutch Baroque steeple dating from 1653. In the 14C the original hall-church was elevated to the rank of basilica, and the spaces between the flying buttresses were filled in to make a ring of 21 radiating chapels. In the 19C two students of Schinkel, Gottlieb Giese and Joachim Christian Friedrich (brother of Caspar David), undertook to remodel the church in the neo-Gothic style in the true spirit of Romanticism. Numerous oil paintings (16C-19C) and tombstones are of interest. Note also the frescoes dating from c 1430.

Universität

Rubenowplatz. The university of Greifswald is the second oldest in northern Europe after Rostock. It was founded in 1456 by local mayor Heinrich Rubenow, who was its first vice-chancellor. The university's most famous student is the poet Ernst Moritz Arndt, after whom the university is named, who went on to hold the university chair in history. The university's elongated main building stands on Rubenowplatz and was built in the mid 18C. The triangular gable bears the coats of arms of the Swedish royal family on the side facing the street, and of Pomerania on the side facing the courtyard.

Pommersches Landesmuseum

Theodor-Pyl-Straße 1. ♿ *May-Oct: Tue-Sun, 10am-6pm; Nov-Apr, Tue-Sun. 10am-5pm. €3.* ☎ *(038 34) 89 43 57.* The well stocked art gallery with works from the 17C to 20C, including paintings by Caspar David Friedrich, is already open to the public.

KLOSTERRUINE ELDENA AND SURROUNDING AREA★

Klosterruine Eldena★

Wolgaster Landstraße. The original Cistercian abbey was founded in 1199, and it appears to have reached the height of its wealth and power around the mid 14C. The Thirty Years War spelled large-scale destruction for it, and the remains were later used as a source of building materials by local people. Of the once splendid building, only fragments of the church, the cloister and the east abbey building

Swing bridge at Wieck.

M. Buffard/MICHELIN

remain. They are nonetheless still as picturesque a scene as they were in the days of Caspar David Friedrich, who not only committed them to canvas, but campaigned for their preservation.

Wieck★

Can easily be reached on foot from the Eldena Abbey ruins.

This little fishing village, now officially classified as a historical site, lies as the mouth of the River Ryck as it flows into Greifswald Bay. The shipmasters' and fishermen's cottages, the latter thatched with reeds, the idyllic little harbour and the **wooden swing bridge★** *(Zugbrücke)* make a delightful scene. The bridge, based on a Dutch design, is a technical monument in itself, dating from 1887.

▶▶ St Jacobikirche – Ehemaliges Hospital St Spiritus – Botanischer Garten★.

Halle★

Halle is a town with a dual identity: on the one hand it is an important industrial centre specialising in mechanical engineering and chemical manufacture; on the other hand, an intellectual enclave whose university traditions go back to the 17C. As early as 806 a fortress was built here to safeguard the sources of salt extraction which formed the basis of Halle's wealth. Halle is also famous as the birthplace of Georg Friedrich Händel, in 1685. The Händel Festival pays tribute to the master of Baroque music every year.

Location

Population: 249 000. Michelin map nº 544 L 19, 20 – Sachsen-Anhalt. Halle is on the banks of the Saale, around thirty kilometres northwest of Leipzig.

🅱 *Roter Turm, Marktplatz, 06108 Halle, ☎ (0345) 47 23 30.*

Surrounding area: see LEIPZIG (34km/21mi east), NAUMBURG (47km/29mi south), DESSAU (53km/33mi north).

Directory

Where to Eat

⊖ Mönchshof – *Talamtstraße 6 – ☎ (0345) 202 17 26 – kontakt@moenchshof-halle.de – Closed Sun evening – €14/25.* This restaurant will suit those who enjoy comfortable country living. The establishment is located next to the cathedral and is panelled in dark wood. Good traditional cuisine of the region is on the menu.

Where to Stay

⊖⊖ **Apart Hotel** – *Kohlschütterstraße 5 – ☎ (0345) 525 90 – fax (0345) 5259200 – info@apart.halle.de – 🅿 ⅹ – 49rm: €64/85 ☐.* This hotel has been formed from an old villa and former hospital. High ceilings and stuccowork characterise the style of both buildings. In the modern and comfortable guestrooms, mahogany and light woods co-exist.

Worth a Visit

Marktplatz★

This huge square is dominated by the belfries of the Marktkirche and by the **Roter Turm** (red tower), built in the 15C and almost 80m/262ft high. An 1859 statue of Händel surveys the square from the centre. The market and the tramway junction there make this the busiest and liveliest part of the town.

Marktkirche★

A triple-aisle hall-church with no chancel, this building was constructed in 1529-54 between the double towers of two Romanesque churhes, whose naves had been torn down. Inside, admire the delicate interlacing of ribs beneath the barrel vaulting, unusual in the absence of transverse arches corresponding to the bays. The side aisles are fitted with stone galleries. The pulpit, dating from 1547 with a sounding board (1596) by Heinrich Heidereiter, blends in harmoniously with its surroundings. The **reredos★** of the high altar carries a Virgin and Child painted by a pupil of the Cranach School.

Behind the altar is kept Luther's death mask.

Moritzkirche

On the Hallorenring. This triple-aisle hall-church, built between 1388 and 1511, displays a network of star-vaulting characteristic of the Late Gothic style. **Works★** by the sculptor **Conrad of Einbeck** are on view in the church, masterpieces

HALLE

Street	Grid
Alter Markt	EZ 3
An der Waisenhausmauer	DEZ 4
Bornknechtstraße	DYZ 14
Brüderstraße	EY 15
Dachritzstraße	DEY 18
Domstraße	DY 27
Friedemann-Bach-Platz	DY 31
Gerberstraße	DY 35
Große Brauhausstraße	EZ 39
Große Märkerstraße	EYZ 42
Große Nikolaistraße	DEY 43
Große Steinstraße	EY
Große Ulrichstraße	DEY
Kellnerstraße	DY 56
Kleine Brauhausstraße	EYZ 57
Kleine Steinstraße	EY 58
Kleinschmieden	EY 60
Leipziger Straße	EYZ
Mauerstraße	EZ 69
Mittelstraße	EY 70
Oleariusstraße	DY 73
Rannische Straße	EZ 78
Rathausstraße	EY 79
Robert-Franz-Ring	DY 86
Rudolf-Breitscheid-Straße	EZ 88
Schmeerstraße	EY 91
Schulstraße	EY 94
Talamtstraße	DY 99
Universitätsring	DEY 100

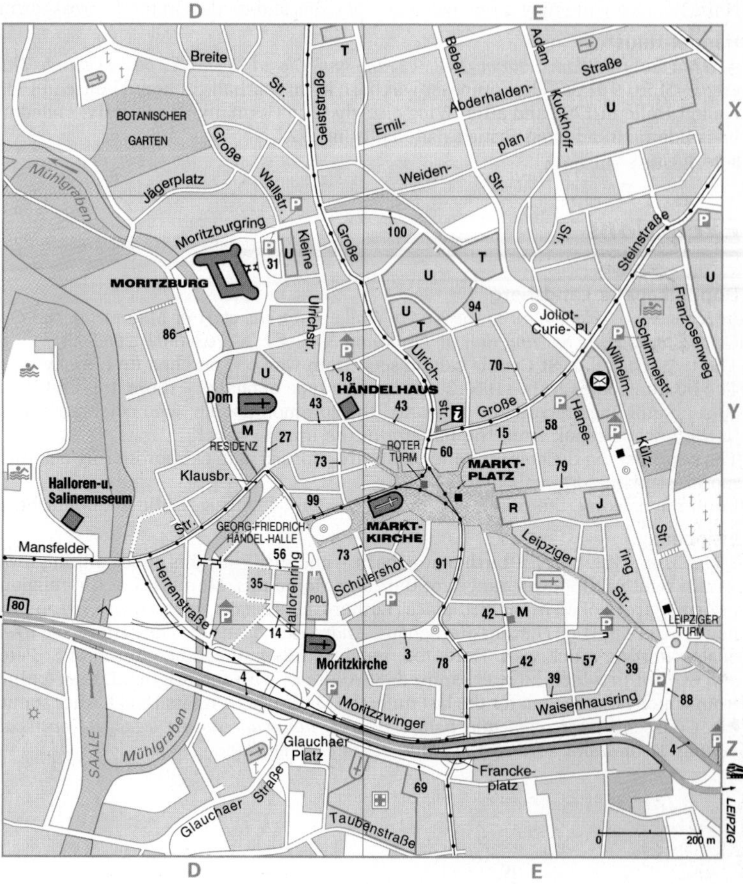

distinguished at the same time by a naive realism and a great power of expression. Note in particular *The Man of Sorrows*, a statue (1411) of St Maurice, and a Pietà (1416).

Dom

Am Domplatz; currently undergoing restoration. The three-naved Gothic hall-church was modified c 1520 by Cardinal Albert of Brandenburg. The interior columns are decorated with statues of Christ, the Apostles and the saints, executed in the studios of Peter Schroh, one of the most talented sculptors of the time. Like the pulpit (c 1525), they already show of a Renaissance influence.

Technisches Halloren- und Salinenmuseum

52 Mansfelder Straße. ♿ Open Tue-Sun, 10am-5pm. Closed 1 Jan., 24, 25 and 31 Dec. €2.10, no charge on Thu. ☎ (0345) 202 50 34. This museum recounts the history of the exploitation of the local salt mines and the cultural development of the "*Halloren*" – the Halle salt miners' guild. An evaporation vessel is demonstrated that still functions and produces regularly.

Staatliche Galerie Moritzburg-Halle★★ (Moritzburg National Gallery)

Friedemann-Bach-Platz. Open Wed-Sun, 10am-6pm, Tue, 11am-8.30pm. Closed 24 and 31 Dec. €4, no charge Tue. ☎ (0345) 21 25 90. In 1484, building began on the Moritzburg, a fortress complex with four wings. Until 1541, it was the preferred residence of the archbishops of Magdeburg and Mainz. Having been destroyed during the Thirty Years War, part of the fortress was restored and converted into a museum at the beginning of the 20C. It now houses the most significant art collection in Sachsen-Anhalt.

19C and 20C German painting – The fine works on display embrace the periods of **Romanticism**, **Impressionism** and **Expressionism**. Works by the artists of the Brücke group, as well as by Kandinsky and Feininger, are on display.
German sculpture of the 19C and 20C – Works by, among others, Wilhelm Lehmbruck and Ernst Barlach are collected here. The museum also displays interesting collections of glassware and ceramics dating from the Middle Ages to the present, and also porcelain and goldware.

Numismatists will enjoy a fine collection of coins and medals in the fortress tower.

Händel Haus★

♿ *Open daily, 9.30am-5.30pm, Thu, 9.30am-7pm. Closed 25 Dec. €2.60, No charge Thu.* ☎ *(0345) 50 09 01 26.* The composer was born in this big half-timbered house in 1685. He left Halle in 1703 and after living elsewhere in Germany and in Italy, ended up in London. He adopted British nationality in 1727.

▶▶ Beatles Museum

Excursions

Doppelkapelle Landsberg

In Landsberg, 19km/12mi to the east of Halle. From the start of May to the end Oct: Guided tours (1hr) Sat and Sun at 11am and 3pm. €2. ☎ *(0346 02) 206 90.*
The twin chapel of **St Crucis** can be seen from way off, perched on a rocky spur. The building dates from 1195-1200. This rare type of chapel – there are only about 30 such buildings recorded – separated the common people, who celebrated Mass in the lower chapel, from the nobility in the upper chapel.
The **capitals**★ on the columns and pillars are adorned with extraordinarily beautiful motifs of plants, animals and figures.
From the balcony, there is a superb **view**★ as far as Leipzig, Halle and Merseburg.

Eisleben

34km/21mi west. **Martin Luther** was born – and died – in this small mining town within sight of the lower ranges of the Harz Mountains. Memories of the religious reformer are evoked in his birthplace (Luther-Geburtshaus, *Lutherstraße 16*) and the house where he died (Luther-Sterbehaus, *Andreaskirchplatz 7*). The historic old town is also worth a quick visit. Here, too, much recalls Luther: the church of St Peter and St Paul in which he was baptised; St Andreas, with the original Luther pulpit, from which he preached for the last time; the Marktplatz with its 1883 Luther statue.
▶▶ Goitzsche (*recreation and nature reserve, landscape as the legacy of open-cast mining; 30km/19mi northeast of Halle, south of Bitterfeld*).

Hamburg★★★

Germany's second largest city after Berlin, Hamburg is one of the most important ports in Europe. Its old title of "Free and Hanseatic Town" and its status as a "City State" (Stadtstaat) testify to its eminence and influence through the centuries. Germany's publishing and media capital, renowned for its commercial dynamism and cosmopolitan atmosphere, is a city of contrasts; not far from the lively – and sometimes rowdy – St Pauli district, residential areas such as Harvestehude and Blankenesee remind the visitor that Hamburg is home to more millionaires than any other city in Germany. Take the time to explore the city, and you will soon fall under its spell.

Location

Population: 1 700 000. Michelin map 541, 542 F 13, 14 – Hamburg. Hamburg stands at the confluence of the Bille and the Alster, on the estuary of the Elbe river, which flows into the North Sea about 100km/62mi to the northwest. The A 1 motorway links the city to Bremen, the A 7 to Hannover and the A 24 to Berlin.

Hauptbahnhof, 20099 Hamburg, ☏ (040) 30 05 13 00.

Surrounding area: see LÜNEBURG (57km/36mi southeast) and the LÜNEBURGER HEIDE, LÜBECK (67km/42mi northeast), KIEL (94km/59mi north), BREMEN (126km/78mi southwest via the A 1).

Background

The Hanseatic Town (13C-15C) – Originally a modest settlement on the banks of the Alster, a small tributary of the Elbe, Hamburg enjoyed its first taste of prosperity when it became a member of the Hanseatic League, headed at that time by Lübeck. It was then that merchants started to organise the banks of the Elbe itself for warehousing and the berthing of ships. The town profited from the particular conditions then of Baltic-North Sea trade: in those days only heavy cargoes of grain and timber took the long sea passage through the Kattegat and the Skagerrak; more valuable material was landed at Lübeck, transported overland to Hamburg, then re-embarked.

Liberty and Neutrality – The great geographic discoveries of the 16C, and the new sea routes they opened up, destroyed existing trade patterns and dislocated the Hanseatic monopoly. Hamburg traders were thus forced to become intermediaries in warehousing and distribution. The foundation of the first German Stock Exchange in 1558 reflected the intense business activity which resulted – a situation in no way worsened by the city's policy of strict neutrality, which kept it out of the Thirty Years' War. In 1618 Hamburg became a Free Imperial City. One year later the Bank of Hamburg was founded. From 1806 to 1814 French troops occupied the town. In 1842 it was ravaged by a disastrous fire. But American independence and the emergence of Latin America lent an added impetus to the extraordinary expansion

The Alster basin right in the heart of the city.

Hamburg Tourismus GmbH

Telephone prefix – 040

Tourist information – For general information or room reservations: *Tourismus-Zentrale Hamburg GmbH, ☎ 30 05 13 00, Fax 30 05 13 33, www.hamburg-tourism.de*. Open Mon-Sun 8am-8pm. Information offices: Main Train Station (Hauptbahnhof), main entrance Kirchenallee, Mon-Sun 7am-11pm; Harbour, St Pauli Landungsbrücken (piers) between piers 4 and 5, Mon-Sun 8am-7pm (Oct-Mar 10am-5.30pm). The fortnightly magazine *Prinz, Szene Hamburg* (every 4 weeks) and the *Hamburger Vorschau* (at the information offices) provide information on all sorts of events. Ticket sales for select events are at the *Tourismus-Zentrale Hamburg*.

Post offices with special opening times – Post office at the main train station (Hachmannplatz) Mon-Fri 8am-8pm, Sat 10am-6pm.

Newspapers – *Hamburger Morgenpost, Hamburger Abendblatt.*

Internet – www.hamburg.de; www.hamburg-intern.de; www.hamburg-web.de; www.hamburg-information.de

Public Transport

Using the buses and underground trains of the HVV (Hamburger Verkehrsverbund, the Hamburg Transit Authority) is recommended. The lines stretch all the way into the surrounding region of Schleswig-Holstein, ☎ 1 94 49, www.hvv.de, open Mon-Sun 7am-8pm. Information at the HVV office at the Hauptbahnhof Mon-Fri, 7am-8pm, Sat-Sun 7am-10pm, Sat 8.30am-5pm, Sun 11am-8pm, and in many U- and S-Bahn stations. Tickets are available from orange vending machines and, for buses, from the drivers. Single tickets for rides in the centre of town from €1.35; a day ticket for one person costs €4.90, a group day ticket for up to five people costs from €7 to €9.35 (the two latter tickets are valid from 9am till the last ride). A 3-day pass costs €12.

The **Hamburg Card** costs €6.40 and is valid for one person, the €12.25 version is for up to five people (card valid on the issue date and from 6pm onward on the day before). The three-day version costs €13.25 (€22.50 for a group). Besides use of the HVV network, free entrance to 11 state-run museums and other discounts, the card also gives discounts for tours on water and on land. The Hamburg Card is available at the tourist information offices, in many hotels, at vending machines and in the HVV customer offices, as well as at many travel agents *(Reisebüros)*.

Sightseeing

City tours – Tours by double-decker bus. Departure and arrivals at the Hauptbahnhof/Kirchenallee, embarkation at several other stops (including St-Pauli Landungsbrücken). The *Top Tour Hamburg*, daily every 15min from 9.30am to 4.45pm (in winter only at 11am and 3pm) lasts about 1hr 30min and costs €11 for adults, half price for children; the *Gala Tour*, departs daily at 10am, 11am, 2pm and 3pm (in winter only at 10am and 2pm), takes in the various districts and lasts about 2hr 30min; details from ☎ 22 71 06 61. Tour with the *Hummel-Bahn* train from Hauptbahnhof/Kirchenallee, Apr-Oct from 10.30am-4.30pm daily every 2hr (lasts about 2hr), Nov-Mar, Sat-Sun every 2hr from 10.30am to 2.30pm; ☎ 7 92 89 79, Fax 7 92 54 15, www.hummelbahn.de. Walking tours of the city under the heading of St Pauli or the Speicherstadt for example: *Tourismus-Zentrale Hamburg* and *Stattreisen Hamburg* ☎ 4 30 34 81, Fax 4 30 74 29, www.stattreisen-hamburg.de.

Boat rides – Tours in boats of various shapes and sizes through the Hamburg Harbour, last anywhere from 1hr, begin and end at the Landungsbrücken 1-9 in St Pauli; full price €7.50, €5.50 with a Hamburg Card; Apr-Oct, daily every 30min 9am-6pm; Nov-Mar, hourly 10.30am-4.30pm. *HADAG* (Hafen-Dampfschiffahrts-Actien-Gesellschaft), is the biggest company ☎ 3 11 70 70, www.hadag.de. In addition there is *Rainer Abicht*, ☎ 3 17 82 20, www.abicht.de; *Kapitän Prüsse*, ☎ 31 31 30, www.kapitaen-pruesse.de and other smaller shipping businesses offering tours of the harbour. Tours of the Alster and canal are also recommendable (departures from Jungfernstieg), by *Alster-Touristik GmbH*, ☎ 3 57 42 40, Fax 35 32 65, www.alstertouristik.de.

Where to Eat

⊖ **Kranzler – CCH Restauarnt** – *Dammtor – ☎ (040) 35 69 32 00 – www.cch-gastronomie.de – ♿ – €12.65/20.90.* Congress-goers and tourists are among the patrons of this very smart, inexpensive self-service restaurant. Located between the Alster and the *Planten un Blomen* park, it has a large open-air terrace surrounded by greenery.

⊖ **Gröninger Haus** – *Ost-West-Straße 47 – Tram 1 Messberg – ☎ (040) 33 00 70 – www.groeninger-hamburg.de – Closed Sat lunchtime and Sun. – ♿ – Reservation recommended – €15/24.50.* This property, first mentioned in a document in 1260, is the city's oldest hotel. The present Gröninger Haus comprises the Gröniger Braukeller, Anno 1750 and the Brauhaus Hanseat. Substantial dishes served here, washed down with beer brewed on the premises.

⊖ **Atlas** – *Schützenstraße 9a – ☎ (040) 851 78 10 – www.atlas.at – Reservation necessary – €15.50/25.50.*
A bistro/restaurant-cum-cocktail bar with an ivy-covered terrace, set in a former factory building somewhat hidden away in Phönixhof. A whole new experience.

⊖⊖ **Café Paris** – *Rathausstraße 4 – ☎ (040) 32 52 77 77 – Reservation recommended – €20.50/28.* The main attraction of this establishment is its location, in the heart of a beautiful building right next to the town hall. The large, attractive dining room has a little balcony, and on the menu: salads, pasta and a selection of international dishes.

Warsteiner Elbspeicher – *Große Elbstraße 39 – Königsstraße – (040) 38 22 42 – www.warsteiner-elbspeicher.de – €22.60/34.* You can choose between the two floors of this old house right next to the harbour: the ground floor houses a laid-back bistro with a large bar and cake buffet, while the rustic restaurant upstairs offers a large choice of fish and meat dishes.

Old Commercial Room – *Englische Planke 10 – Tram Stadthausbrücke – (040) 36 63 19 – www.oldcommercialroom.de – Reservation necessary – €23.50/49.* The Old Commercial Room was founded centuries ago by an English shipowner who has certainly left his mark. English-pub-style decor with mahogany, copper and pictures of sea voyages. Traditional sailors' dishes on the menu *(Labskaus)*, but also lobster, sole and knuckle of ham.

Louis C. Jacob – *Elbchaussee 401 – 22609 Hamburg-Nienstedten – (040) 82 25 50 – jacob@hotel-jacob.de – €48/72.* This Hamburg institution with its spectacular view of the Elbe, elegant upmarket interior and delicious French cuisine is a real delight. The terrace with its lime trees was immortalised in a painting by Max Liebermann in 1902.

Le Canard – *Elbchaussee 139 – 22763 Hamburg-Altona – (040) 880 50 57 – lecanard@viehhauser.de – Closed Sun – €58/69.* This establishment with its stylised white façade, right on the banks of the Elbe, serves excellent classic French-style cuisine – at particularly affordable prices at lunchtime. Modern, bright and elegant dining rooms. The terrace with its wooden flooring offers a remarkable view of the container terminal.

Where to Stay

Hotel Etap Hamburg-City – *Holstenkamp 3, 22525 Hamburg-Eimsbüttel – (040) 85 37 98 20 – www.etaphotel.com – P – 180rm: €42/49 – €4.90.* No surprises at this chain hotel which provides inexpensive accommodation in the city centre. Well-kept, functional, with all mod cons.

Hotel Schwanenwik – *Schwanenwik 29 – (040) 220 09 18 – Fax (040) 2290446 – www.hotel-schwanenwik.de – 18rm: €44/90.* A few offices and a charming boarding house occupy this magnificent 18C white bourgeois house on the banks of the Alster. Simple, modern rooms with a beautiful view of the lake or back garden.

Hotel Brenner Hof 1 – *Brennerstraße 70-72 – Tram Lohmühlenstraße – (040) 280 88 80 – Fax (040) 28088888 – hotel.brennerhof@t-online.de – P – 24rm: €55/95.* This hotel consists of two city centre houses 150m/164yd apart, and offers rooms with modern furnishings. Very good public transport links.

Hotel Yoho – *Moorkamp 5 – (040) 2841910 – Fax (040) 28419141 – www.yoho-hamburg.de – P – booking necessary – 30rm: €57/87 – €9 – restaurant €19.50.* The interior of this white villa was designed by a young team of local architects and now houses a hotel for young people. Plain, pale decor, and a special rate for under 26-year-olds.

Hotel Stephan – *Schmarjestraße 31 – Bahnhof Altona – (040) 389 51 08 – Fax (040) 3895195 – www.hotel-stephan.de – P – 29rm: €65/90.* Very well-kept hotel near the funicular and Altona station, with rather darkly furnished rooms. In summer, breakfast can be taken on the terrace (sheltered from the wind).

Hotel Schmidt – *Reventlowstraße 60, 22605 Hamburg-Othmarschen – (040) 88 90 70 – Fax (040) 8890715 – www.hotel-schmidt.de – P – 45rm: €70/108.* Hotel in a leafy neighbourhood, with rooms spread over several buildings. Variously equipped rooms, some of them particularly comfortable, others more simple. Table service at breakfast.

Hotel Am Elbufer – *Focksweg 40a, 21129 Hamburg-Finkenwerder – (040) 742 19 10 – Fax (040) 74219140 – hotel-@m-elbufer.de – Closed 24 Dec-5 Jan. – P – 14rm: €75/130.* Very pleasant little hotel standing right on the Elbe, with only boats to disturb the peace and quiet. Modern rooms with all mod cons and a lovely view of the river.

Hotel Vier Jahreszeiten – *Neuer Jungfernstieg 9 – (040) 349 40 – Fax (040) 34942600 – emailus.hvj@raffels.com – 156rm: from €215 – €22.* One of the last real grand hotels, on the banks of the Alster, with luxurious Gründerzeit-style decor and charming, modern, comfortable rooms. Quality cuisine in the Haerlin, Doc Cheng's and Jahreszeiten Grill restaurants.

Roller-coaster on the Hamburg "Dom"

Hamburg Tourismus GmbH

Taking a Break

Destille – *Steintorplatz 1 (on the 1st floor in the Museum für Kunst und Gewerbe; entrance via Brockesstraße) – ☎ (040) 2 80 33 54 – 11am-5pm (buffet until 4pm) – Closed same as museum –Free admission if visiting the museum, otherwise €1.* A little café with self-service buffet (home-made salads and cakes) where the owner displays his own collection of decorative arts (objects from the 1930s). Restful view of the leafy courtyard through the glass façade.

Going Out

Useful Tips – Hamburg's night-life has been associated with the name St Pauli since time immemorial. In addition to its old and established temples of eroticism, the area around the Reeperbahn and Große Freiheit has become the site of the "in" scene over the past few years. Around 400 food outlets are squeezed into these cramped quarters. The inner city, too, between the Gänsemarkt and Millerntor (especially around Großneumarkt) offers a great number of opportunities to eat and drink; the passage quarter between Jungfernstieg and Stadthausbrücke is very pleasant. The young, "alternative" crowd gathers around the "Schanzenviertel" west and southwest of the television tower (between Juliusstraße and Neuer Pferdemarkt).

Alex im Alsterpavillon – *Jungfernstieg 54 – ☎ (040) 3 50 18 70 – www.alexgastro.de – Fri-Sat 8am-3am, Mon-Thu 8am-1am, Sun and public holidays 9am-1am.* Not to be missed; no doubt the best terrace in Hamburg with a panoramic view of the Binnenalster. People of all ages gather here throughout the day for a drink or a snack.

Amphore – *Hafenstraße 140 (street that follows the Elbe towards the west from Landungsbrücken) – ☎ (040) 31 79 38 80 – www.cafe-amphore.de – Mon-Fri from 11am, Sat-Sun from 10am.* Friendly little café with a lovely view of the harbour from the terrace above old blockhouses (blankets available). Breakfast served until 3pm.

Café Fees – *Holstenwall 24 (in the Museum für Hamburgische Geschichte; separate entrance) – ☎ (040) 3 17 47 66 – www.fees-hamburg.de – Sun 9.30am-midnight, Fri-Sat 10am-3am, Tue-Thu 10am-2am.* This elegant café has taken up residence in the local history museum. A glass dome houses a pretty winter garden that opens on to the inner courtyard of the museum, and there is also a leafy summer terrace. Also a restaurant from 6pm.

Café Keese – *Reeperbahn 19-21 – ☎ (040) 3 19 93 10 – www.cafe-keese-hamburg.de – Wed-Mon from 11am – dance hall from €5.* A café by day and dance hall by night. Low-key atmosphere and theme evenings: tango on Mondays, jazz on Wednesdays, soul and blues on Sundays. The last Saturday of each month is ladies' night, where the women invite the men to dance.

Christiansen's Fine Drinks & Cocktails – *Pinnasberg 60 (in St Pauli, near the Fischmarkt) – ☎ (040) 3 17 28 63 – www.christiansens.de – Fri 8pm-4am, Sat 8pm-5.30am, Mon-Thu 8pm-3am.* It's difficult to choose between the 250 cocktails, 160 brands of rum and 150 varieties of whisky on offer. Aquarium next to the bar.

Cotton Club – *Alter Steinweg 10 – ☎ (040) 34 38 78 – www.cotton-club.org – Fri-Sat 8pm-1am, Mon-Thu 8pm-midnight; Oct-May Sun 11am-3pm – admission from €5.* Hamburg's local jazz institution was founded in 1959, renamed the "Cotton Club" in 1963 and moved to this address in 1971. Concerts almost every day, attracting jazz lovers of all ages.

Hamborger Veermaster – *Reeperbahn 162 – ☎ (040) 31 65 44 – www.hamborgerveermaster.de – from 5pm (from beginning of Jan to Easter: Fri-Sat only).* It's party time here on Friday and Saturday nights, with much music and cheer. An original setting with maritime decor, also a good place to come for a drink or a meal any other night of the week.

Tower Bar – *Seewartenstraße 9 (in St Pauli, near Landungsbrücken, in the Hafen Hamburg hotel, lift to the 11th floor) – ☎ (040) 31 11 35 24 – www.hotel-hamburg.de – Fri-Sat 6pm-3am, Sun-Thu 6pm-2am (Reservations possible between 6pm-9.30pm).* Near the harbour, on the 12th floor of the Hafen Hamburg hotel, this little cocktail bar has a magnificent panoramic view of the city – especially from the gallery. This is a very popular place, so it is advisable to book.

Culture

Useful Tips – The monthly magazine *Vorschau...* (followed by the month) lists the main events in Hamburg and is available free of charge from the 1st of each month in the tourist information offices, at the central station and at the Landungsbrücken (in St Pauli).

Shopping

Useful Tips – Jungfernstieg, Mönckebergstraße and Spitalerstraße are the main shopping streets with department stores. The many shopping arcades in Hamburg's inner city are especially attractive for shopping, with over 300 speciality stores and boutiques. Exclusive stores have now settled at the Neuer Wall.

Harry's Hamburger Hafenbasar – *Balduinstraße 18 (in St Pauli, at the Erichstraße crossroads) – ☎ (040) 31 24 82 – www.hafenbasar.de – Tue-Sun 12pm-6pm – Closed 2-3 weeks in Jul-Aug – Admission €2.50 (refunded if you make a purchase).* A great jumble of objects brought back by sailors from the four corners of the world; it is more like a museum of ethnology than a shop. You will find mainly wooden sculptures in the labyrinth of little corridors which fill the two floors of this house. Everything is for sale, except the stuffed animals.

Art galleries – In the inner city and various city districts; there is no area with an especially high concentration of galleries.

Antique dealers – Mainly in the *Quartier Satin* on ABC-Straße and the *Antik-Center* of the market hall at Klosterwall.

Flea markets – The *Menschen & Märkte* brochure has all the information on the more spontaneous flea markets in Hamburg (and all across northern Germany). Regular flea markets are held on Saturdays in Barmbek (Hellbrockstraße) 7am-5pm, and in Eppendorf (Nedderfeld/Parkhaus) 4.30pm-7.30pm.

Markets – The fish market is Hamburg's most famous market, held every Sun, in summer from 5.30am-9.30am and in winter from 7am-10am. Weekly markets are held in all of the city's districts. The very typical market held on Mon and Fri under the U-Bahn bridge at Eppendorf is highly recommendable.

of the later 19C. By 1913, the Hamburg-Amerika steamship line was the largest in the world, and shipbuilding was the city's key industry. Today, port traffic in Hamburg has reached an annual turnover of 57 million tons.

Business and Leisure – Like many big ports, Hamburg has a reputation for night-life. This is mainly centred on the St Pauli quarter, to the west of the city centre, where in the side streets flanking the **Reeperbahn** and the Große Freiheit, in the gaudy illumination of multicoloured neon signs, bars, discotheques, exotic restaurants, clubs and the Eros Centre function day and night.

Many Hamburg residents are a little diffident about the fact that their city is known worldwide for the garish Reeperbahn district. They point to the elegance and attraction of the residential area around the northern end, and the business quarter around the southern part, and of Lake Alster which lies like a jewel in the heart of the city.

Between the Staatsoper (Opera House) and the Rathaus (town hall), pedestrian precincts and covered shopping centres form an almost uninterrupted labyrinth of art galleries, fashion boutiques and restaurants. The Mönckebergstraße, which links the Rathaus with the railway station, is the city's other commercial artery.

Antique shops around the Gänsemarkt specialise in oriental art. Between the Rathaus and the station, an impressive variety of old maps, prints, travel works and tourist guides can be found in a number of different booksellers', while philatelists and tobacco lovers will go to the small shops in the printing and counting house quarter.

The people of Hamburg are said to be very "British" Germans, as they tend to be more reserved and serious than their lively southern compatriots. For visitors, Hamburg is among the most welcoming of German cities, and English is spoken in many of the restaurants, stores and wine cellars.

Culinary Specialities – These often mix local produce with Eastern spices, sometimes combining in one dish meat, fruit and sweet-and-sour sauces. Typical are Aalsuppe – eel soup – and Labskaus, a seamen's dish of minced meat, herring, chopped gherkins, beetroot and mashed potato, topped with fried eggs.

Special Features

THE PORT★★

Exploring the port of Hamburg will be one of the highlights of any trip to the city. Apart from the tower of St-Michaelis-Kirche, the best **viewpoint★** from which to see the port as a whole is the Stintfang – a raised terrace below the youth hostel (U/S-Bahn St-Pauli Landungsbrücken).

The Port of Hamburg - A Few Statistics

The Hamburg docks comprise 60 basins and more than 68km/43mi of quays. The overall surface area is more than 75km²/29mi² Thanks to a relatively small tidefall (3m/10ft average), no locks are necessary in the basins accessible to ocean-going traffic able to navigate the Elbe (displacing up to 110 000t and drawing no more than 13.5m/44ft). Some 340 shipping lines call regularly (about 650 departures a month) to transport merchandise to 1 100 all over the world.

Boat Trip Around the Port

Duration: 1hr. Boats leave from the landing stage near the Baumwall U-bahn station. Apr-Oct: 10am-6pm, every 30min; Nov-Mar: at 12pm and 2pm; Sat-Sun: 10.45am-4pm, every 45min. €8.50. ☎ (040) 37 31 68; www.barkassen-centrale.de

Visitors will be astonished by the sheer size of the dockyards and by the extraordinary activity on either side of the Elbe, where every type of vescel is constructed. Motor ferries ply back and forth all day long, transporting south bank workers back to the city during the rush hour. The very lively St Pauli Fischmarkt is held every Sun morning, and on public holidays, until 10am.

Adenauerallee	HY 2	Börsenbrücke	GZ 18	Große Bleichen	FY 33
Alsterarkaden	GY 3	Colonnaden	FY	Große Johannisstr	GZ 34
Bei dem Neuen Krahn	FZ 9	Cremon	FZ 21	Großer Burstah	FZ 35
Bei den St-Pauli-Landungsbrücken	EZ 10	Dammtordamm	FX 23	Große Reichenstr	GZ 37
Bergstraße	GY	Dammtorstraße	FY	Hachmannplatz	HY 39
Böhmkenstraße	EZ 16	Gerhofstraße	FY 29	Helgoländer Allee	EZ 43
		Graskeller	FZ 31	Holstenglacis	EY 46

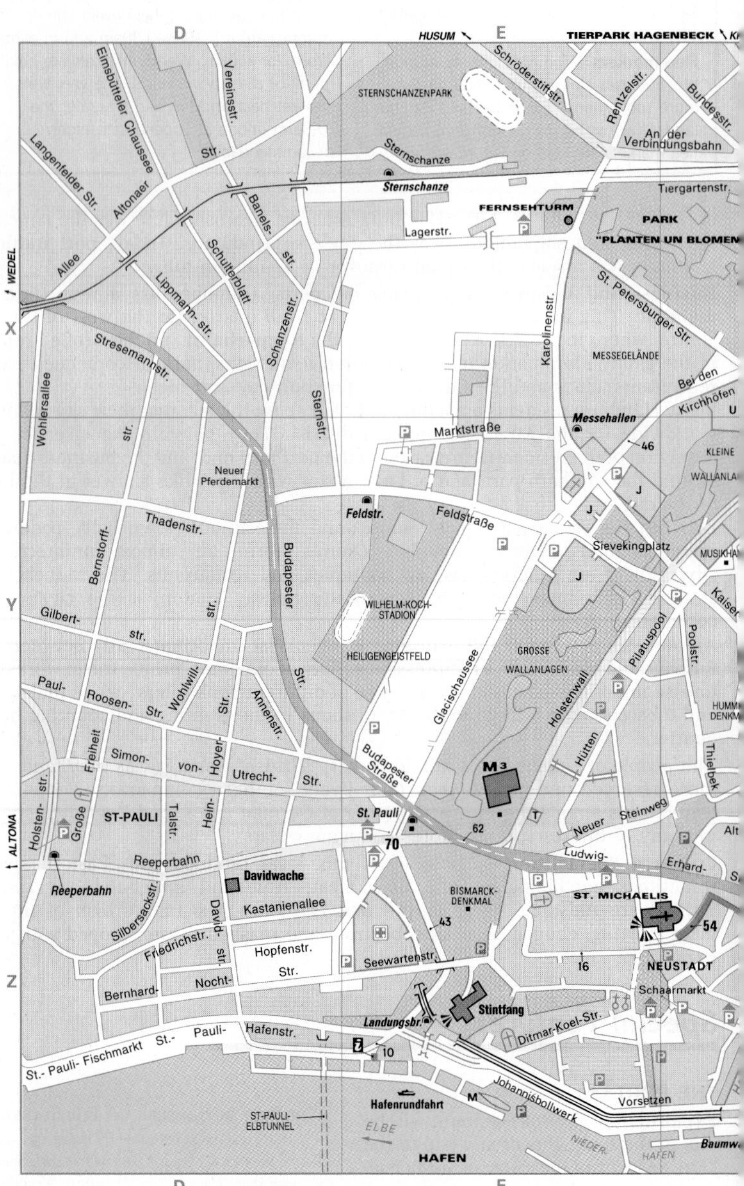

Hamburger Kunsthalle .... HY M¹	Museum für Hamburgische Geschichte .... EYZ M³	Museum für Kunst und Gewerbe .... HY M²

St Pauli District

North of the port and west of the new town. St Pauli had its golden age in the 1960s when the Beatles played the Star Club in **Große Freiheit**. Its image was later considerably tarnished by prostitution and drug trafficking, but over the last few years, this district – which has the city's biggest police station **(Davidwache)** – has undergone a renaissance. Although the sex industry is still prevalent here, the area is now full of bars, cafés and restaurants, many with a genuinely warm atmosphere, making them popular with locals and non-locals alike. St Pauli spreads out around the **Reeperbahn**, the main thoroughfare, which runs parallel to the port.

Jungfernstieg .... GY
Kleine Reichenstraße .... GZ 50
Klingberg .... GZ 51
Krayenkamp .... FZ 54
Millerntordamm .... EZ 63
Mönckebergstraße .... GHY
Neuer Wall .... FYZ
Poststraße .... FY
Pumpen .... HZ 68
Rathausstraße .... GZ 69
Reeperbahn .... EZ 70
Reesendamm .... Gu 71
Rothenbaumchaussee .... FX 72
Schleusenbrücke .... GY 75
Schmiedestraße .... GZ 76
Spitalerstraße .... GHY
Stadthausbrücke .... HY 77
Steintordamm .... HY 79
Steintorplatz .... HY 80
Zippelhaus .... GZ 88

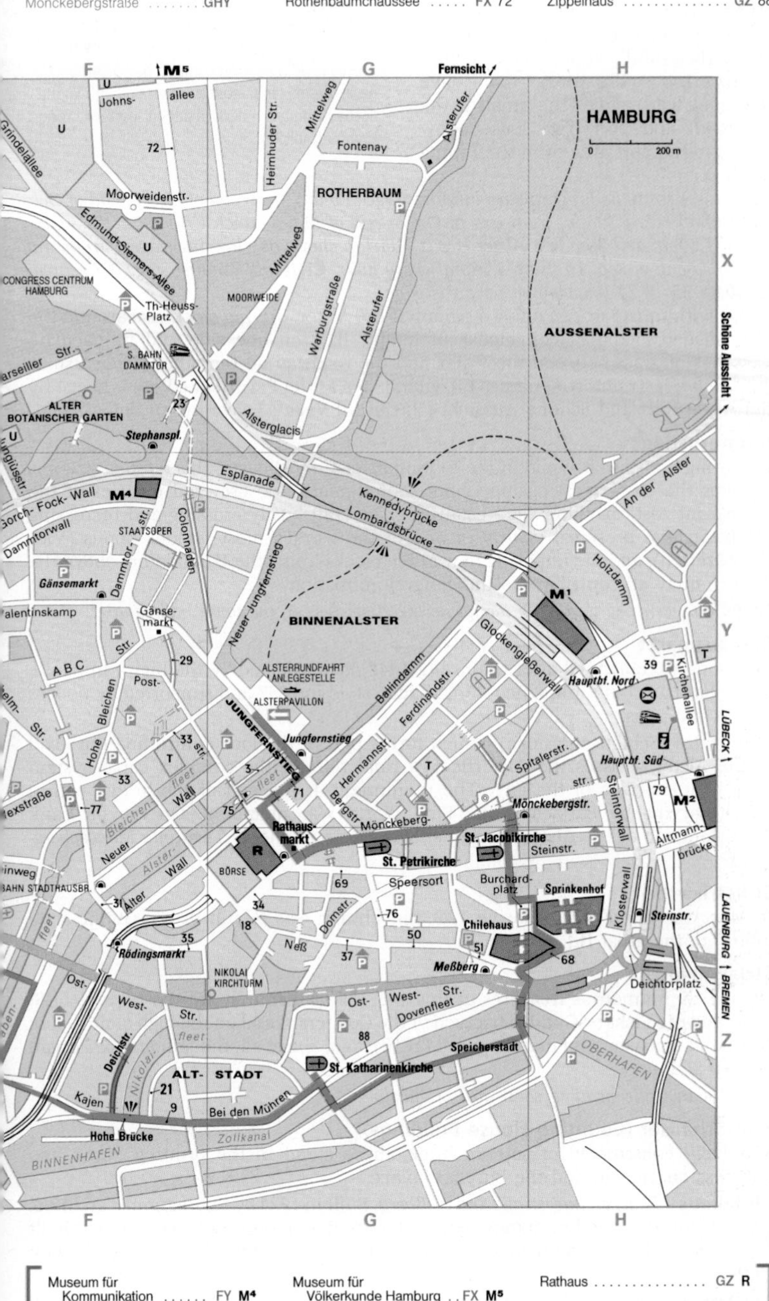

Museum für Kommunikation ...... FY M⁴
Museum für Völkerkunde Hamburg .. FX M⁵
Rathaus .... GZ R

Walking About

CITY CENTRE *allow one day*

Binnenalster and Aussenalster★★★

Lake Alster, north of the old town, is a beautiful stretch of water. It consists of two basins, the Binnenalster and the Aussenalster, the latter – the larger of the two – offering sailing and canoeing possibilities in the centre of the city. A fleet of Alsterschiffahrt motorboats ferries passengers regularly between a series of landing-stages. A boat trip (Alsterrundfahrt) on the lake allows the visitor to get far enough away to appreciate the city skyline punctuated by Hamburg's famous five towers, all of them over 100m/328ft high. They stand above the four main churches and the Rathaus. It is also possible to sail on the Alster canals (beautifully kept parks and villas interspersed with areas that have remained wild) and on the canals in the old town and port (two locks allow access to the port area from the Binnenalster).

The Fish Market

The Hamburg fish market originated in the early 18C and has become a veritable institution. It is held every Sunday morning in the south of the St Pauli district along the Elbe from 5.30am to 9.30am. The cheerful fishmongers, crowds of people of all ages who come to buy or simply to have a look, and musical entertainment in the *Fischauktionhalle*, have made it part of living Hamburg folklore.

Departures from the Jungfernstieg landing stage (50min), from end of Mar to end of Oct: 10am-6pm, every 30min; from end of Oct to end of Mar: "Punch Cruises" at 10.30am, 12pm, 1.30pm and 3pm. €9. Alster-Kreuz-Fahrt (a choice of 9 landing stages), from end of Mar to end of Sep: 10.15am-5.15pm, every hour. €1.10 per landing stage, €7 return. ☎ (040) 35 74 24 19; www.alstertouristik.de

Those with transport can enjoy a circuit of the Alster, driving clockwise around the long shaded avenues with blocks of luxury flats on one side and immaculate stretches of grass between the water and the roadway on the other. Their use as viewpoints has conferred names on such quays as the Fernsicht ("View". Leave by the Alsterufer) and Schöne Aussicht ("Beautiful Vista". Leave by An der Alster).

Jungfernstieg★

Bordering the southern end of the Binnenalster (inner) basin, this famous street is perhaps the city's most cosmopolitan thoroughfare: the crowded terraces of the waterfront Alsterpavillon café-restaurant, the craft busily crossing and recrossing the basin, the presence nearby of one of the world's most famous hotels (Vier Jahreszeiten), and the imposing new office blocks lining the Ballindamm above the eastern quay all contribute to the general animation.

Leave Jungfernstieg and walk alongside the Alsterfleet to the town hall square.

Rathausmarkt

This square, replanned after the fire of 1842, is dominated by the high campanile of the Rathaus, built in the neo-Renaissance style in 1897 and supported by no less than 4 000 piles.

The bridge (Schleusenbrücke), which forms part of the lock controlling the level of the Alster, crosses the Alsterfleet, a final relic of the complex canal system once characteristic of the city. The monument at the end of the bridge with a plinth carving by Barlach is the First World War memorial. On the far bank the colonnade of the Alsterarkaden shelters elegant shops. *Turn into Mönckebergstraße.*

St-Petrikirche

In Mönckebergstraße. Built in the 12C, this church was rebuilt in neo-Gothic style following the great fire of 1842.

St-Jakobikirche

Among the numerous treasures of this 14C-15C hall-church are the reredos of St Luke and the Fishers' Guild; a triptych of the Coopers' Guild on the high altar; Georg Bauman's alabaster and marble pulpit (1610); and, above all, the famous 1693 organ by Arp Schnitger.

Cross Steinstraße heading south to Burchardplatz.

Kontorhäuser (Counting House Buildings)

Massively constructed of sombre brick, these stand in the printing, press and business quarter around the Burchard-platz.

Chilehaus – *Between Burgstraße and Meßberg.* Built in 1924 by Expressionist architect Fritz Höger, this building stands against the sky like the prow of a ship. It was built for a rich local merchant who made his fortune mainly through trade relations with Chile.

The **Sprinkenhof** (1931) is a town within the town, an office complex complete with roadways that can be used by motor cars.

Continue southwards and cross the Auf dem Sande canal to explore Speicherstadt.

Speicherstadt★

After Hamburg – annexed to the Reich in 1871 – joined the German Customs Federation, a free trade zone became necessary. A whole district was destroyed along the Zoll Canal and its secondary channels to make room for the Speicherstadt warehouses in 1885. They still store in their 373 000m^2/447 000sq yd of floor space (the world's largest continuous warehouse complex) such valuable merchandise as coffee, tobacco, spices, raw silk and oriental carpets. With its rows of gabled brick buildings with green copper roofs, Speicherstadt is an original place for a pleasant stroll.

Hamburg Tourismus GmbH

Speicherstadt warehouses

Altstadt

The old town is bounded by the Nikolaifleet, the Binnenhafen (docks reserved for river craft and tugboats) and the Zoll Canal.

St-Katharinenkirche – This Gothic church built of brick during the 14C and 15C, features a bulbous openwork tower that rises above the narrow streets of the old port.

Cremon – From no 33 to no 36, this street is lined by warehouses and former lodging houses, each with dual entrances – one from the street, one from the canal.

Deichstraße – It was in this street that the great fire of 1842 started. The 17C and 18C merchants' houses have today been converted mainly into bars and taverns. The restored façades of warehouses opposite, lining the curve of the Nikolaifleet Canal, recall the Hamburg of yesteryear.

The best view is from the Hohe Brücke, which crosses the Nikolaifleet and lies parallel with the Binnenhafen. The high water marks from the severe floods of 1962 and 1976 are visible on the walls.

St-Michaelis-Kirche★

A brick church, designed in 1762 by Ernst Georg Sonnin, this is one of the finest examples of the Baroque tradition in northern Germany. The church is surprisingly spacious, well proportioned and well lit.

Its famous tower (1786), rising high above the Elbe with a lantern turret in the form of a pillared temple has become the emblem of the city. The **view★** from the platform takes in all the town centre, but most particularly the river, zebra-striped with the wake of ships, and its docks, basins, warehouses and wharves.

Near the east end of the church, pass through the porch at no 10 Am Krayenkamp. The blind alley beyond is lined with astonishing brick and timber houses built in 1670 as almshouses (Krameramtswohnungen) and today transformed into art galleries.

Worth a Visit

Hamburger Kunsthalle★★ (Fine Arts Museum)

♿ *Open every day except Mon, 10am-6pm, Thu 10am-9pm. Closed 24 Dec. €7.50.*
☎ *(040) 428 54 26 12; www.hamburger-kunsthalle.de*

This museum houses one of the largest art collections in Germany. The galleries have correspondingly been recently refitted and the paintings rehung to create a most attractive exhibition.

The exhibition opens with medieval works. The Grabow altarpiece created in 1379 for St Petri, Hamburg, by Master Bertram of Minden is one of the largest and most touching examples of primitive painting in north Germany.

The 17C Dutch School is represented by an early Rembrandt *(Simeon in the Temple)*, and by land- and sea-scapes by Avercamp, Van Goyen, Ruysdael and Van de Velde. Genre paintings by Jan Steen and Pieter de Hooch are also exhibited.

A particular strength of the exhibition is the section of 19C German painting. Prominently displayed are works by the Romantics Caspar David Friedrich *(Ice Field, Rambler above a Sea of Clouds)* and Philipp Otto Runge. The museum also possesses major works by Feuerbach, Von Marées and Böcklin. An entire room is devoted to Menzel. Realists whose works are on display include Wilhelm Leibl, whose famous painting *Three Women in Church* can be found hanging here. There is a dazzling display of work by Max Liebermann *(Women Repairing Nets)*, Lovis Corinth and Edvard Munch *(Madonna)*. The section on the Classical Modern artists is dominated by the works of Max Beckmann and Oskar Kokoschka, as well as the members of the *Brücke* and *Blaue Reiter* groups (Kirchner, Nolde, Marc). Paul Klee's enchanting painting *Goldfish* is also on display in this part of the museum.

In 1997, an extension was added to the art gallery in the form of a building by Oswald Mathias Ungers. The new Galerie der Gegenwart has doubled the amount of exhibition space the gallery can devote to post-1960 art. In keeping with the architect's usual style, squares are a basic element of the design of this building, without in the least becoming monotonous. The effect is particularly charming when seen from the central atrium. Contemporary art is well served in this gallery, not least because many of the artists have taken a hand in setting up the display (Richard Serra, Claes Oldenburg, Hanne Darboven, Jenny Holzer). There are works by many of the famous names of the last few decades (Bruce Naumann, Andy Warhol, Donald Judd, Richard Long). German art is also well represented (Sigmar Polke, Georg Baselitz, Markus Lüpertz, Mario Merz, Gerhard Richter, Rosemarie Trockel). A central room is devoted to the work of Joseph Beuys.

Museum für Kunst und Gewerbe★ (Museum of Decorative Arts)

Steintorplatz 1, opposite the central station. ♿ Open every day except Mon, 10am-6pm, Thu 10am-9pm. Closed 1st Jan, 1st May, 24 and 31 Dec. €7.20. ☎ (040) 428 54 27 32. In a 19C neo-Renaissance-style palace, this vast museum houses superb collections of sculptures, ceramics, furniture, jewellery, musical instruments etc. The exhibition covers periods from Antiquity to the present day and notably includes a remarkable Art Nouveau gallery and a Japanese tea house. Part of the museum is devoted to temporary exhibitions illustrating 20C design trends.

Museum für Hamburgische Geschichte★ (History Museum)

♿ Open every day except Mon, 10am-5pm, Sun 10am-6pm. Closed 1st Jan, 1st May, 24 and 31 Dec. €7.50. ☎ (040) 428 41 23 80. Here the visitor can browse over models of Hamburg in days gone by, a scale model of the city of yore, the harbour and shipping section (over 100 model ships and the impressive 1722 *Wappen von Hamburg*), and a model of the railway system. Other departments include one on clothing and fashion from several centuries and historic apartments with opulent furnishings.

Tierpark Hagenbeck★★ (Zoo)

Leave by the Grindelallee. ♿ Apr-Oct: 9am-5pm (later in good weather); Nov-Mar: 9am-4.30pm. €12.50. ☎ (040) 540 00 10. This wonderful park founded in 1907, with ancient trees, artificial lakes and crags, is a delightful place for a stroll and some communion with nature. Some 2 500 creatures of 360 species from five continents live in open corrals. Over the years, many rare fauna was successfully bred here. The zoo is especially proud of its Asian elephants and the excellent breeding results.

▶▶ Museum für Post und Kommunikation★ – Fernsehturm★ *(television tower: view★★)* – Erholungspark "Planten un Blomen"★ – Museum für Völkerkunde Hamburg★ *(ethnography: gallery of masks from the South Pacific★)*.

Excursions

Altona; Klein Flottbek; Wedel

22km/14mi – allow half a day.

Altonaer Museum in Hamburg und Norddeutsches Landesmuseum★★ (Altona and North German Museum) – *Leave on the Reeperbahn. ♿ Open every day except Mon, 10am-6pm. Closed 1st May, 24 and 31 Dec. €6. ☎ (040) 428 11 35 82.* Art, culture and day-to-day life in the lower Elbe valley and Schleswig-Holstein are illustrated here. Note the exceptional collection of ships' figureheads from the 18C-19C, the models explaining the different kinds of fishing and boats in the North Sea, the ceramics, fine Frisian embroidery and the amazing variety of old toys. The section for decorative arts displays skilfully made utility ware from the Late Renaissance until the Jugendstil period. There is a gallery with paintings of north German landscapes.

An authentic thatched cottage of the Vierlande region, southeast of Hamburg, houses a little restaurant. The 3rd floor is devoted to the history of Altona.

Altonaer Balkon (Altona Balcony) – From a terrace south of Altona's town hall, there is a **view★** of the Köhlbrandbrücke and confluence of the two branches of the Elbe which marks the limit of Hamburg's industrial and port zone. The amount of shipping which passes each hour is astonishing.

Follow the **Elbchaussee★**, a spacious avenue bordered by great houses and superb properties developed since the beginning of the 19C by the grand Hamburg shipowning and trading dynasties.

At Klein Flottbek, turn right and drive along the Baron-Voght-Straße as far as house no. 50.

Jenisch-Haus, in **Klein Flottbek** – *Open every day except Mon, 11am-6pm. Closed 1st May, 24 and 31 Dec. €4.50. ☎ (040) 82 87 90.* A fine landscaped park planted with exotic trees surrounds this pleasant neo-Classical villa built between 1831 and 1834. The luxuriously furnished rooms illustrate the style of German bourgeois interiors from the Late Renaissance to the beginning of the Jugendstil period. Note the splendid marquetry flooring, and the Danish-style furniture manufactured in Altona.

Altonaer Musuem in Hamburg – Norddeutsches Landesmuseum

"Terpsichore" ship's figurehead, Altona Musuem.

Ernst-Barlach-Haus, in **Klein Flottbek** – *Baron-Voght-Straße 50 A. Open every day except Mon, 11am-6pm. Closed 24 and 31 Dec. €4. ☎ (040) 82 60 85; www.barlach-haus.de.* Designed to house cigarette manufacturer Hermann F Reemtsma's private collection, the Ernst-Barlach-Haus contains sculptures, wood engravings and drawings (displayed in rotation) by this artist, born in Wedel. The display, presented in chronological order, includes some powerfully expressive works such as *The Frieze of Listeners*, wall sculptures in oak, *Moses*, and the group of *Three Men Brandishing a Sword*.

Continue along the Elbchaussee, then head for Wedel after driving through the pleasant suburban resort of Blankenese.

Wedel – *Follow the Willkomm-Höft signposts to the café-restaurant beside the Elbe known as the "Schulauer Fährhaus".* Above the terrace is a saluting base for passing ships *(Schiffsbegrüßungsanlage)*. The ceremony involves saluting the colours according to the maritime code, and playing the national anthem of the country represented by the passing ship.

There is an Ernst-Barlach-Museum in the house where the artist was born *(Mühlenstraße 1)* which displays drawings and lithographs as well as fine bronzes, among them the impressive *Old Men Dancing*. The works on display here are a particularly good illustration of the artist's interest in exploring literary motifs and his creative working out of his personal dramas. *Open every day except Mon, 10am-6pm. €5. ☎ (041 03) 91 82 91.*

Stade★

This town with over 1 000 years of history lies on the banks of the navigable stretch of the Schwinge, which flows into the Elbe to the northeast, In the Middle Ages, Stade was a port in the same league as Hamburg. The Swedes occupied the town during the Thirty Years' War and transformed it in the 70 years their troops were stationed here into a garrison stronghold and administrative centre, the capital of their north German territory.

Old Town★★ – Most buildings in the beautiful old town were built after 1659, the date of a great fire that destroyed two thirds of the town's houses. Among the picturesque half-timbered houses, each as fine as the next, note in particular Hökerhaus *(Hökerstraße 27)*, Doppelhaus *(Bäckerstraße 1-3)* and Haus Knechthausen *(Bungenstraße 20)*.

Old Port – An idea of how the port must have looked in the 17C is provided by the fine houses, meticulously restored, which stand on either side of the winding basin. The most magnificent of all is the **Bürgermeister-Hintze-Haus** *(Wasser West)*.

Schwedenspeicher-Museum★ – *Am Wasser West. Open every day except Mon, 10am-5pm, Sat-Sun 10am-6pm. Closed 1st Jan, 25 and 31 Dec. €1, free admission on Thu. ☎ (041 41) 32 22.* Built between 1692 and 1705, this Swedish brick granary now houses a museum illustrating the town's commercial history and its old system of defences. There is also a prehistoric department exhibiting four magnificent **bronze wheels★** (c 700 BC) from a funerary carriage, as well as antique jewellery, weapons and pots.

Hameln★

Hamelin

The town is the setting for the famous Tale of the Pied Piper of Hamelin, as told by the Brothers Grimm in the 19C. Hamelin glories in fine old houses, of which the most typical belong to the Weser Renaissance period, lending the town the air of a fairy tale.

Location

Population: 60 000. Michelin map nº 543 J 12 – Niedersachsen. Built on the banks of the Weser, Hamelin is located at the crossroads of roads 217 (Hannover-Paderborn) and 1 (Minden-Hildesheim). The town extends into the Weserbergland, a hilly expanse intersected by rivers, part of which forms a large nature park.

🅱 *Deisterallee 1, 31785 Hameln, ☎ (051 51) 20 26 17.*

Surrounding area: see LEMGO (41km/26mi southwest), HILDESHEIM (49km/30mi east), HANNOVER (45km/28mi northeast).

Background

A jewel of the Weser Renaissance – The style (late 16-early 17C) is distinguished architecturally by ram's-horn scrollwork and pinnacled gables. Other characteristics include delicately worked stone bands encircling the building, forward projecting pavilions *(Utluchten)*, and large, well-developed dormers *(Zwerchhäuser)* with decorated gables at the base of the roof.

The Pied Piper of Hamelin – In 1284, a mysterious man in multicoloured clothes promised the townspeople that, for a substantial reward, he would free Hamelin from a plague of rats and mice. He played his pipe, and all the rodents emerged to follow him to the banks of the Weser, where they drowned.

But the reward was not forthcoming, so the piper returned on Sunday, when everyone was at church, and played again in revenge. This time it was the children who emerged from their houses. There were 130 of them, and they too followed him, never to be seen again. Only two escaped; one was dumb, the other blind.

The rather less romantic but historically more accurate version of the tale is that overpopulation in the 13C led to a troop of young people being sent by the authorities to colonise territories to the east.

In summer this folktale is acted out every Sunday at midday on the terrace of the Hochzeitshaus.

Walking About

ALTSTADT★ (OLD TOWN)

Rattenfängerhaus★ (The Rat-catcher's House)

It is a large, well-proportioned building dating from 1603. The symmetrical decoration of the façade involves differently sculpted bands of stonework, further adorned with carved busts and masks. Typical Weser Renaissance scrolls and pinnacles enrich the gable.

Directory

WHERE TO EAT

⊜ **Grüner Reiter** – *Kastanienwall 62 – ☎ (05151) 92 62 00 – www.gruenerreiter.de – Mon-Fri. 9.30am-6pm, Sat 9.30am-4pm – ♿ – €15/19.50.* This building was built in 1713 as a chapel for the soldiers of the Hamelin Fortress. A bistro-style restaurant has been sited in a glass extension located in the courtyard.

WHERE TO STAY

⊜ **An der Altstadt** – *Deisterallee 16 – ☎ (05151) 402 40 – fax (05151) 402444 – info@hotel-an-der-altstadt.de – Closed end Dec to mid-Jan – 🅿 ⚞ – 19rm: €50/95 ☕.* This *Jugendstil* hotel in the heart of the legendary "rat catcher's town" has guestrooms furnished in cherrywood.

TAKING A BREAK

Museumscafé – *Osterstraße 8 – ☎ (05151) 215 53 – www.museumscafe.de – Closed Noël and 1 Jan.* The Museumscafé of the Canons' House *(Stiftsherrenhaus)* built in 1562 has without doubt one of the most beautiful half-timbered frontages in the town. Delicious cakes and tarts are on the menu, as are substantial meals. Try the rat catcher's tart *(Rattenfängertorte)*!

Take the Osterstraße, one of the most well-known streets in Hamelin. It is here on 26 July 1284, that the children followed the pipe player... Stop at the top of the Kleine Strasse to look at the splendid Renaissance houses (Haus Osterstrasse 12, Leithaus and Stiftherrenhaus).

Stiftsherrenhaus (Canons' House)

Osterstraße 8. Another remarkable house, this one half-timbered and built in 1558. The sculpted consoles represent biblical figures. This and the Leisthaus next door house the local museum.

Französischen Straße bears testament to the French Huguenots who found refuge in Hamelin at the end of the 17C.

Demptersches Haus

In the market place. An outstanding building, dating from 1607, is noteworthy especially for its fine Weser Renaissance projecting pavilion *(Utlucht)*. The ground and first floors are made of sandstone; the upper floor is half-timbered.

Hochzeitshaus★

On the Markt. The building, constructed between 1610 and 1617, acted as a reception centre for burghers' weddings. Three elegant gables break the horizontals of the façade, themselves emphasised by cornices and lateral bands of stonework.

Take the Fischpfortenstraße and pass in front of Wilhelm-Busch-Haus. From there, continue straight on until you reach the Weser. Retrace your steps until you reach the Wendenstraße where the Burgerhus and the Lückingsches Haus are to be found.

Haus Lücking

Wendenstraße 8. This rich, half-timbered house of 1638 features a rounded doorway and is lavishly adorned with inscriptions and ornamentation.

At the end of the road, turn right into Bäckerstraße.

Rattenkrug

Bäckerstraße 16. A projecting pavilion (Utlucht) and a tall gable of no less than five floors distinguish this 1568 building. Essentially this is an early Gothic building dating from 1250.

Continue until the Münsterkirchhof.

Münsterkirchhof (Collegiate Church)

From the public gardens to the south, the church appears to cower beneath the protection of the massive polygonal tower over the transept – once part of a 12C Romanesque basilica which was transformed a century later into the existing Gothic hall-church. Inside, the layout of the columns and their capitals, checkered or carved with palm leaves, draws attention once more to the raised transept.

Finish the tour by coming back along Alte Markt-Straße, noticing the Kürie Jérusalem passageway.

Excursions

Fischbeck

7km/4mi northwest. The abbey here was officially recognised by Otto I in the year 955 (photocopies of the original documents can be seen in the church). It is now used as a home for elderly Protestant women. ♿ *Open from Easter to end Oct: Guided tour (1hr) Tue and Fri, 9.30-11am, 2-4pm, Wed, Thu, Sat and Sun, 2-4pm. €2.50. ☎ (051 52) 86 03.*

The church itself dates from the 12C. It was equipped in the 19C with partitioned boxes, which allowed the noblewomen to take part in the services.

The crypt is in a pure Romanesque style, with each column topped by a capital embellished with a different motif. Left of the chancel is a moving Ecce Homo in sculpted wood; to the right of it hangs the famous 16C **Fischbeck tapestry** illustrating the foundation of the abbey. The figure of Lady Helmburgis, the founder, dating from the 13C, stands above the entrance to the sacristy.

Hämelschenburg★

11km/7mi south. The **Schloß★**, which boasts both a moat and a lagoon, was built in the shape of a horse-shoe between 1588 and 1616. The wing overlooking the road is the most ornate, with typical alternations of smooth and embossed stone bands, an oriel immediately above the moat, and four decorative gables. Weapons, 18C paintings and furniture (Renaissance, Baroque and Biedermeier) are on view in the interior. ♿ *From Apr to end Oct: Guided tour (45min) Tue-Sun, at 10am, 11am, 12 noon, 2pm, 3pm, 4pm and 5pm. €5. ☎ (051 55) 95 16 90.*

Hannover

Hannover, capital of Lower Saxony, is one of the main economic centres of northern Germany; it is also at the forefront of national politics. The industrial fair and the CeBIT information technology exhibition stimulate an enormous amount of business each year. EXPO 2000 and the additional infrastructure have given the city even greater power of attraction. Hannover also offers plenty of opportunities for a walk: its large waterways (Maschsee), the city forest and the 17C Herrenhausen gardens are all in the heart of the city.

Location

Population: 530 000. Michelin maps 541, 542, 544 I 13 – Niedersachsen. Standing on a plain on the banks of the Leine and the Mittelandkanal, Hannover is halfway between the Baltic Sea and the North Sea. The city is at the intersection of the A2 (Dortmund-Berlin) and A7 (Kassel-Hamburg) motorways.

Ernst-August-Platz 2, 30159 Hannover, ☏ (0511) 16 84 97 00. Open Mon-Fri 9am-7pm and Sat 9.30am-3pm.

Surrounding area: see HILDESHEIM (33km/20.5mi south via the A7), CELLE (41km/25.5mi northeast), HAMELN (45km/28mi southwest), BRAUNSCHWEIG (63km/39mi east via the A2), BREMEN (129km/80mi northwest).

Background

The House of Hanover – When the principality of Hannover fell in the 17C to a branch of the House of Brunswick and Lüneburg, the Court moved to Hannover. The transformation of Herrenhausen began, and the cultured Princess Sophia frequently summoned the composer Händel to give concerts. She also made the philosopher Gottfried Wilhelm Leibniz Court Librarian, a post he held for 40 years. In 1692 the principality became the Electorate of Brunswick and Lüneburg.

Directory

Where to Eat

⊖ **Der Gartensaal** – *Trammplatz 2 – ☏ (0511) 16 84 88 88 – www.gartensaal-hannover.de – Open 11am-6pm, from mid May to mid Sep: 11am-10pm – ♿ – €13.20/26.30.* This bistro-style restaurant is in an unusual location, in the southern entrance hall of the historic town hall. Semicircular arched windows measuring almost the same height as the room offer superb views of a park and pond. In summer you can also enjoy the terrace in front of the restaurant.

⊖⊖ **Broyhan-Haus** – *Kramerstraße 24 – ☏ (0511) 32 39 19 – www.broyhanhaus.de – Closed on public holidays – Reservation necessary – €24.50/35.50.* This building – one of the city's oldest bourgeois houses – was built during the second half of the 14C. It was bought in 1537 by master brewer Cord Broyhan. The Urbock beer bars and cellars inside are spread over three floors.

Where to Stay

⊖⊖ **CVJM City Hotel** – *Limburgstraße 3 – ☏ (0511) 360 70 – Fax (0511) 3607177 – cityhotelh@aol.com – – 47rm: €72.* A pleasant, impeccably run hotel in the pedestrian zone of this trade fair city. Comfortably furnished rooms and breakfast room, with a vaguely Mediterranean feel.

⊖⊖⊖ **Kastens Hotel Luisenhof** – *Luisenstraße 1 – ☏ (0511) 304 40 – Fax (0511) 3044807 – info@kastens-luisenhof.de – P – 152rm: from €139 – Restaurant €28.50/50.50.* Comfort reigns in this hotel, the oldest one in Hannover (1856). Elegant, personalised furnishings, and a "tower" suite with a superb view of the city.

Taking a Break

Holländische Kakao-Stube – *Ständehausstraße 2-3 (street that prolongs Luisenstraße to the southwest) – ☏ (0511) 30 41 00 – Open Mon-Fri 9am-7.30pm, Sat 8.30am-6pm – Closed Sun and public holidays.* If you like hot chocolate you will love this famous establishment decorated with beautiful Dutch ceramics. In addition to a vast selection of hot chocolate – all equally delicious – you will find home-made pastries and confectionery, other drinks and dishes on the menu.

Going Out

heimW – *Theaterstraße 6 – ☏ (0511) 2 35 23 03 – www.heim-w.de – Fri-Sat 9am-2am, Mon-Thu 9am-1am, Sun 10am-1am.* 1970s-style café-bar with a laid-back atmosphere. Even if you are not prone to nostalgia (*Heimweh* in German), the family welcome and refined, seasonal dishes make it worth a visit. The back room with its aquarium looks somewhat like an old sitting room.

Oscar's – *Georgstraße 54 – ☏ (0511) 32 04 08 – www.oscarsbar.de – Sun-Thu 4pm-1am, Fri-Sat 4pm-3am.* Traditional cocktail bar with dark wooden decor. In summer, make the most of the pavement terrace and sample one of the 200 whiskies or other drinks (with or without alcohol) on the menu. An ideal place to stop after exploring the city. Happy hour from 4-8pm.

From the Hanoverian Court to the Court of St James – The marriage in 1658 of the Duke Ernst-Augustus with the Palatine Princess Sophia, granddaughter of the Stuart King James I, had given the Hanoverian succession a claim on the throne of England. So it was that in 1714 the Elector Georg-Ludwig, son of Princess Sophia, did indeed find himself heir to the crown and became George I of England. He still remained Elector of the Electorate of Hannover. George III, who had been King of England since 1760, did not manage to become King of Hannover in his turn (Hannover became a kingdom after the Vienna Congress) until 1814.
The union of Hannover and England ended in 1837, because the Salic Law (forbidding the accession of women to the throne) applied in Hannover. Victoria therefore became Queen of England, while in Hannover it was her uncle Ernst-Augustus who succeeded. Installing his court in Hannover, the new monarch set about restoring the town to its former glory. But the year 1866 saw the fall of the House of Hanover and the annexation of the kingdom by Prussia.

Worth a Visit

Herrenhäuser Gärten★★ (Herrenhausen Gardens) *Allow 1hr 30min*
Leave by the Leibnizufer. This beautiful 17C development, in the northwestern part of the city, comprises four separate and quite different gardens. They are linked by an avenue of lime trees, the Herrenhäuser Allee, laid out in 1726 *(drivers take the Nienburger Straße).*

Over a distance of around 4km/3mi, the "Red Line" leads you through the city from the new town hall (interesting view from the dome), where you can admire models of Hannover in different periods, to the Herrenhausen gardens. ♿ *Open from the end of Mar to the beginning of Nov: 9.30am-6.30pm, Sat-Sun 10am-6.30pm; all other days 11am-4pm. €3. ☎ (0511) 12 34 51 11.*

Großer Garten★★ – Creation of the garden started in 1666. Between 1680 and 1710 Princess Sophia took it over, transformed it, and enlarged it. The oldest part is a formal French pleasure garden divided into flower borders punctuated by statues of allegorical figures and Roman gods. On one side is an open-air theatre, on the other a maze. The paths in the southern part spread out around water features.

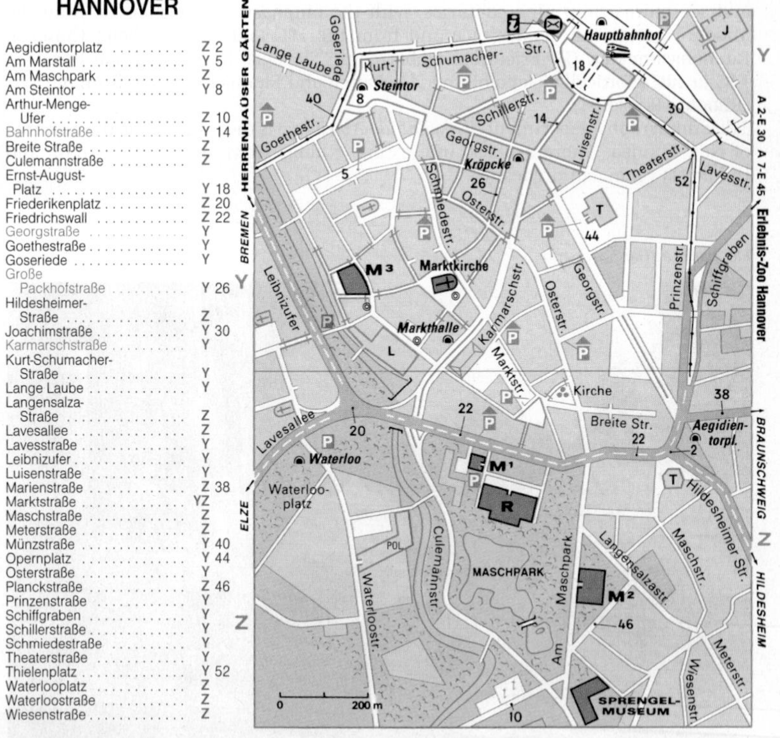

Historisches Museum Hannover Y M³
Kestner-Museum Z M¹
Niedersächsisches Landesmuseum Z M²
Rathaus Z R

Georgengarten – ♿ *Apr-Oct: open every day except Mon, 11am-5pm, Sun 11am-6pm; Nov-Mar: open every day except Mon, 11am-4pm, Sun 11am-6pm. Closed Good Friday, 24 and 31 Dec. €4.50. ☎ (0511) 16 99 99 11.* This romantically landscaped park was laid out between 1835 and 1841 with great expanses of lawn. In its midst is the Leibniztempel and the Wallmodenschlößchen, a pavilion in which you find the small **Wilhelm-Busch-Museum**. It is dedicated to the work of the famous poet, illustrator and humorist (1832-1908), who is immortalised in his illustrated stories such as "Max und Moritz", the forerunners of today's comic strips.

Berggarten★ – The greenhouses of this botanical garden display cactus plants and other succulents, as well as 2 500 varieties of orchid and flora native to the Canary Islands. At the far end of the garden's principal walk is the mausoleum of the Royal House of Hanover.

Welfengarten – The Welfenschloß, today the university, stands in the Welfengaten. In front of the building is the trademark of the state of Niedersachsen, the Saxon Steed, created in 1876 by Friedrich Wolff.

Marktkirche

A four-gabled tower crowned by a sharp pinnacle presides over this Gothic brick church, rebuilt after 1945 in the style of the 14C original. An interesting contrast to the restored Gothic style are the modern (1957) bronze doors by Gerhard Marcks, depicting scenes from recent German history. Inside, note the superb 15C sculpted polychrome **reredos★★**, which represents the Passion. Also noteworthy are the stained-glass windows (14C) and the 15C baptismal font in bronze.

Niedersächsisches Landesmuseum★ (Museum of Lower Saxony)

♿ *Open every day except Mon, 10am-5pm, Thu 10am-7pm. Closed Easter Sunday, Tue after Easter, 1st May, Pentecost, Tue after Pentecost, 24, 25 and 31 Dec. €3. ☎ (0511) 980 75.*

The museum is divided into four departments:

The **prehistoric department★** *(Urgeschichte-Abteilung)*exhibits some significant original artefacts from the prehistory and early history of Lower Saxony, including a well-preserved prehistoric corpse.

The **nature department** *(Naturkunde-Abteilung)* concentrates on the Lower Saxony countryside, but also explains the process of earth's history and how oceans and continents were formed. The exhibition is brought to life by the presence of an aquarium.

The Lower Saxony picture gallery *(Niedersächsische Landesgalerie)* exhibits paintings and sculptures from nine centuries, with the emphasis on German art from the Middle Ages to the Renaissance and from the 19C and 20C (Holbein, Cranach, Riemenschneider, CD Friedrich, Liebermann, Slevogt), Italian painting from the 14C to 18C (Botticelli, Tiepolo) and also Dutch and Flemish painting from the 17C (Rubens, Ruysdael).

The ethnography department *(Völkerkunde-Abteilung)* is thematic, using the example of New Guinea. There are also interesting exhibits from Mexico, Cameroon and Indonesia (gamelan orchestra).

Elephants at Hannover zoo

Zoologischer Garten

Sprengel-Museum Hannover★

♿ *Open every day except Mon, 10am-6pm, Tue 10am-8pm. Closed Good Friday, 1st May, 24 and 25 Dec. €6. ☎ (0511) 16 84 38 75.*

A stabile by Calder, the *Hellebardier*, standing by the Maschsee, serves as a landmark for this museum of 20C art. Cubist works include Picasso's *Three Women* (1908). Some of the main works by artists of the Brücke (Karl Schmidt-Rottluff's *Four Bathers on the Beach*) and the Blaue Reiter (Kandinsky, Jawlensky, Macke's *Nude With Coral Necklace*, Marc's *Horse with Eagle*) movements are on display. Note also several portraits by Max Beckmann *(Woman with a Bouquet of Carnations)*. Surrealism is represented above all by Kurt Schwitters, Hanoverian by birth and the author of many different kinds of work *(Merz-Bau)*. Contemporary tendencies have their spokesmen in Tapiès, Dubuffet and Willi Baumeister.

Zoologischer Garten (Zoological Garden)

Adenauerallee 3. Leave by the Schiffgraben. ♿ *Open Apr-Oct: 9am-7pm; Nov-Mar: 9am-sunset. €14.50. ☎ (0511) 28 07 41 63.*

The zoo has been steering an innovative course in recent times by creating new installations with an eye to the world of experience: the gorilla mountain with its waterfall and natural-looking landscaping; the "evolution path" that traces the Neanderthal; a 12 000m²/120 000sq ft jungle palace for elephants, tigers, leopards and tiger pythons; a Zambezi landscape with lions, giraffes and okapis; the African steppes for zebras, gazelles, antelopes and ostriches; and last but not least, the restored half-timbered barn for poultry and hogs.

▶▶ Kestner-Museum★ *(art of Antiquity, decorative arts, coins and medals)* – Historisches Museum Hannover★.

Harz★★

The wooded heights of the Harz are a popular weekend destination for Germans from the surrounding area. Hiking, mountain biking, canoeing, skiing and rock-climbing are among the many activities on offer.

Location

Michelin map n° 544 K 15, 16 – Niedersachsen and Sachsen-Anhalt. The Harz stands at the southern extremity of the vast Germano-Polish plain, between the rivers Elbe and Weisser extending over 100km/62mi.

Surrounding area (distances from Goslar): see WOLFENBÜTTEL (36km/22mi north), HILDESHEIM (51km/32mi northwest), BRUNSWICK (46km/29mi north), MAGDEBURG (109km/68mi northeast).

Background

Natural environment – The wooded heights of the Harz form the northern foothills of those mountains of central Europe resulting from the Hercynian upthrust in the Primary Era. Almost entirely covered in forests, they break the moisture-laden winds sweeping across from the west to create a hilly region plentifully supplied with watercourses. Numerous dams have transformed the Harz into an exceptional reservoir supplying the nearby areas. The Harz was very rich in mineral ressources and zinc, copper, lead and silver have all been mined here. These mines no longer function but several museums tell the history of mining in the area.

Directory

WHERE TO STAY

⊖ Hotel Zum Brockenbäcker – *Lindenwarte 20, 38875 Tanne – ☎ (039457) 97 60 – fax (039457) 97633 – www.brockenbaecker.de –Closed for a week in Nov – P ⋟ – 16rm: €39/68 ☕.* This establishment is typical of the Harz region and opened as a hotel in 1912. Rustic guestrooms, with hot crusty bread available from the oven at breakfast time.

⊖⊖ Michels Kurhotel Vier Jahreszeiten – *Herzog-Julius-Straße 64b, 38667 Bad Harzburg – ☎ (05322) 78 70 – fax (05322) 787200 – kurhotelvierjahres zeiten@michelshotels.de – P ⛱ ⋟ – 74rm: €75/159 ☕ – Restaurant €21.50/ 35.50.* This establishment's recent renovation has brought this former spa establishment right up to date. Historic architecture and a modern interior are brought together harmoniously. The restaurant is furnished in the style of an elegant tearoom.

A place of legend – The highest point of the range, the **Brocken** (alt 1 142m/3 747ft), attracts a great number of walkers to its windswept slopes. At the summit, according to legend, witches meet on the first night of May *(Walpurgisnacht)* for the Witches' Sabbath, a scene made famous in a chapter of Goethe's *Faust*. The shops of the Harz stock souvenirs relating to the *Walpurgis* legend.

THE HARZQUERBAHN

The Harzquerbahn, a narrow-gauge railway with steam locomotives, penetrates the region from north to south, from Wernigerode to Nordhausen. This provides an excellent way of exploring the heart of the eastern Harz, especially between Wernigerode and the resort of Eisfelder Talmühle, but also from Schierke to the Brocken.

Tour

THE UPPER HARZ 1

81km/50mi – allow half a day

This itinerary follows an admirable road network, passing through vast tracts of rolling country with rounded hills covered in conifers.

Goslar★★ *See GOSLAR.*

Clausthal-Zellerfeld

This is the former mining capital of the Harz. At Zellerfeld, there is the **Upper Harz Mine Museum** *(Oberharzer Bergwerksmuseum)* that illustrates mining techniques until 1930 and documents the technical and cultural history of the region. *9am-5pm. Closed 24 Dec. €4. ☎ (053 23) 989 50.*

At Clausthal, in the *Hindenburgplatz*, the **Pfarrkirche zum Heiligen Geist**, built before 1642, is one of the largest wooden churches in the whole of Europe. Note the majestic positioning of the galleries and the light falling obliquely from windows placed just below the panelled vaulting.

Okertalsperre (Oker Dam)

From the top of the barrage there is a fine **view★** over the widely dispersed waters of the reservoir.

St. Andreasberg

The road leads first to an **old silver mine★** *(Silberbergwerk Samson)* at the bottom of the valley. This was closed in 1910 but has been reopened for tourists.

The *Fahrkunst*, a machine of ingenious simplicity which sent down and brought back the miners, can be seen at work. *Guided tour (75min) 8.30am-4.30pm. Closed 1 Jan and 24 Dec. €4.50. ☎ (055 82) 12 49.*

A museum contains a collection of geological exhibits with Andreasberg calcite and numerous minerals.

Braunlage

Station on the Brocken railway. An important spa resort for its climate and for skiing lies high up on a plateau overlooked by the wooded slopes of the **Wurmberg** (971m/3 186ft).

Harz countryside.

J. Bouraly/MICHELIN

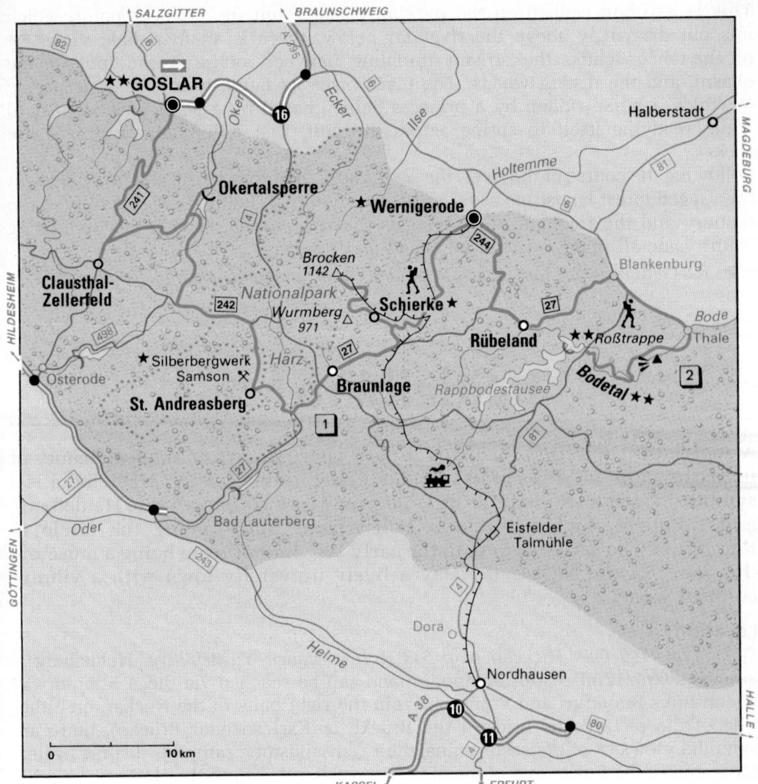

Schierke
Station on the Brocken railway. A magnificent site here: a holiday centre from which many footpaths and ramblers' routes start – most of them leading towards the summit of the **Brocken**.

Wernigerode★
Wernigerode is one of the most delightful small towns in this region. The 16C **Town Hall★★** *(on the Markplatz)* is considered to be one of the finest half-timbered buildings in Germany. The town's narrow streets are bordered by old, **half-timbered houses★★**. The most picturesque group is on the Breite Straße, as it leaves Marktplatz – several rows of town houses built by the rich burghers of Wernigerode in the 16C, 17C and 18C. The wooden sections and joists are often decorated with masks or carved patterns – as for instance on the 1674 house at no 72 known as the "Krummelsches Haus".

THE EASTERN HARZ 2

89km/55mi – allow half a day. In this part of the Harz, the forests have a greater proportion of deciduous trees. Even if it is on a smaller scale, the landscape is at times more spectacular.

Wernigerode★ *(see above)*

Rübeland
In this area, where the chief activity is the exploitation of limestone, tourists enjoy exploring the many caves and grottoes formed by the erosion of the rock. In **Hermann's Grotto★** *(Hermannshöhle)*, note particularly the Chamber of Crystals and the small pool stocked with "cave fish" *(Grottenolmen)* – blind creatures, living out their whole lives in darkness. *Guided tour (45min), Jul to Aug, 9am-5.30pm; Feb to Oct, 9am-4.30pm; Nov to Jan, 9am-3.30pm. Closed 24 Dec. €5. ☎ (0394 54) 491 32.*

Continue via Blankenburg and Thale to reach the Bode Valley.

Bodetal★★
The river here has gouged a passage as best it could through a maze of rock masses and now flows along the foot of impressive cliffs. The most spectacular site, without doubt, is the **Roßtrappe★★** (The Charger's Hoofmark).

This is a 10min walk from the parking place. From the look-out point, which juts out dizzyingly above the river far below, there is an incredible **view★★★** of the sheer cliffs, the stream tumbling between crags at the foot of the chasm, and the distant woods. The place owes its name to a legend, according to which a horse ridden by a princess being chased by a giant pushed so hard while readying itself to spring across the gulf, that it left an imprint in the rock.

Following the course of the river, the scenic stretch of road twists and turns through the rugged forest landscape as far as the junction with Route 81. The beauty of the scenery and the frequent blind spots as the road winds through the undulating countryside all impose a reduced speed on drivers.

►► KZ-Gedenkstätte Mittelbau-Dora *(concentration camp north of Nordhausen)*

Heidelberg★★

A source of inspiration for many a poet, charmed by the natural beauty of its setting and the ruins of its castle clinging to the hillside, Heidelberg is a symbol of German Romanticism. Hölderlin wrote a famous ode to Heidelberg, and Brentano, Eichendorff and Von Arnim were among the circle of Romantics who gathered here in the early 19C. But far from being a museum, this jewel of the Neckar is today a lively university town with a vibrant cultural scene.

Location

Population: 140 000. Michelin map 543 R 10 – Baden-Württemberg. Heidelberg is around 20km/12mi east of Mannheim and can be reached via the A 5 motorway which links Frankfurt and Freiburg. From the right bank of the Neckar, on either side of the picturesque bridge (Alte Brücke or Karl-Theodor Brücke), there are splendid **views★★** of the castle ruins, their red sandstone ramparts distinct against the green of the forest, and of the old town clustered around the Heiliggeistkirche. Further superb views of the castle and the town can be seen from the Philosophenweg (Philosophers' Walk), reached by crossing the Alte Brücke and climbing the Schlangenweg steps.

ℹ Willy-Brandt-Platz 1 (central station), 69115 Heidelberg, ☎ (062 21) 194 33.

Surrounding area: see MANNHEIM (20km/12.5mi northwest via the A 656), SPEYER (27km/17mi southwest), BRUCHSAL (38km/24mi south), WORMS (50km/31mi northwest), Bad WIMPFEN (57km/36mi east).

Background

The Political Capital of the Palatinate – The Rhineland Palatinate, of which Heidelberg was the political centre, owes its name to the title "palatines" given to the highest officers in the Holy Roman Emqire who were in the sovereign's confidence. These functions and dignitaries no longer existed in the 14C, except in the hereditary family ruling a group of territories whose appropriate centre was the confluence of the Neckar with the Rhine. Through the wise government of these palatine-electors *(Kurfürsten)*, the Electoral Palatinate *(Kurpfalz)* became one of the most advanced states of Europe.

The "Orléans War" (1688-97) – In the 16C, the electors, who had become Protestant, were continually reinforcing and embellishing their castle at Heidelberg. The Elector Karl-Ludwig restored his estates in an exemplary manner after the Thirty Years' War.

In the hope of ensuring peace in the Rhineland and extending the influence of his house he married his daughter **Liselotte** (Elisabeth-Charlotte) to Duke Philip of Orléans, brother of Louis XIV. The Palatine Princess did not pass unnoticed at the Court of France. Saint-Simon in his *Memoirs* returns frequently to her loud voice, her endless chatter and her intractable dislike of Mme de Maintenon.

When the son of Karl-Ludwig died without an heir in 1685, the marriage alliance, which was invoked by Louis XIV to assert his claim to the territories on the left bank of the Rhine, proved disastrous to the palatinate and to Heidelberg. The town was laid waste and the castle sacked in the brutal campaign of 1689. Total disaster followed in 1693, when the town was completely destroyed by fire. This catastrophe led to the rebuilding of the town in an uninspired Baroque style on the same foundations and with no thoroughfares. Before long the electors abandoned the ruined castle, turning their attention to their residences at Mannheim and Schwetzingen. Today it's precisely that ruin that makes Heidelberg so attractive.

Directory

Where to Eat

⊖ Kulturbrauerei Heidelberg – *Leyergasse 6 (between Hauptstraße and Am Hachteufel) – ☎ (06221) 50 29 80 – www.heidelberger-kulturbrauerei.de – 11am-1am (food served until 11pm, beer garden until 10pm) – ⊭ ♿ – €18/30 – 20rm: €90/135.* This restaurant, renovated in 2000, has kept its old-style charm, with central columns, old coffered ceiling and cast iron chandeliers. Beer brewed on the premises and regional specialities served here. Spacious well-equipped rooms in the hotel next door (lovely view of the castle from the suite).

⊖⊖⊖ Schlossweinstube – *(in Heidelberg castle) – ☎ (06221) 979 70 – schoenmehl@t-online.de – Closed 23 Dec-15 Jan and Wed – €41.50/57.* Modern black chairs provide a charming contrast with the princely setting; wooden flooring and precious paintings.

Where to Stay

⊖ Hotel-Restaurant Schnookeloch – *Haspelgasse 8 – ☎ (06221) 13 80 80 – Fax (06221) 1380813 – www.schnooke loch.de – Reservation necessary – 11rm: €50/120 ☕ – restaurant €12.50/35.* The Schnookeloch's history is intertwined with the history of this old university town, the restaurant being the traditional student bistro. Some smart, well-equipped rooms upstairs.

⊖⊖ Hotel Backmulde – *Schiffgasse 11 – ☎ (06221) 536 60 – Fax (06221) 536660 – backmulde.heidelberg@t-online.de – P ♿ – 12rm: €62/110 ☕ – Restaurant €24/35.* This old sailors' lodging house has pleasant rooms with distinctive carpets and blue padded chairs. Dark wood and red fabrics in the dining room make for a cosy atmosphere.

⊖⊖⊖ Romantik Hotel Zum Ritter St. Georg – *Hauptstraße 178 – ☎ (06221) 13 50 – Fax (06221) 135230 – info@ritter-heidelberg.de – 39rm: €100/215 ☕ – Restaurant €25/41.* St George the dragon-slayer is patron saint of this hotel set in a superb Renaissance-style house built in 1592. The sandstone façade is typical of the region. The lounge-style Belier restaurant seems rather pompous; the Knights' Room very comfortable.

Taking a Break

Strohauer's Café Alt-Heidelberg – *Hauptstraße 49 – ☎ (06221) 18 90 24 – www.strohauer.de – Open summer: 9am-midnight; winter: 9am-7pm (food served from 11am until 1hr before closing time).* A good place for a snack, with a selection of over 20 homemade tarts and cakes. The dishes of the day depend on the season and cost up to €6.50. Note the counter from 1890 which came from a Viennese coffee house.

Going Out

Café Rossi – *Rohrbacher Straße 4 (near the beginning of the pedestrian zone) – ☎ (06221) 9 74 60 – www.caferossi.de – Mon-Sat 8am-1am, Sun 10am-1am.* Art Deco-style café-bar with a large summer terrace. Try their fresh fruit juice, cocktails and ice cream. Very reasonably priced dishes of the day, and extremely cheap coffee served at the bar (€0.75 for an espresso).

Zum Roten Ochsen – *Hauptstraße 217 – ☎ (06221) 2 09 77 – www.roterochsen.de – Mon-Sat 5pm-midnight (Apr-Oct: also 11am-2pm) – Closed Sun, public holidays and 3 weeks after Christmas.* Once frequented by famous figures such as Bismarck, Mark Twain and Marilyn Monroe, this café-restaurant is a favourite haunt of students. Simple cuisine served on tables where many have left their autograph. The place turns into a piano-bar from 8pm – a pleasant place to enjoy a beer or glass of wine.

Special Features

SCHLOSS★★★ (Castle)

Allow half a day

Cars approach via the Neue Schloßstraße.

Open 8am-6pm. €2.50. ☎ (062 21) 53 84 31; www.schloesser-und-gaerten.de

The red stone of the castle surrounded by greenery makes for a striking contrast. Access by car is via the Neue Schloßstrasse, or on foot by the Kurzer Buckel steps.

Upon entering, turn left as indicated on the plan; this takes you to the Rondell promontory, once the site of a battery of cannons and now a **viewpoint★** looking out over the town, the Neckar Valley and the Rhineland plain. To enter the castle, turn back and go through the **Elisabethentor**, a gate which Friedrich V had built in a single night in 1615, as a surprise for his wife Elizabeth Stuart, daughter of James I of England.

Two gates separated by a moat lead to the inner courtyard; from the fortified bridge that connects the Brückenhaus (Bridge House, 1541) to the Torturm (Gate Tower) you can see the Gesprengter Turm (Shattered Tower) in the southeast

R. Mattès/MICHELIN

Heidelberg and its legendary castle.

corner of the castle. A mine laid by French sappers in 1693 gutted one side of the edifice and destroyed the gun emplacements radiating from a solid central core.

The **gardens★** were laid out in terraces under Friedrich V, after an enormous number of earthworks lasting from 1616 to 1619. The east face of the castle, with its three towers (from right to left: the Glockenturm, the Apothekerturm, the Gesprengter Turm), is visible from the Scheffel terrace.

The courtyard and buildings

The courtyard is on the far side of a fortified bridge guarded by the Torturm. Immediately on the right is the fine Gothic hall of the Brunnenhalle (Well Wing), whose granite Roman columns came from Charlemagne's palace at Ingelheim, near Mainz. Opposite stands a simple residential building, the **Ruprecht**, built by Prince Elector Ruprecht III who became German king in 1400; above the crown are two little angels holding a garland of flowers. Legend has it that they represent the architect's twin children, who died in an accident just before completion of the works.

Library (6) – This Gothic building, set well back from the castle's west wing, is able thus to receive light from windows on all sides. At one time it housed the personal library, art collections and treasure of the princely family. The loggia is charming.

Friedrich Wing★★ *(Friedrichsbau)* **(10)** – The façade design of this wing, with its two festooned gables, retains in its columns the classical orders of antiquity – Doric, Ionic and Corinthian – rediscovered during the Renaissance. But the composition of pilasters and corniches, creating contrasts of light and shade, presages already the subsequent taste for the Baroque. The statues (copies) represent the ancestors of Friedrich IV, who added the wing, among them princes of the house of Wittelsbach.

The rear of the building, the only decorated wall directly facing the town, can best be seen from the Great terrace *(Aldan)*. Looking down on the roofs of old Heidelberg, this is approached via a vaulted passageway to the right of the Friedrich wing.

Hall of Mirrors Wing *(Gläserner Saalbau)* **(8)** – Following a fire, only a shell remains of this building, which retains, nevertheless, a series of tiered galleries in the Italian Renaissance manner.

Ottheinrich Wing *(Ottheinrichsbau)* **(9)** – This palace was built by the Elector Otto-Heinrich (known as Ottheinrich), one of the most enlightened rulers of the Renaissance. During the three years of his reign (1556-59), the sovereign opened the palatinate wide to innovative ideas, notably on religious and artistic matters. The wing inaugurated the fruitful Late Renaissance period in German architecture.

Horizontals predominate in the composition of the façade. In line with contemporary taste, the ornamentation combines biblical and mythological symbols.

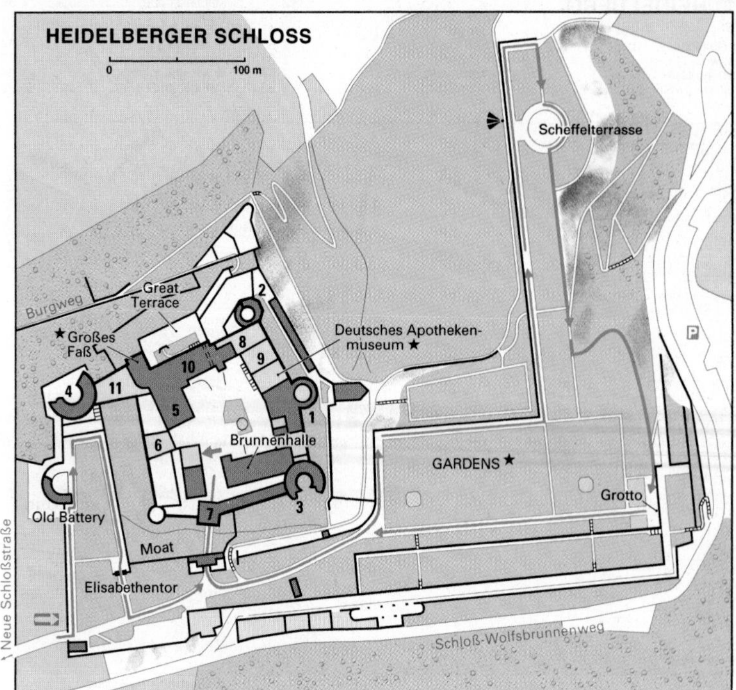

End of Feudal Period (and subsequent altorations)
1) Apothekerturm (14C) - 2) Glockenturm (14C) - 3) Gesprengter Turm (15C)
Gothic-Renaissance Transitional Period (Ludwig V - 1508-1544)
4) Dicker Turm (1533) - 5) Ladles' Wing - 6) Library - 7) Torturm
Renaissance
8) Hall of Mirrors Wing (1549) - 9) Otto-Heinrich Wing (1566)
Renaissance-Baroque Transitional Period
10) Friedrich Wing (Friedrich IV - 1592-1610), and below, Great terrace (Altan)
11) English Wing (Friedrich V - 1610-1632)

The famous sculptor Alexander Colin of Mechelen (1526-1612) collaborated in the design of the entrance, which is in the form of a triumphal arch displaying the elector's armorial bearings: the palatinate lion and the heraldic lozenges of the House of Wittelsbach framing the globe surmounted by a cross symbolising the empire.

Interior

Guided tours only.

Two architectural models allow a comparison between the castle as it is today and as it was in the 17C. So far as the Renaissance decoration of the Friedrich Wing is concerned, this is largely due to a felicitous restoration (c 1900). Statues originally ornamenting the façades can be seen in the corridors. Baroque features were added to the chapel around 1720.

Großes Faß★ (Great Vat) – This colossal cask, with a capacity of 221 726l/48 780gal, was installed in the reign of Charles Theodore at the end of the 18C. Wine can be drawn from it, with the aid of a pump, in the royal banqueting hall (in the Ladies' Wing). The platform above the vat is large enough for dancing as well as wine tasting. The guardian of this Bacchic extravagance – today an idol of local folklore – was the dwarf court jester **Perkeo**, celebrated himself for the astonishing amount he could drink. The memory of Perkeo lives on in a wooden figurine and in the ingenious "surprise" clock he invented.

Deutsches Apothekenmuseum★ (German Pharmaceutical Museum) – *10am-5.30pm. Closed 25 Dec. €2.50, including tour of the courtyard and Great Vat. ☎ (062 21) 258 80. Entrance beneath the steps leading to the Ottheinrich Wing.* This museum contains 18C and 19C apothecaries' equipment, a collection of contemporary chemists' prescriptions and an alchemist's laboratory complete with instruments in the Apothekerturm.

There is an excellent **view★** of the castle from the Molkenkur restaurant, reached via the Molkenkurweg or by funicular railway. The restaurant is built on the site of an ancient fortification.

HEIDELBERG

Street	Grid	Street	Grid	Street	Grid
Bauamtsgasse	Z 5	Hauptstraße	YZ	Marstallstraße	Y 66
Burgweg	Z 19	Heiliggeist-Straße	Y 44	Neue Schloßstraße	Z 74
Grabengasse	Z 36	Jubiläumsplatz	YZ 47	Schloßberg	Z 84
Graimbergweg	Z 39	Karlsplatz	YZ 55	Steingasse	Y 92
		Klingenteichstr.	Z 56	Universitätsplatz	Z 94
		Kornmarkt	Z 57	Zwingerstraße	Z 99
		Marktplatz	Y 63		

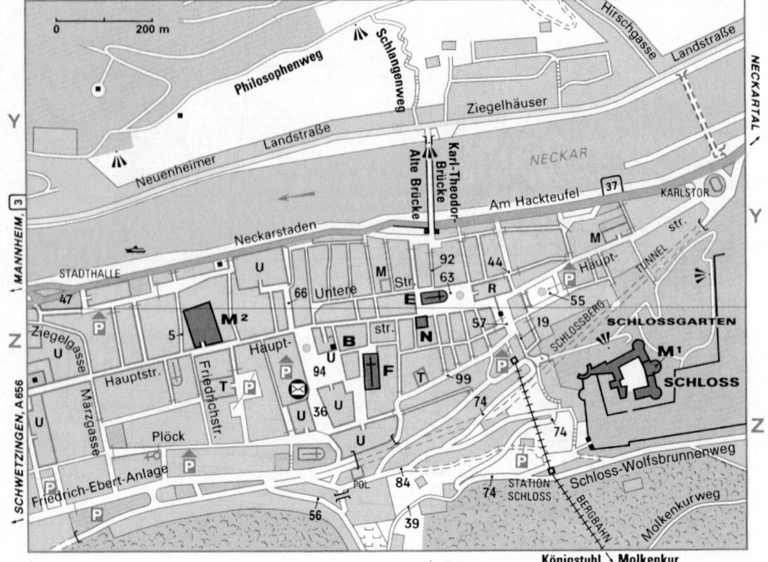

Deutsches Apothekenmuseum	Z	M1
Haus zum Ritter	Z	N
Heiliggeistkirche	Y	E
Jesuitenkirche	Z	F
Kurpfälzisches Museum	Z	M2
Studentenkarzer	Z	B

Walking About

OLD TOWN

Nestling between the Neckar and the hillside, the old town is not very large. The main street, Hauptstraße, runs through it from east to west, parallel to the river. Walk down from the castle via the steps on the west side, then continue straight on to the Kornmarkt. On the far side of the square, on the left, you will come to Marktplatz with the Gothic Heiliggeistkirche at its centre.

Heiliggeistkirche (Church of the Holy Spirit)

The church is an example of the Late Gothic style. As in earlier times, covered stalls hug the walls between buttresses. The galleries in the hall apses were used for the Biblioteca Palatina, which ended up as war booty in the Vatican's possession after Tilly took over Heidelberg in 1623 during the Thirty Years' War. This famous library was considered the best in Europe, now most of it is found in Rome.

The well-lit chancel was formerly the sepulchre of the palatine electors, but since the pillaging wrought during the Orléans War in 1693 only the tomb of Ruprecht III and his wife remains.

Haus zum Ritter★ (The Knight's House)

This magnificent bourgeois house owes its name to a bust of St George in knightly armour which adorns the rich, scrolled pediment. Built in 1592 for the Huguenot merchant Charles Bélier, it was the only Late Renaissance masterpiece to be spared the devastation of 1689-93.

Go along Haupstrasse to Universitätplatz and the old university (Alte Universität), a Baroque building three storeys high. The Palatine lion of the central fountain now stands guard over the square, which is the site of the former St Augustine monastery where Martin Luther was called before his superiors to defend his doctrine in April 1518. Nearby is one of the most popular tourist attractions: the former students' prison.

Studentenkarzer (Students' Prison)

Apr-Oct: open every day except Mon, 10am-4pm; Nov-Mar: open every day except Mon and Sat-Sun, 10am-2pm. Closed on public holidays. €2.50. ☏ (062 21) 54 35 54. From 1712 to 1914, students who were too rowdy or obtrusive ran the risk of incarceration here. Many of them left on the walls inscriptions, outlines darkened with soot, or coats of arms as a reminder to future generations of what they considered a particularly estimable episode in their career.

Jesuitenkirche

This Baroque church was built at the beginning of the 18C from plans drawn up by the Heidelberg architect JA Breunig. The main façade, based on the Gesù Church in Rome, was the work of the Palatinate court architect FW Rabaliatti (1716-82). The luminous triple nave is supported by robust pillars whose capitals are decorated with Rococo stuccowork.

"Homo Heidelbergensis"

In 1907, the jaw of a man who had lived in the early middle Pleistocene period, ie over 500 000 years ago, was found in Mauer, not far from Heidelberg. This Mauer Jaw, also known as **Heidelberg** Man *(Homo heidelbergensis)*, is considered to be the European variety of *Homo erectus*.

The **Museum of Sacred and Liturgical Art** *(Museum für sakrale Kunst und Liturgie)*, which is reached through this church, houses religious artefacts from the 17C to the 19C (Madonnas, altar crosses, liturgical objects). In the museum treasury are examples (including chalices, monstrances) of the goldsmith's and silversmith's art. *Jul-Oct: open every day except Mon, 10am-5pm, Sun 1-5pm; Nov-Jun: Sat 10am-5pm, Sun 1-5pm. Closed 1st Jan, Easter Monday, Pentecost, Christmas. €2. ☎ (062 21) 16 63 91.*

Go west along Hauptstraße. A little further along on the right is the Moraz palace, which houses the Electoral Palatinate Museum.

Kurpfälzisches Museum★ (Electoral Palatinate Museum)

Hauptstraße 97. Open every day except Mon, 10am-5pm, Wed 10am-9pm. Closed 1st Jan, Shrove Tuesday, 24, 25 and 31 Dec. €2.50. ☎ (062 21) 58 34 00.

Part of the collections of this museum is in the Baroque palace built by JA Breunig. The section devoted to the history of the Electoral Palatinate exhibits a cast of the jaw of the prehistoric "Heidelberg Man" (500 000 BC). The department of German Primitives displays the **Altarpiece of the Twelve Apostles★★** (1509 – *Windsheimer Zwölfbotenaltar*) by Tilman Riemenschneider. The collection of **Works from the Romantic Period★★** is devoted essentially to the iconography of the town and castle.

Excursions

Königstuhl

5km/3mi southeast, via Neue Schloßstraße, Molkenkurweg, and then Gaiberger Weg; or take the funicular (stops: Stadt – near the Kornmarkt – Schloß, Molkenkur, Königstuhl). Funicular: summer: 9am-7.20pm, every 10min; winter: 10.50am-5.40pm, Sun 10.10am-5.40pm, every 20min. €5.10 return (from Heidelberg-Kornmarkt station). ☎ (062 21) 227 96; www.hvv-heidelberg.de. From the television tower on the summit (568m/1 864ft) there is a fine panorama of the Neckar Valley, from the Odenwald to the plain of the Rhine.

Schwetzingen★

10km/6mi west via the Friedrich-Ebert-Anlage.

Schwetzingen lies in the Rhine plain with its particularly favourable climate. During the asparagus season, gourmets flock to the town, while in May and June music lovers come for the festivals held here. The town is best known for having been the summer residence of the Palatine electoral princes, as testified by the magnificent palace and gardens.

Schloß★ – The castle, destroyed during the 17C, was rebuilt in 1700-17 as a Baroque palace complex with three wings. The most splendid period of its history was under Prince Elector Karl Theodor, who spent every summer here with his wife Elisabeth Augusta from 1742 to 1778. In 1803, the palace passed to the House of Baden. About forty of the palace rooms are open to the public.

The charming **rococo theatre★** *(Rokokotheater)*, built in the mid 18C by Lorraine architect Nicolas de Pigage (1723-96), is open throughout the summer. During the Schwetzingen Festival it makes an ideal setting for concerts and plays. *From mid-Jun to the beginning of Sep: information ☎ (06202) 12 88 28.*

Schloßgarten★★ – This 72ha/178 acre park was laid out stage by stage and is undoubtedly one of the finest examples of 18C parks in Europe. The French garden, with its rigorously geometric design (circular parterre with fountains along the central axis), is also the work of Nicolas de Pigage. A little later, the English-style gardens were landscaped by Friedrich Ludwig von Sckell, with streams, lakes and trees. The Late Rococo taste for mock ancient buildings gave rise to a number of little temples and artificial ruins dotted around the grounds, such as the Apollo temple, the Mosque, a Roman moated castle and the charming bathing house with a "perspective" (artificial view onto a painted landscape).

Insel Helgoland★★

Helgoland was for a long time the possession of the Danish before becoming British in 1814. The island was exchanged with the Germans for Zanzibar in 1890. Attracted by the idea of a short sea cruise, thousands of tourists each year head for the red-sandstone cliffs of the island of Helgoland, just 70km/43mi out from the estuary of the Elbe.

Location

Population: 1 700. Michelin map nº 541 D 7 – Schleswig Holstein. The island of Helgoland, or Heligoland, as it was known while in British hands, is about 60km from the coast of the Schleswig-Holstein, in an area of the North Sea well-known for its powerful currents and unpredictable climate. There is a daily car ferry service from Cuxhaven *(122km/76mi northwest of Hamburg)* and from the Frisian Islands.
ℹ Rathaus, 27498 Helgoland, ☎ (047 25) 813 70.
Surrounding area: see NORDFRIESISCHE INSELN, Insel SYLT, HUSUM on the mainland (ferry links are subject to change; information available locally).

Worth a Visit

An Unusual Rock

Undermined for centuries by the sea, the island now covers an area of just 2km²/0.8sq mi. In 1947, in accordance with the Potsdam Agreement, German military installations, including a submarine base, were totally destroyed by British sappers using 6 000t of high explosive.
Helgoland was returned to Germany in 1952, since when – thanks to a complete reconstruction of twin built-up areas divided by the form of the cliff (Unterland and Oberland) – it has once more become a tourist centre. An aquarium, an ornithological observatory and a marine biology station make the site of great scientific interest. The island has many attractions to offer the visitor: cliff walks, sea bathing from the lonely but sheltered sands of Düne Beach, even tax-free chocolates, cigarettes and spirits.
Access: From Cuxhaven (2hr30min), from end Feb to beg. Nov: 10.30pm. From Hamburg/St. Pauli-Landungsbrücken, Apr to Oct, 9am. Day return ticket from €51.50. Information from the Reederei Seetouristik: ☎ (0180) 320 20 25; www.helgolandreisen.de

Hildesheim★

Over the centuries Hildesheim managed to preserve its beautiful medieval buildings, until these were destroyed in an Allied Forces air attack in March 1945. After concerted efforts, part of the old town was rebuilt, in particular the historical market square. Today linked by a secondary canal to the Mittellandkanal, the town has developed an economy based largely on ecologically-friendly industries.

Location

Population: 106 500. Michelin map nºs 542, 543, 544 J 13 – Niedersachsen. Hildesheim is around 30km/19mi south of Hannover on the road from Bruges to Novgorod.
ℹ Rathausstraße 18-20, 31134 Hildesheim, ☎ (051 21) 179 80.
Surrounding area: see HANNOVER (33km/21mi north) HAMELN (49km/31mi west), GOSLAR (51km/32mi southeast), HARZ (tour leaves from Goslar).

Background

The Thousand-year-old Rose Tree – As the legend goes, Louis I the Pious, exhausted after a day's hunting, hid his personal reliquary in a rose bush before he lay down to sleep. When he awoke the following morning, the precious casket was nowhere to be found. Interpreting this as a sign from heaven, he founded a chapel – and subsequently a bishopric – on the spot, around which Hildesheim grew up.
The rose bush survived the destruction of the city in 1945 and the burning down of the cathedral; it blooms afresh every year.

Directory

Where to Eat

⊖⊖ **Kupferschmiede** – *Am Steinberg 6 – 31139 Hildesheim-Ochtersum – 5km/3mi southwest via Schützenwiese and the Kurt-Schumacher-Straße, bear right 1km/0.5mi after Ochtersum – ☎ (05121) 26 30 25 – geniesser@kupferschmiede.com – Closed Sun and Mon – €25.50/46.*
This establishment is located in the heart of the forest and was built at the turn of the last century. Various dishes are served in the elegant country-style house. Terrace.

Where to Stay

⊖ **Gästehaus Klocke** – *Humboldtstraße 11 – ☎ (05121) 17 92 13 – fax (05121) 1792140 – www.gaestehaus-klocke.de – P ♿ – 20rm: €52/79* ☕. Built over 100 years ago, this establishment is still run by the same family. The guestrooms are individually designed, but all are quiet and decorated in a functional manner.

Worth a Visit

Marktplatz★

The historical market square has been restored in an exemplary fashion. Visitors are greeted by the sight of buildings spanning eight centuries of architectural styles.

Rathaus – The east side of the square is lined with buildings in the Gothic style predominant between 1246 and 1290. Over the years, the Rathaus underwent numerous modifications and extensions, with the result that it clearly reflects three different periods of construction in three distinct sections. It was rebuilt after 1945 in a simplified form of the original. *There is a carillon at noon, 1pm and 5pm.*

Tempelhaus – This unusual, Oriental-looking building from 1320 to 1330 stands on the south side of the Marktplatz. The crow-stepped gable and two round turrets are probably 16C additions. The most distinctive feature is the ornate Renaissance **oriel★** dating from 1591, on which the parable of the Prodigal Son is depicted.

The nearby **Wedekindhaus** has bay windows projecting from ground level up to the roof gable, a typical feature of the Renaissance architecture of Lower Saxony. The half-timbered building dates from 1598. Note the beautiful carved decoration. Not far off stands the Lüntzelhaus (1755), which now houses a local savings bank, and the 14C Gothic Rolandstift with a Baroque porch (c 1730).

The **Bakers' and Butchers' Guild** houses occupy the west side of the square. The original *Bäckeramtshaus* dated from 1451 but, like the impressive *Knochenhauer-amtshaus★* (1529) next door, it is a faithful reproduction. The Knochenhaueramtshaus is deservedly well-known as the "most beautiful half-timbered house in the world". This eight-storey building is the pride of the local citizens. The five upper floors house the **Municipal Museum** *(Stadtmuseum)*.

The **Rokokohaus** on the north side of the square stands between the *Stadtschänke*, a local restaurant, and the **Weavers' Guild House** *(Wollenwebergildehaus)*.

Dom★ (Cathedral)

♿ *From mid-Mar to end Oct: 9.30am-5pm, Sun, 12 noon-5pm; from Nov to mid-Mar: 10am-4pm, Sat, 9.30am-3pm, Sun, 12 noon-5pm. Closed Good Fri and 24 Dec. €0.50. ☎ (051 21) 179 17 60.*

The present building is a reconstruction, based on the original plans of an 11C Romanesque basilica, with later side chapels faithfully reproduced in the Gothic style and the dome above the transept modelled on the cupola added in the 18C. The interior retains the simplicity of the original. The alternate use of a single pillar and two columns in the nave is typical of the architectural school of Old Saxony. Fine works of **art★** can be seen in the cathedral. A huge chandelier dating from the 11C hangs above the transept crossing. On the north side, the last chapel contains a rare carved baptismal font (13C) supported by four figures representing the rivers of Paradise. In the south transept, an 11C bronze column depicting the life of Christ is displayed.

The two-storey Romanesque **cloister★** abuts the eastern extremity of the cathedral. The legendary rose is trained along the outer wall of the apse.

Scenes from the Old and the New Testament are illustrated in the panels of Bishop Bernward's bronze doors beneath the west front porch – superb examples of early Romanesque sculpture.

Close to the cathedral, a magnificent Renaissance **rood screen★** can be seen in the Antoniuskapelle.

HILDESHEIM

Street	Grid	No.
Almsstraße	Y	
Bahnhofsallee	Y	
Bernwardstraße	Y	
Bergsteinweg	Z	8
Bischof-Janssen-Straße	Y	12
Domhof	Z	20
Eckmekerstraße	YZ	23
Gelber Stern	Z	28
Godehardsplatz	Z	31
Hannoversche Straße	Y	33
Hoher Weg	Z	36
Hohnsen	Z	39
Jacobistraße	Y	41
Judenstraße	Y	44
Kardinal-Bertram-Straße	Y	47
Kläperhagen	Z	49
Mühlenstraße	Z	61
Neue Straße	Z	64
Osterstraße	Y	
Pfaffenstieg	Z	69
Rathausstraße	Y	72
Scheelenstraße	Z	80
Schuhstraße	Z	83
Theaterstraße	Y	91
Zingel	YZ	

Sight	Grid	Key
Antoniuskapelle	Z	A
Heiligkreuzkirche	Z	F
Pelizaeus-Museum und Roemer-Museum	Z	M1
Rathaus	Y	R
St. Andreaskirche	Z	B
Tempelhaus	Y	E

Roemer- und Pelizaeus-Museum★

♿ *Open daily, 10am-6pm. €6.* ☎ *(051 21) 936 90.* The Pelizaeus-Museum houses one of Germany's richest collection of Egyptian antiquities. The life-size seated figure of Heimunu, vizier and nephew of Khufu and the model for Potiphar (Petepré) in Thomas Mann's tetralogy of novels on Joseph, and the statue of the scribe Heti from the excavations near Giza are most impressive.

The Roemer-Museum exhibits rich collections on natural and cultural history. The section on general and cultural history is particularly strong.

St-Michaelis-Kirche★

Dating from the beginning of the 11C, this basilica is typical of Ottonian architecture in Old Saxony, with its double chancel and its alternation of pillars and columns. Note also the 13C painted ceiling depicting the Tree of Jesse in the nave, the two-tier galleries in the transepts, and the simplicity of the cushion capitals – again characteristic of Lower Saxony. Of the original decoration, an Angel Screen remains to the right of the west chancel *(on your left as you enter)*. Above is a balustrade embellished with 13 angels.

St-Godehardikirche★

This 12C church has an elegant silhouette marked by the slender spires crowning its three towers. The church's Romanesque architecture has survived almost intact. Inside, note the richly decorated capitals on the pillars and the treasury.

Andreaskirche

Built by the citizens in the 14C and 15C, this massive Gothic church was destroyed during the Second World War and then rebuilt. It contains the west end of its Romanesque predecessor dating from 1140, whose **façade★** is wonderfully structured in clear lines. The tower, rising with its spire to a height of 114m/355ft, is Niedersachsen's highest and it is the marking feature of the townscape.

The Brühl
Spared by the ravages of war, this quarter is typical of old Hildesheim. Note the Wernersches Haus dating from 1606 in the lower part of the district with a wealth of figurative ornamentation.

Heiligkreuzkirche
Behind the Baroque façade of this building hides an Early Romanesque church (11C) originally refashioned from a fortified gateway. Gothic, Baroque and Ottonian elements jostle each other within.

St-Mauritiuskirche
Leave by the Bergsteinweg. This 11C church, with its 12C cloister, lies in the Moritzberg quarter, on the west side of Hildesheim. The interior was redone in the 18C, a great deal of stucco was added onto it.

Burg Hohenzollern★

Built on a hill separated from the main massif of the Swabian Jura stands Hohenzollern Castle, tall and bristling with turrets; from any angle, it looks like a fortress out of a fairytale. The site★★★ and the history of the dynasty which was born here, even more than the castle itself, is impressive enough to justify its fame.

Location
Michelin map nº 545 V 10 – Baden-Württemberg. 25km/16mi south of Tübingen, the castle is unmissable. Perched on the Zollern hill *(Zollernberg)*, it is reached via route 27 or the A 81 (exit 31).
Surrounding area: see SCHWÄBISCHE ALB (our tour includes the castle), SIGMARINGEN (45km/28mi southeast), HAIGERLOCH (16km/10mi west), ZWIEFALTEN (50km/31mi east), TÜBINGEN (26km/16mi north).

Background

The Cradle of the Hohenzollerns – The dynasty goes back to the counts of Zollern, originally overlords of the Hechingen region, and subsequently divided into several different branches. In 1415, the Hohenzollerns of Franconia became Margraves – and thus elector-princes – of Brandenburg. In 1618 they succeeded to the Duchy of Prussia.
In the 18C, under the rule of the Hohenzollerns, the kingdom of Prussia became a leading power in Europe. It was a Hohenzollern, Wilhelm I, who was placed at the head of the German Empire, founded in 1871 at the instigation of Prussia. But less than half a century later, military defeat in the First World War and the revolution which followed it put an end to the domination of the Hohenzollern dynasty: on 9 November 1918, Kaiser Wilhelm II was forced to abdicate.

The sumptuous interior of Hohenzollern.

Worth a Visit

The Castle
♿ *Guided tour (40min). From mid-Mar to end Oct: 9am-5.30pm; from Nov to mid-Mar: 10am-4.30pm. Closed 24 and 31 Dec. €5. ☎ (074 71) 24 28; www.burg-hohenzollern.com* The castle as it is today was reconstructed from the original plans between 1850 and 1867 by the Prussian architects Von Prittwitz and Stüler. All that remains of the ancient fortress built by the counts of Zollern is the Roman Catholic chapel of **St Michael** *(Michaeliskapelle)*, whose stained-glass windows are said to be the oldest in southern Germany. The neo-Gothic Protestant chapel, in the north

wing of the castle, has housed the tombs of the Friedrich-Wilhelm I, the Soldier-King, and of his son Frederick the Great since 1952, when they were moved there from Potsdam. Mementoes of the latter, including uniforms, decorations, snuffboxes and flutes, can be seen in the collections of the castle **treasury** *(Schatzkammer)*.
Before leaving the castle, make a tour of the ramparts *(start on the left, after the drawbridge)* and enjoy the **panorama★** of the Swabian Jura and the Upper Neckar Valley below.

Husum

The birthplace of the writer Theodor Storm (1817-88), has survived the coastal changes wrought by the North Sea. Today, this "grey city on the sea", as Storm described it in a poem, is the commercial hub of North Friesland thanks to the largest trade and fishing harbour on the west coast of Schleswig-Holstein. By the same token it is a modern holiday region with an abundance of cultural offerings.

Location

Population: 21 000. Michelin map n°° 541 C 11 – Schleswig-Holstein. Husum is one of the last coastal towns before the border with Denmark. The A 23 motorway and the B 5 which connects to it link Hamburg with Schleswig-Holstein's western coast.
🅱 *Großstraße 27, 25813 Husum,* ☎ *(048 41) 898 70.*
Surrounding area: see SCHLESWIG (36km/22mi northeast), KIEL (85km/53mi east), HAMBURG (144km/90mi south), OSTFRIESISCHE INSELN, NORDFRIESISCHE INSELN, Insel HELGOLAND.

Worth a Visit

The port

Right in its midst is the tide-dependent interior harbour: depending on high or low tide, the boats are either afloat or lying in the sand. Some of the old merchants' houses, with their high and in part graduated gables, still stand in the Großstraße. The high attics were originally used as warehouses.

Nordfriesisches Museum★

Herzog-Adolf-Straße 25. ♿ *Open Apr to Oct: 10am-5pm; Nov to Mar: Tue-Sun, 10am-4pm. Closed 1 Jan, 24, 25 and 31 Dec. €3.* ☎ *(048 41) 25 45.* The ground floor of this brick building displays the different types of German coastal landscape (Watt, Geest, Marsch, Polder etc), as well as the life and culture of its inhabitants. The catastrophic consequences of floods are comprehensively explored, as are the construction of dikes and the reclamation of land by polders. A new section deals with emigration from Schleswig-Holstein across the seas from the 17C to the present. There is also an exhibition of Frisian paintings and a section on local history.

Storm-Haus

Wasserreihe 31. Open Apr to Oct: 10am-12 noon, 2-5pm, Mon, Sat and Sun, 2-5pm; Nov-Mar: Tue, Thu and Sat 2-5pm. Closed 24 and 31 Dec. €2. ☎ *(048 41) 66 62 70.* This typical Husum merchant's home was occupied by the writer Theodor Storm from 1866 to 1880; it has furniture from the Biedermeier age, paintings, documents and hand-written manuscripts from the writer's estate.

Marienkirche

This church was built from 1829 to 1832 by the Danish state architect Christian Friedrich Hansen and is a perfect example of a Protestant sermon church in Classicist style. Dorian columns support the galleries, the view of the parishioners is guided towards the gabled pulpit altar.

Schloß vor Husum (Castle before Husum)

Built between 1577 and 1582 by Duke Adolf von Schleswig-Holstein-Gottdorf as a subsidiary residence in the Dutch Renaissance style and later as a widow's residence. The whole complex was renovated in the Baroque style after 1752. The castle park is beautiful, the blooming of the **crocuses★** in spring is especially worth seeing.

THEODOR STORMS

Born in Husum in 1817, Storm regarded his birth town with great affection throughout his life. A deeply sensitive character, Storm contributed to German literature such original works as *Immensee* (1849), a real "poetic jewel" which integrates song and narrative.

Friedrichstadt

15km/9mi south. Dutch refugees, Remonstrants, hounded from their country for religious reasons and given sanctuary here by Duke Friedrich III of Schleswig-Holstein-Gottorf, founded this town in 1621. The duke wanted the city planned along Dutch lines, in the hope of making it a major centre of trade and shipping, and the results were unusual but attractive. Even today, parts of Friedrichstadt look distinctly Dutch: a rectilinear grid of canals with green banks crisscrosses the streets lined with houses topped with stepped gables. The Marktplatz is the heart of the city and the starting point for tours. It is well worth exploring the town from the water.

Eidersperrwerk★ (Eider Dam)

35km/22mi south. Skirting a bird sanctuary, the road arrives at the mouth of the River Eider, closed off by a **dam** constructed between 1967 and 1972, after the catastrophic tidal wave of 1962. The five colossal steel sluice gates remain open when meteorological conditions are normal, permitting the customary rise and fall of tides. But they are closed when storms or abnormally high tides are forecast, preventing the sea from surging up the Eider to invade the low-lying country inland.

Tourist information Friedrichstadt

View of Friedrichstadt.

St-Peter-Ording

37km/23mi south. This well-known seaside town with 22km/14mi of sandy beaches lies to the west of the Eiderstedt peninsula. This spa on the North Sea has some of Germany's most concentrated sulphurous waters. The Seebrücke (Sea Bridge) promenade, 1 012m/3 239ft long, is especially lively.

Nolde-Museum★ at Seebüll

56km/35mi north. Open Mar-Oct, 10am-6pm; Nov, 10am-5pm. €4. ☎ (046 64) 364. Known under the pseudonym of **Nolde**, the painter Emil Nansen (1867-1956), one of the most important representatives of the Expressionist School *(see Art and Architecture)* built himself a house of his own design in the solitude of the Seebüll marshes, between 1927 and 1937. Every year, a different selection of Nolde's works is exhibited there: a changing tribute to one of the most significant masters of German Expressionism. The *Life of Christ*, a series of nine canvases, is on permanent display.

Idar-Oberstein

Since the Middle Ages, the history of Idar-Oberstein has been linked to the production and sale of precious stones. The abundance in earlier times of nearby agate, jasper and amethyst deposits has left the town a centre for the cutting and polishing of the gems. The many jewellery museums, workshops and boutiques bear witness to this trade.

Location

Population: 36 000. Michelin map nº 543 Q 5 – Rheinland-Pfalz. Twin towns here form a single built-up area – picturesque Oberstein lying along the foot of a gorge carved by the River Nahe and Idar spread out around a tributary beyond.

Georg-Maus-Straße 2, 55743 Idar-Oberstein, ☎ (067 81) 644 21.

Surrounding area: see BERNKASTEL-KUES (37km/23mi northwest), MOSELTAL (tour includes Bernkastel Kues), RHEINTAL (Bingen is 60km/37.5mi east), TRIER (64km/40mi west).

Worth a Visit

Deutsches Edelsteinmuseum★★

At Idar, in the Idar-Zentrum (Diamond Exchange), Hauptstraße 118.
The museum presents precious stones from around the world, from agates to diamonds. Some 7 000 cut and polished stones as well as 1 000 intermediate precious stone and crystal phases delight the eye. The Glyptothek is especially interesting, with its 6 000 year history of the gem-cutting industry and the engraving art of the Modern Age.

Felsenkirche★

30min on foot there and back. Access via a stairway (214 steps) rising from the Oberstein Marktplatz.
Framed by a rock overhang in the cliff 50m/164ft above the river, this church, restored several times, is worth a visit for the winged altarpiece (early 15C) alone. The scenes of the Passion represented depict the hatred, the suffering and the annihilation with a ferocious realism.

Museum Idar-Oberstein

At Oberstein, in the Marktplatz (at the foot of the Felsenkirche stairway). Open Apr to Oct, 9am-5.30pm; Nov to Mar, 10am-5.30pm. Closed 1 Jan, 24, 25 and 31 Dec. €3.60, no charge last Sun in Oct. ☎ (067 81) 246 19. Sizeable collections of minerals and precious stones. Note the "Landschaftsachate", which are paper-thin flakes of agate: these translucent slivers reveal extraordinary patterns – like contours or imaginary landscapes – when held to the light. The museum also has displays of crystals, fluorescent stones and locally produced jewellery.

Burgruinen

At Oberstein. Castle ruins with a view of the Nahe Valley.

Weiherschleife (Old Stonecutting Centre)

In the Tiefenstein district. ♿ Guided tour (40min). From mid-Mar to mid-Nov, 10am-6pm; from mid-Nov to mid-Dec and from mid-Feb to mid-Mar, Mon-Fri, 10am-4pm. €3. ☎ (067 81) 315 13. The facetting and polishing of gems can be seen here, from the crude stone to the fine jewel. Skilled craftsmen still work to traditional methods here, in front of sanded grindstones powered by a water-wheel.

Tour

The Hunsrück

Excursion 141km/88mi – allow about 5hr.
The Hunsrück forms the southern rim of the Rhine schist massif. It is a region of low mountains and game-stocked forests, gashed by deep and steep-sided valleys.

Erbeskopf – At 818m/2 660ft, this is the highest summit of the massif. From the wooden tower, there is a panoramic view over the undulating, wooded countryside.

After Thalfang, the **Hunsrückhöhenstraße★** going northward offers fine views of the valleys, the forest-covered hills and numerous villages with ancient houses roofed by slabs of schist. The road passes the Stumpfer Turm, an old Roman watchtower.

Kirchberg – Perched on a hillside, this village boasts many pretty half-timbered houses, especially around the Marktplatz. St Michaelskirche dates back to the pre-Romanesque era, although the present building was constructed in the 15C.

Simmern – The farming centre of the Hunsrück. The parish church of St Stephan (15C), with star-vaulting, houses the **remarkable tombs★** of the Dukes of Pfalz-Simmern. These are some of the finest works of Renaissance sculpture in the middle Rhineland. The Schinderhannesturm, once part of the city fortifications, was named after the bandit Schinderhannes, who was imprisoned here for a time.
It is also well worth exploring the old town centre around the church.

Ravengiersburg – Hidden away at the bottom of a valley, this village boasts a Romanesque church built on top of a spur. The imposing west front has a sculptured cornice and a miniature gallery. Above the porch: Christ in Majesty.

Dhaun – The castle here is built on a remarkable **site★** on top of a sheer rock outcrop. On the esplanade, behind the statue, a staircase leads down to the gun positions.

The road on the final section of the excursion follows the valley of the Nahe before returning to Idar-Oberstein.

Jena

The town has developed steadily ever since the foundation of its university in 1548. From then on, numerous scientists and intellectuals all contributed to Jena's importance. Among them were the philologist and political thinker Wilhelm von Humboldt, his brother Alexander, a geographer, not to mention Goethe, Schiller and Hegel, who worked busily on his philosphical treatise while the French and Prussian armies joined battle outside the city gates in October 1806. The town is also famous for its optical industry, established in the middle of the 19C by Carl Zeiss and Ernst Abbe, the inventors of the microscope. Jena today is a lively and future-oriented city.

Location

Population: 99 000. Michelin maps nº 544 N 18 – Thüringen. Jena is northeast of the forest of Thuringia, midway along the course of the Saale.

Johannisstraße 23, 07743 Jena, ☎ (036 41) 80 64 00.

Surrounding area: see WEIMAR (22km/14mi west), NAUMBURG (31km/19mi north), THÜRINGER WALD (Ilmenau is 92km/57mi southwest).

Worth a Visit

Johannistor

Together with the **Pulverturm** (on the other side of the square), this gate is all that remains of the town's 14C fortifications.

Stadtmuseum Göhre

Open Tue-Sun, 10am-5pm (-6pm Wed). Closed 1 Jan, 24 and 31 Dec. €3. ☎ (036 41) 359 80. This local museum is housed in one of the town's most beautiful buildings, built around 1500. The four floors illustrate the history of Jena since its foundation. The collection includes some beautiful items of art and cultural history.

J. Bouraly/MICHELIN

Statue of the Kurfürst on the Markt.

Stadtkirche St-Michaelis

This ancient collegiate church of the Cistercians was completely transformed in the Gothic mode in the 15C. Note, on the south side, the canopied porch.

Goethe-Gedenkstätte

Open from Apr to end Oct: Tue-Sun, 11am-3pm. Closed 1 May, Ascension, 3 and 31 Oct. €1. ☎ (036 41) 93 11 88. The famous writer always said that it was in Jena that he found the tranquillity essential for literary creation. The inspector's house in the botanical gardens where he lived when he was in the town contains documents and items that recall his work in the field of natural science.

Directory

Where to Eat

Ratszeise – *Markt 1 – ☎ (03641) 42 18 00 – www.ratszeise.net – ♿ – €15.10/31.40.* This restaurant is in the Jena's historic town hall. The interior decoration is rustic in style, in perfect harmony with the exterior. Enjoy the views of the market place (Marktplatz) while sampling pleasant traditional cuisine.

Where to Stay

Hotel Jenaer Hof – *Bachstraße 24 – ☎ (03641) 44 38 55 – fax (03641) 443866 – P – Booking advised – 11rm: €49/69.* A simple, practical hotel located in the heart of the town and set in a *Jugendstil* building. Guestrooms of various sizes are on offer; all of them are furnished in dark wood.

JENA

Alexander-Puschkin-Platz	AZ 3	Goethestraße	AY	Obere Lauengasse	BY 39
Am Planetarium	AY 6	Hainstraße	AZ 18	Rathenaustraße	AZ 40
Bachstraße	AY 9	Johannisplatz	AY 24	Saalstraße	BY 42
Carl-Zeiss-Platz	AY 12	Johannisstraße	AY 25	Schillerstraße	AZ 43
Engelplatz	AZ 13	Löbdergraben	AZ 30	Unterm Markt	ABY 45
		Lutherstraße	AZ 31	Vor dem Neutor	AZ 46
		Markt	AY 34	Weigelstraße	AY 48
		Neugasse	AZ 37	Westbahnhofstraße	AZ 49

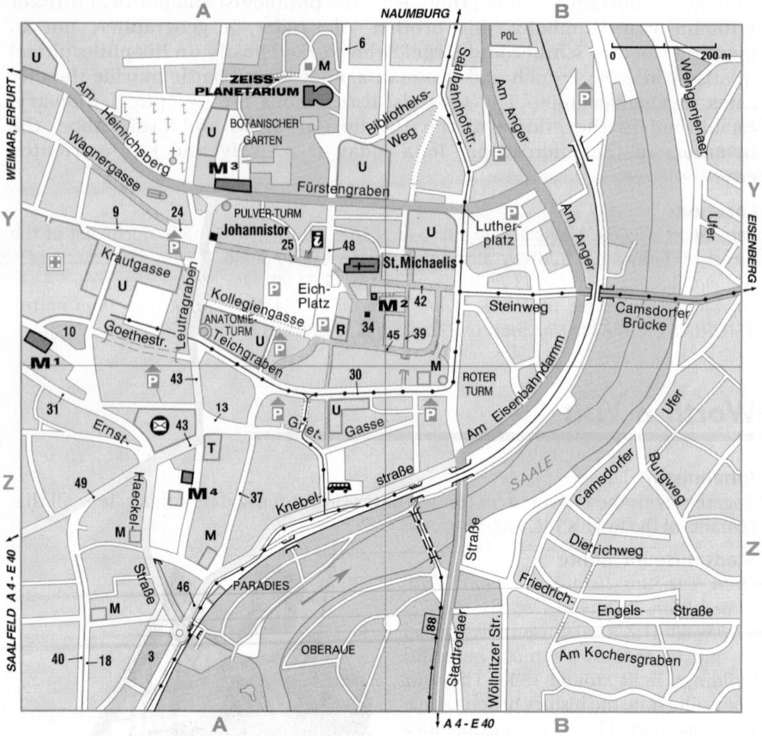

Goethe-Gedenkstätte	AY M³	Schiller-Gedenkstätte	AZ M⁴
Optisches Museum	AY M¹	Stadtmuseum Göhre	ABY M²

Schillers Gartenhaus (Schiller Museum)

Guided tour (20min). Apr.-Oct: Tue-Sun. 11am-3pm; Nov-Mar: Tue-Sat 11am-3pm. Closed public holidays. 1€. ☎ (036 41) 93 11 88. Schiller lived in this summer house from 1797 to 1799 and wrote *Wallenstein* here. It now contains a display of memorabilia from Schiller's "Jena years".

Zeiss Planetarium★ (Zeiss-Planetarium der Ernst-Abbe-Stiftung Jena)

♿ *Closed 1 Jan and 6-8 Jan. €5-8 according to what is showing. Programme changes every month. For information on what is currently showing, ☎ (036 41) 88 54 88.* Built next to the botanical gardens by the Zeiss firm, this scientific spectacle permits visitors to voyage through the cosmos via the artful manipulation and movement of planets and the stellar systems. Varied laser and multi-visual show.

Optisches Museum★

♿ *Open Tue-Sun, 10am-4.30pm, Sat, 11am-5pm. Closed bank holidays. €5. ☎ (036 41) 44 31 65.* The museum retraces 500 years of the history of optics. There is a large collection of spectacles, telescopes, photographic equipment and cameras, and ophthalmological instruments.

Karlsruhe★

Visitors to Karlsruhe will be amazed by the network of streets which radiate from the town's palace, but it is Karlsruhe's three museums which make the town worth a visit. The former seat of the grand dukes today houses Germany's supreme courts (Court of Appeal and the Constitutional Court), together with the country's oldest School of Technology (1825). Among the eminent graduates of the latter are Hertz, who discovered electromagnetic waves, and Carl Benz, the motorcar pioneer.

Location

Population: 270 000. Michelin map nº 545 S 9 – Baden-Württemberg. Situated only a few kilometres from the Rhine, Karlruhe has used the river for its industrial development. The proximity of the Black Forest allows inhabitants to swap this modern town for the fresh air of the countryside.

Bahnhofplatz 6, 76137 Karlsruhe, ☎ (0721) 37 20 53 83.

Surrounding area: see Schloß BRUCHSAL (22km/14mi northeast), Kloster MAULBRONN (34km/21mi east), SCHWARZWALD (starting with BADEN-BADEN, 38km/24mi to the south), PFALZ (Bad Bergzabern is 35km/22mi west).

Background

A star is born – Karlsruhe is one of the "new towns" designed on a geometric plan in the 18C by the princely building enthusiasts of southern Germany. After the devastations of 1689 and the destruction of his family seat at Durlach, the Margrave of Baden decided to build a palace a little further west. The idea, put into operation in 1715 with the construction of an octagonal tower, was for the palace to be the hub of a network of radiating streets. This "town fan" was eventually fully realised in the 19C, when Karlsruhe became the capital of the Grand Duchy of Baden (1806).

The architect **Friedrich Weinbrenner** (1766-1826), a native of the town, was responsible for its neo-Classical aspect. From this period dates the Marktplatz, along with the town hall (Rathaus), the Protestant church *(Evangelische Stadtkirche)*, and the modest pyramid of the founder's mausoleum. The Kaiserstraße *(pedestrian precinct)*, today the city's commercial centre, was also designed by Weinbrenner. Cutting through the "fan" on an east-west axis, it follows the course of the old road from Durlach to the Rhine.

Directory

Where to Eat

Lehners Wirtshaus zum Goldenen Kreuz – *Karlstraße 21a – 76133 Karlsruhe – ☎ (0721) 249 57 20 – – €13.80/22.30.* Those who appreciate good simple food will love this convivial brasserie situated in the town centre. Divided into several rooms, the wooden tables and large bar bring a rustic feel to the place. In the summer a pleasant Biergarten with 300 seats is available.

Where to Stay

Hotel Betzler – *Amalienstraße 3, 76133 Karlsruhe – ☎ (0721) 91 33 60 – fax (0721) 9133625 – www.hotel-betzler.de – – 34rm: €34/72.* Located in the heart of Karlsruhe this establishment is well-placed for access to the public transport network and is equipped with clean and functional guestrooms. The pedestrianised area of the town, as well as most of its sights of interest are easily reached on foot from this hotel.

Worth a Visit

Staatliche Kunsthalle★★ (Fine Arts Museum)

Open Tue-Sun, 10am-5pm, Sat-Sun, 10am-6pm. Closed Shrove Tue, 24 and 31 Dec. €4. ☎ (0721) 926 33 70; www.kunsthalle-karlsruhe.de

The building, erected between 1838 and 1846, houses a remarkable collection of **German Primitives★★** *(Gemälde Altdeutscher Meister)*, including numerous works by Grünewald *(Crucifixion)* and the *Karlsruhe Passion*, a Late Gothic masterpiece executed in c 1450.

The golden age of Flemish and Dutch painting is represented by Rubens, Jordaens and Rembrandt *(Self-Portrait)*. Still-life pictures by Chardin are the highlights of a collection of 17C and 18C French paintings.

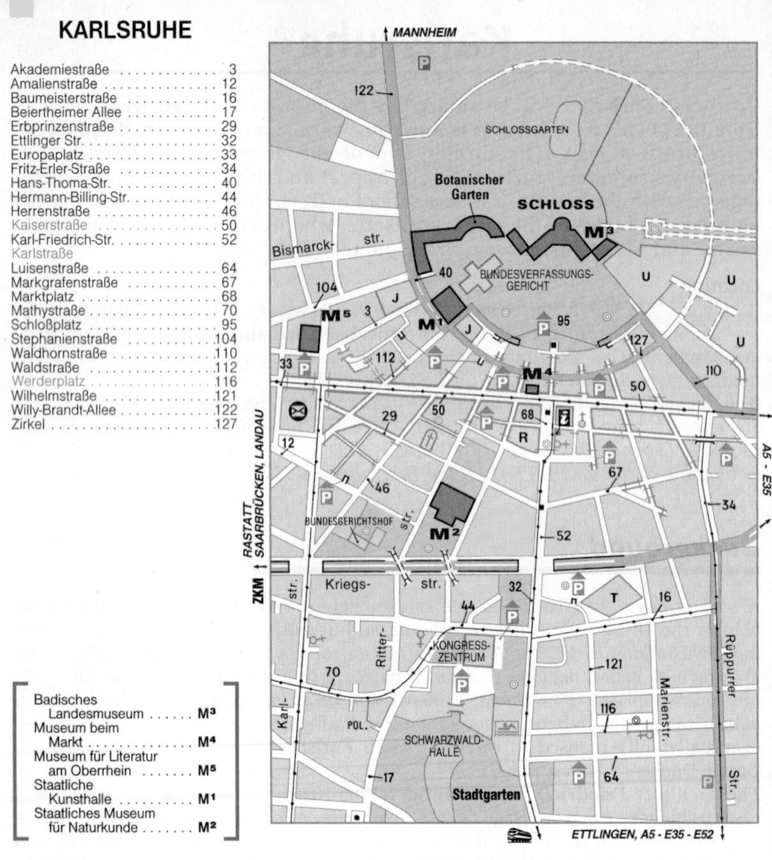

The **Hans Thoma Collection★** occupies a special place in German painting of the 19C. It is embedded in a comprehensive presentation of famous German and French painters from Caspar David Friedrich to Paul Cézanne.

The adjacent **Orangery** houses an outstanding **collection★** of Classical modern and contemporary art. Paintings by German Expressionists (*Deer in the Forest* by Franz Marc), artists who were influenced by Cubism (Léger, Delaunay), but also the *Hurricane* by Max Ernst and *The Seven Deadly Sins* by Otto Dix, stand alongside sculptures by Barlach, Lehmbruck and Henry Moore. The contemporary artists with work on display include Arnulf Rainer, Gerhard Richter, Yves Klein and Antoni Tàpies.

Schloß★ (Palace)

Of the original palace building, only the tall octagonal tower that marks the centre of the city's radiating road system now remains. It was the grand-ducal residence up to 1918.

There is a wonderful view from the **tower** *(Schloßturm, Open Tue-Sun, 10am-4pm, Fri-Sun, 10am-5pm. €4. ☎ (0721) 926 65 14)* over Karlsruhe as far as the northern Black Forest, the Kraich region and the Palatinate mountains.

From the palace park – which gives way, in the north, to a vast wooded area – there is access to the **Botanical Gardens** *(Botanischer Garten)*, where the **greenhouses★** *(Gewächshäuser)* offer a magnificent display of cactuses. *Greenhouses: Open Tue-Sun, 9am-12 noon, 1-4pm (Apr to Sep, 5pm), Sat-Sun, 10am-12 noon, 1-4pm (Apr to Sep, 5pm). €2. ☎ (0721) 926 30 08.*

Badisches Landesmuseum★ (Baden Regional Museum) – ♿ *Open Tue-Sun, 10am-5pm, Fri-Sun, 10am-6pm. Closed 24 and 31 Dec. €4. ☎ (0721) 926 65 14.* This museum has been arranged in the palace and consists of significant collections covering the region's prehistory and early history, the ancient cultures of the Mediterranean area and art, culture and regional history from the Middle Ages to the present. The famous Turkish trophies of the Margrave Ludwig Wilhelm, who was known as **"Louis the Turk"** (1677-1707) are particularly worthy of note. One section is reserved for the history of the palace and the court.

Museum beim Markt – ♿ *Open Tue-Sun, 11am-5pm, Fri-Sun, 10am-6pm. Closed 24 and 31 Dec. €4, no charge Fri. 2-6pm. ☎ (0721) 926 65 78; www.landesmuseum.de. Between Marktplatz and the palace.*

In another building of the Landesmuseum are collections of art from **Jugendstil★** (Art Nouveau) and Art Deco to contemporary craft and design.

ZKM★ (Zentrum für Kunst und Medientechnologie)

Access via Kriegsstraße. ♿ Open Tue-Sun, 10am-6pm, Wed, 10am-8pm. €4.10, no charge 3 Oct (Museumsfest). ☎ (0721) 81 00 13 25; www.mnk.zkm.de. This former weapons and ammunition factory dating from the beginning of the 20C with a total of 10 roofed-in patios now unites research, teaching, workshops and museums revolving around media art.

Museum für Neue Kunst (Museum for New Art) – *Access from Stirnseite, towards Lessingstraße.* European and American art since 1960 (Painting, graphics, sculpture, photography and holography, installations) from private collections in Baden-Württemberg illustrate the most important trends in contemporary art.

T. Krieger/MICHELIN

The former seat of the grand dukes of Baden now houses Germany's supreme courts.

Medienmuseum – *♿ Open Wed-Sun, 10am-6pm, Tue, 10am-8pm, Sat-Sun, 11am-6pm. €5.10. ☎ (0721) 810 00. Access at the level of the blue cube (ZKM music studio).* The visitor must become active here in order to approach the exhibition items. The interactive presentation allows a playful dialogue with forms and effects of new media technologies to take place.

►► Städtische Galerie *(Town Museum, art from Baden after 1850 and post-1945 German art).*

Kassel★

Once the seat of the Landgraves, Kassel is particularly renowned for the Wilhelmshöhe park, with its grottoes, waterfalls and palace. Kassel was bombed in October 1943, and reconstruction of the formerly beautiful town has not always been done in the best taste. However, the town's various sights make it an interesting place to visit.

Location

Population: 196 000. Michelin map nos 543, 544 L, M 12 – Hessen. Kassel is situated on the banks of the River Fulda *(boat trips from Fuldabrücke)*, in the heart of a hilly, lush and wooded countryside, between the Habichtswald and Meißner-Kaufungen Natural Parks. The town is the meeting point for the A 7 motorway (Fulda-Hannover) and A 44 motorway (to Dortmund).

Obere Königstrasse 15, ☎ 0561-7077 07.

Surrounding area: see, GÖTTINGEN (87km/54mi northeast), EISENACH (87km/54mi southeast), THÜRINGER WALD (tour leaves from Eisenach).

Background

The Brothers Grimm – Jakob (1785-1863) and Wilhelm Grimm (1786-1859) lived in Kassel from 1805 to 1830, both employed as Court Librarians. Through their shared work on literature and linguistics (a German basic grammar, the first volume of a German language dictionary) they can be considered the inaugurators of the science of German philology. Fascinated by legends and folklore, the brothers collected from all over the province a wealth of stories which they published between 1812 and 1815 under the general title of *Kinder und Hausmärchen* (Stories for Children and the Home, but better known in English simply as: *Grimms' Fairy Tales*).

Documenta – Famous for its musical and dramatic activities, Kassel is nevertheless known best of all for the Documenta, an international exhibition of contemporary art which has been held every five years since 1955. The main centre for this event is the **Fredericianum**, a pre-Classical building in the vast Friedrichsplatz designed by Simon Louis du Ry to be both museum and library for the Landgrave Frederick II.

The vast – and still very romantic – Wilhelmshöhe park.

Special Features

WILHELMSHÖHE★★ *allow half a day*

Park★★ – The landscaping of this huge 350ha/865-acre park was started in 1701 under the Landgrave Karl. It was based on a design by the Italian architect Guerniero. The Baroque-style park, in which almost 800 different species of trees grow, was transformed in the second half of the 18C into English-style gardens, complete with temples, pavilions, grottoes and artificial ruins. The ruins of **Löwenburg**, a fantasy castle built between 1793 and 1801, is an excellent example of the taste for sentimental Romanticism current in that period (note inside the furnishings and the valuable collection of arms and armour).

At the highest point of the park stands **Hercules★** *(Herkules)*, emblem of the city of Kassel and highlight of the park. This gigantic statue is a copy (1717) of the Farnese Hercules at the National Archaeological Museum in Naples. In the Wilhelmshöhe Park, the figure is placed on top of a pyramid, itself standing on a huge eight-sided pavilion, the Oktogon. The total height of the whole monument is 72m/236ft (Nelson's Column in London's Trafalgar Square measures 52m/170ft). From the base of the statue, there is a very fine **view★★** over the park and the castle to Kassel.

Below the Oktogon is the great **Water Staircase** *(Kaskadentreppe)* – an enormous **cascade★** with huge amounts of water falling in a sequence of steps to the Neptune Pool, before continuing downwards to the Fountain Pool (very high jets) in front of the castle. The Water Staircase falls 200m/656ft from top to bottom.

Schloß (Castle)

♿ *Open Tue-Sun, 10am-5pm. Closed Wed before Ascension, 24, 25 and 31 Dec. €3.50. No charge on Fri. ☎ (0561) 937 77; www.museum-kassel.de*

This building in the Classical style was completed in 1803. The historic salons of the South Wing (museum) display splendid paintings and Louis XV and Empire furniture. Heavily damaged during the Second World War, the building was reconstructed without its central cupola. Extensive renovation work on the central block since June 2000 has created a new setting for the Old Masters Gallery, with a glass saddle roof filling the interior with light.

Antiquities★ – Antique vases (6C and 5C) at the entrance evoke the Classical Greek era. The Roman Empire is represented by the **Kassel Apollo** (2C, after the Athenian sculptor Phydias), a series of busts, a sarcophagus and some urns. Figures of gods and animals in stone and bronze represent art in Ancient Egypt.

Old Masters Gallery★★★ – The rich, world-class exhibits here are derived from collections amassed by the Landgraves. German Primitive painting is represented by some major works: Altdorfer's *Crucifixion*, a triptych *(Reisealtar)* by Cranach the Elder, Dürer's *Portrait of Elizabeth Tucher, Hercules at Antioch* by Hans Baldung Grien.

Dutch works on display include: Rembrandt's *The Blessing of Jacob* (1656), *Portrait of Saskia van Uylenburgh* (the painter's first wife), *The Holy Family at the Screen, A Winter Landscape* and various self-portraits; lifelike portraits by Frans Hals, such as *Man with a Floppy Hat*; Rubens *(Crowning of a Hero; Mary and the Infant Jesus as a Refuge for Sinners)*; Van Dyck *(Sebastian Leerse with his Wife and Son)*; and Jordaens, who pictures himself as a lutenist in *The Painter's Betrothal*. Also on display here are landscapes and scenes of rustic and bourgeois life by Jan Brueghel, Jacob van Ruisdael, Gabriel Metsu and Jan Steen.

Italian (Tintoretto, Titian, Bassano), Spanish (Ribera, Murillo) and French (Poussin's *Cupid's Victory over the god Pan*) works complete the collection.

Worth a Visit

Karlsaue Park★

The most popular parts of this 18C riverside park are the steeply sloping gardens below the Schöne Aussicht terrace, and the Siebenbergen – an artificial island on the Fulda.

In the north corner of the park is the **orangery** (1710), home to the **Museum für Astronomie und Technikgeschichte mit Planetarium**. This museum's rich **collections★★** of old astronomical instruments and clocks are the result of Landgrave Wilhelm IV's interest in astronomy, which led to his founding modern Europe's first permanently equipped observatory in Kassel in 1560. The great clockwork model of the planets was constructed in 1561 based on designs by the "Lord-Astronomer". There are models demonstrating observable scientific phenomena and a display on the evolution of technology from Antiquity to the present (energy technology, data processing). *Open Tue-Sun, 10am-5pm. Closed Wed before Ascension, 24, 25 and 31 Dec. €3.50. No charge on Fri. ☎ (0561) 937 77.*

Not far from the orangery is the **Marmorbad** (1728), marble baths with an interior adorned with reliefs and statues on themes from Greek mythology.

Hessisches Landesmuseum★

Open Tue-Sun, 10am-5pm. Closed Wed before Ascension, 24, 25 and 31 Dec. €3.50. No charge on Fri. ☎ (0561) 937 77; www.museum-kassel.de

The street level is devoted to collections concerned with prehistory. There is a detailed display on the Stone Age. Subsequent periods are evoked by carefully selected exhibits (archeological finds from the Hallstatt and La Tène periods).

On the first floor is the **German Tapestry Museum★★** *(Deutsches Tapetenmuseum)*where more than 600 pieces chart the evolution of wall coverings from the 18C to the 20C: wallpapers with Near- or Far-Eastern motifs, embossed leather, panoramic murals, printed papers with designs from famous workshops in Germany and France (Réveillon, Paris). The techniques of printing are also illustrated.

The second floor covers sculptures and porcelain from the manufacturers of Kassel and Fulda, and decorative art dating from the Middle Ages to the 19C, including coloured crystal and Kassel silverware.

►► Neue Galerie★ *(German and European painting from the mid 18C to the present)* – Brüder-Grimm-Museum – Naturkundemuseum.

Excursions

Schloß Wilhelmsthal★

12km/8mi north on Rasenallee. Guided tour (1hr). Open Mar to Oct: Tue-Sun, 10am-4pm; Nov to Feb: Tue-Sun, 10am-3pm. Closed 1 Jan, 24-26 and 31 Dec. €3.50. ☎ (056 74) 68 98; www.schloesser-hessen.de

This Rococo palace (1747-61), surrounded by a park in the English style, was built by François Cuvilliés the Elder. Interior decoration in the style popular at the time, with fine panelling, elegant furniture (mother-of-pearl inlaid commode), Chinese porcelain and a gallery of beauties painted by JH Tischbein the Elder exemplify the taste of the Court.

Göttingen

47km/29mi north on the A 7. Along with Heidelberg, Tübingen and Marburg, Göttingen is one of the four German towns most deeply imbued with the university tradition. Student life, often highly coloured, lends a particular vivacity to the scene, especially at examination time and on Foundation Days *(Stiftungsfeste)*.

The streets of the old town, bustling with students on their bicycles and with their Gothic churches and neo-Classical university buildings, are a charming scene.

Rathaus *(Town hall)* – Students, tourists and citizens combine to make the market place and the wine cellars *(Ratskeller)* beneath the town hall the animated centre of social life in Göttingen. The 14C-15C building is constructed on the classic

KASSEL

Baunsbergstraße	X 2
Brüder-Grimm-Platz	Z 3
Bürgerm.-Brunner-Str.	Z 5
Dag-Hammarskjöld-Str.	X 6
Demaschkerstr.	X 7
Dresdener Straße	X 8
Fünffensterstraße	Z 12
Fuldabrücke	Z 13
Harleshäuser Str.	X 16
Hugo-Preuß-Str.	X 18
Kölnische Straße	X 20
Königsplatz	Z 21
Kurfürstenstraße	Y 22
Landgraf-Karl-Str.	X 23
Neue Fahrt	Z 25
Obere Königsstraße	Z
Rudolph-Schwander-Str.	Y 27
Scheidemannplatz	Z 28
Schönfelder Str.	X 29
Schützenstraße	X 32
Standeplatz	Z
Treppenstraße	Z
Tulpenallee	X 33
Untere Königsstraße	Y
Werner-Hilpert-Str.	Y 34
Wilhelmstraße	Z 35

Museum		
Brüder-Grimm-Museum	Z	M³
Hessisches Landesmuseum	Z	M¹
Museum für Astronomie und Technikgeschichte	Z	M⁵
Naturkundemuseum	Z	M⁴
Neue Galerie	Z	M²
Schloß Löwenburg	X	A

medieval pattern. In front of it is the modern Goosegirl **Fountain** *(Gänselieselbrunnen)*. Newly anointed PhDs traditionally come to the fountain and give the girl a kiss.

Vierkirchenblick – A church is visible at each point of the compass from the south-east corner of the market: east, the countrified dome of St Albanikirche; south, St Michaelskirche; west, the octagonal towers of St Johannnis; and north, the lofty belfry of St Jakobi – at 72m/236ft the tallest tower in town.

Half-timbered Houses *(Fachwerkhäuser)* – Most of these are in the eastern part of the old town. Note particularly the ancient **Junkernschänke inn★** (near the Rathaus, at the junction of the Barfüßerstraße and the Judenstraße).

Musée municipal (Städtisches Museum) – *Open Tue-Sun, 10am (11am, Sat-Sun)-5pm. Closed 1 Jan, 1 May, Whitsun, 3 Oct, 24, 25 and 31 Dec. €1.50. ☏ (0551) 400 28 43.*

Städtisches Museum (Municipal Museum) – This museum, which is housed in a Renaissance building, is devoted to the historical and cultural development of Göttingen, both town and university. It also exhibits an interesting collection of religious art from the Middle Ages and Modern era, as well as a collection of porcelain of various origins.

Kiel★

As a gateway to Scandinavia, Kiel plays an important role as a hub between north and south. The town's strategic role as a military port meant that it was heavily damaged during the Second World War. Kiel has been largely reconstructed in modern style, its functional urbanism hiding some of its character. But dig a little, and most visitors will find that the capital of Schleswig-Holstein has plenty of style and atmosphere with which to charm visitors.

Location

Population: 240 000. Michelin maps nos 541, 542 D 14 – Schleswig-Holstein. Kiel is located at the end of a 17km/10mi deep inlet in the Baltic Sea at the eastern end of the North Sea-Baltic Sea canal.

Andreas-Gayk-Straße 31, 24103 Kiel, ☏ (0431) 67 91 00.

Surrounding area: see SCHLESWIG (56km/35mi north), LÜBECK (76km/48mi south), HAMBURG (94km/59mi south).

Background

A maritime city – Kiel, founded in the 13C, was always dominated by seafaring and mercantilism – even if this Hanseatic city never achieved more than regional importance, in contrast to Lübeck. For centuries, the city led a tranquil existence. This all changed in 1871, when Kiel was selected to become the main navy base for Germany. Within a few years, the little harbour city grew into a metropolis.

Walking About

Kieler Förde (Roadstead) ★★

The shores of this deep inlet are brightened by a series of sheltered resorts and bathing beaches, among them Schilksee, Strande, Laboe, Stein, Heikendorf and Schönberger Strand. In the northern part of the bay, regattas have been held for more than a century, including the events of the **Kiel Week**.

Kiel Week.

Office de Tourisme de Kiel

Directory

Where to Eat

⊖ Alte Mühle – *An der Holsatiamühle 8 (on the east bank of the Kieler Förde, follow the signs for "Schwentinetal") – ☎ (0431) 2 05 90 01 – www.altemuehle-kiel.de – Mon-Sat, 11.30am-midnight, Sun, 10am-midnight – €18.70/35.* Located in a former 19C mill on the banks of the river Schwentine, this fish restaurant serves traditional, seasonal food. Reasonably-priced set menus are served Monday to Friday at lunchtime.

⊖⊖ Lüneburg-Haus – Zum Hirschen – *Dänische Straße 22 – ☎ (0431) 982 60 00 – 1881@lueneburghaus.com – Closed for 4 weeks in July and August, Sundays – €33/47.* Located on the first floor of the building, modern, bistro-style food is served on elegantly set tables in a pleasantly relaxed atmosphere. Comprehensive wine list and attentive staff.

Where to Stay

⊖⊖ Consul – *Walkerdamm 11 – ☎ (0431) 53 53 70 – fax (0431) 5353770 – hotel-consul-kiel@t-online.de – 40rm: €65/125 – Restaurant €19/33.* Located near to the Kiel's port, this hotel is well served by public transport. Every guestroom is different, but all are clean and well-equipped. Well decorated dining rooms.

⊖⊖⊖ Parkhotel Kieler Kaufmann – *Niemannsweg 102 – ☎ (0431) 881 10 – fax (0431) 8811135 – info@kieler-kaufmann.de – 43rm: from €108 – Restaurant €24/42.* The comfortable entrance hall of this fomer banker's villa sets the scene with its elegant fireplace. Set upstream from the port in a park, the guestrooms are modern and have internet access. Classically-styled restaurant.

Taking a Break

Werkstatt-Café – *Falckstr. 16 (centre-ville) – ☎ (0431) 9 18 65 – Mon-Fri, 10am-8pm, Sat 10am-7pm – Closed Sun and bank holidays.* Pleasant tea room next door to a goldsmith's workshop ("Werkstatt"). Try the delicious home-made cakes or one of the dishes of the day. The café also regularly exhibits the work of local artists. Beautiful garden.

Going Out

Café-Restaurant Schöne Aussichten – *Düsternbrooker Weg 16 (north of the town centre, on the west bank of the Kieler Förde) – ☎ (0431) 2 10 85 85 – from 11.30am (food served until 10.30pm), Sun, from 10.30am (brunch).* This establishment lives after its name: the view over the Förde is superb especially from the terrace in summer months. Mediterranean-inspired food (mainly fish) is on the menu. But you're welcome to stop for just a cake or a beer.

Kieler Brauerei – *Alter Markt 9 (town centre) – ☎ (0431) 90 62 90 – www.kieler-brauerei.de – Fri-Sat, 10-2am, Mon-Thu, 10-1am, Sun, 10am-midnight.* Micro-brewery with salad bar, hot dishes, and well-priced set menus for four people, drinks included (not served on Mondays).

Hindenburgufer★★

This promenade extends for almost 4km/2mi along the shore, with shady parks on one side and extended **views★** of the roadstead on the other.

Rathaus (Town Hall)

Built between 1907 and 1911, the building mixes Baroque and Art nouveau styles and is noteworthy for its 106m/348ft tower. From the upper gallery of this, there is a splendid **view★** of the roadstead as far as the tall Laboe Memorial. *Guided tours of the tower on request, ☎ (0431) 90 10; presseamt1@lhstadt.kiel.de*

Excursions

Schleswig-Holsteinisches Freilichtmuseum★★ (Schleswig-Holstein Open-Air Museum)

6km/4mi south in Molfsee. Open Apr to Oct, 9am-6pm; Nov to Mar, Sun, 11am-4pm. €4.50. ☎ (0431) 65 96 60; www.freilichtmuseum-sh.de

Sixty rural buildings and farms typical of the country north of the Elbe are reconstructed here, arranged in groups according to their geographic origin.

A forge, a potter's workshop, an old-fashioned bakehouse, flour mills and weavers' looms are all operated by local craftsmen in traditional manner.

Laboe★

20km/12mi north. This resort on the Baltic coast has a picturesque fishing and yachting harbour and is very popular with families because of its sandy dunes and calm waters. The memorial tower, 85m/279ft high, offers a wide **view★★** of the outer part of the roadstead and, on a clear day, the Danish archipelago. Together with its underground galleries, the tower – which is built in the form of a ship's stern – constitutes the **German Naval War Memorial★** *(Marine-Ehrenmal).* It includes a museum of navigation. Also on display is the U-995, a submarine launched in Hamburg in 1943, which operated in Norwegian waters and in the Barents Sea. ♿ *From mid-Apr to mid-Oct, 9.30am-6pm; from mid-Oct to mid-Apr, 9.30am-4pm. €2.80. ☎ (043 43) 427 00.*

Nord-Ostsee-Kanal (Kiel Canal)

This link between the Baltic and the North Sea was inaugurated by Wilhelm II in 1895. From Kiel to Brunsbüttel, its 100km/62mi length is the world's busiest waterway: more than 38 000 vessels pass through it annually, not counting sports boats (although from the point of view of tonnage transported, it is relegated to third place).

From the second viaduct from Kiel to Holtenau *(Olympiabrücke, reached from Kiel via Holtenauer Straße and Prinz-Heinrich-Straße)* there is a good view of the **Holtenau** locks, linking the Kiel Canal and the Baltic Sea. On the island formed by the lock (Holtenauer Schleusen) there is an exhibition with a model of the canal and of the mechanics of the lock. Among the structures spanning the canal, the most impressive are the **Rendsburg Railway Viaduct★** *(see below)*, the **Grünental Bridge** on B 204, which has a viewing platform, and the **Hochdonn Railway Bridge**.

Holstein's "Little Switzerland"★ (Holsteinische Schweiz)

51km/32mi – allow 2hr 30min. Between Kiel and the Bay of Lübeck *(Lübecker Bucht)*, not far from the Baltic Sea, Holstein's "Little Switzerland" region is scattered with lakes separated by wooded hills formed from the glacial moraine (highest point: Bungsberg, 168m/550ft).

In the middle of the region, beside the biggest of the lakes (Großer Plöner See) is the town of **Plön**. From the terrace of its Renaissance castle, there is a pretty **view★** of the surrounding lakes. Further east, **Eutin**, birthplace of the composer Carl Maria von Weber, has retained its 17C, brick-built town centre. The moated castle (1723) is surrounded by an English-style park bordering the lake.

Malente-Gremsmühlen, a small resort built on a wooded isthmus, is a departure point for boating trips.

Koblenz★

Established in 9 BC as a Roman camp, the prosperity of Koblenz (from the Latin *confluentia*) derives from its position at the confluence of the Rhine and the Moselle. The town was seriously damaged during the Second World War, but today, after extensive reconstruction, it is a lively place. The departure point for numerous excursions on both the Rhine and the Moselle, Koblenz also offers a summer festival, when the Rhine is set ablaze with flaming torches and there are many open-air concerts.

Location

Population: 108 000. Michelin map nº 543 O 6 – Rheinland-Pfalz. At the confluence of the Rhine and the Moselle, Koblenz is also situated at the point where the Hunsrück, Eifel and Weterwald mountain ranges meet.

🅘 *Bahnhofplatz 17, ☎ (0261) 313 04 or 331 34, or the Rathaus, ☎ (0261) 130 920. Surrounding area: see MOSELTAL, RHEINTAL, (see tour suggestions including Coblence), LIMBURG AN DER LAHN (54km/33mi east), BONN (61km/38mi north).*

Background

A refuge for French aristocracy – The city came under French influence immediately after the 1789 Revolution, when refugees led by the counts of Artois and Provence, brothers of Louis XVI, fled there. From Koblenz, they organised a counter-revolution, appealing for help from the armies of neighbouring kingdoms. But in 1794 troops of the Republic occupied the east bank of the Rhine and in May 1795, the King of Prussia, Frederick-William II, signed the Treaty of Basel in which he recognised the occupation of by the French, and four years later Koblenz became the Prefecture of the French Rhine-and-Moselle department. Subsequently the Prefect Lezay-Marnésia decided to beautify the city, and in 1809 he gave it the impressive **Rheinanlagen**, a splendid riverside promenade. The occupation lasted until 1815, when, following the defeat of Napoleon, the treaty of Vienna assigned the area to the kingdom of Prussia.

Directory

Where to Eat

⊖⊖ **Löffel's Keller** – *Mehlgasse 14 – ☏ (0261) 100 47 15 – info@loeffels-keller.de – fermé 22 juin- 18 août, 21 déc.-5 janv., dim. et lun. – 29/40€.* A regularly changing menu offers a good choice of lighter meals. The three vaulted cellars, which date back to the 13C, have been restored in style.

Where to Stay

⊖⊖ **Continental-Pfälzer Hof** – *Bahnhofsplatz 1 – ☏ (0261) 301 60 – fax (0261) 301610 – info@contihotel.de – Closed 20 Dec to 20 Jan – 35rm: €65/90 – Restaurant €17.50/26.* This modern and centrally-located hotel has functional guestrooms and is a stone's throw from the station. The double-glazing manages to cut out outside noise and ensures a good night's sleep. German and Brazilian specialities available in the Bossa-Nova restaurant.

Walking About

Deutsches Eck★

A gigantic equestrian statue of Wilhelm I presides over this tongue of land which marks the confluence of the Rhine and the Moselle. From the gallery crowning the base of the statue *(107 steps)*, there is a fine view of the town, the port, the Moselle bridges and the east bank of the Rhine, overlooked by the fortress of Ehrenbreitstein.

Stiftskirche St-Kastor

This Romanesque church succeeded an earlier basilica in which the Treaty of Verdun, dividing Charlemagne's empire, was drawn up in 843. Heavy fan vaulting covers the nave and chancel. The furnishings are interesting: the tombs of two archbishops lie at the back of multicoloured Gothic bays and, in the south transept, there is a series of 16 painted wood panels, once part of a rood screen, with a picture of St Castor *(bottom left)*.

Take the promenade along the Moselle and explore the little pedestrianised streets of the old town before arriving at the Liebfrauenkirche.

Liebfrauenkirche

This originally Romanesque church was remodelled in the 13C and given a Late Gothic chancel in the 15C. Beautifully crafted, ornate keystones seem to grow from the ribs of the vault. The belfries were crowned with Baroque roofs towards the end of the 17C. The interesting windows in the chancel are the work of HG Stockhausen in 1992.

Jesuitenplatz

In the courtyard of a 17C Jesuit College, now serving as the town hall, is the *Schängelbrunnen* – a fountain evoking the mischief perpetrated by the street urchins of the city.

Mittelrheinmuseum

Florinsmarkt 15-17. Closer to the Moselle than the Rhine, this museum retraces the history of the town and the surrounding area through paintings, religious artefacts (statues, triptychs and icons) and everyday items dating from the Middle Ages. Finish the walk by walking along the Rhine to the castle.

Excursions

Festung Ehrenbreitstein★ (Citadel)

4.5km/3mi. Cross the Rhine on Pfaffendorfer Brücke then turn left. This strategic stronghold, commanding the confluence of the two rivers, was the possession of the archbishops of Trier from the 10C until 1799, when it was destroyed by the French. Between 1816 and 1832 the Prussians, who had ruled the Rhineland since the Congress of Vienna (1815), constructed the powerful existing fortress.

From the terrace, there is a **view★** of Koblenz, Schloß Stolzenfels to the south, the wooded plateau of Hunsrück and the volcanic massif of the Eifel.

Kloster Maria Laach★

20km/12mi west. The vast crater lake beside which this abbey stands emphasises the monumental air of poise and solidity characterising the abbey buildings. The 12C abbey church is a Romanesque basilica with three naves, whose exterior is reminiscent of the cathedrals of Worms, Speyer and Mainz.

The cloister-type **entrance portico★**, added in the early 13C, has intricately worked capitals. An unusual hexagonal baldaquin – perhaps suggesting a Moorish influence – is stretched over the altar. The crypt is the oldest part of the church.

Rheintal★★★ *(see RHEINTAL)*

Moseltal★★★ *(see MOSELTAL)*

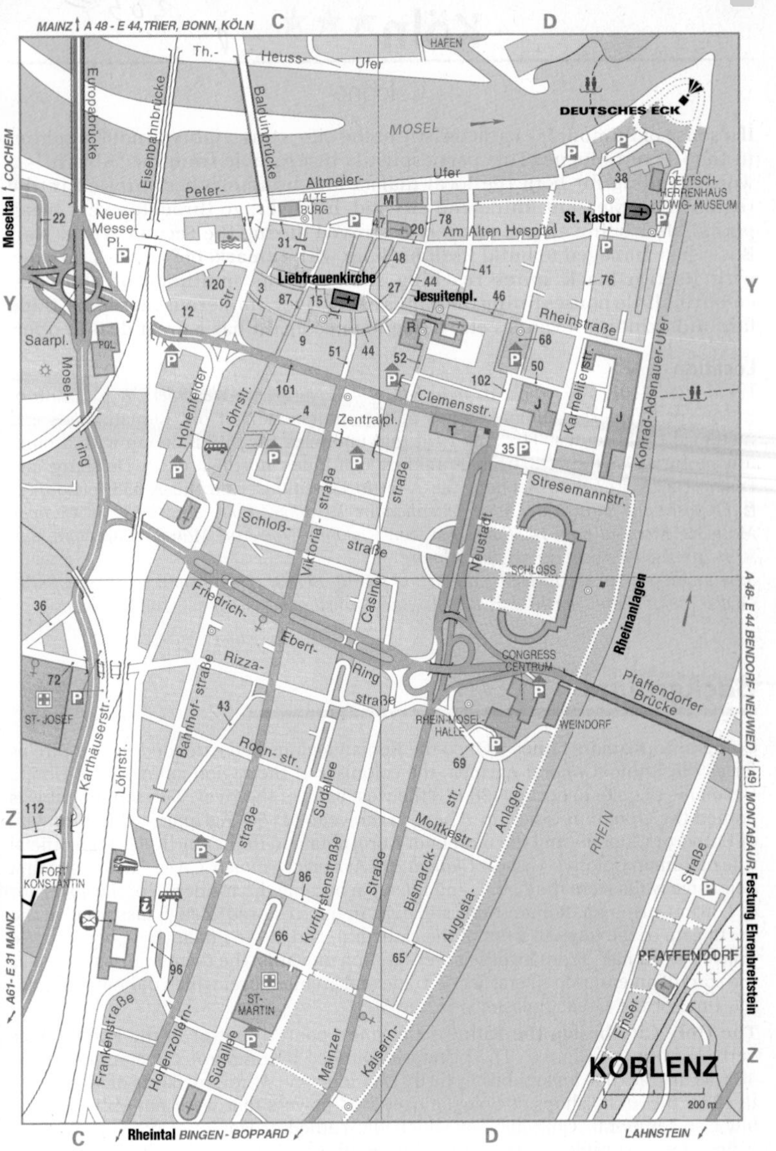

Altengraben . . . . CY 3
Altlöhrtor . . . . CY 4
Am Plan . . . . CY 9
Am Wöllershof . . . . CY 12
An der Liebfrauenkirche . . . . CY 15
An der Moselbrücke . . . . CY 17
Auf der Danne . . . . CY 20
Baedekerstraße . . . . CY 22
Braugasse . . . . DY 27
Burgstraße . . . . CY 31
Clemensplatz . . . . DY 35
Cusanusstraße . . . . CZ 36
Danziger Freiheit . . . . DY 38
Eltzerhofstraße . . . . DY 41
Emil-Schüller-Straße . . . . CZ 43
Entenpfuhl . . . . CDY 44
Firmungstraße . . . . DY 46
Florinsmarkt . . . . CDY 47
Florinspfaffengasse . . . . DY 48
Gerichtsstraße . . . . DY 50
Görgenstraße . . . . CY 51
Gymnasialstraße . . . . DY 52
Januarius-Zick-Straße . . . . . . DZ 65
Johannes-Müller-Straße . . . . . CZ 66
Josef-Görres-Platz . . . . DY 68
Julius-Wegeler-Straße . . . . . . DZ 59
Kardinal-Krementz-Straße . . CZ 72
Kastorpfaffenstraße . . . . DY 76
Kornpfortstraße . . . . DY 78
Löhrstraße . . . . CY
Markenbildchenweg . . . . . . CZ 86
Marktstraße . . . . CY 87
Neversstraße . . . . CZ 96
Pfuhlgasse . . . . CY 101
Poststraße . . . . DY 102
Schlossstraße . . . . CDY
Simmerner Straße . . . . CZ 112
Viktoriastraße . . . . CY
Weißer Gasse . . . . CY 120

Köln★★★

Cologne

If a sense of humour is characteristic of the city, conviviality is not far behind in the life of Cologne. This party spirit is inseparable from the "Kölsch" – a word standing for both the local dialect and a famous beer brewed in the region. This pleasant Rhineland city did, however, go through a very bleak period after being almost entirely destroyed during the Second World War. But it has managed to build itself back up with remarkable vigour and now, with its two black spires reaching skywards, its multitude of churches, colourful little houses lining the banks of the river, numerous museums, trade fair and exhibition venues etc, Cologne once again has a great deal to offer.

Location

Population: 1 017 700. Michelin map 543 N 4 – Nordrhein-Westfalen. A real hub of European business, Cologne stands at the intersection of old Roman roads and medieval trade routes. The ring road that encircles the city links up with around ten motorways: the A 3 from Frankfurt continues northwards to Duisburg and Essen; the A 4 goes to Aachen, the A 59 to Düsseldorf and the A 555 to Bonn.

ℹ *Opposite the cathedral, Unter Fettenhennen 19, 50667 Köln, ☎ 22 132 33 45: open May-Oct, Mon-Sat 8am-10.30pm, Sun 9am-10.30pm; Nov-Apr, Mon-Sat 8am-9pm, Sun 9am-7pm. www.koeln.de; www.koeln.org*

Surrounding area: see BRÜHL (13km/8mi south), BONN (29km/18mi south), DÜSSELDORF (39km/24mi north) and EIFEL (Bad Münstereifel is 49km/31mi southwest).

Background

Cologne in Roman Times – Once the Roman legions had extended the Empire as far as the Rhine, General Agrippa, the coloniser of the region, allowed the Ubii, a Germanic people, to occupy (38 BC) the west bank of the river. The settlement was named the Oppidum Ubiorum. Then, in the year AD 50, Agrippina, the third wife of Emperor Claudius and the mother of Nero, obtained for her birthplace the official title of Roman Colony – *Colonia Claudia Ara Agrippinensium* (CCAA). "Colonia's" first defensive walls were then built, and the town became the residence of the governor of Lower Germania. Roman ruins still exist in the (restored) Zeughausstraße, at the north gate of the town in front of the cathedral, and at the Praetorium, beneath the present town hall. From its official recognition onwards, the town flourished: it was the start of an era, rich in craftwork, trade and architecture, which did not end until the time of the Great Invasions, in the 5C.

The Holy City beside the Rhine – Cologne's political power in the Middle Ages derived from the Church. The bishopric founded by Emperor Constantine in the 4C was upgraded to an archbishopric by Charlemagne. Until the Battle of Worringen in 1288, the archbishops of Cologne exercised powers that were not only spiritual but also temporal. Churches, of which the cathedral was one, monasteries and collegiates rose rapidly – more than 150 in all. In the 13C and at the beginning of the 14C, the city became the enlightened religious, intellectual and artistic centre of the Rhine Valley. Eminent men came to preach: the Dominicans **Albertus Magnus** (the teacher of Thomas Aquinas) and **Master Eckhart**, as well as the Scottish Franciscan, **Duns Scotus**. It was the work of such religious scholars that led in 1388 to the creation of Cologne University by local lay burghers.

Trade and Commerce – Because of its favoured position on the banks of the Rhine and at the crossroads of important trade routes, Cologne soon became a power in the commercial world, imposing its own system of weights and measures over the whole of northern Germany. Such authority derived from a decree known as the **Stapelrecht** (Law of Stockage), under which all foreign merchants passing through the city were obliged to keep their goods there for at least three days, thus allowing Cologne residents a prior right to purchase. The town's first fair was held in 1360. Its elevation to the status of Free City in 1475 did no more than set an official seal on the preponderant role Cologne had in fact been playing since the 13C.

The Modern City – Industrialisation in the second half of the 19C conferred on Cologne an expansion that was both rapid and remarkable. After the Second World War, **Konrad Adenauer** continued the process of modernisation he had inaugurated while he was mayor of the city between 1917 and 1933 – the year in which he was deposed by the Nazis. It was through the man destined to become the Federal Republic's first Chancellor that the university, shut down under the French occupation in 1798, was re-opened (1919); that the Deutz exhibition halls *(Messehallen)* were built; and that the green belts girdling the city were established.

Art and Culture – Diversity is the keyword in any consideration of cultural life in Cologne today. Apart from music and drama, the plastic arts hold pride of place: no fewer than 120 galleries are devoted to the exhibition of contemporary work. Two highly regarded international fairs take place here every year: the *Westdeutsche Kunstmesse* and "Art Cologne", devoted to modern art. Beside the Schnütgen Museum, the **Josef-Haubrich-Halle** mounts important exhibitions.

Heinrich Böll (1917-85), one of the most eminent representatives of German post-war writing and winner of the Nobel Prize for Literature in 1972, was born in Cologne – and his work, sparing neither the Church nor society, is inseparable from his Rhineland birthplace.

Media City – There have been publishing houses and printers in Cologne for centuries. Building on this reputation, a great deal has been done over the past few years in the sphere of electronic media. Cologne, the media city, is currently Germany's TV capital, with eight television stations, including WDR *(Westdeutscher Rundfunk)*, three RTL programmes, *Viva*, *Vox* and five radio stations, recording studios, a media park and an Academy of Media Arts. The media and communications business in Cologne brings in an annual turnover in the region of 10 billion euros.

Town Life – There is a strong sense of neighbourhood – almost rural – unity in the relationship linking the Cologne locals with their "Veedeln": the traditional quarters of the old town, each centred on a parish church, each preserving its own traditions. St Severin is the oldest and most typical *(see below)*. But in addition to their particular district, all Cologne citizens appreciate that part of the old town bordering the Rhine. Remodelled in the 1980s, this is now, night and day, one of the liveliest parts of the city. Since the riverside highway has been diverted through tunnels between the Hohenzollern and Deutzer bridges, land has been freed for the establishment of attractive gardens *(Rheingarten)* where the inhabitants can walk or relax in calm surroundings immediately above the water. Boat excursions leave from this point.

The **Dance Fountain,** which holds open-air events, situated in the 40ha/100-acre **Rheinpark** on the far (eastern) side of the river, continues nevertheless to be very popular.

Special Features

DOM★★★ (CATHEDRAL)

♿ *6am-7.30pm.* ☎ *(0221) 92 58 47 30; www.koelnerdom.de*

It took more than 600 years to complete this gigantic edifice, dedicated to St Ursula. In 1164, when Frederick I Barbarossa donated relics of the Magi to the town of Cologne, an accelerating influx of pilgrims began, and by 1248 the need for a new and larger place of worship had become pressing. Thus began the construction of a new cathedral, the first Gothic church in the Rhineland, its original design based on those in Paris, Amiens and Reims, although the size of its exterior far exceeds theirs. The chancel was completed c 1320. The south tower was built in two levels by 1410 when work was suspended. Work stopped again in 1437, then in 1560 the ground plan of the building had taken shape up to the level of the ground floor when work on the nave and transept was halted. More than three centuries elapsed before the gap between the chancel and tower was filled: it was not until 1842, when

Cologne

Rudolph/Köln Tourismus Office

Directory

Public Transport

The main operator of the local public transport network in Cologne is the *Kölner Verkehrsbetriebe* (KVB), which runs most buses, underground trains (U-Bahn) and trams (Straßenbahn). The KVB is linked with the Rhein-Sieg transport authority (VRS), which covers the area as far as Bonn, among other places.
Cologne is divided into different price zones; the cost of single journeys *(Einzelfahrt)* comes to €1.25, €2 or €3.
A *Minigruppenticket* costs €7.50 and is valid for up to five people after 9am allowing unlimited travel on all of Cologne's public transport for one day. The 24hr ticket for one person costs €5.30, the three-day ticket €13.50. For 24hr information ☎ 50 40 30.
There are KVB information booths *(Informationsstellen)* all over Cologne, the main ones are on the east side of the main railway station *(Hauptbahnhof Ostseite)*, open Mon-Sat 7am-8pm, Sun noon-8pm; and at Neumarkt 25, open Mon-Fri 7am-7pm, Sat 8.30am-4pm, and Ehrenfeldgürtel 14, open Mon-Fri 7am-7pm, Sat 8.30am-2pm.

Internet – www.kvb-koeln.de
The **KölnTourismus Card**, available in hotels for €9.20 (valid 72hr), allows the use of all of Cologne's public transport facilities, including a coach tour of the city, free entry to some of the city's museums and discounts on tickets for the opera, boat trips, ascent of the cathedral tower, chocolate museum etc.

Sightseeing

City tours – Coach trip with guide, including a visit to a museum, available from the *Köln Tourismus* office opposite the cathedral; Apr-Oct, daily at 10am, 11am, 2pm, 3pm, Sat also at 5pm; Nov-Mar at 11am and 2pm. The tour lasts around 2hr and costs €13. Meeting point for tours of the cathedral is by the main door, Mon-Sat at 11am, 12.30pm, 2pm and 3.30pm, Sun at 2pm and 3.30pm only.
City tours on foot organised by *StattReisen Köln, ☎ 732 51 13*, and *Inside Cologne-City Tours, ☎ 52 19 77*, www.stattreisen-koeln.de, www.inside-cologne.de.

Boat trips – The *Köln-Düsseldorfer Deutsche Rheinschiffahrt (KD)* has the largest fleet of excursion boats on the Rhine, *☎ 208 83 18*. Other boat companies include *Dampfschiffahrt Colonia, ☎ 257 42 25*, and *KölnTourist Personenschiffahrt, ☎ 12 16 00*, www.k-d.com

Dates for your Diary

Carnival in Feb (although season traditionally begins on 11 Nov) with the great Rosenmontag (Mon before Lent) parade, **Ringfest der PopKomm** in Aug, **Art Cologne** in Nov.

Where to Eat

⊖ **Brauhaus Goldener Pflug** – *Olpener Straße 421 – 51109 Köln-Merheim – ☎ (0221) 310 56 31 – www.brauhaus-goldener-pflug.de – €10.95/15.80.* A typical Cologne restaurant with a wooden decor that adds warmth to the rustic, comfortable setting. Several bars, a brasserie-style section, dining room, and 240-seat summer beer garden.

⊖⊖ **Hase** – *St.-Apern-Straße 17 – ☎ (0221) 25 43 75 – Closed Sun – ⊭ – €22.50/38.* The pale wooden tables of this restaurant-café add to its rustic charm. A few, generally traditional dishes, marked on a board.

⊖⊖ **Heising und Adelmann** – *Friesenstraße 58-60 – ☎ (0221) 130 94 24 – info@heising-und-adelmann.de – Mon-Thu 6pm-1am, Fri-Sat 6pm-3am, closed Sun and public holidays – €26/39.* A fashionable restaurant serving a variety of dishes in a relaxed atmosphere. 50 different cocktails to choose from at the bar. Lovely terrace at the back.

⊖⊖ **Brasserie Liège** – *Lütticher Straße 30 – ☎ (0221) 952 05 50 – www.liege.de – Closed Sun and public holidays – ⊭ – €26.50/31.50.* A brasserie typical of the Belgian quarter, serving good French cuisine. Sober, modern decor.

⊖⊖ **Em Krützche** – *Am Frankenturm 1 – ☎ (0221) 258 08 39 – info@em-kruetzche.de – Closed Holy Week and Mon – €28.50/43.50.* This family-run restaurant in the old town was founded over 400 years ago and has several dining rooms.

⊖⊖ **Paul's Restaurant** – *Bülowstraße 2 – 50733 Köln-Nippes – ☎ (0221) 76 68 39 – pauls-restaurant@t-online.de – Closed for 1 week during the carnival, 2 weeks in Aug, and Mon – €38.50/46.* A restored house in a residential area with smart rustic interior and well-laid tables. A choice of several original dishes.

⊖⊖ **Le Moissonnier** – *Krefelder Straße 25 – ☎ (0221) 72 94 79 – Closed 24 Dec-3 Jan, 1 week at Easter and 3 weeks in Aug/Sept – ⊭ – €39/57.50.* A typical Art Nouveau *(Jugendstil)* style bistro which occupies an old house in the city centre and pampers its patrons. Creative French cuisine.

⊖⊖⊖ **Hanse Stube** – *Dompropst-Ketzer-Straße 2 – ☎ (0221) 270 34 02 – ehe@excelsiorhotelernst.de – €48/63.* An elegant restaurant in the Excelsior Hotel Ernst. Well-trained staff, French dishes on the menu.

Where to Stay

⊖ **Hotel Im Kupferkessel** – *Probsteigasse 6 (north of Christophstraße near St Gereon's Church) – ☎ (0221) 2 70 79 60 – Fax (0221) 270 79 629 – www.im-kupferkessel.de – 13rm (including 10 single rm) €30/66* ☕. Small, very well-kept hotel with a warm welcome on the edge of the old town. The rooms are small and basic (some with bathroom on the landing). Pleasant breakfast room.

Hotel Brandenburger Hof – *Brandenburger Straße 2 – ☎ (0221) 12 28 89 – Fax (0221) 135304 – www.brandenburgerhof.de – 31rm: €36/140*. North of the old town, this hotel has plain, functional rooms and a small garden. Reasonable prices. The main station *(Hauptbahnhof)* and cathedral are nearby.

Haus an den sieben Wegen – *Grafenmühlenweg 220, 51069 Köln-Dellbrück – ☎ (0221) 689 30 00 – Fax (0221) 68930020 – www.hotel-7-wege.de – Closed from Christmas to beginning of Jan – 15rm: €45/135*. Very neat, well-appointed and well-run hotel set at the heart of a small park in a residential area. Variously decorated rooms, some of them very spacious.

Wippenbekk – *Karlstraße 7, 50996 Köln-Rodenkirchen – ☎ (0221) 935 31 50 – Fax (0221) 93531599 – www.wippenbekk.de – 11rm: €59/149 – Restaurant €10.70/15.50*. This hotel in an ideal location on the banks of the Rhine offers sober, modern rooms equipped with Italian furniture. The restaurant with winter garden affords a delightful view. The hotel also has a beer garden.

Das kleine Hotel – *Wichheimer Straße 200, 51067 Köln-Holweide – ☎ (0221) 691 05 91 – Fax (0221) 6910592 – Reservation necessary – 7rm: €60/80 – Restaurant €27.50/68*. A small well-kept establishment with a boarding-house atmosphere. Cosy rooms with pale wooden furniture and wooden flooring. The Stadtbahn station is on the doorstep.

Hotel Trost – *Vogelsanger Straße 60-62, 50823 Köln-Ehrenfeld – ☎ (0221) 952 91 00 – Fax (0221) 512151 – www.hotel-trost.de – 18rm: €68/99*. This little well-kept family-run hotel occupies an old house that has been renovated. Modern, welcoming rooms.

Hotel Im Wasserturm – *Kaygasse 2 – ☎ (0221) 200 80 – Fax (0221) 2008888 – info@hotel-im-wasserturm.de – 88rm: from €165 – €18 – Restaurant €49/65.50*. This imposing brick building, once the largest water tower in Europe, offers an original setting and personalised rooms. Designer interior for the most part. The 11m/36ft-high entrance lobby is particularly impressive. Magnificent view of the city from the 11th-floor restaurant.

Excelsior Hotel Ernst – *Domplatz – ☎ (0221) 27 01 – Fax (0221) 135150 – ehe@excelsiorhotelernst.de – 152rm: from €210*. The best address in Cologne, right opposite the cathedral. Access to this traditional establishment via a magnificent marble lobby. Highly qualified staff, refined rooms and grand suites, along with a sauna and fitness facilities, to meet the needs of a demanding clientele.

F. Damm/Köln Tourismus Office

Cologne – Hohe Straße

Taking a Break

Café Eigel – *Brückenstraße 1-3 (prolongs Glockengasse to the east) – ☎ (0221) 2 57 58 58 – Mon-Fri 9am-7pm, Sat 9am-6pm, Sun 2-6pm*. This traditional yet modern-looking café serves home-made pralines, cakes and tarts, and exhibits works by modern artists which are also for sale.

Café Reichard – *Unter Fettenhennen 11 (opposite the cathedral) – ☎ (0221) 2 57 85 42 – www.cafe-reichard.de – 8.30am-8pm*. This café with its classic interior has a winter garden and large terrace. Add to that a magnificent view of the cathedral, and it's easy to see why it is so popular. The veranda is undoubtedly the best place to sit and watch the world go by.

Käse-Pavillon – *Breite Straße 29 (access via Opernpassagen or Neue Langgasse) – ☎ (0221) 2 58 01 30 – kaesepavillon@netcologne.de – Mon-Fri 7am-7pm, Sat 7am-4pm*. This unusual fast-food restaurant is a temple to cheese. In winter there is a selection of over 300 varieties (150 in summer) to choose from every day. Make up your own sandwich or choose your favourite dish from the menu. Small selection of wines to accompany your snack.

Going Out

Useful Tips – The old city centre offers a wealth of possibilities when it comes to eating out, having a drink or being otherwise entertained. Areas with the highest density of bars include the Belgian district between Aachener and Venloer Straße, the university district (around Zülpicher Straße), south of town (around Chlodwigplatz) and the district around Friesenstraße. The traditional beer here is "Kölsch", usually served in small 0.2l glasses.

Biergarten im Stadtgarten – *Venloer Straße 40 (street starting from Friesenplatz station to the west) – ☎ (0221) 95 29 94 21 – www.stadtgarten.de – Apr-Oct: noon-11pm (closed in bad weather).* This pleasant beer garden is at the entrance to the "Stadtgarten" park, not far from the city centre. Snacks are served from 3pm. For those with a sweet tooth, a selection of cakes is served at the café next door.

Früh am Dom – *Am Hof 12-14 – ☎ (0221) 2 61 32 11 – www.frueh.de – 8am-12.30am – Closed 24 Dec.* A laid-back restaurant offering a different kind of cuisine on each of its three floors. No need to order your Kölsch – it will be already waiting for you. For peace and quiet, try the 1st floor restaurant; the cellar is more typical.

Päffgen – *Friesenstraße 64-66 (between Friesenplatz and Römerturm) – ☎ (0221) 13 54 61 – www.paeffgen.de – 10am-12.30am.* Traditional restaurant with rustic decor; Kölsch and regional dishes on the menu. In summer, patrons can enjoy the pleasant beer garden at the back.

Papa Joe's Biersalon "Klimperkasten" – *Alter Markt 50-52 – ☎ (0221) 2 58 21 32 – www.papajoes.de – 11am-1am, Fri-Sat until 3am.* Retro atmosphere guaranteed in this restaurant whose walls and even ceiling are covered in old photos. An enjoyable trip down memory lane, to the sounds of piano music or stirring tunes played by musical automatons.

Papa Joe's Jazzlokal "Em Streckstrump" – *Buttermarkt 37 (street parallel to the Rhine, starting from Groß St-Martin to the south) – ☎ (0221) 2 57 79 31 – www.papajoes.de – 8pm-3am, Sun from 3.30pm.* Jazz has reigned supreme over evenings here for more than 25 years. The drinks are admittedly rather expensive but the concerts are free and the atmosphere always good. "Four O'Clock Jazz" every Sunday.

Hyatt-Biergarten – *Kennedyufer 2a (coming from the cathedral, cross the Hohenzollernbrücke) – 50679 Köln-Deutz – ☎ (0221) 82 81 34 – www.cologne.regency.hyatt.de – From end Apr to beginning of Oct, Mon-Sat noon-midnight, Sun 11am-midnight (closed in bad weather).* The beer garden of this luxury hotel on the east bank of the Rhine affords a magnificent view of the cathedral and historic centre of Cologne. From the beginning of May to the end of August, crowds of music-lovers gather to listen to jazz on Sundays (noon-3pm, free admission).

Culture

Useful Tips – Listings of cultural events in the city can be found in the monthly publication *Köln im...* (followed by the month), available from the tourist information office (price €1). Other monthly magazines such as *StadtRevue* and *Prinz* are also valuable sources of information and are sold at bookshops and newspaper kiosks.

Shopping

Useful Tips – The cathedral is the best point of departure for any shopping trip in Cologne. It brings you straight to the main shopping street, the Hohe Straße. This is crossed by Schildergasse, which is lined with department stores. Not far from the Neumarkt are numerous shopping arcades, such as Neumarktpassage and Neumarktgalerie. Exclusive boutiques are centred around Breite Straße, Mittelstraße and Pfeilstraße. There are further shopping opportunities besides these in other parts of town, such as the south around Chlodwigplatz; and in Bonnerstraße and Severinstraße. Antique shops and art galleries are concentrated in St-Apern-Straße; there are more galleries to the north of Neumarkt (Albertusstraße) and in the district around the cathedral.

4711 Echt Kölnisch Wasser – *Glockengasse 4711 – ☎ (0221) 9 25 04 50 – www.4711.com – Mon-Fri 9am-7pm, Sat 9am-6pm.* The traditional home of the famous Eau de Cologne. Here you will find a fountain of *aqua mirabile* where you can freshen up, a historical exhibition, souvenirs and a whole range of beauty products. The carillon on the southern façade of the building plays the *Marseillaise* every hour from 9am to 9pm.

neo-Gothic fever shook Romantic Germany, that work on the original plans was resumed. In 1880 the cathedral was at last ceremoniously consecrated in the presence of Emperor Wilhelm I. UNESCO has declared the cathedral one of the world's cultural heritage sites.

Exterior

The twin-towered western façade marks the peak of achievement in the style known as Flamboyant Gothic. Stepped windows, embellished gables, slender buttresses, burst upwards, ever upwards, slimly in line with the tapering spires that reach a height of 157m/515ft. The apse facing the Rhine, spined with a multitude of turrets and pinnacles is a bravura expression of architectural prowess and enthusiasm. The bronze doors **(1)** in the south transept entrance (1948-54) are by Ewald Mataré (Celestial Jerusalem above; Cologne in flames on the right).

Interior

Entering the cathedral by the west door, one appreciates the sweep of the nave in a single glance, but until the transept is reached, the building's colossal proportions cannot truly be taken in. The nave, as far as the choir, is 144m/472ft long, 45m/148ft wide, and 43.5m/143ft high. Seen from the nave, the choir appears to float at some infinite distance, while the vaulting arched far above seems to reach a height that is completely unreal.

The five Late Gothic **stained-glass windows★** in the north aisle (1507-08) depict the lives of The Virgin and St Peter.

The Kreuzkapelle, a chapel off the north ambulatory, houses the **Cross of Gero★** *(Gerokreuz)* **(3)**, a unique example of 10C Ottonian art. In the axial chapel *(Dreikönigskapelle)* is a very old stained-glass window, the *Älteres Bibelfenster* **(4)**, which was put in place in 1265. Behind the high altar is the shrine of the Three Magi, the **Dreikönigenschrein★★★**. This masterpiece of medieval goldsmithing, intricately decorated with different figures, contains relics said to be of the Three Magi. The reliquary, in the form of a basilica with unusually large dimensions (2.2m/7ft long), was begun in 1190 and completed in 1225 by Cologne master craftsmen. The last chapel in the south ambulatory *(Marienkapelle)* contains the celebrated altarpiece of the city's patrons, the **Altar der Stadtpatrone★★★**, painted c 1440 by **Stefan Lochner** and illustrating The Adoration of the Magi (centre section). Side panels portray the patron saints of the city of Cologne: St Ursula and her Virgins on the left; St Gereon on the right. Against a pillar on the south wall nearby stands a figure of **The Madonna of Milan**, a Virgin and Child which resembles in style the figures on the pillars in the choir which date from 1270 to 1280.

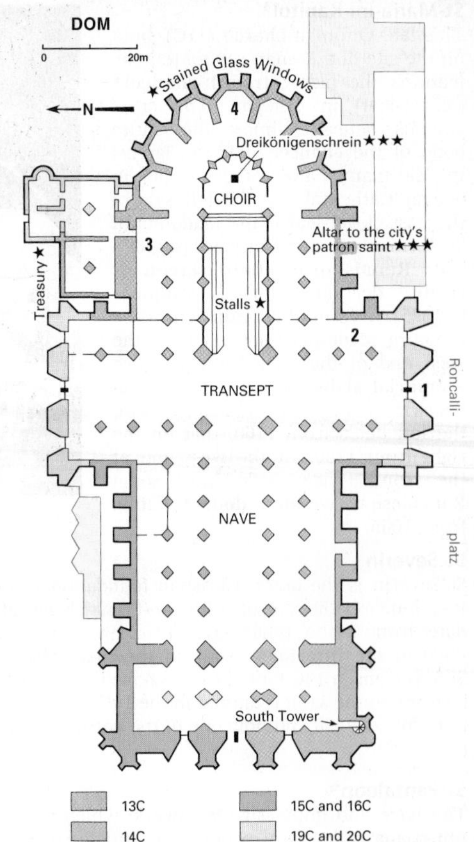

The south transept houses a large Flemish polyptych of 1521 with double side panels known as the **Altarpiece of the Five Moors (2)** *(Agilolphusaltar)*.

Choir – *Same visiting times as the cathedral. The ambulatory is not accessible during services.* ☎ *(0221) 92 58 47 30.* The finely carved **choir stalls★** (14C) *(Chorgestühl)*, the most extensive medieval example in Germany, contain 104 places. High up above the stalls, on each of the chancel walls, frescoes dating from c 1332 to 1340 represent the legends of various saints. The 14 statues incorporated in the pillars of the chancel *(Chorpfeilerstatuen)* are of Jesus, Mary and the 12 Apostles.

South Tower *(Südturm)* – A very steep stairway (509 steps) leads to a platform from which, at a height of 97m/318ft, a splendid panorama of Cologne and the surrounding country can be enjoyed. Do not neglect the belfry *(Glockenstube)*. The largest of the nine bells, St Peter's Bell *(Petersglocke)* was cast in 1923. At an overall weight of 24t (the clapper alone accounts for 800kg/1 763lb) this is the biggest swinging church bell in the world.

Treasury★ *(Domschatzkammer) – Enter from outside via the north side.* ♿ *10am-6pm. €4.* ☎ *(0221) 17 94 05 30.* The cathedral treasury is housed in the Gothic vaults beneath the sacristy and contains gold and silver liturgical plate, crosiers, pectoral crosses, the Baroque shrine to St Engelbert, St Peter's crosier and a reliquary monstrance with St Peter's chain, and Late Antique fabric with the Three Magi.

ROMANESQUE CHURCHES

The Romanesque period in Cologne, from the mid 10C to the mid-13C, saw the construction of numerous churches. In the old town alone, 12 churches from that era are still standing. Strolling through its old streets, therefore, the visitor gets a good idea of the different periods and varying styles of Rhineland Romanesque architecture. Certain concepts of religious design – the trefoil chancel, for instance – originated in the city *(see Art and architecture: Rhineland Romanesque Style)*.

St-Maria-im-Kapitol★

This late Ottonian church (11C), built on the site of a Roman capitol temple, features the oldest **trefoil chancel★** (clover-leaf) in Cologne. The crypt extends beneath almost the entire body of the chancel; it is the largest in Germany after the crypt in Speyer Cathedral. On the left side of the east clover-leaf is the Madonna of St Hermann-Joseph altarpiece (c 1180). The **Renaissance choir screen** is richly decorated with sculpture (c 1525). In front of it, to the left, is the Limburg Madonna (late 13C). At the west end of the nave there are two **memorial slabs** dedicated to Plectrudis, wife of Pepin the Middle; that on the left dates from 1160, that on the right from 1280. At the west end of the south side aisle are some Romanesque **wooden doors★** dating from 1065.

Skylife/Köln Tourismus Office

St-Maria-im-Kapitol

St Severin

St Severin is the oldest Christian foundation in Cologne, dating back to the 4C. It is built on the site of a Roman-Frankish burial ground. The present building dates from the 13C (chancel) and 15C (west tower and nave). There is a fine Gothic nave in the **interior★**. Note, in the main chancel, paintings by the Master of St Severinus; a 13C forked Cross above the parish altar; and behind the high altar, a shrine to the saint (restored in the 19C). The actual tomb of St Severinus, Bishop of Cologne c 400 and now one of the patron saints of the city, is kept in the crypt (11C-13C).

St Pantaleon★

The nave and impressive Westwerk, which originally served as a law court and musicians' gallery, are examples of Ottonian architecture (10C). The **rood screen★** closing off the chancel is Late Gothic. The 10C tombs of Archbishop Bruno of Cologne, brother of Otto the Great, and Empress Theophanu, wife of Otto II, are in the crypt and south side aisle.

Gereonskirche★ (St Gereon)

The originality of this church lies in its elliptical plan and the addition in 1220 of a **decagon★** between its two towers. The crypt with its 11C mosaic floor contains the tombs of Gereon and martyrs of the Theban Legions. The frescoes date from the 13C and the altarpiece is Renaissance style with some Gothic features. In the nave (north side) is an interesting tabernacle (1608), depicting the Last Supper (carved in relief) and the Aubusson tapestry; on the south side is a colourfully painted Virgin and Child (1400).

St Andreas

This Late Romanesque church was built in the first quarter of the 13C, as a vaulted basilica on pillars with a two-storey west transept, short nave, octagonal transept tower and transept with a trefoil apse. It features some remarkable architectural sculpture. At the beginning of the 15C, the chancel was demolished

Eau de Cologne

The people of Cologne were familiar with this *"aqua mirabile"* as early as the 16C, although it did not become a commercial success until the 18C. The fact that it finally did is thanks to the enterprising spirit of a family of Italian immigrants, the Farinas, of whom the most famous is **Johann Maria Farina**. "Cologne water" *(Kölnisch Wasser)* was considered to have medicinal properties and was believed to cure a number of diverse ills. In the wake of the Farina family's success, a number of other producers of the wonder-water sprang up, with the result that "Eau de Cologne" became famous and a best-seller for the export market. The new wave of producers included a certain **Wilhelm Mühlens**, who founded a company in Glockengasse in 1792.

Under Napoleon, the use of Eau de Cologne as a medicine was banned, whereupon the manufacturers hastily began marketing their cure-all as toilet water. Also during the French occupation of Cologne, the city's street numbering was radically altered and as a result the house where Mühlens' business was located became no 4711 Glockengasse. In 1875, this number was registered as a trade mark for authentic Eau de Cologne *(Echt Kölnisch Wasser)*.

The carillon in the gable of no 4711 Glockengasse plays the Marseillaise every hour from 9am to 9pm.

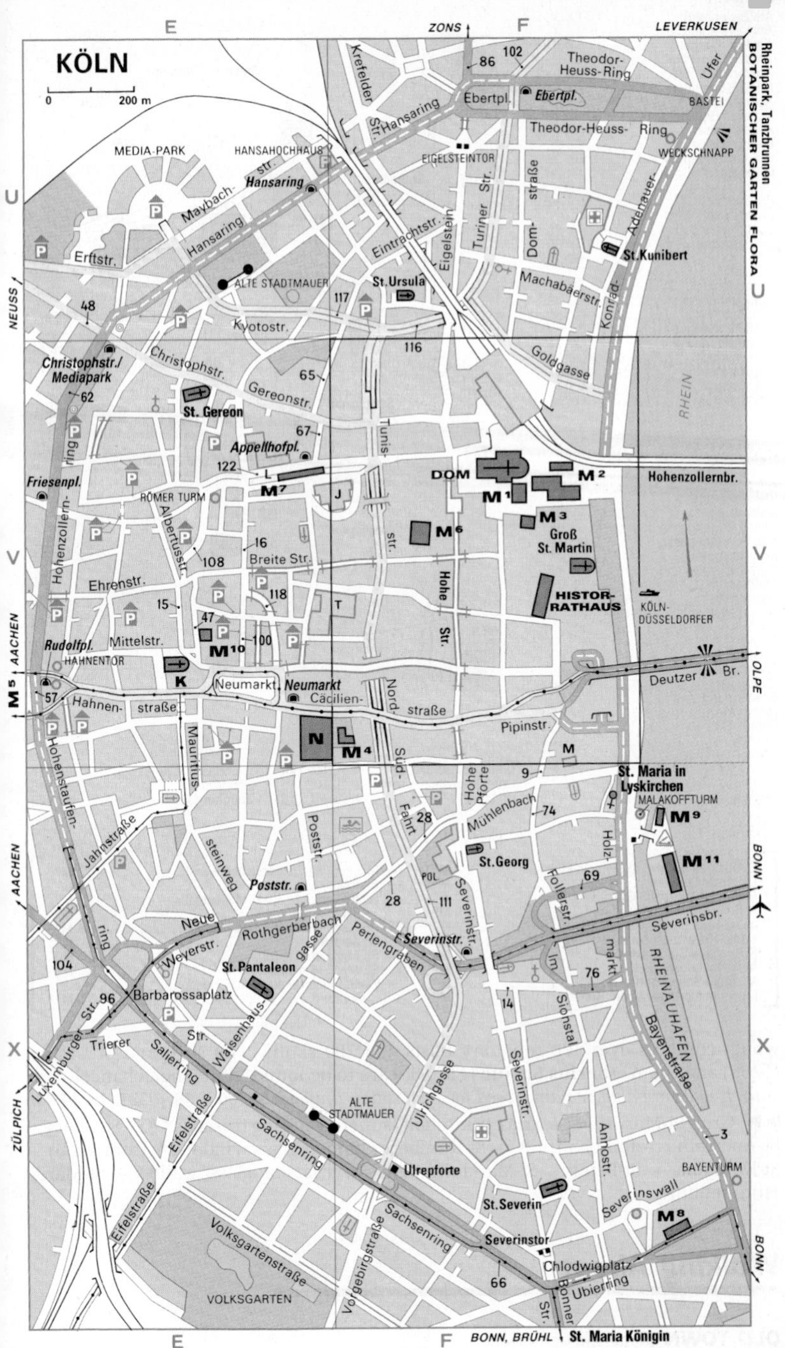

and a Gothic chancel added, modelled on the glass architectural shrine at Aachen (1414-20). The Gothic side chapels contain murals from the first half of the 13C. The sarcophagus of Albert the Great (c 1200-80) lies in the crypt, which also contains the remnants of 14C murals. Elaborate choir stalls dating from c 1430.

St Ursula

In the north aisle are 30 plates (1456) by Stefan Lochner depicting the martyrdom of St Ursula. The daughter of a British king, St Ursula was murdered by Huns along with 10 of her companions in the 5C. As the story was passed down through the ages, the number of martyred maidens increased to 11 000. In the south transept is the **Goldene Kammer**★ (Golden Chamber), built by Johannes Crane in 1643,

Am Bayenturm .... FX 3
Am Leystapel .... GZ 4
Am Malzbüchel .... GZ 5
An den Dominikanern ...... GY 8
An der Malzmühle .... FX 9
An St.-Katharinen .... FX 14
Apostelnstr. .... EV 15
Auf dem Berlich .... EV 16
Augustinerstr .... GZ 19
Bechergasse .... GZ 22
Bischofsgarten-Str. .... GY 26
Blaubach .... FX 28
Breite Str. .... GZ
Brückenstr. .... GZ 32
Dompropst-
Ketzer-Str. .... GY 38
Drusugasse .... GY 39
Ehrenstr. .... EV
Eigelstein .... FU
Gertrudenstr. .... EV 47
Gladbacher Str. .... EU 48
Glockengasse .... GZ 50
Große Budengasse .... GZ 52
Große Neugasse .... GY 54
Gürzenichstr. .... GZ 55
Habsburgerring .... EV 57
Hahnenstr. .... EV
Heinrich-Böll-Pl. .... GY 58
Hohe Str. .... GYZ
Hohenstaufenring .... EX
Hohenzollernring .... EV
Kaiser-Wilhelm-
Ring .... EV 62
Kardinal-Frings-Str. .... EV 65
Karolingerring .... FX 66
Kattenburg .... EV 67
Kleine Budengasse .... GZ 68
Kleine Witschgasse .... FX 69
Komödienstr. .... GY 71
Kurt-Hackenberg-Pl. .... GY 72
Mathiasstr. .... FX 74
Mechtildisstr. .... FX 76
Minoritenstr. .... GZ 79
Mittelstr. .... EV
Neumarkt .... EV
Neusser Str. .... FU 86
Offenbachpl. .... GZ 90
Pfälzer Str. .... EX 96
Quatermarkt .... GZ 99
Richmodstr. .... EV 100
Riehler Str. .... FU 102
Roonstr. .... EX 104
Sankt-Apern-Str. .... EV 108
Schildergasse .... GZ
Severinstr. .... FX
Tel-Aviv-Str. .... FX 111

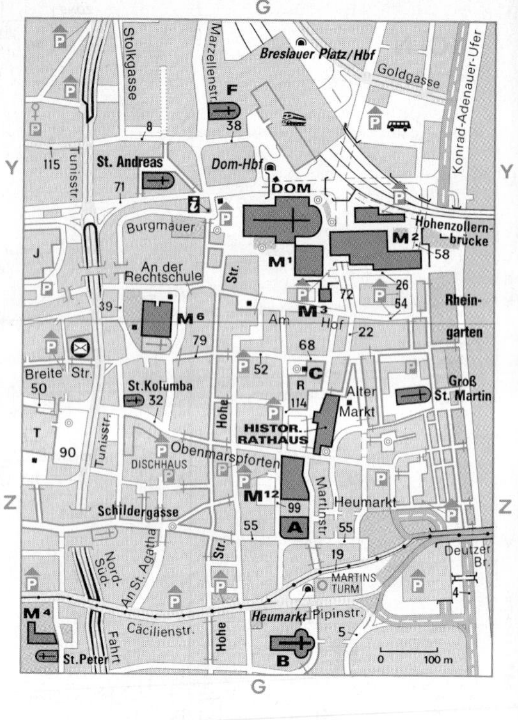

Unter Goldschmied .... GZ 114
Unter Sachsenhausen ...... GY 115
Ursulastr. .... FU 116
Victoriastr. .... FU 117
Zeppelinstr. .... EV 118
Zeughausstr. .... EV 122

Deutsches Sport-und Olympia-Museum ..... FX M11
Diözesanmuseum .... GY M3
Fest- und Tanzhaus Gürzenich .... GZ A
Imhoff-Stollwerck-Museum .... FX M9
Josef-Haubrich-Halle .... EV N
Käthe-Kollwitz-Museum .... EV M10
Kölnisches Stadtmuseum .... EV M7
Museum Ludwig .... GY M2
Museum Schnütgen .... FV M4
Museum für Angewandte Kunst .... GY M6
Museum für Ostasiatische Kunst .... EV M5
Prätorium .... GZ C
Rautenstrauch- Joest-Museum für
Völkerkunde .... FX M8
Römisch-Germanisches Museum .... GY M1
Sr. Aposteln .... EV K
St. Maria im Kapitol .... GZ B
St. Mariä Himmlfahrt .... GY F
Wallraf-Richrtz-Museum Fondation
Corboud .... GZ M12

which contains over 120 reliquary busts and 700 skulls. The shrine of St Ursula (1256) and the **Aetherius Shrine** (1170-80) are to be found in the high chancel. *The church will probably remain closed for restoration until early 2005.* ☎ *(0221) 13 34 00.*

►► Groß St-Martin – St-Maria Lyskirchen (superb vaulting frescoes★★) – St-Georg – St-Aposteln (trefoil chancel★) – St-Kunibert (stained-glass windows★ from 1230) – St-Kolumba – St-Peter – St-Maria Königin (access via glass wall★) – St-Mariä Himmelfahrt.

Walking About

OLD TOWN *allow 2hr*

The cultural heart of Cologne beats in the immediate vicinity of the central station and the Hohenzollernbrücke – the busiest railway bridge in the world, with a train crossing it every two minutes, day and night.

Not far from Germany's best-known church, Cologne Cathedral, are several outstanding museums. The Römisch-Germanisches Museum and Diözesanmuseum rub shoulders with dhe Museum Ludwig, built in 1986 by P Busmann and G Haberer – a piece of modernistic architecture whose saw-tooth roofing contrasts with the Gothic spires of the cathedral and the silhouette of the Gründerzeit railway station. The complex also includes, at basement level, the **Philharmonia** auditorium. From the Heinrich-Böll-Platz, where the museums are located, a series of terraces leads down to the northern part of Rheingarten.

Look back and admire the cathedral's chancel and the forest of flying buttresses surrounding it. When you reach the riverside, take the Frankenwerft which runs alongside the Rhine offering a lovely view of the other bank. The church of Groß St-Martin towers

The Carnival

Celebrations in Cologne start at 11 minutes past 11 on the 11th day of the 11th month, and gradually build up to a climax during the three days preceding Ash Wednesday. Things get under way beforehand with Weiberfastnacht, or the Women's Carnival (on the Thursday before Shrove Tuesday – no man in a tie is safe; women go round indiscriminately cutting them off!). Then there is the people's carnival on the Sunday before Shrove Tuesday with the Veedelszöch and the Schullzöch (dialect words); Rosenmontag, the day before Shrove Tuesday with its legendary procession which includes elaborately decorated floats, bands and a cavalcade of giants, each in its own way caricaturing or parodying some aspects of current affairs; and finally Shrove Tuesday (Fastnachtsdienstag), which ends at midnight with the burning of straw dolls ("Nubbel"). The carnival associations meet up on the evening of Ash Wednesday for a meal of fish. During the carnival season, the inhabitants of Cologne and the many visitors who come for the event go wild, no one gets much sleep and peace and quiet are out of the question.

A brochure and a leaflet detailing the routes of the processions and plenty of other important details, such as stand tickets, traffic direction and room reservation, are obtainable from the Cologne tourist office.

over the charming Fisch-Market with its old reconstructed houses. Between the Alter Markt and the Rhine lies the Martinsviertel, a district famous for its tourist cafés and bars.

Leave the riverside via Lintgasse, a narrow paved street that leads to the Alter Markt, the old market place. It occupies the site of the old Roman port, and in the centre stands a fountain dedicated to Jan von Werth. The carnival starts here.

Altes Rathaus★ (Old Town Hall)

The building with its reconstructed Gothic tower dating from 1407 to 1414 (carillon at noon and 5pm) and the Flemish style Renaissance pavilion (1569-73) lies at the heart of the old Jewish quarter, which is evoked by street names such as Judengasse and Salomonsgasse. In 1349, the ghetto was stormed, despite its defensive gates and curfew system; its inhabitants were murdered and their homes set alight. Right by the town hall, part of the Jewish baths, or **Mikwe** (c 1170), have been preserved and are now covered by a glass pyramid *(it is possible to visit the baths Monday to Friday – the key is held by the porter of the town hall).*

Prätorium

The entrance is a little hard to find as it is tucked away near the underground car park in Kleine Budengasse. Open Tue-Sun, 10am (11am, Sat-Sun)-4pm. ☎ (0221) 22 12 304.
The foundations of the Roman governor's palace (1C-4C) were excavated after the war and are largely preserved. Cracks in the mighty walls suggest that the previous, building on this site must have collapsed. In the antechamber are small sculptures, bricks and receptacles dating from Roman times. Visitors can also view the Roman sewer, which was used as an air-raid shelter by Cologne townspeople during the Second World War.

Head back towards the Alter Markt and go along Martinstraße, until you reach the dance hall.

Gürzenich dance hall

This was one of the first secular Gothic buildings (1441-44) and served as a model for many of the townhouses. The "council's dance hall" was used for receptions and banquets in the Middle Ages and then, after a break, from the 19C on, when the carnival in its present form was born.

Down towards the banks of the Rhine lies the ***Heumarkt*** *(hay market) dominated by the equestrian statue of Frederick William III, king of Prussia between 1770 and 1840. Continuing further south, over the Dutzer Brücke and crossing Cäcilienstrasse, you will reach the church of St-Maria-im-Kapitol with its very attractive cloisters. From here, you can go on to the Reinauhalbinsel (island) and its* ***Chocolate Museum*** *(Imhoff-Stollwerck-Museum). Opposite the island, the church of St-Maria in Lyskirchen boasts some lovely painted vaulting and a Virgin with Child (c 1420), patron saint of boatmen.*

Worth a Visit

Museum Ludwig★★

Tue 10am-8pm, Wed-Fri 10am-6pm, Sat-Sun 11am-6pm. Closed 1st Jan, Thu-Tue during carnival, 24, 25 and 31 Dec. €5.10. ☎ (0221) 22 12 23 79; www.museenkoeln.de
The spacious museum building with its distinctive saw-tooth roof houses an important collection of 20C art, with the Expressionist movement particularly well represented, displaying works by the Brücke and Blaue Reiter groups. There is a good display of art from between the two World Wars: Constructivism, the Bauhaus (for example Klee's *Highway and Byways*), New Objectivity.

One of the museum's strong points is embodied in a collection of Russian Avant-Garde Art. The department devoted to the Surrealists reveals that the Dada movement was in fact born in Cologne, just before the First World War. Besides oil paintings, gouaches and collages by **Max Ernst** *(Friends' Meeting)*, who was born in Brühl, near Cologne, exhibits include work by Hans Arp, Schwitters, Miró, Dalí and Magritte.

French modern art is represented by the **Cubists** Braque, Gris, Léger and Delaunay, and **Nouveau Réalisme** as practised by Arman, Klein, Saint-Phalle, Tinguely, Tàpies, Burri and Dubuffet. A highlight of this section is the display of **Pablo Picasso**'s work, which covers all phases of its development in one of the world's most comprehensive collections.

German post-war and contemporary art on display includes works by the **Gruppe Zero**, but mainly by **Joseph Beuys**, Baselitz, Richter, Polke, Penck and Kiefer. American abstract painting is well represented (Rothko, Newman, de Kooning), as is **Pop Art** (Rauschenberg, Warhol and Segal).

Numerous works by contemporary artists from Europe, America, Japan and China, complete with a whole series of giant installations, illustrate the most recent artistic trends.

Museum Ludwig / Agfa Foto-Historama (Museum of Photography)

Open only during temporary exhibitions. Information, ☎ (0221/22) 12 24 11. Compiled from various private collections), this exhibition presents an overall view of over 150 years of photography. The impact of the displays derives from the juxtaposition of ancient exhibits and photographs of great historical or cultural value. Thus the history of photography can be followed through its various stages – magic lantern, daguerreotype (1839), calotype (Talbot's negative process, 1841), amateur interest, spooled film (Eastman, 1888) – to the invention of microfilm and the small, high-tech cameras of today.

Rheinisches Bildarchiv, Köln

Travelling camera (c 1880)

Römisch-Germanisches Museum

For those preferring to avoid school parties, for which this museum is a popular attraction, we recommend a visit in the afternoon or at weekends. ♿ Open every day except Mon, 10am-5pm. Closed 1st Jan, Thu-Tue during carnival, 24, 25 and 31 Dec. €3.60. ☎ (0221) 22 12 23 04; www.museenkoeln.de

Capital of the Roman province known as Lower Germania, Cologne enjoyed immense prosperity between the 1C and the 4C, due largely to fruitful exchanges between the civilisation of the colonisers and the Germanic culture of the Ubii. Such evidence of the period as has been discovered over the centuries is on display in this very modern museum south of the cathedral. The exhibits are presented thematically.

In the basement is the **Dionysius Mosaic★**, an exceptionally well-preserved Roman mosaic made of one and a 1.5 million fragments of stone (measuring 14.5x7m/48x23ft). The banqueting hall (part of a Roman villa) was uncovered during the construction of an air-raid bunker in 1941 and preserved on its original site. The adjacent rooms evoke not only funerary rites (tombstones and votive items) but also the everyday life of the Ancient Romanc.

Another highlight of the museum is the **Mausoleum of Lucius Poblicius**, an officer of the Roman 5th Legion who settled in Cologne for his retirement in 1C AD. The tomb, which was reconstructed in the 1960s, stands 14.6m/48ft high and is best viewed from the upper floors. It is easy enough to distinguish the original stones from those added during reconstruction.

An interesting exhibit, although it is not the original, is the **Philosophers' Mosaic**: its remarkable geometrical layout represents the Seven Sages of Greece. A valuable collection of **glassware★★** testifies to the incredible wealth of imagination in Roman glassmaking workshops up to the 4C. Note the unique 4C vasa diatreta blown several times to produce a thick glass which is then cut and undercut to give an outer tracery in coloured relief and a Greek inscription on the rim.

The Roman and "Barbaric" engraved gold or cloisonné enamel jewellery is of inestimable archaeological value.

Diözesanmuseum★ (Diocesan Museum)

♿ Open every day except Thu, 11am-6pm. Closed Carnival Monday, 24 and 25 Dec. Free admission. ☎ (0221) 257 76 72. In addition to precious religious objects (liturgical accessories, religious ornaments, rosaries etc), this little museum houses an

interesting collection of religious art from the Middle Ages, notably statues which once decorated part of the cathedral. The most famous piece is Stefan Lochner's **Virgin with Violets**. A particular highlight of the collection is the 11C-16C sculpture and gold work, including the "Herimannkruzifix", a crucifix with little Roman lapis lazuli heads.

Wallraf-Richartz-Museum★★

Open every day except Mon, 10am-6pm, Tues 10am-8pm, Sat-Sun 11am-6pm. Closed 1st Jan, carnival, 24, 25 and 31 Dec. €5.10. ☎ (0221) 22 12 11 19; www.museenkoeln.de

At the beginning of 2001, the Wallraf-Richartz-Museum left the home it shared with the Museum Ludwig to the south of the cathedral and set up residence in this generously proportioned modern building designed by **Oswald M Ungers**.

The priceless Medieval Painters of Cologne collection, culminating with the Late Gothic work of Stefan Lochner and his contemporaries, is unique. Note in particular the **Master of St Veronica** with the early 15C triptych *The Holy Family*; the **Master of Life of the Virgin** with an Annunciation triptych (outside of wing panels); and **Stefan Lochner**'s own **Virgin and the Rose Bush** (c 1450). Works by German, Italian (Martini and Lorenzetti), Flemish and Dutch masters show the pan-European dimension of religious painting in the Middle Ages. Portrait painting is well represented by **Bartholomäus Bruyn the Elder** (portraits of *Gerhard Pilgrim* and *Heinrich Salsburg*). Among the **German Old Masters** on view are **Dürer** *(The Fife Player and The Tambourine Player)* and Lucas Cranach the Elder *(Virgin and Child)*. The 16C Italians are represented by Titian and Tintoretto.

Imhoff-Stollwerck-Museum, Köln

Chocolate-vending machine

Another section is devoted to Baroque art. The collection of Dutch and Flemish painting offers such great names as Rubens (*Venus and Argus, The Holy Family* and *The Stigmata of St Francis*), Ruisdael *(View of a River)*, Frans Hals *(The Fisherman's Daughter)* and **Rembrandt**, with the famous late self-portrait. After this comes the section featuring Spanish (Murillo), Italian (Tiepolo, Bordone), and French (Boucher: *Young Girl Resting*; landscapes by Claude Lorrain) painters.

French and German artists dominate the section devoted to the 18C and 19C. The German Romantics are represented by, among others, CD Friedrich; the **Realists** by the Cologne-born **Wilhelm Leibl** (Portrait of *H Pallenberg*). The German Impressionist School offers work by Liebermann, Corinth and Klinger. With the Romantic movement (Delacroix) as a point of departure, French painting advances via Realism (Courbet) to the **Impressionists**: Renoir, Monet, Sisley, Cézanne, Van Gogh *(The Drawbridge)* and Gauguin. Post 1800 sculptures are also on display.

Schnütgen-Museum★★

Open every day except Mon, 10am-5pm (1st Wed of the month 10am-8pm), Sat-Sun 11am-5pm. Closed 1st Jan, carnival, 24, 25 and 31 Dec. €2.60. ☎ (0221) 22 12 36 20; www.museenkoeln.de

The 12C former Cäcilienkirche, one of the dozen Romanesque religious edifices still standing in the city, makes a suitable site for this museum devoted to sacred art from the 6C to the 19C, but essentially concentrated on the Middle Ages.

Numerous **Madonnas in wood** illustrate the local "tender" style in statuary. St Hieronymus and the Lion (Erkelenz, 1460-70) is a masterpiece of Late Gothic woodcarving. The gold altar panel (c 1170) is from St Ursula's Church.

A collection of medieval items in ivory, most of them from Byzantium, France or other parts of Germany, is of particularly fine workmanship.

The School of Cologne

Manuscript illumination and the decoration of altars were already blossoming local arts in Cologne at the beginning of the 14C. Painting attained its summit in the first half of the 15C, with the works of **The Master of St Veronica** and **Stefan Lochner**, a native of Meersburg. From 1450 onwards, under the influence of the Dutch schools, the artists of Cologne abandoned the idealistic mysticism of the Gothic period in favour of the more gracious realism of the Renaissance. This later work is characterised by a delicacy of colour and a certain suavity in the treatment of subjects. Religious sculpture in Cologne reached its high point between the 14C and the 15C. More than one of the many **Madonnas** on display can be classed as displaying the so-called "style of tenderness" sweeping Europe around 1400 – the hinted smile, a softness of drapery, a lissom stance, these all mark the distinguishing traits of such Virgins of the Late Gothic School.

Goldsmiths' and silversmiths' work on display is equally impressive. Note, too, the items in bronze made by Christians from the East. The museum furthermore boasts a comprehensive collection of textiles dating from the Middle Ages to the 18C.

Museum für Ostasiatische Kunst★★ (Museum of Far Eastern Art)

Universitätsstraße 100. ♿ Open every day except Mon, 11am-5pm, Thu 11am-8pm. Closed 1st Jan, Thu-Tue during carnival, 24, 25 and 31 Dec. €3.60. ☎ (0221) 940 51 80; www.museenkoeln.de

Germany's oldest museum of Far Eastern art (founded in 1909), was relocated in 1977 to a modern building designed by Kunio Maekawa (1905-86), a student of Le Corbusier. The Japanese garden was laid out by contemporary artist Masayuki Nagare (b 1923).

Museum für Ostasiatische Kunst, Köln

Ceremonial urn, Museum für Ostasiastische Kunst

The permanent exhibition displays works of Chinese, Japanese and Korean art, from the Neolithic Age to the present. Among the oldest exhibits are some bronze vessels from China (16C-12C BC). The museum also has a vast collection of Buddhist art from China and Japan. The collection of Chinese ceramics covers all phases of the evolution of this craft until the end of Imperial rule. The reconstruction of the study of a man of letters, complete with 17C Chinese furniture and writing equipment, gives an insight into the culture of the scholarly elite. The Japanese screens decorated with birds and flowers or scenes of *matsuri* (annual festivities) on a gold background *(kimpaku)* and the *ukiyo-e* illustrations provide a glimpse of a vibrant world now long gone.

Museum für Angewandte Kunst★ (Museum of Applied Arts)

♿ Open every day except Mon, 11am-5pm, Wed 11am-8pm. Closed 1st Jan, Thu-Tue during carnival, 24, 25 and 31 Dec. €3.60. ☎ (0221) 22 12 38 60; www.museenkoeln.de

This museum contains a comprehensive collection of applied arts from the Middle Ages to the present. It boasts an extensive collection of furniture, and a ceramics section which gives an overview ranging from stoneware from the Rhineland, to Islamic and Italian majolica, to European porcelain over the last three centuries. As far as metalwork is concerned, there are excellent displays of 16C and 17C pewter and of jewellery. German Waldglas ("forest glass", thick greenish, yellowish or brownish glassware produced in the Middle Ages), Venetian filigree glasses, Baroque goblets and Jugendstil glasses (Emile Gallé) represent some of the glassware on display.

Other interesting departments include **sculpture**, with works by Tilman Riemenschneider, textiles, and large animal figures from the Meissen porcelain manufacture.

The design department gives a comprehensive overview of 20C design right through to the present.

Rautenstrauch-Joest-Museum für Völkerkunde (Ethnographic Museum)

Open every day except Mon, 10am-4pm, Sat 11am-4pm, Sun 11am-6pm. Closed 1st Jan, Thu-Tue during carnival, 24, 25 and 31 Dec €2.60. ☎ (0221) 336 94 13. This museum offers fine displays of Thai and Khmer ceramics and sculpture from the 8C to the 16C, and a good collection of Ancient Egyptian art. There is a new section on the Native American and Inuit civilisations.

Imhoff-Stollwerck-Museum★ (Chocolate Museum)

Rheinauhafen. ♿ Open every day except Mon, 10am-6pm, Sat-Sun 11am-7pm. Closed 1st Jan, Thu-Wed during carnival, 24, 25 and 31 Dec. €5.50. ☎ (0221) 931 88 80. This highly original museum takes as its subject that most fascinating of foodstuffs, chocolate. The museum's architecture and **site★** are fascinating in themselves: a customs warehouse from the Gründerzeit period has been integrated into a modern glass building, which visitors get to across a historical swing bridge over the Rhine. Besides various delicious end-products, the display includes interesting information on the 3 000-year history and production of chocolate, a miniature chocolate factory, and a collection of beautiful silver and porcelain drinking vessels reflecting the fact that chocolate was once an expensive luxury drink enjoyed only by the aristocracy. The museum also recounts the history of the traditional chocolate-making firm of Stollwerck, founded in Cologne in 1839.

Excursions

Schloß Augustusburg★★

13km/8mi south. See BRÜHL.

Altenberger Dom★

20km/12mi northeast. This former Cistercian abbey church (still known locally as the Bergischer Dom – cathedral of the Berg Duchy) lies in a green valley much appreciated by the city dwellers of Cologne. The pure Gothic building (1255-1379) has been celebrating Roman Catholic and Protestant rites alternately since 1857. Note especially the huge (18x8m/59x26ft) coloured glass canopy (c 1400) above the west entrance, considered to be the largest stained-glass window in Germany, and the grisaille stained-glass windows in the chancel.

Zons★

24km/15mi north. This picturesque Rhineland fortified village, a suburb of Dormagen since 1975, had a toll-house added to it in the 14C, which has survived virtually intact and therefore represents a good example of a medieval fortification. Its walls and numerous towers lend particular charm to the site.

Konstanz★

Constance

The foundation of the town – a German enclave on the Swiss shore of Lake Constance – has long been attributed to the Roman emperor Constantius Chlorus (292-306). Konstanz is now a lively holiday town with a large student population. If you wish to further explore the pleasures of the lake, the two tranquil islands of Mainau and Reichenau are perfect for walks away from it all.

Location

Population: 75 000. Michelin map nº 545 X 11 – Baden-Württemberg. Constance occupies an agreeable **site★** opposite the narrows which separate the main body of the lake (known as the Bodensee in German) from its picturesque prolongation (Untersee). The islands of Mainau *(to the north)* and Reichenau *(to the west)* are each linked to the town by a bridge.

Bahnhofplatz 13, 78462 Konstanz, ☎ (075 31) 13 30 30.

Surrounding area: see BODENSEE, SALEM (54km/34mi northeast), SCHWÄBISCHE ALB, SIGMARINGEN (72km/45mi north), SCHWARZWALD (our tour includes Titisee, 96km/60mi west).

Background

Constance, Capital of Christianity – From 1414 to 1418, a council convened in the town to attempt to re-establish the unity of the Church, which had been compromised by the pretentions of three ecclesiastical dignitaries, each claiming the right to be elected to the papal throne. After long negotiations, two of the three rival Popes, Gregory XII and John XXIII, agreed to stand down; only Benedict XIII, who had taken refuge in Spain, remained adamant about the validity of his claim. In 1417, the election of Martin V, who was universally recognised as the true Pope, put an end temporarily to the schism. Three years previously, the council had summoned before it the religious reformer **Jan Hus**, Rector of the University of Prague. Hostile to German influence, Hus expounded his theses – which contested papal primacy and certain rites – was declared a heretic, and burned alive. This precursor of Protestantism was hailed as a national hero in his native Bohemia.

Worth a Visit

The Lake Shore★ (Seeufer)

The charm and ambience of Konstanz is particularly apparent on walking along the lakeside. Just after the landing-stage *(near the tourist office)*, there is the **Konzilgebäude**, a former warehouse built at the end of the 14C, which was used by the Conclave of 1417 which proclaimed the election of Pope Martin V and which today serves as a concert hall. At the bottom of the jetty is the 18m/59ft statue of **Imperia**, by the contemporary sculptor Peter Lenk. The monument represents the 16C Italian courtier that Honoré de Balzac immortalised as Constance in his novel *Ribald Tales*

Directory

Where to Eat

Ostaria Passatempo – *Marktstätte 2 – (07531) 91 79 27 – – €7.99/25.* This restaurant is located where the pedestrianised area of the town begins, in an underground passage leading to the port. The establishment is a youthful, modern set-up, with a relaxed atmosphere and displays of brightly coloured paintings. Italian cuisine.

Where to Stay

Seehotel Siber – *Seestraße 25 – (07531) 996 69 90 – seehotel. siber@t-online.de – €60/85.* Tastefully decorated, Jugendstil villa. The restaurant and terrace offer beautiful views over the lake. Temptingly refined cuisine, presented with irreproachable service.

Hotel Barleben am See – *Seestraße 15, 78464 Konstanz-Staad – (07531) 500 74 – fax (07531) 66973 – www.hotel-barleben.de – – Booking advised – 9rm: from €115 – Restaurant €28/45.* This villa was built in1872, is a listed building and now serves as a small hotel, with lovely, personalised guestrooms. The establishment is particularly well-located, in the heart of parkland, directly adjacent to the lakeside promenade.

Steigenberger Inselhotel – *Auf der Insel 1 – (07531) 12 50 – fax (07531) 125250 – konstanz@steigen berger.de – – 102rm: from €132 .* Set in an old Dominican monastery not far from the old town, this hotel doesn't fail to charm with its tasteful, up-market ambience. Dine in the elegant restaurant or on the splendid terrace with views of the lake.

(Contes drôlatiques). Across the road, in the municipal gardens *(Stadtgarten)*, is a monument to Count Zeppelin (1838-1917), the celebrated airship inventor, who was born in Constance. His *Graf Zeppelin* successfully crossed the Atlantic Ocean in 1928. Carry on down the *Konizilstraße*, where a little bridge allows access to the Insel, home to the former Dominican Monastery founded in 1235 *(now the Steigenberger Inselhotel, see Directory)*. Cross the *Rheinbrücke* and take a short detour along the *Rheinsteig* to admire the old **defensive towers** *(Rheintorturm, Pulverturm)*. On the opposite bank, the Seestraße *(to the right)* is lined with Jugendstil villas culminating in a casino *(Spielbank)*.

The lake itself, busy with all kinds of water traffic, offers numerous opportunities for excursions.

Münster★

Since its construction was spread over a period from the 11C to the 17C, this former **cathedral** lacks any artistic unity.

The **panels★** *(Türflügel)* of the porch doors in the main façade are decorated with bas-relief sculptures representing scenes from the life of Christ (1470).

The 17C vaulting in the central nave rests on the arcades of the original 11C sanctuary, achieving a visual harmony that is completely Romanesque. The decoration of the organ case and the loft itself preview the Renaissance. In the north transept, a spiral staircase turret *(Schnegg)*, finely decorated in the French Late Gothic style, leads to the vault of the east end of the building *(access to the treasury is beneath the Schnegg.)*

The 13C Mauritiuskapelle houses the Münster's most priceless piece of sculpture, the **Holy Tomb★**, a vaulted dodecagon containing three statuary groups. It is one of the few examples of its kind from the High Middle Ages, bearing a stylistic resemblance to the sculpture of Bamberg and Naumburg.

In the crypt are four plaques of gilded copper, each from a different period (11C-13C). They represent Christ in Majesty, the symbolic Eagle of St John, and St Conrad and St Pelagius, patrons of the diocese. They are known as the **Konstanzer Goldscheiben** (gilded plaques of Constance). A staircase to the right of the main door leads to a tower platform from which there is a fine view over the town and the lake.

Between the cathedral and the Rhine snake the streets of the Niederburg, the oldest district of the town, where craftsmen carried out their work in the Middle Ages.

Rathaus

The façade of this Renaissance building is embellished with paintings that illustrate the history of Constance. From the inner courtyard there is a good view of the elegant 16C house between two round towers.

Archäologisches Landesmuseum

Open Tue-Sun, 10am-6pm. Closed 1 Jan, 24, 25 and 31 Dec. €4. (no charge on 1st Sat of month). (075 31) 980 40. This local museum is housed in an old conventual building of the Peterhausen Abbey, which makes a very attractive setting. History comes to life in 3 000m²/32 280sq ft of exhibition space, beginning with the buildings on stilts dating from 4000 BC and continuing to the more recent industrial past.

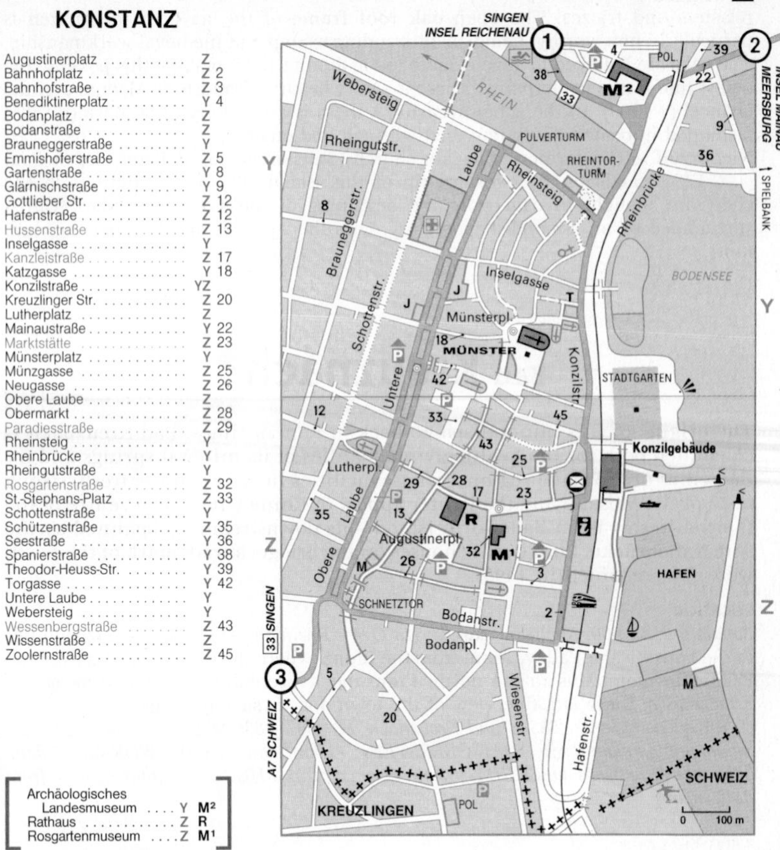

A highlight is the illustration of life in the Middle Ages in the towns of Baden-Württemberg. A section on maritime travel documents early maritime and river boat travel in southwest Germany.

►► Sea Life *(in the centre of Konstanz, near the station)*, Museum of Regional History *(Rosgartenmuseum)*.

Excursions

Mainau Island★★ (Insel Mainau)

7km/4.5mi north. 2hr sightseeing. Exit by ② on the town plan. ♿ *From mid-March to mid-Oct: 7am-8pm; from mid-Oct to mid-Mar: 9am-6pm. €10.50.* ☎ *(075 31) 30 30.* The grand dukes of Baden laid out a large park on this 45ha/110-acre island on Lake Constance. The property of Count Lennart Bernadotte since 1932, it is a paradise for all plant enthusiasts. The juxtaposition of the palace, charming Baroque church and colourful flower beds set in green parkland contributes to the magic of the island. The mild climate means that exotic plants also thrive here. Further attractions include Germany's largest butterfly house and floral displays that change with the seasons.

Reichenau Island★ (Insel Reichenau)

7km/4.5mi west. Exit by ① on the town plan. St Pirmin founded the first German Benedictine monastery to the east of the Rhine on Reichenau Island in 724, and the seeds which he sowed germinated into a centre for arts and science which flourished for centuries. Some quite outstanding book illuminations were produced here during the Ottonian period.

Gardeners have transformed the 430ha/1 063 acres of the island into a fertile market garden. However the three churches are its main attraction.

Oberzell – The late-9C Carolingian St Georgskirche – remarkable for the harmonious design of its stepped elements – contains a series of **wall paintings**★★ (c 1000 AD).

Mittelzell – The chief town on the island, there is an old **abbey**★ (Münster St Maria und Markus) which was built between the 8C and 12C. The robust Romanesque tower of the Westwerk is lightened in appearance by a decorative band of Lombard pilasters and friezes. The open **oak roof frame** of the nave of the church is particularly noteworthy, being an outstanding example of medieval workmanship. The oaks are believed to have been felled in around 1236, making this possibly the oldest roof frame in Germany. There is a very beautiful sandstone Madonna in the chancel (c 1300). In the abbey **treasury★** there is a reliquary of St Mark (c 1305) fashioned in beaten silver enriched with gilt and enamels.

Niederzell – The former collegiate church (Stiftskirche) of St Peter and St Paul (11C-12C) stands on the western tip of this island. The wall paintings in the choir are thought to date from the beginning of the 12C. They show Christ surrounded by an almond-shaped glory, with the Apostles and Prophets beneath him.

Bad Kreuznach★

The origins of this mineral spa go back to Roman times. Bad Kreuznach is celebrated both for the health-giving qualities of its mineral springs and for the wines of the Nahe region – whose qualities lie between the fresh, strong taste of the Moselle and the lighter appeal of Rhine wines. The centre of the thermal resort is on Badewörth Island – its downstream tip spanned by the Alte Nahebrücke. Both Gothic houses on the bridge, a trademark of the town, were first recorded in 1495.

Location

Population: 44 000. Michelin map nº 543 Q 7 – Rheinland-Pfalz. Bad Kreuznach lies in the Lower Nahe Valley, 15km from the Rhine, where the Nahe emerges from the Palatinate mountains to the north. From the Kauzenburg *(café-restaurant on the Kauzenberg)*, there is a fine view of the town and its surroundings.

ℹ *Kurhausstraße 23, 55543 Bad Kreuznach, ☎ (0671) 836 00 50.*

Surrounding area: see IDAR-OBERSTEIN (47km/29mi west), WORMS (56km/35mi southeast), RÜDESHEIM (67km/42mi north), RHEINTAL (tour leaves from Rüdesheim).

Worth a Visit

Römerhalle★

11 Hüffelsheimer Straße. ♿ Open Tue-Sat, 10am-5pm. Closed 24 and 31 Dec. €1.80. ☎ (0671) 92 07 77. The museum is on a former smallholding at the western end of the castle park. Items discovered during archaeological excavations in Bad Kreuznach and the surrounding district are on display. There are two exceptional exhibits, both of them 3C **mosaic floors★★**: one depicts the sea god in his element; the other illustrates wild animals and gladiators in combat. Below, a Roman central heating system has been unearthed (hypocaust).

Nearby, a **Roman villa** has been uncovered. Also close at hand is the **historical Schloßpark** with a small lake, tropical trees and a museum.

Excursions

Bad Münster am Stein-Ebernburg★

By car, 4.5km/3mi. Leave the car near the cure centre (Kurhaus); then 1hr there and back on foot.

Go into the **thermal park★** and walk through the gardens to the Nahe. On the far side of the river is the **Rheingrafenstein★★**, a 136m/446ft rock face surmounted by the ruins of an ancient castle.

Take the ferry across and, from the Hüttental café-restaurant, climb to the panoramic platform on top.

From here, there is a fine **view★** of the Bad Münster basin and, downstream, the Rotenfels, whose sheer porphyry cliffs tower 214m/700ft above the river.

Lahntal

The winding course of the lower Lahn is overlooked by wild scenery and steeply wooded banks. The valley makes a charming setting for excursions to a number of castle ruins, castles and the delightful old towns of Weilburg and Limburg which are steeped in history.

Location

Michelin map nº 543 O 7-9 – Hessen and Rheinland-Pfalz. The Lahn valley cuts through the Taunus-Rhine schist massif and meanders through the forests of the Naussau natural parket, to the east of Koblenz.
Surrounding area: see KOBLENZ (18km/11mi west of Bad Ems), RHEINTAL (tour includes Koblenz), MARBURG (44km/28mi north of Wetzlar), FRANKFURT AM MAIN (66km/41mi south of Wetzlar).

Tour

FROM BAD EMS TO WETZLAR

89km/55mi – about 4hr 30min

Bad Ems

The Lahn valley, separating the Westerwald and the Taunus-Rhine schist massif, is rich in mineral springs, like all areas on the fringe of a volcanic region.
Opposite the assembly rooms, set into the quay-promenade near the Roman springs, is a flagstone *(Benedettistein)* bearing the date 13 July 1870 commemorating the meeting between Wilhelm and the French Ambassador, Benedetti. The Emperor categorically refused the French request that the Hohenzollerns renounce "forever" their claims to the throne of Spain. A report of the meeting, the then-infamous 'Ems Telegram' was distorted and then leaked by Bismarck, ultimately hastening the Franco-Prussian War of 1870-71.

Nassau

This climatic health resort in the Lahn Valley was the cradle of the counts of Laurenburg, from whom the Nassau-Orange royal line of the Netherlands, among them William of Orange, King William III of England, and the current Dutch royalty, is descended. Points of interest include the Adelsheimer Hof (town hall), the Stammburg (ancestral castle) Nassau with its five sided keep and the Steinisches Schloß (birthplace of Prussian Baron von Stein).

Kloster Arnstein

1km/0.6mi by a steep uphill road from the Obernhof bridge. The church of this former Premonstratensian monastery stands alone on a wooded spur. The Romanesque west chancel contrasts with that in the east, which is Gothic.

Balduinstein

Ruins of a castle built in 1320 by Baudouin of Luxembourg, Archbishop of Trier, to rival that of Schaumburg.

Schloß Schaumburg

Open May-Oct, Tue-Sun, 10am-5pm. €2. ☎ (064 32) 810 32. A neo-Gothic reconstitution after the English manner. There is a fine view from the tallest of the crenellated towers overlooking the valley.

Diez

Dominating the small town clustered around its ramparts is the tall mass of the 17C **Schloß Oranienstein**. The castle was built 1672-84 as one of the first ancestral castles of the Nassau-Orange royal house. In 1811, Napoleon dissolved the principality of Orange, as Prince William IV, later King William I of the Netherlands, had not joined the Confederation of the Rhine. In 1867, Schloß Oranienstein was transformed into a cadet school. The modern castle serves as a barracks for an armoured brigade and houses the **Oranien-Nassau-Museum**, devoted to the history of the House of Orange *(apply to the guard). Guided tour (1hr): Apr to Oct, Tue-Sun at 9am, 10.30am, 2pm and 3.30pm, Sat-Sun at 10.30am, 2pm and 3pm; Nov to Mar, Tue-Fri at 9am, 10.30am, 2pm and 3.30pm. Apply to the guard for the guided tour. €3. ☎ (064 32) 940 16 66.*

Limburg an der Lahn★ *See LIMBURG.*

Burg Runkel★

The picturesque **setting★★** of the castle, built into the rock face, and the ancient village below it, can best be appreciated from the 15C bridge over the river.

The Baroque town of Weilburg.

Weilburg

Once the residence of the Counts of Nassau, this Baroque town is built on a promontory enclosed by the Lahn. Of the many different structures which comprised the Renaissance **castle**, note especially the turreted clock tower and the elegant 1573 gallery, where the twinned Ionic columns of the arcades are topped by a glazed gallery with Corinthian columns. About 30 rooms are open to visitors. *Guided tours (45min), Mar to Oct, Tue-Sun, 10am-4pm ; Nov to Feb, Tue-Sun, 10am-3pm. Closed 1 Jan, 24-16 and 31 Dec. €3.50. ☎ (064 71) 22 36.*

The **museum** *(Bergbau- und Stadtmuseum)* is devoted to the history of the local Iron Mountain mining industry and to the culture of the Weilburg region. *Open Apr-Oct, Tue-Sun, 10am-12pm, 2-5pm, Sat-Sun, 10am-5pm; Nov-Mar, Mon-Fri, 10am-12pm, 2-5pm. Closed Jan, Good Fri and at the end of Dec. €3. ☎ (064 71) 37 94 47.*

Schloß Braunfels – This massive castle, built over 800 years, seen unexpectedly after a fork in the road, has a superb and exciting outline with its many towers etched against the sky. The perimeter wall encloses the whole village. Inside the castle are fine pieces of 15C-19C furniture, paintings, Gobelins tapestries and a collection of weaponry. There is an audio-visual presentation on the history of mining, shown in the castle chapel.

Follow the road as far as Wetzlar (see WETZLAR).

Landshut★

Once capital of the Lower Bavaria dukedom, Landshut has kept its medieval centre practically intact. Memories of the Ingoldstadt and Landshut branches of the House of Wittelsbach, whose members until the 16C outshone even their extravagant Munich cousins, remain very much alive in the town.

Location

Population: 59 000. Michelin map n° 546 U 20 – Bayern. Landshut is located in the middle of valleyed countryside on the Isar, a tributary of the Danube which first passes through Munich (75km/46mi southwest via the A 92).

ℹ *Altstadt 315, 84028 Landshut, ☎ (0871) 92 20 50.*

Surrounding area: see REGENSBURG (75km/47mi north), STRAUBING (58km/36mi northeast), MÜNCHEN (72km/45mi southwest).

Worth a Visit

St-Martinskirche★

Designed by Master Hans von Burghausen and built of rose-coloured brick, the most impressive thing about this 14C-15C church is its outstanding elevation. The **tower★★**, square at the base, slims and becomes octagonal as it soars to a height of almost 131m/430ft, making it the world's tallest brick construction. The outside of the building is adorned with tombstones. The five Flamboyant doorways show an Early Renaissance influence.

Directory

WHERE TO EAT

Bernlochner – *Ländtorplatz 3 – (0871) 899 90 – info@bernlochner.com* – – *€18.50/35.50.* Simple, well-prepared, regional cuisine. Accessibly modern styling with rustic touches characterise the interior decoration.

WHERE TO STAY

Gästehaus Elisabeth – *Bernsteinstraße 40 – (0871) 93 25 00 – fax (0871) 34609 – www.hotel-elisabeth-altdorf.de – P – 33rm: €36/90 – Restaurant €6.70/14.80.* Situated on the edge of a business park, guests staying at this hotel have access to the gym facilities located opposite.

TAKING A BREAK

Café Belstner – *Altstadt 295 – (0871) 221 90 – Closed on Sundays.* This classic tea room, is located close to the St. Martinskirche, in the heart of the historic old town. Choose from a wide selection of home-made cakes, tarts and chocolates (to eat in or take away), or have lunch.

The well-lit interior shows a splendid unity of design. Octagonal pillars, deceptively fragile in appearance, support in a single thrust, vaulting which rises to 29m/95ft. There is a delicate Virgin and Child by Leinberger (1518) on the altar in the south aisle, who also executed the choir stalls.

Altstadt★

The town's most important monuments are to be found in this wide, slightly curving main street with its arcaded 15C and 16C houses, between the *Rathaus* and the Martinskirche. Note especially the variety and inventiveness of the gables, which can be seen again – though perhaps to a lesser extent – in the Neustadt, which runs parallel to the Altstadt. The façades in this second street have had many Baroque features added.

Stadtresidenz (Town Palace)

Guided tours (45min), Apr to Sep: Tue-Sun, 9am-6pm; Oct to Mar, Tue-Sun. 10am-4pm. €2.50. (0871) 924 11 44. – Two main blocks linked by narrow wings comprise this charming palace (1536-43) arranged around an arcaded courtyard, which faces the town hall. The German building faces the Altstadt (18C furniture, decorations etc); the 16C Italian Renaissance one looks onto the courtyard (large rooms with painted, coffered ceilings).

PRINCELY MARRIAGE

Every four years, Landshut commemorates with great pomp the marriage in 1475 of the son of Duke Ludwig the Rich with Hedwige, daughter of the king of Poland. Don't miss it if you're in Bavaria at the beginning of summer 2005.

Burg Trausnitz

Guided tours (45min), Apr to Sep, 9am-6pm; Oct to Mar, 10am-4pm. €2.50. (0871) 92 41 10. The fortress founded in 1204 was decorated during the Renaissance with fine arcaded galleries (1579). Interesting features include the chapel, the Gothic hall known as the Alte Dürnitz, and several rooms embellished in 16C style are open to the public. The chapel is remarkable for its Early Gothic statuary. Note also the Jesters' Staircase *(Narrentreppe)*, painted in the 16C with scenes from the Commedia dell'Arte.
From an upper loggia *(Söller)*, there is an exceptional **view** across the town to the spire of the Martinskirche.

Leipzig★

The most highly-populated city in Saxony, Leipzig is particularly renowned as a trade fair and conference centre. It is also an artistic city that can be proud of its exceptional musical heritage; Bach, Wagner and Mendelssohn once lived here, and the city is still very much at the forefront of the German music scene. A centre of cultural exchange with a profusion of publishing houses, Leipzig has also, at times, been a centre of revolution: Liebknecht's Social Democratic Party was founded here, and it was also here, in October 1989, that the silent, peaceful protests – the biggest the German Democratic Republic had ever seen – took place. Today, it is a real pleasure to stroll around this youthful, lively university city, explore its remarkable cultural heritage, or just enjoy a bit of shopping in one of the many covered arcades.

Location

Population: 503 000. Michelin map 544 L, M 21 – Sachsen. Leipzig is in the far west of Saxony, at the confluence of the River Weiße Elster and River Pleiße.
🅱 *Richard-Wagner-Straße 1, 04109 Leipzig, ☎ (0341) 710 40.*
Surrounding area: see HALLE (34km/21mi west), NAUMBURG (63km/39mi south), DRESDEN (113km/70mi east via the A 14 motorway).

Background

The Leipzig Fairs – The first mention of the locality historically was in the Chronicle of Bishop Thietmar of Merseburg (975-1018), who noted the death of the Bishop of Meißen in "Urbs Lipzi". The township of "Lipzk" was granted a city charter c 1165. Subsequently, a situation at the crossing of several important trade routes, plus the bestowal by the Margrave Otto the Rich of the right to levy tolls – one of the oldest feudal privileges enjoyed by burghers – established Leipzig as a commercial centre of more than local influence. From the 12C onwards, markets were held over the Easter period and on the Feast of St Michael. A third event – during the New Year celebrations – was added in 1485. The spring and autumn international trade fairs, symbolised by the famous "Double M", have been held since 1896.

Leipzig, City of Books and Music – One of the world's earliest books, the *Glossa Super Apocalipsim*, was printed in Leipzig in 1481 by an itinerant craftsman. The German Book Exchange was founded in 1825, and this was followed in 1912 by the German Library *(Deutsche Bücherei)* and the Museum of Books and Literature *(Deutsches Buch- und Schriftmuseum)*. More than 35 established publishers are based in Leipzig today, among them Kiepenheuer, Brockhaus and Reclam.

The city also enjoys a fine reputation in the musical world, thanks to the Choir of St Thomas *(Thomanerchor)*, the Gewandhaus Orchestra, and the Mendelssohn-Bartholdy National College of Music.

J. Bouraly/MICHELIN

Leibniz, born in Leipzig in 1646.

A prosperous city – The discovery in the 16C of silver in the neighbouring Erzgebirge mountains was to ensure Leipzig's prosperity for a long time to come. The city is still an important economic centre today and has continued to develop since the reunification; its modern infrastructures (completely renovated station, airport, business centre etc) have helped to attract first-rate investors, such as Porsche and BMW.

Walking About

OLD TOWN★

The historic centre of Leipzig, located south of the impressive central station *(Hauptbanof)*, is clearly defined by a ring road which follows the town's old medieval fortifications.

Augustusplatz

Formerly Karl-Marx-Platz, this square has been entirely renovated and boasts some of the city's most remarkable monuments.

On the north side stands the opera house, built in 1956-60, widely renowned for its acoustics. Further towards the central station is a pleasant park *(Schwanenteich)* with a statue of Wagner.

On the west side of the square is the eye-catching **Krochhaus**, the city's first "skyscraper". It was built in 1928-29 and is crowned by a replica of the Mori, the chime from the belfry in Venice. The building that dominates the west side is however the Leipzig University building, 142m/466ft high, dating from 1973. The Schinkeltor, a gate designed by Karl Friedrich Schinkel and E Rietschel in 1836, has been incorporated in the amphitheatre wing.

On the façade of the university is an impressive bronze diorama celebrating Karl Marx. This remnant from the socialist era was to have been removed following the reunification, but problems mainly related to the weight of the sculpture meant that it has had to stay put.

Directory

Where to Eat

"Zill's Tunnel" Restaurant – *Barfußgässchen 9 – ☎ (0341) 960 20 78 – www.zillstunnel.de – ♿ – €15.40/25.40.* A restaurant-cum-tavern since 1841, with a menu entirely in Saxon (mainly regional dishes). Two charming, comfortable rooms are also available at a very reasonable price considering the central location of the establishment.

Barthels Hof – *Hainstraße 1 – ☎ (0341) 14 13 10 – www.barthels-hof.de – €17.30/33.30.* This hotel, built between 1747 and 1750 for the merchant Gottlieb Barthel, has housed a restaurant for over one hundred years. Simple cuisine (Saxon specialities).

Auerbachs Keller – Historische Weinstuben – *Grimmaische Straße 2 (Mädler-Passage) – ☎ (0341) 21 61 00 – info@auerbachs-keller-leipzig.de – evenings only, closed Sun – €36/62.* This Weinstube has existed since 1525; Goethe frequented this place which is said to have provided inspiration for his *Faust*. Classic cuisine and good traditional dishes. Legend has it that the magician Faust rode upon a cask from this tavern.

Where to Stay

Hotel Am Bayrischen Platz – *Paul-List-Straße 5 – ☎ (0341) 14 08 60 – Fax (0341) 1408648 – P – 32rm: €56/96.* In September 1874, Karl Marx and his daughter Eleanor stayed in this villa-style hotel. If you so wish, you can stay in the same room. Like all the others, it is very tastefully furnished. Rustic, elegant breakfast room.

Hotel Michaelis – *Paul-Gruner-Straße 44 – ☎ (0341) 267 80 – Fax (0341) 2678100 – hotel.michaelis@t-online.de – ♿ – 59rm: €70/100 – Restaurant €25/34.* Built in 1907 and now a listed building, this hotel has been renovated with an eye for detail. Harmonious and elegant individually-styled rooms. Modern, tastefully decorated restaurant.

Hotel Fürstenhof – *Tröndlinring 8 – ☎ (0341) 14 00 – Fax (0341) 1403700 – fuerstenhof.leipzig@arabellasheraton.com – ♿ – 92rm: from €210 – €19 – Restaurant €36/49.* The façade of this classic mansion (1770) conceals a luxuriously elegant interior. Impeccable service and Mediterranean-style spa complex. Very refined restaurant.

Taking a Break

Useful Tips – "Leipziger Lerchen" (Leipzig larks) are a local speciality to be found in all the cake shops. These birds had contributed to the town's culinary reputation, so when the king of Saxony banned lark hunting in 1876, the pastry chefs created a new speciality with the same name, made of shortcrust pastry and almond paste.

Kaffeehaus Riquet – *Schumachergässchen 1-3 – ☎ (0341) 9 61 00 00 – Open Fri-Sat 9am-midnight, Sun-Thu 9am-10pm.* Easy to spot thanks to the two large elephant heads on its façade, this former early 19C trading house has been modelled on a Viennese coffee house since 1996. Seats upstairs.

Zum Arabischen Coffe Baum – *Kleine Fleischergasse 4 (at the junction of Barfußgässchen and Kleine Fleischergasse) – ☎ (0341) 9 61 00 60 – www.coffe-baum.de – ground floor: 11am-midnight, 1st floor: Mon-Sat 12pm-3pm, 6pm-midnight, 2nd floor and museum: 11am-7pm.* One of the oldest coffee houses in Europe. On the ground floor is a café-bistro with terrace, on the 1st floor a restaurant, and on the 2nd floor an oriental-style tea room, Viennese-style café and Parisian-style café. Exhibition on the coffee culture, particularly in Saxony, from the 2nd to the 4th floor.

Going Out

Useful Tips – A large number of lively bars are to be found in the city centre between Brühl and the Neues Rathaus. The most animated place is the Barfußgässchen, an alleyway in the pedestrian zone lined exclusively with bars, restaurants and cafés. Gottschedstrasse, west of the city centre, is another haunt for night owls and very popular with students. This street leads to Dittrichring, level with the Thomaskirche.

Gasthaus & Gosebrauerei Bayerischer Bahnhof – *Bayrischer Platz 1 (at the junction of Windmühlenstraße and Nürnberger Straße) – ☎ (0341) 1 24 57 60 – www.bayerischer-bahnhof.de – 11am-1am – Closed 1st Jan and 25 Dec.* A former station where the traditional beer of Leipzig, *Gose*, is brewed again today (in addition to the usual ingredients: salt, lactic acid and coriander). It had disappeared in the 1960s. Other beers are also available. Rustic setting, lovely beer garden (self-service) and copious dishes.

Kümmel-Apotheke – *Grimmaische Straße 2-4 (in Mädlerpassage) – ☎ (0341) 9 60 87 05 – www.kuemmel-apotheke.de – Open Mon-Sat 9.30am-1am, Sun 10.30am-9pm.* A pleasant place to come at any time for a drink or something to eat and watch the world go by. You can even order a glass of champagne.

Vinothek 1770 – *Tröndlinring 8 (in the Fürstenhof hotel) – ☎ (0341) 1 40 33 33 – www.arabellasheraton.com/fuerstenhof – 12pm-1am.* With over 170 wines from all over the world, this place is very popular with wine drinkers. The bottles on the wall behind the bar give an idea of what you will find on wine list. To accompany your bottle: cheese, antipasti and a few seasonal dishes, as well as some good cigars.

CULTURE

Useful Tips – The monthly programme of events, "Leipzig im..." is available from the Leipzig Tourist Service, €0.50.
The monthly magazine *Prinz* can be bought at kiosks in the city. For online information: www.leipzig.de/touristservice

SHOPPING

Useful Tips – Leipzig is a very pleasant place to shop. A number of glass-roofed arcades house shops and cafés which are appreciated by local residents and tourists alike. You are sure to enjoy a stroll along Mädlerpassage (AZ 24), Specks Hof (ABY 38), Strohsack (BY), Steibs Hof (BY 39) or Jägerhofpassage (AY).

Neues Gewandhaus

This superb auditorium to the south of the square was inaugurated in 1981. More than 1 900 enthusiasts can be seated to hear the famous Gewandhaus Orchestra. The bust of Beethoven (1902) in the foyer is the work of Leipzig-born Max Klinger. In front of the concert hall is a fountain (Mendebrunnen, 1886) which is an allegory on the world of water.

LEIPZIGER GEWANDHAUS ORCHESTRA

Many orchestras were founded as court orchestras, as in the case of the Dresden *Staatskapelle*. Not so the Leipziger Gewandhaus Orchestra, which was founded thanks to a donation by wealthy local burghers and merchants in 1743. In 1781, the 500-seat hall in the Clothworkers' Guildhall was made into a concert hall, and thus the orchestra got its name. Famous composers and performers have appeared in this temple to music over the centuries. Beethoven's *Triple Concerto*, Schubert's *Symphony in C major*, Mendelssohn's *"Scottish" Symphony*, and Brahms' *Violin Concerto in D major*. were all performed for the first time here. In 1884, the city built the orchestra its own concert hall, but the name "Gewandhaus" was retained. This building was destroyed by bombs in 1944. The third "Gewandhaus" was inaugurated in 1981. Since 1998, Swedish conductor Helmut Blomstedt has wielded the baton in the long line of music directors, preceded by such illustrious forebears as Felix Mendelssohn, Arthur Nikisch and Kurt Masur.

Skirt the Neues Gewandhaus and turn in to Schillerstraße. South of the university stands the **Leibniz monument**, *a stone's throw from the Egyptian Museum.*

Aegyptisches Museum★ (Egyptian Museum)

Schillerstraße 6. ♿ Open every day except Mon, 1pm-5pm, Sun 10am-1pm. Closed 1st Jan, 1st May, 24 and 31 Dec. €2, free admission 2nd Sun of Sep. ☎ (0341) 973 70 10. Remarkable collections with around 9 000 exhibits from the Ancient Empire up to the Christian era.

Continue westwards along Schillerstraße to the Neues Rathaus

Neues Rathaus (New Town Hall)

Built between 1899 and 1905 on the foundations of the old Pleißenburg Castle (scene of a famous argument between Luther and Eick in 1519), the town hall marries both Renaissance and Baroque elements with features that are more modern.

Thomaskirche★

Recorded for the first time in 1212 in the foundation charter of the abbey for canons of the Augustinian order, this Late Gothic triple-aisle church took on its present appearance towards the end of the 15C. The church became famous through **Johann Sebastian Bach**, who was *cantor* for 27 years and who is buried opposite the altar (since 1950). The church is also renowned for the **St Thomas children's choir, once directed by** Bach: originating at the School of St Thomas, founded after 1212, this choir at first had no more than 12 singers. It now has about 80 members and performs on Fridays at 6pm, Saturdays at 3pm (sacred choral music and Bach cantatas) and Sundays at 9.30am (main service).

J. Bouraly/MICHELIN

Thomaskirche where Bach was "cantor"

Bachmuseum

Opposite the Thomaskirche, Thomaskirchhof 16. ♿ 10am-5pm. Closed 24, 25 and 31 Dec. €3, free admission 21 Mar. ☎ (0341) 913 72 02; www.bach-leipzig.de.

Musicians in Leipzig

Johann Sebastian Bach worked in Leipzig from 1723 until his death in 1750. As choirmaster and director of music at St Thomas he was responsible for the religious and secular musical life of the entire city. His enormous output includes 200 religious cantatas, three oratorios, two Passions, five masses, one Magnificat, six motets and 190 four-part chorales.

Bach had faded into relative obscurity by the time **Felix Mendelssohn-Bartholdy** took up the post of director of music of the Gewandhaus orchestra in 1835. In the decade he occupied this position he transformed the city into a musical centre of international renown. He decisively turned to reviving forgotten works during this period, including the works of Bach, whose *St Matthew Passion* he had already performed in 1829. Mendelssohn founded Germany's first musical Conservatory in Leipzig in 1843.

Clara Wieck and **Robert Schumann** spent the early years of their marriage in Leipzig. They lived in a fine neo-Classical house at 16 Inselstraße, which is now fitted out as a memorial to them. Among other works, the *'Spring' Symphony* was composed here.

The Bach museum is housed in the former home of the Boses, a family of merchants who had been friends of Bach's. It was built in 1586 and converted in the 18C. Instruments, manuscripts and various documents trace the life, work and legacy of the great composer. The main emphasis is on his Leipzig period (from 1723 to 1750).

Take Thomasgasse eastwards.

Altes Rathaus★ (Old Town Hall)

This long, low building with its fine Renaissance façade is crowned with dwarf gables which are pierced by windows – one of the earliest examples of an architectural style typifying town hall design during the German Renaissance. It was completed in 1556 after plans drawn up by Hieronymous Lotter, architect and burgomaster of Leipzig, and restored for the first time in 1672. The tower above the main doorway features a special balcony for the town pipers or heralds. Today the building houses the local history museum, the Stadtgeschichtliches Museum. ♿ *Open every day except Mon, 10am-6pm. Closed 24, 25 and 31 Dec. €2.50, free admission on 1st Sun of each month. ☎ (0341) 96 51 30.*

Alte Börse★ (Former Produce Exchange)

On the Naschmarkt. Built between 1678 and 1687 after plans by Johann Georg Starcke, this one-time commodity market was Leipzig's first Baroque edifice. It is used today for fairs and festivals.

The statue outside (by Carl Seffner in 1903) represents Goethe as a student.

Katharinenstraße

North of the Alte Börse, Katharinenstaße runs alongside Sachsenplatz. Some Baroque houses survive on the west side of this street. The finest is definitely the Romanushaus *(on the corner with Brühl)*, built in 1701-04 after designs by Johann Gregor Fuchs for burgomaster Franz Conrad Romanus. The neighbouring houses *(nos 21 and 19)* were built in the mid 18C and feature charming façades. The Fregehaus *(no 11)*, also built by Fuchs, belonged to the wealthy banker Christian Gottlob Frege, the Fugger *(see AUGSBURG)* of Leipzig, whose trade emporium stretched across Europe and as far as America.

Skirt Sachsenplatz and head back towards the Alte Börse via Reichsstraße.

Arcades

It is pleasant indeed to stroll through some of Leipzig's characteristic glass-roofed arcades. Many have been remarkably well restored and offer a colourful variety of shops and bars, which are appreciated by local residents and tourists alike.

Mädlerpassage – *Opposite Naschmarkt.* This is the grandest and perhaps the best-known of Leipzig's arcades, not least because it is home to Auerbachs Keller, where Goethe set some of the scenes in his great work *Faust*. There is good food and a great atmosphere in the vaulted underground rooms. Before going downstairs, pause to admire the bronze groups by Matthieu Molitor, depicting Faust, Mephistopheles and revellers.

Specks Hof – *Schuhmachergäßchen.* The restoration of this 1911 trade fair hall provoked some controversy, but the result is a success. Old features have been preserved and new ones added with a sensitive touch. Specks Hof leads into the Hansahaus.

Strohsack – This modern arcade links Nikolaistraße with Ritterstraße. Check the time on the glass-covered clock in the floor.

Steibs Hof – *Between Brühlstraße and Nikolaistraße.* This trade fair house with its blue and white tiled inner courtyards was built in 1907 for a furrier. Leipzig was the European centre for tanned goods until the 1930s.

Jägerhofpassage – *Between Hainstraße and Grosse Fleischergaße.* This arcade with its ivory coloured tiled walls is a late Jugendstil work dating from 1913-14 and houses a cinema.

Nikolaikirche

Nikolaistraße. Standing at the junction of two major trade routes, this church built in 1165 was naturally dedicated to the patron saint of merchants, Saint Nicholas. Originally built in the Romanesque style, the church has since undergone various modifications: the Gothic chancel and west towers date from the 14C, the Late Gothic triple nave surrounded by a double gallery from 1523 to 1526, and the central tower from 1555.

It started with prayer group on Mondays...

From 1982, Christians and non-Christians used to meet at the Nikolaikirche every Monday at 5pm to pray for peace. In summer 1989, as the wave of emigration hit the DDR, this prayer group assumed increasing significance. From May of that year, the streets leading to the Nikolaikirche were guarded by the People's Police. Despite these precautions, a growing number of people flocked there and the 2 000 seats in the church were no longer enough to accommodate those who came. Many people were arrested following the prayer meetings. Tension rose to breaking point. After uniformed troops had attacked unarmed civilians in Leipzig on 7 October, people feared the worst for the prayer meeting scheduled for Monday 9 October, to which 1 000 members of the socialist unity party (SED) had been summoned. When these people left the church, there was a crowd of 10 000 or more waiting for them in the square, all holding candles. The miracle of the peaceful revolution had happened. A member of the SED said afterwards, "We had planned everything. We were ready for anything. But not for candles and prayers."

The church's classical **interior★** (1784-97) by Carl Dauthe is particularly impressive. The effect is simultaneously spacious and dramatic. The pale, fluted pillars end in light green palm leaves. The vaulting is coffered in old rose with stucco flowers. There are 30 paintings hanging in the narthex and chancel by Adam Friedrich Oeser, a contemporary of Dauthe. The Late Romanesque wooden crucifix in the chancel is believed to be the oldest surviving work of art in Leipzig. The organ (1858-62) is the work of renowned Weißenfels organ-builder Friedrich Ladegast.

Worth a Visit

Museum der Bildenden Künste★★ (Fine Arts Museum)

Grimmaische Straße 1-7. ♿ Open every day except Mon, 10am-6pm, Wed 1pm-9.30pm. Closed 24 and 31 Dec. €4, free admission on 2nd Sun of each month. ☎ (0341) 21 69 90.

One of Europe's most important art collections, with works from the Late Middle Ages to the present, is temporarily housed in this trade fair hall until the new building planned on Sachsenplatz, a 34m/112ft high glass cube (designed by a firm of architects from Berlin), can be inaugurated. The works were originally due to be completed in 2002, but owing to delays the transfer date is still uncertain.

The collection notably includes some major works by old German and Dutch masters as well as 19C German paintings.

German Primitives: *The Man of Agonies* (c 1425) by Master Francke; *Portraits of Luther and Junker Jörg* (1521) by Lucas Cranach the Elder; *The Seven Ages of Woman* (1544) by Hans Baldung Grien.

Flemish Painting: *Portrait of an Old Man* (1430-40) by a disciple of Jan van Eyck; *Visitation* (c 1435) by Rogier van der Weyden; a portrait (c 1653) by one of Rembrandt's circle; *The Mulatto* (c 1630) by Frans Hals; and works by Gerard Honthorst, Van Goyen, Van Ostade, Van Ruisdael.

Italian Painting: Cima da Conegliano, Francesco Francia, Tintoretto (*The Resurrection of Lazarus*, c 1565).

German Painting: Anton Graff, JFA Tischbein, JA Koch, CD Friedrich (*The Ages of Life*, c 1835), Carl Spitzweg, Moritz von Schwind, Arnold Böcklin (*The Island of the Dead*, c 1886), Max Liebermann (*The Bottlers*, 1879), Max Klinger (*Blue Hour*, 1890) and Wilhelm Leibl.

In the Sculpture Department there are works by, among others, Balthasar Permoser, Berthel Thorvaldsen, Auguste Rodin and Max Klinger. The museum's collection of prints and drawings offers a virtually unbroken panoramic survey of graphic art from medieval times (Martin Schongauer) to the present.

Grassi-Museum★

East of the historic centre, on Johannisplatz, the Grassi-Museum can be reached via Grimmaischer Steinweg. This impressive complex with its four inner courtyards was built in 1925 to 1929 in the Expressionist style, with echoes of Art Deco, by architects Carl William Zweck and Hans Voigt. Funding has now been found for the urgent renovation of this fine building, so that British architect David Chipperfield's project may be implemented by 2005. *The Grassi-Museum's three collections are housed in other locations during renovation work.*

LEIPZIG

Street	Grid
Am Hallischen Tor	AY 3
Böttchergäßchen	AY 5
Grimmaischer Steinweg	BZ 12
Grimmaische Straße	ABZ 13
Große Fleischergasse	AY 14
Katharinenstraße	AY 18
Klostergasse	AY 21
Kupfergasse	AZ 23
Mädlerpassage	AZ 24
Naschmarkt	AY 26
Otto-Schill-Straße	AZ 27
Preußergäßchen	AZ 29
Ratsfreischulstraße	AZ 30
Reichsstraße	AY 31
Schloßgasse	AZ 33
Schuhmachergäßchen	ABY 34
Specks Hof	ABY 38
Steibs Hof	BY 39
Thomasgasse	BYZ 40

Sight	Grid	Key
Ägyptisches Museum	AZ	M¹
Goethe-Denkmal	AY	A
Museum der bildenden Künste	AY	M³
Museum in der Runden Ecke	AY	M²
Universität	BYZ	U
Zeitgeschichtliches Forum Leipzig	AZ	M⁴

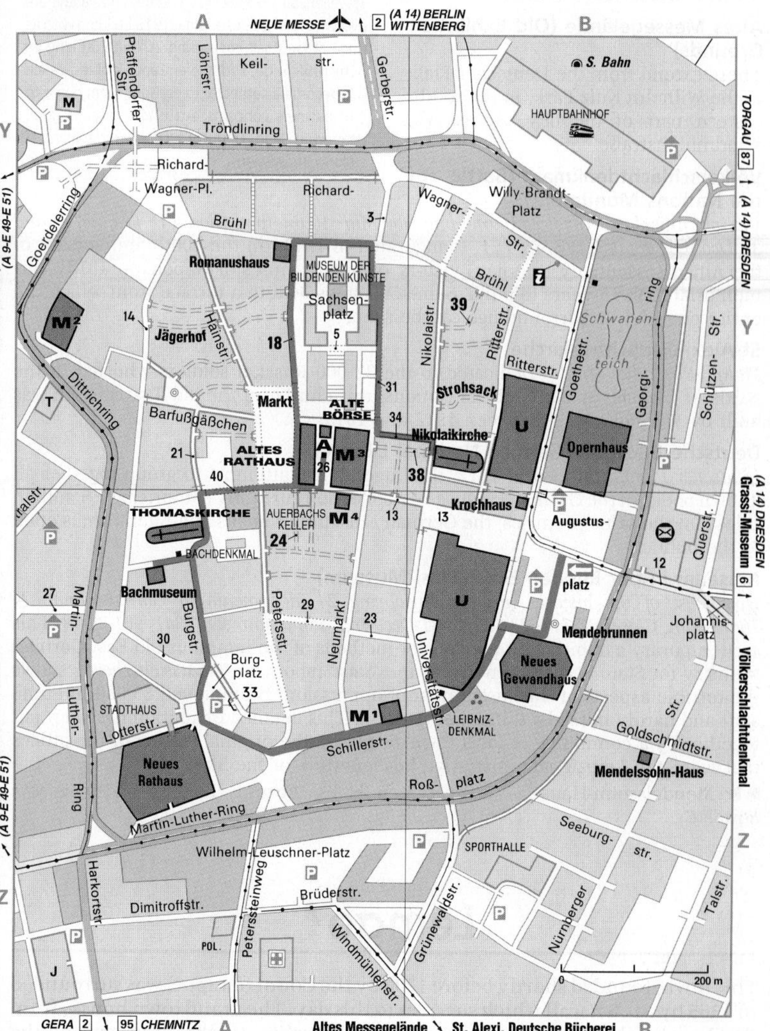

Museum für Kunsthandwerk★ (Museum of Arts and Crafts) – *Neumarkt 20.* ♿ *Open every day except Mon, 10am-6pm, Wed 10am-8pm. Closed 24 and 31 Dec. €4, free admission on 1st Sun of each month.* ☎ *(0341) 213 37 19.* The collection covers European arts and crafts from the Middle Ages right up to the first half of the 20C. Exhibits include furniture (Nuremberg hall cabinet, 16C), porcelain (Meissen), glassware (Venetian, Bohemian), and valuable Jugendstil pieces (Gallé, Lalique). There are also exhibits of work from the Vienna Workshops. An extremely rare objet d'art is the delicate Buchsbaum jointed doll dating from 1521.

Museum für Völkerkunde★ (Museum of Ethnography) – *Berliner Straße 11-13.* ♿ *Open every day except Mon, 10am-6pm, Sat-Sun 10am-5pm. Closed Easter Sunday and Pentecost, 1st May, 24 and 31 Dec. €2, free admission on 1st Sun of each month.* ☎ *(0341) 26 89 56.* This is one of the oldest and most important museums of its kind in Europe. It illustrates the history, culture and way of life of the peoples of Asia, Africa, America, Australia and Oceania by means of a wealth of cultural artefacts and informative documentary photographs and drawings.

Musikinstrumenten-Museum★ (Museum of Musical Instruments) – *Thomaskirchhof 20. Open every day except Mon, 11am-5pm. Closed 1st Jan, Good Friday, 24, 25 and 31 Dec. €3.* ☎ *(0341) 687 07 90.* This is the second most important collection in Europe after Brussels. It displays 5 000 instruments spanning five centuries, including a clavichord, made in Venice in 1543, a spinet (1693) and a hammer piano from Florence (1726). Note the guitar by Antonio Mariani (Venice, 1680) with its finely worked mother-of-pearl inlay.

Railway stations can look good...

Leipzig railway station, which had become seriously rundown, despite being Europe's largest railway terminus, was given a major facelift in 1995. Within two years, the station lobbies had been renovated and a three-storey shopping centre covering 30 000m²/322 800sq ft installed. Travellers arriving in Leipzig by train nowadays are overwhelmed by the original 1915 building with its huge oblong hall, measuring 267m/876ft long by 32m/105ft wide, and two entrance lobbies, which has become a cathedral to consumerism, home to 130 business concerns. Art is also given a good deal, with Jean Tinguely's *Luminator* making a striking impression.

Altes Messegelände (Old Exhibition Grounds)

These extend from the Deutscher Platz to the Wilhelm Külz Park, in the south-eastern part of the city. Access via Windmülenstraße.

Völkerschlachtdenkmal (Battle of the Nations Monument)

Via Johannisplatz. Apr-Oct: 10am-6pm; Nov-Mar: 10am-4pm. Closed 1st Jan, 24, 25 and 31 Dec. €3. ☏ (0341) 878 04 71. Inaugurated in 1913, on the 100th anniversary of the Allied (essentially Prussian) victory over the armies of Napoleon (1813), this memorial took 15 years to build. Some 500 steps lead to a terrace from which the entire city and its surroundings can be seen.

St-Alexi-Gedächtniskirche

Philipp-Rosenthal-Straße. Dedicated to the 22 000 Russian soldiers who fell in the Battle of Leipzig, or Battle of the Nations, this church in the old Tzarist style was built by WA Pokrowski between 1912 and 1913.

Deutsche Bücherei (German National Library)

Deutscher Platz. Founded in 1912, the huge library attempts to group together all known books in the German language – a collection currently comprising 7.5 million titles. On the same premises, the German Museum of Books and Literature is open to the public.

Museum in der Runden Ecke (Stasi Museum)

Northwest of the historic centre, Dittrichring 24, documents in German only. ♿ *10am-6pm. Closed 1st Jan, 23-26 and 31 Dec. Free admission. ☏ (0341) 961 24 43.* This contemporary exhibition on the sinister methods of the infamous old East German Ministry for State Security, known as the *"Stasi"* (short for *"Staatssicherheit"*), shows the terrible aspects of this instrument of oppression. It employed 85 000 full-time staff and hardly missed a thing that went on. This detailed exhibition has been put together by a committee of local townspeople in the original setting of the offices that were the Leipzig administrative headquarters of the Stasi.

►► Mendelssohn-Haus – Zeitgeschichtliches Forum Leipzig (*Grimmaische Straße 6*).

Lemgo★

This town, founded shortly before 1200 by the Count of Lippe, was surrounded in 1365 by a town wall which survives to this day. The grand town houses from the Late Gothic and Renaissance periods testify to the grandeur of the once-wealthy Hanseatic city. Make sure you try the regional speciality, Lemgoer Strohsemmel, created by a local baker's apprentice for Napoleonic troops during their Russian campaign.

Location

Population: 43 000. Michelin maps nº 543 J 10 – Nordrhein-Westfalen. Lemgo is located to the east of Nordrhein-Westphalia, a few kilometres from the A 2 which links Hannover and Dortmund.

Surrounding area: see HAMELN (41km/26mi northeast), HILDESHEIM (91km/57mi east), HANNOVER (92km/58mi northeast), MÜNSTER (107km/67mi west).

Walking About

THE OLD TOWN★

From the Ostertor to the east, approach the Mittelstraße, which is the main street. Grand half-timbered town houses line the street. Note especially the fine façades of nº 17 (with wood carving on all four floors) and nº 36, known as the House of Planets (Planetenhaus).

Rathaus★★

The town hall is a magnificent building. Comprising eight buildings side by side, the civic centre of Lemgo is exceptional for its oriel windows, its arcades and its unique gables. The elegantly worked façade of the old apothecary's shop on the corner of the Marktplatz displays, on the first floor, the sculpted portraits of 10 famous philosopher-physicians, from Aristotle to Paracelsus. Beneath the central arcades, brutal witchcraft trials were held in about 1670.

Bear left into Breite Straße.

Witch-hunting in Lemgo

During the Inquisition, the death penalty existed for heresy and sorcery. Great waves of persecution ran through the country, also affecting the town of Lemgo. They were the result of the "witch-hunt" by the inquisitor J Sprenger. Between 1564 and 1681, more than 200 were persecuted as witches. The accused were tortured and false confessions were wrung out of them. The Lemgo mayor Hermann Cothman ingloriously distinguished himself as a particularly cruel "director of the criminal court".

The persecutions finally came to an end when a young woman withstood the torture, was banished from the region but sued her torturers before the Imperial supreme court.

Hexenbürgermeisterhaus (House of the Witches' Burgomaster)

Temporarily closed. 19 Breite Straße. The house, with its splendid façade, was built between 1568 and 1571 and is an outstanding memorial to Weser Renaissance urban architecture. It houses the city museum, which focuses on housing and everyday culture, craft and trade.

A special exhibition is dedicated to the history of witch-hunting in Lemgo.

Marienkirche

A Renaissance organ with a finely carved case, among the oldest in Germany (1587-1613), adorns this triple-aisle Gothic church constructed at the end of the 13C and the beginning of the 14C (about 1260-1320). Admire too the baptismal font (1592), the pulpit (1644) and the Cross Triumphant (c 1500).

Return to Papenstraße, following it to the right.

St-Nicolaikirche

Appropriately dedicated to the patron saint of merchants, the church (13C onwards) combines features that are both Romanesque (a three-figure tympanum in the south aisle; a stone triptych in the north) and Gothic (frescoes and vault keystones). The pulpit and the font are Late Renaissance (c 1600).

Papenstraße leads back to the starting point.

Worth a visit

Junkerhaus★

Hamelner Straße 36. Guided tour (90min) Sun at 3pm. For information, ☎ (052 61) 21 32 76. **Karl Junker** (1850-1912), painter, sculptor and architect, a contemporary of the blossoming Jugendstil, left in his own house a memorial to his highly personal style. His design is organised around a spiral which relies for its effect on an arcane play of movements alternately balanced and opposed. Surprise is everything in this design: the visitor's perception of Junker's sculpted and painted decor (note the Pointillist medallions adorning the ceilings) is of an infinite diversity, constantly changing with each different point of view.

Schloß Brake

Schloßstrasse 18. ♿ Open Tue-Sun, 10am-6pm. Closed 1 Jan, 24, 25 and 31 Dec. €3. ☎ (052 61) 945 00. This mighty castle was built between the 12C and 19C, although the predominant style is Weser Renaissance. Nothing could be more apt, therefore, than to have a **Weserrenaissance-Museum** here, in which the various aspects of art and culture between the Reformation and the Thirty Years War are clearly explained.

Excursions

Herford

20km/12.5mi west. Town plan in the Michelin Guide Deutschland. This town between Teutoburger Wald and the Weser was a member of the Hanseatic League until the 17C. The historic town centre contains numerous half-timbered houses from the 16C to the 18C.

Münsterkirche – The late Romanesque hall-church (1220-1280) is one of the oldest in Westphalia. Modifications during the Gothic period bequeathed it some beautiful window tracery.

Johanniskirche – The Protestant Johanniskirche is decorated with fine 17C wood **carving★**, both sculpted and painted. Galleries, stalls and pulpit were all donated by different city corporations, whose shields and emblems can be recognised in the design. The chancel has interesting 15C stained-glass windows.

Limburg an der Lahn★

The powerful yet elegant silhouette of the cathedral overhanging the Lahn dominates the Limburg skyline. The town centre, a protected site, consists largely of half-timbered houses with lavish woodcarving dating from the 13C to the 18C.

Location

Population: 35 000. Michelin map nº 543 O 8 – Hessen. On the border of Hessen and Rheinland-Pfalz, Limburg can be reached via the A 3 which links the town to Wiesbaden and Frankfurt to the south and Koblenz, to the north.

Hospitalstraße 2, 65549 Limburg, ☎ (064 31) 61 66.

Surrounding area: see WIESBADEN (39km/24mi south), LAHNTAL (Bad Ems is 41km/26mi west), KOBLENZ (54km/34mi west), FRANKFURT AM MAIN (69km/43mi southeast).

Directory

Where to Stay

Martin – *Holzheimer Straße 2 – ☎ (06431) 948 40 – fax (06431) 43185 – info@hotel-martin.de – P – 30rm: €48/81 – Restaurant €18/36.* This family-run hotel is located in the town centre opposite the station and offers tidy, functionally equipped guestrooms.

Romantik Hotel Zimmermann – *Blumenröder Straße 1 – ☎ (06431) 46 11 – fax (06431) 41314 – zimmermann@romantikhotels.com – Closed 20 Dec-5 Jan – P – 24rm: €80/165.* With furnishings inspired by Enland, the rooms have an air of luxury about them. Huge breakfasts.

Special Features

CATHEDRAL★ (DOM) *allow 30min*

Built on a rocky spur, St Georgsdom is in a picturesque **setting★★**. Apart from that, it is remarkable for the style of its architecture: a classic example of Romanesque-Gothic Transitional, which was prevalent in Germany between 1210 and 1250.

The outside remains Romanesque and closely resembles the Rhineland cathedrals *(see Introduction: Art and architecture)*, but the interior is already Gothic, with a structure directly inspired by the cathedral of Laon, in Picardy, France. Here we find superposed galleries, arcades, a triforium and clerestory windows as typical of the early Gothic period as the distinctive crochet capitals. Diagonal ribs characterise the vaulting. The transept crossing lies beneath a domed lantern tower. The original decoration has been uncovered and restored.

From the cemetery terrace (Friedhofsterrasse) on the north side of the church, there is a good **view★** of the river, the old bridge, and a new motorway viaduct.

Diözesanmuseum★

Domstraße 12. Open from mid-Mar to mid-Nov, Tue-Sun, 10am-1pm, 2pm-5pm, Sun. 11am-5pm. €2. ☎ (064 31) 29 54 82. The 10C Byzantine reliquary cross known as the Limburger Staurothek is the jewel of the religious art collection displayed in this museum, which occupies a historical building along with the cathedral treasury. Another highlight is the sheath encasing the reliquary Staff of St Peter, completed in 980 in Trier under Archbishop Egbert. On display in the medieval sculpture section is an admirable terracotta *Lamentation of Christ*, a moving work that dates from the "soft" style period c 1415.

Worth a Visit

Old Town★ (Alstadt)

In the old town, whole streets are preserved with their original buildings, some of which have fine half-timbering *(Domplatz, Fischmarkt, Brückengasse, Römer, Rütsche, Bischofsplatz)*. Walderdorffer Hof (Fahrgasse) is a Renaissance construction with four wings. Taking time to discover the beautiful old houses in the winding alleys is one of the joys of a visit to Limburg.

Lindau im Bodensee★★

Lindau – *im Bodensee* (in the lake) and not *am Bodensee* (by the lake) like its neighbours Überlingen and Meersburg – boasts a number of fine old gabled burghers' houses in the old town, testifying to the prosperity of bygone days when it was an important trading centre, particularly for commerce with Italy. There is an almost Mediterranean quality to life in this lakeside island resort at the gates of Austria – a atmosphere which can be savoured to the full during an evening stroll between the port and the Maximilianstraße.

Location

Population: 25 000. Michelin map nº 545 X 13. Plan: KONSTANZ – Bayern. Located in a Bavarian enclave at the extreme east of Lake Constance, park the car in one of the car parks on the edge of the lake and follow the signs to "Lindau-Insel" to explore the old town. Ferries link Lindau to Konstanz or Bregenz (in Austria) several times a day.

🅸 *Am Hauptbahnhof, 88131 Lindau, ☎ (083 82) 26 00 30.*

Surrounding area: see BODENSEE, KONSTANZ (94km/59mi in 1hr30min by road or 3hr15min by boat), Deutsch ALPENSTRASSE (tours leaves from Lindau).

Lindau Tourismus

Lindau, an island resort on the Bodensee..

Walking About

THE OLD TOWN★★ *1hr*

Marktplatz

The marketplace surrounds a large circular fountain. The eastern side of the square is dominated by the façades of the Protestant church and the Collegiate church *(Stiftkirche);* the latter contains a beautiful high altar. On the west side of the square, installed in the **Haus zum Cavazzen**★, a typical example of bourgeois Baroque architecture (1729), the **town museum** *(Stadtmuseum)* has an exhibition on home décor, including arts and crafts and an interesting collection of mechanical musical instruments. There is also a gallery of painting and sculpture. *Open from the beginning of Apr to end Oct, Tue-Sun, 11am-5pm, Sat, 2-5pm. Closed Ester Sun and Pentecost, 1 May. €2.50. ☎ (083 82) 77 56 50.*

Maximilianstraße★★

This, the main artery leading through the old town, is a picturesque street lined by old houses and inns. Narrow, half-timbered façades with the oriel windows characteristic of the Alpine Rhine Valley and the Vorarlberg huddle together with the stepped gables of Old Swabia (the former town hall – Altes Rathaus – is a fine example of the latter style). *Turn right into the Zeppelinstraße.*

Directory

Where to Stay

Schachener Hof – *Schachener Straße 76 – 88131 Lindau-Bad Schachen – (08382) 31 16 – info@schachenerhof-lindau.de – Closed 2 Jan-7 Feb – €25/49.* Classically decorated restaurant with dark wood furniture offering succulent dishes mixed with regional and foreign cuisine. Welcoming staff.

Hoyerberg Schlössle – *Hoyerbergstraße 64 (sur la Hoyerberg) – 88131 Lindau-Hoyren – Closed Feb, Mon-Tue lunchtimes – (08382) 252 95 – info@hoyerbergschloessle.de – €40.50/53.50.* Pleasant décor and not a little elegance characterise the renovated rooms of this little castle. There are views over Lindau, the Alps and the lake from the terrace.

Where to Stay

Hotel Köchlin – *Kemptener Straße 41 – (08382) 966 00 – fax (08382) 966943 – www.hotel-koechlin.de – Closed 3 weeks in Nov. – – 21rm: €38.50/82 – Restaurant €10/20.* A small country hotel with shingle roof and flowery façade. Inside, lots of wood and rustic décor. In summer months there is a Biergarten at the back of the establishment, pleasantly shaded by old trees.

Hotel Lindauer Hof – *Seepromenade – (08382) 40 64 – fax (08382) 24203 – info@lindauer-hof.de – – 30rm: €75/195 – Restaurant €18/37.* Modern hotel with particularly comfortable guestrooms. Pleasantly close to the lake. Meals are served on the first floor or on the pretty terrace.

Hotel Bayerischer Hof – *Seepromenade – (08382) 91 50 – fax (08382) 915591 – bayerischerhof-lindau@t-online.de – – 100rm: €106/279 – Restaurant €23/44.* Situated in a very special part of the town, this elegant hotel is comfortable and chic. The restaurant offers good classical cuisine with varied menu and good views.

Schrannenplatz

The Brigands' Tower *(Diebsturm)*, a well-known Lindau silhouette with its crown of bartizans, was the most westerly point of the Medieval fortifications. At the foot of the tower is the small **Peterskirche**, the oldest church in the town (c 1000 AD) and now a monument to those who died in the First World War. Inside there are **frescoes** (15C) by Hans Holbein the Elder.

Go back down Zeppelinstraße towards the port.

Hafen★ (Port)

Tourists crowd the quays, many of them waiting to embark on one of the large white Lake Constance pleasure boats. In the centre of the activity stands the **Mangturm**, a fortified 12C tower once used as a lighthouse. The present lighthouse

LINDAU IM BODENSEE

Bäckergässele . . . . . Y 8
Bahnhofplatz . . . . . Z
Bei der Heidenmauer . . . . . Y 15
Bindergasse . . . . . Z 18
Brettermarkt . . . . . Y 24
Cramergasse . . . . . Y 27
Dammgasse . . . . . Z 30
Fischergasse . . . . . Z 33
Hafenplatz . . . . . Z 38
In der Grub . . . . . Y
Inselgraben . . . . . Z 41
Kirchplatz . . . . . Y 47
Maximilianstraße . . . . . YZ
Paradiesplatz . . . . . Y 62
Reichsplatz . . . . . Z 65
Schafgasse . . . . . YZ 77
Schmiedgasse . . . . . Y 80
Schrannenplatz . . . . . Y 83
Seepromenade . . . . . Z 85
Stiftplatz . . . . . YZ 87
Thierschbrücke . . . . . Y 90
Vordere Metzgergasse . . . . . Z 92

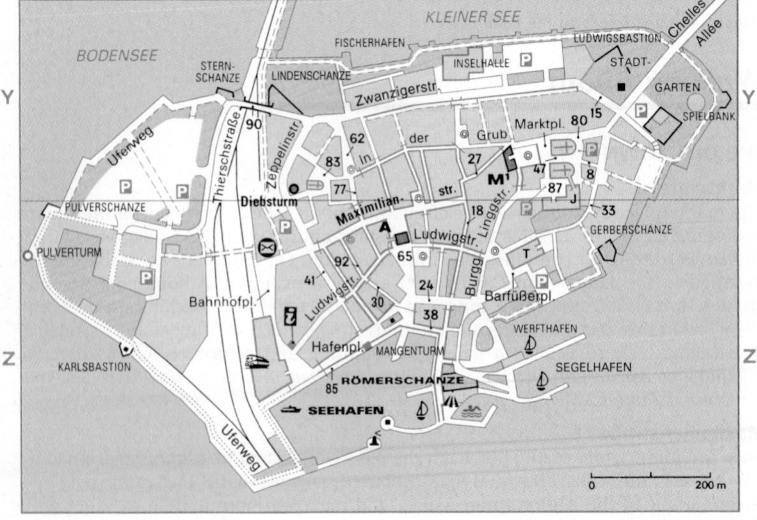

Altes Rathaus . . . . . Z A
Stadtmuseum . . . . . Y M¹

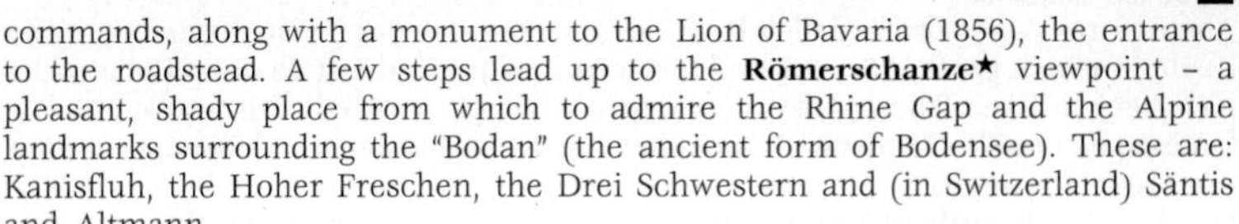

commands, along with a monument to the Lion of Bavaria (1856), the entrance to the roadstead. A few steps lead up to the **Römerschanze★** viewpoint – a pleasant, shady place from which to admire the Rhine Gap and the Alpine landmarks surrounding the "Bodan" (the ancient form of Bodensee). These are: Kanisfluh, the Hoher Freschen, the Drei Schwestern and (in Switzerland) Säntis and Altmann.

Excursions

Wangen im Allgäu★

22 km au Nord. Lying within sight of the first crests of the Allgäu Alps, this small Swabian town has been built with its colourful houses arranged in a simple cruciform plan, the two main streets crossing at right angles in **Marktplatz★**. Herrenstraße, running as it were from side to side, is lined with attractive houses, many with decorative shop signs. At the far end is the *Ravensburger Tor* (or *Frauentor*), a square gateway of which the 17C coping, confined by engaged turrets, is topped by an elegant ribbed roof. Perpendicular to this street, the other main thoroughfare ends at St Martinstor. Painted outside like the Ravensburger Tor, this entrance is crowned with a pyramidal roof, beneath which very finely worked gargoyles jut out.

Schloß Linderhof★★

Deep in the forest, in one of the most secluded valleys of the Ammergau Alps – a region the royal hunters of the House of Bavaria reserved for their own use – Ludwig II had this small villa-like palace built. Designed in the style of the 18C, it served as a backdrop for the romantic fancies of the young king. The extraordinary contrasts provided by a Rococo building surrounded by gardens and terraces inspired by the Italian Renaissance, set in the middle of a park landscaped in the English manner – the whole planted in an Alpine valley – lend the project its own peculiar charm.

Location

Michelin maps n°s 545, 546 X 16 – Bayern. Local map: Deutsche ALPENSTRASSE.
The Ammergau Alps serve as a backdrop to the little valley of the Ammer which provides the Austrian border. Linderhof Palace is slightly removed from the village of the same name *(follows the signs for "Schloß" to the right after you enter the village),* and is framed by majestic mountains covered by huge pine trees.
Surrounding area: see Deutsche ALPENSTRASSE (the tour passes through Linderhof), WIESKIRCHE (38km/24mi northwest), GARMISCH-PARTENKIRCHEN (26km/16mi southeast), Ludwig II's two other palaces (NEUSCHWANSTEIN is 58km/36mi away, and Herrenchiemsee (CHIEMSEE) is 137km/86mi away).

Worth a Visit

2hr. During high season queues can be very long. A walk round the park is a pleasant way to pass the time.

Palace★

Open Apr to mid-Oct; guided tours 9am-5.30pm; from mid-Oct to end Mar, 10am-4pm. Open on Thu until 7.30pm. Closed 1 Jan, Shrove Tue, 24, 25 and 31 Dec. Park and grotto open from mid-Oct to end Mar. Summer €6, winter €4.50. ☎ (088 22) 920 30; www.schloesser.bayern.de

Ludwig II had the castle built between 1874 and 1879, in a style intermingling the second Italian Renaissance and the Baroque. His intention was to achieve a relatively homely atmosphere. Nonetheless, inside, one finds a **state bedchamber** on the upper floor surpassing in luxury even those of Versailles. The magnificent decor in the various rooms, the **hall of mirrors** and the Gobelins room never fails to impress visitors.

Park★★

Open daily from 8.30am to 6pm. No charge, except for the grotto (tickets available from the palace if necessary). Map on the back of the ticket.

The natural slopes of the valley have been used to lay out a vista in line with the castle in which pools, cascades and terraced gardens in the style of an Italian villa have been devised. These strike an unexpectedly upbeat note in this wooded Alpine landscape. The side borders, on the other hand, suggest a more placid approach in the French manner.

Climb to the **Temple of Venus** rotunda, which closes off the perspective above an ornamental lake (a fine view, especially when the fountains play). Then descend, keeping to the right of the castle, and climb the opposite slope to reach the Moorish pavilion and the grotto. It is here that the skill of the landscape gardener, Karl von Effner, is most in evidence, with plantations of trees placed with consummate art against a backdrop of clumps of conifers into which they gradually blend to form a sombre natural density.

Moorish Pavilion *(Maurischer Kiosk)* – Acquired by **Ludwig II** after the 1867 Exposition Universelle in Paris (which was really the world's first International fair), this metallic structure was used by him when he wished to play the oriental potentate.

Grotto of Venus – *By guided tour only.* A cavern, fashioned with the aid of artificial rocks and intended to recreate the atmosphere of the Venusberg sequence in the Wagnerian opera *Tannhäuser*, the conceit here displays once more the king's taste for theatrical effect: by the royal throne is a rock evoking the Loreley, which is set beside a lake, illuminated by the play of coloured lights, on which floats a golden skiff in the form of a huge conch shell.

Hundinghütte – This pavilion was built with the scene in Wagner's opera *The Valkyrie* in mind. It was originally located in the Ammerwald. The present building is a reconstruction (1990) in the castle grounds faithful to the original, which was burned down in 1945.

F. Zaninotto/MICHELIN

The park was designed by the architect Karl von Effner.

Lübeck★★★

Lübeck has retained much of its medieval character as business centre of the Hanseatic League; many of its buildings and monuments are still decorated with alternating bands of red and glazed black-brick courses. Since 1987 the town has been on the UNESCO's World Heritage list. Today the city remains the busiest German port on the Baltic and a focal point for shipbuilding and heavy industry. Don't miss a taste of the delicious local marzipan sweets, one of the town's gastronomic specialities.

Location

Population: 215 300. Michelin map nº 541 E 16 – Schleswig-Holstein. Around 60km northeast of Hamburg, Lübeck has long been in the privileged position of being the hub of trade between the Baltic and western Europe. The river Trave intersects the town. To reach the town from Hamburg, take the A 1 motorway.

Beckergrube 95, 23552 Lübeck, ☎ (0451) 122 54 06.

Surrounding area: see WISMAR (61km/38mi east), HAMBURG (67km/42mi southwest), KIEL (94km/59mi north), SCHWERIN (110km/69mi southeast).

Background

At the Head of the League – The 14C marked the summit of Lübeck's power as Hanseatic capital – the most influential town of that association of Dutch and north German cities which from the 12C to the 16C monopolised trade with Scandinavia and Russia. In the 16C, the business acumen of merchants and shipowners combined to extricate the port from a long period of decline, thanks largely to the

Directory

Where to Eat

Paulaner's – *Breite Straße 1-5 – ☎ (0451) 707 94 50 – www.paulaners.de – ♿ – Booking advised – €16.70/24.10.* Lübeck is one of the most northerly towns in Germany and so it's quite a novelty to be able to try Munich-brewed beer in this Bavarian influenced restaurant. Northern specialities are also served. Pleasant Biergarten in the churchyard of the Jakobikirchhof.

Schiffergesellschaft – *Breite Straße 2 – ☎ (0451) 767 76 – schiffergesellschaft@t-online.de – €26/39.50.* An impressively preserved tavern, built as a sailors' meeting-house, guildhouse and almshouse back in 1535. Take a seat on the old refectory benches and admire countless reminders of Lübeck's maritime past.

Where to Stay

Hotel Jensen – *An der Obertrave 4 – ☎ (0451) 70 24 90 – fax (0451) 73386 – jensen@ringhotels.de – 42rm: €65/108 – Restaurant €21/38.* Located within the historic triangle formed by the Trave, the Holstentor and the *Salzspeicher*, this comfortably appointed, gabled house built in 1307 has modern guestroooms with maritime-themed dining room.

Hotel Kaiserhof – *Kronsforder Allee 11 – ☎ (0451) 70 33 01 – fax (0451) 795083 – service@kaiserhof-luebeck.de – – 60rm: €72/128 – Restaurant €23/48.* Two fine patrician houses have been joined together to form this pleasantly decorated hotel only a few minutes on foot from the town centre. Roman-style steam bath and sound-proofed room available for musicians.

Taking a Break

Café Niederegger – *Breite Str. 89 – ☎ (0451) 5 30 11 26 – www.niederegger.de – Mon-Fri 9am-7pm, Sat 9am-6pm, Sun 10am-6pm.* This café is *the* place to buy marzipan. The shop on the ground floor serves it in all shapes and sizes and the tea room on the ground and first floors serves it in cake form. An exhibition dedicated to the town's speciality *(Marzipansalon)* is on the 2nd floor.

Café Utspann – *Wahmstr. 35-37 (in the Hansehof court) – ☎ (0451) 7 07 06 77 – Mon-Sat, 9am-6pm – Closed Sun and bank holidays.* Friesian-style décor distinguishes this inviting tea room. In the family atmosphere, homemade cakes are served, their appetising smell lingering in the air. In summer months, a few tables are available outside on the old Hansehof court.

Going Out

Brauberger – *Alfstr. 36 (parallel with Meng- and Fischstr.) – ☎ (0451) 7 14 44 – www.brauberger-luebeck.de – Mon-Fri from 5pm, Sat from 6pm, Closed Sun, and for one week in Jan.* This micro-brewery opened in 1988, but its cellar dates from 1225. On the first floor there is a small outdoor terrace. Light snacks are served as are regional specialities, all washed down with beer brewed on the premises.

Metro – *Mühlenbrücke 11 (a continuation of Mühlenstr.) – ☎ (0451) 7 02 06 98 – www.metrocafe.de – Mon-Thu, 12 noon-1am, Fri 12 noon-2am, Sat, 10-2am, Sun, 10-1am.* This café's décor was inspired by the style of Parisian metro stations. Light snacks are on the menu. Beautiful terrace with Biergarten on the water's edge.

establishment of new relations with Holland, and also with France and the Iberian countries, who sent cargoes of wine. For a long time, Dutch architecture was the preferred style for the rich burghers on the banks of the Trave.

Contested supremacy – In the 19C, Lübeck's status as a seaport was rivalled by the Prussian port of Stettin (now Szczecin in Poland) and the opening of the Kiel canal. But the construction of a canal linking the Trave with the Elbe, plus an influx of almost 100 000 refugees in 1945, have together permitted the city to maintain its importance in present-day Germany. Among other assets it has the reputation of being the country's chief importer of the French red wines, which are matured in the celebrated Lübeck Cellars beneath the River Trave.

Walking About

THE OLD TOWN★★★ (Altstadt) *3hr*

Girdled with canals, crowned by belfries and towers, the old town of Lübeck is located on an island which is largely pedestrianised. The west side of the old town is reached throught the Holstentor, a national symbol in Germany.

Leave from the Holstentor (follow the itinerary marked on the town plan)

Holstentor★★

This fortified gate with its enormous twin towers was built between 1466 and 1478, before the construction of the city's perimeter wall, more as a matter of prestige than protection. The most impressively decorated façade, that towards the town, has three tiers of blind arcades with ornamented ceramic friezes. The building houses the **Local History Museum**. *(Stadtgeschichtliche Museum). Apr-Sep, 10am-5pm; Oct-Mar, 10am-4pm. Closed 25, 26 and 31 Dec. €3. ☏ (451) 122 41 34.*

M. Hertlein/MICHELIN

The Holstentor used to appear on the 50 Deutschmark note.

Rathaus★

Built from 1250 onwards, on two sides of the Marktplatz, the town hall is an elegant edifice in dark glazed brick, supported on a gallery of arcades. Note the high protective walls, sometimes pierced with blind arcades or by gaping round openings decorated and strengthened by slender turrets with "candle-snuffer" roofs. In front of the north wing, a Renaissance superstructure in ornately carved sandstone has been added. The building at the extremity of the east wing, the Neues Gemach (1440), is interesting for the heightened effect lent to it by an imaginative openwork wall.

Pass beneath the arcades to see, on the Breite Straße, a stone staircase (1594) in Dutch Renaissance style.

Continuing the circuit of the Rathaus, arrive at the foot of the north façade.

The wall here displays an impressive layout, with immense bays lined up across almost its entire height.

Marienkirche★★

The Rathaus at Lübeck.

One of the finest brick-built Gothic churches in Germany. The original designers in 1250 planned a hall-type church without a transept *(see Art and Architecture chapter)*, but the concept was changed while work was in progress. Subsequently, under the influence of French cathedral architecture, the main buttress-supported vaulting was raised to a height of 38.5m/126ft. The 125m/410ft spires were completed in 1350. The composer Dietrich Buxtehude (1637-1707) was the church's official organist. The interior, audacious in design, has grandiose proportions. A fire, started by an air raid in 1942, exposed the original polychromatic 13C and 14C decoration. At the west end of the south aisle is an elegant 14C chapel, the Briefkapelle, with tall lancet windows recalling the High Gothic style. The star vaulting rests on two monolithic columns of granite. Inside the south tower, two huge church bells, which were brought down during the raid, remain embedded in the ground.

The ambulatory vaulting covers in a single sweep both the radial apsidal chapels and the axial Lady Chapel, which contains an altarpiece to the Virgin made in Antwerp in 1518.

Outside the church, walk around the east end and go through the arcade of the former town hall Chancellery (15C-16C) to the Mengstraße.

Buddenbrookhaus

Mengstraße 4. ♿ Apr to Nov, 10am-5pm; Dec-Mar, 11am-5pm. €4.10. ☎ (0451) 122 41 90. However attractive the concept may be, Heinrich and Thomas Mann were unfortunately not born in Buddenbrookhaus. It is however a fact that in 1841 their grandfather Johann Siegmund Mann bought the Baroque house with its beautiful façade, which was built in 1758 and the brothers were frequently guests there during their childhood and adolescence. Thomas Mann used the house in his world-renowned book *Buddenbrooks*, in which he described the greatness and fall of a patrician family in Lübeck. The house is now the home of the Heinrich and Thomas Mann Centre, which is dedicated to the life and works of Lübeck's most famous sons.

Follow the Mengstraße until the Schabbelhaus and then retrace your steps. Take the BreiteStraße north.

Haus der Schiffergesellschaft★ (House of the Seamen's Guild)

Behind the stepped Renaissance gable, the **interior★★** *(now a restaurant, see Where to Eat above)* still preserves the picturesque furnishings of a seamen's tavern, with rough wooden tables, copper lamps and model ships hanging from the beams.

Jakobikirche★

Opposite the Haus der Schiffergesellschaft. The magnificent woodwork of the two organ **lofts★★** (16C-17C) in this small Gothic hall-church is noteworthy. Larger than life-size representations of apostles and saints adorn the pillars of the central nave. A chapel on the south aisle contains an altar known as the "Brömbse" (c 1500), with bas-relief sculptures of very fine workmanship. The chapel to the north of the tower is arranged as a memorial to the shipwrecked, and displays a lifeboat from the *Pamir*, the full-rigged Lübeck training ship lost with all hands in 1957.

Follow the promenade to the northernmost part of the old town marked by the Burgtor.

Burgtor★

This fortified gateway defended the narrow isthmus – now cut by a canal – which was once the only land approach to Lübeck. The structure is a fine example of military architecture (13C-15C) with a design of superimposed tierce point bays.

Return towards the centre of the old town along Große Burgstraße.

Heiligen-Geist-Hospital★ (Hospice of the Holy Spirit)

Since the end of the 13C, the three turret-bordered gables of this almshouse have stood above the Koberg. The chapel, a large Gothic hall embellished with 13C and 14C paintings, is just outside the even bigger Great Hall of the hospice (Langes Haus).

Katharinenkirche★

♿ *Open Apr to Sep Tue-Sun, 10a-5pm. €0.50, no charge on first Fri of the month.* ☎ *(0451) 122 41 34.* The lower niches of the 14C façade contain modern **statues★**, the first three on the left being by Ernst Barlach. Inside the church, which is a museum, note, on the right side as you enter, *The Resurrection of Lazarus* by Tintoretto.

The "Höfe und Gänge"

At the corner of the church, turn left into the Glockengießerstraße, on which open the courts *(Höfe)*, set back from the street, which are typical of Lübeck – social amenities donated in the 17C by local benefactors. Note, successively, the delightful **Füchtingshof★** (n° 25 – **Y S**), with its Baroque doorway dating from 1639; the *Glandorps-Gang*, a simple alignment of small houses along an alley (n° 41); and, from n°s 49 to 51, the *Glandorps-Hof*.

Explore this picturesque district south of the Glockengießerstraße, then go to the south of the old town to the cathedral district.

St-Annen-Museum★

Open Apr to Sep, Tue-Sun, 10am-5pm; Oct to Mar, 10am-4pm. Closed 25, 26 and 31 Dec. €3, no charge on last Fri of each month. ☎ *(0451) 122 41 34.* This former convent has a large collection of 15C and 16C paintings and sculpture which originate from the churches of Lübeck, as well as decorative artefacts which bear witness to the huge wealth of local notables in the past. German modern art is also on display.

Dom

The 14C enlargement of the chancel in the Gothic style transformed this Romanesque church. A covered entrance and a very fine porch were added to the north transept in the mid 13C. Inside, there is an imposing monumental Late Gothic **Crucifix★** made between 1470-77 by Bernt Notke. A stone screen (first half of the 14C) with a wooden tracery balustrade closes off the choir. There are some fine altarpieces against the pillars in the transept: the altarpiece of the Merchants of Stecknitz (1422); the altarpiece of the canonical daily offices, from the early 15C; altarpiece of the millhands (c 1460); and the altarpiece of Our Lady (1506).

▶▶ Petrikirche (**view★** of city from tower) – Behnhaus und Drägerhaus (painting and crafts from Romanticism to the present).

Excursions

Travemünde★

20km/12.5mi northeast. Town plan in the Michelin Guide Deutschland. This smart Baltic health resort boasts a fine sandy beach, a 2.5km/1.5mi-long promenade and a casino. **Travemünde week** is an annual event for German and foreign yachtsmen. Travemünde is also a well-known port, with links to Scandinavia and Estonia.

The old town, with its half-timbered houses and the fishermen's church of St Lorenz, is charming. Along the seafront there are some typical local gabled houses dating from the 18C and 19C. The four-masted bark *Passat*, a former trading ship, lies at anchor on the **Priwall** peninsula, on the opposite bank *(accessible by ferry)*.

The steep coastline of the **Brodten shore** stretches for several miles behind the promenade. A walk as far as **Niendorf** affords wonderful views over Lübeck Bay and the coastline. The popular Baltic Sea resort of **Timmendorfer Strand** lies further to the north.

Ratzeburg★

23 km/14mi southeast. The island town of Ratzeburg is built attractively in the middle of a **lake★**, the biggest of many in the morainal hills between the Elbe and Lübeck. The Schöne Aussicht viewpoint in Bäk on the east shore of the lake provides the best **view★** of the town dominated by the squat outline of its cathedral.

Dom★ – ♿ *Open Apr to Sep, 10am-12 noon, 2-6pm, Sun, 2-6pm; Oct to Mar, Tue-Sun, 10am-12 noon, 2-4pm, Sun, 2-4pm.* ☎ *(045 41) 34 06.* Brick-built and Romanesque in style, this 12C cathedral lies in a stretch of parkland on the northern point of the island. Outside, note the lavish gable decorations of the south porch, remodelled as a chapel. The entrance now is through doors beneath the tower. Above the high altar is an altarpiece in the form of a triptych, illustrating the **Crucifixion★** (1430), on the superb central shrine. Beautiful ecclesiastic vestments embroidered with gold thread may be seen in a chapel off the north aisle.

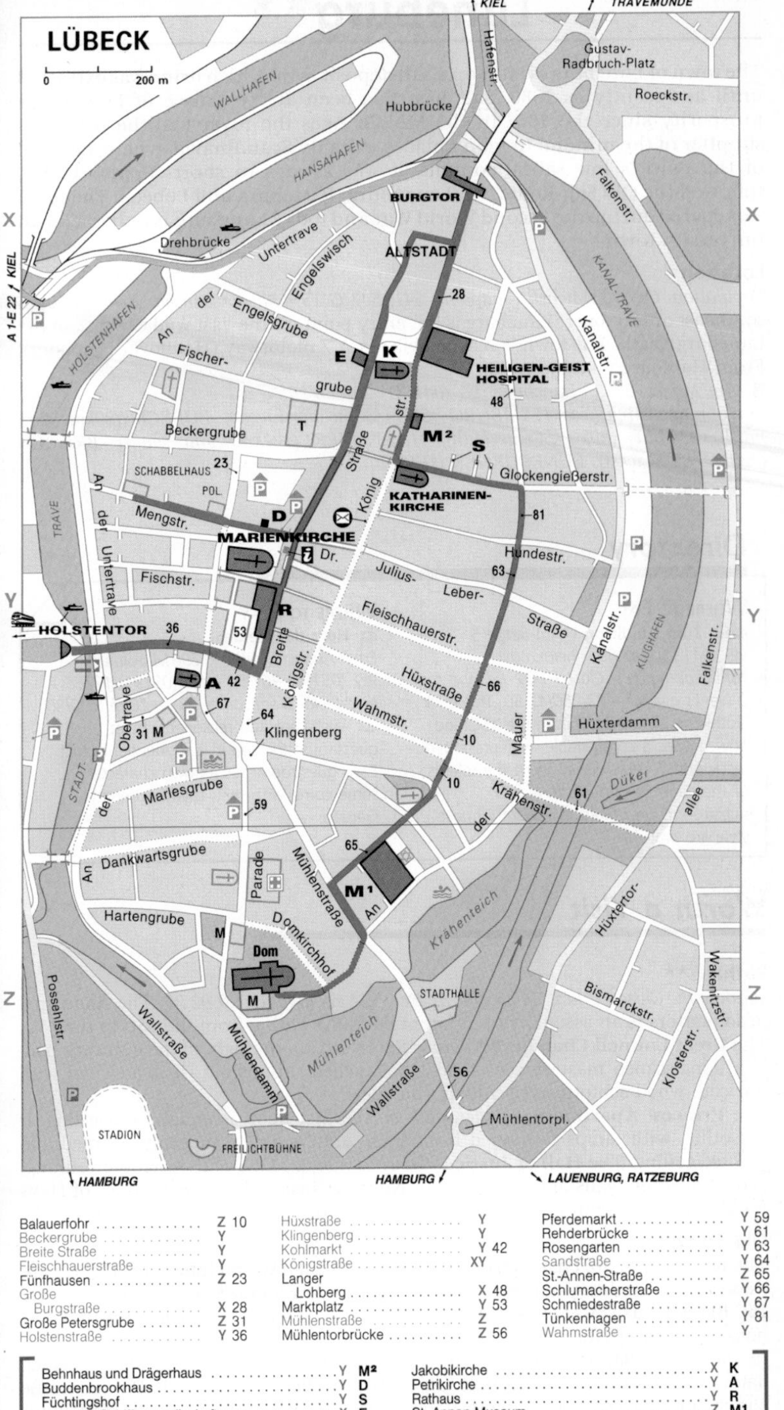

Balauerfohr	Z 10	Hüxstraße	Y	Pferdemarkt	Y 59
Beckergrube	Y	Klingenberg	Y	Rehderbrücke	Y 61
Breite Straße	Y	Kohlmarkt	Y 42	Rosengarten	Y 63
Fleischhauerstraße	Y	Königstraße	XY	Sandstraße	Y 64
Fünfhausen	Z 23	Langer Lohberg	X 48	St.-Annen-Straße	Z 65
Große Burgstraße	X 28	Marktplatz	Y 53	Schlumacherstraße	Y 66
Große Petersgrube	Z 31	Mühlenstraße	Z	Schmiedestraße	Y 67
Holstenstraße	Y 36	Mühlentorbrücke	Z 56	Tünkenhagen	Y 81
				Wahmstraße	Y

Behnhaus und Drägerhaus	Y	M²	Jakobikirche	X	K
Buddenbrookhaus	Y	D	Petrikirche	Y	A
Füchtingshof	Y	S	Rathaus	Y	R
Haus der Schiffergesellschaft	X	E	St. Annen-Museum	Z	M¹

Ernst Barlach Museum (Ernst-Barlach-Museum 'AltesVaterhaus') – *At no 3 Barlachplatz, beside the Petrikirche. Open from Mar to beginning Oct, Tue-Sun, 10am-1pm, 2-5pm. €3. ☎ (045 41) 37 89.* The sculptor, artist, graphic designer and playwright Ernst Barlach (1870-1938), one of the leading exponents of German Expressionism, spent part of his youth in Ratzeburg and was buried here at his own request (suburban cemetery, Schweriner/Seedorfer Straße).

The original bronze sculptures on display include *The Singer*, *The Flautist* and *Mother Earth*. There are also lithographs, drawings and woodcuts to be seen. The exhibition includes examples both of the artist's early work and from his years in Güstrow.

Lüneburg★★

The town of Lüneburg is built on a salt deposit from which brine was extracted until as recently as 1980. Salt has thus been at the source of Lüneburg's prosperity since the 10C: In the Middle Ages the town was the principal supplier of the mineral to many places, notably Scandinavia, where, because of the Baltic's low saline content, it was always in short supply. Traffic followed the Old Salt Route, via Lauenburg, Ratzeburg and Lübeck. The town was spared during the Second World War and today Lüneburg is a characterful university town.

Location

Population: 68 000. Michelin maps n°s 541, 542 G 15 – Niedersachsen. Around 50km southeast of Hamburg, Lüneburg is the entry point for the vast wild expanse of the Lüneburg heath. The town is reached via the A 7 motorway (Hannover-Hamburg). From Hamburg take the A 250.

Am Markt, 21335 Lüneburg, ☎ (041 31) 207 66 20.

Surrounding area: see HAMBURG (57km/36mi northwest), LÜBECK (89km/56mi north), CELLE (89km/56mi south), HANNOVER (127km/79mi south), BREMEN (139km/87mi west), LÜNEBURGER HEIDE.

Directory

Where to Eat

Zum Heidkrug – *Am Berge 5 – ☎ (04131) 241 60 – heidkrug@zumheidkrug.de – Closed 1-22 Jan and for 2 weeks in Aug – €34.50/42.50.* This brick Gothic building was built in the 15C and now houses a comfortable, well-presented restaurant. Classic dishes show the talents of the chefs to perfection. A few guestrooms decorated in "country house" style are available.

Where to Stay

Herz der Heide – *Ernst-August-Straße 7, 29614 Soltau – ☎ (05191) 967 50 – fax (05191) 17765 – herzdheide@aol.com – – 16rm: €39/80* . Well-kept and reasonably quiet guesthouse located in a residential district. Each guestroom has its own character; some come with their own kitchenette. Garden.

Worth a Visit

Rathaus★★

10am-5pm. Closed 1 Jan, 24-26 and 31 Dec. €3. ☎ (041 31) 30 92 30. The municipal headquarters is an assembly of different buildings dating from the 13C to the 18C. The **Great Council Chamber★★** *(Große Ratsstube)*, on the right of the entrance hall, is a Renaissance masterpiece (1566-84). Panelled throughout, it is adorned with intricate wood sculptures by Albert von Soest.

The **Princes' Apartment** *(Fürstensaal)*, on the first floor, is equally rewarding. It is Gothic, with lamps fashioned from stags' antlers and a superbly beamed and painted ceiling. The **Hall of Justice** (*Gerichtslaube*, c 1330), with its cradle vaulting, is decorated on walls and ceilings with paintings inspired by the etchings of Hans Burgkmair and Heinrich Aldegrever.

Old Town★

The houses here are characterised by the traditional brick architecture. Typical are those lining the long, narrow square known as **Am Sande★**, especially no 1, the 16C **Black House** (*Schwarzes Haus* or *Schütting*), which was once a brewery and now houses the International Chamber of Commerce.

In the Große Bäckerstraße (n° 10) stands the *Rathsapotheke* (pharmacy), which dates, with its fine twisted brick gables, from 1598. The Reitende-Diener-Straße comprises a double row of identical low houses, each embellished with medallions and, again, twisted brick cornices.

Rotehahnstraße is a particularly picturesque street. Note especially n° 14, the **Haus Roter Hahn**, a former 16C hospice with three half-timbered gables and a pretty inner courtyard.

St-Johanniskirche

The robust **west tower** (108m/354ft high) is displaced from the vertical at the top by 2m/6ft 6in and has been refurbished several times. The church itself dates from the 13C. The huge interior, with five naves and two rows of side chapels, forms a perfect square, closed at the east end by plain polygonal apses.

LÜNEBURG

Street	Grid	No.
Altenbrücker Damm	Y	2
Altenbrückertor-Straße	Z	3
Am Markt	Y	5
Am Ochsenmarkt	Y	6
Am Sande	Z	
Am Schifferwall	Y	7
Am Werder	Y	8
An den Brodbänken	Y	9
An den Reeperbahnen	Z	10
An der Münze	Y	12
Auf dem Meere	Y	14
Bahnhofstraße	Y	16
Bardowicker Str.	Y	17
Bei der Abtspferdetränke	Y	18
B.d. St. Johanniskirche	Z	19
Beim Benedikt	YZ	21
Bockelmannstraße	Y	24
Egersdorffstraße	Y	27
Görgesstraße	Y	28
Grapengießerstraße	Z	
Große Bäckerstraße	Y	30
Kaufhausstraße	Y	32
Kleine Bäckerstraße	Z	34
Kuhstraße	Z	35
Lüner Straße	Y	36
Neue Torstraße	Y	38
Reitende-Diener-Str.	Y	40
Rosenstraße	Y	42
Rotehahnstraße	Y	43
Rote Str.	Z	
Schießgrabenstraße	YZ	44
Schröderstraße	YZ	45
Sülfmeisterstraße	Z	46
Uelzener Str.	Z	47
Vor dem Bardowicker Tore	Y	48
Waagestraße	Y	49

Building	Grid	Key
Brauhaus	Y	F
Haus Roter Hahn	Y	D
Rathaus	Y	R
Rathsapotheke	YZ	A
Staatshochbauamt	Y	K

The most valuable item of the furnishings is the sculpted reredos of the high altar, which has painted panels depicting scenes from the lives of St John the Baptist, St Cecilia, St Ursula and St George (late 15C). The 16C organ, enlarged in the early 18C, is one of the oldest in Germany. Note also the 15C candelabra in honour of the Virgin Mary (north side aisle) and sandstone epitaphs by Albert von Soest.

Old Port Quarter★ (Wasserviertel)

There is a particularly fine view of this district from the bridge across the Ilmenau. To the left is the *Alter Kran*, a crane dating from the 14C, converted in the 18C. Looking upstream, there is a good view of the Lüner Mühle, a grand half-timbered mill building dating from the 16C, of the *Abtswasserturm* (water-tower) in the centre and, to the right, of the rear of the old houses along Am Stintmarkt. A **brewery★** *(Brauhaus)* stands at the corner of the Am Werder square and Lünertorstraße. This is a Renaissance building, its gables once more decorated with medallions and twisted brick motifs. The oriel construction on the front of this 1550 building was not added until the 17C. Further on, at the corner of Lünertorstraße and Kaufhausstraße, is a striking house *(Staatshochbauamt)* built in 1574 with remarkable rusticated half-pilasters in sandstone and a solid cornice. Beside it, note the Baroque façade (1741-45) of an old warehouse *(Altes Kaufhaus)*.

Excursions

Kloster Lüne

2km/1.2mi via ① on the plan. This **abbey** dates from the 15C and makes a harmonious complex set among its conventual buildings. It has housed a community of Protestant nuns since the Reformation. Particularly fine features include the Gothic cloister and fountain, the nuns' choir, the refectory and the summer refectory. Inside the abbey church are a fine altarpiece from 1524 and a Baroque organ from 1645. There is an interesting little tapestry **museum★** with Gothic tapestries and finely worked embroidery.

Lauenburg an der Elbe

25km/15.5mi north via ① (B 209) on the plan. A sleepy township today, Lauenburg commands a point where the ancient salt route from Lüneburg to Lübeck crossed the Elbe. At the foot of a steep, wooded slope, lie old **half-timbered houses** clustered along Elbstraße. These were built from the 16C to the 19C. They are dwarfed by the tower of the Maria-Magdalena-Kirche dating from the first half of the 13C. All that remains of the mighty fortress begun in 1182 is the castle tower of 1477. The other extant parts of the castle date from the late 17C and early 18C.

The **Elbe Navigation Museum** *(Elbschiffahrtsmuseum)* – in the lower town, at no 59 Elbstraße – relates the history of river traffic between Bohemia and Hamburg with the help of models, documents, illustrated panels and even ships' engines *(demonstrations).* Open Mar to Oct, *10am-1pm, 2-5pm, Sat and Sun, 10am-5pm; Nov to Feb, Wed, Fri, Sat and Sun, 10am-1pm, 2pm-4.30pm. Closed 1 Jan and 24-26 Dec.* €2. ☎ *(041 53) 512 51.*

Lüneburger Heide

Lüneburg Heath

It is the pastor of the heath Wilhelm Bode (1860-1927), who initiated the transformation of the Lüneburg Heath into a nature reserve, whom visitors have to thank for the fact that they are able to enjoy the delights of this once undervalued region. To preserve the heath from the increasing advances of agriculture and forestry, a 200km²/77sq mi nature reserve has been created in the neighbourhood of the Wilseder Berg, where the flora and fauna are protected and cars are only permitted on the main roads which cross the heath. Considerable effort is being made to preserve the rural character of Lower Saxony housing, and even outside the reserve villages on the heath have retained much of their old-world charm – notably in the case of their wooden belfries, separated from the church and half hidden in plantations of trees.

Location

Michelin maps n°s 541, 542 G 13 to 15 – Niedersachsen. The great expanse of Lüneburg Heath stretches between the glacial valleys of the Aller to the south and the Elbe to the north.

Surrounding area (distances from Undeloh): LÜNEBURG (37km/23mi east), BREMEN (99km/62mi west), HAMBURG (53km/33mi north).

Worth a Visit

Bergen-Belsen

7km/4mi southwest of Bergen. The **memorial** *(Gedenkstätte)* raised to the victims of the Bergen-Belsen concentration camp was erected in 1946 on the orders of the British Military Government and stands in solitude in a clearing on Lüneburg Heath, surrounded by pines and birch trees. There is a **documentation centre** *(Dokumentenhaus)* at the entrance, with a permanent exhibition retracing the history of the camp.

The Monument – *From the car park, 45min there and back on foot.* The monument is beyond the tumulus which marks the site of the mass graves. It is a simple obelisk in pale volcanic tufa, with inscriptions in 13 languages honouring the memory of those who fell victim to the Nazis' "extermination" policy.

Celle★★ – *See CELLE.*

Kloster Ebstorf

26km/16mi south of Luneburg. Guided visit (75min). Apr to mid-Oct, Tue-Sun, 10-11am, 2-5pm, Sun at 11.15am, 2-5pm; mid-Oct to end Oct, Tue-Fri, 2pm. Closed Good Fri. €3. ☎ *(058 22) 23 04.* Do not miss the former Benedictine abbey in the small town of

Ebstorf, where the 14C and 15C cloister and nuns' gallery are the most impressive features among the ruins. A life-size wooden statue of St Maurice (1300) and several Romanesque and Gothic Virgins can be seen in the gallery. Visitors interested in cartography can see a reproduction **Mappa Mundi★** *(Ebstorfer Weltkarte)*. The famous 13C original, once preserved in the abbey, was destroyed during the Second World War.

Lönsgrab

Between Fallingbostel and Walsrode, in the bird reserve (Vogelpark-Region).

The tomb of the poet Hermann Löns (1866-1914), who celebrated the beauties of Lüneburg Heath with extravagant lyricism, can be seen here in a setting of junipers.

Lönsstein

30min there and back. Leave the car halfway between Baven and Müden and climb up to the left of a row of birch trees. This monument to the poet of Lüneburg Heath stands in the middle of typical heathland vegetation; one of the few places in the south area of Lüneburg Heath of which this can be said.

Handwerksmuseum am Mühlenberg, in Suhlendorf

♿ *Open Feb to mid-Dec, Tue-Sat, 10am-4.30pm; from mid-Mar to mid-Nov, Tue-Sun 10am-6pm. €2.50. ☎ (058 20) 370.* The location of this craft museum is indicated by a tall windmill visible from some way off. The museum, which has a sizeable collection of mills, documents the work of a miller. Various workshops contain displays on other professions, including the work of the saddler, smith and cobbler.

Heide-Park Soltau

♿ *Open from Apr to end Oct, 9am-6pm. €24. ☎ (051 91) 912 48.* This well-maintained leisure park offers 40 different kinds of ride. It is organised into areas on various themes, such as Lüneburg Heath itself, a Dutch village, or Little America, and some

The Heath

In the Middle Ages, the name "Heide" signified the boundary of a village. Only later did it come to mean the common heather *(Calluna vulgaris)* which carpets such areas with its rose-pink hue in August and September. The bell-heather *(Erica tetralix)* which blooms in July is also found on Lüneburg Heath, but it is very rare, preferring marshy and damp areas.

Although we may be tempted to think of the term heath as the epitome of a natural landscape, in reality it is man-made dwarf shrubland. 5 000 years ago Lüneburg Heath was covered in forest, which was uprooted by farmers. Cattle were then driven into the forest to finish off the farmers' work. Only then was the light-hungry heath able to spread. To prevent the forest taking hold again, the practices of burning, allowing cropping by moorland sheep, or lifting turf (the heath was grubbed up using a hoe) were employed.

Flora and Fauna – The Juniper *(Juniperus communis)* gives Lüneburg Heath a quite special character. The bushes appear either individually or in groups. The heath is also home to birch, mountain ash, pine and oak, together with common gorse and broom, silver grass and matgrass, crowberries, bilberries and cranberries.

The moorland sheep are "living mowers". Where they are still used as such, they maintain the heath heather at an optimum height of 20cm/8in. Both the males and the females have horns, those of the male being spectacularly coiled. They have dark heads and legs. There were one million moorland sheep on Lüneburg Heath around 1800, when it was much larger, but there are only a few thousand head left today.

Bees are also an intrinsic feature of Lüneburg Heath. They frequently belong to travelling beekeepers, who bring their swarms to the heath flowers, sometimes in the baskets known as "Lüneburg Bogenstülpern". The largest bird seen on the heath is the blackcock or capercaillie with its lyre-shaped tail, although it is now virtually extinct. There are plenty of buzzards, red kites, hobbies and kestrels, not forgetting the herons and snipes in the lowlands and high moors. Autumn visitors include flocks of fieldfares.

Boulders – Large and small boulders made of granite, and in some cases porphyry, are scattered all over Lüneburg Heath. They came from Scandinavia as boulder clay and were left behind when the glaciers of the last Ice Age retreated over 18 000 years ago. The angular or sharp polished stones known in German as Windkanter were formed by corrosion.

of the attractions on offer involve roller-coasters, cable railways and water flumes. The park is home to animals such as dolphins, sea-lions and crocodiles. A particular favourite with visitors is the mountain rafting in circular rafts, or a breathtaking ride on the "Limit" roller-coaster.

Undeloh★

The charming village of Undeloh, with its old houses sheltered beneath huge oak trees, is the departure point for the 4km/2.5mi trip to Wilsede, a nature reserve village which has been kept untouched by the onward march of a mechanised civilisation *(cars are not allowed: there is a service of horse-drawn vehicles from Undeloh)*.

Vogelpark Walsrode

Follow the waymarked itinerary.

Almost 5 000 birds (850 species, from all parts of the world) live in this fine 22ha/54-acre **ornithological park**, most of them in their natural habitat and at semi-liberty. Waders and web-footed birds, as well as parrots and budgerigars, are particularly well represented in the ornithological park, the largest of its kind in the world. A tropical plant house is occupied by a range of exotic bird-life unlike any to be found in a zoo. ♿ *Open Mar to Oct, 9am-7pm; Nov to Feb, 10am-4pm. Summer, €12, winter, €8. ☎ (051 61) 604 40.*

A historic half-timbered house (1717) contains the **German Birdcage Museum** *(Deutsches Vogelbauermuseum)*, where an incredible number of birdcages are on display.

Kloster Wienhausen★ *See CELLE: Excursions.*

Wilseder Berg★

From the summit (there is a marker post: 169m/554ft), a vast **panorama★** of heath and woodlands is visible. On a clear day, the spires of the churches of Hamburg can be seen, 40km/25mi away to the north.

Magdeburg★★

Magdeburg grew up on an important trade crossroads and to this day is a thriving cultural and economic centre. The town became known as the "pearl of Europe" around the turn of the 19C-20C, but has suffered destruction over the course of the centuries. Magdeburg was largely rebuilt after the Second World War and with many parks and open spaces the city offers a high standard of quality of life to its inhabitants.

Location

Population: 231 000. Michelin map nos 542, 544 J 18 – Sachsen-Anhalt. Magdeburg is in the heart of Sachsen-Anhalt, situated mid-way along the course of the Elbe. The town is easily reached, situated at the crossroads of the A 2 (Berlin-Hannover) and A 14 motorways (for Leipzig).

ℹ *Julius-Bremer-Straße 10, 39104 Magdeburg, ☎ (0391) 540 49 03.*

Surrounding area: see DESSAU (63km/39mi southeast), WÖRLITZER PARK (79km/49mi southeast), WITTENBERG (85km/53mi southeast), WOLFENBÜTTEL (96km/60mi west).

Background

A steadfast merchant city – Magdeburg was founded by Emperor Otto I, who built his favourite Imperial palace here and raised the town to the status of archbishopric in 968. The early success of this commercial centre, which declared its support for Martin Luther in 1524, was brought to an end in 1631 when Imperial troops laid siege to the town before destroying it. Famous local figures include Bürgermeister Otto von Guericke (1602-86) who carried out experiments on creating vacuums using water pumps (the legendary Magdeburg hemisphere experiment using 16 horses in 1659), and the Baroque composer Georg Philipp Telemann (1681-1767).

In the 19C, industrialisation and the removal of the fortifications allowed the city on the Elbe to expand and flourish once more, becoming known as the "pearl of Europe" around the turn of the 19C-20C.

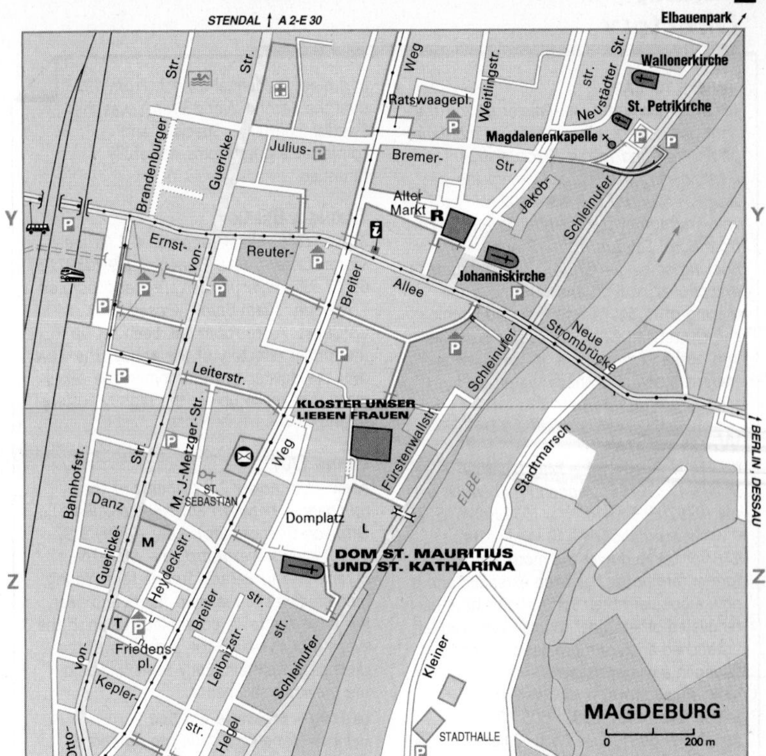

Special Features

DOM ST MAURITIUS UND ST KATHARINA★★★

Situated to the south of the old town. Entrance through the north doorway.

At a time when the Romanesque style in Germany was losing its impetus, the construction of Magdeburg Cathedral at the beginning of the 13C marked the first attempt to impose a Gothic style derived from the architectural precepts of the great French cathedrals. The decision was taken by Archbishop Albrecht II, who had studied in France and witnessed the new cathedrals being built there, and following a fire in the original Ottonian building the foundation stone of the new cathedral was laid in 1209.

Magdeburg Cathedral, completed in 1520 with the erection of the 103m/338ft high west towers, can be considered the first great German Gothic religious building.

Outside, the three levels of the east end (absidioles, ambulatory, apse) at once give an impression of power. On the north side, the **Paradise Doorway** *(reached from inside the cathedral)* displays **statues★★** of the Wise and Foolish Virgins. Dating from c 1250, these, in common with statuary at Bamberg and Naumburg, mark a stage in the evolution of Gothic sculpture, which became more and more inclined towards the expression of emotional feeling.

Interior – The tall well-lit nave features wide bays. The **bronze tomb★** of Archbishop Ernst of Saxony *(between the towers)* was cast in 1495 in the workshop of Peter Vischer the Elder of Nuremberg. A small 16-sided chapel (mid-13C) off the north aisle houses seated **statues★** that represent Christ and the Church, or otherwise interpreted, Otto I and his wife the Anglo-Saxon princess Edith. Behind this chapel is the Late Renaissance **alabaster pulpit★** (late 16C) with its wealth of decorative figures. The High Gothic choir screen gives access to the high chancel, which contains Emperor Otto I's elegant tomb and the choir stalls dating from 1363 with outstanding carved ornamentation. To the right is a **statue★** (c 1250) of St Maurice, with black African features. In the north transept is a carved wooden memorial to those who fell in the First World War by Ernst Barlach (1929). The south transept gives access to the cloister and the chapel of the fountains with its delicate rib vaulting.

Directory

Where to Eat

⊖ St. Immanuel – *Alt-Prester 86 (on the right bank of the Elbe, cross two tributaries of the river and follow Cracauerstr., Genthinerstr. and Pechauerstr. to the south) – ☏ (0172) 3 05 40 02 – www.restaurant-st-immanuel.de – Mon-Fri from 6pm, Sat-Sun from 12 noon – ⌿ – Booking advised – €20/45.* This restaurant's exceptional location and building is the making of it. Set in a former neo-Gothic church, refined, seasonal cuisine is served in a hushed atmosphere. In the summer there is a beautiful shady waterside terrace.

Where to Stay

⊖ Hotel Bördehof – *Magdeburger Straße 42, 39179 Magdeburg-Ebendorf – ☏ (039203) 515 10 – fax (039203) 515125 – www.boerdehof.de – P – 42rm: €46/75.* Located near the motorway, this former farmhouse has been extended and is now a popular hotel. Some rooms have been renovated other, older rooms have been left untouched and are more basic. Dinner is served in a winter garden.

⊖⊖ Plaza Hotel – *Halberstädter Straße 146 – ☏ (0391) 605 10 – fax (0391) 605110 – www.12plaza.de – P ♿ – 103rm: €65/85 – Restaurant €13/28.* This hotel is located on the outskirts of the town and is well served by public transport. Behind its modern, white façade, this hotel has comfortable, tastefully decorated guestrooms and a bistro-style restaurant with courtyard terrace.

⊖⊖ Residenz Joop – *Jean-Burger-Str. 16 – ☏ (0391) 6 26 20 – fax (0391) 6262100 – info@residenzjoop.de – P – 25rm: €84/146.* This villa hotel is located in a quiet residential district. From 1903 until the Second World War it was the Swedish consulate. Spacious and comfortable guestrooms, tastefully furnished.

Taking a Break

Klostercafé – *Regierungsstr. 4-6 (in the Kloster Unser Lieben Frauen) – ☏ (0391) 5 65 02 33 – www.klostercafe-magdeburg.de – Tue-Sun, 10am-6pm – Closed at Christmas.* A tea room has been set up in the former refectory of the abbey. The view over the cloister and the homemade cakes more than make up for the slightly austere setting.

Going Out

Alex – *Ulrichplatz 2 (southeast of the roundabout between Ernst-Reuter-Allee and Otto-von-Guericke-Str.) – ☏ (0391) 5 97 49 11 – www.alexgastro.de – Mon-Thu, 8-1am, Fri-Sat, 8-3am, Sun, 9-1am.* Young, modern café set over two floors and near the town centre. A good place to finish the evening or to watch the sun set over the Ulrichplatz fountain. Early risers will enjoy the breakfast set menus.

Le Frog – Brasserie am See – *Heinrich-Heine-Platz 1 (in the Rotehorn public park on the right bank of the Elbe near the Stadthalle; cross the river and take Kleiner Stadtmarsch) – ☏ (0391) 5 31 35 56 – www.lefrog-md.de –Mon-Sat 11am-midnight, Sun, 10am-midnight.* Glass pavillion set on the edge of lake in the pretty Rotehorn park. Whether it's coffee and cake, a mediterranean-inspired meal or a late-night cocktail... there's something for everyone here. When the weather allows, there is a pleasant Biergarten.

Worth a Visit

OLD TOWN★

The historic centre of Magdeburg is dominated by the tower of the cathedral and extends west of the Elbe. The sights described below are located from the south to the north along the riverbank, from the Kloster to the Petriberg.

Kloster Unser Lieben Frauen★★

Regierungstraße. Open Tue-Sun, 10am-5pm. €2, no charge first Fri of the month. ☏ (0391) 56 50 20; www.kunstmuseum-magdeburg.de This abbey was consecrated in the early 11C and taken over by the Premonstratensian Order, who then gave it up in 1632 during the Thirty Years War. After they moved out the abbey was used as a seminary and school until 1945. Since 1974 it has been an art museum (interesting collection of sculpture from Antiquity to the present in a triple vault). The **abbey church★** has been used as a concert venue since 1977.

Gothic vaulting was added to the triple-aisled basilica in 1220-40. The hall crypt beneath the chancel, also with three aisles, is the oldest part of the church. The **cloister★** is particularly harmonious in style. The lavabo with its conical stone roof is thought to be the oldest of its kind in Germany.

Rathaus

In front of the two-storey Baroque town hall (1691-98) stands a gilded copy of the famous statue of The Magdeburg Knight, one of the oldest equestrian sculptures in Germany *(the c 1240 original is in the Kulturhistorisches Museum).*

Since 1974 the Kloster Unser Lieben Frauen has been an art museum.

Johanniskirche

Open May to Sep, 10am-7pm; Feb to Apr and Oct, Tue-Sun, 10am-6pm; Nov to Jan, Tue-Sun, 10am-5pm. Closed 24 and 31 Dec. €1, no charge on 3 Oct. ☎ (0391) 593 45 48. Magdeburg's oldest parish church (documented in 941), in which Martin Luther preached (memorial in front of church), was destroyed apart from its exterior walls during the Second World War. It is now used as a venue for various events and exhibitions. Visitors can climb the south tower *(take care, as the steps are uneven)* and enjoy a superb **view★★** over Magdeburg from 60m/200ft up.

Petriberg

North of the town hall, on the banks of the Elbe. Three churches adorn this riverside hill: the **Magdalenenkapelle** (built 1315), with a single Gothic nave; **St Petrikirche**, a Gothic hall-church with three aisles and a fine south narthex in the brick Gothic style (14-15C); and the **Wallonenkirche**, a former abbey church (founded 1285) used by a Reformed community from the French-speaking Netherlands from 1694-1945.

Elbauenpark★

Northeast of the old town, to the east of the Elbe. Access from the centre of town via Schleinufer and Markgrafenstraße. ♿ Open Summer, 9am-8pm; Winter, 10am-4pm. €2.60. ☎ (018 05) 25 19 99. This 140ha/345 acre park was created for the 1999 national garden show, and features such attractions as open-air stages, gardens on different themes, a butterfly house, a summer toboggan run and a panoramic railway (recommended to get an overview of the park). There are child-care facilities in an imaginatively decorated playhouse. The highlight of the park is the **Millennium Tower★★**, at 60m/200ft the world's tallest timber-built tower. Inside, there is a very creatively designed interactive exhibition retracing 6 000 years of history of humankind and science. Beginning at the "pre- and early history pit" you work your way up a spiral of six floors to the "window into the future".

►► Museum of Cultural History *(Kulturhistorisches Museum)*.

Excursions

Halberstadt

45km/28mi southwest. In 804, Charlemagne raised the mission of Halberstadt to the rank of bishopric. In the Middle Ages, this former Hanseatic city was a major economic centre whose main activity focused on the textile and linen trade. An aerial bombardment shortly before the end of the Second World War destroyed most of the inner city.

Dom St-Stephanus★★ – *Open May-Oct, 10am-5pm, Sat, 10am-4.30pm, Sun, 11am-5.30pm; Nov to Apr, 10am-4pm, Sun, 11am-4pm. ☎ (039 41) 242 37.* In its opulence and the spirit of its design, this cathedral recalls the Gothic cathedrals of France. Building began in 1240 and the nave was completed towards the end of the 15C.

The **rood-screen hall★** is finely worked in the High Gothic style (c 1510). Above it, a group representing the **Triumphal Cross★** is a splendid example of Late Romanesque sculpture. A cloister decorated with 13C Stations of the Cross opens off the southern part of the nave.

Domschatz★★ (Treasury) – *Guided visit (75min). Apr-Oct, Tue-Sun at 10am, 11.30am, 2pm and 3.30pm, Sat at 10am, 12 noon and 2pm, Sun at 11.30am and 2.30pm; Nov to Mar, Mon to Sun, at 11.30am and 2.30pm, additional weekend visit at 1pm. €3.50. ☎ (039 41) 242 37.* Rare liturgical vestments and religious vessels from the 12C to the 16C are displayed here with a precious collection of altar paintings, manuscripts, and 12C tapestries, in particular the Abraham Tapestry, which is more than 10m/33ft long.

Mainz★

Mainz was elevated in 1949 to the capital of the Land of Rheinland-Pfalz and is Germany's largest and most important wine market. The town is home to ZDF, Germany's second TV channel and SAT1, a privately-owned channel. Although 80 per cent of the old town was destroyed during the Second World War, a large part of it has now been reconstructed and makes for some interesting walks. It is also the site of a famous annual carnival, which draws hundreds of visitors to its procession on the Monday before Shrove Tuesday *(see Calendar of events).*

Location

Population: 186 000 – Michelin map nº 543 Q 8 – Rheinland-Pfalz. Situated at the confluence of the Rhine and the Main, Mainz is ideally placed for trade. The town has a simple signposting system: roadsigns in red and white lead to the Rhine and those in blue and white run parallel to it.

Brückenturm, 55116 Mainz, ☎ (061 31) 28 62 10.

Surrounding area: see WIESBADEN (on the opposite bank of the Rhine, 11km/7mi further north), FRANKFURT AM MAIN (42km/26mi northeast), RHEINTAL (Rüdesheim is 44km/28mi west).

Directory

Where to Eat

Weinhaus Schreiner – *Rheinstraße 38 – ☎ (061 31) 22 57 20 – Closed 2 weeks in July and Aug, Sun and bank holidays – €16/29.* A typical local wine bar with plain, rustic decor and lively atmosphere. Seasonal dishes with a regional flavour are on the menu.

Where to Stay

Stiftswingert – *Am Stiftswingert 4 – ☎ (061 31) 98 26 40 – fax (061 31) 832478 – hotel-stiftswingert@t-online.de – P – 30rm: €76* . Keenly managed hotel, with cherrywood furnished guestroooms, well-presented bathrooms and modern facilities.

Walking About

CATHEDRAL QUARTER

Leaving the Liebfrauenplatz, walk down the Domstraße and then left around the cathedral.

Dom★

From the Leichhof square, there is a **view★★** of the cathedral in its entirety, the west chancel and transept rising loftily, their complex ridge roofs overlooked by the lantern tower which crowns the transept crossing. Baroque as well as Gothic elements adorn the upper part of this tower, which rests on a Romanesque base showing a Lombard influence.

The adjoining square, known as the Höfchen, is extended towards the south by the Gutenbergplatz (containing Thorvaldsen's statue of the craftsman printer, a theatre and the House of German Wines) and to the northeast by the market square, embellished with a **Renaissance fountain** *(Renaissancebrunnen).*

Enter via the doorway opening onto the market square (Marktportal).

The **cathedral** is an enormous restored Romanesque building – a basilica with two chancels, one in the west, leading off a wide transept whose crossing is illuminated by a fine Rhenish dome and one in the east of simpler architectural style. Fixed to the massive Romanesque columns is a collection of archiepiscopal **funerary monuments★** *(Grabdenkmäler der Erzbischöfe).*

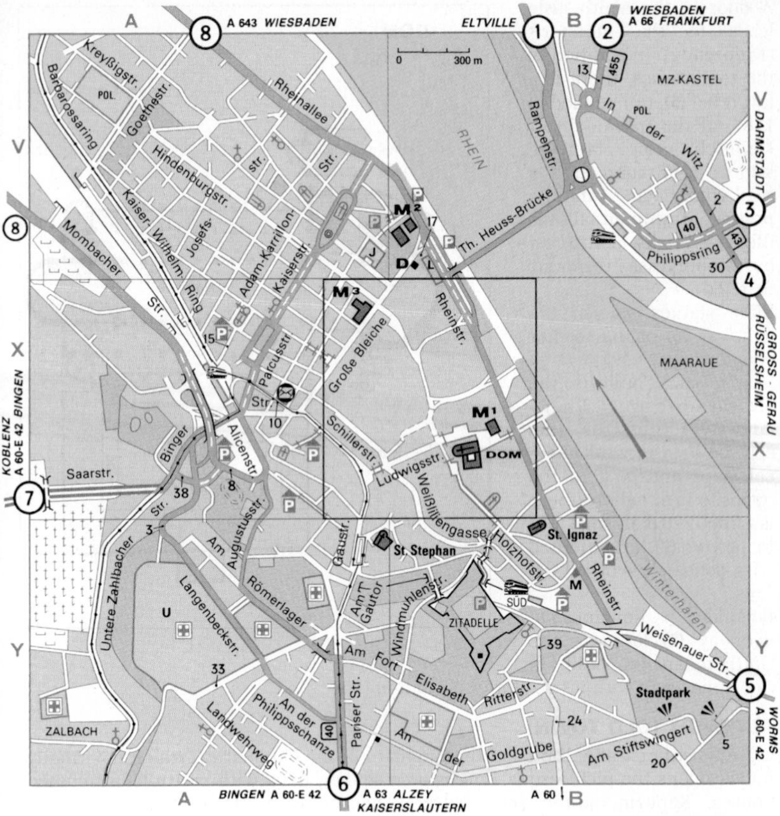

MAINZ

Street	Ref
Admiral-Scheer-Str.	BV 2
Am Lisenberg	AY 3
An der Favorite	BY 5
Augustinerstr	Z 6
Augustusstr.	AX 8
Bahnhofstr.	AX 10
Bischofsplatz	Z 12
Boelckestr.	BV 13
Bonifaziusstr.	AX 15
Christofsstr.	Z 16
Deutschhaus-Platz	BV 17
Fischtorstr	Z 21
Flachsmarkstr.	Z
Göttelmannstr.	BY 20
Große Bleiche	Z
Gutenbergplatz	Z 23
Hechtsheimer-Straße	BY 24
Höfchen	Z 26
Karmeliterstr.	Z 27
Kirschgarten	Z 29
Kostheimer Landstr.	BV 30
Liebfrauenplatz	Z 32
Ludwigsstr.	Z
Markt	Z
Obere Zahlbacher Str.	AY 33
Peter-Altmeier-Allee	Z 35
Quintinsstr.	Z 36
Römerwall	AX 38
Salvatorstr.	BY 39
Schillerstr.	Z
Schöfferstr.	Z 40
Schusterstr.	Z
Zeughausgasse	Z 43

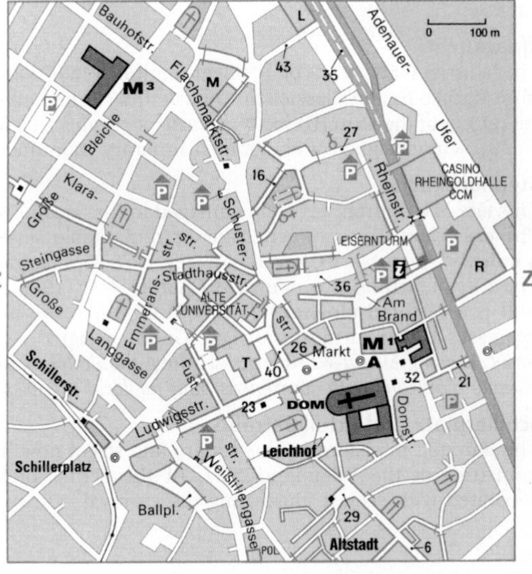

Gutenberg-Museum	Z	M¹
Jupitersäule	BV	D
Landesmuseum Mains	Z	M³
Renaissancebrunnen	Z	A
Römisch-Germanisches Zentralmuseum	BV	M²

Turn left into the north aisle on entering the church.

In the second chapel **(1)**, there is a moving late-15C Entombment. A multicoloured Gothic funerary monument is attached to one of the main pillars **(2)**.

In the east crypt, beneath the chancel, a modern **gold reliquary (3)** of the Saints of Mainz stands upon the altar.

A pillar **(4)** on the south side of the east chancel steps bears another Gothic funerary monument in many colours, surrounded by statuettes of St Benedict, St Catherine, St Maurice and St Clare.

A door in the south aisle leads to the **cloister**★ (Kreuzgang). In addition to the tombstones, there is a low relief **(5)**, remodelled in 1783, of the master-singer Heinrich von Meißen, known as "Frauenlob" – a man who, having sung the praises of women all his life, was finally laid to rest by the burgesses of Mainz in 1323.

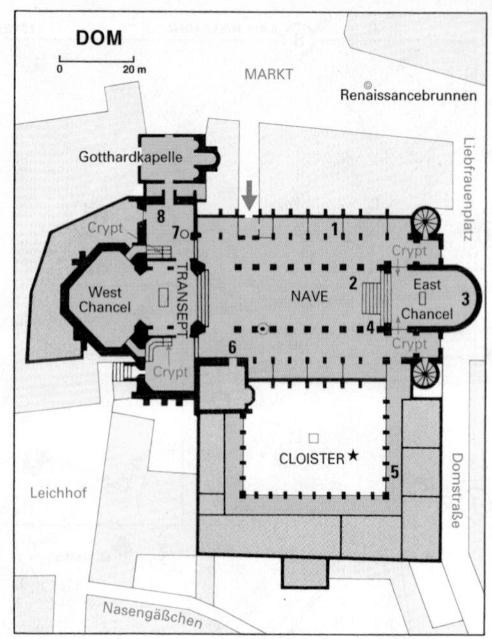

Fine statues adorn the doorway **(6)** of the former chapter-house (Kapitelsaal), built in the 15C in an elegant Rhineland style. Cross the transept below the west chancel steps and go into the opposite arm, where there is a fine 1328 baptismal font in pewter **(7)**, ornamented with delicately worked figures.

Beyond, a Romanesque doorway **(8)** leads to the Gotthardkapelle, built in the same style with a two-storey elevation.

ALTSTADT (OLD TOWN)

Off Augustinerstraße, the chief thoroughfare of the old quarter, which is virtually intact, opens the picturesque *Kirschgarten* square, lined with pretty half-timbered houses. Kapuzinerstraße (note several houses with sandstone door frames and Rococo panels) leads to the church of St Ignaz, past several inviting little streets.

Ignazkirche

This church is the work of JP Jäger, built in 1763-75 and illustrating the transition from Rococo to neo-Classicism. Outside the church, on the left, stands an imposing 16C group of the **Crucifixion**★ *(Kreuzigungsgruppe)*, by Mainz artist Hans Backoffen (1519), who designed it as his own funerary monument.

Stephanskirche

This late 13C church, severely damaged in the Second World War, has been rebuilt. The east chancel is renowned for its remarkable series of modern **stained-glass windows**★★, by Marc Chagall between 1978-85, illustrating themes from the Bible. There are a further 19 windows by Charles Marq (1989-2000). Built against the south wall is a restored **cloister**★ (1465-99) of which the intricate and varied vaulting expresses all the virtuosity of Late Gothic design.

Go back along Maria-Ward-Strasse. Along the Ballplatz and the Schillerplatz, note the various mansions with courtyards built for local notables.

Schillerplatz and Schillerstraße

The Baroque mansions in this square and street now house (after restoration) the ministries of the Rheinland-Pfalz. In the centre of Schillerplatz, a fountain is decorated with scenes illustrating the carnival.

Worth a Visit

Gutenberg-Museum★★

♿ *Open Tue-Sun, 9am-5pm, Sun, 11am-3pm. Closed bank holidays. €3. ☎ (061 31) 12 26 40.*

The visitor to this museum is reminded how, over the centuries, men of taste and discrimination have nurtured the art of the printed word, regarding it as one of the most precious treasures of civilisation, to be guarded and passed on as a sacred trust as its usage developed and spread.

A reconstruction of an early print shop (15C) gives an idea of the developments in working conditions and technology in the world of printing. The museum's prize exhibit, two original editions of the world-famous **Gutenberg Bible**★★★ (1452-55),

with 42 lines to the page, are on display in a strong room. Further exhibits of interest include incunabula and a collection of editions published between the 16C and the 19C, ancient presses and typesetting machines, and a section on modern book production and paper.
Polychromatic wood engravings and printed works from China, Japan and Korea can be seen in the Far East Department on the third floor.

Gutenberg

Johannes Gutenberg (c 1394-1468), the father of modern printing, is the city's most prominent son. Born in Mainz in 1395, he worked for a long time in Strasbourg on a revolutionary printing technique using moveable characters. This technique allowed large volumes of books to be printed at low cost. Gutenberg did not profit from his infention, however, and, unable to repay his creditors, he died in poverty in 1468.

Römisch-Germanisches Museum★ (Romano-German Museum)

Open Tue-Sun, 10am-6pm. Closed Shrove Tue, 24 and 31 Dec. No charge. ☎ (061 31) 912 40. Installed in the one-time Electors' Palace (15C-17C), the three departments of this museum house collections on the pre- and proto-history of ancient Europe and the advanced Mediterranean civilisations, and Ancient Roman and early medieval archaeology.

Landesmuseum Mainz★

Open Tue-Sun, 10am-5pm, Thu, 10am-8pm. Closed 1 Jan, Carnival, Ascension, Pentecost, 3 Oct, 24, 25 and 31 Dec. €3, no charge on Sat. ☎ (061 31) 285 70.
The Department of Antiquities traces Rhineland civilisation from prehistory to the present.
Of particular interest is the Steinhalle which houses some 300 stone memorials dating from the Roman colonisation of Germany, including Jupiter's Column *(Jupitersäule)*. A copy of this column stands in the Deutschhaus-Platz, in front of the old Teutonic Order commandery which now houses the state parliament for Rheinland-Pfalz.
The museum's medieval and Baroque sections and its extensive collections of Höchst porcelain and Jugendstil glassware are also well worth seeing. The 20C Department houses the largest collection of works by Tàpies in Germany.

Mannheim

The town, founded in 1606 by the Palatine elector Friedrich IV, was conceived as a fortified residential enclave. Conforming to a rigid plan, the centre comprises a chessboard of 142 identical blocks (Quadratstadt), each identified only by a letter and number according to its coordinates on the city plan. Local enthusiasm for the arts – especially the theatre, where the works of Schiller were first performed – soon made Mannheim a cultural as well as a trade centre. The town today is a lively industrial centre.

Location

Population: 324 000. Michelin maps n°s 543, 545 R 9 – Baden-Württemberg. A few kilometres to the northwest of Heidelberg, Mannheim is located at the confluence of the Rhine and the Neckar *(large river port, with motorboat trips around the port area from the Kurpfalzbrücke, the bridge spanning the Neckar).*
Willy-Brandt-Platz 3, 68161 Mannheim, ☎ (0190) 77 00 20.
Surrounding area: HEIDELBERG (20km/16mi southeast), SPEYER (22km/14mi south), WORMS (23km/14mi northwest).

Directory

Where to Eat

Martin – *Lange Rötterstraße 53 – ☎ (0621) 33 38 14 – Closed 25 Aug-17 Sep, Mon, Sat lunchtimes – €25/52.*
A family-run establishment: the well-managed restaurant was constructed in the old German style and offers fish specialities. Attention and service beyond compare.

Where to Stay

Mack – *Mozartstraße 14 – ☎ (0621) 124 20 – fax (0621) 1242399 – hotelmack@t-online.de – – 50rm: €64/100* . From the outside, this former town house topped with a pinnacle doesn't seem to have much going for it. Once inside, however, the well-kept, personalised guestrooms and succulent breakfast will ensure a pleasant stay.

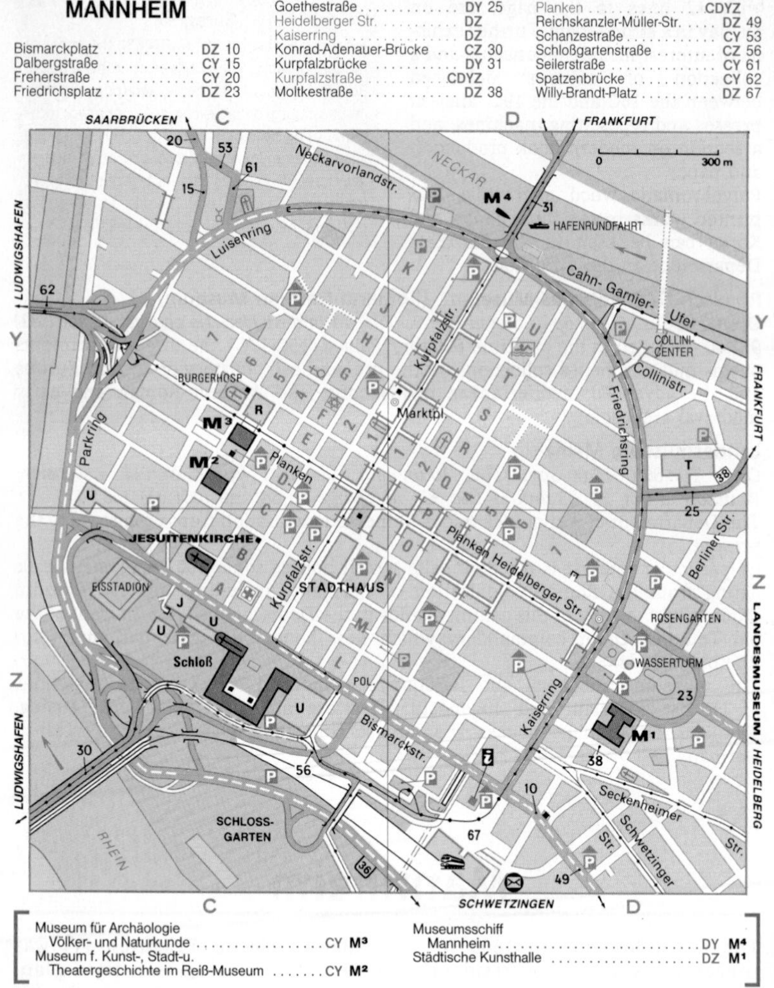

Worth a Visit

Städtische Kunsthalle★★ (Fine Arts Museum)

♿ *Open Tue-Sun, 11am-6pm. Closed Carnival, Good Fri, 1 May, first Tue in May, 24 and 31 Dec. €2.10. ☎ (0621) 293 64 30.* Installed in a Jugendstil building designed by H Billing in 1907, the museum concentrates on works of the 19C and 20C. Sculpture, including works by Rodin, Lehmbruck, Barlach, Brancusi, Giacometti, Moore, Nam June Paik, Richard Long and Mario Merz, form the focal point of the art collection. Important works from the collection of paintings include the *Execution of Emperor Maximilian* by Manet and *The Pipe Smoker* by Cézanne, together with paintings by Corot, Monet and Pissarro.

The German Secession artists are represented by Slevogt and Corinth, and the Expressionists by Beckmann, Heckel *(Sunflowers)*, Kokoschka *(View of Amsterdam)* and the Belgian James Ensor *(Still-life)*. Other departments exhibit works from the New Objectivity period and post-1945 art.

Museum für Kunst-, Stadt- und Theatergeschichte im Reiß-Museum★

Closed for an indeterminate period. ☎ (0621) 293 31 51. In the Arsenal (Zeughaus, built 1777-79).

The Art History department houses mainly sculpture and painting of the Palatinate electorate dating from the 18C, together with Baroque and Rococo furniture. There is an outstanding, even on an international scale, collection of **European porcelain and faience★**, with the highlight of this comprehensive display being Frankenthal porcelain from the Palatinate.

The **local history collections** chronicle the development of the town.

The theatre collection retraces the history of the Mannheim national theatre through costumes, props and audio-visual media.

Museum für Archäologie, Völker- und Naturkunde★ (Museum of Archaeology, Ethnology and Natural History)

♿ *Open Tue-Sun, 11am-6pm. Closed 1 May, 24 and 31 Dec. €2.10. ☎ (0621) 293 31 51. In the Mutschler-Bau opposite the arsenal.*

The archaeology collections include important artefacts from the Paleolithic and Mesolithic eras to the Carolingian period, as well as finds from Ancient Greece, Antique Italy and the Roman Empire. The Middle Ages are represented, as is the archaeology of the modern period with town centre excavations.

The exhibition of **folklore★** is conceived as a tour around the Old World, from the Tuareg in North Africa via the Islamic cultures of the Near East, to India. The **Benin collection★** is of international significance.

Schloß (Palace)

Probably closed until 2007.

The building of this Baroque palace, the biggest in all of Germany (400 rooms, 2 000 windows), lasted from 1720 to 1760. Restored after the Second World War, the palace is now occupied by departments of the university. Two wings at right angles to the central block enclose an enormous main courtyard. The palace church terminates the right wing, the former palace library the left.

From the state staircase inside, there is a view down the entire perspective of Kurpfalzstraße, the street that bisects the chessboard centre from one end to the other, as far as the River Neckar.

The painted ceilings have been restored after the original work of Cosmas Damian Asam. The same artist was responsible for the ceiling of the church *(Schloßkirche)* and the frescoes in the Knights' Hall *(Rittersaal)*. The most interesting apartment is the green and rose Rococo library in the university wing, which is embellished with stuccowork, panelling and *camaïeu* (monochrome) paintings.

Jesuitenkirche★

Founded at the same time as the palace (building in fact lasted from 1733 to 1769), this massive edifice is said to be the biggest Baroque church in south-west Germany. The façade is Classical with the three orders superposed. The green and red marble stuccowork lends colour to the well-lit interior. The high altar by Peter Anton von Verschaffelt, which was destroyed in the Second World War, is currently being rebuilt, as are the former electoral court galleries. The Silver Virgin with her Crown of Light *(Silbermadonna im Strahlenkranz)*, in the northern aisle, is the work of the Augsburg silversmith JI Saler (1747).

Landesmuseum für Technik und Arbeit in Mannheim★ (Regional Museum of Industrial Techniques)

At Museumsstraße 1. ♿ *Open Tue-Sun, 9am-5pm, Wed, 9am-8pm, Sun, 10am-6pm. Closed Good Fri, 24, 25 and 30 Dec. €3, no charge on Wed from 12 noon. ☎ (0621) 429 87 50.*

Two hundred and fifty years of industrial development in south-west Germany are retraced in this modernistic building, which impresses with the elegance, lightness and transparency of its architecture. The museum illustrates the effect of industrialisation on people's lives. History is presented in a chronological spiral, from enlightened absolutism on the fifth floor to the 20C in the basement. Visitors can be carried around the grounds on a steam railway.

▶▶ Museumsschiff Mannheim *(museum boat)*

Marburg★★

Built on the side of a hill, this charming town was once a great pilgrimage centre, with crowds being drawn to the town to venerate the relics of St Elizabeth of Hungary. Since the Reformation, and still maintaining the magnificent Gothic church dedicated to the saint and the equally impressive Landgraves' castle, Marburg has, thanks to its university founded in 1527, become a centre of Protestant scholarship and theology. It is largely because of its prestigious university that this medieval town projects such youth and dynamism.

Location

Population: 80 000. Michelin map nº 543 N 10 – Hessen. Marburg is located on a rocky outcrop on the edge of the Lahn in a land of forests and crystal-clear streams. The town occupies the centre of a triangle with the towns of Frankfort, Kassel and Cologne at the end of each point.

ℹ *Pilgrimstein 26, 35037 Marburg, ☎ (064 21) 991 20.*

Surrounding area: see LAHNTAL (Wetzlar is 44km/28mi southwest), SAUERLAND (Bad Berleburg is 49km/31mi north).

Background

St Elizabeth (1207-31) – Princess Elizabeth, daughter of the King of Hungary and the intended bride of the Landgrave Ludwig of Thuringia, was brought to the Thuringian court at Wartburg Castle near Eisenach at the age of four. Early in her life she became known for her kindness to the sick and unfortunate. She married Ludwig in 1221, but in 1227 he died of the plague, and Elizabeth resolved to withdraw from the world. She withdrew to Marburg, in the far west of Thuringian territory. The hard work of her daughter Sophie of Brabant later made this into the seed from which Hessen would grow. Elizabeth died of exhaustion at the age of 24.

A place of pilgrimage – Canonised only four years later (1235), she was to have her remains exhumed the following year in the presence of Emperor Friedrich II, to be immortalised in the superb Gothic church built by the members of the Teutonic Order to receive them. This attracted so many pilgrims that it became one of the largest centres of pilgrimage in Western Christianity.

Seat of the Reformation – In 1529 one of her descendants, the **Landgrave Philip the Magnanimous**, one of the most important Protestant princes of the Reformation period, decided to abolish the cult of relics. He had the shrine forced open and personally removed his ancestor's bones to bury them in a nearby cemetery. This is the same Philip who invited the Reformers Luther and Zwingli to a meeting that was to become known as the "Marburg Religious Discussion" (1529).

Directory

WHERE TO EAT

Zur Sonne – *Markt 14 – ☎ (064 21) 171 90 – €17.50/29.50.* This 16C building houses various dining rooms, all with immaculately-set tables, low ceilings and rustic-style decor. A variety of dishes are on offer.

WHERE TO STAY

Dammühle – *Dammühlenstraße 1, 35041 Marburg-Wehrshausen-Dammühle – 5km to the west along Barfüßertor – ☎ (064 21) 935 60 – fax (064 21) 36118 – dammuehle@t-online.de – P – 21rm: €50/90 – Restaurant €15/30.* This small half-timbered 14C mill, in a charming location has prettily-decorated, comfortable guestrooms. There is also a dining room with country-style decor, a Biergarten, mini-golf and games area.

Special Features

OLD MARBURG AND THE ELISABETHKIRCHE★★ *2hr*

Elisabethkirche★★

Open Apr to Sep, 9am-6pm, Sat, 9am-5pm, Sun, 11.15am-5pm; Oct, 9am-5pm, Sun, 11.15am-5pm; Nov-Mar, 10am-4pm, Sat, 9am-5pm, Sun 11.15am-5pm. Shrine: €2. ☎ (064 21) 655 73. The first truly Gothic church in Germany, this was built between 1235 and 1283. Its regional character derives from the stylistic unity of the chancel and transepts, each terminating in an apse, and from its three aisles of equal height – making it in fact the first hall-church. Transverse roof timbers covering the side aisles are typically Hessian. The towers, surmounted by stone spires, rest on massive buttresses.

Enter through the main doorway.

The church possesses some exceptional works of art.

Nave – Note the following works:

1) A statue of St Elizabeth (c 1470) wearing an elegant court gown.

2) An openwork Gothic rood with finely decorated consoles; on the altar *(nave side)*, a modern Crucifix by Ernst Barlach.

Chancel and transepts – A collection of exceptional works of art★★★:

3) Altarpiece of the Virgin; 1360 Pietà in the predella.

4) Tomb of St Elizabeth (after 1250). The 14C bas-relief on the sarcophagus represents the saint's burial.

5) The remains of frescoes visible in the niches date from the 14C and 15C. On the right, a scene evoking St Elizabeth's charitable activities (the Landgrave sees in his imagination the Saviour, in a bed in which Elizabeth placed a sick man); the formal exhumation of 1236.

6) St Elizabeth's Shrine★★ *(Elisabethschrein)* in the old sacristy. This masterpiece of the goldsmith's art was completed by craftsmen from the Rhineland c 1250. Scenes from the saint's life enrich the casket's sloping panels.

7) St Elizabeth's Window. Assembled from a collection of 13C medallions, this illustrates the charitable works of the saint.

8) Above the former priest's seat, a statue of St Elizabeth as the personification of Charity (the work, dating from 1510, is attributed to Ludwig Juppe, one of the most illustrious Marburg artists).

9) "The Landgraves' Chancel" *(in fact the south transept)*. Necropolis of the Landgraves of Hessen descended from St Elizabeth.

Leaving the church, climb up into the old town by way of the Steinweg – an unusual ramp with three different levels, which continues as the Neustadt and then the Wettergasse.

Turn right into the Marktgasse.

Marktplatz★

Only the upper part, the Obermarkt, has retained its original old houses. Particularly outstanding examples among them include nos 14 and 21, dating from 1560, no 23, and no 18, a stone house of 1323 and the oldest preserved house still inhabited.

The market fountain, dedicated to St George who is depicted vanquishing the dragon, is a popular meeting place.

Rathaus – A Gothic building built in 1512-27. Above a door in the staircase tower is a fine carving by Ludwig Juppe, representing Elizabeth bearing her coat of arms of the House of Hessen-Thuringia. A mechanical cock crows the hours from the gable.

The Nikolaistraße now leads to the forecourt of the Marienkirche.

This dates from the end of the 13C and is preceded to the right by the Gothic building of the former ossuary (Karner). From the terrace, there is a fine view over the roofs of the old town to the valley beyond. Past the church façade, at the top of a steep slope, there is a glimpse of the castle above.

At the end of the esplanade, a passage leads down to the *Kugelkirche*, a fine small church in the Late Gothic (end of the 15C) style.

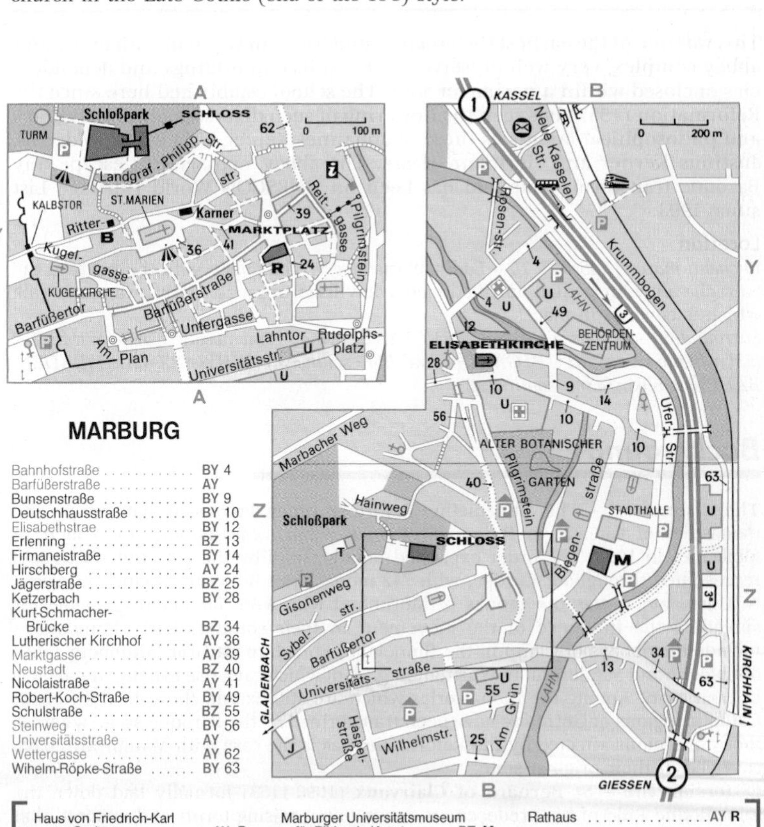

Haus von Friedrich-Karl von Savigny .... AY B
Marburger Universitätsmuseum für Bildende Kunst ...... BZ M
Rathaus .... AY R

Climbing again, this time to the top of the Kugelgasse. Before the Kalbstor fortified gate, turn right into Ritterstraße.

In Ritterstraße, at no 15, is the house which belonged to the famous legal historian Friedrich Karl von Savigny (1779-1861), one of the founders of the "historical school" of the study of law and a man who was the nucleus of the Marburg Romantics (Clemens von Brentano, Achim and Bettina von Arnim, Jakob and Wilhelm Grimm).

Worth a Visit

Schloß★ (Castle)

Open Apr to Oct, Tue-Sun, 10am-6pm; Nov to Mar, Tue-Sun, 11am-5pm. Closed 1 Jan, 24, 25 and 31 Dec. €2.60. ☎ (064 21) 282 58 71.

From the 13C to the 17C, the castle was the home of the Landgraves of Hessen. From the terrace there is a view along the Lahn Valley.

The historic buildings (13C-15C) on top of the spur include the Gothic Princes' Hall with its double nave, the west hall which gives a view of the excavations of the remains of the previous fortress (9C and 11C), the south hall with its memorials of the founding of the university (1527) and of the religious debates that took place in Marburg in 1529, and finally the castle chapel with its medieval ceramic floor. The **Regional and Art History Museum★** (Museum für Kulturgeschichte), housed in the 15C Wilhelmsbau wing, displays among other things precious artefacts from the Elisabethkirche (fragments of stained glass, a 15C tapestry depicting the story of the Prodigal Son). There is also an exhibition of medieval shields.

There is a pleasant walk through the **park** at the foot of the buttress.

Marburger Universitätsmuseum für bildende Kunst (Fine Arts Museum)

Open Tue-Sun, 11am-1pm, 2-5pm. Closed 1 Jan, 24-25 and 31 Dec. No charge. ☎ (064 21/2) 82 23 55. Mainly German paintings from the 16C to the present are on view here, including Carl Spitzweg's *Der Briefbote*.

Kloster Maulbronn★★

This was one of the earliest Cistercian foundations in Germany, an enormous abbey complex, very well preserved, with all its outbuildings and dependencies enclosed within a perimeter wall. The school established here since the Reformation (1557) has seen the flowering of such diverse scientific, literary and philosophical talents as those of Johannes Kepler, Friedrich Hölderlin, Justinus Kerner and Hermann Hesse. The abbey managed to escape any Baroque transformations and has been on UNESCO's World Heritage List since 1993.

Location

Michelin map n° 545 S, T 10 – Baden-Württemberg. The abbey is in the heart of the Salzach valley, in a small, fortified medieval village, approached by a rampart walk which is covered in places.

Surrounding area: see Schloß BRUCHSAL (24km/15mi west), BAD WIMPFEN (53km/33mi north), STUTTGART (47km/29mi southeast), SCHWARZWALD (BADEN-BADEN is 69km/43mi southwest).

Background

The Cistercians – This Benedictine Reformist order derives its name from the monastery of Cîteaux in Burgundy, France, which was founded by Robert of Molesmes in 1098. The order expanded rapidly, until by the 12C and 13C it was represented throughout Europe, with 742 monasteries between Ireland and Syria. In Germany, it was the monks of Morimond who were largely responsible for spreading the influence of the movement in their country. Early foundations include the abbeys of Camp in the Rhineland, Ebrach in Bavaria, Altenberg south of Cologne and Maulbronn in Württemberg, all of which gave rise to daughter abbeys in their turn. Among the monasteries which are still extant, those in the Roman Catholic regions of Germany have been transformed by the Baroque style, whereas those in regions affected by the Reformation, as is the case with Maulbronn, have survived in their original state.

Cistercian life – St Bernard of Clairvaux (1090-1153) formally laid down the Benedictine Rule of his predecessors in uncompromising terms and ensured that his monks followed it to the letter. Cistercian rule tolerates only what is essential

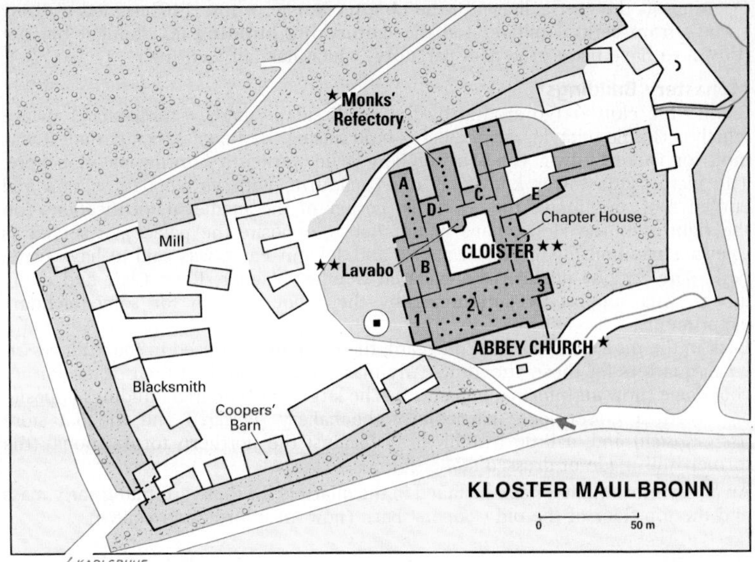

to the development and expansion of the monastic way of life, hence the strict discipline imposed on the monks and the extreme austerity of their abbeys. These tend to be located in isolated spots, tucked at the bottom of a secluded valley or in a forest clearing, and they share practically identical architectural features: blind nave, barrel-vaulted side aisles, a square and not very deep chancel ending in a flat east end, no bell-tower (a discreet lantern turret above the transept crossing would be all that signalled the abbey's presence). In the absence of any decorative elements, such as sculpted or painted motifs, or stained-glass windows, the characteristic beauty of Cistercian architecture is embodied in its well-proportioned dimensions and clarity of line.

Special Features

ABBEY★★ *2hr*

Open Mar-Oct, 9am-5.30pm; Nov-Feb, Tue-Sun, 9.30am-5pm. Closed 24, 25 and 31 Dec. €4.50. ☎ (070 43) 92 66 10; www.schloesser-und-gaerten.de

Abbey Church★

This was consecrated in 1178. The early 13C Paradise Porch **(1)** is the first German example of the Romanesque-Gothic transition.

Inside, the **fan vaulting** of the nave and south aisle, which was not added until the 15C, changes the impact of the original flat ceiling of Romanesque design. The nave is separated into two sections – one for the monks, the other for the lay brothers – by a Romanesque rood screen **(2)**, which is topped by a dog-tooth frieze. A large Crucifix (1473) sculpted from a single stone stands before the screen. To the left, in the north side aisle is a set of choir stalls with 23 seats dating from the early 15C. More impressive still are the richly carved monks' choir stalls (behind the choir screen), to seat 92, made in c 1450 and clearly influenced by the Ulm School. Note a beautiful 14C **Virgin** *(to the left of the high altar)* **(3)**, probably from the Cologne school.

Cloister★★

The west gallery leads to the **lay brothers' refectory (A)** (rebuilt in 1869-70), where groined vaulting arches low over the two aisles, and to the Romanesque **storeroom (B)**, now a *lapidarium*. The storeroom vaulting is square-ribbed. The **monks' refectory★**, completed c 1220-30 by the master who did the Paradise Porch, is flanked by the *calefactory* **(C)** and the kitchens **(D)** to the north. With its tall columns, featuring an annulet halfway up, and its early Gothic vaulting, the refectory is one of the most impressive rooms in the abbey complex. Opposite the entrance door, a charming **lavabo★★** (*Brunnenkapelle*, c 1350) with quadri-lobed blind arcades juts out into the cloister garden.

Scarlet Traces

The red crayon sketches that can be seen here and there on the vaulted ceilings of the monks' refectory are in fact the outlines of a fresco that was never painted. Jörg Ratgeb, the artist who sketched them, was taken away in 1526 for having led a peasants' revolt.

Opening off the east gallery are the **chapter-house**, whose 14C groined vaulting springs from central pillars, and the **connecting building (E)**, thought but not proven to have been used as a parlatory, which has fan vaulting.

Monastery Buildings★

Behind the cloister (go around by the north side), stands a three-storey palace which is Gothic in style, despite being built during the Renaissance period. It was built for Duke Ludwig von Württemberg, who wanted a hunting pavilion here. The picturesque tower known as the Faustturm, with its wooden section and curved roof, dominates the southeast corner of the medieval fortifications (on the right after the Herrenhaus manor house, opposite the palace); it served as a leisure pavilion for the ducal palace and Johann Faust was said to have come here. The famous doctor, who inspired Goethe, Wagner, René Clair and many others, was supposedly summoned by the abbot in 1516 for some alchemy experiments.

Back in the monastery's main courtyard, the museum is housed in the *Frühmesserhaus* (quarters for those attending early mass) and on the first floor of the former cooperage (now an information centre). The large half-timbered buildings opposite are worth a closer look, particularly the bakery *(Pfisterei)* and the oat store *(Heberkasten)* and, a little further away (against the northern fortifications), the former mill made of dressed stone.

An abbey museum has been installed in the quarters for those attending early mass and the top floor of the old Coopers' Barn (now an information centre).

Mecklemburgische Seenplatte★★★

This unique region contains over 1 000 lakes, most of which are linked by natural or artificially created canals, making it a paradise for water sports enthusiasts. The area has not yet been particularly developed as a tourist attraction or marketed in the same way as the lakes of Upper Bavaria. Nor has it yet been taken over by motor boats. Only a very few lakes have roads along their shores, and motorists only get the odd magical glimpse across a shining expanse of water. It is almost as if the lakes were hiding, despite the fact that most are quite large.

Location

Michelin map nº 542 folds 20 to 22 – Mecklenburg-Vorpommern. The Mecklenburg lake district was formed during the last Ice Age and lies in the area between the Elbe-Lübeck canal and the Ucker march.

Surrounding area: see NEUBRANDENBURG (43km/27mi east of Waren), SCHWERIN, ROSTOCK (89km/55mi north of Waren).

Directory

WHERE TO STAY

⊖ Hotel Seestern – *Müritzpromenade, 17207 Röbel – ☎ (039931) 580 30 – fax (039931) 580339 – Closed from mid-Jan to end Feb – P – 27rm: €45/88 ☕ – Restaurant €19/26.* This hotel is located on a small tongue of land jutting out onto the lake. Ask for one of the larger rooms with superb views. The restaurant is situated in a welcoming annexe of the hotel with a winter garden. Pleasant terrace.

⊖ Insel-Hotel – *An der Drehbrücke, 17213 Malchow – ☎ (039932) 86 00 – fax (039932) 86030 – P – 16rm: €46/76 ☕ – Restaurant €12/24.* Situated in the old town of Malchow and on the edge of a swing bridge *(Drehbrücke)*. Well turned-out guestrooms, some of them with views over the lake. On the menu in the restaurant: traditional dishes, served on wooden tables.

⊖ Hotel Paulshöhe – *Falkenhäger Weg, 17192 Waren – ☎ (03991) 171 40 – fax (03991) 171444 – info@hotel-paulshoehe.de – P – 14rm: €46/77 ☕ – Restaurant €16/27.* This hotel and its 7 bungalows are located in a pleasant location 200m from the Müritz lake. Hotel has all mod-cons, with welcoming, well-presented restaurant.

⊖⊖ Hotel Kleines Meer – *Alter Markt 7, 17192 Waren – ☎ (03991) 64 80 – fax (03991) 648222 – info@kleinesmeer.com – 30rm: €79/119 ☕ – Restaurant €31/41.* Contemporary-style hotel on the former marketplace, not far from the port. Beautifully presented guestrooms; restaurant with light, modern decor.

Tour

FROM SCHWERIN TO THE MÜRITZ LAKE

150km/94mi – One day.

The **Schweriner See**, forms an idyllic backdrop to the provincial capital **Schwerin★** *(see SCHWERIN)* and castle of this name, which is reflected in its waters. The Krakower See, is home to the Mecklenburg regional poet Fritz Reuter, who dreamt of paradise on its peaceful wooded shores. The area is a bird sanctuary and therefore paradise for bird-watchers.

The **Plauer See**, the third largest lake in Mecklenburg-Vorpommern, offers flat shores to the north and thick forest to the south. Together with the **Müritz**, it forms the heart of the Mecklenburg lake district.

Northeast of these lies **Mecklenburg's "Switzerland"**, stretching north of the **Malchiner See** and the **Kummerower See** and earning its name from the numerous outcrops that characterise it. To the west of the **Malchiner See** *(on the B 108)* stands Mecklenburg's largest classic castle complex, **Burg Schlitz**, set in a wonderful park. The road leads through the town of **Malchin**, with its fine brick basilica, to the Kummerower See. On the way, a short detour leads to the 1 000-year-old oak tree known as the Ivenacher Eichen (near Reuter's town of Stavenhagen).

The pearl of the Mecklenburg lake district is **Müritz**, the second largest lake in Germany, 110km^2/42sq mi in size. The name comes from the Slavonic word *"morcze"* meaning small sea. The town of **Waren**, the main tourist centre of the region, lies on its northern shores. In addition to the two parish churches of St Georg and St Maria, the old and new town halls and the Löwenapotheke (pharmacy) draw the eye. **Röbel** is developing into a pretty marina, with its attractive boathouses on the shores of the lake.

Müritz-Nationalpark★

This 310km^2/194mi^2 nature reserve stretches eastwards from the east bank of the Müritz. Two thirds of its surface area are covered by forest, 12% by lakes and 8% by marshland. This park, 25 000ha/61 775 acres of which were state hunting grounds under the socialist regime, is now the realm of ramblers and cyclists. With a pair of binoculars you may be able to spot a rare osprey (on the road from Federow to Speck); the high-voltage metal pylons seem to be one of their preferred nesting grounds (parking is not permitted near nests). The sea eagle, **Germany's heraldic bird of prey, can also be spotted near the fish pools at Boek:** its territory extends for 50km^2/31mi^2. White storks nest at Kargow, and the nature reserve is also home to a number of black storks and cranes. The dry areas of ground are covered mainly by pines with some beech trees, while alders, birch and ash dominate the marshes and bogs of the east bank of the Müritz. To find out more about the wealth of flora and fauna (150 bird and 700 plant species), it is well worth going on one of the guided tours which explain the natural history of the reserve.

Lakeside houses on piles, Müritzsee

K. Thiele

Meißen★

Meißen is famous for its porcelain, distinguished by a pair of crossed swords in blue. From the vineyards in the river valley it also produces a pleasantly fruity dry white wine. Meißen's historic centre is remarkably well preserved and is dominated by the flamboyant Albrechtsburg and the cathedral.

Location

Population: 30 000. Michelin map nº 544 M 24 – Sachsen. Located not far from Dresden, the town of Meißen grew up around a rocky plateau in the picturesque Elbe valley.
Markt 3, 01662 Meissen, ☎ (035 21) 419 40.
Surrounding area: see DRESDEN (23km/14mi east), LEIPZIG (100km/63mi west).

Directory

Where to Eat

Romantik Restaurant Vincenz Richter – *An der Frauenkirche 12 – ☎ (03521) 45 32 85 – restaurant@vincenz-richter.de – Closed 4 Jan-22 Jan, Sun evenings and Mon – – €20/29.* It's easy to be charmed by this restaurant set in a former draper's house built in 1523. Numerous utensils and paintings decorate the dining room of this rustic-style restaurant. In the summer, the interior courtyard is a pleasant place to enjoy a meal.

Where to Stay

Hotel Am Talkenberger Hof – *Am Talkenberger Hof 15, 01640 Coswig Kreis Meissen – ☎ (03523) 743 17 – fax (03523) 74379 – P – Booking advised – 9rm: €31/47 – Restaurant €9.30/19.* Pleasant little guesthouse, nestling among the vineyards. The clean, well cared-for guestrooms have country-style furnishings. Superb view over the local area from the terrace.

Background

Historical notes – To understand the development of Meißen, the foundation of the town has to be placed in the military and historical context of the campaigns waged against the Slav tribes east of the Saale and the Elbe by King Heinrich I. In 929, he fortified a height commanding a strategic ford crossing the Elbe. The fortress was built on a rocky plateau where a tributary, the Triebisch, precipitated itself into the main river. The town grew up around the foot of the castle hill from the 12C. Since the 18C, of course, Meißen has been famous worldwide for its porcelain.

The porcelain of Saxony – It was in the reign of Augustus the Strong that the alchemist **Johann Friedrich Böttger** (1682-1719) revealed that he had discovered the formula for creating the white hard-paste porcelain until then made only in China. The formula is based on kaolin (china clay), large quantities of which could be – and still are – mined only a short distance northwest of Meißen. Böttger made the discovery in 1708, although he did not reveal the secret until 29 March 1709. A year later, Augustus, Elector of Saxony and King of Poland, founded the Royal Saxon Porcelain Manufactory, which he installed in the castle – an isolated, well-guarded site, ideal for the protection of secrets. Böttger, who had until then produced only hard red stoneware, was its first director.

The Motifs – Initially, the lavish decoration imitated Chinese and Japanese models. The period of plant designs, red and green dragons, a yellow lion, flowers, birds and mythical creatures dates from the directorship of Böttger's successor, Johann Gregorius Höroldt (1720-55), who was responsible for the factory's first flush of prosperity (Old Saxony).

It was Höroldt who produced the famous "Blue Onion" *(Zwiebelmuster)* tableware design, based on the use of cobalt, which was to become one of the most celebrated glazed designs in the world. Innumerable elegant services, along with individual vases, pots, giant animals and "conversation pieces", were also created by Johann Joachim Kändler (1706-75). The factory mark distinguishing Meissen porcelain is a pair of crossed swords in blue.

Walking About

OLD MEISSEN

The old town has plenty of witnesses to the Gothic and Renaissance periods. On **Marktplatz**, stand the Late Gothic *Rathaus* (town hall, 1470-86), the *Bennohaus* from the second half of the 15C, the *Marktapotheke*, a Renaissance building from 1555-60, and the *Hirschhaus* with a fine 1642 doorway. Not far from this is the *Tuchmachertor*, a Late Renaissance gateway (c 1600), and the 16C *Brauhaus* (brewery).

MEISSEN

Am Lommatzscher Tor	AX 3	Fleischergasse	AY 9	Markt	AY 22
An der Frauenkirche	AY 4	Gerbergasse	BY	Marktgasse	ABY 24
Baderberg	AXY 6	Hahnemannspl.	BY 10	Martinstraße	BY 25
Elbstraße	BY 7	Heinrichsplatz	BY 12	Ratsweinberg	BY 28
		Justusstufen	AY 15	Schloßberg	AX 31
		Kerstingstraße	AY 16	Vorbrücker-Str.	BX 33
		Lorenzgasse	AY 19	Weinberggasse	BX 34

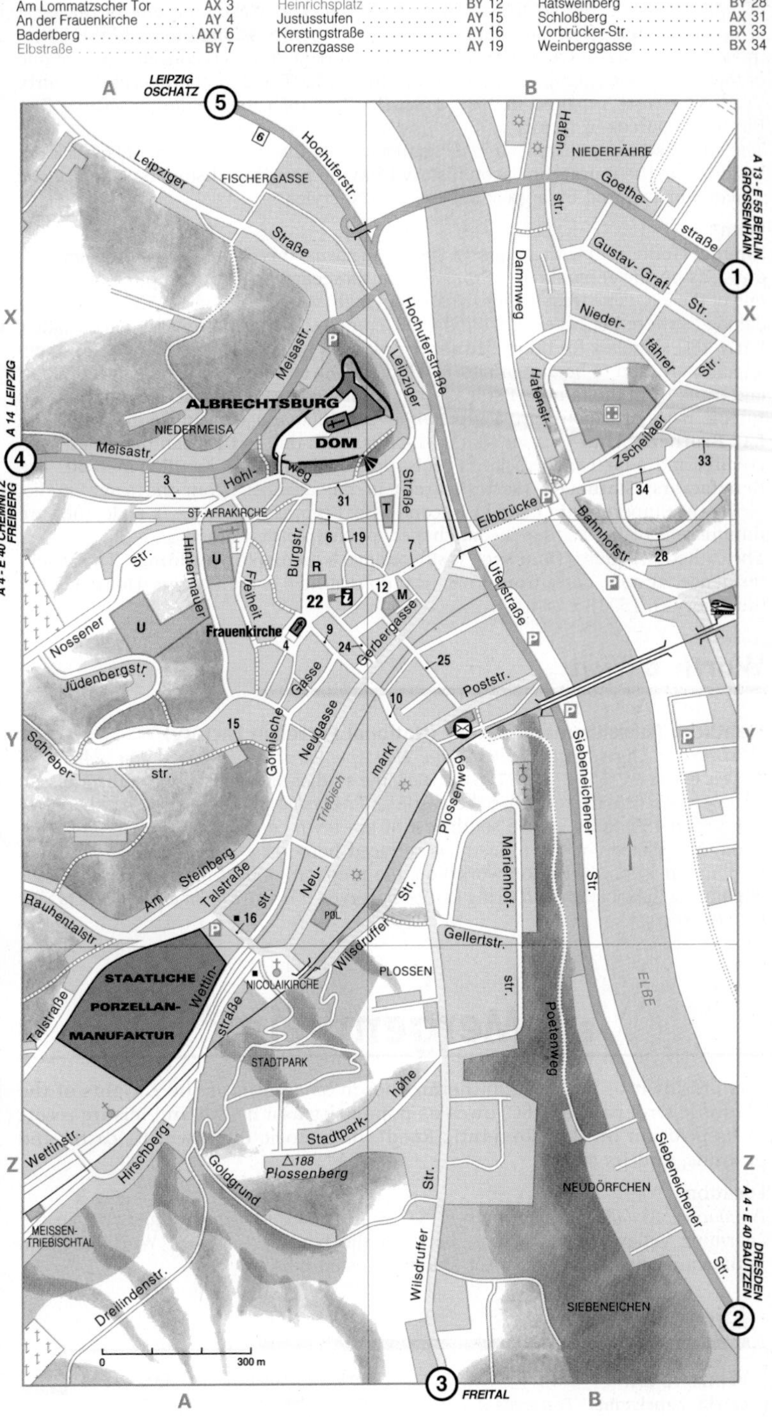

Frauenkirche

Also standing on the Marktplatz is this three-aisle Late Gothic hall-church with its fine star-vaulting dating from the late 15C. The bells of the carillon are made of Meissen porcelain.

BURGBERG ★★

The castle, the cathedral and its subsidiary buildings are all grouped on this hill which was the original site of the town.

Albrechtsburg★

Open Mar to Oct, 10am-6pm; Nov-Feb, 10am-5pm. Closed 1 Jan, last 3 weeks of Jan, 24, 25 and 31 Dec. €3.50. ☏ (035 21) 470 70. Arnold von Westfalen, one of the most esteemed architects of late medieval times, was commissioned to build this castle in 1471 by the Margrave Albert. The finished work (1521-24) is considered to be one of the finest civic examples of the Late Gothic style. The depredations of the Thirty Years War were repaired in 1662. From 1710 to 1865 the castle housed the first European porcelain factory.

The **spiral staircase** *(Großer Wendelstein)* adorning the façade is a model of its kind. Inside, note the murals on Saxon history from the period of Historicism, an eclectic movement inspired by a great variety of past styles.

Dom★

Another Gothic hall with a transept and three naves, this church was built from 1250 onwards on the remains of a Romanesque sanctuary and not completed until the end of the 15C. The west towers (81m/265ft high) were begun in 1315 and, following damage suffered between 1904 and 1908, completed after designs by Carl Schäfer. Early 16C sketches for bronze **funerary plaques★** in the Dukes' Chapel (Fürstenkapelle) are said to be due in part to Albrecht Dürer and Lucas Cranach the Elder, and came from the famous Peter Vischer studio in Nuremberg. In front of the rood screen, parts of which were sculpted between 1260 and 1270 in Naumburg, is the **Lay Brothers' Altar★** (Laienaltar), which is again due to Cranach the Elder, with crucifix and altar candlesticks in Meissen porcelain by JJ Kändler in 1760. The **Benefactors' Statues★★** (Stifterfiguren) in the chancel, from the same studio, represent Emperor Otto I and his second wife, Empress Adelaide. In style, they are reminiscent of the statues in the chancel of Naumburg Cathedral.

The cathedral square (Domplatz) is surrounded by **monastic buildings**. The Dean's residence, at no 5, dates from 1526; next door at no 6 is the Canons' House (1728); the Priory (c 1500) is at no 7.

Worth a Visit

Staatliche Porzellanmanufaktur★ (National Porcelain Factory)

Talstrasse 9. Open May-Oct, 9am-6pm; Nov-Apr, 9am-5pm. Closed 1 Jan, 24-26 and 31 Dec. €7.50. ☏ (035 21) 46 82 08. In 1865, the studios and workshops of the Meissen factory were transferred from the castle *(Albrechtsburg)*, where they had been for more than 150 years, to the southwest of the town centre.

Today the history of the industry is retraced here via a large number of superb exhibits. In a demonstration workshop, the preparation of paste and the processes of painting, fabrication and firing can be observed *(there are often long queues to visit the workshop).*

Bad Mergentheim★

The old town of Bad Mergentheim, chosen as a base for the Knights of the Teutonic Order in the 16C, owes its popularity as a health and leisure resort to its position on the "Romantic Road", its historic old town, its castle and grounds, and its spa.

Location

Population: 23 000. Michelin map nº 545 R 13 – Baden-Württemberg. Lying in the charming valley of the Tauber, between the popular towns of Wurtzburg and Rothenburg, this spa town is set among forested hills.

Directory

WHERE TO EAT

⊖⊖⊖ Zirbelstube – *Poststraße 2 – ☏ (079 31) 59 36 07 – Closed Sun and bank holidays – €54/62.* Walls clad in dark pine and hung with attractive pictures, not to mention the prettily set tables give this restaurant an air of elegance and comfort.

WHERE TO STAY

⊖ Hotel Bundschu – *Cronbergstraße 15 – ☏ (079 31) 93 30 – fax (079 31) 933633 – info@hotel-bundschu.de – Closed from the beginning of Jan to mid-Jan – P – 50rm: €56/100 – Restaurant €21.50/41.50.* This well-kept hotel is run by the Bundschu family and is located in the middle of a quiet residential district. Comfortable, modern guestrooms. Convivial restaurant serving Mediterranean flavours, with pleasant terrace garden.

🅱 *Marktplatz 3, 97980 Bad Mergentheim,* ☎ *(079 31) 571 31.*
Surrounding area: see ROMANTISCHE STRASSE, HOHENLOHER LAND *(15km/9mi south).*

Worth a Visit

Deutschordensschloß (Castle of the Teutonic Order)

Deutscheordenmuseums Bad Mergentheim GmbH
Castle of the Teutonic Order.

♿ *Open Tue-Sun, 10am-5pm. Closed 24, 25 and 31 Dec. €3.50.* ☎ *(079 31) 522 12.*
The castle, which was built in the 12C as a moated castle, was extended in the mid-16C to become the residence of the Teutonic Order and its Grand Master, following which other structural changes were gradually made. The coat of arms of the Grand Master Maximilian, Archduke of Austria (1590-1618), is displayed above the richly decorated main entrance to the inner courtyard, whilst the corner towers in the inner courtyard house intricate Renaissance spiral stairways.
The museum of the Teutonic Order occupies three floors of the castle. On the second floor, the royal apartments with their Baroque stucco ceilings and the classical chapter-house form the setting for a presentation on the history of the order. The department on the history of the town focuses on local history from its beginnings until the present. The Adelsheim antiques collection includes porcelain, faience, carved ivory pieces and religious works of art.
An extensive and attractive **dolls' house collection** includes 40 exhibits from the 19C and 20C.

The Teutonic Order

The order was founded as a Germanic hospitaller community in the Holy Land and became a religious order in 1198 after the fall of the Kingdom of Jerusalem, when the knights were forced to return home. They became princes in their own right of sizeable territories and estates, either by conquering them (Prussia and Livonia) or by accepting them as gifts.
In 1525 the Grand Master of the order, Albrecht von Brandenburg-Ansbach, who resided in Königsberg, adopted the teaching of Luther and suppressed the religious side of the organisation. The community's patrimony of Prussia became a secular principality.
Dispossessed of its seat, the Teutonic Order elected Schloß Mergentheim in Franconia as its new headquarters during the same year. The castle had been in its possession since 1219 and remained the residence of the Teutonic and Grand Master for almost three centuries. In 1809 the order was abolished by Napoleon throughout all the states of the Rhine Confederation.
Nowadays the order has resumed existence as a religious and charitable body, and has its headquarters in Vienna.

Excursions

Stuppach

6km/4mi on the Schwäbisch Hall road. The parish church of this village now boasts the central panel of the celebrated altarpiece from the Chapel of Our Lady of the Snow in Aschaffenburg, kept in a side chapel. The panel, known as the **Stuppacher Madonna**★★ (1519), depicts a Virgin and Child and is the work of Matthias Grünewald. ♿ *Open Mar to Apr, Tue-Sun, 10am-5pm; May to Oct, Tue-Sun, 9.30am-5.30pm; Nov, Tue-Sun, 11am-4pm. €1.50.* ☎ *(079 31) 26 05.*

Monschau★★

Before 1919, the small town of Monschau was called Montjoie. This ancient Eifel village, with its tall, narrow, slate-roofed houses huddled together at one end of a winding gorge carved from the rock by the river is famous for its culinary specialities, in particular the Montjoier Düttchen (Montjoie croissants).

Location

Population: 12 600 – Michelin map nº 543 O 2 – Nordrhein-Westfalen. Monschau is located to the west of the Eifel massif, only a few kilometres from the Belgian border. From a lay-by viewpoint on Bundesstraße 258, coming from Aachen, there is a superb **view★★** of the town.

Stadtstraße 1, 52156 Monschau, ☎ (024 72) 194 33.

Surrounding area: see AACHEN (38km/24mi north), EIFEL (Bad Münstereifel, our tour's departure point, is 56km/35mi to the east).

Background

Drapers' town – Monschau owes its wealth, apparent from the considerable number of grand houses, to the clothmaking industry brought to the small farming town by Protestants from Aachen in c 1600. The town flourished in the 18C and its buildings are therefore predominantly Baroque in style. Visitors should keep an eye open for the wonderful Baroque doors which can adorn even the most modest of houses, contributing to the overall charm of the locality.

Walking About

Leaving the market place via the Unterer Mühlenberg slope, on the right of the Kaular café, turn right again along the Knieberg and climb to the chapel (Friedhofkapelle) which lies beyond the cemetery. From here, again, there is a good **view★** of the town, the castle, and the ruins of the Haller watchtower.

The oldest part of Monschau is in the Kirchstraße quarter (note especially the period house at no 33).

Rotes Haus★ (Red House)

Open from Good Fri to the end of Nov, Tue-Sun, at 10am, 11am, 2pm, 3pm and 4pm. The number of visitors permitted inside the Red House is limited, so the doors are closed 5min after these times to allow visitors an hour inside the house. €2.50. ☎ (024 72) 50 71.

The draper and merchant Johann Heinrich Scheibler had this house built in 1762-65 as his place of residence and business. He paid 90 000 Thaler, a considerable sum in those days. However, Scheibler was well able to afford this, with about 6 000 people working for him. The remarkable interior **decor★** has a harmoniousness rare for the time and is an exceptional example of middle-class home decor in the 18C and 19C: fine collection of oak furniture from Aachen and Lüttich; hand-painted wall-hangings; and 6 000 textile designs from the heyday of Monschau's draper's industry. All this is overshadowed by the magnificent **Rococo staircase★**, however, probably the work of craftsmen from Lüttich. The free-standing staircase serves three storeys and features rocaille cartouches illustrating the various stages of the clothworker's trade.

Haus Troistorff

Laufenstraße 18. This magnificent house was built by a cloth manufacturer in 1783. In comparison with the Rotes Haus, it takes architectural evolution a step further. It is much more like a town house, and its central façade with heraldic gables and balconies supported by atlantes stands apart from the otherwise more rustic architecture of the rest of the town.

▶▶ Musée Felsenkeller Brauerei *(local beers)* – Monschauer handwerkermarkt (Monschau Craft Museum) – Eifeler Photographica und Filmmuseum (Eifel Museum of Photography and Film).

Excursions

The North Eifel Lakes

85km/53mi – allow half a day.

Leave Monschau on B 258. The road rises rapidly, and after a mile there is yet another **look-out point★** giving a good view over the village. From Imgenbroich onwards, particularly between Strauch and Schmidt, there are attractive glimpses, on the right, of the Rur lake region. Leaving Schmidt, the Nideggen ruin lies straight ahead.

Burg Nideggen – Until the 15C the rose-coloured sandstone castle – a true "eagle's eyrie" site – was the residence of the counts and dukes of Jülich, after which it fell into disuse. From the 12C keep (partially restored and turned into a museum – Burgenmuseum – devoted to the castles and fortresses of the Eifel), there are fine **views★** to the south of the Rur Valley cutting into the Eifel plateau, and of the Aachen basin to the north. The restored 12C church has a Romanesque chancel with frescoes.

Rurtalsperre★ (Rur Dam) – In a wild stretch of country, the reservoir here, known also as the "Stausee Schwammenauel", forms with the Urft reservoir to the south the largest stretch of water in the Eifel. Motor boat services operate on each of them. The road crosses the dam to enter the Kermeter forest. From Einruhr, the route skirts the southern end of the Rursee, which is overlooked from a viewpoint laid out at the top of the hill beyond.

Moseltal★★★

Moselle Valley

Dotted with picturesque villages and renowned for its wines, the Moselle Valley is an enchanting region. Over 195km/121mi from Trier to Koblenz, the river's winding course runs through the very heart of the German countryside, with castles and vineyards to explore, and cruises, hiking and cycling among the activities on offer.

Location

Moselle Valley – Michelin map 543 Q 3 – P 5 – O 6 – Rheinland-Pfalz. The wide, peaceful curves of the River Moselle flow between two massifs of Rhineland schist, the Eifel to the northwest and the Hunsrück to the southeast. The river, canalised from Thionville onwards, comprises 12 separate sectors, the locks beside each dam taking barges of up to 1 500t, or towed convoys of 3 200t.

Surrounding area: see EIFEL (Manderscheid is 56km/35mi north of Trier), IDAR-OBERSTEIN (37km/23mi south of Bernkastel-Kues), RHEINTAL (our suggested touring programme includes Koblenz).

Directory

Cruises

Cruises between Koblenz and Cochem, from the end of April to mid October: Mon, Fri, Sat-Sun from Koblenz 9.45am and from Cochem 3.40pm (from end of June to beginning of Oct). Closed 11-19 June. €23.60 return. Information from the offices at the landing stages or from Köln-Düsseldorfer, Frankenwerft 35, 50667 Köln, ☎ (0221) 208 83 18; www.k-d.com

Where to Stay

Reichsschenke "Zum Ritter Götz" – *Robert-Schuman-Straße 57, 54536 Kröv – ☎ (06541) 816 60 – Fax (06541) 8166105 – Closed 2 weeks in Feb and 3 weeks in Nov – 16rm: €28/80 – Restaurant €17.50.* This old inn-style hotel with its smart, rather soberly furnished rooms, is set in the heart of the vineyards. The small, low-ceilinged dining rooms of the restaurant, decorated with dark wood and some wood carvings, give it a rustic air.

Wein- und Gästehaus Port – *Weingartenstraße 57, 54470 Bernkastel-Kues – ☎ (06531) 911 73 – Fax (06531) 91175 – weingutport@t-online.de – P – 5rm, 4 holiday apartments €30/50 – €6.50.* Peace and quiet guaranteed in this establishment surrounded by vineyards. Comfortable rooms and holiday apartments available. Guests start the day with a hearty breakfast and end it with wine and *Schwenkbraten* (pork chops marinaded and grilled).

Hotel Bären – *Gestade 4, 54470 Bernkastel-Kues – ☎ (06531) 25 52 – Fax (06531) 915547 – www.hotel-baeren.de – closed Nov-Mar Sun-Tue – 33rm: €48/110 – Restaurant €15/85.* Rooms furnished with care, offering magnificent views. The rustic restaurant next door to the hotel has an elegant terrace with a view of the river.

Steigenberger Esprix – *Am Flughafen Hahn – Gebäude 1380, 55483 Hahn – ☎ (06543) 50 98 00 – Fax (06543) 509820 – www.hahn.esprix-hotels.de – P – 35rm: €61/81.* This hotel next to Hahn airport is particularly well suited to the needs of travellers in transit. Plain, well-equipped rooms.

Background

Moselle wines – Most of the steep slopes of the Moselle Valley are planted with wonderful vines, producing dry white wines largely from Riesling stock. Here the schistous subsoil plays a vital part in the maturing of the grapes, the decomposed rock absorbing heat during the day and breathing it out at night among the vines. The harvest is late and sometimes continues until the Feast of St Nicholas (6 December). The wines are light, sometimes pungent, but with an extremely delicate bouquet. The further north the vines are planted, the more acid the wine becomes.

Tour

FROM TRIER TO KOBLENZ

195km/121mi – one day

Trier★★ – *See TRIER.*

Neumagen-Dhron

This town is known for its Roman discoveries, which have been transported to the Rhineland Museum at Trier. A copy of the famous *Wine Ship* can be seen beside the chapel opposite the Am Römerweinschiff café.

Bernkastel-Kues★– *See BERNKASTEL-KUES.*

One magnificent vineyard follows another on this route. Note the oversize sundials *(Sonnenuhren)* fixed here and there to bare rock outcrops, which have given their names to some of the better-known vintages (Wehlen and Zeltingen, for instance).

The road passes through many villages typical of this wine-growing region: **Ürzig**, **Kröv**, **Enkirch** and **Pünderich** among them. From Enkirch, make a 5km/3mi detour to **Starkenburg**. From the terrace, there is a splendid **view★** over the river's lazy Mont-Royal meanders.

Some 3km/2mi after the bridge at **Zell**, which offers a fine perspective of the riverside houses lining the bank on the far side of the water, take the left turn in the direction of Marienburg.

S. Ollivier/MICHELIN

Cruise boat at Bernkastel-Kues

Marienburg

The old convent here stood in an exceptional **setting★★** overlooking the narrowest stretch of land enclosed by the river bend at Zell. From the restaurant terrace and the wooden "Prinzenkopf" look-out tower *(follow the footpath: 45min there and back)*, there are impressive **views★★** of the various curves in the course of the river and the vineyards on either bank, the Kondel forest and the Hunsrück slopes.

Beilstein

This tiny fortified town, whose last squire was the Chancellor Metternich, is huddled at the foot of a huge church and a castle. From the ruins of the **castle** *(Burgruine); 30min on foot there and back, from the banks of the Moselle via Bachstraße)* there is, again, a splendid **view★** of the ever-curving valley. *From Easter to end of Oct: 9am-6pm. €2. ☎ (026 73) 936 39.*

Cochem

We recommend leaving the car on the outskirts and following the river bank on foot to discover one of the most celebrated **sites★★** of the region: towering above the river, the **castle** crowns a conical hill entirely covered with vines.

Of the original castle, the Reichsburg, *(30min on foot there and back, from Marktplatz)*, only the keep and the foundations of the walls remained after the destruction of 1689 – but the ruins were rebuilt in 14C style during the 19C, bristling with turrets and pinnacles. The **interior** has been refurnished in an opulent "feudal" manner. *Guided tour. From mid Mar to mid Nov: 9am-5pm. €4. ☎ (026 71) 255.*

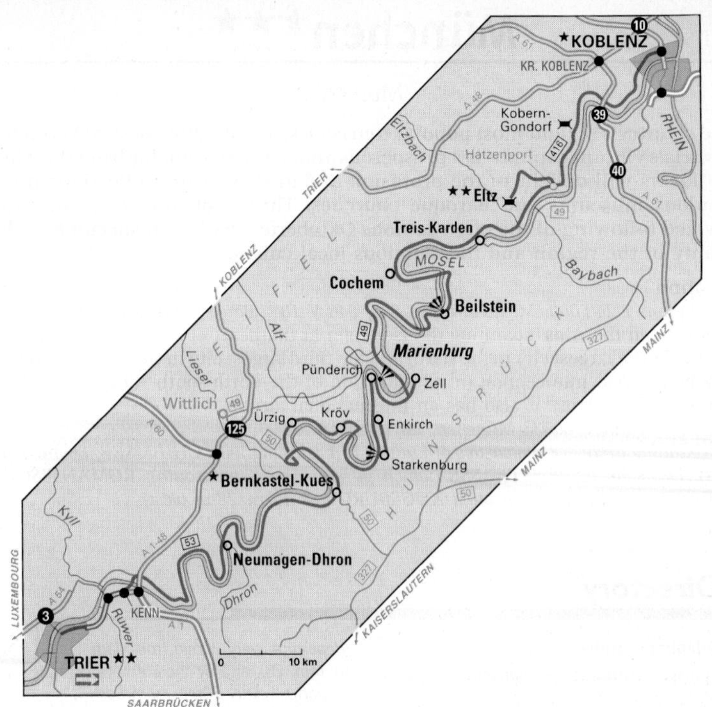

Treis-Karden

The **church of St Castor**, in the Karden quarter, exemplifies a transitional style halfway between Rhineland Romanesque (the "dwarf gallery" in the apse) and Gothic (ribbed vaulting).

Inside, there is a 1420 high altarpiece in carved wood representing the Three Magi and, in the chapel on the left-hand side of the chancel, a small wooden shrine to St Castor in the Gothic style (1490).

Burg Eltz★★

10km/6mi from Hatzenport, plus 15min on foot or 5min by bus. From the promontory at the first hairpin bend after the car park, there is an awe-inspiring view looking down on this romantic **site★★**: the fortress, bristling with eight towers and numerous turrets, pinnacles and spires, rises majestically above the trees at the far end of the wild Eltz Valley. *Guided tour (40min). From Apr to end of Oct: 9.30am-5.30pm. €6. ☎ (026 72) 95 05 00.* The castle courtyard also makes an impressive scene.

There are period furnishings inside, as well as a treasury. Not to be missed are the Rübenach lower hall with a 15C timber ceiling and the upper hall with Gothic ornamentation, the knights' hall and the late medieval Rodendorf kitchen, still intact. Among the paintings, note Lucas Cranach's *Madonna with Grapes*.

Returning to the main road, the visitor soon sees the twin-tower silhouette of Thurant Castle on the east bank of the river. At **Kobern-Gondorf**, not long before the final twist in the river, the road passes right through an enormous restored 15C-17C castle – one of two overlooking this stylish small town and blending remarkably well with the landscape. Opposite the upper castle and the plain square keep stands the hexagonal Romanesque chapel of St Matthias.

Koblenz★ – *See KOBLENZ.*

München★★★

Munich

The country's second most popular tourist destination after Berlin, Munich – Bavaria's vibrant capital – is a prosperous and lively city not far from the Alps. Art lovers will delight in the profusion and quality of the collections in its fabulous museums and Baroque churches. Those not already among the devoted following of the city's famous Oktoberfest will soon succumb to the beauty of the region and the delicious local cuisine.

Location

Population: 1 248 000. Michelin maps 545, 546 V 18 – Bayern. Equidistant from the Danube and the Alps, spanning the Isar river at the heart of the Bavarian plateau, Munich is the largest city in the south and the third largest city in Germany. Standing at a major road intersection (at the junction of the north-south A9 and the A8 to France and Austria), it also has an international airport.

🅱 *Hauptbahnhof, 80335 München, ☎ (089) 233 03 00.*

Surrounding area: see the castles of Ludwig II (beginning with CHIEMSEE, 85km/53mi east), Deutsche ALPENSTRASSE (which passes 45km/28mi south), ROMANTISCHE STRASSE (which passes through AUGSBURG just 45km/28mi west).

Directory

Telephone prefix – 089

Tourist information – *Fremdenverkehrsamt München*, ☎ 23 33 03 00, Fax 23 33 02 33, Mon-Thu 9am-3pm, Fri 9am-12.30pm. Information points: Tourist information at the Hauptbahnhof, Mon-Sat 9am-8pm, Sun 10am-6pm, ☎ 23 33 02 57/58; Tourist information in the Neues Rathaus (Marienplatz), Mon-Fri 10am-8pm, Sat 10am-4pm, ☎ 23 33 02 72/73. A detailed overview of events is given in the following local newspapers available from news kiosks: *Prinz and Münchner*. Every four weeks the tourist office publishes a calendar of events. Advance ticket bookings via the tourist information point in the Neues Rathaus or at the numerous advance tickets booths. It is well worth making sure you buy tickets in plenty of time.

Post offices with extended opening hours – Postfiliale 32, Bahnhofsplatz, Mon-Fri 7am-8pm, Sat 9am-4pm, Sun 10am-3pm. Postfiliale 24 at the airport (central area level 3) in McPaper, Mon-Sat 7.30am-9pm.

Daily newspapers – Süddeutsche Zeitung. Münchner Merkur, AZ

Internet sites: www.intermunich.de; www.munich-online.de; www.munich-info.de; www.muenchen-tourist.de

Getting About

Much of the centre of Munich is a pedestrian and bicycle zone. Many sights are within walking distance and the city's main museums can be easily reached by tram from Karlsplatz *(lines 17, 18 and 27 stop at Nationalmuseum, Deutsches Museum and Pinakotheken)*. Munich's railway station *(Hauptbahnhof)*, a 10min walk from the centre, is also the main public transport hub.

Airport – ☎ 975 00. The FJ Strauss Flughafen, 34km/21mi north, is linked to the city by S-Bahn lines S1 and S8 *(departure every 20min from 4am to 1am, €8)*, and by the Lufthansa shuttle *(departure every 20min from 5am to 8pm, €9)*.

Public Transport – Munich and its surroundings are divided into four ring-shaped price zones. The local transport and fare association MVV (Münchner Verkehrs- und Tarifverbund) covers underground trains (U-Bahn), SWM (Stadtwerke München) buses and trams (Straßenbahn), rail (S-Bahn) and the transport authorities for the surrounding area; ☎ 41 42 43 44. Information at the tourist information office or main railway station *(Hauptbahnhof)* on the mezzanine level, Mon-Sat 9am-6pm. Tickets are available from any underground or rail station and in trams, from ticket machines or from bus drivers.

Tickets – Tickets for the central zone (Münchner Innenraum), which includes Munich city centre: Single tickets (*Einzelfahrt*) cost €2, 10-trip tickets: €9 (*10er Streifenkarte*, can be used by more than one person, in Munich city centre two strips on this ticket must be validated); travellers can change lines with these tickets. Single day tickets (*Single-Tageskarte*), €4.50, and "Partner" day tickets (*Partner-Tageskarte*, for up to five people), €8, are valid from when they are stamped to 6am the following day. There is also a three-day ticket costing €11 for one person, and €18.50 for two to five people.
Internet – www.mvv-muenchen.de

Combination ticket – There are four varieties of **München Welcome Card**: one-day single *(Single 1 Tag)* €6.50, three-day single *(Single 3 Tage)* €15.50, one-day "Partner" (for five adults – two children between 6 and 14 years old equal one adult) *(Partner 1 Tag)* €9.50; three-day "Partner" *(Partner 3 Tage)* €22.50. The ticket is valid for use of public transport in

Munich city centre and gives discounts of up to 50% for more than 30 sights, museums, castles and palaces, tourist attractions, city tours and bicycle hire. It is available from tourist information offices, in many hotels, and at the airport (where it will cost €10 more but includes a return to the city centre).

Bicycle hire – *Radius Bike Tours*, ☎ 55 02 93 74, rents out bicycles for €14 per day. Munich is a very bicycle-friendly city, so this is an ideal – and very popular – form of transport.

Sightseeing

Theme tours – The tourist office can organise tours with an English-speaking guide for groups, on request, ☎ 23 33 234. *Stattreisen* also offers a programme of city tours on 60 different themes, eg beer, tours on foot, by tram or by bicycle, ☎ 54 40 42 30, www.stattreisen-muenchen.de. Regular guided tours in English are also available from *Munich Walks*, ☎ 55 02 93 74, www.munichwalks.com.

Coach tours – *Münchner Stadt-Rundfahrten – Panorama Tours*, ☎ 55 02 89 95, stadtrundfahrten@t-online.de: *Höhepunkte Münchens* (1hr, €11), daily at 10am, 11am, 12pm, 1pm, 2pm, 2.30pm, 3pm and 4pm (1st Apr to 31 Oct also at 11.30am and 5pm); the city centre and Schloß Nymphenburg (2hr 30min, €19), daily at 2.30pm; departure from Bahnhofplatz (in front of Hertie department store), all tours accompanied by a guide. Tickets also available from hotels.

Finding your Way

The most animated part of the city is concentrated in the pedestrian precincts of Neuhauser Straße and Kaufingerstraße, between Karlsplatz (or "Stachus") and Marienplatz. Elegant boutiques are mainly to be found in Maffeistraße, Pacellistraße, Maximilianstraße and Brienner Straße; antique dealers in Ottostraße near Maximilianplatz; art galleries under the arcades of Hofgartenstraße. The Schwabing quarter *(via Ludwigstraße)*, deployed around Leopoldstraße, enjoyed its hour of glory as the city's artistic and intellectual hub at the turn of the 20C – but with its boutiques, its pavement cafés and its night-spots remains one of the most brilliant and lively after-dark centres in Germany.

Regional Specialities

The most famous local specialities include the white sausages known as *Weißwurst*, roast knuckle of pork *(Schweinshaxe)* and *Leberkäs*, a meat and offal pâté which can be bought hot any time after 11am. At the beer festivals, a favourite offering is *Steckerlfisch*, small fish grilled on a skewer. *Bretzels*, *Salzstangen* (small salt rolls) and white radishes *(Radi)* are often served with beer.

Munich is also the capital of beer: Five and a half million hectolitres – 110 000 000 gallons – of beer are brewed here every year, most of it being drunk in the beer cellars, taverns and beer gardens *(Biergarten)* of the town itself.

Dates for your Diary

The origins of the famous early autumn *Oktoberfest*, which is held on the **Theresienwiese** *(via Mozartstraße)*, go back to the marriage of the heir to the throne, Prince Ludwig (future Ludwig I of Bavaria), and Princess Theresa in 1810. Around six and a half million visitors flock to Munich each year for this gigantic public fair, from the second last Saturday in September to the first Sunday in October.

Although there are parades through the streets of the city during the first two days, the festivities mainly involve a big booze-up; under canvas marquees and in stands ranged around the base of a huge statue representing Bavaria, around five million tankards of *Wiesenbier* – a beer specially brewed for the occasion and delivered in the old style by horse-drawn drays – are served. The party is complemented by roasts of poultry and beef (two entire oxen are cooked on a spit each day). The hotels are all full at this time of year, so it is advisable to book a year in advance.

The **Fasching** carnival is celebrated with high spirits and much merriment and ends with the traditional dance of the market women at the Viktualienmarkt. The religious festival of Corpus Christi *(Fronleichnam)* involves a procession of clergy and members of the religious orders, Roman Catholic personalities, Catholic student organisations and representatives of the various city guilds through beflagged streets garlanded with branches of young birch trees.

Other festivals include *Starkbierzeit* (Stark beer festival) in March; *Auer Dult* (local festival) from late April to early May, late July and mid October; *TollWood Sommerfestival* (music and theatre) from mid June to mid July and in December; *Opernfestspiele* (opera festival) in July; and the *Christkindlmarkt* (Christmas market) in December.

All the cultural activities in Munich (exhibitions, concerts, theatre, cinemas) are listed in two monthly publications: *Offizielles Monatsprogramm* (in German, €1.55) and *Munich Found* (in English, €3), both available from the tourist information office.

A very big flower show is due to be held on the site of the former Riem airport in 2005. Munich is also set to host the opening match of the Football World Cup in June 2006, which will be a major event for the entire country.

Where to Eat

⊖ **Metzgerbräu** – *Klammergasse 4 – 83646 Bad Tölz – ☎ (08041) 706 11 – www.augustiner-wirtschaft.de – closed Thu – ⊭ – €10/25.* An introduction to the Bavarian way of life. Rustic decor and a large choice of traditional dishes, including calf's head, tripe and oxtail.

Dürnbräu – *Dürnbräugasse 2 – ☎ (089) 22 21 95 – €10.70/17.* A brasserie-style establishment in a little street near the city centre. Dark wood and long tables give the room a very rustic look. In summer, patrons can make the most of the terrace in front of the restaurant and the little garden in the inner courtyard.

Karawanserei – *Pettenkoferstraße 1 – ☎ (089) 54 54 19 54 – www.karawanserei-muenchen.de – open 11.30am-3pm et 5pm-midnight – Reservation required – €15.90/24.90.* An oriental-sounding name for this Persian restaurant in a little palace in the city centre. Persian cuisine and decor.

Gasthaus zur Alten Schule – *Rathausstraße 3 – 82194 Olching-Gröbenzell – ☎ (08142) 50 46 60 – closed Mon – ♿ – reservation necessary – €18.90/27.50.* As its name suggests, this simple restaurant opposite the town hall is set in an old school *(alte Schule)*. Meals are served in what was once the classroom, in a well-kept, rustic setting. In summer you can also enjoy the garden.

Lenbach – *Ottostraße 6 – ☎ (089) 549 13 00 – info@lenbach.de – closed Sun – €30.50/48.50.* The interior design of this restaurant in the Lenbach palace is the work of the famous designer Sir Terence Conran. The concept: modern cuisine on a vast scale – the restaurant covers a surface area of 2 200m²/2 630yd²! A glass walkway with a splendid stuccoed ceiling leads to the restaurant.

Käfer Schänke – *Prinzregentenstraße 73 – 81675 München-Bogenhausen – ☎ (089) 416 82 47 – kaeferschaenke@feinkost-kaefer.de – closed Sun and public holidays – €35/52.* A pleasant restaurant with small, variously decorated rooms: the Meissen room, for example, is adorned with around 300 pieces of porcelain. The establishment also has a large delicatessen.

Bogenhauser Hof – *Ismaninger Straße 85 – 81675 München-Bogenhausen – ☎ (089) 9855 86 – bogenhauser-hof@t-online.de – closed 24 Dec-8 Jan, Sun and public holidays – €41.50/60.* This former henting lodge dating from 1825 is now a traditional gourmet restaurant. In an elegant decor – or an idyllic summer garden – attentive waiters serve delicious classic cuisine.

Tantris – *Johann-Fichte-Straße 7 – 80805 München-Schwabing – ☎ (089) 361 95 90 – tantris@t-online.de – closed 1 week in Jan, Sun-Mon and public holidays – €55/89.* Guarded by mythical monsters, this temple of delight with its predominantly avant-garde decoration in black and orange is the best gourmet restaurant in Munich. Hans Haas charms the palate with his classical and innovative dishes.

Nationaltheater

R. Chéret/MICHELIN

Where to Stay

Hotel Lutter – *Eversbuschstraße 109, 80999 München-Allach – ☎ (089) 812 70 04 – Fax (089) 8129584 – hotel-lutter@t-online.de – closed 20 Dec-7 Jan – P – 26rm: €67/82.* A very well-run hotel in the northwest of Munich, providing cheap accommodation. The rooms are functional and breakfast is served in a very bright and charming winter garden.

Hotel Uhland – *Uhlandstraße 1 – ☎ (089) 54 33 50 – Fax (089) 54335250 – info@hotel-uhland.de – P – 25rm: €72/165.* This hotel with its hundred-year-old neo-Renaissance façade in a leafy residential quarter along the Theresienwiese has rooms to suit all tastes, some with modern water beds, some with rustic furniture.

Hotel Schlicker – *Tal 8 – ☎ (089) 242 88 70 – Fax (089) 296059 – schlicker-munich@t-online.de – closed 23 Dec-7 Jan – P – 69rm: €78/180.* In the heart of the old town, this hotel set in a 16C building offers personalised rooms, some of them with great style. View of the new town hall *(Neues Rathaus)* and its world-famous carillon.

Müller – *Fliegenstraße 4 – ☎ (089) 232 38 60 – Fax (089) 268624 – closed 23 Dec- 6 Jan – P – 44rm: €79/109.* A hotel with refurbished rooms, attentive service and a pleasant setting, located near the Sendlinger Tor, directly opposite Matthäuskirche.

Drei Löwen Hotel – *Schillerstraße 8 – ☎ (089) 55 10 40 – Fax (089) 55104905 – hotel-drei-loewen-muc@t-online.de – 97rm: from €105.* A welcoming hotel in the heart of the city centre, near the main railway station *(Hauptbahnhof)*. Access through a vast panelled lobby with plenty of seats. The rooms are bright with modern furnishings.

Hotel Platzl – *Sparkassenstraße 10 – ☎ (089) 23 70 30 – Fax (089) 23703800 – info@platzl.de – ♿ – 167rm: from €106.* Comfortable rooms in traditional Bavarian style – right in the heart of the historic old town: Marienplatz with its famous carillon and the food market *(Viktualienmarkt)* can be easily reached on foot. The vaulting of the Pfistermühle restaurant gives the place an air of "old Munich", while the smart Ayingers restaurant is more in the bistro-style.

Hotel Bayerischer Hof – *Promenadenplatz 2 – ☎ (089) 212 00 – Fax (089) 2120906 – info@bayerischerhof.de – – 395rm: from €150 – €21.* A luxurious, traditional grand hotel with personalised rooms (rustic, nostalgic or modern) and a remarkable function room. The elegant Garden-Restaurant serves gastronomic specialities and you can enjoy a South Pacific ambience in the Trader Vic's. The Palais Keller is also part of this establishment.

Mandarin Oriental Hotel – *Neuturmstraße 1 – ☎ (089) 29 09 80 – Fax (089) 222539 – momuc-reservation@mohg.com – 73rm: from €280 – €24.* This luxury hotel has retained the past splendour of the temple of dance it once was. The view from the covered terrace with swimming pool stretches as far as the Alps. A marble staircase leads to the elegant Mark's restaurant.

Taking a Break

Café Arzmiller – *Theatinerstraße 22 – ☎ (089) 29 42 73 – 8.30am-6.30pm.* A good place to relax and forget the stress of the city. Coffee, cakes and dishes of the day are served in the lovely, peaceful Theatinerhof. The house speciality, *Strudel*, is definitely not to be missed.

Café Luitpold Palmengarten – *Brienner Straße 11 – ☎ (089) 29 28 65 – www.cafe-luitpold.de – Mon-Fri 9am-8pm, Sat 9am-7pm, closed Sun and public holidays.* Over the year, this café offers a choice of more than 300 different tarts. The house speciality is, of course, Luitpold tart, which can be sampled under the glass dome in the palm-filled inner courtyard or on the terrace on Maximilianplatz and in Brienner Straße.

Confiserie Rottenhöfer – *Residenzstraße 25/26 – ☎ (089) 22 29 15 – www.rottenhoefer.de – Mon-Fri 8.45am-7pm, Sat 8am-6pm, closed Sun and public holidays.* Boutique (over 160 kinds of chocolates) and tea room on the ground floor, non-smoking room upstairs. Founded in 1825, this shop was once official supplier to the kings of Bavaria.

Arzmiller café and confectioner's

M. Hertlein/MICHELIN

Viktualienmarkt – *Viktualienmarkt – ☎ (089) 23 32 34 73 – www.viktualienmarkt.de – Mon-Fri 10am-6pm, Sat 10am-3pm.* This traditional market dates back to 1807 and offers a wide variety of goods, including beer, wine, sausages and oysters. The beer garden in the centre is very popular in good weather.

Going Out

Useful Tips – Beer gardens are an integral part of life in Bavaria, especially in Munich. Many of these shaded gardens and terraces are open even in winter; the slightest ray of sunshine will bring the regulars flocking to the wooden tables. Although the prices are rather high and the service limited or non-existent (often self-service), people come here to enjoy the unique atmosphere. Munich's café and bar scene is not concentrated only in the old town. The best-known area for spending leisure time is Schwabing. Around the university there is a plethora of student bars, and along Leopoldstraße south of Münchner Freiheit a range of smarter establishments where people go to "see and be seen". Other parts of town which offer a good evening out are Haidhausen (around Pariser and Weißenburger Platz) and the area around Gärtnerplatz. For online information: www.where2go.de, www.nightlife-munich.de

Alter Simpl – *Türkenstraße 57 – ☎ (089) 2 72 30 83 – www.altersimpl.de – Sun-Thu 11am-3am, Fri-Sat 11am-4am.* This laid-back bar with its partly stuccoed ceilings has been a student haunt for over one hundred years. Mainly Bavarian specialities served here (up to 1hr before closing time).

Brasserie Tresznjewski – *Theresienstraße 72 – ☎ (089) 28 23 49 – www.tresznjewski.de – Sun-Thu 8am-3am, Fri-Sat 8am-4am.* Opposite the Neue Pinakothek, this smart, tastefully decorated restaurant offers a wide choice of hot and cold drinks as well as Mediterranean-style cuisine.

Hirschgarten – *Hirschgarten 1 – Tram 16, 17 Romanplatz (then go down Guntherstraße) – ☎ (089) 17 25 91 – www.hirschgarten.de – 9am-midnight (beer garden from Mar to Oct).* This beer garden (with rustic restaurant next door) near Schloß Nymphenburg is probably the biggest one in Munich, and even in Bavaria. 8 000 seats outside including 1 200 with table service.

Hofbräuhaus – *Am Platzl 9 – ☎ (089) 2 90 13 60 – www.hofbraeuhaus.de – Sun-Thu 9am-midnight, Fri-Sat 9am-1.30am (1st-floor restaurant until 11.30pm).* This place is so famous that it attracts rather too many tourists, but its unique atmosphere makes it really worth a visit. Music (wind instruments) in the ever noisy *Schwemme* on the ground floor *(Mon-Fri 12-4pm and 6-11pm, Sat-Sun 11.30am-3pm and 6-11pm).* It is quieter on the first floor *(Trinkstube, music 6-11.30pm)* and in the beer garden in the inner courtyard.

L-Opera – *Maximilianstraße 2 – ☎ (089) 54 44 46 44 – www.l-opera.de – 8am-1am.* Opposite the Residenz, under the arcades of a 19C building with Pompeiian paintings, this place is open all year round (heating in winter) from breakfast time to late at night. An ideal spot to watch the comings and goings on one of Munich's most beautiful squares.

Seehaus – *Kleinhesselohe 3 (in the Englischer Garten) – Tram Münchner Freiheit (then follow Haidhauser Straße) – ☎ (089) 3 81 61 30 – www.kuffler-gastronomie.de – Beer garden, weather permitting 11am-midnight, restaurant 11.30am-midnight.* A dream location for this idyllic beer garden (self-service) and restaurant, on the shores of Lake Kleinhesselohe in the English Garden. Boat hire nearby.

R. Chéret/MICHELIN

Maypole at the Viktualienmarkt.

Culture

Useful Tips – You will find all the necessary information in the monthly programme "München im..." (followed by the month) published by the tourist office and available from its offices or from kiosks. This programme is also in the monthly magazines "Go!" and "Prinz", on sale in kiosks and bookshops. Every Thursday, the "SZ-extra" supplement of the "Süddeutsche Zeitung" newspaper gives details of various cultural events. The free listings magazine "In" is available at locations throughout the city.
Internet sites: www.muenchenticket.de, www.ticketbox.de, www.muenchenbeinacht.de, www.prinz.de, www.kunstpark.de

Shopping

Useful Tips – Many consider Munich to be Germany's best city by far for shopping. The old town has numerous shopping arcades and boutiques to cater for all budgets. *Beck am Rathauseck* and other department stores are located between Marienplatz and Stachus. Another good shopping district is Schwabing (on and to the west of Leopoldstraße). Exclusive boutiques are to be found in Residenzstraße, Brienner Straße and Maximilianstraße.
There is also the *Fünf Höfe* shopping centre in stylish Theatinerstraße.

Art galleries – Most of Munich's galleries are in Maximilianstraße and the nearby streets, also in Residenzstraße and on Odeonsplatz. In the old artists' district of Schwabing, the most interesting streets in this respect are Türken-, Schelling- and Franz-Joseph-Straße.

Antiques – Munich covers the whole range from elegant, exclusive antique dealers' establishments to inexpensive bric-à-brac shops. Schwabing boasts a wealth of antique shops in Amalien-, Türken-, Barer-, Kurfürsten- and Hohenzollernstraße, as does the city centre around Maximiliansplatz, Lenbachplatz and Promenadenplatz.

Background

The Foundation of the Town – A small village founded in the 9C near a Benedictine abbey identified itself by taking the name of the monks – in German Mönch, in Old High German Munich. Ever since, the town's emblem has been a little monk *(Münchner Kindl)*.

In 1156 Emperor Frederick I Barbarossa ceded a part of Bavaria to Henry the Lion, Duke of Saxony. Two years later, the duke decided to take for himself the salt trade taxes formerly levied by the bishop of Freising, and to this end destroyed the bridge, warehouse and customs building set up 9.5km/6mi from the town. He then built a new bridge over which traders had to pass, forcing all commercial transactions into the town. The stratagem, subsequently legalised by Barbarossa, proved to be the beginning of a long and flourishing history for Munich, which until then had been no more than a cluster of unimportant houses.

The Rise of the Wittelsbachs – In 1180 Henry the Lion was stripped of his titles and banished from his lands in southern Germany. Barbarossa replaced him with the Palatine count Otto von Wittelsbach, and from then on that house became closely linked with Bavaria. In 1225 Munich became the ducal seat. In 1314 one of the dukes, Ludwig the Bavarian, became King of Germany, and then Emperor (1328). After the demise of the Wittelsbachs of Landshut in 1503, Munich was created the sole capital of the Bavarian duchy, rivalling as a trade centre both Augsburg and Nuremberg.

In 1623, Duke Maximilian I exercised the function of prince-elector and made the town, during the turbulence of the Thirty Years' War, the bastion of German Catholicism.

The Kings of Bavaria – Max Joseph (1799-1825, Elector until 1806), who had at first remained neutral in the conflict opposing Napoleon and the European coalition, finally took sides with Napoleon – a ploy which rewarded him in 1806 with the crown of Bavaria under the name of Maximilian I. Despite the Napoleonic Wars, in which large numbers of Bavarian troops were involved, Munich continued to flourish, embellished now with monuments in the Classical style, such as the palace of Prince Karl and the buildings of Karolinenplatz and Brienner Straße.

Maximilian's son, **Ludwig I** (1825-48), a great admirer of Classical Antiquity, welcomed to his court the best of Europe's architects (Leo von Klenze), painters and sculptors. In his desire to make his capital the most beautiful in Europe, he enriched the city with the Alte and the Neue Pinakothek, the university, the Glyptothek and the Propylaea. He cut a swathe through the old town with the construction of Ludwigstraße and had the ducal residence greatly enlarged. But in 1848, faced with a rebel movement provoked by the scandal of his liaison with the Spanish dancer Lola Montez, he was obliged to abdicate in favour of his son, Maximilian. A younger son, Otto, had already become King of Greece (1832).

Maximilian II (1848-64) continued the artistic traditions of his father, founding in 1855 the Bavarian National Museum.

In the history of the Wittelsbach dynasty, a special place must be reserved for **Ludwig II** (1864-86). This tormented romantic, a passionate admirer of Wagner, succeeded to the throne at the age of 18. Beloved by his subjects, he was nevertheless restless and unpredictable, a young man prey to extreme depression – especially in the face of political setbacks. After his disastrous choice of an alliance with Austria (their combined armies were beaten by the Prussians at Sadowa in 1866), he switched sides a year later and supported the proclamation of Prussia's Wilhelm I as Emperor of all Germany. But the young ruler, craving solitude and living in a fantasy world, largely withdrew from his court and built himself the three extravagant and isolated castles of Neuschwanstein, Linderhof and Herrenchiemsee. Mentally unstable, Ludwig II (whose tragic life has been the subject of books and films) was deposed in 1886 and confined to Schloß Berg, on the shores of Lake Starnberg. He was found drowned there shortly afterwards.

In the absence of a direct heir – and in face of the fact that the younger brother Otto, the King of Greece, was also mentally ill – the son of Ludwig I, **Prince Luitpold**, assumed the Regency. An able and inventive man, always open to new ideas, the Regent improved the Bavarian capital with a zoological garden, an ethnographic museum, a new town hall, the German Museum and the impressive avenue named after him, Prinzregentenstraße. His son, crowned as Ludwig III (1912-18), was the last king of Bavaria: under pressure from a workers' revolutionary movement after the defeat of Germany in the First World War, he was forced to abdicate.

In Between Two Wars – The months following the cessation of hostilities were turbulent with strife, nowhere more so than Munich. In February 1919 **Kurt Eisner**, the social democrat Bavarian President, was assassinated. A month earlier, **Adolf Hitler**'s German Workers' party had been formed and its aims announced by the leader at the Munich Hofbräuhaus. Meanwhile, a republican Council of State had been proclaimed, only to be annihilated by Imperial troops in May of the same year.

In 1923, Hitler and Ludendorff fomented a popular uprising (the Munich Putsch), but it was unsuccessful, the party was dissolved and Hitler imprisoned. Released before the sentence had run its term, he reorganised the group as the National Socialist (Nazi) Party. After he had become Chancellor, it was Munich that Hitler chose in 1938 for the notorious meeting with Chamberlain, Daladier and Mussolini at which the annexation by Germany of the Sudetenland was agreed.

"Simplicissimus"

A satirical literary journal created in Munich in 1896, *Simplicissimus* rapidly became famous throughout Germany for its caricatures and audacity. Writers such as Thomas Mann and Frank Wedekind took an active part in it, as did some avant-garde and Expressionist artists. In the 1930s, the Nazis took over this weekly publication and turned it into an instrument of propaganda. It disappeared along with the Nazis in 1945.

Munich today – After being heavily bombed during the war, Munich rapidly got back on its feet and became the most important economic zone in southern Germany. Large industrial companies (Siemens, BMW) set up their headquarters in the city, congress-goers and tourists flocked there, and modern buildings – including two new art galleries – were built. The stadium built for the 20th summer Olympic Games now hosts the matches of the famous Bayern Munich team. In recent years, the industrial high-technology sectors have undergone rapid growth.

MÜNCHEN

Am Gasteig .... LZ 4
Amiraplatz .... KY 6
An der Hauptfeuerwache .... JZ 7
Beethovenstraße .... JZ 20
Brienner Straße .... JKY
Burgstraße .... KZ 30
Damenstiftstraße .... JZ 32
Dienerstraße .... KZ 36
Eisenmannstraße .... KZ 39
Franz-Joseph-Strauß-Ring .... LY 50
Hofgraben .... KZ 75
Innere Wiener Straße .... LZ 79
Kardinal-Faulhaber-Straße .... KY 88
Karlsplatz (Stachus) .... JY 91
Kaufingerstraße .... KZ
Ledererstraße .... KZ 100
Lenbachplatz .... KY 101
Lerchenfeldstraße .... LY 102
Maffeistraße .... KY 106
Marienplatz .... KZ
Maximiliansbrücke .... LZ 119
Maximiliansplatz .... KY 121
Maximilianstraße .... KYZ
Max-Joseph-Platz .... KY 125
Max-Joseph-Straße .... KY 127
Mozartstraße .... JY 138
Neuhauser Straße .... JZ 147
Oettingenstraße .... LY 151
Orlandostraße .... KZ 157
Pacellistraße .... KY 160
Papa-Schmid-Straße .... KZ 162
Pfisterstraße .... KZ 164
Platzl .... KZ 165
Prinzregentenstraße .... LY 170
Promenadeplatz .... KY 171
Residenzstraße .... KY 177
Rindermarkt .... KZ 179
Rosenstraße .... KZ 182
Salvatorstraße .... KY 184
Schleißheimer Straße .... JY 192
Sendlinger Straße .... KZ
Sendlinger-Tor-Platz .... JZ 194
Sonnenstraße .... JZ
Sternstraße .... LZ 202
Theatinerstraße .... KY 206
Triftstraße .... LY 214
Veterinärstraße .... LY 221
Wagmüllerstraße .... LY 224
Weinstraße .... KZ 228
Wittelsbacherstraße .... KZ 231

Alter Hof .... KZ N
Antikensammlungen JY M3
Bayerisches Nationalmuseum .. LY M5
Deutsches Jagd-und Fischereimuseum . KZ M1
Erzbischöfliches Palais .... KY Y
Feldherrnhalle ...... KY S
Glyptothek .... JY M2
Heiliggeistkirche .... KZ F
Michaelskirche ..... KZ B
Münchner Stadtmuseum ..... KZ M7
Neues Rathaus ..... KZ R
Palais Portia .... KY Z
Peterskirche .... KZ E
Richard-Strauss-Brunnen .... KZ A
Städtische Galerie Im Lenbachhaus .. JY M4
Theatinerkirche ..... KY V
Viktualienmarkt ..... KZ Q
Völkerkundemuseum LZ M8
Weinstadl .... KZ K

Special Features

ART COLLECTIONS★★★

The state of Bavaria's three art galleries together house a highly impressive and very comprehensive collection. The *Alte Pinakothek* (from the Middle Ages to the 18C), the *Neue Pinakothek* (19C works) and the new *Pinakothek der Moderne* (modern works) offer an all-encompassing overview of European painting, with an impressive number of masterpieces. *A combined ticket allows entry to the three art galleries in one day for €12; however, considering the size of the collections, it is advisable to spread your visit over several days.*

Alte Pinakothek★★★ *3hr*

♿ *Open every day except Mon, 10am-5pm; Tue 10am-8pm. Closed 1st Jan, Shrove Tuesday, Easter Sun, 1st May, 24, 25 and 31 Dec €5, free admission on Sundays. Plan available at the entrance, free audio guide recommended. ☎ (089) 23 80 52 16.*

The **Alte Pinakothek**, a colossal building destined to house the collections of paintings amassed by the House of Wittelsbach, was built between 1826 and 1836 by the architect Leo von Klenze, in the Venetian Renaissance style.

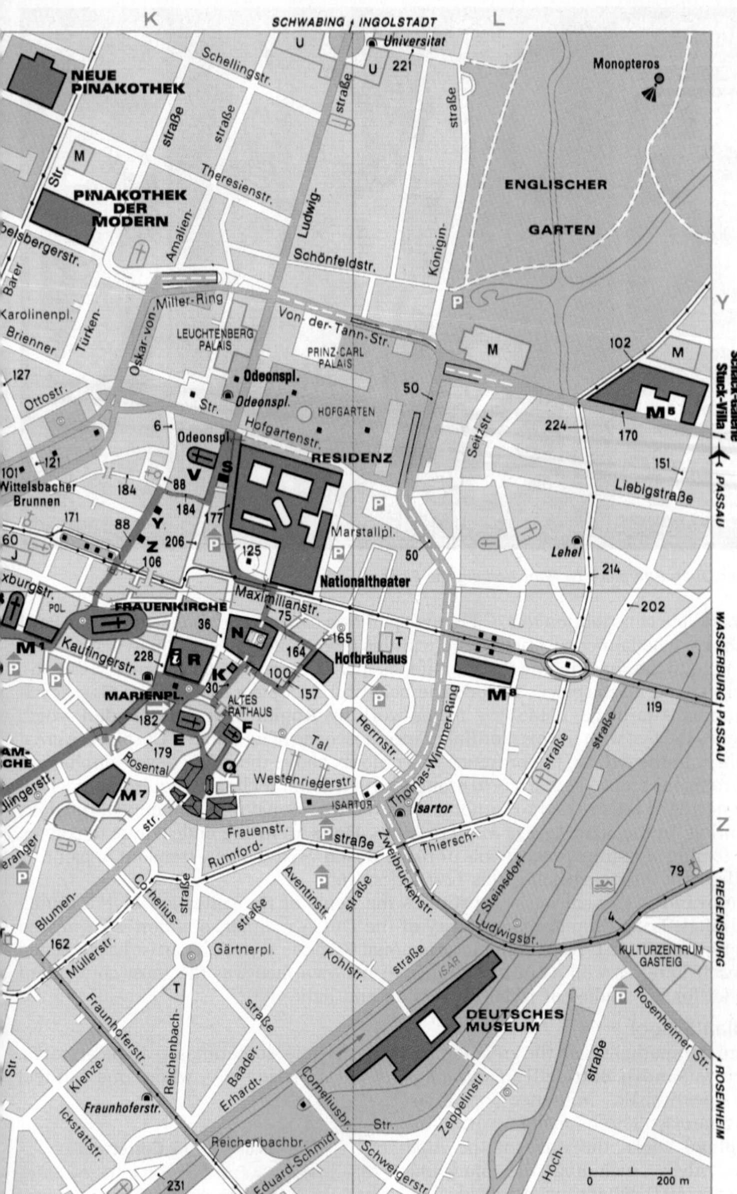

German School

The section devoted to German Primitives is the Pinakothek**'s** most extensive one, thanks to the Wittelsbach's policy of systematic acquisition. Alongside sacred 15C paintings illustrating the Late Gothic style are works by the painters who brought the Renaissance north of the Alps. The most outstanding works include **Albrecht Dürer**'s *Four Apostles* (1526), where the boldness of the composition and the voluminous robes make the subjects both accessible and imposing. **Albrecht Atldorfer's** *Landscape* (1528), shows for the first time a landscape with no human figures, ie a painting whose sole subject is nature. The themes remain religious in general, but the treatment of costume is more modern, as in **Hans Holbein the Elder**'s *St Sebastian Altarpiece* (1516). Other painters, such as those from the Cologne School, learnt the new techniques of spatial representation around the main figure but stuck with the classic fashion for Gothic religious images against a gold background.

Dutch and Flemish Schools

The Land of Milk and Honey (1566) by **Pieter Bruegel the Elder**, painter of country scenes, depicts three representatives from different social classes after feasting together. Besides the many paintings by **Sir Anthony Van Dyck**, the most

Bayerische Staatsgemäldesammlung, Alte Pinakothek Münich

St Sebastian Altarpiece by Hans Holbein the Elder.

remarkable contribution to 17C Flemish painting came from his master, **Peter Paul Rubens**, who launched a new trend with his large paintings with many figures and his unique gift for bringing them to life, as in *The Great Last Judgement* (c 1614-16). Early Dutch masterpieces include the beautiful *Altarpiece of the Three Magi* (or St Columba Altarpiece, c 1455), a major work by **Rogier Van der Weyden** which catches the eye with the extraordinary luminescence of its colours. Despite the great realism in the details, the presence of a crucifix above the infant Jesus emphasises the religious scene. This art form brought with it a new technical requirement which the northern artists tried to combine with the traditional requirements of religious painting. In the *Seven Joys of Mary* (c 1480), **Hans Memling** endeavours to convey the feeling of omnipotence, while **Jérôme Bosch** used the new freedom in painting to depict a terrifying hell in his *Last Judgement*.

Rembrandt's Passion cycle constitutes the heart of the collection of 17C Dutch paintings; here, despite the austerity of the Dutch manner, emotion is expressed in grand gestures typical of the international Baroque style. The artist has depicted himself here, as well as in a self-portrait; his own face was the most convenient model for his studies of facial expression and light.

Italian School

Here the spotlight is on the great Renaissance masters, sometimes in atypical works, such as **Sandro Botticelli**'s *Lamentation of Christ* (post 1490), where one can feel the pessimistic influence of Friar Savonarola. Three major works by **Raphael** adorn the walls of the Alte Pinakothek, including the *Madonna Tempi* (1507), where the artist's ideal of beauty appears to be very human: it is more mother and son than the Virgin and Child of his predecessors.

The Wittelsbachs show a consistent interest in Venetian painting. *The Crowning of Thorns* (1560) by **Titian** – the most famous painter of Venice – demonstrates his characteristic creation of colour and light by seemingly rough and scintillating touches. Two centuries later, the Venetian School is back in the limelight with the increasing complexity and originality of the Baroque style, as illustrated by two typical examples of **Tiepolo**'s work: the *Veneration of the Holy Trinity by Pope Clemens* (1739) and the *Adoration of the Magi* (1753). Fine works by **Antonio Canaletto** and **Francesco Guardi** celebrate the art of the Venetian *vedutisti* (urban landscape painters).

The Origins of the Collection

The collection was started in the 16C by Duke Wilhelm IV, who commissioned historical scenes from the most eminent painters of his time, Altdorfer and Burgkmair. In the 17C, the Elector Maximilian I founded the Kammergalerie which, under King Ludwig I, developed into the finest exhibition of art in the whole of Europe. The building suffered severe damage in 1943, but the paintings had already been moved to a safe location.

French School

French classicism is illustrated by great landscape painter **Claude Lorrain**'s *Sea Port at Sunrise* (1674) and paintings by **Nicolas Poussin**, who takes his subjects from Ovid's *Metamorphoses* (1627). Among the 18C painters, François Boucher's *Madame*

Pompadour is on display, executed at her request – and by her favourite painter – in 1756. The sensual *Nude Lying on a Sofa* (1752), another work by Boucher, was very fashionable during the Rococo period.

Spanish School

This school is notably represented by **Murillo**'s lively genre paintings; the Alte Pinakothek alone has no less than five of them.

The museum's major works

	First Floor
Galleries I and IIa Dutch Primitives	Rogier Van der Weyden: *Altarpiece of the Three Magi, St Luke drawing the Madonna.* Dirck Bouts: *Imprisonment and Resurrection of Christ.* Hans Memling: *Seven Joys of Mary.*
Galleries II, IIb and III German Primitives	Albrecht Dürer: *Self-portrait in Fur Coat, Lamentation of Christ, Four Apostles, Portrait of Oswolt Krel.* Hans Holbein the Elder: *St Sebastian Altarpiece.* Lucas Cranach the Elder: *The Crucifixion, Suicide of Lucretia, The Golden Age.* Albrecht Altdorfer: *Susanna Bathing, Landscape, Virgin Mary and Child in Glory, Battle of Alexander.* Mathias Grünewald: *St Erasmus and St Mauritius, Mocking of Christ.*
Galleries IV and V 15C and 16C Italian Painting	Sandro Botticelli**:** *Lamentation of Christ.* Ghirlandaio: *High altar from Santa Maria Novella in Florence.* Raphael: *Madonna Tempi, Holy Family from the Canigiani House, Madonna della Tenda.* Leonardo da Vinci: *Madonna and Child.* Veronese: *Cupid with two Hounds, Portrait of a Lady.* Tintoretto: *Vulcan surprising Venus and Mars.* Titian: *Crowning of Thorns, Madonna and Child in an Evening Landscape.*
Rooms 1-6 14C-17C Italian Painting	Fra Angelico: Four small-format predella paintings. Jacopo de Barbari: *Still-life with Partridge.* Fra Filippo Lippi: *Virgin Mary and Child.* Tintoretto: *Portrait of a Sculptor.* Johann Liss: *Death of Cleopatra.*
Galleries VI-VIII 17C Flemish Painting	Anthony van Dyck: *St Sebastian, Susanna Bathing, Rest on the Flight to Egypt.* Jacob Jordaens: *Allegory of Fertility, Satyr and Peasant.* Peter Paul Rubens: *Self-portrait with Isabella Brant in a Honeysuckle Bower, The Great Last Judgement, Hunt Scene with Hippopotamuses and Crocodiles, Drunken Silenus, Hélène Fourment in her Wedding Dress, Descent into Hell, Massacre of the Innocents at Bethlehem.* Jacques d'Arthois: *Woodland Path, Canal through Woods, Ford in Woods.*
Rooms 7-12 17C Flemish Painting	Anthony van Dyck: *Lamentation of Christ, Self-portrait as a Young Man.*Peter Paul Rubens: *Hélène Fourment putting on a Glove,* the Medici cycle and *The Small Last Judgement.* Adriaen Brouwer: series of small-format peasant scenes. David Teniers the Younger**:** genre paintings.
Room 13 16C and 17C German Painting	Adam Elsheimer, *Flight into Egypt.* Johann Rottenhammer, *Victory of Truth* and *Birth of Christ.*
Gallery IX 17C Dutch Painting	Rembrandt: *Portrait of a Man in Oriental Costume, The Holy Family, Sacrifice of Isaac.* Ferdinand Bol: *Leaders of the Amsterdam Wine Merchants' Guild.* Frans Hals: his only full-length portrait, *Willem van Heythuyzen.*
Rooms 14-23 17C Dutch Painting	Rembrandt**:** *Self-portrait*, Passion cycle. Willem van de Velde: *Calm Sea.* Gerard ter Borch: *Portrait of a Gentleman and a Lady, Boy whipping his Dog* (c 1655). Jacob van Ruisdael: *Sand Dunes*, painted when he was about 18 or 19 years old. Gabriel Metsu: *The Cook, Bean Feast,* two genre scenes. Jan Davidsz de Heem: Vanitas still-life painting full of hidden symbolism.

Galleries X and XIIb 17C and 18C Italian Painting	Giovanni Battista Tiepolo: *Veneration of the Holy Trinity by Pope Clemens, Adoration of the Magi.* Guido Reni: *Ascension of the Blessed Virgin Mary.*
Galleries XI-XIIa 17C and 18C French Painting	Claude Lorrain: *Sea Port at Sunrise.* Nicolas Poussin: *Midas and Bacchus, The Lamentation over Christ.* François Boucher: *Portrait of Madame Pompadour, Nude Lying on a Sofa*; *Rural Idyll* is typical of Boucher's landscape painting. Hubert Robert: *Landscape with Roman Temple Ruin.* Maurice Quentin de La Tour: *Abbé Nollet, Mademoiselle Ferrand* Jean-Étienne Liotard: *Breakfast*, a very realistic painting for the time.
Gallery XIII Spanish Painting	El Greco: *Stripping of Christ.* Velázquez: *Young Spaniard.* Bartolomé Esteban Murillo: *Grape and Watermelon Eater.*
	Ground Floor
Galleries I-III German Primitives	Hans Pleidenwurff: the *Hofer Altarpiece*, a landscape stretching over four panels. Hans Baldung Grien: *Palatine Count Philip the Warlike.* Lucas Cranach the Elder: *St Anne, Virgin and Child* (c 1516), *Adam and Eve.* Bernhard Strigel: *Hans Funk Diptych, Sleeping Grave Attendants.* Hans Holbein the Elder: *Kaisheimer Altarpiece.* Martin Schaffner: *Wettenhausen Altarpiece.*
Rooms 1-9 Primitives from the Cologne School	Bartholomäus Bruyn the Elder: *Crucifixion Altarpiece.* Stefan Lochner: outer panels of the *Last Judgement Altarpiece, Virgin Mary and Child in front of a Grassy Bank, Adoration of the Child by Mary.* Martin Schongauer: *The Holy Family.*
Rooms 16-23 The Bruegel Family	Pieter Bruegel the Elder: *The Land of Milk and Honey.* Jan Bruegel the Elder: *Bouquet of Flowers, Large Fish Market, Fish Market on the Bank of a River, Sea Port with the Sermon of Christ.*

Galleries **XI-XIII** are reserved for temporary exhibitions.

Neue Pinakothek★★ *2hr*

♿ *Open every day except Tue, 10am-5pm; Wed-Thu 10am-10pm. Closed 1st Jan, Shrove Tuesday, Easter Sunday, 1st May, 24, 25 and 31 Dec. €5. Free admission on Sundays. Plan available at the entrance, free audio guide recommended. ☎ (089) 23 80 51 95. www.neue-pinakothek.de*

The Post-Modernist style **Neue Pinakothek** building, completed in 1981 and faced with light sandstone, was designed by Alexander von Brancas. This well-proportioned construction with charming light effects replaces the building erected under Ludwig I, which had to be demolished due to serious war damage.

Early 19C

Galleries **1, 2 and 2a** are devoted to international art c 1800. **Thomas Gainsborough**'s portraits and landscapes are characterised by delicate colour tones and a return to nature inspired by the enlightened philosophers; **Jacques-Louis David** painted the *Marquise de Sorcy* without the usual constraints of representation of rank, and works by **Joshua Reynolds** *(Captain Pownall)*, **William Turner** *(Ostend)* and **Francisco Goya** (*Marquesa de Caballero*, 1807) are also on display.

German painters from the first half of the 19C

On display in Galleries **3 and 3a** are early Romantic works from Dresden, Berlin and Munich, with highly spiritual symbolic landscapes by **Caspar David Friedrich** and other paintings with contrasting light effects and exotic, undulating scenery: Johann Christian Dahl (*Frederiksholm Canal in Copenhagen*, 1817), Karl Blechen (*View of Assisi*, 1830). Ludwig I of Bavaria was a great patron of the arts who commissioned many paintings, including those on display in Galleries **4 and 4a:** his son Otto arriving in Greece was immortalised by Peter von Hess and there is also a famous portrait of the great German poet, Johann Wolfgang von Goethe, painted **in** 1828 by **Joseph Karl Stieler**, who is known mainly for the captivating portraits in the "Gallery of Beauties" in Schloß Nymphenburg. Galleries **5 and 5a** are devoted to the German neo-Classicists in Rome, including a very well-known landscape by **Ludwig Richter**, *The Night-Watchman* (*Watzmann*, 1824), which endeavours to express the joyous communion of man and nature. This artist also produced the four large paintings of the *View of Rome from Villa Malta* (between 1829 and 1835), transporting the visitor to Italy for the space of a gallery.

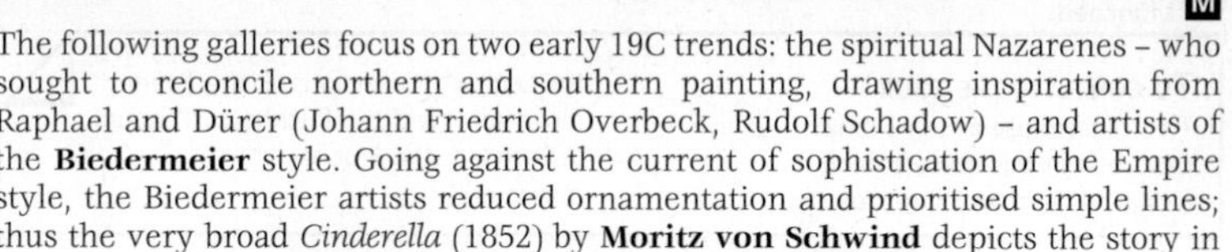

The following galleries focus on two early 19C trends: the spiritual Nazarenes – who sought to reconcile northern and southern painting, drawing inspiration from Raphael and Dürer (Johann Friedrich Overbeck, Rudolf Schadow) – and artists of the **Biedermeier** style. Going against the current of sophistication of the Empire style, the Biedermeier artists reduced ornamentation and prioritised simple lines; thus the very broad *Cinderella* (1852) by **Moritz von Schwind** depicts the story in an original arrangement of four paintings and fifteen vignettes.

From Romanticism to Realism

Pride of place is given to French painters in Galleries **10 and 10a**. The Romantics are represented by **Théodore Géricault** (*Artillery Moving to the Front*, 1814) and his admirer **Eugène Delacroix**. Of the Naturalist painters, who left their studios to go out and capture the reality of nature, there are paintings by **Gustave Courbet** *(Horse in Motion, River Landscape)* and Camille Corot.

In Galleries **11 and 11a,** Andreas Achenbach (*Landscape with Rune-Stone*, 1841; *Beach Scene*, 1880) and **Carl Spitzweg** (*The Hussar, The Poor Poet*, 1839, *The Writer*, 1850) represent late German Romanticism, and **Adolf von Menzel** realism, with *Menzel's Sister* (1847) and *Procession in Hofgastein* (1880).

Galleries **12 to 14a are reserved for temporary exhibitions.**

German painters from the second half of the 19C

Gallery **15** is entirely devoted to **Hans von Marées** (1837-87), a great portrait painter inspired by Renaissance art; works include *Three Boys beneath Orange Trees* and the *Hesperides* triptych. Gallery 16 contains works by a group of German painters who went to live and work in Rome. Arnold Böcklin and Hans Thoma are there, along with **Anselm Feuerbach** whose famous painting *Medea's Farewell* (1870) depicts very sculptural figures. Paintings by **Leibl –** leading light of the Bavarian school of Realism – are on display in Gallery **17:** *Portrait of Mina Gedon* (1868), *Girl with White Headscarf* (1875) and *In the Farmer's Parlour* (1890).

Impressionists, post-Impressionists and Symbolists

Galleries **18 and 19 contain** paintings by German Impressionists, notably *Summer Holiday* by Friedrich von Uhde and *Portrait of the Writer Eduard Graf von Keyserling* (1901) by Lovis Corinth.

Symbolism and Jugendstil provide the theme of Galleries **20 and 21a**. *Margarethe Stonborough-Wittgenstein*, the philosopher's sister, appears to be floating in the ethereal whiteness of her dress in **Gustav Klimt**'s superb portrait (1905). The mysterious lady with the bare stomach watching from the shadows with a half-smile is none other than *War* (1894) by Franz von Stuck. **Auguste Rodin**'s marble bust of *Helene von Nostitz* is surrounded by works by Ferdinand Hodler (*Disappointed*, five old men with resigned expressions), Egon Schiele (*Agony*, 1912) and Giovanni Segantini (*Ploughing*, 1890).

Post-Impressionists Toulouse-Lautrec, Vuillard and Ensor share Gallery **21** with a large painting of *Waterlilies* by **Claude Monet** (1918). Galleries **22** and **22a** are occupied by, among others, **French Impressionists**: **Paul Gauguin**'s somewhat disconcerting *Birth of Christ* combines Christian and Polynesian symbols (1896) and *Breakfast in the Studio* (1868) and *Barque* (1874) are by **Édouard Manet**. Also on display is a painting by **Vincent Van Gogh** from the *Sunflowers* series (1888) revealing the influence of Japanese art and works by **Camille Pissarro** (*Street in Upper Norwood*, 1871), **Edgar Degas** (*Woman Ironing*, c 1869) and **Paul Cézanne** (*Still-life with Chest of Drawers*, c 1885; *Railway Cutting*, 1870).

Pinakothek der Moderne★★ *2hr*

Barer Straße 40. ♿ Open every day except Mon, 10am-5pm, Thu-Fri 10am-8pm. Closed Shrove Tuesday, 1st May, 24 and 31 Dec. €9, free admission on Sundays. ☎ (089) 23 80 53 60; www.pinakothek-der-moderne.de

The building, designed by Munich architect Stephan Braunfels, is known as the "Cathedral of Light" because of its glass rotunda and glazed saw-tooth roofs. It opened in September 2002 and houses four museums *(the entrance ticket allows access to all departments)* focusing on 20C art, with paintings, sculptures, photographs, drawings, models and design objects.

Staatsgalerie moderner Kunst (Modern Art Collection)

3rd floor. The question of form and content in modern art is the underlying theme of the permanent exhibition. It is arranged in chronological order and by cross-influence, so it is not essential to follow the numbering.

"Classic" Modern Art (Galleries 1-17) – A large section is devoted to German Expressionism, which took aestheticism to a new height, and to the various Expressionist movements: "Die Brücke" *(The Bridge*, whose tortured subjects set them apart from the Fauves) with **Ernst Ludwig Kirchner**, and "Der Blaue Reiter" (*The Blue Rider*, focusing on abstraction and spiritualisation of form) with Franz Marc and **Wassily Kandinsky**. Works by another Expressionist, **Max Beckmann**, characterised by strident colours and thick contours, include the *Temptation of St Anthony* triptych and a striking self-portrait. In a radically different approach, the Cubists and Futurists moved towards autonomous art, as illustrated in numerous

To complete the tour
Two other museums in Munich described in this guide exhibit works by German Expressionists: the Lenbach Collections (*Blaue Reiter* movement) and the Buchheim Museum in Bernried (*Die Brücke* movement).

works by **Pablo Picasso** (including *Madame Soler*) and **Georges Braque**. Surrealism is represented by Max Ernst, René Magritte and Salvador Dali, and Bauhaus by Feininger *(Halle Church)* and Paul Klee.

Modern Art (Galleries 20-36) – Important themes in art during the second half of the 20C – informal art, celebration of the trivial, rise of pop culture etc – are broached in artists' monographs. One can thus follow the works of **Joseph Beuys** (whose unusual sculpture *The End of the 20th Century* defends the ability of man and nature to communicate), Lucio Fontana (with *Attese*, one of his spatial concept paintings), **Francis Bacon** (*Crucifixion*), Georg Baselitz and Willem de Kooning. The museum also displays some remarkable works by American artists, with paintings by **Andy Warhol**, photographs by Jeff Wall and videos by Bruce Nauman.

Other departments

Neue Sammlung (Craft and Design, basement) – In addition to objects of industrial design, sports accessories, cars and computer equipment, the museum presents prototypes of objects designed since the industrial revolution up to the 1960s, including Bahaus and Art Nouveau. Furniture design classics as well as works by visionaries such as Colani and John Maeda are incorporated in a presentation combining interactive screens, models and finished objects.

The collections of the Graphic Art department *(Grafische Sammlung)* and Architecture **Museum** *(Architekturmuseum der Technischen Universität)* are shown in temporary exhibitions on the ground floor owing to their great sensitivity to light.

DEUTSCHES MUSEUM★★★ *Allow half a day*

In view of the huge scope of subjects covered, visitors are advised to choose a particular theme to follow. There are some 16 000 exhibits displayed over an area of 46 000m²/495 150sq ft. A brochure in English and a plan of the museum's layout are available at the entrance. 9am-5pm. Closed 1st Jan, Shrove Tuesday, Good Friday, 1st May, 1st Nov, 24, 25 and 31 Dec. €7.50. ☎ (089) 21 791; www.deutsches-museum.de

Founded in 1903, this museum – one of the most important in the world for scientific and technical matters – is built on an isle in the Isar *(Museumsinsel)*. It traces the history of science and technology from the beginning of time to the present day and explains physical processes and phenomena. Around 1.3 million people visit it each year.

Besides a large number of original items and reconstructions, most of them of great value, the exhibits comprise dioramas and scale models. In line with the expressed wish of the museum's founder, the Bavarian pioneer of electricity **Oskar von Miller**, the display system is pedagogic: the visitor is there to inquire, to touch, and to discover. Thus there are innumerable working models and workshop and laboratory demonstrations to explain the relevant techniques in a way that even a beginner can understand. Such physics experiments as Faraday's Cage and Foucault's Pendulum, for example, are reproduced. And there are regular performances illustrating such manufacturing processes as papermaking, glass-blowing, smelting and the fabrication of tiles. Some of the demonstrations are accompanied by a commentary on film.

A library endowed with 900 000 different volumes is associated with the museum, as well as privately donated collections and archives including documents, plans, maps, blueprints and drawings.

Ground Floor

Environment; metallurgy; machine tools; machines powered by different types of energy (wind, water, steam); applications of electrical current; bicycles and barouches; civil engineering (roads, bridges, tunnels, railways, canals etc). In the Railway Hall, there are famous steam engines, including the 1912 S-3/6 which powered the Bavarian Express, and the first electric locomotive *(Siemens, 1879)*. The Aeronautical Section (Modern Division) exhibits early jet planes, including the Messerschmitt Me-262, the first jet fighter made on a production line, helicopters, gliders and vertical take-off machines.

An Elbe sailing ship (1880) and an Italian steam tug (1932) stand at the entrance to the Navigation Department *(continued in the basement)*.

Basement

Among many other displays, the Navigation Section highlights naval construction, warships (including U-1, the first German submarine, built in 1906), methods of navigation, fishing techniques, and Jacques Picard's 1958 bathysphere.

A section on mining details the working of a coal mine, the extraction of salt, and the treatment of ores. There is a model salt mine.

Deutsches Museum

First electric locomotive (1879).

The Automobile Department shows an 1885 carriage with a Benz engine, an 1891 steam-driven Serpollet, luxury cars of the 1920s and 1930s (Daimler, Opel, Horch, Bugatti), utility vehicles, racing cars (1936 Auto-Union Grand Prix Type-C), an assembly line, and motorcycles. Note the 1885 Daimler-Maybach (a replica, built in 1906).

First Floor

The most interesting section here is perhaps Aeronautics. Gliders built by the engineer Lilienthal (c 1885), the pioneer of this form of flight, can be seen. Also a 1917 Fokker Dr I Triplane, of the type made famous by Baron von Richthofen's "circus" in the First World War a replica including parts from the original). Note also the Wright Brothers' Type-A Standard (USA, 1909), a Blériot Type XI (1909), a Junkers F-13 (the first true airliner, 1919), and the legendary Junkers Ju-52 (built under licence in France, 1947). Military aircraft of the 1930s and 1940s are on show, including the Messerschmitt Bf-109.

From this most recent gallery devoted to aeronautics, there is direct access *(by escalator)* to the second floor section on space flights. Technologies from the earliest attempts at rocketry (Hitler's V2, code-named A4) to the current Spacelab are illustrated.

Department of Physics – Physical laws and their application: optics, mechanics, electronics, thermology, nuclear physics; chemistry: alchemy, Liebig's laboratory, pharmacy, biochemistry; media technology; musical instruments.

Second Floor – Manufacture of glass and ceramics (beautiful 17C earthenware stove from the Thurgau area in Switzerland); paper, printing; photography (Daguerre's apparatus, 1839); textile processes (Jacquard's 1860 loom); environment.

Third Floor – Weights and measures; climatic forecasts; agriculture (dairy farming, flour milling, breweries); data processing and computer science, robotics and microelectronics. Access to the fourth floor observatory *(visits must be booked in advance)*.

Fifth Floor – Astronomy (celestial globes, sundials, astrolabes, quadrants etc).

Sixth Floor – Planetarium.

In 2003 the museum opened an annex devoted to the history of transport development from the first engine to the space shuttle; it is located in the old trade fair centre *(Verkehrszentrum, Theresienhöle 14)*.

RESIDENZ★★ *Allow half a day*

From the beginning of Apr to mid Oct: 9am-6pm; from mid Oct to Mar: 10am-4pm. Open until 8pm on Thu. Combined ticket for the Residenzmuseum and Schatzkammer €8.50. ☎ (089) 29 06 71; www.schloesser.bayern.de

In 1385, the Wittelsbachs started the building of this new royal palace *(Neuveste)*, which, with the passing of time, expanded into an ever more vast complex around seven courtyards. Work was well advanced in the Renaissance period (Antiquarium, Kaiserhof, the Residenzstraße façade) and the subsequent Classical era (Festsaalbau, Königsbau). This tremendous building now houses the municipal collection of

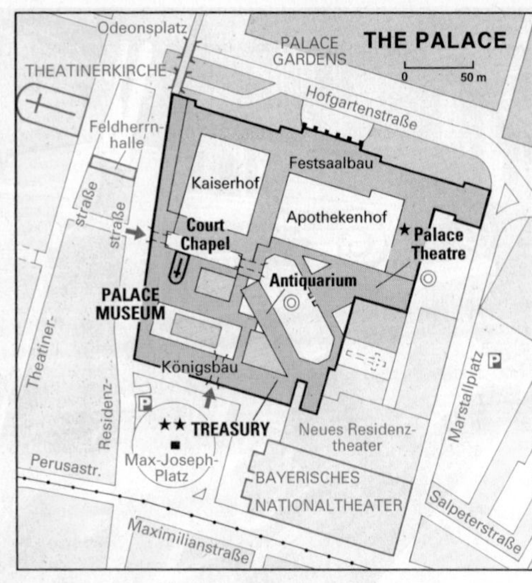

Egyptian art and the municipal numismatic collection. Visitors who are pressed for time, however, should direct their attentions first of all to the treasury and the palace museum. The 130 rooms of this museum contain trappings of royal domestic life spanning four centuries.

Schatzkammer★★ (Treasury) *1hr*

Same opening times as the Residenz. €5. Free audio guide recommended.

This is one of the most fascinating collections of its kind in Europe, a testimony to three centuries of Bavarian rulers' passion for collecting things. The magnificent displays of gold work, enamels, crystal ware and carved ivories will fascinate every visitor. Among the highlights of the collection are the superb cross executed for Queen Gisela of Hungary (after 1006), Heinrich's crown from 1280, a domestic altar depicting the Flagellation of Christ (c 1580-85) and a dazzling example of the goldsmith's art inlaid with precious stones, a statue of St George (1586-97). The royal insignia of the House of Bavaria – crown, orb, sceptre, royal sword, and chest of seals – were made in Paris in 1806-07 for the first king of Bavaria, Maximilian I.

Residenzmuseum★★

€5. The tour changes at 1.30pm. Plan available at the entrance.

Visitors should do both the morning and afternoon guided tours (which are different) if nothing is to be missed. Both tours include the most important rooms, such as the Ancestors' Gallery or Antiquarium. It is possible that the tours may be modified. *Since the rooms contain such a wealth of material, we recommend that visitors hire an official guide for detailed information on the fittings and furnishings.*

Morning tour – The enormous **Antiquarium** (c 1570) inlaid with marble, the oldest part of the palace, impresses with its painted ceilings and innumerable Antique busts. The **State Rooms** (*Die Reichen Zimmer* – 1730-37), decorated by Effner and Cuvilliés, illustrate in great style the early version of the Rococo style. A particular highlight of the tour is the **Royal Apartments** in the Königsbau (King's Wing), which Ludwig I had built by court architect Leo von Klenze between 1826 and 1835. The building suffered extensive damage in the Second World War. However the contents that were not permanent fixtures were removed in time, so that the rooms can once more be viewed in their former glory, since exemplary restoration work, as a complete work of art including paintings, sculpture and furniture. A room embellished with gilded stuccowork and carvings houses the Wittelsbach **Ancestors' Gallery**.

Afternoon Tour – Masterpieces from the workshops of Meissen, Nymphenburg, Frankenthal and Sèvres ("Bird Service" of 1759) are on display in the **Porcelain Rooms**. The 17C **Hofkapelle** (Court Chapel) is dedicated to the Virgin Mary, patron saint of Bavaria. The **Reiche Kapelle**, severely damaged in 1944 but whose furnishings it was possible to save, now lives up to its name. Close at hand is the **Reliquary Room** *(Reliquienkammer)*, with valuable exhibits of 16C-18C gold and silver plate.

The **Silver Rooms** *(Silberkammer)*, magnificent **Stone Room** *(Steinzimmer)* with its marble, stucco and scagliola decor, and reconstructed **Imperial Room** *(Kaisersaal)* are also worth seeing.

Altes Residenztheater★

Access from outside the Residenz. Same opening times as the Treasury. Closed during rehearsals. €2.

This enchanting Rococo theatre was built by **François de Cuvilliés** between 1751 and 1753 (and is therefore also known as Cuvilliéstheater), with four tiers of Court boxes, each different from the others in design and decoration. The prince-elector's box, in the centre, is set apart by the elegance and richness of its hangings, marble and stuccowork. The harmonisation of colours in red, gold and ivory is particularly beautiful.

Walking About

OLD TOWN★★ (ALTSTADT)

See itinerary on the plan – allow half a day.

Marienplatz★

This square is the heart of Munich. In the centre rises the **Mariensäule**, a column erected by the Prince-Elector Maximilian in 1638, in honour of Mary, patron saint of Bavaria. The north side is occupied by the neo-Gothic **Neues Rathaus** (1867-1908), whose **carillon** *(Glockenspiel)* installed in the tower's oriel window, is a favourite tourist attraction. When the mechanism is activated *(at 11am, noon and 5pm)*, brightly coloured figures in enamelled copper emerge and enact the Dance of the Coopers *(Schäfflertanz, below)* and the Tournament which accompanied royal weddings in the 16C *(above)*. The cobbled courtyard with its spiral staircase turret is worth a look. From the town hall tower (85m/279ft: *lift*) there is another lovely view of the city.

The façade of the **Altes Rathaus**, with its stepped gables and bell turrets, occupies the eastern side of the square. There is a toy museum *(Spielzeugmuseum)* in the tower.

Peterskirche

Baroque vaulting remodelled this 13C, three-aisle Gothic church in the 17C and 18C. The centre section of the enormous high altar is occupied by an Erasmus Grasser statue of St Peter (1492). Slightly lower down, the flanking figures representing the four Fathers of the Church were sculpted by Egid Quirin Asam in 1732.

The church's 1386 bell-tower is affectionately nicknamed "Old Pete" by the people of Munich. Visitors braving the climb to the top *(306 steps)* are rewarded with a splendid view of the city.

Viktualienmarkt (Food Market)

This market can certainly claim to have tradition; it has been held here since 1807. Fresh fruit and vegetables, meat and fish are on sale here every day. The market stalls and kiosks, not to mention the beer garden during warm weather, ensure that the atmosphere on this centrally located square is always lively. Two of the six fountains recall the famous local comedian Karl Valentin and his partner Liesl Karlstadt.

KARL VALENTIN

The comedic talent of Valentin Ludwig Fey (1882-1948) – nurtured since his childhood in the Munich suburbs – rapidly brought him international acclaim. This nonconformist actor, author and friend of Brecht produced sketches that were both grotesque and tragic, earning him the nickname of "metaphysical clown". A trip to the Valentin-Karlstadt museum (Tal 50, near the Isartor) will take you into the world of this local star.

Heiliggeistkirche

Another Gothic original which paid later tribute to the local taste for the Baroque, this hall-church was completely transformed between 1723 and 1730. The façade however is neo-Baroque, and dates from 1888.

The painting above the **high altar** is by Ulrich Loth (1644), and the two angels with large wings in front of the altar pillars are the work of Johann Georg Greiff (1730). The mid-15C Virgin in the north aisle, said to be by Hammerthal, was once in the Benedictine abbey at Tegernsee.

Cross the Talstraße, take the passage beneath the old town hall, and turn right into Burgstraße.

Weinstadel

Burgstraße 5. The oldest house (1552) in Munich, in days gone by the municipal office of the Clerk of the Court. The façade is decorated in *trompe-l'œil.* The fine doorway has a basket-handle arch.

At no 10 Burgstraße opposite the Weinstadel, take the vaulted passageway to reach Ledererstraße, then cross diagonally (left) into Orlandostraße.

Hofbräuhaus

The best-known of the famous Munich beer halls stands on Platzl and dates from 1589. The present building was constructed at the end of the 19C, the original brewery having already been transferred to the east bank of the Isar through lack of space.

Every day, in this great temple of beer, waiters serve 100 hectolitres (17 500 pints) of beer in one-litre (1.75 pints) tankards *(Maßkrug)*. In many of the rooms and in the shaded courtyard, orchestras add to the festive atmosphere with renditions of popular songs. The huge vaulted **Bierschwemme**, on the ground floor, where the odours of strong tobacco mingle with those of sausages and beer, is the rowdiest part of the building; here tourists and locals out with their families sit around large wooden tables eating sausages and drinking beer. Customarily there is a police presence to ensure that high spirits do not degenerate into brawls.

At the far end of the square, turn left into Pfisterstraße.

Alter Hof (Old Castle)

This building, a quadrilateral opening onto an inner courtyard, was the official Wittelsbach residence from 1253 to 1474. The south wing has an elegant tower with half-timbered corbelling (late 15C), known locally as the *Affenturm* (monkey tower). The courtyard with its fountain is charming.

The Hofgraben leads to Max-Joseph-Platz, enclosed on the north and east by the imposing mass of the palace.

March Beer

The strong-beer season starts in March: in order to get through Lent, the Franciscan monks, traditional brewers, invented a beer with a higher alcohol content – which was therefore more energising – in the 17C. Having some scruples on account of such a literal interpretation of the Bible (which only forbids eating), they took a barrel to the Vatican to seek the Pope's approval. The Pope generously gave his blessing, in the belief that drinking such a bad beer – it was very strong and probably damaged by the journey – was punishment in itself. The names of these spring beers traditionally end in "ator".

Nationaltheater

Built between 1811 and 1818, the national theatre, home to the Bavarian State Opera, was endowed with one of the largest stages in the world. The five-tier auditorium can seat 2 100 spectators.

Residenz★★ *(See p 379)*

Continue to the left of the Residenz via Residenzstraße.

Odeonsplatz

On the westside of this square stands the Leuchtenberg-Palais, built for Eugène de Beauharnais, Count of Leuchtenberg, in 1816-21 by Leo von Klenze. It now houses the Bavarian Finance Ministry. To the south, the **Feldherrnhalle** portico, erected in 1840-44 by Friedrich von Gärtner in imitation of the Loggia dei Lanzi in Florence, Italy, closes the long perspective of Ludwigstraße. The far (northern) end of this splendid avenue leads in a straight line to a triumphal arch *(Siegestor)*.

Theatinerkirche★

A fine example of Baroque ecclesiastical architecture, this church was built between 1663 and 1688, first under the direction of the Italian Barelli and later by Zuccalli, who came from Graubünden. The well-proportioned Late Rococo façade was added a century afterwards, by Cuvilliés.

Inside, the dome of this very tall building, which rises to a height of 71m/233ft, emphasises a grandiose impression of space. The stuccowork is particularly rich, the Italian stuccodore having paid special attention to the smaller load-bearing arches and the pendentives. The wreathed double colonnade of the monumental high altar is also very generously embellished. The dark wood of the pulpit, designed in 1681 by Andreas Faistenberger, makes a striking contrast with the whites and greys in the nave and elsewhere. Princes from the Wittelsbach dynasty are buried in the crypt beneath the chancel.

From Salvatorstraße, go to Kardinal-Faulhaber-Straße.

Erzbischöfliches Palais (Episcopal Palace)

Kardinal-Faulhaber-Straße 7. **François de Cuvilliés** built his finest palace between 1733-37, once called the Palais Holnstein and destined for the natural son of Electoral Prince Karl Albrecht. Now an Archbishop's Palace, it is set out around a rectangular courtyard and boasts a magnificent pink and white façade with a rounded balcony supported by cherubs.

Palais Portia

Kardinal-Faulhaber-Straße 12. This mansion, designed by Enrico Zuccalli in 1694, was transformed in the Rococo style by Cuvilliés in 1735, for one of Karl Albrecht's favourites, later to become Countess Portia. The façade, in tones of pink and grey, is charming.

Take the alley at the end of Kardinal-Faulhaber-Straße.

Frauenkirche★

The architect of this vast Late Gothic hall-church (1468-88) was **Jörg von Halspach**, who also designed the old town hall. The exterior of the church, in dark-red brick, is extremely sober; only the side entrances and tombstones built into the walls break the tall façades. The onion domes, which since 1525 have crowned the two towers at the west end (just over 98m/320ft high), have become the symbol of the city.

Interior – In striking contrast to the exterior, the brilliant white nave makes an immediate impression with its simplicity and its height. Eleven pairs of powerful octagonal pillars support the reticulated vaulting. Seen from the entrance, the perspective of these columns forms a continuous line, effectively hiding the aisles. The south side aisle contains the lavishly built monumental **cenotaph★** to Emperor Ludwig of Bavaria, worked in black marble by Hans Krumper (1619-22). The four knights in armour come from another funerary monument (c 1595).

Furnishing and works of art blend the old and the new. Thus the 32 carved wood busts representing the Apostles, the Saints and the Prophets, attributed to the sculptor **Erasmus Grasser** (c 1500), are placed immediately above the modern choir stalls. All the chapels contain high quality paintings and altarpieces. The main

chapel off the chancel contains a fine Robed Madonna by Jan Polack, c 1510; the image of Our Lady of Mercy in the shrine was donated by the citizens of Munich in 1659. Above the retable in the chapel of Our Lady's Sacrifice *(to the right of the main chapel)* is an altar panel dating from 1445 with a Crucifixion and scenes from the life of Christ.

The chapels off the ambulatory contain 15C **stained-glass windows**; that in the main chapel is the work of Alsatian stained-glass artist Peter Hemmel of Andlau. A staircase at the far end of the choir leads to the Bishops' and Princes' Crypt *(Bischofs- und Fürstengruft)*, with the burial vaults of certain cardinals of Munich and Wittelsbach princelings.

In the south tower, there is now a lift taking visitors to the platform *(April to October)*, from which there is a fine **view★** of the town.

Take the busy shopping street Neuhauser Straße towards the Karlstor.

Office de Tourisme de Münich

Frauenkirche and Neues Rathaus on Marienplatz

Michaelskirche★

This Jesuit sanctuary was built between 1583 and 1597 on the model of the society's Roman church *(Gesù)*. It was the first Renaissance church north of the Alps. The façade is decorated with pilasters and bands of script. The 15 statues are of sovereigns descended from the church's patron, the Archangel Michael, who is depicted between the two entrances. This superb Mannerist statue in bronze is the work of Hubert Gerhard (1588).

The single nave – which inspired many builders of the Baroque School in south Germany – is covered by a 20m/65ft wide cradle vault resting on massive pillars abutting the walls. At the far end of the well-lit chancel the high altar rises to the level of the vaulting like a triumphal arch. The pulpit and seven side altars date from 1697. The tomb of Eugène de Beauharnais, stepson to Napoleon and son-in-law to King Maximilian I, who died in Munich in 1824, is in the north transept. Thirty of the Wittelsbach princes, including Ludwig II of Bavaria, are buried in the crypt *(Fürstengruft)*.

Richard-Strauss-Brunnen

Bas-relief sculptures on the central column of this fountain illustrate scenes from the opera *Salome*, which the famous Munich composer wrote in 1905.

Take Eisenmannstraße which turns into Damenstiftstraße, then take the first alley on the left after Brunnstraße to Sendlingerstraße.

Asamkirche★ (St Johannes Nepomuk)

The church, built in 1733, is always referred to locally under the name of the men who constructed it, the **Asam Brothers**: Cosmas Damian Asam, who specialised in the painting of frescoes, and Egid Quirin Asam, sculptor and stuccoworker. The church's remarkable unity of style is due to the fact that the two brothers drew up the plans themselves, and both executed and supervised every stage of the work. The design of the interior is strikingly harmonious. A curved gallery links the choir, the nave and the organ loft; above, supported on pillars, a second gallery is adorned with stuccowork and statues of angels or cherubim. The frescoed ceiling, lit by windows concealed behind mouldings, depicts episodes in the life of St John of Nepomuk.

Return to Marienplatz via Sendligerstraße and Rosenstraße.

Worth a Visit

CENTRAL DISTRICT

Schack-Galerie★

Prinzregentenstraße 9. Open every day except Tue, 10am-5pm. Closed 1st Jan, Shrove Tuesday, 1st May, Ascension Day, Corpus Christi, Assumption. 3 Oct, 24, 25 and 31 Dec. €2.50, free admission on Sundays. ☎ (089) 23 80 52 24.

Those interested in 19C German painting must not fail to visit this collection, which is exceptionally comprehensive. It is on display in a house that was built especially for the purpose and therefore provides the perfect setting for it.

The collection, assembled by Count Adolf Friedrich von Schack (1815-94), spans Early to Late Romanticism and includes numerous works by landscape painter **Carl Rottmann** *(Kochelsee)*, **Moritz von Schwind** *(Rübezahl, Morning Hour)*, **Carl Spitzweg** *(Hermit, A Hypochondriac)*, **Arnold Böcklin** *(Spring Landscape Ideal, Villa by the Sea I and II)*, **Franz von Lenbach** *(Shepherd Boy, Self-portrait)*, **Anselm Feuerbach** *(Paolo and Francesca, Hafis by the Well, Portrait of Nanna)*, Georg Köbel *(Nymph Egeria's Spring near Rome)*.

Münchner Stadtmuseum★ (City Historical Museum)

St.-Jacobs-Platz 1, in the stables of the old Arsenal. ♿ Open every day except Mon, 10am-6pm. Closed Shrove Tuesday, 24 and 31 Dec. €2.50, free admission on Sundays. ☎ (089) 23 32 23 70. This museum houses comprehensive collections on local history, including a display of home decor in Munich, crafts, paintings, musical instruments, marionette theatres, photography and film. Do not fail to see the **Moorish Dancers★★** *(Moriskentänzer)*, 10 carved wooden figures painted and gilded in 1480 by **Erasmus Grasser** *(ground floor)*.

Deutsches Jagd- und Fischereimuseum★ (German Hunting and Fishing Museum)

Neuhauserstraße 2. 9.30am-5pm, Thu 9.30am-9pm. Closed Shrove Tuesday, 24 and 31 Dec. €3.50. ☎ (089) 22 05 22. The museum, housed in a disused Augustinian church, displays on three different levels a splendid collection of ancient and modern arms, trophies, paintings and drawings of hunting scenes, and stuffed animals. Different species of freshwater fish are shown in their separate groups against a diorama. One section of the museum looks at beings from the world of legends *("Wolperdinger")*.

Wittelsbacher Brunnen (Wittelsbach Fountain)

Between Lenbachplatz and Maximiliansplatz. **Adolf von Hildebrand** built this neo-Baroque fountain in 1895 to mark the completion of a water canalisation programme which provided the city with clean drinking water.

▶▶ Staatliches Museum für Völkerkunde *(Ethnology Museum)*, Spielzeugmuseum *(Toy Museum)*, ZAM *("Centre for Unusual Museums")*.

PINAKOTHEK QUARTER

Propyläen

West side of Königsplatz. This imposing gateway by Leo von Klenze (1784-1864) was completed two years before the Munich architect died. Inspired by the Propylaea of the Acropolis, it stands on the west side of the Königsplatz (which is thus flanked on three sides by monuments in the Classical style). The frieze represents the Greek war of liberation against the Turks; Otto I of Wittelsbach, King of Greece from 1832 to 1862, is commemorated in a statue on the pediment above the Doric colonnade.

Glyptothek★ (Sculpture Museum) *45min*

♿ Tue, Thu 10am-8pm, Wed, Fri and Sat-Sun 10am-5pm. €3. ☎ (089) 28 61 00. One thousand years of Greek and Roman sculpture are gathered together under the roof of this museum, built with its Classical porch and Ionic colonnade, by the architect Leo von Klenze (1816-30). The scarcity of Greek statues (generally designed in bronze and unfortunately later melted down) makes the original marble statues here even more remarkable. The **Tenea Apollo** *(Gallery I)*, with his handsome, smiling face, is typical of the Kouroi – those large naked figures, half human, half divine, who spread through Greece in the 6C BC. The **Barberini Faun** (c 220 BC) *(Gallery II)*, which appears sated with drink and half asleep, dates from the Hellenistic epoque (c 220 BC). Note the **bas-relief by Mnesarete** *(Gallery IV)*, which is said to have adorned the tomb of Socrates' daughter, and the statue of *Irene*, the Goddess of Peace *(Gallery V)*.

A CULTURAL CENTRE

Ludwig I wanted **Königsplatz** to be the cultural heart of his "Athens on the Isar". The ancient model provided architect Leo von Klenze with inspiration (1816-30) for the "orders" of the buildings bordering the square: Doric for the Propylaea, Ionic for the Glypthothek, and Corinthian for the collection of antiquities.

Note too, in the original works from the east and west pediments of the Temple of Aphaia on the island of Aegina, which were sculpted from Paros marble *(Galleries VIII-IX)*.

Staatliche Antikensammlungen★ (State Collection of Antiquities) *45min*

Opposite the Glypthothek. Open every day except Mon, 10am-5pm (Wed 10am-8pm). €3. ☏ (089/59) 98 88 30. A building by GF Ziebland (1838-48) which, with its Corinthian colonnade, forms an architectural counterpart to the sculpture museum across the road.

An important display of ceramics on the ground floor traces the evolution of pottery and the painting of vases in Greece, which reached its zenith during the 6C and 5C BC. Geometric decoration was succeeded by the representation of black figures on a red background – illustrated by an amphora and a goblet by the painter Exekias. The amphora depicts Ajax carrying the body of Achilles; Dionysius decorates the goblet, in a boat escorted by dolphins *(Gallery II, showcases 10 and 12)*. The transition towards the use of red figures against a background of varnished black can be seen on another amphora, where a single subject – Hercules' banquet in the presence of Athena – is treated in the two styles *(Gallery III, showcase 6)*.

Certain vases (*loutrophora* and *lecythus* on a white ground) were destined for funerary worship; others – such as the elegant *canthare* (drinking vessel in the shape of a female head) – for domestic use *(Gallery II, showcase 7 – 540 BC)*.

Bronzes on the first floor (ceremonial vessels, engraved plaques, statuettes), and particularly the **Etruscan jewellery** in the basement *(Galleries VII and X)* testify to the enormous craftsmanship enjoyed by these workers in metal: necklaces, fibula, rings, in filigree or with granulations, rival each other in the delicacy and elegance of their execution.

Städtische Galerie im Lenbachhaus★ (Lenbach Collections)

Open every day except Mon, 10am-6pm. Closed Shrove Tuesday and 24 Dec. €4. ☏ (089) 23 33 20 00. Built between 1883 and 1889 in the style of a Florentine villa, the house containing the Lenbach collections is devoted mainly to the works of **Munich painters of the 19C**. Among these are the landscapes of EB Morgenstern *(Starnberg Lake)* and portraits by FA von Kaulbach and F von Defregger. There is also a set of powerful portraits by **Franz von Lenbach** himself *(King Ludwig I, Bismarck, Wagner)*.

But the gallery's international reputation is built above all on the avant-garde **Blaue Reiter** collection. Born in the tumultuous period just before the First World War, the movement is represented by its founder members, Kandinsky, Marc *(Blue Horse)* and Kubin, as well as by paintings from the hands of Jawlensky, Klee and Macke. Contemporary art is also displayed in the Lenbach villa.

ENGLISCHER GARTEN QUARTER

Englischer Garten★ (English Garden)

Not far from the city centre, this park, with its broad sweeps of tree-bordered lawn, its streams and its lake, was designed in the late 18C by **Friedrich Ludwig von Sckell** and the British-American scientist Sir Benjamin Thompson, Count Rumford. It is particularly popular in summer, when a beer garden seating 7 000 people is open near the **Chinese Tower** *(Chinesischer Turm)*. From the **Monopteros**, a circular temple built on a knoll by Leo von Klenze, there is a fine **view★** of the belfries in Munich's old town.

Chinese Tower in the English Garden

M. Hertlein/MICHELIN

Bayerisches Nationalmuseum★★ (Bavarian National Museum) *2hr*

Plan (in German) available at reception. Open every day except Mon, 10am-5pm, Thu 10am-8pm. Closed Shrove Tuesday, 1st May, Pentecost, 1st Nov, 24, 25 and 31 Dec. €3, free admission on Sundays. ☏ (089) 211 24 01; www.bayerisches-nationalmuseum.de

Maximilian II created this museum in 1885 with the aim of preserving Bavaria's artistic heritage. The exhibition is very well laid-out (although with little commentary) and it is possible to unearth treasures in almost every room from among the wealth of objects on show. The rooms on the ground floor offer a survey of Bavarian arts and crafts from Romanesque to Renaissance *(Galleries 1-19)*, including silver and gold plate and religious statuary, furniture and paintings, among them an altarpiece by Gabriel Engler (1445) and works by Multscher *(Gallery 8)*, the interior of an Augsburg weaver's studio *(Gallery 9)* and an armoury *(Gallery 18)*. The Renaissance *(Galleries 21-31)* and Baroque *(Galleries 32-46)* periods are illustrated by magnificent tapestries *(Gallery 22)*, models of medieval towns, Italian bronzes *(Gallery 25)*, earthenware and pewter, jewellery and costumes.

A Little Exercise

The people of Munich practise all kinds of sports in the English Garden: besides joggers, cyclists and basketball players, you may even see surfers on the large artificial wave which starts from one of the bridges on Prinzregentenstraße.

On the first floor, there are displays of musical instruments, silverware and porcelain from different periods. The basement contains an exhibition of folk art (collection of Christmas cribs).

Museum Villa Stuck

Prinzregentenstraße 60. Professor at the Munich Academy of Fine Arts from 1895 and one of the founding members of the Munich Secession, **Franz Stuck** (1863-1928) built this Jugendstil villa with an Italian influence after his own plans. The interior of the house is impressive: it was Stuck himself who made the furniture, the panelling, the bas-reliefs, sculptures and coffered ceilings. Note in particular the famous canvases by the artist, including *The Guardian of Paradise* and *The Sin,* and his sculptures *(Dancer, Amazon)*. The museum also hosts temporary exhibitions.

▶▶ Prähistorische Staatssammlung *(Archaeology Museum)*, Haus der Kunst *(temporary modern art exhibitions)*.

Excursions

SCHLOSS NYMPHENBURG★★ *Allow half a day*

6km/4mi west of the city centre, leaving Munich on Marsstraße.

From Apr to mid Oct: 9am-6pm; from mid Oct to end of Mar: 10am-4pm. €3.50. ☏ (089) 17 90 80; www.schloesser.bayern.de

The oldest part of the palace, once the summer residence of the Bavarian sovereigns and prince-electors, is the five-storey central pavilion, built by Barelli between 1664 and 1674 in the style of an Italian palazzo. The Prince-Elector Max Emmanuel, who reigned from 1679 to 1726, added two lateral pavilions on either side which were linked to the main building by arcaded galleries. At the same time he remodelled the central block, accentuating the verticals by the addition of pilasters. His successors, Karl-Albrecht (1726-45) and Max III Josef (1745-77), then constructed a semicircle of outbuildings and dependencies, which underlined the palace's resemblance to Versailles.

From 1701 onwards, the surrounding park too was enlarged under the direction of Carbonet and Girard, pupils of Le Nôtre. The formal French gardens date from this period, as do the various park pavilions: Pagodenburg (1719), Badenburg (1721), Magdalenenklause (1728) and Amalienburg (1739).

Palace★

The splendid **banqueting hall**, a symphony of white, gold and pale green, was richly adorned with coloured stuccowork and frescoes by Johann Baptist Zimmermann and his son Franz.

The rooms in the north wing of the central block are panelled, with tapestry hangings and paintings. Beyond this the north pavilion contains views of the castle and park in the early 18C.

The most fascinating room in the main block's south wing is the one devoted to a **collection of Chinese lacquer**. In the south pavilion, the apartments of Queen Carolina contain the famous **Gallery of Beauties** conceived by King Ludwig I. Commissioned by the King to immortalise the most beautiful women of the epoch (Lola Montez, among others), these paintings were executed by the portraitist Joseph Karl Stieler (1781-1858).

Park★

See itinerary on Nymphenburg map. Most of the park can be seen from the top of the steps in front of the palace's main entrance. Below the steps, beyond the formal rectilinear flower gardens lined with white marble urns and the statues of gods, the Grand Canal, which ends in a waterfall, flows straight as an arrow away into the distance.

Amalienburg★★ – *Same opening times as Schloß Nymphenburg. €1.50. ☏ (089) 17 90 80.* This charming little hunting lodge by **Cuvilliés** is one of his most accomplished designs – a model for the many Rococo country pavilions which so delighted the courts of 18C Germany. The simplicity and sobriety of the exterior is in vivid contrast with the extraordinary richness of the interior. The Blue Room

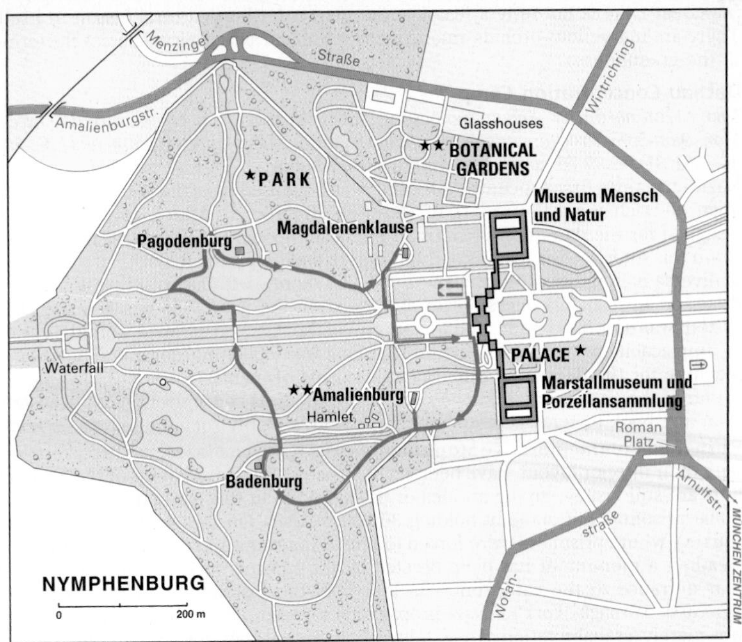

and a beautiful bedchamber, with silver woodwork on a background of lemon yellow, lead into the **Hall of Mirrors** rotunda. Here the combination of blue walls and ceiling, silver-plated stucco and wood-framed glass forms a marvellous ensemble. A Hunting Room, the Pheasant Room, and kitchens whose walls are tiled with blue Delft complete this masterpiece of Bavarian Rococo.

Badenburg – A luxurious heated swimming pool, with a ceiling decorated by mythological motifs, is the centrepiece of this 18C bathhouse. A dressing-room, and an antechamber serving as games and rest room are also included in the pavilion.

Pagodenburg – The 18C taste for exoticism and the Far East is exemplified in the design of this octagonal tea house. A drawing room, a Chinese room and a boudoir occupy the first floor.

Magdalenenklause – A "hermitage" or folly built in the then popular style of "artificial ruins", this pavilion is dedicated to St Mary Magdalene.

Marstallmuseum und Porzellansammlung (Carriage Museum and Porcelain Collection)

Same opening times as Schloß Nymphenburg. €2.50. ☎ (089) 17 90 80.
The museum is housed in the castle's former stables. Besides superb 18C and 19C harnesses, broughams, coaches, carts, sledges and sedan chairs used by the Wittelsbachs are on display. Note especially the coronation coach of Emperor Karl VII, and the state coach and personal sleigh of Ludwig II, all of them equipped with quite incredible luxury.
Above the old stables, a series of rooms exhibits the **Bäuml Collection of Nymphenburg Porcelain**. Painted figurines by Franz Anton Bustelli, master modellist of the factory between 1754 and 1763, are particularly fine. The **reproductions in porcelain★** – miniature copies in extraordinary detail of paintings in the Alte Pinakothek – were commissioned by King Ludwig I.

Museum "Mensch und Natur" ("Man and Nature" Natural History Museum)

♿ *Open every day except Mon, 9am-5pm. Closed Shrove Tuesday, 24, 25 and 31 Dec. €2.50, free admission on Sundays. ☎ (089) 17 13 82. In the north wing of Nymphenburg Palace.* Rarely is a natural history museum so interesting and accessible, especially to younger visitors. The museum provides information on the origins and internal structure of planet Earth, and on the evolution of life forms during the Earth's history. It also explains the evolution of agriculture as a source of food for a human popelation now numbering billions. There are informative interactive games on the plant and animal kingdoms to encourage visitors to get involved.

Botanischer Garten★★ (Botanical Gardens)

♿ *May-Aug: 9am-7pm; Apr and Sep: 9am-6pm; Feb-Mar and Oct: 9am-5pm; Jan, Nov-Dec: 9am-4.30pm. Closed 24 and 31 Dec. €2. ☎ (089) 17 86 13 10.* Reputed to be among the finest and most richly stocked in Europe. A stroll through the Schmuckhof *(opposite the main building)*, the Spring Garden and the Rose Garden, past masses of rhododendrons shaded by pines and around the Alpine Garden by the Great Lake is not only a feast for the eyes but a horticultural lesson in itself. There are marvellous orchids among the tropical and sub-tropical species flowering in the greenhouses.

Dachau Concentration Camp *2hr*

*19km/12mi northwest. Follow signposting "**KZ**-Gedenkstätte". ♿ Open every day except Mon, 9am-5pm. Free (donations gratefully received). Audio guide recommended (€2.50). ☎ (081 31) 66 99 70; www.kz-gedenkstaette-dachau.de*

Nazi Germany's first concentration camp was organised near the pleasant, terraced town of Dachau on the orders of Heinrich Himmler in March 1933. Originally designed for the detention of German political opponents of the Nazi regime, the camp was soon flooded by tens of thousands of deportees, the majority of them Jews of diverse nationalities. More than 32 000 died there – without counting the several thousand Russian prisoners-of-war shot dead on the nearby SS firing range. The system was described by Joseph Rovan, one of the few who escaped from the camp, as "implacable, perverted, an organisation that was totally murderous, a marvellous machine for the debasement and dehumanising of man".

A tour of the site provides a better account of the Nazi concentration camp system than any book or television documentary, and is highly recommended.

Ruins and Commemorative Monuments – The huts were razed, but two, complete with their interior layout, have been reconstructed. The foundations of the 32 other huts are still visible, giving an idea of the daily life in this camp designed to hold 5 000 prisoners but actually holding 30 000 in 1944. On the Appellplatz (roll-call square), where prisoners were forced to muster morning and evening whatever the weather, a monument has been erected by the International Community. At the rear entrance to the camp one can still read the inscription *"Arbeit macht frei" ("Freedom Through Work")* – Nazi propaganda to make people believe that Dachau was merely a rehabilitation camp. A Jewish memorial, a Protestant commemorative sanctuary and a Catholic expiatory chapel in the form of an open tower have been built within the precincts of the old camp. Land surrounding the cremation ovens, beyond the camp *(on the left)*, has been turned into a park-necropolis. The bodies of other victims have been buried in the cemeteries of Dachau *(Waldfriedhof)* and Leitenberg, 2km/1.2mi northeast. Outside the camp perimeter, is a Carmelite convent with a chapel which may be visited.

Dachau Memorial – The museum housed in the former camp administration buildings outlines the punitive penal system established there by the Nazis. The recently refurbished exhibition is sober and very comprehensive *(in English and German)*. It outlines the organisation of the concentration camps in Germany and Europe, looking closely at their model, Dachau. Statements, photographs and documents dating from that time illustrate the thematic descriptions of the camp's history, the prisoners' daily life, hard labour, "medical" experiments, mass executions and the liberation of the camp.

OTHER SIGHTS

Olympiapark

5km/3mi northwest of the centre, via Dachauer Straße. ♿ Freely accessible all year round. From Apr to beginning of Oct: guided tour at 11am (Fußballtour) and 2pm (Erlebnistour). €5 (Fußballtour), €7 (Erlebnistour). Olympiaturm: 9am-midnight. €3. ☎ (089) 30 67 24 14. Munich was host to the 20th Olympic Games in 1972. The many sports and leisure facilities continue to be used for international events. There is a museum on the Olympic Games in the old cycling stadium. The 1968 Olympiaturm (television tower) is no less than 290m/951ft high. At the 190m/623ft level *(lift)*, there is a terrace with **panorama★★★**, which offers an exceptional view over the city to the Bavarian Alps.

BMW-Museum

Petuelring 130. 5km/3mi north of the centre, via Schleißheimer Straße and Lerchenauer Straße. ♿ 9am-5pm. Closed 24 and 31 Dec. €3. ☎ (089) 38 22 56 57. This strange silver building shaped like a cup lies at the foot of the administration tower – which enhances the futuristic effect by being built in the form of four linked cylinders. The guided tour, which progresses in a spiral, retraces technical developments, social history of the 20C and examines prognoses for the future. Examples from BMW used to illustrate each of these themes include aircraft engines (from 1916), motorcycles (from 1923) and motor cars (from 1928), and besides the exhibits there are explanatory films, videos and slide shows.

Tierpark Hellabrunn★ (Hellabrunn Zoological Gardens)

6km/4mi from the city centre, leaving via Wittelsbacherstraße. ♿ Apr-Sep: 8am-6pm; Oct-Mar: 9am-5pm. €7. ☎ (089) 62 50 80; www.zoo-munich.de. Munich's zoo was founded as the world's first nature reserve and zoo combined in 1911, occupying an idyllic site on the banks of the Isar. The generous enclosures are home to about 5 000 animals. Main attractions include the giant aviary, elephant house, jungle pavilion with primeval forest biotope, tortoise house, polar zone and children's zoo.

The Villa Dracula may well send a shiver down your spine with its resident bats, although they are only the plant-eating variety. The zoo is world-famous for its breeding programmes for Przewalski's horses and Mhorr gazelles.

Bavaria-Filmstadt (Bavaria Film Studios) *1hr 30min*

10km/6mi south of the centre via Hochstraße, Grünwalderstraße and Geiselgasteigstraße. ♿ Guided tour (1hr 30min). From Mar to beginning of Nov: 9am-4pm; from beginning of Nov to end of Feb: 10am-3pm. Closed 24 and 25 Dec. €10. ☎ (089) 64 99 20 00. Visitors here will learn all about film and television and be able to admire the original sets for famous features such as *The Boat* and *Neverending Story*. They can even visit the set of the Asterix film shot here.

During the tour of the studios, visitors are shown what goes on behind the cameras. In the Showscan-Kino, the seats move in coordination with the action on the screen. Stuntspeople demonstrate their dangerous work in the Action Show.

Schloß Schleißheim★

15km/9mi north. Leave via Schleißheimer Straße. ♿ Apr-Sep: open every day except Mon, 9am-6pm; Oct-Mar: open every day except Mon, 10am-4pm. Closed 1st Jan, Shrove Tuesday, 24 and 25 Dec. €3. ☎ (089) 315 87 20. **Neues Schloß**, the so-called "new" palace, a majestic 330m/1 083ft in length, was built between 1701 and 1727 under Elector Max II Emanuel. The grand staircase leads to the State Apartments on the upper floor, the highlight of which is the huge banqueting hall in dazzling white. The adjacent Hall of Victory is adorned with gleaming gold stuccowork by JB Zimmermann. Next come the princely apartments and **galleries**, hung with European Baroque painting and works by 16C and 17C Dutch and Flemish masters, including the great gallery taking up the whole of the garden side of the central block.

On the ground floor, a second series of galleries follows on from the music room. The palace **grounds** are laid out in formal geometric French style by Carbonet and Girard, with a central canal as their main axis. At the far end of the park, enclosed by a circular canal, stands a small Baroque folly, the **Lustheim**, built by Zuccali in 1684-89; it houses a collection of Meissen porcelain.

Flugwerft Schleißheim★

Right next to Schloß Schleißheim. ♿ 9am-5pm. Closed 1st Jan, Shrove Tuesday, Good Friday, 1st May, 1st Nov, 24, 25 and 31 Dec. €3.50. ☎ (089) 315 71 40. The hangar was built between 1912 and 1919 for the Bavarian air corps. The Deutsches Museum has set up a new branch in the historic hangar and the newly built glass exhibition hall, the **Museum of Air and Space Travel** *(Museum für Luft- und Raumfahrt)*, which has proved popular with the public. It houses a wealth of historic aircraft of all kinds.

Buchheim Museum★, in Bernried

45km/28mi southwest. Take the A95 to Starnberg then the lakeside road. ♿ Apr-Oct: 10am-6pm, Sat-Sun 10am-8pm; Nov-Mar: open every day except Mon, 10am-5pm, Sat-Sun 10am-6pm. €7.80. ☎ (081 58) 99 70 60. This museum, founded by Günter Behnisch on the shores of the Starnberger See, houses the vast private collection of the German writer and painter Lothar-Günther Buchheim (author of *Das Boot*). The highlights of the collection are examples of German Expressionism, in particular painters of the *Die Brücke* movement such Kirchner, Heckel, Pechstein and Schmidt-Rottluff (paintings, engravings, watercolours, drawings). Bavarian folk art and crafts, and items from Africa and other countries are also on display.

Tours

AROUND AMMERSEE

Round tour of 116km/72mi – allow half a day.

Ammersee★

Lying at an altitude of 533m/1 749ft, this lake of glacial origin is cradled in a pretty landscape of wooded hills. Swimming, sailing and boat trips can be enjoyed at small resorts such as Dießen and Herrsching. Enthusiasts of the Rococo style must be sure to visit the abbey church at Andechs.

Follow the western lake shore to reach Dießen.

Dießen – The **church★** *(Marienmünster)* was built between 1732 and 1739 to replace a former monastery collegiate. The architect was Johann Michael Fischer, one of the most celebrated of the late, south German Baroque. The Asam brothers and François de Cuvilliés also contributed to the design.

The church is an impressively harmonious blend of rich decoration, in the stuccowork, frescoes and valuable altarpieces crafted by south German and Italian masters (including Straub and Tiepolo). The imposing chancel altar, over 20m/65ft high, with a fold-away image, unusually features a Mysteries stage.

The climb from Fischen to Andechs offers fine views of the lake.

Andechs★ – Crowning the Heiliger Berg ("holy hill"), this abbey *(Kloster Andechs)* overlooks the Ammersee from more than 200m/656ft. Its **church★★**, erected on a Gothic base, was remodelled as a Rococo building between 1751 and 1755. The architect JB Zimmermann (1680-1758), then at the height of his powers as a mature artist, was responsible both for the frescoes and the stuccowork. An elegant gallery, its balustrade decorated with painted panels evoking the history of the abbey, surrounds the main body of the church. The treatment of the vault frescoes, in various shades of pastel, shows an exceptional talent in the handling of colour. Bavarian composer Carl Orff, famous for the *Carmina Burana*, is buried in the Chapel of Suffering. About 1.5 million visitors come to Andechs every year to visit the church (and sample the famous local beer). *Only the abbey church and brewery are open to the public. Guided tour (1hr): every day except Sat-Sun, at 3pm. €2.50. ☎ (081 52) 37 60.*

Return to Munich via Herrsching and Seefeld.

EXPLORING THE BAVARIAN ALPS

172km/107mi-tour. Allow one day.

This route links up with the German Alpine Road *(see Deutsche ALPENSTRASSE)* at Wallgau.

Head south on the A8 until you reach exit 97, then join the B13 at Holzkirchen.

Bad Tölz – The discovery of exceptionally pure iodine springs, the richest in Germany, in 1845 transformed Tölz into a spa town famous throughout Europe. The wide curve and steep slope of the **Marktstraße★**, bordered by multicoloured façades beneath overhanging eaves, give the old town its special charm. At the top of the path which climbs up **Calvary Hill** *(Kalvarienberg)* stands a small chapel (1743) dedicated to St Leonard, whose powers are still widely revered among the peasants of Bavaria and Austria. The saint's anniversary, 6 November, is celebrated each year by a parade of rustic wagons and carts and drawn by teams of brilliantly harnessed horses *(see Events and Festivals)*. The Blomberg peak (1 248m/4 095ft) is a favourite day-trip destination *(chair-lift)*.

Head westwards on the B472 for 13km/8mi, then take the left fork to join the B11.

Benediktbeuern – Built on the lower slopes of the Bavarian Alps foothills, the monastery *(Kloster)*, founded in 739, has been the home of St John Bosco's Salesians since 1930. The **abbey church** as it is now was remodelled between 1681 and 1686. On those parts of the intersecting vaulting left free of stuccowork, Georg Asam – father of the famous Asam Brothers – painted the first complete cycle of frescoes dating from the beginning of the Bavarian Baroque period: the Birth, Baptism, Transfiguration and Resurrection of the Saviour, the Descent of the Holy Spirit and the Last Judgement.

Elegant frescoes and finely worked stucco make the **Anastasiakapelle★** (1751-53), a chapel a little to the north of the old church, one of the most charming examples of Rococo art. The designer, Johann Michael Fischer, and the craftsmen who carried out the work for him, were commissioned a few years later to repeat their artistry at Ottobeuren *(see Ottobeuren)*.

Continue southwards on the B11 for 21km/13mi.

Walchensee★ – *40km/25mi southwest.* Framed by dense woods, this deep blue reservoir lake is one of the beauties of the Bavarian Alps. Its waters serve the power station on the Kochelsee, some 200m/650ft lower down.

A chair-lift rises to the Fahrenberg, from which a path leads in 30min to the summit of the **Herzogstand** (1 731m/5 679ft). From the observation deck, there is a superb **all-round view★★** taking in the Walchensee, the Kochelsee, the Karwendel massif and the rock wall of the Wetterstein, which culminates in the Zugspitze.

Head north on the B11 and return to Munich via the A95 at Sindelsdorf.

Landsberg am Lech★

62km/39mi east via the A 96. A fortified frontier town between Swabia and Bavaria in the Middle Ages, Landsberg – on the old road from Salzburg to Memmingen – prospered through trade and the levying of tolls. Fortress gates, towers and perimeter walls still preserve a most attractive medieval atmosphere.

There is a fine view of the tiered **site★** from the shady riverside promenade on the west bank of the Lech, where it meets the Karolinenbrücke *(the best place to park if the Marktplatz below is full)*.

Marktplatz★ – Triangular in shape, the market place is surrounded by a remarkable group of gaily coloured roughcast town houses. The **fountain** *(Marienbrunnen)*, in the centre, falls into a marble basin surmounted by a statue of the Virgin Mary.

Rathaus – The façade of this building was executed c 1720 by Dominikus Zimmermann, one of the greatest artists of the Wessobrunn School *(see Wessobrunn)*, who built the Wies church and went on to be burgomaster of Landsberg (1749-54). The gable of the elegant structure is ornamented with finely worked stucco. The rest of the town hall was built between 1699 and 1702.

In the far corner of the square stands the **Schmalztor**, through which the upper town can be reached. Hemmed in on all sides by old houses, the 14C tower-gate is topped by a lantern turret roofed with glazed tiles.
The Alte Bergstraße climbs steeply to the "Bavarian Gate".
Bayertor (Bavarian Gate) – With its projecting porch flanked by turrets and sculptures, this 1425 town gateway is one of the best preserved of its period in the whole of Germany. Outside the ramparts, which continue on either side, the gateway is embellished with carved and painted coats of arms and with a Crucifixion.
Landsberg is on the Romantic Road (see ROMANTISCHE STRASSE) which continues northwards.

Münsterländer Wasserburgen★

Moated Castles of the Münster Region

There are around 100 moated castles to be found all over the Münster region, an area of low-relief. Most of them are privately-owned and can only be viewed from the outside, but some are open to visitors. Such well-preserved moated castles, situated in pleasant landscapes, fascinate still with their old-world charm.

Location

Michelin map n° 543 K 3 to 8 – Nordrhein-Westfalen. The castles are spread over about 100km/63mi around the town of Münster. Few can be reached by public transport. The best ways of getting to them are by car or bicycle.
Surrounding area (distances from Münster): see MÜNSTER, ESSEN (85km/53mi southwest), SAUERLAND (Soest is 63km/39mi southeast)

Background

Remains of Medieval wars – The charming **Wasserburgen** – literally "water castles" – are to be found all over the Münster region. Witness to the incessant fighting between rival nobles in order to protect their territories, they are built on the sites of temporary encampments set up by the Teutons. They first appeared in the 12C in the form of wooden strongholds erected on artificial hills ("Motten") which were protected at the base by a surrounding stockade or defensive wall and a moat full of water. The invention of firearms at the beginning of the 16C made this system of defence precarious, and it was replaced, little by little, with proper fortifications isolated still more by moats or lagoons.
Many of these fortresses spread over two islands, joined by a bridge. The first isle, or "Vorburg", would be used for the outbuildings; the second, or "Hauptburg" for the dwelling. Subsequently, two separate influences could be detected in their design: that of the Weser Renaissance from the east, and that of the Dutch architectural school coming from the west. Their defensive character became less distinct over the centuries, and especially after the Thirty Years War (1618-48). After that, virtual palaces set in formal gardens began to appear.
In the 18C, a taste for the Baroque manifested itself in the treatment of façades and gateways. Descriptions of several of the castles are given below.

Worth a Visit

Anholt★

Guided tour (1hr). Apr to Sep, Tue-Sun, 11am-5pm; Oct to Mar, Sat-Sun, 11am-5pm. Closed 1 Jan, 24-26 and 31 Dec. €5, combined ticket for guided tour and park, €6. ☎ (028 74) 453 53.
Surrounded by a 34ha/84-acre landscaped park and restored Baroque garden, this moated castle (Hauptburg and Vorburg 12C-17C, converted into a Baroque place in c 1700) is built around a square inner courtyard. The museum contains evidence of three centuries of royal home decor: collection of paintings (Rembrandt, Brueghel, Murillo), tapestries, furniture, porcelain and weapons. Note the large oak staircase, the Knights Room with gallery, the reception hall decorated with Flemish tapestries, the porcelain collection and the gallery of Dutch masterpieces.

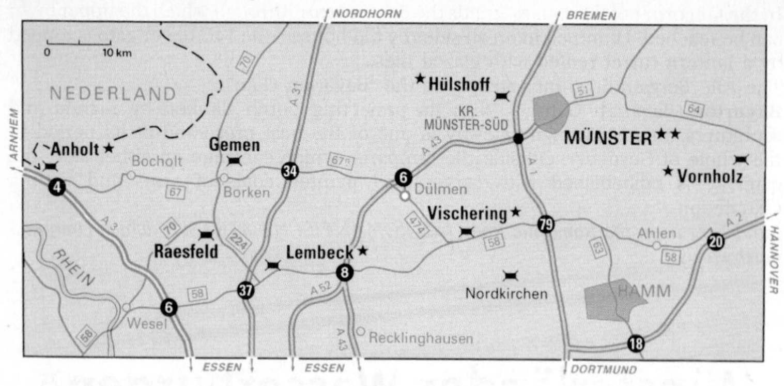

Gemen

This castle is a training centre; visits on request only: ☎ (028 61) 922 00.
The towers, battlements and buildings of this castle (15C, remodelled in the 17C) are grouped on a fortified islet which arises from beautiful, shaded stretches of water. The original keep was later crowned with a Baroque roof. Today, the moated castle is a youth centre.

Hülshoff★

Open from Feb to mid-Dec, 9.30am-6pm. €3. ☎ (025 34) 10 52. The massive square towers of the outbuildings (first island) complement a manor-house (second island) constructed in 1545. The brick and stonework manor is distinguished by gable ends and a turret with cupola and lantern. A neo-Gothic chapel was added in 1870. The poetess **Annette von Droste-Hülshoff** was born here in 1797 (small museum).

Lembeck★

Guided visit (45min). From Mar to end Oct, 10am-6pm. €4. ☎ (023 69) 71 67.
The approach to this castle is impressive – a long perspective of driveway punctuated by a series of Baroque gateways and flanked by the arched entrances to various parts of the central complex. The monumental edifice spread over two islands today was built at the end of the 17C on the site of a 14C fortress. Huge towers with Baroque roofs stand at every corner. A few rooms inside can be visited. The biggest (Großer Saal) is embellished with fine panelling and stuccowork. Valuable furniture, Gobelins tapestries, porcelain and paintings from the 17C to the 19C are on display.
In the spring the rhododendron park is an absolute riot of colour.

Raesfeld

Guided tour (1hr) by appointment with the Tourist Office only. ☎ (028 65) 95 51 27.
Raesfeld castle, built between 1643 and 1658 by Alexander von Velen, now consists only of a building with two wings, the Vorburg and the castle chapel. The tower (49.5m/162ft) and onion dome are visible from afar.

Vischering★

Open Apr-Oct, Tue-Sun, 10am-12.30pm, 1.30-5.30pm; Nov-Mar, Tue-Sun, 10am-12.30pm, 1.30-4.30pm. Closed 1 Jan and 24-26 Dec. €2.50. ☎ (025 91) 79 90 11.
Built on two islands and protected by a double fortified wall, Vischering is still one of the most formidable **fortresses** in the Münster region. A Renaissance building has been constructed on the medieval foundations of the Rundburg. The fortress now houses a museum, with special emphasis on furniture from various eras, for example a state bed from the 16C. The wall and ceiling paintings and splendid sandstone fireplaces are particularly impressive.
The Vorburg, which stands on a separate island, used to house the fortress' farm outbuildings. Today visitors can see an exhibition of life and work in the rural environment. There is also a richly decorated carriage house.
Not far from Vischering, 8km/5mi south-east of Lündinghausen, is the impressive 18C moated castle of **Nordkirchen**, known as "Westphalia's miniature Versailles". This beautiful palace also houses a school of finance.

Vornholz★ *see MÜNSTER: Excursions*

Münster★★

Münster, the historical capital of Westphalia, where the local lords used to stay in winter, lies in the middle of a wooded plain studded with castles and manor houses. The city, one of Germany's most important university centres, has been restored to give full value to its many fine Gothic, Baroque and Renaissance façades. Cyclists will adore this city: its little streets throng with bikes (*Leeze* in the local dialect) whatever the weather.

Location

Population: 280 000. Michelin map n° 543 K 6 – Nordrhein-Westfalen. Münster can be reached via the A 1 (Dortmund-Bremen), and is one hour by car from the big towns of the Ruhr.

Klemensstraße 9, 48127 Münster, ☎ (0251) 492 27 10.

Surrounding area: see MÜNSTERLÄNDER WASSERBURGEN, OSNABRÜCK (56km/35mi north via the A 1), RUHRGEBIET (Dortmund is 67km/42mi south via the A 1).

Directory

Where to Eat

Kleines Restaurant im Oer'schen Hof – *Königsstraße 42 – ☎ (0251) 484 10 83 – Closed Sun-Mon – €30/43.50.* This establishment is spread over three floors of an old glazed brick house. Pleasant ambience, where rustic furniture is mixed with modern paintings.

Where to Stay

Hotel-Restaurant Hiltruper Hof – *Westfalenstraße 148, 48165 Münster-Hiltrup – ☎ (0251) 278 80 – fax (0251) 7878 – www.hiltruper-hof.de – 17rm: €40/70 – Restaurant €9/25.* For 150 years this little family-run hotel has welcomed guests into well-cared for guestrooms. Sports and leisure equipment is available locally and the hotel is a good departure point for bike trips.

Background

The Peace of Westphalia – This treaty, signed on 24 October 1648, ended the Thirty Years War. During the five years of negotiations, the Emperor shuttled between the plenipotentiaries of the Protestant states in Osnabrück and those from the Catholic states in Münster, where the documents were finally agreed. As a result, much of Germany was carved up, to the detriment of Imperial prestige. The treaty recognised and confirmed the cession to France of Alsace and the bishoprics of Metz, Toul and Verdun, guaranteed the independence of Switzerland and the Netherlands, and favoured the development of Prussia. Three religious faiths were recognised, the Calvinists receiving the same rights as the Lutherans and Roman Catholics.

Worth a Visit

Dom★★

A squat building with two towers, two chancels and two transepts, this church is in the transitional style typical of Westphalia in the 13C.

Entering via the 16C south porch, the visitor sees that the inner door is surrounded by 13C statues and overlooked by a Christ in Judgement. A 16C statue of St Paul, patron saint of the cathedral, looks down from the pier.

Visit the interior anti-clockwise.

The wide central nave and its bays lie beneath rounded vaulting. The side aisles are very low. In the ambulatory there is a 1540 **astronomical clock★** in which the hours are struck by metal figurines wielding hammers. The spectators' gallery, high up in the church, was painted by Tom Ring the Elder.

The Chapel of the Holy Sacrament, left of the entrance to the cloister, is richly **furnished★** (note especially an 18C silver tabernacle, made by a craftsman in Augsburg). The cloister entrance is reached through the north transept crossing.

Treasury★★ (Domkammer) – *Off the cloister. Open Tue-Sun, 11am-4pm. Closed 1 Jan, Good Fri-Easter Sun, 1 May, Pentecost, 24-26 and 31 Dec. €1. ☎ (0251) 49 53 33.* This is a modern building, blending perfectly with the structure of the cathedral, to which it is indirectly attached by the cloister.

On the ground floor, fourteen 15C reliquary-busts of the Prophets in copper and silver, the 11C head-reliquary of St Paul, together with a 13C Virgin – both of them in chased gold – surround the **Processional Cross** of the Chapter, which is the focal

MÜNSTER

Street	Grid
Alter Fischmarkt	Y 2
Alter Steinweg	Y 5
An der Apostel kirche	Y 8
Bahnhofstraße	Z
Bogenstraße	Y 12
Drubbel	Y 16
Eisenbahnstraße	Z 20
Hammer Straße	Z 30
Johannisstraße	Z 39
Ludgeristraße	Z
Mauritzstraße	Y 48
Mauritztor	Y 51
Pferdegasse	Y 63
Prinzipalmarkt	YZ
Rothenburg	Z 69
Salzstraße	YZ 72
Spiekerhof	Y 78
Steinfürter Straße	Y 80
Überwasserstraße	Y 83
Universitätsstraße	YZ 86
Verspoel	Z 89
Wasserstraße	Y 92
Wolbecker Straße	Z 96

Sight	Grid
Domkammer	Y M²
Rathaus	YZR
Westfälisches Landesmuseum für Kunst und Kulturgeschichte	YZM¹

point of the whole treasure house. In the basement there is a fine collection of liturgical vestments, particularly from the 17C and 18C, and ritual items. In the centre stands a portable altar (12C) hung with a cloth embroidered in pearls. Noteworthy on the first floor, amid a collection of Gothic and Baroque statuary, is the 1520 **Altarpiece of St John**.

Westfälisches Landesmuseum für Kunst und Kulturgeschichte★ (Fine Arts Museum)

♿ *Open Tue-Sun, 10am-6pm. Closed 24, 25 and 31 Dec. €2.60, no charge Fri.* ☎ *(0251) 59 07 01.* The medieval art of Westphalia lives on, thanks to the Gothic statuary of the cathedral and churches of Münster, a series of stained-glass windows in this museum, and the sculptures of Johann and Heinrich Brabender. There is a remarkable collection of **altarpieces★★** by Konrad von Soest, Koerbecke and the Masters of Liesborn and Schöppingen. Flemish influence is noticeable in the works of the tom Ring family (Ludger tom Ring's painting was a precursor of the still-life). Interesting portraits of Luther and his wife are by Lucas Cranach. 20C masterpieces by August Macke, Ernst Ludwig Kirchner and Josef Albers, among others, round off this overview of artistic creativity from the Middle Ages to the present.

Prinzipalmarkt★

Running in a semicircle to the east of the cathedral, this is the busiest – and at the same time the most historic – street in town. The elegant houses, with Late Gothic or Renaissance gables, which have been restored since the Second World War, were once the homes of rich burghers. Under the arcades, attractive shops compete for space with restaurants and beer halls. The northern end of the street opens into the Bogenstraße, a wide space inviting for both window-shoppers and strollers (the statue halfway up, a pedlar with his basket, is known as the *Kiepernkerl*).

Rathaus

♿ *Open Tue-Sun, 10am-5pm, Sat-Sun, 10am-4pm. €1.50. ☎ (0251) 492 27 24.* The late-14C gabled façade of the town hall, with pinnacles and fine stone window tracery, is one of the most impressive examples of Gothic civic architecture.

Friedenssaal★ (Peace Hall) – The wood-panelled council chamber, now named after the peace treaty, dates from the second half of the 12C. In 1648 it was the backdrop to the peace between Spain and the Netherlands, which heralded the whole Treaty of Westphalia. The original fittings, which were put out to store during the Second World War, are preserved just as they were recorded in the painting of the peace treaty by Gerhard Terborch.

The woodwork on the doors of the filing cabinet behind the burgomaster's table are some of the most original produced by German sculptors at the beginning of the 16C. The colourful mixture of religious and amusing motifs nonetheless raises the suspicion that the present arrangement is not that of the original.

Lambertikirche

Groined vaulting over the centre nave and star vaults above the side aisles are the striking features of this Gothic hall-church. The neo-Gothic tower with its openwork **spire★** was added in the 19C. It stands 99m/324ft tall. Still visible hanging from the tower are the iron cages in which the bodies of the Anabaptist rebel leaders were displayed to the public following the defeat of their uprising in 1536. Behind the east end of the church is the Krameramtshaus, a fine guild house with a gable end (1588).

Residenzschloß★

Once the prince-bishops' residence, this Baroque palace is now part of the university. The red brick of the elegant three-part façade designed by Johann Conrad Schlaun is variegated with sandstone facings which enliven any monotony of style. At the back, surrounded by water, lies a park *(Schloßgarten)* with an adjoining botanical garden. This green space is continued south of the palace by the Rampart Walk *(Wallpromenade)*, from which there is a view of Lake Aasee.

Erbdrostenhof

This palace, dating from 1757, was built with a majestic concave façade and a triangular forecourt testifying to the skill of architect Johann Conrad Schlaun.

The Anabaptists

This Reformist movement, which refused to acknowledge infant baptism, advocating baptism for believing adults only, originated in Zürich. What began as a peaceful movement aiming to change the Church from within, evolved over time into a more radical revolutionary sect under the pressure of savage persecution (since they dared to voice criticism of the state). One of the places they achieved supremacy was Münster, where one of their more radical branches effectively set up a reign of terror in 1534, which was brought to an end only after a 16-month state of siege; whereupon its ringleaders were hung. The Anabaptists, or Rebaptists, were in some ways the spiritual forerunners of the Baptists.

►► Ludgerikirche – Westfälisches Museum für Naturkunde★ (*planetarium★*) – Mühlenhof-Freilichtmuseum★ *(access via Hüfferstraße)* – Museum Pablo Picasso (exhibition of 800 lithographs by the artist)

Excursions

Telgte

12km/8mi east on B 51. In the historic town centre of Telgte, next to the Baroque pilgrimage chapel in which there is a Pietà dating from 1370 visited by numerous pilgrims, is the local museum, Heimathaus Münsterland. One of its prize exhibits is a folk art masterpiece on cloth, the **Lenten Veil★** (*Hungertuch*, 1623), which measures no less than 32m²/344sq ft. Both the Heimathaus and the nearby **Christmas crib museum** explore the way religious faith is expressed in local art and customs.

Freckenhorst

26km/16mi east on B 51. **The Collegiate Church★** (Stiftskirche) with its fortified façade, is a fine example of pre-Romanesque German architecture *(see Introduction)*. Note the magnificent **baptismal font★** in the north aisle, inscribed with the date of the church's consecration (1129). On a tomb in the crypt is the recumbent statue of Geva, the church's founder.

Fine twinned columns support the remaining (west) gallery of the cloister.

Ostenfelde

36km/22mi east on B 51. The graceful **Vornholz Castle★** (1666) stands in a rolling landscape forested with ancient oaks. Built on two islets, its tall, roofed main block flanked by two wings, this is a typical Münsterland "water castle" (Münsterländer Wasserburg – *see below*).

Münsterländer Wasserburgen – *see MÜNSTERLÄNDER WASSERBURGEN*

Naumburg★

The pretty town of Naumburg lies on the edge of the Thuringian basin, surrounded by vineyards and wooded hillsides. The town's exceptional cathedral marries Roman and Gothic architecture. The philosopher Friedrich Nietzsche spent a lot of time in the town at various stages of his life. During the last weekend in June the town celebrates the kirsch festival.

Location

Population: 31 400. Michelin map nº 544 M 19 – Sachsen-Anhalt. Naumburg is in the middle of the "Saale-Unstrut-Triasland" National Park and makes a pleasant and practical base for exploring the region.

Markt 6, 06618 Namburg, ☎ (034 45) 20 16 14.

Surrounding area: see HALLE (47km/29mi north), WEIMAR (50km/31mi southwest), LEIPZIG (63km/39mi northeast).

Background

Important trading centre – The seat of a bishopric since 1028, by the 12C, Naumburg was already developing as a civic entity independent of the cathedral city. The city was an important trading centre in the Late Middle Ages and Renaissance period. The "Peter-Pauls-Messe" held here was a serious rival to the trade fair in Leipzig. Naumburg became part of Prussiaunder the Vienna Congress and was transformed into a local government and administration centre for the provinceof Saxony.

A model town – Largely spared damage during the Second World War, in 1991 Naumburg was one of five cities in the nine new Federal German states selected as a model for restoring old city centres. Its economic structure is essentially composed of administration and service facilities, and small- and medium-sized craft industries.

Worth a Visit

Dom St. Peter und Paul★★

Access via Domplatz. This double-chancel church is a perfect example of the architectural evolution from Late Romanesque to Early Gothic. The Romanesque nave was built in the beginning to mid-13C. Between 1250 and 1270, the western section was completed by a chancel already displaying certain Early Gothic features. The east chancel, under which there is still a Romanesque crypt, was itself transformed into a Gothic structure in the 14C. The eastern chancel is separated from the central nave by the eastern rood screen, the only remaining hall-church rood screen in Germany.

West Chancel – The western **rood screen★★** is a magnificent work by the Master of Naumburg, who created it as a partition wall, in which the incredibly poignant, life-like scenes represent the Passion as a human tragedy. The splendid central portal depicts a Crucifixion group, surmounted by the Majesty of God as a fresco in a quatrefoil. The same master also created the famous **statues of the cathedral's benefactors★★★**, which decorate the chancel and which undoubtedly took medieval sculpture in Germany to the summit of its glory. The individual personification of these figures and their penetrating expressions all add up to an exceptional effect of humanity and grandeur. The best known are those of the founders of the town, Margrave Ekkehard and his wife Uta *(centre, right)*.

View of Naumburg with the cathedral in the background.

J. Bouraly/MICHELIN

Marktplatz

The large **market square** is edged with 16C-17C houses. The **town hall**, a Late Gothic building with a beautiful portal dating from 1612, boasts six transverse gables with tracery decoration. The same façade design is repeated on the *Schlößchen* (1543), behind which towers the church of St Wenzel. The "Hohe Lilie" (municipal museum), with its Late Gothic corbie gable and traced transom, stands at the entrance to Herrenstraße.

St-Wenzel★

The original church on this site was first recorded in 1228. The present building was constructed as a Late Gothic hall-church with an unusual floor plan in the 15C. The width of the west octagon matches the distance west to east as far as the junction with the east chancel, to which extra elevation has been added (33m/108ft). Between 1610 and 1618, five Renaissance tribunes were added, and up to the mid-18C the interior was transformed into the Baroque style with a mirror-vaulted ceiling, magnificent carved altar, pulpit and organ. This instrument is one of the largest surviving works by **Zacharias Hildebrand**. It was put through its paces by Johann Sebastian Bach, no less.

There are two fine paintings by **Lucas Cranach the Elder**: *The Adoration of the Magi* (1522) facing the choir and, on the south side of the choir, *The Blessing of the Children* (1529). The artist is supposed to have portrayed himself in both these scenes.

Townhouses

In Jakobstraße note the Alte Post (1574) with its three-storey oriel. In **Marienstraße** there are plenty of interesting old houses to look at. The extravagantly ornate portals, testify to the town's prosperity, for example the Samson portal on Peter-Pauls-Haus illustrating the fight between Samson and the lion. **Herrenstraße** features some fine oriels, for example the oldest in Naumburg at house no 1. The *"Lorbeerapotheke"*, chemist's shop adjacent to it also boasts a splendid oriel, as does the house at no 8 (1525).

Marientor

This is the only one of the five original town gates to have survived. It is a rare example of a double gate with gatehouses, a courtyard with a bend in it to trap intruders, and a watchpath. Its nucleus dates from the 14C, but it was extended in the 15C.

►► Nietzsche-Haus

(Am Weingarten) From 1890 until 1897, during his collapse into mental and physical decline, Nietzsche was cared for in this house by his mother. Photos and documents (in German) evoke the intellectual life and works of the traveller-philosopher.

Excursions

Freyburg

7km/4.5mi north. This wine-growing centre stands in a picturesque location on the banks of the Unstrut, dominated by the Neuenburg which stands high above the town. Visitors can travel by steamer along the river through attractive countryside as far as the Naumburg flower fields.

Shloß Neuenburg★ – *Open Apr to Oct, Tue-Sun, 10am-6pm; Nov to Mar, Tue-Sun, 10am-5pm. €3. ☎ (0344 64) 355 30.* The Neuenburg was founded in 1090 by Ludwig der Springer, the Landgrave of Thuringia. It represented the eastern counterpart to the Wartburg fortress in the west. The double **chapel★**, an extremely unusual type of building, of which the lower floor was reserved for the people and the upper floor for the higher nobility, is of considerable interest. Its origins date back to c 1230. The two floors are linked by a small grille in the ceiling. The rich architectural design and ornamentation is copied from the Lower Rhine area. The serrated transverse arches of the upper floor are in the same style, as is the splendid gilded **capital★** with its decorative figures. The superb Renaissance spiral staircase, which leads from the lower to the upper floor, was moved here in the 19C.

There are around a dozen beautifully furnished rooms to visit in the royal apartments, including the banqueting hall and the royal hall with a whole series of portraits of various princes and a portal which dates from 1552.

The **Dicker Wilhelm**, a Romanesque keep with a domed slate roof, is said to have been built at the end of the 12C. An exhibition retraces the history of the tower and the town.

Schulpforta, near Bad Kösen

On B 87, just before Bad Kösen, around 6km/3.5mi west. Cistercian abbey church and estate, open Apr to Aug, 10am-6pm; Sep to Mar, 10am-4pm. Closed 24 Dec-6 Jan. No charge. Guided tours only of historic buildings (75min), from Apr to beginning Oct, Sat at 10.30am and 2pm. €2.50. ☎ (0344 63) 351 10.

The **Cistercian monastery**, which was founded in 1137, was closed in 1540. Since then it has been the home of the renowned provincial school, whose famous scholars include Schlegel, Fichte and Klopstock, together with Friedrich Nietzsche, who joined the school in 1858 ("I longed for Pforta, only for Pforta") and which is still in existence today. The **monastery church**, with its imposing west façade dating from c 1300 has been under restoration for some considerable time. The well maintained monastery contains the interesting **Panster mill★**, a technically most impressive monument to the technology of its era *(the mill is put into operation during guided tours)*.

Bad Kösen★

On B 87, around 7km/4.25mi west. This attractive little health resort on the Saale boasts a **technical monument** which is quite unique in Europe, the **brine extraction unit★**, which comprises an undershot water wheel, a 180m/590ft-long double set of artificial rods which originates from 1780, and a 320m/1 050ft refinery.

The **Romanesque house** *(by the double set of rods)*, now used as a museum, was first recorded in 1138 as the Schulpforte monastery guesthouse. The exhibits illustrate this past, for example there is a Romanesque store cabinet from the 13C. Since there was a doll workshop run in Bad Kösen by Käthe Kruse between 1912 and 1950, there is also an area of the museum given over to a display of dolls of yesteryear. *Open May to Oct, Tue-Sun, 10am-12 noon, 1-5pm, Sat-Sun, 10am-5pm; Nov to Apr, Wed, 10am-12 noon, 1-4pm, Sat-Sun, 10am-4pm. Closed from mid-Dec to mid-Jan. €2. ☎ (0344 63) 276 68.*

The ruined fortresses of **Rudelsburg** and **Burg Saaleck**, which were destroyed during the Thirty Years War, lie in an attractive **site★** high above the Saale 3km/2mi to the south of Bad Kösen. They are a popular tourist destination. Built in the 12C, they have fallen into disrepair over the years, but the walls were repaired and the towers made safe during the castle blessing which took place in the 19C.

Neubrandenburg

The town was founded in 1248 at the behest of Margrave Johann von Brandenburg. Built on an almost circular ground plan, criss-crossed by a grid-like network of streets, the town has retained its original layout. Its later development took place outside the town walls. When 80% of the old town was destroyed in 1945, the fortifications with their four unique gates were quite remarkably spared from damage, making them a principal point of attraction to the tourist, in conjunction with the Tollensesee close by.

Location

Population: 70 000. Michelin map n° 542 F 23 – Mecklemburg-Vorpommern. Mid-way between Berlin and the Baltic coast, Neubrandenburg is to the northeast of the pretty lake of Tollense.

🅱 *Marktplatz 1, 17033 Neubrandenburg, ☎ (0395) 194 33.*

Surrounding area: see MECKLEMBURGISCHE SEENPLATTE (Waren is 43km/27mi west via the 192 road), GREIFSWALD (66km/41mi north), Insel USEDOM (Mellenthin is 79km/49mi northeast).

Worth a Visit

Fortifications★★

Some 50 years after the town was founded, it became obvious that considerable defences were needed to protect it. Consequently, work was begun on a 2.3km/1.4mi-long town wall, over 7m/23 ft in height, 1.40m/4ft 7in wide at the base and 0.60m/1ft 10in at the top. Boulders from the vicinity were used to build the wall, capped by several rows of bricks. Four gates were incorporated into the wall, and these were closed every evening and only opened in return for payment. These remained the only access to the town right up to the mid-19C.

The gates are all of the same design. The main gate is inside the wall, and is connected with an outer gate via keep walls. Each gate constitutes an individual fortification. The outer gates were secured with portcullises. As if this was insufficient to secure the town, a semicircular battle tower with 4m/13ft-thick walls, the Zingel or circular wall, was erected 19m/62ft away from the outer gate.

So that the town could be safely defended, 3- to 4-floor bastions, known as **Wiekhäuser**, were built into the town wall every 30m/98ft. There were 56 of them in the 16C, 25 of which have been reconstructed. All the able-bodied citizens were called upon to maintain the Wiekhäuser, whilst defence of the gates was the duty of the four principal guilds: Bakers, Wool Weavers, Shoemakers and Blacksmiths.

NEUBRANDENBURG

An der Marienkirche .... AY 3
Beguinenstraße .... AY 4
Behmenstraße .... BY 5
Bernhardstraße .... AY 7
Bussardstraße .... BY 8
Darrenstraße .... AY 9
Friedländer Straße .... BY 12
Herbordstraße .... BY 13
Lerchenstraße .... AY 14
Marktplatz .... AY 17
Mühlenholz straße .... .BYZ 18
Post Boulevard .... AY 19
Poststraße .... BY 20
Sonnenkamp .... BZ 21
Torgelower Straße .... BY 22
Treptower Straße .... AY 23
Turmstraße .... BY
Voßstraße .... AY 22
Waagestraße .... AY 4
5. Ringstraße .... BY 30

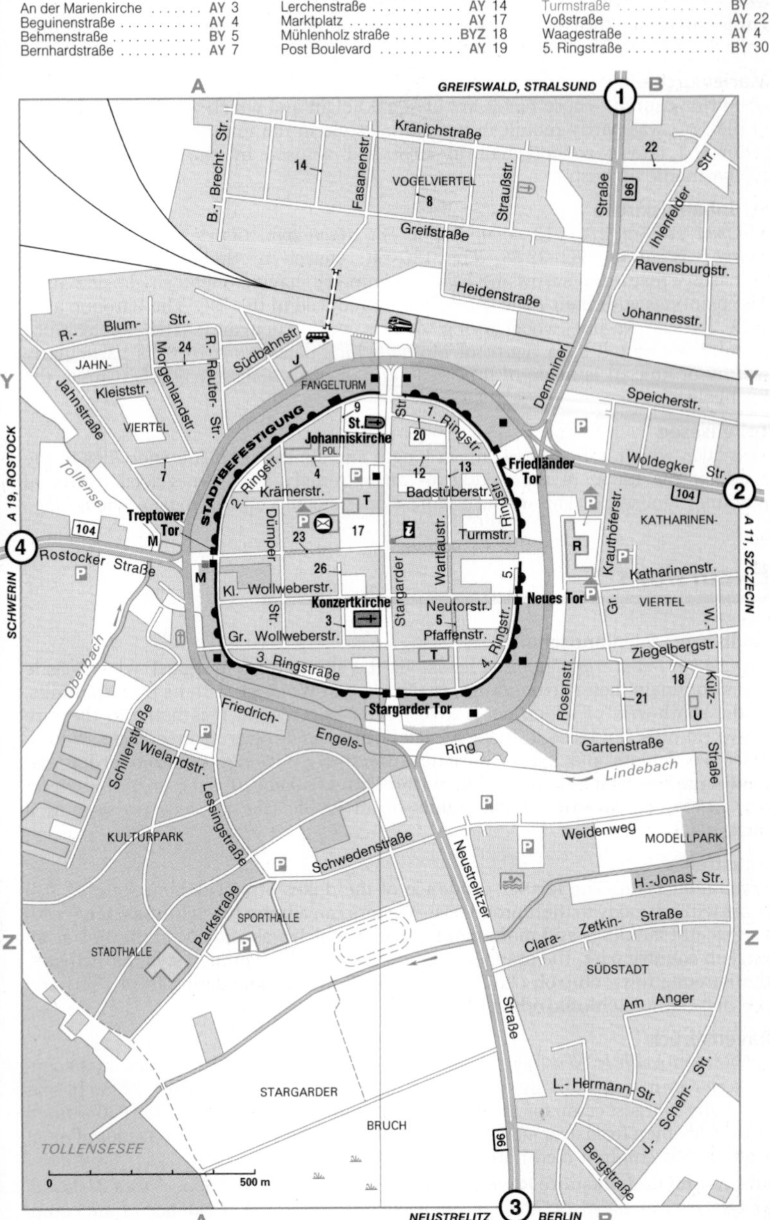

Friedländer Tor – This is the oldest gate, built just after 1300. It is 19m/62ft high. On the outside it is possible to see the transition from the Romantic to the Gothic period, whilst the town side, built later, is entirely Gothic. The houses of the former keeper of the circular defence wall, the gate recorder and the tax collector are incorporated into the 48m/157ft-long wall between the main gate and the outer gate.

Stargarder Tor – Built during the first half of the 14C. The body of the tower and the gable ends form a unit in which the Perpendicular style is emphasised by nine terracotta figures characterised by long stiffly-pleated robes, known as "Die Jungfrauen" *(the maids)*. The outer gate is especially sumptuously decorated.

Treptower Tor – Built c 1400. At 32m/105ft, this is the highest of the gate towers. Both the main gate and the outer gate are sumptuously decorated with brick tracery. On this High Gothic masterpiece, the outside is for the first time more highly decorated than the inside, an expression of the town's desire to appear imposing.

Neues Tor – Built after 1550. The Late Gothic structure features no fresh influences, but instead combines the decorative elements of the other three gates. The outer gate no longer exists.

Fangelturm – Of the two towers which provided reinforcement to the fortifications, only the 19m/62ft-high Fangelturm remains. The spire was added in 1845.

Marienkirche

The brick church, whose naves are of equal height and which was built at the end of the 13C, was partly rebuilt in neo-Gothic style in the mid-19C. The church was renovated into a concert hall in 1996 and is used by the Neubrandenburg philharmonic orchestra.

St. Johanniskirche

♿ *Open Tue-Sat, 10am-12 noon, 1-6pm, Sat, 10am-4pm. Closed bank holidays. No charge.* ☎ *(0395) 582 22 88.* The 13C-14C church of the former Franciscan monastery features a surprising lack of symmetry, having only a single side aisle. The paintings with their plant motifs were produced in the 19C. The Baroque altar with its extravagant woodcarving depicts the Crucifixion. The Renaissance **pulpit★** supported by a figure of Moses, which dates from 1598, is particularly worthy of note. It is made of limestone and displays alabaster reliefs (Christ, the Evangelists).

Tollensesee

This lake, which is 10.4km/6.5mi in length and almost 3km/2mi wide, lies to the south of the town, in the middle of an extremely attractive glacial (terminal moraine) landscape. The western bank slopes steeply up to Brodaer woods.

Excursions

Feldberger Seenlandschaft★

75km/47mi round trip. The road leads, via the site of **Burg Stargard**, whose castle ruins dominate their surroundings, to the town of **Woldegk** with its five windmills, to the south-west of which lies a lovely hilly lake region. It is home to the rare old-world otter, and also to the sea eagle, osprey and lesser spotted eagle. Woods, meadows, moors and lakes alternate attractively between **Fürstenwerder** and **Feldberg**. The former house of the writer **Hans Fallada** (*If you ever eat from a tin bowl*, 1934) in **Carwitz**, which stands in an idyllic lakeside location, is now a memorial.

Neustrelitz

27km/17mi south. The former residence of the dukes of Mecklenburg-Strelitz still bears witness today to their proud past. Visitors can admire the **Schloßgarten★** with its graceful buildings and monuments, part of which was laid out in the 19C as an English country park, the orangerie with its remarkable Pompeii-style **paintings★**, the Baroque town **church** (1768-78), the classical **Rathaus** dating from 1841, and the neo-Gothic **Schloßkirche** (1855-59).

Ravensbrück

19km/11mi south of Neustrelitz, 1km/0.6mi from Fürstenberg. Ravensbrück concentration camp was built on the shores of Lake Schwedtsee after 1938. It was Germany's largest camp for the detention of women. Up until 1945, 132 000 women and 20 000 men from over 40 nations were deported here. Tens of thousands of men, women and children died here.

Mahn- und Gedenkstätte Ravensbrück – *Open Tue-Sun, 9am-5pm. Closed 24-26 and 31 Dec. No charge.* ☎ *(0330 93) 60 80; www.ravensbrueck.de.* Evidence of the camp, such as the crematorium and the cell block, has been included in the memorial. A permanent exhibition in the old SS camp commander's headquarters documents the history of the camp and the lives and deaths of its victims.

Schloß Neuschwanstein★★★

Neuschwanstein castle, with its countless towers and light limestone merlons, is a fairy-tale castle come true, and is a product of the imagination of King Ludwig II of Bavaria (1845-86). The young ruler was an ardent admirer of the composer Richard Wagner, whose theatrical world he wished to recreate in this castle "in the true style of the old German knights' castles". Neuschwanstein is the most popular tourist sight in Bavaria and visitors should be prepared to queue for several hours in high season. However, the many footpaths near the castle will allow visitors to escape the crowds and find some tranquillity.

Location

Michelin maps nos 545, 546 X 16 – Bayern. Five kilometres to the east of Füssen, the castle is located on a rocky ridge 200m above the Pöllat gorge, making an impressive **site★★**. From the windows of the castle or from one of the surrounding walkways, there are arresting panoramic views of the Alpes, the Allgäu plain, the Alpsee lake and the deep gorges of the Pöllat.

Surrounding area: see ROMANTISCHE STRASSE, Deutsche ALPENSTRASSE, FÜSSEN (5km/3mi east), WIESKIRCHE (25km/16mi northeast).

Background

The construction – **King Ludwig** *(see MÜNCHEN)* found the ideal location for "Neu-Hohenschwangau" (which did not become commonly known as Neuschwanstein until after 1890) not far from Hohenschwangau castle *(see below)*, where he had spent part of his childhood and youth. He was unquestionably inspired, when planning Neuschwanstein, by the **Wartburg**, which he had seen in 1867.

In 1868 he commissioned Eduard Riedel to design the castle. The foundation stone was laid a year later. In view of the fact that three architects were involved in the building (Georg Dolmann from 1874 and Julius Hoffmann from 1886), each of whom had to adapt to the king's ideas, the consistency of the building work is quite impressive.

The end of a dream – Ludwig II only lived at Neuschwanstein for 170 days. The work on the castle had left the royal coffers empty and the king's increasingly unpredictable behaviour led a government commission from Munich to bring him news of his dethronement on 10 June 1886. The king was found dead three days later in Lake Starnberg. The circumstances of his death, and that of his doctor, who had accompanied him on a walk that fateful night, never became clear. The castle was not quite complete when Ludwig died, but the great hall was finished and the interior of the 3rd and 4th floors were almost ready.

The wonderful Neuschwanstein castle which ruined Ludwig II of Bavaria.

F. Zaninotto/MICHELIN

Special Features

CASTLE★★★

Guided tour (35min, commentary available in English). Apr to Sep, 9am-6pm (-8pm, Thu), Oct to Mar, 10am-4pm. Closed 1 Jan, Shrove Tue, 24, 25 and 31 Dec. Ticket booths open at 7.30am in season. €8. ☎ (083 62) 810 35, www.neuschwanstein.com. Combined ticket with Hohenschwangau: €15. Tickets are purchased before going up to the castle: 30min walk up gentle slope; by bus (10min, leaves every 30min, €1.80); on horseback (30min, stops mid-way, €5). Visitors should be prepared to queue for several hours in high season.

The castle is only seen in all its grandeur at the end of the climb where, for most people, the queueing begins. The interior, with its profusion of gilded panelling and wall paintings, seems almost unreal. The most distinctive rooms are, on the third floor, the **throne room★** (unfinished), the **bed chamber★** furnished with Gothic pieces, the **sitting room★** with its decor inspired by the Lohengrin legend, and the artificial stalactite cave with the adjacent small winter garden, evoking the Tannhäuser legend. The design of the **minstrels' room★★** *(Sängersaal)* is based on the Wartburg *(see EISENACH)*, where the legendary poetry contest featured in Wagner's opera Tannhäuser was said to have taken place in the early 13C.

Visitors can also watch a film (20min, in English or German) on the king's life.

After the tour, visitors can go up to the Marien bridge (Marienbrücke, 10min on foot, steep slope) to watch the Pöllat river cascade down a deep gorge and admire a splendid **view★★** of the castle. Ludwig II would sometimes gaze at the silent, empty castle from this bridge in the dark, having had the lights in the minstrels' room lit earlier. The walk continues around the wooded slopes, with an ever-changing view of the castle.

After heading back down, a short detour to the shores of the **Alpsee★** (100m/109yd behind the ticket offices) with the Tyrol in the background provides an opportunity for a quiet stroll along banks frequented by the swans that Ludwig II's family loved so much. .

Gothic with All Mod Cons

Ludwig II's plans for a home recreating Germanic mythology through Gothic architecture also took into account the latest scientific developments. The cranes used to build the castle were steam powered, a steel frame was used in the throne room, and the windows held broad panes of glass that were uncommon even in the 19C. Other features included a floor-based central heating system, flushing toilets, a lift, electric bells to summon servants, and telephones on the third and fourth floors. Not so much the "Fairytale King" *(Märchenkönig)* as a man with his own private theme park...

Excursions

Schloß Hohenschwangau★

Guided visit (35min). Apr to Sep, 9am-6pm; Oct to Mar, 10am-4pm. Closed 24 Dec. €8. ☎ (083 62) 93 08 30; www.ticket-center-hohenschwangau.de

Maximilian II of Bavaria, who was at the time still the Crown Prince, had this castle built between 1833 and 1837 on the remains of a fortress dating from the 12C. The neo-Gothic style, which was highly influenced by English castle and fortress architecture, was in accordance with current taste, which tended to be medieval, and the Prince's predilection for chivalric romance. It was in these surroundings that the unfortunate King Ludwig II of Bavaria spent most of his youth.

The **castle** stands in a picturesque setting on a wooded hill. It is best to skirt this, following the road round to a beautiful **viewpoint★** on a shaded rocky spur of the **Pindarplatz** on the north bank of the Alpsee, from where it is possible to look out over the lake and its surroundings dotted with pines, which is overlooked by the steep slopes of the Säuling. Then cross the avenue to reach the castle.

In comparison to Neuschwanstein and despite many exaggerated features (there is an almost compulsive repetition of the etymological swan – *Schwan* – motif throughout the interior) and an accumulation of rather cumbersome objets d'art, Hohenschwangau has retained a very homely character. The length of time spent here by Queen Maria, Ludwig II's mother, explains the relatively personal atmosphere of the castle.

Having endured the mania for over-decoration characteristic of the period, especially the High Gothic ceilings, visitors will welcome with relief the clean lines of the maple and cherrywood Biedermeier furniture. Oriental art, to which a great deal of space is given over, rubs shoulders with impressive murals, based on designs

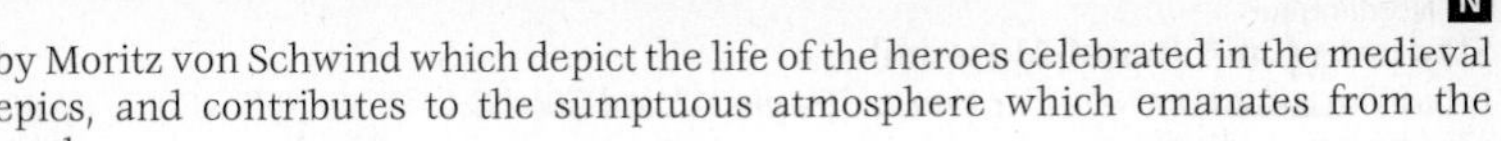
by Moritz von Schwind which depict the life of the heroes celebrated in the medieval epics, and contributes to the sumptuous atmosphere which emanates from the castle.
The old **music room** on the second floor contains evidence of the high esteem in which Ludwig II held Richard Wagner: the grand piano on which they both played, and also extracts from their correspondence. The fantastic and extravagantly romantic is again in evidence in the King's bedchamber, where the ceiling is painted to represent the stars in the night sky, which can be lit up like lamps. King Ludwig II was able to monitor the progress of the building work on Schloß Neuschwanstein with a telescope from his window.

Nördlingen★

The former Free Imperial Town of Nördlingen lies in the middle of the Ries basin, along the Romantic Road. It is first mentioned in records in 898. Its development throughout the centuries has been by concentric extension, witnessed by the street pattern and the ring of fortifications. The town's medieval houses, some of them a little lopsided, are for the most part extremely well preserved.
Nördlingen saw the armies of the French subdue the Austrians in 1796 and 1800.

Location

Population: 21 000. Michelin maps nos 545, 546 T 15 – Bayern. Nördlingen occupies an important position at the gates of the Bavarian Plateau, in the centre of the Ries basin, a crater 25km/16mi in diameter and formed by a meteorite *(see Rieskrater-Museum).*
Marktplatz 2, 86720 Nördlingen, ☎ (090 81) 43 80.
Surrounding area: see ROMANTISCHE STRASSE, EICHSTÄTT (65km/41mi northeast), ULM (73km/46mi southwest).

Directory

WHERE TO EAT

Meyer's Keller – *Marienhöhe 8 – ☎ (090 81) 44 93 – meyers.keller@t-online.de – Closed for 2 weeks in Feb and Mon and Tue lunchtimes – €30/79.* Parquet flooring, modern artworks and contemporary decor sets the tone here – sit out on the pleasant terrace, under the old trees. Tasteful, regional dishes are served in the brasserie.

WHERE TO STAY

Hotel Sonne – *Marktplatz 3 – ☎ (090 81) 50 67 – fax (090 81) 23999 – kaiserhof-hotel-sonne@t-online.de – Closed for 2 weeks in Nov – P – 29rm: €55/120 – Restaurant €14/26.* This traditional hotel in the heart of Nördlingen, dates from 1477. Behind its pretty façade are comfortable but functional guestrooms. Higgledy-piggledy original corridors and stairways. Rural decor with vaulted ceiling in the pleasant dining room.

Worth a Visit

St-Georgskirche★

This late-15C hall-church is surmounted by a majestic, 90m/295ft-high bell-tower, known as Daniel, on which a look-out still keeps watch round the clock. Climbing the 350 steps to the top of the tower allows visitors a view of the Ries crater. Fan vaulting covers the interior in splendid style. The pulpit (1499) is reached via a corbelled staircase with only three steps. Note the curious little **organ** on the finely worked baldaquin *(on the right hand side).* The **Crucifixion group★** and the statues of St George and Mary Magdalene, created by Niclaus Gerhaert von Leyden, still remain on the Baroque altar replacement. Note the expression of the Saviour, moving in its sweetness and humility.

Stadtmauer★ (Town Walls)

The Nördlingen town walls are the only remaining fully accessible walls of their kind in Germany. Access to the historic, picturesque old town is possible through just one of the five gates, and a walk right around the town walls, which are for the most part covered, reveals 11 watchtowers. One of the most attractive parts of the walk is along the battlements from the Berger Gate via the Alte Bastei, or old bastion, to the Reimlinger Gate. The history of the town wall is documented in the Löpsinger gate tower.

Stadtmuseum★ (Local Museum)

From Mar to start of Nov, Tue-Sun, 1.30-4pm. Closed Good Fri. €3. ☎ (090 81) 273 82 30. The museum displays cover the pre- and early history of the Ries basin, along with the history of the Imperial Town of Nördlingen. There is a collection of 19C painting, and altar panels by Old German masters, such as the wings (1462-77) of the altarpiece from St Georgskirche by Friedrich Herlin. The display includes other panel paintings by Hans Schäufelin and Sebastian Taig. The "Battle of Nördlingen" (1634) is reproduced in the form of a pewter figure diorama.

Rieskrater-Museum★

Next to the Stadtmuseum. May to Oct, Tue-Sun, 10am-4.30pm; Nov to Apr, Tue-Sun, 10am-12 noon, 1.30-4.30pm. Closed 1 Jan, Shrove Tue, Good Fri, 24-26 and 31 Dec. €3. ☎ (090 81) 273 82 20. The Nördlingen Giant Crater was formed approximately 15 million years ago when a meteorite hit the earth. Just imagine it – a giant stone sphere, 1km/0.6mi in diameter, leaves its orbit between Mars and Jupiter and hits the earth at a speed of 70 000kph/44 000mph, penetrating up to 1km/0.6mi into the rock! The energy of 250 000 Hiroshima atom bombs is released, and a wave of pressure and heat extinguishes all life within a range of 100km/62mi. The heat generated by the impact is so great that the meteorite evaporates. A crater 14km/9mi in diameter is formed, which eventually spreads to 25km/16mi due to all the rock that subsequently falls in. The crater, which was originally 4km/2.5mi deep, is gradually filled in over the course of millions of years, but later partially excavated and opened out again.

The Rieskrater-Museum, which is housed in a carefully restored barn (1503), attempts to give the general public an understanding of this scarcely imaginable phenomenon. An ambitious venture, which succeeds admirably using modern didactic methods (a slide show and videos to watch, stone to touch). There is even a lump of moon rock, which is on permanent loan to the museum from NASA.

Excursions

Neresheim Abbey★

19km/12mi southwest. The abbey church (Klosterkirche), started in 1745 under the direction of Balthasar Neumann, was the last work of the great Baroque architect. It was not finished until 1792. Inside, the seemingly weightless ceiling decoration painted between 1771 and 1775 by Martin Knoller is entirely in keeping with the tremendous sense of light in the building's interior.

Nordfriesische Inseln★

Northern Frisians

This group of wild islands, in perpetual battle against marine erosion, makes up part of the Schleswig-Holsteinisches Wattenmeer national park which was created in 1985. The fragile sand dunes of the islands are protected from the ravages of the North Sea by dykes and artificial banks. Beach life and the fresh North Sea air make the Northern Frisians a popular holiday destination.

Location

Michelin maps nº 541 A-C 8-10 – Schleswig Holstein. The Northern Frisians face the west coast of Schleswig-Holstein, in the North Sea, next to the border with Denmark. The islands are reached by ferry and the departure point depends on the destination: for the islands of Föhr and Amrun, ferries leave from Dagebüll-Hafen (43km/27mi north of Husum). For Pellworm, ferries leave from Nordstrand. Ferries for the Halligen islands leave from Husum and Nordstrand.

Surrounding area: see HUSUM on the mainland (ferries for Dagebüll from Amrum and the Halligen islands), Insel HELGOLAND (ferries from Dagebüll, Husum and Hörnum on the isle of Sylt, among others).

Background

Islands battling against the elements – Since the melting of the great Quaternary Era glaciers, the wind and sea have been the agents crafting the landscape of the Northern Frisians, restoring islands to the mainland and breaking chunks off the mainland to become islands. These islands in the mudflats off the Danish-German coast fall into two groups: the islands of Sylt, Föhr and Amrum, consisting mainly of sandy moorland *(Geest)* formed by moraine deposits from the Ice Age, and Pellworm and Nordstrand, island strips of marshland *(Marschen)* which were formed during the great storm floods of 1634.

Worth a Visit

Sylt★★ *(see Insel SYLT)*

Föhr

Ferries to Föhr: Dagebüll-Föhr (45min): about 9 to 12 ferries a day. €9.70 there and back. Dagebüll-Amrum (90min): around 6 to 10 ferries a day. €14.40 there and back. Timetables vary. Information and car reservations from Wyker Dampfschiffs-Reederei Föhr-Amrum GmbH, in Wyk, on Föhr. ☎ 018 05 08 01 40.

This is a peaceful, charming island which boasts an exceptionally mild climate thanks to its sheltered site in the mudflats behind a protective outer circle of smaller islands and the Halligens. The second largest island off the west Schleswig-Holstein coast consists of broad expanses of green marshland and gently undulating moorland, dotted with pretty villages, their houses thatched with reeds (eg Nieblum, Süderende or Oldsum). The beaches stretch round the south of the island. The small, windswept woods frequented by bird colonies are in the more remote north of the island.

The delightful port and main town of the island, **Wyk**, is located in the southeast. It features well-tended narrow streets which are a pleasure to explore, and the tree-lined promenade (Sandwall) above the beach, laid in honour of summer visits by the Danish royal family. Visitors interested in the nature, history and culture of the Northern Frisians should not miss the **Friesenmuseum** *(Open Jul to Aug, 10am-5pm; Mar to Oct, Tue-Sun, 10am-5pm; Nov-Feb, Tue-Sun, 2-5pm. Closed 24 and 31 Dec. €2.50. ☎ (046 81) 25 71)*. In Boldixum, St Nikolaikirche dates from the second half of the 13C with the original painted vaulted ceiling. **Dunsum** is the departure point for a walk across the mudflats to Amrum.

Amrum

Ferries to Amrum: Schlüttsiel-Amrum (2hr 30min): 1 to 2 ferries daily. €14.40 there and back. Timetable varies. Information and car reservations from Wyker Dampfschiffs-Reederei Föhr-Amrum GmbH, in Wyk, on Föhr. ☎ 018 05 08 01 40.

Amrum is possibly the oldest and certainly the most unspoiled of the Northern Frisians. The west coast is protected from the full force of the North Sea by a 1.5km/1mi-wide strip of sand. Behind this lie sand dunes, heaths, woods, farmland and finally the mudflats of the east coast, a rich habitat for sea birds.

There have been various pre- and early historical artefacts found near the hamlet of Steenodde, which make the island culturally and historically interesting. The **Esenhugh**, measuring 4.7m/15ft high and with a diameter of 26.5m/87ft, is the largest stone grave site on the island. The prettiest hamlet on the island is **Nebel**, which grew up around the **medieval church of St Clemens** in the 16C. The graveyard contains some interesting tombstones with inscriptions dating back to the 18C. Also of interest is the **Öömrang Hüs**, a sea captain's house built in 1736. The far north of the island, in the bird sanctuary area of **Amrum Odde**, is the departure point for walks across the mudflats to Föhr.

Halligen★

This collection of tiny islands is all that remains of mainland marshes that were once part of the much more extensive coastal region in prehistoric times. In c 1600, there were more than 25 documented islands here, but the number has since fallen to 10, of widely differing sizes. The other Halligen fell victim to storm floods or simply merged into one another over the centuries. In contrast to the other North Sea islands, most of the Halligens are not protected by sea dikes, with the result that it can be a case of "total submersion" up to 50 times a year. At these times only the houses on the man-made mounds (terps) can be seen above water level. A total of about 400 people inhabit the Halligens; the largest with 18 mounds is **Langeneß**, linked with **Oland** (mainland connection), and **Hooge** (Queen of the Halligens). Various shipping companies offer boat trips to the Halligens.

Pellworm

Ferries for Pellworm: Leaving Nordstrand/Strucklahnungshörn, Pellworm. Ferries (35min): between 3 and 7 ferries a day according to the tide. €9 per person, €45 per car not including passengers there and back. ☎ (048 44) 753.

Those who are looking first and foremost for peace and quiet, rather than sandy beaches, should go to Pellworm. The island is enclosed by a 25km/15mi-long and 8m/20ft-high dike, without which Pellworm would be inundated twice a day, since the island lies below sea level. Sheep graze on the dikes, as much a part of the island landscape as the distinctive black-and-white cows.

The island's main feature is the mighty ruined tower of the **Alte Kirche St Salvator**, whose origins date back to the 11C-12C. Nearby lies the **Friedhof der Heimatlosen**, where the bodies of strangers washed up on the island's shores by the sea are buried. Traces and artefacts from the settlement inundated in 1634 are on display, along with other exhibits, in the **Wattenmuseum Liermann**.

Nordstrand

This marshland island is now linked to the mainland by a 4km/2mi causeway. Nordstrand consists of a tapestry of reclaimed farmland (polders) and villages on man-made mounds (terps). Arable fields rub shoulders with fertile pastureland in what was once a landscape crisscrossed with sea dikes. The island's centre is at **Süden**, in one of the most picturesque stretches of countryside, where many craftspeople have made their home. Part of the bird-nesting area set up in 1905 and then allowed to become overgrown with woods again since 1930 has now been restored as a cultural and historical monument, while an area has been sectioned off as a completely untouched microclimate of indigenous island vegetation.

Nürnberg★★

Nuremberg

Before the Second World War, the capital of Franconia was so typically "Germanic" that the city was chosen by the Nazi party for its huge annual rallies each September. In the medieval centre there are still some half-timbered burghers' houses with embellished gables, the remains of what was once one of the most beautiful medieval cities in Germany. Today, the old bronze caster's and gold-beaters' town is one of the main industrial centres of southern Germany and a capital of culture, thanks to its outstanding Nationalmuseum. The city's culinary delights include grilled sausages and Lebkuchen – fragrant gingerbread sold in attractive coloured boxes. From the Friday before the first Sunday in Advent until Christmas Eve the marketplace is taken over by the famous Christkindlesmarkt.

Location

Population: 500 000. Michelin maps 545, 546 R 17 – Bayern. The second largest city in Bavaria after Munich, Nuremberg stands in the centre of the Franconian plateau. The major north-south (A 9) and east-west (A 3) motorways make it an obligatory point of passage on tourist itineraries.

Hauptmarkt 18, 90403 Nürnberg, ☎ (0911) 233 61 35.

Surrounding area: see BAYREUTH (82km/51mi northeast), BAMBERG (63km/39mi northwest), ROTHENBURG (83km/51.5mi west), REGENSBURG (103km/64mi south-east).

Background

The Golden Age – Nuremberg was at the peak of its fame and fortune during the 15C and 16C. Located at the crossroads of major trade routes and a shop window for Franconian craftsmanship, the city at that time rivalled Augsburg in importance. Nor was its renown purely commercial; literature, the arts and sciences flourished. The first German science university was founded in Nuremberg in 1526. From 1510

The Pegnitz river and Heilig-Geist-Spital, in the heart of old Nuremberg

M. Hertlein/MICHELIN

onwards the locksmith Peter Henlein manufactured fob watches. In the world of art, the audacious sculptors **Veit Stoß** (c 1445-1533) and **Adam Krafft** (c 1460-1508/09); the talented bronze caster **Peter Vischer the Elder** (c 1460-1529); **Michael Wolgemut** (1434-1519), the painter of altarpieces – and above all his pupil **Albrecht Dürer** (1471-1528) – all profoundly influenced the German scene with their works. From the 13C, **Hans Sachs** and the *Meistersinger* (mastersingers) brought new life to German poetic form; they provided the inspiration for Wagner's opera *The Mastersingers of Nuremberg* in 1868.

The Nuremberg Trials – It was in Hitler's "ideological capital" of the Third Reich that the notorious anti-Semitic laws were promulgated in 1935; and it was here, too, that the Allies brought 24 high-ranking officials and eight Nazi organisations (including the Gestapo and the SS) before an international military tribunal when the fighting was over. These men were accused of war crimes and crimes against peace and against humanity. The trials took place between 20 November 1945 and 1st October 1946 in the Palace of Justice on Fürther Straße, which is now a Civil Court.

Special Features

Germanisches Nationalmuseum★★★

♿ *Open every day except Mon, 10am-6pm, Wed 10am-9pm. Closed Shrove Tuesday, 24, 25 and 31 Dec. €5, free admission on Wed 6-9pm. Plan available at reception. Allow half a day.* ☎ *(0911) 133 10; www.gnm.de*

The museum, which was founded in 1852, houses the largest collection of art and antiquities in Germany, with 20 000 of the millions of exhibits it possesses on permanent display. The heart of the massive collection is a former Carthusian monastery dating from the 14C; the museum subsequently spread to the neighbouring Augustinian monastery and then across the Kartäusergasse. The Israeli artist Dani Karavan has redesigned the street itself, which is fully integrated into the museum complex, as a street of human rights.

In view of the extent of the collections, visitors are advised to choose a particular theme to follow. As in all museums in Germany, don't be put off by a closed door: all the rooms are open unless otherwise indicated.

Upper Floors – The **picture gallery** *(first floor, Section B)* displays works by **Albrecht Dürer** *(Portrait of Michael Wolgemut, Emperor Charles the Great in his Coronation Robes)*, Hans Baldung Grien (religious scenes), Hans Holbein the Elder (portraits), Albrecht Altdorfer and Lucas Cranach the Elder *(Portrait of Martin Luther, Venus with Cupid the Honey Thief)*. There are also some later works, including a *Self-portrait* by Rembrandt. Works by **Veit Stoß** *(The Archangel Raphael and The Young Tobias)*, Tilman Riemenschneider *(The Lamentation of Christ)* and Ignaz Günther are especially outstanding within the sculpture collection. The most noteworthy of the very many **scientific instruments** *(Section A)* is the so-called **Behaim terrestrial globe**, dating from 1492 to 1493, which is the oldest surviving depiction of the earth in globe form. An area of the museum is devoted to sets of apothecary's equipment and old medical and pharmaceutical instruments *(Section C)*, a collection of toys and doll's houses (including one dating from 1639), and an impressive folk art collection *(Section D)* with many traditional costumes and reconstructed peasant dwellings. The second-floor galleries include an excellent exhibition of 19C and 20C art and design *(Section E)*, notably including Ernst Ludwig Kirchner's Expressionist *Self-portrait* (1914).

Ground Floor – The impressive collection of medieval religious art treasures *(Section C)* illustrates the work of craftsmen from the Carolingians to the early Renaissance, who vied with one another in reproducing the same scenes. Sometimes varying only a gesture or piece of clothing until the mid 15C, they then boldly turned their hands to the new techniques inspired by the Italians. Many types of decorative arts are represented, including glass, ceramics, furniture and textiles. The gold and silversmith's work should not be missed. The section on ancient musical instruments *(Section D)* boasts the largest collection in the world of historical pianos. In addition to a collection of historical arms and hunting pieces *(Section E)*, the museum has a section devoted to **prehistory** *(Section B)*; here the golden cone from **Ezelsdorf**, dating from around 1100 BC, takes pride of place. There is also an extensive prints and drawings section and a numismatic collection *(Section F)*.

The Germanisches Nationalmuseum complex also houses the **Industrial Museum** *(Section D)*, which is linked with the Bavarian Industrial Institute. Its exhibits include examples of craftsmanship, commercial art and design dating from Antiquity right up to the 20C.

Directory

Where to Eat

Useful Tips – The city's culinary speciality – the famous grilled sausages or *Nürnberger Rostbratwürste* – can be sampled at booths in the city centre (often sold as *Drei in an Weckla*: three sausages in a roll) and in most restaurants serving traditional fare.

⊖ **Historische Bratwurstküche Zum Gulden Stern** – *Zirkelschmiedsgasse 26 – ☎ (0911) 205 92 88 – info@bratwurstkuec he.de – €12/16.* The oldest *Bratwurstküche* is set in this historic house dating from 1419, with its country-style, wooden decor. Nuremberg sausage grilled over beech-wood charcoal served here.

⊖⊖ **Sebald** – *Weinmarkt 14 – ☎ (09101) 38 13 03 – info@restaurant-seb ald.de – Closed Sun – ⊠ – €27/37.* This charming house in the old town harbours a modern restaurant and bistro. Yellow marble walls and warm shades give the place something of a Tuscan atmosphere.

⊖⊖⊖ **Essigbrätlein** – *Weinmarkt 3 – Closed 24 Dec-1st Jan, Easter, 1 week in Aug and Sun-Mon – ☎ (0911) 22 51 31 – €37/79.* This inn dating from 1550, preserved in its original state and set in an old building made of Franconian sandstone, exudes a certain air of nostalgia. Andree Koethe serves ambitious dishes of his own invention.

Where to Stay

⊖⊖ **Hotel-Restaurant Jägerheim** – *Valznerweiherstraße 75, 90480 Nürnberg-Zerzabelshof – ☎ (0911) 94 08 50 – Fax (0911) 9408585 – www.hotel-jaegerheim.de – P – 33rm: €64/82 ☕ – Restaurant €19/29.* A quiet hotel near the exhibition grounds, well served by public transport. Smart rooms with pale wooden furniture. Traditional restaurant.

⊖⊖ **Hotel Am Jakobsmarkt** – *Schottengasse 5 – ☎ (0911) 200 70 – Fax (0911) 2007200 – info@hotel-am-jakobs markt.de – Closed 24 Dec-2 Jan – P ⊁ – 77rm: €83/115 – ☕ €9.* The functional, modern rooms of this smart hotel are spread over two buildings: the main building and a half-timbered annex reached via an inner courtyard. Breakfast is served in a pleasant room with a glass façade.

⊖⊖⊖ **Le Méridien Grand-Hotel** – *Bahnhofstraße 1 – ☎ (0911) 2 32 20 – Fax (0911) 2 32 24 44 – lemeridien@grand-hotel.de – ⊁ – 186rm. €120 – ☕ €15 – Restaurant €30/50.* The hotel is located next to the central station, a stone's throw away from the old town. A luxurious setting, with refined Art Nouveau-style rooms: marble bathrooms and air conditioning are standard.

Taking a Break

Konditorei-Café Beer – *Breite Gasse 79 – ☎ (0911) 2 30 84 20 – www.cafebeer.de – Mon-Sat 8.30am-7pm.* This classic tea room with terrace gives on to one of the city's busiest shopping streets. Ornamental cakes have always been the speciality of this bakery and sweet shop founded in 1864 and still run by the same family.

Going Out

Altstadthof – Braustüberl "Schwarzer Bauer" – *Bergstraße 19-21 – ☎ (0911) 22 72 17 – www.altstadthof.de – Open 11am-1am (terrace until 10pm).* Different kinds of beer brewed on the premises (using traditional recipes) and home-made brandy are served here. They can be sampled in the small bar itself or in the beer garden in the rear courtyard, or you can even take them away.

Biergarten Am Hexenhäusle – *Vestnertorgraben 4 – ☎ (0911) 36 73 24 – www.sudhausnuernberg.de – Open 11am-11pm.* This former guardhouse – known as the Witch's House – with its lovely shaded garden and friendly atmosphere, is just north of the palace. Refreshing drinks and local specialities can be enjoyed in the beer garden with its beautiful view.

Blauer Adler – *Bahnhofsplatz 5 (in the west wing of the central station) – ☎ (0911) 2 42 62 90 – www.blaueradler.com – Open Sun-Thur 9am-1am, Fri-Sat 9am-4am.* The modern design of this immense bar, tastefully laid out over various levels, presents an interesting contrast with the station's historic architecture. House speciality: brochettes.

Culture

Useful Tips – Events are listed in the monthly magazines *Plärrer* and *Prinz*, available from the city's bookshops and newspaper kiosks. The free monthly listings magazine *doppelpunkt* can be found in bars, cinemas and shops. Online information: www.kubiss.de, www.events-nuernberg.de, www.congressing.de

Shopping

Useful Tips – Karolinenstraße, Breite Gasse and Königsstraße are the city's busiest shopping streets, with department stores and a wide variety of specialist shops. If you're looking for small gifts to take home, *Lebkuchen* are ideal; traditionally made during Advent, this gingerbread is now available all year round and is often packaged in attractive metal boxes (for example at *Lebkuchen Schmidt* on the southeast corner of Hauptmarkt/ Plobenhofstraße 6).

Handwerkerhof – *Königstor (opposite the central station; near the Frauentorturm) – ☎ (0911) 8 60 70 – www.handwerkerhof.de – Mar-Dec: boutiques: Mon-Fri 10am-6.30pm, Sat 10am-4pm, Restaurant: Mon-Sat 10.30am-10pm.* Small crafts shops and traditional restaurants in a picturesque walled-in courtyard. Ideal for souvenir-hunting (gingerbread) and a pleasant place for a short break.

Walking About

OLD TOWN★★ *Allow half a day*

Hauptmarkt (Marketplace) and Schöner Brunnen★ (Beautiful Fountain)

The 14C Gothic **fountain,** comprising 40 figures (copies) over four levels, dominates the marketplace. At the top of the 19m/62ft-high pyramid-shaped structure, Moses is surrounded by the Prophets; around the base are the seven Electors and a series of nine Old Testament and medieval heroes: three forefathers, three Jews and three Christians. A seamless gold ring is held captive in the railing *(on the upper part)*, where an apprentice locksmith is said to have placed it in the 17C. The hustle and bustle of the square, particularly during the Christmas market, masks the grisly origins of this place: the Jewish quarter stood there until 1349, when it was razed to the ground and its occupants burnt to death by the local inhabitants.

Frauenkirche★

A Gothic church on the east side of the market, built on the site of a destroyed synagogue; it was a gift from Karl IV and was built between 1350 and 1358. The gable, with its pinnacles and niches, was designed by Adam Krafft (early 16C) and crowns the beautiful façade, which is one of the only original parts. Dating from 1509, the clock above the balcony attracts visitors each day at noon, when a series of jacks appear to strike the hour. These colourful metal figures *(Männleinlaufen)* represent the seven Electors coming to swear allegiance to the Emperor after the enactment of the Golden Bull in Nuremberg in 1356.

Inside, the roof above the main body of the church, which is almost square in plan, is supported by four columns. On the north wall of the building is Adam Krafft's **Peringsdorffer Epitaph** (a robed Madonna), which dates from 1498. The **Tucher Altar** in the chancel, garnished with human figures, is a masterpiece of the pre-Albrecht Dürer Nuremberg school of painting: the triptych (c 1445-50) depicts the Crucifixion, the Annunciation and the Resurrection. Note the depiction of Jesus on his way to school, in the chancel.

Sebalduskirche★

This church with two chancels was built in the 13C and enlarged in the 14C in honour of a clergyman from Nuremberg who was canonised in 1425. The towers, which burned down during the Second World War, and the major part of the east chancel, which was also destroyed, have been rebuilt. The sobriety of the Romanesque west front is in vivid contrast with the huge Gothic east chancel, intricately worked and adorned with statues and pinnacles. Inside, the Romanesque and transitional Gothic western section (13C central and side aisles) is easily distinguished from the High Gothic style of the 14C east chancel and its ambulatory.

To the right of the entrance, at the far end of the first chancel, the **St Peter Altarpiece** (1485) takes pride of place, painted on a gold background in Michael Wolgemut's studio. In the centre, the richly decorated bronze **baptismal font★** (Gothic, c 1430), including a hearth, is the oldest religious work cast in bronze in Nuremberg. In the nave, on the inner side of the great left pillar, is the painted statue of St Sebald (1390) and on the next column, the **Virgin Mary in Glory★** made of pear-tree wood.

The magnificent **tomb of St Sebald★★** stands in the centre of the west chancel. The Gothic shrine is part of a bronze display shelf by Peter Vischer (1519), supported by dolphins and snails and adorned with a host of statuettes. On the side panels, St Sebald is represented, and the artist himself in working clothes. The ambulatory contains two oak statues (*St John* and *The Virgin Mary*) and a bas-relief in sandstone *(The Last Supper, The Mount of Olives and Christ Taken Prisoner)* by **Veit Stoß**; it is illuminated by some fine stained-glass windows (14C and 15C).

Outside the church, on the side of the east chancel, Adam Krafft sculpted a magnificent bas-relief in 1492 depicting the Passion and the Resurrection on the **funerary monument of the Schreyer family★**.

Adam Krafft

Born in Nuremberg around 1460, Krafft left his mark on every church in the city. His early works – typical of the Late Gothic style – portrayed very expressive figures with tumultuous draperies, and rich decorative reliefs. He then moved towards greater clarity and his later, more monumental works, assume more rounded and restrained poses (see the Stations of the Cross from St John's cemetery, dating from 1505, in the Germanisches Nationalmuseum).

Stadtmuseum Fembohaus (Fembo Municipal Museum)

♿ *Open every day except Mon, 10am-5pm, Thur 10am-8pm. Closed 1st Jan, Shrove Tuesday, Good Friday, 24-26 and 31 Dec. €4. ☎ (0911) 231 25 95.* The **museum** is housed in a sandstone Renaissance mansion with a scrolled gable embellished by cornucopiae and obelisks. It is the only patrician mansion in the city to survive in its entirety and dominates the Burgstraße. Typically, it is grouped around an inner courtyard. The museum is concerned with the history of Nuremberg, and in particular the home life of the town's gentry between the 16C and the 19C.

Burg (Castle)

Guided tour (1hr 30min). Apr-Sep: 9am-6pm; Oct-Mar: 10am-4pm. €4.50. ☎ *(0911) 22 57 26.* Symbol of the city, the castle stands proudly on a sandstone outcrop a little way to the north. The original **castle of the Burgraves** *(Burggrafenburg)*, almost entirely destroyed in 1420, had been completed in the 12C by the part known as the **Kaiserburg**; its present appearance dates from the 15C and 16C. From the outside terrace or the **Sinwellturm**, a 25m/82ft high keep, there is an exceptional **view★** of the steeply sloped roofs and towers of the old town. In an adjoining courtyard, the **well** *(under cover inside the building)* is an impressive 50m/165ft deep.

Among the dependencies near the apartments, the **Imperial Chapel**, a Romanesque double-chapel, is particularly interesting with its special Imperial Gallery from which the Emperor could survey his court assembled below. The castle contains an exhibition on the significance of the Imperial Palace in the history of the Empire and a display of historical weapons.

NÜRNBERG

Äußere Laufer Gasse	KY 5
Albrecht-Dürer-Str.	JY 6
An der Fleischbrücke	JY 10
An der Karlsbrücke	JY 13
Bahnhofsplatz	KZ 16
Beckschlagergasse	KY 17
Bergstraße	JY 18
Bischof-Meiser-Str.	JY 24

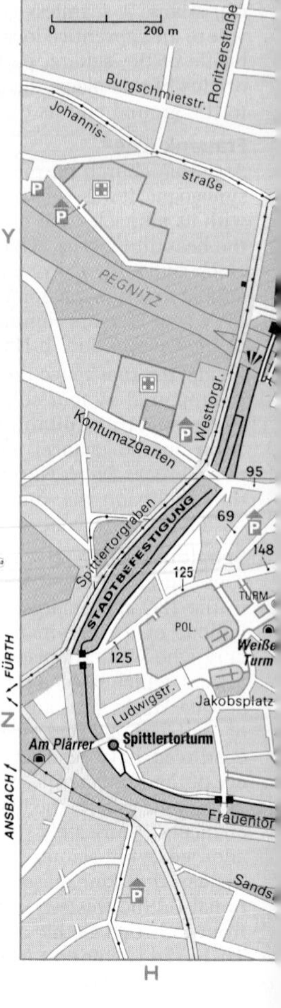

Frauenkirche	JY E
Heilich-Geist-Spital	JY F

Tiergärtnertorplatz

The half-timbered houses around the picturesque Tiergärtnertor square suffered the least damage during the Second World War. The statue of St George in armour decorates **Pilate's House**, which was once the home of an armourer. The 15C burgher's residence with jutting eaves standing opposite on the other side of the square is Dürer's house.

Albrecht-Dürer-Haus★ (Dürer's House)

Open every day except Mon, 10am-5pm, Thur 10am-8pm. Closed 1st Jan, Shrove Tuesday, Good Friday, 24-26 and 31 Dec. €4. ☎ *(0911) 231 25 68.* **Dürer** bought this house in 1509 and lived here until his death in 1528. The soberly furnished interior gives some idea of the life and work of the artist through films, demonstrations of the printing of engravings on a period press, and reproductions of works by the artist and his disciples, both past and present.

Stadtbefestigung★ (Fortifications)

Completed in the mid 15C, these have remained practically intact. They comprised an inner and an outer ring *(Zwingermauer)*, the ramparts of the former with a covered parapet walk. A wide dry moat (in which modern avenues now run) lay outside the latter. No less than 67 defensive towers still exist. Among them are the four **Great Towers**, dating from the 16C and protected by colossal shells of cannon-proof masonry, sometimes 6m/20ft thick (Frauentor, Spittlertor, Neutor, Laufertor).

The most interesting sector lies between the Kaiserburg and the Spittlertor *(west side)*. An instructive 30min walk starts from the castle gardens *(Burggarten) (outside, below the Kaiserburg)*. From the ramparts it is possible to reach the watch-path, which can be followed as far as the Neutorzwinger. Continue inside the ramparts. The River Pegnitz is crossed via a suspension footbridge beside the fortifications, before the promenade is concluded, once more on the outside (there is an attractive view of the castle from this point).

Banks of the Pegnitz

Parts of the old city still standing can be seen by crossing between the two banks of the river from bridge to bridge as far as the Heilig-Geist-Spital. From the Maxbrücke there is a fine **view** of the half-timbered wine hall *(Weinstadel)* and its flanking tower, the water tower and the executioner's footbridge *(Henkersteg)*.

Heilig-Geist-Spital (Hospital)

This 14C-15C building, spread over two wide arches, spans a branch of the Pegnitz. Its graceful corbelled tower, and the oriel window embellishing the façade, can be seen from the Museumsbrücke. The covered part of the bridge *(reached from an islet upstream)*, known as the **Crucifixion** Courtyard on account of the *Crucifixion group* by A Krafft on the north side, has wooden galleries above wide sandstone arches, and used to be a home for the elderly.

Street	Grid
Breite Gasse	JZ
Findelgasse	JZ 38
Grübelstraße	KY 50
Hans-Sachs-Gasse	JY 53
Henkersteg	JY 58
Inn. - Cramer-Klett-Str.	KY 62
Johannesgasse	KZ 64
Kaiserstraße	JZ 67
K.-Grillenberger-Str.	HZ 69
Karlstraße	JY 72
Karolinenstraße	JZ
Katharinengasse	KZ 73
Königstorgraben	KZ 77
Königstraße	JZ 78
Lessingstraße	JZ 82
Lorenzer Str.	KZ 84
Ludwigstraße	HZ
Luitpoldstraße	JZ 86
Marientorgraben	KZ 87
Maxbrücke	JY 90
Mohrengasse	HYZ 95
Museumsbrücke	JY 99
Obere Krämersgasse	JY 105
Obere Wörthstraße	JY 106
Obstmarkt	JY 107
Pfannenschmiedsgasse	JZ 110
Prinzregentenufer	KZ 116
Rathausplatz	JY 117
Richard-Wagner-Platz	JZ 121
Schlotfegergasse	HZ 125
Steubenbrücke	KY 138
Sulzbacher Str.	KY 140
Tafelhofstraße	JZ 142
Vordere Ledergasse	HZ 148
Vordere Sterngasse	JZ 149
Weißgerbergasse	JY 154

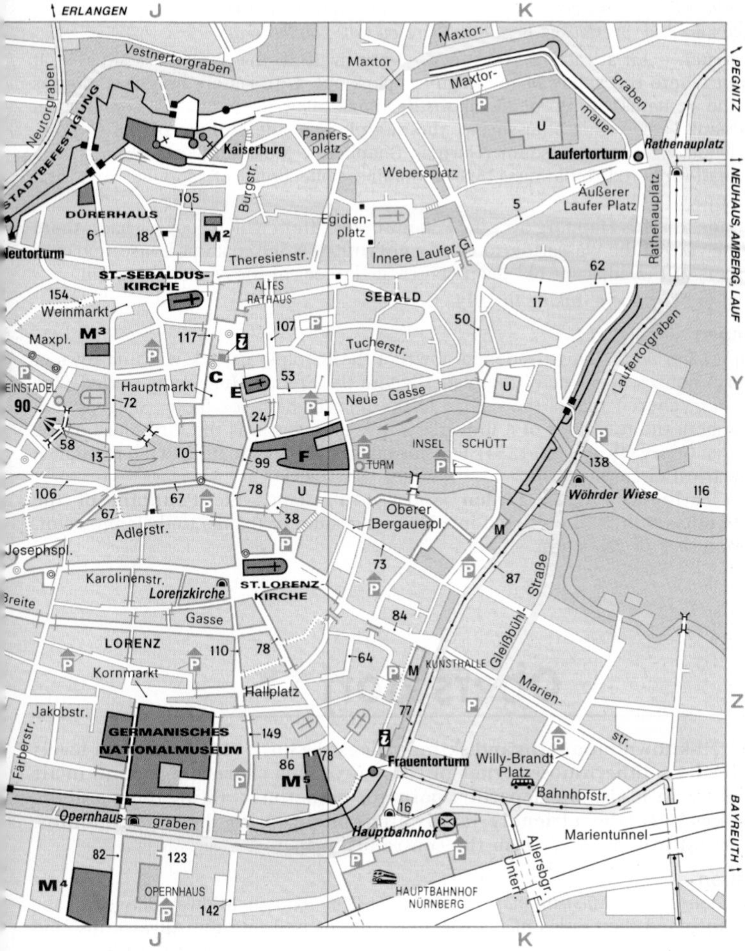

Sight	Grid
Neues Museum/Staatl. Museum Für Kunst und Design	JZ M⁵
Schöner Brunnen	JY C
Spielzeugmuseum	JY M³
Stadtmuseum Fembohaus	JY M²
Verkehrsmuseum	JZ M⁴

Lorenzkirche★

A magnificent rose window enlivens the west face of this 13C-14C Gothic church and crowns the tympanum of the door depicting the life of Jesus. The impressive hall-type chancel was added in the 15C. Inside *(enter via the south door)*, from the nave, two outstanding works of art can be seen: the 1400 rood-beam Crucifix and Veit Stoß's **Annunciation★★** (1517-18), a masterpiece in carved wood: the archangel Gabriel's annunciation to Mary is set in a crown of 55 roses evoking the Rosary of five series of ten *Ave Marias* and one *Pater Noster*.

The richly ornamented **tabernacle★★** (1493-96) by Adam Krafft stands to the left of the main altar, with statues evoking the Passion of Christ. The stonemason has depicted himself life-sized beneath the gallery. The ambulatory is lit by superb stained-glass windows from the workshop of the Alsatian Peter Hemmel of Andlau, notably that representing the Tree of Jesse (1487, *second on the right, starting from the central window*).

►► Spielzeugmuseum★ *(Toy Museum)* – Verkehrsmuseum★ *(Transport Museum, see the railway section in particular)* – Neues Museum *(Modern Art Museum)* – Old Nazi rally grounds and commemorative museum *(at Luitpoldhain)*.

Tours

Hersbrucker Alb

Round tour of 109km/68mi – allow half a day. Leave on Sulzbacher Straße, then take the A9 motorway in the direction of Bayreuth, leaving at the Plech exit.

Neuhaus an der Pegnitz★ – This charming locality comes suddenly into view after a bend in the road, with the tall tower of Burg Veldenstein dominating the town.

Continue following the course of the Pegnitz in the direction of Hersbruck. The valley is steeply enclosed, overlooked here and there by tall, pointed crags.

Hersbruck – An attractive little town – very lively in the summer – situated at a point where the valley of the Pegnitz opens out, with stately burghers' houses and the remains of its medieval fortifications. The town church contains an important Late Gothic altar-shrine, the altarpiece of the Fathers of the Church. The Deutsche Hirtenmuseum (German Shepherds' Museum, *Eishüttlein 7*) in a fine half-timbered building (1524) contains collections of popular arts and traditions.

Continue towards Happurg over the Pegnitz bridge, from which, looking back, there is a fine view of the Wassertor (fortified gate) with its stone customs house, and over the roofs of the adjacent old town centre at the foot of the Michelsberg hill.

Return to Nuremberg, taking the B14.

Erlangen

17km/10.5mi north. This residential town of the Baroque period, widh its rows of uniform houses, was one of the places where the French Huguenots settled. The Protestant church marks the centre of the quarter built for them. Sharing with Nuremberg the functions of a university city, Erlangen was the birthplace of the physicist **Georg Ohm** (1789-1854), who formulated the law relating to the resistance of electrical circuits.

In an early-18C English **garden** *(Schloßgarten)* stands the **Fountain of the Huguenots**, built by the French in 1706 as a gesture of thanks to their protector, the Margrave of Bayreuth.

Oberstdorf★★

The well-known mountain and skiing village (843m/2 765ft above sea level) lies in the southernmost corner of Germany. This charming mountain-air health resort is also the departure point for numerous walking tours and the ski slopes engender a friendly, family atmosphere during the winter months. Motor traffic is banned from the centre of town.

Location

Population: 11 000. Michelin maps nos 545, 546 X 14 – Bayern. Midway between Lake Constance and the castles of Ludwig II, deeply incised into the Allgäu Alps, and seven other valleys, the town lies at the junction of the valley of the Iller.

Marktplatz 7, 87561 Oberstdorf, ☎ (083 22) 70 00.

Surrounding area: see Deutsche ALPENSTRASSE (15km/9mi north), LINDAU (76km/48mi west), FÜSSEN (60km/38mi east) or the paths around GARMISCH-PARTENKIRCHEN (105km/66mi east).

Walks

Nebelhorn★★

1hr 30min there and back, of which 20min are by cable-car (3 stages to the trip).

Operates every 10min. First departure is at 8.30am, last trip down from Höfatsblick is at 4.50pm (summer) or 4.30pm (winter). Closed 4-24 May, and 3 Nov to mid-Dec. Summer: €18 return trip, winter: €28.50 return trip. ☎ (083 22) 960 00.

The highest cable railway in the Allgäu leads to the 2 224m/7 296ft-high summit of the Nebelhorn, from where, in clear weather, there is a panoramic **view★★** over more than 400 Alpine summits: extending from the Zugspitze in the east to the Säntis (the Swiss Appenzell Alps) in the west and, beyond the bold outlines of the Allgäu itself, even the snows of the Bernese Oberland can be seen.

The destination of numerous hikes, the Nebelhorn is also the point of departure for the demanding "Hindelang climb". A geological footpath explains the origins and structure of the Alps.

Directory

Where to Eat

⊖ **Oberstdorfer Einkehr** – *Pfarrstraße 9 – ☎ (083 22) 97 78 50 – www.oberstdorf.net/einkehr – Booking advised – €14/35.* The Oberstdorfer Einkehr is popular with locals as well as visitors. A traditional establishment with comfortable, panelled dining rooms, with local specialities on the menu.

⊖⊖ **Maximilians** – *Freibergstraße 21 – ☎ (083 22) 967 80 – info@maximilians-restaurant.de – Closed for 3 weeks in May and Jun, and for 3 weeks in Nov and Sundays – – €25/60.* Elegant restaurant furnished in country-house style typical of the region. Seasonal food is served with delicious refinement.

Where to Stay

⊖ **Hotel Traube** – *Hauptstraße 6 – ☎ (083 22) 80 99 40 –fax (083 22) 3168 – www.hotel-traube.de – P – 20rm: €59/149 – Restaurant €8. 90/29.80.* Situated in the centre of the town this traditional hotel has comfortable guestrooms furnished in country style. A sauna and a solarium are available for use and in the restaurant, a large choice of regional and foreign dishes are on offer. In summer months, check out the pleasant Biergarten.

⊖ **Hotel Scheibenhaus** – *Scheibenstraße 1 – ☎ (083 22) 95 93 02 – fax (083 22) 95336 – ashhorlacher@t-online.de – Closed Apr and Nov – P – 8rm: €60/124 .* Hospitality in the proper sense of the word, with minute attention to detail, including complimentary refreshments and homemade cakes, make this place stand out. Beautiful view of the Trettachtal and surrounding mountains.

Fellhorn★★

Take the Fellhorn cable-car in two stages up to the station at the summit (1 967m/6 452ft). Operates beginning May to late Oct, 8.20am-4.50pm; mid-Dec to mid-late Apr (depending on snow) 8.30am-4.30pm. Summer: €16 return trip, winter: €29.50 return trip. ☎ (083 22) 960 00.

There is a wonderful panoramic **view★★** over the Allgäu mountains, the Austrian and Swiss Alps, from the 2 037m/6 683ft-high summit of the Fellhorn.

The Fellhorn has an easily accessible network of paths for hikes 1 500-2 000m/4 922-6 562ft long, including a very interesting flower footpath *(Blumen- und Wanderlehrpfad)*, with rare Alpine flowers, including orchids, to be seen along it. In summer these bloom all the way to the summit. The Alpine Rose, which blooms between about mid-June to mid-July, is particularly captivating.

Excursions

Breitachklamm★★

6.5km/4mi southwest, plus a 1hr 30min walk there and back. Accessible May to Sep daily 8am–5pm; Oct to Apr daily 9am–4pm. Closed from beginning Nov to mid-Dec. €2.50. ☎ (083 22) 48 87.

In the lower gorge, galleries lead down to a cutting with sheer, polished walls, where the turbulent mountain stream has carved a course 100m/300ft deep into the bedrock. At the foot of this path it is possible to turn back and re-mount by the long series of stairways that lead to the upper gorge (which is, however, less impressive). To return to Oberstdorf without a car, leave the gorge path at the top of these stairways. Walkers will then arrive at the Walserschanze, on the Kleinwalsertal road, from which there is a frequent bus service to the resort.

The Kleinwalsertal

17km/11mi – allow 30min. The name identifies a high valley of the River Breitach, a mountain area some 100km^2/38sq mi in size, which was settled in the 13C by the **Walsers**, emigrants of Germanic origin from the Upper Valais. Cut off from the rest of the Vorarlberg by the peaks of the Allgäu, the Walsers found themselves Austrian subjects when national frontiers were established in 1453, although such culture and traditions as they had were oriented exclusively towards Germany.

In 1891 the area was granted a special status whereby, still under Austrian sovereignty, it was nevertheless economically regarded as part of Germany.

Today the Kleinwalsertal has Austrian police, German customs, a German postal service but Austrian stamps, and the only legal tender is the German mark. Until a modern road was built in 1930, the valley remained isolated and the Walsers, like other hardy pioneers, retained a reputation of grim individualism and dourness of character – traits still reflected in the sombre buildings of their scattered homesteads.

Riezlern, **Hirschegg** and **Mittelberg** are the main resorts of the Kleinwalsertal, popular with tourists everywhere.

Oldenburg

Steeped in tradition, this capital and lively university city is the cultural and economic focus of the region. Seat of government for the Weser-Ems region of Lower Saxony, Oldenburg is becoming an increasingly popular and successful commercial centre.

Location

Population: 155 000. Michelin map nº 541 G 8 – Niedersachsen. Oldenburg is about 70km/44 mi west of the Dutch border. Its river port is linked to the Weser and the North Sea by the Hunte, and to the Benelux countries by a coastal canal *(Küstenkanal).*

Wallstraße 14, 26122 Oldenburg, ☎ (0441) 157 44

Surrounding area: see BREMEN (48km/30mi east), EMDEN (84km/53mi northwest), OSNABRÜCK (110km/69mi south).

Walking About

TOWN CENTRE

The old city, which includes Germany's oldest pedestrian precinct, also houses monumental buildings spanning five centuries, generous parkland and its former ramparts.

Schloßgarten★ (Castle Park)

A mild, moist coastal climate has favoured the growth of magnificent trees and shrubs in this landscaped garden, such as rhododendrons and tulip trees. From the weeping willows on the lake shore there is an attractive view of the towers of the Lambertikirche.

Schloß (Castle) – Landesmuseum für Kunst und Kulturgeschichte (Regional Art and History Museum)

♿ *Open Tue-Sun, 9am-5pm, Thu, 9am-8pm, Sat-Sun, 10am-5pm. Closed 1 Jan, Good Fri, Easter Sun, 1 May, Pentecost, 24, 25 and 31 Dec. €3. ☎ (0441) 220 73 00.* The museum, housed since 1923 in the former seat of the counts and grand dukes of Oldenburg, was built in the 17C and remodelled in the 18C and again the 19C.

The first floor houses among other things the Old Masters' gallery, which includes mainly 16C-18C Italian and Dutch masters and 18C-19C European paintings. The series of small pictures depicting idyllic scenes by Johann Heinrich Wilhelm Tischbein (1751-1829) is particularly interesting.

Items relating to Oldenburg's provincial history and culture are exhibited with commentaries on several floors.

Stadtmuseum★

♿ *Tue-Sun, 10am-6pm. €1.50. ☎ (0441) 235 28 81.* Of interest here are rooms from the villas Francksen (1877), Jürgens and Ballin, with paintings, furnishings and decor dating from the 17C to the early 20C. There are also departments on local history and an antiques collection.

Right next door to the Stadtmuseum is the Horsst-Janssen-Museum, opened in 2000. The illustrator and graphic artist, who died in 1995, was born and is buried in Oldenburg. His talented drawings are displayed to good advantage in this well designed building. ♿ *Tue-Sun, 10am-6pm. Closed Good Fri, 1 May, 24 and 31 Dec. €3.50. ☎ (0441) 235 28 91.*

Augusteum

Elisabethstraße 1. ♿ *Open Tue-Sun, 9am-5pm, Thu, 9am-8pm, Sat-Sun, 10am-5pm. Closed 1 Jan, Good Fri, Easter Sun, 1 May, Pentecost, 24, 25 and 31 Dec. €3. ☎ (0441) 220 73 00.* Works by painters from the Worpswede colony are on show here along with such German Expressionists as Erich Heckel. Among the Surrealists, note Franz Radziwill – who classes himself as a "symbolic realist".

Landesmuseum für Natur und Mensch Oldenburg

Damm 40-44. ♿ *Open Tue-Sun, 9am-5pm, Fri, 9am-3pm, Sat-Sun, 10am-5pm. Closed 1 Jan, 1 May, Pentecost, 24, 25 and 31 Dec. €2. ☎ (0441) 924 43 00.* These exhibitions are focused on the northwest region of Germany with its varied landscapes and traces of pre- and early historic settlements. Natural, archeological and cultural aspects are presented in a display entitled "Neither sea nor land – the peat bogs, a lost landscape". A huge block of peat, in which ancient bodies were found buried, always attracts attention.

Landesmuseum Oldenburg

The former seat of the counts and dukes of Oldenburg, now home to the Regional Art and History Museum.

Excursions

Museumsdorf Cloppenburg★

31km/19mi south. ♿ Open Mar to Oct, 9am-6pm; Nov to Feb, 9am-4.30pm. Closed 24 and 31 Dec. €4.10. ☎ (044 71) 948 40.

In an area of about 20ha/50 acres, 53 historic buildings from the 15C to the 19C have been constructed around a lake and a church. Most of the reconstructed buildings come from the region between the River Weser and River Ems. Large farmsteads, two types of mill, peasants' and tenants' houses, a blacksmith's and a bleachery illustrate aspects of the history of everyday life in Lower Saxony. The houses are fitted out with furnishings, household goods, clothing and work tools.

Steindenkmäler von Visbek (Megalithic Monuments)

38km/24mi south. In this group collectively known as **"The Intended"**, the Bride *(Visbeker Braut)* is a collection of granite blocks arranged in a rectangular pattern in a clearing that measures 80x7m/262x23ft.

The Groom *(Visbeker Bräutigam)* comprises a dolmen, considered as a sacrificial altar *(Opfertisch)*, and, again, an alignment of 80 blocks in a rectangle 108x10m/354x33ft. At the western extremity of the site a funerary chamber recalls – it is thought – the dwellings of this period. *The site is a 30min walk, there and back, from the Engelmannsbäke inn.*

Osnabrück

Preliminaries to the Peace of Westphalia started in Osnabrück and in the neighbouring town of Münster. A member of the *Hanseatic League,* the town's speciality lay in the textile and linen trade; this has now been supplanted by metallurgy (cables and coachbuilding) and paper mills.

Location

Population: 166 000. Michelin map n° 541 J 8. – Niedersachsen. Lying between the Teutoburger Wald and the Wiehengebirge heights, Osnabrück developed around two separate centres: in the 9C the old town spread from the ancient market and the episcopal quarter; and from the 11C onwards, a new town proliferated around the Johanniskirche. When they united within a single city wall (c 1300), Osnabrück became an important commercial centre.

Krahnstrasse 58, 49074 Osnabrück, ☎ (0541) 323 22 02.

Surrounding area: see MÜNSTER (56km south via the A 1), MÜNSTERLÄNDER WASSERBURGEN.

Worth a Visit

Rathaus (Town Hall)

8am-6pm, Sat, 9am-4pm, Sun, 10am-4pm. Closed 1 Jan, 24 and 31 Dec. No charge. ☎ (0541) 323 21 52. This early-16C building had to be restored after the Second World War, but still retains its Gothic look beneath a wide pavilion roof. The peace of 1648 was announced from its steps. The statue of Charlemagne, above the entrance, is surrounded by the effigies of eight other emperors and kings.

Friedenssaal★ (The Peace Chamber) – The hall in which the long-drawn-out peace negotiations were held is adorned with portraits of the heads of state and their delegates. The floor and ceiling have been rebuilt; the carved wooden seats and the chandelier are authentic and date from 1554.

Among the gold plate in the **Treasury** is the priceless 14C *Kaiserpokal* (Imperial goblet).

Marienkirche

A 13C-14C Gothic hall-church which, with its elegant transverse gables, closes off the northern end of the Marktplatz. Its most interesting work of art is the early-16C **Altarpiece of the Passion★**, originally from Antwerp.

Dom St. Peter

The squat outline of this 13C Transitional Gothic church is distinguished by large towers differing both in shape and size. The north face boasts a fine Romanesque embellishment of blind arcades and cornices. The ogive vaulting in the nave is rounded; from the triumphal arch hangs an early-13C crucifix.

The interior is equally unusual, with a flat chevet and squared-off ambulatory. The chapels leading off this contain a few works of art, notably a 15C Pietà and a 16C stone Crucifixion. There is a good view of the two towers from the asymmetrical cloister, entered via the south aisle.

Before the Peace in 1648

Preliminaries to the **Peace of Westphalia** started in Osnabrück between the Emperor and the Protestant belligerents (Sweden and the Lutheran princes of Germany) five years before the end of the Thirty Years War. On the other side, the Roman Catholic powers negotiated with the Emperor in Münster. News of the treaties' final signature was announced in Osnabrück on 25 October 1648 to a crowd, at first incredulous and then bursting into a spontaneous hymn of thanksgiving.

Johanniskirche

This Early Gothic hall-church dates from the 13C and served as parish church for the new town. Architectural and decorative effects have all been reduced to the essential. The carved Passion altarpiece (16C) is the work of Edvard van Rodens. The church also features some interesting figures sculpted in stone: Christ, the Virgin Mary and the Apostles (c 1400-40). The cloister encloses a graveyard.

Felix-Nussbaum-Haus

Lotter Strasse 2. ♿ Open Tue-Sun, 11am-6pm, Sat-Sun, 10am-6pm. Closed 1 Jan, Good Fri, 1 May, 1 Nov, 24 and 31 Dec. €4. ☎ (0541) 323 22 07.

This Deconstructivist museum building (1998) was designed by **Daniel Libeskind**. Its broken architectural lines and other resolutely non-standard details all combine to disorientate the visitor. This language turned to stone is supposed to symbolise the turmoil and disorientation in the life of Jewish painter **Felix Nussbaum**.

The artist was born in Osnabrück in 1904, and his work ranks him under Neue Sachlichkeit (New Objectivity), although it also contains echoes of Surrealism. After years of productive creativity in Berlin, Nussbaum emigrated to Belgium in 1935. His short life ended in 1944 in Auschwitz. Anticipating his tragic early death, Nussbaum had expressed the wish that his paintings not be allowed to die with him, but that they be shown to posterity. Some 160 paintings from his huge output are on display in this building.

Excursions

Tecklenburg★

23km/14mi southwest – around 90min. Leave the car in the car park at the entrance to the town. Famous for its half-timbered houses and its position on the crest of the Teutoburger Wald, this is a very popular small town. We recommend heading for the main square and then west, through the Legge gateway, to the oldest part, at the foot of the castle. Of this, nothing remains but a monumental Renaissance gateway and a look-out tower.

Ostfriesische Inseln★

Eastern Frisians

The Eastern Frisian islands' evolution is by no means finished; due to the prevailing northwesterly tides and winds, they are drifting ever further southeast. To the north and east of land formations dating from the modern era and ranging in area from 6.5km²/2.5sq mi to 30.5km²/12sq mi, stretch sandy beaches, which are covered with wicker-hooded deck chairs and windbreaks during the summer. Dune formations grouped by age are characteristic of the island interiors, while to the south of the sea is reclaimed fertile pastureland.

Location

Michelin map nº 541-E-F 3-7 – Niedersachsen. The seven inhabited Eastern Frisian islands lie between the Ems and the Weser deltas off the North Sea coast of Germany. Between the islands and the mainland are the mudflats which were declared a national park in 1986. The islands are reached by ferry; the departure point varies depending on the destination.
Surrounding area: see EMDEM (ferry from Borkum), BREMEN (98km/61mi from Wilhelmshaven, 131km/82mi from Emden).

Fremdenverkehrsbüro, Hallig Langeness

Langeness: Sand undulations on the North Sea coast.

Worth a Visit

Borkum

3 ferries a day (about 2hr) from Emden. €13.50 there and back. ☎ (049 21) 890 70.
The largest of the Eastern Frisians (c 30km²/12sq mi) boasts an impressive beach promenade with grand hotel façades from the turn of the century. In fine weather, there is a good view of the mainland and the "Hohes Riff" (high reef) seal bank from the 60m/200ft tall **Neuer Leuchtturm**, a lighthouse built in 1879 *(315 steps)*.

Juist

From Norddeich (around 75min). €16 there and back. Timetable information from ☎ (049 31) 98 70.
This island (17km/11mi long) is home to an interesting **Küstenmuseum** *(Coastal Museum)* in the attractive village of Loog. The museum documents the local daily life on the coast, the history of the lifeboat service and the importance of dike building and includes literature on drilling for oil and gas in the North Sea. At the exit of the village of Loog is the start of the nature conservation zone of **Bill**, a windswept but fascinating landscape of sand dunes.

Norderney

From Norddeich (around 1hr) Daily ferries with variable timetables according to the season. €13 there and back. Timetable information from ☎ (049 31) 98 70.
The most urbanised of the Eastern Frisians was once the summer residence of the royal House of Hanover. Its main town still has much of its old charm with the spa rooms on the Kurplatz, well-tended spa gardens and 19C houses in some of the side streets.

Baltrum

Landing-stages: Neßmersiel and Baltrum. 2 to 3 ferries (30min) according to the tide. €15 there and back. ☎ (049 33) 99 16 06.

On the smallest of the Eastern Frisians, it is relatively calm even in high season. The main sight here is the **old church** in Westdorf, built one year after the great floods of 1826. The church bell next to the simple place of worship was originally a ship's bell, which was washed up as jetsam on the coast of Baltrum. Nature has been left to its own devices on the east side of the island and the impressive valley of **sand dunes** *(Großes Dünental)* here is well worth a visit.

Langeoog

From Bensersiel (around 1hr): 9.30am-5.30pm. €19 there and back (day ticket). ☎ (049 72) 69 30.

The house on this island houses the **Schiffahrtsmuseum** (Museum of Seafaring). In front of the building is Langeoog's lifeboat, in service between 1945 and 1980. From the raised promenade along the chain of sand dunes, near Ebbe, there is a fine view of 14km/9mi of beach and sand banks many hundred yards long.

Spiekeroog

Landing-stages: Neuharlingersiel and Spiekeroog. 1 to 4 ferries daily (allow 45min). €20 there and back. ☎ (049 76) 919 31 01.

The striking thing about this island is the fact that, despite the numerous contemporary spa and holiday facilities, the traditional village and island infrastructure has remained virtually intact. The **Alte Inselkirche** of 1696 is the oldest surviving place of worship in the Eastern Frisians. A Pietà made of wood and fragments of a pulpit are said to have come from a ship in the Spanish Armada that sank in 1588. One of the island's more unusual sights is the **Muschelmuseum** (Mussel Museum) in the basement of the seaside hall.

Wangerooge

From Harlesiel (around 80min). Timetable information from ☎ (044 64) 94 94 11.

Over the course of history, the furthest east of the Eastern Frisians has belonged to Holland, France, Russia (twice) and since 1818 to the Grand Duchy of Oldenburg. This much sought after island is now a peaceful family holiday destination. The colourful island train runs from the isolated port on the southwest point past lagoons rich in bird life straight to the centre of the village.

The local brew

Statistics show that the inhabitants of the Eastern Frisians drink 14 times more tea per head than the inhabitants of the whole of the rest of Germany. Tea-drinking is a way of life here (so British visitors will feel quite at home). The beverage was introduced to the region by the Dutch in c 1670 and soon caught on. Frederick the Great attempted to implement a tea ban in 1777, but was forced to repeal it two years later as so many people were leaving the region. Even during rationing in the Second World War, the Eastern Frisians were allocated a much more generous tea allowance than elsewhere.

An essential aspect of the Eastern Frisian "tea ceremony" is the sequence of events: first warm the teapot, then pour boiling (not just hot) water onto the tea leaves in the pot and leave to draw for 5min. Place a piece of white sugar crystal into a porcelain cup and pour on the strong, hot tea, which will make an enticing crackling sound as it hits the sugar. Finally, with infinite care, add the merest splash of cream over the back of a special curved spoon made for this purpose. On no account should the cup of tea be stirred; in Eastern Frisian circles this would be a grave breach of etiquette.

Ottobeuren★★★

The Benedictine abbey of Ottobeuren, founded in 764 under the patronage of Charlemagne, was transformed into the Baroque style in the 18C. It is not undeservedly known as the "Swabian Escorial". The overall plan is in the shape of a Christ on the cross with the head (the church) slightly bowed.

Location

Population: 8 000. Michelin map 545 W 14 – Bayern. Ottobeuren is a charming village surrounded by forests and pasture land. The A 96 which links Memmingen to Munich is 11km/7mi to the north.

Surrounding area: see Deutsche ALPENSTRASSE (Füssen is 67km/42mi south), ULM (69km/43mi north), WIESKIRCHE (71km/44mi south).

T. Krieger/MICHELIN

The church and abbey buildings

Worth a Visit

Abbey church★★★ – *Brochure available at the entrance (€2.30).* ♿ *Apr-Oct: 8.30am-6pm; Nov-Mar: 8.30am-4pm. Closed 1 week in Jun, Jul and Sep, Thu pm. No charge.* ☎ *(083 32) 79 80; www.abtei-ottobeuren.de.* In 1748, **Johann Michael Fischer**, the great architect of southern Germany, put the finishing touches on this jewel of German Baroque, which was to be his masterpiece. He was assisted by equally gifted masters for the church's Rococo interior ornamentation: Johann Jakob Zeiller and his cousin Franz Anton Zeiller for the frescoes, Johann Michael Feichtmayr for the stuccowork, and Johann Joseph Christian for the figurative sculptures.

The church's astonishing dimensions are only really evident once inside. The impression of space is enhanced by the unusual amount of light, a result of the church's north-south orientation. The architecture of the entire church is focused on the flattened central dome, amid a proliferation of paintings, stuccowork and sculptures with their wonderfully depicted cherubs, draperies, and lighting effects. This profusion and the structure itself form an inseparable whole that is skilfully organised to symbolise the proclamation of the Apostles' Creed.

The four altars, of St Michael – patron saint of the Ottobeuren area and the Empire – of the Holy Guardian Angels, of St Joseph and of St John the Baptist, are remarkable features, as are also the outstanding works of art that are the **pulpit** and, opposite, the representation of the **Baptism of Christ**, executed by Feichtmayr in red and marble stucco after designs by Zeiller.

On the altar of the Holy Sacrament at the entrance to the chancel stands a much venerated **crucifix** dating from 1220, the Ottobeurer Gnadenheiland (Merciful Redeemer). The **high altar**, with paintings of the Holy Trinity by Zeiller and larger than life-size figures of the Apostles and saints by Christian is an outstanding composition. The walnut **choir stalls★★** (1764) are a masterpiece of the wood-carver's art. The high backs to the stalls are decorated with gilded lime-wood low reliefs by Joseph Christian (depicting scenes from the life of St Benedict on the right and scenes from the Old Testament on the left).

Karl Joseph Riepp, a pupil of the famous organ builder Silbermann, built both the **chancel organs★★** in 1766.

Abbey buildings – *Feb-Mar: Sat-Sun 2-4pm; Apr-Oct: 10am-12pm, 2-5pm; Nov-Jan: 2-4pm. Closed Good Friday and Holy Saturday, 24 and 31 Dec. €3. ☎ (083 32) 79 80.* These were constructed between 1711 and 1725. Inside the **museum★** admire the superb decoration of the rooms, in keeping with the architecture of the church; the abbatial palace *(Prälatur)*, magnificent **library**, theatre and **Emperor's Hall** *(Kaisersaal)*, with a frescoed ceiling depicting the coronation of Emperor Charlemagne, are well worth a visit. The museum also houses some interesting medieval works of art and 15C-17C paintings.

Excursions

Memmingen

11km/7mi northwest. In the **old town**, surrounded by a largely preserved fortified wall, the characteristic appearance of a medieval trading centre remains. On either side of the stream canalised through the city centre stand such ancient buildings as the **Siebendächerhaus** (House with Seven Roofs), once the tanners' headquarters. Interesting buildings also surround the **Marktplatz**: the **Steuerhaus** (1495), with its ground floor opened by arcades; the 1589 **Rathaus**, which was remodelled in the Rococo style in 1765. The design of this is unusual, with three oriel windows on different floors, each with an onion dome. A further highlight is the Late Gothic Antonierhaus with an arcaded courtyard, which houses a museum with works by Memmingen painter Bernhard Strigel (1460-1528) and another on the Antonine Order.

The Gothic basilica **Martinskirche** dates from the 14C and 15C. It has a fine chancel (1496-1500), a masterpiece by architect of the Münster at Ulm, Matthias Böblinger. The **choir stalls★** *(Chorgestühl)*, dating from 1501 to 1507, are intricately carved with 68 figures of the Prophets, sibyls and church benefactors.

On Hallhof square, the final octagon on the 1617 belfry of the **Kreuzherrenkirche** surpasses the town's other towers in the refinement of its decoration.

F. Zaninotto/MICHELIN

Interior view of Ottobeuren abbey church.

Passau★★

Passau, a frontier town between Bavaria and Austria and known as the "Town of the Three Rivers", lies in a marvellous setting★★ at the junction of the Inn, the Danube (Donau) and the small River Ilz. The old town, with its Baroque churches and patrician houses, lies crowded onto the narrow tongue of land separating the Inn and the Danube. Northwards, on the far bank of the Danube, rises the wooded bluff on which the Oberhaus fortress is built. Passau's cultural and economic influence on eastern Bavaria was reinforced in 1978, when a new university was opened. In summertime, the European Weeks attract a large number of music – and theatre – lovers.

Location

Population: 50 000. Michelin map nº 546 U 24 – Bayern. Situated in eastern Bavaria Passau is actually made up of 3 towns: Ilzsdadt to the north, Innsdadt to the south, and the peninsula of Altstadt. The A 3 passes near the town and the Czech Republic is only 50km/31mi away.

Rathausplatz 3, 94032 Passau, ☎ (0851) 95 59 80.

Surrounding area: see BURGHAUSEN (80km/50mi south), STRAUBING (80km/50mi northwest), LANDSHUT (120km/75mi southwest).

Background

A Powerful Bishopric – The see was founded in the 8C by St Boniface, the English-born "Apostle of Germany" *(see FULDA)*. By the end of the 10C it had become so powerful that it rivalled that of Salzburg. In 1217 the bishops were created by princes of the Empire. Until the 15C the diocese was so huge that it encompassed the entire Danube Valley in Austria, even including Vienna.

Directory

Where to Eat

Heilig-Geist-Stift-Schenke – *Heiliggeistgasse 4 – ☎ (0851) 26 07 – Closed 9 Jan-1 Feb and Wednesdays – €14/27.* This establishment built in 1358 has a cosy, rustic atmosphere due in part to the combination of its beautiful vaulted ceiling and panelling, open fire and charming vine-covered garden.

Where to Stay

Rotel Inn – *Donauufer – 50m/55yds from the main station (Hauptbahnhof) – ☎ (0851) 951 60 – fax (0851) 9516100 – www.rotel-inn.de – May-Sep – – 96rm: €25/30 – €5.* Viewed from the outside, this hotel on the bank of the Danube looks like a sleeping man. Inside there is a choice of double or single guestrooms. Bathrooms are off the corridor.

Euro-Hotel Passau – *Neuburger Straße 128 – ☎ (0851) 98 84 20 – fax (0851) 98842111 – www.euro-hotel-passau.de – – Booking advised – 73rm: €44/57.* This multi-storied hotel is not far from the conference hall. This has its advantages: it is near the A3 motorway (Passau-Süd exit). Modern and functional guestrooms.

Hotel Passauer Wolf – *Rindermarkt 6 – ☎ (0851) 931 51 10 – fax (0851) 9315150 – 40rm: €64/144 – Restaurant €23/46.* This traditional establishment is mid-way between the Danube and the pedestrianised part of town. The guestrooms are all different, but all are well-furnished. Rustic-style restaurant with beautiful view of the river.

Taking a Break

Atelier Café – *Ort 2 (between Schaiblingsturm and Dreiflüsseeck) – ☎ (0851) 9 34 66 11 – www.ort2.de – Mar-Oct, Wed-Sun, 11.30am-7.30pm; Nov-Feb, Sat-Sun, 11.30am-7.30pm.* Astrid Störzer, the Austrian proprietor, is proof of the professionalism and enthusiasm behind this café. Her gastronomic background comes to the fore as she prepares cakes and cold dishes in her workshop. There are Austrian specialities on offer and everything can be enjoyed in the idyllic garden.

Café Greindl – *Wittgasse 8 – ☎ (0851) 3 56 77 – Mon-Sat, 6.30am-6pm, Sun, 11am-6pm.* Tea room offering tarts, cakes, ice-creams, and home-made chocolates. In good weather, there is a little terrace outside. There is another branch in the pedestrian district *(Theresienstr. 8).*

Going Out

Café Duft – *Theresienstr. 22 – ☎ (0851) 3 46 66 – www.cafeduft.de – Mon-Sat, 9am-1am, Sundays and bank holidays, 10am-1am.* A former stable is the setting for this café. There is also a terrace onto the pedestrian district and at the back of the establishment there is a beautifully verdant courtyard. Regional cuisine is served as is *tapas*. Cosy candlelit atmosphere at night.

A Commercial Base – The arrival of the Inn waters at Passau almost doubles the flow volume of the Danube; from there on it becomes a really big river. From the Middle Ages, river trade played an important role in the town's prosperity. Today, when barges can go upriver as far as Kelheim, the "Town of Three Rivers" also offers excursions, cruises and passenger traffic to Vienna and Budapest.

Worth a Visit

Veste Oberhaus (Fortress)

Work on this imposing citadel, which served the bishops as a refuge against continuous rebellions by the burghers, started in 1219. It is linked with the Veste Niederhaus by a fortified road along the spit of land separating the Danube and the Ilz. From the belvedere marked Zur Aussicht, near the car park – or from the top of a tower inside the compound *(142 steps)* – there are magnificent **views★★** over the rocky promontory dividing the Inn from the Danube, with the town's churches and houses jumbled close together upon it. Some of the houses, following a former Inn Valley tradition, have ridge roofs behind façades – masking the many sloping angles from street level.

The history of the town and its craftwork, folk art, and religious past are traced in a small **museum** which also displays paintings of the Danube School.

M. Hertlein/MICHELIN

Passau and its cathedral.

Dom St. Stephan

Apart from the east chancel and the transept, the original Late Gothic **cathedral** was destroyed by fire in the 17C. Once rebuilt, the greater part of it was in the Baroque style. The majestic west front is so severe in concept that the late 19C addition to the two towers of a final, octagonal stage seems almost frivolous.

The huge interior is richly decorated with frescoes and stuccowork. There are four **lateral chapels** with fine paintings by the Austrian artist JM Rottmayr (1654-1730). The organ, with 17 774 pipes and 233 stops, is the largest in the world *(organ recitals)*. From the Residenzplatz, visitors can admire the cathedral's **east end★★**, a remarkable Late Gothic work (1407-1530) whose slender outline is emphasised by the domed belfry which tops the transept cupola.

Residenzplatz

The square is bordered on the south by the bishops' **New Residence**, which dates from the beginning of the neo-Classical period. The surrounding streets are still lined with many old houses above arcades, with corbelling and concealed Inn valley ridge roofs.

Rathausplatz

One of the town's most picturesque squares. The painted façade of the Rathaus (D) dates from the 14C; the building's tower was built in the late 18C.

Glasmuseum★★

In the "Wilder Mann" hotel on Rathausplatz. Apr-Sep, 10am-4pm; Oct-Mar, 1-4pm. €4. ☎ (0851) 350 71. Glassware from Bohemia, Bavaria and Austria, from the late 18C to the 1930s, makes up most of this fine collection of 20 000 pieces evoking 250 years of the history of glass.

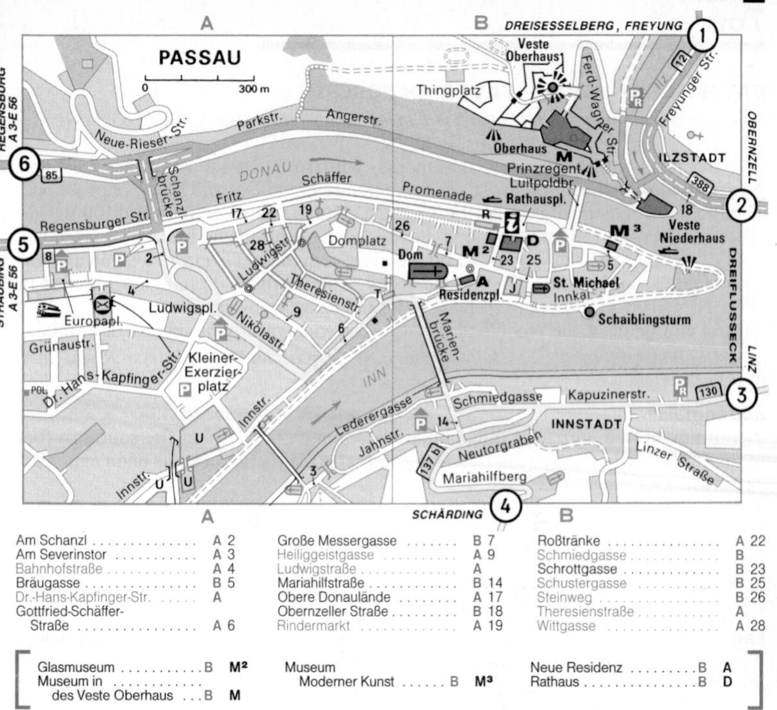

The most important display comes from **Bohemia** (Biedermeier, Historicism, Jugendstil); note especially the Lobmeyr state goblet created in 1878-81 and depicting the *Marriage of Neptune with Amphitrite*; it is considered to be the most significant glass work of the 19C.

St-Michaels-Kirche

This 17C **church** built by the Jesuits overlooks the north bank of the Inn. The over-rich gilding and stuccowork date from c 1670. A reredos painted by Carlo Innocenzo Carlone hides the squared-off chevet.

Dreiflußeck★ (Three Rivers Walk)

From St Michaels-Kirche, go down to the Inn quayside.

The fast-flowing, at times almost torrential, river runs at the foot of the Schaiblingsturm (1481), which was once used to store salt. At the confluence, the green current of the Inn can be seen running alongside the brown Danube waters and dark water of the Ilz before they mingle. From the Danube bank, on the far side of the promontory, there is a fine viewpoint, looking across the river at the wooded, rocky height of the Oberhaus fortress.

▶▶ *Stiftung Wörlen Museum Moderner Kunst* (Modern Art Museum).

Excursions

Dreisesselberg★

48km/30mi northeast, 3km/2mi from the Czech border. The drive to this curious group of granite rocks, eroded into flat, saucer-like shapes, runs through some of the wildest regions of the Bavarian forest. The inn at the foot of the formation is soon reached from the road. Green triangles bordered with white waymark the path leading to the lowest rock outcrop. From there, steps rise to the **Hochstein** (1 332m/4 370ft). The viewpoint at the summit affords a splendid **panorama**★ which reveals the immensity of this Bohemian forest.

Osterhofen Church

36km/22mi NW. Leave Passau by ⑥ on the town plan. Three great names of the Bavarian Baroque style have expressed the fullness of their talent here in this suburb of Altenmarkt: Johann Michael Fischer in the architecture and the Asam brothers in the decoration. The alternation of the convex lines of the balustrades and concave lines of the pilasters as well as the almost total absence of right angles gives many contours to the buildings. Note in particular the monumental high altar with its wreathed columns and its angels with enraptured smiles surrounding a radiant almond-shaped glory.

▶▶ Museumsdorf Bayerischer Wald in Tittling (*20km/12mi north*).

Tour

BAYERISCHER WALD★ (BAVARIAN FOREST)

Round tour leaving from Bodenmais (70km/44mi north of Passau). About 65km/41mi – 3hr.

The Bavarian forest is of low mountains, with rounded off summits, wild and romantic rock bastions and isolated, comb-like river valleys and broad depressions. The Pfahl is a geological peculiarity, a stretch of quartz between 50m and 100m wide (164 by 328ft) and 150km/90mi long. Europe's largest protected forest area stretches over 13 300ha/32 865 acres on both sides of the German-Czech border over an ancient base of gneiss and granite. The centre of the region is the National Park founded in 1970. Forestry was gradually stopped to let the forest grow as nature intended. The natural character of the woodland has drawn a wide variety of species of animals.

To get to Bodenmais from Passau, take the B 85 (Bayerische Ostmarkstr) to Regen, then fork to the right.

Bodenmais★

This unique town with a healing climate lies in a pastureland at the southern foot of the Großer Arber. A subsoil rich in sulphur and magnetic rock has been exploited since the 15C.

Travel 23km/14mi along the massif towards Kötzting

From Kötzting onwards, the road mounts the pastoral Weißer Regen Valley within sight of the peaks of the Osser.

Lam

This charming holiday resort is situated on a broad valley floor.

Motorists continue climbing as far as the Lamer Winkel, a hollow of woods and upland meadows at the head of the valley. A panoramic drive across the mountainside, enlivened by a closer view of the Großer Arber, terminates this part of the journey (highest point: Brennes-Sattel, at 1 030m/3 380ft).

Danube School

The German painters working in the Danube Valley in the 16C were among the first to depict landscape for its own sake. The best masters of this so-called school were Albrecht Altdorfer, Lucas Cranach the Elder, Wolf Huber and Jörg Breu the Elder.

Hindenburg-Kanzel★

A **look-out point★** offers a fine view of the Lamer Winkel and the Arber.

Großer Arber★★

From the lower cable railway terminal, 1hr there and back, including 20min on foot. Summer: 8.30am-4.45pm; Winter: 8.30am-4.30pm. Closed 2 weeks in Apr and from Nov to the start of Dec. €8 round trip. ☎ (099 25) 941 40.

From the upper terminal, continue to climb on foot. At the top there are two rocky crags. That on the left (above a small chapel) overlooks the Schwarzer Regen depression, with an extended **view★★** of the frontier region of the south-east. The right-hand rock (surmounted by a cross) affords a splendid view of the Lamer Winkel and the wooded undulations of the forest to the north.

The **Großer Arbersee★**, a dark, romantic lake surrounded by pines, is passed on the right as the road goes down, winding through the tree-covered foothills on the southern slopes of the Arber. On the way, there are several magnificent **viewpoints★** commanding the Zwiesel basin, the Falkenstein and the Großer Rachel.

Pfalz★

Rheinland Palatinate

One of the largest wooded areas of Germany, the Palatinate massif is also a protected botanical and zoological park. The northern part of the massif is popular with walkers; to the east, the mild climate encourages the growth of exotic fruit. The climatic health resort of Dahn and the German Wine Road are two good reasons to explore further the Pfalz region.

Location

Michelin maps n°s 543, 545 S 7 – R 9 – Rheinland-Pfalz. The Palatinate mountains stretch from the Rhine plains to the Vosges. The massif is reached via the A 65 motorway from Mannheim, a few kilometres to the west, or from Karlsruhe, further south. The German Wine Road starts 15km/9mi to the west of Worms, at Bockenheim *(B 271)* and winds 80km/50mi south towards the French border.

Surrounding area: see MANNHEIM (23km/14mi east of Bad Dürkheim), HEIDELBERG (42km/26mi east of Bad Dürkheim), KARLSRUHE (35km/22mi south of Bad Bergzabern).

Directory

Where to Eat

Weinstube Ester – *Triftweg 21 – 67098 Bad Dürkheim – ☏ (06322) 98 90 65 – Closed for 2 weeks in Sep and Mon and Tue – €14/25.50.* Many regulars come to this rustic tavern, which is typical of the Palatinate region. Regional dishes, mostly the establishment's meat and sausage specialities, are on the menu.
The wines mostly come from the vineyards which surround the restaurant.

⊖⊖ Reuters Holzappel – *Hauptstraße 11 – 76889 Bad Bergzabern – ☏ (06343) 42 45 – www.reuters-holzappel.de – ⊠ – €28/60.* Typical local style, welcoming wine cellar in a 250-year-old farmhouse with courtyard. Wooden furniture and collections of objets make this place cosy and comfortable. Local and international dishes are on the menu.

Where to Stay

⊖ Hotel Zum Lam – *Winzergasse 37, 76889 Bad Bergzabern – ☏ (06343) 93 92 12 – fax (06343) 939213 – info@zum-lam.de – Closed 2-23 Jan – P – 11rm: €55/85 – Restaurant €22/36.* As well as being a charming resort, Bad Bergzabern is well-known for its 18C half-timbered houses; this hotel is one of them. Very pleasant garden terrace and local-style room furnishings. Charming peaceful setting in a typical wine growers' area.

⊖⊖⊖ Hotel Deidesheimer Hof – *Am Marktplatz 1, 67146 Deidesheim – ☏ (06326) 968 70 – fax (06326) 7685 – info@deidesheimerhof.de – Closed 1-3 Jan – P – 28rm: €105/200 – €14.* Elegant inn with tastefully furnished rooms. Gourmet restaurant on the premises as well as lounge offering regional specialities. The former Chancellor Helmut Kohl liked to receive official guests at this establishment.

Background

The palatinate mountains are a continuation of the northern Vosges, with a similar forested aspect broken up by escarpments of red sandstone.
The *Pfälzer Wald*, densely wooded and sparsely inhabited, is a huge natural park in the northern part of the massif much favoured by walkers; further south lies the broken country of the **Wasgau**, where tree-clad heights crowned by castle ruins or rock outcrops overlook the valley clearings which shelter the villages.
The Wines of the Palatinate – The most extensive wine-growing region of the country, the Palatinate produces almost one-third of Germany's total output: a long reach of suitable country, calcareous, protected and facing the sun, it stretches along the foot of the **Haardt** – the steep eastern flank of the massif overlooking the Rhine.
The highest point of the Haardt is the Kalmit, at 673m/2 208ft. The strip below being almost flat, vines can be cultivated in the traditional way on low cordons. This permits late-harvested grapes to ripen more and produce fruity wines of fairly high alcoholic content, the most appreciated being the whites. The most famous vintages come from the villages of Bad Dürkheim, Forst, Deidesheim and Wachenheim. The itinerary suggested below follows part of the celebrated Deutsche Weinstraße (German Wine Road), which begins at Schweigen, on the French frontier, and ends at Bockenheim, west of Worms.

Tour

FROM WORMS TO BAD BERGZABERN

151km/91mi – allow one day

Worms★ *see WORMS*
South of Worms, still part of Rhineland Hessen, cultivation of the Rhine plain becomes progressively devoted to the vine. Soon, the steep barrier of the Haardt appears in the distance.

Freinsheim
A large wine town, encircled by ramparts. The town hall, beside a 15C church, occupies an elegant Baroque house with an overhanging roof that protects an outside staircase.
The road continues through vineyards, past pretty villages.

Bad Dürkheim
Sheltered by the Pfälzer Wald, this thermal cure town enjoys a mild climate in which fig, almond and chestnut trees in the Spa Park flower early. A couple of miles west *(via Schillerstraße and Luitpoldweg)* are the ruins of Limburg abbey. From here there are picturesque views – to the east across the vineyards of the Rhine plain; westwards along the Isenach Valley to the Hardenburg ruins.

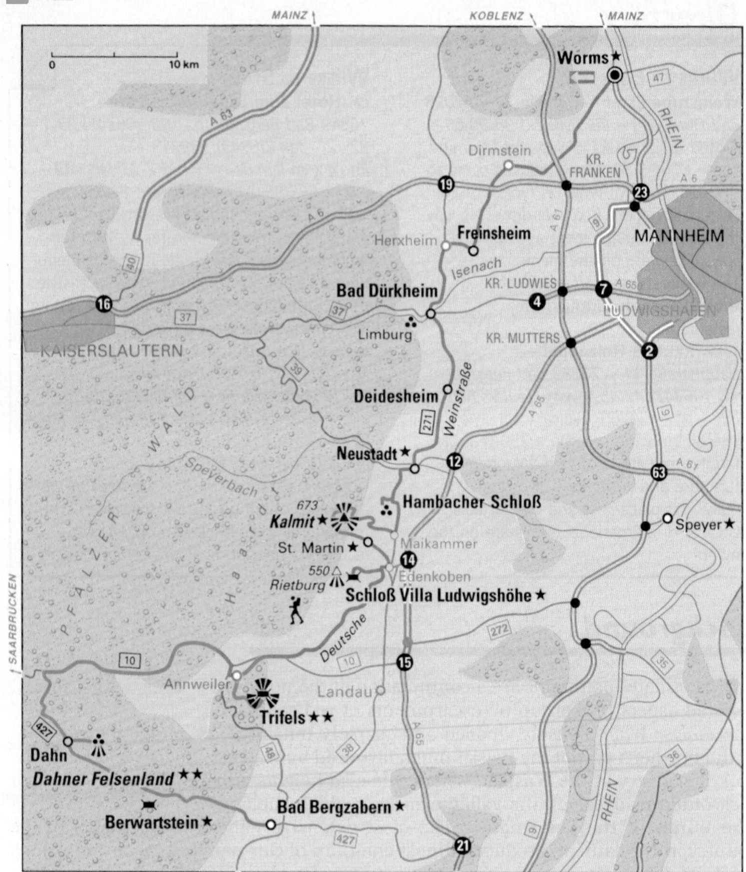

Deidesheim

One of the most typical and prosperous towns on the German Wine Road with its smart market place, bordered by half-timbered and patrician houses.
The traditional goat auction, which takes place in historical costumes on the steps of the town hall (16C), is held every year on Whit Tuesday.

Neustadt an der Weinstraße – Narrow, picturesque lanes in this small town surround a pretty market place with an 18C town hall. The old **town★** is attractive and boasts the largest number of old houses in the region.

Hambacher Schloß

On the outskirts of Hambach. From Mar to end Nov: 10am-6pm. €4.50. ☎ (063 21) 308 81.

Founded by the Salian Franks in the 11C, this castle was for some considerable time the summer residence of the Speyer bishops before being destroyed in 1688. The ruins of this old fortress are famous in Germany because it was here, in 1832, that militant patriots demanding a more liberal approach raised for the first time the black, red and gold flag adopted as the German national emblem in 1919, and again in 1949. A permanent exhibition in the fully restored ruins commemorates this event, the first major rally in German history.

Kalmit

8km/5mi, leaving from Maikammer, then 15min on foot there and back. At 673m/2 208ft above sea level, the Kalmit is the highest outcrop in the Rhineland Palatinate. It is a good departure point for numerous walks through beautiful woodland. There is a viewpoint at the summit. From the Kalmithaus terrace, there is a splendid **view★★** of the Rhine plain and, in the east, Speyer cathedral. Return to the Wine Road via the charming village of **St Martin★**.

Schloß-Villa Ludwigshöhe★

2km/1mi from Edenkoben. Guided tours of historic rooms only. From holy week until the end of Sep, 10am-6pm; Oct-Nov and Jan-Palm Sun, 10am-5pm. The Max-Slevogt-Galerie can be visited independently of the guided tour. €2.60. ☎ (063 23) 930 16.

Built by Ludwig I of Bavaria in the "Italian villa" style, this stately home now houses a **gallery★** devoted to the works of the German Impressionist painter Max Slevogt (1868-1932). The apartments with Pompeian-style murals and fine parquet **flooring★** are also open to the public. There is a superb **view★** of the River Rhine plain from the terrace.
A chair-lift carries sightseers to the Rietburg (550m/1 804ft), departure point for forest walks. The return journey in the chair-lift affords superb views over the vine-covered slopes.

Trifels★

7km/4.5mi from Annweiler, plus 1hr 30min walking and sightseeing. From holy week until end Sep, 10am-6pm; Oct-Nov and Palm Sun, 10am-5pm. €2.60. ☎ (063 46) 84 70.
This castle is of considerable historic importance and dates back to a foundation by the Salian Franks. It was the Hohenstaufen imperial stronghold and in the 12C and 13C, the temporary residence of the crown jewels and royal treasury. Legend even has it that the Holy Grail was found here. It is proven fact, however, that Emperor Henry IV held **Richard the Lionheart** prisoner in the fort, while the latter was returning from the Third Crusade in 1193. The enormous ransom that Henry IV received for Richard's release enabled him to fund a military campaign against the Norman kingdom in south Italy. He set off from Trifels on 9 May 1194.
On a superb **site★★** crowning the summit of a bluff, Trifels makes an imposing sight even from a distance. It is clear to see how strategic a role the fortress played in protecting the route from Metz via Pirmasens to the Rhine plain. The sandstone outcrop on which it rests, seemingly fused at the base, is 1 450m/4 765ft long and only 40m/130ft wide.

Dahner Felsenland★★

The climatic health resort of **Dahn** is surrounded by one of the best areas for walking in Germany, featuring breathtaking mountains and numerous interesting rock formations from red sandstone, of which 47 have been singled out as protected natural monuments. The **castle ruins★** of Altdahn dominate the town. Flights of steps and guard rooms hewn into the rocks add to the charm of the castle, the heart of which probably dates from c 1100. From the towers, there are fine **views★** of the Wasgau.

Burg Berwartstein★

Turn off towards Erlenbach (B 427). Open Mar to Oct, 9am-6pm; Nov to Feb, Sat-Sun, 11am-6pm. €2.50. ☎ (063 98) 210.
This former robber baron's lair, situated at the intersection of several valleys, is perched 100m/330ft above the village of Erlenbach. The upper castle dates back to the 12C, and the lower to the 15C. The castle was destroyed by a fire in 1591, and then rebuilt at the end of the 19C. The knights' hall, hunting room, a 104m/340ft deep well, the old kitchen, casemates and subterranean passages cut into the rock are open to the public. From the terrace there is a **view★** "beyond frontiers" of the undulating Wasgau landscape as far as France.
Winding through a landscape scattered with rock outcrops, the road arrives at Bad Bergzabern.

Bad Bergzabern★

This charming health resort features numerous half-timbered houses (Königstraße, Marktstraße). Among the ornate residences dating from the 17C and 18C, note in particular the **Gasthaus zum Engel★** (1579), which is said to be the finest Renaissance building in the region. The palace with its sturdy round towers was built in 1720-25. All that remains of the previous building is a polygonal staircase tower on the courtyard side, dating from 1530.

Rhine-Main-Danube Canal

Ever since Roman times emperors, kings, engineers and visionaries have dreamt of linking the Rhine and Danube waterways. Charlemagne began the great enterprise, hence the name Charlemagne's Ditch (Fossa Carolina). Bavaria's Ludwig I made another attempt when he built the Ludwig Canal. However it was barge loads of 20C dignitaries who were the first to cross the watershed between the Rhine and the Danube on 25 September 1992.
The 177km/110mi canal with its hundreds of locks takes the barges up and down the 245m/800ft climb. Some 12 centuries after it was originally conceived, the idea of a waterway linking Europe from the North Sea to the Black Sea has become a reality.

Potsdam★★★

Located in delightful countryside only a few miles west of Berlin, Potsdam was chosen at the beginning of the 17C as the official residence of the electors of Brandenburg because of its ideal setting – a natural wooded site dotted with lakes and crisscrossed by canals and arms of the River Havel. Sacked by Swedish troops during the Thirty Years War (1618-48), the town was revived by Friedrich Wilhelm I. After the Revocation of the Edict of Nantes, many French Huguenots emigrated to Potsdam, among them merchants and craftsmen who contributed to the subsequent economic development of the area. But it is to Frederick the Great (Friedrich II) that Potsdam owes its renown as "rococo jewel".

Location

Population: 129 000. Michelin maps n°s 542, 544 I 23 – Brandenburg. The capital of Brandenburg is a few kilometres to the west of Berlin, in the heart of the Havelland, an area of canals and lakes.

Friedrich-Ebert-Straße 5, 14467 Potsdam, ☎ (0331) 27 55 80.

Surrounding area: see BERLIN (30km/19mi), WITTENBERG (78km/49mi southwest), WÖRLITZ (85km/53mi southwest), DESSAU (95km/59mi southwest).

Background

A Prussian Versailles – Under the rule of Friedrich Wilhelm, "the King-Sergeant" (1713-40), Potsdam became an administrative centre and above all a garrison town (to the extent that at one time three-quarters of the population were military). The King's son, **Frederick the Great** (Friedrich II: 1712-86, reigned from 1740), was on the contrary a patron of the arts and man of letters. Most of the prestigious monuments for which the city is famous today were due to him, notably Sanssouci and the Neues Palais. Frederick, as eloquent in French as in his own language, welcomed many eminent Frenchmen to his court, among them **Voltaire**, who lived in Potsdam for three years.

In 1991, 205 years after his death, the remains of Frederick the Great were reinterred in the crypt of his beloved palace of Sanssouci in Potsdam.

The Potsdam Conference – The treaty defining the role of the victors in the occupation and future of Germany after the Second World War was signed here at Cecilienhof Palace on 2 August 1945 by the leaders of the Allied powers (Churchill – subsequently Attlee – Truman and Stalin).

Special Features

SANSSOUCI PALACE AND PARK★★★

Follow the itinerary suggested on the map.

Designed in part by Peter Joseph Lenné (1789-1866), the most talented landscape gardener in Prussia, the 300ha/740-acre park contains several hundred different species of tree. The various palaces and pavilions were all built between 1744 and 1860. This huge complex marrying architecture with the landscape is undoubtedly the best example of its kind in Germany.

Sanssouci Palace and terraced gardens, dear to the heart of Frederick the Great.

J. Malburet/MICHELIN

Directory

Where to Eat

⊖⊖ **La Maison du Chocolat** – *Benkertstraße 20 – ☎ (0331) 237 07 30 – schoko_haus@gmx.de – ⊭ ♿ – €26/34.* This restaurant has a boutique attached where customers can buy all manner of succulent cakes and chocolate truffles. A little corner of France in the Dutch quarter of Potsdam.

Where to Stay

⊖ **Bed and Breakfast am Luisenplatz** – *Zimmerstraße 1 – ☎ (0331) 971 90 20 – fax (0331) 9719019 – www.bed-breakfast-potsdam.de – ⊭ – 15rm: €49/79 – ☕ €6.* The relatively central situation and reasonable prices makes this little hotel a useful address to know about. The welcoming guestrooms are modern and furnished in light wood; breakfast is served on the Luisenplatz.

Wandering here and there it is easy to understand why Frederick the Great, turning his back momentarily on affairs of state, took such delight coming here to steep himself in the arts, especially music. In fact, Sanssouci has become his final resting place. His body was brought from Burg Hohenzollern in 1991 and interred in a vault above the terraces of the palace. His father, Friedrich Wilhelm I, is buried in a mausoleum in the Friedenskirche near the Marly Gardens.

Friedenskirche

This **church** was built under Friedrich Wilhelm IV, who is buried here, in 1844-54. It was modelled on the basilica of San Clemente in Rome. The apse contains a fine **mosaic★** made during the first half of the 18C and from the island of Murano. The mausoleum houses the recumbent statues of Emperor Friedrich III and his wife, and the sarcophagus of Friedrich Wilhelm I, the King-Sergeant.

Neptungrotte (Neptune's Grotto) – This is the last building (1751-57) designed by Georg Wenzelaus von Knobelsdorff. The fountain decorated with shell motifs was not installed until the 19C.

Bildergalerie★ (Paintings Gallery)

From mid-May to mid-Oct, Tue-Sun, 10am-5pm. €2. ☎ (0331) 969 42 02.

This was built between 1755 and 1763. Amid the rich Rococo decor of the great rooms visitors can admire works mainly from the Italian (Bassano, Tintoretto and Caravaggio), Flemish (Van Dyck, Rubens and Terbrugghen) and French (Simon Vouet and Van Loo) schools, all acquired by Friedrich II.

Schloß Sanssouci★★★

There may be a wait, because only a limited number of visitors are allowed in at once. Guided visit (40min). Open Apr to Oct, Tue-Sun, 9am-5pm; Nov to Mar, Tue-Sun, 9am-4pm. Closed 24, 25 and 31 Dec. €8. ☎ (0331) 969 42 02; www.spsg.de

It is impossible to remain unmoved by the progressive appearance of this majestic façade as one climbs the great staircase rising through the tiers of terraces before it. The original idea of the architect (Knobelsdorff again) was for the façade, adorned with 36 atlantes, to encompass the entire terrace area. But the king preferred a generous proportion of space which indeed became one of his favourite places to relax in. On the far side of the palace the state entrance is flanked by an elegant semicircular colonnade.

A walk through the rooms inside reveals the enormous skill and artistry in the Rococo style of the craftsmen who

The historic mill.

Ph. Gajic/MICHELIN

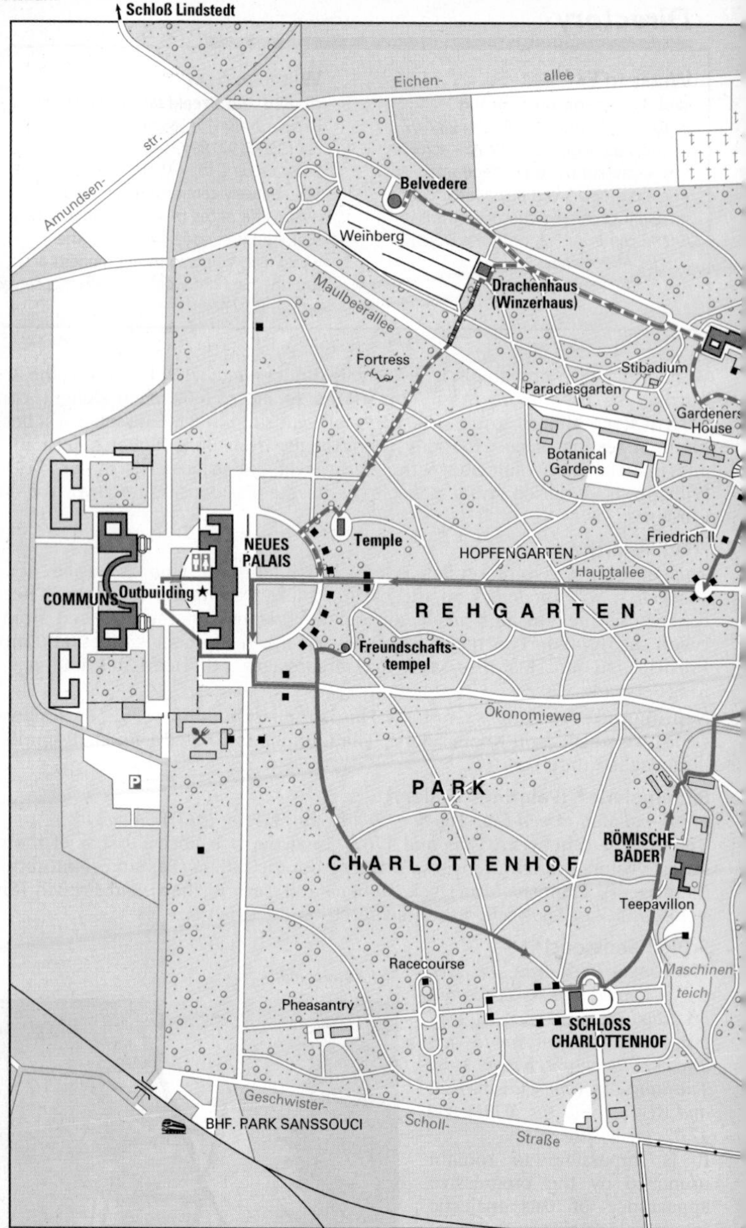

decorated them. In the study and bedchamber Frederick the Great's desk and the chair in which he died are on display. The monarch's favourite room was the Music Room, a masterpiece of Prussian Rococo. The Marble Hall is also impressive, with great French windows opening out onto the terrace; this is where the "philosophical discussions" took place.

Neue Kammern★ (New Rooms)

♿ *Open Apr to mid-May, Sat-Sun, 10am-5pm; mid-May to mid-Oct, Tue-Sun, 10am-5pm. €2. ☎ (0331) 969 42 02.*

Designed in 1747 by Knobelsdorff in the form of an orangery, this block was transformed into the palace guesthouse by Georg Christian Unger from 1771 to 1774. The Rococo interior decor is bright and captivating. Note in particular the **Ovid-Galerie★**, in which the panelling is decorated with scenes from Ovid's *Metamorphoses*.

Historische Mühle

This mill is the subject of a well-known anecdote, which is an excellent observation on the role of the State and of Frederick the Great's enlightened despotism. The

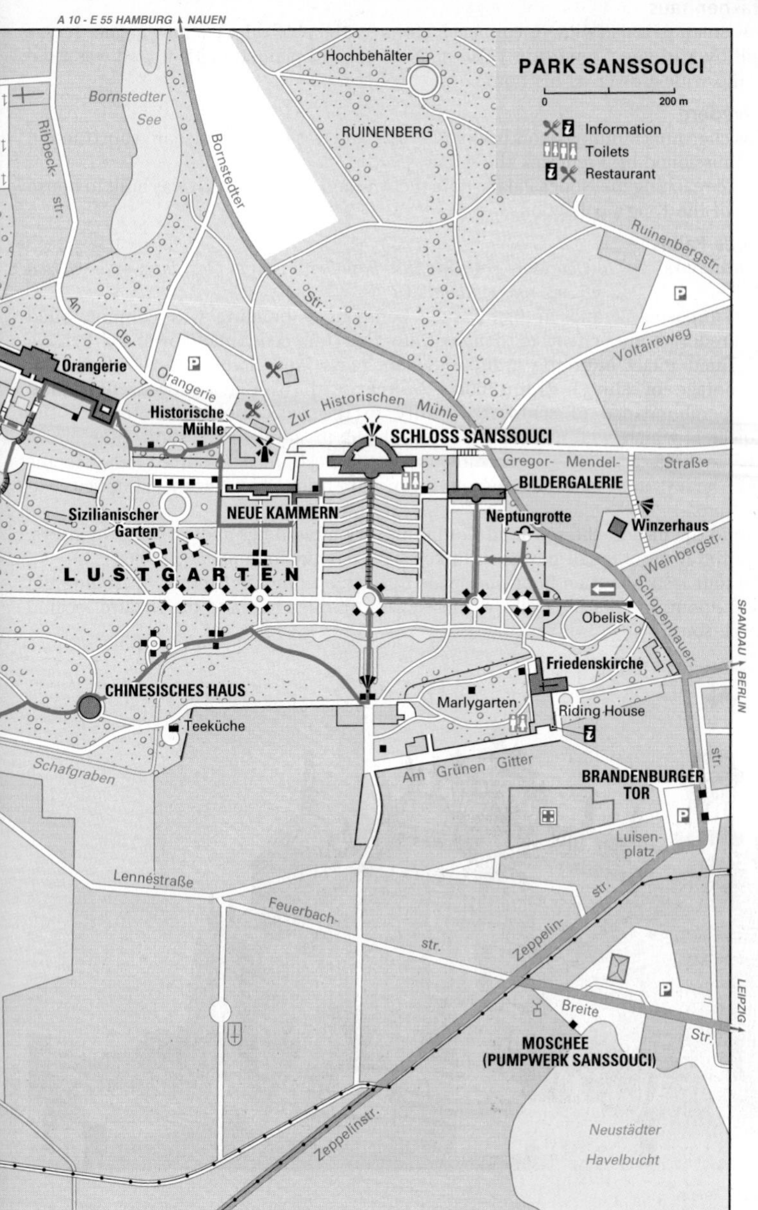

King was disturbed by the noise of the mill, so made efforts to persuade the miller to discontinue his business or go somewhere else. He began by offering compensation, and when this did not work proceeded to threats, but to no avail. The King then took the miller to court, but lost the civil case, on the principle that in a court of law it is the law that speaks while the King must remain silent.

Sizilianischer Garten

These charming gardens were designed in the Renaissance style by Lenné.

Neue Orangerie

♿ *Guided visit from mid-May to mid-Oct, Tue-Sun. 10am-5pm. €3. ☎ (0331) 969 42 02.* The orangery was built in the style of an Italian Renaissance palace between 1851 and 1860, after plans by Friedrich Wilhelm IV. Among the magnificent apartments occupied by Czar Nicolas I and his wife, the malachite hall is particularly impressive. Even more of a find, however, is the Raphael Hall★, which houses 47 copies of paintings by Raphael.

Drachenhaus

This small pagoda (with 16 copper dragons on the roof ridge) is now a café. It was built by Karl von Gontard in 1770, near a vineyard planted in 1769, and was used by the wine-grower as his home.

Belvédère

This charming building dates back to 1770-72 and was the last Potsdam construction commissioned by Frederick the Great.
Before reaching the Neues Palais, note the Antique temple, which was built to house part of the King's collections.

Neues Palais★★

Guided tours, Apr to Oct, Mon-Thu, Sat-Sun, 9am-5pm; Nov to Mar, 9am-4pm. Closed 24, 25 and 31 Dec. €5. ☎ (0331) 969 42 02.
This imposing – and in fact rather pompous – building was commissioned by Frederick the Great to demonstrate that the economic power of Prussia remained intact after the arduous Seven Years War. Some 400 rooms behind a frontage of almost 213m/700ft, together with over-lavish decorations and a superabundance of sculpture, testify to the over-ambitious nature of the project – which was nevertheless completed in a relatively short time, from 1763 to 1769. The style of architecture, an unrestrained Baroque, today seems both heavy and over mannered, very far from the elegant simplicity of Sanssouci.
Behind the palace, the so-called Communs, or outbuildings and servants' quarters, take the form of small pavilions linked by a curved colonnade (1766-69).
The tour lasts about an hour and leads through a number of rooms, including the Shell Room, the Marble Gallery, the elegant Marble Hall, and the theatre located in the south wing.

Ph. Gajic/MICHELIN

Neues Palais.

Schloß Charlottenhof★

Guided tour (45min). From mid-May to mid-Oct, Tue-Sun. 10am-5pm. €4. ☎ (0331) 969 42 02. Karl-Friedrich Schinkel and his pupil Ludwig Perseus drew up the plans for this palace, which was built in the Classical Italian style between 1826 and 1829. Visitors can see, among other things, the bedchamber and office of Alexander von Humboldt.

Römische Bäder (Roman Baths)

Schinkel designed this group of buildings, Perseus executed it between 1829 and 1835, and Lenné planted the garden. The guiding principle was to blend a group of different buildings harmoniously with their natural setting. The **interior decor★** of the baths is tastefully done.
A pergola leads to the Tea Pavilion, not unlike a temple, with a single room decorated all in blue, which has a good view of the lake and gardens.

Chinesisches Teehaus★★ (Chinese Tea House)

A circular pavilion decorated with gilded statues, this structure arose from the "Sino-mania" so popular in 18C Germany. There is an exhibition of Chinese porcelain inside.

Worth a Visit

THE TOWN

Brandenburger Tor★

Luisenplatz. A monumental gateway in the form of a triumphal arch, Roman style, built in the Baroque fashion in 1770 based on designs by Karl von Gontard and Georg Friedrich Unger.

Dampfmaschinenhaus★ (Steam-powered pumping station)

Take Schopenhauerstraße, and then, on the right, Breite Straße. Guided tour (30min). From mid-May to mid-Oct, Sat-Sun, 10am-5pm. €2. ☎ (0331) 969 42 02.
Installed in a most unusual building imitating a mosque, complete with minarets, this pumping station (1841-43) supplies water to the fountains, pools and cascades in Sanssouci Park. The ingenious machinery can be seen at work.

Marstall (Old Stables)

Breite Straße. Dating from 1685 and modified by Knobelsdorff in 1746. Groups of horse trainers decorate the attics. There is an interesting film **museum★** here with reconstructions of Marlene Dietrich's and Lilian Harvey's dressing-rooms. The museum also contains a lot of literature on German Expressionist films and émigré film directors.

Nikolaikirche★

Built on the site of an old Baroque church destroyed by fire in 1795, this is a perfect example of German Classicism as conceived by Karl Friedrich Schinkel. Construction lasted from 1830 to 1850. The cupola was added in 1849.

Holländisches Viertel★ (Dutch Quarter)

It is on each side of the Mittelstraße that one can still see these gabled houses in varying colours, built by the Dutch architect Boumann around 1740 for Netherlands artisans working in Potsdam. There is a good view of the row of houses from the corner of Benkerstraße and Mittelstraße.

LE NOUVEAU PARC★★

This park was laid out at the end of the 18C by Peter Lenné on the shore of Heiliger See for Frederick the Great, who was a great fan of English-style landscaped gardens. Interesting follies and features in the park include the Holländisches Etablissement, where servants were quartered; the orangery; the pyramid; the kitchens, which Langhans incorporated into a building in the style of an ancient ruin; and finally the marble palace.

Marmorpalais

♿ *Open Apr to Oct, Tue-Sun, 10am-5pm; Nov to Mar (guided tour only), Sat-Sun, 10am-4pm. Closed 24, 25 and 31 Dec. €2. ☎ (0331) 969 42 02.* This marble palace was built by Karl von Gontard and converted into a summer residence for Friedrich Wilhelm II by Langhans (1744-97). The king's private apartments with their beautiful furnishings and the state apartments are open to visitors. The concert hall, with a view of the lake from three sides, and the Oriental Room are particularly delightful.

Schloß Cecilienhof★

♿ *Open Apr to Oct, Tue-Sun, 9am-5pm; Nov to Mar (guided tours only), Tue-Sun, 9am-4pm. €4. ☎ (0331) 969 42 02.* This English-style country residence built during the First World War for Crown Prince Wilhelm (1882-1951) and his wife Cecilia of Mecklenburg-Schwerin (1886-1954) houses the historic meeting rooms of the Potsdam conference of 1945 and the Schloßhotel Cecilienhof, a luxury hotel.
Historische Stätte der Potsdamer Konferenz – Besides the conference and meeting rooms used by the members of the Allied delegations and where the Potsdam Agreements were signed (2 August 1945), visitors can see Crown Princess Cecilia's private office, furnished like a ship's cabin.

Excursions

Brandenburg

38km/24mi west. It was in the 14C that this small town in the heart of the Havelland (an area of scattered lakes fed by the River Havel) began to prosper, mainly through the cloth trade. The **Dom St Peter und St Paul★**, founded in 1165 and remodelled in the 14C, is furnished with several Gothic altarpieces. In the two-aisle crypt there is a mausoleum in memory of the clergy murdered during the Nazi regime.
Rich exterior decoration distinguishes the 15C **St Katharinenkirche★**, which boasts a hall chancel with an ambulatory *(currently under restoration)* that is a typical example of brick-built Gothic.

POTSDAM

Am Alten Markt .... BY 6
Benkerstraße .... BX 15
Brandenburger Straße .... ABXY
Ebräerstraße .... BY 21
Französische Straße .... BY 25
Hermann-Elflein-Straße .... AX 31
Luisenplatz .... AY 42
Mühlenbergweg .... AX 48
Platz der Einheit .... BY 54
Schloßstraße .... BY 60
Siefertstraße .... BY 64
Wilhelm-Staab-Straße .... BY 67

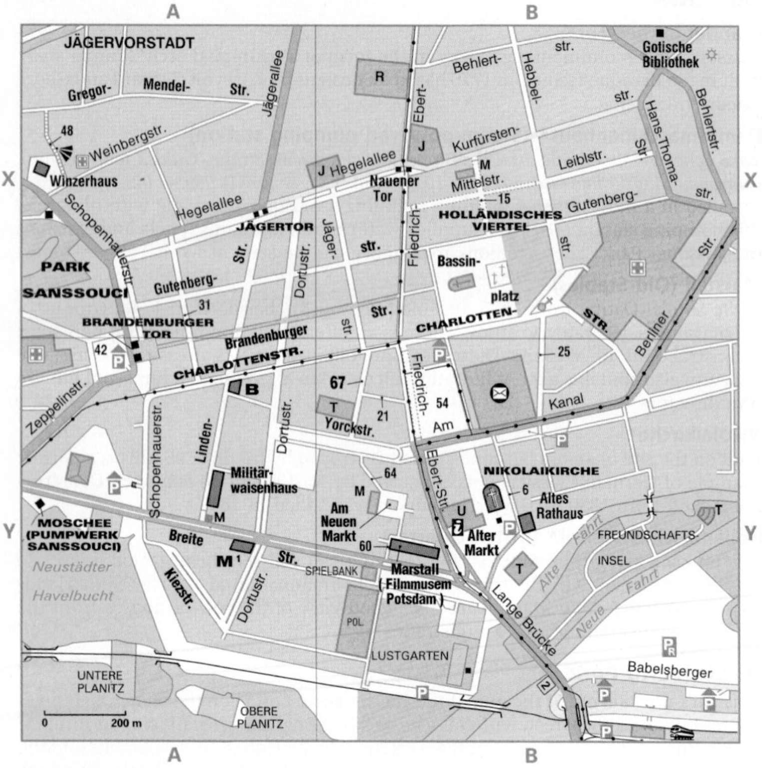

Ehemalige Hauptwache .... AY**B**
Hiller-Brandtsche Häuser .... AY**M¹**

Kloster Lehnin★ (Abbey)

28km/17m southwest. ♿ Open Apr to Oct, Mon-Fri, 9am-noon and 1-4pm, Sat, 11am-noon and 1-5pm, Sun, 11.30am-noon and 1-5pm; Nov to Mar, Mon-Fri 10am-noon and 1-4pm, Sat, 11am-noon and 1-5pm, Sun, 11.30am-noon and 1-5pm. Closed 1 Jan, 24-26 and 31 Dec. No charge. ☎ (033 82) 76 88 55.

Brick-built again, this three-aisle basilica, commissioned by Otto I and occupied in 1180 by the Cistercian Order, has all the hallmarks of Early Gothic. Worth seeing: a Triumphal Cross dating from 1225 and the funerary stone of the Margrave Otto IV.

Quedlinburg★

Nestling at the foot of a rock pinnacle crowned by a castle and an abbey church, the picturesque half-timbered houses and narrow, winding streets of Quedlinburg, which hosted a number of Imperial diets, form a picture that corresponds to everyone's idea of a 17C German town. The old town, in which no less than 770 houses are classified as historical monuments, has been inscribed on UNESCO's World Heritage List since 1994.

Location

Population: 23 800. Michelin map nº 544 K 17 – Sachsen-Anhalt. Quedlinburg is a few kilometres north of the Harz massif. The town is close to the A 14 motorway which leads to Leipzig (to the south) and Magdeburg (to the north), making it an ideal base for exploring the Harz mountains.

ℹ Markt 2, 06484 Quedlinburg, ☎ (039 46) 77 30 00.

Surrounding area: see HARZ (Wernigerode is 32km/20mi west), HALLE (75km/47mi southeast), DESSAU (85km/53mi east), MAGDEBURG (56km/35mi northeast).

Directory

Where to Stay

⊖⊖ **Romantik Hotel Theophano** – *Markt 14 – ☎ (039 46) 963 00 – fax (039 46) 963036 – theophano@t-online.de – P – 22rm: €62/113 ☐.* The guestrooms in this hotel are particularly smart, with tasteful pastel tones and good-quality soft furnishings, many of them with four-poster beds. The restaurant is in the vaulted wine-cellar of the half-timbered building.

⊖⊖ **Schlosshotel Zum Markgrafen** – *Weingarten 30 – ☎ (039 46) 811 40 – fax (039 46) 811444 – www.schlosshotel-zum-markgrafen.de – P – 12rm: €90/160 ☐.* Built in 1898, this beautiful villa with a turbulent past is in the centre of a small park. All the elegant guestrooms come with Italian furnishings.

Special Features

THE OLD TOWN★

Markt★ (Market Place)

The early-17C Renaissance **Rathaus**, a two-storey building flanked by a gateway showing the town's armorial bearings, borders the northern side of the market place. On the left of the façade is a statue of Roland (c 1440). Houses built in the 17C and 18C line the other three sides of the square.

Old Streets★

Circle St Benediktkirche via Marktstraße and Kornmarkt to explore the cobbled lanes behind the Rathaus, then return to the Markt along Breitstraße, which has several picturesque alleyways opening off it. On the far side of the square, stroll to the hill that leads up to the castle by way of Wordgasse (museum on half-timbering), Hohe Straße and Blasiistraße. On one side of the charming **Schloßbergplatz★** stands the late-16C house (Klopstock-Haus, *no 12*) in which the poet **Friedrich Gottlieb Klopstock**, author of epic poems and odes, was born in 1724. The various rooms in the house contain pictures, personal effects and books recalling the poet's life and work. *Open Tue-Sun, 10am-5pm. Closed 24 and 31 Dec. €2.50. ☎ (039 46) 26 10.*

Feininger-Galerie

Behind the Klopstock Museum, entry at no 5A, Finkenherd. ♿ Open Apr to Oct, Tue-Sun, 10am-6pm; Nov to Mar, Tue-Sun, 10am-5pm. Closed 1 Jan, 24 and 31 Dec. €6. ☎ (039 46) 23 84; www.feininger-galerie.de. This small gallery houses an interesting collection of drawings and water-colours by the Expressionist painter Lyonel Feininger. Born in New York City, Feininger trained in France and Germany, where he exhibited with the Blaue Reiter group in 1913. After the First World War he joined the staff of the Bauhaus.

Lyonel Feininger (1871-1956)

Born in New York to musician parents, Feininger was fascinated from a very young age by the visual universe of the American metropolis. At the age of 16 he was sent to Germany to study music, but quickly became interested in sculpture and started a career in drawing for picture books. Walter Gropius invited him to join the Bauhaus in 1919. Feininger taught there until the closure of the school by the Nazis. He was a modern-life painter who brought together Expressionism and Cubism, with a predilection for the representation of apparently banal subject matter (factories, boats, ports, buildings, etc).

SCHLOSSBERG★

The ramp leading up to the castle ends in a wide terrace with a fine general **view★** of the town.

Stiftskirche St-Servatius★★

On the site of the original 9C church, the present basilica, in the form of a Latin cross, was started in 1070 and consecrated in 1129. The **capitals★** and friezes above the central nave were sculpted by craftsmen brought especially from northern Italy. Beneath the chancel, the **crypt★★** is divided by three aisles with diagonal rib vaulting decorated by **frescoes★** depicting scenes from the Bible. Note the sarcophagi of King Heinrich I and his wife Matilda, interred here in the 10C, and the funerary stones of abbesses. The **treasury★★** (Domschatz) – manuscripts, 10C Gospel, and, above all, the **Quedlinburg Knotted Carpet★** – is kept in the sacristy.

Schloß

Construction of the castle building, which formed part of the abbey, extended from the late 16C to the mid-17C. The irregularity of the floor plan was imposed on the architects by the nature of the rocky base onto which the castle was built.

The **Schloßmuseum★** presents the history of Quedlinburg. The Abbess' Reception Room, the Throne Room and the Princes' Hall (mid-18C) can be visited. *Open daily, 10am-5pm (-8pm, Wed). Closed 24 and 31 Dec. €2.50. ☎ (039 46) 27 30.*

H. Champollion/MICHELIN

The interior of the Stiftskirche St-Servatius.

Excursions

Gernrode

7km/4.5mi south. Here, the collegiate church of **St Cyriacus★**, first documented in 961, was designed with the three-aisle nave, flat ceiling and upper galleries characteristic of the Ottonian basilica. The hall crypt is among the earliest of its type in Germany. The west section was modified in the mid-12C. The funerary plaque of the founder and patron Margrave Gero can be seen in the transept crossing. The late-12C baptismal font is in the Romanesque style. Upstairs, in the south aisle, is the **Holy Sepulchre group★**, a handsome and rare example of Romanesque sculpture.

Rastatt★

The Margrave Ludwig of Baden (1665-1707), known as Ludwig the Turk turned Rastatt into a stronghold at the same time building a castle designed to replace his seat at Baden-Baden. To this day, the town retains traces of its prestigious past, which lasted until this line of margraves of the House of Baden died out in 1771. Since 2000 a street theatre festival has taken place annually at the end of May.

Location

Population: 48 000. Michelin map n° 545 T 8 – Baden-Württemberg. Less than 10 kilometres from the French border, Rastatt straddles the Murg just before it enters the Rhine, and is the harbour for the Black Forest region.

Herrenstraße 18, 76437 Rastatt, ☎ (072 22) 97 24 62.

Surrounding area: see KARLSRUHE (21km/13mi north), BADEN-BADEN (8km/5mi south), SCHWARZWALD.

Worth a Visit

Schloß★

Guided tour (45min). Apr-Oct, Tue-Sun, 10am-5pm; Nov to Mar, Tue-Sun, 10am-4pm. Closed 24, 25 and 31 Dec. €4. ☎ (072 22) 97 83 85.

This harmonious palace complex with three wings and a vast courtyard facing the town was built 1698-1707 by Italian master architect Domenico Egidio Rossi. After Ludwig the Turk's death in 1707, his widow Sibylla Augusta dismissed the architect and summoned as his successor **Michael Ludwig Rohrer** from her Bohemian homeland who thereafter took charge of the construction of the palace.

Royal Apartments – The nucleus of the central block is the tall, sumptuous Hall of Ancestors (Ahnensaal), with the column capitals decorated with stucco figures representing Turkish prisoners. The Margrave's apartments are in the south wing, those of his wife in the north. Both are richly embellished with frescoes and stuccowork. The Collection of Porcelain (Porzellankabinett) is worth seeing.

The origin of the Margraves

Charlemagne set up border marches *(Mark)* to secure vulnerable borders against attack, in contrast with the counties of the internal regions of the Carolingian Kingdom. These hostile borders were watched over by a *marchione* (military governor), a term derived from the words margrave *(Markgraf)* and marquis. This title then became honorific and hereditary.

Wehrgeschichtliches Museum (Military Museum) – *Access via the south wing.* ♿ *Open Tue-Sun, 9.30am-5pm. Closed 24 and 31 Dec. €3. ☎ (072 22) 342 44.* German military and general history from 1500 up to the end of the First World War is displayed here. The exhibits include weapons, uniforms and pictures.

Erinnerungsstätte für die Freiheitsbewegungen in der deutschen Geschichte (German Freedom Movements Memorial Museum) – *Access via the north wing.* ♿ *Tue-Sun, 9.30am-5pm. Closed 1 Jan, 24, 25 and 31 Dec. No charge. ☎ (072 22) 77 13 90; www.erinnerungsstaette-rastatt.de.* The displays here follow freedom movements in Germany from c 1500 to the resistance in former East Germany up to 1990, charting the people's initiatives so vital to German democracy. The focal point of the exhibition is the period leading from 1815 up to the March revolution of 1848 (Vormärz) and the revolution of 1848-49 itself, which was particularly fierce in Baden.

Excursions

Schloß Favorite★★

5km/3mi southeast. Guided visit (1hr). From mid-Mar to end Sep, Tue-Sun, 10am-5pm; Oct to mid-Nov, Tue-Sun, 10am-4pm. €4.50. ☎ (072 22) 412 07.

This charming Baroque palace was built between 1710 and 1712 for the Margravine Sybilla Augusta, widow of Ludwig the Turk. The architect was again Michael Ludwig Rohrer, who had designed the church attached to her old apartments in Rastatt Palace. He coated the outside of this much smaller building with an unusual matrix of roughcast gravel and granite chips. The **interior★★** is particularly fine: floors of brilliant scagliola (stucco imitating encrusted marble), shiny as glass; mirror decorations; mosaics; chinoiserie. Note especially the Florentine Room, embellished with miniatures; the Mirror Study; Sybilla Augusta's apartments; sumptuous kitchen quarters with pottery from Frankfurt, Delft and Strasbourg; and a collection of Meissen, Nymphenburg and Chelsea porcelain.

Regensburg★★

The extraordinary density of religious buildings in the city centre justifies Regensburg's popularity among visitors. Walk through the medieval town centre on the bank of the Danube to discover remarkably well-preserved treasures. Nowadays Regensburg is the economic and, not least thanks to its university, the cultural hub of eastern Bavaria, but the town's position, well off the tourist trail, lends the town a relaxed and welcoming air.

Location

Population: 127 000. Michelin map n° 546 S20 – Bayern. Regensburg is located in eastern Bavaria and spans the Danube at the crossroads of the A 3 and A 93.

Altes Rathaus, 93047 Regensburg, ☎ (0941) 507 34 16.

Surrounding area: see STRAUBING (41km/25mi east), EICHSTÄTT (100km/63mi west), NUREMBERG (100km/63mi northwest).

Background

Preserved by time – Regensburg became a Roman garrison town *(Castra Regina)* guarding the natural frontier of the Danube at its most northerly point. Some evidence of Roman occupation remains (Porta Praetoria). The town was converted to Christianity by St Emmeram in the 7C, and St Boniface founded a bishopric there in 739, making it a centre for religious life in the Middle Ages, a role reflected by the extraordinary density of religious buildings in the city centre. As the seat of the Bavarian dukes (6C-13C), the town developed into an important trading post, and

Directory

Where to Eat

Haus Heuport – *Domplatz 7 – (0941) 599 92 97 – www.heuport.de – Closed for 2 weeks in Jan – €13/30.* This 13C mansion house is located in the centre of the old town, opposite the cathedral. Behind the beautiful façade is a small restaurant and cocktail bar. Simple cuisine is served in the dining room or on the terrace.

David – *Watmarkt 5 (5th floor) – (0941) 56 18 58 – Closed Sun and Mon – €35/48.* This establishment is accessed by lift (elevator) due to its position on the 5th floor of a historic mansion house. French and Italian-influenced cuisine is served in a romantic atmosphere. Beautiful covered terrace with view of the town.

Where to Stay

Hotel Wiendl – *Universitätsstraße 9 – (0941) 92 02 70 – fax (0941) 9202728 – www.hotelwiendl.de – 35rm: €38/80 – Restaurant €8.50/25.80.* This small, unpretentious hotel has simple guestrooms furnished in pale chestnut wood. Country-style restaurant.

Hotel Kaiserhof – *Kramgasse 10 – (0941) 58 53 50 – fax (0941) 58 53 595 – info@kaiserhof-am-dom.de – 30rm: €55/118.* Welcoming guestrooms, all with views of the twin towers of the cathedral. A high vaulted ceiling overhangs the breakfast room set in what was a chapel built in the 14C.

Taking a Break

Café Goldenes Kreuz – *Haidplatz 7 – (0941) 5 72 32 – Mon-Sat, 7am-7pm, Sun and bank holidays, 9am-7pm.* This elegant tea room is set in a historic building with abundant Gothic architecture. In summer months there is a vibrant terrace on the Haidplatz.

Going Out

Brauhaus Joh. Albrecht – *Schwarze-Bären-Str. 6 – (0941) 5 10 55 – www.brauhaus-joh-albrecht.de – 12pm-1am.* Convivial micro-brewery set over 2 floors. Try home-brewed beers in a pleasant ambience with hearty regional dishes.

Félix – *Fröhliche-Türken-Str. 6 – (0941) 59 0 59 – www.cafefelix.de – Mon-Sat, 9am-1am, Sun and bank holidays, 10am-1am.* This posh café is always lively. Service from breakfast (served till 3pm) until evening cocktails.

in 1245 it was made a Free Imperial City. The wealth and ambition of local merchants was manifested in the Italian-style towers (Goldener Turm, Baumburger Turm) they had built all over town between the 12C and 14C. A 14C fortified gateway, the Ostentor, is all that remains of the medieval fortifications. The town became part of Bavaria in the 19C and lost influence to Munich, which saved it from being bombed during the Second World War. Today its city centre remains miraculously intact.

The City of Diets – Once a Free Imperial City, Regensburg was privileged on occasion to be the seat of plenary sessions of the Royal Diet (Reichstag), which was charged with responsibility for the internal peace and external security of the immense and confused federation of states forming the Holy Roman Empire. From 1663 to 1806 the city was the seat of a Permanent Diet – the first indication of a continuing, overall German government. The Diet drew representatives from up to 70 other states to Regensburg.

Walking About

THE OLD QUARTER

Allow half a day – follow the itinerary suggested on the town plan.

Dom St. Peter★

Open Apr to Oct, 6.30am-6pm; Nov to Mar, 6.30am-5pm. (0941) 507 10 02.

Based on the design of certain French cathedrals, this pillared Gothic church has three naves and a non-projecting transept. Building began after 1260 but was essentially brought to a halt in 1525; the spires were not added until the 19C. The **Donkey Tower** *(Eselsturm)*, above the northern part of the transept, is all that remains of the original Romanesque sanctuary built on this site.

The **west front**, richly decorated, is the work of a local family of sculptors named Roritzer. The main entrance, flanked by two neo-Gothic towers, is unusual, with a triangular, jutting porch. St Peter can be seen on the pier, and there are beautiful statues in the niches – particularly the meeting of the Virgin and St Elizabeth.

Go inside via the south porch.

The huge Late Gothic nave measures: 85m/279ft long and 32m/105ft high. On each side of the nave, the aisles are encircled by a gallery; that on the south side is supported by fine carved consoles. Two masterpieces of local Gothic statuary – the

Archangel Gabriel, and Mary at the Annunciation, by the Master of Erminold (c 1280) – stand in front of the west transept pillars. The three chancel windows are adorned with beautiful 14C stained **glass★★**.

Domschatz – *In the south wing of the former bishops' residence (Bischofshof), entrance via the courtyard. Open Apr to Oct, Tue-Sun, 10am-5pm, Sun, 12 noon-5pm; Dec to Mar, Fri and Sat, 10am-4pm, Sun, 12 noon-4pm. Closed 1 Jan, Nov, 24 Dec. €1.50. ☎ (0941) 595 32 25 30.* Among the liturgical items, reliquaries and vestments from the 11C to the 18C on display here are the Ottocar Cross (mid-13C), a Venetian reliquary chest in the form of a tiny house (1400-10), and the Schaumberg Altar (1534-40), in the Zwölf-Boten-Kapelle.

Kreuzgang (Cloister) – *Access through the cathedral garden. Guided tour (75min, cathedral visit included). May to Oct, at 10am, 11am and 2pm, Sun, at 12 noon and 2pm; Nov to Apr, Mon-Sat, at 11am, Sun at 12 noon. €2.50. ☎ (0941) 507 10 02.* – This is divided by a central gallery paved with tombstones. On the right is the Romanesque *Allerheiligenkapelle*, on the walls of which are traces of ancient frescoes. Another gallery leads to the Alter Dom – the old 11C Stefanskapelle, with an altar reliquary. This is a box-shaped, limestone monolith, hollow underneath, with blind windows, thought to date from the 5C-8C.

Diözesanmuseum – *Open Apr to Oct, Tue-Sun, 10am-5pm. €1.50. ☎ (0941) 595 32 25 30.* The museum is installed in the **Ulrichskirche**, an Early Gothic galleried church (c 1225-40) decorated with 1 571 murals. Among other exhibits, visitors can see antique bishops' crosses (including the 12C Cross of St Emmerammus), fine medieval reliquaries, gold and silver plate, and religious paintings.

Taking the covebed passageway that links the **Herzogshof** (Ducal Palace) with the massive quadrilateral of the **Römerturm** (Roman tower), visitors arrive at a wide, paved square, **Alter Kornmarkt★**, where a grain market used to be held.

M. Hertlein/MICHELIN

Detail of Dom St Peter.

Alte Kapelle★

The basilica of Our Lady associated with this chapel stands on the south side of Alter Kornmarkt. Originally Carolingian, Alte Kapelle was completely transformed in the Rococo style in the 18C. The two double oratories in the chancel, the splendid reredos, the painted ceiling and the gilded stuccowork executed by a Master of Wessobrunn, Anton Landes, combine to form a harmonious ensemble admirably set off by the light penetrating the tall windows.

Kassianskirche

Enter by the west door. A Romanesque basilica with pillars and later (18C) Rococo decoration. On the left of the main doorway, a Gothic low relief represents the Visitation. On an altar in the south aisle is a *Schöne Maria* (Lovely Mary) sculpture by Hans Leinberger, the Master of Landshut (1520).

Hinter der Grieb

In this ancient alleyway with its old burghers' houses, the visitor is transported back to the Middle Ages. Looking back from the far end, there is a fine view of one of the cathedral spires.

Haidplatz★
A square surrounded by historic buildings, among which (at *no 7*) is an inn, Zum Goldenen Kreuz, with a grey-stone tower and façade, and a crenellated pediment. In the centre of the square is the 1656 **Justitiabrunnen** (Fountain of Justice).

Altes Rathaus★
The eight-storey tower of the old town hall dates from c 1250. The Gothic western section (Reichssaalbau) was built c 1360. The façade includes a gabled doorway and a pedestal supporting a charming oriel window which lights the Imperial Hall (Reichssaal).

Reichstagsmuseum – *Guided tour, Apr to Oct, 9.30am-12 noon, 2-4pm, Sun, 10am-12 noon, 2-4pm, every half hour; Nov to Mar, 9.30-11.30am, 2-4pm, Sun, 10am-12 noon, every half hour. Closed 1 Jan and 24 Dec. €2.50. ☎ (0941) 507 44 10.* The museum is set in the splendid Gothic hall, where the "Permanent Diet" used to meet. In the same building the Reichsstädtisches Kollegium houses an exhibition tracing the history of all the Regensburg Diets.

On the ground floor, the interrogation room (Fragestatt) and the dungeons are also open to the public.

Fischmarkt (Fish Market)
This is one of Regensburg's oldest market squares. It was built in 1529 in Italian style, as the original stone benches indicate. The fountain, *Fischbrunnen* or *Georgsbrunnen*, is one of three in Regensburg depicting local virtues; this one represents Fortitude.

Steinerne Brücke
Built between 1135 and 1146, this 310m/1 017ft bridge rests on no less than 16 arches. From the middle, there is a fine **view★** of the old town, its medieval roofs dominated by the cathedral's spires. In the foreground is the 14C Brückturm gateway (Brückturm museum), flanked, on the left, by the huge roof of the Salzstadel (early-17C salt loft). Beside this building, on the quayside, is the **Historische Wurstküche**, the oldest cooked sausage kitchen in Germany.

REGENSBURG

Brückstraße	E 7
Domgarten	E 12
Fröhliche-Türken- Straße	E 15

Porta Praetoria
These are the remains of the walls and north gateway of the ancient Roman stronghold *Castra Regina*, a garrison which covered an area of almost 25ha/62 acres. The west arch of the gateway and the east corner tower are all that are still standing.

Niedermünster
A Romanesque basilica with two towers that was originally the church of a convent of nuns. The interior was remodelled in the Baroque style in the 17C and 18C. The stuccowork is good. The tomb of St Erhard, surmounted by an altar and baldaquin (c 1330), is in the north aisle.

Regensburg mustard

Nothing goes better with Bavarian *Bratwurst* than *Händlmaier's süßer Hausmachersenf*, the sweet, smoky mustard which is the speciality of Regensburg. Johanna Haendlmaier concocted it in 1914 to sell in her butcher's shop as the perfect accompaniment to her husband's sausages.

Worth a Visit

St Emmeram★
This was once the abbey church of an 8C Benedictine monastery. A Gothic gateway on **Emmeramsplatz** leads to a close from which visitors pass through the huge Romanesque porch (12C) to the double doors at the church entrance. The 11C sculptures by these doors (Jesus Christ, St Emmeram and St Dionysius) are among the oldest in Germany.

The original Romanesque aspect of the church was lost when the Asam brothers introduced a Baroque decorative scheme. Light from the clerestory windows highlights the ceiling's frescoes and stuccowork.

Street	Grid	Street	Grid	Street	Grid
Gesandtenstraße	D	Luitpoldstraße	E 26	Viereimergasse	E 43
Goldene-Bären-Straße	D 17	Maximilianstraße	E	Weiße-Hahnen-Gasse	E 46
Goliathstraße	DE	Neue-Waag-Gasse	D 28	Weiße-Lilien-Straße	E 48
Haidplatz	D	Neupfarrplatz	DE	Historisches Museum	E M[1]
Königsstraße	E 21	Pfauengasse	E 30	Marstallmuseum Thurn und Taxis Museum	D M[2]
Landshuter Straße	E 22	Rathausplatz	D 34		
Ludwigstraße	D 24	Thundorfer Straße	E 42		

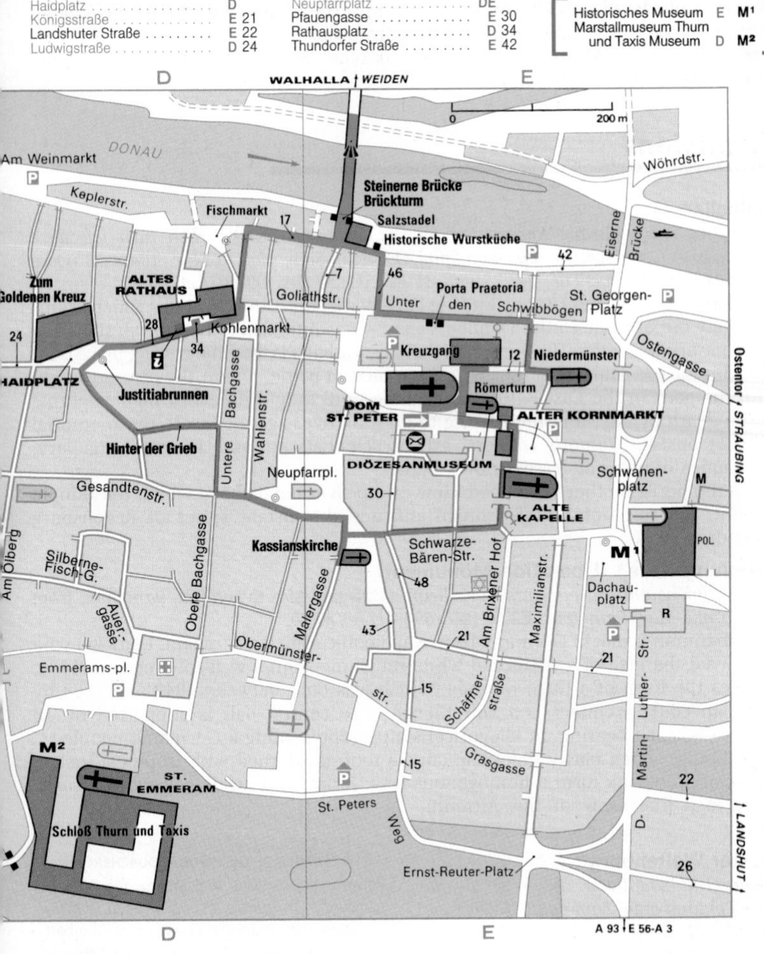

Among the numerous tombs, more of artistic than historic importance, since most were rebuilt several centuries after the death, is the tombstone of **Queen Hemma★** (c 1280), by the north wall, depicting the queen with an expression of profound sadness.

Schloß Thurn und Taxis

Guided visit (90min). Open Apr to Oct, at 11am, 2pm, 3pm and 4pm, in addition Sat-Sun at 10am; Nov to Mar, Sat-Sun, at 10am, 11am, 2pm and 3pm; 26 Dec-6 Jan, Mon-Fri at 2pm and 3pm in addition. Closed 24 and 25 Dec. €8, Castle and Cloister. ☎ (0941) 504 81 33.

The Thurn and Taxis princes held the monopoly of German postal services until the 19C. As partial compensation for losing the monopoly, they were given the St Emmeram abbey buildings. They occupied these as their home from 1816 and converted them into a good example of Historicist style. Visitors can visit the state apartments (including the ballroom and throne room), with their fine fittings and furnishings, as part of a guided tour.

The Romanesque-Gothic **cloister**, built between the 12C and 14C, can be visited separately. The Benedictus portal dating from the first half of the 13C is especially impressive. *Guided visit (30min). Open Apr to Oct, at 11am, 2pm, 3pm and 4pm, in addition Sat-Sun at 10am; Nov to Mar, Sat-Sun, at 10am, 11am, 2pm and 3pm; 26 Dec-6 Jan, Mon-Fri at 2pm and 3pm in addition. Closed 24 and 25 Dec. €4.*

Marstallmuseum – ♿ *Open Apr to Oct, 11am-5pm, Sat-Sun, 10am-5pm; Nov to Mar, guided visit only, Sat-Sun, at 11.30am and 2pm; 26 Dec-6 Jan, additionally Mon-Fri at 2pm. Closed 24 and 25 Dec. €4.50. ☎ (0941) 504 81 33.* The museum houses a fine collection of coaches, sleighs and sedan chairs, with space allocated to ceremonial harnesses and riding accessories.

Thurn und Taxis Museum – *Apr to Oct, 11am-5pm, Sat-Sun, 10am-5pm; Nov to Mar, Sat-Sun, 10am-5pm. Apr to Oct: €4.50 (combined ticket with the Marstallmuseum); Nov to Mar: €3.50. ☎ (0941) 504 81 33.* This branch of the Bavarian Nationalmuseum was installed in the north wing of the coach house in 1998, and regroups numerous handcraft items from the royal family's possessions. The collection is well presented in the available space. The most interesting exhibits are the gold work, clocks, furniture, porcelain and valuables dating from the 17C to the 19C.

►► Historisches Museum★ – Schottenkirche St Jakob *(Romanesque main entrance★)* – Dominikanerkirche.

Excursions

Walhalla★

11km/7mi east – Leave Regensburg on the Steinerne Brücke, then turn left after Donaustauf. Open Apr to Sep: 9am-6pm; Oct, 9am-5pm; Nov to Mar, 10am-12 noon, 1-4pm. Closed Shrove Tue, 24, 25 and 31 Dec. €2.50. ☎ (094 03) 96 16 80.

Built between 1830 and 1842 by Ludwig I of Bavaria, this Doric temple – which seems strangely out of place in the Danube Valley – was intended to honour all the great men in German history (in Nordic mythology, Valhalla is the final resting place built by Odin for the souls of heroes who have died in battle, where they train to fight with the gods in the Last Battle by drinking until they drop every night, fighting to the death by day, and then rising to do it all over again). Inside the memorial are 124 busts of famous soldiers, artists, scientists etc and, beneath a gallery, 64 plaques of older or lesser-known heroes.

From the peristyle there is a good **view** of the river bend above which the temple is built, the ruins of Schloß Donaustauf, and the distant spires of Regensburg Cathedral.

Befreiungshalle★ (Liberation Monument)

28km/18mi southwest, just outside Kelheim. From mid-Mar to end Oct, 9am-6pm; from Nov to mid-Mar, 9am-4pm. €2.50. ☎ (094 41) 68 20 70.

The liberation is that of Germany from Napoleonic rule. It was, again, Ludwig I who conceived the idea of a memorial while returning from a visit to Greece in 1836. It takes the form of a huge rotunda, which was built between 1842 and 1863 by Bavarian court architect Leo von Klenze. The central hall is supported by 18 buttresses, each bearing an allegorical statue representing a Germanic people.

The coping, which partly hides the cupola roof, is adorned with trophies. Inside, 34 victory tableaux form a homogenous ring. From the outside gallery *(staircase)*, there is a fine **view** of the Altmühl Valley.

Kloster Weltenburg★

33km/21mi southwest. ♿ Visit to the abbey church only, 8am-6pm. No charge. ☎ (094 41) 20 40.

Set in a delightful landscape, right on the banks of the Danube, Weltenburg Abbey has a truly majestic appearance. The abbey church was built by Cosmas Damian Asam in 1718, with an ante-nave – or narthex – and a nave proper, both of them oval. The attention is drawn immediately to a statue of St George, theatrically illuminated in the central arch of the reredos by light from a hidden source. Visible through an aperture in the lower dome is a *trompe-l'œil* Asam composition in the upper dome on the theme of the Church Triumphant. Most of the sculptural decoration is the work of Cosmas's brother Egid Quirin Asam.

THE GORGES OF THE "DONAUDURCHBRUCH"

Between Kelheim and Weltenburg, the Danube narrows as it "breaks through" steep, narrow limestone cliffs in a series of meanders. The best way to view these gorges is to take a boat between the two towns. Excursions leave from Kelheim from mid-March to October and timetables are available from the Tourist Office. €7 return trip.

Rheintal★★★

Rhine Valley

The Rhine is 1 320km/820mi long and flows through four different countries. Since the Middle Ages, it has been a unique highway for the exchange of commercial, intellectual and artistic ideas, a vital artery of the West. With its alternation of vineyards and impressive escarpments, punctuated by castles perched on rock spurs, the stretch between Rüdesheim or Bingen to Koblenz offers some magnificent views.

Location

Michelin map 543 O6 – Q 7 – Rheinland-Pfalz and Hessen. Roads run along both river banks, allowing travellers to admire the scenery from the water's edge. There are no bridges between Koblenz and Mainz; ferries are the only way to cross the river. Shipping companies organise cruises and regular services on the Rhine, leaving from most of the larger towns.

Surrounding area: see Bad KREUZNACH (16km/10mi south of Bingen), MAINZ (44km/27mi east of Rüdesheim), BONN (61km/38mi north of Koblenz), MOSELTAL (our suggested touring programme includes Koblenz).

Background

The Rhine Legends – There is not, along the whole length of the river, a castle, an island, even a rock without its tale of chivalry or legend. **Lohengrin**, the Knight of the Swan, appeared at the foot of the castle of Kleve (Cleves); Roland escaped from Roncesvalles to arrive too late before the island of Nonnenworth, where his fiancée, inconsolable at the rumour of his death, had taken the veil (Roland in despair withdrew to the neighbouring castle of Rolandsbogen); at the **Loreley**, the Rock of Lore, a beautiful enchantress bewitched boatmen with her song, leading their vessels to disaster.

The outstanding legend associated with the Rhine however is the story of the Nibelungen, an inexhaustible source of inspiration from which Wagner borrowed both names and ideas for his opera tetralogy *The Ring Cycle* (*Walküre, Siegfried, Götterdämmerung* and *Rheingold* as introduction). Inspired by Germanic and Scandinavian myths, the **Song of the Nibelungen** was probably composed towards the end of the 12C. It tells of the splendours of the 5C Burgundian court at Worms, and of the passions inflaming the hearts of its heroes, known also under the name of Nibelungen.

From the Alps to the North Sea – The Rhine rises in the Swiss Alps. Gushing down the mountainsides it quickly reaches Lake Constance *(Bodensee)*, which it crosses at a sluggish pace. The lakes of the Swiss plateau which drain into its tributary, the Aar, and the reception of the Neckar at Mannheim and the Main at Frankfurt, help to moderate and even out the irregularity of its flow caused by the melting snow in springtime.

The treacherous Loreley and the Goethe pleasure boat.

D. Scherf/MICHELIN

After the exit from Lake Constance, rock outcrops from the Black Forest and the foothills of the Jura produce the famous Rhine Falls at Schaffhausen *(see The Green Guide Switzerland)*. Further downstream, limestone strata result in rapids *(Laufen)*. These obstacles, although they inhibit the use of shipping, do allow the installation of powerful hydroelectric projects.

At Basle, the Rhine abruptly changes direction, veering north to follow and fertilise the subsidence fault separating the Vosges and the Black Forest. In Alsace, a canal draws off some of the excess water, but after Breisach this is fed only from power station dams.

From Bingen to Neuwied, north of Koblenz, the Rhine cuts its way through the Rhineland schist massif, where the hard rock – especially the quartzite exposed in the neighbourhood of the Loreley – can foment dangerous whirlpools. This so-called "romantic" stretch of river valley, with its alternation of vineyards, woods and impressive escarpments, punctuated by ruins perched on rock spurs, is the most picturesque part of what is known as the Rhine Gorge. Later, having passed through the industrial region around Duisburg, the river turns west and curls slowly across the plain towards the sea.

An Exceptional Shipping Lane – The traditional strings of Rhine barges, displacing anything from 1 000 to 2 000t each as they are towed, have been supplanted latterly by self-powered "auto-barges" and convoys towed or pushed by tugs which can comprise anything up to six 2 000 or 3 000t freight carriers. Recent work carried out on the more difficult reaches upstream from St Goar have guaranteed shipping a uniform navigation channel 120m/394ft wide.

Today, the Rhine, navigable over almost 1 000km/620mi between Rotterdam and Rheinfelden (upstream from Basle), handles an annual traffic of 265 million tons. Linked both to Rotterdam and to Antwerp, it boasts also in Duisburg-Ruhrort the world's largest river port (18 million tons annually).

Next in order of importance, on the river's German sector, are Cologne-Godorf, Karlsruhe, Ludwigshafen and Mannheim.

Tours

THE LORELEY★★ – from Rüdesheim to Koblenz 1

75km/47mi – about 4hr.

This route, following the Rhine's east bank, passes through the wildest and steepest part of the valley, with splendid views of the castles and fortresses on the far side of the river.

After **Rüdesheim★** *(see entry)*, the road runs at the foot of terraced vineyards overlooked by the ruins of Burg Ehrenfels, built by the archbishops of Mainz at the same time as the Mäuseturm, a tower on the opposite bank to supervise the collection of tolls from shipping on the river.

After Assmannshausen, silhouetted high up on the opposite bank, the castles of Rheinstein, Reichenstein and Sooneck with their crenellated towers appear one after the other. The tower of Fürstenberg, on the wooded slopes facing Lorch, marks the start of a more open stretch. And then the vineyards and towers of Bacharach slide into view. After that the fortified isle of Pfalz comes into view in the middle of the river.

The Mäuseturm

According to legend, the Archbishop of Mainz, Hatto, had this tower built to collect tolls from boatmen. However, when the region was hit by famine, the peasants flocked to Mainz to demand wheat. Hatto sent them to the barn where the wheat was stored, closed the doors behind them and set fire to the building. Soon nothing remained. Only a few mice managed to escape, scuttling over to the archbishop's palace, where they ate everything they could find. Hatto decided to take refuge in the tower on the Rhine. But the mice climbed into the boat with him and, when they landed, polished him off.

Kaub

One of the outstanding landmarks in the valley, this village dominated by the restored ruins of Gutenfels is worth exploring on foot by way of Metzgerstraße, the picturesque main street.

Pfalz bei Kaub★ (Pfalzgrafenstein) – *Opposite Kaub. Apr-Sep: open every day except Mon, 10am-1pm, 2-6pm; Oct-Nov and Jan-Mar: open every day except Mon, 10am-1pm. Last admission 1hr before closing time. Closed Dec. €2.10.* The massive five-sided keep of this toll fortress rises from the centre of the river, encircled by a turreted fortified wall. Its position and the thickness of its walls always kept it beyond the reach of its assailants.

Before a sharp, almost right-angled bend in the river, admire the **setting★★** of the towers of Oberwesel as they succeed one another at the foot of the Schönburg, on the far side of the water. The sharp bend, veering northeast and then northwest, leads to the most untamed stretch on this part of the Rhine.

D. Scherf/MICHELIN

Burg Gutenfels and the fortified island of Pfalz on the Rhine

The Loreley★★★

This legendary spur, 132m/433ft high, has become the symbol of the Romantic Rhine and has a very special place in German literature. It juts out, reducing the river's width by one quarter. According to legend, the Loreley was a blonde water sprite who bewitched boatmen with her feminine charms and melodious songs at the most dangerous spot on the river. Heine based a poem on this legend, *I Know Not Whence Cometh My Sadness*, which was set to music by Friedrich Silcher.

St Goarshausen

The town, strung out along the river bank (which makes a very pleasant walk), is dominated by the **Katz** (Cat) stronghold *(not open to the public)*, said to have been built to neutralise the **Maus** (Mouse), a little further downstream.

Loreley viewpoint★★

From St Goarshausen take the road signposted "Loreley-Burgenstraße". During high season there are shuttle buses between St Goarshausen/Schiffsanleger and the Loreley Plateau. There are impressive **views★★** plunging down into the "romantic gorge" from several accessible spurs here. On the plateau a landscape garden with waymarked footpaths has been laid out and a Loreley centre set up, in which interactive displays cover the Loreley legend, and local geology, flora and fauna. ♿ *From Apr to end of Oct: 10am-6pm. €1. ☎ (067 71) 59 90 93; www.loreley-touristik.de*

Wellmich

In the church of this small riverside town, there are traces (restored) of 15C wall paintings. Note: in the nave, the Crucifixion, the Last Judgement and the Martyrdom of the Apostles.

The Rival Brothers

At Kamp-Bornhofen, turn right towards Dahlheim, and then right again at the sign "Zu den Burgen".

The hill slopes become wild again. Beyond Kestert there is a fine **panorama★★**; from the ruins of **Liebenstein Fortress**, **Sterrenberg** and the valley below can be admired (the two castles are traditionally linked to an ancient legend concerning two rival brothers).

From Boppard *(see below)* onwards, where the Rhine swings lazily into a huge double loop, dense cultivation of vines appears and the landscape becomes less wild. Soon the fortress of Marksburg emerges on its promontory.

At Braubach, take the road to Nastätten.

Marksburg★

Guided tour (50min). From Easter to Oct: 10am-5pm; from Nov to Easter: 11am-4pm. Closed 24-31 Dec. €4.50. ☎ (026 27) 206. The **castle**, the only one in the whole Rhine Valley never to have been destroyed, is built on a **site★★** above the river that is almost aerial. Particularly notable are the fortress' great battery, a medieval garden with more than 170 different species of plant, and a collection of armour ranging from 600 BC to the 15C. The guided tour explains the way of life in a medieval fortress.

Burg Lahneck

3km/2mi from Lahnstein, near the confluence of the Rhine and the Lahn. Guided tour (40min). Apr-Oct: 10am-5pm. €3. ☎ (026 21) 91 41 71.

Directory

Where to Eat

⊜⊜ Tannenheim – *Bahnhof Buchholz 3 (B 327) – 56154 Boppard-Buchholz – ☎ (06742) 22 81 – hoteltannenheim@aol.com – Closed 1st-18 Jan, Sat lunchtime, Thur, Sun and public holidays – €21/35.* This charming restaurant has been run by the Fuchs family for four generations. It also has a few rooms and a pretty garden. Comfortable little Jagdstübchen (hunting room) where varied seasonal dishes are served.

⊜⊜ Gasthaus Hirsch – *Rheinstraße 17 – 56154 Boppard-Hirzenach – ☎ (06741) 26 01 – Closed 2 weeks after Easter and from mid Nov to 25 Nov – €22.50.* A tasteful, rustic establishment: the entirely panelled dining room is adorned with many paintings. Tasty dishes made with market produce.

⊜⊜ Zum Turm – *Zollstraße 50 – 56349 Kaub – ☎ (06774) 922 00 – info@rhein-hotel-turm.com – Closed 1 week at the beginning of Jan, 1 week at the end of July, and from mid to end Nov – €26/46.* This establishment near the old tower was founded over 300 years ago and has housed a small family-run restaurant for over a century. Carefully prepared dishes served in a rustic setting.

Where to Stay

⊜ Hotel Altkölnischer Hof – *Blücherstraße 2, 55422 Bacharach – ☎ (06743) 13 39 – Fax (06743) 2793 – altkoelnischer-hof@t-online.de – Open Apr-Oct – 20rm: €48/98 – Restaurant €21/35.* This family-run hotel is set in an old half-timbered house that has been restored. Charming rooms with wooden furniture. Meals are served in the panelled dining room or tavern. Rhineland specialities.

⊜ Hotel Zum Goldenen Löwen – *Heerstraße 82, 56329 St. Goar – ☎ (06741) 16 74 – Fax (06741) 2852 – 12rm: €49/110 – Restaurant €18.50/38.* A convenient little hotel with well-kept rooms of varying size and furnishings. Old-German-style rustic restaurant.

⊜ Hotel Ebertor – *Heerstraße 172, 56154 Boppard – ☎ (06742) 80 70 – Fax (06742) 807100 – www.ebertor.de – P – 66rm: €50.50/78 – €8.50 – Restaurant €11/28.* This hotel offers simple rooms and will supply an extra bed on request. The "Brasserie Eberbach" serves specialities made with wild boar from the Boppard forest.

⊜ Hotel Landsknecht – *An der Rheinufer-Straße (B 9), 56329 St. Goar-Fellen – ☎ (06741) 20 11 – Fax (06741) 7499 – info@hotel-landsknecht.de – Closed Jan-Feb – P – 15rm: €55/115 – Restaurant €20/33.50.* A pleasant, modern hotel with comfortable rooms and standard furnishings. Attractive garden next to the establishment. Rustic restaurant with a fine view of the Rhine from its terrace.

⊜⊜ Park-Hotel – *Marktstraße 8, 55422 Bacharach – ☎ (06743) 14 22 – Fax (06743) 1541 – park-hotel-bacharach@t-online.de – Open mid Mar to mid Nov – P – 25rm: €65/135 – restaurant €20/35.* This establishment has been run by the same family for years and offers comfortable rooms, some with a splendid view of the Rhine. Regional specialities are served in the Counts Palatine Room (Pfalzgrafen).

⊜⊜ Schloßhotel und Villa Rheinfels – *Schloßberg 47, 56329 St. Goar – ☎ (06741) 80 20 – Fax (06741) 802802 – info@burgrheinfels.de – P – 56rm: €85/150 – Restaurant €35/48.* In a great location in the Loreley Valley, in front of the impressive castle, the Schloßhotel und Villa Rheinfels offers pleasant accommodation in comfortable rooms. Lovely view from the classic restaurant.

The ruins of this fortress, originally built in the 13C to protect neighbouring silver mines, were reconstructed in neo-Gothic style in the 19C. From the keep there is a **view** of the junction of the two rivers and the troubadour castle of Stolzenfels, on the far side of the Rhine.

THE RHINE CASTLES★★★ – from Koblenz to Bingen 2

63km/39mi – Allow one day.

This itinerary in effect retraces the previous one, in the opposite direction, on the other side of the river. Soon after leaving Koblenz, Lahneck comes into view again, with its tower overlooking the river confluence. Above, on the right, is Stolzenfels.

Stolzenfels

Guided tour (45min). From mid Apr to end of Sep: open every day except Mon, 10am-6pm; from Oct to mid Apr: open every day except Mon, 10am-5pm. €2.60. ☎ (0261) 516 56.

This enormous **castle** was reconstructed, with its many crenellations, by Friedrich Wilhelm IV in 1842. The style is now neo-Gothic, inspired by certain English manor houses. The sumptuous **interior★** is arranged as a museum.

The Rhine Valley Castles

The Rhine Valley boasts an impressive number of castles. Stately residences, defensive castles, toll castles, refuges for travellers, each served a purpose. Many of them lost their crenellated towers in fires started by the French army under Louis XIV then, in the 18C, during fighting between the French revolutionaries and the émigré nobles who had taken refuge at Koblenz. Many castles were rebuilt in the 19C following the creation of the German Confederation in 1815.

From the slope against which Stolzenfels is built, the terrace offers a view of Koblenz and the citadel of Ehrenbreitstein.

Rhens

A town of pretty colour-washed houses with half-timbered facades. The old town hall juts out into the main street.

Gedeonseck

1hr there and back, including 20min on a chair-lift. From end of Mar to beginning of Apr: 10am-5pm, Sat-Sun 10am-5.30pm; from beginning to end of Apr: 10am-5.30pm, Sat-Sun 10am-6pm; 1st May and from mid Jun to end of Aug: 9.30am-6.30pm; from 2 May to mid Jun and Sep: 10am-6pm, Sat-Sun 10am-6.30pm; from beginning to mid Oct: 10am-5.30pm; from mid to end Oct: 10am-5pm. €6.20 return. ☎ (067 42) 25 10.

Southwards, there is a superb **view★** of the great convex loop of the Rhine as it flows around the Boppard curve.

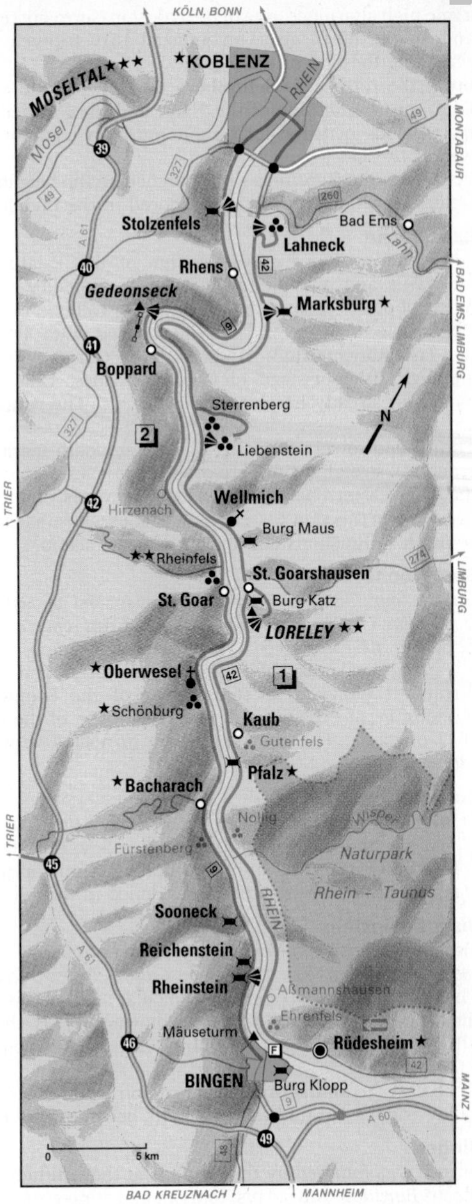

Boppard

Originally a Roman camp, Boppard became a Free Imperial City in the Middle Ages. Interesting sights in the town include the Late Romanesque Severuskirche and the Gothic Carmelite church with its rich interior fittings: choir stalls (c 1460) and Renaissance tombs. The museum in the fortress (14C) displays, among other things, some wooden furniture by local artist Michael Thonet. Pleasant riverside walk.

The beginning of the "romantic" Rhine Gorge is marked by the two Rival Brothers fortresses *(see above)* on the opposite slopes. After Hirzenach, the Cat and Mouse towers are visible, standing above St Goarshausen.

St-Goar

The village, clinging to the hillside at the foot of the impressive **Rheinfels Castle★★**, *(Burg Rheinfels: Mar-Sep 9am-6pm; Oct 9am-5pm. €4. ☎ (067 41) 383)* commands with St Goarshausen the Loreley passage. The river here, obstructed and narrowed by the legendary rock, swirls and eddies dangerously as it races through the defile. Rheinfels, which threw back the assaults of Louis XIV, was until it fell to the French in 1797 the most powerful fortress in the whole valley. It is worth climbing to the top of the clock tower to get an overall view of the turbulent Rhine, the Cat and Mouse castles, and the maze of towers, gates, courts and casemates comprising the Rheinfels complex.

The banks of the river remain steep and heavily wooded until Oberwesel.

Oberwesel

Sixteen towers survive of the original fortifications around this idyllic wine-growing village. It is possible to walk along part of the medieval wall, from where there is a good view of the Rhine. South of the town, the Gothic **Liebfrauenkirche★** has a fine high altarpiece, one of the oldest in Germany (early 14C), a Gothic rood screen and, in the north aisle, an unusual 1510 triptych illustrating the 15 cataclysms presaging the end of the world.

From the terrace of **Schönberg Castle★**, a little further on, there is a view of Kaub, on the far side of the river, and the fortified isle of Pfalz. Schönberg is in fact a block of three forts sheltered by a common – and impressive – defence wall.

Pfalz, with the Gutenfels ruins perched on the heights far above it, is an astonishing sight: a massive stone ship, anchored in the middle of the fast-running river.

Bacharach★

Once the property of the counts of the Palatinate, Bacharach – a town of vineyards and ancient towers, relics of medieval fortifications – is one of the most popular resorts in the Rhine Valley. The houses in Marktplatz and Oberstraße, wooden-walled and decked with flowers, are a delight. One of the last Romanesque naves built in Germany can be seen in Peterskirche, although its four-stage elevation (arcades, galleries, triforium and clerestory windows) already heralds French Gothic. The ruins of the Gothic Wemerkapelle are nearby.

The ruined towers of Nollig and Fürstenberg mark the end of the valley's most grandiose stretch; from here onwards it is less winding, the river running between the steep eastern bank, topped by a few vines, and the cliffs on the opposite shore. The road on this side passes below castles whose sites are ever more audacious, from Sooneck to Reichenstein and finally Rheinstein.

Burg Sooneck

Guided tour (45min). From mid Apr to end of Sep: open every day except Mon, 10am-6pm; Oct-Nov and from Jan to mid Apr: open every day except Mon, 10am-5pm. €2.60. ☎ (067 43) 60 64. This **fortress** is much restored and tiered to suit the terrain with a maze of staircases, platforms and terraced gardens beneath the turrets. It clings to a steep slope of the Soonwald outcrop. King Friedrich Wilhelm IV of Prussia made the conversion of the castle ruins his business from 1842 onwards. The apartments are furnished with neo-Gothic and Biedermeier furniture.

Burg Reichenstein

From Mar to mid Nov: open every day except Mon, 10am-6pm. €3.40. ☎ (067 21) 61 17. Well-situated at the mouth of a rural valley, this 10C neo-feudal **castle** has a fine collection of arms and hunting trophies. After serving as an imperial tollhouse, it was converted into a summer residence in the 19C.

Burg Rheinstein

From mid Mar to mid Nov: 9.30am-5.30pm; from mid Nov to mid Mar: open every day except Sat, 2-5pm, Sun 10am-5pm. Closed 20 Dec-5 Jan. €3.50. ☎ (067 21) 63 48. The **castle** is perched on a perpendicular rock spur, in a commanding position above the Rhine. From the foremost watchtower there is a bird's-eye **view★★** of the valley. Rheinstein was the first of the Rhine castles to be rebuilt by the Hohenzollerns (after 1823).

Once past the **Mäuseturm**, balanced on its tiny islet in the middle of the river, the valley widens out and the east bank becomes covered with terraced vines.

Bingen

Bingen was founded by the Romans at the confluence of the Rhine and the Nahe *(Castel Bingium)*. Nowadays, tourism and wine-growing are the town's main sources of income.

Burg Klopp, an ancient stronghold built by the bishops of Mainz, has been razed to the ground more than once – in particular by the troops of Louis XIV in 1689, during the "Orléans War". From the terrace there is a fine **view★** of the Binger Loch, between Hunsrück and the hills of the Rheingau, upstream from the Niederwald monument on the outskirts of Rüdesheim.

Romantische Straße★★

By way of river valleys and an idyllic, rolling countryside, the "Romantic Road" tourist itinerary recalls at every stage of its course some aspect of the past that could only belong to the history of Germany. As the route unfolds, it evokes life in the great medieval cities (Rothenburg, Nördlingen and Dinkelsbühl), the religious sensibility of artists like Tilman Riemenschneider, the prestige of German chivalry (Bad Mergentheim), the sumptuously Baroque character of the old episcopal courts and such Imperial towns as Würzburg and Augsburg.

Location

Michelin maps nos 545 folds 6, 17, 18, 28, 29, 420 folds 9, 17, 21, 25, 26, 30, 34, 37, 41 – Baden-Württemberg and Bayern. From the Main Valley to the foot of the Bavarian Alps stretches Germany's most popular tourist itinerary, crossing diverse landscapes of valleys, prairies, forests and cereal and fruit fields, and pretty little towns, most of them with car-free town centres.

Waaggässlein 1, 91550 Dinkelsbühl, ☎ (09851) 902 71. Internet site: www.romantischestrasse.com

The entire route is signposted "Romantische Straße". From April to October, the Europabus travels between the towns of the Romantic Road in both directions once a day. Information from: Deutsche Touring ☎ (069) 790 32 56; www.deutsche-touring.com

Surrounding area: see Deutsche ALPENSTRASSE, MÜNCHEN (66km/41mi east of AUGSBURG).

Tours

FROM WÜRZBURG TO ROTHENBURG o. d. T.

100km/62mi – about 4hr

Leaving **Würzburg★★** *(see entry)*, B 27 winds down towards the valley of the Tauber, which it reaches at Tauberbischofsheim.

Bad Mergentheim★ – *See Bad MERGENTHEIM.*

Weikersheim

Guided tour (1hr). Open Apr to Nov, 9am-6pm; Dec-Mar, 10am-12 noon, 1.30-4.30pm. Closed 24 and 31 Dec. €4. ☎ (079 34) 83 64.

Once the seat of the counts of Hohenlohe, this small town has retained its 18C architectural unity, especially noticeable in the layout of the market, built in a semicircle on the palace side to provide a splendid vista.

The castle was built between 1580 and 1680 on the banks of the Tauber, in a sober style divorced from Baroque influences. Two hundred years of decorative art (c 1550-1750) are illustrated by the remarkable collection of **furniture★★**. The magnificent **Knights' Hall★★** *(Rittersaal)*, completed in 1603, is typical of the

Directory

Where to Stay

Hotel Goldener Anker – *Untere Schmiedgasse 22, 91550 Dinkelsbühl – ☎ (09851) 578 00 – fax (09851) 578080 – goldener.anker@t-online.de – 25rm: €39/77 – Restaurant €18/32.50.* This old inn has a neat façade and good, spacious rooms decorated in a rustic style. Traditional Franconian cooking.

Hotel Kunst-Stuben – *Segringer Straße 52, 91550 Dinkelsbühl – ☎ (09851) 67 50 – fax (09851) 553527 – info@kunst-stuben.de – Closed Feb – 5rm: €50/70.* A very friendly small hotel incorporating an artist's workshop. Spick and span rooms and library guarantee a restful stay.

Hotel Blauer Hecht – *Schweinemarkt 1, 91550 Dinkelsbühl – ☎ (09851) 58 10 – fax (09851) 581170 – blauerhecht@ringhotels.de – Closed Jan – 44rm: €55/90 – Restaurant €17/32.* Smart hotel in a former brewery inn dating from 1684. Beautifully furnished and personalised guestrooms. Rustic old German restaurant.

Laurentius – *Marktplatz 5, 97990 Weikersheim – ☎ (07934) 910 80 – fax (07934) 910818 – info@hotel-laurentius.de – 11rm: €60 – Restaurant €30/64.* Behind this establishment's charming yellow façade are immaculate guestrooms with Italian furnishings. The restaurant with visible kitchen is in a beautiful vaulted cellar.

Romantik Hotel Greifen-Post – *Marktplatz 8, 91555 Feuchtwangen – ☎ (09852) 68 00 – fax (09852) 68068 – hotel@greifen.de – 35rm: €75/150 – Restaurant €27/40.* This 600-year-old establishment knows the true meaning of hospitality. Guestrooms are elegantly furnished and personalised and the dining rooms reflect the building's historic charm.

transition between the Renaissance style and the Baroque. Note the sculptured figures above the monumental doorway of emperors and empresses. The perspective of **formal gardens** (1710), peopled with grotesque statues in the style favoured by the Franconian courts of the period, ends in a charming perforated orangery. *The picturesque section of the run, in the narrow part of the Tauber Valley, begins above the attractive town of Bieberehren. The road rises and falls over slopes covered at times by natural woodland, at times by orchards, above the willow-fringed river banks. Occasionally the stream forms a loop to feed a sawmill or watermill. This countryside is at its loveliest in springtime.*

Creglingen

The isolated Herrgottskirche – about 1.5km/1mi along the road to Blaufelden – contains the precious **Altarpiece of the Virgin Mary★★** sculpted by Tilman Riemenschneider. The theme of the Assumption in the central motif has permitted the artist to translate all his own sensitivity into the attitude and expression of the Madonna.

Opposite the church is a **thimble museum** *(Fingerhutmuseum)*, the only one of its kind in Germany.

Detwang

In the church at Detwang another **Riemenschneider altarpiece★** portrays the *Crucifixion*.

Rothenburg ob der Tauber★★★ – *See ROTHENBURG OB DER TAUBER.*

T. Krieger/MICHELIN

Dinkelsbühl.

FROM ROTHENBURG o. d. T. TO DONAUWÖRTH

105km/64mi – about 5hr.

Feuchtwangen

Once a Free Imperial City, and also birthplace of the troubadour Walther von der Vogelweide, this town features an attractive market place surrounded by pretty houses and overlooked by a parish church housing another Altarpiece of the Virgin – this time the work of Albrecht Dürer's teacher, Michael Wolgemut. Near the café Am Kreuzgang there is a Romanesque cloister. Installed in a 17C burgher's house is a **Museum of Franconian Folklore** *(Fränkisches Museum)* displaying a comprehensive collection of fine rustic furniture with regional pottery and costumes.

Dinkelsbühl★

Ramparts and watchtowers still surround this idyllic medieval town which wakes up every year in mid-July with a colourful children's festival *(Kinderzeche)* commemorating the relief of Dinkelsbühl in the Thirty Years War *(see Calendar of events)*.

The **Georgskirche★** has retained its Romanesque tower. The interior is a remarkable sight, with all three naves decorated with skilfully designed fan vaulting.

Among the town's many ancient buildings, note the **Deutsches Haus★** *(Am Weinmarkt)*, and its richly decorated Renaissance façade, as well as the Hezelhof *(Segringer Straße 7)*, remarkable for the long, two-tiered balconies hung with flowers that overlook its inner courtyard.

The undulating landscape of the Feuchtwangen-Dinkelsbühl region is supplanted, after Nördlingen, by the bleak wastes of the Ries basin$. This practically treeless depression amid the heights of the Swabian Jura forms a symmetrical bowl 20km/12mi across and a regular 240m/656ft deep, which is thought by some geologists to have been caused millions of years ago by the fall of a gigantic meteorite.

Wallerstein

From the summit of the rock, reached by a pathway and then steps cut in the strata, there is a vast panorama over the Ries Basin *(access via the Fürstlicher Keller)*.

Nördlingen★ – *See NÖRDLINGEN*

Schloß Harburg

Guided visit (1hr). Mid-Mar to end Oct, Tue-Sun, 10am-5pm. €4.50. ☎ (090 80) 968 60. A large fortified castle whose buildings, considerably enlarged and remodelled in the 18C, look down on the picturesque houses of a village tightly packed along the banks of the Wörnitz.

Leave on the Mündlingerstraße, to the left, and take the Romantic Road to Mündling for Kaisheim. The valley of the Wörnitz, commanded by Schloß Harburg, peters out after a final, narrow, twisting section, allowing the Ries to connect with the Danube Valley.

Kaisheim

The former Cistercian abbey church *(Zisterzienserkloster)* was built at the end of the 14C in the full flower of the Gothic era (the abbey itself is now a penal institution). Around the chancel, very pure in style, is a 12-sided **ambulatory★** with ogive vaulting, divided into two galleries *(to visit, apply at the presbytery.)* The emperor's room in the old Imperial foundation was built by Vorarlberg architect Franz Beer from 1716-23 and is open to the public *(on request)*.

Donauwörth

The old Free Imperial City is proud of its pastel-coloured historic buildings, principally lining the Reichsstraße; the most impressive are the town hall and *Fuggerhaus* (1543). The Late Baroque abbey and pilgrimage church of Heilig Kreuz (constructed from 1717-22) is adorned with Wessobrunn stuccowork. The Gothic Liebfrauenmünster has rich interior decoration (15C murals). Parts of the town's fortifications are still standing.

FROM DONAUWÖRTH TO FÜSSEN

148km/92mi – about one day

This drive along the ancient *Via Claudia*, one of the main arteries of the old Holy Roman Empire, owes its interest less to the route (which follows the Lech Valley, by now largely widened) than to the historical souvenirs evoked by the sites on the way. These include **Augsburg★★**, **Landsberg★**, **Neuschwanstein★★★** and **Hohenschwangau★**, and *(well worth the price of a small detour)* the **Wieskirche★★**.

Rostock★

A particularly choice situation on the wide Warnow estuary favoured the development of Rostock from its earliest days: the town was a member of the Hanseatic League and the town's port still plays an important part in international maritime commerce. Rostock is certainly worth a visit, even more so now that a substantial programme of rehabilitation has returned its historic centre to the glory of its splendid past.

Location

Population: 200 000. Michelin map nº 542 D 20 – Schleswig-Holstein. One of the most important Baltic ports, Rostock also has one the highest populations in the Mecklemburg area. The A 19 and its continuation, the A 24, link the town to Berlin (allow 2hr 30min); the A 20 links the town with Lübeck.

ℹ *Neuer Markt 3, 18055 Rostock, ☎ (0381) 194 33.*

Surrounding area: see Bad DOBERAN (16km/10mi west), STRALSUND (75km/47mi east), MECKLEMBURGISCHE SEENPLATTE (accessible via the A 19 to the south).

M. Hertlein/MICHELIN

Traditional wicker beach-chairs on the sands.

Background

Object of desire – By the beginning of the 13C, the town was already a member of the Hanseatic League, was minting its own money and was in the process of asserting its independence from the princes of Mecklenburg. In 1419, Rostock founded the first Baltic university, which earned it the nickname of "Light of the North". Such a position and such a reputation soon excited the envy of powerful and covetous neighbours, with the result that it failed to escape damage during the Thirty Years War (1618-48), and during the Nordic countries' struggle for supremacy in the war raging from 1700 to 1721. Nor was the port spared during the **Napoleonic Wars**; it was occupied by French troops until 1813.

Until German **Reunification**, Rostock with its port installations, shipyards and fishing fleet was the former East German Republic's only significant outlet to the Baltic, and to the rest of the world.

Walking About

THE OLD TOWN★

The oval-shaped historic district of Rostock extends south from the Warnow. In the centre is the Marienkirche; to the west of the church is the Kröpeliner Tor, to the south the Navigational Museum.

Marienkirche★★

The building as it is today – an imposing basilica in the form of a cross – results from a transformation in the second half of the 15C of a hall-church built in the previous century. It is one of the biggest churches in northern Germany.

The massive tower, lightened by pierced sections, was not completed until the end of the 18C. From the top there is a **panorama**★ of the city and the dock area.

Inside the church, the overriding impression is one of height and verticality. Note especially the 1472 **astronomic clock**★★ (its face was remodelled in 1643), which comprises a calendar valid until the year 2017. The delicately worked bronze **baptismal font**★, decorated with scenes from the life of Christ, is supported by the figures of four men. The Baroque organ dates from 1770.

Rathaus (Town Hall)

Neuer Markt. This is composed of three 13C-14C gabled houses topped by a brick-built arcaded gallery supporting seven towers. In front of the Gothic block is a Baroque façade added in 1727. Across the square stand some fine gabled houses.

Schiffahrtsmuseum★ (Navigational Museum)

At the corner of August-Bebel-Straße and Richard-Wagner-Straße. Open Tue-Sun, 10am-6pm. €3. ☎ (0381) 25 20 60.

The museum charts the history of maritime travel in the Baltic region from its earliest days to the present. Models of ships, paintings, navigational instruments and photographs document life and work on board ship. Note in particular the reconstruction of a tramp steamer bridge.

Directory

Tour of the Harbour

Visitors are recommended to take a tour of the harbour, in order to gain full appreciation of the importance of international shipping and maritime trade to the city.
Departures from landing-stages Stadthafen, by Schnickmannstraße, and Warnemünde/Alter und Neuer Strom. Details of timetables and fares from the tourist office: ☎ (0381) 381 22 22.

Where to Eat

⊖ **Seekiste zur Krim** – *Am Strom 47 – 18119 Rostock-Warnemünde – ☎ (0381) 5 21 14 – From end-May to beginning Oct, 11am-midnight, Oct-Apr, Mon-Fri, 5pm-midnight, Sat-Sun, 11am-midnight – ♿ – €14.70/26.10 – 4rm: €20/40.* Before he moved to Warnemünde, the proprietor of this establishment was a sailor. So this place is full of souvenirs from every corner of the world. Traditional dishes are served, with the accent on fish from the Baltic.

⊖⊖ **Zur Gartenlaube 1888** – *Anastasiastraße 24 – 18119 Rostock-Warnemünde – 11km/7mi northwest – ☎ (0381) 526 61 – Closed Sundays – €33/46.* Those nostalgic for days gone by will love this place: behind its painted façade, have a seat on the old church pews and enjoy varied cuisine in a rustic atmosphere.

Where to Stay

⊖ **Hotel & Appartementhaus Fischerhus** – *Alexandrinenstr. 124, 18119 Rostock-Warnemünde – ☎ (0381) 54 83 10 – fax (0381) 5 191 041 – www.hotel-fischerhus.de – P ♿ – 24 apartments: €50/100.* Modern apartments with all modern comforts, most of them in former fishermens' huts and complete with kitchens. Breakfast is served on the white porcelain of the Wellenspiel Café.

⊖⊖ **InterCityHotel** – *Herweghstraße 51 – ☎ (0381) 495 00 – fax (0381) 4950999 – rostock@intercityhotel.de – P ♿ – 174rm: €85/126 – Restaurant €16/26.* A few feet from the main station *(Hauptbahnhof)*, functional rooms with light-coloured furniture. The hotel pass *(Hotelausweis)* entitles you to reduced fares on public transport.

Taking a Break

Marientreff – *Bei der Marienkirche 27 – ☎ (0381) 4 92 23 89 – Mon-Sat, 11.30am-5.30pm – Closed 25 Dec-1 Jan.* This meeting place cum tea room has been set up as a charitable concern in the former sacristan's house near the Marienkirche. Homemade cakes and drinks are served in a cosy atmosphere. Unbeatable prices, but donations are always welcome.

Going Out

Useful tips – There are plenty of restaurants along Kröpeliner Str., in the streets around it, and in the Kröpeliner Tor-Vorstadt district to the west of the old town. Young people and students frequent the latter in particular. There is a seaside resort at Warnemünde, located 11km/7mi to the north of the town centre, with promenades along the estuary of the Warnow (Am Strom) and Baltic sea beach (Seestr. and Seepromenade) edged with cafés, restaurants and bars which are lively in season.

Szenario – *Friedhofsweg 44a – ☎ (0381) 5 10 84 22 – Mon-Sat, 11am-11pm.* The proprietor's Swiss heritage is in evidence with *röstis* on the menu of this bistro, which used to be a school (built in 1878). *Tapas* is served from 6pm, together with a large selection of drinks including cocktails. Contemporary art is displayed.

Zur Kogge – *Wokrenter Str. 27 – ☎ (0381) 4 93 44 93 – www.zur-kogge.m-vp.de – 11.30am-midnight.* The interior of this one-off restaurant reminds the visitor of being on a ship. Lifebelts are attached to the balustrade of the gallery and there is plenty of bric-a-brac with a maritime theme. Accordion player most Friday and Saturday nights.

Kröpeliner Straße

This pedestrian precinct, crossing the inner city from the Rathaus to the Kröpeliner Tor, has become the town's shop-window and commercial centre. It is bordered by the familiar essentially Gothic gabled houses with façades dating from Baroque and Renaissance times. At no 82, the brick façade of the old (late 15C) Heilig-Geist-Spital presbytery is distinguished from the other buildings by a stepped gable.

Kröpeliner Tor★

The 14C brick gate, six floors high, closes off the western end of Kröpeliner-Straße. The interior houses the cultural history museum's local **history collections**.

Kulturhistorisches Museum★ (Cultural history museum)

♿ *Open Tue-Sun, 10am-6pm. €3. ☎ (0381) 20 35 90.* This former Cistercian convent, founded in 1270 by the Danish queen Margarethe, and its triple-aisled hall church in the brick Gothic style offer a rare impression of unity, as the only completely preserved convent complex in the region. Besides medieval religious art, including the **Altarpiece of the Three Kings★** (late 15C), the museum displays highlights from its sizeable collections on folklore and art.

ROSTOCK

Street	Grid
Arnold-Bernhart-Str.	BX 2
Badstüberstr.	BX 4
Beim Grünen Tor	BX 8
Breite Str.	BX
Buchbinderstr.	CX 9
Friedhofsweg	BX 14
Gertrudenplatz	BX 16
Große Wasserstr.	CX 17
Kleine Wasserstr.	CX 19
Krämerstr.	CX 21
Kröpeliner Str.	BCX
Mönchentor	CX 24
Pädagogienstr.	BX 26
Richard-Wagner-Str.	CX 28
Rungestr.	BCX 29
Schwaansche Str.	BX 31
Strandstr.	BCX 34
Vogelsang	CX 38
Wendenstr.	CX 41

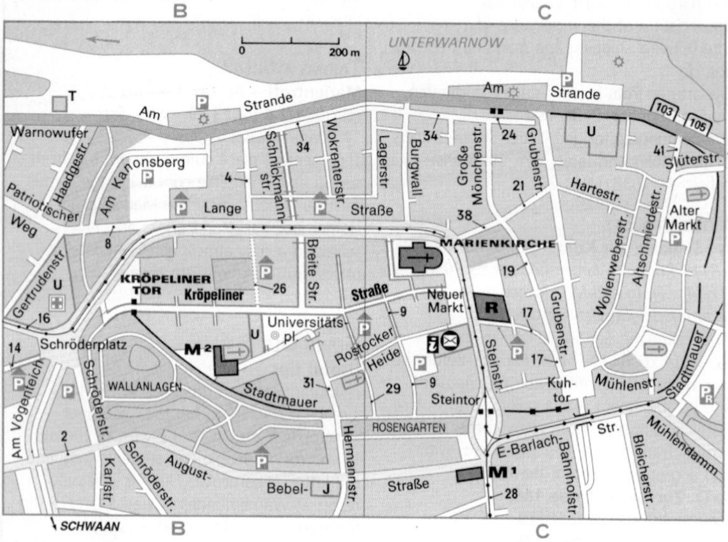

Kulturhistorisches Museum . BX **M²** Rathaus . . . . CX **R** Schiffahrtsmuseum . . . . CX **M¹**

Excursions

Warnemünde★

11km/7mi north. This one-time fishing village, "bought" by the town from the Prince of Mecklenburg in 1323, has become Rostock's most popular holiday beach, with charming little streets and pleasant sea front. From the ferry terminal, services run to Denmark. Warnemünde has also become the most important German destination port for cruisers from all over the world. In summer, some 50 such floating hotels are moored here.

Fischland, Darß and Zingst

Northeast of Rostock. The peninsular chain of Fischland-Darß-Zingst is an attractive natural area in which woods, salt-marshes, moorland and broad stretches of water alternate. The narrow tongue of land extends northwards and eastwards parallel to the mainland, separated from it by a lagoon (flat bays) in which brackish water from the Baltic and freshwater from the rivers leading down to it mingle. The artists' village of **Ahrenshoop** in the slightly hilly **Fischland** is a very popular Baltic resort. **Darß** and **Zingst** form part of the National Park of the West Pomeranian lagoon area. The contemplative nature of the little villages and seaside resorts with their reed-covered houses and cottages makes them especially attractive.

Güstrow★

50km/31mi south of Rostock. Güstrow was granted the civic charter in 1228 and went on from this promising start to become the residence of the dukes of Mecklenburg-Güstrow between 1556 and 1695. The wealth that accompanied this status continued to accumulate over the next few centuries, as can be seen from the elegant burghers' houses which line the **cathedral** and **market squares** and the streets surrounding them.

Schloß★ – *Open Tue-Sun, 9am-5pm. Closed 24 Dec. €3. ☎ (038 43) 75 20.* This Renaissance palace is one of the most important examples of its type in north Germany. Combining Italian, French and German stylistic features, it was built from 1558 onwards for Duke Ulrich

The Schloß contains a branch of the **State Museum of Schwerin** *(Staatliches Museum Schwerin).*

Dom★ – This Gothic brick **basilica**, consecrated in 1335, is richly endowed with works of art, having been the court church of the dukes of Mecklenburg. The elaborately designed **Renaissance tombs★** on the north side of the choir are the work of Philipp Brandin. A particular highlight among the cathedral's collection of art treasures are the **Güstrow Apostles★**, 12 almost life-size oak figures made by Claus Berg of Lübeck in c 1530. A stark contrast to these is Ernst Barlach's *Der Schwebende*.

Ernst-Barlach Stiftung★ (Barlach Museum) – ♿ *Open Apr to Oct, Tue-Sun, 10am-5pm; Nov to Mar, Tue-Sun, 11am-4pm. Closed 1 Jan, 24 and 31 Dec. €3.50. ☎ (038 43) 822 99.* This museum in honour of Barlach is located in three different parts of Güstrow: his religious works are exhibited in the Late Gothic **Gertrudenkapelle**, which the artist had always longed in vain to use as a studio. The "Barlachweg" leads to Barlach's **Heidberg studio**, on the shores of the Inselsee just outside the town: a collection of studio models is exhibited here. A few yards away is another building used for rotating exhibitions, in fact it was the first brand new museum to be built in the former states of East Germany.

Rothenburg ob der Tauber★★★

One of the oldest towns on the "Romantic" tourist road, Rothenburg overlooks the winding course of the River Tauber from its rocky crag. Once behind the ramparts in the car-less central enclave, the visitor faced with Rothenburg's ancient houses, street signs, fountains and narrow, cobbled lanes seems all at once in some kind of time-warp, plunged back into the mid 16C.

Location

Population: 11 000. Michelin maps 545, 420 R 14 – Bayern. The old town stands on a steep promontory overlooking a meander in the River Tauber, its sides cloaked in vineyards. An ideal stopping place on the Romantic Road, Rothenburg offers striking views of landscapes that seem to belong to another age.

ℹ Marktplatz 2, 91541 Rothenburg, ☎ (098 61) 404 92. The tourist office publishes a very informative free booklet which explains the history of the town's buildings.

Surrounding area: see ROMANTISCHE STRASSE, HOHENLOHER LAND (Langenburg is 30km/19mi west), NUREMBERG (83km/52mi east).

Background

Medieval grandeur – In the 12C, King Conrad III built an imperial castle on the Burggarten spur, a rock platform providing an ideal defensive position. At first the town itself was small; the outline of its earliest circle of fortifications can be seen, with two towers (*Markusturm* and *Weißer Turm*), in the arc formed by the Judengasse and the Alter Stadtgraben. Granted the status of free town in 1274, it spread out... then lost both its castles, destroyed in an earthquake in 1356. From then on the ambition of the local Rothenburg worthies inclined more and more towards the building, and then the embellishment, of such public works as might enhance their own importance: the Rathaus, Jakobskirche, the long line of merchants' houses especially on the Herrngasse.

A Long Drink *(Meistertrunk)* – During the Thirty Years' War, the Protestant Rothenburg was unable to withstand the siege by the Catholic Imperial army commanded by General Tilly, and opened its gates to the 40 000 victorious mercenaries. After occupying and pillaging the town for three months, Tilly decided to raze the town. This is where the legend begins: all pleas for mercy having been rejected, the burgomaster as a last resort offered the victorious general a goblet of the very best local wine... and the miracle occurred. His heart warmed by generosity, Tilly offered a way out. He would spare the town if some eminent local could empty in a single draught a hanap (a 6-pint/3.4litre tankard) of the same wine. A man named Nusch, a former burgomaster, succeeded in this exploit and Rothenburg was saved (the after-effects on the courageous drinker are not recorded); ever since then, the population of Rothenburg takes part in a huge reconstruction of this event every year at Pentecost.

Saved once again – Too poor even to rebuild its houses in line with the prevailing taste, the town vegetated throughout the 17C and 18C, unable to expand beyond its own walls. In the 19C, however, its steep-roofed houses with their tall gables, staircase turrets and corner oriels were rediscovered by some Romantic painters,

Rothenburg: a striking illustration of the Middle Ages

T. Krieger/MICHELIN

Directory

Where to Eat

⊖ **Baumeisterhaus** – *Obere Schmiedgasse 3 – ☎ (09861) 947 00 – €16/27.* This Renaissance treasure was built opposite the town hall in 1596. Within its venerable walls, a restaurant is laid out over two floors and adorned with beautiful old wall paintings. The courtyard is surrounded by half-timbered galleries.

Where to Stay

⊖ **Hotel-Gasthof Schwarzes Lamm** – *Detwang 21, 91541 Rothenburg-Detwang – from Rothenburg: Romantische Straße towards Bad Mergentheim – ☎ (09861) 6727 – Fax (09861) 86899 – www.HotelSchwarzesLamm-rothenburg.de – Closed from mid Jan to mid Feb – P – 30rm: €45/75 – Restaurant €13.50/19.* A smart establishment with a long family tradition, set in the oldest part of Rothenburg. The hotel has quiet, modern rooms with balconies. The lime-tree garden *(Lindengarten)* is particularly charming in good weather.

⊖ **Mittermeier** – *Vorm Würzburger Tor 9 – ☎ (09861) 945 40 – info@mittermeier.rothenburg.de – Restaurant closed Sun – P – 27rm: €55/125 – Restaurant €26/46.* Guests here can sleep in "Africa" or "Spain" – the names of two of the rooms and suites in this charming hotel with personalised furnishings. The restaurant reflects a youthful, fresh, rustic style. Delicious, refined cuisine.

⊖ **Hotel Spitzweg** – *Paradeisgasse 2 – ☎ (09861) 942 90 – Fax (09861) 1412 – info@hotel-spitzweg.de – P – 10rm: €60/85.* This little hotel with comfortable, rustic rooms is full of souvenirs of the Rothenburg painter Spitzweg. It is set in a carefully restored listed building dating from 1536.

Taking a Break

Useful Tips – Almost all of the cafés in town sell *Schneeballen* (snowballs), traditional regional cakes made with shortcrust pastry. Originally covered only with icing sugar or cinnamon, they now come in a variety of forms, for example covered or filled with chocolate.

Caféhaus – *Untere Schmiedgasse 18 – ☎ (09861) 9 39 85 – 9.30am-6pm, terrace/winter garden closed Jan-Easter.* Over one hundred speciality coffees and a wide variety of *Schneeballen* are served here. The café's glass-fronted winter garden affords a magnificent view of the green Tauber valley.

Going Out

Zur Höll – *Burggasse 8 – ☎ (09861) 42 29 – www.rothenburg.hoell.de – 6pm-1am.* This picturesque half-timbered house now harbours a weinstube serving mainly local wines and brandies as well as traditional dishes.

Shopping

Käthe Wohlfahrt – *Herrngasse 1 – ☎ (09861) 40 90 – www.wohlfahrt.com – Mon-Fri 9am-6.30pm, Sat-Sun 9am-6pm (closed Sun from Christmas to mid May); museum from mid Apr to beginning of Jan 10am-5.30pm (last admission 5pm) – museum: €4.* Here it's Christmas all year round – choose your favourite decorations (from over 65 000 items) by the light of the candles of the "Christmas Village". The museum on the 1st floor presents the historical evolution of Christmas decorations.

and the town soon became a tourist attraction. One third of the town (mainly the north and east) was destroyed on 31 March 1945 by bombs targeting a Nazi general who had taken refuge there; the intervention of a British officer familiar with Rothenburg fortunately prevented its total destruction, and the generosity of local inhabitants and private donors enabled the exact reconstruction of the town.

Walking About

OLD TOWN★★★ (ALTSTADT) *allow 3hr 30min*

Starting at Marktplatz, follow the itinerary marked on the town plan.

Rathaus★ (Town Hall)

The Gothic part, its gable topped by a 60m/197ft belfry, is 14C, while that facing Marktplatz, with its octagonal staircase tower, is a Renaissance work, completed by an 18C portico. Visitors can inspect the historic vaults *(Historiengewölbe, on the left)* now a history museum, or climb the tower for a **view★** of the fortified town. North of Marktplatz is the gable of an ancient inn, the Ratstrinkstube, on which the figures of a clock re-enact mechanically *(at 11am, noon, 1pm, 2pm, 3pm, 8pm, 9pm and 10pm)* the famous legend of the Long Drink *(Meistertrunk)*.

Baumeisterhaus

The steps on the gables of this Renaissance house serve as pedestals for dragon motifs. Statues on the first floor represent the seven cardinal virtues, those on the second the seven deadly sins.

ROTHENBURG OB DER TAUBER

Alter Stadtgraben	5
Georgengasse	3
Grüner Markt	6
Hafengasse	
Herrngasse	
Heugasse	8
Kapellenplatz	9
Kirchgasse	10
Kirchplatz	12
Markt	15
Marktplatz	16
Obere Schmiedgasse	18
Rödergasse	
Untere Schmiedgasse	23
Vorm Würzburger Tor	24

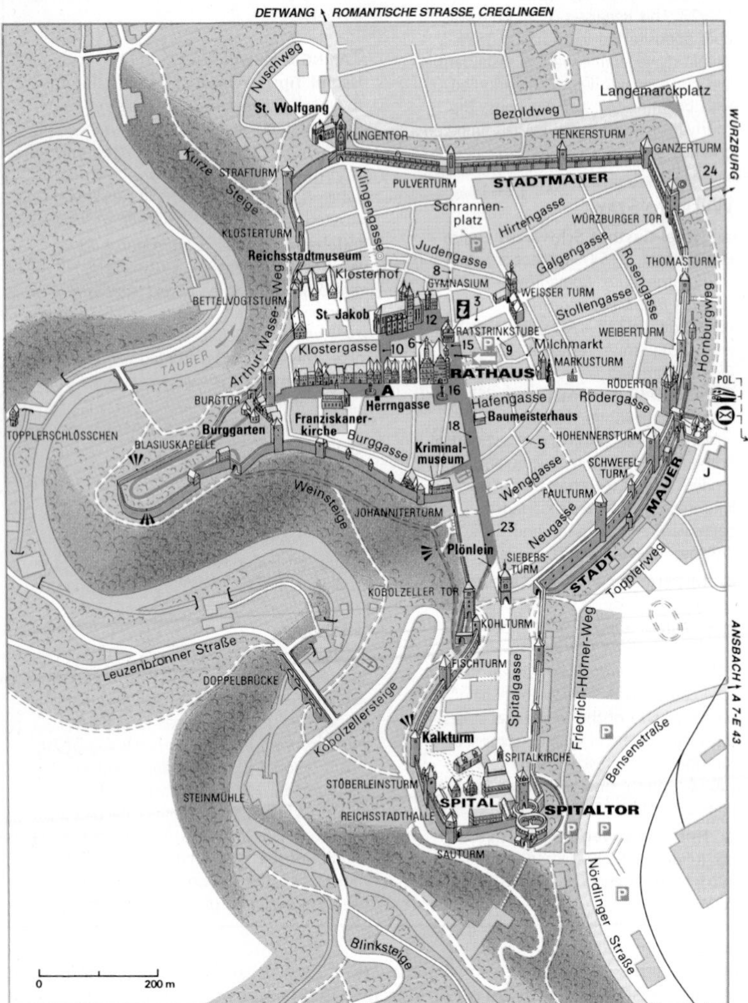

Mittelalterliches Kriminalmuseum (Museum of Medieval Justice)

Apr-Oct: 9.30am-5.15pm; Nov and Jan-Feb: 2-3.30pm; Mar and Dec: 10am-3.30pm. €3.20. ☎ (098 61) 53 59. Medieval attitudes towards crime and dissidence are reflected in this museum installed in the former headquarters of the Knights of the Order of St John of Jerusalem.

Law books, seals, engravings, along with instruments of public humiliation, torture and execution are exhibited on four different floors.

Plönlein

A picturesque corner formed by the bifurcation of two streets, one level, leading to the Siebers tower (1385), one descending. They both end at another fortified gateway, to the south. The fountain once fed the two fish stocks used by Tauber fishermen for their trade.

Leave the town by the Koboldzell gate, on the right, turn sharp right again, and follow the path circling the spur some way below the ramparts.

In the valley below, there is a remarkable arched, two-storey **viaduct** *(Doppelbrücke)* which crosses the Tauber. Return to the old town via the Burggarten.

Burggarten

All that remains of the double fortress erected on this promontory is a chapel, the Blasiuskapelle, which has been turned into a war memorial, and a fortified gateway, the Burgtor. The area is now a large public garden with **views★** of the Spital quarter (to the south), the river, the Topplerschlößchen (a riverside tower oddly topped by apartments) and, to the north, the village of Detwang *(see the ROMANTISCHE STRASSE)*.

Return to the town via the Burgtor; assailants unaware of the grimacing mask above the second gate risked being drenched in boiling oil here.

Herrngasse★

The mansions of formerly well-known personages line this busy commercial street. In the **Franziskanerkirche,** the rood screen, as well as walls and columns in this church, are decorated with fine 15C and 16C sculptures. Note also, on the left above a funerary niche, the Creglingen Madonna (1400). Back in Herrngasse, those interested can look into some of the courtyards, for instance no 15, where the half-timbered gallery rests on embossed wooden pillars.

Turn left into Kirchgasse after the round fountain.

St Jakobskirche★

Admission charge €1.50. Building of the Gothic church started in 1311, but the western part *(on the left)* was not completed until 1471. The works of art adorning the interior include Tilman Riemenschneider's magnificent **"Holy Blood" altarpiece★★** (1504), in the west chancel *(up to the left after the entrance)*. The composition of the main scene, the Last Supper, is original. Judas is the focal point of the composition, looking at Christ. The expressions are tense and perplexed, except for that of Jesus, which is full of compassion. Also of note are the altar with the crowning of the Virgin *(on the left before the east chancel)* and the 17m/56ft stained-glass windows (1350-1400) which illuminate the high altar.

The east chancel overlooks a square on which stands the 1593 Renaissance building of the former **college** *(Altes Gymnasium) (Altes Gymnasium)*, with its beautiful octagonal stairwell.

Worth a Visit

Spital★ (Hospital)

A picturesque group of buildings, mostly 16C and 17C, built on the southern extremity of the plateau known locally as the Kappenzipfel (peak of the cap). There are works of art in the Gothic chapel *(Spitalkirche)* and, in the middle of the courtyard, the Hegereiterhäuschen – a graceful pavilion with a pointed roof and turrets.

The hospital courtyards provide access to the **Kalkturm** viewpoint *(also accessible from outside)*, with its **view★** over the town's monuments, and to the watch-path linking the Stöberleinsturm and the Sauturm.

Stadtmauer★ (The Ramparts)

Constructed in the 13C and 14C, these ramparts, complete with gates and towers, are still in a state of perfect preservation. Long stretches are open to the public. Near the hospital, the southern entry to the town is defended by the **Spitaltor★**, a massive 17C bastion enclosing two inner courtyards, both oval.

Wolfgangskirche

North of the Klingentor. A curious Gothic church (1475-93), fortified and incorporated into the barbican doubling the defences of the gateway. The casemates and the parapet walk can still be viewed.

Reichsstadtmuseum

Apr-Oct: 9.30am-5.30pm; Nov-Mar: 1-4pm. Closed Shrove Tuesday, 24 and 31 Dec. €3. ☎ (098 61) 93 90 43. A Dominican monastery from 1258 to 1554, this building is now a local museum showing, among other collections in its spacious, oak-beamed rooms, the Rothenburg Stations of the Cross (1494). Perhaps the most fascinating exhibit is the original hanap drained by ex-Burgomaster Nusch in front of General Tilly *(see above)*. The tankard's design depicts the emperor and the seven electors. It was made in 1616.

►► Rödertor *(Röder gate and tower)*, Puppen- und Spielzeugmuseum *(toy and doll museum)*.

Rottweil★

A charming, fortified town founded in 1140 by the Zähring duke Konrad, Rottweil became a Free Imperial City in 1268. In the 15C it joined in an "everlasting league" with the Swiss Confederation. Traces of the Baroque era are still evident, in the church buildings in particular. Part of Württemburg since 1802, Rottweil has become a tourist centre.

Old Alemannic customs still dictate events on Shrove Tuesday, with the celebrations culminating in the famous Rottweiler Narrensprung (fools' parade) when traditional carved wooden masks are worn.

Location

Population: 24 000. Michelin map n° 545 V 9 – Baden-Württemberg. Rottweil occupies a pleasant site on a spur circled by a meander in the Upper Neckar, between the Swabian Jura and the Black Forest and near the A 81 motorway.

Hauptstraße 21, 78628 Rottweil, ☎ (0741) 49 42 80.

Surrounding area: see DONAUESCHINGEN (31km/19mi south), TÜBINGEN (56km/35mi northeast), SCHWARWALD, SCHWÄBISCHE ALP.

THE ROTTWEILER

The rottweiler is descended from a race of sheepdogs used by the Roman legions. The breed was particularly widespread in the region from the Middle Ages. Robust and powerful, with distinctive black and tan markings, the police use them for their strength and intelligence.

Worth a Visit

It is best to park in car park P 1 (Kriegsdamm) or P 2 (Nägelesgraben). Both are only around 2min walk from the town centre.

Old Town★

The almost fully preserved late-medieval town centre with its burghers' houses adorned with oriels *(Hauptstraße)* and its fountains is just as remarkable as the churches and museums. From Hauptstraße there is a delightful **view★** of the distant Swabian Alps.

Turn left at the Rathaus.

Heiligkreuzmünster

The Late Gothic minster was built between 1430 and 1534. The high altar is adorned with a crucifix which is attributed to the leading Nuremberg master Veit Stoß (1447/48-1533). Splendid **altarpieces★** from various periods decorate the side chapels. These include the Late Gothic St Peter's altarpiece in the north side aisle, the St Nicholas altarpiece in the south side aisle and the Virgin Mary and Apostles altarpieces, both dating from the 15C. The 17C chancel is richly decorated.

Go through the Pfarrgasse, left along Schulgasse and then onto Kriegsdamm.

Dominikanermuseum

♿ *Open Tue-Sun, 10am-1pm, 2-5pm. Closed on all public holidays that fall on weekdays. €1.50. ☎ (0741) 49 43 30.* The museum owes its name to a Dominican monastery which was founded on this site in 1266. Of the monastery buildings, only the Baroque church remains. The architecturally attractive museum, which was built in 1992, exhibits the most important local finds dating from Roman times. The beautiful **Orpheus Mosaic★** from the 2C AD, which is composed of 570 000 small stones, is well worth seeing. In addition the museum houses a high quality collection of **Swabian sculptures★** from the 14C to the 16C with works by famous artists (Hans Multscher, Michel Erhart).

Take Lorenzgasse to Lorenzkapelle.

Lorenzkapelle

This former cemetery chapel was built in c 1580, and now houses a collection of **Rottweil stonemasonry**. It displays the best work produced by the Rottweil stonemason's lodge in late medieval Swabia.

Turn left, and take Hauptstraße back to the town's central crossroads.

Kapellenkirche

The **tower★** of this Gothic church, Baroque on the inside, is a splendid example of the Flamboyant style. The square base, quartered with graceful staircase turrets, supports on the façade an unusual pierced loggia. The upper part of the tower, in two octagonal tiers, is lit by windows with a fine tracery of stonework.

The three entrances retain their original Gothic carvings: the Last Judgement (west face) and the Knight's Betrothal (right corner turret) are outstanding.

Excursions

Dreifaltigkeitsberg★ (Trinity Hill)

20km/12mi southeast; about 30min. A minor road leads up to the pilgrimage church here from Spaichingen, on the edge of the Swabian Jura. From the top of the hill a wide **panorama★** includes the Baar Depression and, in the distance, the dark outline of the Black Forest.

Rüdesheim am Rhein★

The wine town of Rüdesheim lies between the Rhine and the mountains. Here at the Bingen Gap, gateway to the "Romantic Rhine", Rüdesheim has become the most popular tourist centre in the whole valley: the narrow streets, including the famous Drosselgasse, are crammed with visitors, attracted by the wine bars offering a taste of the celebrated local Riesling. There are also distilleries to be visited and cellars where sparkling wine can be drunk.

Location

Population: 10 000 – Michelin map n° 543 Q 7 – Hessen. Rüdesheim lies at the southern end of the Rhine Gorge – where the river, deflected westwards through the Rheingau vineyards by the Taunus massif, decides to turn north again.

Geisenheimerstraße 22, 65385 Rüdesheim, ☎ (067 22) 29 62.

Surrounding area: see RHEINTAL (suggested itinerary includes Rüdesheim), WIESBADEN (28km/18mi east), MAINZ (32km/20mi east), Bad KREUZNACH (67km/42mi south).

Directory

Where to Eat

Hotel Trapp – *Kirchstraße 7, 65385 Rüdesheim – ☎ (067 22) 911 40 – fax (067 22) 47745 – hotel-trapp@t-online.de – Open from mid-Mar to mid-Dec – P – 38rm: €65/130.* Located in the heart of this romantic little town, this family-run establishment offers characterful guestrooms, most of them furnished in light wood. Welcoming atmosphere.

Hotel Rüdesheimer Schloss – *Steingasse 10, 65385 Rüdesheim – ☎ (067 22) 905 00 – fax (067 22) 47960 – ruedesheimer-schloss@t-online.de – Closed from Christmas to the beginning of Jan – P – 21rm: €95/135 – Restaurant €16/32.* Historic building dating from 1729, with pretty interior courtyard and vineyard. Designer furnishings in rooms. The restaurant is laid out along the lines of a traditional taverna.

Worth a Visit

Brömserburg

Rheinstrasse 2. Residence-cum-refuge for the bishops of Mainz until the 13C, this stronghold passed into the hands of the knights of Rüdesheim, and then became a meeting-place for brigands. It was retaken in 1281 by Archbishop Wernherr. Today, it is arranged as a **wine museum**. The outstanding exhibits are 21 old winepresses and a collection of amphorae (vases, jars, bins for storage or transport of wine).

Niederwald Monument

Access by road (2km/1mi) or by cable-car (terminal on the Oberstraße: 20min there and back). Built (1877-83) to commemorate the re-establishment of the German Empire in 1871, the monument comprises a statue of Germania (which alone weighs 32t) on a plinth with bronze bas-relief sculptures showing Bismarck, Emperor Wilhelm I, the German princes and their armies. From the terrace there is a view of the vineyards, Bingen, and the confluence of the Rhine and Nahe. The heights of the Palatinate are visible in the distance.

Tour

The Rheingau

23km/14mi – allow 2hr. A southern exposure allows successful cultivation of vines high up on the foothills of the Taunus. Before passing through these vineyards to reach Eberbach Abbey, the road passes the picturesque villages of Geisenheim, Winkel and Hattenheim.

Kloster Eberbach★★ – *See Kloster EBERBACH*

Kiedrich – The 15C **church** in this wine-growers' market town is still furnished in its original, rare Flamboyant form: the c 1510 carved **pews★★** and choir stalls are still adorned with polychromatic embellishment; they still have their Gothic inscriptions. The **Kiedrich Madonna★** (c 1333), beneath the rood screen, is by an unknown Rhenish master. The organ is one of the oldest in Germany (c 1500-20). Gregorian chant in a Gothic german dialect has been practised in Kiedrich since 1333.

Eltville – The oldest town in the Rheingau makes a picturesque scene with its narrow streets and fine old town houses dating from the 16C and 17C. Built beside the Rhine, the castle here was the residence of the prince-electors of Mainz in the 14C and 15C. Living quarters in the tower can still be viewed. The Johannes Gutenberg memorial in the castle is testimony to the fact that the inventor of book printing was honoured in Eltville during his lifetime. In the church of St Peter and St Paul *(Rosengasse 5)*, there is a very fine baptistery from the Mainz studio of Hans Backhoffen, with the symbols of the Four Apostles worked into the base.

Insel Rügen★

Rügen is Germany's largest island. In a total area of 926km²/358sq mi, the Baltic island offers a surprising variety of scenery. In the west, as the straits widen towards the open sea, the coastline is indented, following the irregular contours of many inlets. Chalk cliffs and sandy beaches in the east attract summer crowds; the wooded southern shores face the wide, shallow waters of the Greifswalder Bodden (Gulf); and to the north Rügen is cut almost in two by the deep, extraordinarily jagged penetration of the Jasmunder Bodden – which is practically an inland sea.
The poet, travel writer, historian and polemicist Ernst Moritz Arndt (1769-1860) was born on Rügen.

Location

Michelin map n° 542 C 23 to 25 – Mecklemburg-Vorpommen. Rügen is joined to the mainland by a long bridge (2.5km/1.5mi) straddling the straits opposite the town of Stralsund. The island can be reached by train as well as car.
Surrounding area: see GREIFSWALD (33km/21mi south of Stralsund), ROSTOCK (75km/47mi to the west of Stralsund), Insel USEDOM.

Directory

Where to Stay

⊖⊖ Strandhotel Lissek – *Strandpromenade 33, 18609 Binz – ☎ (038393) 38 10 – fax (038393) 381430 – strandhotel-lissek@t-online.de – P – 40rm: €67/148* ☕. Carefully restored spa architecture with great attention to detail. Modern comforts, some rooms with fine views of the Baltic Sea. The marine-style restaurant, carries the name of the fish market *(Fischmarkt)*.

⊖⊖ Wreecher Hof – *Kastanienallee, 18581 Putbus-Wreechen – ☎ (038301) 850 – fax (038301) 85100 – info@wreecher-hof.de – P – 43rm: €80 ☕ – Restaurant €24/44.* Peaceful hotel village located off the beaten track, with reed-thatched buildings. Modern comfortable rooms, many with living room area. The restaurant has a winter garden and beautiful terrace.

Tour

FROM PUTBUS TO KAP ARKONA

75km/47mi – Half a day.

Putbus★

The "white town" in the south-east of the island was founded in 1810 by Prince William Malte of Putbus, in imitation of Bad Doberan, as a royal seat and bathing resort. Although the princely castle was demolished in 1960, the neo-Classical town has miraculously remained. A surprisingly harmonious picture of a homogenous whole, such as is rarely found in Germany, greets the visitor. It is not without justification that Putbus is known as "the pearl of Rügen".

Circus★ – The round circus is surrounded by houses with eaves, many with neo-Classical ornamentation. Finished in dazzling white, they stand out from the green of the oaks. The 21m/69ft-high obelisk, which bears the Prince's crown on the top, stands in the centre of the circus.

Theatre★ – *Alleestraße.* The building was erected between 1819 and 1821 by the Berlin architect Steinmeyer (a student of Schinkel). The portico is made up of four Tuscan columns. Above the entrance, a stucco frieze depicts Apollo and the Muses. The theatre is famous for its acoustics.

Schloßpark★ – The 75ha/185-acre Schloßpark with its orangery (converted in 1853 by Friedrich August Stüler), royal stables and parish church, is laid out in the style of an English landscape garden.

Jagdschloß Granitz

12km/7.5mi east of Putbus, south of Binz. Open May to Sep, 9am-6pm; Oct to Apr, Tue-Sun, 10am-4pm. Closed 25 Dec. €3. ☎ (0383 93) 22 63. In 1837 Prince William Malte I of Putbus had a hunting lodge, the most important secular building on the island, built in the neo-Gothic Tudor style on the 107m/351ft high Tempelberg, the highest point in Eastern Rügen. The four crenellated corner towers of the square "castle" rise up in the middle of Granitz woods. A 38m/125ft high viewing tower was built in the inner courtyard in 1844, based on plans by Karl Friedrich Schinkel. The viewing platform is reached up the 154 steps of the fine cast-iron **spiral staircase** (recommended as a subject for amateur photographers). From the top, the **view★★** of Rügen Island is breathtaking. The rooms inside the house are open to the public.

Bathing Resorts★

These are all in the southwest of the island. **Binz**, **Sellin**, **Baabe** and **Göhren** await the visitor with their inviting sandy beaches, beautiful seaside resort architecture and a woodland backdrop.
They can be reached in the "**Rasender Roland**", a little train that connects Putbus to Göhren (via Granitz).

Saßnitz

Ferries to Scandinavia leave from this port. There are very beautiful beech forests in the north.

Stubbenkammer★★

The **Königsstuhl**, a 117m/384ft-high cliff, towers over the impressive chalk bluff which projects out into the sea. If you are lucky enough to visit on a sunny day you will see the breathtaking sight of the white cliff, surrounded by green foliage, shining brightly above the deep blue sea. This postcard idyll (marred nowadays only by the many visitors) also inspired the painter Caspar David Friedrich.

Kap Arkona★

Kap Arkona, with its 50m/164ft-high chalk cliffs, is the northernmost point of the island. The **old lighthouse** *(Alte Leuchtturm: Jul to Aug, 10am-7pm; May to Jun and Sep, 10am-6pm; Mar to Apr and Oct, 10am-5pm; Jan to Feb and Nov, 11am-4pm. €2)* a square three-storeyed brick building on a granite base, was built in 1826-29 based on plans by Karl Friedrich Schinkel. There is a wonderful **view★★** from here right across to the neighbouring island of Hiddensee. Not far from the lighthouse, an embankment recalls the Jaromarsburg fortification, which was built there by the Slavs, but was destroyed by the Danes in 1168. Next to the castle wall stands the naval direction-finding tower built in 1927; it houses the international Baltic Coast exhibition centre.

Excursions

Hiddensee Island★

Ferry connections – Boat trips to the island from Wiek and Schaprode on Rügen and from Stralsund, journey time 30min-2hr 30min. Details from Reederei Hiddensee GmbH, Büro Hiddensee, Achtern Diek 4, 18565 Vitte/Hiddensee, ☎ (0383 00) 501 69; www.frs.de/hiddensee/start.htm
Motor traffic (except service vehicles) is forbidden on the island. We recommend catching the ferry from Kloster and hiring a bicycle once on Hiddensee. Allow 5hr to visit the island.
Hiddensee Island, the little "pearl of the Baltic", is to be found 17km/10mi off the west coast of its larger neighbour, Rügen. Like the neighbouring peninsula of Fischland, Darß and Zingst *(see ROSTOCK)*, it falls almost entirely within the boundaries of the Nationalpark Vorpommersche Boddenlandschaft. The island belongs to the few Central European natural coastal landscapes, with towering cliffs,

Störtebeker

Klaus Störtebeker is one of the more colourful characters from this stretch of the Baltic coast. This notorious pirate is said to have been born in the village of Ruschwitz on Rügen in 1370. As a young man, feeling thirsty one day while at work, he seized his master's tankard of beer and took a generous gulp of the contents. Unfortunately, he was seen by his employer, who had him chained up and beaten. Störtebeker was so strong, however, that he managed to break free of his chains and set about thrashing his tormentors. He then fled in a fishing boat which took him as far as the cape of Arkona, where he made the acquaintance of a certain Michael Gödecke, leader of a band of brigands whose reputation struck terror into all those who sailed the seas anywhere near this stretch of coast. He passed a number of trials of strength with flying colours, thus qualifying to join the band. Having embarked on his new career, he became one of the most feared buccaneers of his age as he proceeded to scour the seas, until he was betrayed by one of his followers, eventually being run to ground in Hamburg in 1401 and condemned to death beneath the guillotine. As a mark of the respect he commanded, his last request, that the lives of some of his companions arrested with him should be saved, was granted.
Legend has it that Störtebeker hid his booty beneath the cliffs of the Stubbenkammer, and once a year a ship in full sail, steered by a phantom crew of buccaneers, is said to haunt this part of the coast. Every summer, at Ralswiek, several of the islanders put on a play commemorating the adventurous life of this local anti-hero, scourge of the rich and benefactor of the poor.

land spits, lagoons and deeply incised coastal inlets, which are all undergoing continual change. The island's relief was sculpted by retreating Scandinavian glaciers some 10 000 years ago and rises to its highest point in the north, at the Dornbusch peak (72m/236ft), site of the island's trademark lighthouse, put into operation in 1888 and measuring 28m/90ft in height. There is a good view from the top terrace of the lighthouse of the Bessin sand spits stretching away along the coastline. This landscape is ideal habitat for migrating birds in the spring and autumn. The Neue Bessin is growing at a rate of 30-60m/100-200ft a year, due to accretion.
Hiddensee Island is crisscrossed by footpaths and cycle paths, giving visitors ample opportunity to explore the individual villages and other sights. The small village of **Grieben** is famous on the island for its fine thatched houses. The village of **Kloster** has developed into a pleasant bathing resort. The graveyard next to the church here is the final resting place of writer **Gerhart Hauptmann** (1862-1946), best-known for his Naturalist dramas. Hauptmann's summer residence, Haus Seedorn on Kirchweg street, is open to the public. The island's administrative centre is at **Vitte**, which has evolved from a fishing village to a tourist resort. Heading south from Vitte, the countryside is a charming one of vast dunes interspersed with marshland *(Dünenheide)*. **Neuendorf**, the island's most southerly village, has its fishermen's houses arranged along an east-west axis, so that the living area is facing the sun. The island's most southerly point is Gellen, formed of shifting sands and growing at an annual rate of 5m/16ft.

Ruhrgebiet

Ruhr Basin

The infrastructure provided by the rivers encouraged settlement here in pre-Roman times. However, it is the last one and a half centuries with the rise of mining and heavy industry that left their mark most noticeably on the landscape and employment structures of the Ruhr Basin. This has tended to overshadow the fact that, for example, Duisburg already had a town charter by the 12C and Dortmund was a member of the Hanseatic League.
Since the period following the Second World War, the Ruhrfestspiele have held a special place in the Ruhr-Rhine region's annual calendar of events. Theatres, opera houses, and even local churches host national and international figures in performances of theatre or classical music.

Location

Michelin map n° 543 L 4 – M 9, folds 1 and 2 – Nordrhein-Westfalen. The Ruhr Basin region (4 400km^2/1 700sq mi) lies between three rivers: the Ruhr, the Rhine and the Lippe, and is home to a total population of 5.5 million. The large towns of Duisburg, Essen and Dortmund are in the region.
Ruhrgebiet Tourismus GmbH, service-center, Königswall 21, 44137 Dortmund ☎ 0231 18 16 186.
Surrounding area: see KÖLN (66km/41mi south of Duisburg via the A 3), MÜNSTER (67km/42mi north of Dortmund via the A 1).

Background

Important industrial centre – The Ruhr is still one of the world's most important industrial centres. A large proportion of German steel is manufactured here; Duisburg inland port is the largest in Europe and the largest river port in the world. The landscape in the north of the region is shaped by the chemical industry and ultra-modern mining operations, reaching depths of 1 000m/3 300ft or more. To the south, the perimeter strip is home to staff-intensive businesses, heralding the light industry of the hillsides delimiting the Ruhr Valley, the Bergisches Land.

A New Image – The reorganisation of the Ruhr Basin has been and is being implemented in a variety of ways. The legacy of heavy industry has been seized upon as an opportunity of reworking the Ruhr's old "Black Country" image and using it to create a region characterised by a new culture and activities. The Emscherpark international construction exhibition, the Westphalian and Rhineland countryside associations, and the Ruhr Basin municipal association have agreed upon and implemented year-long projects for reconstructing countless industrial plants that had been closed down.

In this way, for example, one of Europe's most modern shopping centres has sprung up on a disused factory site in Oberhausen, occupying 70 000m²/753 200sq ft and offering shoppers some 200 shops and boutiques. For those vital breaks, there are 20 restaurants and bars, as well as variety performances, jazz, cinema and concerts. Old pits and factories are not only doing business, but have been converted in many cases into industrial museums. In this way they give educational insight into the production methods and social history of heavy industry.

Worth a Visit

Museums and sights of the Ruhr Basin and Bergisches Land (in alphabetical order of the main towns of the region).

BOCHUM

Kunstsammlung Museum Bochum

Kortumstrasse 147, opposite the Stadtpark. ♿ Open Tue-Sun, 11am-5pm, (-8pm Wed; -6pm Sun). €3, no charge 1st Wed of the month. Closed 1 Jan, Good Fri, 1 May, 24, 25 and 31 Dec. ☎ (0234) 516 00 30. The collections in this spacious, airy modern building concentrate mainly on contemporary international art.

Deutsches Bergbau-Museum★★ (German Mining Museum)

Am Bergbaumuseum 28. ♿ Tue-Sun, 8.30am-5pm, Sat-Sun, 10am-5pm. Closed 1 Jan, 1 May, 24-26 and 31 Dec. €6. ☎ (0234) 587 70. Founded in 1930, this museum is on the edge of the town centre. It gives a complete picture of the evolution of mining from Antiquity to the present. Models, reconstructions, graphics and original equipment cover every aspect of extraction. Fifty feet underground, in the **Schaubergwerk**, more than 2.5km/1.5mi of abandoned workings have been restored to illustrate various methods of coalface extraction and transport. The tour of the mine workings ends with a trip to the top of the 71m/233ft-high mining tower. There is a good view of Bochum and the surrounding area from the platform.

Deutsches Bergbau-Museum

German Mining Museum in Bochum.

Eisenbahnmuseum★ (Railway Museum)

At Bochum-Dahlhausen, C-Otto-Straße 191, halfway between Essen and Bochum. Car park. Open Apr to Oct, Wed and Thu, 10am-5pm, Sun, 10am-3pm; Nov to Mar, Wed and Fri, 10am-5pm, Sun, 10am-1pm. €5. ☎ (0234) 49 25 16 (Wed and Fri).

Founded by a society of railway enthusiasts, this museum is installed in a disused station and rolling-stock repair shop on the north bank of the Ruhr. Equipment dating from 1914 (an engine house, a turntable, a hydraulic crane) is for the most part still in mint condition. More than 180 machines that ran on rails retrace the evolution of this form of transport from the beginnings to the end of the steam era. The highlights of the collection are 15 **steam locomotives**. Special vehicles (railcars, hand-operated gangers' trucks) and many types of wagon can also be seen.

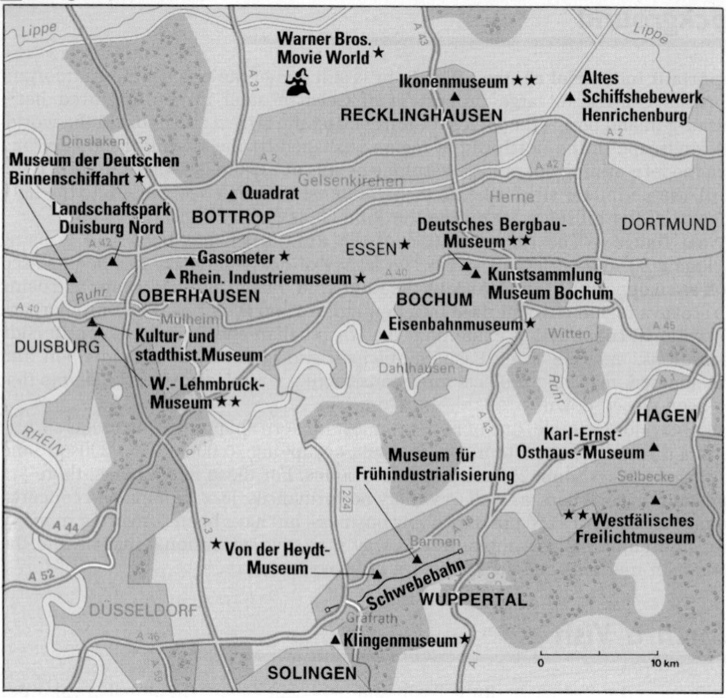

BOTTROP

Quadrat Museum Centre

Im Stadtgarten 20 (near town centre). ♿ *Open Tue-Sun, 10am-6pm. Closed 1 Jan, 24, 25 and 31 Dec. Museum für Ur- und Ortsgeschichte and Josef Albers Museum no charge.* ☎ *(020 41) 297 16.* The Constructivist work of Bottrop painter and educational art theorist Josef Alber gave rise to the name of this museum centre. The former Bauhaus lecturer called the pictorial results of his research on changing effects of colour *Hommage an das Quadrat* (Homage to the Square). True to its origins, the museum is dedicated to Constructivism. The adjoining sculpture park contains works by Max Bill, Donald Judd, Norbert Kricke etc.

Next to the Quadrat is the **Museum of Pre- and Local History** *(Museum für Ur- und Ortsgeschichte)*. The **Ice Age Hall★** houses Germany's largest Quaternary Era collection.

Warner Bros. Movie World★

In Bottrop-Kirchhellen, via A 31, exit Kirchhellen. Open Aug, 10am-9pm; mid-Apr to end Sep, 10am-6pm, Sat-Sun, 10am-7pm; Oct, Mon-Thu, 10am-6pm, Fri-Sun, 10am-10pm. Closed Mon in Apr, May, Sep and Oct. Day ticket €23. ☎ *(020 45) 89 90.* This 45ha/110-acre film and amusement park, under the motto "Hollywood in Germany", will take your breath away, with more than 35 different attractions and shows. They include the **Bermuda Triangle** with its rapids and raging waterfalls, the **Batman adventure** in the breathtaking flight simulator, the *Police Academy* Stunt Show, which presents a robbery with plenty of thrills and surprises, a 3D animated film theatre, the *Neverending Story*, which includes a trip on rapids through caverns and gorges, the breakneck *Lethal Weapon* roller-coaster and many more.

Visitors finding themselves in need of a little peace and quiet can visit the **Museum of German Film History★**, a look back over 100 years of film in Germany, which also traces the development of photographic and film cameras, beginning with the camera obscura.

DORTMUND

Dortmund was first mentioned around 885 and was given market rights before the year 900. Documents prove its status as an Imperial City since 1220, and as such it was a flourishing town during the Middle Ages. As in many places, however, the Thirty Years War left deep scars, so that by 1648 only 2 000 people lived here.

The actual boom period began in the mid-19C with the start of the Industrial Revolution. Ever since, Dortmund has been marked by coal, steel and beer. Nevertheless, as an economic hub, the city did put its money on innovation and research. Trade, insurance companies and the service sector have now long been economic buttresses for the city.

Directory

Tourist office – *opposite Hauptbahnof Süd, Königswall 18a, 44137 Dortmund ☎ (0049) 231/5025656.*

Where to Eat

Pfefferkorn – *Hoher Wall 38 – ☎ (0231) 14 36 44 – www.pfefferkorn-dortmund.de – Booking advised – €16/34.* This restaurant's old German-style decor together with its pleasant atmosphere make this a good address to know about; friendly service.

Where to Stay

Haus Überacker – *Wittbräucker Straße 504 (B 234), 44267 Dortmund-Höchsten – ☎ (02304) 807 06 – fax (02304) 86844 – Closed 3 weeks in Aug/Sep – P – 17rm: €40/80 – Restaurant €19/39.* Good family-run hotel set in a neat half-timbered house. Partly panelled guestrooms with solid wooden furnishings. A new heated winter garden and pleasant terrace complete the restaurant.

Westfalenpark★

10am-11pm (automatic ticket booths). €1.80. ☎ (0231) 502 61 00. The two main centres of attraction in this 70ha/173-acre park are the **Television Tower** (Fernsehturm "Florian") and the **Rose Garden** *(Deutsches Rosarium)*, which cultivates some 3 200 varieties from all over the world. The tower is 220m/722ft high (31m/102ft higher than the Telecom Tower in London). At a height of 137m/450ft there is a revolving platform with a restaurant and a terrace from which there is a superb **panorama★** of the Ruhr and the Sauerland.

Reinoldikirche★

In the Ostenhellweg, near the market.

This triple-aisle basilica dating from the early Gothic period has interesting furnishings, which include a 15C sculpted reredos, probably a Burgundian work, that represents the life of Christ and the Crucifixion. Of particular interest is the highly skilled bronze eagle pulpit (Adlerpult), a work originating in the Maas Valley around 1450. Note the 14C wood statue of St Reynold, patron saint of the town, on the north side of the chancel, and a late-15C statue of Charlemagne on the south.

Museum für Kunst und Kulturgeschichte (Museum of Art and Civilisation)

At no 3, Hansastraße. ♿ Open Tue-Sun, 10am-5pm, Thu, 10am-8pm, Sat, 12 noon-5pm. Closed 1 Jan, 24, 25 and 31 Dec. €3. ☎ (0231) 502 55 22. The exhibits here, displayed chronologically, cover such diverse subjects as the history of Dortmund (many items from archeological digs); religious art at the end of the Middle Ages; houses and furniture in different periods; and 19C painting (Berlin Secession, CD Friedrich, 20C design). The section devoted to the Romanesque epoch contains the **Dortmund Treasure★** *(Dortmunder Goldschatz)* – a collection of 444 gold coins, dating for the most part from the 4C AD.

►► Marienkirche – Petrikirche *(carved altarpiece★)* – Probsteikirche – Brauerei-Museum – Museum am Ostwall *(modern art)*.

DUISBURG

Wilhelm-Lehmbruck-Museum★★

In Duisburg town centre, Kantpark. ♿ Tue-Sun, 11am-5pm, Sun, 10am-6pm. Closed 1 Jan, 1 May, 24, 25 and 31 Dec. €4. ☎ (0203) 283 31 38. The "Centre for International Sculpture" is home to over 700 20C sculptures and objets (Arp, Barlach, Beuys, Calder, Dalí, Giacometti, Kollwitz, Kricke, LeWitt, Magritte, Moore, Tinguely, Uecker etc). One wing of the museum is given over to an exhibition of major works by Duisburg sculptor **Wilhelm Lehmbruck** (1881-1919). The surrounding park (7ha/17 acre) contains outdoor sculptures by international artists against a backdrop of the area's original trees.

Museum der Deutschen Binnenschiffahrt★

Duisburg-Ruhrort, Apostelstraße 84. ♿ Open Tue-Sun, 10am-5pm. Closed 1 Jan, 24, 25 and 31 Dec. €3. ☎ (0203) 80 88 90. The former Jugendstil swimming pool at Ruhrort has become the home of Germany's largest museum on the economy, technology and social history of inland shipping. Visitors are treated to a comprehensive presentation of developments from dug-outs to the modern association of tugs. Life on board ship and in the ports is also elaborated. Two museum ships (dating from 1882 and 1922) are near the maritime stock exchange, 10min walk away along a path through Ruhrort port.

Landschaftspark Duisburg Nord

In Duisburg-Meiderich, Emscherstraße 71. Car park.

The centrepiece of the park is the disused iron and steel works with its blast furnaces and chimneys towering skywards. The old industrial hangars now host a variety of events. Lighting effects by British artist Jonathan Park transform the old works into a fascinating show of light and colour in the evening. *Sound and light shows at dusk. No charge. ☎ (0203) 429 19 42; www.landschaftspark.de*

ESSEN★

Essen no longer lives up to its coal-bowl image. Three-quarters of the people in Europe's formerly largest mining town work in administration, service, and retail. The main industry is now the manufacture of machine tools. Typical of the region is the reusing of industrial complexes for other purposes such as in Essen-Katernberg: the Zollverein Colliery *(Gelsenkirchener Staße 181)* is now home to the Design-Zentrum Nordrhein-Westfalen, located in the old boiler house, which was rebuilt by Sir Norman Foster.

The capital of the Ruhr has the air of a residential town, with attractive pedestrian precincts bordered by elegant shops, a lovely art gallery and pleasant suburbs in green surroundings (Grugapark, RS). Woods, extending southwards, border the Baldeneysee.

Museum Folkwang★★

Museumszentrum. ♿ Open Tue-Sun, 10am-6pm, Fri, 10am-midnight. Closed 1 Jan, 1 May, 24 and 31 Dec. €5. ☎ (0201) 884 53 1401. Museumszentrum.

This museum houses a major collection of 19C and 20C painting, sculpture, graphic art and photography, particularly rich in works of art from Germany and France. Besides the German Romantics and Realists of the 19C are the French Realists and Impressionists, as well as the French Cubists and Surrealists.

Works by the artists of the Brücke group, the Blaue Reiter (Kandinsky, Macke, Marc) and the Bauhaus demonstrate the tremendous variety of German Impressionism and art of the 20C.

Note also the collection of post-1945 art, with works by Baselitz, Kiefer, Lüpertz, Penck and Richter, as well as Americans Pollock, Newman and Stella.

Ruhrlandmuseum★

♿ Open Tue-Sun, 10am-6pm, Fri, 10am-midnight. Closed 1 Jan, 1 May and 31 Dec. €5. ☎ (0201) 884 52 00. Besides its geological and archaeological collections, the focus of the museum is on the social history of industrialisation. The conditions of a working-class family and the lifestyle of the bourgeoisie in the Ruhr region around the turn of the century are depicted.

Münster (Cathedral)

The 10C **west chancel★**, with three angled side walls, is the oldest part of the building. It was directly influenced by that in the cathedral at Aachen. The nave, a Gothic hall, dates from the end of the 13C; the Ottonian crypt now has stained-glass windows by Manessier. Off the northern aisle, there is a lateral chapel housing a priceless work: The **Golden Madonna★★★**, said to be the oldest (AD 980) statue of the Virgin in the West. In the western part of the church there is a gigantic seven-branch candelabra (c 1000) decorated with geometric motifs. The **cathedral treasury★** *(Domschatzkammer)* (DZ M[1]) holds among other things four splendid **processional crosses★★★** (10C and 11C), the Golden Madonna's crown, gospels, and the "sword of the martyr-saints Cosmas and Damian" (parade sword from Otto III's treasure). *Open Tue-Sun, 10am-5pm, Sun, 11.30am-5pm. Closed 1 Jan, Good Fri, Easter Sun and Pentecost, 1 Nov, 24, 25 and 31 Dec. €2.50. ☎ (0201) 220 42 06.*

Villa Hügel★

♿ Open Tue-Sun, 10am-6pm. Closed 1 Jan and 24-26 Dec. €1. ☎ (0201) 188 48 23.

This imposing Gründerzeit mansion stands in an attractive park on the north shore of Lake Baldeney. The original house was built in 1870-73, after designs by Alfred Krupp. The complex included a residential wing and a guest wing, and could boast 269 bedrooms. Until 1945, the Villa Hügel was home to three successive generations of the Krupp family. Since 1953, it has been open to the public.

The construction and fittings of the present great house date from 1915. The 15C-18C tapestries are one of the main features to have survived from the mansion's earlier magnificent decor. The villa now houses temporary exhibitions. The smaller house is used for permanent exhibitions. They offer an insight into the extraordinary success story of this family business, which started in 1811 with Friedrich Krupp's construction of the first steel-casting crucible and subsequently reflected the entire growth and development of heavy industry in Germany.

▶▶ Johanniskirche – Abteikirche St-Ludger

HAGEN

Karl-Ernst-Osthaus-Museum

Hochstraße 73. Open Tue-Sun, 11am-6pm, Thu, 11am-8pm. Closed 1 Jan, 1 May, 24, 25 and 31 Dec. ☎ (023 31) 207 31 38.

This museum steeped in tradition dates back to industrialist and patron Karl Ernst Osthaus, who founded the Museum Folkwang for art and crafts here in 1902 (the collections were donated to the city of Essen in 1922). The museum building was fitted out with Jugendstil interior decor designed by Henry van de Velde. The collection covers Classical Modern and contemporary works of art.

The Museum des Hagener Impulses *(Stirnband 10)*, an annexe of the museum, contains a particularly impressive original interior by Van der Velde, as well as works by Ferdinand Hodler, Henri Matisse and items from the Hagen silversmithing workshops.
Part of the 20C German art collection is given over to the artist Christian Rohlfs, who worked in Hagen until his death in 1938.

Westfälisches Freilichtmuseum★★ (Open-Air Technical Museum)

At Hagen-Selbecke, in the valley of Mäckingerbachtal. Leave Hagen heading south on the Frankfurt, then the Eilpe road. At Eilpe, turn right towards Breckerfeld-Halver and continue for just over 1.5km/1mi to Selbecke. From the museum car park (Museum-sparkplatz), on the left of the road, 10min on foot. Open from Apr to end Oct, Tue-Sun, 9am-5pm. €5. ☎ (023 31) 780 70.
Along 2.5km/1.5mi of this valley, more than 70 installations or buildings have been reconstructed to illustrate the evolution of crafts and techniques in Westphalian industry (mid-17C to late 19C). Traditional metalwork displays (at the foot of the valley) include giant iron and copper hammers activated by water from artificial lakes. A half-timbered 18C house has been turned into a **Blacksmith Museum** with a working forge. There are also examples of James Nasmyth's steam hammer (c 1840) and the zinc rolling mill of Hoesch (1841), both of which marked the start of true industrialisation.
Higher up the valley an 18C **paper mill** houses a Printing Museum. Finally there is a whole village of traditional craftsmen, where not only saddlers and smiths and rope makers and dyers, but also bakers and brewers ply their trade (their products may be purchased). *We recommend visiting on weekday mornings to see the craftsmen in action.*

OBERHAUSEN

Gasometer★

Oberhausen new town centre (near CentrO shopping centre). ♿ Panoramic viewpoint on the roof, Jan to Mar and Nov to Dec, Tue-Sun, 10am-5pm, Wed, 10am-3pm. Roof and tour of inside, Jan to Mar and Nov to Dec, Sat-Sun, 10am-5pm. Closed 1 Jan, Apr to mid-May and Oct, 24-26 and 31 Dec. Roof €2, inside €3. ☎ (0208) 850 37 33.
The present exhibition hall used to be Europe's largest blast furnace gas storage tank in its heyday (117.5m/385ft high, 68m/220ft in diameter, built in 1928-29). The outside staircase has 592 steps leading up to the viewing platform, from where there is a view over the site of the 1999 regional garden show towards the lower Rhine. Inside, a panoramic lift takes visitors up to a height of 106m/350ft. The impressive spatial effect of the rotunda opens out from the second level.

Rheinisches Industriemuseum★

In Oberhausen town centre (behind the main station), Hansastraße 20. Tue-Sun, 10am-5pm, Thu, 10am-8pm. Closed 1 Jan, 24, 25 and 31 Dec. €4. ☎ (0208) 857 92 81.
The Altenberg zinc works was closed down in 1981, after 130 years of processing raw zinc from Mülheim and Essen. The heavy industry museum was housed in the old rolling hall. It is dedicated not only to the history of technological progress since the mid-19C, but also underlines the political and economical importance of iron and steel production to the Rhine and Ruhr regions. Original components from the factory building have been retained and incorporated into the exhibition, eg the 9m/30ft high steam power hammer dating from 1900.

RECKLINGHAUSEN

Ikonen-Museum★★ (Icon Museum)

Kirchplatz 2a. Tue-Sun. 1am-6pm. €2.50. ☎ (023 61) 50 19 41. The marvellous specimens exhibited here are arranged by theme: the Holy Trinity and the Celestial Hierarchy (a theme rich in symbolism); the Virgin Mary; the Saints and their Days (a splendid calendar of all the religious feasts). To these are added a collection of iconostases (screens separating the sanctuary from the rest of the church).

Altes Schiffshebewerk Henrichenburg

In Waltrop, Am Hebewerk 2. ♿ Open Tue-Sun, 10am-6pm. Closed 1 Jan, 24, 25 and 31 Dec. €2.60, no charge on Fri. ☎ (023 63) 970 70.
In 1899 Emperor Wilhelm II inaugurated this construction, which was one of a kind at the time. It provided a means of bridging a stretch of land with a 14m/46ft difference in height via the Dortmund-Ems canal (1892-99), the waterway to the North Sea. The Westphalian industrial museum now illustrates how the ship's hoist, which has been restored, works. It also contains displays on the technical, political and economical requirements of canal building, and life and work on and along the canal. The museum ship **MS Franz Christian** gives an insight into life aboard a canal boat.

SOLINGEN

Deutsches Klingenmuseum★ (Blade Museum)

At Solingen-Gräfrath. ♿ Open Tue-Sun, 10am-5pm, Fri, 2-5pm. Closed 1 Jan, 24, 25 and 31 Dec. €3. ☎ (0212) 25 83 60.

Known the world over for its knives and its scissors, Solingen is the centre of fine metalwork in Germany. The museum is located in the former Gräfrath Abbey, an elegant Baroque building charmingly converted with considerable imagination by Joseph Paul Kleihues, making the architectural backdrop to the exhibits well worth taking note of. The museum traces the history of side arms (magnificent dress swords). A further highlight of the collections is the cutlery, and by extension tableware, from the 18C, which give those visitors less interested in matters military plenty to admire. The museum basement houses the treasury of the neighbouring church of St Maria Himmelfahrt.

From the abbey gardens, go down some steps to the historic **Marktplatz**. The houses around the square have been restored in the traditional half-timbered style of the Bergisches Land, with slate shingles cladding roofs and walls and green wooden shutters at the windows.

WUPPERTAL

Von der Heydt-Museum★

At Wuppertal-Elberfeld. ♿ Open Tue-Sun, 11am-6pm, Thu 11am-8pm. Closed 1 Jan, 1 May, 24, 25 and 31 Dec. €1. ☎ (0202) 563 62 31. This museum, housed in the old Elberfeld town hall (1827-42), has an interesting collection of paintings and sculpture. The museum is named after the Wuppertal family of bankers, the Von der Heydts, who were its generous patrons. The collections include 16C and 17C Flemish and Dutch painting; French and German painting from the 19C to Impressionism, Expressionism (Kirchner, Beckmann), Fauvism, Cubism (Braque) and the present. Sculptures from the 19C and 20C are also on display (Rodin, Maillol). The cafeteria was designed by French artist Daniel Buren.

Museum für Frühindustrialisierung

At Wuppertal-Barmen. Open Tue-Sun, 10am-1pm, 3pm-6pm ☎ (0202) 563 64 98. Housed in a disused factory, this museum traces the economic and social history of the Wupper Valley since the mid-18C.

Schwebebahn (Cable railway)

An interesting mode of transport for getting around Wuppertal is the cable railway (1898-1903). This is the world's oldest suspended railway for transporting passengers and is also one of the safest means of public transport, carrying 22.6 million passengers a year. Most of the station buildings date from the turn of the century.

Oberes Saaletal★

Saale Valley

The winding course of the Saale forms a natural link between such towns as Jena and Halle, masterpieces of sacred architecture like Merseburg and Naumburg, and the innumerable castles built on its banks.

The itinerary suggested below heads south through a countryside of woods and fields and small market towns to an attractive upland region dotted with lakes, in a corner formed by the old East- and West-German demarcation line and the Czech frontier.

Location

Michelin map n° 544 N, O 18 – Thüringen. Rising on high ground at the eastern extremity of the Thüringer Wald, the River Saale flows 427km/265mi to the north before joining the Elbe upstream from Magdeburg.

Surrounding area: see (distances from Rudolstadt): WEIMAR (37km/23mi north), JENA (38km/24mi north), THÜRINGER WALD (Ilmenau is 43km/27mi west).

Tour

FROM RUDOLSTADT TO SAALBURG

61km/38mi – allow 4hr

Rudolstadt

Once the seat of the princes of Schwarzburg-Rudolstadt, this town is dominated by the fine silhouette of **Schloß Heidecksburg★**, which dates from 1737. Several **rooms★★** magnificently decorated in the Rococo style are open to the public. *Open Tue-Sun, 10am-6pm. €4. ☎ (036 72) 429 00.*

Saalfeld

Saalfeld Fairy Grottoes.

Saalfelder Feengrotten

In medieval times, Saalfeld was among the most important towns in Thuringia, thanks to local silver and copper mines and a position on the main trade route to Bohemia which assured its commercial prosperity. Modern Saalfeld contains an impressive number of historic buildings.

The Renaissance **Rathaus** in Marktplatz is designed around a façade that centres on a staircase tower with two oriel windows. On the other side of the square, the *Stadtmarktapotheke* (pharmacy) is one of the rare Romanesque (restored) buildings in the area. The *Johanniskirche* features a late-14C Last Judgement above its main entrance. The historic rooms of an old Francisan abbey house the local **museum** *(Stadtmuseum Saalfeld im Franziskanerkloster)* with collections on local history and folklore, as well as several Late Gothic altarpieces from Saalfeld studios. ♿ *Open Tue-Sun, 10am-5pm. Closed 24 and 31 Dec. €2.50. ☎ (036 71) 59 84 71.*

Feengrotten★ (Fairy Grottoes)

1km/0.6mi southeast of Saalfeld on B 281. Guided tour (45min). Open Mar to Oct, 9am-5pm; Nov, Sat-Sun, 10am-3.30pm; Dec to Feb, 10am-3.30pm. €5. ☎ (036 71) 550 40; www.feengrotten.de

Stalactites, stalagmites, concretions and petrifications... such near-magical subterranean decor can be found in the abandoned galleries of this disused slate mine.

Leave Saalfeld on B 85. Cross the Saale at the Hohenwarte dam.

The artificial lake at **Hohenwarte** (Hohenwarte-Talsperre) curves for 10km/6mi, in a series of wide arcs magnificently incorporated into the existing landscape. Woodland scenery alternates with crops as the road crosses the plateau.

Via Drognitz and Remptendorf, the suggested route arrives at the Bleiloch reservoir. Driving across the dam, sightseers regain the river's east bank.

This reservoir, 29km/18mi long, with an enormous volume of water retained, is the largest of the five artificial lakes between Saalfeld and Blankenstein.

Saalburg

Now a lakeside town, Saalburg lost part of its outskirts when the valley was flooded. Remains of the 16C fortifications, however, can still be seen.

Saarbrücken★

Although it was seriously damaged during the Second World War, the capital of the Saarland has developed into a regional metropolis, especially since 1950, when it became the capital of the 11th German province and completed the secession of the Saarland from France. It has since taken full advantage of its border situation. The city's architecture today owes its character to the large number of Baroque buildings that have been preserved from the time of Count Wilhelm Heinrich von Nassau.

Location

Population: 200 000 – Michelin map nº 543 S 5 – Saarland. Saarbrücken is in the Saar valley, on the border with France and at the crossroads of the A 6 motorway to Mannheim and the A 4 motorway to Metz in France.

ℹ *Reichstrasse 1, 66111 Saarbrücken, ☎ (0681) 93 80 90.*

Surrounding area: see Unteres SAARTAL (Mettlach is 53km/33mi north), PFALZ (Dahn is 78km/49mi east), TRIER (96km/60mi north), WORMS (124km/76mi northeast via the A 6).

Background

From market town to Royal Seat – Saarbrücken was first mentioned in the record books in AD 999, although it dates back to Celtic and Roman times. During the 1C, the Romans built a *vicus* (small market town) at a river crossing of the Saar, crossroads of the Metz to Worms road and the link between Trier and Strasbourg. They also built a stone bridge over the river, which was used right up to the Middle

Directory

WHERE TO EAT

Hauck – Das Weinhaus – *St.-Johanner-Markt 7 – ☎ (0681) 319 19 – www.weinhaus-hauck.de – €15/50.* Only the first floor still retains something of the old tavern dating from 1856. A fine selection of wines, most of them also available in carafes, to accompany simple dishes, including a number of regional specialities.

WHERE TO STAY

Hotel Schlosskrug – *Schmollerstraße 14 – ☎ (0681) 354 48 – Fax (0681) 375022 – www.hotel-schlosskrug.de – Closed from Christmas to beginning of Jan – P – 20rm: €23/59 – Restaurant €25/35.* This boarding-house-style hotel is set in an old town house. Functional rooms, some with their own bathroom, and some family rooms with several beds available. Cyclists will appreciate the workshop and shed.

Ages. The medieval settlement was the seat of the counts of Saarbrücken. In 1321 it was given the status of a town, together with St Johann on the north bank of the Saar. It came to the house of Nassau by marriage in 1381.

Fit for a Prince – In 1738 Count Wilhelm Heinrich von Nassau summoned the master builder **Friedrich Joachim Stengel**, who originally came from Zerbst, to the court in Saarbrücken. A time of intensive and fruitful building activity began, and the city's architecture today owes its character to the large number of buildings that have been preserved. The castle, the Ludwigskirche, the collegiate church in St Johann, all originate from this period. Under the influence of Palladio, Stengel created impressive works in a Classical Late Baroque style.

Walking About

ALT-SAARBRÜCKEN *(on the south bank of the Saar)*

Friedrich Joachim Stengel was charged with transforming the old centre of Saarbrücken into a harmonious Baroque ensemble.

Schloß

The medieval fortress was succeeded at the beginning of the 17C by a Renaissance castle, which was demolished in 1738 to make way for a Baroque castle designed by the court architect Friedrich Joachim Stengel. Wars and conversion work left deep marks, so that reconstruction was necessary in 1982 and the new design was entrusted to **Gottfried Böhm**. The Classical three-winged structure was renovated and the central façade was determinedly given a modern look, becoming a glass building through which the light floods. The banqueting hall is a successful symbiosis of glass and colour.

The Saar Historical Museum, a glass and steel construction and a further creation of Gottfried Böhm, adjoins the right wing of the castle. Its permanent exhibition deals with the First World War and National Socialism in the Saar region. Another important exhibition shows development since the post-war era and during the 1950s, up to the point at which the Saarland became part of Germany on 1 January 1957. ♿ *Tue-Sun, 10am-6pm (-8pm, Thu), Sat, 12 noon-6pm. €2.50, no charge Thu from 5pm. ☎ (0681) 506 45 01.*

Museum für Vor- und Frühgeschichte

First building on the left in Schloßplatz. ♿ Open Tue-Sun, 9am-5pm, Sun, 10am-6pm. Closed bank holidays. No charge. ☎ (0681) 954 05 11.

Housed in the former district Parliament house, a neo-Baroque building. Inside there is a remarkable cast iron bannister from a Saarbrücken wealthy middle-class house, the Bodesch Palais *(25 Altneugasse)*, created by court blacksmith Höer. On the ground floor, finds mainly from Roman times can be admired. The central feature of the museum is however the **Celtic princess's grave★★** from Reinheim, which dates back to 400 BC. The find is considered one of the most important in Central Europe from the Early Celtic period. The princess' jewellery and the tomb furnishings, which include a gilded bronze pitcher, are wonderfully well preserved.

Altes Rathaus

To the far west of the Schloßplatz. The old town hall, or Altes Rathaus, with its clock tower and its imperial roof (1748-50) stands at the western end of the Schloßplatz. The Saarbrücken city coat of arms is visible on the gable end. The *Abenteuermuseum (Museum of Adventure)* housed on the upper storey contributes to an understanding of foreign peoples and foreign countries.

The Erbprinzenpalais stands on the southern side of Schloßplatz. It was a building converted by Stengel for the hereditary prince Ludwig von Nassau between 1760 and 1766 from three older houses and adapted to the style of the castle, with a triaxial central projection and a mansard roof. It has been used for many purposes since the French Revolution, for example as the seat of the Prussian mountain authority, the mining administration or police headquarters, and today the offices of municipal institutions.

Ludwigsplatz★★ and Ludwigskirche

This is Stengel's masterpiece, one of the most beautiful and uniform Late Baroque complexes in Germany, erected between 1762 and 1775.

Ludwigsplatz – The square is bordered in the north, south and west by eight palaces of various sizes. All with three storeys and mansard roofs, they illustrate the transition from the Late Baroque to the neo-Classical style. Their white and silver-grey colouring enhances the effect of the Ludwigskirche, which is built in yellow and red sandstone in the centre of the square. The long building (front elevation) on the western side is the former orphanage. The minister-president also has his offices in Ludwigsplatz.

Ludwigskirche – ♿ *Open Oct to Mar, Tue, 3-5pm, Wed, 10am-12 noon (in addition Apr to Sep, 4-5.30pm), Sat, 4-6pm, Sun, 11am-12 noon. Often closed on Sat for wedding ceremonies. €0.50. ☎ (0681) 525 24.* A successful restoration project has allowed this unique Baroque Protestant church to radiate its former glory once again. The east end exhibits a degree of splendour which is quite unusual in a Protestant church, with elaborate window frames and statues of the Evangelists by Franziskus Bingh in the splays either side of the projecting building.

The **interior**, with its restrained elegance, forms a contrast to the sumptuous iconological exterior.

ST JOHANN

St Johanner Markt★

The old city around the market is the true heart of Saarbrücken. The focal point is the beautiful market fountain, with its obelisk and cast-iron railing, which was built in 1759-60. Life pulses in the crooked streets and the numerous bistros (France is very close by).

Basilika St. Johann★

Open Mon, Wed and Fri, 8.30am-6pm, Tue, Thu and Sun, 9.30am-6pm, Sat, 9am-6pm. ☎ (0681) 329 64. Built by the princely master builder Stengel between 1754 and 1758, and consecrated to St John the Baptist and St Ludwig, this church with its onion tower and lantern is another jewel of the Late Baroque period. The tympanum over the main doorway shows the Synagogue and the Church. The balconies were built in 1789 by Heinrich Heidehoff. The four **confessionals**, which date back to original plans by Stengel and already hint at the Louis XVI style, are noteworthy.

Worth a Visit

Saarland Museum – Alte Sammlung

Karlstraße 1 (opposite the Moderne Galerie). Open Tue-Sun, 10am-6pm, Wed, 10am-10pm. Closed Tue after Easter and Pentecost, 24, 25 and 31 Dec. €1.50, no charge Sat. ☎ (0681) 996 40. Paintings and decorative arts (including a remarkable Renaissance cabinet from Limburg Monastery) from south-west Germany and Lorraine from the Middle Ages up to early modern times. There is an extensive collection of ceramics and porcelain.

Saarland Museum – Moderne Galerie

Bismarckstraße, on the banks of the Saar. ♿ Open Tue-Sun, 10am-6pm, Wed, 10am-10pm. Closed Tue after Easter and Pentecost, 24, 25 and 31 Dec. €1.50, no charge Sat.

20C art (paintings, sculptures, graphic art). The main emphasis is on German Impressionism and above all **Expressionism★**. There are major works by artists of international stature, such as Picasso, Léger, Tàpies, Beuys, Polke.

Stiftskirche St-Arnual★

In the district of St Arnual, via Talstraße and Saargemünder Straße. The Gothic church was erected between the end of the 13C and the end of the 14C, and was given a Baroque domed roof in 1746, based on plans by Stengel. It was named after Bishop Arnuald von Metz, who lived in the 7C. The cross-shaped three naved vaulted basilica which incorporates the west tower and the projecting porch is one of the most important religious buildings in south-west Germany, a transitional building of French Gothic design in the east, but restrained by influence from Trier.

Having been the burial place of the dukes of Nassau-Saarbrücken since the 15C, the church houses 50 **tombs★★** dating from the 13C to the 18C, some of which are masterly and are decorated in colour. The tomb of Elisabeth von Lothringen (who died in 1446 and won a name for herself as a translator and writer of medieval prose) is to be found in the chancel. The northern wall of the chancel features the larger than life-size Renaissance grave of Count Philipp von Nassau-Saarbrücken (who died in 1621) with his mother Anna Maria von Hesse and his sisters Dorothea and Luise Juliane. In the northern transept, note the altar tomb of Count Johann III (who died in 1472), in full armour, with his two wives Johanna von Heinsberg and Elisabeth von Württemberg, a work of considerable artistic merit. Above it stands the wall tomb of Count Johann Ludwig (who died in 1545) with his two sons. The octagonal **font★** (15C) made of red sandstone shows the *Ecce Homo* motif and an angel with the instruments of the Passion.

Deutsch-Französischer Garten

Deutschmühltal, in the direction of Forbach. A park (50ha/124 acres) with a Lilliputian world straight out of Gulliver's Travels, chair-lift and Europe's largest water organ beckons visitors to promenade outside the gates of Saarbrücken.

Excursions

Weltkulturerbe Völklinger Hütte★

In Völklingen, 10km/6mi west of Saarbrücken. ♿ Open Apr to Oct, 10am-7pm; Nov to Mar, 10am-6pm. Closed 25 and 31 Dec. €7.50. ☎ (068 98) 910 00; www.voelklinger-huette.org

This iron and steel works was established in 1873. After being taken over by the Röchling family in 1881, it developed into a major industrial centre, ultimately covering all stages of iron and steel manufacture. For over a century the town of Völklingen was dominated by the iron and steel works, which brought work and prosperity to the whole region. When the blast furnaces were closed down in 1986, it signalled the end of an era. During its heyday, the monumental works employed more than 16 000 people.

This plant, with its six blast furnaces and blast preheaters, is quite unique within Europe, and in 1994 it became the first industrial monument to be included in the UNESCO world cultural heritage list.

Under expert guidance, visitors are familiarised with the various stages of pig iron manufacture, namely the sintering plant, coking plant, blast furnaces. The high spot of the tour is the visit to the vast gas **blower hall★**, a cathedral of industrial culture with its heavy machinery dating from the early 20C.

Homburg : Schloßberghöhlen

20km/12mi east on the A 6 motorway. Open Apr to Oct, 9am-6pm; Nov-Mar, 9am-4pm. Closed last 2 weeks in Dec to first week in Jan inclusive. €3. ☎ (068 41) 20 64; www.homburg.de

The largest coloured sandstone caves in Europe are man-made. Mile long corridors, 2km/1mi of which can be visited, extend over 12 levels. The caves were built between the 11C and 17C and were mainly used for defence purposes. They served as munitions and food stores, and during the Second World War they were used as air raid shelters. At a constant temperature of 10°C/50°F, the humidity is between 80 and 90%. Ventilation is natural.

Römermuseum Schwarzenacker

2km/1mi east of Homburg, on the B 423. Open Mar to Oct, Tue-Sun, 9am-6pm; Nov to Feb, Sat-Sun, 10am-4.30pm. Closed 24 Dec-1 Jan. €3. ☎ (068 48) 875.

The **Roman settlement of Schwarzenacker** was apparently as large as the medieval town of Worms. It was founded at around the time of the birth of Christ and was destroyed by the Alemanni in AD 275. The excavations uncovered roads, buildings and also many examples of different skills. The house of an optician and a columned house with a cellar have been reconstructed and are graphic examples of Roman architecture. The finds are exhibited in a Baroque house, the *Edelhof*, from where a Baroque garden leads to the open-air museum.

Unteres Saartal

Saar Valley

The region of the Saar Valley, far from the tourist routes, has remained unspoilt. Between Mettlach and Konz, where it flows into the Moselle, the River Saar cuts its way through the crystalline Hunsrück massif, the resistance of which reduces this stretch of the river valley to a winding defile. Ten percent of the total vineyard coverage of the area between the Moselle, Saar and Ruwer rivers lies between Konz and Serring. Grapes, predominantly Riesling, have been cultivated here since the 18C.

Location

Michelin map n° 543 Q 3 – R 3 – Rheinland-Pfalz and Saarland. To the south of the Moselle Valley, the Saar valley runs along the French and Belgian borders. The B 51 road links the curves of the Saar to Saarburg and on to Trier.
Surrounding area: see MOSELTAL (suggested itinerary includes Trier), SAARBRÜCKEN (53km/33mi southeast), EIFEL (Manderscheid is 56km/35mi north).

Tour

FROM METTLACH TO TRIER

57km/35mi – about 2hr

Mettlach

The Baroque, red sandstone façade of the old abbey – now the headquarters of Villeroy & Boch ceramics company – rises above the trees bordering the road leading uphill towards Merzig. Downstream, in the historic abbey gardens, stands the "Alter Turm", a ruined octagonal funerary chapel for Lutwinus the abbey's founder which dates from 989.

Cloef★★

7km/4mi west of Mettlach then 15min on foot there and back.
From a viewpoint high above the river, there is a breathtaking view of the Montclair loop, a hairpin curve enclosing a long, densely wooded promontory.
From Cloef or Orscholz it is possible to take a detour *(about 30km/18mi there and back, via L 177 and B 406)* towards the Moselle valley and the Roman villa of Nennig.

Römisches Mosaik in Nennig★★

♿ *From mid-Jan to end Sep, Tue-Sun, 8.30am-12 noon, 1-6pm; Oct-Nov, Tue-Sun, 9am-12 noon, 1-4.30pm. Closed 1 Nov. €1.50. ☎ (068 66) 13 29; www.nennig.de*
In 1852 the remains of an enormous Roman villa thought to date from the 2C or 3C AD with a 120m/394ft-long façade were discovered. A superb floor mosaic survives (16x10m/52x33ft). It consists of eight medallions framed by intricate geometric designs and illustrating combat scenes between gladiators and animals in the arena of Trier amphitheatre.
Return to Mettlach.
From Mettlach to Saarburg, the road runs at the foot of the valley, forested on the lower slopes, with tall escarpments above. Vines appear as the valley widens.

Saarburg

This picturesque town on the banks of the Saar is dominated by its mighty ruined fortress. This was first recorded in 964 and later belonged to the electoral princes of Trier. It was blown up by the French in 1705. There is a good view of the town and Saar valley from the site.
The **old town**, listed as protected, with its charming medieval alleyways and half-timbered houses and a 20m/65ft waterfall right in the centre of town, makes a delightful scene. The local museum (Amüseum am Wasserfall), the Hackenberger Mühle watermill museum by Leukbach and a bell-casting foundry are further attractions.
After Konz, where the Saar joins the Moselle, follow the river to Trier.

Trier★★ *See TRIER*

German wines

Since legislation passed in 1971 and 1982, German wines can be divided into four categories:
(Deutscher) Tafelwein – table wine with no clearly defined region of origin, which may in fact be a blending of other Common Market wines or of purely German ones,
Landwein – medium quality wine which carries a general indication of origin (eg Pfälzer Landwein) and can only be made from officially approved grapes; it must have at least 55° Öchsle and be dry or medium dry,
Qualitätswein bestimmter Anbaugebiete – wine of superior quality which carries an allocated control number and originates from one of the officially recognised regions (Gebiet), eg Moselle, Baden, Rhine,
Qualitätswein mit Prädikat – strictly regulated wine of prime quality, grown and made in a clearly defined and limited area or vineyard and generally carrying one of the following descriptions: Kabinett (a perfect reserve wine), Spätlese (wine from late-harvest grapes), Auslese (wine from specially selected grapes), Beerenauslese and Trockenbeerenauslese (sweet wine) or Eiswein (wine produced from grapes harvested after a minimum -7°C frost).

Sächsische Schweiz★★★

Swiss Saxony

The region known as Swiss Saxony is one of Germany's most popular – and most spectacular – natural wonders. It is an area of sheer sandstone cliffs, of table-shaped outcrops and isolated pillars, of deep gorges gouged from the rock and fantastically shaped formations through which the upper reaches of the Elbe flow in wide curves between Bad Schandau and Stadt Wehlen. The valley can be explored by road, following the suggested itinerary below, or by river, on one of the "Weiße Flotte" boats which link Dresden and Bad Schandau.

Location

Michelin map nº 544 M 15, 16 – Sachsen. Swiss Saxony lies between Dresden and the Czech frontier, on the upper course of the Elbe.

Surrounding areas (distances from Dresden): see DRESDEN, MEISSEN (23km/14mi northwest), BAUTZEN (64km/40mi east), GORLITZ (107km/67mi east).

Background

Geological formation – The Elbe sandstone massif *(Elbsandsteingebirge)* is part of the Mittelgebirge range on whose edge it stands. This was formed by a fault in the Earth's crust between the Lausitz mountains to the northeast and the Erzgebirge range to the southwest. The highest summit is the Großer Winterberg (552m/1 810ft). At the beginning of the Late Cretaceous period about 100 million years ago, Swiss Saxony was part of a sea of limestone.

Tour

ROUND TOUR FROM DRESDEN

78km/49mi – one day

Dresden★★★ *See DRESDEN.*

Leave the city to the east by Pillnitzer Landstraße on the town plan.

Pillnitz Schloß★ *See DRESDEN: Excursions.*

Bastei★★★

The **view★★** from this rocky spine across the Elbe Valley to the table mountains of Swiss Saxony is famous. The top of the ridge is split by numerous fissures. The narrow rocky outcrop projecting furthest towards the Elbe is the Bastei itself, the top of which towers 190m/620ft above river level. The spectacular, almost lunar, landscape of these unusual rock formations is all the more impressive for being seen close at hand, with visitors actually able to touch the rocks that make up this dramatic scenery.

A short stretch downhill leads to the 76m/250ft long Basteibrücke. There are numerous waymarked footpaths through the surrounding rocks.

Bad Schandau★

Apart from being the main tourist centre of the region, Bad Schandau is also a spa renowned for the properties of its iron-rich waters, which have been exploited since 1730. At the exit from the town, in the direction of Schmilka, a lift and a footpath lead to the Ostrauer Scheibe, from which there is a superb **view★** of the Schrammsteine – a chaotic rock massif much favoured by amateur mountaineers.

The **Kirnitzsch Valley★** *(Kirnitzschtal)*, which can be followed by mountain railway, is hemmed in by steep cliffs.

Cross the Elbe at Bad Schandau and turn right along the south bank (B 172) towards Königstein fortress.

The Bastei viewpoint, Swiss Saxony

D. Scherf/MICHELIN

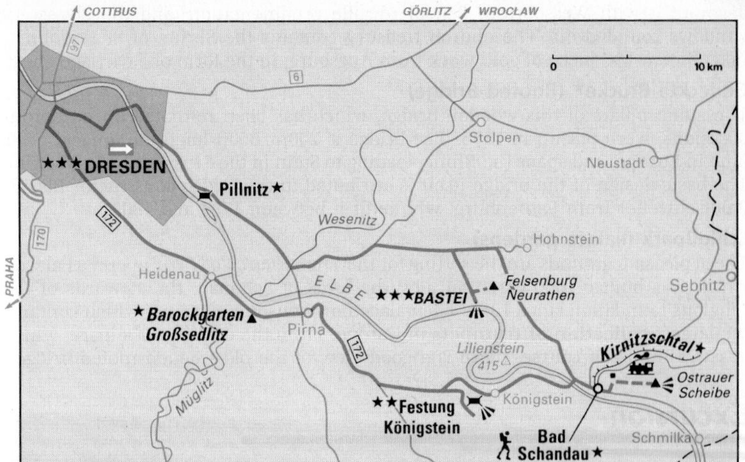

Festung Königstein★★

The great sweep of the Elbe here is overlooked by the 415m/1 362ft Lilienstein on the east bank, and the **Königstein** (360m/1 181ft) on the west. The formidable **fortress** crowning the latter was built between the 13C and the 16C, strengthened and enlarged in the 17C and 18C, and served several times as a refuge for the Court of Saxony. Prisoners held there had very little chance of escaping. Among the most famous internees were JF Böttger, the inventor of hard-paste porcelain *(see MEISSEN)*; August Bebel, founder with Karl Liebknecht of the Social Democrat party in 1869; and Fritz Heckert, co-founder of the Spartacists and later prominent German Communist party member. From the old rampart walk, which follows the edge of the Erzgebirge, there are splendid **views★★** of the Lausitz foothills and the distant mountains of Bohemia.

Barockgarten Großsedlitz★

♿ *Open from mid-Mar to end Sep, 8am-8pm; Oct, 8am-5pm. €2.60. ☎ (035 29) 563 90.*
This **garden** pleasure ground was commissioned in 1719 by Count Wackerbarth and laid out in the French style by some of the famous artists of the day: Pöppelmann, Knöffel and Longuelune. August the Strong took the project over in 1723 and it was completed in 1732. Großsedlitz still ranks among the finest achievements of Baroque German landscape gardening. Features include gardens delineated by patterns of hedges, ornamental flower beds, sandstone sculptures, numerous water features, two orangeries and a miniature palace.
Return to Dresden on B 172.

Bad Säckingen★

Säckingen and its Benedictine convent passed into the hands of the Habsburgs in 1173 where they remained until 1805. The warm springs at Bad Säckingen were no doubt already in use in the Middle Ages, although the town was only officially dubbed "Bad" (the German prefix for a spa town) in 1978. There is clear evidence of the architectural influence of nearby Switzerland in the buildings of this town on the banks of the Rhine south of the Black Forest.

Location

Population: 16 800. Michelin map nº 545 X 7 – Baden-Württemberg. The town has grown up around the 9C Benedictine convent and is located on the edge of the Black Forest near Switzerland.
🅸 *Waldshuter Straße 20, 79713 Bad Säckingen, ☎ (077 61) 568 30.*
Surrounding area: see ST BLASIEN (40km/25mi north), BADENWEILER (46km/29mi northwest), SCHWARZWALD (Belchen is 47km/29mi north).

Worth a Visit

Fridolinsmünster★

This church is named after St Fridolin, the missionary who converted the Alemanni, and who founded a missionary cell here in 522. The barrel-vaulted processional crypt has survived from the Carolingian era. The present basilica was built in the Gothic style in the 14C and later had Baroque features added to it: the once pointed arcades were filled in to become round arches; the vaulting lowered in order to decorate it with Wessobrunn School rocaille ornamentation; and the clerestory windows rounded off. The church treasury contains the Shrine of St Fridolin, a magnificent 18C piece of gold work from Augsburg, in the form of a carriage chest.

Gedeckte Brücke★ (Roofed Bridge)

The stone pillars of this wooden bridge, which has been re-roofed on numerous occasions, were put up in 1575. The bridge is 200m/650ft long, the longest of its kind in Europe, and spans the Rhine, leading to Stein in the Swiss canton of Aargau. The basic design of the bridge itself is attributed to the bridge constructor Blasius Baldischweiler from Laufenburg, who built it between 1785 and 1803.

Schloßpark (Palace gardens)

These pleasant grounds are the setting for the *Trompeterschloß* (Trumpeter's Palace), which was built c 1600 essentially by the lords of Schönau, the stewards of the religious foundation since 1360. The palace now houses a museum, which contains the largest **collection of trumpets** in Europe. From the corner of the park, which boasts a mini-golf course, there is a good view of the old wooden roofed bridge.

Excursion

Waldshut

26km/16mi west. Halfway up a wooded, semicircular slope rising from a curve in the Rhine, this small town retains its two fortified gateways. The heart of the historic **old town★** is **Kaiserstraße** – a street whose orderly line of houses is broken only by overhanging eaves. It is delimited to the west by the Lower or Basle Gate and to the east by the Upper or Schaffhaus Gate.

The Late Baroque **town hall**, built in 1770, is thought to have been designed by Johann Caspar Bagnato. This fine building boasts a magnificent doorway with cartouches and a turret with a sundial. Among the grand houses along Kaiserstraße, note in particular the *"Wilder Mann"*, a 16C town house with a typical overhanging gable. The *"Alte Metzig"* (Butcher's Gateway) built in 1588 now houses the **Local Museum** *(Heimatmuseum)*.

Salem★

Salem was founded in 1134 by the Cistercian Order and remained one of the the most important foundations of this Order on German soil for over 650 years. As a self-governing institution it was answerable only to the Emperor and the Pope. It was at its most influential under Abbot Anselm II (1746-78), the builder of the pilgrimage church at Birnau. Since 1802, it has been the property of the Margraves of Baden.

Location

Population: 11 000. Michelin map nº 545 W 11 – Baden-Württemberg. Salem is to the extreme south of Baden-Württemberg, on the edge of a small lake, only 7km/4mi away from its larger cousin, Bodensee (Lake Constance).

Surrounding area: see BODENSEE (tour passes through Birnau, 8km/5mi south), KONSTANZ (54km/34mi southeast), WEINGARTEN (36km/23mi east), SIGMARINGEN, SCHWÄBISCHE ALB (40km/25mi north).

Worth a Visit

Münster★

The central part of the complex is the High Gothic abbey church. Construction was begun in 1297, and the church was consecrated at the start of the Council of Constance in 1414. The austerity of the exterior is tempered by the delicate tracery of the bays lighting the east and west gables.

Inside, the design is typical Cistercian Gothic, with a large chancel and flattened chevet, soaring vaults and side aisles supporting the nave through walls abutting on wide arcades. The unusual alabaster decoration is thanks to Abbot Anselm II.

Schloß★

♿ *Open Apr-Oct, 9.30am-6pm, Sun, 10.30am-6pm. €5.50. ☎ (075 53) 814 37.*

The old abbey buildings and present palace, almost completely destroyed by fire in 1697, were rebuilt by Franz Beer as the third of the Salem abbey buildings. The complex encompasses three inner courtyards. Its size and decoration testify to the tremendous wealth that Salem abbey accumulated over the course of its history. The ceiling of the old summer refectory still boasts its fine Wessobrunn stucco ornamentation, the work of the Schmuzer brothers. These artists were also responsible for decorating the library ceiling with its fine basket-handle vaulting. Further highlights of a tour round the palace must include the Bernardus passage, the Imperial Hall completed in 1707 – the first great State Hall in the Baroque style in any German abbey – and the Rococo study of Abbot Anselm II.

Untertor-Haus (Lower Gatehouse)

Between the pilasters of this strikingly elegant Baroque entrance, the decorative window lintels have a different design on each storey.

Feuerwehr-Museum

500 years of the history of the fire brigade is brought to life here, with equipment from around the world.

A distillery museum in a show distillery explains the production of spirits *(Branntwein)*, while the Cooperage Museum, housed in an old winepressing room with a huge winepress dating from 1706, sheds light on this old profession. Craftsmen and women demonstrate their art in a special handicrafts village.

▶▶ Distillery Museum *(Brennereimuseum)*, Cooperage Museum *(Küfereimuseum)*, Animal park *(Affenberg, 4km/2.5mi south)*.

Sauerland★

The meanders of the Lenne and the Rhur rivers cut through the forest-covered mountain range of the Sauerland. The picture-postcard countryside is popular with visitors all year round: skiers converge on the town of Wintenberg in winter months, and in the summer, as well as walkers and cyclists, the region's many lakes also make it popular with water sports enthusiasts.

Location

Michelin map n° 543 L 6 – M 7 to 9 – Nordrhein-Westfalen. The Sauerland stretches from the southeast of Rhineland to north Westfalen. The region is easily reached via the A 46 and the A 44 to the north and by the A 46 to the south.

Surrounding area: see MÜNSTER (63km/39mi north of Soest), ESSEN (83km/52mi west of Soest), KÖLN (86km/54mi southwest of Attendorn), DÜSSELDORF (119km/74mi west of Attendorn), KASSEL (122km/76mi east of Soest via the A 44).

Background

Mountains, lakes and forests – The Sauerland, which forms the hinterland to the Ruhr Basin, is the most mountainous, if not actually the highest part, of the Rhineland Schist Massif. It is crowned by the **Langenberg** (843m/2 766ft), near Niedersfeld, which is already in effect a transitional area linking the Sauerland with the Waldeck heights.

Numerous artificial lakes in the region supply water and hydroelectric energy to the industrial towns of the Ruhr, serving also as centres for water sports. The Upper Sauerland, especially the Rothaargebirge, a range covered by forests of beech and fir, is very popular with tourists.

Tour

FROM SOEST TO BAD BERLEBURG

181km/112mi – allow one day

Soest★

The famous German **Pumpernickel**, dense black rye bread which is baked for 16-24 hours, is made in Soest. The townscape is characterised by half-timbered buildings lining radiating streets. Various church towers can be seen above the wall surrounding the town centre.

Patroklidom – The interest in this massive 11C-12C Romanesque building lies entirely in the **Westwerk★★** and its perfectly balanced square **tower★★** austerely decorated with blind arcades and blind rose windows. The two tiers of arcades lightening the upper part of the tower are matched by two more at the base, the lower of which is furnished with very delicate small columns. The Romanesque frescoes in the apse of the north transept are original, having survived the Second World War. The others were restored to Romanesque designs in 1950.

Wiesenkirche★ – Length, width and height are virtually identical in the nave of this beautifully-lit 14C Gothic hall-church. A late-14C Virgin and Child can be seen at the pier of the south doorway. The 1520 **stained-glass window** of the Last Supper, above the north doorway, gave the artist the chance to advertise some local specialities: boar's head, ham, pitchers of beer and small loaves of rye bread can be recognised on the table. The most important work of art in the church is the 1525 **Aldegrever Altarpiece**★ – the Virgin Mary between St Anthony and St Agatha, bathed in a halo of light – in the south apsidal chapel.

Möhnesee★

This artificial lake on the northern edge of the Sauerland is 10km/6mi long. The dam retaining the reservoir is 650m/700yd across and almost 40m/131ft high. To the north, the lakeshore is open to tourists and those practising water sports. On the other hand, the south bank, which is well forested, is a nature reserve harbouring many species of birds, some of them very rare.

Arnsberg

The old town is built on a spur enclosed by a bend in the River Ruhr, rising in tiers above the waterside. To the north, a clock tower commands the approach to the Schloßberg ruins; to the south, near the old abbey, stands a superb Rococo gate, the *Hirschberger Tor*, decorated with hunting scenes.

Beyond Arnsberg, the road skirts the right bank of the Sorpesee reservoir (water sports) and then crosses the Lennegebirge massif. There are many attractive viewpoints, particularly near the pass. On the far side of Finnentrop, the Bigge Valley is punctuated by a number of rock-strewn passages.

Attahöhle★ (Grotto)

On the right-hand side of the road (signposted), just before Attendorn. Guided tour (40min). Open Mar to Apr and Oct, 10am-4pm; May to Sep, 9.30am-4.30pm; Nov to Feb, Tue-Sun, 10.30am-3.30pm. Closed 24 and 25 Dec. €5.50. ☎ (027 22) 937 50.

This strange cavern eroded from the limestone cuts into the bedrock for no less than 3km/2mi. Apart from a multitude of stalactites and stalagmites, curious stone "draperies" are visible, some of them translucent.

Attendorn

The reputation of Attendorn was at its height in the Middle Ages, as witnessed by the splendid 14C town hall (Historisches Rathaus) with its stepped gable, the open, arcaded hall of the old covered market (Alter Markt), and the **"Sauerland cathedral"** (Sauerländer Dom). This Gothic hall-church has magnificent 14C interior decorations.

Southeast of Attendorn, on the other side of the Bigge, is **Burg Schnellenberg**, which dates, in its present form, largely from the 17C.

Biggetalsperre

This dam, in service since 1964, forms with the **Lister barrage** – which has flooded an adjacent valley – the largest reservoir in Westphalia.

About 2km/1mi before Olpe, fork left on the B 55. Soon after Bilstein, on a small mountain road, take a right turn in the direction of the Hohe Bracht.

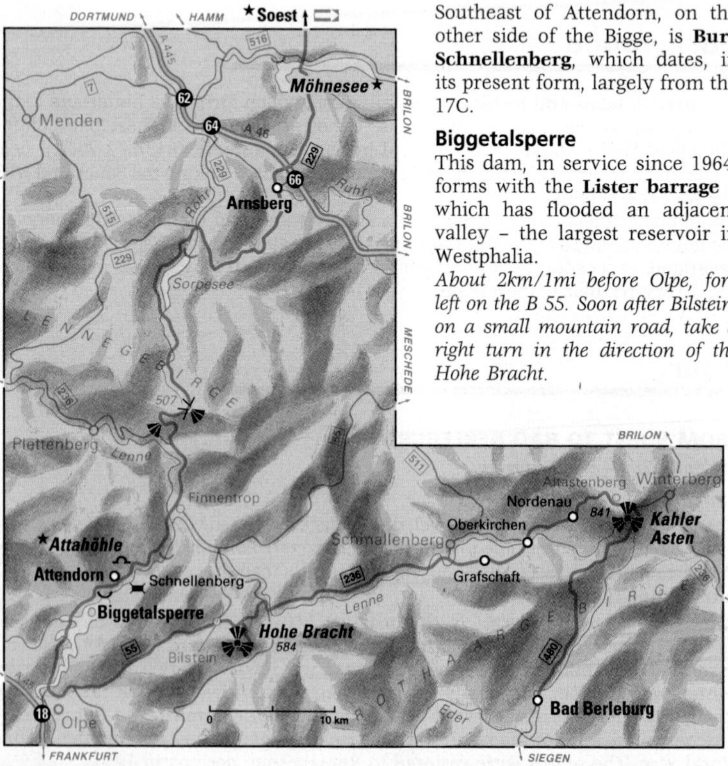

Hohe Bracht

Alt 584m/1 916ft. From the viewing tower (620m/2 034ft above sea level), there is a fine panorama, including the hummocked Rothaargebirge massif as far as Kahler Asten.

After crossing the rural landscape of the Lenne Valley, the route passes **Grafschaft** *and* **Oberkirchen**, *two villages with charming half-timbered houses, and then the country becomes wilder and more hilly. Beyond* **Nordenau**, *a typical Upper Sauerland village where the houses are roofed with slate, is the ski station of Altastenberg. Finally, on the far side of an open upland plateau with splendid views all around, the road arrives at Kahler Asten.*

Kahler Asten

At 841m/2 759ft above sea level, this is the highest point of the Rothaargebirge. From the look-out tower, as might be expected, there is a superb view all around. To the northeast is the spa and winter-sports centre of Winterberg.

Slate quarries flank the road back down, which twists and turns but is well made. There are many attractive views towards the south.

Bad Berleburg

The townscape of the Kneipp spa resort Bad Berleburg is definitively characterised by the castle of the princes of Sayn-Wittgenstein at the heart of the historic town centre. The origins of the castle date from the 13C, although the present building's appearance bears the stamp of later Baroque additions. The castle now serves as a venue for concerts.

Schleswig★

Schleswig-Holstein's oldest town makes a striking impression with its bright welcoming houses when approached from the south. Smaller in size than the rival towns of Lübeck or Kiel, Schleswig has a number of interesting sights. The town's relaxing atmosphere makes it a particularly pleasant stop for those in search of discovery and relaxation.

Location

Population: 26 000. Michelin map nº 541 C 2 – Schleswig-Holstein. Schleswig was built on low-lying banks at the inner end of an arm of the sea, the Schlei, which penetrates the coast for 43km/27mi. From the car park on the B 76, there is an attractive **view**★ of the old town below the cathedral, on the far side of the water.

Plessenstraße 7, 24837 Schleswig, ☎ (046 21) 98 16 16.

Surrounding area: see HUSUM (36km/23mi west), KIEL (56km/35mi south), HAMBURG (124km/78mi south, direct route via the A 7 motorway).

Directory

Where to Eat

⊖ Eckernförder Fischdeel – *Kattsund 22 – 24340 Eckernförde – Follow the signposts to the port (Hafen) – ☎ (04351) 56 51 – www.eckernfoerder-fischdeel.de – Open Thu-Tue, 11.30am-2.30pm, 6-10pm, Closed Wed and 1 Nov – no credit cards – Booking advised – €17.50/32.* Specialising in fish dishes, this restaurant is in the heart of the charming old town of Eckernförde, near the harbour. Tasty, traditional cuisine in a comfortable environment.

Where to Stay

⊖⊖ Zollhaus – *Lollfuß 110 – ☎ (04621) 29 03 40 – fax (04621) 290373 – info@zollhaus-schleswig.de – Closed Jan and from mid-Nov to mid-Dec – P – 9rm: €65 – Restaurant €21/33.50.* Set in a lively street near the Schlei, with bright, functional rooms furnished in beechwood. Temporary art exhibitions are held in the restaurant-bistro.

Background

The Vikings – Merchants were settled on the south bank of the Schlei at the beginning of the 9C. Their favoured position at the crossroads of the old north-south road to Jutland and the east-west route used to transport light loads from the Baltic to the North Sea, soon made the settlement an important North European trade centre. Some 1 000 people lived here on an area of 24ha/60 acres. The area, Haithabu ("the town in the heather"), was encircled with a vast defence system of which the semicircular retrenchment beside the Haddebyer Noor remains today. Further evidence of the settlement, for example stones with runic carvings such as the Busdorfer Runenstein, is to be found in the Wikinger Museum Haithabu. In the 11C, the townspeople of Haithabu, seeking better defences against attack, crossed back to the north bank of the Schlei to found the town of Schleswig.

Special Features

SCHLOß GOTTORF

The collections merit at least half a day to be fully appreciated. ♿ *Open Apr to Oct, 10am-6pm; Nov to Mar, Tue-Fri, 10am-4pm, Sat-Sun, 10am-5pm. Closed 1 Jan, 24, 25 and 31 Dec. €5.* ☎ *(046 21) 81 32 22; www.schloss-gottorf.de*

Two large museums devoted to the Schleswig-Holstein Land are housed in this 16C-18C palace, once the seat of the Holstein-Gottorf ducal family, which in 1762 became the Imperial House of the Czars of Russia.

Landesmuseum für Kunst und Kultur★★

This museum contains extensive cultural and historical collections (local arts, crafts and traditions). Note in particular the Gothic hall (medieval religious art), the **collections of porcelain and faience★**, the sizeable Cranach collection and the antique furniture. Another highlight is the **Renaissance chapel★★** with its ducal loggia and oratory. Finally, visitors should be sure not to miss the remarkable **Jugendstil collection★**.

An adjacent building houses Rolf Horn's fine collection of works spanning Expressionism to the present. The luminosity of the paintings by Emil Nolde and Alexei von Jawlensky are especially striking. One room is given over to sculptures by Ernst Barlach.

Works by artists of the Brücke are on display on two floors in the old stable – this is the largest collection after the *Brücke-Museum* in Berlin.

Wikinger Museum Haithabu

Terslev fibula in the Viking museum

Archäologisches Landesmuseum★

This museum offers a systematic presentation of Schleswig-Holstein's pre- and early history from the Paleolithic Age to the time of the Vikings. There are spectacular finds dating from the 4C (bodies found perfectly preserved, fragments of clothing, shoes, weapons) rescued from the peatbogs before their decay.

Schloß Gottorf also houses an impressive **ethnological collection,** including Germany's largest display of Japanese weapons.

Nydam-Boot

In the Nydam Hall. This oak-hulled longship with its fine lines dates from about 320 AD and was excavated in 1863 from the Nydam marshes, on Danish territory. It is some 23m/75ft long by 3m/10ft wide and was powered by 36 oarsmen. It is the oldest surviving Germanic longship, and was probably sunk in the peatbogs as a sacrifice in c 350 AD. Further artefacts from Nydam and Thorsberg are on display in the hall.

Worth a Visit

Dom St-Peter★

Thanks to its graceful spire, this brick-built Gothic hall-church can be seen from far off. Enter by the south doorway (St Peter's), which is of stone, with a carved tympanum dating from 1170. The most remarkable work of art is the 1521 **Bordesholm Altarpiece★★**, which can be seen in the chancel. Northwest of the nave lies the 14C cloister, with stylised vine-leaf motifs painted on the vaulting.

The Holm★

This picturesque old sailors' and fishermen's quarter with its low houses (18C and 19C) is centred around a small cemetery and chapel.

Wikinger Museum Haithabu (Viking Museum)

Access via B 76, direction Kiel. ♿ *Open Apr to Oct, 9am-5pm; Nov to Mar, Tue-Sun, 10am-4pm. Closed 1 Jan, 24, 25 and 31 Dec. €3.* ☎ *(046 21) 81 30.*

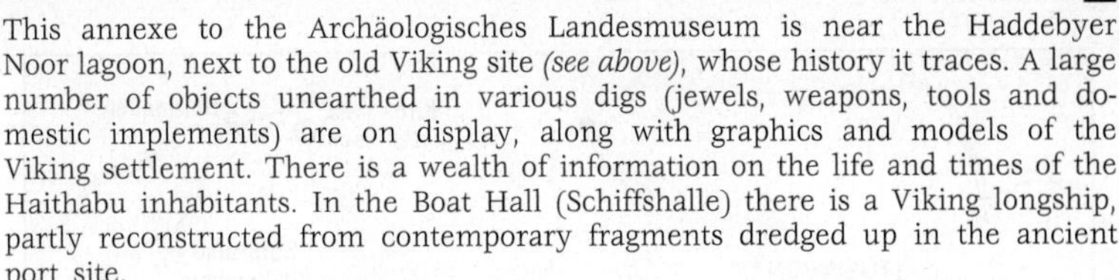
This annexe to the Archäologisches Landesmuseum is near the Haddebyer Noor lagoon, next to the old Viking site *(see above)*, whose history it traces. A large number of objects unearthed in various digs (jewels, weapons, tools and domestic implements) are on display, along with graphics and models of the Viking settlement. There is a wealth of information on the life and times of the Haithabu inhabitants. In the Boat Hall (Schiffshalle) there is a Viking longship, partly reconstructed from contemporary fragments dredged up in the ancient port site.

Schwäbische Alb★

Swabian Jura

The Swabian Jura region is a paradise for walkers, cyclists and those who love old buildings. The highest point is at Lemberg (1 015m/3 330ft). From this summit, the Jura plateaux drop no less than 400m/1 312ft to the Neckar Basin in the northwest.
Mountain outcrops, detached from the main block, form natural fortresses; some were chosen as castle sites by families who went on to enjoy great glory and dynastic fame, among them the Hohenstaufens and the Hohenzollerns.

Location

Michelin maps nos 545 V 10 – T 15, 546 U 13 – T 15 – Baden-Württemberg. To the east of the Black Forest, between Stuttgart and Lake Constance, this itinerary will take you through a karst landscape punctuated by caves, dry valleys and steep-sided gorges.
Surrounding area: see TÜBINGEN (14km/9mi from Lichtenstein), STUTTGART (31km/19mi north), ZWIEFALTEN (35km/22mi northeast of Sigmaringen), KONSTANZ (Constance is 41km/26mi south of Sigmaringen).

Tours

FROM KIRCHHEIM UNTER TECK TO BURG HOHENZOLLERN *125km/78mi – allow one day* 1

Kirchheim unter Teck

The pinnacled tower of the half-timbered Rathaus overlooks the main crossroads. The building dates from 1724.

Holzmaden

The **Hauff Museum★** *(Urwelt-Museum Hauff, follow the arrows)* displays dinosaurs, fish, sea lilies and ammonites found in the 180 million year old Jurassic slate strata locally. *Open Tue-Sun, 9am-5pm. Closed 1 Jan, 24 and 25 Dec. €4.50. ☎ (070 23) 28 73.*

Burgruine Reußenstein (Castle ruins)

45min on foot there and back. Make for the edge of the escarpment to appreciate to the full the **setting★★** of Reußenstein as it dominates the Neidlingen valley. From the look-out point built into the castle ruins, there is a **view★** of the whole narrow valley and, beyond it, the plain of Teck.
After Wiesenstein, with its half-timbered houses, the route follows one section of the Schwäbische Albstraße, *which is marked by blue-green arrows.*

Bad Urach

A pretty town, enclosed deep in the Erms Valley, with half-timbered houses clustered round a central Marktplatz.

Uracher Wasserfall (Urach Falls)

15min on foot there and back. Leave the car in the parking area marked "Aussicht 350m". Impressive **view★** of the valley and the waterfall (flow reduced in summer).

Schloß Lichtenstein

Guided tours (30min). Open Apr to Oct, 9am-12 noon, 1pm-5.30pm, Sun, 9am-5.30; Nov and Feb to Mar: Sat and Sun, 9am-12 noon, 1-5pm. €4. ☎ (071 29) 41 02.
Built on a rock spur protected by a natural cleft, Lichtenstein was completely redesigned and decorated in the "troubadour" style in 1842. Before crossing the entrance bridge, turn right and make for two viewpoints: one overlooks the Echaz Valley, the other the castle itself.

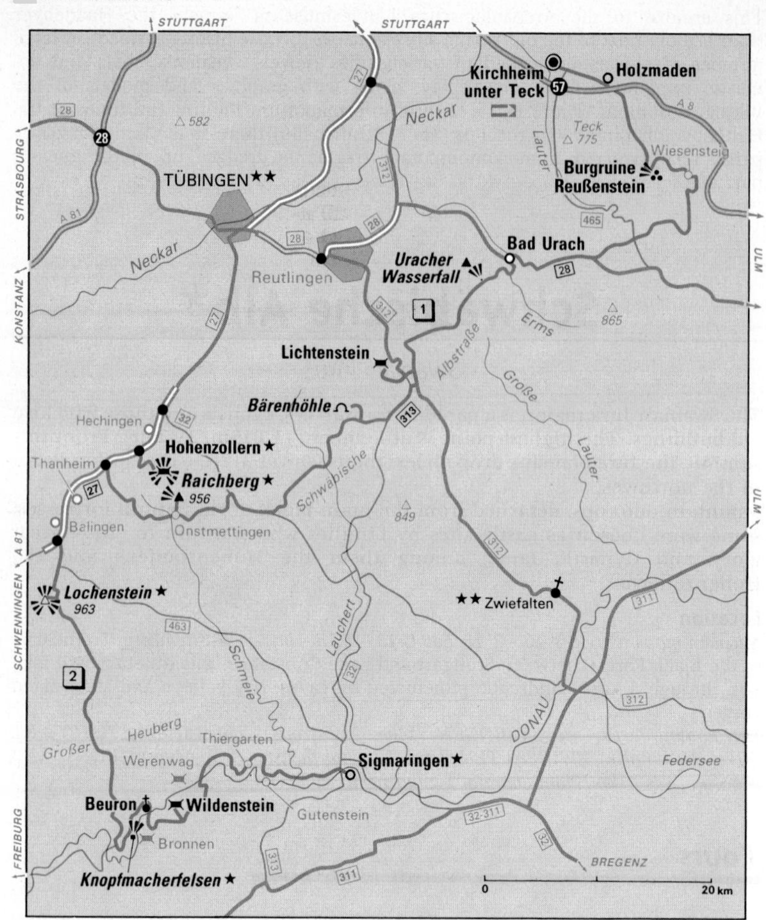

Bärenhöhle

In Erpfingen. Guided tour (30min). Open Apr to Oct, 9am-5.30pm; Mar and Nov, Sat-Sun 9am-5pm. €3. ☎ (071 28) 925 18. The biggest cavern in this "Bear Grotto" contains well-preserved fossilised bear skeletons, as well as the skeleton of a bear on its feet.

At Onstmettingen, follow the signs "Nädelehaus" and "Raichberg".

Raichberg★

30min on foot there and back. Leave the car at the hotel and walk past a brownstone tower, across the fields to the lip of the plateau. From here there is a fine **view★** of the downward sweep of the Jura and, 3km/2mi away, Burg Hohenzollern.

Return to Burg Hohenzollern★ (see entry) via Tannheim and Hechingen.

FROM HOHENZOLLERN TO THE DANUBE GAP★ 2

89km/55mi – allow half a day

Burg Hohenzollern★ – *See Burg HOHENZOLLERN.*

Lochenstein★

30min on foot there and back. Leave the car at the saddle *(Lochenpaß)* and climb to the summit (alt 963m/3 160ft) of the Lochenstein, which is surmounted by a Cross. From here there is a **view★** of the Balingen-Hechingen depression, and still – away in the distance – Hohenzollern Castle.

Beyond the pass, the road sweeps downhill in tight curves and then crosses the bare, rolling uplands of the Großer Heuberg plateau.

Knopfmacherfelsen★

Below the car park, make your way to a viewpoint from which there is a **view★** of the Danube Valley as far as Beuron Abbey and, on the right, Schloß Bronnen.

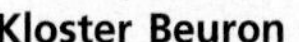

Kloster Beuron

♿ *6am-8pm. No charge.* ☎ *(074 66) 170.* A flourishing Benedictine congregation at Beuron contributed greatly to the revival of monastic life, the liturgy and the use of the Gregorian chant in Germany. The Gnadenkapelle, added to the Baroque abbey church in 1898, is treated in the "Beuron style" – derived from a late-19C school of sacred art much influenced by Byzantium.

Burg Wildenstein

7km/4.5mi from Beuron via Leibertingen. This small citadel commanding the Danube was designed with two moats and a forward defence system on the plateau side comprising two towers linked by a long wall.

Below Beuron, the road follows the **Danube Valley★** *past the rocky fortresses of Wildenstein and Werenwag on the way to Sigmaringen. Approaching the town, the cliffs give way to curious rock needles which form a fantastic ensemble between Thiergarten and Gutenstein.*

Sigmaringen★ – *See SIGMARINGEN.*

Schwäbisch Hall★★

This old town, built in tiers up the steep flank of the Kocher Valley, grew up around salt springs known as far back as Celtic times. In the Middle Ages, it was famous for the Imperial silver coins, the Heller, minted there. The town's well-preserved half-timbered houses and tranquillity make this a pleasant stopping point.

Location

Population: 33 000. Michelin map nº 545 S13 – Baden-Württemberg. Schwäbisch Hall is hidden in the Kocher valley, to the south of the Hohenlohe plain.

ℹ *Am Markt 9, 74523 Schwäbisch Hall,* ☎ *(0791) 75 12 46.*

Surrounding area: see STUTTGART (69km/43mi southwest), ROMANTISCHE STRASSE (ROTHENBURG is 69km/43mi northeast).

Directory

Where to Eat

⊖⊖ **Sonne** – *Gelbinger Gasse 2 –* ☎ *(0791) 97 08 40 – www.hogain.de – Closed Mon – Reservation advised – €21/29.* Pleasant restaurant in the centre of Schwäbisch Hall, with two panelled dining rooms. Regional specialities are on the menu. Enjoy the Biergarten, weather permitting.

Where to Stay

⊖ **Hotel Sölch** – *Hauffstraße 14 –* ☎ *(0791) 518 07 – fax (0791) 54404 – www.hotel-soelch.de – Closed 24 Dec-6 Jan – P ⅹ – 24rm: €39/59 ☕.* This welcoming hotel is located fifteen-minutes' walk away from the old town. Guestrooms are furnished in oak and home-made breads are served at breakfast.

Worth a Visit

Marktplatz★★

Laid out on a slope, this square is dominated by the monumental stone steps of Michaelskirche (where actors, during a festival from June to August each year, perform a repertory of the world's theatre classics). The fine square is flanked by houses in a variety of architectural styles from Gothic to Baroque.

Dating from 1509, the **fountain** *(Marktbrunnen)* stands against a decorative wall adorned with statues of Samson, St Michael and St George *(copies, originals in the Hällisch-Fränkisches Museum)*. The rectangular design, unusual in a Gothic work, includes the old pillory post. The elegant **town hall★** in the Late Baroque style (1730-35) with a slightly bowed central block and beautiful clock tower stands opposite the church.

The two parallel streets of the **Obere** and the **Untere Herrengasse**, linked by stone stairways, are bordered by numerous 15C and 16C half-timbered houses.

Michaelskirche

The church occupies an imposing position at the top of 53 steps. The porch, opening beneath a Romanesque tower with a Renaissance top, has a statue of its patron saint in front of its central pillar. The **interior★**, originally Romanesque also, was transformed into a Gothic hall-church in the 15C. The Flamboyant chancel was added in the 16C. Fine interior fittings.

Hällisch-Fränkisches Museum (Regional Museum)

Open Tue-Sun, 10am-5pm, Wed, 10am-8pm. Closed Good Fri, 24, 25 and 31 Dec. €2. ☎ *(0791) 75 13 60.* This museum is housed in six historical buildings, one of which is an 8-storey tower. The collections cover geology, prehistory and early history from the Middle Ages to the Thirty Years War and the history of Hall until the end of its Imperial City status in 1802, concentrating on the art, culture and everyday life of the townspeople. There is information on the history of the Heller, the region's salt trade, the large fire which almost destroyed the town in 1728 and there is an exhibition of ivory figurines by the 17C sculptor Leonhard Kern, inspired by his travels in Italy and Africa.

The White Gold of Hall

The word Hala means "salt" in old German. The Celts found a salt water spring here and were using it as far back as c 500 BC. Rediscovered in AD 800, the salt works quickly brought fame and fortune to the town of Hall. Green brine was pumped from a well that was dug where Haalplatz now stands, then processed by "distillers" who fed huge wood fires to evaporate the water. The resulting salt – said to be very white, very fine and of high quality – was used until 1924. The town was renamed Schwäbisch Hall in 1934.

Gräterhaus

This beautiful half-timbered house, so exquisitely decorated with diagonal crosses, stands alongside further fine half-timbered buildings in Gelbinger Gasse. It dates from 1605.

T. Krieger/MICHELIN

Half-timbered houses on the banks of the Kocher.

The banks of the Kocher★

From the Henkersbrücke bridge there is an attractive view of the mass of half-timbered buildings on the opposite river bank, and their reflection in the waters of the Kocher. The view is perhaps even better from the junction of the street named Am Spitalbach and the Salinenstraße quay, from which the east end of the old church of St Johann can also be seen. From Unterwöhrd island in the river Kocher and Mauerstraße (the quay on the west bank), there is a fine general **view★** of the old town, with its roofs stepped one above the other at the foot of Michaelskirche, and the imposing 1527 **Büchsenhaus** or *Neubau* (the former arsenal). Below, the arms of the river are spanned by attractive roofed wooden bridges.

►► Galerie Würth *(Modern art, Picasso and German expressionist works)*, Katharinenkirche.

Excursions

Benediktinerkloster Großcomburg★

3km/2mi south. Guided tour (30min). Open from Apr to end Oct, Tue-Fri, at 10am, 11am, 2pm, 3pm and 4pm, Sat-Sun at 2pm, 3pm and 4pm. €2.30.

The church of this old fortified Benedictine abbey still has its three Romanesque towers. The rest of the building was reconstructed before 1715, the interior taking the form of a Baroque hall. Along with those of Aachen and Hildesheim, the church's chandelier is one of the most precious in the West. Dating from 1130 and designed in the shape of a crown, the **chandelier★★★** *(Radleuchter)* is made of iron, subsequently copper-plated and then gilded. In front of the high altar is an **antependium★** of the same period, made of gilded beaten copper representing Christ among the Apostles. The framework supporting this is treated with *cloisonné* enamel and filigree work.

Hohenloher Freilandmuseum★ (Hohenlohe Open-Air Museum)

At Wackershofen, 5km/3mi northwest. Open Jun-Aug, 9am-6pm; mid-Mar to end Apr, Tue-Sun, 10am-5pm; May to beginning Nov, Tue-Sun, 9am-6pm. €5. ☎ (0791) 97 10 10.
Over 50 buildings from the 16C to the 19C, which originally stood in different locations, have been moved to here and faithfully recapture the rural life of this area from the mid-16C to the 19C. There is an exhibition of furniture and agricultural implements.

Schwarzwald★★★

Black Forest

Although it was named after its dark forests of tall conifers steeped in legend, the Black Forest also boasts lakes, pasture land, vineyards, steep roads, and a surprising variety of scenery for such a small region. Add to that its picturesque villages, a passion for cuckoo clocks and the possibilities of hiking in summer and skiing in winter, and it is easy to see why this mountainous region has become one of Germany's most popular tourist destinations.

Location

Michelin map 545 W 8 – Baden-Württemberg. In the southwest corner of Germany, the Black Forest stretches for 170km/106mi from Karlsruhe to Basle and is separated from the Vosges by the subsided plain of the Rhine. It is easily accessible from Stuttgart via the A81, and from Strasbourg or Freiburg via the A5.
Surrounding area: see RASTATT (to the north), ROTTWEIL and DONAUESCHINGEN (to the east), ST BLASIEN and Bad SÄCKINGEN (to the south).

Background

Twin sister of the Vosges – The Vosges and Black Forest ranges both rise from a crystalline base to summits of a similar altitude (the Feldberg at 1 493m/4 899ft and the Grand Ballon at 1 424m/4 674ft). Both drop steeply in the direction of the Rhine, and less abruptly down to the Swabian plateaux in one case, to Lorraine in the other.
The Black Forest, on the other hand, displays no marked north-south line of crests, and no coherent east-west arrangement of passes.

The mountain landscape – The contrast, within a few miles, between the orchards and vineyards flourishing south of Baden-Baden and the upper pasture land *(Grinde)* of the moors crossed by the famous crest road, is remarkable. The primitive conifer forest stretches out in the north and centre of the massif. Everywhere there are lakes and rivers, and the deep valleys that cut into the Upper Black Forest in the south form an almost Alpine landscape.

Varied resources – The economy of the region has always been linked to the forest, wood being practically the sole construction material and the base of all crafts. The trunks of trees, often 50m/165ft long, were floated away as far as the Netherlands, where they were much in demand by boat builders. Clock-making, symbolised among other things by the famous cuckoo clock, remains a fruitful activity. Much of the region's wealth today comes from the spa and winter sports resorts.

Tours

CREST ROAD★★★ 1 (Schwarzwald-Hochstraße)

From Baden-Baden to Freudenstadt. 80km/50mi – about 4hr.

Amply provided with viewpoints and car parks, the Black Forest crest road, or Hochstraße, runs past many winter ski slopes with ski lifts. Much of the route is at heights approaching 1 000m/3 280ft.

Baden-Baden★★ – *See BADEN-BADEN.*

Follow signs "Schwarzwald-Hochstraße/B500".
The road gradually climbs, passing through quiet health resorts such as Bühlerhöhe, at an altitude of 750m/2 460ft.

Black Forest landscape

Mummelsee

This small, dark glacial lake is at the foot of the **Hornisgrinde** (1 164m/3 819ft), the highest point of the northern Black Forest. It is named after the "Mümmeln" (water sprites) that inhabit its icy depths, according to local legend. In days gone by, the Black Forest breweries would obtain blocks of ice chopped out of the frozen lake until well into spring.

At Ruhestein, leave the Hochstraße temporarily to plunge towards the Allerheiligen Valley★ and then climb back from Oppenau towards Zuflucht by way of an extremely steep mountain road.

Allerheiligen★

The ruins of a late-13C church, built for a Premonstratensian monastery, add a romantic touch to this lonely dell. The vaulted porch and the walls of the transept are still standing, together with a Gothic chapel leading off them. A footpath leads from the ruins to the celebrated waterfall.

Allerheiligen-Wasserfälle★ – *45min on foot there and back from the car park at the foot of the falls (2km/1mi beyond the abbey ruins).* A series of seven waterfalls with a total drop of 90m/295ft, along a steep, stepped path between rock walls.

Continue along the Hochstraße towards Freudenstadt.

From Zuflucht to Kniebis, the route crosses an upland plateau, most of it marshy moorland typical of the Grinde.

Freudenstadt★

At the crossing of several tourist routes, the town, built after 1599 by order of the Duke of Württemberg, was destroyed by fire in 1945. Rebuilt since, it now follows a chessboard plan centred on the **Marktplatz★**, a huge square surrounded by houses with arcades.

The 17C church *(Stadtkirche)* is oddly placed: its two naves, arranged at right-angles, form one corner of Marktplatz. Note the carved Romanesque **lectern★★** (12C) supported by the Four Apostles. A further treasure is the **font★** dating from c 1100 and decorated with masks and depictions of animals.

CENTRAL BLACK FOREST★★ 2

From Freudenstadt to Freiburg. 152km/94mi – one day.

The itinerary follows the foot of the Kinzig and Elt valleys, passing through a number of busy villages before reaching the Upper Black Forest at Mount Kandel.

Alpirsbach★

The church, joined to the old Benedictine **abbey★** buildings, is the Black Forest's oldest Romanesque monument (early 12C) and has an unusual layout: the Romanesque base supports a Gothic chancel in which the buttresses do not reach the ground but stand on free columns. The interior is more austere. The deepest niche after the altar bears traces of 12C wall paintings: Christ in Glory between the Chosen and the Damned on the vaulting, and Christ on the Cross between the Virgin and St John on the hemispherical surface. Access to the cloister (late 15C Gothic Flamboyant style) is via the reception area.

Schiltach★★

At the confluence of the Schiltach and the Kinzig lies this picturesque half-timbered village. Its location and a collection of 16C half-timbered houses around the steeply sloping **Marktplatz★** lend this village an idyllic aspect. The town's streets and alleys afford lovely views and beg to be explored.

Directory

Where to Eat

Löffelschmiede – *Löffelschmiede 1 – 79853 Lenzkirch – ☎ (07653) 279 – www.sbo.de/loeffelschmiede – Closed from Nov to mid Dec – €13.50/35.* This little well-kept family-run restaurant is set in a small valley near Lenzkirch. Trout and simple regional dishes are served in the bright and welcoming restaurant with its earthenware stove. A few rooms are also available.

Gasthof Gedächtnishaus – *Fohrenbühl 12 – 78730 Lauterbach – ☎ (07422) 44 61 – www.king-gastro.de – Closed from beginning of Jan to mid Feb – – €14.50/29.* This guesthouse, built in regional style, is in an ideal mountaintop location. The rustic restaurant is decorated in dark wood. Simple accommodation for tired hikers.

Jägerstüble – *Marktplatz 12 – 72250 Freudenstadt – ☎ (07441) 23 87 – info@jaegerstueble-fds.de – Closed from mid Oct to beginning of Nov – €18.50/37.* The rustic setting and relaxed atmosphere of the Jägerstüble, a traditional establishment set in the marketplace, make it popular with locals and visitors alike.

Dorfstuben – *Gärtenbühlweg 14 – 72270 Baiersbronn-Mitteltal – ☎ (07442) 470 – info@bareiss.com – €27/41.50.* Its charming decor and creaking wood make the Dorfstuben a delightful place of refuge. The cuisine is just as delicious, with succulent Black Forest specialities.

Where to Stay

Berggasthaus Gisiboden – *79674 Todtnau-Gschwend – ☎ (7671) 99 98 21 – Fax (07671) 999821 – P – 16rm: €18/36 – Restaurant €11.30/21.60.* Guaranteed peace and quiet at an altitude of 1 200m/3 937ft. This mountain hotel offers simple rooms with showers and a pleasant restaurant with a charming garden. An ideal starting point for hikes and mountain-bike rides.

Hotel Hirsch – *Haus Nr. 10, 72250 Freudenstadt-Zwieselberg – ☎ (07441) 86 01 90 – Fax (07441) 8601959 – info@zwieselhirsch.de – Closed from beginning of Nov to mid Dec – P – 29rm: €30/81 – Restaurant €17/26.* A typical Black Forest hotel which looks quite old from the outside, in an ideal location in the heart of nature. Much of the interior looks brand new. Bright, welcoming restaurant.

Hotel Sonne – *Krumlinden 44, 79244 Münstertal-Obermünstertal – ☎ (07636) 319 – Fax (07636) 377 – www.sonne-muenstertal.de – Closed from mid Nov to mid Dec – P – 13rm: €31/70 – Restaurant €15.20/25.50.* A pleasant little hotel with a new extension, set in the romantic Münstertal. The rooms in the new building, with wooden flooring and furniture, are very comfortable. The restaurant with its partly panelled walls is also pleasant.

Hotel Belchen-Multen – *79677 Schönau-Aitern-Multen – ☎ (07673) 209 – Fax (07673) 7039 – www.belchen-multen.de – Closed from mid Nov to mid Dec – P – 22rm: €32/90 – Restaurant €15/38.* A well-kept hotel in the wilds of the Upper Black Forest, with simple, functional rooms. The covered swimming pool, solarium and sauna are particularly appreciable in bad weather.

Schwarzwaldhaus – *Am Kurpark 26, 79872 Bernau-Innerlehen – Closed from mid Nov to mid Dec – ☎ (07675) 365 – Fax (07675) 1371 – schwarzwaldhaus@freenet.de – P – 15rm: €32/78 – Restaurant €13/32.* This farmhouse covered in wooden shingles is a typical Black Forest establishment. Well-kept and efficiently run with rustic-style rooms. The restaurant is housed in the former stables and serves mainly regional fare.

Hotel Alemannenhof – *Bruderhalde 21, 79822 Titisee – ☎ (07652) 911 80 – Fax (07652) 705 – www.hotel-alemannenhof.de – P – 22rm: €54/154 – Restaurant €20/45.* In a good location on the shores of the Titisee, this modern Black Forest hotel boasts a private beach and landing stage. In addition to the comfortable rooms, the establishment has a pleasant restaurant with two dining rooms, one of them decorated with a stove. The terrace overlooking the lake is particularly inviting.

Freilitchtmuseum Vogtsbauernhof★★ (Black Forest Open-Air Museum), in Gutach

From the end of Mar to the beginning of Nov: 9am-6pm. €4.50. ☎ (078 31) 935 60. The skills of the people of the Black Forest in matters of rural building, craftwork and agriculture are celebrated in this admirable open-air museum in the Gutach Valley. The Vogtsbauern farm, still in its original (1612) state, is set amid six more reconstituted farmhouses with their outbuildings.

Continue towards Triberg.

The road leading through the Landwassereck pass offers a number of fine **views★** over the undulating landscapes of the central Black Forest. Upstream from Oberprechtal, the beautiful cascades of the Elz border the route.

Triberg★

This centre of the clock-making industry is also a favourite health resort. The **Waterfall Walk★** *(1hr on foot there and back)* follows the Gutach rapids in a natural setting of boulders and tall trees. The **Schwarzwald Museum** specialises in the

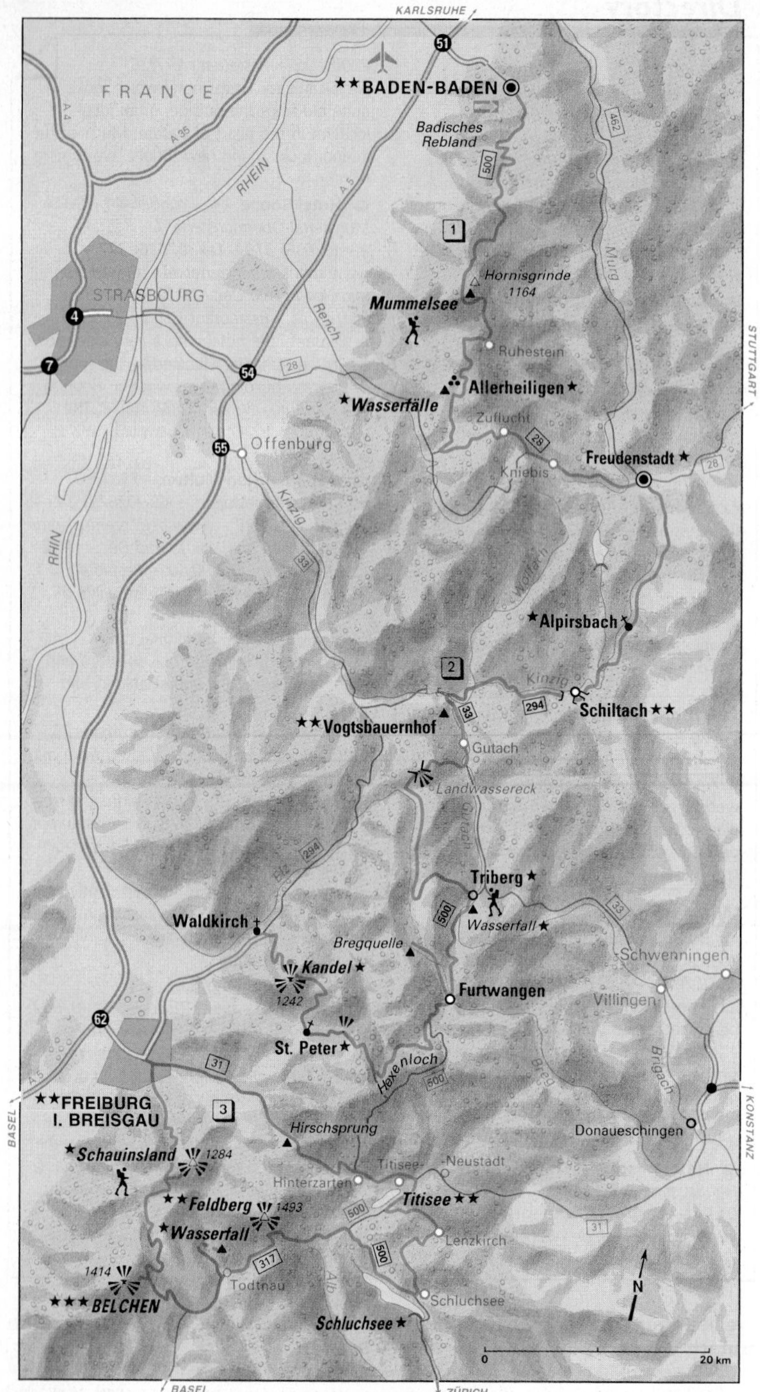

exhibition of traditional costumes and local craftwork. It contains one of Europe's largest collections of barrel-organs. *From the beginning of Apr to mid Nov: 10am-5pm. €3.90.*

The church of **Maria der Tannen (Our Lady of the Firs)**, one of the most popular pilgrims' sanctuaries in the Black Forest, displays carved and painted Baroque **furnishings★** in an exuberant rustic style.

Furtwangen

This health resort lies in a mountain valley 850m/2 790ft above sea level. It has a population of 10 000 and is the cultural and economic centre of this agricultural region. The **Deutsches Uhrenmuseum** displays the world's largest collection of

Black Forest clocks. The exhibition explores the themes of the art, history and technology of clock-making, and presents timepieces from all over the world and from every age. ♿ *Apr-Oct: 9am-6pm; Nov-Mar: 10am-5pm. Closed 24-26 Dec. €3. ☎ (077 23) 92 01 17.*
From the town it is only 6km/4mi to the source of the Breg *(signposts "Katzensteig-Martinskapelle" and then "Donauquelle")*. The Breg, one of the rivers flowing into the Danube which lies furthest from its mouth, rises here at a height of 1 078m/3 537ft. The source of the Danube itself is located at Donaueschingen.

R. Corbel/MICHELIN
A traditional Black Forest house

Soon after leaving Furtwangen, turn right for Hexenloch.
Pass through a deep, steeply wooded gorge enlivened by many waterfalls. Between St Märgen and St Peter, the twists and turns of the road allow plenty of clear **views★★** of the central Black Forest.

St Peter★
Two onion-domed towers top the **church★** of this Benedictine abbey built between 1724 à 1754 after plans by Peter Thumb. The statues by Johann Anton Feuchtmayer inside the church represent the Dukes of Zähringen, a reminder that the abbey was built on the burial place of the founders of Freiburg, dating back to the 11C.
The **library★**, decorated in typical Brigsau Baroque style, boasts a curved gallery punctuated with statues by Christian Wentzinger personifying Science, and a ceiling painted by Benedikt Gambs. ♿ *Guided tour (1hr) Tue 11am, Thu 2.30pm, Sun 11.30am. Closed Good Fri and 3rd Sunday in Advent. €3. ☎ (076 60) 910 10.*
Hikes of all levels of difficulty leave from the various car parks.

Mount Kandel★
From the viewing table here *(30min on foot there and back)* there is a splendid **panorama★** taking in the Vosges, the Feldberg, the Belchen, and the isolated Kaiserstuhl massif.

Waldkirch★
Lovely 18C houses, once the property of the abbey, surround the former collegiate church of St Margaretha in a tranquil, shady quarter of this small industrial town. The Baroque **interior★** of the church is richly furnished.

Freiburg★★ – *See FREIBURG.*

UPPER BLACK FOREST★★★ 3 (Hochschwarzwald)
Round tour leaving from Freiburg im Breisgau. 142km/88mi – one day.

This circuit, mountainous in the first part, passes the three principal summits of the Black Forest (Schauinsland, Belchen and Feldberg), and then the two best-known lakes (Schluchsee and Titisee) in the massif. Since much of the region is a nature reserve, you will often come across rare species of wildflowers, and sometimes chamois. The main health resorts, on the other hand, are overrun with tourists in summer.

Off the Beaten Track

To explore the region in a different light, the "German Clock Road" *(Deutsche Uhrenstraße)* – over a distance of around 320km/199mi – takes you to various sights connected to cuckoo-clocks: museums, factories open to the public, and remarkable clocks (details available from information offices in the region). For railway fans, the Black Forest **train** *(Schwarzwaldbahn)* negotiates a 670m/2 198ft variation in level following the forms of the landscape on a route planned to avoid having to build bridges. Despite the 39 tunnels required to avoid the largest natural obstacles, the journey takes you through some magnificent scenery. The most interesting section (27km/17mi) is between Hornberg and St-Georgen.

Schauinsland★
The mountain road, extremely twisty, leads to the upper cable-car station. From the car park, climb to the top of the viewing tower *(91 steps)* after following the signs "Rundweg" and "Schauinsland Gipfel" *(30min on foot there and back)*. The lookout point offers a **view★** across upland meadows to the Feldberg.
Follow the road for 1km/0.5mi, and take the right-hand fork towards Stohren and the Münstertal.
Winding down through the meadows, the route finally plunges once more into the forest.
At Wiedener Eck, turn right towards the Belchen.

Mount Belchen★★★

From the end of the road, walk (30min there and back) to the viewing table.
This rounded mountain with its steep, bare flanks, dominates the Wiesenthal and the valleys which, like the Münstertal, interlace the western fringe of the Black Forest. The Belchen summit is at a height of 1 414m/4 637ft. When visibility is good, it makes a magnificent **observation point★★★** over the Rhine plain, the rounded heights of the High Vosges, and the Alps from Säntis (Swiss Alps at Appenzell) to Mont Blanc.

The Falls of Todtnau★

1.5km/1mi from Todtnau. Climbing through a wooded combe, a footpath leads *(60min there and back)* to an impressive series of cascades *(Wasserfall)*, gushing down over 97m/318ft.

Feldberg Massif★★

A chair lift *(Feldbergbahn)* conveys sightseers to Mount Seebuck (1 448m/4 750ft), which is crowned by the Bismarck monument. From here there is a **view★** of the symmetrically perfect, circular bowl of the Feldsee, a small lake in the hollow of a glacial cirque. It is possible to reach the bare Feldberg summit at 1 493m/4 897ft *(1hr 30min there and back)* to enjoy, again, a vast **panorama★★** stretching as far as the Alps.

Schluchsee★

This lake, originally glacial, has become – thanks to a dam built in 1932 – the most immense stretch of water in the Black Forest. On its shore is a small climatic health resort which shares its name.
The Titisee is reached via Lenzkirch. During the final part of the descent, the road overlooks the lake.

Titisee★★

This pretty glacial lake with its clear water is at the junction of several tourist routes. Because of its position, it has developed both into a popular tourist centre – Titisee-Neustadt and **Hinterzarten★** – with people drawn by the healthy Black Forest air and climate, and a departure point for many Black Forest excursions.
The return to Freiburg is through the **Höllental★** ("The Vale of Hell"), which – except perhaps in the Hirschsprung Gorge – does nothing to justify its nickname.

Schwerin★

Schwerin renewed its links with an administrative past by becoming a Land capital in 1990 and is without doubt one of the most pleasant towns of northern Germany. With its refined architecture and castle reigning majestically on an island opposite the old town, Schwerin is a city full of character.

Location

Population: 98 000. Michelin map nº 542 F 18 – Mecklemburg-Vorpommern. The town of Schwerin is magnificently situated in a landscape of lakes and forests. The A 24 motorway which links Hamburg and Berlin is about 20km to the south.
Am Markt 10, 19055 Schwerin, ☎ (0385) 592 52 12.
Surrounding area: see MECKLENBURGISCHE SEENPLATTE, WISMAR (31km/19mi north), LÜBECK (66km/41mi northwest).

Background

The oldest town in Mecklenburg – The origins of the town go back to the 11C, when the Slavs built a fortress on what is now an island – Schloßinsel. It was not long, however, before they were expelled by Henry the Lion, the Duke of Saxony, who used the emplacement as a base for the construction of the first German town east of the Elbe. For almost five centuries after that (1358-1918 with interruptions), Schwerin was capital of the Duchy of Mecklenburg. The town escaped for the most part the ravages of war and a major restoration programme has brought out all the character of the old part of the town.

Special Features

SCHLOSSINSEL★★ *allow 2hr*

The island, and the two bridges linking it with the town, separate the smaller Burgsee from the 21km/13mi stretch of Lake Schwerin.

Schloß★

Open from mid-May to mid-Sep, Tue-Sun, 10am-6pm; from mid-Oct to mid-Apr, Tue-Mon, 10am-5pm. €4. ☎ (0385) 525 29 20; www.schloss-schwerin.de

Built between 1845 and 1857 as the residence of the Grand Dukes of Mecklenburg-Schwerin in the neo-Renaissance style – with elements borrowed from the Gothic and the Baroque styles – this is one of the most important civic constructions of 19C Germany. From the outside, it recalls the Château of Chambord on the Loire, which the architects Friedrich August Stüler and Georg Adolph Demmler were in fact inspired by. The museum occupies the old state rooms and apartments with their rich interior decor, paintings and decorative arts from the 18C and 19C. In the former childrens' rooms is an exhibition of European porcelain and court paintings. The **Throne Room**★, the Ancestors' Gallery *(Ahnengalerie)* and the Smoking Room are especially fine. Note also the beautiful **parquet** floors.

J. Bouraly/MICHELIN

The Castle.

Schloßkirche★

The church was built between 1560-63 and was the first newly built Protestant church in Mecklenburg. It was modified in the 19C. The Renaissance galleries and vaulting are supported by Tuscan columns.

Schloßgarten★

Created in the 19C, this formal Baroque garden is organised around canals in the form of a cross and features stands of lime trees and ornamental flowerbeds. The canals are peopled with statues (copies) by Balthazar Permoser.

Worth a Visit

ALTSTADT

Markt

Four late-17C half-timbered houses with gables have been preserved next to the town hall. On the north side of the square, the so-called New Building (Neues Gebäude) was erected between 1783 and 1785 in the Classic style, with Doric columns and attics, to be used as a chamber of commerce.

Directory

Where to Eat

Weinhaus Uhle – *Schusterstraße 15 – ☎ (0385) 56 29 56 – weinhaus-uhle@t-online.de – €19.50/32.50.* Located near the market place, this neat town house is home to a well-run, elegant restaurant (18C vaulted ceiling and pretty arched windows). Huge wine list.

Where to Stay

Niederländischer Hof – *Karl-Marx-Straße 12 – ☎ (0385) 59 11 00 – fax (0385) 59110999 – hotel@niederlaen discher-hof.de – P – 33rm: €90/128 – Restaurant €24/32.* In an old building with listed façade, this hotel fits perfectly into the surrounding urban landscape. The tasteful interior is elegantly furnished and the parquet flooring and warm tones of the restaurant add up to a refined atmosphere.

SCHWERIN

Street	Grid ref.
Alter Garten	CY 3
Apothekerstraße	BY 10
Bischofstraße	BY 15
Enge Straße	BY 25
Franz-Mehring-Straße	BY 27
Friedrichstraße	BY 28
Heinrich-Mann- Straße	BZ 40
Helenenstraße	BY 42
Hermann-Straße	BZ 43
Jägerweg	BZ 46
Jahnstraße	CY 48
Kleiner Moor	CY 57
Lennéstraße	CZ 58
Lobedanzgang	BY 61
Ludwigsluster Chaussee	BZ 63
Mecklenburgstraße	BYZ 66
Puschkinstraße	BY 78
Ritterstraße	BY 84
Schloßgartenallee	CZ 91
Schmiedestraße	BY 94

Dom★
Brick-built in the Gothic style during the 14C and 15C, the church contains several works of art worth a visit. They include a Gothic altarpiece (from a Lübeck workshop, c 1440); a number of 14C funerary plaques; a processional cross (1420) from the Marienkirche in Wismar; and, in the Chapel of the Assumption, frescoes dating from c 1335.

Staatliches Museum★
Werderstraße. ♿ Open from mid-Apr to mid-Oct, Tue 10am-8pm, Wed-Sun, 10am-6pm, Tue; from mid-Oct to mid-Apr, Tue 10am-8pm, Wed-Sun, 10am-5pm. Closed 24 and 31 Dec. €6. ☎ (0385) 595 80.

The **national museum** is near the castle and theatre, by Alter Garten park, in a neo-Classical building (1877-82) with Italian Renaissance ornamentation. It houses important Flemish and Dutch paintings of the 17C (Brueghel, Rembrandt, Rubens, Hals), European painting from the 16C to the 20C (Cranach, Oudry, Gainsborough, Friedrich, Stuck, Corinth) and contemporary art (Cage, Polke). There is also Schwerin's collection of works by Marcel Duchamp. The prehistory section has stone-age remains.

Excursions

Ludwigslust★
The town was founded by Duke Friedrich von Mecklenburg, who moved his residence from Schwerin to Ludwigslust in 1764. The palace and town were built at the same time, under the supervision of the court master builder Johann Joachim Busch.

Schloß★ – The E-shaped Late Baroque building (1772-76) already features some Classical elements. Made of brick, the façade was faced with Pirnau sandstone. Three projections divide the frontage, with the portico in the centre extending over the side sections. The attic parapet which crowns the roof is still adorned with the original 18 vases and 40 statues, produced by the Bohemian sculptor Rudolph Kaplunger. The figures represent the arts, sciences and virtues, and symbolise the special interests of the Duke, so that at his request, allegories were even invented to convey hydraulics and hydrostatics!

Ludwigslust Cardboard Decor

Duke Friedrich's intensive building activity exhausted his funds, but he was determined to decorate his palace in an appropriate, not to say sumptuous manner. The precious and expensive materials used elsewhere were substituted at Ludwigslust by papier mâché. A malleable substance was produced from used paper, glue and water in a time-consuming process, and after it had set, it could be ground, polished and painted. Works of art made of it were even able to withstand the weather. The Ludwigslust workshop achieved such mastery that its products were exported as far afield as Russia. Production stopped in 1835 through lack of demand, and the original recipe was kept a closely guarded secret and has never yet been divulged.

The Interior – White and gold dominate the rooms which are decorated in the German version of the Louis XVI style, with tendrils and shells being replaced by medallions and festoons. The furniture is original. Oil paintings above the doors show countryside and animal motifs.

The **Golden Room★**, which is two storeys high and contains exclusively papier mâché ornamentation, is particularly sumptuous. The Venus Medici in the salon just before the gallery, is in fact also made of papier mâché though it looks deceptively like marble.

An oval lake with a waterfall lies in front of the palace, with a sandstone sculpture by Rudolph Kaplunger displaying two river gods on either side of the Mecklenburg coat of arms. *Open from mid-Apr to mid-Oct, Tue-Sun, 10am-6pm; mid-Oct to mid-Apr, Tue-Sun, 10am-5pm. Closed 24 Dec. €3. ☎ (038 74) 571 90; www.museum-schwerin.de*

Schloßpark – The park covers an area of 135ha/334 acres and is one of the largest of its kind in Mecklenburg-Vorpommern. It was originally created by Johann Joachim Busch, and was transformed in the mid-19C by Peter Josef Lenné. Take a stroll around the park and you will constantly discover new points of interest, including streams, monuments, mausoleums and a limonite grotto (earth containing iron, which produces a porous stone when dried out).

Sigmaringen★

The strong defensive position of Sigmaringen made the town an ideal choice as minor capital of the principality ruled by the Swabian (Catholic) branch of the Hohenzollerns. The castle rises in traditional style from the edge of the cliff, but the only feudal parts remaining are the site and its general appearance: all the buildings and their interior decoration are pastiches of different styles.

Location

Population: 16 600. Michelin map nº 545 V 11 – Local map see SCHWÄBISCHE ALB – Baden-Württemberg. Sigmaringen castle is located on a rocky spur rising from the valley at the mouth of the Upper Danube Gap. The old town developed around a meander in the river framed by forested hills.

🅱 *Schwabstraße 1, 72488 Sigmaringen, ☎ (075 71) 10 62 23.*

Surrounding area: see SCHWÄBISCHE ALB (suggested itinerary leaves from Sigmaringen), ZWIEFALTEN (35km/22mi northeast), BODENSEE (Überlingen is only 41km/26mi south).

Worth a Visit

Schloß

Guided tour (1hr). Feb to Apr and Nov, 9.45am-4.30pm; May to Oct, 9am-4.45pm. Closed Shrove Tue. €6. ☎ (075 71) 72 92 30; www.hohenzollern.com

The State Apartments are adorned in the 16C style with coffered ceilings and tapestries (Portuguese Room, Ancestral Hall etc) and contain valuable furniture and paintings. The weaponry boasts one of Europe's largest collection of arms and armour (15C-19C).

Marstallmuseum – *Under renovation; by appointment only.* The Marstallmuseum houses a display of carriages, sleighs, litters and a collection of works by 15C and 16C Swabian painters and sculptors.

Pfarrkirche St Johann

Luminous with Rococo stuccowork, the church clings to the castle rock. A shrine in a transept chapel on the left contains the cradle of St Fidelio of Sigmaringen (1577-1622), first Capuchin martyr, Patron of the Order and local patron saint.

Speyer★

The old Imperial City of Speyer lies in the Rhine plain and is easily distinguished from some way off by its belfries. A historic city with a prestigious past, the town's cathedral, with its outstanding crypt, is the largest Romanesque building in Europe. Long the object of dispute between France and Germany, Speyer is today a charming town, popular with visitors.

Location

Population: 50 000 – Michelin maps n°s 543, 545 S 9 – Rheinland-Pfalz. To the south of Heidelberg, Speyer is located between the wooded mountains of the Odenwald to the east and those of the Pfalz to the west. The town effectively has its back to the Rhine, which cuts a meander at this point, and is linked to the river only by the Rheinallee and the port.

Maximilianstraße 13, 67346 Speyer, ☎ 06232 – 14 23 92.

Surrounding area: see HEIDELBERG (27km/17mi northeast), BRUCHSAL (35km/22mi southeast), KARLSRUHE (51km/32mi south), PFALZ (Dahn is 64km/40mi southwest).

Directory

WHERE TO EAT

Kutscherhaus – *Am Fischmarkt 5a – ☎ (06232) 705 92 – Closed for 3 weeks in Aug – €21/36.* Behind the half-timbered façade of this old house, meals are enjoyed in comfortably furnished dining rooms. The Biergarten – one of the most charming in the town – has a relaxing atmosphere.

WHERE TO STAY

Hotel Goldener Engel – *Mühlturmstraße 5 – ☎ (06232) 132 60 – fax (06232) 132695 – Closed 23 Dec-7 Jan – P – 46rm: €55/102.* Hotel in the centre of town with individually furnished rooms ranging from rustic to modern in style.

Background

Imperial city – Once favoured as a place to stay by the Salian emperors, and having been an episcopal seat since the 4C, Speyer enjoyed considerable importance from the 11C on. It was made Imperial City in 1294. More than 50 Imperial Diets were held here, the last one taking place in 1570. Speyer was the seat of the Imperial Council from 1526 to 1688. However, Speyer was burned to the ground in 1689 by Louis XIV's troops during the Orléans War. For this reason, the only evidence of its medieval splendour that survives is the Kaiserdom, fragments of the town wall in the cathedral grounds and the *Altpörtel*, a tall tower at the west end of Maximilianstraße that was once the town's main gateway.

Administrative centre – After a brief period under French rule – the town was handed over to France in 1797 – Speyer passed into the hands of the Bavarian monarchs, along with the rest of the Palatinate east of the Rhine. During this period, numerous authorities were based here, including archives and libraries, with the result that Speyer now has a reputation as an administrative centre.

Special Features

KAISERDOM★★

Open Apr to Oct, 9am-7pm; Nov to Mar, 9am-5pm. Donations requested. ☎ (062 32) 100 92 18.

This fine cathedral building, founded by Konrad II in 1030 and remodelled at the end of the 11C, is a Romanesque basilica with four towers and two domes. It is the largest Romanesque building in Europe.

Exterior

There is an interesting **view★★** of the east end from the garden approach to the 13C **Heidentürmchen** (Pagan Tower). An elegant dwarf gallery circles the nave and transept just below the roof. The finely carved capitals display a wide variety of motifs on the garden side of the apse. On the lower part of one of the blind arcades, in the centre, a worn 11C relief depicting the Kingdom of Peace can be distinguished. The window arches of the east transept show Lombard influence and – especially on the south side – a lavish decoration of palm leaves and scrollwork. Similar motifs are repeated on the cornice below the roof.

T. Krieger/MICHELIN

Speyer Cathedral.

Interior

The most impressive way to enter is via the door in the west face (rebuilt in the mid-19C). On the right of the porch is a statue of Rudolph of Habsburg. The huge, well-lit nave has groined vaulting with prominent transverse arches. The half columns engaged in the main pillars are cut by rings and capitals with acanthus leaves.

The sobriety of the side aisles, also with groined vaulting, is remarkable. There is a good view of the building's harmonious proportions from the top of the south aisle stairway.

The raised **transept★★** is a masterpiece of unity and balance. Note particularly, above the transept crossing, the octagonal cupola on squinches with its small lantern tower. The lack of texture and ornamentation on the walls emphasises the natural decorative character of the architecture itself. The central nave was painted (1845-53) under King Ludwig I of Bavaria.

The **Chapel of the Holy Sacrament** *(Afrakapelle, on the left, before the north transept)* houses two 15C low-relief sculptures: the Bearing of the Cross and the Annunciation. Opposite, before the south transept, eight groined vaults surround a two-tier central rotunda in which are the **baptistery** (Chapel of St Emmerammus) and, above, a chapel dedicated to St Catherine.

Crypt★★★

This is probably the finest and largest Romanesque crypt in Germany. Beneath the chancel and the transept, whose crossing above is marked by four columns with splendid cushion capitals, Romanesque groined vaulting spreads out like a net supported by transverse arches of alternately pink and white sandstone.

Four Holy Roman Emperors and four German Kings are buried in the impressive **Royal Vault**. The 13C tombstone of Rudolph of Habsburg stands guard at the entrance.

In the gardens south of the cathedral is the **Ölberg** (1502-12), once the centre of the cloister. A large stone trough – the **Domnapf** – stands in the forecourt. In days gone by, each time a bishop was enthroned, it was filled with wine and anyone who wished to could drink until he dropped.

Worth a Visit

Old Town

This stretches from the cathedral west towards the **Altpörtel★**, a fine 12C-13C gateway tower. Maximilianstraße is a lively street, whose crowning glory is the Late Baroque town hall. At the fork with Korngasse stands the "Alte Münze" (Old Mint) built in 1748; its name is derived from the coin minters' guildhall which stood on this spot in the Middle Ages. There are old houses to be admired in Kleine and Große Greifengasse, Hagedorngasse and Gutenberggasse. The district around the timber and fish market is also picturesque.

The "Protestants"

The Edict of Worms, in fact never enacted, was confirmed by the Diet of Speyer in 1529. The Lutheran states then made a solemn protest against the Diet's decisions, from which derives the label "Protestant" to identify partisans of the Reformation. The fact is commemorated by the existence of a neo-Gothic church, Gedächtnikirche, built early this century on Bartholomäus-Weltz-Platz.

Judenbad (Jewish Baths)

Access via Judengasse, southwest of the cathedral (signposted). Ritual ablutions were performed here. The building *(Judenhof)*, in the centre of the medieval Jewish quarter, was erected in the 12C, by workmen engaged in the construction of the cathedral.

A stairway with double doors leads down to the first chamber, which has groined vaulting and, on the left, an anteroom for changing. A second, semicircular staircase then descends to the level of the water-table, where the actual bath is situated.

Dreifaltigkeitskirche

In Große Himmelsgasse. The **interior★** of this enormous Baroque church (1701-17) is surrounded by a two-storey gallery with a balustrade adorned by paintings. The wooden capped vaulting is painted too.

Historisches Museum der Pfalz★ (Palatinate Museum)

♿ *Open Tue-Sun, 10am-6pm. Closed 25 and 31 Dec. €4.50. ☎ (062 32) 62 02 22; www.museum.speyer.de*

In Gallery 4 on the ground floor of this museum is the celebrated **Golden Hat★** of Schifferstadt, the rarest, most valuable item in the Prehistoric Department. In the shape of a cone, this solid gold religious cult object dates from the 12C BC.

Domschatzkammer (Cathedral Treasury) – *In both the basement storeys of the new building.* There is no doubt that the tomb furnishings of the emperors and kings from the vault of the cathedral are the main points of attraction; for example, the funerary crown of Konrad II, the first Salian emperor, the Imperial orb of Heinrich III, the crown of the Canossa penance of Heinrich IV. There are some magnificent liturgical robes and articles. A little piece of German history is brought to light in a multi-media presentation.

Weinmuseum – *In the cellar.* The museum presents 2 000 years of wine history. The showpiece is the **Roman wine★**, which is the oldest still liquid wine in the world, in its amphora-like bottle. It was found in the Palatinate in a Roman stone sarcophagus dating from the 3C AD. There is a sumptuous collection of decorated barrels, and imposing winepresses dating from the 16C and 18C.

Technik-Museum★

♿ *9am-6pm. €9. ☎ (062 32) 670 80; www.technik-museum.de*

The Technology Museum situated south of the cathedral will interest young and old alike. Displayed in exhibition halls and the open air are an impressive number of aircraft, railway engines, and mainly classic or veteran cars by every famous manufacturer, not forgetting a whole range of fire engines. There is a submarine with which visitors can enjoy a hands-on visit. Being able to go inside the U 9, built in 1966, gives visitors a vivid insight into how terribly cramped conditions are inside a submarine. Further attractions on offer at this museum include a maritime display with model ships and an extensive collection of historical musical instruments.

Those who enjoy big-screen thrills must be sure not to miss the **IMAX-Filmtheater★**, either for conventional cinema or the dome version with an 800m²/8 600sq ft screen.

▶▶ Purrmann-Haus *(birthplace of painter Hans Purrmann, Kl. Greifengasse 14)* – Feuerbachhaus *(birthplace of painter Anselm Feuerbach, Allerheiligenstraße 9).*

Spreewald★★

A network of more than 300 waterways crisscrosses this lush countryside, declared a biosphere reserve by UNESCO – the site of an ancient forest swamp painstakingly cleared and drained – lending it the appearance of a "Venice in the Woods". The region's special interest lies also in its Sorbian minority, descendants of western Slav people who settled in the Lausitz area of Germany after the migrations of the 6C and who remain fiercely proud of their language, traditions and culture today *(see BRANITZ).*

Location

Michelin map n° 544 K 25 – Brandenburg. Spreewald is nearly 100km/62mi to the southeast of Berlin, near the Polish border. The region covers about 260km²/100sq mi and Lübbenau is its capital.

Surrounding area: see BRANITZ (37km/23mi southeast), FRANKFURT AN DER ODER (76km/48mi northeast, see Berlin "Excursions"), BERLIN (93km/58mi northwest).

Worth a Visit

Barge Trip (Kahnfahrt)

Boat trips are available in most places in the Spreewald, although **Lübbenau** *has established itself as the centre for such trips. In Lübbenau, leave the main road opposite the railway station and take Maxim-Gorki-Straße to one of the car parks near the landing-stage.*

Embarkation in Lübbenau harbour. Apr to Oct (weather permitting). Duration: 2-9hr, with a stopover. From €7. ☎ (035 42) 22 25; www.spreewaldexpress.de

Boating in the Spreewald.

Boatmen/guides organise excursions aboard flat-bottomed craft which ferry passengers to the heart of a leafy paradise shaped by man into a limitless garden. Only the ripple of water, the singing of birds and the quacking of ducks break the silence.

A stop at **Lehde★**, a tiny lagoon village with a population of 150 and which boasts almost as many islands as houses, allows sightseers to visit the Open-Air Museum (Freilandmuseum Lehde). Here, three early-19C farms, complete with living quarters and outbuildings, display rustic furniture, folk art, costumes and agricultural implements. Visitors to the museum can learn about barge-building in the Spreewald and about matters related to nature conservation.

Visitors preferring to make these discoveries on foot can choose between three different footpaths starting from Lübbenau: one leading towards Lehde *(1hr there and back)*, another to Wotschofska and a third to Leipe *(3hr there and back)*.

Lübbenau

In addition to a visit to the old town, the town church of **St Nikolai★**, built in 1738-41 by the Dresden master and fortifications builder Findeisen, is well worth a visit. The interior is in an impressively harmonious Dresden Baroque style. Two-storey galleries extend along the sides, opening out into glazed loges in the chancel. There are some impressive tombs, including the high **tomb** (c 1765) of the mediatised (ie no longer an immediate vassal of the Holy Roman Empire and thus deprived of some of his rights of government) Prince Moritz Carl, Count of Lynaer. ♿ *Open from May until the local Autumn school holidays, Tue-Sun, 2-4pm. Closed bank holidays. Donation requested. ☎ (035 42) 36 68.*

Lübbenau castle and grounds are well worth a trip, for the chancellery building (1745, now a museum), the neo-Classical castle (1817, now a hotel) and the orangery.

St Blasien★

The majestic domed church dedicated to St Blaise comes suddenly into view in the southern part of the Black Forest. It stands in the grounds of a medieval monastery founded in 835 by a brotherhood of hermit monks whose influence extended all over the southern part of Germany. The area is characterised by its fresh air and peace and quiet.

Location

Population: 4 200. Michelin map n° 545 W 8 – Baden-Württemberg. St Blasien is located at the far end of a wooded valley in the Hotzenwald and is dominated by the peaks of the Feldberg.

ℹ Am Kurgarten, 79837 St Blasien, ☎ (076 72) 414 30.

Surrounding area: see SCHWARZWALD (Schluchsee is 15km/9mi away), Bad SÄCKINGEN (40km/25mi south), DONAUESCHINGEN (62km/39mi northeast), BODENSEE (115km/72mi east).

Worth a Visit

Dom★★

This Baroque church, following a ground plan much favoured during that period, is built in the middle of what would have been the north wing of the old abbey complex, which had four wings.

The French architect, Pierre-Michel d'Ixnard (1723-95), graced it with a central dome, which rises 64m/210ft from the ground, behind a peristyle. After those of St Peter's in Rome and Les Invalides in Paris this is the third largest dome in Europe (33.5m/110ft in diameter). Inside the dome, which is lit through windows set in deep niches, is a false cupola, suspended from the true dome although it appears to be supported by the columns of the central rotunda. Behind the high altar lies the chancel, which is quite long and roofed with cradle vaulting.

The church and its impressive dome.

T. Krieger/MICHELIN

Excursions

The Hochkopf Massif

45km/28mi west. Drive via Todtmoos to the Weißenbachsattel pass.

Hochkopf – *1hr on foot there and back.* From the car park, to the right of the road, a footpath leads up to the look-out tower, from which there are superb **views**★★ of the barren peaks of the Belchen and the Feldberg, to the west, and – on clear days – the Alps to the southeast.

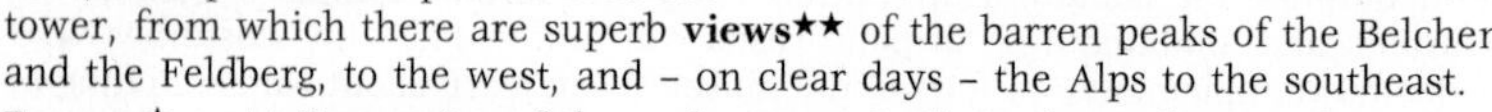

Bernau★ – At Bernau-Innerlehen, the **town hall** (Rathaus) houses the **Hans-Thoma-Museum**, an exhibition of paintings by this local artist, notably some of his Black Forest landscapes executed with great sensitivity.

The Alb Valley (Albtal)

30km/18.5mi south.

The road runs high above the Alb gorges, alternating stretches along the edge of the cliffs with tunnels through the rock, before it reaches the Rhine at Albbruck.

Stendal

Founded c 1160 by the Margrave Albrecht the Bear, Stendal soon developed into an important trade centre. The town was a member of the Hanseatic League from 1358 to 1518, and until the mid-16C remained the most influential in the Brandenburg March. The ravages of the Thirty Years War, however finally dealt it a death blow. Several monuments typical of Gothic brick architecture can still be seen from its period of prosperity. Stendal was the birthplace of Johann Joachim Winckelmann (1717-68), considered to be the founder of a scientific approach to archeology. One of his admirers, the French novelist Henri Beyle (1783-1842), liked the name of the town so much that he adopted it as a pseudonym, adding an extra "h" to become world famous as Stendhal.

Location

Population: 38 000. Michelin maps n°s 542, 544 I 19 – Sachsen-Anhalt. Stendal is on the B 189 road which links it to Magdeburg to the south.

Surrounding area: see MAGDEBURG (64km/40mi south), POTSDAM (101km/63mi east) BERLIN (125km/78mi east).

Worth a Visit

Rathaus

Markt. The oldest part of the town hall, in exposed brick, dates from the beginning of the 15C. The gables are stepped. Added at the end of that century, the main wing was later remodelled in the Renaissance style. The council chamber features richly carved ornamental wall panelling dating from 1462. In front of the court arcade belonging to the town hall stands a statue of Roland, the third largest in Germany and a copy of the original from 1525.

Marienkirche

Behind the Markt. The triple-aisle hall-church was built between 1435 and 1447. The chancel, surrounded by an ambulatory, is separated from the nave by a delicately worked partition. The high altar (Coronation and Death of the Virgin) is in the Flamboyant Gothic style.

Dom St Nikolaus★

The former Augustinian monks' church was supplanted in the 15C by a cathedral of much larger size, the square ground-plan recalling the hall-churches of Lower Saxony, in particular St Johanniskirche in Lüneburg. The 22 stained-glass **windows★** (1420-60) are remarkable. Note especially those in the chancel, which, because of the amount of wall they replace, suggest a huge conservatory.

Uenglinger Tor★ (Uenglingen Gate)

Northwest of the old town. Dating from c 1380, this is one of the most interesting fortified medieval gateways in the region. From the outside, the two lower storeys present an aspect that is purely defensive, while the upper part, added in the 15C, is much more decorative.

Excursions

Tangermünde★

10km/6mi southeast.

Situated, as its name suggests, where the waters of the River Tanger join those of the Elbe, Tangermünde's history closely follows the history of Stendal. The small town, still enclosed within its late-14C ramparts, is crossed by two parallel streets, bordered by half-timbered houses with finely worked doorways. The brick-built Late Gothic (1430) **Rathaus★** has a three-gable façade garnished with a superb lacework of carved decorations.

The town's ancient gateways retain their monumental aspect, particularly the **Neustädter Tor★**, an imposing circular tower on the south side and one of the finest brick tower constructions in north Germany.

Havelberg★

46km North, cross the Elbe at Tangermünde. Overlooking this small, pretty town on the banks of the River Havel is the **Cathedral of St Marien★** consecrated in 1170. The nave was almost entirely rebuilt in the Gothic style between 1279 and 1330 following a fire. The sculpturing of the chancel partition and the **rood-screen panels★★** (1396-1411) is very fine indeed. Illustrating scenes from the life of Jesus, these were probably the work of craftsmen from the Parler studio in Prague. Note also three **sandstone candelabra** and a **Triumphal Cross** (c 1300). The Early Gothic cloister dates from the 13C.

Stralsund★

Separated from the island of Rügen by a narrow sea channel and surrounded by lakes, the Baltic town of Stralsund has developed since the earliest times as a centre of maritime navigation and long-distance trade. Its Gothic brick buildings, inspired by those of Lübeck, its more powerful neighbour, are a distinguishing feature of the townscape.

Location

Population: 59 800. Michelin map nº 542 D 23 – Mecklemburg-Vorpommern. The town of Stralsund is on the Baltic at the far northeasterly point of mainland Germany. A 2.5km/1.6mi bridge links the town to the island of Rügen.

🛈 *Alter Markt 9, 18409 Stralsund,* ☎ *(038 31) 246 90.*

Surrounding area: see Insel RÜGEN, GREIFSWALD (33km south), ROSTOCK (75km west).

Background

A Coveted City – From the moment of its foundation by Prince Wizlaw I of Rügen in 1209, Stralsund was subjected to assaults from envious neighbours: from Lübeck, from Denmark, from Sweden and even Holland they came with their troops to seize this port, so admirably situated. Protected by its massive rampart belt, the town was able during the Thirty Years War to beat off the

Directory

Where to Stay

An den Bleichen – *An den Bleichen 45 – ☎ (03831) 39 06 75 – fax (03831) 392153 – P – 23rm: €55 ☕.* Located in a residential area on the edge of the town centre, this family-run establishment is surrounded by pretty gardens. Close to the old town, port and beach. Practical and comfortable guestrooms.

Steigenberger Hotel Baltic – *Frankendamm 22 – ☎ (03831) 20 40 – fax (03831) 204999 – stralsund@steigenberger.de – 134rm: €99/154 ☕ – Restaurant €20/36.* This hotel is located in a former barracks renovated in an elegantly modern style. Contemporary bistro-restaurant.

forces of the all-conquering Imperial General Albrecht von Wallenstein. Having belonged to Sweden since 1648, it returned to Prussian rule after the Napoleonic Wars. Today, Stralsund's prosperity depends mainly on its shipyards, service industries and administration; tourism is also an important source of the town's income.

Walking About

THE OLD TOWN★

Rathaus★ (Town hall)

Alter Markt. Built in the 13C and 14C, this splendid edifice comprises two separate, parallel blocks. The magnificent **north façade★★**, crowned by a pediment with openwork gables – again, inspired by the Rathaus in Lübeck – was added c 1450. The ground floor arcades open onto a covered market hall. From this a passageway leads to the west porch of Nikolaikirche. Among the old houses bordering the market place, the Wulflammhaus *(no 5)*, brick built in the mid-15C, features an unusual three-storey gable. It is named after a former mayor of the town.

Nikolaikirche★

Alter Markt, opposite the town hall. Modelled on the Marienkirche at Lübeck, this 13C hall-church has seen its central nave raised and its single tower replaced by a powerful façade with two towers. The relatively low ambulatory at the east end is dominated by solid buttresses.

Inside, there is a striking contrast between the modest height of the side aisles, flanked by low chapels, and the spectacular, soaring nave. Certain columns and several chapels still have Late Gothic frescoes. Among the works of art, note the six medieval carved altarpieces, a stone group depicting St Anne (c 1290) and the reredos separating chancel and nave, made at the beginning of the 18C based on designs by Andreas Schlüter.

Leave the Alter Markt and take Mönchstrasse south.

Deutsches Meeresmuseum★ (Oceanographic Museum)

Mönchstraße. Open Jul to Aug, 9am-6pm; rest of the year, 10am-5pm. Closed 24 and 31 Dec. €4.50. ☎ (038 31) 26 50 10; www.meeresmuseum.de

Buildings which once belonged to a former abbey (the Katharinenkloster) have been transformed into galleries devoted to topics relating to oceanography, the sea fishing industry, and to the flora and fauna of the Baltic Sea. Among the aquariums is a huge 50 000l/11 000gal tank stocked with sharks. In the old chancel hangs the eye-catching 15m/50ft long skeleton of a fin-back whale that was stranded on the west coast of Rügen in 1825.

Kulturhistorisches Museum (Historical Museum)

Mönchstraße. Open Tue-Sun, 10am-5pm. Closed 24 and 31 Dec. €3. ☎ (038 31) 287 90.

Sacred art from the Middle Ages, gold and silver plate from the isle of Hiddensee (Rügen), and the history of Stralsund itself, are among the diverse exhibits displayed here.

Continue south until the Neuer Markt.

Marienkirche★

Neuer Markt. Apart from the impressive 104m/340ft west tower, which was added between 1416 and 1478, this church was built towards the end of the 14C. Its originality lies in the fact that the flying buttresses of the chancel are concealed

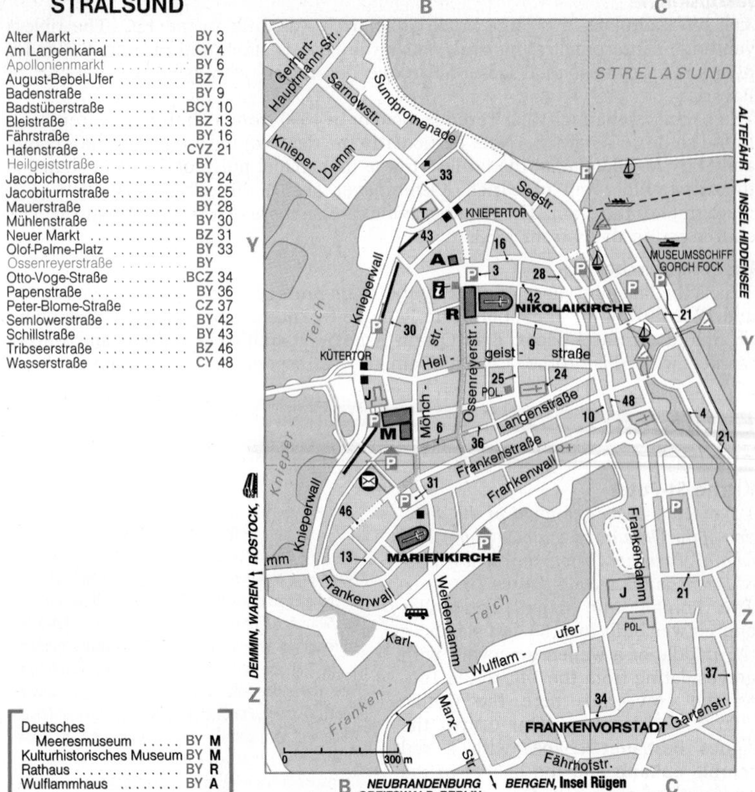

below the roof. The interior of the west tower comprises a central portion flanked by side aisles, in the manner of a transept. There is a Gothic High Altar with the Coronation of the Virgin Mary (15C) and an organ (c 1659) by organ builder Friedrich Stellwagen from Lübeck.

Stadtbefestigung (Ramparts)

The sections on the west side of the town are in the best condition, between the Kniepertor and the Kütertor, beside the lake.

Straubing

Straubing evolved from a Roman military camp. The present town centre, the Neustadt, is however a Wittelsbach addition dating from the early 13C. Straubing was the governmental seat of the dukes of Straubing-Holland between 1353 and 1425 and an important administrative centre for the old kingdom of Bavaria until the early 19C. Modern Straubing is still the economic focus of the region which goes deep into the Bavarian Forest.

Location

Population: 44 000. Michelin map nº 546 T 21 – Bayern. Embraced by a loop of the Danube, Straubing's site in the fertile Gäuboden region, the granary of Bavaria, contributed in no small terms to its prosperity.

Theresienplatz 20, 94315 Straubing, ☎ (094 21) 94 43 07.

Surrounding area: see REGENSBURG (41km/26mi west), LANDSHUT (58km/36mi south), PASSAU (80km/50mi east).

Worth a Visit

Stadtplatz★

The elongated town square is divided into the Theresienplatz *(West)*, with a Trinity column wonderfully adorned with statues and the Tiburtibus fountain (1685), and the Ludwigsplatz *(East)* with the Jakobsbrunnen fountain dating from 1644. In the centre stands an original 14C tower crowned by five pointed turrets, the town's emblem.

Jakobskirche

Just off Stadtplatz, this large brick hall-church was built in the 15C. The ribless vaulting of interpenetrating ovals above the nave is supported on round, slender pillars. This almost total lack of Baroque decoration is unusual for this part of Bavaria.

The panels of the high altar **reredos**, bought in 1590 from a church in Nuremberg, frame some 16C statuary. Note particularly the figure of the Virgin, in the middle, and Mary Magdalene, at the far left. In the first chapel north of the axial chapel is the admirable tomb of Ulrich Kastenmayer (1430), his effigy costumed as a magistrate of the town. The features and expression are of a poignant realism. The church pulpit dates from 1753.

Ursulinenkirche

This is the last joint piece of work by the Asam brothers. It was built between 1736 and 1741 during the transition from Baroque to Rococo and features a rare blend of architecture and decor. Egid Quirin Asam was architect, sculptor and stucco-worker, while his brother Cosmas Damian was responsible for the paintwork.

Excursions

Kirche St-Peter

1.5km/1mi. Leave the town in the direction of the Danube by route 20 (signposted Cham). Turn right before the castle bridge. St Peter's is the second church.

The Romanesque triple-aisled pillar church was built in 1180 and stands in the middle of a walled graveyard with graves dating from the 14C to the 19C. In the graveyard, note the Gothic chapel dedicated to Our Lady, the Agnes Bernauer chapel with a red marble epitaph and the chapel of the dead with a fresco of the Dance of Death by local painter Felix Hölzl (1763).

Agnes Bernauer

Agnes, a beautiful young barber's daughter from Augsburg, was married in secret to Albrecht III, son of Duke Ernst of Bavaria. The Duke took exception to the match, for reasons of State, and had Agnes condemned as a witch. In 1435 she was drowned in the Danube not far from Straubing. The tragic fate of this beautiful country girl captured many a heart, inspiring Friedrich Hebbel to write a political tragedy (1855) and Carl Orff to compose an opera (1947). Every four years there is a festival (Agnes-Bernauer-Festspiele) in her memory (next one in 2007).

Stuttgart★

The capital of the Baden-Württemberg Land is a commercial and industrial centre whose name is often associated with automobile production. The name of the city, originally Stutengarten, derives from a 10C seigniorial stud farm which flourished in the region. In the 14C the town became the home of the dukes and kings of Württemberg, and prospered during the industrial revolution. Its quality museums and wide choice of excursions counter the impression left by an overly commercial city centre.

Location

Population: 550 000. Michelin map 545 T 11 – Baden-Württemberg. Stuttgart lies in a valley surrounded by vineyards and wooded hills opening to the northeast onto the Neckar. The finest overall **view★** of Stuttgart is from the upper platform of the **Fernsehturm** (television tower) *(access via the Hohenheimer Straße)*, which soars 400m/1 312ft above the woods on the southern side of town.

Königstraße 1 a, 70173 Stuttgart, ☎ (0711) 222 82 40.

Surrounding area: see TÜBINGEN (45km/28mi south), SCHWÄBISCH ALB (at Kirchheim, 31km/19mi southeast), SCHWÄBISCH HALL (69km/43mi northeast) or MAULBRONN Abbey (47km/29mi west).

Background

Two Motor Car Pioneers – An engineer who lived in Bad Cannstatt, **Gottfried Daimler** (1834-1900) pioneered the adaptation of the internal combustion engine to the powering of vehicles. Collaborating with the brilliant designer Wilhelm Maybach, he developed a vertical motor which was patented in 1883.

Unlike Daimler, **Carl Benz** (1844-1929) was less concerned with the actual invention of a new motor than with its universal application. Born and educated at Karlsruhe, he envisaged an entire motor vehicle, which he elaborated himself in every detail at Mannheim. Soon he was able to start manufacturing in series and put his cars

Directory

Where to Eat

Jägerhaus – *Obere Waiblinger Straße 110 – 70374 Stuttgart-Bad Canstatt – ☎ (0711) 52 60 90 – www.krehl-gastronomie.de – Closed 1 week beginning of Jan, and Tue – ♿ – €8.70/15.30.* You will be given a warm welcome in this pleasant restaurant in the Canstatt quarter. The rooms are divided into alcoves where you can sample regional dishes. There is also a beer garden here.

Amici – *Lautenschlagerstraße 2 – ☎ (0711) 227 02 92 – info@amici.de – Mon-Thu 11am-2am, Fri and Sat 11am-4am, Sun 5pm-2am – ♿ – Reservation necessary – €19/23.* A restaurant, café, bar and lounge – the choice is yours. Its spectacular architecture and striking lighting effects set it apart from the rest. The decor also includes an original racing car. Mediterranean dishes prepared in the glass-fronted kitchen and live music at weekends are among the highlights of this very trendy place.

Weber's Gourmet im Turm – *Jahnstraße 120 – 70597 Stuttgart-Degerloch – ☎ (0711) 24 89 96 10 – restaurant@fernsehturm-stgt.de – Closed 2 weeks in Jan, 3 weeks in Aug, and Sun-Mon – €54/70.* First you need a boarding pass, then you can take the lift up to the restaurant in the television tower *(Fernsehturmrestaurant)*, 144m/472ft up. The creative cuisine and fine wines make it well worth the trip.

Where to Stay

Hotel Geroksruhe – *Pischekstraße 70 – ☎ (0711) 23 86 90 – Fax (0711) 2360023 – www.smg.nethotels.com/geroksruhe – P – 19rm: €30/70.* Very smart, functional rooms make this a convenient place to spend the night, near the city centre. The breakfast room with its terrace is particularly pleasant. Apartments are also available for longer stays.

Hotel Bergmeister – *Rotenbergstraße 16 – ☎ (0711) 268 48 50 – Fax (0711) 283719 – info@hotel-bergmeister.de – Closed 23 Dec-6 Jan – – 46rm: €71/123.* Bright, comfortable rooms, many with a large balcony and all of them functional. Mahogany or cherrywood furniture and cheerful blue decor.

Hotel Abalon – *Zimmermannstraße 7 (access via no 79 Olgastraße) – ☎ (0711) 217 10 – Fax (0711) 2171217 – info@abalon.de – – 42rm: €82/119.* A modern building with covered terrace – where guests take breakfast – and spacious rooms. Near the city centre, but away from the hustle and bustle.

Taking a Break

irma la douce – café & suppenbar – *Neue Brücke 8 (behind the Karstadt department store in Königstraße) – ☎ (0711) 2 84 88 21 – Open Mon-Sat 11am-1am.* If you like soup, go and see what's cooking at this little self-service restaurant. In addition to delicious seasonal soups, there are home-made sandwiches and desserts to eat in or take away. Make the most of the large terrace in summer.

Weinhaus Stetter – *Rosenstraße 32. (south of and parallel to Charlottenstraße) – ☎ (0711) 24 01 63 – www.weinhaus-stetter.de – Weinstub: Open Mon-Fri 3-11pm, Sat 11am-3pm, wine cellar: Mon-Fri 10am-12.30pm and from 2.30pm, Sat 11am-3pm; Closed 25 Dec-8 Jan, 2 weeks between end of Aug and beginning of Sep.* For over one hundred years this rustic establishment has been offering its clients an excellent choice of mainly regional wines to accompany typical dishes. At the wine cellar you are sure to find a good bottle to take home.

Going Out

Useful Tips – The *Bohnenviertel* between Charlotten- and Pfarrstraße is a charming district with a profusion of restaurants and bars. The mainly cobbled streets are partly reserved for pedestrians.

Biergarten Karlshöhe – *Humboldtstraße 44 (the path through the vineyards – No signposting – Leaves from the first bend in the street coming from Marienstraße and Mörikestraße; around 10min on foot) – ☎ (0711) 6 20 06 66 – Mar-Oct: 12-11.30pm (in good weather).* This beer garden (self-service) is certainly not easy to find. However, many people make their way here in summer to enjoy the view of the city, which is particularly stunning at sunset.

Brasserie Flo – *Marktstraße 1 – ☎ (0711) 211 16 61 – www.breuninger.de – Closed Sun and public holidays.* This modern bistro-style establishment is in Karlspassage in the Breuninger department store. Serving breakfast, lunch, cakes and fancy dinners, there is something here for everyone. A pleasant place to go for a break from shopping.

Teehaus – *Im Weißenburgpark (access via Hohenheimer Straße and Bopserwaldstraße – near Bopser station; walk up from Bopserwaldstraße: 5min) – ☎ (0711) 2 36 73 60 – May-Oct: 11am-11pm (times may vary depending on the weather; open at weekends from Mar).* Set in a public park, this little Art Deco pavilion (built in 1912-13 by a detergent manufacturer) with its terrace is an idyllic and peaceful place to enjoy a coffee, cake, ice cream or cold drink.

Culture

Useful Tips – *Highlightbroschüre* (annual) and *Highlightflyer* (six-monthly) are available from Stuttgart Marketing's offices and provide information on the main events in the city. The monthly magazines *Lift* and *Prinz* are more in touch with current happenings and are on sale in bookshops and newspaper kiosks.

SHOPPING
Useful Tips – Stuttgart's shopping centre (department stores and specialised shops) is based on Königstraße and the neighbouring streets. The city's main department store is *Breuninger (Marktplatz)*. South of the *Altes Schloß* on the other side of Dorotheenstraße is the *Markthalle*, an Art-Deco-style covered market. Crafts shops and antique dealers are to be found in the *Bohnenviertel* (between Charlotten- and Pfarrstraße).

on the market. In 1899 he sold his 2 000th vehicle and thus became the world's leading automobile manufacturer. Then, in 1901, Daimler's company marketed a model baptised **Mercedes**, after the daughter of its most important foreign agent. The name was to make a fortune. And since the two firms amalgamated to form Daimler-Benz AG in 1926 Mercedes-Benz has been synonymous with luxury cars built to a high standard of excellence and technical prowess. In 1998 the firm merged again with American car manufacturer Chrysler to form DaimlerChrysler. Today, above the roofs of the city, the night sky over Stuttgart blazes with the illuminated three-point-star within a circle – the firm's world-famous trademark.

Urban Landscape – The former appearance of the city is only apparent nowadays on Schillerplatz, which is flanked by the Stiftskirche (collegiate church) and the Altes Schloß (Old Castle). The statue of Schiller in the centre of the square is the work of the Danish sculptor Thorwaldsen (1839).

In front of the Baroque Neues Schloß (New Palace) is the wide Schloßplatz, off which a tree-lined avenue leads through the 8km/5mi long castle gardens to the Höhenpark Killesberg. The Neues Schloß was built between 1746 and 1807 after a design by L Retti. It is now the home of regional ministerial departments. Modern Stuttgart's business and shopping centre is based on Königstraße, in the pedestrian zone.

Worth a Visit

Staatsgalerie★★ (Art Gallery)

♿ *Open every day except Mon, 10am-6pm; Thu 10am-9pm, 1st Sat of the month 10am-midnight. Closed Good Friday, 24 and 25 Dec. €4.50, free admission on Wed. ☎ (0711) 47 04 00; www.staatsgalerie.de*

The building commissioned under King Wilhelm I of Württemberg in 1838-43 houses European painting from medieval times to Impressionism. Note especially the **Old German Masters Section★★**, in which Swabian painting from the 14C to the 16C is pre-eminent. One of the masterpieces exhibited is the **Herrenberg Altar** by Jerg Ratgeb (1519), which portrays – from left to right – the Last Supper, the Martyrisation of Jesus, the Crucifixion and the Resurrection.

Venetians and Florentines from the 14C dominate an excellent collection of Italian painters. Among the Dutch Old Masters are Hans Memling *(Bethsheba Bathing)*, Rembrandt *(St Paul In Prison)*, Jacob van Ruisdael and Rubens.

The 19C art department contains a special display on "Swabian Classicism" and works from the most important artistic movements of the age, from the Pre-Raphaelites to the Impressionists.

An annexe (opened in 1984), designed by the British architect James Stirling, houses the department of 20C Art. Among the "modern classics" on display are works by the Fauvists and French Cubists (Matisse, Braque, Juan Gris), the Expressionists (a fine selection of Kokoschka paintings), the artists of Neue Sachlichkeit (Dix, Grosz) and artists of the Bauhaus School. A special place is reserved for the work of **Willi Baumeister** (1889-1955) and **Oskar Schlemmer** (1888-1943) of the Bauhaus, both natives of Stuttgart. Schlemmer's famous six-figure *Triadic Ballet* is on view, as well as certain enormous sketches for murals (the finished works, painted in 1929, were victims of the Nazi crusade against the so-called "degenerate art"). Another highlight of this museum is a collection of 12 works by **Picasso** covering every period of his creative life. Among them is the world-famous sculpture group in wood, *The Bathers*.

The section on contemporary art covers the half century since the Second World War, starting with Dubuffet and Giacometti and ending with the latest works of Baselitz and Kiefer, by way of American Pop Art (Warhol, Segal), Italy's Arte Povere and the "installations" of Beuys.

Linden-Museum★★

♿ *Open every day except Mon, 10am-5pm; Wed 10am-8pm. Closed Mon and Shrove Tuesday, Good Friday, 1st May, 24, 25 and 31 Dec. €3, free admission on Wed from 5pm. ☎ (0711) 202 23; www.lindenmuseum.de*

Exhibits in this museum consecrated to ethnology worldwide are beautifully presented, falling under six main headings.

STUTTGART

Arnulf-Klett-Platz . . . . LY 6
Augustenstraße . . . . KZ 7
Blumenstraße . . . . LZ 10
Bolzstraße . . . . LY 15
Calwer Str. . . . . .KYZ 18
Charlottenplatz . . . . LZ 20
Dorotheenstraße . . . . LZ 24
Eberhardstraße . . . . .KLZ 25
Friedrichsplatz . . . . KY 27
Hauptstätter Str. . . . . KZ 30
Hegelplatz . . . . KY 32
Heilbronner Str. . . . . LY 34
Holzstraße . . . . LZ 40
Karlsplatz . . . . LY 43
Karlstraße . . . . LZ 44
Katharinenplatz . . . . LZ 45
Kirchstraße . . . . LZ 46
Königstraße . . . . .KLYZ
Konrad-Adenauer-Straße . . . . LY 47
Kronenstraße . . . . .KLY 48
Kronprinzstraße . . . . .KYZ 49
Leonhardsplatz . . . . LZ 50
Marktplatz . . . . .KLZ 52
Marktstraße . . . . LZ 53
Österreichscher Platz . . . . KZ 57
Pfarrstraße . . . . LZ 61
Rotebühlplatz . . . . KZ 66
Rotebühlstraße . . . . KZ 70
Schloßplatz . . . . LY 72
Schulstraße . . . . KZ 75
Silberburgstraße . . . . KZ 76
Sophienstraße . . . . KZ 78
Theodor-Heuss-Str. . . . . .KYZ 80
Torstraße . . . . KZ 82
Wilhelmsplatz . . . . LZ 86
Wilhelmstraße . . . . LZ 88
Willi-Bleicher-Str. . . . . KY 91

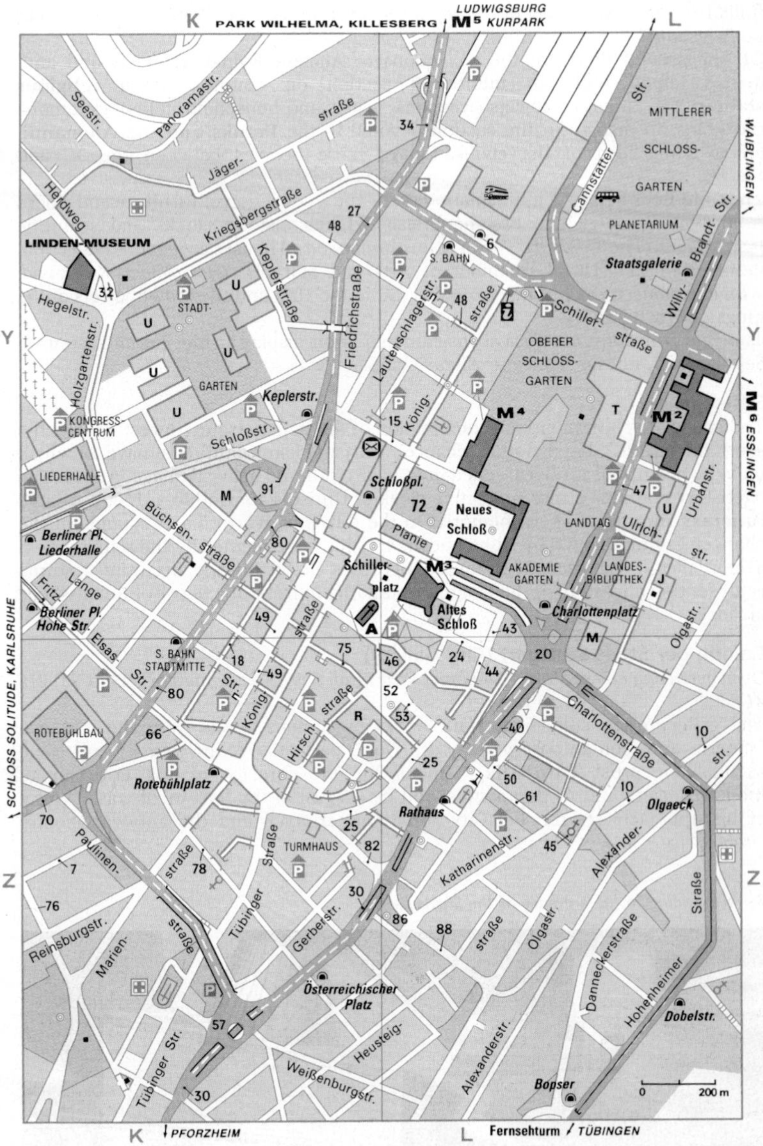

Galerie der Stadt Stuttgart . . LY M4
Mercedes-Benz- Museum . . LY M6
Museum am Löwentor . . . . LY M5
Staatsgalerie . . . . LY M2
Stiftskirche . . . . KY A
Württembergisches Landesmuseum . . . . LY M3

On the ground floor: America (Native Americans, Ancient Peruvian cultures) and the Pacific (Melanesia, cult of the ancestors and spirit beliefs in Papua and New Guinea, Australia).

On the first floor: Africa (royal palace, masks) and the Middle East (Islamic culture and history).

On the second floor: the Far East and South Asia (the cultures of Japan, China, India, Nepal and Tibet, the evolution of Buddhism and Hinduism, shadow theatre puppets from Indonesia).

Altes Schloß (Old Castle)

Four wings flanked by round towers comprise this building, most of which dates from the 16C. The **Renaissance Courtyard★** *(gives access to the Schloßkirche)* is surrounded by three floors of arcaded galleries.

Württembergisches Landesmuseum★

Inside the Altes Schloß. Open every day except Mon, 10am-5pm, Tue 10am-1pm. Closed 1st Jan, Good Friday, 24, 25 and 31 Dec. €2.60. ☎ (0711) 27 90; www.landesmuseum-stuttgart.de

The first floor displays collections from the Bronze and Iron Ages, with important finds from the excavation of the royal tomb★, a mid-6C BC Celtic burial site near Ludwigsburg.

On the second floor are the collections of Ancient Roman artefacts and antiquities, along with an interesting section on South German **religious statuary★★**. Funerary objects (weapons, jewels and household items) are among the items on display in the section devoted to the **Franks and the Alemanni**, giving some idea of the civilisation of these peoples between the 3C and the 8C.

The third floor houses a numismatic gallery and a collection of furniture and clocks from Württemberg. The basement also exhibits historic clocks and scientific instruments. The Treasury Tower *(Kunstkammerturm)* houses a weapons collection, items from the "Ducal Chamber of Arts and Marvels" *(Herzogliche Kunst-und-Wunderkammer)* which range from the 15C to the 18C, and the crown jewels of the kings of Württemberg.

The fine collection of musical instruments is on display in the Fruchtkasten on Schillerplatz, not far from the Altes Schloß.

Stiftskirche

The collegiate church with its combination of the Romanesque (lowest floor of the south tower, 12C), Early Gothic (chancel, 14C) and Late Gothic (the nave, of which only the north wall survives, added in 1436-55), suffered heavy damage in 1944. The baptistery contains a rare protective cloak of Christ (Late Gothic, c 1500). A large **funerary monument★**, a memorial to the dukes of Württemberg, stands in the chancel. Commissioned by Duke Ludwig III, this was executed by the sculptor Sem Schlör after 1576. Eleven armoured figurines in historically accurate costume representing ancestors of the Duke are standing in front of a decor of Renaissance arcades.

Galerie der Stadt Stuttgart (City Gallery)

Open every day except Mon, 11am-6pm, Wed 11am-8pm. Free admission. ☎ (0711) 216 21 88.

The gallery owns some important works by famous artists from the Classical Modern and contemporary periods. Note particularly the **work★** of Neue Sachlichkeit artist **Otto Dix**, famous for the ferocity of his criticism of modern society and its depravities, and his disgust at the horrors of war. Typical of his approach are the Big City *(Großstadt)* triptych and the anti-war picture *Grabenkrieg*.

Terrace leading to the entrance of the Staatsgalerie

Staatsgalerie Stuttgart

Excursions

Mercedes-Benz Museum★

Leave by Schillerstraße. At Mercedesstraße 136, in a block of the company's main factory, located at Stuttgart-Untertürkheim. ♿ Open every day except Mon, 9am-5pm. Closed public holidays. Free admission. ☎ (0711) 172 25 78.

The museum boasts the world's largest collection of vehicles of a single marque. Beginning with the oldest automobiles by Karl Benz and Gottlieb Daimler right up to today's models hot off the production line, the display retraces the highlights of the company's manufacture. The legendary early racing cars, such as the Silver Arrows of the 1930s and 1950s, testify to the success of the Mercedes marque as much as the modern McClaren-Mercedes.

Porsche Museum★

Leave on Heilbronner Straße, in the direction of the motorway. Before the motorway, take the exit signposted Zuffenhausen-Industriegebiet, and then turn right into Porschestraße. The museum is at no 42. ♿ 9am-4pm, Sat-Sun 9am-5pm. Closed 24 Dec-1st Jan. Free admission. ☎ (0711) 911 56 85.

In 1934, the engineer **Ferdinand Porsche** (1875-1951), already distinguished by his work at Daimler-Benz, produced a design for the famous "people's car" – the *Volkswagen*. His prototype evolved into the celebrated "Beetle". Porsche, from 1948 onwards, devoted himself to a sports model bearing his own name, which was developed from the original VW chassis and engine and subsequently manufactured at Zuffenhausen. In one of the factory buildings 30 different Porsches are now on show, along with a display of high-performance engines.

Wilhelma Park and Zoo★

4km/2.5mi northeast of the centre. Leave by Heilbronner Straße. ♿ May-Aug: 8.15am-6pm; Apr and Sep: 8.15am-5.30pm; Mar and Oct: 8.15am-5pm; Nov-Feb: 8.15am-4pm. €9. ☎ (0711) 540 20; www.wilhelma.de

This botanical and zoological garden (one of Europe's finest) laid out at the request of King Wilhelm I in the mid 19C is furnished with hothouses displaying many fascinating tropical plants and a celebrated exhibition of orchids and cacti. The zoo is home to more than 8 000 animals (1 000 species). Worth seeing also: the **aquarium and terrarium** and the **Amazonian house** with flora and fauna from this region.

Höhenpark Killesberg

4km/3mi north of the centre. Leave by Heilbronner Straße. A little way to the west of the Rosenstein, this park is a continuation of the green belt encircling the inner city. Laid out on a height to the north of the centre, it integrates perfectly with the undulating terrain. Terraced cascades, fountains and brilliantly coloured flower beds invite the visitor to relax and admire, and there is a **miniature train** on which a tour of the whole park can be made. A panoramic view of Stuttgart can be enjoyed from a look-out tower at the highest point *(Aussichtsturm).*

Schloß Solitude★

9km/5.5mi southwest. Leave by Rotebühlstraße. Apr-Oct: open every day except Mon, 9am-12pm, 1.30-5pm; Nov-Mar: open every day except Mon, 10am-12pm, 1.30-4pm. €3. ☎ (0711) 69 66 99; www.schloesser-und-gaerten.de

The former summer residence of the Württemberg court stands on the edge of a plateau. Flanked by lateral wings, the palace is centred on an oval pavilion with a cupola, the whole being majestically raised on a base of open arcades. Around this, the lower outbuildings lie in an immense arc. The design was by the French court architect, La Guépière, who supervised construction between 1763 and 1769.

Inside, the decorations of the central rotunda *(Weißer Saal)* and the small marble room are in the neo-Classical tradition. The other apartments, which are panelled, are French Rococo. One of the more bizarre items on view is the desk used by Friedrich I of Württemberg – generously hollowed out to accommodate the corpulent figure of its owner.

►► Staatliches Museum für Naturkunde *(National Museum of Natural Sciences, in Rosenstein Park)*, Museum am Löwentor *(collection of prehistoric fossils, also in Rosenstein Park).*

Esslingen am Neckar

13km/8mi southeast. The very busy road linking northern Italy to Flanders passed through this 1 220-year-old Swabian town. The finest ornament to the picturesque **Marktplatz★**, which dates from the 19C, is the Kielmeyer house. All the streets leading into the square are bordered by old houses decorated with wood carvings. The Gothic **Stadtkirche** contains fine 13C and 14C **stained glass★**. The 15C and 16C **Altes Rathaus★** (old town hall) combines the charm of old half-timbering with the gracefulness of decorated Renaissance façades. The curvilinear stepped gable overlooking the Rathausplatz is surmounted by a double lantern (carillon), vibrant with colour. But it is the other gable above all which must be seen – an outstanding feature typical of Swabian half-timbering, with heavy corbels and obliquely crossed beams. The Gothic **Frauenkirche**, which stands on a hillside *(reached from the Marktplatz via the Untere Beutau rise)*, has a beautiful ornate **church tower★**, flanked by slender staircase turrets.

Schloß Ludwigsburg★

15km/9.5mi north. Built by Duke Eberhard Ludwig von Württemberg along the lines of Versailles in the early 18C, this monumental quadrilateral has no less than 452 rooms, 75 of them open to the public.

Tour of the Apartments – Inside, the "best rooms" (on the first floor of the new building, facing the park) are the apartments of the first king of Württemberg, furnished in the Empire style. Through the Ancestors' Gallery *(Ahnengalerie)* and the castle's Catholic church *(Schloßkirche)*, decorated with lavish Italian stucco, visitors arrive at the Fürstenbau state apartments. These are in the oldest and highest part of the palace, which closes off the north side of the court. *Guided tour (1hr 15min). From mid Mar to end of Oct: 10am-5pm; from Nov to mid Mar: 10am-12pm, 1-4pm. €4. ☎ (071 41) 18 64 40; www.schloss-ludwigsburg.de*

Blühendes Barock★ (Park) – Green Baroque arbours and terraces clothed with an embroidery of flowers have been reconstituted in the southern part of the park, in front of the newest part of the palace. The terrain to the north and east, more broken up, has been landscaped in the English manner. In the **Märchengarten★★** (Fairytale Garden), fairy stories, legends and folk tales from Germany (the Brothers Grimm) and elsewhere are illustrated. ♿ *From mid Mar to beginning of Nov: 7.30am-8.30pm. €6.50. ☎ (071 41) 97 56 50; www.blueba.de*

Tiefenbronn★

38km/24mi west. This village is home to the **Pfarrkirche St Maria Magdalena**, which boasts an unusually rich interior decor. Besides murals (late-14C *Last Judgement* above the interior of the triumphal arch; altar murals on the east wall of the nave from c 1400), stained-glass windows (late 14C) and numerous tombs, there are some particularly fine Late Gothic altarpieces. The high altar by Ulm master Hans Schüchlin (1469) depicts scenes from the life of the Virgin Mary and the Passion of Christ. On the end wall of the south side aisle there is a magnificent **altarpiece of St Mary Magdalene★★** (1432) by **Lucas Moser**, illustrating various episodes from the life of the saint. In the chancel, to the left of the high altar, is a **monstrance★** dating from c 1500, which must be a masterpiece of Late Gothic gold- and silversmiths judging by its shape and wealth of figures.

Schwäbisch Gmünd

54km/34mi east. Traditionally Schwäbisch Gmund is a centre for the working of precious metals; there are still about 70 gold- and silver-working firms in business here. The Baroque character of the huge **Marktplatz** (marketplace) is emphasised by the prosperous-looking houses surrounding it and a twin-statue fountain dedicated to the Virgin Mary. Several half-timbered buildings, including the Heilig-Geist-Spital hospital and the *Gräth* (old town hall) nevertheless recall the medieval existence of the town. The beautiful 14C **Heiligkreuzmünster★** surprisingly has a ridge turret instead of towers. The interior is a hall-church with chapels rich in statuary; note especially, in the axial chapel, a Holy Sepulchre (c 1350) with the sleeping guards and the three Marys, and the Tree of Jesse (1520) in the Batpismal Chapel, composed of 40 sculpted figurines.

Hohenstaufen★ – *14km/9mi southwest, plus 30min on foot there and back. Park the car in the village square.* From the two churches at the top of the town, a shady footpath leads to the summit at 684m/2 244ft.

Nothing remains of the castle, the onetime seat of the Staufer, but the climb is worthwhile for the **panorama★** of the two remaining Kaiserberge, Stuifen and Rechberg, and, on the horizon, the "blue wall" of the Swabian Jura.

Insel Sylt★★

Despite its modest area (100km²/39sq mi) the landscape of this long, narrow island, with origins in the Geest is varied. The west coast features a long stretch of fine sandy beach running for miles. The rest of the island landscape is characterised by dunes and marshes, salt pastures and mudflats (Watt, or Wadden), fields and meadows, open heathland and primeval burial mounds. The island's spas, North Sea bathing and climatic health resorts make it popular with holidaymakers.

Location

Michelin map n° 541 B 8-9 – Schleswig-Holstein. Sylt stretches in a north-south direction for 40km/25mi, although in parts it is less than 457m/500yd across. The island is the largest of the Northern Frisian Islands and the most northerly part of German territory. Since 1927, it has been connected to the mainland via a rail link across the Hindenburgdamm causeway. It is possible to reach Sylt via train-car ferries from Niebüll *(Westerland, 35min: car with passagers €77 return. ☎ (046 61) 93 45 67)*, or by ferry: there is a seaborne car ferry service from Havneby *(on the Danish island of Römö – accessible by road): 5 to 7 ferries a day, up to 12 daily in July and Aug. Journey time about 50min. €53 return per vehicle including passengers, €6.20 return for foot passengers. Information and reservations: ☎ (0180) 310 30 30)* and from List, on the northern tip of Sylt.

Surrounding area: see NORDFRIESISCHE INSELN, Insel HELGOLAND (via ferry from Hörnum).

Directory

Where to Eat

Webchristel – *Süderstraße 11 – 25980 Sylt-Westerland – ☎ (04651) 229 00 – Closed 20 Nov-24 Dec and Wed – €24/48.* Frisian house with rustic decor. This restaurant serves refined regional dishes.

Landhaus Nösse – *Nösistig 13 – 25980 Sylt-Ost-Morsum – ☎ (04651) 972 20 – info@landhaus-noesse.de – Closed Mon – €47/59.* Reed-thatched house in a wonderfully isolated cliff-top location. Gourmet restaurant and bistro. Most of the neat guestrooms have a view over the Watt.

Where to Stay

Parkhotel am Südwäldchen – *Fischerweg 45, 25980 Sylt-Westerland – ☎ (04651) 83 63 00 – fax (04651) 8363063 – www.parkhotel-sylt.de – 24 rm: €50/160.* Situated in a quiet location in a residential area, this manicured hotel has an indoor pool and sauna.

Hotel Seiler Hof – *Gurtstig 7, 25980 Sylt-Ost-Keitum – ☎ (04651) 933 40 – fax (04651) 933444 – info@seilerhofsylt.de – 11rm: from €90.* This former captain's house dates from 1761 and has a beautiful garden. Comfortable guestrooms.

Taking a Break

Kupferkanne – *Stapelhooger Wai – 25999 Sylt-Kampen – ☎ (04651) 41010 – www.kupferkanne-sylt.de – Open 10am-6pm.* This slightly surreal everyday café in a former bunker serves excellent coffee and cakes (small menu). Large coffee garden with view of the mud-flats.

Going Out

Salon 1900 – *Süderstraße 40 – 25980 Sylt-Ost-Keitum – ☎ (04651) 93 60 00 – www.salon1900.de – Closed from mid-Jan to mid-Feb.* A café, restaurant, bar and disco are all under one thatched roof. Parts of this establishment are decorated in the *Jugendstil* and the garden is particarly pleasant.

Worth a Visit

Westerland★

This is the largest resort on the island and the most popular North Sea spa and cure establishment in Germany. The cure establishment boasts a leisure pool – the *Sylter Welle* – in the form of a ship and a 7km/4mi-long sandy beach with foaming breakers. The aim is to see and be seen on the promenade, which is centred around the large music hall. There is also plenty of action in the bars, bistros and nightclubs. As the island's metropolis, Westerland has everything visitors could desire, from window-shopping *(Strandstraße and Friedrichstraße)*, galleries and boutiques to a casino (in the old *Jugendstil* spa building). There are also various sports facilities and cultural events to be enjoyed.

Keitum

This idyllic village with numerous craft workshops is the other face of the island. Keitum's ancient traditional thatched Frisian houses, almost hidden among trees and lilac bushes, the drystone embankments overgrown with dog roses, and the view from the *Grünes Kliff* over endless miles of water and the mudflats of the Schleswig-Holstein National Park have earned it the nickname of being the island's "green heart". At the edge of the village, on the side towards Munkmarschen, lies the early-13C seafarers' church of St Severin with a Late Romanesque font.

South of **Kampen**, a resort favoured by VIPs and artists, the **Rotes Kliff★** towers above the sea. In Wenningstedt-Braderup, the **Denghoog** is a megalithic grave over 4 000 years old which is open to the public. Three massive roof stones weighing 2t each are supported by 12 load-bearing stones. **Morsum-Kliff**, on which 10 million years of geological history can be seen, is an interesting geological feature.

To the north of Sylt, near the port of **List**, lie the **Wanderdüne**, 1 000m/3 280ft-long and 30m/10ft-high dunes made of quartz sand and moving several metres further east every year.

Thüringer Wald★★

Thuringia Forest

Much in the same way as the Harz, the Thuringia Forest is a wooded massif, orientated northwest-southeast, with an average height of 1 000m/3 300ft. This is one of the most beautiful natural regions in Germany, and the massif is scattered with charming villages whose inhabitants still retain their traditional skills and craftsmanship. A wealth of tourist amenities, particularly at Oberhof, and the development of several resorts have made the region popular with a large number of ramblers and summer holidaymakers.

Location

Michelin map nº 544 N14–O16 – Thuringia. Around 100km/63mi in length, the Thuringia Forest separates the valleys of Swiss-Franconia from Thuringia.

Surrounding area (distances from Eisenach): see ERFURT (61km/38mi), WEIMAR (77km/48mi), Oberes SAALETAL.

Background

Flora and Fauna – The forest covering practically the whole area is largely a mixture of beech, pine and fir. Marshy plateaux have developed in some of the higher reaches, and there is moorland on the approaches to some crests. Among the larger varieties of game, stags, roe deer and wild boar are abundant.

Forest under threat – Acid rain and industrialisation have damaged some of the trees of the Thuringia Forest. However, the massif remains generally well-preserved as the "lungs" of Germany.

Tour

THÜRINGER HOCHSTRASSE: FROM EISENACH TO ILMENAU

110km/68mi – one day

This fascinating forest road mainly follows the **Rennsteig**, a ramblers' path 160km/100mi long which keeps to the highest parts of the forest and includes such major summits as the Großer Inselsberg and the Großer Beerberg.

Eisenach★ *see EISENACH*

Leave Eisenach in the direction of Gotha.

Großer Inselsberg

1hr on foot there and back.

The **panorama★★** extending from the summit takes in the greater part of the forest.

Marienglashöhle★

Guided visit (45min). Open Apr to Oct, 9am-5pm; Nov to Mar, 9am-4pm. €4. ☎ (036 23) 332 00.

Crystalline gypsum is extracted from this natural **cavity**. The use of this mineral in the decoration of church altars has led to the grotto's unusual name (*Marienglas* means Glass of Mary).

The road cuts across the Rennsteig and twists between the Regenberg (727m/2 385ft) and the Spießberg (749m/2 457ft), offering numerous possibilities for sightseeing and walks, especially in the direction of **Ebertswiese**, a zone of marsh

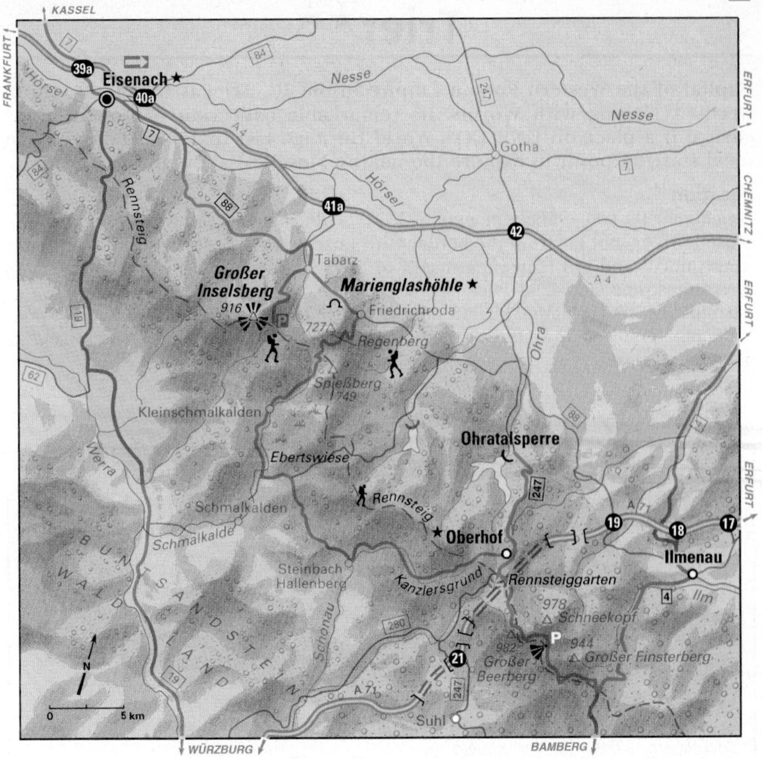

and meadows. Steinbach is overlooked by the Hallenburg ruins. The road continues towards Oberhof via the Kanzlergrund, a valley with wide stretches of grass and meadowland.

Oberhof★

At 800m/2 625ft altitude, this town is the most important leisure centre and winter-sports station in the Thuringia Forest, and the training ground for international toboggan and bobsleigh racers.

In the **Rennsteiggarten**, a botanical park specialising in Alpines and the flora of Central European heights, more than 4 000 varieties of plant can be seen.

Ohratalsperre

Follow the B 247 to the large car park. The reservoir dammed by this **barrage**, the surface of which extends over 88ha/218 acres, supplies water to Weimar, Jena, Gotha and the Thuringian capital, Erfurt.

Leave Oberhof in the direction of Schmücke

The country road winds once again sinuously between the Großer Beerberg and the Schneekopf. From the hotel car park at Schmücke, there is a fine viewpoint looking out over the valley. The Finsterberg is visible on the left.

Ilmenau

This locality on the northern fringe of the Thuringia Forest has always been associated with Goethe, who is said to have been particularly fond of its natural beauties. There is a plaque in his memory on the wall of the town's municipal headquarters (Amtshaus, in Marktplatz), which has been transformed into a Goethe museum, and another in the Gabelbach hunting lodge. A pathway called **"In Goethe's Footsteps"** *(Auf Goethes Spuren)* links the places associated with the great writer.

Trier★★

Capital of the Western Roman Empire in the 3C, Trier is the oldest city in Germany, along with Worms. Its remarkable collection of Roman ruins earned it a place on UNESCO's World Heritage List in 1992. The city is an ideal starting point to explore the nearby Moselle Valley or Luxembourg.

Location

Population: 99 000 – Michelin map 543 Q 3 – Rheinland-Pfalz. Trier straddles the Moselle river, not far from the border with Luxembourg, with the Eifel mountains to the north and the Hunsrück massif to the southeast.

Simeonstraße 60, 54290 Trier, ☎ (0651) 97 80 80.

Surrounding area: see MOSELTAL (tour leaving from Trier), Unteres SAARTAL (tour including Trier), IDAR-OBERSTEIN (64km/40mi east), EIFEL (Manderscheid is 60km/37mi north).

Directory

Where to Eat

Palais Kesselstatt – *Liebfrauenstraße 9 – ☎ (0651) 402 04 – kesselstatt@aol.com – Closed 12-30 Jan, Sun-Mon – €28/42.* The restaurant of this Baroque palace is tastefully decorated with stuccowork, paintings and chandeliers, providing a princely setting and very refined cuisine.

Where to Stay

Berghotel Kockelsberg – *Auf dem Kockelsberg, 54293 Trier-Kockelsberg – ☎ (0651) 824 80 00 – Fax (0651) 8248290 – hokotr@aol.com – P – 30rm: €36/80 – Restaurant €15/32.* A late 19C-early 20C hotel with a lovely view of Trier. Behind the white façade with its little tower are smart, comfortable rooms. Very pleasant restaurant with a delightful view.

Hotel Alte Villa – *Saarstraße 133 – ☎ (0651) 93 81 20 – Fax (0651) 9381212 – hotelaltevilla@t-online.de – P – 20rm: €56/128.* A hotel on the outskirts of the city, set in a villa dating from 1743 (a listed building). Functional rooms, with modern furniture in the new building.

Hotel Petrisberg – *Sickingenstraße 11 – ☎ (0651) 46 40 – Fax (0651) 46450 – www.hotel-petrisberg.de – P – 34rm: €60/95.* The rooms in this hotel are smart and well equipped, but its idyllic, peaceful location and magnificent view are what really set it apart. Pleasant footpaths lead to the city centre.

Taking a Break

Café Bley – *Simeonstraße 19 – ☎ (0651) 7 36 80 – Mon-Sat 9.30am-6.30pm, Sun 1-6pm.* A classic café in the 13C *Dreikönigenhaus*, with a large choice of cakes. You can buy the house speciality – Riesling truffles – to take away; they are even packaged in bottles.

Going Out

Historischer Keller – *Simeonstraße 46 (beneath the Karstadt department store) – ☎ (0651) 46 94 96 – www.historischer-keller.de – Mon-Fri 9.30am-7.30pm, Sat 9.30am-6pm.* The décor of this cellar built c 1200 recalls the knights' era. Coffee, cakes and various dishes are served here.

Walderdorff's – *Domfreihof 1a – ☎ (0651) 9 94 44 12 – www.walder dorffs.de – Open Sun-Thur 9am-1am, Fri-Sat 10am-2am, wine cellar: from 5pm, Sat-Sun from 11am, club: Tue 8pm-1am (jazz), Wed-Sat 10pm-4am.* This place has something for everyone: a bistro with attractively priced dishes, a bar with over 80 cocktails, a wine cellar where you can sample the excellent local wines and, for night owls, a club in the basement. Very pleasant setting, quiet terrace with a view of the cathedral.

Background

The oldest city in Germany – Trier became the meeting point very early on for the Celtic, Germanic and Latin cultures which evolved to form Western civilisation. After the conquest of the Treveri, a Celtic tribe from the eastern part of Gaul, the Roman Emperor Augustus founded on their territory the town of **Augusta Treverorum** (c 16 BC), which soon became a centre of intense economic, cultural and intellectual activity, continuing to develop until the invasion of Germanic tribes in AD 274. Essentially a civic and residential settlement, the town fell before the onslaught.

A second Rome – Later, however, when Diocletian reorganised the Roman Empire, Trier was retaken and became capital of the western territories (Gaul, Spain, Germania and Britain). As the town regained its former eminence, the Emperor Constantine (306-37) surrounded it with a defensive wall within which magnificent buildings were erected. In this second period of prosperity, Trier was given the status of Imperial Residence.

In the year 313, the Edict of Milan put an end to the persecution of Christians, and a year later the See of Trier, the oldest in Germany, was created. But towards the end of the 4C, renewed pressure from the Germanic tribes became so strong that the Imperial residence was transferred to Milan and the prefecture to Arles. In 470, Trier finally fell into the hands of the Franks.

Between the Germanic Empire and the French Republic – After the status of prince-electors was conferred upon the archbishops of Trier in the 14C, the city on the banks of the Moselle flourished for a second time. In the wake of the French Revolution, it was made capital of the French administrative region of Saar (from 1794 to 1814) before falling into the hands of Prussia in 1815. It was occupied by the French again from 1918 to 1930, and from 1945 to 1955. Trier is now a focal point of the region, not only as a major centre of wine production and trade but also of culture, and attracts a large number of tourists.
The philosopher and economist **Karl Marx** (1818-83) was born in Trier.

Special Features

OLD TOWN *allow one day*

Porta Nigra★★

From mid Apr to end of Sep: 10am-6pm; Oct-Nov and from Jan to mid Apr: 10am-5pm; Dec: 10am-4pm. €2.10. ☎ (0651) 754 24.
Perhaps the most memorable sight in Trier is the *Porta Nigra*, the largest Roman edifice on German soil. This monumental gateway (late 2C), built to defend the northern part of the town wall, is made of stones fitted together without mortar, held only here and there with iron crampons. The gateway was designed for military use: the double arcade of the central block, flanked by two massive towers, leads to an inner court where only the upper arcades are pierced – and assailants forcing the outer gates would find themselves exposed here to attack from all sides.
In the 11C, the fortified gateway was transformed into a church on two levels, dedicated to St Simeon. The Romanesque apse can still be seen on the east side, and there are other traces of St Simeon's church, including Rococo decoration, for example – in the upper galleries *(on the inner courtyard side)*. It was Napoleon who ordered the monument to be restored to its original form in 1804. There is a fine view from the tower terrace.

M. Hertlein/MICHELIN

The Porta Nigra

Städtisches Museum Simeonstift

Open Mar-Oct: 9am-5pm; Nov-Feb: open every day except Mon, 9am-5pm, Sat-Sun 9am-3pm. Closed 1st Jan, 24, 25 and 31 Dec. €2.60. ☎ (0651) 718 14 59; www.museum-trier.de
This municipal museum is installed in a Romanesque convent, the Simeonstift, built beside the Porta Nigra at the same time as the church (11C). The history of Trier is illustrated with models, paintings, engravings, maps and sculptures, among them the original figures surrounding the fountain in the market place (the Four Virtues and St Peter, late 16C). It also encompasses a double storey Romanesque **cloister** surrounding Germany's oldest cloister garth.

TRIER

Street	Grid
Ausoniusstraße	CX 3
Bismarckstr.	DX 4
Bruchhausen-straße	CX 6
Brückenstraße	CY 7
Brotstraße	CDY
Deutschherrenstr.	CX 9
Dietrichstraße	CX 10
Domfreihof	DX 12
Fahrstraße	CY 15
Fleischstraße	CXY
Grabenstraße	DX 16
Hauptmarkt	DX
Kornmarkt	CY
Liebfrauenstr.	DXY 24
Lindenstraße	CX 25
Nagelstraße	CY
Neustraße	CY
Simeonstraße	DX
Stresemann-Straße	CY 34
Walramsneustr.	CX 35

Place	Grid	Key
Bischöfliches Museum	DX	M1
Die Steipe	DX	D
Dreikönigenhaus	DX	K
Rotes Haus	DX	E
Schatzkammer der Stadtbibliothek	DY	B
Städtisches Museum	DX	M2

Dreikönigenhaus★ (House of the Three Kings)

This Early Gothic town house (c 1230), with its arched windows, recalls the Italianate towers of the patricians of Regensburg.

Hauptmarkt★

One of the finest old squares in Germany. In the middle is the **Market Cross★** *(Marktkreuz)*, erected in the year 958 when the town was granted the right to hold a market. The **fountain**, with its figures representing the cardinal virtues, dates from the late 16C.

Standing by the Cross (which was restored in the 18C), the visitor can see 15 centuries of history encapsulated in the monuments around the square. To the north is the Porta Nigra, to the east the Romanesque cathedral, to the south the Gothic **Gangolfkirche**, whose early 16C tower was once used as a look-out post. Picturesque half-timbered houses, both Renaissance and Baroque, stand on the west side. The **Steipe**, a medieval (15C) municipal building with a steep, tall roof, is elegantly built over an open gallery. Beside it, the 17C **Rotes Haus** (Red House), bears the proud inscription: "There was life in Trier for 1 300 years before Rome even existed".

Frankenturm

This heavily built Romanesque tower (c 1100) with battlements and small windows is named after one of its early owners, Franco of Senheim (14C).

Dom★ (Cathedral)

Seen from its forecourt *(Domfreihof)*, Trier Cathedral with its six towers looks more like a fortress than a church. A rounded apse projects from a massive, austere façade which, with its squat, square towers, is a fine example of Early Romanesque architecture. From the north side, different stages in the construction are evident. A flattened gable and rectangular plan distinguish the 4C Roman heart of the building. West of this

central block is the 11C Romanesque section; east of it the polygonal chancel, which is furnished with a dwarf gallery and dates from the 12C. A Baroque axial chapel crowned by a dome was added to this in the 18C.
Entering the cathedral from the forecourt, note near the main door the fallen section *(Domstein)* of a Roman column which supported part of the former church.
Inside, the decoration is principally Baroque and includes some interesting altarpieces. In the west chancel *(on the left of the entrance)* there is a Gothic funerary monument dedicated to the Archbishop and Prince-Elector Baldwin of Luxembourg. A splendid **tympanum★** in the south aisle depicts Christ between the Virgin Mary and St Peter. Another Madonna, a graceful 16C example, stands in the stuccoed chapel on the right of the chancel.

Domschatz★ (Treasury) – *Apr-Oct: 10am-4.45pm, Sun 2-4.45pm; Nov-Mar: 11am-3.45pm, Sun 2-3.45pm. Closed 1st Jan, Easter Sun, 25 Dec. €1.50. ☎ (0651) 979 07 90.* Silver and gold plate including the portable altar of St Andrew, richly enamelled, valuable ivories, and magnificently illuminated Gospels are on view here, in the domed axial chapel.

Cloister (Kreuzgang) – In the northeast corner, the 15C Malberg Madonna watches over this Gothic cloister which offers a good **view★** of the cathedral and the Liebfrauenkirche.

Liebfrauenkirche★ (Church of Our Lady)

One of the earliest Gothic sanctuaries in Germany (1235-60), this church was directly inspired by one in the Champagne region of France, with the ground plan in the form of a Greek cross. There are four apsidal chapels, between each pair of which two smaller, three-sided chapels have been interposed, giving the whole church the highly original form of a rose with 12 petals. The **tympanum** over the west porch shows the Virgin Mary Enthroned, the Annunciation, the Adoration of the Magi, the Massacre of the Innocents and the Presentation in the Temple. The Coronation of the Virgin is represented at the north entrance.
The interior has an incomparable elegance, enhanced by rings of foliage carved around each column, by the finesse of the public gallery, and the richness of the high central vaulting. There is a fine 17C **funerary monument★** (north chapel) to Metternich's personal canon.

Bischöfliches Dom- und Diözesanmuseum★ (Episcopal Museum)

♿ *Apr-Oct: 9am-5pm, Sun 1-5pm; Nov-Mar: open every day except Mon, 9am-5pm, Sun 1-5pm. Closed 1st Jan, 24-26 and 31 Dec. €2. ☎ (0651) 710 52 55.* The most interesting exhibits here are the frescoes (*Deckenmalerei*, 4C) which decorated the Palace of Constantine, discovered beneath the cathedral. It is supposed that the central picture represents Constantine's wife Fausta. The colours are extraordinarily fresh and the technique highly skilled. The rest of the museum is mainly devoted to sacred art.

Basilika★

This large rectangular brick building was once the main hall *(Aula Palatina)* of the Imperial palace, built by Constantine c 310. Modified many times over the centuries, it was rebuilt in 1954 and is used today as a Protestant church. The basilica is used today as a Protestant church. The sheer size of the interior is breath-taking, although the decor is restrained.

Ehemaliges Kurfürstliches Schloß

Only the north and east wings remain of the former Renaissance electoral castle, on which building was begun in 1615. The Rococo wings were built between 1756 and 1762, based on plans by the court master builder Johannes Seitz. His virtuosity (he was a student of Balthasar Neumann) is expressed in a magnificent staircase, one of the most beautiful creations of its kind in Germany. The south façade with its gentle colouring looks out over the **Palastgarten★** (palace gardens), laid out in the French style with ponds, flower borders and Baroque statues.

Rheinisches Landesmuseum★★ (Rhineland Museum)

Open every day except Mon, 9.30am-5pm (May-Oct: open every day), Sat-Sun 10.30am-5pm. Closed 1st Jan, carnival, 24-26 Dec. €5.50. ☎ (0651) 977 40; www.landes-museum-trier.de
The department of prehistory *(ground floor)* and a section on Roman antiquities are particularly interesting.
Paleolithic Age: Stone Age implements and ceramics; objects from the Bronze Age; jewels set in gold from Iron Age sepulchres.
Roman Period: marvellous mosaics; bronze statuettes and bas-reliefs (including a school scene and one depicting the payment of farm rent). Among the sculpture discovered at Neumagen is the representation of a ship sailing down the Moselle loaded with wine. Included in this **Neumagen ship carving** is the figure of "the jolly sailor" – a mariner with a broad grin who has passed into the folklore of the Moselle. Regional ceramics and jewels and glassware found in Frankish tombs are also on display, along with medieval, Renaissance and Baroque works of art.

Kaiserthermen★★ (Imperial Roman Baths)

Same opening times as the Porta Nigra. €2.10. ☎ (0651) 442 62.

Among the largest in the Roman Empire, these baths date from the time of Constantine, but appear never to have been used. The construction of the rounded walls – alternate layers of brick and rubble – is typically Roman. The window openings are wide and arched. Inside, the hot water caldarium is preceded by a tepidarium (warm water baths), a frigidarium (cold) and a gymnasium for physical exercises. The two floors below ground where the heating and circulating plant were installed are particularly interesting to see.

Schatzkammer der Stadtbibliothek★★ (Municipal Library Treasury)

Open only during exhibitions. ☎ (0651) 718 14 29.

Fascinating exhibits are on view here. The collection includes rare ancient manuscripts, beautifully illuminated (medieval Bibles, homilies, fables etc); examples of the earliest books to be illustrated (Gospels, teaching manuals, legal volumes); and many old documents, treaties, letters of credit and safe conduct passes.

Karl-Marx-Haus

Brückenstraße 10. Open Apr-Oct: 10am-6pm, Mon 1-6pm; Nov-Mar: 10am-1pm, 2-5pm, Mon 2-5pm. Closed 1st Jan, 24-26 and 31 Dec. €2. ☎ (0651) 97 06 80.

The birthplace of the socialist theoretician has been turned into a museum, displaying letters, manuscripts, first edition of Communist Manifesto etc.

Worth a Visit

Basilika St Paulin★

Access via Thebäerstraße. Tall windows illuminate the single nave of this church, the interior of which was designed by Balthasar Neumann and completed in 1754. Masterly stuccowork joins the nave to the vaulting. The martyrdom of St Paulin, citizens of Trier, and of the Theban Legion (AD 286) are illustrated in paintings on the ceiling by Christoph Thomas Scheffler of Augsburg. The high altar was based on Neumann's designs with the woodcarving by Trier artist Ferdinand Tietz.

Barbarathermen

Same opening times as the Porta Nigra, *but closed Mon. ☎ (0651) 442 62.*

Roman baths from the 2C, used for several centuries, are now in ruins.

Amphitheater (Roman Amphitheatre)

Same opening times as the Porta Nigra. *€2.10. ☎ (0651) 730 10.*

Once seating 20 000 spectators, this hillside arena was used as a quarry in the Middle Ages, and became so damaged by the 18C that vines were grown on the terraces. The cellars below ground housed theatrical equipment and machinery. The amphitheatre now houses the Antikenfestspiele (festival) every summer.

Kirche St Matthias

Access via Saarstraße. A 12C pillared Romanesque basilica, now a Benedictine convent church housing the St Matthias reliquary shrine. Apart from Romanesque, the façade shows traces of Baroque and neo-Classical influence.

Tübingen★★

Tübingen was lucky enough to escape undamaged during the Second World War. It therefore gives an unbroken picture of its evolution from the Middle Ages to the 19C. The labyrinth of narrow sloping streets lined with ancient half-timbered houses and its animated student life combine to create a delightful atmosphere, making Tübingen one of the most attractive towns in south Germany.

Location

Population: 83 000. Michelin map nº 545 U 11 – Baden-Württemberg. Tübingen is near Stuttgart, on the banks of the Neckar and Ammer, between the slopes of Schloßberg and Österberg.

ℹ *An der Eberhardsbrücke, 72072 Tübingen, ☎ (070 71) 913 60.*

Surrounding area: see STUTTGART (40km/25mi north), SCHWÄBISCHE ALB (Liechtenstein is 14km/9mi away), SCHWARZWALD (60km/38mi west).

H. Champollion/MICHELIN

Neckar riverfront, Tübingen.

Background

The University – The saying goes that, rather than having a university, Tübingen is a university, so closely linked are the town's history and cultural life with its Alma Mater. It all began in 1477, when Count Eberhard took the risk of founding a university in a small town with only 3 000 inhabitants. A success story that is still going strong started with 300 matriculations. Tübingen University now has 16 faculties, and 23 000 students registered in 74 different subjects.

The university and the Protestant "seminary" founded in 1536 have schooled important figures such as the poets Hölderlin, Mörike and Uhland, and the philosophers Hegel and Schilling. The astronomer Kepler worked here, as did Greek scholar and theologian Melanchthon. It was here in 1623 that Wilhelm Schickard invented the first calculating machine, which was attributed to Blaise Pascal for many years. In 1869, 25-year-old Friedrich Miescher discovered deoxyribonucleic acid, or DNA, here.

Walking About

THE OLD TOWN★★

Eberhardsbrücke

This bridge gives a scenic **view★** over the Neckar. The roofs of the houses and the Hölderlin Tower rise above the light foliage of the weeping willows. The **Platanenallee** leads off to the left, a beautiful walkway along the bank of the Neckar. From here visitors may be fortunate enough to see some punts, the gondolas of Tübingen, which make trips from the Hölderlin Tower along past the river front and round the island in the Neckar. To the right, a small path leads along the river front.

Hölderlinturm

Open Tue-Sun, 10am-12 noon, 3-5pm, Sat-Sun, 2-5pm. €1.50. ☎ (070 71) 220 40. Once part of the fortifications, this tower was turned into a residence and inhabited by Friedrich Hölderlin from 1807 until his death in 1843. Now a museum, it displays many souvenirs of the poet.

FRIEDRICH HÖLDERLIN IN TÜBINGEN

Friedrich Hölderlin was born at Lauffen am Neckar in 1770. He studied theology at the Protestant seminary in Tübingen in preparation for entering the church as a minister, a vocation chosen for him by his mother. Here he befriended the philosophers Hegel and Schelling. He had begun writing poetry while still at school (in Maulbronn), and continued to write at Tübingen, finally rebelling against a career in the Church. He spent some time in Frankfurt, Switzerland and Bordeaux as a private tutor. The first signs of his mental illness (he is thought to have been suffering from schizophrenia) manifested themselves in 1802. In 1806, he returned to Tübingen where he was promised a recovery from his condition if he put himself into the hands of the professor of medicine, Autenrieth, at the residential home (in the former hostel, the oldest surviving original university building). When the treatment failed to produce any results, he went to stay with a family of carpenters called Zimmer at no 6 Bursagasse. He spent the remaining 36 years of his life in the tower room at this address.

Directory

Where to Eat

Schwärzlocher Hof – *Schwärzloch 1 (2.5km/1.5mi west of the town, leave Tübingen via Schwärzlocher Str. between Schleifmühleweg and Burgholzweg – ☎ (07071) 4 33 62 – www.schwaerzlocher-hof.de – Wed-Sun 11am-10pm – Closed from 25 Dec to mid-Feb – €13.50/22.* The chancel of a 12C church has been incorporated into this farm-inn. There is a beautiful view of the surrounding area from the terrace, shaded by lime trees. Sample the *Most* (dry cider) while enjoying traditional dishes.

Weinstube Forelle – *Kronenstraße 8 – ☎ (07071) 240 94 – www.weinstube-forelle.de – €17.60/30.40.* This restaurant is very popular with students as well as tourists in the evenings. Welcoming staff serve typically Swabian dishes in a pleasant environment.

Where to Stay

Hotel Am Bad – *Am Freibad 2 – ☎ (07071) 797 40 – fax (07071) 75336 – info@hotel-am-bad.de – Closed 18 Dec-6 Jan – P – 35rm: €47/98.* Well-kept hotel located very near Tübingen's open-air swimming pool. Some of the guestrooms have dark-wood furniture, others have a more natural look. Family rooms are available.

Hotel Metropol – *Reutlinger Straße 7 – ☎ (07071) 910 10 – fax (07071) 910125 – P – 12rm: €49/75.* This little hotel is located on the edge of the town and dominates the Tübingen skyline. Guestrooms are clean, modern and functional and the old town is easily accessible on foot.

Taking a Break

Die Kelter – *Schmiedtorstr. 17 – ☎ (07071) 25 46 90 – www.diekelter.de – Café: Mon-Fri 9.30am-11pm, Sat 9.30am-4pm, Bar: Mon-Wed until 1am, Thu-Sat until 2am, Sun, 5pm-1am – Closed the first two weeks in Jan.* This half-timbered building brings together a café-restaurant, bar, delicatessen and wine shop (tastings available) all under the one roof.

Going Out

Schöne Aussichten – *Wilhelmstr. 16 – ☎ (07071) 2 28 84 – www.schoene-aussichten-tuebingen.de – Mon-Thu, 10am-midnight, Fri and Sat, 10am-1am, Sun and bank holidays, 2pm-midnight.* This café has a selection of sweet and savoury nibbles and breakfasts (served between 10am and 6pm, various set menus available). The relaxed atmosphere helps guests forget the stresses of daily life.

Sport and Leisure

Bootsvermietung H. Märkle – *Eberhardsbrücke (behind the tourist office) – ☎ (07071) 3 15 29 – www.bootsvermietung-tuebingen.de – Apr-Sep: 11am-8pm (closed in bad weather or times of flood) – rowing boat from €6.90, pedalo from €9.20, Stocherkahn from €45.60.* Row around Neckar island *(journey time: 1hr)* and enjoy beautiful views of the old town. Or go for a trip in *Stocherkahn*, a type of gondola piloted by a boatman (booking 2-3 days in advance advised).

Schloß Hohentübingen

The present building was built during the Renaissance on the foundations of an earlier 11C fortress built by the archdukes of Tübingen. It houses several university institutes. A magnificent Renaissance portal, the work of sculptor Christoph Jelin, gives access to the four-wing complex.

Museum★ – *Open May-Sep, Wed-Sun, 10am-6pm; Oct-Apr, Wed-Sun, 10am-5pm. Closed 24, 25 and 31 Dec. €3. ☎ (070 71) 297 73 84.* The pre- and early history department displays numerous exhibits, such as the tiny ivory **"Vogelherdpferdchen"★**, the figure of a horse named after the cave near Ulm in which it was discovered in 1931, which is one of the oldest works of art on display from the New Paleolithic Age. There are outstanding exhibits from Classical Antiquity, Ancient Egypt and the Ancient Orient. Note in particular the **religious chamber★** from a tomb dating from the Old Kingdom (3rd millennium BC), which is completely covered in bas-relief sculptures. There is an interesting collection of castings of ancient sculpture in the knights' hall, which features a state oriel with stellar rib vaulting dating from 1537. The museum also has an ethnology department.

There is a good view of the Neckar and the roofs of the old town from the castle terrace.

Castle Residents

Schloß Hohentübingen is home to south Germany's largest colony of bats. Disturbed by the renovation of the roof framework in 1995, the bats decided to move home, choosing the castle cellars as their new abode. For this reason, it is no longer possible for visitors to see the giant vat dating from 1548 which has a capacity of 850hl/18 700gal.

Marktplatz★

An old square, very animated on market days *(Mondays, Wednesdays and Fridays)*. In the centre are a Renaissance fountain and a statue of Neptune. The old half-timbered houses which surround it add to the charm. The sgraffito decoration

TÜBINGEN

Am Markt	Y	Froschgasse	Y 15	Mühlstraße	Y
Ammergasse	Y 5	Hirschgasse	Y 21	Münzgasse	Y 39
Derendinger Straße	Z 8	Holzmarkt	Y 27	Neckargasse	Y 42
Friedrichstraße	Z 12	Karlstraße	Z	Pfleghofstraße	Y 48
		Kirchgasse	Y 30	Poststraße	Z 54
		Kronenstraße	Y 33	Schmiedtorstraße	Y 60
		Lange Gasse	Y	Wilhelmstraße	Y

Bebenhausener Pfleghof . . . Y **B**	Hölderlinturm . . . . Z **A**	Rathaus . . . . Y **R**

on the 15C **Rathaus** dates from 1876 and depicts the allegories of Justice, Agriculture and Science, as well as famous local figures. The astronomic clock (1511) on the façade is the work of Johann Stöfler.

Fruchtschranne

The roof of this imposing 15C half-timbered house is broken by four rows of shed dormers. The house, now a grammar school, was once a ducal grain store

Bebenhausener Pfleghof (Bebenhausen Hospital)

This 15C building was once the administrative seat and tithe barn of Bebenhausen Abbey *(see below)*. Jutting from the tall, steep roof is a three-storey dormer through the windows of which the grain was passed into the lofts.

Stiftskirche

Rood screen and Tower, open from Easter to Harvest Festival (Erntedank) in early October; Fri and Sat, 11.30am-5pm, Sun, 12.45-5pm; during local school summer holidays, Tue-Sun, 11.30am-5pm. €1.

A Gothic hall-church built in the 15C. The rood screen (1490) and the **pulpit**★ (1509) are Flamboyant in origin. Beneath the rood screen with its reticulated rib vaulting stands a fine three-panelled Passion altarpiece (1520), attributed to Dürer's pupil Hans Leonhard Schäufelein. The chancel is in fact the burial place of the princes of Württemberg. Note the funerary monument of Eberhard the Bearded, original founder of the university, and the **Renaissance tombs**★★ of Duke Ludwig and his wife, adorned with fine alabaster relief work.

From the top of the church tower, there is an interesting **view**★ of the river, the castle promontory and, in the distance, the Swabian Jura.

At the foot of the perron leading to Stiftskirche stretches the *Holzmarkt* (woodwork market) with the Georgsbrunnen fountain lending added charm to the scene. The old Heckenhauer bookshop (now a travel agent) is where the writer and poet Hermann Hesse spent his apprenticeship from 1895 to 1899.

►► Neuer Botanischer Garten★ *(greenhouses★)* – Auto- und Spielzeugmuseum Boxenstop *(car and toy museum, Brunnenstraße 18).*

Excursion

Kloster Bebenhausen★

6km north via the Wilhelmstraße. Open Apr to Oct, 9am-6pm, Mon, 9am-12 noon, 1-6pm; Nov to Mar, Tue-Sun, 9am-12 noon, 1-5pm. Closed 1 Jan, 24, 25 and 31 Dec. €3. ☎ (070 71) 60 28 02.

This ancient monastery, founded in c 1180 in the solitude of Schönbuch Forest, is an interesting example of Romanesque-Gothic architecture in Germany. Together with Maulbronn and Eberbach, it is the best preserved Cistercian monastery in Germany. Built to the classic Cistercian plan, but much restored, the abbey church still shows traces of Romanesque design.

In the 15C, Bebenhausen was the wealthiest monastery in Württemberg, owning a vast estate (over 30 000ha/74 000 acres). The famous roof **turret★**, which has become the monastery's trademark, dates from this period of prosperity. It was built by a lay-brother from Salem Abbey between 1407 and 1409 and its filigree stonemasonry is a masterpiece of Gothic architecture. In 1535, the monastery was dissolved, but a Roman Catholic convent remained here with interruptions until 1648. In 1556, a Protestant monastic school was founded here, which remained in place until 1807. Finally, between 1947 and 1952, these historic walls housed the State Parliament *(Landtag)* of the then mini-state of Württemberg-Hohenzollern.

The **cloister** (1475-1500), in the Flamboyant style, has splendid fan vaulting. Facing the lavabo is the summer **refectory★** with delicate painted ornamentation; it was built in c 1335 and its vaulting is supported by three detached pillars. The chapter-house, parlatory and common eating room *(frater)* are also worth a closer look. The west wing houses the winter refectory, which is like a small slice of history from 1490. The tiled stove dates from the mid-16C. On the first floor is the monks' dormitory, which was divided into separate cells in the early 16C.

Schloß Bebenhausen – *Guided tour (45min, leaves hourly). Open Apr to Oct, Tue-Sun, 9am-12 noon, 2-5pm, Sat-Sun, 10am-12 noon, 2-5pm; Nov-Mar, Tue-Sun, 9am-12 noon, 2-4pm, Sat-Sun, 10am-12 noon, 2-4pm. Closed 1 Jan, 24, 25 and 31 Dec. €3. ☎ (070 71) 60 28 02.*

King Karl of Württemberg had a hunting lodge built in the old monastery manor house after 1870. This is where the last king of Württemberg, Wilhelm II, retired after his abdication. His widow, Charlotte, lived here until her death in 1946. The rooms have a homely atmosphere, as Charlotte lived modestly, in a style far removed from royal pomp and splendour.

Überlingen★

This former Imperial City on the northwest arm of Lake Constance was founded c 1180 by Frederick I Barbarossa. Its growth and prosperity in the Middle Ages were largely due to harvests from the vineyards and trade in salt and grain. In 1379 Überlingen was granted Imperial freedom, a status that it retained until 1802. From the mid 19C, the tourist industry, fostered by the mild climate, played an increasingly important role in local economy. Überlingen has been an officially recognised Kneipp spa resort since 1956.

Location

Population: 21 000. Michelin map nº 545 W 11 – Baden-Württemberg. The town is situated on the northwest bank of Bodensee surrounded by orchards and benefits from a mild climate. West of the town there is a pleasant **moat walk** *(Stadtbefestigungsanlagen)* which leads to the lakeside **Seepromenade**.

Landungsplatz 14, 88662 Überlingen, ☎ (075 51) 99 11 22.

Surrounding area: see BODENSEE, KONSTANZ (41km/26mi south), SALEM (13km/8mi east).

Directory

Where to Stay

Hotel Seegarten – *Seepromenade 7 – ☎ (07551) 91 88 90 – fax (07551) 3981 – Closed from Dec to 1 Mar – 21rm: €49/140 – Restaurant €18.50/32.50.* Hotel right by the lake, with a terrace shaded by chestnut trees. Comfortable guestrooms; ask for one with a view of the Überlinger See. Beautiful terrace.

Hotel Rosengarten – *Bahnhofstraße 12 – ☎ (07551) 928 20 – fax (07551) 928239 – info@haus-rosengarten.com – 15rm: €70/135.* Modernised Jugendstil villa peacefully located in the park (Stadtgarten) not far from the lake. Rooms fitted with every comfort.

ÜBERLINGEN

Bahnhofstraße .... A 2
Christophstraße .... A 3
Franziskanerstraße .... B 5
Gradebergstraße .... B 6
Hafenstraße .... B 8
Hizlerstraße .... B 9
Hochbildstraße .... B 10
Hofstatt .... B
Jakob-Kessenring-Str. ...... A 12
Klosterstraße .... A 14
Krummebergstraße .... B 15
Landungsplatz .... B 17
Lindenstraße .... B 19
Luziengasse .... B 20
Marktstraße .... AB 22
Münsterstraße .... B
Obertorstraße .... B 23
Owinger Straße .... B 25
Pfarrhofstraße .... B 26
St.-Ulrich-Straße .... B 28
Seestraße .... B 29

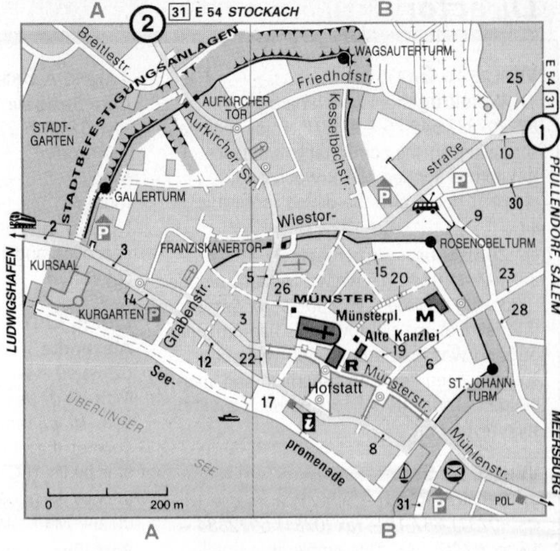

Rathaus .... B R
Städtisches Museum .... B M

Worth a Visit

Münsterplatz

The square lies between the Gothic cathedral, the north façade of the town hall, and the Renaissance municipal chancellery (Alte Kanzlei).

Münster★

The Gothic cathedral, or minster, has an enormous central portion with five aisles covered by painted fan vaulting. The influence of this place of worship is underlined by the number of donor altarpieces including the High Altar by the Brothers Zürn in 1616. A graceful Swabian work of 1510, the Virgin of the Crescent Moon, stands in St Elizabeth Chapel off the south aisle.

Rathaus

Enter through the turret on the right and walk up to the first floor. Open Mai to Oct, Tue-Sun, 9am-12 noon, 2.30-5pm, Sat, 9am-12 noon; Nov to Apr, Mon-Fri, 9am-12 noon, 2.30-5pm. No charge. ☎ (075 51) 99 10 11.

The **Council Chamber★** *(Ratssaal)* is decorated with great finesse in the Gothic manner: panelled walls embellished with projecting arches; ribbed, and slightly rounded, wooden ceiling; a series of 15C statuettes.

Städtisches Museum

Open Tue-Sun, 9am-12.30pm, 2-5pm (Apr to Oct, additionally Sun, 10am-3pm). Closed Tue after Easter and Pentecost. €2. ☎ (075 51) 99 10 79.

Among the exhibits, housed in a late-15C mansion with Baroque modifications, are paintings and sculpture by local artists from the Gothic period to Classicism, a collection of 18C cribs (Krippen) and 50 dolls' houses from the Renaissance to Jugendstil.

Ulm★★

The royal palace of "Hulma", recorded for the first time in 854, was one of Europe's most important cities in the Middle Ages and acknowledged leader of the Swabian League of Cities. Between 1842 and 1859 Ulm and Neu-Ulm, on the opposite bank of the Danube and now part of Bavaria, were made into a stronghold as part of the German Federation and enclosed in a 9km/6mi-long fortified wall. Blessed with an exceptional cathedral, visitors also enjoy walks between the canals and the Danube. Ulm's most famous local figure is Albert Einstein, born here in 1879.

Location

Population: 115 000. Michelin maps nos 545, 546 U 13 – Baden-Württemberg. Ulm is separated from Neu Ulm by the river Danube, mid-way between Munich and Stuttgart on the A 8. Trade and industry, especially in the manufacturing sector, have long been established in these sister cities situated at the crossroads of several major communications routes.

i Münsterplatz, 89073 Ulm, ☎ (0731) 161 28 30.

Surrounding area: see ZWIEFALTEN (50km/31mi southwest), SCHWÄBISCHE ALB (50km/31mi west), ROMANTISCHE STRASSE – join it at AUGSBURG (77km/48mi east) or at NÖRDLINGEN (73km/46mi north).

Directory

Where to Eat

⊖ Weinkrüger – *Weinhofberg 7 – ☎ (0731) 649 76 – €12/17.* Enjoy regional specialities in the comfortable ambience of this former tannery. Dark wood and pleasant decor give the dining room a rustic air.

⊖ Zunfthaus – *Fischergasse 31 – ☎ (0731) 644 11 – www.zunfthaus-ulm.de – Booking advised – €19.30/39.10.* Set in the heart of the old town this half-timbered building was built around 600 years ago and has been home to fishermen and shipbuilders. Today its 3 floors house a country-style restaurant.

Where to Stay

⊖ Pension Rösch – *Schwörhausgasse 18 – ☎ (0731) 657 18 – fax (0731) 6022584 – 16rm: €24/72.* This simple little hotel, good value and very clean, is located at the entrance to the fishermen's district. Neat little guestrooms.

⊖⊖⊖ Schiefes Haus – *Schwörhausgasse 6 – ☎ (0731) 96 79 30 – fax (0731) 9679333 – hotelschiefeshausulm @t-online.de – 11rm: from €103.* This medieval house has been restored and filled with designer furniture. Comfortable water beds in the guestrooms.

Taking a Break

Café Ströbele – *Hirschstr. 4 – ☎ (0731) 6 37 79 – Mon-Sat, 7.30am-8pm, Sun, 11am-6pm, Shop. Mon-Fri, 8am-6pm, Sat, 8am-4pm.* Tea room (on the first floor) with 10 different types of tart, more than 40 types of chocolate and freshly baked cakes. Delicious coffee.

Going Out

Alexandre – *Marktplatz 1 – ☎ (0731) 6 02 74 90 – www.alexandre-welt.de – Mon-Wed, 9am-1am, Thu-Sat,)am-2am, Sun, 10am-1am.* French café on the ground floor of the old town hall, recognisable from afar by its 16C murals and with *Jugendstil* interior. In good weather, there is a terrace on the Marktplatz.

Barfüßer – *Paulstr. 4 (to the northeast of Augsburger-Tor-Platz) – 89231 Neu-Ulm – ☎ (0731) 97 44 80 – www.barfuesser-brauhaus.de – 11.30am-11.30pm.* Glass-fronted micro-brewery with tasteful decor and enormous Biergarten on the banks of the Danube. Nibbles and traditional dishes are served to accompany the beer.

Special Features

MÜNSTER★★★

45min (not counting ascent of the spire)

At a total height of 161m/528ft, Ulm cathedral spire is the tallest in the world. It appears to arrow the entire Gothic building skywards in its slender trajectory. The church's sweeping vertical lines, added to the lightness of the pierced masonry, are wholly admirable. Although the foundation stone was laid in 1377, the two towers and the spire were not erected until 1890. A beautiful porch with three arcades and a very fine profile precedes the double Renaissance entrance doors, with a copy of Hans Multscher's arresting *Man of Sorrows* (1429) adorning the central jamb.

Interior

The upswept nave, with sharply pointed arches, is emphasised in its soaring flight by the absence of a transept, which also concentrates attention on the chancel. The chancel arch bears the largest fresco north of the Alps. It depicts the Last Judgement and was created in 1471. To the right on the chancel arch stands the *Man of Sorrows*, an early work by Hans Multscher, a native of Ulm (1429).

The pillars of the central nave support a series of graceful early-15C consoles. The pulpit is surmounted by a splendid wooden sounding board dating from 1510, the work of Jörg Syrlin the Younger, and above this is what appears to be a second pulpit in the Late Gothic style. This is intended for the Holy Spirit, the invisible preacher. The four side aisles feature fine Late Gothic fan vaulting.

At 161m, the spire of Ulm catherdral is the tallest in the world.

M. Hertlein/MICHELIN

Tabernacle★ – *Left of the entrance to the chancel.* At 26m/85ft it is the tallest in Germany. The masterpiece, chiselled out of limestone and sandstone, was produced c 1460-70. Three rows of wooden figures depict the prophets and lawbringers. Visitors should note the small figures of people and animals, which have been carved into the hand-rail of the banister and on which the artist has allowed his imagination to run riot.

Chorgestühl★★★ (Choir stalls) – A marvellous example of wood carving, executed by Jörg Syrlin the Elder between 1469 and 1474, faces two series of characters, from the Bible and from pagan antiquity, one opposite the other. Men are grouped on the left, women on the right, the upper gables being devoted to the Church's apostles and martyrs, and the high backs of the stalls to Old Testament figures.

The most expressive sculptures are carved from the sides of the stalls and include sibyls on the right, busts of Greek and Latin philosophers and writers (Pythagoras, Cicero etc) on the left. Figures probably representing the sculptor and his wife head the ranks nearest the nave.

The triple throne, which Jörg Syrlin the Elder created in 1468 as a test of his skill, stands beneath the chancel arch. Only after completing this work was he commissioned to produce the choir stalls.

The Iconoclasts

Konrad Sam, a virulent preacher, brought the Swiss Reformation movement to Ulm in 1530, advocating the destruction of imagery in the church. Following a referendum, and with the approval of 87% of the population, he turned the cathedral into a Protestant building. The town council advised private donors to take their altars home and had the most precious parts concealed: the central door, the stalls and the tabernacle (particularly targeted since it contained the blood and body of Christ by virtue of a transubstantiation that was refuted by the Reformers). Some altars were even given to neighbouring villages, where they have remained to this day. The rage of the iconoclasts was unleashed on 21 June 1531: what remained in the cathedral – sixty altars, numerous statues, and probably a large number of altarpieces and hangings – was savagely destroyed.

Ascent of the Spire

768 steps. The climb to the top of the spire is an experience in itself: the structure takes on the appearance of stone lacework. From the tower platform or the bulb of the spire, the extraordinary all-round **panorama★★** includes the town, the Danube, the plateaux of the Swabian Jura and the Alps.

Walking About

Fischerviertel★

The little alleys which extend along the Blau in the quarter formerly inhabited by millers, fishermen and tanners, are very appealing. A good place to start an exploration is Fischerplätzle, a small square shaded by a lime tree. Turn left into a narrow street and pass over the little bridge, which leads to the so-called **crooked house** (*Schiefes Haus*, mid-15C) on the banks of the *Blau*. The tiny alley opposite is known as the "kissing alley" *(Kußgasse)*, because the roofs of the houses touch one another. The house of oaths *(Schwörhaus)* nearby (the main part of which originates from 1613) is the scene every year on Oath Monday of the ceremonial statement of account by the chief burgomaster and of the renewal of his oath.

Deutsches Brotmuseum, Ulm

Baker's sign dating from 1820.

The town **walls** afford a wonderful close-up view of the gables of the old houses. Visitors cannot fail to notice the crooked **Metzger tower**, erected in 1349, since it stands 2.05m/nearly 7ft out of true. Go through the rose garden to reach the eagle bastion *(Adlerbastei)*, where the unfortunate tailor of Ulm attempted to fly in 1811.

South bank of the Danube★

A walk along the Jahnufer (the south bank of the Danube) gives a fine view of gabled houses crowning the ramparts on the far side of the river, of the Metzgerturm (Butchers' Tower) and the cathedral.

ULM

Bahnhofstr.	Y	Gideon-Bacher-Str.	Y 23	Münsterpl.	Y 43
Dreikönigasse	Y 16	Glöcklerstraße	Z 24	Neue Str.	Z
Fischergasse	Z 19	Herdbruckerstr.	Z 25	Neuer Graben	Y 44
Fischerplätzle	Z 20	Hirschstr.	Y 29	Platzgasse	Y
Friedrich-Ebert-Str.	Z 21	Kornhausgasse	Y 33	Schuhhausgasse	Y 52
		Krampgasse	Z 34	Schweinemarkt	Z 54
		Kronengasse	Z 35	Schwilmengasse	Z 55
		Marienstr.	Z 38	Schwörhausgasse	Z 56
		Marktpl.	Z 39	Stadmauer	Z 59

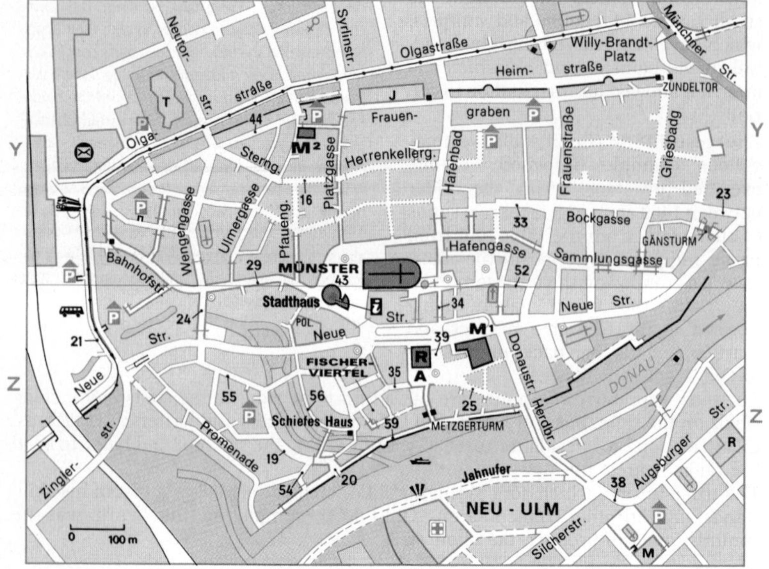

Deutsches Brotmuseum	Y	M²	Rathaus	Z	R
Fischerkasten	Z	A	Ulmer Museum	Z	M¹

Worth a Visit

Stadthaus

The gleaming white town hall (1991-93) with its avant-garde architecture, has been the subject of controversy. It was unquestionably somewhat daring to erect this work, by the American architect **Richard Meier**, right next to the venerable cathedral. However it provides an exciting link between the past and the present, takes away a little of the severity of the cathedral square, and brings a cheerful note, especially in the summer, when the terrace is full of young and old.

Ulmer Museum★

Open Tue-Sun, 11am-5pm. Closed 24, 25 and 31 Dec. €2.50, no charge on Fri. ☎ (0731) 161 43 00; www.museum.ulm.de

The museum consists of a complex of four adjacent houses. The works by the Ulm masters are particularly noteworthy, and include the Virgin Mary of Bihlafingen by Hans Multscher.

One of the most arresting exhibits is the charming *Mary of Sorrows*, edged in blue and gold, the work of a master from the Lake Constance area of Upper Swabia (early 13C). The easternmost of the houses, the Kiechelhaus, is the only one among the very many Ulm mansions from the 16C and 17C which has survived fully intact. It features, among other things, a beautiful Renaissance coffered ceiling on the second floor. Several rooms are dedicated to the guilds, which were of course especially important in a rich town like Ulm. The master craftsman's plaques, which date from the 16C to the 18C, bear witness to the strict guild regulations.

The museum boasts an archaeological section with an interesting statuette, one of the oldest representations of man (about 32 000 years old). There is a collection of 20C art, including works by Klee, Kandinsky, Kirchner and Rothko as well as the **Kurt Fried collection**.

Altes Rathaus

An elegant Gothic and Renaissance building with pierced gables and painted façades. An astronomic clock adorns the fine west façade.

On the market square in front of the town hall is the *Fischerkasten*, a fountain thus named because fishermen would cool their wares in it. The spiral stem was fashioned by Jörg Syrlin the Elder in 1482.

Deutsches Brotmuseum★

♿ Open daily, 10am-5pm (-8.30pm, Wed). Closed Good Fri and 24 Dec. €2.50, no charge on 3rd Sun of May. ☎ (0731) 699 55; www.museum-brotkultur.de

This collection, unique in Germany, has found a worthy setting in the Salzstadel or salt barn, a Renaissance building dating from 1592. It was established when an Ulm entrepreneur realised that no museum existed for bread, which is so important to humanity. Starting around 1950 he and his son meticulously put together a collection, with enormous professional and artistic understanding, which represents **8 000 years** of the cultural and social history of bread. Videos and dioramas contribute towards a better understanding of the subject.

Exhibits range from ovens, models, guild symbols, coins and stamps, to specially selected works of art (by Brueghel, Corinth, Kollwitz, Picasso). Everything in the museum is related to grain (its cultivation and trade) or bread. A critical examination is made of the world food situation.

Olympic Designs

The pictograms representing each of the Olympic disciplines were designed at the Ulm School of Design by German designer Otl Aicher for the Olympic Games in Munich in 1972. They have been used at each subsequent Games and are reproduced on the medals, to the great pride of the city.

►► Heilig-Geist-Kirche *(modern church with beautiful view over the town)* – Donauschwäbisches Zentralmuseum *(history and culture)*.

Excursions

Kloster Wiblingen (Abbey)

5km/3mi south. Open Apr to Oct, Tue-Sun, 10am-12 noon, 2-5pm, Sat-Sun, 10am-5pm; Nov to Mar, Sat-Sun, 2-4pm. Closed 24, 25 and 31 Dec. €2. ☎ (0731) 502 89 75; www.kloster-wiblingen.de

Although its foundation dates back to the 11C, the final touches were not put to the abbey church until the 18C. As at Vierzehnheiligen *(see Wallfahrtskirche VIERZEHNHEILIGEN)*, more than a third of the abbey church's floor plan is occupied by the transept, where pilgrims worshipped relics of the Holy Rood. The flattened domes of this Baroque building could give visitors the impression of being crushed, but this is compensated for by the illusion of height provided by the painter Januarius Zick in the frescoes which cover them. This artist is also responsible for the high altar. The **abbey library★**, completed in 1760, is one of the finest examples of the Rococo in Swabia.

The main interest lies in a gallery, supported by 32 columns, which projects into the centre of the room and at each end. The rhythmically placed columns, painted alternately pink and blue, combine with the large false-relief fresco on the ceiling to create an ensemble rich in colour and movement.

Blaubeuren★

18km/11mi west. Follow the signposts for Blautopf-Hochaltar, in this village of the Swabian Jura renowned for its fine setting among the rocks, then leave the car near the monumental abbey entrance.

Blautopf – *15min on foot there and back.* This deep blue pool was formed by a natural embankment of glacial origin. The shady approaches have been laid out as walks.

Old Benedictine Abbey – *Allow 30min. Follow the "Hochaltar" signs.* The premises include a picturesque group of ancient half-timbered buildings. In the chancel of the old abbey church (Klosterkirche) is a magnificent **altarpiece★★** (Hochaltar), a masterpiece of Gothic sculpture and a collective work created by the principal studios of Ulm in the 15C. The themes treated are Christ's Birth and Passion, the life of St John the Baptist, and the Virgin Mary between the saints. The beautiful choir **stalls★** of 1493 and the triple throne are the work of Ulm master Jörg Syrlin the Younger.

Insel Usedom★

Usedom displays a wonderfully unspoilt natural landscape, alternating between moors, inland seas, forest, dunes, sandy beaches, with steep cliffs here and there. The island is part of the Usedom-Oderhaff Nature Reserve. Its extremely irregular outline can best be compared with a wide-open crocodile's jaw. Its main industry is tourism, since the elegant bathing resorts on the Baltic coast developed after 1820. At the turn of the century it became known as "Berlin's bathtub", since it was mainly the residents of the capital who came here to relax and recuperate. Notable bathing resort architecture from this period remains, and has been carefully restored everywhere.

Directory

Where to Stay

⊜⊜ **Hotel Zur Post** – *Seestraße 5, 17429 Usedom-Bansin – ☎ (038378) 560 – fax (038378) 56220 – hzp_usedom@t-online.de – P ♿ – 60rm: €65/130 ☕ – Restaurant €17.50/35.* A beautiful example of coastal architecture, this hotel is reached via an exterior staircase. The two tower guestrooms have particularly attractive furnishings, while the restaurant serves good traditional cuisine.

⊜⊜⊜ **Romantik Seehotel Ahlbecker Hof** – *Dünenstraße 47, 17419 Usedom-Ahlbeck – ☎ (038378) 620 – fax (038378) 62100 – ahlbecker-hof@seetel.de – P – 66rm: €145/200 ☕ – Restaurant €36/52.* Set in a beautiful building which has been brought bang-up-to-date, this hotel will satisfy the most demanding guest: guestrooms and spa complex are elegantly arranged. The crystal chandeliers and timeless ambience of the restaurant make this an unforgetable place to stay.

Location

Michelin map nº 542 D 25, E 26 – Mecklemburg-Vorpommen. Usedom is Germany's easternmost island. The eastern part of the island, with the town of Swinoujscie, covering around one fifth of the total area, belongs to Poland. The flat northwest contrasts with the hilly southeast part, which likes to be known as Usedom's Switzerland.

Surrounding area: see GREIFSWALD (30km/19mi north of Wolgast), STRALSUND (63km/39mi north of Wolgast), Insel RÜGEN.

Worth a Visit

Wolgast

On the mainland. One point of access to Usedom is in the south at Zecherin, and the other lies in the northwest, from Wolgast over the River Peene. The **parish church**, Pfarrkirche St Petri in the birthplace of the Romantic painter Philipp Otto Runge, with its formidable octangular tower, dating back to the year 1370, is a must for visitors. Its unadorned exterior contrasts with its sumptuous interior. There are wall paintings from the 15C and 16C, a danse macabre cycle, which was painted around 1700 by Caspar Sigmund Köppe based on a woodcut by Hans Holbein the Younger, and a Renaissance gravestone. ♿ *Open from May to end Sep, 10am-12.30pm, 1.30pm-5pm, Sun after the church service until 12 noon. ☎ (038 36) 20 22 69.*

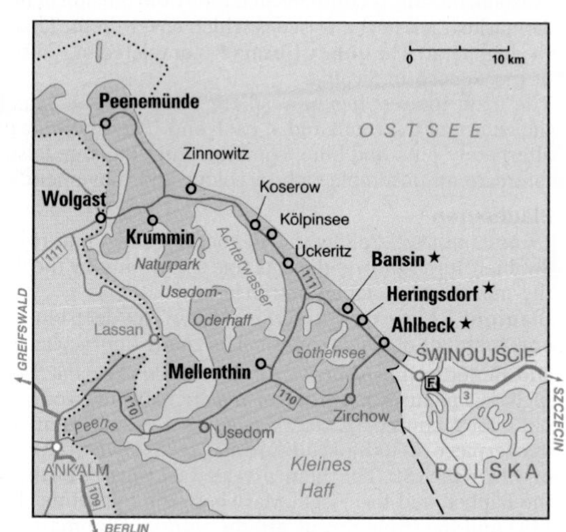

Krummin

East of Wolgast. The most beautiful avenue of **lime trees★** *(Lindenallee)* in Usedom leads to the right off the main B 111 road, down to the little fishing village which lies on the Krummin cove.

The surfaced road is only just two kilometres long, but it is quite marvellous. The rounded canopy formed by the leaves overhead gives one the impression of being in a high Gothic cathedral.

Peenemünde

Historisch-technisches Informationszentrum – ♿ *Open Apr to Oct, Tue-Sun, 9am-6pm; Jun to Sep, 9am-6pm; Nov to Mar, Tue-Sun, 10am-4pm. Closed 24-26 Dec. €5. ☎ (0383 71) 50 50.* The army test-establishment of Peenemünde, the development site of the V2 rockets among others, which cost thousands their lives during the Second World War, but which signalled the beginning of modern space travel, was built right in the north of the island in 1936. An exhibition in the old power station retraces the history of rocket development and its associated dilemmas.

The "Taille" Usedoms

At the narrowest point or waist of the island, the white sandy beaches of the resorts of **Zinnowitz**, **Koserow**, **Kölpinsee** and **Ückeritz** stretch out, protected from time by the steep cliff. At Koserow, the island is barely 200m/220yd wide.

Bansin, Heringsdorf, Ahlbeck

These "three sisters" in the southeast of the island, are linked by a 10km/6mi-long beach promenade. During the 19C these were fashionable resorts, the rendezvous of the aristocracy and the wealthy. The many imposing villas and hotels, which have happily stood the test of time and make these resorts so attractive, bear witness to the past. Despite its rather ordinary name, **Heringsdorf** was an extraordinarily fashionable resort, and Emperor Wilhelm II was a regular visitor. He resided in the Villa Staudt *(Delbrückstraße 6)*, which still stands today. At 508m/1 666ft long, the pier is the longest on mainland Europe. **Ahlbeck** is also justifiably proud of its attractive **historical pier★**, which was built in 1898. A restaurant was added in 1902, and with its white walls, red roof and the four green-roofed corner towers, it is one of the most favoured photographic subjects on the island.

Mellenthin

Northeast of the town of Usedom, 2km/1mi north of the B 110. This little-visited village radiates peace, and with its Renaissance castle, it forms a rural idyll. The three winged building surrounded by a moat is unadorned, whilst a colourfully mounted Renaissance fireplace from the year 1613 in the entrance hall is quite magnificent. The 14C village church in the centre of a cemetery full of 600-year-old oak trees is seriously damaged, but it is still a little pearl with its interior **decoration★** dating from the 17C. The painted Baroque gallery from 1755 in particular radiates fresh and simple belief. The offertory dates from 1125.

Wallfahrtskirche Vierzehnheiligen★★

This pilgrimage church dedicated to the 14 Auxiliary Saints is a marvel of Baroque architecture certain to entrance any visitor. The bold concepts of Balthasar Neumann, master of the Baroque, are evident in the interior.

Location

Michelin maps nos 544, 546 P17 – Bayern. The church is 26km/16mi southeast of Coburg, on an open hillside overlooking the beautiful Upper Main Valley, opposite Kloster Banz *(see BAMBERG: excursions)*.
Surrounding area: see BAMBERG (32km/20mi south), BAYREUTH (56km/35mi east), THÜRINGER WALD.

Background

The Pilgrimage – In 1445 and 1446, a herdsman on this hillside was blessed with a number of visions, the last of them identified as the Christ Child among the "Fourteen Holy Helpers". The worship of this group of saints, actively encouraged by German Dominicans and Cistercians, must be seen in the context of the mysticism which prevailed at the beginning of the 15C, when "visions" were frequent (the "voices" heard by Joan of Arc – born in 1412 – were those of St Catherine and St Margaret, themselves members of this group of Auxiliary Saints). This devotion to the Holy Helpers remained alive for many years among local people, attracting crowds of pilgrims to a chapel which was to be superseded, in the 18C, by a sumptuous Rococo church.

Worth a Visit

THE CHURCH★★

The church was built in handsome yellow ochre sandstone following designs by Balthasar Neumann between 1743 and 1772. The west façade is framed by domed towers unusually tall for a Baroque building. The ornately decorated gables are adorned with a statue of Christ between allegorical figures of Faith and Charity (the statues were once gilded).

Interior – The interior layout is organised as a succession of three oval bays framed by colonnades and covered by low inner domes. The true centre of the church is the bay containing the altar to the Auxiliary Saints – to the detriment of the transept crossing, which is invaded by the bay's colonnade.

Circular domes, again, cover the transepts. Such geometric subtleties create an overall perspective concentrating the worshippers' view relentlessly on a central focal point – an ideal striven for by 18C architects who wearied of an endless succession of rectangular bays.

Many visitors will be surprised by the restraint and elegance of the church's Rococo interior decoration. Outstanding are the colour combinations of the painting inside the domes, the lightness of the stuccowork, the richness of the gold outlines defining the woodwork of the galleries, and the grace of putti surmounting confessionals and cornice.

Nothelfer-Altar★★ (Altar to the Fourteen Auxiliary Saints)

A Rococo pyramid with a pierced baldaquin, where every line is nevertheless convex or concave, this remarkable work was executed by Johann Michael Feuchtmayr and stucco-workers of the Wessobrunn School in 1764. It stands on the spot where the herdsman's visions are said to have occurred.

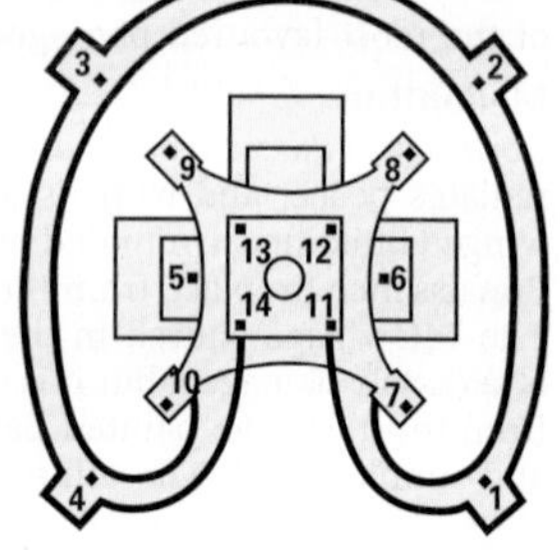

Balustrade: **1**) St Denys – **2**) St Blaise – **3**) St Erasmus – **4**) St Cyriacus (delivery from the Devil at the final hour).

Altar niches: **5**) St Catherine, patron saint of the learned, of students and girls wishing to get married (the model of Christian wisdom) – **6**) St Barbara, patron saint of miners, artillerymen and prisoners (the grace of a noble death).

Buttresses: **7**) St Acacius (the agonies of death) – **8**) St Giles, the only intercessor not to suffer martyrdom (to obtain the grace of a true confession) – **9**) St Eustace (converted by the vision of a stag with a Cross between its antlers) – 10) St Christopher, patron saint of travellers.

On top of the baldaquin: **11**) St Vitus (epilepsy) – **12**) St Margaret (intercession for the forgiveness of sins) – **13**) St George, patron saint of peasants and their possessions – **14**) St Pantaleon.

Those who enjoy seeing – or photographing – unusual views should climb the slopes above the church. Before long, Banz Abbey comes into view on the far side of the valley, framed by the Vierzehnheiligen towers, in line with – and apparently resting on – the ridge pole of the church roof.

Weimar★★

To most non-Germans, the name of Weimar recalls the ill-fated republic which existed uneasily between the end of the First World War and the Hitler years. But the city's claim to a place in European history rests unshakeably on the extraordinary flowering of intellectual and artistic talent here over the centuries, as it attracted great names as diverse as Luther, Cranach, Bach, Wieland, Schiller and Liszt. The one genius whose traces it is impossible to escape in Weimar, however, is that greatest of all German classicists, Johann Wolfgang von Goethe.

The first historical mention of Weimar occurs in a document dated 899. By 1410 the town had been granted an urban charter, and in 1547 it became the capital of the Duchy of Saxe-Weimar. From this time onwards dates the formidable cultural expansion which made the town the true spiritual capital of Germany.

Location

Population: 62 000. Michelin map nº 544 N 8 – Thüringen. Set on the banks of the Ilm, Weimar is in the heart of Thuringia, around 20km/13mi from Erfurt, the capital of the Land. The A 4 motorway links the town to Dresden to the east and Frankfurt to the southwest.

🅸 *Markt 10, 99423 Weimar, ☎ (036 43) 240 00.*

Surrounding area: see ERFURT (20km/13mi west), JENA (22km/14mi east), NAUMBURG (50km/31mi north).

Background

The "German Athens" – Weimar's claim to a place in European history rests unshakeably on the extraordinary flowering of intellectual and artistic talent here over the centuries, as it attracted great names as diverse as Luther, Cranach, Bach, Wieland, Schiller and Liszt. However, the one genius whose traces it is impossible to escape in Weimar is the greatest of all German classicists, Johann Wolfgang von Goethe.

Directory

Where to Eat

Sommer's Weinstube Restaurant – *Humboldtstr. 2 – ☎ (03643) 40 06 91 – www.wein-sommer.com – Closed Sun – €11/17.50.* This restaurant has been run for over 130 years by the Sommer family, and has managed to keep its old-fashioned charm. Thuringian specialites, often potato-based, are served. Large choice of regional and international wines.

Bratwurstglöck'l – *Carl-August-Allee 17a – ☎ (03643) 20 28 75 – Closed Mon – ♿ – €13/18.* Built in 1870, this traditional German inn is situated close to the station. The panelling and beautiful decor make this little town house really comfortable. Regional specialities are on the menu.

Where to Stay

Hotel Zur Sonne – *Rollplatz 2 – ☎ (03643) 80 04 10 – fax (03643) 862932 – hotelzursonne@web.de – 21rm: €51/81 – Restaurant €10/17.50.* The neat brick house is located in the heart of the old town. Inside the style is modern, with practical, welcoming guestrooms. The pleasant restaurant is set out in the style of an old German inn.

Romantik Hotel Dorotheenhof – *Dorotheenhof 1, 99427 Weimar-Schöndorf – ☎ (03643) 45 90 – fax (03643) 459200 – info@dorotheenhof.com – P ♿ – 60rm: €68/145 – Restaurant €21.50/32.50.* Country house hotel set above the city in a quiet location in a small park. Elegant restaurant with charming vaulted ceiling.

Going Out

Café Louis – *Jakobstr. 10 (in the courtyard of the Kirms-Krackow) – ☎ (03643) 80 16 81 – www.cafe-louis-weimar.de – Tue-Sun, 11am-midnight (dinner served until 11pm).* Hidden away in the courtyard of an old house, this establishment's atmosphere is quite unique, with its terrace, 19C Goethe drawing room and idyllic garden. Thai cuisine and cakes are on the menu. Local wine list and cocktails.

Crêperie du palais – *Am Palais 1 (east of Wittumspalais) – ☎ (03643) 40 15 81 – www.creperie-weimar.de – 9.30am-midnight; closed the second week in Jan).* This French-style crêperie has pancakes, crêpes, cider, wine, aperitifs and even a selection of French cigarettes on the menu. Small shady terrace on the other side of the road.

Residenz-Café – *Grüner Markt 4 (near Stadtschloss) – ☎ (03643) 5 94 08 – www.residenz-cafe.de – Mon-Fri, 8am-1am, Sat-Sun, 9am-1am.* This building dates from 1839 and before it became a café, the *Goethezimmer* room was Goethe's living room. Today it is a modern establishment with pleasant ambience where refreshments are served all day long.

An Intellectual and Cultural Centre – Weimar's hour of glory coincided with the succession, in 1758, of the Duchess Anna Amalia. It was during her reign that the town's intellectual reputation grew, largely because of **Goethe** (1749-1832). He had first been summoned to the court at the age of 26 by Amalia's son, Duke Carl August. In the small provincial capital – at that time numbering no more than 5 000 inhabitants – he was appointed Minister and raised to a peerage, and it was in Weimar that he produced the majority of his life's work, including his dramatic masterpiece *Faust*. Goethe's reputation and influence spread far beyond the city's boundaries. For more than 25 years he directed the Weimar Theatre, which soon became accepted as the German National Theatre, renowned for its staging of international classics. This was the result of a fruitful collaboration with **Friedrich von Schiller**, who moved permanently to Weimar in 1799. The work produced by these two friends, along with the writings of the theologian **Johann Gottfried Herder** (1744-1803, moved to Weimar in 1776), a disciple of Kant, raised Weimar's literary reputation to the point where the town was considered "the home of German classicism". In the Goethe-Schiller Archives *(Jener Straße)*, which are among the most important literary collections in the country, several posthumous works are conserved, together with letters from almost 1 000 personalities worldwide.

Art and Music in Weimar – It was in Weimar that **Lucas Cranach the Elder** worked – from 1552 until his death a year later – on his final masterpiece: the altarpiece triptych for the local church of St Peter and St Paul *(see Stadtkirche below)*. **Johann Sebastian Bach** was organist and choirmaster there from 1708 to 1717. In 1848 **Franz Liszt** in his turn became choirmaster and surrounded himself with the artistic elite of the period. It was Liszt who was the driving force behind the creation of Weimar's famous School of Music, which still bears his name today.

In 1860, an establishment was founded which left an indelible mark on 20C German painting. This was the School of Fine Arts – later to be transformed into the Bauhaus University, a College of Architecture and Design. It was under the influence of such celebrated graduates as **Arnold Böcklin** (1827-1901) that painters spearheading the contemporary avant-garde movement developed what is known as "the Weimar School".

Jugendstil and Bauhaus – The famous Belgian exponent of Jugendstil, or Art Nouveau, **Henri van de Velde**, was called to Weimar in 1902. In the company of other artists he stood for the "new Weimar", founded an applied arts school (the

WEIMAR

present day Van-de-Velde building in the Bauhaus University) and built a number of Jugendstil houses, examples of which are at *nos 15 and 47 Cranachstraße*. His own house, the "Hohe Pappeln" house *(Belvederer Allee 58)*, completed in 1907 and recently restored, is a fine example of his work.

Further Jugendstil buildings by other architects can be seen in Gutenbergstraße and Humboldtstraße.

In 1919 the State Bauhaus was established in Weimar under the management of Walter Gropius. The interdisciplinary interaction between artists and craftsmen was to lead to a new style of building and living. This "Bauhaus style" took shape in Weimar, where beauty of form and practicality were expressed in cubic architectural and commercial art designs. Traditional Weimar was not capable of taking advantage of this opportunity for radical renewal, with the result that the Bauhaus was obliged to cease its work in 1925 and moved to Dessau *(see DESSAU)*.

The Weimar Republic (1919-33) – The constitution of the ill-fated Weimar Republic was set up in 1919 by the German National Assembly, which sat at that time in the theatre of the town. However, the government was never really based in Weimar and returned to Berlin one week after adoption of the text. The humanist tradition of Goethe's town had merely provided the budding democracy with a welcome counterpoint to the politically oppressive atmosphere of post-war Berlin.

Walking About

THE HISTORIC CENTRE★★

Some of the main sights of Weimar – mostly related to great figures of the German Renaissance or Enlightenment – are to be found within a small area in the lively and essentially pedestrian city centre, around two large, neighbouring squares: Theaterplatz – with the National Theatre and Bauhaus Museum – and Marktplatz.

Goethes Wohnhaus und Goethe Museum★★

Frauenplan. Open Apr to Oct, Tue-Sun, 9am-6pm; Nov to Mar, Tue-Sun, 9am-4pm. Closed 24 Dec. €6. ☏ (036 43) 54 54 01; www.weimar-klassik.de

The dramatist-politician lived in this Baroque mansion (1709) for over 20 years, from 1809 until his death in 1832. The interior is for the most part the way he left it. The living rooms, workroom, library (5 400 volumes) and garden can all be visited. Each room has its own particular decoration with paintings and sculptures amassed by the great man during his travels. The national Goethe museum's permanent exhibition puts the work of Goethe in the context of Weimar Classicism from the end of the 18C to the beginning of the 19C. Manuscripts, letters and *objets d'art* evoke his contemporaries: men of letters such as Wieland, Herder and Schiller, or patrons like the Duchess Anna Amalia and her son the Duke Carl August.

J. Bouraly/MICHELIN

Garden of Goethes Wohnhaus.

Go to Haus der Frau von Stein via Ackerwand.

Haus der Frau von Stein

Ackerwand 25. Goethe met Charlotte von Stein, lady-in-waiting to the Duchess Anna Amalia, in November 1775. The first 10 years of his stay in Weimar were profoundly influenced by his feelings for her. The house was remodelled in 1776 to his own design. Today the building is home to the Goethe Institute as well as a language school and cultural centre.

Platz der Demokratie

The equestrian statue of the Grand Duke Carl August of Saxe-Weimar-Eisenach (1757-1828), executed by Adolf von Donndorf, stands in this square. On the south side, the former palace (1757-74) is occupied by the **Franz Liszt Hochschule für Musik**. The 16C-18C *Grünes Schloß* today houses the **Duchess Anna Amalia Library**. It contains medieval manuscripts, very early printed works, rare documents dating from the 16C and 17C, and above all original, priceless 18C volumes. For many years now, the museum has been collecting manuscripts, publications and translations relating to the "Age of Enlightenment" *(Aufklärung)* – Kant, Locke, Leibniz etc.

From Platz der Demokratie go to the neighbouring market place

Cranach-Haus

The famous painter spent the last year of his life in this Renaissance house (1549) adorned with scrolled gables. His studio was on the third floor.

The Rathaus, opposite, was built c 1500 but heavily remodelled in the mid-19C.

Take Schillerstraße towards Theaterplatz.

Schillers Wohnhaus★

Schillerstraße 12. Open Apr to Oct, Tue-Sun, 9am-6pm; Nov to Mar, Tue-Sun, 9am-4pm. Closed 24 Dec. €3.50. ☎ (036 43) 54 54 01. The writer moved here in 1802 to be nearer to his great friend Goethe. It was here that *William Tell* and *The Bride of Messina* were written. The Schiller Museum offers a rundown on his life and his work.

Follow Schillerstraße until Theaterplatz.

Deutsches Nationaltheater

The present structure, which dates from 1907, was built on the site of a 1779 Baroque building. It was in this old theatre that Schiller's great plays were staged and directed by Goethe; it was here, in 1850, that the first performance of Richard Wagner's *Lohengrin* was given. In 1919 the constitution of the Weimar Republic was adopted by the German National Assembly which sat here.

In front of the present building stand the **statues★★** of Goethe and Schiller, sculpted in 1857 by Ernst Rietschel.

H. Champollion/MICHELIN

Goethe and Schiller, Weimar.

Bauhaus-Museum

Open Apr to Oct, Tue-Sun, 10am-6pm; Nov to Mar, Tue-Sun, 10am-4.30pm. €3. ☎ (036 43) 54 61 30; www.kunstsammlungen-weimar.de
The Bauhaus School occupied this building from 1919 until 1925, when it moved to Dessau. The museum brings together designs and finished work from Henry Van de Velde's School of Applied Arts. The main collection is that accumulated by Walter Gropius.

Wittumspalais

Open Apr to Oct, Tue-Sun, 9am-6pm; Nov to Mar, Tue-Sun. 10am-4pm. Closed 24 Dec. €3.50. ☎ (036 43) 54 54 01. After the death of her husband the Duchess Anna Amalia moved to this 1767 Baroque palace with two wings; it was here that she organised the famous salons of which Goethe, Schiller, Herder and Wieland were so important a part. The **Wielandmuseum** illustrates the life and work of this fervent supporter of German classicism, translator and spokeswoman for the *Aufklärung* (German Enlightenment).

Go to Herderplatz via Zeughof then Rittergasse.

Stadtkirche or Herderkirche

Am Herderplatz. This triple-nave Gothic hall-church *(see Art and Music in Weimar above)* was built between 1498 and 1500 and much remodelled in the Baroque style between 1735 and 1745. It is also known as the Herderkirche, in memory of the sermons preached there by the philosopher, who is buried in the church. The famous **Cranach Triptych★★**, started by Lucas Cranach the Elder and finished by his son in 1555, represents the Crucifixion on its central panel. This is surrounded by scenes from the Old and New Testmanents. On the right, Luther and Cranach the Elder himself are depicted.
Sumptuous **Renaissance gravestones★** adorn the chancel of this otherwise relatively plainly decorated church.

Stadtschloß und Kunstsammlungen zu Weimar

The original palace burned down in 1774 and was rebuilt in the neo-Classical style under Duke Carl August from 1789 to 1803. The addition of a south wing in 1914 completed the four-wing layout. Some of the apartments, among Germany's finest examples of early and late neo-Classicism, are open to the public: the banqueting hall, the great gallery and rooms dedicated to the writers Goethe, Schiller, Wieland and Herder. The galleries house the Weimar art collections. Here, visitors can see: an important **Cranach collection★★** *(Sybil of Cleves, Portrait of Luther)*; Flemish and Italian paintings; and work by Hans Baldung Grien, Albrecht Dürer and Bartholomäus Bruyn the Elder. The Weimar School and German Impressionists and Expressionists (Max Beckmann, Max Liebermann) are also represented.
In the southwest wing of the complex is the main tower (1729-32) with its Baroque cupola, and the 1545 (renovated) keep. *Open Apr to Oct, Tue-Sun, 10am-6pm; Nov to Mar, Tue-Sun, 10am-4.30pm. €4. ☎ (036 43) 54 61 30.*

ILM PARK★★

Weimar is in fact a park in which they happened to build a town: this approving comment was written by Adolf Stahr in 1851 – and indeed modern Weimar is still a city of green spaces, indissolubly linked with its riverside park. From the palace of Tiefurt to the Belvedere, there is a single stretch of greenery centred on the gardens laid out on each side of the Ilm. There was no intention of restraining nature – said Goethe, planning the English-style landscaping – but simply of guiding and at the same time respecting her. The gardens are only a few yards from the city centre.

Goethes Gartenhaus★★

Duke Carl August made a present of this summer residence to Goethe, and the great man liked it so much that he lived there permanently from 1776 to 1782. It remained his favourite retreat until the end of his life.
Among his works there is even a short poem recording his delight in the place:

"It is an unpretentious
Small house beneath a tall roof.
Everyone who came there
Felt light-hearted;
Trees I had planted grew strong and green,
And the spirit as well
Thrived on this blessed ground."

It was in this house that Goethe wrote *Wilhelm Meister's Theatrical Mission*, major parts of *Iphigenia*, and early drafts of *Egmont* and *Torquato Tasso*. The house has been converted into a museum with examples of Goethe's furniture and drawings. Facing it is the **Borkenhäuschen**, Augusts' own favourite retreat. Only 10min walk away is the **Römisches Haus**, a classical building (1791-97) designed by Goethe for the Grand Duke.

Cross the park now in the direction of the Belvederer Allee.

Liszt-Haus

On the west side of the park along the Belvederer Allee. Open Apr to Oct, Tue-Sun, 9am-1pm, 2-6pm; Nov to Mar, Tue-Sun, 10am-1pm, 2-4pm. Closed 24 Dec. €2. ☎ (036 43) 54 54 01; www.weimar-klassik.de

In this one-time gardeners' lodge at the entrance to the park it is possible to visit the apartments lived in by the composer during his second stay in Weimar, from 1869 to 1886.

Worth a Visit

Neues Museum

Rathenauplatz. ♿ Open Apr to Oct, Tue-Sun, 10am-6pm; Nov to Mar, Tue-Sun. 10am-4.30pm. €3. ☎ (036 43) 54 61 30. The grand neo-Renaissance building was put up as an archducal museum between 1863 and 1869. During the Third Reich it was the headquarters of the Nazi administration for Thuringia. It has now been restored to its original vocation as a museum, thanks to the collection of gallery owner Paul Maenz from Cologne. The museum is dedicated to the international Avant-Garde since 1960 with special emphasis on German art and Italian *Arte Povera*, and American Minimal and Conceptual Art.

Historischer Friedhof und Fürstengruft

This is the central focus of the ancient cemetery and was built in 1825-27 by CW Coudray as the burial place of the princely family. It is the last resting place for Goethe, Schiller and Grand Duke Carl August, who lie here side by side. The **Russian Orthodox Church** nearby was built between 1859 and 1862 specially for Maria Pavlova, Grand Duchess and daughter-in-law of Carl August. Goethe's muse, Frau von Stein, also lies in the cemetery.

Nietzsche Archiv

Open Apr to Oct, Tue-Sun, 1-6pm; Nov to Mar, Tue-Sun, 1-4pm. Closed 24 Dec. €2. ☎ (036 43) 54 54 01.

The philosopher **Friedrich Nietzsche** spent the last three years of his life, until his death in 1900, in this house. During this final stage of his 12-year decline into paralysis and madness he was cared for by his sister Elisabeth. After Nietzsche's death, Elisabeth set up an archive on her brother's work and commissioned Van de Velde to adapt the ground floor of the house to accommodate it in 1903. Appropriating her brother's intellectual legacy, Elisabeth was far from conveying the true essence of his work and thinking; she was in fact instrumental in creating the erroneous image of Nietzsche as anti-Semitic and pro-German, opening the way for the ideology of the Third Reich.
A highlight of the visit has to be the **library★**, in which the furniture and fittings combine to make the room a work of art in itself. Note the bust of Nietzsche by Max Klinger. The archive houses literature on the life and work of this brilliant, although tragically misinterpreted, philosopher.

►► *Haus Unter den Hohen Pappeln* (House of Henry Van de Velde, Belvederer Allee 58; take bus 1 or 12 towards Papiergraben).

Excursions

Schloß Tiefurt

2km/1mi east. Open Apr to Oct, Tue-Sun, 9am-6pm; Nov to Mar, Tue-Sun, 10am-4pm. Closed 24 Dec. €3.50. ☎ (036 43) 54 54 01. The former summer residence (18C) of Duchess Amalia is surrounded by English-style gardens. Both palace and gardens were frequently the scene of the literary gatherings she loved. Goethe, the Humboldt brothers and the other members of her cultural coterie were welcome guests.

Schloß Belvedere

4km/3mi southeast. Open Apr to mid-Oct, Tue-Sun, 10am-6pm; mid- to end Oct, Tue-Sun, 10am-4.30pm. €3. ☎ (036 43) 54 61 30.
This is one of the most delightful – and the most artistically successful – stately homes of Thuringia. Comprising a large central block flanked by two low wings, the mansion is completed by four outbuildings and an orangery harbouring a collection of carriages and barouches. The beautifully restored interior is open to visitors. There is an outstanding collection of 17C-19C porcelain and glassware.
The grounds, originally formal in the Baroque style, were redesigned and laid out as an English garden between 1814 and 1840.

Buchenwald

8km/5mi northwest. ♿ Open May to Sep, Tue-Sun, 9.45am-5.15pm; Oct to Apr, Tue-Sun, 8.45am-4.15pm. Closed 22 Dec-1 Jan. No charge. ☎ (036 43) 43 02 00; www.buchenwald.de
Only a few miles from Weimar, cradle of Humanism and first capital (1918) of a democratic Germany, the Ettersberg beech forests concealed for eight years one of the largest concentration camps of the Hitler regime. Established in July 1937 for the internment of Germans who opposed the Nazi ethos, the camp was quick to take the Jews and gypsies persecuted by the National Socialists – and then, as the invasion of Europe expanded, victims from the occupied countries. A total of some 250 000 human beings, including innumerable children, took the road that led to Buchenwald; more than 50 000 of them died there. The camp was liberated by the Americans on 11 April 1945 at 3.15pm.
In August 1943, about 100km/60mi north of Weimar near Nordhausen, an auxiliary camp to that of Buchenwald was set up, called **Dora** *(see HARZ)*. From October 1944 this was run as an independent labour camp with auxiliary camps of its own. Internees had to convert existing shafts into an underground factory for the manufacture of V-2 rockets and undertake rocket production itself. The construction of the factory in what was essentially an unsuitable location, coupled with catastrophic standards of hygiene and appalling working conditions resulted in a very high death toll among the prisoners. In the 20 months of the camp's existence, some 20 000 people met their death there. Dora is now a memorial site and museum, with some of the shafts open to visitors as part of a guided tour.

Gedenkstätte Buchenwald (Memorial Centre) – *Map and descriptive brochure at entrance.* The Information Centre shows a film tracing the history of the camp. A tour of the camp starts at the gatehouse, which still retains above the entrance the chilling slogan: "Jedem das Seine" ("You get what you deserve").
The position of each hut is marked out on the ground; at the far end, on the right, is the building which was used for storing the inmates' possessions and effects, now transformed into a museum. Outside the camp, a road leads to the quarry where excessively rigorous working conditions resulted in a particularly high death rate among those sent there.

Special camp 2 – From 1945 to 1950, the Soviet occupation force set up a special camp here, in which Nazi criminals and officials, and also political prisoners, were interned. According to Soviet sources, over 7 000 people died in this camp.

Buchenwald Memorial (Mahnmal Buchenwald) – *1km/0.6mi in the direction of Weimar.* From the entrance, the Steles' Way leads to the Avenue of Nations, which links three mass graves. The last of these brings you to the memorial bell-tower, in front of which is the statuary group by Fritz Cremer, representing resistance in the camp.

Wiesbaden★

Lying at the foot of the Taunus mountains and favoured by the mild climate of the Rhine Valley, the capital city of Hessen has great variety to offer visitors. The refined atmosphere of a spa town, the flair of an elegant city, its proximity to the Rhine region, its attractive surroundings, all serve to contribute to its special attraction.

Location

Population: 270 000. Michelin map n° 543 P 8 – Hessen. Located around 40km to the west of Frankfurt and close to Mainz on the opposite bank of the Rhein, Wiesbaden can be reached via the A 63 or the A 67 to the south and via the A 3 or the A 5 to the north. Take the A 66 if you are coming from Frankfurt.

🅱 *Marktstrasse 6, 65183 Wiesbaden, ☏ (0611) 172 97 80.*

Surrounding area: see MAINZ (11km/7mi south), FRANKFURT AM MAIN (41km/26mi northeast), RHEINTAL (Rüdesheim is 48km/30mi west).

Background

Ancient success – First mentioned during the 9C as "Wisibada" (spa in the meadows), the city was owned from the 13C on by the House of Nassau, and from 1806 it became the seat of government of the newly founded Duchy of Nassau. For a time the city blossomed and enjoyed an upturn in its economy, which is evident from the generous layout of the roads and in the spa quarter built by Christian Zais in the Classical style. During the time of Emperor William II, when the Emperor brought his court to Wiesbaden every summer, new quarters with elegant villas and new roads were built, for example Wilhelmstraße and Ringstraße, which still afford visitors an insight into the city's original style.

The "World Spa Town" – The ancient Romans were aware of the benefits of the 26 hot sodium chloride springs (46-66°C/115-150°F), and Pliny noted with surprise that the water from the springs stayed warm for three days. The middle of the 19C saw the start of Wiesbaden's heyday as a spa town, when it became a rendezvous for the crowned heads and higher nobility of the world. Modern Wiesbaden enjoys an excellent reputation as a spa resort specialising in rheumatism with a modern rehabilitation clinic.

Directory

Where to Eat

⊜⊜ Käfer's Bistro – *Kurhausplatz 1 (inside the spa complex) – ☏ (0611) 53 62 00 – info@kurhaus-gastronomie.de – €28/47.* This restaurant is located in the spa complex *(Kurhaus)* and offers a varied menu. The building was constructed in 1907 in Wilhelminian style. Paintings and wood dominate the decor of the beautiful dining room. Access to the casino.

Where to Stay

⊜⊜ Drei Lilien – *Spiegelgasse 3 – ☏ (0611) 99 17 80 – fax (0611) 9917888 – info@dreililien.de – Closed from Christmas until the start of Jan – ⅍ – 15rm: €79/139* ☕. Modern, well-presented guestrooms. *Jugendstil* features were injected when the building was restored in 1905, but older historical details were preserved.

Walking About

OLD TOWN

The town centre is largely pedestrianised and is organised around the *Schlossplatz.* The shop-lined Landgasse and Neugasse are two particularly lively streets.

Schlossplatz

This elegant and well-proportioned square is the heart of the town. It is lined with beautiful buildings and is the setting for the market which takes place here twice a week around an imposing fountain designed by Johannes Barger in 1753.

Schloß (Castle) – The former residence of the dukes of Nassau was built between 1837 and 1841 in the unadorned Classical style. The main entrance lies on the diagonal and is emphasised by a rotunda. Today the palace is the seat of the Hessen Provincial Parliament.

Altes Rathaus (Old town hall) – The oldest building in the city, whose ground floor has been kept in the Late Renaissance style, it was built in 1609-10, whilst the upper storey in the Romantic Historicist style originates from the year 1828.

Neues Rathaus (New town hall) – Georg Hauberisser, the architect of the Munich town hall, erected this building in the German Renaissance style, divided by oriels and projecting bays, in 1886-87. It was destroyed in the Second World War and has been rebuilt since. It is somewhat free of adornment, but is impressive due to the considerable use of sandstone and the beautiful proportions on the ground floor and in the central part.

Marktkirche – This first brick-built church in the Nassau region was erected in the mid-19C. Its architect, Carl Boos, copied the Friedrichwerder church in Berlin which was created by Schinkel. *Carillon rung daily at 9am, noon and 5pm.*

SPA QUARTER

The spa quarter has developed to the west of the old town.

Kaiser-Friedrich-Bad – *Langgasse 38-42.* The Jugendstil building built at the beginning of the 20C cost 3 million Gold Marks. The Late Jugendstil frescoes in the entrance hall are worth seeing, as is the Roman-Irish steam bath with its majolica glazed tiles manufactured in Darmstadt and Karlsruhe.

Kochbrunnen – This fountain is made up of 15 springs. Its hot salty water contains iron, as is easy to tell from the reddish scale deposit on the granite fountain basin. Among Roman women the reddish powder was highly regarded, as they used it to colour their hair red. The octangular Kochbrunnen Temple dates from 1854.

Kurhaus★ (Spa house) – A lawn as flat as a bowling green, flanked on either side by the hydro and the theatre colonnades and by lofty plane trees, planted at the beginning of the 19C, leads up to what is, according to Emperor Wilhelm II, "the most beautiful spa house in the world".

The spa house itself was built in 1907. The inscription "Aquis Mattiacis" refers to the springs and the Germanic Mattiaker tribe who settled here in Roman times. The sumptuous interior decoration was restored to its original state in 1987. Although visitors don't get to see the magnificent rooms, unless they are attending an event or trying their luck in the casino which is located in the left wing, they should at least have a look in the foyer, in order to get a glimpse of the splendid decor.

Staatstheater – The impressive Renaissance style building, built in 1892-94, lies to the south of the theatre colonnade. The taste for lavish decoration which existed at the turn of the century is evident in its foyer, redolent of the Rococo, with a double flight of outdoor stairs.

Kurpark und Kuranlagen★ (Spa park and grounds) – A vast park, laid out in 1852, stretches away to the east behind the spa house. Sonnenberger Straße *(to the north)* and Parkstraße *(to the south)* feature magnificent villas dating from the Gründerzeit.

FROM WILHELMSTRASSE TO THE NEROBERG

Museum Wiesbaden

♿ *Open Tue-Sun, 10am-5pm, Tue, 10am-8pm. Closed 1 Jan, Tue after Easter and Pentecost, 1 May, 24, 25 and 31 Dec. €2.50.* ☎ *(0611) 335 22 50; www.museum-wiesbaden.de*

This museum is in fact made up of three separate museums: the **natural sciences collection**, the **collection of Nassau antiquities** and most importantly the **art collections**, which proudly boast the largest **Jawlensky collection★** in the world. The artist lived in Wiesbaden from 1921 up to his death in 1941. The exhibition includes significant works from the 16C and 17C as well as Classical modern paintings and contemporary art. Substantial renovation has made this museum into a real treasure, in which works of art are displayed to their optimum advantage.

Wiesbaden's main street, the **Wilhelmstraße**, is flanked on one side by elegant shops and on the other by the "Warmer Damm" park, which leads to the Staatstheater.

Taunusstraße, which leads to the **Nerotal** park, will make the heart of every lover of antiques beat faster, since a large number of antique dealers have set up shop here.

Whilst walking through the Nerotal, a beautiful park with a lake, it is impossible not to admire the magnificent Gründerzeit villas along Wilhelminenstraße.

Russian Orthodox Church, Wiesbaden

Kurbetriebe Wiesbaden

Nerobergbahn★

Open Apr (from Good Fri) and Sep, Wed-Sun, 12 noon-7pm, Sun, 10am-7pm; May to Aug, 9.30am-8pm; Oct, Wed, Sat-Sun, 12 noon-6pm; services every 15min. €1.80 round trip. ☎ (0611) 780 22 22. The cable-rack railway, which still runs as well and safely today as it did when it was built in 1888, is a very special monument to technical achievement. It leads up the Neroberg, Wiesbaden's local mountain, 245m/804ft in height. Driven with water ballast (a 7 000l/1 540gal tank), the car descending into the valley hauls the car going up the mountain. When it arrives at the bottom, the water is pumped back up to the top to be re-used. It couldn't be more environmentally friendly!

Russische Orthodoxe Kirche

Open May to Oct, 11am-6pm; Nov to Apr, Sat-Sun, 11am-4pm. €0.60. ☎ (0611) 52 84 94. Also known as the Griechische Kapelle, or Greek Chapel. It was built by Duke Adolf of Nassau in 1847-55 in memory of his wife Elisabeth, a Russian grand duchess, who died at the tender age of 19. It includes a central building with five gilded cupolas, which overlook the whole of the city. The elegant marble tomb, a copy of Rauch's tomb for Queen Luise in Berlin-Charlottenburg, was created by Emil Alexander Hopfgarten.

Wieskirche★★

Wies Church

A masterpiece of Bavarian Rococo, the Wieskirche was built by the architect Dominikus Zimmermann in the middle of the 18C. This huge pilgrimage church nestles in a charming Alpine valley setting and is on the UNESCO World Heritage List.

Location

Michelin map n°s 545, 546 W 16 – Bayern. The Wieskirche stands 25km/16mi to the northeast of Füssen, amid the forests, meadows and peatbogs whose gentle undulations characterise the final slopes of the Ammergau Alps between the Lech and the Ammer.

Surrounding area: see Deutsche ALPENSTRASSE (The Ammergau tour includes Wies), FÜSSEN (25km/16mi southwest), Schloß NEUSCHWANSTEIN (25 km/16mi southwest), Schloß LINDERHOF (38km/24mi southeast), GARMISCH-PARTENKIRCHEN (43km/27mi southeast).

Background

The Architect – It was **Dominikus Zimmermann** (1685-1766), one of the most gifted members of the Wessobrunn School *(see ZWIEFALTEN)*, who was entrusted with the task of building this pilgrimage church "in der Wies" (in the meadow), and dedicated to Jesus Scourged. Aided by his brother Johann Baptist, a painter at the Bavarian court, Zimmermann started the work in 1746, soon after he finished Steinhausen, and completed it in 1754. Indeed, much of the church was based on the Steinhausen design *(see ZWIEFALTEN)*: the focal point, as in the earlier edifice, was an oval cupola, which lent itself to painted decorations. The Wies church, more than any other, embodies the Rococo style in its purest form. Zimmermann was so pleased with the result, which he considered the most successful of all his works, that he spent the last 10 years of his life in a small house near the church.

Worth a Visit

Exterior and Interior

♿ *Open May to Oct, 8am-7pm; Nov to Apr, 8am-5pm. Donation requested. ☎ (088 62) 93 29 30; www.wieskirche.de*

A certain sobriety in the church exterior leaves the visitor unprepared for the splendour and magnificence of the oval bay and the long, narrow chancel which prolongs it. Gilded stucco, wood carvings and vividly coloured frescoes stand out from the whitewashed walls, while the richly glowing effect is enhanced by an abundance of **light** entering through windows whose elaborate design is typical of the architect – an essential feature of the whole, both inside and out.

It is in fact this same finesse in the adaptation of detail to the global effect that strengthens the balance between architecture and ornamentation and achieves that visual harmony for which Wieskirche is renowned. The lower parts of the interior,

for example – the walls and paired pillars defining the ambulatory in the usual manner of pilgrimage churches – are deliberately sparsely decorated because they symbolise, in the mind of the designer, the Earth. The upper reaches, on the other hand, symbolising the heavens, vibrate with a profusion of paintings, stucco and gilded work. The immense **cupola fresco** represents the Second Coming, the Gates of Paradise (still closed) and the Court of the Last Judgement with the throne of the Judge himself yet to be occupied.
The decoration of the **choir** is unparalleled: columns, balustrades, statues, gilded stuccoes and frescoes combine to form a symphony of colour. The wide reredos painting is of Christ Made Man. The richness and delicacy of the lavish ornamentation adorning the organ loft and pulpit mark the high point of the Rococo style in southern Germany.

Bad Wimpfen★★

Imperial residence of the Hohenstaufens in the 13C, this small fortified town, with its network of narrow streets lined with numerous old half-timbered houses, is built on a rise overlooking the River Neckar. Along the foot of the hill stretch the Ludwigshalle salt works, the product of which once brought prosperity to the whole surrounding region, and the built-up area of Bad Wimpfen im Tal, which grew up around an old collegiate church.

Location

Population: 6 000. Michelin maps n°s 543, 545 S 11 – Baden-Württemberg. Bad Wimpfen is a few kilometres from the A 6 motorway which links Mannheim with the west and Nuremberg with the east. From Heidelberg the town can be reached along the Neckar valley via the stunning route 37.
ℹ *Carl-Ulrich-Straße 1, 74206 Bad Wimpfen, ☎ (07063) 9 72 00.*
Surrounding area: see Kloster MAULBRONN (53km/33mi southwest), Schloß BRUCHSAL (54km/34mi southwest), HEIDELBERG (57km/36mi northwest), SCHWÄBISCH HALL (59km/37mi east).

Directory

Where to Stay

Am Kurpark – *Kirschenweg 16, 74206 Bad Wimpfen – ☎ (07063) 977 70 – fax (07063) 977721 – rezeption@amkurpark.de – Closed from mid-Dec to mid-Jan – P – 9rm: €47/104.* This hotel-guesthouse has many things going for it: its quiet location near the spa park, the comfortably-furnished guestrooms (six double rooms with balcony), not to mention the friendly welcome.

Sonne – *Hauptstraße 87, 74206 Bad Wimpfen – ☎ (07063) 245 – fax (07063) 6591 – info@sonne-wimpfen.de – Closed 21 Dec-18 Jan – 18rm: €50 – Restaurant €30/41.* This hotel is in the old town and consists of two beautiful half-timbered houses with rustic, but functional guestrooms – modern comforts in a quaint setting. The restaurant has a small, shady terrace.

Walking About

BAD WIMPFEN AM BERG★★ (UPPER TOWN)

Allow 1hr 30min. Follow the itinerary on the town plan, starting at Marktplatz.

Kaiserpfalz (Remains of the Imperial Palace)

Standing behind the Rathaus are the remains of the Imperial Palace with the **Blauer Turm** (Blue Tower), whose "neo-feudal" top dates only from the 19C. From the top of the tower – occupied today as in medieval times by a watchman – there is a panoramic view of the town and the Neckar Valley. A little further on is the Romanesque **Steinhaus**, with its 16C stepped gable, where there is a museum tracing the history of Bad Wimpfen since the Roman occupation.
Eight steps down from the Steinhaus terrace, on the right at the foot of the wall, note the twin-columned Romanesque arcading through which light entered the gallery of the old palace. The decorative intricacy of the arcades demonstrates the building talents of the Hohenstaufens, under whose rule Romanesque civic architecture reached its peak.
Continue to follow the wall as far as a flight of steps, on the right, which leads to the tip of the spur on which the town is built, at the foot of the **Roter Turm** (Red Tower), the fortress' final defensive point.

Return to the town centre, descending to pass beneath the **Hohenstaufentor**, which was the castle's main entrance in medieval times, and join Klostergasse.

Old Streets

In **Klostergasse**, which has considerable rustic charm, there are a number of half-timbered houses standing in their own gardens. On the left are the former spa bathhouses, recognisable by their outside galleries. To explore more of the town's old streets, return to the Langgasse crossroads and take a narrow alley on the right which leads to **Hauptstraße★**. At *no 45* is the courtyard of a former hospital *(Spitalhof)*, with beautiful half-timbered houses which are among the oldest buildings in Bad Wimpfen. Return along Hauptstraße, with its many picturesque, finely worked signs, and pass the beautiful 1576 Eagle Fountain *(Adlerbrunnen)* before regaining Marktplatz via Salzgasse.

BAD WIMPFEN IM TAL (LOWER TOWN)

Stiftskirche St Peter und St Paul

This Gothic parish church has retained a strikingly plain Westwerk from an earlier Romanesque building. The **cloister★★** (Kreuzgang) clearly shows the evolution of the Gothic style, though the late-13C east gallery is an example of the period at its best: a true purity of line informs the sculpted decor and the tri- and quadri-lobed windows. The north gallery (c 1350), already more angular in design, marks the transition to the style of the west gallery, heralding the sober forms of the Renaissance. *Guided tour (1hr): by prior written appointment. ☎ (070 63) 970 40.*

Excursions

Neckarsulm

10km/6mi southeast. The castle once belonged to the Teutonic Order. It now houses the **German Cycle and Motorcycle Museum** *(Deutsches Zweiradmuseum, NSU-Museum)*. Nearby is the Audi factory, originally the NSU motor factory which produced the first bicycles in Germany. The museum explores the development of the bicycle. ♿ *Open Tue-Sun, 9am-5pm (-7pm, Thu). Closed 24 and 31 Dec. €4. ☎ (071 32) 352 71.*

Sinsheim

25km/15.5mi west via Steinweg.

Auto- und Technikmuseum (Automobile and Technical Museum) – Mechanised vehicles of many types are brought together in this collection. In the first building are impressive early-20C tractors, steam locomotives, luxury

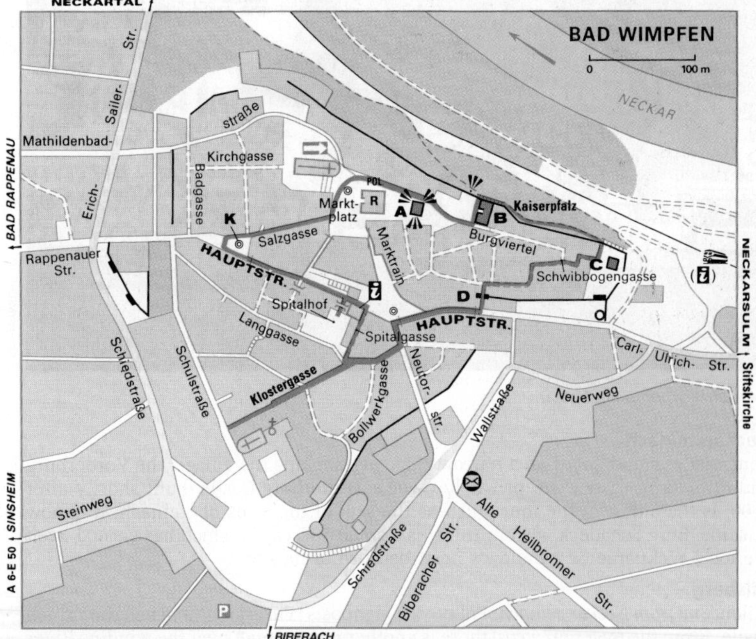

motor cars (Bugatti, Mercedes), and a replica of the first hang-glider to be commercially marketed, the Lilienthal, which dates from the late 19C. A second building exhibits a collection of mainly military vehicles (tanks, motorised artillery, aeroplanes). ♿ *Open daily, 9am-6pm, Sat-Sun, 9am-7pm. €10. ☎ (072 61) 929 90.*

Tour

NECKARTAL★ (THE NECKAR VALLEY)

Round tour of 74km/46mi – about 4hr.

Downstream from Bad Wimpfen, the Neckar, cutting once more through the sandstone massif of the Odenwald, runs through an area of wooded hills, many of them crowned by castles. Linked now with the great flow of navigation on the Rhine, river traffic is heavy.

Burg Guttenberg

Open Mar and Nov, Sun, 11am-5pm; Apr to Oct, 10am-6pm. €4. ☎ (062 66) 910 22. A massive defence wall protects this **castle** on the side facing the mountain. Inside, there are rare collections of ***objets d'art***★ and a series of archives. Note especially the odd 18C "Library-Herbarium", in which the plants are encased in 92 pseudo-"books" made of wood. A 15C altarpiece, The Virgin Mary in her Cloak, is on display. There is a fine view of the river from the keep.

Burg Hornberg

1.5km/1mi outside Neckarzimmern. 10am-5pm. €3. ☎ (062 61) 50 01; www.burg-hornberg.de Crowning a hill planted with vines, this **castle** – now partly in ruins – can be recognised from far away by its tall keep. In the part now turned into a history **museum**, note the body armour of Götz von Berlichingen, who died here in 1562. This knight, popularised in German folklore as a Robin Hood figure, was immortalised in a play by Goethe. From the keep, the **view**★ stretches a long way down the valley.

Hirschhorn am Neckar★

The castle stands on a fortified spur. From the terrace and tower *(121 steps, a difficult climb)* the **view**★ extends over the meander and wooded slopes of the Neckar Valley.

T. Krieger/MICHELIN

View of Hirschhorn am Neckar.

Neckarsteinach

Four castles stand guard on a narrow ridge overlooking the village: the Vorderburg and Mittelburg castlec are privately owned. Hinterburg Castle, built shortly after 1100, is the oldest of the four and was the seat of the lords of Steinach; it is now in ruins. Burg Schadeck, also in ruins, is a small 13C castle which has earned itself the local nickname of "swallow's nest" because of its site.

Dilsberg

4.5km/3mi from Neckarsteinach. Follow the signposts "Burgruine" to reach the ruined castle. From the tower *(97 steps)* there is another **panorama**★ over the winding River Neckar.

The best way to get to **Heidelberg**★★ *(see entry)* is along the east bank road, which leads straight to the castle.

Wismar★

Mid-way between Rostock and Lübeck, Wismar is an important economic centre known for its fisheries and naval dockyards. Sweden reigned over the town during the 17C and 18C and evidence of this occupation remains in Wismar today. The historic town centre with its characteristic red-brick houses and other admirable buildings was added to the UNESCO World Heritage List in June 2002.

Location

Population 47 300 – Michelin map nos 541, 542 E18 – Mecklemburg-Vorpommern. Wismar stands on a bay in the Baltic Sea, looking out towards the island of Poel. The A 20 runs west to link the town to Lübeck.

Am Markt 11, 23966 Wismar, ☎ (038 41) 194 33.

Surrounding area: see Bad DOBERAN (43km/27mi northwest), ROSTOCK (57km/36mi northeast), LÜBECK (61km/38mi west), SCHWERIN (31km/19mi south).

Directory

Where to Stay

Willert – *Schweriner Straße 9 – ☎ (03841) 261 20 – fax (03841) 210059 – hotel-willert@t-online.de – P – 17rm: €58/86.* Built in 1910, this Jugendstil villa was meticulously restored after the fall of the Berlin Wall. The stucco ceilings in the breakfast room and stairwell have been left in their original state.

Reuterhaus – *Am Markt 19 – ☎ (03841) 222 30 – fax (03841) 222324 – 10rm: €60/90 – Restaurant €20/31.* A small hotel in a renovated building on the market place with rather large, comfortable guestrooms and Italian furnishings.

Background

A trading town – Wismar dates back to the year 1229. It enjoyed its heyday for a time as a Hanseatic city, relying principally on trade with the main countries in Europe. The brewery trade (Wismar was known for its excellent beer) and wool weaving were further sources of wealth.

The ravages of war – Its downfall came with the **Thirty Years War**. The peace of Osnabrück meant that the town came under Swedish rule in 1648, under which it remained until 1803. Industrial operations only started up at the end of the 19C, and the town revived again as merchant shipping grew in importance.

Walking About

OLD TOWN★

Remarkable houses can be discovered everywhere in the old town. They are either noticeable because they have been renovated, or are still eking out their humble existence. With a little imagination, the visitor will be able to picture what a treasure Wismar once was and promises to become again once all the restoration is complete.

Marktplatz★

Of considerable size (10 000m^2/107 600sq ft), this square is dominated to the north by the white silhouette of the neo-Classical **Rathaus**, which dates from 1817 to 1819. The gabled houses date from a number of different periods, each of them recording a chapter of architectural and art history. On the eastern side stands the oldest well-to-do middle-class house in the town, an eye-catching red-brick building, known as the "Old Swede" *(Alter Schwede)* and built around 1380. On its right stands the Reuterhaus, where the works of the Mecklenburg writer Fritz Reuter were published and on its left, a house with charming Jugendstil ornamentation. On the south-east side of the market place stands an eye-catching artistic pavilion, the **waterworks★**. It was built in 1580-1602 in the Dutch Renaissance style and served to supply the town with water for centuries.

Marienkirchturm

Only the 80m/262ft-high **tower** remains of the mighty Marienkirche which was built during the first half of the 13C and destroyed during the Second World War *(carillon at noon, 3pm and 7pm)*. The brick built **archdeaconry** at the corner of Marienkirchhof and Sargmacherstraße dates from 1450.

Fürstenhof

To the west of the Marienkirchturm.

The building, which was erected in two phases, is thought to be the northernmost Renaissance castle in Europe. The more recent, long section in particular, built in 1553-54 by Gabriel von Aken and Valentin von Lyra, is impressive with the ornaments on the pilaster and friezes. Those facing the road represent the Trojan Wars, and those facing the courtyard represent the parable of the Prodigal Son. The gateway and window frames are sumptuously decorated.

St-Georgen-Kirche

The Late Gothic brick church (begun in 1290 and completed during the 15C) was seriously damaged during the Second World War. Extensive restoration work currently underway should help to restore it to its former splendour and dignity.

Grube

The "Grube" is a watercourse laid in 1255, where washing was done right up into the 20C. It is the only artificial stream of its kind still existing in Germany. After careful renovation, the streets which flank it could become one of the most picturesque corners of Wismar.

Schabbellhaus★

Open May-Oct, Tue-Sun, 10am-8pm; Nov to Apr, Tue-Sun, 10am-5pm. Closed Good Fri, 24 and 31 Dec. €2, No charge on Fri. ☎ (038 41) 28 23 50. The sumptuously decorated red-brick building in the Dutch Renaissance style, which stands on the corner of Schweinsbrücke and Frische Grube, was erected between 1569 and 1571 by the Dutch master builder Philipp Brandin for Hinrich Schabell. It bears witness to the wealth of the owner, a respected merchant and mayor of the town (his gravestone is in the Nikolaikirche). The house is home to a Museum of Local History *(Stadtgeschichtliches Museum).*

Nikolaikirche★

♿ *Open Apr and Oct, 10am-6pm, Sun, 11.30am-6pm; May-Sep, 8am-8pm, Sun, 11.30am-8pm; Nov to Mar, 11am-4pm, Sun, 11.30am-4pm. Donation requested, suggested amount: €1 per person.*

Beyond the *Grube* looms the dark mass of this, the highest brick church in the world, after the Marienkirche in Lübeck. The basilica was built between 1381 and 1487. Arched buttresses over the side aisles support the considerable pressure and at the same time alleviate the austere appearance of the building. The southern gable with its glazed figures is attractive. The interior is impressive with its sumptuous decor, with some valuable pieces from both the other destroyed churches contributing to the decorations. The **Altar der Krämergilde★** (Grocers' Guild Altarpiece), a hinged, panelled altarpiece in a later softer style, erected in 1430, is worth a closer look. The figures on the central panel, the Virgin Mary, the Archangel Michael and St Mauritius, exude a strong, expressive sensitivity. A bronze font cast in 1335 depicts the Life of Christ, the Last Judgement and the Wise and Foolish Virgins. The "Devil's railing" around the font originates from the 16C. The Triumphal Cross group (15C) is captivating, thanks to the quality of the crucifix. The frescoes in the side halls of the tower, including an immense St Christopher, date from the period around 1450.

Wismar harbour.

D. Scherf/MICHELIN

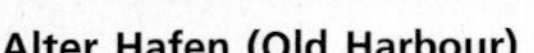

Alter Hafen (Old Harbour)

From the Grube and the idyllic street Am Lohberg, just a few steps lead to the harbour, at the end of which stands an unadorned Baroque building, the *Baumhaus* (tree house). Here the harbour used to be locked by the lock keeper at fixed times with a tree trunk. The function of the two "Swedish heads" executed in colour is not clear. Were they intended to frighten people off? In any event, they are known to date from 1672.

Excursions

Insel Poel

This little Baltic island to the north of Wismar makes a pleasant day trip. Poel's charming seaside villages and wild coastal stretches invite exploration. The flat relief makes it perfect for cycling and the local tourist office has bikes for hire.

Lutherstadt Wittenberg

Birthplace of Luther, who spent many years here, Wittenberg provided the stage for some of the major events in the Reformation. In summer, thousands of "pilgrims" flock here to walk in the footsteps of the great man. Also a renowned university town, Wittenberg attracted many people of great talent, including Lucas Cranach the Elder, who lived here for 43 years.

Location

Population: 48 000. Michelin map n° 544 K 21 – Sachsen-Anhalt. Wittenberg enjoys a pleasant location between the wooded hills of Fläming and the Elbe. To reach the town from the A 9 motorway, take exit 8 and follow B 187, towards Coswig then Wittenberg.

Schloßplatz 2, 06886 Wittenberg, ☏ (034 91) 49 86 10.

Surrounding area: see WÖRLITZER PARK (20km/13mi south), DESSAU (32km/20mi west).

Background

A Key Town in the Reformation – Summoned by the Elector Friedrich the Wise (1502) to teach philosophy in the university he had just founded, **Martin Luther** was at the same time appointed the town preacher. After the celebrated public burning of a Papal Bull, Luther was forced to appear before the Imperial Diet at Worms. Then, installed again in Wittenberg in 1522, he was obliged to temper the excesses of his own followers, especially Thomas Müntzer. A year after Luther's death, in 1546 at Eisleben, and eight years before he signed the Peace of Augsburg, allowing freedom of worship to the Lutherans, **Emperor Charles V** seized Wittenberg and is said to have meditated over the tomb of the great Reformer. The Lutherstadt prefix was added to Wittenberg in 1938.

Worth a Visit

Schloßkirche★ (Castle Church)

Am Schloßplatz, in the west of town. The church attached to the royal residence was burned down in 1760 and rebuilt. It was on the original doors that Luther had pinned up his famous 95 Articles condemning the abuses practised by the Church (1517). The new church contains the text, which was cast in bronze in 1855. Luther's tomb is also in this church, as is that of Melanchthon *(see below)*, as well as the bronze epitaph to Friedrich the Wise executed in 1527 by Peter Vischer.

Markt★

In front of the Late Gothic (1440) town hall stand statues of Luther (by Schadow, 1821) and of his friend and disciple Melanchthon (Drake, 1860). The square is bordered by houses with gables, that in the southwest corner *(Markt 4)* having been the birthplace of the painter Lucas Cranach the Elder. The artist lived and worked not far from here between 1513-50 *(Schloßstraße 1)*.

Stadtkirche St-Marien

On Kirchplatz, east of the market square. This triple-aisle Gothic (14C-15C) **church** was redecorated in neo-Gothic style in the 18C. The fact that Luther preached here is celebrated in one panel of the 1547 **Cranach Reformation Altarpiece★**. Melanchthon is depicted on the left-hand panel. Luther married Katharina von Bora here in 1525.

Melanchthon-Haus

Collegienstraße 60. Open Apr to Oct, 10am-6pm; Nov to Mar, Tue-Sun, 10am-5pm. €2.50. ☎ (034 91) 40 32 79.

The building in which Luther's companion lived and died is a Renaissance edifice topped by a gable of particularly elegant form. A man of moderate temperament, more tolerant than Luther, the author of the Confession of Augsburg worked for most of his life trying to reconcile the different factions of the Reformation. His study, and many documents relating to his work, can be seen in this house.

PHILIPP MELANCHTHON$ (1497-1560)

A gifted humanist with a perfect command of Greek and Latin, Philipp Melanchthon was closely associated with the Reformation. Admitted to Heidelberg University at the age of twelve, he finished his studies at the Faculty of Philosophy in Tübingen. He became professor of Greek at Wittenberg in 1518, and made a strong impression on Luther who came to hear him speak. The two men became close friends and Melanchthon soon became an ardent defender of the Reformation. The force of argument of his Loci communes (theological common places) (1521) contributed greatly towards the spread of Protestantism. Melanchthon, who became head of the Lutheran church after Luther's death, was an open and tolerant man; driven by a desire to reconcile the Protestant and Catholic dogmas, he was resented by the most orthodox Lutherans.

Luther-Haus★

At the far end of Collegienstraße. Occupied by Luther from 1524 onwards, this house faces the courtyard of the Collegium Augusteum, the town's old university. The Reformation Museum, housed here since 1883, exhibits collections of antique Bibles, manuscripts, and original editions of Luther's works. One department displays a selection of fine arts from Luther's time: portraits of the Reformer, prints and paintings by Lucas Cranach the Elder, canvases by Hans Baldung Grien etc. *Open from Mar to Oct, 9am-6pm; Nov to Mar, Tue-Sun. 10am-5pm. €5. ☎ (034 91) 420 30; www.martinluther.de*

Excursions

Wörlitz Park★★

18km/11mi west. Take the car ferry across the Elbe in Coswig. *See WÖRLITZER PARK.*

Wolfenbüttel★★

For three centuries, until the court transferred to Brunswick in 1753, Wolfenbüttel was the seat of the dukes of Brunswick and Lüneburg. The precise, spacious plan of the small town, with die-straight streets linking large symmetrical squares, makes it one of the most successful examples of Renaissance town planning in Germany.

Location

Population: 55 000. Michelin maps n°s 542, 544 J 15 – Niedersachsen. Built on the banks of the Oker, in the duchy of Brunswick, a few kilometres from the border between Lower-Saxony and Sachsen-Anhalt, Wolfenbüttel is the ideal base for exploring the Harz massif.

Stadtmarkt 3-6, 38100 Wolfenbüttel, ☎ (053 31) 29 83 46.

Surrounding area: see BRAUNSCHWEIG (11km/7mi north), GOSLAR (36km/23mi south), HARZ, HILDESHEIM (49km/30mi west).

Directory

Where to Eat

Ratskeller – *Stadtmarkt 2 – ☎ (05331) 98 47 11 – www.ratskeller-wolfenbuettel.de – Closed Mon – ♿ – Reservation – €24/28.50.* This pleasant establishment is located in the basement of a house which is over 400 years old. Its brick façade and grey-blue half-timbered frontage is typical of the region. Characterful guestrooms and beautiful library.

Where to Stay

Parkhotel Altes Kaffeehaus – *Harztorwall 18 – ☎ (05331) 88 80 – fax (05331) 888100 – info@parkhotel-wolfenbuettel.de – P – 74rm: €69/126 – Restaurant €15.50/30.* Modern hotel with well-presented guestrooms which are comfortable and furnished in light wood. Dine in the bright restaurant or in the wine cellar *(Weingrotte).*

Walking About

Half-timbered Houses ★★ (Fachwerkhäuser)

Picturesque groups of these houses in different styles reflect the town's social structure under the dukes. The homes of High Court officials lining Kanzleistraße, Reichstraße and the west end of Harzstraße, most of them built c 1600, are distinguished by majestic façades with overhangs on either side of the main entrance. The corbelled upper floors of these houses are supported on brackets. At no 12 Harzstraße, note the curious grimacing heads above cornices carved with biblical inscriptions. The decoration of smaller houses owned by lesser dignitaries and merchants, oddly enough, is more elaborate. A single gable normally tops their wide, flat façades (Lange Herzogstraße, Brauergildenstraße, Holzmarkt, Krambuden). The simpler, two-storey houses of the less well-to-do (Krumme Straße, Stobenstraße) are prettily ornamented with coloured fan designs.

The corner houses with only slightly projecting oriels are a particular characteristic of Wolfenbüttel. The most harmonious single group of these half-timbered houses is to be found surrounding the main town square *(Stadtmarkt).*

Stadtmarkt★

The town hall (Rathaus) occupies a number of 16C and 17C buildings on the north and west side of the square. The Weights and Measures Office has a distinctive arched doorway surmounted by King Solomon's Edict and the Wolfenbüttel coat of arms. A statue of Duke Augustus the Young (1635-66) honours one of the most cultivated princes of the Brunswick-Wolfenbüttel line of the House of Guelph.

Schloß★

♿ *Open Tue-Sun, 10am-5pm. Closed 1 Jan, Good Fri, 1 May, 24, 25 and 31 Dec. €3. ☎ (053 31) 924 60.* This is reached via an attractive narrow street bordered by arcades known as the Krambuden. Originally a 12C stronghold conquered by Henry the Lion of Brunswick, the building was the subject of many transformations before it evolved into Lower Saxony's second largest palace (after the *Leineschloß* in Hannover), complete with an imposing Baroque façade

WOLFENBÜTTEL

Street	Grid	No.
Am Herzogtore	BY	2
Anna-Vorwerk-Str.	AY	3
Bahnhofstraße	AZ	5
Brauergildenstraße	BZ	6
Breite Herzogstraße	BYZ	
Dr.-Heinrich-Jasper-Str.	AZ	8
Enge Str.	BZ	9
Große Kirchstraße	BZ	12
Großer Zimmerhof	AX	13
Holzmarkt	BZ	15
Jägermeisterstraße	BY	16
Jägerstraße	AZ	17
Kanzleistraße	AZ	19
Kleine Kirchstraße	ABZ	21
Klosterstraße	AZ	23
Kommißstraße	AZ	24
Kornmarkt	AZ	26
Krambuden	AZ	27
Landeshuter Platz	BZ	29
Lange Herzogstraße	ABYZ	
Lange Str.	BZ	
Leopoldstraße	BY	32
Löwenstraße	AZ	33
Marktstraße	BZ	35
Okerstraße	BYZ	
Reichsstraße	BZ	36
Schiffwall	AYZ	37
Schloßplatz	AZ	39
Sophienstraße	AY	40
Stadtmarkt	AZ	
Stobenstraße	AYZ	42
Ziegenmarkt	BYZ	43

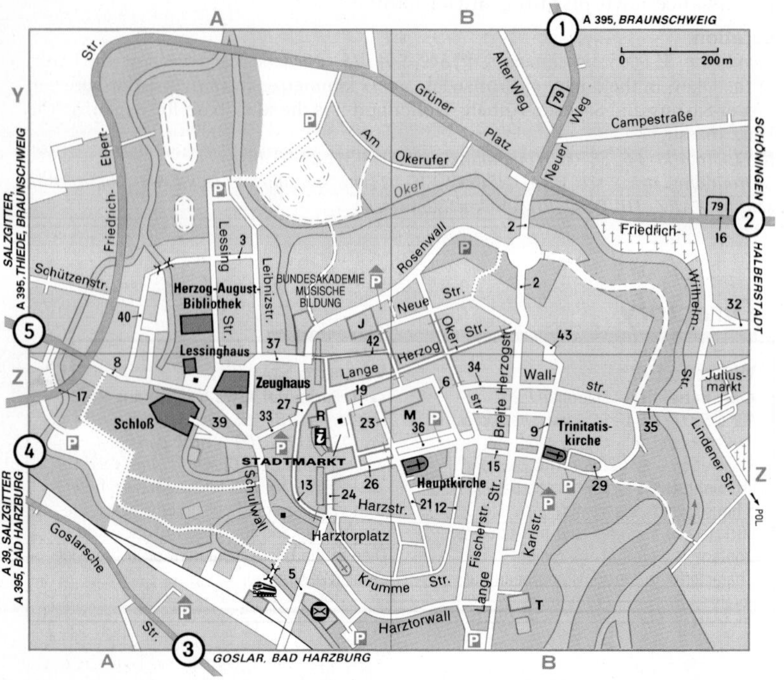

and overlooked by a fine Renaissance **tower★**. In the 16C and 17C, under the rule of several ducal patrons, the Guelph seat became a cultural centre of the region.

The Ducal Apartments – *Access via the central courtyard and main stairway.* The palace museum consists of the ducal apartments as they were 1690-1750. Rare furniture, tapestries and paintings, along with valuable porcelain give the visitor a good impression of High and Late Baroque court life. Note the scenes, executed in marquetry with an ivory inlay, adorning the walls of the small study.

Herzog-August-Bibliothek★ (Library)

Open Tue-Sun, 10am-5pm. Closed Good Fri, 24, 25 and 31 Dec. €3. ☎ (053 31) 80 82 14.

Founded in 1572 by Augustus the Young, this was the largest, most important library in Europe in the 17C. Still an invaluable treasure house for researchers and scholars, it houses today some 860 000 volumes. Among the priceless manuscripts and illuminated documents from the Middle Ages are a rare example of the 14C *Saxon Mirror*, and the first *Helmarshausen Gospel* (12C) said to have belonged to Henry the Lion. These are exhibited in the Augusteer-Halle or new treasury. In the Globe Room are two globes, terrestrial and celestial, as well as ancient maps and a *portolan* (marine chart) which provide interesting information on the state of geographic knowledge and the advances in cartography during the 15C, 16C and 17C. The Malerbuchsaal contains books illustrated by great artists of the 20C *(shown in rotation)*.

The Town of Jägermeister

Jägermeister ("Hunt Master") made its first appearance in Wolfenbüttel in 1935. This alcoholic drink with a unique taste is made from 56 plants, roots and extracts of fruit left to ripen for twelve months. The stag on the label is a reference to St Hubert, the patron saint of hunters. Legend has it that King Hubert, who lived in the 7C, turned his back on the splendours of royalty following the death of his wife Floribana, and devoted himself to hunting. During one of his solitary outings, a stag with a cross floating between its antlers appeared to him. This vision gave him a new calling; he immediately forsake his wealth and title and founded several monasteries.

Lessinghaus

Open Tue-Sun, 10am-5pm. Closed Good Fri, 24, 25 and 31 Dec. €3. ☎ (053 31) 80 82 14. **Gotthold Ephraim Lessing**, the great innovator of German drama, spent eleven years working as official ducal librarian in Wolfenbüttel (1770-81) and writing, among other works, *Emilia Galotti* and *Nathan the Wise*. His former home here is now a museum containing an evocation of his life and works.

Right by the Lessing house is the Zeughaus (Arsenal, 1613), a distinctive Renaissance building with projecting gables flanked by obelisks and scrolls. Note the fine rusticated west doorway.

Hauptkirche

Built on Kornmarkt in 1608, this Protestant church was clearly influenced by the Late Gothic hall-church tradition. The ornamental features of the Late Gothic are mingled with Mannerist elements. The massive tower with its Baroque roof resembles the castle tower in shape. The altar, pulpit and organ case in the Baroque interior date from the Late Renaissance.

Trinitatiskirche

The church, which closes off the east end of the *Holzmarkt*, was built in 1719. In its construction, the architects made use of an existing, twin-towered structure which was once a city gate. This explains the strangely flat silhouette of the church. Near the church is a **park**, formed from the old city walls.

Wörlitzer Park★★

Wörlitz Park

Wörlitz Park was the first landscaped park on the European mainland and served as a model for the gardens which were later created in Prussia. The park extends over 112 hectares/277 acres between the towns of Dessau and Wittenberg and has retained all its original magic. Visitors are free to wander the canalside pathways and to explore by boat the small islands on the lake.

Location

Michelin map n° 544 K 21 – Sachsen-Anhalt. Wörlitz Park is 17km/11mi west of Dessau. From the A 9 motorway (Leipzig-Berlin), take exit 10 and follow B 185 to Orienbaum. Take B 107 to Wörlitz.

Surrounding area: see DESSAU (17km/11mi west), WITTENBERG (20km/13mi northeast), LEIPZIG (77km/48mi south), MAGDEBURG (79km/49mi northwest).

Background

Prince Leopold III Friedrich Franz von Anhalt-Dessau (1740-1817), known as "Father Franz" to his subjects, was an enlightened ruler, to whom the welfare of his small state was paramount *(see DESSAU)*. However his endeavours extended far beyond merely material matters, and he sought to link the beautiful with the useful and promoted literature, music, architecture and garden design.

A number of trips to England provided him with food for progressive thought and paved the way for his planned reforms. It was also in England that he saw his first landscaped parks, which with their attempt to create unity between nature and reason were so in keeping with his own beliefs and with the fundamental tenets of the Enlightenment. He wanted to create such a park environment in his own kingdom. His friend, the master builder **Friedrich Wilhelm von Erdmannsdorff**, who had accompanied him on his trips, was to act as his assistant and like-minded adviser.

After 1764 a garden was laid out which appears natural at first sight, but which is in reality nature shaped by artifice. In the park, axes of vision were created (sometimes up to 14 sightlines). A palace and a Gothic house were the most striking buildings here, and a whole series of smaller buildings and numerous bridges in a whole range of designs, created a kind of Arcadian paradise. This work of art took shape during three stages of building, which extended to around 1800.

Walking About

Allow at least half a day to view the entire park and also the palace and Gothic house.

Schloß★

Guided tour (1hr). Apr and Oct, Tue-Sun, 10am-5pm; May to Sep, Tue-Sun, 10am-6pm. €4.50. ☎ (0340) 64 61 50; www.gartenreich.com

Erdmannsdorf built the palace between 1769 and 1773, making it the earliest neo-Classical building in Germany. He modelled it on Claremont Castle in Surrey, which was inspired by Andrea Palladio (1508-80). The splendid two-storey yellow and white plastered building stands out boldly against a backdrop of trees. The entrance hall, supported by four Corinthian pillars, is crowned by a simple tympanum. An inscription explains that Prince Franz had the palace built for his wife Luise. He attached great importance to practical accoutrements, as indicated by the water pipes, lifts, folding beds and cupboards fitted into the walls. All the sculpture and carpentry work was undertaken by local people, whom Erdmannsdorff insisted, as far as he was able, on having properly trained.

Luckily the original interior and artistic decoration have survived virtually intact. The elegant **dining room** *(Speisesaal)* with its elaborate stucco decoration and slim Corinthian pillars, and the great **banqueting hall** *(Großer Festsaal)*, which is two storeys high, are particularly striking. In the latter, the eye is drawn to the beautiful coffered ceiling and murals in the style of Carracci. The **library** is as successful a composition as the rest of the rooms, richly hung with paintings (Snyders, Van

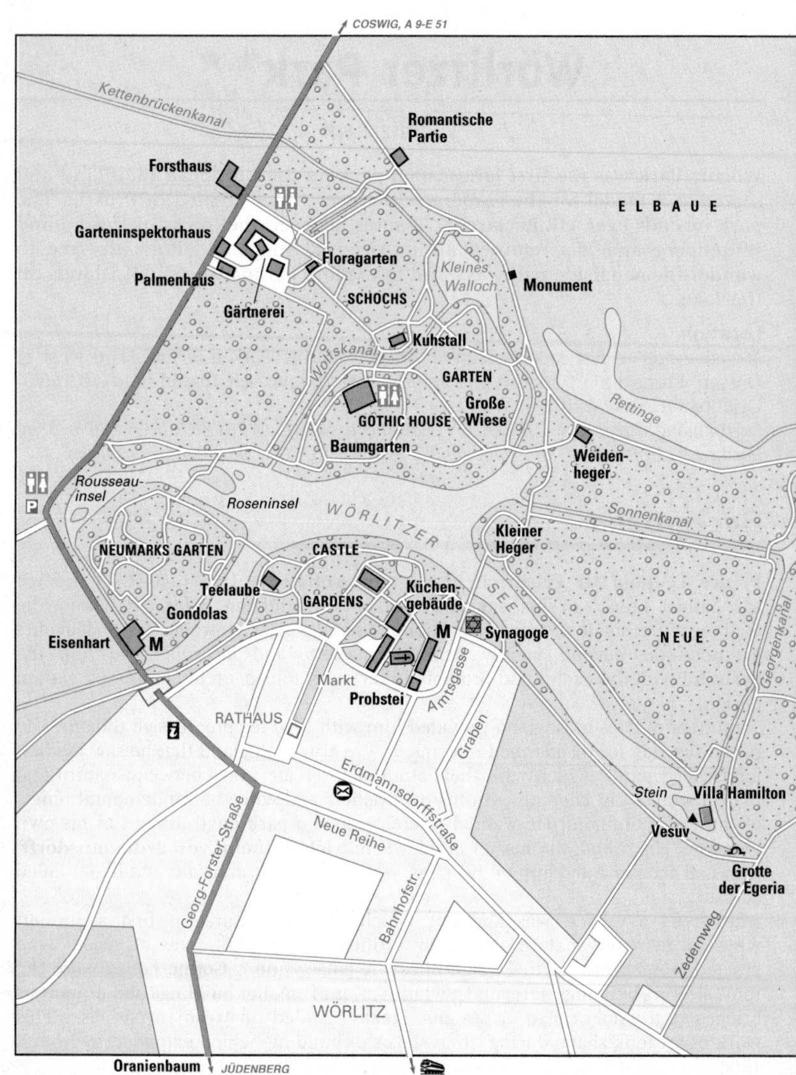

Ruysdael, Antoine Pesne) and fitted with furniture, the highlight of which is unquestionably the suite of furniture from the Roentgen workshop, which can be found in the Princess' cabinet.

Gotisches Haus★ (Gothic House)
Guided tour (1hr). Apr and Oct, Tue-Sun, 10am-5pm; May to Sep, Tue-Sun, 10am-6pm. €4.50. ☎ (0340) 64 61 50.

The canal-side façade of this building, built in several stages between 1773 and 1813, is modelled on the Gothic church of Santa Maria dell'Oro in Venice; the side facing the garden, with its brick façade and the white pointed arch windows, tends towards the English Tudor style. This "Gothic house" is the first neo-Gothic building in Germany, with the exception of the Nauener Gate in Potsdam.

R. Chéret/MICHELIN

The Pantheon in Wörlitz Park

While the palace served for official purposes, the Gothic house was a refuge for the prince, to which he could withdraw and in which he would frequently come and live for a spell. Through the mediation of the Swiss scholar Johann Caspar Lavater he was able to acquire an outstanding collection of **Swiss stained glass★** dating from the 15C to the 17C. This has survived intact and adorns the windows of the Gothic house.

All the rooms house numerous paintings (male portrait by Tintoretto in the war cabinet and several works by Lucas Cranach the Elder in the library).

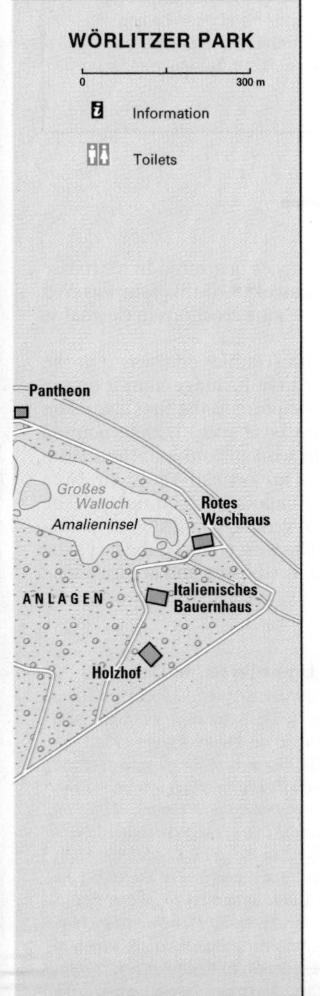

Worms★

The city of Worms was, like Speyer and Mainz, an Imperial residence on the banks of the Rhine, a town with a legendary past (the Song of the Nibelungen), a town of history and prestige. Today it extends along the river irrigating the rich soil of the Palatinate plain vineyards. Worms is a good point of departure for exploring the local vineyards and the Rhineland Palatinate region.

Location

Population: 82 000. Michelin maps n°s 543, 545 R 9 – Rheinland-Pfalz. Worms sits on the left bank of the Rhine, around 20km/13mi to the north of Mannheim. The Liebfrauenkirche *(leave on Remeyerhofstraße)*, which stands amid the vines in the northern suburb, has given its name to the wine sold only outside Germany as *Liebfraumilch.*

Neumarkt 14, 67547 Worms, ☎ (06241) 250 45.

Surrounding area: see PFALZ (suggested tour leaves from Worms), MANNHEIM (23km/14mi southeast), MAINZ (47km/29mi north), HEIDELBERG (50km/31mi south-east).

Directory

Where to Eat

Rôtisserie Dubs – *Kirchstraße 6 – 67550 Worms-Rheindürkheim – 9km/6mi north, via the Nibelungenring – ☎ (06242) 20 23 – rotisseriedubs@web.de – Closed for 3 weeks in Jan, Tuesdays and Saturday lunchtime – €27/48.* Small country restaurant with elegant interior. Wolfgang Dubs, the owner, treats guests to refined and varied cooking.

Where to Stay

Kriemhilde – *Hofgasse 2 – ☎ (06241) 911 50 – fax (06241) 9115310 – hotelkriem@aol.com – 19rm: €46/75 – Restaurant €14/30.* A small hotel in the town centre with friendly service and practical guestrooms, with pine or oak wood furniture. Rustic, tastefully-designed restaurant.

Worth a Visit

Dom St-Peter★★ *allow 30min*

Worms Cathedral is a Romanesque building with two apses quartered in each case by two round towers. From the outside, the **west chancel★★** of this four-towered structure, completed in 1181, is one of the finest Romanesque creations in Germany, with its double tier of Rhenish dwarf galleries.

Interior – The best way to go in is through the south (Gothic) doorway. On the tympanum: the Coronation of the Virgin. A splendid Christ In Judgement is on the far side of the door, dating from the 12C. A very old sculpture in the first chapel on the south side represents Daniel in the Lions' Den. The east chancel, with its pointed vaulting, is the older of the chancels: the high altar is the work of Balthasar Neumann. Nine Imperial tombs of relatives of Emperor Konrad II are beneath the choir. Note the transept crossing, surmounted by a Rhenish cupola on squinches. The Romanesque nave, which has five bays with diagonally ribbed vaulting, is embellished with blind arcades featuring intricate carving. The west chancel, the last to be built, is extremely elegant, with rose windows, a chequered frieze and arches added to its blind arcades. Five **Gothic relief sculptures★** in the north aisle *(Scenes from the Life of Christ)* represent the Annunciation, the Nativity, the Entombment, the Resurrection and the Tree of Jesse.

Lutherdenkmal (Luther Monument)

Unveiled in 1868, the **monument** commemorates the Reformer's appearance before the Diet. Luther himself, in the centre, is surrounded by the precursors of the Reformation: Pietro Valdo, John Wycliffe, Jan Hus and Savonarola. At the four corners are *(back)* the Reformist theologians Melanchthon and Reuchlin, *(front)* the Landgrave of Hessen Philip the Magnanimous *(see MARBURG)* and the Elector of Saxony who protected Luther. Seated women symbolise the towns of Speyer, Augsburg and Magdeburg.

Luther Before the Diet

Everyone knows the old chestnut about Luther and the "diet of worms", bandied about to much hilarity during school history lessons. In fact this particular Diet had perhaps the most far-reaching consequences of any conference before the two world wars *(see Introduction: History – "The Reformation and the Thirty Years War: Luther")*. Summoned before it by the young Charles V in 1521, after a Papal Bull condemning everything he believed in, Luther arrived in Worms "as though going to the torture chamber". He went nevertheless without hesitation, held back by the anxiety of his friends but acclaimed by enthusiastic crowds. Refusing to retract his beliefs, he was banned to the outer parts of the empire *(see Introduction)*.

WORMS

Street	Grid	Street	Grid	Street	Grid
Adenauerring	A 2	Friedrichstraße	A 13	Marktplatz	A 25
Allmendgasse	B 3	Friedrich-Ebert-Str.	A 14	Martinsgasse	A 26
Am Römischen Kaiser	A 5	Hardtgasse	A 15	Neumarkt	A 30
Bärengasse	B 6	Heinrichstraße	B 16	Petersstraße	A 32
Bauhofgasse	B	Herzogenstraße	B 18	Pfauenpforte	A 34
Fischmarkt	A 9	Kämmererstraße	A 20	Pfauentorstraße	A 35
Folzstraße	A 12	Karolingerstraße	B 22	Remeyerhofstraße	B 36
		Ludwigsplatz	A 23	Stephansgasse	A 38
		Mähgasse	B 24	Valckenbergstraße	A 39
		Mainzer Straße	A 25	Wilhelm-Leuschner-Str.	A 40

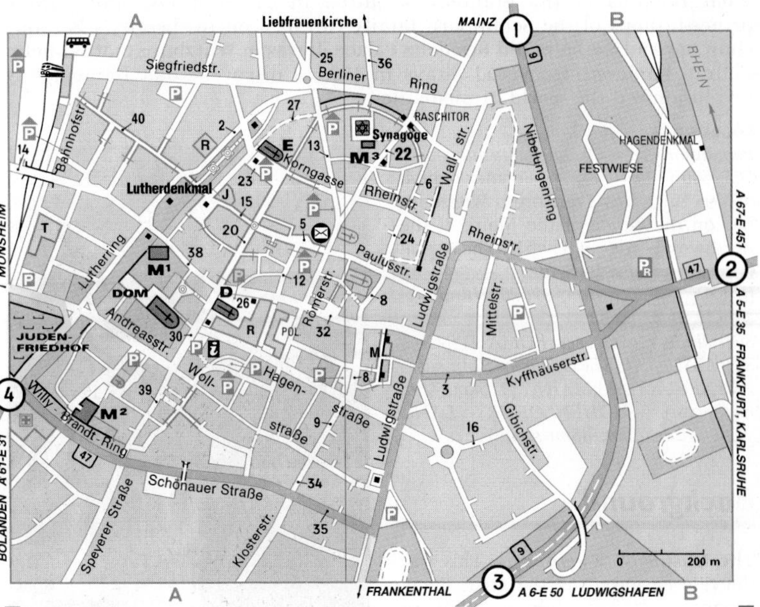

Sight	Grid	Key	Sight	Grid	Key	Sight	Grid	Key
Dreifaltigkeitskirche	A	D	Raschi-Haus	B	M³	St. Martinskirche	A	E
Museum Heylshof	A	M¹	Städtisches Museum	A	M²			

Museum Heylshof★

Open May to Sep, Tue-Sun, 11am-5pm; Oct to Apr, Tue-Sun, 2-5pm, Sun, 11am-5pm. Closed Jan to mid-Feb, Good Fri, 24, 25 and 31 Dec. €2.50. ☎ (062 41) 220 00.
This museum installed in the salons of a Gründerzeit mansion displays **paintings★** from the 15C to the 19C, including works by Rubens, Van Loo and Tintoretto, among others. Also on view are ceramics, glassware and crystal, valuable porcelain, and examples of 15C and 16C stained-glass windows.

Judenfriedhof★ (Jewish Cemetery)

Worms was one of the great centres of Jewish culture in Germany. This is Europe's most ancient Jewish burial ground, in use since the 11C, and studded with more than 2 000 steles carved in Hebrew.

Synagogue

Dating also from the 11C (and rebuilt in 1961), this is the oldest synagogue in Germany. Nearby is the *Mikwe* (Women's Bathhouse) and the *Raschi-Haus*, an old Jewish school restored to exhibit archives, ceremonial items and other examples of life in the Rhineland Jewish community.

Städtisches Museum

Open Tue-Sun, 10am-5pm. Closed 1 Jan, Good Fri, 1 May, 24-26 Dec and 31 Dec. €2. ☎ (062 41) 94 63 90. Five thousand years' worth of artefacts are displayed in the Romanesque buildings of a former monastery. The Ancient Roman section is a highlight, with one of the largest collections of glassware from this period in Germany. There is a lapidary museum in the picturesque cloister.

Dreifaltigkeitskirche

Only the tower and façade of the original Baroque (18C) church buildings remain. The interior commemorates the Reformation.

St-Martinskirche

The Romanesque west door is flanked by eight columns with crocketed capitals. Note the decorative interlacing of vine stems and leaves on the tympanum.

Excursions

Rhineland Palatinate★ – *See PFALZ*

Würzburg★★

Würzburg lies at the foot of the episcopal citadel of Marienberg, at the starting point of the Romantic Road; unfortunately most of the city's treasures were destroyed by bombs on 16 March 1945 in the space of just twenty-two minutes. What remains of the grandeur acquired in the mid 17C under three prince-bishops of the Schönborn family can be seen in the city's Baroque churches and the splendid Residenz Palace. It was in Würzburg that Wilhelm Conrad Röntgen discovered X-rays in 1895, a discovery that immediately revolutionised the world of medicine.

Location

Population: 129 000. Michelin maps 543, 545, 546 Q 13 – Bayern. Former capital of the Duchy of Franconia, Würzburg lies on the banks of the Main, at the northwest border of Bavaria. The region is renowned for its wine.

Congress Centrum, 97070 Würzburg, ☎ (0931) 37 25 35.

Surrounding area: see ROMANTISCHE STRASSE, BAMBERG (99km/62mi east), FRANKFURT-AM-MAIN (115km/72mi northwest), HOHENLOHER LAND (Schöntal is 72km/45mi south).

M. Hertlein/MICHELIN

The old bridge across the Main and Marienberg Fortress.

Background

The Master of Würzburg – This was the title bestowed on the great Flamboyant Gothic sculptor **Tilman Riemenschneider** (1460-1531), who came to live in Würzburg in 1483 and who was also the town's mayor in 1520 and 1521. Riemenschneider's work was never purely decorative: his whole interest centred on human beings, whose faces and hands – even their clothes – served as vehicles to express emotion and sensitivity. A gravity that is almost melancholy distinguishes his finest work, which includes the magnificent altarpieces at Creglingen and Rothenburg, the statues in Würzburg's local museum, and the tomb of Heinrich II in Bamberg cathedral – all priceless treasures of Franconian art.

Special Features

RESIDENZ★★ *1hr*

Apr-Oct 9am-6pm; Nov-Mar 10am-4pm. €4. ☎ (0931) 35 51 70; www.schloesser.bayern.de

This superb Baroque palace, one of the biggest in Germany, was built between 1720 and 1744 under the direction of that architect of genius, **Balthasar Neumann**, supplanting the old Marienberg stronghold as the bishops' residence.

A Masterpiece in 210 Days

Having initially commissioned an artist from Milan to paint the palace, who "painted it so atrociously badly", Prince-Bishop Carl Philipp von Greiffenclau hesitated no longer: only **Giovanni Battista Tiepolo**, the best fresco painter of his age, could meet his demands. The painter arrived, in the company of his two sons aged 23 and 14, on 12 December 1750. He was entertained in a princely style, "... and was given eight courses at lunch and seven in the evening. In other respects, he wanted for nothing and was generally treated quite admirably". He was to receive 10 000 Gulden for his work, three times more than he earned in Venice. During the barely three years he stayed in Würzburg, Tiepolo created the frescoes adorning the Imperial Hall and the staircase, two altars for the Würzburg court church, one for Schwarzach Abbey (now located in the Alte Pinakothek in Munich) and also worked for some other families in Würzburg. Since he was not able to paint his frescoes during the winter months, he must have worked day and night for the rest of the year. It took him only 210 days to complete the staircase fresco, which is 32x19m/105x62ft in size and features an overwhelming range of people, allegories and details, virtually a theatre of the world. In the frescoes in the Würzburg Residenz the artist, who was well known in his youth for the amazing speed at which he painted and for his creativity, produced his greatest and most important work.

Directory

Where to Eat

Bürgerspital – *Theaterstraße 19 – ☎ (0931) 35 28 80 – Closed 3 weeks in Aug – ⊭ – €16/27.50.* One of Germany's major taverns, belonging to the Bürgerspital wine estate. Impeccable tables in a historic setting – beneath a lovely groined vault – and Franconian specialities to go with the local wine.

Weinhaus zum Stachel – *Gressengasse 1 (near the Marktplatz) – ☎ (0931) 5 27 70 – webmaster@weinhaus-stachel.de – Closed Sun, Mon and Tue lunchtime – ⊭ – Reservation recommended – €20.50/38.50.* This traditional Weinstube in a rustic setting with an idyllic courtyard dates back to the 15C. Excellent wines, mainly Franconian, and refined regional cuisine.

Where to Stay

Hotel Alter Kranen – *Kärnergasse 11 (street parallel to Mainkai) – ☎ (0931) 3 51 80 – Fax (0931) 50010 – www.hotel-alter-kranen.de – P – 14rm: €60/84.* A hotel standing on the banks of the Main, a stone's throw from the old town. Magnificent view of Marienberg Fortress from the breakfast room and from some of the rooms. Cyclists welcome.

Hotel Rebstock – *Neubaustraße 7 – ☎ (0931) 309 30 – Fax (0931) 3093100 – rebstock@rebstock.com – 72rm: €98/210 – Restaurant €36.50/46.50.* Behind the Rococo façade dating from 1737, elegant, modern and even rustic rooms. Charming restaurant with panelling and a coffered ceiling. Bistro-style winter garden.

Taking a Break

Café Michel – *Marktplatz 11 – ☎ (0931) 5 37 76 – mmichel@cafe-michel.de – Open Mon-Fri 8am-6pm, Sat 7.30am-6pm, Sun and public holidays 1.30-5.30pm; Brasilino: Mon-Tue 9am-6pm.* This café spreads over two floors and offers a wide variety of cakes and tarts as well as a selection of savoury dishes. You can also go for a drink in the more modern café-bar next door, the Brasilino.

Going Out

Useful Tips – Many bars frequented mainly by young people and students are to be found along Juliuspromenade north of the city centre and in Sanderstraße south of the city centre.

Gutsschenke Schützenhof – *Mainleitenweg 48 (near the Käppele) – BUS 35 Käppele – ☎ (0931) 7 24 22 – Open 9am-1am, closed from mid Dec to beginning of Mar.* Peace and quiet and a panoramic terrace shaded by trees, slightly outside the city. You can come here for coffee and cake or a proper meal. Produce from the garden is used to prepare the dishes.

Schönborn – *Marktplatz 30 – ☎ (0931) 4 04 48 18 – Open Mon-Sat 8am-1am, Sun 10am-1am.* Always very busy, whatever the hour, this café has a large terrace on Marktplatz. On the menu: a wide choice of drinks, from coffee to cocktails, as well as a variety of dishes.

Palace★★

Open every day except Mon, 9am-6pm from Apr to Sep, 10am-4pm from Oct to Mar. €4.
The monumental **Grand Staircase★★** *(Treppenhaus)* occupies the whole northern part of the vestibule and is one of Neumann's masterpieces. The huge **fresco★★** ($600m^2$/6 400sq ft) decorating the vaulted ceiling is by the Venetian, **Tiepolo** (1753). This gigantic work depicts the homage of the four then known continents to the Prince-Bishop Carl Philipp von Greiffenclau. In the White Room *(Weißer Saal)*, between the Grand Staircase and the Imperial Hall, the brilliant **stuccoes**, also Italian, are the work of Antonio Bossi.
The oval **Imperial Hall★★** *(Kaisersaal)* is splendid. Situated on the first floor, it, too, is adorned with **frescoes by Tiepolo**. The elements in relief (cornices, sculptures, stuccowork) blend in extremely well with the sculptural paintings set in trompe-l'œil architecture, following a fashion current in the Baroque period.
It is also possible to visit the **Imperial Apartments** *(Paradezimmer)*, a luxurious suite of rooms restored in all their splendour with Rococo stuccowork, tapestries and German furniture. In 1812, Napoleon and his wife Marie-Louise slept in the **bed chamber** (the Duke of Würzburg at that time was Marie-Louise's uncle). The museum also houses a **picture gallery with some fine 17C and 18C Italian paintings, among them** *Amor and Psyche* by Antonio Bellucci, some *"vedute"* (views of Venice) by Canaletto, and works from the school of Veronese.

Hofkirche★

The Residenz church reflects the customary originality of the architect Balthasar Neumann; the curved lines of force supporting the vaulting, like those guiding the balustrade that overhangs the high altar, present a structure that is complex yet easy on the eye. The different varieties of marble, the gilding – discreet at the lower level and omnipresent on the ceiling – the warm tints of frescoes by the court painter Rudolf Byss – all of these combine to form a colourful composition rich in contrasts. Two more **Tiepolo** paintings hang above the side altars: *The Assumption* and *The Fall of the Angels*.

WÜRZBURG

Street	Grid
Am Studentenhaus	X 2
Augustinerstr.	Z
Auverastr.	X 3
Bahnhofstr.	Y 5
Balthasar-Neumann-Promenade	Z 6
Barbarossapl.	Y 7
Deutsche Einheit (Brücke)	X 8
Domstr.	Z
Eichhornstr.	Y
Friedensbrücke	X 9
Georg-Eydel-Str.	X 10
Haugerring	X 12
Hofstallstr.	Y 13
Juliuspromenade	Y 15
Kaiserstr.	Y 16
Kantstr.	X 18
Kürschnerhof	YZ 23
Leistenstr.	X 24
Ludwigsbrücke	X 25
Marienpl.	Y 27
Marktpl.	Y 29
Martin-Luther-Str.	X 30
Mergentheimer Str.	X 32
Nürnberger Str.	X 34
Peterstr.	Z 35
Raiffeisenstr.	X 37
Rimparer Str.	X 38
Sanderglacisstr.	X 40
Schönbornstr.	Y 42
Schweinfurter Str.	X 43
Seinsheimstr.	X 45
Semmelstr.	Y 46
Sieboldstr.	X 48
Spiegelstr.	Y 50
Textorstr.	Y 52
Theaterstr.	YZ
Urlaubstr.	X 54
Valentin-Becker-Str.	X 55
Veitshöchheimer Str.	X 58
Virchowstr.	X 60
Wirsbergstr.	Z 64

Sight	Grid	Key
Haus Zum Falken	Y	D
Mainfränkisches Museum	X	M[1]
Marienkapelle	Y	E
Museum am Dom	Z	M[2]
Neumünster	YZ	B
Rathaus	YZ	R
Vierröhrenbrunnen	Z	F

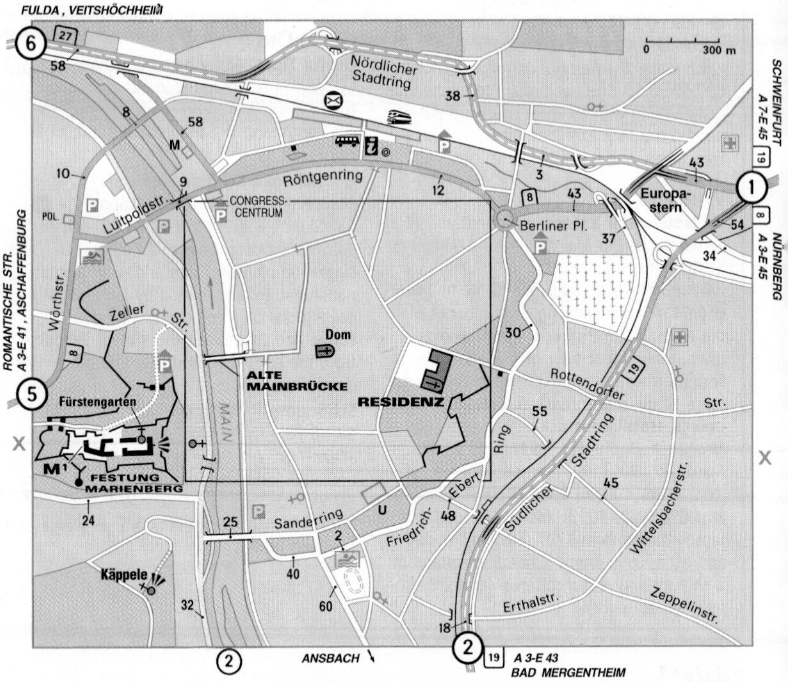

FULDA, VEITSHÖCHHEIM
0 300 m
Nördlicher Stadtring
Röntgenring
CONGRESS-CENTRUM
Luitpoldstr.
Berliner Pl.
Europastern
SCHWEINFURT A 7-E 45 19
NÜRNBERG A 3-E 45 8
ROMANTISCHE STR. A 3-E 41, ASCHAFFENBURG
Wörthstr.
Zeller Str.
Dom
ALTE MAINBRÜCKE
RESIDENZ
Fürstengarten
FESTUNG MARIENBERG
MAIN
Rottendorfer Str.
Ring
Südlicher Stadtring
Sanderring
Friedrich-Ebert
Wittelsbacherstr.
Erthalstr.
Zeppelinstr.
Käppele
ANSBACH
A 3-E 43 BAD MERGENTHEIM

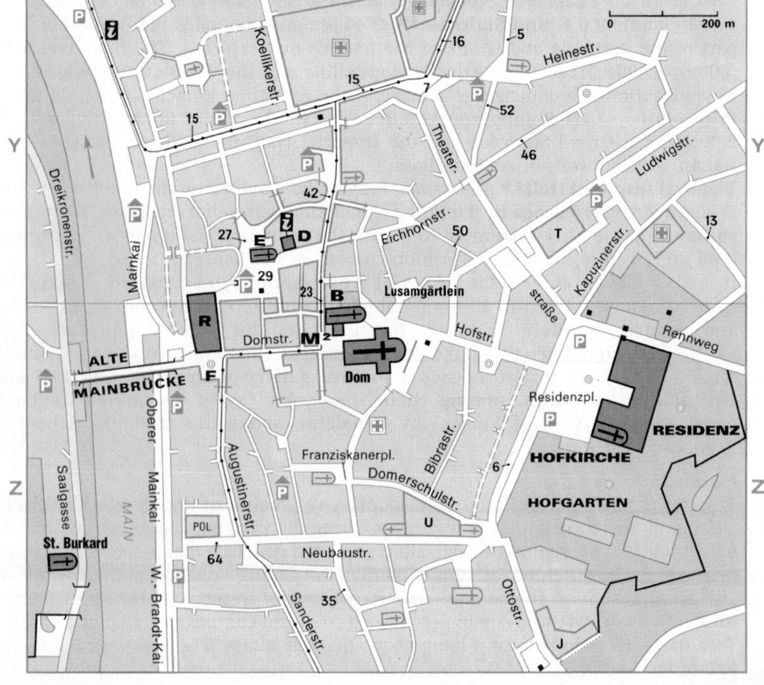

Hofgarten★

Astute use of old, stepped bastions has produced a layout of terraced **gardens** with majestic ramp approaches. From the eastern side, the whole 167m/545ft of the palace façade, with its elegant central block, is visible. The stucco is the work of Johann Peter Wagner.

Martin-von-Wagner-Museum★

In the south wing. Picture gallery: open every day except Mon and Sun, 9.30am-12.30pm, collection of antiquities: open every day except Mon, 2-5pm, Sun 9.30am-12.30pm; picture gallery and collection of antiquities open alternately. Closed 1st Jan, Good Friday, 1st May, 3 Oct, 1st Nov, 24 and 31 Dec. Free admission. ☎ (0931) 31 28 66.

On the second floor there is a **picture gallery★** exhibiting German and other European work from the 14C to the 20C. The most interesting exhibits include altar paintings by the masters of Würzburg (14C-16C) and Franconian sculpture, especially that of Riemenschneider. Dutch and Italian painters from the 16C to the 18C are well represented (Tiepolo again).

On the third floor, there is a **collection of antiquities★** displaying an interesting series of **painted Greek vases★★** (predominantly from the 6C to the 4C BC). Note the Greek and Roman marble sculpture and antiquities from Ancient Etruria, the Middle East and Egypt.

Worth a Visit

Dom St. Kilian (Cathedral of St Kilian)

This basilica with columns and four towers, rebuilt after 1945, has retained its original (11C-13C) silhouette, although the interior is marked by many other centuries. The Baroque stuccowork of the chancel contrasts with the high ceiling and simplicity of the Romanesque nave; the modern **Altar of the Apostles** in the south transept was conceived in 1967 by H Weber as a resting place for three **sandstone sculptures★** by Riemenschneider which were created between 1502 and 1506. Against the pillars on either side of the great nave, **funerary monuments★** to the prince-bishops, ranging from the 12C to the 17C, stand in proud array. Those by the seventh and eighth pillar on the left side (*Rudolf von Scherenberg* and *Lorenz von Bibra*) are also by Riemenschneider. The crypt, accessible via the north transept, houses a monument (13C) to the founder of the cathedral, Archbishop Bruno. Off the left transept is the **Schönborn Chapel**, built between 1721 and 1736 by Balthasar Neumann and the architect Maximilian von Welsch to take the tombs of the prince-bishops of that house. The 15C Gothic **cloister** and exhibition of relics and ornaments abuts on the right side of the cathedral.

Neumünster (New Cathedral)

The imposing Baroque **west façade** of this church (1710-16) is attributed to Johann Dientzenhofer. The only colour in the interior, which was also modified in the early 18C, is beneath the **vaulting; the** decoration there contrasts with the overall austerity. In niches below the cupola are a Riemenschneider *Virgin and Child* and a Christ in an unusual pose with arms folded below the chest (14C).

In the west crypt is the **tomb of St Kilian**, apostle, patron of Franconia and missionary, executed in Würzburg in 689.

On the left of the chancel is the entrance to the Lusamgärtlein, a small garden where the troubadour-poet Walther von der Vogelweide, who died in 1231, is said to be buried.

Museum am Dom (Cathedral Museum)

Between the two cathedrals. Open every day except Mon, 10am-7pm from Apr to Oct, 10am-5pm from Nov to Mar. €3. Opened in 2003, this museum houses mainly works of modern art (Joseph Beuys, Otto Dix) but also, in a surprising juxtaposition, some works by masters of Romanesque, Gothic and Baroque art (Tilman Riemenschneider, Georg Anton Urlaub).

Marienkapelle

This fine Gothic chapel with its lovely upswept lines was built by the town burghers in the 14C and 15C and boasts an attractive *Annunciation* on the tympanum of the north doorway (c 1420). Inside the west front is the 1502 tombstone of Konrad von Schaumberg (1502), carved by Riemenschneider and, on the north side, a **silver Madonna** made by the Master of Augsburg, J Kilian, in 1680.

East of the chapel is the **Haus zum Falken★** (Falcon House), with its graceful 1752 façade decorated in the Rococo style (reconstructed after the war).

Alte Mainbrücke★

Built between 1473 and 1543, the bridge over the Main was adorned in the Baroque era with 12 huge sandstone statues of saints.

Rathaus (Town Hall)

A 13C building, once an episcopal residence. The painted façade dates from the 16C. The interior courtyard is charming. The western part, known as the **red building** *(Roter Bau)*, is an example of the Late Renaissance (1659) architectural art.
The Baroque **fountain** *(Vierröhrenbrunnen)* in front of the town hall dates from 1765.

Festung Marienberg★ (Marienberg Fortress)

♿ *Apr-Oct: open every day except Mon, 9am-6pm; Nov-Mar: open every day except Mon, 10am-4pm. €2.50. ☎ (0931) 35 51 70; www.schloesser.bayern.de*
From 1253 to 1719, this stronghold was the home of the prince-bishops of Würzburg. Built on a commanding height above the west bank of the Main, the original early-13C medieval castle was transformed into a Renaissance palace by Julius Echter c 1600. It was under the Schönborn bishops that it became one of the fortresses of the empire from 1650 onwards.
Marienberg forms a complex around a rectangular central courtyard in which stand a fine 13C circular keep, a **circular chapel** dedicated to the Virgin Mary *(Marienkirche)* and a Renaissance covered well that is 104m/341ft deep. The chapel, crowned by an impressive cupola decorated with Baroque stuccowork, dates back to the early 8C (it was consecrated in 706). It houses many episcopal tombstones. From the terrace of the **Fürstengarten** (Princes' Garden) there is a fine **view★** of the town.

Fürstenbaumuseum – *Same opening times as the Residenz. €2.50. ☎ (0931) 35 51 70.* This comprises the prince-bishops' apartments, richly furnished and hung with paintings and tapestries. These include the huge Echter family tapestry dating from 1564. The treasury contains valuable items (church plate etc) from the cathedral, royal chapel and Marienberg Chapel.

Mainfränkisches Museum★★ (Franconian Museum of the Main)
The entrance is on the right in the fortress' first courtyard. Apr-Oct: open every day except Mon, 10am-5pm; Nov-Mar: open every day except Mon, 10am-4pm. Closed Shrove Tuesday, 24, 25 and 31 Dec. €3. ☎ (0931) 20 59 40. Among the displays of local art and crafts in this former arsenal (Zeughaus, 1702-12) is an important collection of **Riemenschneider sculptures** *(first floor)*, with 80 of his works including Adam and Eve, Virgin Mary and Child and The Apostles.
In the splendid vaulted galleries of the **Echterbastei**, statues, gold and silver religious plate, Gothic easel paintings and examples of Franconian folk art can be seen. In the cellars are old winepresses.

Käppele (Chapel)

At the top of a monumental Way of the Cross, this well-situated Baroque pilgrim sanctuary with curious bulbous domes was built by Balthasar Neumann in 1748. The adjoining chapel of mercy is connected via a "miracle passage". The finest **view★★** of Würzburg and the river is from the chapel terrace, with the fortress of Marienberg rising from the vineyards in the foreground.

Excursions

Schloß Veitshöchheim★

7km/4mi northwest via ⑥ on the town plan. Closed probably until 2005. Fountains, Apr-end of Oct: 1-5pm. Free admission. ☎ (0931) 35 51 70.
The **palace**, built at the end of the 17C and enlarged around 1750 after plans drawn up by Balthasar Neumann, contains splendid Rococo and Empire furniture.
But it was above all the **park★** that received particular attention from the prince-bishops, who improved it so consistently that by the end of the 18C it was an entirely Rococo creation. In the southern part, formalised in the French manner, about 200 statues people the shaded walks and leafy arbours, brightening avenues bordered by artistically clipped lime trees. In the middle of the great lake stands the superb **Parnassus Group** (Pegasus, the Muses and Apollo) which was carved in 1766.

Tour

FRANCONIAN WINE ROUTE★ (BOCKSBEUTELSTRASSE)

Round tour of 87km/55mi – allow 1 day. Leave Würzburg via ③ on the town plan.
It was monks at the beginning of the Middle Ages who introduced viticulture to the Franconian region of the Main – an area with a mild climate and hot, dry summers. The 4 500ha/11 115 acres under the vine produce mainly dry white wines from the **Müller-Thurgau** and traditionally fruity **Silvaner** grape stock. Such wines adapt perfectly to the essentially rich Franconian cooking.

Sommerhausen

A small Franconian walled town. The picturesque gables of the 16C town hall and the castle overlook the main street.

Ochsenfurt

Another town still encircled by ancient **ramparts★** punctuated by gates. In the centre, many old half-timbered houses and hotels are adorned with wrought-iron statuettes or signs. A clock in the lantern turret with mechanical figurines striking the hours is an attraction at the **Neues Rathaus** (late 15C). The **Stadtpfarrkirche St Andreas**, built between the 13C and the 15C, is noteworthy for its interior decoration.

Turn left off the B13 and drive alongside the Main on the U47.

Marktbreit

Here there is a fine **Renaissance ensemble★** formed by the town hall, dating from 1579, a bridge (Breitbachbrücke) and the gateway beyond it (Maintor, c 1600). Two Baroque houses with corner oriels complete the scene.

Sulzfeld

Fortified historic town centre featuring towers and gateways, numerous half-timbered houses and idyllic out-of-the-way spots. A highlight of this pretty wine-growing village is the Renaissance **town hall** with its scrolled gables.

Pass through Kitzingen and Mainstockheim (on the east bank of the Main), and take the road for Dettelbach.

Dettelbach★

A fortified market town clinging to the northern slopes of the Main Valley. Its charm lies in its Late Gothic (c 1500) town hall and the mid-15C parish church, whose principal tower is linked by a wooden bridge to the smaller staircase tower.

Northeast of the upper town is the **pilgrimage church "Maria im Sand"** (1608-13), an interesting example of the transition between Flamboyant Gothic and a Renaissance already tainted by the Baroque. The 1623 **Renaissance doorway★** was made by Michael Kern, who was also responsible for the sandstone and alabaster **pulpit★** (1626).

From Dettelbach to Neuses am Berg, the road crosses an open plateau planted with vines, with good views of the neighbouring slopes. It then drops down again to the valley of the Main; follow a meander before crossing to the other bank.

Volkach★

This delightful little wine-growing town lies on the east (outer) side of a wide oxbow curve in the Main. Of the original medieval enclave only two gates remain: the **Gaibacher Tor** and the **Sommeracher Tor**, one at each end of the main street. On one side of Marktplatz is the **Renaissance town hall** *(Tourist Information Centre)*, built – with its double-flight outside stairway and corner turret – in the mid 16C. In front of it is a 15C fountain with a statue of the Virgin Mary and slightly further south is the **Bartholomäuskirche**, a Late Gothic building with Baroque and Rococo interior decor.

The building known as the **Schelfenhaus**, a civic mansion in the Baroque style dating from c 1720, is worth seeing for its interior decorations *(in the Schelfengasse, north of the market place)*.

At the northwestern limit of the town *(about 1km/0.5mi, in the direction of Fahr)* stands the 15C **pilgrimage church "Maria im Weingarten"**, in the middle of vineyards covering the Kirchberg. Inside is the famous **Virgin with Rosary★** *(Rosenkranzmadonna)*, a late work (1512-24) of Tilman Riemenschneider, in carved limewood.

From the Kirchberg there is a superb **panorama** including Volkach, the vineyards and the valley of the Main.

Return to Würzburg via Schwarzach, turning right onto the B 22.

Zugspitze★★★

With a summit at 2 964m/9 724ft above sea level, the Zugspitze is the highest peak in Germany. The matchless panorama it offers, added to extensive ski slopes which can be used up to the beginning of summer in the Schneeferner corrie, have meant that the mountain is particularly well served so far as tourist facilities are concerned.

Location

Michelin maps n°s 545, 546 X 16 – Bayern. The Zugspitze is the northwest pillar of the Wetterstein limestone massif, a rocky barrier enclosing the valley of the Loisach and on the border with Austria. On clear days, 4 countries can be seen from the summit, including Munich in Germany, the Dolomites in Italy, the Piz Bernina in Switzerland and the Groß Venediger in Austria.

Surrounding area: see Deutsche ALPENSTRASSE, Schloß LINDERHOF and Schloß NEUSCHWANSTEIN (to the west of Garmisch). Walks are also possible from GARMISCH-PARTENKIRCHEN.

Special Features

Ascent

Be sure to wear warm clothing. From Eibsee by cable-car (Journey time: 10min, departs every 30min). Jul to Aug, 8am-5.30pm; Sep to Jun, 8am-4.45pm. Closed for 2 weeks in spring and autumn. Summer: €43 round trip, winter: €34 round trip. ☎ (088 21) 79 70; www.zugspitze.de Note that a reduced service may run in bad weather conditions.

The summit can be reached by cable-car *(Gletscherbahn)* from Zugspitzplatt station, the terminus of the rack railway rising from Garmisch, or directly from the Eibsee, or again from Ehrwald with the Tyrolean Zugspitz train (carriages carry up to 100 people). Only very experienced and well-equipped walkers are advised to undertake the ascent on foot.

From Garmisch-Partenkirchen – *The whole trip lasts 1hr 15min. Departs every hour from 8.15am to 2.15pm. €43 round trip (€34 in winter). Last train back: 4.30pm. ☎ (08821) 79 10.* A 4.6km/2.9mi tunnel bored through the mountain ending the rack-railway climb to Zugspitzplatt station. As long as the snow is good (from October to May), the lower part of the corrie known as the Zugspitzplatt offers a skiing area of some 7.5km^2/almost 3sq mi, equipped with many ski-tow installations. The cable-car *(Gletscherbahn)* from Zugspitzplatt station climbs the last 350m/1 148ft to the summit.

From the Eibsee – *Cable-car direct to the summit in 10min. Departs every 30min from 8am to 5.15pm (4.15pm in winter). Same price (see above).*

From the Austrian Tyrolese side – *From Ehrwald, the Tyrolean cable-car (which carries 100 people) takes you from the valley station to the summit in 10min.*

Zugspitzgipfel★★★ (The Summit)

The upper terminals of the Gletscherbahn and the Eibsee cable-car are on the German side, next to the eastern peak of the mountain where a cross has been planted. After that come the "Münchner Haus" refuge and an observatory. The look-out terrace by the Gipfelbahn is at an altitude of 2 964m/9 724ft. On the Austrian side is the upper station of the Tyrolean Zugspitzbahn. The crossing from Austria to Germany at the summit has been redesigned and revised.

The **panorama★★★** to the east reveals the forward bastions of the Kaisergebirge, the Dachstein and the Karwendel, the glacial peaks of the Hohe Tauern (Großglockner, Groß Venediger), the High Alps of the Tirol (Zillertal, then Stubai and Ötztal to the south) as well as the Ortler and the Bernina massifs.

Nearer, towards the south-west, the mountains of the Arlberg (Silvretta, Rätikon) stand in front of the Säntis in the Appenzell Alps and, further away to the west and northwest, the Allgäu and Ammergau ranges. To the north, the Bavarian lowlands are visible, together with the lakes, the Ammersee and Starnberger See.

Those who wish to spend longer at the summit can visit a gallery of modern art (temporary exhibitions) or have a snack at the restaurant.

Zwiefalten★★

The Upper Swabian Plateau is scattered with beautiful Baroque churches whose fluid, low-key decorations in pastel tints harmonise perfectly with the landscape. The unmatched prosperity and cultural influence of the Benedictine abbeys in the 18C meant that updating their churches became a priority – regardless of whether they were in good condition. Thanks to the abbots' patronage of the arts, the great artists of the time were able to create these magnificent buildings, built "so that God may be glorified in all things", according to the inscription on the Weingarten façade.

Location

Population: 2 300. Michelin map n° 545 V 12 – Baden-Württemberg. Between Ulm and Lake Constance (Bodensee), this tour crosses the Upper Swabian Plateau, with its gentle hills and soft light.

Surrounding area: see SALEM (32km/20mi southwest of Ravensburg), LINDAU IM BODENSEE (32km/20mi south of Ravensburg), ULM (50km/31mi northeast of Zwiefalten), SCHWÄBISCHE ALB (35km/22mi west of Zwiefalten).

Tour

85km/53mi – half a day.

Ravensburg

This ancient Swabian town still shelters behind a well-preserved city wall bristling with towers and fortified gateways. The road from Wangen passes beneath the Obertor, a gateway with stepped gables. At the end of Marktstraße is a block of old buildings comprising the Rathaus (14C-15C) and the weigh-house with the Blaserturm, a 15C-16C tower. In order to overlook and spy on the activities of the constables of Veitsburg, on a nearby hill, the burghers of Ravensburg erected **The Mehlsack** ("Sack of Flour") – a stone tower, originally whitewashed, which rises to a height of 50m/164ft. Looking out over the city wall from the top *(240 steps)*, the **view** extends as far as the church at Weingarten.

CESA, Marburg

Interior of Zwiefalten Church.

The 14C **Liebfrauenkirche** is worth visiting for its best-known work of art, which is exposed on an altar in the south aisle. This is a copy of **The Ravensburg Madonna★★**, a poignant 15C sculpture of the Virgin Mary in a mantle (the original is in the Gemäldegalerie in Berlin). Note also the triptych in Limoges enamel dating from the second half of the 15C.

Exit via the B 30 towards Weingarten.

Weingarten★★

A dominant position in this town is held by the abbey church, with its fine bare-sandstone façade. Consecrated in 1724, the church rivals Ottobeuren as the largest Baroque sanctuary in Germany. It is 102m/335ft long and 44m/144ft wide at the transepts. The west front, framed by two short but elegant towers, is rounded. This, with the construction of a dome on a drum with wide window openings above the transept crossing, betrays an Italian influence transmitted by way of Salzburg.

The interior vistas are amplified by openings pierced through the dividing piers in a manner typical of the Vorar-

The Devil to Pay

Of the 66 stops (sets of pipes) of the Weingarten organ, the 46th is called Vox Humana. Gabler's ambition was to build an organ combining man and machine in resounding praise of God. After countless attempts to perfect a process to achieve a human sound, he is said to have sold his soul to the devil; in return, he received a piece of metal which he melted down to make the pipes. However, the monks were so enthralled by the beauty of the organ's song that they were unable to pray, whereupon the abbot ordered an inquiry. Gabler was found out, confessed and then sentenced to death. But since the only sounds produced by the organ now sounded like wailing, Gabler was reprieved.

lberg School. The painting and stuccowork, relatively restrained, were entrusted to the masters of the day. Scenes on the vaulting by Cosmas Damien Asam are full of virtuosity. The choir stalls by Joseph Anton Feuchtmayer are also interesting. The superb **organ★★** is due to Joseph Gabler (1700-71) and fits in perfectly with the rest of the decoration: its 6 666 pipes follow the line of the windows and mix with the columns of pink marble.

The tour continues along the Upper Swabian Baroque Road (signposted 'Oberschäbische Barockstraße') via the B 30 until Bad Waldsee, where you should turn left onto the L 275 towards Bad Schussenried.

Bad Schussenried

A pleasant small town. The **old abbey buildings** (now a conference and exhibition centre) and the abbey church owe their sumptuous Baroque appearance to former Premonstratensian abbots. In the church, the upper panels of the intricately decorated choir stalls (1717) are separated by 28 statuettes representing men and women who founded religious orders. The **library★** has a huge painted ceiling by Franz Georg Herrmann, court painter to the Prince-Abbot of Kempten, and a sinuous gallery and Rococo balustrade supported by twin columns, the work of Fidelis Sporer. The column pedestals are embellished alternately with vivacious cherubim in burlesque costumes and effigies of Fathers of the Church. *Open Apr to Oct, Tue-Fri, 2-5pm, Sat-Sun and bank holidays, 10am-5pm; Nov to Mar, Sat-Sun and bank holidays, 2-4pm. Closed 24, 25 and 31 Dec. €3. ☎ (073 15) 02 89 75.*

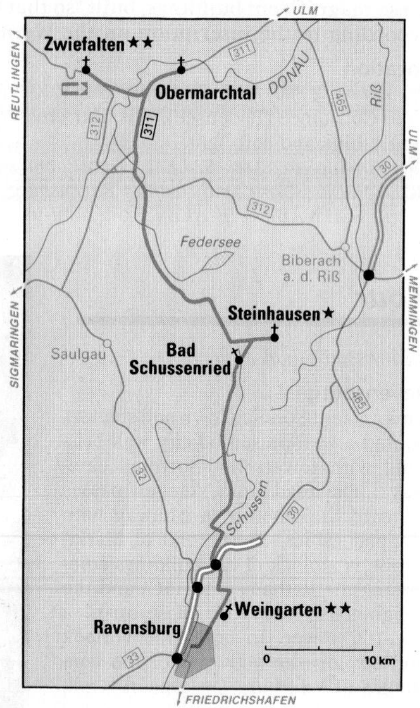

Steinhausen★

Designed by Dominikus and Johann Zimmermann, the pilgrimage church in this hamlet comprises a single nave and a small chancel, both of them oval in shape. A crown of pillars, which supports the inner shell of the vaulting, marks the limit of a gallery circling the nave. The capitals, cornices and window embrasures, carved and coloured, are adorned with birds and insects or flowers with heavy corollas. There is a Pietà dating from 1415.

Follow the L 275 until Riedlingen, then join the B 312 to Zwiefalten.

Zwiefalten★★

This village, on the Danubian edge of the Swabian Jura, has a remarkable Baroque **church**. Like most Baroque edifices in this region, the church's sober exterior conceals a lavishly decorated interior.

Entering the church, which was built by **Johann Michael Fischer** between 1739 and 1753, the initial impression is of an extraordinary profusion of luminous colours, a richness and exuberance in the decoration and an extreme virtuosity on the part of the stuccoworkers. The eye, intoxicated at first by this deluge of painting, stucco and statues, finally settles on the details: the beautiful ceiling paintings devoted to the Virgin Mary by Franz Joseph Spiegler (1691-1757), the pulpit decorated by Johann Michael Feuchtmayer (uncle of the sculptor and stuccoworker Joseph Anton Feuchtmayer), the angels and cherubs, in every attitude and from every corner, addressing themselves to the pilgrims.

The choir is separated from the nave by an altar to the Virgin surrounded by

School of Wessobrunns

In the 17C and 18C, the little town of Wessobrunn produced a series of architects and artists of multiple talents who, according to the needs of construction projects or the dictates of their own inspiration, were able to exchange the compass at will for the paintbrush or the tools of the stuccoworker. Working in a corporate and family framework known as the Wessobrunn School, these artists of Baroque genius, who were in no way specialists, beautified churches and civic buildings all over Bavaria, Swabia and the Tyrol. The names of the **Feuchtmayer** and **Schmuzer** families are eminent within the group, though the most celebrated is perhaps **Dominikus Zimmermann**, who was responsible for the church at Wies *(see entry)*.

superb grilles dating from 1757. The stalls were richly carved and gilded by Joseph Christian. Before leaving the church, note the most unusual confessionals built to resemble grottoes.

Go back to Zwiefaltendorf then take the B 311 to the left.

Obermarchtal

The old **abbey church** in this small town, dating from 1686, was one of the first to be completed by the Vorarlberg School. The rigidity of the architecture – a Baroque still undeveloped – is accentuated by the heaviness of the furnishings: only the Wessobrunn stuccowork lightens the overall effect. *Tour on request. ☎ (073 75) 95 91 00.*

Index

Leipzig *Sachsen* .... Towns, sights and tourist regions followed by the name of the *Land*.
Goethe, Johann Wolfgang von ..... People, events and artistic styles mentioned in the guide.
Botanical Gardens .... Sights in major cities.

Notes

Travel Publications

Hannay House, 39 Clarendon Road
Watford, Herts WD17 1JA, UK
☎ 01923 205 240 - Fax 01923 205 241
www.ViaMichelin.com
TheGreenGuide-uk@uk.michelin.com

Manufacture française des pneumatiques Michelin
Société en commandite par actions au capital de 304 000 000 EUR
Place des Carmes-Déchaux – 63 Clermont-Ferrand (France)
R.C.S. Clermont-Fd B 855 200 507

No part of this publication may be reproduced in any form
without the prior permission of the publisher

© Michelin et Cie, Propriétaires-éditeurs
Dépôt légal février 2005 – ISBN 2-06-711027-6 – ISSN 0763.1383
Printed in France 01-05/4.1

Typesetting: MAURY, Malesherbes
Printing and Binding:: AUBIN, Ligugé

Graphics: Christiane Beylier, Paris 12e arr.
Cover design: Carré Noir, Paris 17e arr.